CRITICAL SURVEY
OF
DRAMA

CRITICAL SURVEY

OF

DRAMA

Second Revised Edition

Volume 1
Kōbō Abe - Albert Camus

Editor, Second Revised Edition
Carl Rollyson
Baruch College, City University of New York

Editor, First Editions, English and Foreign Language Series
Frank N. Magill

SALEM PRESS, INC.
Pasadena, California   Hackensack, New Jersey

Editor in Chief: Dawn P. Dawson
Managing Editor: Christina J. Moose
Developmental Editor: R. Kent Rasmussen
Project Editor: Rowena Wildin
Research Supervisor: Jeffry Jensen
Research Assistant: Michelle Murphy

Acquisitions Editor: Mark Rehn
Photograph Editor: Philip Bader
Manuscript Editor: Sarah Hilbert
Assistant Editor: Andrea E. Miller
Production Editor: Cynthia Beres
Layout: Eddie Murillo and William Zimmerman

Library of Congress Cataloging-in-Publication Data

Critical survey of drama / edited by Carl Rollyson.-- 2nd rev. ed.
    p. cm.
Previous edition edited by Frank Northen Magill in 1994.
"Combines, updates, and expands two earlier Salem Press reference sets: Critical survey of drama, revised edition, English language series, published in 1994, and Critical survey of drama, foreign language series, published in 1986"--Pref.
Includes bibliographical references and index.
ISBN 1-58765-102-5 (set : alk. paper) -- ISBN 1-58765-103-3 (vol. 1 : alk. paper) --
1. Drama--Dictionaries. 2. Drama--History and criticism--Dictionaries. 3. Drama--Bio-bibliography. 4. English drama--Dictionaries. 5. American drama--Dictionaries. 6. Commonwealth drama (English)--Dictionaries. 7. English drama--Bio-bibliography. 8. American drama--Bio-bibliography. 9. Commonwealth drama (English)--Bio-bibliography. I. Rollyson, Carl E. (Carl Edmund) II. Magill, Frank Northen, 1907-1997.
PN1625 .C68 2003
809.2'003—dc21
    2003002190

Fourth Printing

PRINTED IN THE UNITED STATES OF AMERICA

PUBLISHER'S NOTE

Critical Survey of Drama, Second Revised Edition continues the Magill tradition of *Critical Surveys*: *Long Fiction, Short Fiction, Drama,* and *Poetry*. All these multivolume reference sets offer in-depth treatments of the world's major writers—novelists, short-fiction writers, dramatists, and poets—in essays ranging from four or five to more than a dozen pages, with full biographical, bibliographical, and analytical coverage. Supplemental volumes and revised editions of the *Critical Surveys* began to appear in the late 1980's. Then, beginning in 2000, the editors of Salem Press, in collaboration with academic genre-experts acting as editors, began to issue the heavily revised and expanded *Second Revised Editions*.

Critical Survey of Long Fiction, Second Revised Edition (appearing in 2000 at 8 volumes) increased the 401 previously covered novelists to 463 and updated, revised, or expanded the previously published essays, also adding a full volume of "overview essays" on major theories, world and ethnic literatures, and research aids. *Critical Survey of Short Fiction* (7 volumes) appeared in 2001, increasing the previous coverage of short-story writers from 347 to 480, with 133 new writers and 29 overview essays, more than half new. The third of the *Second Revised Editions*, the 8-volume *Critical Survey of Poetry* featured more than 20 percent new material, 20 percent revised material, more than 740 heavily revised or completely new essay-bibliographies. The new revised editions use a format that allows easy access to listings and text discussions, several new research tools and indexes, and photographs of more than 450 poets.

Publication of *Critical Survey of Drama, Second Revised Edition*, completes the series of new editions. It combines, updates, and expands two earlier Salem Press reference sets: *Critical Survey of Drama, Revised Edition, English Language Series*, published in 1994, and *Critical Survey of Drama, Foreign Language Series*, published in 1986. The new 8-volume set contains 602 essays, of which 538 discuss individual dramatists and 64 cover broad overview topics.

The dramatist profiles contain more than 310 photographs and drawings.

Of the revised edition's 538 profiles of individual dramatists, 79 are completely new essays—mostly on playwrights who have recently come to be regarded as established figures in the theater. Included in this group are dramatists such as Kōbō Abe, Eric Bogosian, Marina Carr, Alice Childress, Spalding Gray, Jessica Hagedorn, Elizabeth Jolley, Tony Kushner, Kenneth Lonergan, Earl Lovelace, Antonio Machado, Jane Martin, Yury Olesha, Yasmina Reza, Alfred Uhry, Fay Weldon, and Yevgeny Zamyatin.

In addition to the entirely new author profiles, 88 profiles have been updated and revised to include the authors' new works and achievements, as well as developments in their personal lives. Besides listing new productions and publications and honors and awards, the updated essays provide analyses of significant new works. Among the playwrights who merited such treatment are Jon Robin Baitz, Mart Crowley, Marguerite Duras, Dario Fo, Václav Havel, Arthur Kopit, Terrence McNally, David Rabe, Ntozake Shange, Sam Shepard, Megan Terry, and Derek Walcott. The remaining profiles were checked for accuracy and, if needed, updated to reflect current research and the publication of plays or significant compilations as well as English translations of previously untranslated works. The bibliographies in all the dramatist profiles have been updated and annotated.

The 538 essays on dramatists, alphabetically arranged, include playwrights as ancient as Aeschylus and Euripides and as recent as Jon Robin Baitz and Sarah Kane. Geographically, the largest number of dramatists are North Americans, including 142 from the United States and 6 from Canada. The next largest group of playwrights are associated with the British Isles: 132 from England, 26 from Ireland, 3 from Scotland, and 2 from Wales. In Western and southern Europe, France is represented by 67 dramatists; Germany and Prussia by 47; Italy, Sicily, and Rome by 35; Spain and Portugal by 34; Austria and the Austro-

Hungarian Empire by 21; Switzerland by 6; and Greece by 5. Of the Scandinavian nations, Denmark is represented by 6 dramatists, Sweden by 5, Norway by 4, and Finland by 2. Iceland and the Netherlands are each represented by 1 dramatist. In Eastern and southeastern Europe, the Soviet Union, Russia, and the Ukraine are represented by 27 dramatists, followed by Poland and Silesia with 11, Czechoslovakia and Bohemia with 5, Hungary with 4, Romania with 2, and Yugoslavia with 1. Africa is represented by 15 ancient and modern dramatists, including 4 from Nigeria, and 1 each from modern Algeria, Kenya, Egypt, and South Africa. Asian dramatists include 4 from Japan, 2 from India, and 1 each from China and the Philippines. Australia is represented by 5 dramatists, with one from New Zealand. Latin American dramatists included 4 from Mexico, 2 from Argentina, and 1 each from Chile and Guatemala. The West Indies is represented by 9 dramatists, including 2 from Cuba, and one each from Martinique, St. Lucia, Trinidad, and Puerto Rico.

The 538 dramatists, who have been selected to reflect those most often addressed in North American secondary and university curricula, include 45 women, more than 15 openly gay writers, 14 African Americans, 3 Asian Americans, 1 Native American, and 1 Latino. The work of minority group dramatists as well as those out of the mainstream are covered in essays on topics such as Asian American drama, Latino drama, Native American drama, American regional theater, and New York theater. Lesser-known world dramas are covered in essays on subjects such as postcolonial theater, theater of the Islamic world, and the drama of Asia, Africa, and Latin America.

Every essay on a dramatist provides such ready-reference material as birth and death dates and places and lists of the author's major dramatic works (with dates of first production and publication). Each essay opens with a brief survey of the author's publications in literary forms other than drama, a summary of the writer's professional achievements and awards, an extended biographical sketch that centers on the writer's development as a dramatist, and an extensive critical analysis of the writer's major dramatic works. Each major analysis of a play is headed by the work's

title. Following this discussion is a list of major publications in fields other than drama and an annotated bibliography of critical works about the author.

The format of the articles is standardized to allow predictable and easy access to the types of information of interest to a variety of users. Each dramatist essay is broken into the following sections:

Principal drama: Lists the author's major plays through mid-2002, including titles and dates of production (pr.) and publication (pb.).

Other literary forms: Describes the author's work in genres other than drama, helping students to identify those authors known primarily as dramatists, as opposed to those whose work in other genres has garnered equal or greater fame.

Achievements: Lists honors, awards, and other tangible recognitions, as well as a summation of the writer's influence and contributions to drama and literature, where appropriate.

Biography: A condensed biographical sketch with vital information from birth through (if applicable) death or the author's current activities.

Analysis: An overview of the dramatist's favorite themes, genres, and development, leading into subsections on major plays or aspects of the person's work as a dramatist.

Other major works: Principal works in other genres, by genre and, within each genre-subsection, chronologically listed by year of publication.

Bibliography: Secondary print sources for further study, annotated to assist students and librarians in evaluating focus and usefulness. All these bibliographies have been updated and annotated.

Contributor byline: Name of the original contributor of the article and that of the scholar who updated it, where relevant.

In the 538 dramatist profiles, the dates of both first production (pr.) and first publication (pb.) are given for each play mentioned, whether in the principal drama listing or in the discussion of the dramatist's life and works. On first mention of a play, the drama's title and its first production and first publications dates are provided, as well as the title of the first English translation and its date of publication or first production (whichever is earlier), where appropriate.

In overview essays—which focus on broader issues rather than individual dramatists—on first mention of a play, its title and its first production or publication date are given, as well as the first English translation and its date of publication, as appropriate.

The 64 overview essays are arranged under broad subject headings in volume 8. They cover dramatic traditions in the United States, the British Isles, Europe, Africa, Asia, Australia, and other parts of the world, as well as various genres and techniques. Among the 27 new overview essays added to this edition are original articles on Native American Drama, American Regional Theater, Asian Drama, Southeast Asian Drama, Melodrama, Deaf Theater, Feminist Theater, Political Theater, and Gay and Lesbian Theater. Of the original overview essays, 26 have been updated to reflect current trends in the theater. These revised essays include African American Drama, Irish Drama, French Drama Since the 1600's, Chinese Drama, Australian Drama, Musical Drama, and Experimental Theater.

All the essays in the set have individual bibliographies that have been annotated and updated. Finally, all the articles are signed by the scholars who wrote and or updated them.

Appendix material in volume 8 includes lists of major dramatic awards (Pulitzer Prize in Drama and Obie and Tony awards), a detailed time line of world drama history, a glossary of dramatic terms and movements, and an annotated bibliography. This bibliography differs from those in the essays in covering broader themes.

Additional perspectives on the individual dramatists who appear in this set are provided by a chronological listing (by birth dates), a geographical index that separates dramatists by the geographical areas in which they have lived or worked, and a categorized index that separates dramatists by the movements, genres, cultures, or historical ages represented by their works. A subject index to all eight volumes rounds out the set.

This set would not have been possible without the efforts of the many academicians and area experts who contributed to both the original editions and this revised edition. Wherever possible, the original contributors of these essays were invited to update their work. The names and affiliations of all contributors are listed in the first volume of this set. This edition also owes much to its editor, Carl Rollyson, Baruch College, City University of New York.

CONTRIBUTORS

Carl Rollyson
Editor, Second Revised Edition

Claude Abraham
University of California, Davis

Howard C. Adams
Frostburg State University

Patrick Adcock
Henderson State University

Jacob H. Adler
Purdue University

Thomas P. Adler
Purdue University

Kwaku Amoabeng
*State University of New York,
   Stony Brook*

Elba Andrade
The Citadel

Andrew J. Angyal
Elon College

Norman Araujo
Boston College

Joseph R. Arboleda
Original Contributor

Stanley Archer
Texas A&M University

Frank Ardolino
University of Hawaii at Manoa

Gerald S. Argetsinger
Rochester Institute of Technology

Ricardo Arias
Fordham University

Edwin T. Arnold
Appalachian State University

Herbert A. Arnold
Wesleyan University

Bryan Aubrey
Independent Scholar

Philip Bader
Independent Scholar

Ehrhard Bahr
University of California, Los Angeles

William M. Baillie
Bloomsburg State College

Margaret Ann Baker
Iowa State University

William Baker
Northern Illinois University

Lowell A. Bangerter
Original Contributor

Thomas Banks
Ohio Northern University

Henry J. Baron
Calvin College

Theodore Baroody
American Psychological Foundation

Milly S. Barranger
*University of North Carolina,
   Chapel Hill*

David Barratt
Independent Scholar

Jean-Pierre Barricelli
University of California, Riverside

Thomas Barry
Himeji Dokkyo University

Fiora A. Bassanese
University of Massachusetts, Boston

Ronald H. Bayes
Original Contributor

Kirk H. Beetz
Original Contributor

Rebecca Bell-Metereau
Original Contributor

Jacques Benay
Original Contributor

Robert Bensen
Hartwick College

Richard P. Benton
Trinity College

Milton Berman
University of Rochester

Anthony Bernardo
Cecil Community College

Antony van Beysterveldt
Original Contributor

Cynthia A. Bily
Adrian College

Margaret Boe Birns
New York University

Nicholas Birns
New School University

Franz G. Blaha
University of Nebraska, Lincoln

Robert Blake
Elon University

Keith Bowen
Original Contributor

Jay Boyer
Arizona State University

Harold Branam
Savannah State University

Gerhard Brand
*California State University,
    Los Angeles*

Timothy Brennan
University of Minnesota

Ward W. Briggs
University of South Carolina

J. R. Broadus
Original Contributor

David Brodsky
Independent Scholar

Kenneth Brown
*Northwestern Oklahoma State
    University*

Mitzi Brunsdale
Mayville State College

Hallman B. Bryant
Clemson University

Lorne M. Buchman
California College of Arts & Crafts

Elizabeth Buckmaster
Pennsylvania State University

Suzanne Burgoyne
University of Missouri, Columbia

Donald Burness
Franklin Pierce College

Douglas R. Butler
Iowa State University

Edmund J. Campion
University of Tennessee

Pamela Canal
Original Contributor

Ayne Cantrell
Middle Tennessee State University

Ralph S. Carlson
Azusa Pacific University

Susan Carlson
Iowa State University

John Carpenter
University of Michigan

Thomas Gregory Carpenter
Lipscomb University

Linda M. Carter
Morgan State University

Frank P. Casa
University of Michigan

Carole A. Champagne
*University of Maryland, Eastern
    Shore*

Michael M. Chemers
University of Washington

Vera V. Chernysheva
Independent Scholar

C. L. Chua
California State University, Fresno

Alfred Cismaru
Original Contributor

John R. Clark
University of South Florida

Lorna Clarke
Original Contributor

Ada Coe
University of California, Davis

Richard N. Coe
Original Contributor

Lina L. Cofresí
Original Contributor

John J. Conlon
University of Massachusetts, Boston

Robert T. Corum, Jr.
Independent Scholar

Natalia Costa-Zalessow
San Francisco State University

Edward V. Coughlin
Original Contributor

John W. Crawford
Henderson State University

Carol Croxton
University of Southern Colorado

LouAnn Faris Culley
Kansas State University

Sandra Messinger Cypess
*State University of New York,
    Binghamton*

J. D. Daubs
Independent Scholar

J. Madison Davis
Original Contributor

William A. Davis
University of Delaware

Frank Day
Clemson University

Joan F. Dean
Original Contributor

Elliott A. Denniston
Missouri Southern State College

Giuseppe C. DiScipio
Original Contributor

Margaret A. Dodson
Independent Scholar

Lillian Doherty
University of Maryland

Jill Dolan
University of Texas at Austin

Henry J. Donaghy
Idaho State University

Reade W. Dornan
Original Contributor

Susan Duffy
Original Contributor

Ayne C. Durham
Original Contributor

Paul F. Dvorak
Original Contributor

Stefan Dziemianowicz
Independent Scholar

Ted R. Ellis III
East Carolina University

Jon Erickson
Ohio State University

Thomas L. Erskine
Salisbury University

Manuel A. Esteban
California State University, Bakersfield

Christoph Eykman
Original Contributor

Jane Falco
Virginia Polytechnic Institute and State University

Rodney Farnsworth
Original Contributor

Patricia A. Farrant
Independent Scholar

James Feast
Baruch College, City University of New York

Jarre Fees
Independent Scholar

Thomas R. Feller
Independent Scholar

Gastón F. Fernández
Original Contributor

Gerald A. Fetz
University of Montana, Missoula

John W. Fiero
University of Louisiana at Lafayette

Edward Fiorelli
St. John's University

Benjamin Fisher
University of Mississippi

Seymour L. Flaxman
City University of New York

Anne Fletcher
Southern Illinois University, Carbondale

Howard L. Ford
University of North Texas

Robert J. Forman
St. John's University

Margot K. Frank
Randolph-Macon Women's College

William Frankfather
Independent Scholar

Lawrence S. Friedman
Indiana University

Steven H. Gale
Kentucky State University

Janet E. Gardner
University of Massachusetts, Dartmouth

Keith Garebian
Independent Scholar

Daniel H. Garrison
Northwestern University

Henry A. Garrity
St. Lawrence University

Edward V. Geist
Original Contributor

U. Henry Gerlach
University of Illinois

Donna Gerstenberger
University of Washington

Perry Gethner
University of Chicago

Scott Giantvalley
Original Contributor

Richard B. Gidez
Pennsylvania State University

Jill Barnum Gidmark
University of Minnesota

E. Bryan Gillespie
Stetson University

Irene Gnarra
Kean College of New Jersey

Eleanor R. Goldhar
Independent Scholar

C. Peter Goslett
Independent Scholar

Peter W. Graham
Virginia Polytechnic Institute and State University

William Grange
Florida Southern College

Sharon L. Gravett
Valdosta State College

Leah Green
The Kansas City Star

Christopher Griffin
Original Contributor

William C. Griffin
Appalachian State University

Ira Grushow
Franklin and Marshall College

Clara Györgyey
Original Contributor

Franz P. Haberl
Original Contributor

Angela Hague
Middle Tennessee State University

Elsie Galbreath Haley
Metropolitan State College of Denver

Shelley P. Haley
Original Contributor

Jay Halio
University of Delaware

Martha T. Halsey
Pennsylvania State University

Gertrude K. Hamilton
St. John's University

Robert D. Hamner
Hardin-Simmons University

Klaus D. Hanson
Original Contributor

Maryhelen C. Harmon
Original Contributor

Steven Hart
Original Contributor

Zia Hasan
King Faisal University

Robert W. Haynes
Texas A&M International University

William J. Heim
University of South Florida

Gordon Henderson
West Chester University

Michael Hennessy
Southwest Texas State University

Janet S. Hertzbach
Gettysburg College

Ann R. Hill
Original Contributor

Holly Hill
John Jay College

Peter C. Holloran
New England Historical Association

John R. Holmes
Franciscan University of Steubenville

Joan Hope
Independent Scholar

Glenn Hopp
Howard Payne University

William L. Howard
Chicago State University

Kenneth A. Howe
Original Contributor

Eril Barnett Hughes
East Central University

E. D. Huntley
Appalachian State University

Mary Hurd
East Tennessee State University

William Hutchings
University of Alabama, Birmingham

Allen E. Hye
Wright State University

Evelyn Uhrhan Irving
Original Contributor

Miglena Ivanova
*University of Illinois at Urbana-
Champaign*

Per Schelde Jacobsen
Original Contributor

Paul A. Jagasich
Original Contributor

Philip K. Jason
U.S. Naval Academy

Vera Jiji
Independent Scholar

Millard T. Jones
McNeese State University

David Jortner
University of Pittsburgh

Rhona Justice-Malloy
Central Michigan University

B. A. Kachur
University of Missouri, St. Louis

Albert E. Kalson
Purdue University

Irma M. Kashuba
Original Contributor

Hideyuki Kasuga
Aichi Prefectural University

Nancy Kearns
Mercer University, Atlanta

Richard Keenan
*University of Maryland, Eastern
Shore*

Howard A. Kerner
Polk Community College

Leigh Husband Kimmel
Independent Scholar

Arthur Kincaid
Original Contributor

Anne Mills King
Prince George's Community College

Charles L. King
Original Contributor

B. G. Knepper
Original Contributor

Jane E. Knox
Original Contributor

Grove Koger
Boise Public Library

Matthew J. Kopans
University of Pittsburgh

Philip Krummrich
Original Contributor

Mildred C. Kuner
*Hunter College, City University of
New York*

Lieselotte A. Kuntz
Original Contributor

Joseph E. Laggini
Rutgers University

Ananda Lal
Independent Scholar

Frank S. Lambasa
Original Contributor

Gregory W. Lanier
University of West Florida

Carrol Lasker
*State University of New York,
    Stony Brook*

Kathleen Latimer
Original Contributor

Norman Lavers
Arkansas State University

Carolina Donadio Lawson
Original Contributor

Katherine Lederer
Southwest Missouri State University

John M. Lee
Original Contributor

Raymond LePage
George Mason University

Ralph Ley
Rutgers University

Emanuele Licastro
Original Contributor

Randall W. Listerman
Miami University

Corinna del Greco Lobner
Independent Scholar

Stanley Longman
University of Georgia

Janet Lorenz
Independent Scholar

Dieter P. Lotze
Original Contributor

Michael Loudon
Eastern Illinois University

Bernadette Flynn Low
*Community College of Baltimore
    County*

John R. Lucas
Brown University

Carol Luther
*Pellissippi State Technical Community
    College*

R. C. Lutz
University of the Pacific

Robert McClenaghan
Independent Scholar

Michael McCully
Bloomsburg University

John F. McDiarmid
New College

James C. MacDonald
Humber College

Richard D. McGhee
Arkansas State University

Sheila McKenna
University of Pittsburgh

Alan L. McLeod
Rider University

S. Thomas Mack
University of South Carolina, Aiken

Christopher R. McRae
Original Contributor

Christina Hunt Mahony
Catholic University

Cherie Maiden
Furman University

James E. Maloney
Original Contributor

Stella Maloney
Independent Scholar

Franco Manca
University of Nevada, Reno

Martha Manheim
Original Contributor

Barry Mann
Independent Scholar

Lois A. Marchino
University of Texas at El Paso

Jonathan Marks
American Repertory Theatre

Patricia Marks
Valdosta State College

Joseph Marohl
Original Contributor

John L. Marsden
Indiana University of Pennsylvania

Anne Laura Mattrella
Original Contributor

Richard A. Mazzara
Original Contributor

Walter J. Meserve
Independent Scholar

Siegfried Mews
*University of North Carolina,
    Chapel Hill*

Nicholas J. Meyerhofer
Saint Mary's College

Julia M. Meyers
Duquesne University

Jennifer Michaels
Grinnell College

Vasa D. Mihailovich
*University of North Carolina,
    Chapel Hill*

Andrea E. Miller
Independent Scholar

Raymond Miller, Jr.
University of Delaware

Leslie B. Mittleman
*California State University,
Long Beach*

Christian H. Moe
*Southern Illinois University,
Carbondale*

Michael D. Moore
Wilfrid Laurier University

Michael G. Moran
Clemson University

Laurie P. Morrow
Louisiana State University

Robert E. Morsberger
*California State Polytechnic
University, Pomona*

Gerald W. Morton
Auburn University, Montgomery

Anna Lydia Motto
Original Contributor

Barbara Mujica
Georgetown University

Mary C. Murphy
U.S. Naval Academy

Moses M. Nagy
Original Contributor

José María Naharro-Calderón
University of Maryland

Wayne Narey
Arkansas State University

Helen H. Naugle
Original Contributor

Gregory Nehler
Original Contributor

Anne Newgarden
Independent Scholar

Evelyn S. Newlyn
*Virginia Polytechnic Institute and
State University*

Hanh N. Nguyen
University of California, Riverside

Kirsten F. Nigro
Arizona State University

Sally Osborne Norton
University of Redlands

George O'Brien
Georgetown University

Robert H. O'Connor
North Dakota State University

Leslie O'Dell
Wilfrid Laurier University

Michael C. O'Neill
Wilkes College

Margarita Ortiz-Swetman
Original Contributor

Thórir Oskarsson
Independent Scholar

Elizabeth Spalding Otten
Independent Scholar

Robert M. Otten
Marymount University

Cóilín D. Owens
George Mason University

Philip Oxley
Original Contributor

Anthony F. R. Palmieri
George Mason University

David J. Parent
Independent Scholar

Sidney F. Parham
St. Cloud State University

James Allan Parr
Original Contributor

David B. Parsell
Furman University

Glenn Patterson
Independent Scholar

Lisë Pedersen
McNeese State University

Peter N. Pedroni
Miami University

Vibeke R. Petersen
Original Contributor

Peter Petro
University of British Columbia

H. Alan Pickrell
Emory & Henry College

Peter L. Podol
*Lock Haven University of
Pennsylvania*

Marjorie Podolsky
*Pennsylvania State University,
Behrend College*

John Povey
Original Contributor

Victoria Price
Lamar University

Maureen Puffer-Rothenberg
Valdosta State University

Diane Quinn
Original Contributor

Michael L. Quinn
University of Washington

Richard N. Ramsey
Original Contributor

Donald A. Randolph
Original Contributor

Bette Adams Reagan
Kutztown University of Pennsylvania

James R. Reece
University of Idaho

Steven Reese
Independent Scholar

Rosemary M. Canfield Reisman
Charleston Southern University

Helene M. Kastinger Riley
Original Contributor

J. Thomas Rimer
University of Pittsburgh

Theodosia Smith Robertson
Independent Scholar

James W. Robinson, Jr.
Independent Scholar

Carl Rollyson
Baruch College, City University of New York

Paul Rosefeldt
Delgado Community College

Joseph Rosenblum
University of North Carolina, Greensboro

Diane M. Ross
Independent Scholar

Robert Ross
University of Texas at Austin

Sven H. Rossel
University of Vienna

Patrizio Rossi
Original Contributor

Matthew C. Roudané
Independent Scholar

Valerie C. Rudolph
Purdue University

Victor Anthony Rudowski
Clemson University

Loren Ruff
Western Kentucky University

Irene Struthers Rush
Independent Scholar

Susan Rusinko
Bloomsburg University

Murray Sachs
Brandeis University

Claire Brandicourt Saint-Léon
Original Contributor

Jan St. Martin
Salisbury State College

Arthur M. Saltzman
Missouri Southern State College

Vicki A. Sanders
Riverside Military Academy

Francesca L. Savoia
Original Contributor

Barry Scherr
Dartmouth College

June Schlueter
Lafayette College

Fredericka A. Schmadel
Indiana State University

James Schmitt
Original Contributor

George C. Schoolfield
Yale University

Laurence Senelick
Original Contributor

Roberto Severino
Georgetown University

Walter Shear
Pittsburg State University

Chenliang Sheng
Northern Kentucky University

Richard J. Sherry
Asbury College

John C. Shields
Independent Scholar

Hugh Short
Original Contributor

Jack Shreve
Original Contributor

R. Baird Shuman
University of Illinois at Urbana-Champaign

K. M. Sibbald
Original Contributor

Thomas J. Sienkewicz
Monmouth College

Charles L. P. Silet
Iowa State University

Dale Silviria
University of California, Los Angeles

John D. Simons
Florida State University

Jan Sjåvik
University of Washington

Genevieve Slomski
Independent Scholar

Philip E. Smith II
University of Pittsburgh

Ingeborg H. Solbrig
Original Contributor

Madison U. Sowell
Brigham Young University

Jerry S. Spencer
University of Massachusetts

P. Jane Splawn
Purdue University

Jill Stapleton-Bergeron
Pellissippi State Technical Community College

August W. Staub
University of Georgia

Judith Steininger
Milwaukee School of Engineering

Anthony Stephenson
York University

Eric Sterling
Auburn University

Roger J. Stilling
Appalachian State University

Joseph H. Stodder
*California State Polytechnic
University, Pomona*

Ingo R. Stoehr
Kilgore College

Laura M. Stone
Original Contributor

Gerald H. Strauss
Bloomsburg University

Paul Stuewe
St. Jerome's University

George A. Sumnik
Independent Scholar

Charlene E. Suscavage
University of Southern Maine

Roy Arthur Swanson
University of Wisconsin

Glenn R. Swetman
Original Contributor

Edmund M. Taft
Independent Scholar

Ted T. Takaya
University of the Pacific

Daniel Taylor
Bethel College

Judith K. Taylor
Northern Kentucky University

Thomas J. Taylor
University of Akron

Hans Ternes
Lawrence University

Christopher J. Thaiss
George Mason University

Currie K. Thompson
Gettysburg College

Jonathan L. Thorndike
Belmont University

Ian C. Todd
Original Contributor

Rosco N. Tolman
Original Contributor

Edna M. Troiano
Original Contributor

E. F. J. Tucker
The Citadel

Janet G. Tucker
University of Arkansas

John Van Cleve
Mississippi State University

A. Gordon Van Ness III
University of South Carolina

Richard B. Vowles
University of Wisconsin

Mara R. Wade
University of Illinois

Doris Walters
Missouri Southern State College

Gordon Walters
Independent Scholar

Elissa B. Weaver
University of Chicago

Judith A. Weiss
Mount Allison University

James M. Welsh
Salisbury State University

Craig Werner
University of Wisconsin

Joan M. West
Original Contributor

David Wheeler
University of Southern Mississippi

David Allen White
Original Contributor

Duffield White
Wesleyan University

Barbara Wiedeman
Auburn University, Montgomery

Edwin W. Williams
East Tennessee State University

Eric Williams
Lehigh University

David Willinger
City College of New York

Robert F. Willson, Jr.
University of Missouri

Ann Wilson
University of Guelph

Thomas N. Winter
University of Nebraska

Barry B. Witham
Original Contributor

Eugene P. Wright
North Texas State University

Liliana Zancu
Original Contributor

Michael Zeitlin
University of Toronto

Harry Zohn
Brandeis University

Virpi Zuck
University of Oregon

CONTENTS

VOLUME 1

COMPLETE LIST OF CONTENTS

VOLUME 1

VOLUME 3

VOLUME 4

VOLUME 5

VOLUME 6

VOLUME 8

CRITICAL SURVEY

OF

DRAMA

A

KŌBŌ ABE

Born: Tokyo, Japan; March 7, 1924
Died: Tokyo, Japan; January 22, 1993

PRINCIPAL DRAMA

Seifuku, pr., pb. 1955

Yūrei wa koko ni iru, pr. 1958, pb. 1959 (*The Ghost is Here*, 1993)

Omae ni mo tsumi ga aru, pr., pb. 1965 (*You, Too, Are Guilty*, 1978)

Tomodachi, pr., pb. 1967 (*Friends*, 1969)

Bō ni natta otoko, pr., pb. 1969 (*The Man Who Turned into a Stick*, 1975)

Gikyoku zenshū, pb. 1970

Imeiji no tenrankai, pr. 1971 (pr. in U.S. as *The Little Elephant Is Dead*, 1979)

Mihitsu no koi, pr., pb. 1971 (*Involuntary Homicide*, 1993)

Gaido bukku, pr. 1971

Midoriiro no sutokkingu, pr., pb. 1974 (*The Green Stockings*, 1993)

Ue: Shin doreigari, pr., pb. 1975

Three Plays, pb. 1993

OTHER LITERARY FORMS

A man of myriad talents, Kōbō Abe first established himself in the literary world as a novelist, but his reputation rests almost equally on his dramatic works. His first published work, in 1947, was a collection of poetry entitled *Mumei shishū* (collection of nameless poems). His best-known novel is *Suna no onna* (1962; *The Woman in the Dunes*, 1964), and his *Daiyon kanpyōki* (1958-1959, serial; 1959, book; *Inter Ice Age 4*, 1970) is science fiction. Abe also wrote short stories, some of which are collected in *Four Stories by Kōbō Abe* (1973), political essays, screenplays, film scripts, and film criticism.

ACHIEVEMENTS

Kōbō Abe received the Second Postwar Literary Prize (1951) for his short story "Akai mayu" (1950; "The Red Cocoon," 1966). Later in the same year, he was given the twenty-fifth Akutagawa Prize for the title story in his collection *Kabe* (1951; walls), a surrealistic work. The 1967 his play *Friends* was awarded the Tanizaki Jun'ichirō Prize. For most of the forty years preceding his death in 1993, Abe was a central figure among avant-garde artists in Japan. In 1975, Columbia University conferred on him the honorary degree Doctor of Humane Letters. He was frequently mentioned as a likely Nobel Prize candidate, but his death in 1993 prevented realization of that honor.

BIOGRAPHY

Although Kōbō (Kimifusa) Abe's parents lived in Manchuria, China, where his father worked as a doctor, he was born in Tokyo in 1924 because his father had brought the family back to Japan in order to conduct some research. His mother, like his father, was from the northern Japanese island of Hokkaido, and she had written novels as a young woman. The young Abe and his mother moved to Hokkaido temporarily in 1931 to avoid the Japanese invasion of the Chinese mainland.

Both Manchuria and Hokkaido are important in that they represent the only frontier lands that many Japanese would ever have the opportunity to experience, and they were also the only places where the significance of "being Japanese" was not a given. Those living in these marginal places were not completely excluded nor were they wholly accepted by mainstream Japanese society. This fact is reflected in Abe's writings, in which he portrays Manchuria as a

Kōbō Abe (Library of Congress)

tional detachment. He remarked jokingly that he was allowed to graduate only on the condition that he never practice medicine. Abe began writing fiction upon his graduation from medical school. His first long work, *Owarishi michi shirube ni* (the road sign at the end of the road) was published in 1948.

When Abe was in his early twenties, he met and married Machiko Yamada, who would be his lifelong companion and artistic collaborator. A brilliant artist in her own right, she designed the covers for most of Abe's books as well as sets for the Abe Studio productions. They had one child, a daughter, Neri, who became a physician and writer in Tokyo.

In Manchuria the concept of the "harmony of the five races" had instilled in Abe a sense of the equality of all peoples, but when he watched the behavior of the Japanese, which contrasted so greatly with what he had been taught, he felt frustration and anger. This experience may have contributed to his attraction to the Japanese Communist Party, which he joined. Even before his writing began to receive literary awards, Abe was involved with party operations. Trips to Eastern Europe in the late 1950's provided direct exposure to a communistic society, and he became disillusioned. It was, however, in this part of the world that his work first received international attention. Abe's play *Friends*, the story of a man whose home is invaded by unwanted visitors, slipped past the censors and provided its audiences with an allegorical comment on their own situation. His criticism of the Japanese Communist Party led to his expulsion from the party.

Following a period of poverty and hardship in which he and his young wife lived in Tokyo and sold charcoal and pickles on the street, the 1950's proved to be very productive and increasingly prosperous for Abe. He published more than a dozen short stories, four major novels, a collection of political essays, and a collection of film criticism. He also staged seven plays, released a film that he had written, and broadcast a dozen radio plays or teleplays.

The 1960's were also successful, and his work included the works for which he is best known: the stage play *Friends* and the novel *The Woman in the Dunes*. Other major works of the period include the

bleak, flat, hostile place and Hokkaido as a land of promise, a Japanese "wild west."

Though Abe grew up in a colonial setting, his school books were those issued by the Ministry of Education in Japan, so he had read textbook descriptions about the landscape of Japan with its mountains, rivers, and cherry blossoms, but in Manchuria, he knew only plains and no cherry trees. On occasions when he was scolded by teachers, he was told that "a child back home would never do such a thing," reinforcing in Abe's mind the fact that he was not a typical Japanese. Abe has commented on how he grew to doubt the significance of belonging to any nation or to any society.

In 1943, Abe entered medical school in Tokyo at the strong urging of his father, and although Abe took no pleasure in his studies, the training may have contributed to his ability to make precise descriptions and to look on situations and on people with emo-

novels *Inter Ice Age 4*, *Tanin no kao* (1964; *The Face of Another*, 1966), and *Moetsukita chizu* (1967; *The Ruined Map*, 1969); the stage play *You, Too, Are Guilty*; and the film versions of *The Woman in the Dunes* and *The Face of Another*.

In 1971, Abe formed his own theater troupe, the Abe Studio. For the next seven years, the studio held one or two productions a year, most of them written by Abe. He worked not only on scripts but also on sets, lighting, direction, and musical scores. Abe continued his work in various genres throughout the 1980's, but in the early 1990's, his health began to fail. The last novel he would see in print, *Kangarū nōto* (*The Kangaroo Notebook*, 1996), was published in 1991. In 1992, he was hospitalized and died of heart failure on January 22, 1993.

ANALYSIS

Kōbō Abe's background may have been a prime influence in his coming to occupy a central position among Japanese avant-garde writers. Though he was born in Japan, being brought up in Manchuria isolated him from mainstream Japanese life. The sense of alienation and utter isolation he experienced provided one of the most powerful themes that would emerge in almost all of his work. Many of Abe's sources were not Japanese; therefore, his work appealed to an international audience, and a substantial number of his plays were translated into English and other languages.

Although Abe's earlier works were relatively structured and linear, they were characterized by social satire, allegory, and black humor. The later experimental plays moved away from allegorical social criticism toward allegories involving dream imagery, and some of the later plays were freely created in rehearsals.

SEIFUKU

Two themes that would be evident in much of Abe's later work, the censure of others' suffering and the rejection of what Abe felt to be Japan's self-victimization, are particularly clear in this 1955 play, *Seifuku* (uniform). In this allegorical play, a broken old soldier who wears the ragged uniform of a colonial police officer and is stranded at a port in North

Korea in 1945 represents Japan's colonial experience, which left the nation impoverished and unable to shed its disgrace. In the old solider, the play depicts the Japanese colonial spirit, which has been broken and is stranded on a foreign shore, unable to return home. All the characters fulfill an allegorical role: the innocent youth of Korea, the conscience of Japan, and the spirit of Japanese womanhood, symbol of hearth and home.

FRIENDS

In *Friends*, his most successful play, Abe critiques Japanese communal values, which he views as stifling of individual creativity. One evening, a family of strangers bursts into the apartment of a man who enjoys his solitude in order, they say, to save him from his loneliness. Although he resists their forced companionship, he is unable to remove them from his home. Finally, he dies, a victim of their aggressive communality. The play portrays the consequences of social pressures and the kind of mandatory communal spirit a communist totalitarianism would inflict on the citizenry. Abe had broken with the Communist Party just a few years before the play appeared.

THE MAN WHO TURNED INTO A STICK

Abe dealt with the theme of the exploitation of one group of people by another in a number of his plays, but perhaps the consequences of this behavior are most clearly investigated in *The Man Who Turned into a Stick*. Abe explained the play as depicting the alienation occurring in modern society, in which a sticklike man who has no reason for existence except being used by others is punished from within himself precisely for being a stick. The man turns into an actual stick, falling from the roof of a department store as his son watches. Two characters have to find the stick and take it with them to Hell, where they are employed specifically to gather up all the sticks into which many people have turned. The message is clear: In a world in which people are merely tools—the source of another's livelihood—there is no room for mercy or sentimentality.

THE GREEN STOCKINGS

By depicting characters who could not possibly exist, Abe intended to administer a shock to the theatrical form. *The Green Stockings* moves away from

Abe's socially critical works toward interior-oriented plays with dreamlike allegorical qualities with no obvious reference to the exterior, real world. Pajama-clad Man stands center stage against the backdrop of a dreamscape of an immense wild field. Man, initially a narrator, turns into a nameless main character, a go-between for the performers and the audience.

Man is obsessed with lingerie and, in an effort to transcend everyday existence, raids clotheslines for items, including green stockings, on Mondays and Fridays. Not satisfied, Man attempts suicide, and although a doctor offers him a new life as a grass-eating man, his emptiness prevails. The play poses the difficult question of whether reality, fiction, and dream are distinguishable even in one's mind.

UE: SHIN DOREIGARI

Built around a hoax in which two characters pretend to be an exotic species of animal, *Ue: Shin doreigari* (the new slave hunters) may be the quintessential Abe Studio production. A professor receives a box containing a pair of *ue* along with instructions and a note reading "Limited only by your imagination! You may put these remarkable creatures to any use you wish." Actually, the *ue* are the sister of the professor's daughter-in-law and her husband, participating in a game to extort money from the professor by his son. At first dubious, the professor succumbs to a yearning to believe that animals that look just like human beings could exist. The fake *ue* become human, and the rest of the household also assume animal identities that correspond to their latent qualities.

THE LITTLE ELEPHANT IS DEAD

The full Japanese title for this play when it was performed in the United States is *Kozō wa shinda: Nikutai + ongaku + kotoba + imeiji no shi* (*The Little Elephant Is Dead: Bodies + music + words = image poem*). This title demonstrates what happens when words are supplanted by integrated but diffuse information. As Abe's last play, it provides a good means of measuring the departures from his earliest works as well as the continuities. The play is especially difficult to comprehend, for the underlying "logic" is not logic, but the illogic of a world of dreams. *The Little Elephant Is Dead* comes as close to a purely gestural theater as is possible.

OTHER MAJOR WORKS

LONG FICTION: *Owarishi michi shirube ni*, 1948; *Baberu no tō no tanuki*, 1951; *Mahō no chōku*, 1951; *Kiga dōmei*, 1954; *Kemonotachi wa kokyō o mezasu*, 1957; *Daiyon kanpyōki*, 1958-1959 (serial), 1959 (book; *Inter Ice Age 4*, 1970); *Ishi no me*, 1960; *Suna no onna*, 1962 (*The Woman in the Dunes*, 1964); *Tanin no kao*, 1964 (*The Face of Another*, 1966); *Moetsukita chizu*, 1967 (*The Ruined Map*, 1969); *Hako otoko*, 1973 (*The Box Man*, 1974); *Mikkai*, 1977 (*Secret Rendezvous*, 1979); *Hakobune sakura-maru*, 1984 (*The Ark Sakura*, 1988); *Kangarū nōto*, 1991 (*The Kangaroo Notebook*, 1996); *Tobu otoko*, 1994.

SHORT FICTION: *Kabe*, 1951; *Suichū toshi*, 1964; *Yume no tōbō*, 1968; *Four Stories by Kōbō Abe*, 1973; *Beyond the Curve*, 1991.

POETRY: *Mumei shishū*, 1947.

NONFICTION: *Uchinaru henkyō*, 1971.

MISCELLANEOUS: *Abe Kobo zenshū*, 1972-1997 (30 volumes).

BIBLIOGRAPHY

Goodman, David. *Japanese Drama and Culture in the 1960's: The Return of the Gods*. Armonk: M. E. Sharpe, 1988. This translation of five plays representative of the period provides commentary by a leading Japanese critic. The central thesis is that the decade of the 1960's was characterized by disillusionment with the radical politics of the pre-World War II era and a quest for viable alternatives.

Olsen, Lance. *Ellipse of Uncertainty: An Introduction to Post-modern Fantasy*. New York: Greenwood Press, 1987. The first study to examine the intersection of fantasy and postmodernism in literature. Olsen develops working definitions of these terms and then analyses various postmodernist fantasy works. Accessible to intellectually mature undergraduates.

Shields, Nancy K. *Fake Fish: The Theater of Kōbō Abe*. New York: Weatherhill, 1996. Provides plot summaries of the plays that were produced in the Abe Studio, the theater group that Abe began in 1971. Also discusses techniques used and themes developed in the plays and provides descriptions of Abe's rehearsal sessions.

Yamanoguchi, Hisaaki. "In Search of Identity: Abe Kōbō and Ōe Kenzaburō." In *The Search for Authenticity in Modern Japanese Literature.* Cambridge, England: Cambridge University Press, 1978. Compares and contrasts works of Abe Kōbō

and Ōe Kenzaburō, both of whom are concerned with the solitude of men and women alienated from contemporary society and suffering from a loss of identity. Notes that Abe shares a greater kinship with contemporary European writers such as Franz Kafka than other Japanese writers do.

Victoria Price

KJELD ABELL

Born: Ribe, Denmark; August 25, 1901
Died: Copenhagen, Denmark; March 5, 1961

PRINCIPAL DRAMA

Enken i spejlet, pr. 1934 (ballet scenario)
Melodien, der blev væk, pr., pb. 1935 (lyrics by Sven Møller Kristensen; *The Melody That Got Lost*, 1939)
Eva aftjener sin barnepligt, pr., pb. 1936
Anna Sophie Hedvig, pb. 1938, pr. 1939 (English translation, 1944)
Judith, pr., pb. 1940
Dronning går igen, pr. 1943, pb. 1955 (*The Queen on Tour*, 1953)
Silkeborg, pr., pb. 1946
Dage på en sky, pr., pb. 1947 (*Days on a Cloud*, 1964)
Ejendommen matr. nr. 267 østre kvarter, pr., pb. 1948
Miss Plinckby's kabale: Eller, En Juninat, pr., pb. 1949
Vetsera blomstrer ikke for enhver, pr., pb. 1950
Den blå pekingeser, pr., pb. 1954
Andersen: Eller, Hans livs eventyr, pr., pb. 1955
Kameliadamen, pr., pb. 1959 (based on Alexandre Dumas, *fils*'s novel *La Dame aux camélias*)
Skriget, pr., pb. 1961

OTHER LITERARY FORMS

In addition to writing his own plays, Kjeld Abell translated several others into Danish. Two of those, *Columbe* (pr. 1951; *Mademoiselle Colombe*, 1954) and *Beckett: Ou, L'Honneur de Dieu* (pr., pb. 1959;

Beckett: Or, The Honor of God, 1962), were by Jean Anouilh. Others were Robert E. Sherwood's *Idiot's Delight* (pr., pb. 1936), Jean Giraudoux's *Pour Lucrèce* (wr. 1944, pr., pb. 1953; *Duel of Angels*, 1958), and William Shakespeare's *A Midsummer Night's Dream* (pr. c. 1595-1596). Abell wrote scenarios for ballets, screenplays for motion pictures, and numerous revue sketches.

Abell wrote a children's book, *Paraplyernes oprør* (1937; the revolt of the umbrellas), which he also illustrated, several short tales, and a small number of published poems. His most significant nondramatic writings were many essays on the nature of the theater, especially the autobiographical *Teaterstrejf i paaskevejr* (1948; theater sketches in Easter weather) and two travel books, *Fodnoter i støvet* (1951; footnotes in the dust) and *De tre fra Minikoi* (1957; *Three from Minikoi*, 1960). The latter is a fanciful account of the author's two trips to China, while the former travel book chronicles his first journey to the Far East in 1950-1951.

ACHIEVEMENTS

Along with the playwright-pastor Kaj Munk, Kjeld Abell was known as one of Denmark's leading dramatists of the twentieth century. After Munk's death at the hands of the Nazis in 1944, Abell stood alone as the prime standard-bearer of Danish theater. His career spanned more than a quarter of a century, and his artistic presence was only increased by the fact that he was active in so many creative fields—literature, ballet, film, painting, and journalism. Not even his critics would deny that Abell's consistent production dominated the middle third of the twentieth century, and no one has emerged to assume his mantle in the subsequent years.

While Abell, like his kindred spirit Hans Christian Andersen, was thoroughly Danish in his style and outlook, he enriched his nation's culture by incorporating other European impulses into his work. His exposure to Sergei Diaghilev's Ballets Russes in Paris and his subsequent work in Copenhagen as assistant to George Balanchine, Diaghilev's last ballet master, helped bring the Diaghilev style to the Danish stage: a synthesis of several creative forces—music, art, choreography, athleticism—to produce a unified artistic whole. The French presence was also felt in Abell's indebtedness to the great director Louis Jouvet and the playwright Jean Giraudoux, both of whose work he admired. The works of other Scandinavian playwrights, such as August Strindberg and Nordahl Grieg, are also represented in Abell's œuvre, as are the foreign playwrights whose works he translated for the Danish stage.

Another well-deserved title for Abell was that of liberator—he, more than anyone else, has been credited with freeing Danish theater from its slavish adherence to the naturalistic tradition. Even though few Danish plays were written in the naturalistic style, virtually all those produced in the first part of the twentieth century followed the strict naturalistic demands: almost photographic reproduction of "real life," strong audience identification with the characters onstage, the imaginary "fourth wall" to create the illusion that the audience is not witnessing a play but is privy to a "real" event, and the Aristotelian unities of time, place, and action. Naturalism represented more than a convention; it had become a form of artistic tyranny, and though others spoke out, Abell took the lead in liberating the Danish stage from its strictures.

The form of his plays is open and innovative. His works are loosely constructed (too loosely, said his critics) and episodic, particularly his debut piece, *The Melody That Got Lost*, which teems with song, dance, and revue-style humor. Abell's later plays appeal to the senses, as light, color, music, movement, sym-

bols, and the spoken word blend to encourage the most important element of his theater: fantasy. Many of his plays possess a dreamlike quality that destroys the bonds of time and space and frees the spectator to enjoy a subjective theater experience.

Abell was also innovative in the content of his plays, the consistent theme of which is freedom. The three stages of his dramatic career proclaim three types of freedom: from bourgeois culture, from political tyranny, and from fear and isolation. Because he fought for freedom, not with heavy-handed rhetoric but with grace, wit, and nostalgia, one critic has aptly named him "the revolutionary romanticist," while another called him "an artist with a witticism in one hand and a smoking bomb in the other."

In freeing Danish culture from the hold of naturalism, Abell gave it a new concept of theater. Theater, he said, possessed a "soul," born of the communication between stage and audience. Questions posed by the playwright and suggestively transmitted through dialogue, movement, and symbols are answered only when the audience is an active participant in the experience of theater, "the fantastic sanctuary of free thought."

BIOGRAPHY

Kjeld Abell's life was marked by controversy and contradictions. Called Denmark's leading modern dramatist, he was also at times vilified by the public for his leftist political sympathies and mocked by the literary critics for his strangely symbolic, highly personal plays. Friends and critics alike seemed divided about Abell's true calling as an artist, and the playwright himself did little to resolve their questions. On the one hand, Abell was called "above all a playwright of ideas," on the other, "a great writer for the theater but a weak thinker." Both Abell's moody, capricious temperament and his unwillingness to give an unambiguous explanation of his art contributed to the paradoxical quality that marked his thirty-year career in the theater.

Abell was born August 25, 1901, in the provincial town of Ribe on the Danish west coast. The son of a schoolteacher, he dutifully completed his studies in economics and political science at Copenhagen University, but his previous work at the Royal Academy of Art and a growing fascination with the theater exerted a greater hold on him. Above all, it was a 1920 production of Strindberg's *Spöksonaten* (pb. 1907; *The Ghost Sonata*, 1916) that served as the catalyst for Abell's lifelong commitment to theater. In *Teaterstrejf i paaskevejr*, he wrote of this experience, "I stopped thinking. In the brief moments in which the catastrophe took place, there was only time to feel. I felt with my eyes, my ears, my whole being."

Immediately after graduation in 1927, Abell was married and traveled to Paris for what amounted to an apprenticeship in the theater. He painted scenery and absorbed the artistic impulses of the Paris theater and ballet world. His entrée to Danish theater came in 1930-1931, as stage designer for Balanchine's guest season in Copenhagen, after which he worked for three years as a graphic artist with an advertising agency.

After writing the scenario for the experimental ballet *Enken i spejlet* (1934; the widow in the mirror),

Kjeld Abell (Kongelige Bibliotek)

Abell scored his professional breakthrough with the enormously successful *The Melody That Got Lost.* Other plays followed, as did film manuscripts, revue sketches, and leadership in Tivoli Gardens, Copenhagen's elegant amusement park. In 1944, Abell was forced to go underground in occupied Denmark and later in neutral Sweden. He had interrupted a production at the Royal Theater to bid his countrymen to pay tribute to the martyred Kaj Munk.

After the war, Abell's dramas continued to deal with current topics: the resistance movement, the dawning of the atomic age, and a sense of growing isolation, fear, and despair. The playwright and his wife were fascinated by the Far East and made three trips there that resulted in two colorful travel books. Abell's final plays continued to provide fine theater, but their often obscure symbolism left many critics and spectators confused about their meaning. To some, their proclamations of life and vitality seemed unconvincing and forced.

On March 5, 1961, Abell died suddenly of a stroke suffered at his home in Copenhagen. His final play *Skriget* (the scream), was produced posthumously in November of that year.

ANALYSIS

Common to virtually all Kjeld Abell's plays are the qualities of innovation, fantasy, and delight in the possibilities of the theater. Because of his background as a stage and graphic artist, his was a visually oriented drama, drawing on clever sets, stage tricks, and symbols to create the atmosphere he believed necessary to activate the audience. From sight gags in his early works through flashbacks, dream sequences, and the blending of past, present, and future time in his later ones, Abell consistently explored the rich possibilities of the stage. All too frequently, however, the formal structure of the play was subordinated to the author's pleasure in creating a theater experience. Throughout his career, Abell was praised for his devotion to the magic of theater while being faulted for unclear or unresolved plots.

Also common to most of his plays is the theme of rebellion against the prevailing social structure and the praise of human freedom and fellowship. Abell's variations on this theme roughly correspond to the concerns of Danish and European society in the 1930's, 1940's, and 1950's, and for each decade there is a single drama that best represents Abell's work of that era. *The Melody That Got Lost* reflects the concern of the 1930's with the tyranny of bourgeois life and the appeal of leftist politics as a possible alternative. *Anna Sophie Hedvig*, written only months before the outbreak of World War II, challenges the political tyranny and public apathy that marked the prewar and war years. Finally, *Den blå pekingeser* (the blue Pekinese) seeks to combat the feeling of fear and isolation that arose after the war and persisted into the 1950's.

THE MELODY THAT GOT LOST

Abell burst onto the scene in the 1930's with three social satires—a ballet, *Enken i spejlet*; a musical, *The Melody That Got Lost*; and a comedy, *Eva aftjener sin barnepligt* (Eve serves her childhood duty)—the second of which attained the greatest success and became the signature work of Abell's career. *The Melody That Got Lost* was staged at a small experimental theater in Copenhagen that was well suited to its light, colloquial tone. Danish audiences, accustomed as they were to ponderous, naturalistic productions, were enchanted by the inventive vitality of this work and responded by attending a record-breaking 594 performances.

The play, which has two acts containing twenty-one loosely connected revue or cabaret-style scenes, is enlivened by songs, the lyrics of which were composed by Sven Møller Kristensen, later a professor of literature. It is marked by numerous scenic plays calculated to entertain and stimulate the audience. Characters in the play directly address the audience, and a spectator climbs onto the stage to express his concern about the development of the play. Wedding plans, ceremony, reception, and honeymoon are telescoped into one brief, symbolic scene, with the ceremony itself represented by a spotlighted bridal veil, bouquet, and top hat passing across an empty stage. The dreariness of a typical day at the office is similarly compressed into brief but revealing scenes of song, dance, and mime, while offstage voices, wires, and rolling sets generate further novelty.

In addition to entertaining, Abell's gimmicks also illustrate the depersonalized nature of the characters. The protagonist is Larsen, an undistinguished member of the "white-collar proletariat," a "very nicely dressed" product of "very nice" parents and schools. His hope for a more exciting life is represented by a recurring light melody and a gaudy sheik's costume, but this hope is threatened by the tyranny of conformity at work and at home.

The three typists at his office, all called Miss Møller, wear identical photographic masks and refer to themselves as copies and automatons. Their employer gruffly tells them not to expect any change in their dull routine and tries to stifle Larsen's enjoyment of life's melody by threatening to fire him.

Similar pressure is exerted by the parents of Larsen's fiancée, Edith. They are first seen in a giant photograph of their living room, with only the actors' faces visible through holes cut out of the screen. The father is small and timid, the mother, large and domineering, and she manipulates Larsen and Edith so that they renounce life's melody. In their desire to obtain the material gifts proffered by the parents, they agree to conform to the middle-class conventions that celebrate niceness, order, and cleanliness at the expense of joy and adventure, and with that agreement, the sheik's costume symbolically sails upward.

Larsen and Edith's miserable life without the melody is brilliantly depicted by Abell in the last several scenes of act 1. Dull routine at the breakfast table, in the office, and during the obligatory Sunday visits with the parents drain all the vitality from Larsen and his marriage. Cozy evenings are not cozy, and Sunday is exhausting, not a day of rest. Larsen is passive and without energy. He is no longer the same man whom Edith married, and she resolves at all costs to rediscover Larsen's melody.

Act 2 shows the family rushing about seeking the melody, which is now represented by three elusive young girls, who are seen and heard by the audience but not by the characters. The search proceeds to the police, the church, and to caricatured representations of death and nature, with little success. Edith finally discovers the melody with a little girl skipping rope, Little Edith, presumably her youthful, uncorrupted self. She also encounters others who know the melody—a worker, a cyclist, and a soccer-playing scientist—and hurries to share her discovery with Larsen, who resolves to abandon his "nice" self and repossess the melody of life.

The final scenes have been faulted for being artificial and dramatically inconsistent with the rest of the play, but such an avant-garde production cannot be expected to follow the conventions of traditional dramatic structure. To be sure, there may be too many consecutive scenes in which characters search for the melody, but the greater problem is the clumsy insertion of social and political commentary—on war and peace, class struggle, and child rearing—which distracts from the story of Larsen's fate. One comment by Little Edith—"You can bet it's tough being a child"—leads directly to Abell's next play, *Eva aftjener sin barnepligt*, a critique of traditional child-rearing practices, but it is out of place in *The Melody That Got Lost*.

ANNA SOPHIE HEDVIG

With the growing political and military menace in Europe, Abell turned his attention to the issue of totalitarianism and the citizen's response to its dangers. In *Judith*, a drama inspired by Giraudoux's play of the same name, Abell challenges the audience to deal with the tyrant Holofernes. In *The Queen on Tour*, the issue is free speech in the theater, and *Silkeborg* documents the courage and conflict of the resistance movement in occupied Denmark. Unquestionably, however, Abell's most memorable play of this period was *Anna Sophie Hedvig*, which centers on a country schoolteacher who reveals at a family dinner party that she has murdered the evil colleague who was tyrannizing the school in the hope of becoming principal.

In many respects, *Anna Sophie Hedvig* is Abell's simplest and most naturalistic play—its primary setting is the living room of a middle-class Copenhagen family—but even without resorting to the technical tricks of his earliest works, the playwright again produces innovative drama. He employs several devices—such as a power failure and a mysterious telegram—to heighten the suspense of the play, and much like the mystery novelist, he uses flashbacks to reveal key elements of the plot. These are accomplished by the stage equivalent of the cinematic cross-fade technique, the blending of one scene into another, changing sets by open curtain and a moment of darkness. The final scene of the play is something of a flash-forward of great dramatic effect. To the rising sound of drums, Anna Sophie Hedvig is symbolically executed with the doomed Spanish Republican rebel whose picture she had seen in the newspaper.

The unreal blending of time, place, and plot in this scene is typical of the play's multileveled structure. The narrative frame overarching the play is a maid's recounting of the previous night's events to two young people, while the family dinner party, at which Anna Sophie Hedvig announces her crime, is the primary level of the plot. The party frames yet another level of action, two flashbacks to the school on the night of the murder.

This entire story line of Anna Sophie Hedvig and her Copenhagen relatives—their "little world"—is also juxtaposed with the political events of the "big world" outside, as represented by newspaper accounts of civil war in Spain, the menacing voice of Adolf Hitler on the radio, and the execution scene. In tying together the two worlds of the provincial teacher and European Fascism, Abell makes his point about the need to resist aggressors at whatever level they appear. Humankind, he suggests, not only has a right but also a duty to resist. In pushing Mrs. Møller down the long school staircase, Anna Sophie Hedvig was not only defending her own interests but also those of the colleagues and students who were cowed by the evil would-be principal.

The appearance of Anna Sophie Hedvig at the family's dinner party is the catalyst for the political debate that assumes more of the drama as the mystery is unraveled. The discussion moves across a spectrum of political attitudes. The dinner guest Hoff, an arch capitalist, rejects involvement in unpleasant events, claiming that "an enlightened, cultivated modern man cannot kill!" The father and Karmach, two business associates of Hoff, are typically conservative bourgeois who are reluctant to discuss sensitive issues, especially when a business deal might suffer as a result. The father's son, John, assumes the radical role at the other end of the political spectrum. As the playwright's mouthpiece, he challenges the passivity and avarice of the businessmen and staunchly defends the premeditated act of Anna Sophie Hedvig. The behavior of John's mother illustrates the intended result of Abell's dramatic activism. At first, she tries to remain neutral, unwilling to offend her husband and his clients and repulsed at the idea of murder. Caught between the men's view and that of her son, she soon realizes the necessity of taking a stand in the death struggle between good and evil and sides with John.

As with most of Abell's works, the critical response to *Anna Sophie Hedvig* was not commensurate with the popular acclaim. Some reviewers found that such a forceful theme as the murder of tyrants was not well served by the suspenseful revelations of a multileveled murder mystery. Moreover, because most of the action—including the murder of Mrs. Møller—is told rather than shown, there is no direct connection between the little world of Anna Sophie Hedvig and the larger world of prewar Europe. Although it is clear that the playwright intends the teacher's violent act to be symbolic of all resistance, he does appear to be endorsing a vigilante reaction that is far out of proportion to the provocation.

Performed in the wake of civil war, military takeovers, and unsuccessful appeasement policies, this play struck a responsive chord among Scandinavian audiences and provided a clear platform for the debates that raged in the late 1930's. Yet just as the popularity of *Anna Sophie Hedvig* was assured by its treatment of these dynamic events, so its relevance to later generations is somewhat limited. Abell himself recognized this limitation in 1957, when, in a revival of the play, he altered the heroine's final speech, omitting the Utopian references to "a time when it is wrong to kill—when no one will need to die for others or believe blindly without knowing." Postwar experience had shown him that when one set of life's problems is conquered, another arises. Still, *Anna Sophie Hedvig* is an interesting play whose basic premise, the citizen's need for action in the face of tyranny, endures.

POSTWAR PLAYS

Abell's postwar dramatic production was of two types: light revels in the art of the theater and fantas-

tic yet serious encounters with the problem of human isolation and despair. The former group includes an incidental drawing room comedy, *Miss Plinckby's kabale* (Miss Plinckby's solitaire), and two festival plays, *Ejendommen matr. nr. 267 østre kvarter* (lot no. 267 east district), a tribute to the bicentennial of the Danish Royal Theater in 1948, and *Andersen: Eller, Hans livs eventyr* (Andersen: or, the fairy tale of his life), celebrating the one hundred and fiftieth birthday of Hans Christian Andersen in 1955.

The more serious plays of his last years all deal in imaginative ways with the same question: How can an individual in today's world overcome fear, alienation, and despair, and does that person have a responsibility to lead others from death to life, from isolation to community? *Days on a Cloud* challenges the scientist who would work on awesome new weapons but refuse to get involved with decisions about their use. The title refers to the moments during which a scientist, contemplating suicide, decides whether to open his parachute. *Vetsera blomstrer ikke for enhver* (Vetsera does not bloom for everyone), only loosely based on the double suicide of Austria's Crown Prince Rudolf and his mistress Maria Vetsera, also rejects suicide as an answer to life's trials. *Kameliadamen* (the lady of the camellias) is an innovative version of the celebrated work by Alexandre Dumas, *fils*, and *Skriget*, Abell's final work, is a multileveled, often obscure fantasy that revives many of the themes and motifs of his entire career.

DEN BLÅ PEKINGESER

The most prominent work of Abell's last years is *Den blå pekingeser*, a theatrical tour de force that charmed his audiences and bewildered his critics. It is a lovely work with a rich blend of light, color, music, sound effects, and verbal and visual symbols, yet these many stimuli and the unconventional structure made it difficult for audiences to follow. The plot itself is reasonably simple, though its exposition is not. Tired of her egotistic, isolated existence, a young heiress, Tordis Eck, attempts suicide on the remote island where she has inherited an old villa. As she lingers between life and death, with a physician seeking to revive her, the spirits of persons from different time frames—past, present, and future—hover about her. With the intercession of others, her initial impulse to die yields to an affirmation of life and human fellowship.

The past in *Den blå pekingeser* is represented by the ghost of Isabella de Creuith, owner of the fanciful dog of the title and the deceased aunt who bequeathed Tordis both her villa and her lonely fate on the island of Iselø. The author uses these names to suggest the isolation and the cold (in Danish *is* means "ice") which characterize and threaten human relationships: Tord*is*, *Is*abella, *Is*elø.) Present time includes Tordis's crisis and the effort by her former lover, André (in Danish *andre* means "others"), to will her back to life, a psychic rescue directed from the café where he has learned of her suicide attempt. Thus space, as well as time, is dissolved in this exotic dream play. The future is represented by Esmond, the named but as yet unborn son of the lighthouse keeper's wife. His reluctance to enter what he perceives as a hopeless existence prompts Tordis to tell him that life is indeed a gift to be cherished, and with that she wishes to reclaim her own life.

In addition to the three time frames that merge on the island, the play presents the plot from three dramatic perspectives with differing blends of action and dialogue. First, André's activity in the café is dramatic action in the present, but there is no dialogue. Second, his narrative recollections of earlier encounters with Tordis are spoken in the past tense. Although they are monologues that represent his thoughts, they often replay past dialogues in his mind, and they entail no action. Finally, the fantastic realm in which past, present, and future meet on Iselø contains both action and dialogue.

Time is a major theme of this play, expressed not only in its creative structure but also in its story. There are numerous references to the fluid nature of time, in which a second is an eternity and a few years become a thousand. Time is also of the essence to the dying Tordis, as symbolized by the incessant turning of the lighthouse lamp. Only when she resolves to live does it stop, and with it the crisis of time.

As always with Abell, the theme of freedom is also prominent in the play. Yet while the playwright ultimately believes in humankind's right to freedom

from fear and loneliness, he also warns that freedom is not absolute. For Tordis, freedom had come to represent a retreat to Iselø and the refusal to commit herself to another person. Freedom was what she valued most, and it almost cost her her life. For Abell, as he says through André and Esmond, freedom is one's life, and there is a responsibility to live it in fellowship with others.

Abell's repeated assertions that life was not hopeless, that faith in human fellowship was not in vain, should be seen against a growing sense of apprehension and preoccupation with death in postwar Europe. There was tremendous disappointment that World War II had not resulted in a lasting peace but only in the division of the world into hostile camps armed with nuclear weapons. Pessimism also reigned in cultural affairs, in which alienation, angst, and the absurd were watchwords. It was Abell's dream to neutralize such despair by uplifting his audience through the stimulation of their fantasy, but although he forcefully proclaimed his faith in humankind's ability to overcome despair, his preoccupation with that theme in his last years created the impression that his faith was more a wish than a firm conviction.

OTHER MAJOR WORKS

LONG FICTION: *De tre fra Minikoi*, 1957 (*Three from Minikoi*, 1960).

SCREENPLAYS: *Millionærdrengen*, 1936; *Tak fordi du kom, Nick-!*, 1941; *Regnen holdt op-*, 1942; *Ta' briller på-!*, 1942.

NONFICTION: *Teaterstrejf i paaskevejr*, 1948; *Fodnoter i støvet*, 1951.

CHILDREN'S LITERATURE: *Paraplyernes oprør*, 1937.

MISCELLANEOUS: *Synskhedens Gave*, 1962.

BIBLIOGRAPHY

Hye, Allen E. "Fantasy Plus Involvement Equals Thought: Kjeld Abell's Conception of Theater." *Scandinavian Studies* 63 (Winter, 1991): 30-49. An examination of the Scandinavian playwright's view of theater.

Lingard, John. "Kjeld Abell." In *Twentieth Century Danish Writers*, edited by Marianne Stecher-

Hansen. Vol. 214 in *Dictionary of Literary Biography*. Detroit, Mich.: The Gale Group, 1999. A brief biography of Abell plus a listing of major works.

Marker, Frederick J. *Kjeld Abell*. Boston: Twayne, 1976. A basic but comprehensive study of Abell's life and works.

Marker, Frederick J., and Lise-Lone Marker. "Playwriting in Transition" and "Three New Voices." In *A History of Scandinavian Theatre*. Cambridge, England: Cambridge University Press, 1996. A look at Abell from the perspective of the history of the theater in Scandinavia.

Allen E. Hye

ARTHUR ADAMOV

Born: Kislovodsk, Russia; August 23, 1908
Died: Paris, France; March 16, 1970

PRINCIPAL DRAMA

La Parodie, pb. 1950, pr. 1952

L'Invasion, pr., pb. 1950

La Grande et la petite manœuvre, pr. 1950, pb. 1951

Le Professeur Taranne, pr., pb. 1953 (*Professor Taranne*, 1960)

Le Sens de la marche, pr., pb. 1953

Tous contre tous, pr., pb. 1953

Théâtre, pb. 1953-1968 (4 volumes)

Le Ping-Pong, pr., pb. 1955 (*Ping-Pong*, 1959)

Paolo Paoli, pr., pb. 1957 (*Paolo Paoli: The Year of the Butterfly*, 1959)

Le Printemps '71, pb. 1960, pr. 1962

Two Plays, pb. 1962

La Politique des restes, pr. 1963, pb. 1966

M. le modere, pr. 1967, pb. 1968

Off Limits, pr. 1967, pb. 1969

OTHER LITERARY FORMS

Arthur Adamov is best remembered for his plays, despite the fact that his long and checkered career began with the writing of Surrealist poetry as early as 1924. His autobiographical volume *L'Aveu* (1946; confession) is described by critic Martin Esslin as "among the most terrifying and ruthless documents of self-revelation in the whole of world literature."

ACHIEVEMENTS

Together with Samuel Beckett, Eugène Ionesco, and, to a lesser degree, Jean Genet, Arthur Adamov helped define and develop new directions in French drama during the early 1950's. His early works contributed significantly to what Esslin has called the Theater of the Absurd. Drawn in large measure from his own experience of emotional disturbance, informed by his acquaintance with the works of Sigmund Freud and Carl Jung, Adamov's earliest and best-known plays were hailed for their striking and memorable imagery, and he was ranked briefly with Ionesco and Beckett as a master of the new, nonrepresentational theater. Around 1956, however, Adamov suddenly and resolutely turned his back on the type of playwriting that had brought him fame and success, preferring instead to follow in the footsteps of Bertolt Brecht. Going so far as to repudiate all his earlier work as irrelevant, Adamov in his fifties devoted his not inconsiderable energy and talents to the further development of a committed, didactic theater—with results that were judged generally inferior to even the lesser works of his earlier mode. Of his later efforts, only the first, *Paolo Paoli*, in fact a transitional work, bears comparison with such earlier works as *Ping-Pong* and *Professor Taranne*. Never able to recover the spirit or momentum of his earlier success, Adamov committed suicide at the age of sixty-one.

Even at the height of his powers, Adamov remained relatively unknown in the English-speaking world, despite the vigorous efforts of such critics as Esslin, George Wellwarth, and Jacques Guicharnaud. Among the few of his works to be translated into English (and performed by university drama groups) were *Professor Taranne*, *Tous contre tous* (all against all), and *Ping-Pong*. Since his death, Adamov's reputation as a dramatist has dwindled considerably, suggesting that the reputation of his early plays may have been inflated. Today, few critics, even among Adamov's erstwhile champions, would consider his work to be on a par with that of Beckett, Ionesco, or even Genet. His importance must thus be seen as primarily historical: He helped define the form, shape, and fortune of contemporary drama.

BIOGRAPHY

Born in 1908 to prosperous Russian parents of Armenian extraction, Arthur Adamov was educated primarily in French. The outbreak of World War I found the Adamov family on vacation in Germany, from which they escaped, with royal intervention, in order to seek refuge in Geneva, Switzerland, where the young Adamov was to receive much of his formal education. After a brief residence in Mainz, Germany, the sixteen-year-old Adamov found his way to Paris, where he was soon befriended by the early Surrealists and became editor of the periodical *Discontinuité*. Before long, however, Adamov's writing career was interrupted by his first experience of the recurring mental and emotional disturbance later to be described at some length in *L'Aveu*. It was probably during this period that Adamov made the acquaintance of the brilliant, eccentric Antonin Artaud, now esteemed as one of the foremost theoreticians of contemporary drama, who shared with Adamov the affliction of mental illness.

During this period, Adamov first conceived a number of theories and positions that would stand him in good stead around the onset of middle age, when he began to write for the theater. Never really free of his Surrealist origins, Adamov as an artist came to value the lucidity provided by his neurosis, going so far as to assert that his madness gave him a visionary power denied to ordinary mortals. By the end of World War II, after a brief period of intern-

ment and two years' residence in occupied Paris, Adamov had worked out his personal response to changes both internal (psychological) and external (political), a response articulated both in essays and in attempts at playwriting.

Unsuccessful in the effort to get his first plays staged, despite the encouragement and backing of prominent writers, Adamov in 1950 took the unusual step of publishing two of his plays as a book. One of these, *L'Invasion*, was performed soon thereafter, while the other, *La Parodie* (in fact the first of Adamov's plays to be written), was not staged until 1952. In the meantime, however, Adamov had written a third play, *La Grande et la petite manœuvre*, which was performed almost immediately. Adamov's fortunes as a dramatist thus rose almost simultaneously with those of Ionesco, who followed the qualified success of *La Cantatrice chauve* in 1950 (*The Bald Soprano*, 1956) with *La Leçon* in 1951 (*The Lesson*, 1955) and *Les Chaises* in 1952 (*The Chairs*, 1957). Samuel Beckett, at that time known exclusively (if at all) as a novelist, was not to emerge as a dramatist until the 1952-1953 theatrical season, which also witnessed the production of three new plays by Adamov: *Le Sens de la marche*, *Professor Taranne*, and *Tous contre tous*. By the time he turned forty-five, Adamov was clearly at the forefront of the new French drama. The resounding success of *Ping-Pong* in 1955 served only to consolidate his reputation.

Pending a full-scale biography of Adamov, it is hard to say precisely how and why he reoriented his creative efforts toward didactic, politically "committed" drama in the mode of Bertolt Brecht. It is clear in any case that Adamov's political sympathies, such as they were, had long lain with the extreme Left. His early plays, however, are resolutely devoid of any topical reference. Adamov recalls that for the longest time he was unable even to name a real place in any of his plays. In the mid-1950's, however, he abruptly renounced his characteristic mode of expression and repudiated all his earlier efforts. At first, it seemed as though Adamov's new direction would prove as fruitful as his previous one: His first play after his "conversion," *Paolo Paoli*, brought to the service of didactic drama a strong infusion of absurdist irony and technique. Adamov's subsequent plays, however, turned ever more sharply away from his proven talents, seeming to be little more than slavish imitations of Brecht, and inferior ones at that. For a while, Adamov clearly enjoyed his elder-statesman status as what Esslin called "the main spokesman of the committed, political theater in France." On March 16, 1970, however, Adamov took his own life; the survival of even his best work is uncertain.

ANALYSIS

Formed in a climate of soul-searching, intensive reading, and recurring bouts of madness, Arthur Adamov's early plays offer an original, highly personal (if depersonalized) artistic deformation of perceived reality, rivaling in their finest moments the dramatized nightmares of Eugène Ionesco. As with Ionesco, the dialogue is more often serviceable than memorable; in transcribing his disturbing visions, Adamov was less concerned with prose style than with the evocation of memorable scenes. Adamov's first play, *La Parodie* (although third or fourth to be performed), is his most derivative; although based on personal experience, it relies heavily on August Strindberg and on the conventions of German expressionism. By contrast, *L'Invasion*, *Le Sens de la marche*, *Professor Taranne*, and especially *Ping-Pong* bear the mark of a singular, mature talent, breaking new ground in the development of contemporary drama. Although comparable in many ways to the works of Ionesco and Beckett, they could have been written only by Adamov. *Professor Taranne*, offering the unforgettable spectacle of an apparently distinguished man systematically and symbolically stripped of his identity, is by any standard a landmark in the evolution of contemporary drama. So also is *Ping-Pong*, with its portrayal of humankind's fascination with games and machines that effectively predicted and parodied the era of computers and video games that would surface a quarter-century later.

As noted above, Adamov's later, didactic plays, with the exception of *Paolo Paoli*, his first venture into the new mode, were at best qualified failures: *Le Printemps '71*, a dioramic re-creation of the Paris Commune, preserved some element of the author's ob-

jectivity and trenchant irony; *La Politique des restes*, a similar attempt to portray American racism between the two world wars, failed even to match Jean-Paul Sartre's severely flawed *La Putain respectueuse* (pr., pb. 1946; *The Respectful Prostitute*, 1947), loosely based on the famed Scottsboro case. *M. le modere*, although acclaimed for its innovative infusion of humor, failed to deliver the promise of a "third style" that critics of the time thought to be in the offing. Adamov's reputation therefore rests primarily on three or four plays from his earliest mode, partially augmented by the brilliance and relative success of *Paolo Paoli*.

L'INVASION

The second of Adamov's plays to be written, by only three days the second to be produced (Paris, November 14, 1950), *L'Invasion* was nevertheless the first Adamov effort to reach a wide audience and served as the basis for much of his growing reputation. The search for identity, perhaps the dominant theme of all Adamov's early work, here finds expression in the mixed, mysterious legacy of a deceased writer known only as Jean. Jean, it seems, has left behind in his apartment a bewildering assortment of unpublished papers, most of them penned in an illegible hand in rapidly fading ink. The legatee of record is Jean's disciple and brother-in-law, Pierre, who now lives in the apartment with his mother and his wife, Agnès, sister of the dead man. It is imperative that Jean's work, now in great disorder, be preserved intact, against the danger that some well-meaning disciple might invent new passages or improvise unintended meanings in order to suit his own fancies.

As the cataloging process gets under way, disorder inside the apartment is mirrored by disorder outside; there is a war or revolution in progress, and the unnamed country is being overrun by refugees. Pierre, meanwhile, must contend not only with his wife and mother but also with Tradel, a rival disciple with his own strong convictions concerning the organization of Jean's legacy. Soon, a man who is supposedly looking for someone in the apartment next door strikes up a flirtation with Agnès and becomes, in effect, her live-in lover as Pierre spends more and more time trying to make sense of her brother's papers. In time, Agnès elopes with the man, known only as *le premier venu* ("the first one who comes along"). By the time she returns, ostensibly to borrow Pierre's typewriter, order has been restored both inside and outside the apartment; Pierre is nearing the end of his task, with all Jean's writings arranged in neat stacks. Before he can be told of Agnès's return, however, Pierre is found dead in his downstairs study by Tradel, to whom he has confided his decision to abandon what remains of the project.

Clearly, the dead man's papers represent for Pierre both an occupation and a search for meaning—despite ironic suggestions scattered throughout the play that there may well be less to Jean's literary legacy than meets the eye. It is Pierre's preoccupation with his lifework that costs him the affection of his wife, although, as Esslin observed, Agnès herself appears to stand for disorder: It is, after all, through her that Pierre has become involved with her brother and his papers; when she leaves with *le premier venu*, order returns to Pierre's life and work in direct proportion to the disorder that begins to plague the life of her new lover. Yet as soon as Pierre questions and begins to renounce his long-term project, he dies, having apparently failed both in his work and in his interpersonal relationships. Implicitly, *L'Invasion* casts serious doubt on the validity of work, as well as that of love and friendship. Such, Adamov seems to be saying, is the eventual result of all human endeavor: futility.

Like *L'Invasion*—the title presumably refers to the intrusion of each person's life into the life and pursuits of others—all Adamov's best plays graphically illustrate the isolation and alienation that he sees as defining human life, both individual and social. His main characters, usually sketched rather than fully drawn (yet still more rounded than, for example, those of Ionesco), are seemingly adrift in a sea of humanity, desperately seeking some meaning that would give confirmation to their identity.

PROFESSOR TARANNE

Professor Taranne, perhaps Adamov's best-known play, was said by the author to have come to him in a dream, requiring only transcription and a few minor changes in the main character. To an even greater degree than *L'Invasion*, *Professor Taranne* describes in unforgettable imagery the isolation of each individual, even with regard to himself.

The action of *Professor Taranne* begins when the title character, a distinguished-looking man of about forty, is accused of indecent exposure on a public beach. Incensed, the professor points with pride to his reputation as an internationally famous scholar, claiming with righteous indignation that no man in his position would be capable of such a deed. Turning for help to a number of familiar faces, he is met only with blank stares as each person, in turn, denies ever having seen him before. One woman, at last, appears to recognize Taranne, only to reveal that she has mistaken him for his arch rival, Professor Menard. With each successive denial, the accused appears to dig himself in deeper, casting serious doubt on his very identity as well as on his innocence. As the action proceeds, even his existence is called into question. At one point, Taranne's sister arrives with a letter from the university in Belgium where Taranne claims that he has been invited to lecture. Sure at last that his identity is about to be proven to the satisfaction of local authorities, Taranne rips open the envelope and pulls out a letter rescinding the earlier invitation. Taranne, it seems, has been exposed as an academic fraud, guilty of plagiarizing the work of the eminent Professor Menard. Before long, having utterly failed to furnish evidence of his identity to satisfy even himself, the professor slowly begins to take off his clothes, performing the same offense of which he stands accused in the first place.

As Esslin observes, "It is by no means clear whether the play is meant to show a fraud unmasked, or an innocent man confronted by a monstrous conspiracy of circumstances engineered to destroy his claims." Such ambiguity, presumably preserved intact from Adamov's original dream, endows *Professor Taranne* with a rare evocative and associative power, casting serious doubt on even the most elementary assumptions of human identity or worth. Here especially, the neurosis that is said to have inspired Adamov's best work becomes almost contagious, inviting the spectator to share fully in the nightmare haunting Taranne and his creator.

TOUS CONTRE TOUS

Considered by George Wellwarth to be the finest of Adamov's plays, *Tous contre tous* combines much of the ambiguity of *Professor Taranne* with the sense of disorder that underlies the action of *L'Invasion*. Although it predates by several years the "committed" phase of Adamov's dramatic career, *Tous contre tous* functions on at least one level as an ingenious social and political satire. In later years, Adamov would repudiate the play for not coming to grips with the problem of racial and religious persecution by naming actual names and places. Like much of Ionesco's best work, however, *Tous contre tous* derives no small measure of power from the implication that the action described could happen anywhere, at any time, in any society. In the opinion of most of Adamov's critics, *Tous contre tous* remains his most effective expression of social criticism, considerably stronger than the deliberately didactic efforts of his later period.

Like *L'Invasion*, *Tous contre tous* takes place in a country overrun by refugees, many of whom are identifiable by a pronounced limp. The audience is warned, however, that not all refugees limp; conversely, not all those who limp are necessarily refugees. The main character is one Jean Rist, who becomes an antirefugee rabble-rouser for intensely personal, nonpolitical reasons: His wife has eloped with a refugee. Riding the wave of political fortune, Jean ascends briefly to power as a result of his views; before long, however, a shift in public opinion grants power to the refugees, and it is Jean who faces persecution; perhaps not surprisingly, he then affects a limp and masquerades as a refugee in order to escape detection. Presumably, a subsequent shift in political fortunes will enable him to break cover and profit from his earlier reputation. In the meantime, however, Jean has fallen in love with a refugee girl, Noémi, with whom he lives in relatively happy obscurity. When another revolution occurs, Jean chooses to die with Noémi rather than to save his life by disclosing his true identity, a gesture that would also cost him Noémi's trust and affection.

The ending of *Tous contre tous*, criticized by some observers as a peculiar, sentimental lapse into the conventions of such subgenres as the romantic war film, may also be seen as the gesture of a man who, having at last perceived the cyclical nature of history, has simply grown tired of playing "the game." Sentimental or not, Jean's liaison with Noémi is at the very least to be seen as a value more permanent than the variable fortunes of politics.

On balance, the refusal of the pre-Brechtian Adamov to anchor *Tous contre tous* in place and time seems to have been a wise, if unconscious, decision. Although obviously inspired by the persecution of Jews and other minorities before and during World War II, *Tous contre tous* remains suggestively afloat, still applicable to the fickleness of human behavior—both individual and social—some thirty years after it was written.

PING-PONG

The last of Adamov's plays to be written before his well-publicized commitment to the Brechtian mode, *Ping-Pong* is regarded by a majority of his critics as his finest achievement. The genesis of *Ping-Pong* appears to have been atypical. Adamov said that he wrote the last scene first, having simply envisioned two decrepit old men playing a seemingly endless game of table tennis. Indeed, even in final versions of the play, the concluding scene is discontinuous with what has gone before, although in a way quite fitting.

The action of *Ping-Pong* begins with two young men—Victor, a medical student, and Arthur, an art student—whiling away their precious idle hours over the pinball machines in Mme. Duranty's café. Before long, the pinball machine comes to dominate their conversation, their thinking, and eventually their lives. Applying their intellectual curiosity to the machine both as a game and as an artifact, they begin to devise better marketing procedures as well as better-engineered machines and are soon taken into the employ of the consortium that owns and distributes the machines. Abandoning their studies, they devote their lives to their work for the consortium, which in turn defines and circumscribes their behavior. When they quarrel, it is either about the design of the machine, its marketing, or a girl who works for the consortium and appears to distribute her favors equally between them. History and politics, meanwhile, are of interest to them only insofar as they affect the use, distribution, or development of bigger and better pinball machines.

In the final scene, Arthur and Victor are presumably retired, discarded by the consortium to which they have obsessively devoted the best years of their lives. They are playing Ping-Pong, arguing over the rules of the game just as, years earlier, they argued over the flippers and flashing lights of the pinball machine. Discarding net and paddles, they are volleying the tiny ball with their bare hands when Victor falls dead of an apparent heart attack, leaving Arthur utterly alone.

Like *L'Invasion*, *Ping-Pong* questions humankind's relationship to work, especially insofar as work relates to an innate quest or need for meaning. As Esslin observes, "*Le Ping-pong* is a powerful image of the alienation of modern man through the worship of a false objective, the deification of a machine, an ambition, or an ideology." By allowing the pinball machine to invade every dimension of their lives, Arthur and Victor are quite graphically and convincingly dehumanized, exchanging passionately technical dialogue as if its subject were a matter of life and death. Of all Adamov's plays, *Ping-Pong* is the most effective, and the most deserving of survival.

PAOLO PAOLI

Conceived in a spirit of fidelity to Marxist ideals as fulfilled by the Brechtian epic theater, *Paolo Paoli* nevertheless incorporates many elements characteristic of Adamov's earlier "poetic," nonrepresentational mode. In retrospect, this first of Adamov's "later" plays is probably also the best, although it falls far short of the standard set by *Ping-Pong* or *Professor Taranne*. Unfortunately, Adamov's personal concept of ideological drama appears to have entailed a nearly absolute suppression of originality; to the extent that *Paolo Paoli* succeeds, it does so because Adamov's wild originality had yet to be thoroughly tamed.

Purporting to describe in detail the political and socioeconomic causes of World War I, *Paolo Paoli* is an epic drama in twelve scenes covering the period from 1900 to 1914. The title character is a dealer in rare butterflies; his friend and customer, Florent Hulot-

Vasseur, is a prosperous purveyor of ostrich feathers, indispensable to the fashions of the period. The author of *L'Invasion* and *Ping-Pong* is thus very much still in evidence, choosing such bizarre commodities as his examples of international trade. Adamov is careful, however, to document his choices, showing that ostrich feathers constituted France's fourth largest export in 1900 and relating Paolo's butterfly trade to the exploitation of prisoners on Devil's Island, where Paolo's Corsican father was employed for years as a civil servant.

Unlike many epic dramas, *Paolo Paoli* is notable for its economy of distribution. Thanks, no doubt, to his apprenticeship in absurdist drama, Adamov managed somehow to compress his historical parable into the lives of only seven characters. A priest, a union leader, and Paolo's German wife (on occasion, Florent's mistress) suffice to close the interlocking circles of exploitation, privilege, and economic interest. Unfortunately, the brilliance of the play's conception is frequently vitiated by trite and longwinded speeches that detract from the otherwise wellmanaged action. Once the initial novelty has passed, moreover, it is difficult to sustain interest in such characters as Paolo and Florent, regardless of their occupations. "The idea is excellent," acknowledges George Wellwarth, "but the actual story of Paolo Paoli is simply dull. In turning from the general to the specific, Adamov has paradoxically lost the knack of telling a story in dramatic terms."

LATER PLAYS

Indeed, whatever remained of Adamov's creative vitality had disappeared completely by the time of *Le Printemps '71*, a drab, utterly humorless reconstruction of the Paris commune, or *La Politique des restes*, an intentionally doctrinaire Marxist account of racism in the United States between the two world wars. Perhaps the greatest loss sustained by Adamov in his shift to Brechtian realism was that of his ironic distance. Unlike Brecht, he was never able to reconcile subjective observation with the sought ideal of objectivity.

OTHER MAJOR WORK
    NONFICTION: *L'Aveu*, 1946.

BIBLIOGRAPHY

Adamov, Arthur. *Man and Child: The Autobiography of Arthur Adamov*. Translated by Jo Levy. New York: Riverrun Press, 1991. The playwright's life, as told by Adamov himself.

Bradby, David. *Adamov*. London: Grant and Cutler, 1975. A bibliography of works concerning the playwright Adamov.

Esslin, Martin. *The Theatre of the Absurd*. 3d ed. New York: Penguin Books, 1991. A classic history of the Theater of the Absurd and the drama associated with it. Index.

Gaensbauer, Deborah B. *The French Theater of the Absurd*. Boston: Twayne, 1991. An examination of French drama in the twentieth century, focusing on the Theater of the Absurd. Bibliography and index.

McCann, John Joseph. *The Theater of Arthur Adamov*. Chapel Hill: University of North Carolina Press, 1975. A collection of essays on the works of the French playwright. Indexes and bibliography.

Reilly, John H. *Arthur Adamov*. New York: Twayne, 1974. A basic examination of the life and work of the French dramatist. Bibliography.

David B. Parsell

JOSEPH ADDISON

Born: Milston, Wiltshire, England; May 1, 1672
Died: London, England; June 17, 1719

PRINCIPAL DRAMA

Rosamond, pr., pb. 1707 (libretto; music by Thomas Clayton)

Cato, pr., pb. 1713

The Drummer: Or, The Haunted House, pr., pb. 1716

OTHER LITERARY FORMS

Joseph Addison wrote in almost every genre flourishing in British literature during the reigns of William III and Queen Anne. In addition to his three plays, Addison wrote verse in Latin and in English, a travel book, a scholarly account of ancient Roman coins, political pamphlets, and hundreds of essays for *The Tatler*, *The Spectator*, and other periodicals. This variety reflects the active literary culture of the time, Addison's own wide learning, and his search for his proper niche.

Because of Addison's varied canon, there has yet to be a satisfactory complete edition. The first attempt, by Thomas Tickell in 1721, omitted some embarrassing early works and many of the periodical essays. Another collected edition a century later restored some early works and offered a fuller selection of essays. Two good modern critical editions cover most of Addison's corpus: A. C. Guthkelch's *The Miscellaneous Works* (1914) includes the plays as well as the poetry and nonperiodical prose works, and Donald Bond's *The Spectator* (1965) covers Addison's essays for the most famous periodical to which he contributed. Essays written for other journals await modern editions. Addison's *Letters*, an unrevealing collection, was published in 1941.

ACHIEVEMENTS

Joseph Addison's literary reputation has risen and fallen cyclically for reasons that have little to do with his artistic achievement. His contemporaries and the next generation praised Addison highly for expressing not only Whig political principles but also classical qualities that gave English literature a dignity it previously lacked. Readers and writers in the Romantic age, however, found Addison unoriginal and conventional. The Victorians restored Addison to the pedestal because he spoke well of virtue and painted the portrait of the Christian gentleman. Twentieth century critics often treat his work as a reflec-

Joseph Addison (Library of Congress)

If Addison's primary achievement was in periodical prose, his plays rank second, his scholarly prose third, and his poetry last. His plays do not have all the virtues of successful drama but do show that two qualities of his prose—a light comic touch and a skill at putting the best words in the best order—were partially transferable to another genre. There is a consistency to Addison's drama: All three plays are quite competent and worth reading. Historically, the plays received varied reactions: *Rosamond* was a disaster, *Cato* was a huge success, and *The Drummer* was hardly noticed. The reactions to *Rosamond* and *Cato* had little to do with their literary merit, a fate common to other imaginative works in Augustan London, where politics, authorial popularity, and prejudice were often decisive.

BIOGRAPHY

Joseph Addison might easily have followed in his father's footsteps: attending Oxford University, becoming a minister of the Anglican Church, pursuing a series of increasingly important ecclesiastical posts, and supporting the divine right of Stuart kings. Addison, however, took a different path.

Two revolutionary currents swept up Addison while he was at Oxford. The first was an enthusiasm for the "New Philosophy," the scientific method that was challenging the supremacy of classical philosophy; the second was the Glorious Revolution of 1688, which brought William III to the throne in place of James II and established the principle that Parliament's choice for a king weighed equally with God's anointing of his earthly representative. Addison followed the traditional classical curriculum at Oxford (where he achieved his first literary reputation for Latin poetry), but with the idea of supporting a new English culture and political order. Based on the Roman concept of an educated citizenry, this new order, Addison and like-minded revolutionaries hoped, would be the greatest civilization England had yet known: A literate and cultured populace would sensibly cooperate in their own government to develop a thriving commercial economy at home and to achieve leadership among European nations.

While at Oxford, Addison expressed his enthusi-

tion of the values of the ascendant bourgeoisie; many dislike the man for accommodating himself to the class structure of eighteenth century England.

Although such judgments affect how often Addison is reprinted and how much he is read, his place in literary history rests firmly on two achievements: his role in the development of the periodical essay and his prose style. Through his collaboration with Richard Steele on *The Tatler* (1709-1711), *The Spectator* (1711-1712, 1714), and *The Guardian* (1713), Addison helped establish the periodical essay as a literary form. Seemingly informal and natural yet shaped by conscious art, Addison's prose style became for the next two centuries a model for novice writers: Stylists as diverse as Benjamin Franklin and Thomas Hardy began by imitating Addison. Samuel Johnson defined Addison's style in an immortal assessment: "Whoever wishes to attain an English style, familiar but not coarse, and elegant but not ostentatious, must give his days and nights to the volumes of Addison."

asm for this new concept of England in poems that brought him to the attention of leading Whig politicians. In 1699, Lord Somers and Lord Halifax secured for Addison a grant from William III, allowing Addison to travel throughout the Continent in preparation for government service. Addison remained abroad until late 1703, when William's death ended the pension. He produced little for the next year until, at the request of two of Queen Anne's ministers, he wrote *The Campaign* to celebrate the military victories of the duke of Marlborough against the French. This successful poem, which was published in 1705, won for Addison a position as commissioner of appeals.

This post placed Addison in a circle of Whig politicians and writers called the Kit-Kat Club. The powerful politicians supported the writers by patronage; the writers helped the politicians gain or keep power by penning public-relations puffs and persuasive pamphlets. Addison's new acquaintances spurred his literary efforts. A Kit-Kat publisher brought out Addison's travels in 1705 to capitalize on the reputation of the author of *The Campaign*. Richard Steele, a Kit-Kat writer, urged Addison to dabble in drama and to try his hand at an English opera to counteract London's then current passion for Italian opera. Addison's opera, *Rosamond*, was a failure, however, primarily because of Thomas Clayton's poor musical score.

Nevertheless, *Rosamond* was the only setback for Addison between 1705 and 1711. Political contacts at the Kit-Kat Club provided him with increasingly responsible appointments. He served as secretary to a number of important ministers and was elected to Parliament in 1708. His literary output in these years was limited to several political tracts and to a few contributions to the early numbers of Steele's *The Tatler*.

After the Whig ministry lost power in 1710, Addison became a regular partner with Steele in the later issues of *The Tatler* and shared responsibility for founding its successor, *The Spectator*. The new paper was spectacularly successful and was the talk of London's polite society; Addison provided most of the variety in the paper, writing sketches, fables, short stories, and poems in addition to the expository essays that were its staple.

Political events and Addison's high literary reputation conspired to return him to the theater in 1713. The country was torn by the question of the aging Queen Anne's successor: Would the Protestant Prince George of Hanover succeed to the throne according to Parliament's wish, or would a Catholic Stuart attempt to assert his hereditary right by military force? Addison had begun sometime earlier a play about the Roman patriot Cato, who had resisted the dictatorial ambitions of Julius Caesar. His Whig friends encouraged Addison to finish the play and produce it as a clarion call to resist the return of Stuart absolutism. Addison reluctantly agreed and saw the play received with a passionate response from the party faithful. The Whigs' opponents, the Tories, ironically clapped up the play just as loudly, hailing it as a patriotic summons to resist a foreign prince. The play was produced at both London and Oxford with great success, although few paid attention to its literary qualities.

In 1714, the Protestant prince did ascend the English throne as George I, and Addison served as secretary to the council that oversaw the transition. Addison supported the new government with several poems and a political journal, *The Freeholder*. He tried his hand at the theater once more with *The Drummer* in 1716, but it ran for only three nights. Although not roundly scorned, as *Rosamond* had been, this "delicate" comedy (as Steele called it) did not impress audiences. In 1717, Addison reached the height of his political career by becoming secretary of state.

Political and literary success brought substantial rewards. Addison purchased a pleasant estate, Bilton Hall; married the widowed countess of Warwick; and fathered a daughter, Charlotte. In 1718, however, illness forced him to resign from the government, and the last months of his life were marred by a pamphlet war with his former partner Steele over the Peerage Bill. On his deathbed, legend holds, Addison summoned his dissolute stepson to witness "how a Christian can die." Addison never lacked confidence in his religious, political, or literary convictions.

ANALYSIS

Joseph Addison's three plays indicate important trends in eighteenth century British theater. *Rosamond* attempts to combine music and drama as a domestic alternative to Italian opera, an ambition not realized until two decades later, with the success of John Gay's *The Beggar's Opera* (pr., pb. 1728). *Cato* represents a strain of classical tragedy that produced much declamation and little worth, "immortal in the closet" (as the saying went) but stale on the stage. *The Drummer* is an early sentimental comedy whose primary virtue was in being less maudlin than its successors.

None of Addison's plays is a landmark of drama—except *Cato*, by political accident—but none is bad. In fact, each play has its interesting aspects. All of them suffer from a common flaw, the lack of a central character whose plight engages the audience's sympathy, and each play suffers individual minor difficulties. Yet each play has distinctive virtues. *Rosamond* and *The Drummer* have enough comic characters and dialogue to justify, in conjunction with Addison's humorous papers in *The Spectator*, Samuel Johnson's observation: "If Addison had cultivated the lighter parts of poetry, he would probably have excelled." *Cato*'s blank verse, while no rival to Christopher Marlowe's or William Shakespeare's, is a solid achievement and is the best poetry that Addison ever wrote.

ROSAMOND

Rosamond's three acts tell of the love affair between Henry II and Rosamond Clifford. The main plot concerns Henry's conflict, his love for Rosamond against his duty to Queen Elinor, and the subplot concerns the man whom Henry has set to watch over Rosamond, Sir Trusty, himself in love with his charge and plagued with a shrewish wife, Grideline. Act 1 displays the characters in their frustrations: the queen jealous, the mistress guilty and lonely, and the guardian melancholy. Only Henry, returning from France and eager to see Rosamond, seems pleased with the situation. In act 2, Grideline sends a page to spy on Sir Trusty, but the young man discovers instead Queen Elinor plotting to kill her husband's mistress. Hesitating for a moment because Rosamond's death may lead to Henry's, Elinor finally issues an ultimatum to her rival: be stabbed or drink

poison. Rosamond chooses poison, and when Sir Trusty finds the corpse, he likewise drinks the fatal concoction. Act 3 begins with Henry asleep and dreaming of martial conquest. Spirits grant him a vision of England's future glory if he gives up his illicit love. Henry awakens and resolves to put Rosamond aside, but hearing of her death, he vows to die in battle. Elinor counters his rashness by revealing that the poison was only a sleeping potion and that Rosamond lives. She retires to a convent to expiate her sin, and Henry returns to Elinor and reestablishes domestic accord. Sir Trusty, awakening to find king and queen happily reunited, now devotes himself wholeheartedly to Grideline.

Addison's opera had several elements that ought to have made it congenial to audiences of the day. The plot came from English history, a strong appeal to the patriotic instincts of a generation locked in a long war with France. The characters were familiar dramatic types: The royal leads experienced the conflicts of love and honor so common to the protagonists of Restoration heroic tragedy, while Sir Trusty and Grideline knew the jealousies and philanderings fundamental to the Restoration comedy of manners. Finally, the play's third act offered a spectacular effect: In Henry's vision, there was a backdrop featuring Blenheim Castle, which was at that moment under construction. The play's theme—that married love conquers all—likewise accorded well with the sentiments for reform that had been growing increasingly fashionable since the accession of William III.

Contemporaries agreed that an atrocious musical score doomed the play, but it must also be admitted that Addison's arrangement of the parts must have seemed odd to his audience no matter how mellifluous the music. A plot recitation indicates those elements that were supposed to predominate: several romantic conflicts, a patriotic theme, and an uplifting moral. A close reading of *Rosamond*, however, reveals that the author's best effects are in the comic elements. If the London stage of 1707 had been familiar with the musical comedy, as Bonamy Dobrée points out, Addison's opera would have been comprehensible. It is a play in which the major ingredients are wholesome and bland while the subplot and supporting characters are what the audience enjoys and remembers. The witty but foolish Sir Trusty steals the show. His superficial passion and foolish suicide, meant to contrast with Henry's love and Elinor's jealousy, instead made the royal lovers look like caricatures. Surely the effect was unintentional; not until W. S. Gilbert and Sir Arthur Sullivan's operettas would ridiculing the aristocracy become public dramatic entertainment.

THE DRUMMER

The Drummer does not suffer from the same tension between main plot and subplot; in fact, the two are nicely harmonized, although the best character in the play is still the male protagonist of the subplot. What *The Drummer* lacks, in fact, is any strong tension at all. Although its situations and language produce numerous smiles, the play lacks the sharpness that memorable comedy demands.

Addison, drawing on his classical learning, borrowed the plot of *The Drummer* from the last several books of Homer's *Odyssey* (c. 725 B.C.E.; English translation, 1614). Like Homer's epic, Addison's play is about a soldier, supposedly dead in a war, who comes home in disguise to find his wife besieged by suitors and his only ally in a faithful servant.

Act 1 depicts the estate of Lady Trueman, supposedly haunted by the drumbeating ghost of her husband, Sir George, killed fourteen months before in battle. The ghost is actually a disguised suitor for the widow's hand in marriage, the London beau Fantome, who has secured the help of a servant, Abigail, in his plot to drive away another suitor, the foppish Tinsel. Though Lady Trueman acts kindly toward Tinsel, she in fact despises both men. When the real Sir George turns up alive in act 2, he enters the household disguised as a conjurer in order to observe his wife's behavior. Throughout act 3, Vellum, Sir George's faithful steward, attempts to help his master expose Tinsel and subvert Fantome by wooing Abigail. In act 4, Fantome disposes of his rival but unknowingly loses Abigail's assistance. In act 5, Sir George tests his wife to determine if she still loves her husband; convinced by her reaction, the real Sir George routs the pseudo-Sir George by appearing as the drumbeating ghost of himself. Sir George and

Lady Trueman are reunited, and Vellum earns Abigail's love as well as her rich bribe from Fantome.

Sir George and Lady Trueman are more convincing lovers than Henry and Elinor. Because they do not begin so very far apart, reconciliation is natural. Though fearful that his widow may have been too quick to forget him, Sir George really knows all along that his spouse has more heart than the typically coquettish wife. Though Lady Trueman is quick to have suitors, she keeps them at a distance.

Vellum, not in love with the same woman as his lord, does not undercut Sir George's character as Trusty undercut Henry's. Vellum, in fact, is a reluctant lover, becoming a wooer of Abigail only to help his master and only after he discovers that she responds to his stewardly approach to love. A steward is a careful man who always itemizes and lists what is valuable and keeps an eye on it. Addison skillfully uses the steward mentality both to depict Vellum as a delightful eccentric and to use him as a weapon against the unstewardly figures Tinsel and Fantome, who know how to value nothing.

In addition to Vellum, who is the highlight of the play, Addison creates some humor with three bumbling servants—a butler, a coachman, and a gardener—of whose credulity Sir George takes advantage in order to pass himself off as a conjurer. These four, however, do not have enough stage lines to offset the blandness of the major characters. Sir George and Lady Trueman are loving but not very witty with each other, and the fops Tinsel and Fantome are without any distinguishing or distinctive foolishness. Abigail, who has some tendency to be vixenish, slides without ado from corrupted betrayer to protective intriguer. *The Drummer* on the whole does not disappoint the reader, but it cannot lure one back for a second encounter.

CATO

If *Rosamond* and *The Drummer* show Addison's comic touch, *Cato* contains his best poetry. For several decades after its first performance, *Cato* maintained a firm stage reputation as well as a solid critical repute, but largely on the strength of its political appeal, the high esteem in which Addison was generally held, and a weakness for declamation among audiences that should have known better. In more recent times, the glaring discrepancy between the main plot and the subplot has become impossible to ignore and the absence of human feeling in the tragic protagonist too obvious to be obscured by the play's virtues. Only the language, which develops subtle and rich image patterns, saves the play from being a mere museum piece.

The main plot and subplot are so different that the play is better summarized in two parts than act by act. The hero is Cato, often praised as the ideal Roman magistrate, who as consul and senator opposed the dictatorial ambitions of Julius Caesar. Cato has led a senatorial army in defense of the Republic, but it is now reduced to a small force trapped at Utica. Like many other cornered generals, Cato confronts, in addition to the enemy, mutiny among his own troops and desertion by allied contingents. Cato personally faces a severe dilemma. Should he fight a glorious but futile battle, dying in defense of his principles? Should he slink out of Utica alone in hopes of raising new allies and a new army elsewhere so that he can carry on the struggle? Should he surrender his troops to avoid senseless bloodshed but commit suicide to prevent falling into his enemy's hands? After successfully combating mutiny in the ranks, Cato chooses suicide in order to remain the master of his own destiny.

The subplot, patterned after the romantic dilemmas of Restoration heroic tragedy, seems today to be made out of soap-opera materials. With Cato at Utica are his two sons Marcus and Portius, both of whom are in love with Lucia, the daughter of a Roman general. Portius knows he is his brother's rival and feels badly; Marcus does not know and spills his heart's love to Portius; Lucia knows that both men love her and refuses to choose one lest she make the other despair. With Cato, too, is his daughter Marcia, herself pursued by two suitors: the Roman senator Sempronius and the Numidian prince Juba. Marcia refuses to consider either until the army's fate is decided. Sempronius, however, refuses to wait and plans to revolt against Cato and carry off Marcia. The mutiny helps bring out all the lovers' true feelings. Marcia resists Sempronius and confesses to loving Juba, whom she mistakenly believes has been killed

in the rebellion. Lucia refuses Marcus's proposal—painfully delivered by the torn Portius—and the rejected suitor throws himself bravely but recklessly into battle against Sempronius's rebels. Marcus's heroic death leaves Portius and Lucia free to wed, as are Juba and Marcia.

That Cato should have to see to his children happily married as the Republic collapses about him indicates one of the imbalances in the play. Addison, in apparent deference to the theatrical taste of the time, tried to combine a complicated love plot with a tragedy in the Senecan mold that discusses important political issues through declamation. The two plots never mix onstage: The oil of romance remains atop and befouls the waters of political philosophy.

Cato himself is a paragon of virtue. Addison follows most classical authors in depicting the Roman senator as the epitome of Stoic virtue. Seneca, Cicero, and Plutarch all described Cato as a human rock steadfast amid the storms of Fortune. Cato was an attractive model of secular, civic virtue to eighteenth century Englishmen who had seen the results of religious, sectarian virtue in the religious civil wars of the seventeenth century. Reviewing the text of *Cato* before its production, Lady Mary Wortley Montagu praised Cato's plain and great sentiments.

Yet for all the ideals that Cato represented to a contemporary audience, the dramatic fact is that he does not engage one's sympathy. As Samuel Johnson put it, the play's "hopes and fears communicate no vibrancy to the heart." Although Addison has created in the first three acts enough dilemmas to bring out a character's humanity, Cato shows none of it in the last two acts. His reaction to Marcus's death in act 4, glorying in the corpse's wounds as a sign of virtue, seems exaggerated and monstrous. In act 5, he contemplates the immortality of the soul before he commits suicide, but so superficially that he seems to be carrying out a ritual rather than reflecting on eternity. He advises Portius to retire to his estate—prudential wisdom indeed, but not consistent with his own fate or that of Marcus. Worst of all, as a contemporary reviewer observed, *Cato* lacks the reversal of fortune, the moment of realization by a despairing protagonist such as Oedipus that strikes an audience with terror and pity. Cato suffers throughout the play, but he never contributes to his downfall. He stands against superior armed forces and malevolent fate until he chooses no longer to be overwhelmed.

Although Cato's story is not tragic, it is not unmoving. It is a brave tale, a portrait of human greatness, and a paean to devotion to principle. The audience senses these qualities, however, more through the language of the play than through its action. Addison builds around a central metaphor a pattern of imagery that makes sense of otherwise discordant love complications and cardboard characters.

The central metaphor is that of the man who stands so calmly and resolutely amid the storms of civil war that his virtue shines like a beacon through the darkness, the wind, and the rain. Throughout the play, Addison images the forces of rebellion—Caesar, Sempronius, the mutinous troops—as storms that batter Cato. In contrast stands Cato's soul, whose virtuous flame never flickers amid the external mayhem. Shielded by virtue, Cato's soul is all placidity. In each act, this opposition of internal harmony and external chaos becomes an index by which the other characters in the play can be judged.

In language rich with contrasting images of harmony and discord, calm and storm, peace and battle, Addison measures each character against the standard, and with each character the loftiness of the standard becomes more apparent. Sempronius, though like Cato a senator, proves un-Roman because the outer storm of Caesar's rebellion sets off in him corresponding inner storms of rebellion against Cato and of lustful passion for Marcia. Marcus is inwardly as blown about by passion and resentment as is Sempronius, but at least Marcus directs his untamable energies into his country's cause. Juba, prince of a desert kingdom, accustomed to riding the whirlwind of his own desires, gradually acquires a Cato-like serenity by learning the Stoic philosophy.

The remaining characters—Portius, Marcia, and Lucia—are already Cato-like as the play opens. Despite their personal dilemmas about love, each focuses more on Cato's plight and resolves not to let personal fears or jealousies conquer as long as the great man's fate hangs in the balance. In the course of

the play, none is lost to frustrated passion; having withstood the storms of civil war as well, each emerges at the play's end pure and rejuvenated:

So the pure limpid stream when foul with stains,
Of rushing torrents, and descending rains,
Works itself clear, and as it runs, refines;
'Till by degrees, the floating mirrour shines,
Reflects each flow'r that on the border grows,
And a new Heaven in its fair bosom shows.

As is revealed in *Cato* and his other plays, in keeping with the increasingly intellectual preoccupations of the middle class, Addison tried his hand at both the comic and the serious, the delicate and the moral, and the domestic and the philosophical. Even when light in tone, his works reflect the polite society of the day, while revealing an underlying common sense that informs his essays and drama alike. Drawing on his scholarly background, Addison synthesized popular and learned aspects of Augustan society. As a stylist, he gained the respect of his era, and he has continued to exert a formidable influence on later writers.

OTHER MAJOR WORKS

POETRY: "To Mr. Dryden," 1693; *A Poem to His Majesty*, 1695; *Praelum Inter Pygmaeos et Grues Commisum*, 1699; "A Letter from Italy," 1703; *The Campaign*, 1705; "To Her Royal Highness," 1716; "To Sir Godfrey Kneller on His Portrait of the King," 1716.

NONFICTION: *Remarks upon Italy*, 1705; *The Tatler*, 1709-1711 (with Richard Steele); *The Whig Examiner*, 1710; *The Spectator*, 1711-1712, 1714 (with Steele); *The Guardian*, 1713 (with Steele); *The Lover*, 1714 (as Marmaduke Myrtle, Gent.; with Steele); *The Reader*, 1714 (with Steele); *The Freeholder: Or, Political Essays*, 1715-1716; *The Old Whig*, 1719; *Dialogues upon the Usefulness of Ancient Medals*, 1721; *The Letters of Joseph Addison*, 1941 (Walter Graham, editor); *The Spectator*, 1965 (Donald Bond, editor).

TRANSLATION: *Fourth Georgic*, 1694 (of Vergil's *Georgics*).

MISCELLANEOUS: *The Miscellaneous Works*, 1914 (A. C. Guthkelch, editor).

BIBLIOGRAPHY

Bloom, Edward A., and Lillian D. Bloom, eds. *Joseph Addison and Richard Steele: The Critical Heritage*. 1986. Reprint. London: Routledge, 1997. These essays examine Addison and Steele from a contemporary perspective, better enabling the reader to understand their original works. Includes index and bibliography.

Bloom, Edward A., Lillian D. Bloom, and Edmund Leites. *Educating an Audience: Addison, Steele, and Eighteenth Century Culture*. Los Angeles: William Andrews Clark Memorial Library, 1984. An examination of Addison and Sir Richard Steele and the culture of their time.

Ellison, Julie. *Cato's Tears and the Making of Anglo-American Emotion*. Chicago: University of Chicago Press, 2000. Ellison examines politics, sensibility, and masculinity from the 1600's to the early 1800's through an analysis of early popular dramas, including Addison's *Cato*.

Knight, Charles A. *Joseph Addison and Richard Steele: A Reference Guide, 1730-1991*. New York: G. K. Hall, 1994. A listing of all substantial scholarly works on Addison and Steele, from after Steele's death in 1729 through 1991. Also lists works by Addison and Steele. Includes indexes and bibliographies.

Otten, Robert M. *Joseph Addison*. Boston: Twayne, 1982. A basic biography of Addison that covers his life and works. Bibliography and index.

Robert M. Otten,
updated by Frank Day

AESCHYLUS

Born: Eleusis, Greece; 525-524 B.C.E.
Died: Gela, Sicily; 456-455 B.C.E.

PRINCIPAL DRAMA

Of the more than 80 known plays of Aeschylus, only 7 tragedies survive in more or less complete form.

Persai, 472 B.C.E. (*The Persians*, 1777)
Hepta epi Thēbas, 467 B.C.E. (*Seven Against Thebes*, 1777)
Hiketides, 463 B.C.E.? (*The Suppliants*, 1777)
Oresteia, 458 B.C.E. (English translation, 1777; includes *Agamemnōn* [*Agamemnon*], *Choēphoroi* [*Libation Bearers*], and *Eumenides*)
Prometheus desmōtēs, date unknown (*Prometheus Bound*, 1777)

OTHER LITERARY FORMS

A few surviving epigrams and elegiac fragments show that Aeschylus did not limit himself to drama but also experimented with other forms of poetic expression. The ancient *Life of Aeschylus* mentions that the playwright lost a competition with the poet Simonides to compose an elegy for the heroes of Marathon. Although Aeschylus's entry was judged to lack the "sympathetic delicacy" of that of Simonides, the elegy, fragments of which were discovered in the Athenian agora in 1933, projects the dignity and the majesty that mark Aeschylus's dramatic style. It is doubtful that Aeschylus's surviving tombstone inscription is autobiographical, despite such ancient authorities as Athenaeus and Pausanias, because the epigram mentions the place of Aeschylus's death.

ACHIEVEMENTS

The earliest of the three ancient Greek tragedians whose work is extant, Aeschylus made major contributions to the development of fifth century B.C.E. Athenian tragedy. According to Aristotle's *De poetica* (c. 334-323 B.C.E.; *Poetics*, 1705), it was Aeschylus who "first introduced a second actor to tragedy and lessened the role of the chorus and made dialogue take the lead." This innovation marks a principal stage in the evolution of Greek tragedy, for although one actor could interact with the chorus, the addition by Aeschylus of a second actor made possible the great dramatic agons, or debates between actors, for which Greek tragedy is noted.

Aeschylus also is the probable inventor of the connected trilogy/tetralogy. Before Aeschylus, the three tragedies and one satyr play that traditionally constituted a tragic production at the festival of the Greater Dionysia in Athens were unconnected in theme and plot, and Aeschylus's earliest extant play, *The Persians*, was not linked with the other plays in its group. All the other surviving plays of Aeschylus were almost certainly part of connected groups, although the *Oresteia*, composed of the extant *Agamemnon*, *Libation Bearers*, and *Eumenides*, is the only connected tragic trilogy that survived intact. However, the loss of the *Oresteia*'s satyr play, *Proteus*, makes observations on Aeschylus's use of connected tetralogies (three tragedies and one satyr play) nearly impossible. In fact, there is no certain evidence that Aeschylus always used the connected group in his later productions, and imitations of this dramatic form by other fifth century B.C.E. play-wrights are not firmly documented. The triadic form of the *Oresteia*, however, has certainly had a great influence on the development of modern dramatic trilogies.

Aeschylus's brilliant use of the chorus as protagonist in *The Suppliants* may have been another significant innovation. Until the discovery in 1952 of a papyrus text, this play was universally considered the earliest surviving Greek tragedy, and the central place of the chorus of Danaids was thought to reflect the choral role of early tragedy. As a result of the play's revised dating to 463 B.C.E., *The Suppliants*' chorus is now viewed as demonstrating a deliberate attempt to make the chorus a part of the action of the tragedy. Certainly, the chorus of *The Suppliants* is the earliest known example of a Greek tragic chorus, traditionally nondramatic and reflective, transformed into a significant dramatic participant. Although later dramatists rarely borrowed this choral technique, *The Suppliants*' chorus underscores Aeschylus's originality and experimentation in the development of Greek tragedy.

Aeschylus's historical play *Persai* (472 B.C.E.; *The Persians*, 1777) must also be mentioned as the only extant Greek tragedy based directly on historical events rather than on mythology. At least two other historical tragedies are known to have been produced in the early fifth century B.C.E., both by Phrynichus: *Capture of Miletus* (492 B.C.E.), based on the fall of that Greek city to the Persians in 494, and *Phoenissae* (c. 476 B.C.E.), based on the naval battle of Salamis in 480. Themistocles, the Athenian victor at Salamis, was Phrynichus's *choregus*, or producer. Aeschylus's *The Persians*, then, is clearly an imitation in the main of Phrynichus's *Phoenissae*, but it is impossible to judge whether Aeschylus derived from the play the idea to depict the Greek victory from the perspective of the defeated Persians. This ability to divest his historical tragedy of jingoism and propaganda makes Aeschylus's *The Persians* a universal statement on the tragic cause and meaning of defeat.

Aeschylus was known in antiquity for his spectacular stagecraft and especially for his use of stage trappings, special effects, and costuming. Examples of Aeschylus's skilled attention to such visual elements

Aeschylus (Library of Congress)

of drama include his dramatic employment in *Agamemnon* and *Libation Bearers* of stage machinery such as the *eccyclema*, a wheeled vehicle used to display the interior; his striking use of altars and tombs in *The Suppliants* and in *Libation Bearers*; his fondness for spectral appearances, such as the ghosts of Darius in *The Persians* and of Clytemnestra in *Eumenides*; and the terrifying costuming of the chorus of Furies in *Eumenides*, said to have been so effective that it caused miscarriages among pregnant spectators.

Aeschylus's plays were held in such great esteem in the late fifth and fourth centuries B.C.E. that posthumous revivals of his works were granted special license to compete at the Greater Dionysia and often won first prize. The famous debate between the ghosts of Aeschylus and Euripides in Aristophanes' comedy *Batrachoi* (405 B.C.E.; *The Frogs*, 1780) is perhaps the best ancient statement of Aeschylus's dramatic and literary significance. Aeschylus's plays were widely adapted by Roman tragedians, who in the second and first centuries B.C.E. still had access to the entire Aeschylean corpus, but Seneca's *Agamemnon* (c. 40-55 C.E.; English translation, 1581) is the only surviving example of such Roman imitation.

The first complete ancient edition of the Aeschylean corpus was not made until the late fourth century B.C.E. by the orator Lycurgus. This edition became the basis of the definitive Alexandrian edition by Aristophanes of Byzantium in the second century B.C.E. The seven surviving plays are probably the result of a school selection made by the fifth century C.E. The work of Aeschylus was unknown in Western Europe from early medieval times until the fifteenth century, when the impending fall of Constantinople to the Turks brought many Byzantine scholars to the West. The first printed edition of the extant plays was the Aldine edition of Venice, in 1518.

Perhaps because of the difficulty of Aeschylus's poetic language, which is generally indirect and metaphoric, Aeschylus's extant corpus has not been as directly influential as the works of Sophocles and Euripides have been on the history of tragedy since the Renaissance. Nevertheless, Aeschylus is recognized today as a brilliant dramatist whose contributions to the fifth century B.C.E. Athenian theater have made him a "father of Western tragedy."

BIOGRAPHY

The life of Aeschylus can be pieced together from ancient sources, especially from several biographies that survive in the manuscript tradition that are probably derived from an Alexandrian volume of biographies, perhaps by Chamaeloon. Aeschylus was born in about 525-524 B.C.E. in the Attic town of Eleusis. His father, Euphorion, was a Eupatrid (an aristocrat) and probably very wealthy. As a youth, Aeschylus witnessed the fall of Pisistratid tyranny in Athens and the beginnings of Athenian democracy, and he later lived through the Persian invasions of mainland Greece in 490 and 480 B.C.E. He is said to have fought at Marathon in 490, where he lost a brother, Cynegirus, and at Salamis in 480. Aeschylus's description in *The Persians* of the great sea battle of Salamis suggests that he was an eyewitness. Ancient reports that Aeschylus also fought in other battles of the Persian Wars, including Artemisium in 480 and Plataea in 479, are more doubtful. Aeschylus's well-known patriotism may have led to the tradition of his being involved in all these battles. Aesychlus lived in an age not only of the citizen-soldier but also of nationalistic and political poetry, and allusions to contemporary issues can be found in Aeschylus's plays. In addition to the historical play *The Persians*, other political references in the extant Aeschylean corpus include those in *Eumenides* to the reform of the Athenian Areopagus by Ephialtes in 462 and to the Athenian alliance with Argos in 458.

Evidence for Aeschylus's connections with the Eleusinian Mysteries is contradictory. In *The Frogs*, Aristophanes implies that Aeschylus was initiated into this famous mystery cult of his native city; however, in *Ethica Nicomachea* (335-323 B.C.E.; *Nicomachean Ethics*, 1797), Aristotle states that Aeschylus was accused of revealing the secrets of the mysteries in a play, and Clement of Alexandria asserts that Aeschylus was acquitted of this charge by proving that he had not been initiated. Scholars have searched the surviving plays and fragments for such a revelation, but none has been found. Certainly, the religious piety that pervades the extant plays makes conscious revelation most unlikely.

Aeschylus's dramatic career probably began very early in the fifth century B.C.E. with his first dramatic production at the Greater Dionysia between 499 and 496. His first tragic victory, for unknown plays, was won in 484, and he earned at least twelve more victories in his lifetime and several more posthumously. *The Persians*, presented in 472 together with the lost *Phineus* and *Glaucus Potnieus*, is Aeschylus's earliest extant play and won first prize. That the *choragus* of this group was Pericles, the great Athenian general and statesman, may suggest Aeschylean sympathy for Periclean political reforms.

A second production of *The Persians* was probably made within a few years at the court of Hieron, tyrant of Gela in Sicily, where Aeschylus also wrote a play called *Aetnae*, now lost, in honor of Hieron's founding of the city of Aetna in 476 B.C.E. Aeschylus's Sicilian connections can be readily explained by noting that Hieron, like other Greek tyrants, such as Polycrates of Samos and the Pisistratids of Athens, was a great patron of the arts and attracted to his court many poets and philosophers, including Pindar, Bacchylides, Simonides, and Xenophanes.

Aeschylus had certainly returned to Athens by 468 B.C.E., for he lost in the Greater Dionysia of that year to Sophocles, who won his first tragic victory. In the next year, however, Aeschylus was victorious with *Laius*, *Oedipus*, and the extant *Seven Against Thebes*, a tragic group often called Aeschylus's Theban trilogy. Evidence suggests that Aeschylus produced his Danaid trilogy, including the extant *The Suppliants* and the lost *Egyptians* and *Danaids*, in 463, when he was victorious over Sophocles. This trilogy was formerly dated on stylistic grounds as early as 490, but subsequently discovered evidence has caused scholars to revise their conclusions about Aeschylus's dramatic development and about the evolution of Greek tragedy in general.

Aeschylus's surviving trilogy, the *Oresteia*, was produced in Athens in 458 B.C.E. and was followed shortly by the poet's second trip to Gela, where he died and was buried in 456-455. The Gelans erected the following tombstone inscription in the poet's honor:

This memorial hides Aeschylus, the Athenian, son of Euphorion
Who died in wheat-bearing Gela.
The sacred battlefield of Marathon may tell of his great valor.
So, too, can the long-haired Mede, who knows it well.

Conspicuously absent from this epitaph is any reference to the literary accomplishments of Aeschylus, who is remembered only as a patriotic Athenian. The author of *The Persians* and *Eumenides* would have wanted no other eulogy.

Aeschylus had at least two sons, Euaeon and Euphorion, both of whom wrote tragedies. In 431 B.C.E., Euphorion defeated Sophocles as well as Euripides, who produced his *Mēdeia* (*Medea*, 1781) in that year. Aeschylus's nephew Philocles was also a tragedian; according to an ancient hypothesis (an introductory note providing information about the play) to Sophocles' *Oidipous Tyrannos* (c. 429 B.C.E.; *Oedipus Tyrannus*, 1715), one of Philocles' productions was even considered better than Sophocles' play.

ANALYSIS

Despite the fifth century B.C.E. Athenian political and religious issues that are diffused more often in Aeschylus's tragedies than in those of Sophocles and Euripides and that demand some historical explanation for the modern reader, the plays of Aeschylus still possess that timeless quality of thought and form that is the hallmark of classical Greek literature and that has made the themes of Aeschylean drama forever contemporary. Although Aeschylus's intense Athenian patriotism and probable support for Periclean democratic reforms is fairly well documented in his biographical sources and is reinforced by the dramatic evidence, it is his attention to theological and ethical issues and especially to the connection between Zeus and justice and to the rules governing relationships among humans and between humanity and divinity that provide a central focus for his tragedies. It cannot be a coincidence that all seven extant tragedies, while less than one-twelfth of his total corpus, reflect a constant Aeschylean concern with the theme of human suffering and its causes. Again and again, the plays of Aeschylus suggest that human suffering is divine punishment caused by human transgressions and that people bring on themselves their own sorrows by overstepping their human bounds through *hybris*, hubris or excessive pride. At the same time, the role of the gods, and especially of Zeus, in this sequence of human action and human suffering is of particular interest to Aeschylus, whose plays seek in Zeus a source of justice and of fair retribution despite the vagaries of an apparently unjust world.

THE PERSIANS

The Persians, Aeschylus's earliest surviving tragedy, analyzes this system of divine retribution in the context of the unsuccessful invasion of Greece by the Persian king Xerxes in 480-479 B.C.E. Instead of the jubilant Greek victory ode that this drama could have become in the hands of a less perceptive artist, *The Persians*, presenting events from the viewpoint of the defeated Persians rather than that of the victorious Greeks, transforms the specific, historical events into a general, universal dramatization of defeat and its causes, of hubristic actions and their punishment. The tragedy, set in the palace of Xerxes at Sousa, far from the events with which it is concerned, sacrifices the immediacy of the battlefield for a broadened perspective.

The Persian defeat at Salamis is dramatically foreshadowed in the parodos, or choral entrance song, in which description of the magnificent departure of the Persian forces contrasts with the chorus's fear of impending disaster. A central cause of this apprehension is the yoking of the Hellespont, which the Persian king had ordered to facilitate departure, and, with overweening pride, to punish the sea for inhibiting Darius's earlier expedition against Greece. The chorus of elders does not speak here specifically of hubris, but of *ate*, an untranslatable Greek word implying "blindness," "delusion," "reckless sin," and "ruin." At the climax of the parodos, the ropes that bind the Hellespont become a metaphor for the nets of *ate* from which no mortal "who enters is able to escape."

Foreshadowing is continued in the first episode, in which the queen mother Atossa describes to the cho-

rus a vision of Xerxes' defeat, which has troubled her at night. The chorus's response to this dream is the suggestion that the queen sacrifice to the chthonic powers and especially to the dead Darius, but before Atossa can act on this advice, a messenger arrives with news of the disaster at Salamis. This scene is an example of the structural and dramatic variety open to the Greek dramatist with Aeschylus's introduction of the second actor. The messenger's opening lines are in the traditional anapestic meter reserved for entrances and are followed by an epirrhematic passage in which the messenger speaks in iambic trimeter while the chorus responds in sung lyrics. No details of the battle are provided by the messenger until the queen requests them, and there follow several messenger reports, one listing Persian losses, another describing the sea battle at Salamis, a third the nearby land battle, and, finally, one announcing the losses in the fleet on the return journey. These reports are interrupted by brief interchanges between the messenger and the queen, in which both speakers respond in two or more lines of trimeter. Rarely in this early play can be found the rapid stichomythia, or conversation in alternate lines of trimeter, that is later used so effectively by two or more speakers in Greek tragedy. The messenger scene substantiates the earlier fears of the queen and the chorus with the reality of defeat, and the dramatic effect of the series of speeches is like a sequence of disastrous waves on the Persian nation. The choral ode that follows the messenger scene is a lyric lament over the disaster and contrasts vividly in its pathos with the majesty of the parodos, in which the expedition's departure was described.

The messenger scene dramatizes the actuality of the Persian defeat, but the causes of this defeat are not explained until the second episode, in which Atossa and the chorus call forth the ghost of Darius as they had planned to do before the arrival of the messenger. It is Darius who, as a ghost, has the atemporal perspective to link cause and effect and to explain the defeat of his son Xerxes. When the disaster of Salamis is announced to him, Darius's initial response is that "some great divine force has made Xerxes unable to think clearly," and he then elaborates by linking both Zeus and Xerxes himself as agents in the disaster. Darius says that Xerxes' senses were diseased when he yoked the Hellespont: "Although a mortal, he thought to have power over all the gods, but not with good counsel." Zeus did not stop Xerxes in his folly because "god joins in when a man hastens [his own destruction]," a doom that Xerxes "in his youthful boldness unwittedly accomplished." Thus, it is Xerxes' senseless pride, his haughty attempt to become more than human, which is his downfall, and the gods, especially Zeus, not only acquiesce but also assist in this downfall. Darius makes this most explicit in his prophecy of the Persian defeat at Plataea (479 B.C.E.), in which he speaks specifically of "*hybris* blossoming forth and having the fruit of *ate*" and of Zeus who is "a harsh accountant and punisher of excessively arrogant thoughts." This dramatically central episode ends with Darius advising the absent Xerxes to be more moderate.

The arrival of the defeated Xerxes in the exodos, or last scene, is, in a sense, an undramatic but necessary anticlimax to the psychopomp of Darius in the second episode. The scene with Xerxes is a purely lyric lament in which no further dramatic or thematic development is achieved. There is, in fact, no reference in the exodos to the appearance of Darius or to his explanation of events. The drama ends with Xerxes, still unconscious of his own fatal role in the disaster, giving himself over to uninhibited lamentation. This ignorance is a significant feature of Greek tragedy, and of Aeschylean tragedy in particular, a fact that has been obfuscated by Aristotelian criticism. In his *Poetics*, Aristotle placed great emphasis on a tragic fall (peripeteia) linked with recognition (anagnorisis) and tragic flaw (hamartia). Most Greek tragedies cannot be successfully interpreted through Aristotelian terminology; certainly not *The Persians*, in which there is no recognition (anagnorisis) of his tragic flaw (hamartia) by Xerxes. The disastrous effects of Xerxes' pride are well developed in *The Persians*, but they are developed for Atossa, the chorus, and the audience, not for Xerxes.

AGAMEMNON

The theological and ethical system suggested in *The Persians* can also be seen in *Agamemnon*, a play in which the theme of pride and its punishment is complicated by the issues of blood guilt and family curse. The plot is not historical in the modern sense of the word, but rather mythical, which, for the Greeks, was also historical, and it is concerned with the homecoming of Agamemnon, the leader of the Greek forces in the Trojan War, and with his subsequent brutal murder by his wife, Clytemnestra, and his cousin Aegisthus. The story is at least as old as Homer, who uses it in the *Odyssey* (c. 725 B.C.E.; English translation, 1614), but it is impossible to determine whether the stark thematic contrasts between the Aeschylean and Homeric versions are a result of an intermediary source or Aeschylean innovation. In Homer, the tale is used as an exemplum of filial duty and feminine deception: Telemachus should show as much fidelity to his missing father as Orestes did to his late father, Agamemnon, and on his visit to Hades, Odysseus is warned by the ghost of Agamemnon to beware of the guile of women. In Aeschylus's *Agamemnon*, the death of the king is not simply a result of the deception of Clytemnestra; rather, the play is a dramatized quest for the deeper causes of events, causes that are seen as a combination of past and present deeds, individual and collective guilt, and human and divine motivation.

The parodos of *Agamemnon* deals with the past. In this unusually long entrance song, the chorus of elders reflects forebodingly on the crucial event surrounding Agamemnon's departure for Troy—the sacrifice by Agamemnon of his own daughter Iphigenia. This sacrifice presented a dilemma for Agamemnon. On the one hand, it was clear that Zeus was sending him against Troy because Troy broke the Greek custom of *xenia*, or guest-friendship, in the theft of Helen, wife of Agamemnon's brother Menelaus, by the Trojan prince Paris. On the other hand, the departing Greeks had offended the goddess Artemis, who would not permit departure until Iphigenia was sacrificed. Agamemnon was thus placed in the impossible situation of either offending Zeus or killing his own daughter. He reluctantly chose the latter course. Significantly, the chorus's narration of these events is broken by the famous "Hymn to Zeus." In this prayer, occurring at the narrative point at which Agamemnon must make his decision, the chorus turns to Zeus as a source of wisdom, as a god who "has led men to think, who has set down the rule that wisdom comes through suffering." These lines, often considered the heart of *Agamemnon*, if not of the entire *Oresteia*, underscore Zeus's central role in dramatic events. Agamemnon dies not only because he killed Iphigenia, but also because of Zeus's didactic system of learning through suffering (*pathei mathos*).

The lessons of Zeus's instruction are explained in the first choral ode, a song of victory for the fall of Troy in which the chorus argues that the city fell by the lightning stroke of Zeus because of Paris's insolence in stealing Helen. It is in reference to Paris that the chorus says that "someone has denied that the gods deign to care about mortals who trample upon the beauty of holy things." Yet, by the end of the ode, Zeus's anger is not only directed toward Paris but also toward someone else who has caused so many war dead, who has become "prosperous beyond justice." Although his name is not mentioned, it is clear that this man is Agamemnon. The hubris of Agamemnon, implied in the first ode, becomes more explicit in the second episode, when a messenger arrives to confirm the fall of Troy and to report that even the temples of the gods at Troy have been destroyed. The burden for this unwarranted and insolent offense against the gods must fall squarely on the shoulders of Agamemnon, as commander, and is an act of hubris similar to Xerxes' yoking of the Hellespont.

Agamemnon's hubris is dramatically confirmed in the famous third episode, often called the "Carpet Scene" because of the purple carpet that Clytemnestra craftily laid in the path of her returning husband, supposedly as a gesture of respect but actually for Agamemnon's spiritual destruction. Agamemnon himself refers to this carpet as an honor befitting the gods alone and asks that he should be respected as a mortal, not a god. Nevertheless, Clytemnestra is able to coax her husband across the fatal tapestry by the mention of Priam, Agamemnon's defeated Trojan rival, who, in his Eastern opulence, would certainly have accepted the honor. So, the Greek king walks on the carpet into his palace and his death, not without

an apotropaic prayer that "no god strike him from afar" as he does so. Although hubris is not mentioned in this scene, there is no need to do so. Agamemnon's act is in itself visual proof of the king's overweening pride, of his excessive self-esteem. Agamemnon dies, then, for his own sins.

There are, however, further considerations: There is Cassandra, a Trojan princess whom Agamemnon has brought home as his slave and mistress. Cassandra is another proof of Agamemnon's pride; he has what a god could not have. Cassandra, a prophetess of Apollo, had dedicated her virginity to the god. When she refused the god's sexual advances, Apollo punished her by making her prophecies never believed but always true. Aeschylus uses this prophetic skill of Cassandra to great effect in the climactic fourth episode, in which the prophetess repeatedly predicts the king's and her own imminent deaths, but no one believes her. At the same time, Cassandra adds another perspective to the death of Agamemnon by mentioning "small children crying for their own death." This is a reference to the crime of Agamemnon's father, Atreus, who had killed his nephews, Aegisthus's brothers, and served them for dinner to their father, Thyestes. Cassandra's prophetic abilities thus serve to clarify the causes of Agamemnon's death, just as the ghost of Darius did Xerxes' downfall. In this way, Aeschylus manipulates Greek belief in prophecy and in ghosts to great dramatic effect.

By the time that Agamemnon's death cries ring from the palace, the king's death has been shown to be not only the result of his own sins of pride but also the result of blood guilt, of the sins of his father. The net in which Clytemnestra and Aegisthus capture Agamemnon is no simple affair, but an entangled web of his own and his father's making, of human and divine cause and effect. This web engulfs Agamemnon in the first play of the *Oresteia* and engulfs his son in the remaining two plays.

Xerxes in *The Persians* had been caught in a similar net of pride, and such links of theme and imagery between these two plays, which together represent Aeschylus's earliest and latest extant plays, suggest a continuity of thought in the Aeschylean corpus centered around hubris and its consequences. Variations on this theme can be found in the other surviving plays, such as *The Suppliants*, in which a just but mysterious Zeus is seen as the protector of the good and the punisher of evil, and *Seven Against Thebes*, in which human and divine will together with blood guilt again coalesce into disaster. Despite its diversity, the Aeschylean corpus presents a peculiar cohesion of thought. Although the lessons derived from dramatic events may be lost on Aeschylus's main characters, such as Xerxes and Agamemnon, for whom there is no "learning through suffering," the lesson of Aeschylus's plays is directed especially to the audience, not only a fifth century B.C.E. Athenian audience but also a more universal one for whom the Aeschylean play is a timeless attempt to explain the causes of human suffering through a complicated chain of cause and effect, of human action and divine punishment. Through a masterful combination of great poetry and ingenious stagecraft, Aeschylus presents in his plays the outstanding moral issues of his day and of all time.

PROMETHEUS BOUND

Prometheus Bound, the seventh play in Aeschylus's manuscript tradition, cannot be firmly dated and contains so many problems and idiosyncrasies of meter, languages, staging, and structure that a large number of modern scholars have come to question Aeschylean authorship. The arguments on both sides of the authorship debate have been thoroughly discussed by C. J. Herington in *The Author of the "Prometheus Bound"* (1970) and by M. Griffith in *The Authenticity of "Prometheus Bound"* (1977), and the debate has remained a stalemate. If this play was written by Aeschylus, it must have been written toward the end of Aeschylus's lifetime, probably after 460, and may have been part of a connected trilogy including the lost *Prometheus Lyomenos* (unbound) and *Prometheus Pyrphoros* (fire-bearer).

BIBLIOGRAPHY

Bloom, Harold, ed. *Aeschylus*. Philadelphia: Chelsea House, 2001. Part of a series on dramatists meant for secondary school students, this book contains essays examining the work and life of Aeschylus. Includes bibliography and index.

Connacher, D. J. *Aeschylus: The Earlier Plays and Related Studies*. Buffalo, N.Y.: University of Toronto Press, 1996. A study of the Greek dramatist's earlier works, with particular emphasis on his technique. Includes bibliography.

Goward, Barbara. *Telling Tragedy: Narrative Technique in Aeschylus, Sophocles, and Euripides*. London: Duckworth, 1999. The author examines the function of narrative in the works of Aeschylus, Sophocles, and Euripides. Includes bibliography and index.

Griffith, M. *The Authenticity of "Prometheus Bound."* New York: Cambridge University Press, 1977. Discusses the question of whether Aeschylus wrote *Prometheus Bound*.

Harrison, Thomas E. H. *The Emptiness of Asia: Aeschylus' "Persians" and the History of the Fifth Century*. London: Duckworth, 2000. An examination of Aeschylus's *The Persians* from the historical perspective. Includes bibliography and index.

Herington, C. J. *The Author of the "Prometheus Bound."* Austin: University of Texas Press, 1970. An examination of the authorship question regarding *Prometheus Bound*.

Podlecki, Anthony J. *The Political Background of Aeschylean Tragedy*. 2d ed. London: Bristol Classical Press, 1999. In addition to providing literary criticism, the author looks at the politics that pervades much of Aeschylus's work. Includes bibliography and index.

Sullivan, Shirley Darcus. *Aeschylus's Use of Psychological Terminology: Traditional and New*. Montreal: McGill-Queen's University Press, 1997. Sullivan examines the psychological aspects of the language used in Aeschylus's tragedies. Includes bibliography and index.

Taplin, Oliver. *The Stagecraft of Aeschylus: The Dramatic Use of Exits and Entrances in Greek Tragedy*. Reprint. Oxford: Clarendon, 1989. Taplin focuses on Aeschylus's stagecraft, particularly his use of dramatic visual devices.

Thomas J. Sienkewicz

ISIDORA AGUIRRE

Born: Santiago, Chile; March 22, 1919

PRINCIPAL DRAMA

Pacto de medianoche, pr. 1954

Carolina, pr., pb. 1955 (*Express for Santiago*, 1961)

Entre dos trenes, pb. 1955, pr. 1956

Selecciones, pb. 1955

La micro, pr. 1956

Las sardinas: O, La supressión de Amanda, pr. 1956

Anacleto Chin, Chin, pr. 1956, pb. 1982

Dos mys dos son cinco, pr. 1956

Las tres Pascualas, pr., pb. 1957 (*The Three Pascualas*, 1965)

La población Esperanza, pr. 1959 (with Manuel Rojas)

La pérgola de las flores, pr. 1959, pb. 1986

Los papeleros, pb. 1964, pr. 1965

La dama del canasto, pr. 1965

Magy ante el espejo, pr. 1968

Los que van quedando en el camino, pr. 1969, pb. 1970 (*Ranquil*, 1988)

Quien tuvo la culpa de la muerte de la María González, pr. 1970

Los Cabezones de la Feria, pr. 1972

En aquellos locos años veinte, pr. 1974

Lautaro, pr., pb. 1982

Amor a la africana, pr. 1986

Federico, hermano, pr. 1986

Retablo de Yumbel, pr. 1986, pb. 1987 (*Altarpiece of Yumbel*, 1991)

Diálogos de fin de siglo, pr., pb. 1989

Los libertadores, Bolívar y Miranda, pr. 1989, pb. 1993

Diego de Almagro, pr. 1995

Manuel, pr., pb. 2000

OTHER LITERARY FORMS

Isidora Aguirre began her literary career writing stories and novels for children. In 1954, she began concentrating on drama, for which she is best known.

She has also written for the cinema. She collaborated on the script for *Alsino and the Condor* (1982; *Alsino y el cóndor*, 1983), a Chilean film made in Mexico under the direction of Miguel Littin, which received international acclaim.

ACHIEVEMENTS

Critics of the Chilean theater recognize Isidora Aguirre as one of the most important figures among a group of dramatists who appeared on the national scene during the 1950's. The members of this group, known as the Generation of the 1950's, had as a common characteristic the rejection of the old naturalistic models that had dominated (and continue to dominate) the Chilean theater since the beginning of the twentieth century. Seeking new forms of aesthetic expression, these dramatists came in contact with the latest theatrical innovations in Europe, which were quickly assimilated into their plays. Aguirre's works reflect these new aesthetic tendencies. In thematic, formal, and technical aspects, as well as in her inclination toward realism and expressionism, Aguirre reveals a close link to the theater of Bertolt Brecht.

Aguirre's plays have enjoyed great popularity in Chile, making her one of the best-known dramatists of recent decades. She has also gained critical acclaim and won various national awards. *La población Esperanza* received the Golden Laurel Prize in 1960. Aguirre was given the Santiago Municipal Prize twice, for *Los papeleros* in 1966 and *Ranquil* in 1972. Aguirre won honorable mention for *Ranquil* from the Casa de las Américas in 1969, the Catholic University's Eugenio Dittborn award in 1983 for *Lautaro*, and the prestigious award Casa de las Américas in La Habana in 1987 for *Altarpiece of Yumbel*. In 2000, *Manuel* received an Honorary Award from the Catholic University of Santiago.

Aguirre began writing light comedies and later moved toward a theater closely tied to the sociopolitical situation in Chile and throughout Latin America. During a decade of rapid social change, this playwright took a stand sympathetic to the oppressed classes and in opposition to the status quo. This political position is demonstrated in her selection of characters who represent the struggle of common people demanding a just place in society. Implicitly or explicitly, these plays decry poverty and denounce institutionalized violence in state organizations, misuse of power, and other forms of social injustice. As a playwright, Aguirre studies in depth the conflicts that animate her plays. On the basis of her own experiences and observations, she creates authentic characters, through whom she issues a call for social change, while holding the audience's interest.

Aguirre acknowledges the influence on her work of numerous dramatists, including Anton Chekhov, Arthur Miller, Eugene O'Neill, William Shakespeare, Armand Gatti, and Jean Genet. It is Brecht, however, whom she names as her mentor because of his assertion that ideology enhances the theater. Brecht's influence on her work has been noted primarily in the formal aspect, and to a lesser extent in the use of epic distance, which limits the audience's sense of identification with the dramatic world. Nevertheless, recognizing that works with social themes are the most interesting to her "because they are a living testimony which obligates the audience to become aware of the problems," Aguirre has adopted one of Brecht's principle strategies: using the theater to arouse the viewer's critical intelligence in order to promote social change.

BIOGRAPHY

Isidora Aguirre was born in 1919 into an upper-middle-class family in Santiago. She completed her high school education at Jean D'Arc, a private French high school, and later entered the university to pursue a career in social service, which she abandoned two years later to study the fine arts. Aguirre completed studies in drawing at the University of Chile School of Fine Arts; ballet at the Andrée Haas Academy of Dance; drama at the Ministry of Education Theater Academy; and cinematography at the Institute for the Advanced Study of Cinematography in Paris.

During the mid-1950's, Aguirre focused her creative energies on drama. As a result, she had a pro-

found influence on the public, which few playwrights can match. Over a period of six years, from the first performance of one of her works in 1954 to the first performance of *La pérgola de las flores* in 1959, the prolific Aguirre wrote ten plays, all of which were performed for the first time by professional and amateur companies in central and neighborhood theaters. *La pérgola de las flores* was Aguirre's first play to win for her recognition as a dramatist, and it became the most popular musical comedy in Chile; it was also a great financial success. After *La pérgola de las flores*, Aguirre began writing plays containing stronger social messages, though she continued to use comedy to some extent. The work that marked the beginning of this trend was *La población esperanza*.

Gifted with a lively spirit and an abundance of energy, Aguirre has succeeded over the years in combining her work as a playwright with a number of activities related to the theater. In 1959, she began teaching drama at the University of Chile and at the State Technical University. During this period, she also developed theatrical workshops on contemporary playwriting techniques, dramatic improvisation, and popular and didactic theater in Santiago and other cities. In 1973, she left her university position to pursue other activities related to the theater.

Aguirre's eagerness to meet and establish contacts with other Latin American writers and dramatists led to her participation in international theater conventions and festivals. During the 1970's she traveled to Cuba, where on two separate occasions she was chosen as a member of the Casa de Las Américas panel of judges. She participated as a representative of Chile in international theater encounters in Ecuador, Peru, and Colombia, where she also taught courses in playwriting.

During the 1980's, Aguirre's reputation and activity in the theater showed no signs of diminishing. On the contrary, the staging of some of her early plays, and Aguirre's free adaptations of classical dramas such as Lope de Vega Carpio's *Fuenteovejuna* (wr. 1611-1618, pb. 1619; *The Sheep Well*, 1936), Shakespeare's *Richard III* (pr. c. 1592-1593), the anonymous work *Lazarillo de Tormes*, and Sophocles' tragedy

Oidipous Tyrannos (c. 429 B.C.E.; *Oedipus Tyrannus*, 1715), the latter of which she adapted in 1984, evidenced a renewed national interest in her work. Through the 1990's Aguirre continued writing and winning national and international recognition for her plays.

ANALYSIS

The majority of Isidora Aguirre's short comedies have shared neither the high quality nor the success of her plays with social themes. The one exception, *La pérgola de las flores*, has been the greatest success in the history of Chilean theater. It has also been well received in Mexico, Cuba, Spain, Bolivia, and Argentina, where it was made into a film.

LA PÉRGOLA DE LAS FLORES

The popularity of the musical comedy as a genre directly descending from the Spanish *zarzuela* motivated Aguirre to write *La pérgola de las flores*. This light comedy satirizes the upper strata of Santiago society during the 1920's while depicting the common people sympathetically. A spontaneous country girl in love with a young peasant and a florist fighting to defend a flower stand in the snobbish Santiago environment are notable examples of Aguirre's portrayal of common folk.

Aguirre used a factual event as the basis for *La pérgola de las flores*: the change in location of the flower market, which was situated on an important avenue in Santiago. Needing to remodel this important thoroughfare, the City of Santiago issued a decree for the transfer of the flower market to another neighborhood in the city. Because the market was very popular, however, the decision to move it was met with heavy opposition, which delayed the move for more than twenty years.

La pérgola de las flores is a delightful, entertaining work dominated by sentiment and a portrayal of the cultural environment. It is brimming with scintillating and ingenious dialogue, which captures the language and expressions of the upper class and the spirit of popular humor with all its colorful figures of speech. Nevertheless, Aguirre does not ignore social issues in preference for pleasantry; she focuses on the people's fight in defense of the florists.

The social implications of the play have been recognized in Mexico and in Cuba, though in Chile, critics have placed more emphasis on the work's comedic aspect.

LA POBLACIÓN ESPERANZA

Aguirre's interest in writing plays with a social theme began with *La población Esperanza*, in which she, along with Manuel Rojas, attempts to portray the miserable life of the slums: Its central theme is the unsuccessful struggle of a thief to improve the conditions of his life. The play has a weak plot, and its characters are not fully developed, but Aguirre overcomes these problems in the staging of *Los papeleros*, a realistic epic drama.

LOS PAPELEROS

In *Los papeleros*, Aguirre portrays in nine scenes the living conditions of various sectors of the working class, conditions similar to those of the *Lumpenproletariat*. Using Brecht's theatrical techniques to invoke in the audience a sense of alienation, or *Verfremdungseffekt*, Aguirre tells the story of the garbage collectors who subsist under intolerable conditions at the dump.

In this play, the playwright breaks away from the traditional Chilean dramatic schema: the stereotypical image of the woman as weak and passive and completely removed from the process of social change. This type of artificial aesthetic portrayal changes drastically in *Los papeleros*, in which Aguirre creates a new female character, whose development is related to the historical context of the play, which takes place in a decade of social unrest and popular struggles.

The play is set in a poverty-stricken suburb of Santiago, where the lives of the garbagemen are being destroyed by alcohol, inertia, and passivity. The conflict of the play is between the proprietor of the dump, who sells the junk collected by the garbagemen, and the leaders of the garbage collectors, represented by Romilia and Rucio. The protagonist of *Los papeleros* is Romilia, whose most pronounced trait is the great combative strength that she displays in her struggle to defend her rights. Her transformation is brought about by the appearance of the son whom she had abandoned in the provinces. The son arouses her dormant maternal conscience and causes her to begin the difficult struggle to attain the houses that the proprietor had once promised the garbagemen. The proprietor is inaccessible to the workers; all they know of him is the large fence surrounding his house and the sound of his voice barking orders through a megaphone. He has a man, nicknamed "El Perro" (the dog), who represents him and carries out his orders. To achieve her purpose, Romilia bravely organizes the people in the dump for the fight to claim their union rights. They form a committee, whose task is to confront the proprietor with the serious housing problems of the people living at the dump. The group is received with threats of violence. The committee members become discouraged; they follow the proprietor's orders to return to their homes. Romilia persists, alone in her struggle, until she can fight no longer. She is made powerless by the indifference of her fellow workers and by the proprietor's insensitivity, and after the birth of a child at the dump, she decides to set fire to the houses. El Perro, the proprietor's representative, threatens her with a weapon and orders her to surrender. Everyone says that she has gone crazy. Defended only by Rucio and her son, Romilia screams an impassioned defense of her cause. The play ends with a song that arouses the audience's critical reflection on the problem.

Using the Brechtian concept of epic theater, Aguirre tries in this play to appeal to the audience's sense of reason rather than to their emotions to present convincingly her social message. This attempt to create alienation can be perceived in the songs, the narrator's account of the action, the unresolved conflict, and the exposure of the society's faults. Aguirre manages to keep the play balanced by avoiding sentimental melodrama and superficial simplification of the situation, and by showing logically why it is difficult for the garbagemen to organize themselves and what their real alternatives are. Thus, rather than trying to define the problem clearly, the play simply depicts an actual situation. It does this by criticizing the regime then in power, the politicians' demagogic promises, and the lack of laws protecting the public welfare. Although *Los papeleros* ends with the conflict unresolved, leaving the audience with the task of thinking about a solution, the play suggests that the key to resolving the problem lies in organization and moral courage.

RANQUIL

Ranquil follows essentially the same formal structure as *Los papeleros*. In contrast to *Los papeleros*, however, *Ranquil* provides an explicit, didactic political message. In effect, the play is a call to social consciousness through the dramatization of an event that occurred in Chile in 1934. Aguirre chose as the central theme of her play a peasants' rebellion that took place in the town of Ranquil. Several peasant families were killed when the police suppressed the rebellion. The insurrection was in response to a government order to evict the peasants from their lands and relocate them in the hills. In writing her play, Aguirre used real accounts of the rebellion by peasants in the region, spoke with some of the actual survivors, collected data, and researched the history of the Chilean peasantry. She used analogies to relate this historic event to contemporary peasant struggles. In this way, she offers the audience a specific political and ideological option.

The play, which is divided into two parts, begins with the announcement that land will be given to the poor. Thus, in the prologue, the tone for the entire production is set by Actor 1 and the chorus, who project the dramatic synthesis of events that link historic events to the present. Lorenza Uribe, the protagonist, is the character who links the chronicles of the past with the present as she tells her grandnephew Juanucho about the insurrection that had occurred during her childhood. A group of peasants marching past her house demanding that the government give them the land that they were promised serves as the associative element between the two historical periods. To tie together successfully two separate dates, Aguirre resorts to a simple dramatic device: She transforms Mama Lorenza into the young Lorenza with a simple change of clothing and minor set changes. In this way, the protagonist continues to be haunted by the memory of the dead: her three brothers, who were murdered; a teacher, Juan Leiva, who had informed the workers of their union rights; and her lover, Rogelio. She remembers also the attitude of the landowners, and the revolt of the sixty men and women armed only with sticks and machetes.

In the dramatic plot, Lorenza is the conscious voice of the peasants fighting for their rights and their dignity. Like Romilia in *Los papeleros*, Lorenza is characterized by a combative spirit, strong moral convictions, and courage. The antagonistic force opposing her and the other peasants is represented by the landowners, the government officials, the police, and the military. The state is portrayed as the ally of the ruling class, which opposes the people struggling to defend themselves against the decree to expel them from their land. Presenting this strong conflict of interest, the play is an active incitement to the peasants to expropriate the land when the possibilities for legal recourse have been exhausted and the living conditions are unbearable.

In contrast to *Los papeleros*, which leaves the resolution of the conflict in the audience's hands, *Ranquil* provides a definite solution to the problem. In this respect, *Ranquil* offers a Manichaean representation of reality, lauding the characters who represent good, and criticizing those who represent evil. This Manichaeanism removes any subtlety from the social message. Rather than appealing to the audience's critical reasoning, the personification of the characters approaches the realm of melodrama, which leads the audience to an emotional commitment—the anti-Brechtian concept. Nevertheless, Aguirre successfully employs Brechtian techniques in lighting, sound effects, chorus, offstage narration, placards which announce the action, and music. These audiovisual resources significantly enhance the staging of the play.

The close correspondence between contemporary political events, particularly to the agrarian reform promoted by the government, and the events in the play caused heated public debate among the supporters and opponents of the government policies when *Ranquil* premiered. Yet it received honorable mention from the Casa de las Américas in 1969 and received the Santiago Municipal Prize in 1972. The play has been performed in Germany under the title *Die guten Tage, die schlechten Tage*, as well as in Austria, Switzerland, the former Czechoslovakia, Cuba, Mexico, Colombia, and the Netherlands. In spite of its contro-

versial nature—its open criticism of the government at that time—the play was presented by the drama department at the theater of the University of Chile, the state's main educational institution.

LAUTARO

In *Lautaro*, Aguirre once again uses historical events for the setting of her dramatic work: Spain's conquest of Chile is the subject of this play. The play is structured around two main characters: Pedro de Valdivia, the Spanish captain, and Lautaro, who, at the age of eighteen, is the congenial guerrilla leader of the Mapuches tribe, one of the tribes of the Araucanian Indians. Aguirre attempts to narrate the epic of the Araucanian people, who, in their refusal to submit, struggled for three centuries against the Spanish conquerors. No war of the Spanish conquest was as long and bitter as the Araucanian War. During the height of the war, Chile was referred to on the Iberian peninsula as the graveyard of the Spaniards. This struggle, which began as a war of self-defense and resistance on the part of the Araucanians, evolved into Indian insurrections throughout the country.

To dramatize these events, Aguirre divides the play into two parts, each of which consists of a number of scenes subtly separated by changes in lighting and instrumental music. As she had done with *Ranquil*, which she had researched for four years, Aguirre documented this play with written sources on Lautaro and on Pedro de Valdivia. In addition, she established contact with the Mapuche Indians in the south of the country, transforming historical information into personal experience.

The first part of the play opens with the depiction of an idyllic world: a forest in southern Chile, where the young Lautaro is playing happily with his future wife, Guacolda. This harmonious life is abruptly disrupted by the arrival of the conqueror. Lautaro is taken prisoner and placed in the service of Pedro de Valdivia as a stable boy. During his years of captivity as Valdivia's servant, Lautaro learns horsemanship, the handling of weapons, and the Spanish way of life. As a result, a father-son relationship develops between him and Valdivia. The first part ends with Lautaro's flight to his people's camp. This is the point at which Lautaro's definitive character transformation takes place, as he is chosen chief of his people. In the second part, Lautaro is at the center of the dramatic action, not only as chief warrior but also in his role as Guacolda's loving husband. In this manner, the development of the military conflict is interrupted by love scenes in which both Lautaro and Valdivia are portrayed as ordinary human beings with everyday concerns. Thus, Aguirre succeeds in combining scenes that develop in a realistic, familiar, and intimate manner with scenes that reach epic proportions. Valdivia's defeat in Tucapel is narrated alternately by Guacolda and by Doña Sol, Valdivia's wife. Using this original technique, Aguirre has each woman describe the fate of her loved one in the battle. Valdivia's death precedes the death of Lautaro, which is recounted in the epilogue by the actors and the chorus.

Performed for the first time in 1982, *Lautaro* was the first theatrical success of that season. It received the Catholic University's Eugenio Dittborn award in 1983. Although the play is a reminder of the heroic fight of the Araucanians and their guerrilla leader, it has a universal message because it symbolizes the conflict between native and colonizer—a conflict that could take place anywhere at any time.

ALTARPIECE OF YUMBEL

In 1986 Aguirre wrote *Altarpiece of Yumbel*, relying on different metadramatic conventions to encode its political protest. Specifically, the play uses metadramatic strategies such as the play-within-the-play, role playing within the role, and the real-life reference within the play to instill the playwright's point of view in the reader/spectator's consciousness.

Inspired by the martyrdom of Saint Sebastian under the reign of Emperor Diocletian, Aguirre creates an allegory between the Christian persecution during the Roman Empire and the political persecution suffered by the opponents of General Augusto Pinochet's regime. Using the metadramatic technique of the play-within-the-play, the author portrays the reenactment of the martyrdom of Saint Sebastian, patron saint of Yumbel, by the families of nineteen political prisoners who had disappeared in September, 1973, and whose remains were found in Yumbel in 1979. The result is a fascinating view on the stage of three meta-

dramatic planes: the workshop where the actors rehearse, the plaza of the town of Yumbel, and the dungeons of the Roman Empire, where Christians are interrogated and tortured.

This play occupies a place in the history of Chilean theatre during the dictatorship not only because it is a work rich in theatrical signs but also because, through the reflection of Chilean political events, it reaches an audience that can recognize itself in the world of the play.

In 1987, *Altarpiece of Yumbel* was published in Cuba and in Chile. Four years later, it was published in Madrid, Spain, and again in Chile during 1994. This play was performed for only a few days in Concepción because of the violent political repression that followed the assassination attempt on General Pinochet in 1986. Years later the play was succesfully performed in Nicaragua and Montreal, Canada.

MANUEL AND OTHER PLAYS

During the last years of the 1980's and the 1990's, Aguirre continued writing plays that portray historical and political figures such as the president of Chile José Manuel Balmaceda (1840-1891) in *Diálogos de fin de siglo, Los libertadores: Bolívar y Miranda*, which received the Annual Award of the Chilean National Book Council in 1993, *Diego de Almagro*, a play dedicated to the discoverer of Chile, and the last version of *Manuel*, which depicts the patriotism of the guerrilla leader Manuel Rodríguez during the War of Independence with Spain. The romantic adventures of Rodríguez's life along with his tragic death sparked an emotional reaction in the audience, a good example of the anti-Brechtian concept, although Aguirre continued employing Brechtian techniques such as the lighting and the chorus. In this play, the author succeeds once again in combining scenes with music created by Manuel López, and several songs received acclaimed performances in Chile.

OTHER MAJOR WORKS

LONG FICTION: *Doy por vivido todo lo soñado*, 1987; *Carta a Roque Dalton*, 1990; *Santiago de diciembre a diciembre*, 1998.

CHILDREN'S LITERATURE: *Ocho cuentos*, 1945; *Waikii*, 1948.

BIBLIOGRAPHY

Andrade, Elba, and Hilde Cramsie, eds. *Dramaturgas latinoamericanas contemporáneas.* Madrid: Verbum, 1991. Anthology dedicated to the works and life of Aguirre and six other women playwrights. Contains an analysis of each of the plays reproduced in the volume and the playwrights' individual responses to a series of questions dealing with their conceptions about theater. In Spanish.

Andrade, Elba, and Walter Fuentes, eds. *Teatro y dictadura en Chile.* Santiago, Chile: Documentas, 1994. Critical anthology that includes essays about representative authors, including Aguirre, and their plays that were written under the dictatorship of Chilean general Augusto Pinochet. It also includes the testimonies of the playwrights about the history of the Chilean theater during that controversial historical period. In Spanish.

Castedo-Ellerman, Elena. *El teatro chileno de mediados del siglo veinte.* Santiago, Chile: Andres Bello, 1982. Castedo attempts to characterize the Chilean theater during the 1980's by categorizing playwrights (including Aguirre) and their works into six groups, which are related to the influence of a particular dramatist such as Henrik Ibsen, Tennessee Williams, and Bertolt Brecht, among others. In Spanish.

Hurtado, María de la Luz. *Dramaturgia chilena, 1960-1973.* Santiago, Chile: CENECA, 1983. The book offers a critical analysis of the theater written in Chile between 1960 and 1973. It focuses on plays and authors, including Aguirre, who depict in their works the social problems of the decade and suggest political solutions. In Spanish.

Piga, Domingo, and Orlando Rodríguez. *Teatro chileno del siglo veinte.* Santiago, Chile: Lathrop, 1964. Comprehensive overview of the development of the Chilean theater from 1900 to 1964. Authors such as Isidora Aguirre, Luis Alberto Heiremans, Alejandro Sieveking, and Egon Wolff are recognized as the most important playwrights of the decade of the 1960's for their role as renovators. In Spanish.

Salas, Teresa Cajiao, and Margarita Vargas, eds. *Women Writing Women: An Anthology of Spanish-American Theater of the 1980's.* Albany: State University of New York Press, 1997. The first anthology in English dedicated exclusively to Spanish American women playwrights, including Aguirre. Includes eight plays by award-winning authors who have received national and international acclaim.

Elba Andrade,
updated by Elba Andrade

JOANNE AKALAITIS

Born: Cicero, Illinois; June 29, 1937

PRINCIPAL DRAMA
Dressed Like an Egg, pr. 1977, pb. 1984
Southern Exposure, pr. 1979
Dead End Kids: A History of Nuclear Power, pr. 1980, pb. 1982
Green Card, pr. 1986, pb. 1987

OTHER LITERARY FORMS

JoAnne Akalaitis is known primarily as a playwright, director, and actor. Her tribute, "Meeting Beckett," appeared in the Fall, 1990, issue of *The Drama Review.* She directed the film version of *Dead End Kids* in 1986.

ACHIEVEMENTS

JoAnne Akalaitis and Mabou Mines, the theater company that she helped form in 1969, are best known for their contributions to multimedia, collaborative work. Akalaitis has received support from the National Endowment for the Arts, the Rockefeller Foundation, and the New York State Creative Artists Public Service Program. Mabou Mines did not originally consider itself to be performance theater. Its conceptual collaborations, such as *Red Horse Anima-*

tion (1970) and *The Saint and the Football Player* (1976), evolved slowly, taking place first as visual performance pieces in New York's Solomon R. Guggenheim Museum, the Museum of Modern Art, and the Berkeley and Pasadena art museums. Other multimedia events by Akalaitis include performances with the 1976 American Dance Festival. Composer Philip Glass, who was once married to Akalaitis, provided music for Mabou Mines in such productions as *Dressed Like an Egg* and *Dead End Kids*, which was the only New York avant-garde play included in the Toronto Theatre Festival in 1980. She has won three Obie Awards and in August, 1991, succeeded Joseph Papp as director of the New York Shakespeare Festival at the Public Theatre, a position she maintained until early 1993.

BIOGRAPHY

The influence of JoAnne Akalaitis's background appears in various forms in her work. Born in Chicago, Illinois, in 1937, she was reared in a predominantly Lithuanian Catholic neighborhood. She studied philosophy at the University of Chicago and Stanford University, training that emerges in her constant fascination with the nature of being. She worked at the Actors' Workshop in San Francisco in 1962, where she first met Lee Breuer and Ruth Maleczech, with whom she formed the theater collective Mabou Mines in 1969. Her acting teachers included Herbert Berghof, Bill Hickey, and later Spalding Gray and Joyce Aaron of Open Theatre. She has commented in an interview with Jonathan Kalb that having two children with her former husband, composer Philip Glass, may have kept her from doing more work, but that she would not be who she is without them.

In 1993, only twenty months after being appointed artistic director of the Public Theatre by Joseph Papp, Akalaitis was dismissed from that position in a sudden Public Theatre Board decision. Although the board's decision may have been partly based on Akalaitis's performance of her administrative duties as artistic director, her political agenda, her working style, and various theater business issues, Akalaitis remains an artist who is on the cutting edge of theater.

ANALYSIS

JoAnne Akalaitis's place in the history of theater is, according to her own assessment, not connected with the American theater tradition of such artists as Tennessee Williams, Arthur Miller, and Edward Albee, who, despite their apparent differences, all have family and relationships at the core of their work. Solidly nested in avant-garde theater, Akalaitis's work with Mabou Mines is more international and multimedia in flavor. Surrealist and expressionist elements appear in nontraditional use of objects and lighting. Like Bertolt Brecht, Mabou Mines creates a reflexive world in which the actors call attention to the existence of the stage and their own acting, through nonconcealment of set changes, onstage narration, shifting of character portrayal among various actors, and partial set designs that reveal the bare bones of the stage.

At once grounded in history and deliberately detached from context, Akalaitis's work is highly conceptual, tempting the audience to decipher or create the play's patterns while deconstructing these patterns, even as they grow. Her views on acting include a firm determination not to manipulate actors or audiences but rather to allow whatever works for the moment to happen. The methods of Akalaitis and Mabou Mines stem from their notions of group consciousness, and they aim to create theater from the dialectic between past and present, traditional theater and nontheatrical media, and group and individual.

DRESSED LIKE AN EGG

Akalaitis's first widely successful production, *Dressed Like an Egg*, first presented by the New York Shakespeare Festival in May of 1977, is a collage piece with ten segments: "Prologue," "The Dance," "The Cage," "The Bath," "The Seaside," "The Cage (Part II)," "The Pantomime," "Opium," "The Novel," and "Age." Based on the writings of Colette, each of the segments deals in some manner with the issue of gender. The prologue begins with a brief recitation on carrying a child high in the womb. The play moves quickly to "The Dance," which explores relationships between men and women, juxtaposing such romantic elements as a Chopin polonaise to the obvious movements of a stagehand who offhandedly whistles the tune as he works. Flowers and lines about the ecstasy of love are delivered by males and females wearing turn-of-the-century undergarments and gazing into hand mirrors as they speak, thus undercutting the emotion and sentimentality of their words. "The Cage" and "The Bath" feature trapeze work and a bathing scene, followed by "The Seaside," in which a man claims that he writes out titles the library should have, a service he claims preserves the honor of the catalogue. These comic scenes focus audience attention on the concept of the ideal in sexuality, romance, and intellect.

The structure of the play is not at first apparent, but on closer inspection, the second half seems more serious, less playful, despite occasional absurdities that may draw audience laughter. "The Cage (Part II)" deals with the ending of romance, and the last line, "I'm cold," hints at death, a line reiterated as the last phrase of the final scene. In absurd recapitulation of the theme of physical passion, a stagehand commands a woman to "let loose a breast!" in "The Pantomime." "Opium" and "The Novel" quote extensively from Colette on the topics of opium dens and the power play of romantic involvements. These two segments both depict decadent phases of development, one within an individual or culture and one within a relationship. The historical connections and recurrence of themes achieve full circle in "Age," which combines images of American planes and the cycle of Venus, a planet that grows into its period of greatest brilliance every eight years. The section on Venus indirectly comments on the waxing and waning of romantic impulses, at both an individual and a cultural level.

As in most of Akalaitis's works, visual and aural richness play an integral role in the production. *Dressed Like an Egg* contrasts the soft romantic elements of seashell footlights, pastel pinks, blues, and grays, with the crudity of modern fabrics, silver lamé, a Celastic dress, a mylar rug, and the startling image of hairy male arms and hands dancing in women's shoes. Stereotypically feminine symbols, such as carnations and irises, act as counterpoint to a woman snoring loudly. *Dressed Like an Egg* explores sexual ambiguity in other visually shocking scenes: For example, a woman dressed as a mummy passionately kisses another woman who is dressed as a man in an allusion to Colette's intimate friendships with other women.

SOUTHERN EXPOSURE

Akalaitis works well with historical information, weaving facts into the fabric of a purely modern vision, including abstract philosophy and absurdist elements of theater performance. *Southern Exposure*, performed at The New Theatre Festival, Baltimore, in 1979, is an exploration of exterior and interior poles. The play offers tribute to early explorers of the Antarctic at the same time that it explores interior or mental uncharted territory, areas of the mind untouched by civilization, perhaps seeking the blank spot of pure being, nonbeing, or Nirvana. As in *Dressed Like an Egg*, past and present commingle in delightful ways, with the idea of blankness as the element that draws people to superimpose definitions and "culture" on empty space. In the prologue, a woman dressed in Edwardian style builds a penguin nest as she explains the penguin family system, in which the father warms the eggs. Blackout follows this touching scene, after which a film of a modern couple visiting aquarium penguins appears, accompanied by a female voiceover describing the timeless penguin burial ground, where dead penguins float, layer on layer, preserved in the ice of Antarctica.

In the "Shackleton Story," a scene in *Southern Exposure*, a couple in bed recount the disastrous mission of Ernest Shackleton's Trans-Antarctic Expedition from 1914 to 1917. The melancholy quality of this historical document diminishes as the woman drops black cubes into the man's lap. In "Mirage," a man draws the word "horizon" on a blank paper, then rips and crinkles it, underscoring the failure of art to capture the immediate quality of the environment, just as the explorer fails to encompass the vastness of physical space. "Bed" and "Food" bring the play to a humorous, mundane level, with the account of the Shackleton party's obsession with fantasies of huge repasts. The next segment, "Quilt," takes the audience to the domestic scene of a man and a woman sewing a pattern on a quilt as they discuss the failure of Robert Falcon Scott and Roald Amundsen, as slides are projected onto the background. The quilt and the final reading from the explorer's journal point to humanity's drive to trace the pattern of life, even if this attempt is utterly futile.

The stark set serves as an additional character in the piece. Whites predominate, with only the gray stones of a penguin nest, a book, a grayish chair, and the gray shadow of a canted bed offering contrast to the stark simplicity of the set. The set, costumes, slides, film, and props all call attention to the connections between art and life, between the exploration of geographical domains and the intellectual and spiritual realms of art. Human beings' attempts to impose a design on this blank space are portrayed simultaneously as the origin of nobility and the destruction of the very openness necessary to creativity.

DEAD END KIDS

Dead End Kids, one of the group's most widely publicized works and clearly its most didactic, is worthy of detailed analysis. The play's opening at The Public Theatre in November of 1980 exemplifies the group's attempt to break down boundaries between audience and performers, between theater and life, with the performance beginning even before the audience enters the theater. In the lobby, patrons view a 1950's-style science fair, whose theme is "Atoms for Peace." As people enter the theater, they hear the droning voice of a girl describing effective construction and use of home bomb shelters, a haunting recapitulation of many of the defense department films of the 1950's. The girl's speech ends with an admonition to be prepared and to remember President Franklin D. Roosevelt's famous line, "There is nothing to fear but fear itself," a statement whose irony becomes more apparent as the play continues.

The appearance of such characters as alchemists, Madame Marie Curie, Albert Einstein, a lecturer, a magician, a young female doctoral student, and an announcer underscore humanity's communal responsibility for the development of nuclear energy and weapons. When Mephistopheles and Faust appear, reciting in German as Madame Curie conducts a simultaneous commentary, the link between nuclear power and the desire for metaphysical power becomes apparent. In the next scene, army generals and a sexy stenographer join with Mephistopheles, sitting around a conference table, smoking and guffawing at double entendres laced through descriptions of the first nuclear explosion. This scene portrays military knowledge as a means to establish virility and provide male bonding.

After this relatively comic interlude, the intermission actually returns the audience to more sober aspects of the play's nuclear theme, with the fallout shelter tape continuing throughout. On return to their seats, audiences witness a film compilation of 1950's government propaganda films for nuclear power and arms. A man and woman recite back and forth all that they have seen in the universe, and they are then joined by a series of characters, including a boy nerd, a Cub Scout, an older woman, and a teenager, all of whom begin dancing the Jerk, until the music ceases and they end frozen in grotesque, strained poses, as a voice recites statistics about the risk of lung cancer caused by plutonium particles. The lecturer continues with graphic information about the effects of radiation sickness, as various listeners display a disturbing lack of emotion. The play closes much as it began, with voices of two girls reciting definitions of nuclear terms; as the audience exits, the fallout shelter tape resumes. The play accomplishes its purpose quite effectively, showing at once the absurdity and logic behind the development of nuclear power, as a natural outgrowth of human intellectual curiosity and the self-destructive impulse toward ultimate domination over life itself.

GREEN CARD

In keeping with Akalaitis's interest in social responsibility for individual suffering, *Green Card* addresses the issue of United States immigration policies. Through what Akalaitis calls a "collage" of characters, the play presents information about the lives and viewpoints of aliens, from a Salvadoran refugee to a Jewish immigrant of the late 1900's. As with *Dead End Kids*, the opening occurs as the audience enters, with loudspeaker voices delivering lines relevant to the play's theme. A woman's recitation of Emma Lazarus's poem, "Send these, the homeless, tempest-tost to me," fades under a booming male voice reeling off racial slurs and epithets. A spotlight shines on a master of ceremonies who cheerfully calls out insulting terms for different ethnic and racial groups. As if in answer, the light on him fades and another appears, highlighting a collection of men and women grouped together. To the sound of blasting rock music, they break into dance, and then, just as suddenly, stop, paralyzed and frightened-looking, as before.

Green Card opened in Los Angeles' Mark Taper Forum in 1986, a location appropriate to the play's immediate concern. At one point the Salvadoran refugee comments that El Centro, near Los Angeles, is "really a jail," thus bringing the play's suffering into the backyard of the audience. Personal histories of individual men and women interweave with ethnic tidbits in this sometimes humorous, always biting, commentary on the new "melting pot" on the West Coast. The play repeatedly suggests the United States' complicity in the bloody wars and political repression that has driven people from their homelands in Central America and elsewhere in the world. The issue of citizen and government responsibility is not resolved, nor is the fate of the aliens whose lives have been briefly displayed. *Green Card* closes with a line of men and women waiting at a bus stop, all gazing hopefully down the line into a less than rosy future. Some viewers find the play painful to watch, oppressive in its grim depiction of apparently futile struggles. Others see more optimism and a call for action, but regardless of one's interpretation, Akalaitis's work demands that its audience grapple with disturbing political realities.

AKALAITIS AS DIRECTOR

If Akalaitis creates a stir by her selection of controversial subject matter, she creates an even greater controversy in her treatment of other playwrights' work in her role as director. The most outstanding case is the much-disputed American Repertory Theater production of Samuel Beckett's 1957 *Endgame*, performed in Cambridge, Massachusetts, in 1984. Beckett's stage directions call for an empty room with two small windows, but director Akalaitis placed the work in a subway station with a derailed train in the background. Beckett threatened to halt production but finally agreed to allow the performance to take place with his disclaimer attached to the playbill. Such conflicts between playwrights and performers appeared frequently in the theater of the 1980's, particularly in the protests of minorities seek-

ing more casting of nontraditional actors in traditional roles. Akalaitis later met Beckett, an encounter that she described in a memoriam to him in *The Drama Review*. Profoundly impressed by the sparsity and intense purposefulness of all of his communication, Akalaitis and the Mabou Mines company informed Beckett that they wished to perform his radio play *Cascando* (1963) in Geneva and Zurich. Beckett's agent had earlier denied them permission, but Beckett told them not to worry and handed Akalaitis a napkin signed with his name and his permission to perform the play in Switzerland.

Throughout the 1980's, Akalaitis gained the respect of the theatrical community, eventually working at the Guthrie Theater in Minneapolis, the Goodman Theatre in Chicago, and the New York Shakespeare Festival, directing more traditional works such as Shakespeare's *Cymbeline* (pr. c. 1609-1610, pb. 1623) and John Ford's *'Tis Pity She's a Whore* (pr. 1629[?]-1633, pb. 1633). As with her earlier work, her direction of *Cymbeline* in 1990 caused a critical furor, with much criticism of Akalaitis's liberal interpretation of Shakespeare's intent. Joseph Papp appointed her his successor when his struggle with cancer caused him to give up his directorship of the New York Shakespeare Festival. In spite of entering this mainstream position, Akalaitis maintained a politically activist stance, as demonstrated by her visit to the Middle East to talk with Palestinian dramatists in September of 1991. Her unorthodox interpretations of conventional theater pieces continued to arouse interest and controversy.

The whole issue of the nature of performance, the extent to which directors and actors may tamper with original casting, set design, and text, is central to the fate of directors and groups such as Akalaitis and Mabou Mines. As is the case with many artists, within the strengths of works by Akalaitis reside her limitations and perhaps her downfall. Dedication to timely topics and a collaborative theater style make her work vibrant and electric, but these virtues may condemn her to the same kind of relative obscurity endured by such innovative and polemical artists as Clifford Odets and Elmer Rice. Indeed, Akalaitis and Mabou Mines hope that *Dead End Kids* will become dated, that the dangerous use of nuclear power that inspired their work may someday be eliminated, erasing any need for protest. At the same time, all of their works deal with concepts and human concerns that are timeless. The survival of their plays, however, may not be assured without a change in the very nature of the theater canon. As long as it is a body of literature created by individuals and preserved through conventional publishing methods, dynamic groups such as Mabou Mines and truly collaborative artists may remain in the realm of theater ephemera—which may be exactly where they wish to reside. As a director, however, Akalaitis has established her reputation as a powerful and lasting influence in American theater.

BIBLIOGRAPHY

Akalaitis, JoAnne. "JoAnne Akalaitis." Interview by Jonathan Kalb. *Theatre Magazine* 15 (May, 1984): 6-13. Contains photographs of Akalaitis and productions of *Dressed Like an Egg*, *Dead End Kids*, and *Southern Exposure*. The interview deals with Akalaitis's work on the filming of *Dead End Kids*, and she discusses her collaboration with Ruth Maleczech, Women's Interart, and Mabou Mines. Akalaitis describes her work on an opera written with John Gibson.

Gussow, Mel. "Other Ways at the Shakespeare Festival." *The New York Times*, June 17, 1991, p. B5. Gussow devotes a page with photographs to a relatively sympathetic description of Akalaitis's career, as director, playwright, collaborative performance artist, and Joseph Papp's successor as director of the New York Shakespeare Festival. He briefly reviews the critical reception of her writing and directorial career, mentioning the negative critical reception of Akalaitis's direction of Shakespeare's *Cymbeline*.

Lacayo, Richard. "Directors Fiddle, Authors Burn." *Time*, January, 1985, 75. Lacayo's article describes Samuel Beckett's objections to Akalaitis's setting of *Endgame* in a subway station with a derailed train. The article places the event in a larger context of modification of well-established plays. Lacayo discusses the legal and artistic dimensions of directorial discretion, with reference to works by Arthur Miller and Edward Albee.

Mehta, Xerxes. "Some Versions of Performance Art." *Theatre Journal* 36 (May, 1984): 164-191. Mehta gives a thorough, scene-by-scene description of *Southern Exposure*, which was not a production of Mabou Mines. Photographs and notes assist the general reader to picture the simple, almost harsh, set of the play. Mehta places the work in the context of Surrealist and cubist art movements.

Pressley, Nelson. "Director Bearing Greek Gifts: JoAnne Akalaitis Puts a New Face on the Classics." *The Washington Post*, March 27, 1999, p. C01. Pressley's article, full of quotes from Akalaitis, delves into her directing of various writers' plays, focusing on her interpretations of Euripides.

Saivetz, Deborah. *An Event in Space: JoAnne Akalaitis in Rehearsal*. Hanover, N.H.: Smith and Kraus, 2000. Saivetz looks at Akalaitis as a playwright and director and also examines her role in Mabou Mines. Bibliography.

Rebecca Bell-Metereau

VASSILY AKSYONOV

Born: August 20, 1932; Kazan, U.S.S.R.

PRINCIPAL DRAMA

Potselui, Orkestr, Ryba, Kolbasa . . ., pb. 1964
Chetyre temperamenta, pb. 1965 (*The Four Temperaments*, 1987)
Vsegda v prodazhe, pr. 1965
Aristofaniana s lygushkami, pb. 1967-1968
Vash ubiytsa, pb. 1977 (*Your Murderer*, 1999)
Tsaplya, pb. 1979, pr. 1984 (*The Heron*, 1987)
Aristofaniana s lygushkami: Sobranie pes, pb. 1981 (includes *Potselui, Orkestr, Ryba,*

Kolbasa . . . , *Vsegda v prodazhe*, *Chetyre temperamenta*, *Aristofaniana s lygushkami*, and *Tsaplya*)

OTHER LITERARY FORMS

Although Vassily Aksyonov has written five plays, he is actually more widely known for his prose works, in particular his novels. These range from the historical realism of *Voina i tiurma* (1993; *Generations of Winter*, 1994), a harsh look at the effects of Stalinism on a physician, to the satirical alternate history of *Ostrov Krym* (1981; *The Island of Crimea*, 1983), which features a Crimean peninsula with its narrow land bridge broken, freed to explore capitalist democracy.

Aksyonov has also written numerous short stories and several screenplays, as well as a fictionalized travelogue, *Kruglye sutki: Non-stop* (1976), based on his experiences as a visiting professor at the University of California in Los Angeles in the 1970's. His autobiography *Vpoiskakh grustnogo bebi* (1987; *In Search of Melancholy Baby*, 1987) simultaneously celebrates the freedom of American society and mourns the loss of Americans' moral fiber. He has served as an editor for the literary journal *Youth* and the anthology *Metropol*.

ACHIEVEMENTS

Vassily Aksyonov has been well recognized for his works. In 1967 he received a Golden Prize in the International Competition of Satirical Authors in Bulgaria. In 1982 he was made a fellow of the Woodrow Wilson International Center. He has also been made a member of the French, Swedish, and Danish chapters of the International Association of Poets, Playwrights, Editors, Essayists, and Novelists (PENs).

BIOGRAPHY

Vassily Pavlovich Aksyonov, the son of Pavel Vassilievich and Evgenia Semyonovna (Ginzburg) Aksyonov, was born on August 20, 1932, in Kazan, a provincial city of the Soviet Union. Almost from the beginning, he was at odds with the Soviet government. Both his parents were arrested as enemies of the people during the Great Purges. His father was

Vassily Aksyonov in 1984. (AP/Wide World Photos)

shot, and his mother was sentenced to hard labor in the prison camps of Siberia, leaving him effectively an orphan. He was placed in an institution for the children of enemies of the state, where he remained until relatives retrieved him.

When he was a teenager, his mother was released from the prison camp to begin a period of internal exile in the remote Magadan region. She managed to locate her son and bring him to her place of exile, where they made a precarious life for themselves. Young Aksyonov learned not to cry in the face of indignities heaped on him and his mother by drunken state security personnel, and his experiences while in exile both forged his unyielding moral character and sparked his interest in writing.

However, his formal education was as a physician,

and his medical experience was the basis of his first novel, *Kollegi* (1961; *Colleagues*, 1962), which was published during the height of the thaw, a period of cultural liberalization under Nikita Khrushchev. Over the next several years, Aksyonov established his literary reputation with additional novels, short stories, and his play *Vsegda v prodazhe* (always on sale), which was staged in Moscow at the Sovremennik Theater in 1965.

After Khrushchev's fall, the political climate turned more doctrinaire, and Aksyonov shared the fate of many Soviet writers of conscience. He found it steadily more difficult to publish, until he compared himself to an iceberg, his published works only a small portion of his total literary works. In 1979 he joined twenty-two other writers in challenging Soviet censorship by requesting that an anthology of their banned works be published. It resulted in his being stripped of his Soviet citizenship and hounded into emigrating to the United States.

Aksyonov traveled and lectured throughout the United States and Western Europe, eventually making Washington, D.C., his base. Even in exile, he remained prolific, drawing on memory to work away from his native land. In 1990, following the breakup of the Soviet Union, Aksyonov's Russian citizenship was restored. However, unlike such writers as Aleksandr Solzhenitsyn, he did not return to Russia. Instead he remained in the United States, where he became the Clarence Robinson Professor in Slavic studies at George Mason University, a leading conservative university with a strong classical-liberal emphasis, located in Fairfax, Virginia.

ANALYSIS

Vassily Aksyonov uses his dramatic works as vehicles for criticism of the Soviet government and Soviet society, which did not endear him to the authorities of his native land. All five of his plays are heavily satirical, holding the follies and foibles of his targets up to ridicule, often indirectly through comedic stereotypes. Yet the actual targets of his wit remain obvious enough to offend the powers that be in an authoritarian society. Therefore, only one of his plays, *Vsegda v prodazhe*, was produced within the Soviet

Union. Director Olega Efremov staged the drama in Moscow's Sovremennik Theater in 1965. Plans were made to stage three of his other plays in the Soviet Union, but none of these plans were realized. *The Heron* was produced abroad, in Paris in 1984.

Attempts to publish his plays met with similar difficulty. In 1977, *Your Murderer* was published abroad. In 1979 Aksyonov published *The Four Temperaments* in the literary almanac *Metropol*, of which he was an editor. Because Aksyonov published *Metropol* in defiance of Soviet censorship, he was exiled to the United States. However, his play *The Heron* was published in the journal *Kontinent* later that year. In 1981 a collection of his plays was published by Hermitage, a Russian emigré publishing house.

Aksyonov's work has consistently shown a strong awareness of his literary predecessors, including such specifically Russian playwrights as Yuri Olesha and Mikhail Bulgakov, but also dramatists of other cultures and ages. Aksyonov has described *The Heron* as a "paraphrase" of Anton Chekhov's *Chayka* (pr. 1896, rev. pr. 1898; *The Seagull*, 1909), but the play also is heavily informed by *Tri sestry* (pr., pb. 1901, rev. pb. 1904; *Three Sisters*, 1920), another of Chekhov's well-known dramatic works. *Aristofaniana s lygushkami* directly borrows the plots of two plays by the ancient Greek dramatist Aristophanes, namely *Batrachoi* (405 B.C.E.; *The Frogs*, 1780) and *Lysistratē* (411 B.C.E.; *Lysistratē*, 1837), and even quotes whole lines from the originals. Although *The Heron* can be understood without any reference to the Chekhov plays, it is essential to have some familiarity with the works of Aristophanes to appreciate *Aristofaniana s lygushkami*.

VSEGDA V PRODAZHE

In *Vsegda v prodazhe*, the young mining engineer Treugolnikov returns to Moscow to confront an old friend, Kistochkin. The action takes place primarily in the apartment house in which Kistochkin has created his own private empire, corrupting those with whom he deals. There are hints that he is not human at all but an alien from another dimension. When a young neighbor asks an innocent question about unidentified flying objects (UFOs), Kistochkin panics guiltily. However, Treugolnikov manages to rally the other tenants, and they rebel against Kistochkin's control. Kistochkin then flees in a UFO.

The first of the two brief epilogues shows Kistochkin's dimension, in which the inhabitants have been reduced to robotlike slaves under the tyranny of him and his epicene assistant, the Waitress. The second shows Treugolnikov's world, in which humanity and love have triumphed, and Kistochkin, cut off from the source of his malevolent power, has become a courteous keeper of a food kiosk.

The play is rich with political meaning, particularly the criticism of tyranny and those who support it. Kistochkin can be seen as one of the "heirs of Stalin," individuals who lived after Stalin's death but continued to support and propagate many of his policies and programs, in particular the repression of dissent. The Waitress can be interpreted as a retired member of the NKVD (Stalin's secret police, a precursor of the KGB), who now controls a younger generation of informers and repressors. By contrast, Treugolnikov represents the young generation of romantic writers who believe that the Soviet Union can be cleansed of the lingering contagion of Stalin's crimes.

YOUR MURDERER

In *Your Murderer*, Aksyonov sharpens his satirical wit and takes on alcoholism, which was one of the major social problems of the Soviet Union and has remained a problem in Russia. However, by locating his play on an imaginary tropical island instead of somewhere in the Soviet Union, Aksyonov gives it a universality of theme, acknowledging that the problems of which he speaks are not specific to any one culture.

Your Murderer is the story of Alexandro, a writer who stubbornly resists the Masculinus alcohol conglomerate's attempts to take over the island's society by bullying everyone into drinking their product. However, his principled fight results only in his progressive isolation from everyone around him, and in despair, he flings himself under the wheels of a fancy car driven by his former friends. When he survives, he interprets this as a sign that he should join the forces of Masculinus and creates an advertising campaign around a tough-talking folk hero he calls Pork

Sausage. However, his success is short lived, for he is soon horrified by the violence that his character is provoking and resolves to destroy his creation.

That proves more easily said than done, and the monster keeps coming back in a multitude of disguises. Finally it is Alexandro himself who is killed, in a bizarre and farcical electrocution scene. His body is tossed over the stage's proscenium and his girlfriend Maria asks if he is dead. He answers that it depends entirely on the characters of the novel he was writing—if they have survived, he will survive as well. In the brief epilogue, the island has become an alternative paradise to which Alexandro and his friends flee to escape the besotted dominance of Masculinus. However, when they shake the beautiful Tree of Freedom to gain its bounty, the hideous head of Pork Sausage falls out and mocks them.

Although on its most obvious level *Your Murderer* is a criticism of the rampant alcoholism in Soviet society and the Soviet government's financial interest in selling liquor to the populace, it also works on several other levels. Alexandro's struggle with Masculinus Corporation can be seen as the struggles of the artist to maintain integrity in the face of Soviet censorship and the pressures of Socialist Realist doctrine that art must support the purposes of the state. Aksyonov makes personal barbs against individual Soviet leaders of the time through Masculinus Stockholder, whose consistent mispronunciation of certain words was intended to hint at Khrushchev's similar speech habits and whose chatter about sending the "national cavalry" against the United States military was a sly jab at the appallingly incompetent Marshal Klimenty Voroshilov, who sent Soviet cavalry against Nazi tanks. Even the principal antagonist, Pork Sausage, is a reference to the common perception that Khrushchev resembled a pig.

THE FOUR TEMPERAMENTS

Drawing on the ancient Greek tradition of four basic temperaments, Aksyonov creates another meditation on the nature of tyranny and freedom in *The Four Temperaments*. The four allegorical characters, Chol Erik, Sng Vinik, Phleg Matik, and Melan Cholik, begin the story with a suicide attempt, from which they are rescued by the mysterious Razrailov. He then persuades them to climb a tall tower, away from Earth's influence, to participate in an experiment in linking human beings to a computer, the Cyber.

As the four protagonists begin to shake off their passivity, they are approached by an old soldier, the Eagle, who tells them that he fights the Steel Bird (a symbolic figure that represents Stalinism in a number of Aksyonov's works). He also tells them that Razrailov has lied to them and that they have in fact died and the tower is part of the land of the dead. Subsequently another subject, Nina, arrives after being murdered by a jealous husband. She causes all four of the protagonists and the Cyber to fall in love with her, and that love humanizes the Cyber. Razrailov then crushes their rebellion by strangling Nina.

The last scene shows the characters in a café, waiting for someone. Razrailov and Nina arrive and battle for control. In the end, Razrailov drags Nina away, but the other characters settle back in to wait, certain she will return. Nina can be interpreted as the Muse, the source of artistic inspiration who has been squelched by the Soviet government but can never be truly eliminated.

ARISTOFANIANA S LYGUSHKAMI

In this play, which draws heavily on the works of the playwright Aristophanes, ancient Greece stands for the modern Soviet Union. In Hades, the dead of various professions are gathered in "living rooms," including the one shared by poets Alexander Pushkin, William Shakespeare, and various moderns, even a far-future poet known only as Boo. In the world above, Athens is ruled by the dictator Alcibiades, who has driven out true poets and replaced them with graphomaniacs, hacks who churn out praises for the tyrant. The god Dionysus, aided by Aristophanes, descends into Hades to take Aeschylus to the upper world and confront Alcibiades. However, they are instead attacked by the hacks, until they are rescued by a chorus of frogs, representing true poetry. In the final scene, back in Hades, Dionysus and his poets are greeted with cheers by the other poets.

OTHER MAJOR WORKS

LONG FICTION: *Kollegi*, 1961 (*Colleagues*, 1962);

Zvezdenyi bilet, 1961 (*A Starry Ticket*, 1962; also as *A Ticket to the Stars*); *Apel'siny iz Marokko*, 1963 (*Oranges from Morocco*, 1979); *Pora, moi drug, pora*, 1965 (*It's Time, My Friend, It's Time*, 1969); *Zatovarennaya bochkotara*, 1968 (*Surplussed Barrelware*, 1985); *Stalnaya ptistsa*, 1977 (novella; *The Steel Bird*, 1979); *Zolotaya nasha Zhelezk*, 1979 (*Our Golden Ironburg*, 1986); *Ozhog*, 1980 (*The Burn*, 1984); *Ostrov Krym*, 1981 (*The Island of Crimea*, 1983); *Szazhi izyum*, 1985 (*Say Cheese!*, 1989); *Moskovskaia saga: Trilogiia*, 1993-1994 (includes *Pokolenie zimy*, *Voina i tiurma* [*Generations of Winter*, 1994], and *Tiruma i mir* [*The Winter's Hero*, 1996]); *Novyi sladostnyi stil*, 1997 (*The New Sweet Style*, 1999).

SHORT FICTION: *Katapul'ta*, 1964; *Na polputi k lune*, 1965; *The Steel Bird and Other Stories*, 1979; *Pravo na ostrov*, 1983; *The Destruction of Pompeii and Other Stories*, 1991; *Negativ polozhitel'nogo geroia*, 1996.

NONFICTION: *Lyubov k elektrichestvu*, 1971 (biography); *Kruglye sutki: Non-stop*, 1976; *Vpoiskakh grustnogo bebi*, 1987 (*In Search of Melancholy Baby*, 1987).

EDITED TEXT: *Metropol: Literaturnyi almanakh*, 1979 (*Metropol: Literary Almanac*, 1982).

MISCELLANEOUS: *Quest for an Island*, 1987 (plays and short stories); *Sobranie sochinenii*, 1994 (works; 4 volumes).

BIBLIOGRAPHY

Dalgard, Per. *Function of the Grotesque in Vasilij Aksenov*. Aarhus, Denmark: Arkona, 1982. Discussion of how Aksyonov portrays commonplace things and events as grotesque or ridiculous, often as a method of social criticism.

Kustovich, Konstantin. *The Artist and the Tyrant: Vassily Aksenov's Works in the Brezhnev Era*. Columbus, Ohio: Slavica, 1992. An in-depth study of how Aksyonov uses satirical and fantastical motifs to criticize the Soviet regime. Includes analysis of several of his plays and comparison of motifs found in them with those in his prose works.

Mozejko, Edward. *Vasily Pavlovich Aksenov: A Writer in Quest of Himself*. Columbia, Ohio:

Slavica, 1986. A collection of articles about various aspects of Aksyonov's writing, including his plays. One contributor's article appears both in English translation and in the Russian original.

Simmons, Cynthia. *Their Fathers' Voice: Vassily*

Aksyonov, Venedikt Erofeev, Eduard Lemonov, and Sasha Sokolov. New York: Peter Long, 1994. Compares and contrasts three leading writers of the post-Stalin generation.

Leigh Husband Kimmel

EDWARD ALBEE

Born: Virginia; March 12, 1928

PRINCIPAL DRAMA

The Zoo Story, pr. 1959, pb. 1960

The Death of Bessie Smith, pr., pb. 1960

The Sandbox, pr., pb. 1960

Fam and Yam, pr., pb. 1960

The American Dream, pr., pb. 1961

Bartleby, pr. 1961 (libretto, with James Hinton, Jr.; music by William Flanagan; adaptation of Herman Melville's "Bartleby the Scrivener")

Who's Afraid of Virginia Woolf?, pr., pb. 1962

The Ballad of the Sad Café, pr., pb. 1963 (adaptation of Carson McCullers's novel)

Tiny Alice, pr. 1964, pb. 1965

A Delicate Balance, pr., pb. 1966

Malcolm, pr., pb. 1966 (adaptation of James Purdy's novel *Malcolm*)

Everything in the Garden, pr. 1967, pb. 1968 (adaptation of Giles Cooper's play *Everything in the Garden*)

Box and Quotations from Chairman Mao Tse-tung, pr. 1968, pb. 1969 (2 one-acts)

All Over, pr., pb. 1971

Seascape, pr., pb. 1975

Counting the Ways, pr. 1976, pb. 1977

Listening, pr., pb. 1977

The Lady from Dubuque, pr., pb. 1980

Lolita, pr. 1981, pb. 1984 (adaptation of Vladimir Nabokov's novel)

The Man Who Had Three Arms, pr., pb. 1982

Finding the Sun, pr. 1983, pb. 1994

Marriage Play, pr. 1987, pb. 1995

Three Tall Women, pr. 1991, pb. 1994

The Lorca Play, pr. 1992

Fragments: A Sit Around, pr. 1993, pb. 1995

The Play About the Baby, pr. 1998, pb. 2002

The Goat: Or, Who Is Sylvia?, pr., pb. 2002

Occupant, pr. 2002

OTHER LITERARY FORMS

Although Edward Albee has written the libretto for an unsuccessful operatic version of Herman Melville's story "Bartleby the Scrivener," as well as some occasional essays and a few adaptations, he is known primarily for his plays. Albee's unpublished works include a short story and at least one novel written while he was a teenager. *Esquire* published the first chapter of a novel he began writing in 1963 but never completed.

ACHIEVEMENTS

Edward Albee is, with David Mamet, Sam Shepard, and August Wilson, one of the few American playwrights to emerge since the 1950's with any claim to being considered a major dramatist ranked among the pantheon of Eugene O'Neill, Thornton Wilder, Arthur Miller, and Tennessee Williams. Since *The Zoo Story* first appeared, Albee has produced a sustained and varied body of work, often of considerably higher quality than his critical and popular reputation would suggest. In the introduction to his most experimental works, the two one-acts published together in *Box and Quotations from Chairman Mao Tse-tung*, Albee sets forth the two "obligations" of a playwright: to illuminate the human condition and to make some statement about the art form itself by altering "the forms within which his precursors have had to work." Like O'Neill before him, Albee has always been an experimentalist, refusing to go back and repeat the earlier formulas simply because they have proved commercially and critically successful. Although acutely disturbed by the downward spiral and paralysis of will that seem to have overtaken modern civilization and committed to charting these in his work, Albee is not primarily a social playwright, and there is hardly one of his plays that is totally naturalistic or realistic. In form and style, they range, indeed, from surrealism (*The Sandbox*) to allegory (*Tiny Alice*), from the quasi-religious drawing-room play (*A Delicate Balance*) to the fable (*Seascape*), from the picaresque journey (*Malcolm*) to the ritual deathwatch (both *All Over* and *The Lady from Dubuque*), from scenes linked by cinematic techniques (*The Death of Bessie Smith*) to monodrama for a disembodied voice (*Box*), and from traditional memory play (*Three Tall Women*) to postmodern burlesque (*The Play About the Baby*).

Albee has received numerous awards and honors, including two Obie Awards, one in 1959-1960 for *The Zoo Story* and a second in 1993-1994 for sustained achievement, and two Tony Awards for best play, for *Who's Afraid of Virginia Woolf?* in 1963 and for *The Goat: Or, Who Is Sylvia?* in 2002. He was awarded three Pulitzer Prizes in Drama, for *A Delicate Balance* in 1967, *Seascape* in 1975, and *Three Tall Women* in 1994. The New York Drama Critics Circle Award for Best Play was given to three of Albee's dramas: *Who's Afraid of Virginia Woolf?* (1963), *Three Tall Women* (1994), and *The Goat* (2002). Other honors include the Kennedy Center Lifetime Achievement Award (1996) and the National Medal of Arts (1997).

BIOGRAPHY

Born on March 12, 1928, Edward Franklin Albee was adopted at the age of two weeks by the socially prominent and wealthy New Yorkers Reed and Frances Albee. His adoptive father was the scion of the family who owned the Keith-Albee chain of vaudeville houses; his adoptive mother was a former Bergdorf

high-fashion model. Albee's deep-seated resentment of the natural parents who abandoned him finds reflection in the child motifs that pervade both his original plays and his adaptations: the orphan in *The Zoo Story* and *The Ballad of the Sad Café*, the mutilated twin in *The American Dream*, the intensely hoped-for child who is never conceived and the conceived child who is unwanted in *Who's Afraid of Virginia Woolf?*, the dead son in *A Delicate Balance*, the child in search of his father in *Malcolm*, the prodigal son detested by a haughty mother in *Three Tall Women,* and the apparently kidnapped child in *The Play About the Baby*.

Living with the Albees was Edward's maternal grandmother, Grandma Cotta, whom he revered and would later memorialize in *The Sandbox* and *The American Dream*. After his primary education at the Rye Country Day School, Albee attended a succession of prep schools (Lawrenceville School for Boys, Valley Forge Military Academy), finally graduating from Choate in 1946 before enrolling at Trinity Col-

Edward Albee in 2002. (AP/Wide World Photos)

lege in Hartford, Connecticut, where he studied for a year and a half. While in high school, he wrote both poetry and plays.

In 1953, Albee was living in Greenwich Village and working at a variety of odd jobs when, with the encouragement of Thornton Wilder, he committed himself to the theater. *The Zoo Story*, written in only two weeks, premiered in Berlin on September 28, 1959; when it opened Off-Broadway at the Provincetown Playhouse on a double bill with Beckett's *Krapp's Last Tape* (pr., pb. 1958) in January, 1960, it brought Albee immediate acclaim as the most promising of the new playwrights and won for him an Obie Award as Best Play of the Year. *Who's Afraid of Virginia Woolf?*, his first full-length work—and still his most famous—opened on Broadway in October, 1962, winning for him both the Drama Critics Circle Award and the Tony Award for the Best American Play of that season; the Drama Jury voted it the Pulitzer Prize, but the Advisory Board of Columbia University overturned the nomination because of the play's strong language, and, as a result, John Gassner and John Mason Brown resigned from the jury in protest. Albee went on, however, to win three Pulitzers, for *A Delicate Balance*, *Seascape*, and *Three Tall Women*. Along with the New York productions of numerous original one-act plays and original full-length works, Albee has done four adaptations for the stage: of Carson McCullers's 1951 novella *The Ballad of the Sad Café*; of James Purdy's 1959 novel *Malcolm*; of Giles Cooper's 1962 play *Everything in the Garden*; and of Vladimir Nabokov's 1955 novel *Lolita*.

From the time of his own early successes, Albee has actively encouraged the development of other young dramatists and, as part of a production team, has also brought the work of major avant-garde foreign dramatists to New York. Under the auspices of the State Department, he toured behind the Iron Curtain and in South America, and he has become a frequent and popular lecturer on the college circuit, as well as a director of revivals of his own plays. He is an impassioned defender of the National Endowment for the Arts. He has also been actively involved with the international writers association PEN and served as president of the International Theater Institute.

After a residency at the University of Houston, Albee directed the world premieres of *Marriage Play* and *Three Tall Women*, both at the English Theatre in Vienna; he also directed *Marriage Play* at the Alley Theatre in 1991 and at the McCarter Theatre in 1992. Between 1993 and 1994, the Signature Theatre Company presented a season of plays by Albee that included the New York premieres of *Finding the Sun, Marriage Play* and *Fragments*. Albee's plays and the actors who perform in them are perennial nominees for Tony and Obie Awards. *The Goat*, Albee's nineteenth play produced on Broadway, won the Tony Award for Best Play in 2002 as well as a New York Drama Critics Circle Award for Best Play. In 1996, he became only the fourth playwright to receive a Kennedy Center Honor. Critic David Richards of *The New York Times* noted that Albee, "increasingly introspective over the years," has countered his disappointment with Broadway (*The Man Who Had Three Arms* saw only sixteen performances in 1983) by becoming "a European playwright."

ANALYSIS

Though he is touted sometimes as the chief American practitioner of the absurd in drama, Edward Albee only rarely combines in a single work both the techniques and the philosophy associated with that movement and is seldom as unremittingly bleak and despairing an author as Samuel Beckett. Yet the influence of Eugène Ionesco's humor and of Jean Genet's rituals can be discerned in isolated works, as can the battle of the sexes and the voracious, emasculating female from August Strindberg, the illusion/reality motif from Luigi Pirandello and O'Neill, and the poetic language of T. S. Eliot, Beckett, and Harold Pinter, as well as the recessive action and lack of definite resolution and closure often found in Beckett and Pinter. As the only avant-garde American dramatist of his generation to attain a wide measure of popular success, Albee sometimes demonstrates, especially in the plays from the first decade of his career, the rather strident and accusatory voice of the angry young man. The outlook in his later works, however, is more that of the compassionate moralist, linking him—perhaps unexpectedly—with Anton Chekhov;

one of the characters in *All Over*, recognizing the disparity between what human beings could become and what they have settled for, even echoes the Russian master's Madame Ranevsky when she says, "How dull our lives are." Even in his most technically and stylistically avant-garde dramas, however, Albee remains essentially very traditional in the values he espouses, as he underlines the necessity for human contact and communion, for family ties and friendships, which provide individuals with the courage to grow and face the unknown. Always prodding people to become more, yet, at the same time, sympathetically accepting their fear and anxiety over change, Albee has increasingly become a gentle apologist for human beings, who need one crutch after another, who need one illusion after another, so that—in a paraphrase of O'Neill's words—they can make it through life and comfort their fears of death.

Despite a lengthy career that has, especially in its second half, been marked by more critical downs than ups, Albee has not been satisfied to rest on his successes, such as *Who's Afraid of Virginia Woolf?*, nor has he been content simply to repeat the formulas that have worked for him in the past. Instead, he has continued to experiment with dramatic form, to venture into new structures and styles. In so doing, he has grown into a major voice in dramatic literature, the progress of whose career in itself reflects his overriding theme: No emotional or artistic or spiritual growth is possible without embracing the terror—and perhaps the glory—of tomorrow's unknown, for the unknown is contemporary humanity's only certainty.

The major recurrent pattern in Albee's plays finds his characters facing a test or a challenge to become more fully human. In *The Zoo Story*, Jerry arrives at a bench in Central Park to jar Peter out of his passivity and Madison Avenue complacence; in *The Death of Bessie Smith*, the black blues singer arrives dying at a Southern hospital only to be turned away because of racial prejudice; in *Tiny Alice*, Brother Julian arrives at Miss Alice's mansion to undergo his dark night of the soul; in *A Delicate Balance*, Harry and Edna arrive at the home of their dearest friends to test the limits of friendship and measure the quality of Agnes and Tobias's life; in *Seascape*, the lizards Leslie and

Sarah come up from the sea to challenge Charlie to renewed activity and to try their own readiness for the human adventure; and in *The Lady from Dubuque*, the Lady and her black traveling companion arrive to ease Jo to her death and help her husband learn to let go.

To effect the desired change in Peter, Jerry in *The Zoo Story* must first break down the barriers that hinder communication. Accomplishing this might even require deliberate cruelty, because kindness by itself may no longer be enough: Oftentimes in Albee, one character needs to hurt another before he can help, the hurt then becoming a creative rather than a destructive force. Along with the focus on lack of communication and on a love and concern that dare to be critical, Albee consistently pursues several additional thematic emphases throughout his works. *The American Dream*, which comments on the decline and fall from grace of Western civilization and on the spiritual aridity of a society that lives solely by a materialistic ethic, also decries the emasculation of Daddy at the hands of Mommy; to a greater or lesser degree. *The Death of Bessie Smith*, *Who's Afraid of Virginia Woolf?*, and *A Delicate Balance* all speak as well to what Albee sees as a disturbing reversal of gender roles (a motif he inherits from Strindberg), though Albee does become increasingly understanding of the female characters in his later works. Several plays, among them *Who's Afraid of Virginia Woolf?* and *A Delicate Balance*, consider the delimiting effect of time on human choice and the way in which man's potential for constructive change decreases as time goes on. Characters in both *A Delicate Balance* and *Tiny Alice* face the existential void, suffering the anxiety that arises over the possibility of there being a meaninglessness at the very core of existence, while characters in several others, including *Box and Quotations from Chairman Mao Tse-tung*, *All Over*, and *The Lady from Dubuque*, confront mortality as they ponder the distinction between dying (which ends) and death (which goes on) and the suffering of the survivor. Elsewhere, particularly in *Counting the Ways*, Albee insists on the difficulty of ever arriving at certainty in matters of the heart, which cannot be known or proved quantitatively. Finally, in such works as *Malcolm* and *Seascape*, he explores the notion that innocence must be lost—or at least risked—before there can be any hope of achieving a paradise regained.

If the mood of many Albee works is autumnal, even wintry, it is because the dramatist continually prods his audiences into questioning whether the answers that the characters put forward in response to the human dilemma—such panaceas as religion (*Tiny Alice*) or formulaic social rituals (*All Over*)—might not in themselves all be simply illusions in which human beings hide from a confrontation with the ultimate nothingness of existence. In this, he comes closer to the absurdists, though he is more positive in his holding out of salvific acts: the sacrifice to save the other that ends *The Zoo Story*, the gesture of communion that concludes *Who's Afraid of Virginia Woolf?*, the affirmation of shared humanness that ends *Seascape*, and the merciful comforting of the survivor that concludes *The Lady from Dubuque*. If Albee's characters often live a death-in-life existence, it is equally evident that human beings, God's only metaphor-making animals, can sometimes achieve a breakthrough by coming to full consciousness of their condition and by recognizing the symbolic, allegorical, and anagogical planes of existence.

WHO'S AFRAID OF VIRGINIA WOOLF?

Who's Afraid of Virginia Woolf?, which brought Albee immediate fame as the most important American dramatist since Williams and Miller, is probably also the single most important American play of the 1960's, the only one from that decade with any likelihood of becoming a classic work of dramatic literature. In this, his first full-length drama, Albee continues several strands from his one-act plays—including the need to hurt in order to help from *The Zoo Story*, the criticism of Western civilization from *The American Dream*, and the Strindbergian battle of the sexes from that play and *The Death of Bessie Smith*—while weaving in several others that become increasingly prominent in his work: excoriating wit, a concern with illusion/reality, the structuring of action through games and game-playing (here, "Humiliate the Host," "Hump the Hostess," "Get the Guests," and "Bringing Up Baby"), and a mature emphasis on the need to ac-

cept change and the potentially creative possibilities it offers.

Tightly unified in time, place, and action, *Who's Afraid of Virginia Woolf?* occurs in the early hours of Sunday morning in the home of George, a professor of history, and his wife, Martha, in the mythical eastern town of New Carthage. After a party given by her father, the college president, Martha invites Nick, a young biology teacher, and his wife, Honey, back home for a nightcap. Through the ensuing confrontations and games that occasionally turn bitter and vicious, both the older and the younger couples experience a radical, regenerative transformation. George, who sees himself as a humanist who lives for the multiplicity and infinite variety that have always characterized history, immediately sets himself up against Nick, the man of science, or, better yet, of scientism, whose narrow, amoral view of inevitability—wherein every creature would be determined down to color of hair and eyes—would sound the death knell for civilization. Like the attractive, muscular young men from *The American Dream* and *The Sandbox*, Nick is appealing on the outside but spiritually vapid within. If his ethical sense is undeveloped, even nonexistent, and his intellect sterile, he is also physically impotent when he and Martha go off to bed, though his temporary impotence should probably be regarded mainly as symbolic of the general sterility of his entire life. George apparently intends, much as Jerry had in *The Zoo Story*, to jar Nick out of his present condition, which involves being overly solicitous of his mousey, infantile wife. Though experiencing a false pregnancy when Nick married her, Honey, slim-hipped and unable to hold her liquor—her repeated exits to the bathroom are adroitly managed to move characters on and off the stage—is frightened of childbirth. As George detects, she has been preventing conception or aborting without Nick's knowledge, and in this way unmanning her husband, preventing him from transmitting his genes. By the play's end, Nick and Honey have seen the intense emptiness that can infect a marriage without children, and Honey three times cries out that she wants a child. George and Martha were unable to have children—neither will cast blame on the other for this—

and so, twenty-one years earlier, they created an imaginary son, an illusion so powerful that it has become, for all intents and purposes, a reality for them.

If not intellectually weak, George, who is in fact Albee's spokesperson in the play, does share with Nick the condition of being under the emotional and physical control of his wife. Ever since the time when Martha's Daddy insisted that his faculty participate in an exhibition sparring match to demonstrate their readiness to fight in the war and Martha knocked George down in the huckleberry bush, she has taunted George with being a blank and a cipher. It is unlikely that he will ever succeed her father as college president—he will not even become head of the history department. Martha claims that George married her to be humiliated and that she has worn the pants in the family not by choice but because someone must be stronger in any relationship. George realizes that if he does not act decisively to change his life by taking control, the time for any possible action will have passed.

In a formulation of the evolutionary metaphor that Albee recurrently employs, George, who, like civilization, is facing a watershed, remarks that a person can descend only so many rungs on the ladder before there can be no turning back; he must stop contemplating the past and decide to "alter the future." Martha, too, seems to want George to take hold and become more forceful; she, indeed, is openly happy when he exerts himself, as when he frightens them all with a rifle that shoots a parasol proclaiming "Bang," in one of the absurd jokes of which Albee is fond. Martha, despite being loud and brash and vulgar, is also sensual and extremely vulnerable. She does indeed love George, who is the only man she has ever loved, and fears that someday she will go so far in belittling him that she will lose him forever.

The imaginary son has served not only as a uniting force in their marriage but also as a beanbag they can toss against each other. When George decides to kill the son whom they mutually created through an act of imagination, Martha desperately insists that he does not have the right to do this on his own, but to no avail. Even if the child, who was to have reached his twenty-first birthday and legal maturity on the day

of the play, had been real, the parents would have had to let go and continue alone, facing the future with only each other. As George says, "It was time." He kills the illusion, intoning the mass for the dead. It is Sunday morning, and Martha is still frightened of "Virginia Woolf," of living without illusion, and of facing the unknown. "*Maybe* it will be better," George tells her, for one can never be totally certain of what is to come. Just as there can be no assurance—though all signs point in that direction—that Nick and Honey's marriage will be firmer with a child, there can be no certainty that George and Martha's will be better without their imaginary son, though George is now prepared to offer Martha the strength and support needed to see her through her fear. Finally, Albee seems to be saying, human beings must not only accept change but also actively embrace it for the possibilities it presents for growth. The future is always terrifying, an uncharted territory, yet if one does not walk into it, one has no other choice but death.

TINY ALICE

Tiny Alice is Albee's richest work from a philosophical point of view; it also represents his most explicit excursion into the realm of the absurd. In it, Albee addresses the problem of how human beings come to know the reality outside themselves, even questioning whether there is, finally, any reality to know. To do this, Albee builds his play around a series of dichotomies: between faith and reason, between present memory and past occurrence, and between symbol and substance. The play opens with a scene that could almost stand on its own as a little one-act play, demonstrating Albee's wit at its virulent best. A Lawyer and a Cardinal, old school chums and, apparently, homosexual lovers in their adolescence, attack each other verbally, revealing the venery of both civil and religious authority. The Lawyer has come as the emissary of Miss Alice, ready to bequeath to the Church one hundred million dollars a year for the next twenty years; the Cardinal's secretary, the lay Brother Julian, will be sent to her castle to complete the transaction. For Julian, this becomes an allegorical dark night of the soul, a period when his religious faith will be tempted and tested. On the literal level, the play seems preposterous at times and even muddled; the suspicion that all this has been planned by some extortion ring, though it is unclear what they hope to gain by involving Julian, or even, perhaps, that all this is a charade devised by Julian to provide himself with an opportunity for sacrifice, is never quite dispelled. On the metaphoric and symbolic levels, however, as a religious drama about contemporary man's need to make the abstract concrete in order to have some object to worship, *Tiny Alice* is clear and consistent and succeeds admirably.

Julian, who earlier suffered a temporary loss of sanity over the disparity between his own conception of God and the false gods that human beings create in their own image, is now undergoing a further crisis. His temptation now is to search out a personification of the Godhead in order to make the Unknowable knowable, by making it concrete through a symbol; he hopes to prove that God exists by making contact with an experiential representation of him. To represent the Deity in this manner is, however, as the Lawyer insists, to distort and diminish it so that it can be understood in human terms. Up to this point, Julian has always fought against precisely such a reduction of the divine. The symbol that Julian now literally embraces—through a sexual consummation and marriage that is both religious and erotic—is Miss Alice, the surrogate for Tiny Alice. That God in Albee's play is named "*Tiny* Alice" points, in itself, to the strange modern phenomenon of a reduced and delimited rather than an expansive deity. Instead of the real (Miss Alice) being a pale shadowing forth of the ideal form (Tiny Alice), here the symbol (Alice) is *larger* than what it represents, just as the mansion in which the action after scene 1 occurs is larger than its replica, exact down to the last detail, that is onstage in the library. The Lawyer insists that human beings can never worship an abstraction, for to do so always results in worshiping only the symbol and never the substance or the thing symbolized. Furthermore, he causes Julian to question whether that substance has any tangible existence: Is it only the symbol, and not the thing symbolized, that exists? If so, then Julian faces the possibility of nothingness, of there being *nothing there*, of there being only the finite, sense-

accessible dimension in which people live and no higher order that provides meaning.

In the face of this dilemma, Brother Julian can either despair of ever knowing his God or make a leap of faith. When the financial arrangements have been completed, the Lawyer, who—like the Butler—has had Miss Alice as his mistress, shoots Julian, who has always dreamed of sacrificing himself for his faith. Martyrdom, the ultimate form of service to one's God, always involves questions of suicidal intent, of doing, as Eliot's hero in *Murder in the Cathedral* (pr., pb. 1935) knows, "the right deed for the wrong reason." Is one dying for self, or as a totally submissive instrument of God? As Julian dies in the posture of one crucified, he demands, in a paroxysm blending sexual hysteria and religious ecstasy, that the transcendent personify itself; indeed, a shadow moves through the mansion, accompanied by an ever-increasing heartbeat and ever-louder breathing, until it totally envelops the room. As Albee himself commented, two possibilities present themselves: Either the transcendent is real, and the God Tiny Alice actually manifests itself to Brother Julian at the moment of his death, or Julian's desire for transcendence is so great that he deceives himself. Thus, the play's ending, while allowing for the person of faith to be confirmed in his or her belief about the spiritual reality behind the physical symbol, is at the same time disquieting in that it insists on the equally possible option that the revelation of transcendence is merely a figment of one's imagination. What Albee may well be suggesting, then, and what brings him to the doorstep of the absurdists in this provocative work, is that there is, finally, nothing there except what human beings, through their illusions, are able to call up as a shield against the void.

A DELICATE BALANCE

A Delicate Balance, for which Albee deservedly won the Pulitzer Prize denied him by the Advisory Board four seasons earlier for *Who's Afraid of Virginia Woolf?*, is an autumnal play about death-in-life. A metaphysical drawing-room drama in the manner of Eliot and Graham Greene, it focuses on a well-to-do middle-aged couple, Agnes and Tobias, who are forced one October weekend to assess their lives by the unexpected visit of their closest friends, Harry and Edna (characters in Albee traditionally lack surnames). The latter couple arrives on Friday night, frightened by a sudden perception of emptiness. Having faced the existential void, they flee, terrified, to the warmth and succor of Agnes and Tobias's home, trusting that they will discover there some shelter from meaninglessness, some proof that at least the personal values of friendship and love remain. As the stage directions imply, an audience should not measure these visitors-in-the-night against the requirements of realistic character portrayal; they function, instead, as mirror images for their hosts, who, by looking at them, are forced to confront the emotional and spiritual malaise of their own lives. Agnes's live-in sister, the self-proclaimed alcoholic Claire—whose name suggests the clear-sightedness of this woman who stands on the sidelines and sees things as they are—understands the threat that Harry and Edna bring with them. Agnes fears that their guests come bearing the "plague," and Claire understands that this weekend will be spent waiting for the biopsy, for confirmation of whether some dread, terminal disease afflicts this family.

Agnes not only has no desire for self-knowledge but also deliberately guards against any diagnosis of the family's ills. As the fulcrum, she is able to maintain the family's status quo only by keeping herself and Tobias in a condition of stasis, insulated from the currents that threaten to upset the "delicate balance" that allows them to go on without ever questioning their assumptions. A somewhat haughty though gracious woman, whose highly artificial and carefully measured language reflects the controlled pattern of her existence and her inability to tolerate or handle the unexpected, Agnes muses frequently on sex roles. A dramatic descendant of Strindberg's male characters rather than of his female characters, she decries all of those things that have made the sexes too similar and have thus threatened the stability of the traditional family unit.

From her perspective, it is the wife's function to maintain the family *after* the husband has made the decisions: She only holds the reins; Tobias decides the route. It is Tobias's house that is not in order, and

only he, she says, can decide what should be done. Tobias himself would claim that Agnes rules, but Agnes would counter that this is only his illusion. Clearly, Tobias seems to have relinquished his position of authority after the death of their son, Teddy; at that point, according to their oft-divorced daughter, Julia, now inopportunely home again after a fourth failed marriage, Tobias became a pleasant, ineffectual, gray *non*eminence. Undoubtedly, his insufficiencies as a father have had an adverse effect upon his daughter's relationships with men, and although Tobias rationalizes that he did not want another son because of the potential suffering it might have caused for Agnes, he might equally have feared his own inadequacy as a role model.

That Tobias lacks essential self-criticism and decisiveness is suggested by the motto he has cheerfully adopted: "We do what we can." In other words, he takes the path of least resistance, no longer exerting himself to do more than the minimum in his personal relationships. At one point in the play, Tobias tells a story about his cat and him—a parable similar to Jerry's tale of the dog in *The Zoo Story*—which illustrates Tobias's attitude toward having demands placed on him and being judged. Believing that the cat was accusing him of being neglectful, and resenting this assessment, he turned to hating the cat, which he finally had put to sleep in an act Claire terms the "least ugly" choice.

Now, with Harry and Edna's visit, Tobias is again having his motives and the depth of his concern measured. He realizes that if he does not respond positively to their needs, he will be tacitly admitting that his whole life, even his marriage to Agnes, has been empty. In one of the verbal arias for which Albee is justly famous, Tobias begs, even demands, that they remain, though he does not want this burden and disruption. When, despite his desperate entreaties, they insist on leaving, Agnes can calmly remark, "Come now; we can begin the day," satisfied that the dark night of terror is safely passed. Her closing line must, however, be understood as ironic. Although it is Sunday morning, there has been no resurrection or renewal; the opportunity for salvation has been missed, and Tobias must now live on with the knowledge that he has failed, that much of his life has been a sham.

As is true of the characters at the end of O'Neill's *Long Day's Journey into Night* (pr., pb. 1956) Tobias's tragedy is that he has come to self-knowledge too late to act upon the new recognition. This is perhaps Albee's central perception in *A Delicate Balance*: that time diminishes the possibilities for human choice and change. Try as he might, it is now too late for Tobias to break out of the pattern, and so he is condemned to living out his days with an awareness of how little he has become because he lacks the comforting illusions of propriety and magnanimity that Agnes can call on for solace. He has seen his soul and has found it wanting, and things can never be the same again. For Tobias, in what is Albee's most beautiful play, the "delicate balance" that everyone erects as a shelter has tipped, but not in his favor. As Agnes muses, "Time happens," and all that remains is rust, bones, and wind. These are Albee's hollow people for whom the dark never ends.

Seascape

If *Tiny Alice* and *A Delicate Balance* are dark plays, *Seascape* is a play of light, Albee's most luminous work to date. An optimistic tone poem that won for Albee his second Pulitzer, *Seascape* might, indeed, profitably be seen as a reverse image of *A Delicate Balance*, which won for him his first. In the later play, Albee again focuses on a couple in their middle age who ask: Where do we go from here? Are change and growth still possible, or is all that remains a gradual process of physical and spiritual atrophy until death? Nearly the entire first act of *Seascape*—which is primarily a play of scintillating discussion rather than action—is a two-character drama, with the diametrically opposed viewpoints of Nancy and Charlie temporarily poised in a tenuous equilibrium. Nancy's inclination is to follow the urge to ever fuller life, while Charlie is seduced by the prospect of a painless withdrawal from all purposive activity.

The "seascape" of the play's title is the literal setting, but it is also an "escape," for the sea lying beyond the dunes is the archetype of both life and death; if it once symbolized Charlie's will-to-life, it now communicates his willed desire for the inertia of

death or, at least, for a kind of premoral existence in which life simply passes. The shadow of Albee's dark plays still falls over *Seascape* in Charlie's initial stance as a man experiencing existential angst, terrified by the premonition of loneliness if Nancy should no longer be with him, fearful that even life itself may be only an illusion. In the face of these terrors—symbolized by the recurrent sound of the jet planes passing overhead—death beckons as a welcome release for Charlie because he has lived well. As his watchword, he chooses "we'll see," just another way of saying that things will be put off until they are blessedly forgotten.

Nancy, on the other hand, refuses to vegetate by retreating from life and living out her remaining days in a condition equivalent to "purgatory *before* purgatory," insisting instead that they "*do something.*" She understands that if nothing is ever ventured, nothing can be gained. If Charlie, like Agnes in *A Delicate Balance*, desires stasis, a condition comfortable precisely because it is known and therefore can be controlled, Nancy will make the leap of faith into the unknown, accepting change and flux as a necessary precondition for progress and growth. Nancy accuses Charlie of a lack of "interest in imagery"; if, as Albee has frequently said, it is man's metaphor-making ability that renders him truly human, then Charlie's deficiency in this regard signals his diminished condition.

No sooner has Nancy finished her admonition to Charlie that they "*try* something new" than the opportunity presents itself in the appearance of Leslie and Sarah, two great green talking lizards come up from the sea. Their arrival, a startling yet delightful *coup de théâtre*, raises the work to the level of parable and allegory: Leslie and Sarah, existing at some prehuman stage on the evolutionary scale, serve as recollections of what the older couple's heritage was eons ago—as well as of what Charlie desires to become once again. Leslie and Sarah, like Harry and Edna in *A Delicate Balance*, are afraid not of the prospect of dying and finding nothingness or the void but of the challenge of becoming more highly developed, which is to say more human and morally responsible creatures. Life in the sea, unterrifying because a known quantity, was also more restricted and limiting. What

inspires them to seek something more are the in-
klings of a sense of wonder, of awe, and of a childlike
enthusiasm—qualities Nancy possesses in abundance.
Their choice, then, exactly parallels Charlie's: They
can make do by settling for less than a full life, or
they can expand their lives qualitatively by becoming
conscious of themselves as thinking and feeling beings, though that, of course, requires a willingness to
experience consciously suffering as well as joy.

Significantly, it is Charlie, himself afraid, who
convinces Leslie and Sarah to remain up on earth
rather than descend back into the deep. In the moment of convincing them, he himself undergoes a regenerative epiphany that saves him, too. At the climactic point in *Seascape*, Charlie, like Jerry in *The
Zoo Story* and George in *Who's Afraid of Virginia
Woolf?* before him, gives Leslie and Sarah a "survival
kit." To accomplish this requires that he hurt them,
especially Sarah. Because what separates human beings from the lower animals is precisely their consciousness of being alive, of being vulnerable, and of
finally being mortal, Charlie realizes that he can help
Leslie and Sarah complete their transformation from
beast to human only by making them feel truly human emotions. Playing on Sarah's fear that Leslie
might someday leave her and never return, he deliberately, in an action that recalls the necessary violence
of Jerry toward Peter, makes Sarah cry; that, in turn,
makes Leslie so defensive and angry that he hits and
chokes Charlie. Having tasted these human emotions
of sorrow and wrath, Sarah and Leslie at first desire
more than ever to return to the ooze, to the prehuman
security of the sea. What quenches their fears is
Nancy and Charlie pleading with them not to retreat,
extending their hands to the younger couple in a gesture of compassion and human solidarity. In aiding
Leslie and Sarah on the mythic journey from the
womb into the world that, no matter how traumatic,
must in time be taken, Charlie simultaneously leaves
behind his desire to escape from life and asserts once
more his will to live. If Charlie is a representative
Everyman, fallen prey to ennui and despair, then
Leslie's "Begin," on which the curtain falls, is a declaration of faith, trust, and determination, uttered not
only for himself and Sarah but also for all human-

kind, who must periodically be roused and inspired to
continue their journey.

THE MAN WHO HAD THREE ARMS

In *The Man Who Had Three Arms*, Albee abolished the fourth wall of the theater in a manner that
reminded many critics of the works of Luigi Pirandello. The play's protagonist, coyly named "Himself," spends much of the drama lecturing to the audience. Himself claims to have been an ordinary man
who aspired to little more in life than his marriage,
family, and success at work until the morning he discovered a third arm growing out of his back. Seduced
by his newfound celebrity, he embarks on a lucrative
and highly conspicuous career, exploiting his anoma-
lous "talent" and indulging morally challenging impulses with the seeming approval of an admiring
public. One day, however, the third arm mysteriously
withers away and disappears, leaving him financially
bankrupt, spiritually broken and forsaken by his supporters.

Coming on the heels of *The Lady from Dubuque*,
which garnered mixed reviews and closed after only
twelve performances on Broadway, and the failed adaptation of *Lolita*, which earned Albee some of the
worst reviews of his stage career (as well as criticism
by the Nabokov estate and the condemnation of several special interest groups), *The Man Who Had Three
Arms* struck many critics as a transparently autobiographical play in which a self-pitying Albee lashed
out at a public that he felt had celebrated him during
his successful years, then abandoned him. Many reviewers, in fact, decried *The Man Who Had Three
Arms* as a virtual attack on its audience. Albee con-
curred, noting that he agreed with Atonin Artaud that
at times a dramatist must "literally draw blood." He
admitted that the drama was "an act of aggression"
and "probably the most violent play I've written," but
he also disputed the autobiographical allusions many
saw in the play. *The Man Who Had Three Arms*
closed after sixteen performances, capping a period
that marks a low point both personally and professionally for Albee, in which it seemed his relevance
and ability to enlighten as well as provoke theater audiences had, like the symbolic third arm of his protagonist, withered away to nothing.

THREE TALL WOMEN

With *Three Tall Women,* Albee proved that second acts are possible in a theater career. The play earned him his third Pulitzer Prize and inaugurated a revival of interest in his work that continued through the 1990's and beyond. It is a touchstone for many themes that he has tackled in other dramas, notably the illusions people cling to to distract them from the emptiness of their lives and the disillusionment that comes as aging gradually shuts off the individual's capacity for change and redemption. The play also reflects a highly original melding of Albee's influences. It is a Chekhovian play in its compassion for its characters, and might almost be seen as Albee's rendition of *Tri sestry* (pr., pb. 1901, revised pb. 1904; *The Three Sisters*, 1920) in its treatment of three heroines who reflect with nostalgia and regret on the choices they have made in their lives. At the same time, its observations on personal decline and its minimalist staging techniques suggest the spare and despairing spirit of the plays of Beckett.

The first act establishes the personalities of three distinct characters who are on stage for the entire play. Woman A is a frail and needy woman in her early nineties. Described in the character notes as "thin, autocratic, proud," she radiates fading glory and dominates the dialogue with memories of her life as a girl from an ordinary family who married into wealth and soon learned the self-deceiving social rituals and hypocrisies of the moneyed class. A has outlived the philandering husband she once loved by more than thirty years. She speaks proudly of her accomplishments but grows childish and petulant when her memory fails or she finds herself physically incapable of activities she could once perform. B, who "looks rather as A would have at fifty-two," serves A as a nurse and caretaker. She is dutiful and understanding and calm to the point of seeming enigmatic. B serves as a buffer between A and C, who "looks rather as B would have at twenty-six" and who shows all the impatience and selfishness one associates with youth. Though serving A in a vaguely legal capacity, C taunts A with the deficiencies of her age and openly expresses her exasperation with the older woman. There is no action per se in the first act, only verbal

exchanges between the three women, who oscillate back and forth between heated, catty arguments with each other and conspiratorial schoolgirl confidences until A suffers an apparent stroke that brings down the curtain on first act.

The seemingly naturalistic development of the play collapses in the second half when it becomes apparent that A, B, and C are actually different incarnations of the same character at different ages in her life, a nod (as some critics have suggested) to Beckett's *Krapp's Last Tape* (pr., pb. 1958), in which an aging man labors to reconcile his current self with tape-recorded messages that reflect the person he was on several different birthdays at earlier times in his life. The emotional makeup and personalities of these three tall women are shaped by their expectations and experiences of the moment. A has come to accept that the arc of her life has gradually moved her away from the attractive fantasy of things she hoped for as a young woman—love and happiness—to the cold reality of things she settled for: financial security and social status. B is embittered by the fresh memory (for her) of the son who despised her for her compromises and acquiescence to disappointment and who ran away from home (and who visits A and curries her favor, much to B's dismay). C is two years younger than the woman she will be when she marries; she clings desperately to the belief that the best times of her life are all ahead of her, when in fact observations from A and B suggest that the best years of her life—the years that A and B might look back on wistfully—are soon to end. Despite the fact that these three women are the same character, each has no sympathy for the others and either resists or repudiates the person that the other is. However, though they act as if irreconcilable toward one another, the three provide one of Albee's most elaborate character mirrorings, yielding a single sympathetic reflection of someone once young, beautiful, and full of hope whose life has devolved into a simple, seemingly pointless struggle to survive.

As in previous plays, Albee provides his characters with an illusion that serves them as a crutch for getting through life: the jewelry the three women are given by their husband. Each interprets the illusion and its significance differently, based on her different self-awareness. C, who is still beholden to the illusions of youth, cherishes her jewelry as "tangible proof . . . that we're valuable." B is of a more cynical frame shaped by her disillusionments and disappointments: She sees no difference between real and fake jewelry "because the fake looks as good as the real, even feels the same, and why should anybody know our business?" Virtually all of A's jewelry is fake: Over the years, she has had to sell her real jewelry to support herself, a type of self-cannibalization that crystallizes the decline into emotional and spiritual entropy at the play's core.

In his introduction to the published edition of the play, Albee reveals that *Three Tall Women* grew out of his troubled relationship with his adoptive mother Frankie, whom the characters are meant to represent. Albee himself appears in the play as the prodigal son, who is present at A's sickbed but does not speak a line. He writes, "As she moved toward ninety, began rapidly failing both physically and mentally, I was touched by the survivor, the figure clinging to the wreckage only partly of her own making, refusing to go under." The play thus makes an interesting bookend to *The Man Who Had Three Arms,* for which Albee appears to have drawn from his personal life to craft a theatrical act of revenge. With *Three Tall Women,* he showed it was possible to draw from the same life and fashion a compassionate reflection equally devastating in its honesty.

MARRIAGE PLAY

Marriage Play confines its violence to the stage, where the protagonists, a married couple named Jack and Gillian, alternate between bouts of physical abuse and scenes of tenderness and physical attraction. Jack and Gillian are in some ways reminiscent of the battling couples of *Who's Afraid of Virginia Woolf?,* but the newer play also incorporates the sort of metaphysical speculation that marks much of Albee's later work. *Marriage Play* encapsulates many of the principal themes of Albee's dramatic career.

THE PLAY ABOUT THE BABY

With *The Play About the Baby,* Albee's career came full circle. The play reprises ideas and themes from earlier plays, albeit in a synthesis that makes it stand apart from the works from which it borrows. Its central conceit, a baby that may just be a figment of the characters' imaginations, seems a self-conscious nod to *Who's Afraid of Virginia Woolf?* and is reinforced by the pairing of a younger and older couple. At the same time, the free-form absurdism of the play calls to mind Albee's debut *The Zoo Story,* with its escalation to an act of dramatic provocation to shock a character out of a complacent frame of mind.

Girl and Boy, the younger couple, have apparently had a baby together. Their nemeses are Man and Woman, an older couple—possibly married, possibly not—who first claim to have taken the baby, then proceed to call the baby's very reality in question. While the young couple plead for the return of their child, the older couple taunt them with word games, false memories, and similar challenges that hinder the younger couple's ability to prove who they are and the reality of their child. The play ends with them agreeing—possibly under emotional duress, possibly faced with irrefutable proof—that there is no baby. Although very much a chamber piece, the play shows Albee at his wittiest and builds on distillations of trademark ideas in his dramas, including the notion that individual reality is shaped by needs, and the therapeutic value of an act of cruelty to save people from the illusions that focus their life.

THE GOAT

Albee's award-winning *The Goat* is, on the surface, a comedy, but it has an underlying tone of tragedy. Like *Who's Afraid of Virginia Woolf?*, it centers on a married couple, successful upper-class New York architect Martin, who has just won the Pritzker Prize, and Stevie, his wife of more than twenty years. This couple, however, has a seventeen-year-old gay son, and the center of their conflict involves Martin's infidelity. His infidelity is revealed during the course of a television interview. Martin explains that although he loves his wife, he fell in love while visiting property in upstate New York. When Martin shows the interviewer, his friend Ross, a photograph of his new love, Ross is shocked to see a photo of a goat—Sylvia.

The second act deals, largely humorously, with Stevie's feelings as she comes to terms with Martin's infidelity; she is especially angry and feels unclean when she realizes that Martin had been having sex with both her and the goat for several months. She complains that he has brought her down, and as she exits, she threatens to bring him down as well. The couple's son, Billy, argues with his father, comparing their sexual preferences, and when they reconcile, a kiss turns sexual. When Ross walks in and sees the kiss, he expresses his disgust, and in return, Martin describes a father being sexually aroused after bouncing his baby on his lap. It is this scene rather than, as might be expected, the references to bestiality that brought shocked responses from the audience. Some critics suggest that this is because Albee's treatment of bestiality is similar to the early treatment of homosexuality in its vagueness.

In the last act, Stevie returns, dragging along the body of Sylvia. Martin is grief-stricken, able only to say "I'm sorry." A reviewer for *The New Republic* noted that Albee manages to sympathetically portray Martin, the goat-lover, despite the repugnance that many people feel for those who engage in bestiality.

BIBLIOGRAPHY

Amacher, Richard E. *Edward Albee*. Rev. ed. Boston: Twayne, 1982. Taking Albee's career through *The Man Who Had Three Arms*, this study is part biography, part script analysis, and part career assessment. Amacher is best at discussing Albee's "place in the theatre" and his marriage of the well-made play form with the formless Theater of the Absurd. Good second opinion after C. W. E. Bigsby's edition of essays in 1975. Chronology, notes, bibliography.

Bigsby, C. W. E., ed. *Edward Albee: A Collection of Critical Essays*. Englewood Cliffs, N.J.: Prentice-Hall, 1975. Part of the Twentieth Century Views series, this collection includes notable names in theater and scholarship, such as Gerald Weales, Martin Esslin, Richard Schechner, Alan Schneider, Harold Clurman, Philip Roth, and Robert Brustein. They contribute several interpretations of the symbolic aspect of Albee's plays, usually, but not always, in single-play discussions. Chronology and select bibliography.

Bottoms, Stephen J. *Albee: "Who's Afraid of Virginia Woolf?"* New York: Cambridge University Press, 2000. A thorough study of Albee's best-known play.

Bryer, Jackson R. "Edward Albee." In *The Playwright's Art*. New Brunswick, N.J.: Rutgers University Press, 1995. Interview conducted in 1991 that discusses most of Albee's major plays at the time, both successes and failures. Albee reveals himself as clever and articulate as the characters in his plays, and makes pointed statements about the Broadway establishment and its impact on playwriting in America.

"Edward Albee." In *Playwrights at Work*. New York: Modern Library, 2000. Although this interview appeared in the *Paris Review* in 1966, when Albee had taken several critical hits in the wake of his success with *Who's Afraid of Virginia Woolf?*, it captures him in the full flush of his "angry young man" interval and records observations on the art and craft of playwriting that continue to inform his work.

Gussow, Mel. *Edward Albee: A Singular Journey*. New York: Simon & Schuster, 1999. A comprehensive biocritical study of the playwright by a leading cultural critic of *The New York Times*, whose association with Albee extends back to 1962. Written with Albee's cooperation and input, it discusses all of his plays in the context of his life and his beliefs as an artist. With photos, bibliography, and index.

Kolin, Philip C., and J. Madison Davis. *Critical Essays on Edward Albee*. Boston: G. K. Hall, 1986. Part of a series of critical essays on American literature, this collection of original reviews (from *The Zoo Story* to *Counting the Ways*), general criticism, and an overview of Albee's importance to world theater is comprehensive and thorough, with some thirty-seven articles, as well as an annotated bibliography of Albee interviews (with its own index).

McCarthy, Gerry. *Edward Albee*. New York: St. Martin's Press, 1987. Stronger than other studies on Albee's theater sense, as opposed to his plays as dramatic literature, this brief but informative overview puts the work in a dynamic, action-and-reaction-oriented structural perspective. Some production stills, index, and brief bibliography.

Roudané, Matthew. *Understanding Edward Albee.* Columbia: University of South Carolina Press, 1987. Organized chronologically, and pairing the plays in each chapter (*Who's Afraid of Virginia Woolf?* gets its own), this study focuses on Albee's plays in a "culture seeking to locate its identity through the ritualized action implicit in the art of theater." Bibliography and index.

_____. *Who's Afraid of Virginia Woolf?: Necessary Fictions, Terrifying Realities.* Boston: Twayne, 1990. A close study of Albee's landmark drama, by one of Albee's most perceptive critics. A followup to the author's *Understanding Edward Albee,* with particular emphasis on the function

and purpose of illusion in Albee's dramas.

Wasserman, Julian, ed. *Edward Albee: An Interview and Essays.* Houston, Tex.: University of St. Thomas, 1983. This 1981 interview, on translations, audiences, and similar earthly subjects, has a show-biz tone to it, without much of the transcendental abstractions of later interviews. A good place to start a study of Albee because he articulates his intentions here with some clarity and grace. Wasserman contributes an essay on language; seven other authors offer single-play discussions, not including *Who's Afraid of Virginia Woolf?* but including *The Lady from Dubuque, Seascape,* and *Counting the Ways.*

Thomas P. Adler,
updated by Thomas J. Taylor,
Robert McClenaghan, and Stefan Dziemianowicz

VITTORIO ALFIERI

Born: Asti, Piedmont (now in Italy); January 16, 1749

Died: Florence (now in Italy); October 8, 1803

PRINCIPAL DRAMA

Antonio e Cleopatra, pr. 1775, pb. 1804 (*Antony and Cleopatra*, 1876)

Polinice, wr. 1775-1781, pb. 1784, pr. 1824 (*Polynices*, 1815)

Filippo, wr. 1775-1781, pb. 1784, pr. 1825 (*Phillip II*, 1815)

Antigone, wr. 1777, pr. 1782, pb. 1784 (English translation, 1815)

Agamennone, wr. 1778, pb. 1784, pr. 1842 (*Agamemnon*, 1815)

Virginia, wr. 1778, pr., pb. 1784 (English translation, 1815)

Don Garzia, wr. 1779, pb. 1788 (English translation, 1815)

La congiura dei Pazzi, wr. 1779, pb. 1788 (*The Conspiracy of the Pazzi*, 1815)

Maria Stuarda, wr. 1780, pb. 1788 (*Mary Stuart*, 1815)

Oreste, pr. 1781, pb. 1784 (*Orestes*, 1815)

Saul, wr. 1782, pb. 1788, pr. 1794 (English translation, 1815)

Tragedie, pb. 1783-1789 (*The Tragedies of Vittorio Alfieri*, 1815)

Rosmunda, pb. 1784, pr. 1841 (English translation, 1815)

Ottavia, pb. 1784 (*Octavia*, 1815)

Timoleone, pr. 1784 (*Timoleon*, 1815)

Merope, pb. 1784 (English translation, 1815)

Agide, pb. 1788 (*Agis*, 1815)

Sofonisba, pb. 1788, pr. 1824 (*Sophonisba*, 1815)

Bruto primo, pb. 1788 (*The First Brutus*, 1815)

Bruto secondo, pb. 1788, pr. 1848 (*The Second Brutus*, 1815)

Mirra, pb. 1789, pr. 1819 (*Myrrha*, 1815)

Abele, wr. 1790, pb. 1804 (*Abel*, 1815)

Alceste seconda, wr. 1798, pb. 1804, pr. 1831
  (*Alcestis II*, 1876)

L'uno, pb. 1804

I pochi, pb. 1804

I troppi, pb. 1804

L'antidoto, pb. 1804

La finestra, pb. 1804

Il divorzio, pb. 1804

*The Tragedies of Vittorio Alfieri, Complete, Includ-
  ing His Posthumous Works*, pb. 1876 (2 volumes)

O<small>THER LITERARY FORMS</small>

Vittorio Alfieri's love of liberty and hate of tyranny resulted in several poetic works. In *L'America
libera* (1784; *Alfieri's Ode to America's Independence*, 1976), the poet exalts the Americans who rebelled against English tyranny. He wrote the first four
odes in 1781 and added one more in 1783. The first
describes the reasons for the American War of Independence, the second enumerates the participants, the
third speaks about the Marquis de Lafayette, the
fourth praises George Washington, and the fifth is
dedicated to the peace of 1783 and ends with a pessimistic note: What is there to rejoice about? asks the
author—only force reigns. Alfieri also glorified the
fall of the Bastille in the ode *Parigi sbastigliata*
(1789; Paris without the Bastille).

Alfieri expressed the same sentiments about freedom in his political prose, but more coherently and
systematically. The treatise *Della tirannide* (1789; *Of
Tyranny*, 1961), written in 1777, condemns even the
most reformed monarchs as wanting only obedient
subjects: From the highest nobleman to the poorest
peasant, all must follow orders; the king's subjects
are mere victims. Alfieri concludes that it is better
not to marry, in order not to create new victims. *Del
principe e delle lettere* (1789; *The Prince and Letters*,
1972) expounds the same theme with equal passion.
It deals with the relationship between a prince and
men of letters. A poet protected by a prince can bring
glory to tyranny, but a writer, according to Alfieri,
should be free to fight tyranny with his pen and cannot accept any kind of protection.

Il misogallo (1799) consists of five prose passages
and more than a hundred poems, in which Alfieri ex-
aggerates his anti-French sentiments, for he considered the post-revolutionary French rulers as tyrannical as France's former kings, only more vulgar.

Rime (1789, 1804, published in two parts) is a poetic diary of Alfieri's intimate feelings, consisting of
compositions in the traditional Arcadian style, bizarre epigrams, and passionate sonnets written for the
countess of Albany. The most original poems are
those in which Alfieri laments the forced separation
from his beloved countess. Alone, he ponders the nul-
lity of life and longs for death, evincing a new sensi-
tivity that is Romantic in quality. Petrarch's influence
resulted in a new spirit and experience that reached
the tragic and sublime, making Alfieri not unlike his
tragic characters. In some poems, he describes or,
rather, defines himself as a person; in others, he
points out the contradictions of life—"to hope, to
fear, to remember, to lament"—and pays tribute to
the great men of the past, even if always overcome by
a profound pessimism.

His *Vita di Vittorio Alfieri* (1804; *Memoirs*, 1810),
written in 1790 and subsequently repeatedly revised

Vittorio Alfieri (Library of Congress)

and enlarged, is a prototype of the Romantic autobiography, which aims to understand intimately the development and growth of the artist. The book is divided into four significant periods of Alfieri's life, and each event and emotion is scrutinized with psychological insight. In his effort to portray himself as an artist, Alfieri comes close to the German Romantics of the Sturm und Drang movement.

Achievements

The Italy of Vittorio Alfieri's time was made up of several independent states and kingdoms. Alfieri was reared in Piedmont, a cultural environment strongly affected by French traditions, and French, rather than Italian, was the language of the nobility. By the second half of the eighteenth century, Piedmont's territorial expansion had come to a halt, and Charles Emanuel III of Savoy dedicated himself entirely to the administration of internal affairs with an austere sense of morality that was also imposed on all his subjects. Alfieri's personal, aristocratic, and independent concept of liberty made him rebel against all kinds of control with a typical proto-Romantic spirit. Incapable of accepting the political realities of his day, Alfieri passionately advocated the overthrow of tyranny with the consciousness of a libertarian, but he never proposed a practical alternative. Imbued with the progressive ideals of European Enlightenment, he was a true cosmopolitan in the tradition of the eighteenth century, yet from the day he decided to become a writer, he spent all his time searching for his Italian roots and trying to shed his Piedmontese ways, repressing his cosmopolitanism in the process. The result was that he created a national spirit that was to influence the following generations of the Italian Risorgimento.

Alfieri is classified as pre-Romantic, only because his tragedies are classical in form, strictly adherent to the rules on the unity of time, place, and action—even if their context is Romantic, something that was unknown to his contemporaries. His tragedies, written with the intent of giving Italy dramas comparable to those of other European nations, seemed too austere to his contemporaries, but in the twentieth century, because of their concentration on a few characters, they strike audiences as being modern. Alfieri

achieved what he set out to do: He became the greatest Italian tragic writer. His prose, especially in his autobiography, is of a masterly quality, and his influence, as both a poet and a prose writer, on style and content is evident in Ugo Foscolo and Giacomo Leopardi, the two great Italian Romantics.

Biography

Vittorio Alfieri was born on January 16, 1749, in Asti, Piedmont, to Count Antonio Alfieri and his wife, Monica Maillard de Tournon, a Turinese lady of Savoyard origin and the widow of Marquis Cacherano. His mother was much younger than his father, who married when he was in his late fifties and died before Vittorio was a year old. Later, Alfieri's mother remarried a man her own age, Giacinto Alfieri, from a different branch of the same family, with whom she lived in perfect harmony.

Alfieri and his older sister, Giulia, lived with their mother and stepfather, but when Giulia was sent to the convent boarding school, Alfieri, although living at home, felt very lonely under the care of his private teacher, and he developed a melancholy that was to accompany him for the greater part of his life.

At the age of nine, Alfieri was sent to the military academy in Turin, where he stayed from 1758 to 1766. Although this school enjoyed a good reputation in eighteenth century Europe and counted prominent foreigners among its graduates, Alfieri condemned it as a horrible institution with an antiquated and useless system of education. On graduating, he received the military degree of ensign and joined the provincial regiment in Asti. Intolerant of any kind of subordination, he could not adapt to military life and asked permission from the king to travel. His first journey took him through various Italian cities and was followed by a trip abroad from 1767 to 1768 to France, England, Holland, and Switzerland. Half a year later, he departed again, this time for Austria, the German states, Denmark, Sweden, and Russia. In 1771, he was again in England. Then, passing through Holland and France, he visited Spain and Portugal. He returned to Italy only in 1772 and settled in Turin for a time. His restless travels reflect his desire to conquer the melancholy and boredom that oppressed him. His uneasy spirit found comfort in constant motion. He did not actually visit these countries, he flew through them, stopping only to admire that which caught his fancy and affected his sensibility, such as the immensity of the sea, the deep silence of the forests, the spectacle of a frozen Nordic sea, the danger involved in passing in a boat through floating ice, and the desolate beauty of the Spanish desert. Intolerant of all authoritarianism, Alfieri was quick to criticize the French court, Prussian militarism, Pietro Metastasio's servile genuflections in the presence of Empress Maria Theresa, and Russian primitivism. This period, through 1774, was also a period of unrestrained passions, which made him suffer to the degree of attempting suicide, as in Holland, when Cristina Emerenzia Imhof abruptly ended their relationship. In England, his liaison with Penelope Pitt ended in a duel with the lady's husband, who was generous enough to spare the Italian's life.

Although Alfieri's travels were carried out with impatience, they served not only to acquaint him with his world and its problems but also to bring him in contact with many European diplomats, some of whom shared their cultural opinions with him, becoming his close friends. While abroad, Alfieri avidly read the works of Voltaire, Jean-Jacques Rousseau, Charles de Montesquieu, and Claude-Adrien Helvétius. Once settled in Turin, he started to write. His desire to polish his Italian, contaminated by French and the Piedmontese dialect, brought him to Tuscany. In 1776, he took up residence in Siena, where he enjoyed the friendship of Francesco Gori-Gandellini, who gave him moral support and practical advice, encouraging his literary creativity and love for liberty.

In Florence in 1777, Alfieri met Louise Stolberg Gedern, countess of Albany, wife of Charles Edward Stuart, pretender to the English throne. His devotion to this woman became a great, inspiring, and lasting love. He saw in her his ideal tragic woman: beautiful, intelligent, kind, and the victim of a cruel and unreasonable husband, who was a heavy drinker and impatient with his much younger wife. Alfieri helped her escape to a convent, from where she proceeded to Rome under the protection of her brother-in-law, Cardinal Henry Benedict Stuart, duke of York.

Pressed for an absolute need to be free from all civil obligations, Alfieri decided in 1778 to give all his possessions to his sister, Giulia, reserving for himself only an annual pension. While in Florence from 1778 to 1780, he worked diligently on his tragedies. He left Florence for Rome to be closer to the countess of Albany and stayed there two years. He frequented the salons of Roman society, where he read his tragedy *Virginia* and recited from his *Antigone*, which was also performed by a group of amateur actors. It was in Rome that he was recognized and admired as Italy's great tragic writer. After the reading of his *Saul* on April 8, 1783, he became a member of the Academy of Arcadia. Alfieri was at this time also preparing his complete tragedies for publication, excluding, for political reasons, *Mary Stuart*, *The Conspiracy of the Pazzi*, and *Don Garzia*.

Yet no lasting peace was destined for Alfieri. When Cardinal York learned of Alfieri's true relationship to his sister-in-law, the playwright was diplomatically asked to leave Rome, which he did on May 4, 1783, while the countess stayed. A clamorous scandal resulted. Someone circulated a satiric sonnet written by Alfieri a few years earlier on the Papal States. Roman literati vented their ill feelings against him, and critics, too, were not kind to his tragedies when the first volume appeared in print. Alfieri fought back with epigrams and expressed his love-grief in sonnets written during his wanderings through Italy, which became a pilgrimage of sorts, not only of an unhappy lover but also of a writer now completely consecrated to his poetic work. He visited illustrious writers such as Melchiorre Cesarotti in Padua and Giuseppe Parini and Pietro Verri in Milan. He departed for France with letters for Carlo Goldoni and Louis-Sébastien Mercier, and he went to England for the sole reason of buying horses. Meanwhile the countess of Albany had obtained a legal separation from her husband, and Alfieri was able to see her in August, 1784, in Alsace, in Martinsburg near Colmar, but the two were again separated. She, being obliged to live in the Papal States, chose to go to Bologna, while he settled in Pisa.

When the countess went to France, Alfieri returned to Martinsburg, experiencing a renewed creativity and attending to the publication of the definite and final version of his tragedies. To be closer to his French publisher, Didot, Alfieri moved to Paris, where he met the playwright Pierre-Augustin Caron de Beaumarchais and the poet André Chénier and witnessed with enthusiasm the events leading to the French Revolution. In 1791, he accompanied the countess, whose husband had died in 1788, to England. After returning to France with the hope of taking up his literary activities, Alfieri and the countess had to flee Paris. The violent and bloody acts of the French Revolution, in which he had lost all his books, shattered his ideal and abstract notion of liberty and made his former admiration turn into hate for the new French rulers.

Alfieri returned to Florence in 1792 and spent the rest of his life in ever-increasing semiseclusion. His anti-Gallic attitude, reinforced by the French occupation of Florence in 1799, found its way into his writings. His last years were dedicated to his six comedies, on which he worked with such fervor that the countess attributed his death to them. Alfieri died on October 8, 1803, and was buried in the church of Santa Croce in Florence.

ANALYSIS

Vittorio Alfieri's nineteen tragedies were written between 1775 and 1786. They all underwent three stages of composition: first a division of subject matter into five acts, then the writing of prose dialogue, and finally versification. Moreover, they were all revised by the author for the definite and complete edition that appeared in Paris between 1787 and 1789. Alfieri strictly applied the rules of the classical theater, never transgressing the Aristotelian unities of time, place, and action. Indeed, he carried the unity of action to an extreme through frequent use of monologues and the elimination of all secondary events, including the traditional narration to or by confidants, so as not to distract the spectator, who must concentrate fully on the rapidly unfolding catastrophe centered on the protagonist. The first and the fifth acts are very short. Moreover, the last act emphasizes the action of death and keeps the dying hero's (or heroine's) speech to a bare minimum.

Alfieri, true to eighteenth century classical tradition, did not invent any subjects for his tragedies. He based them on three sources only: antiquity, the Bible, and European history. He did, however, modify historical or mythological events to suit his artistic needs, thus giving an originality all his own to well-known stories. His main characters, full of virtues, are sublime heroes and heroines, incapable of even one low thought. Their perfection brings them into acute contrast with the ugly tyrannical powers that rule the world, but against which they rebel and succumb. This basic theme is characteristic of all his tragedies, although tyranny can appear in various forms. In the so-called tragedies of liberty, such as *Virginia*, *Timoleon*, *The Conspiracy of the Pazzi*, *The First Brutus*, and *The Second Brutus*, the struggle is against political tyranny, in which Alfieri sanctifies tyrannicide. Paternal tyranny brings about death to the noble sons in *Phillip II* and *Don Garzia*. Octavia is a victim of Nero, her cruel husband. Antigone is crushed by a terribly destiny, while Saul and Myrrha face a supernatural power: Saul must yield his throne to David, as is the will of God interpreted by the high priests, and Myrrha falls victim to the vengeance of Venus, goddess of love.

VIRGINIA

In nineteenth century Italy, Alfieri's tragedies of liberty were preferred on account of their political message, since Italians were striving for freedom and unification. In *Virginia*, Alfieri chose a grandiose and terrifying episode taken from Roman history. Virginia, daughter of the respected soldier Virginius and his wife, Numitoria, is bride to Icilius, a former tribune, but is desired by Appius, chief of the Decemvirs governing Rome. Appius, unable to seduce the virtuous girl, orders his henchman, Marcus, to abduct her. Marcus claims that Virginia is his former slave taken by Numitoria and appeals for arbitration to the Roman law. With fearless courage, the two virtuous heroes, Virginius and Icilius, denounce tyranny, but they are betrayed and lose their battle. Icilius, rather than accept disgrace, stabs himself to death. Virginius, seeing that all is lost, kills his own daughter before the passive Roman people, who, moved by this utmost example of virtue, rebel against Appius and overcome him and his followers. Here the classical beauty of the virtuous, austerely noble characters, typical of Alfieri's heroes, seems somewhat artificial. The evil characters lack individuality but fit the Alfierian scheme. There is also in this tragedy an implicit criticism of the nobility for its abuses and excesses—a criticism that Alfieri, as a nobleman himself, could make without being dismissed as merely envious.

TIMOLEON

In *Timoleon*, derived from Plutarch's *Bioi paralleloi* (c. 105-115 C.E.; *Parallel Lives*, 1579), the protagonist is even more idealized, and the plot is complicated by the fact that the antagonist is the hero's brother, Timophanes, who is about to seize absolute power in the city of Corinth. The action of the play is actually based on dramatic dialogue expressing opposing ideals; in addition to the two brothers, the principal characters are their mother, Demariste, and Aeschylus, Timophanes' brother-in-law. Timophanes loves his brother, but he cannot comprehend the latter's love of liberty and offers to share his new powers with him, which is not acceptable to the hero. Yet at the end, before he is slain by Aeschylus, Timophanes recognizes his brother's ideal and forgives all those plotting against him, thus from tyrant becoming human again.

THE CONSPIRACY OF THE PAZZI

With *The Conspiracy of the Pazzi*, Alfieri turned to a relatively modern period: 1478, and the revolt led by Raymond of the Pazzi family against the Medici, rulers of Florence, in which Lorenzo managed to save himself while his younger brother Julian was slain. In the play, Raymond, who is plotting against the two tyrants, is married to Bianca, sister to the two Medici brothers, but keeps her in the dark. He and his father form a unity against the two tyrants, who also complement each other, almost reducing the number of characters. Concentration, however, is on the tragic figure of Raymond, while Bianca provides relief from the ferocity of the action with her personal drama of a woman seen as sister, wife, and mother. In this tragedy, Alfieri succeeded in making his republican hero more human by having him agonize over what will happen to his wife and children if the plot should fail. The result is a new pathos in a play in which the protagonist's pessimistic outlook on life is stressed. Raymond assassinates his opponent Julian, but Lorenzo, assigned to Salviati, is only wounded. There is no other way of escape for the hero but to commit suicide, an act of liberation. When Bianca asks Raymond who the traitor is, he answers, "The traitor . . . is . . . the vanquished," a response that is typical of the forceful brevity of style found in all Alfieri's tragedies. After *The Conspiracy of the Pazzi*, generally considered his best play about liberty, Alfieri returned to Roman subjects with *The First Brutus*, leader of the revolt against the Tarquins, and *The Second Brutus*, principal assassin of Caesar.

PHILLIP II

In the twentieth century, literary critics shifted their attention to Alfieri's other tragedies, singling out *Phillip II*, *Antigone*, *Saul*, and *Myrrha* as true masterpieces. In the first tragedy, King Philip II of Spain embodies a double tyrant, as father and king to his virtuous son Carlos, whom he hates for his perfect virtue and as a possible rival in the heart of his young second wife, Isabella, originally promised to Carlos. Isabella, indeed, spiritually belongs to Carlos, for she has the same virtuous soul and suffers in the oppressive Spanish court. Accused of treason under trumped-up charges to mask the king's jealousy, Carlos stabs himself to death, and Isabella follows suit to escape the tyrannical clutches of Philip.

Hate is the main force that governs *Phillip II*. The two victims, Carlos and Isabella, who embody virtue and beauty, are masterfully trapped by Philip and his sinister adviser, Gomez, with Alfieri's rapid and concise theatrical technique. In the end, however, the king finds no joy in his vengeance.

Philip II, although ranked as Alfieri's first tragedy, since *Antony and Cleopatra* was repudiated, should not be considered a work from Alfieri's early period because it was revised very carefully for the final edition and bears the stamp of the master's maturity. (This is also true of the other tragedies and makes a chronological study of Alfieri's plays based on the final editions somewhat arbitrary.)

ANTIGONE

Antigone, the sequel to *Polynices*, is a perfect example of Alfieri's ability to create a new interpretation of an old myth. Alfieri creates a powerful drama in concentrating all his attention on the heroine, who has throughout the centuries been reinterpreted as a character by many playwrights, from the times of Aeschylus and Sophocles forward, because of her tragic lot as the daughter of Oedipus. Alfieri's Antigone, after witnessing her father's banishment, her brothers' violent deaths inflicted on each other, and her mother's suicide, finds herself the sole survivor of a family predestined to a terrible fate. As the first act opens, the heroine is presented as a courageous young woman who has decided to administer burial rites to her brother Polynices, explicitly forbidden under penalty of death by her uncle Creon, the new tyrant of Thebes. She transgresses the law, aimed solely at her, with the full knowledge that her punishment will be death. Moreover, she wants to die, for the sins of her family weigh heavily on her. Argeia, her sister-in-law, is not Oedipus's daughter and can live on, but Antigone must refuse all earthly ties, including the love of Haemon, Creon's virtuous son. Antigone's desire to die dominates the play. She is strong and unfaltering in her determination yet afraid that she will not achieve her goal. In the end, she indeed finds liberation from a cruel destiny in death.

Critics were slow in giving credit to Alfieri for his new interpretation of the Antigone myth. In his tragedy, Antigone becomes a sublime heroine who cannot accept compromise. She is horrified by the sins committed by her kindred. She is the only member not yet fallen and is determined to preserve her own purity by sacrificing herself and redeeming her family through her own death, a death seen as a liberating and purifying force of redemption. This makes her an exceptional heroine and a pre-Romantic figure, one who comes close to a Christian interpretation of the old myth, not as a resigned but as a fighting Christian who prefers death to the burden of sin.

Saul

Saul, a tragedy based on the story of the biblical king destined to yield his throne to David, the new hero, is considered by some to be Alfieri's best work. Saul has the unusual double role of tyrant and victim. Human strength and weakness are centered on one character who symbolizes, in a Romantic way, the struggle a great man must undergo to find himself.

Saul, encamped in Gilboa in preparation for a battle against the Philistines, is torn between his former love for David, to whom he gave his own daughter, Michal, in marriage, and his hate for him, since David, not his son, Jonathan, is destined to ascend to the throne as the Anointed of the Lord. This complexity of inner torments leads Saul to folly. He had sent David into exile but then makes peace with him on the latter's secret return, only to give way yet again to his violent impulses. He orders the death of the priest Ahimelech, whom he suspects of planning his overthrow in favor of David. No calm comes to Saul, whose anguish only increases, and David determines to leave the camp. When the Philistines attack, Saul's forces are completely destroyed; his son, Jonathan, is killed, and the king takes his own life, finding peace only in death.

Saul embodies human torment brought about by the desire to rule, which isolates him and cuts him off from all others, including his children, Jonathan and Michal, who, together with David, embody love and righteousness, true to the Alfierian pattern. In no other tragedy has Alfieri's interest in the tyrant found such a perfect poetic presentation as in *Saul*, where the tyrant becomes victim and, thus, fully human.

Myrrha

In *Myrrha*, no tyrant is visible onstage. King Cinyras of Cyprus and his wife, Cenchreis (called Cecris in the play), are gentle and loving parents to their only child, Myrrha, engaged to virtuous Pereus, heir to the throne of Epirus. Yet Myrrha from the beginning appears very unhappy, to the point of agonizing and invoking death. When questioned about her strange manners not becoming a happy bride, she denies being in love with someone else and repeats her willingness to marry Pereus, who is also perplexed by her behavior. During the wedding ceremony, Myrrha is seized with an attack of frenzy and yells that the Furies have taken hold of her. Pereus interprets this as a refusal on the part of Myrrha to marry him, and he rushes off in despair. When his suicide is announced to the king, he confronts his daughter and demands an explanation. Hard-pressed, Myrrha confesses that she loves him, her own father, and stabs herself to death, lamenting that she was unable to die with her secret, the incestuous passion bestowed on her as a curse by Venus, offended by Myrrha's mother.

Myrrha's confession comes as a surprise, for nothing in the play points to it. All attention is concentrated on the effort of the loving group of people surrounding the wretched girl to learn her secret and help her. Myrrha dies like all other Alfierian heroes and heroines, but her death is not a heroic one: She is abandoned by her horrified parents. Her death is useless, for she gives away her secret before dying. Her story of incest (even if not committed), a daring subject in the eighteenth century, but delicately handled by Alfieri, concludes the cycle of the author's opposing forces. The invisible tyrant is a supernatural power against which there is no defense.

THE COMEDIES

Alfieri's comedies, his final works, are read only by scholars of Italian literature. *L'uno* (the one), *I pochi* (the few), and *I troppi* (the many) are satires on the three main forms of government: monarchy, oligarchy, and democracy, respectively. Because they are all defective, a solution is proposed in *L'antidoto* (the antidote): Combine all three. In *La finestra* (the little window), Mercury investigates the merits of the souls admitted to the Elysian Field but is scrutinized in turn and has to flee. *Il divorzio* (the divorce), Alfieri's only comedy set in his contemporary Italy, criticizes the social acceptance of *cicisbei*, or gallant escorts of ladies, and comes to the conclusion that there is no need for divorce, since marriage is a union in name only.

OTHER MAJOR WORKS

POETRY: *L'America libera*, 1784 (*Alfieri's Ode to America's Independence*, 1976); *Parigi sbastigliata*, 1789; *Rime*, 1789, 1804 (two parts); *Il misogallo*, 1799.

NONFICTION: *Panegirico di Plinio e Trajano*, 1787; *Della tirannide*, 1789 (*Of Tyranny*, 1961); *Del principe e delle lettere*, 1789 (*The Prince and Letters*, 1972); *Vita di Vittorio Alfieri*, 1804 (*Memoirs*, 1810).

MISCELLANEOUS: *Opere postume di Vittorio Alfieri*, 1804; *Opere di Vittorio Alfieri da Asti*, 1951.

BIBLIOGRAPHY

Betti, Franco. *Vittorio Alfieri*. Boston: Twayne, 1984. A basic biography of Alfieri that covers his life and works. Bibliography and index.

Costa-Zalessow, Natalia. "Alfieri's *Antigone*: A Review of Previous Interpretations and a New Proposal." *Italian Quarterly* 23 (1982): 91-99. A study of interpretations of the Antigone story, with particular emphasis on Alfieri's treatment.

Lees, Barrie. "Birth of Vittorio Alfieri: January 16th, 1749." *History Today* 49, no. 1 (January, 1999): 53. This short essay on Alfieri examines his life, in particular his affairs, as well as his motivation for writing drama.

Mazzaro, Jerome. "Alfieri's *Saul* as Enlightenment Tragedy." *Comparative Drama* 33, no. 1 (Spring, 1999): 125-139. In this examination of *Saul*, Mazzaro points out that Alfieri observes the unities of plot, time, and action made prominent by dramatist Jean Racine.

Megaro, Gaudens. *Vittorio Alfieri: Forerunner of Italian Nationalism*. 1930. Reprint. New York: Octagon Books, 1975. This study of Alfieri focuses on his political thoughts and actions, while shedding light on his literary output. Bibliography and index.

Natalia Costa-Zalessow

CARL JONAS LOVE ALMQVIST

Born: Stockholm, Sweden; November 28, 1793
Died: Bremen, Germany; September 26, 1866

PRINCIPAL DRAMA
Ramido Marinesco, pb. 1834, pr. 1952
Signora Luna, pb. 1835

Colombine, pb. 1835, pr. 1982
Godolphin, pb. 1838
Ferrando Bruno, pb. 1839
Isidoros av Tadmor, pb. 1839
Marjam, pb. 1839
Svangrottan på Ipsara, pb. 1839
Den sensade kritiken, pb. 1849
Silkesharen på Hagalund, pb. 1850
Purpurgrefven, pb. 1850

OTHER LITERARY FORMS

Carl Jonas Love Almqvist is known primarily for his fiction and nonfiction. His major works, including his plays, were organized within a frame narrative called *Törnrosens bok* (the book of the friar rose), which he published in two editions: The fourteen volumes of the duodecimo edition appeared between 1832 and 1851 and the imperial octave edition's three volumes between 1839 and 1850. Inspired by a characteristically romantic aspiration toward an organic unity among the genres and probably also by frame narratives such as *Alf layla wa-layla* (15 C.E.; *The Arabian Nights' Entertainments*, 1706-1708), Giovanni Boccaccio's *Decameron: O, Prencipe Galetto* (1349-1351; *The Decameron*, 1620), and Johann Wolfgang von Goethe's *Unterhaltungen deutscher Ausgewanderten* (1795; *Conversations of German Emigrants*, 1854), Almqvist combined stories and fairy tales, novels and novellas, dramatic and lyric pieces, treatises and lectures, tracts and speeches, and essays on a wide range of sociopolitical, economic, and religious topics in his *Törnrosens bok*. These works are not connected thematically and bridge two movements in Swedish literature, Romanticism and realism. However, Almqvist succeeds in creating an organic whole, which has unity despite its heterogeneity, and ambivalence. A firm supporter of liberalism in Swedish society and in education, Almqvist also published a series of influential textbooks in science and grammar books in Swedish, Greek, and French.

ACHIEVEMENTS

Because of his legal problems and flight from Sweden, Carl Jonas Love Almqvist failed to receive formal recognition of his innovative work and daring ideas during his lifetime from either the Swedish public or the literary establishment, both of which failed to draw a distinction between Almqvist the man and the writer. It was not until 1894 when Ellen Key published her influential article calling Almqvist Sweden's most modern poet that Almqvist's literary and nonliterary production enjoyed popularity and acclaim. He has come to be regarded as one of the most talented and intrepid Romantic writers in Swedish literature. Though he was one of the founders of the Stockholm center of Romanticism, he was a keen cultural reformer and liberal who never joined the Swedish Academy, the most prestigious literary establishment at the time.

In the 1830's, Almqvist introduced *folklivsskildring*, stories that featured realistic representations of life in rural Sweden, into Swedish literature. In the 1880's, this art form would come back in vogue and shape the poetry and prose of a whole generation of Swedish writers. In the 1890's, the influence of Almqvist's peasant stories could be clearly seen in the tales of Selma Lagerlöf, the first woman writer to win the Nobel Prize, and in the works of many other writers.

Almqvist's masterpiece, *Det går an* (1839; *Sara Videbeck*, 1919; also as *Why Not! A Picture Out of Life*, 1994), a didactic and radical yet lively and enjoyable novel, was his response to the debates on the function of weddings; the rights of unmarried women, especially their right to work; and the Lutheran doctrine of marriage. His rather daring ideas of "free marriage" made the novel one of the first significant feminist texts in Swedish literature. It anticipated the arrival forty years later of the strong feminist voices of Det Unga Sverige, a group that opposed traditional social and religious conventions in the so-called Great Scandinavian Morality Debate.

BIOGRAPHY

Carl Jonas Love Almqvist was born in Stockholm in 1793 to Carl Gustaf Almqvist, an army paymaster, and Brigitta Lovisa Gjörwell, daughter of a famous publicist. Almqvist's ancestors included a theology professor and a dean on his father's side, and his mother came from a famous middle-class Stockholm family. He attended Uppsala University, where he studied history and philosophy. It was there that he became familiar with German Romanticism and with the works of the Uppsala center of Romanticism.

Having earned his master of arts degree from Uppsala in 1815, Almqvist embarked on a career as a civil servant, which he grew to dislike and abandoned in 1823. In the meantime, however, he started publishing theological and philosophical tracts, one of which, *Vad är kärlek?* (1816; what is love?), provided a theme for his future writing. In 1817, he helped found Manna Samfundet, a Romantic circle dominated by the ideas of Emanuel Swedenborg (1688-1772), a Swedish Enlightenment thinker, noteworthy scientist, and theological writer. Almqvist's Romantic ideas and social criticism were manifested in 1822 in the novel *Amorina* (1822, 1839). However, Almqvist's uncle, who was a bishop, had the book destroyed, fearing the ideas expressed within it would have negative consequences for his nephew.

In 1824, Almqvist started another romantic experiment: Drawn by the Romantic dream of living the idyllic life of a peasant, he became a farmer in Värmland. He married a peasant girl and devoted his time equally to writing and farming. However, his enthusiasm for the rural life did not last long, and in August, 1825, he returned to Stockholm and started a new career, becoming a teacher. Financial difficulties dominated the next few years, until in 1828 when he became the principal of a famous experimental school in Stockholm. Between 1829 and 1841, in addition to his philosophic, religious, and literary works, he wrote textbooks in a wide range of subjects and introduced a number of educational reforms. In 1832, Almqvist began his lifelong literary project, *Törnrosens bok*. Well received by the public, the first volumes were quickly followed in 1834 by another success, the novel *Drottningens juvelsmycke: Eller Azouras Lazuli Tintomara* (1834; *The Queen's Diadem*, 1992).

Toward the end of the 1830's, however, Almqvist's views on art, religion, society, and politics turned away from Romanticism and toward realism. A Neoplatonic Romantic and an ordained minister, Almqvist was disappointed by his unsuccessful application for the chair of aesthetics and modern languages at Lund University in 1838. A year later, the publication of his realistic novel *Sara Videbeck* caused a big stir among his contemporaries as they found Almqvist's liberal treatment of the marriage controversy too radical and morally damaging. He was questioned by the Cathedral Chapter of Uppsala because of both the novel and the theological drama *Marjam* and was soon dismissed from his position as a principal. In 1846, he joined the staff of *Aftonbladet*, Sweden's liberal newspaper, to which he had been contributing since 1839.

Almqvist's financial difficulties persisted despite his position at the newspaper. In 1851, he was accused of having attempted to poison a creditor and of having forged and stolen promissory notes. Although these crimes were never proved or disproved, they resulted in Almqvist's exile from Sweden in August, 1851. The next fourteen years Almqvist spent in the United States, where, after extensive travels, he settled in Philadelphia and married a second time under a false name. In 1865, the seventy-two-year-old Almqvist left the United States for Bremen, Germany, under the name Professor Carl Westermann. He never saw his native country again, dying in Bremen on September 26, 1866.

ANALYSIS

Carl Jonas Love Almqvist's work, both Romantic and realistic, is dominated by the conflict between the individual and society, specifically the conflict between an enlightened intellectual with liberal and radical views and the society of early nineteenth century Sweden, with its traditional, conservative social and religious beliefs. In artistic terms, this is expressed in Almqvist's Romantic aesthetic of the poetic fugue, a combination of drama and epic with dance and music. Two of his early works, *Amorina* and *The Queen's Diadem*, are novels in dramatic form: Dramatic monologues or dialogues, accompanied by dance and music pieces, make up about 90 percent of the former and 60 percent of the latter. A contemporary reader may see in this an anticipation of modernism; however, Almqvist's works use older narrative techniques that would later be replaced by the use of an omniscient third-person narrative and interior monologue. Still, the pronounced dramatic aspects of both works attracted the attention of Alf Sjöberg, a gifted Swedish director, who successfully produced dramatic adaptations of *Amorina* and *The Queen's Diadem* at the Royal Dramatic Theater in 1951 and 1957, respectively. Almqvist's Romantic aesthetic could also be seen in his creation of a new genre, his *songes*, short poems that aimed at an organic unity between poetry, drama, and music. These *songes* were presented as short stage plays, or living pictures, in famous literary salons as well as in the theater during the 1820's and gained enormous popularity.

Almqvist experimented with a variety of dramatic forms: verse and prose drama, comedy, tragedy, tragicomedy, melodrama, classical and theological drama, and pieces in which he discussed aesthetic and philosophical principles. At the beginning of his literary career Almqvist tried to escape from the immediate present by exploring different time periods and geographical locations, including the Celtic and Nordic past, the early Christian period and the Middle Ages, and the Mediterranean and other exotic locales; however, in his treatment of both subject matter and characters, it is possible to discern a subtext that reveals his awareness of contemporary political, economic, social, and aesthetic problems. Therefore, some of Almqvist's major themes and motifs center on the interactions between demonic and heavenly forces, saints and sinners, lovers and criminals, and spiritual and earthly principles.

RAMIDO MARINESCO

This short verse drama contains seven scenes and a tight plot line, a rather original rendering of Don Juan's story in which his son, Don Ramido, pays with his life for the sins of his father. It also introduces some of Almqvist's favorite motifs: the rather unpredictable relationships between parents and children (Don Ramido's teacher, the monk Anselmo, turns out to be his father, Don Juan), the threat of incest (four times Don Ramido falls in love with a different half-sister), and the nature of love and the tragedy of beauty.

The work also serves as an illustration of Almqvist's aesthetic principle of the collaborative relationship between a piece of art and its audience. Although he was praised by contemporary reviewers for the rich poetic sound of his verse and his masterful female characterizations, he was criticized for the rather ambiguous and open ending of his play, in which Don Ramido becomes a victim of demonic art. The young man dies at the very climax of experiencing love and beauty as he kisses the poisonous portrait of his beloved, painted by his own father. Almqvist defended his artistic method in a work titled *Om sättet att sluta stycken* (1835; dialogue on how to finish pieces), in which he presented his Romantic theory of the participatory reader. By not saying everything and by refusing to provide a clear ending to his drama, the author encourages the reader to enter the world of the play, to participate in its life by looking for aesthetic patterns. Although it was widely read, *Ramido Marinesco* was never staged during Almqvist's lifetime.

MARJAM

Like Almqvist's earlier work *Ferrando Bruno*, which presents a quest for truth and one's (Christian) self, the theological play *Marjam* explores themes and motifs from the times of early Christianity. The play's rather unorthodox message that Christianity has lost its original purity and close connections with nature, which have been replaced by rigid Christian dogma, is in accord with both Almqvist's journalistic and literary work in the late 1830's and early 1840's. The playwright's nostalgia for the richness and simplicity of the Christian past is presented through his portrait of the opposition between a nameless stranger, easily identifiable as Saint Paul, and Saint John. Saint Paul's preaching sounds affected and hollow in comparison with the ease and straightforwardness of Saint John's address because Saint John stands much closer to Christ's legacy. The Lutheran Church found Almqvist's ideas extremely disturbing and morally denigrating, and *Marjam*, together with the novel *Sara Videbeck*, contributed significantly to Almqvist's being perceived as a corruptor of morals. This would eventually cost him his position as a principal and result in a rather strained relationship with his contemporaries.

PURPURGREFVEN

Like *Silkesharen på Hagalund* (the silk hare of Hagalund), *Purpurgrefven* (the purple count) is a comedy in prose and one of Almqvist's last plays.

Almqvist called them "dramatic stories" and used them to introduce utopian solutions to current socioeconomic problems. In *Purpurgrefven*, the playwright envisions the construction of an enormous hotel, which brings together all families and households in a collective whole. The enterprise's leaders are young and noble, intelligent and enlightened people, who, entangled in comic love affairs, come to share even love. The play was staged successfully in the 1950's. It was also a popular radio play.

OTHER MAJOR WORKS

LONG FICTION: *Amorina*, 1822, 1839; *Drottningens juvelsmycke: Eller Azouras Lazuli Tintomara*, 1834 (*The Queen's Diadem*, 1992); *Kapellet*, 1838 (*The Chapel*, 1919); *Det går an*, 1839 (*Sara Videbeck*, 1919; also as *Why Not! A Picture Out of Life*, 1994); *Grimstahamns nybygge*, 1839; *Ladugårdsarrendet*, 1840; *Gabrièle Mimanso: Sista mordförsöket emot konung Ludvig Filip i Frankrike, hösten 1840*, 1841-1842 (*Gabriele Mimanso, The Niece of Abd-el-Kader: Or, An Attempt to Assassinate Louis Philippe, King of France*, 1846).

SHORT FICTION: "Jaktslottet," 1832; "Araminta May," 1838; "Skällnora kvarn," 1838; "Palaset," 1838; "Ormus och Ariman," 1839; "Målaren," 1840.

POETRY: *Songes*, 1849; *Dikter i landsflykt*, 1956.

NONFICTION: *Om enheten av epism och dramatism*, 1821; *Svensk rättstafningslära*, 1829; *Om sättet att sluta stycken*, 1835; *Grekist språklära till ungdomens tjenst vid högre och lägre undervisningsverk*, 1837; *Det europeiska missnöjets grunder*, 1838; *Praktisk lärobok i franska språket*, 1838; *Skönhetens tårar*, 1839; *Den svenska fattigdomens betydelse*, 1839; *Poesi i sak*, 1839; *Ordbok öfver svenska språket i dess närvarande skick*, 1842, 1844; *Monografi*, 1844-1845; *Om Skandinavismens utförbarhet*, 1846.

MISCELLANEOUS: *Törnrosens bok*, 1832-1851, 1839-1850.

BIBLIOGRAPHY

Blackwell, Marilyn. *C. J. L. Almqvist and Romantic Irony: The Aesthetics of Self-Consciousness*. Stockholm, Sweden: Almqvist & Wiksell International, 1983. Examines Almqvist's Romantic production with special emphasis on his dramatic novels and early fiction and nonfiction.

_____. "Friedrich Schlegel and C. J. L. Almqvist: Romantic Irony and Textual Artifice." *Scandinavian Studies* 52, no. 2 (1980). Places Almqvist within the context of German Romanticism. Sees a common Romantic search for a higher unity of genres (drama, epic, and lyric poetry) and emphasizes the importance of the Romantic fragment.

Nolin, Bertil. "The Romantic Period." In *A History of Swedish Literature*, edited by Lars G. Warme. Lincoln: University of Nebraska Press, 1996. A chapter on Almqvist presents a brief biographical introduction, followed by an overview of his major works. A chapter on Romantic plays situates Almqvist within the context of nineteenth century Swedish drama, highlighting his influences.

Romberg, Bertil. *Carl Jonas Love Almqvist*. Boston: Twayne, 1977. A detailed and laudatory study of Almqvist's life and work. Contains close readings of major works and useful summaries of the rest, all of which are accompanied by generous examples from Almqvist's correspondence and nonliterary writing.

Miglena Ivanova

SERAFÍN ÁLVAREZ QUINTERO *and* JOAQUÍN ÁLVAREZ QUINTERO

Serafín Álvarez Quintero
Born: Utrera, Spain; March 26, 1871
Died: Madrid, Spain; April 12, 1938

Joaquín Álvarez Quintero
Born: Utrera, Spain; January 20, 1873
Died: Madrid, Spain; June 14, 1944

PRINCIPAL DRAMA

Esgrima y amor, pr., pb. 1888

Gilito, pr., pb. 1889

La media naranja, pr., pb. 1894

El ojito derecho, pr., pb. 1897

La reja, pr., pb. 1897

La buena sombra, pr., pb. 1898

Las casas de cartón, pr., pb. 1899

El patio, pr., pb. 1900

Los galeotes, pr., pb. 1900

Las flores, pr., pb. 1901

La zagala, pr., pb. 1904

La casa de García, pr. 1904, pb. 1906

Mañana de sol, pr., pb. 1905 (*A Sunny Morning*, 1914)

El genio alegre, pr., pb. 1906

El centenario, pr., pb. 1909 (*A Hundred Years Old*, 1918)

Doña Clarines, pr., pb. 1909 (*Lady Clarines*, 1932)

La rima eterna, pr., pb. 1910

Malvaloca, pr., pb. 1912 (English translation, 1916)

Puebla de las mujeres, pr., pb. 1912 (*The Women's Town*, 1919)

La consulesa, pr., pb. 1914 (*The Lady from Alfaqueque*, 1927)

OTHER LITERARY FORMS

The brothers Serafín Álvarez Quintero and Joaquín Álvarez Quintero were best known for their comedies, many of which were translated from the original Spanish into several other languages. They also, however, contributed work in other literary genres. Working together, they produced a novel, a number of fine short stories, and many poems, some of which were incorporated into their plays. Furthermore, as young men still developing their dramatic talent, they published theater reviews and other pieces of literary journalism.

One of the best known of their nondramatic works, *La madrecita* (1919; the little mother), is a short novel whose profound structure and sensibility achieved wide acclaim from the literary public. Also, their collection of short stories *Con los ojos* (1938; with the eyes) shows, as much as their plays, the graceful life lived around the patios of the Spanish province of Andalucía. Although these stories were written during the most fruitful period of the authors' lives and achieved general acceptance, some critics found fault with the Álvarez Quintero brothers' portrayal of Spanish life and customs, charging them with inaccuracies. Some critics singled out the brothers' dialogue, which, the critics alleged, did not reflect the actual speech patterns of the various types of characters who are portrayed in their works. Such criticisms, however, miss the point: The aim of the Álvarez Quinteros was to create, in the various genres in which they wrote, a *sui generis* reality—a self-contained imaginary world.

ACHIEVEMENTS

Because Serafín Álvarez Quintero and his brother Joaquín Álvarez Quintero always worked together, it is difficult to separate their achievements. Comedy was their strong suit, and their interest in it began when they were quite young. In fact, when the brothers were still in their teens, they had the privilege of having one of their farces, *Esgrima y amor*, a one-act play, performed in the Seville Theatre. The success of this venture persuaded them to go to Madrid, where the Teatro español accepted their second farce, *Gilito*, for production. Madrid, however, was not Seville, and the Álvarez Quinteros suffered a waiting period before they were recognized.

In 1897, however, they established a reputation as comic playwrights with the reception of *El ojito derecho* and *La reja*. These plays won for them some favorable attention. Then, in 1898, with the presentation of *La buena sombra*, their reputations were assured. Literary and worldly reputation, fame, fortune, and popularity were theirs. During the prolific period between 1898 and 1920, the brothers saw more than one hundred comedies, farces, and *zarzuelas* (musical comedies) performed.

Perhaps the greatest achievement of the brothers was their perfect coordination as collaborators. They continued to work in harmony throughout their lives; indeed in almost every case it is impossible to separate the ideas or content of one brother from the other. This preternatural harmony is illustrated by an incident that happened when the brothers were still in high school: Serafín, being given only part of a stanza written by Joaquín, finished the verse. On comparing the completed stanzas, it was found that the brothers had, without knowledge of each other's version, completed the stanza with identical words.

Their method of collaboration was quite simple. They would walk together, talk together, and discuss such items as dialogue, characterization, and plot. Then, once these details were worked out, Serafín would pen the actual lines. As he wrote, he would read the results to Joaquín, who would make comments and corrections on the spot. All details and matters of style were settled in this manner.

A second notable achievement of the Álvarez Quintero brothers was their great prolificacy without loss of quality. After their initial opportunity to show their talent in 1897 and to prove it in 1898, they often averaged five *estrenos* (debuts) per year. At that time, Spain was producing many new playwrights each year, and novelty was much in vogue. To have more than one success in a year was a remarkable achievement. Furthermore, in most cases, a play's initial run was its final run, but many of the Quinteros' plays remained in the theaters' repertoires.

Altogether, the brothers saw 220 of their works performed during their lifetimes; eight others (authored solely by Joaquín) were never produced. This extensive volume of work, especially work widely acclaimed by both popular and intellectual circles, is an achievement not often equaled in literary history.

A third notable achievement of the Álvarez Quinteros was the variety of their works. They wrote in both the *género chico* (light drama, usually brief) and the *género grande* (more serious drama, usually full length), and they also wrote in both prose and verse. They were recognized for their farces, such as *Las casas de cartón* and *El ojito derecho*, as well as for their more profound dramas, such as *La casa de García* and *La zagala*, in which there is a well-developed tragic element.

The Álvarez Quinteros were especially fond of the *sainete*, a one-act farce depicting manners and customs of the lower classes. In this genre, the brothers followed the pattern of such distinguished predecessors as Lope de Rueda, Miguel de Cervantes, Ramón de la Cruz, and Ricardo de la Vega.

Another achievement of the Álvarez Quintero brothers was their success—despite the critical objections noted above—in capturing the speech of their native Andalucía and, without losing the vigor and harmony of local dialect or the vitality of the local color, making this speech seem clear, fresh, and comprehensive to the nation at large. In fact, the Álvarez Quinteros have been said by some to have begun a mode of writing called *Andalucismo*, although it should again be noted that, however vivid was their evocation of Andalucía, their aim was not documentary realism but imaginative coherence: Their Andalucía exists nowhere but on the stage.

As far as new forms, genres, or novel techniques are concerned, the Álvarez Quinteros did not use innovative devices in structure, plot, or characterization; rather, their genius lay in working within traditional limits to exploit the rich heritage of Spanish drama. Inspired by the ideals and methods of Lope de Vega Carpio, Pedro Calderón de la Barca, and others, the Álvarez Quintero brothers achieved a harmony of past and present.

Culturally, too, the brothers are significant. Deeply in love with their hometown Utrera, with Seville, Andalucía, and Spain, the Álvarez Quinteros present even the oddest speech and customs with a touch that is at once both familiar and new. The technique used is one of implied comparison: Andalucía is both an antithesis of the rest of Spain and a part of it; Spain is both different from and very much like the rest of the world. The Álvarez Quinteros capture universal aspects of human nature by focusing on particular aspects of a unique culture.

During their lifetimes, the Álvarez Quinteros were awarded the highest honors. After the production of *Los galeotes*, the brothers achieved recognition by the Real Academía Española, putting them on the same level as Jacinto Benavente y Martínez. In 1902, the Piquer Award was presented to them for the same play, and the city of Utrera erected a stone at the house of their birth. In 1907, they received the Cross of Alfonso. Streets and parks were named for them in

Madrid, Murcia, Fuenterrabia, Seville, and Utrera. Three times the Álvarez Quinteros declined membership in the Real Academía Española because they believed that there were other writers who deserved the honor more, but Serafín finally entered into membership in that prestigious organization on November 21, 1920, and Joaquín, on April 23, 1925.

BIOGRAPHY

Serafín Álvarez Quintero was born on March 26, 1871, and his brother Joaquín Álvarez Quintero, on January 20, 1873, both in the Andalusian town of Utrera in the hinterland of Seville. Their early years were spent in Utrera, where they enjoyed, according to their own testimony, a happy and tranquil childhood with all the comforts that middle-class life could offer in their sleepy little hometown: in the spring—horses, a young donkey, and kites; and at Christmas—a nativity scene with the three Wise Men, a toy train, and a velocipede. Their youth, however, was not without that healthy conflict that molds character. There were two factions among the children of the town, and conflict, though never malicious, was inevitable.

Given two brothers whose backgrounds and artistic temperaments were so alike as to be almost identical, one might conclude that they would be similar in personality as well, but such was not the case. Serafín was extroverted, happy, and talkative; Joaquín was introverted, melancholy, and quiet. They were both, however, mischievous, dynamic, and wholesome.

In 1878, because of financial reverses, the family moved to Seville, a city where the patios were filled with roses, jasmine, and rose blossoms. The boys first attended the Colegio de San Lorenzo and then the Instituto Provincial. It was in the institute that Serafín began composing poetry and Joaquín began writing short theatrical works. Their association with the little magazine *Perecito* began at this time also. In this venture, the boys had the support of their older brother Pedro, and they found in Manuel Díaz Martín, the magazine's editor, a benefactor and spiritual guide. A journalist, Martín had also a passion for folklore, and his influence on the brothers was significant. It was in Seville, also, that their first play,

Esgrima y amor, was performed in 1888. They then moved to Madrid where *Gilito* was produced in 1889; however, this initial success was followed by a lean period, during which the brothers supported themselves by working in the treasury. Finally, however, with the success of *El ojito derecho* and *La reja* in 1897 and *La buena sombra* in 1898, the brothers' reputation was not only established but also secure. As noted above, they saw at least one new play produced each year during their lifetimes and often averaged as many as five debuts each year for a total of 220 plays. Also, they lived to see 106 of their plays translated and published in other languages.

Although few dramatists have enjoyed such tremendous success, acclaim, and adulation, their lives were not without sorrow. In 1905, Serafín met Dolores Sanchez Mora. Even though she was at that time seriously ill and likely to die at any moment, Serafín married her on September 15, 1905.

After the marriage, her health seemed to improve, but soon she found it impossible to adapt to the life that the theater imposed on Serafín. Finally, through mutual agreement, they separated, Serafín remaining in Madrid, and Dolores returning to her parents' home in Huelva. Nevertheless, they wrote to each other daily, until September of 1907, when Serafín received a dramatic letter in which Dolores avowed that she could no longer live without him and be separated from him. Serafín went to her immediately, but when he arrived he found that she had died even as he was rushing to her side.

The brothers were not exempt from the tragedy of the Spanish Civil War. Many of their fellow writers were killed or exiled; they themselves were jailed but were freed the next day. The brothers believed themselves to be under surveillance, and finally, in order to be left alone and to avoid persecution, they agreed to make the following forced declaration: "The brothers Álvarez Quintero, who are surrounded by respect and admiration, exhibit to the world how the Loyalist Government treats its writers."

In January of 1928, the brothers had celebrated the fortieth anniversary of their debut in the theater, amid the glitter and trappings of success. It was an occasion of national homage. Their first play,

Esgrima y amor, was again presented in the Teatro de Lara by an extraordinary cast of actors and actresses. After the performance, Joaquín read his poem "De ayer a hoy" ("from yesterday to today"). In January, 1938, they celebrated their golden anniversary in the theater under much different circumstances. It was in the middle of the Spanish Civil War; at noon on the day of the celebration, the brothers learned that a close friend had died. Because of the *maldita guerra* (damned war), the festivities were muted. The brothers met with other notables, other literary figures of their time, friends, and fellow writers after visiting the Teatro de María Isabel. A few months later, Serafín was dead of cerebral congestion.

Even after Serafín's death, Joaquín continued to write in collaboration with his brother: Using notes, unfinished manuscripts, and memory, he continued to produce successful work, always signing both names or using the pen name El Diablo Cojuelo (the limping devil) that the two had used years earlier.

On his seventy-first birthday, Joaquín composed a long, melancholy poetic composition in which he expressed a premonition of his own death. Less than six months later, he was dead from cancer. On his desk he left nine unpublished works—their authorship, a mystery. Even after death, their works remained inseparable.

ANALYSIS

The brothers Serafín Álvarez Quintero and Joaquín Álvarez Quintero, as playwrights, can best be described as being realistic without being realists, for, although their depictions of life-as-it-is are extremely accurate in the details, taken as a whole, their perspective is not objective but subjective. Their viewpoint is positive and optimistic, and their plays celebrate the joy of life and the power of human love and understanding. Their comedy can best be described as delicate and delightful. Their serious drama tends toward an exploration of the beauty of life even in the midst of sorrow, and their satire, rather than presenting the biting excoriations of some of their predecessors in the Spanish drama, is a gentle and indulgent reminder of the many foibles of human life.

Although critical opinion does not rank the Álvarez Quinteros with the great names of Spanish literature—Miguel de Cervantes, Lope de Vega Carpio, Jacinto Benavente y Martinez—when one considers the usual rankings of collaborators who write primarily light comedy, it is a genuine tribute to their abilities that they rank as high as they do. Although there is no doubt that the brothers strove first to entertain and to delight, they also achieved something more: They brought to the stage dramas that did not have something to say but something to show. What their dramas show is that although life can have its misfortunes and people can do petty, silly, even evil things, those who live with patience, understanding, and the redeeming power of love will find that life can be not merely worthwhile, but also joyous.

THE WOMEN'S TOWN

In all probability, the two best-known, and most characteristic, of the brothers' plays are the light comedy *The Women's Town* and the serious drama *Malvaloca*. A close analysis of these two plays reveals not only correspondences between them but also certain characteristic methods, motifs, symbols, and themes that run throughout the Álvarez Quinteros' works.

The Women's Town, a brief two-act comedy, was first presented in the Teatro Lara of Madrid, January 17, 1912. Highly successful, this pleasant and humane satire was twice translated into English—by Charles A. Turrell in 1919, and by Helen and Harley Granville-Barker as *The Women Have Their Way* in 1927. This play begins, as many of the Álvarez Quinteros' plays do, with the appearance of a stranger in a small Andalucian town, thus giving both an internal and external view of the play's milieu. The stranger in this case is Adolfo, the hero, a young lawyer who has come to the town on behalf of his aunt in order to settle the affairs of his late uncle's entangled estate. Before the handsome young man is introduced to the pretty young heroine, Juanita, however, the women of the town, by means of rumor and gossip, have already established that the two young people are quite in love with each other. The women, therefore, connive to bring the young couple together, much to the discomfiture of Adolfo, who finds that he is constantly thrust into Juanita's presence but is always under the prying eyes of the women. This situation brings about much hilarity involving Concha, the town gossip; Pepe Laura, a bungling rejected suitor; Don Julian, the village priest; and many others. Eventually and inevitably, however, Adolfo and Juanita are brought together through the women's machination—or perhaps in spite of them—and the ending, like most of the Álvarez Quinteros' endings, is one of undiluted happiness.

Also, as with many of their plays, there is an undercurrent of symbolism that is so natural and appropriate that it passes almost unnoticed by the conscious mind, serving to accentuate the values inherent in the plot and structure. The play opens to a scene in which the image of the Virgin (natural in a priest's patio, but especially appropriate to the "women's town") dominates the setting. Both acts begin with discussions of the flies and mosquitoes that are symbolic of gossip: The town priest tells young Adolfo that the insects are not so bad for townspeople, but strangers in town are fresh food, a real delicacy. Similarly, the constant clanging of the church bells is analogous to the clacking of the women's tongues.

As with all the Álvarez Quinteros' dramas, the symbolism is not heavy-handed. When Concha (the town gossip) enters, the stage directions observe that dramatists given to symbolism might insist that she represents the spirit of the village, but since they (the Álvarez Quinteros) are not so inclined, they will only say that she is very pretty, very meddlesome, and knows everybody's business. It is, however, obvious that in the Álvarez Quinteros' plays, poetry and song symbolize the joy of life. It is ironic in *The Women's Town* that Santita, the priest's deaf sister, is constantly on the alert to prevent the servant girls from singing the songs that she alone cannot hear.

Intermixed with the symbolism of song and verse is the symbolism of flowers. Juanita is called "La Rosa" on more than one occasion in the play, and the rose figures prominently in a love song central to the significance of the drama. When Juanita recites some verses to Adolfo, he declares his love for her, and Pepe Lara, who rejects all "poetry," is himself rejected by La Rosa. Thus, the symbols intertwine and

interlace like the flowers that are so often themselves symbolic in the Alvarez Quinteros' works.

MALVALOCA

Except for the essential difference between light comedy and domestic drama, *Malvaloca* is very surprisingly similar to *The Women's Town*. The best-known of the Álvarez Quinteros' serious dramas, *Malvaloca* was first performed by the Compañia Guerrero-Mendoza at the Teatro de la Princesa, on April 6, 1912. It was the first of the brothers' plays to be translated into English, although their plays had previously been translated into many other languages.

Like *The Women's Town*, *Malvaloca* begins with a young outsider who has come to a small Andalusian town: Leonardo, passing through the village, has remained to reopen a brass foundry there. Some time later, after he has established himself in the town, he goes to the convent of the Sisters of Charity to look in on his partner Salvador, who was burned in a foundry accident. At the convent, Leonardo meets a young woman called Malvaloca, to whom he is immediately attracted. As in *The Women's Town*, there are complications. Rumor and gossip figure prominently in the plot, especially in that Malvaloca has a bad reputation she is trying to overcome. Also, there is a former suitor, in this case Leonardo's friend and partner Salvador. Finally, in spite of, or perhaps because of, the problems encountered, the lovers are united in a happy ending—except that, in this case, although the ending is certainly joyous, the happiness is not unmitigated; as Malvaloca says, one cannot love without tears.

The symbols in the plays are also similar. Again, there is symbolism involving bells, but this time it is silence rather than constant ringing that serves the playwrights' needs. The great bell of the convent has been cracked—damaged—just as Malvaloca has been injured by her past. It is Leonardo, through his charity, who recasts the bell and makes it whole, just as it is Leonardo, through his love, who brings about Malvaloca's rebirth.

Flowers are also symbolic in this more serious drama. For example, the real name of Malvaloca (mallow) is Rosa (rose), a name she lost as a child, but a name she still holds within, just as she still clings to the hope of redemption. Yet the flower symbolism in this play is much more profuse than in the simple comedies and other less complex works. Here is seen the willow (sadness) and the orange tree (love). In a very touching scene near the end of the play, Leonardo's daughter Juanela brings flowers to Malvaloca (as a gesture of forgiveness and acceptance) so that Malvaloca can throw them before the image of Jesus Christ as the religious procession passes.

The curtain of this play, also, opens on a religious icon, but in this case it is a wooden cross, emblematic of Christ's forgiveness—and the play ends with the Procession of Thorns, in which Leonardo is united with the reborn Malvaloca as a woman holding a child in her arms signs a song to Christ the Redeemer, and the great bell of the convent—once again whole—peals its first golden notes.

OTHER PLAYS

Other Álvarez Quintero plays that have attracted wide recognition are *Las flores* (the flowers), a comedy about a widow and the romances of her three daughters; *A Sunny Morning*, about an old couple who meet in the park and, finding that they had once loved each other, try unsuccessfully, each of them, to hide the truth; *El genio alegre* (the happy heart), a ro-

mantic comedy about the beneficial effect of love on a wayward son; and *La zagala*, a serious drama about the social pressures on a widower who loves a girl beneath his social station.

OTHER MAJOR WORKS

LONG FICTION: *La madrecita*, 1919.
SHORT FICTION: *Con los ojos*, 1938.

BIBLIOGRAPHY

Halsey, Martha T., and Phyllis Zatlin, eds. *The Contemporary Spanish Theater: A Collection of Critical Essays*. Lanham, Md.: University Press of America, 1988. These essays provide general information on the state of the Spanish theater in the twentieth century. Bibliography and index.

McCarthy, Jim. *Political Theatre During the Spanish Civil War*. Cardiff: University of Wales Press, 1999. Although the Álvarez Quintero brothers were not political writers, they were also influenced by the civil war. Bibliography and index.

Sánchez de Palacios, Mariano. *Serafín y Joaquín Álvarez Quintero*. Madrid: Gráf. Valera, 1971. A basic biography of the Álvarez Quintero brothers that examines their lives and work. In Spanish.

Glenn R. Swetman and Margarita Ortiz-Swetman

MAXWELL ANDERSON

Born: Atlantic, Pennsylvania; December 15, 1888
Died: Stamford, Connecticut; February 28, 1959

PRINCIPAL DRAMA

White Desert, pr. 1923
What Price Glory?, pr. 1924, pb. 1926 (with
    Laurence Stallings)
Outside Looking In, pr. 1925, pb. 1929
First Flight, pr. 1925, pb. 1926 (with Stallings)
Three American Plays, pb. 1926

Saturday's Children, pr., pb. 1927
Gypsy, pr. 1929
Elizabeth the Queen, pr., pb. 1930 (adaptation of
    Lytton Strachey's history *Elizabeth and Essex*)
Night over Taos, pr., pb. 1932
Both Your Houses, pr., pb. 1933
Mary of Scotland, pr., pb. 1933
Valley Forge, pr., pb. 1934
Winterset, pr., pb. 1935
The Masque of Kings, pb. 1936, pr. 1937

High Tor, pr., pb. 1937

Knickerbocker Holiday, pr., pb. 1938 (lyrics; music by Kurt Weill)

Key Largo, pr., pb. 1939

Eleven Verse Plays, 1929-1939, pb. 1940

Joan of Lorraine, pr., pb. 1946

Anne of the Thousand Days, pr., pb. 1948

Lost in the Stars, pr., pb. 1949 (lyrics; music by Weill; adaptation of Alan Paton's novel *Cry, the Beloved Country*)

Barefoot in Athens, pr., pb. 1951

Bad Seed, pr. 1954, pb. 1955 (adaptation of William March's novel)

The Day the Money Stopped, pr., pb. 1958 (adaptation of Brendan Gill's novel)

The Golden Six, pr. 1958, pb. 1961

Four Verse Plays, pb. 1959

OTHER LITERARY FORMS

Maxwell Anderson's reputation rests exclusively on his dramatic works. In addition to his works in various forms of drama, he wrote a number of essays on the theater, some of which are collected in *The Essence of Tragedy and Other Footnotes and Papers* (1939) and *Off Broadway: Essays About the Theatre* (1947). Anderson also published two collections of poetry: *You Who Have Dreams* (1925) and *Notes on a Dream* (1971). Finally, he wrote a number of screenplays, including the screenplay for the film adaptation of the play *Joan of Lorraine*, entitled *Joan of Arc* (1948).

ACHIEVEMENTS

Maxwell Anderson was a prolific and versatile playwright, the author of poetic drama and historical drama, realistic plays and thesis plays, radio drama, screenplays, and musical drama (including two collaborations with composer Kurt Weill). At the peak of his success, during one season in the 1930's, he had three plays running on Broadway at the same time. In 1933, he received a Pulitzer Prize for *Both Your Houses*. He received New York Drama Critics Circle Awards in the 1935-1936 Broadway season for *Winterset* and in the following season for *High Tor*.

Maxwell Anderson in 1956. (Library of Congress)

Of the twelve Anderson plays produced on Broadway in his lifetime, nine are verse dramas—a remarkable feat in itself in the twentieth century, with verse drama long an endangered species. Indeed, it is as a rare modern practitioner of that form that Anderson is likely to be remembered.

Even Anderson's lesser achievements attest the enormous vitality of the American theater in his time: The sheer range of his work, including both failed experiments and commercial successes, the stretch of his ambition (even when one concedes that his theory of tragedy, for example, is an intellectual embarrassment)—all of this makes him one of the representative figures of a key period in the history of American drama.

BIOGRAPHY

James Maxwell Anderson was born the son of a Baptist minister in Atlantic, Pennsylvania, on December 15, 1888. The family moved frequently, but in time, Maxwell enrolled at the University of North Dakota, where he wrote poetry and drama. Following graduation, in 1911, he married Margaret Haskett. After two years of teaching high school, he enrolled at Stanford University, where he earned a master's degree in 1914. After having taught for five years, Anderson went into journalism, working for the *Chronicle* and the *Bulletin* in San Francisco. In 1918, he moved to New York, where he worked on the editorial staffs of *The New Republic*, *New York Evening Globe*, and *New York World*.

Anderson's playwriting did not begin until 1923, when, at the age of thirty-five, he wrote the verse tragedy *White Desert*. Although that play flopped, it impressed fellow playwright Laurence Stallings enough to begin collaborating with him. In 1924, the two collaborated on *What Price Glory?*, a realistic antiwar play that was well received.

Following this success, Anderson began to broaden his techniques, writing in both verse and prose. After subsequent collaborations with Stallings did not prove successful, Anderson parted company with him. He was to write six more plays before he achieved another success, with *Elizabeth the Queen* in 1930.

Through the 1940's and 1950's, Anderson devoted much of his time to matters outside the theater and produced fewer plays than he had during the 1930's. In 1940, he campaigned for Republican presidential candidate Wendell Willkie against Franklin D. Roosevelt. Two years later, he helped to raise money to buy High Tor, which in 1943 was given to the state of New York for a park, thus saving the real mountain from the unhappy fate it suffered in Anderson's play of the same title. Anderson spent part of 1943 touring army bases in the eastern United States, England, and North Africa. The following year, he helped run a successful campaign against the U.S. congressman from his New York home district. He toured Greece in 1947 and wrote several essays about the political situation there.

Anderson married three times. Two years after his first wife died in 1931, he married actress Gertrude Maynard. Years later, they became estranged, and in March, 1953, she committed suicide. The following year, Anderson married Gilda Oakleaf, with whom he established a new home in Stamford, Connecticut.

Burdened with tax problems during the 1950's, Anderson wrote three plays primarily to bring in money. However, of these plays, only *Bad Seed* (1954) proved to be a commercial success. After suffering a stroke at his home in Stamford, Connecticut, he died on February 28, 1959.

ANALYSIS

Maxwell Anderson was one among several playwrights, including Eugene O'Neill, Elmer Rice, Sidney Howard, Robert E. Sherwood, George S. Kaufman, and Paul Green, who changed perceptions of American drama. Before World War I, American drama was purely of local interest, and no great playwrights had appeared in the United States. By the end of the 1920's, however, New York City ranked as one of the most vital theater centers in the world, and American dramatists were enjoying a period of extraordinary creative flowering.

Although American playwrights of that period presented diverse views, many reflected the disillusionment that followed World War I. Anderson was among these; the basic philosophy of life that informs his drama is typical of the 1920's. In this view, the modern individual is deprived of religious faith or the opportunity for meaningful social action. Love, although fleeting, is the only thing that gives life meaning.

Throughout his dramatic works, Anderson adhered to the Aristotelian principles of unity and the tragic hero as he explored the myths of his times. Producing the most important body of his work during the Great Depression years of the 1930's, he addressed social issues and injustices, though his primary purpose seems to have been to place them in their historical, literary, and mythological contexts rather than to raise the audience's awareness of such problems. Clearly, Anderson was interested in dramatic theory and history, and his plays exemplify his concerns with form as well as with theme.

WHAT PRICE GLORY?

Anderson's first successful play, *What Price Glory?*, on which he collaborated with Stallings, has affinities with many works of the 1920's. Its critical look at the myths surrounding war brings to mind Ernest Hemingway's novel *A Farewell to Arms* (1929). The play centers on a squad of U.S. marines in the midst of some of the heaviest fighting in World War I.

The play's disillusioned attitude and profane dialogue may seem mild to modern readers accustomed to stronger stuff, but to audiences of the 1920's, the play was shocking. Its soldiers talked like real soldiers, and their profanity (toned down after objections from various groups, including the Marine Corps) epitomized a thoroughgoing irreverence among the characters toward matters that traditionally had been treated with greater respect.

The play uses the war as a symbol for a world that is purposeless and chaotic. Act 1 shows the U.S. Marines awaiting a battle with the Germans in a French town; act 2 centers on the battle, emphasizing the suffering of Americans and Germans alike; and act 3 reveals the futility of the conflict.

ELIZABETH THE QUEEN

The opening of *Elizabeth the Queen* on November 3, 1930, launched Anderson on the most productive decade of his career and for the first time showed the public the nature of his concern with poetic tragedy. The play was both a popular and critical success—surprising, perhaps, considering that it was written in verse. The controlled expression of emotion through rhythm and image is well handled in the play, perhaps contributing to the acceptance of its poetic form by the audience. Anderson got his idea for the play from Lytton Strachey's history *Elizabeth and Essex* (1928) but shifted the story's focus from historical transition to individual character. Evident here is a recurring theme in Anderson's Tudor plays: the lust for power in conflict with sexual passion. In this play, the central theme is the aging Queen Elizabeth I's suspicion that her youthful lover, Essex, is as enamored of her throne as he is of her person.

Anderson distrusted government systems and power politics in the United States and elsewhere. He believed that people of goodwill are usually destroyed by evil ones—a sentiment expressed in this play in the line "The rats inherit the earth." He saw, however, in the struggle of humankind against powerful forces a magnificence in which he found inspiration. *Elizabeth the Queen* revolves around strong characters motivated by great passion, flawed characters who are nevertheless dignified through suffering. Their sense of loneliness and alienation reflects the fragmentation and isolation of modern society; Elizabeth says, "The years are long living among strangers." Such recognition of the lonely state of human beings in a society in which evil is a dominant force recurs throughout Anderson's work.

BOTH YOUR HOUSES

Shortly after *Elizabeth the Queen*'s success, Anderson returned to prose drama with the political satire *Both Your Houses*, which brought him his Pulitzer Prize in 1933. Although this play's setting is modern Washington, D.C., rather than historical England, it, like its predecessor, centers on the isolation of the honest individual in a predominantly evil society. Its protagonist, Alan McClean, is a freshman congressman who is appalled by the graft and corruption he finds to be commonplace in Washington. As he explores this rampant corruption, he discovers not only that his own election campaign is tainted but also that if he votes according to his conscience, he risks financially ruining his fiancé's father, a man whom he admires.

HIGH TOR

Among Anderson's many plays of the 1930's, one of the most interesting is *High Tor*, whose environmental theme is an enduring one in American literature. High Tor is a real mountain peak overlooking the Hudson River, near which Anderson lived at the time he wrote the play. Van Van Dorn, the individualistic owner of High Tor, is determined not to sell his mountain despite the threats of two men who represent a mining company that wants to buy it.

The play blends realism, fantasy, farce, and satire in a delightfully theatrical mix; it won for Anderson the New York Drama Critics Circle Award. Despite the play's entertaining qualities, however, it reminds the audience that the materialistic modern world will not allow the free and natural to survive.

OTHER MAJOR WORKS

LONG FICTION: *Morning Winter and Night*, 1952 (as John Nairne Michaelson).

POETRY: *You Who Have Dreams*, 1925; *Notes on a Dream*, 1971.

SCREENPLAYS: *All Quiet on the Western Front*, 1930 (with others; adaptation of Erich Maria Remarque's novel); *Joan of Arc*, 1948 (with Andrew Solt; adaptation of his play *Joan of Lorraine*); *The Wrong Man*, 1956 (with Angus MacPhail).

NONFICTION: *The Essence of Tragedy and Other Footnotes and Papers*, 1939; *Off Broadway: Essays About the Theatre*, 1947; *Dramatist in America: Letters of Maxwell Anderson, 1912-1958*, 1977.

BIBLIOGRAPHY

Adam, Julie. *Versions of Heroism in Modern American Drama: Redefinitions by Miller, Williams, O'Neill, and Anderson*. New York: St. Martin's Press, 1991. Adam argues that Maxwell Anderson, Arthur Miller, Tennessee Williams, and Eugene O'Neill often ignore the formal aspects and philosophical dimension of traditional tragedy and instead identify tragedy with dramatization of heroism and redefine it as primarily a dramatic tribute to individualism and human potential. Excellent bibliography and index.

Anderson, Maxwell. *Dramatist in America: Letters of Maxwell Anderson, 1912-1958*. Edited by Laurence G. Avery. Chapel Hill: University of North Carolina Press, 1977. Collection of 212 annotated letters, few of which come from Anderson's early life or the period when he suffered a nervous breakdown. Contains a chronology, a list of letters, and appendices.

Bailey, Mabel D. *Maxwell Anderson: The Playwright as Prophet*. New York: Abelard-Schuman, 1957. Brief but well-written study for general readers. Bailey tests the validity of Anderson's creative principles—particularly his dramatic theory—by critically examining the plays that Anderson produced in accordance with that theory. Central to this theory is the notion that theme is the thing for which the work of art exists. Particularly useful on *Barefoot in Athens*.

Shivers, Alfred S. *The Life of Maxwell Anderson*. New York: Stein and Day, 1983. This first full-length biography of Anderson is based on his correspondence, diaries, business documents, notes, and legal documents, as well as oral and unpublished written reminiscences of relatives and friends. It includes a family genealogy, lengthy bibliography, list of the Playwrights' Producing Company productions, and list of Anderson's addresses. Shivers also published *Maxwell Anderson: An Annotated Bibliography of Primary and Secondary Works* (1985).

_____. *Maxwell Anderson*. Boston: Twayne, 1976. Based not only on a study of the dramatic works themselves and on the published secondary sources but also on new archival materials and correspondence with Anderson's relatives and friends, who volunteered much fresh information about him and his art. As a result, the first chapter offers much more biographical material than had previously appeared in print. The other chapters contain critical studies of his plays.

John W. Crawford,
updated by Genevieve Slomski

ROBERT ANDERSON

Born: New York, New York; April 28, 1917

PRINCIPAL DRAMA

Come Marching Home, pr. 1945
All Summer Long, pr. 1953, pb. 1955
Tea and Sympathy, pr., pb. 1953
Silent Night, Lonely Night, pr. 1955, pb. 1960
The Days Between, pr., pb. 1965
You Know I Can't Hear You When the Water's Running, pr., pb. 1967 (includes four one-act plays: *The Footsteps of Doves*, *I'm Herbert*, *The Shock of Recognition*, and *I'll Be Home for Christmas*)
I Never Sang for My Father, pr., pb. 1968

Solitaire/Double Solitaire, pr. 1971, pb. 1972
Free and Clear, pr. 1983
A Discarded Rose Petal, pb. 1997

OTHER LITERARY FORMS

Robert Anderson has written numerous radio, television, and film scripts, including screen adaptations of Kathryn Hulme's 1956 novel *The Nun's Story* (1959), of Richard McKenna's 1962 novel *The Sand Pebbles* (1966), and of his own *I Never Sang for My Father* (1970). The only one of these that has been published, however, is the screenplay of *I Never Sang for My Father*. Many interviews with Anderson and essays by him on the practice of playwriting and the state of the theater have been published in various newspapers and journals. He has also published the novels *After* (1973) and *Getting Up and Going Home* (1978).

ACHIEVEMENTS

Considering Robert Anderson's lifelong devotion to the theater, the number of his plays receiving wide

Robert Anderson in 1953. (Library of Congress)

notice has been relatively small. Although he wrote *The Days Between* with Broadway in mind, Anderson offered it to the newly formed American Playwrights Theater when that organization was having difficulty getting good new plays to offer its member theaters. As a result, *The Days Between* was produced during 1965-1966 in fifty regional theaters but was never produced on Broadway. *Come Marching Home*, which did have a short New York run, was never published.

Although Anderson's plays are to some extent marred by imitativeness and by a lack of variation in theme and motif, they nevertheless represent a solid, if modest, achievement. Anderson has created several memorable characters—for example, the rigid, domineering, irascible, charming, and pathetic Tom Garrison of *I Never Sang for My Father*, a self-made man who in his old age is unable to admit to himself, much less communicate to his family, his need for them and his loneliness; the comic, anxiously adaptable actor Richard Pawling of *The Shock of Recognition*, also pathetic in his eagerness to be or to do anything at all in order to get a part in a play; and the middle-class, middle-aged, anguished Chuck of *I'll Be Home for Christmas*, suddenly, by a letter from his son, brought face to face with his own fears about the meaninglessness of his existence.

In addition, Anderson has been willing to take chances in his plays, and in so doing has helped enrich both in subject and in technique the possibilities open to the theater. In subject, for example, *Tea and Sympathy* was the first American play to deal explicitly with homosexuality, and *Double Solitaire* carries frankness in the discussion of sexual experiences to what is probably the limit of public acceptability on the stage. In stage technique, *The Shock of Recognition* introduced for the first time the possibility of presenting male frontal nudity in the theater (though not itself actually presenting such nudity); and in format, his *You Know I Can't Hear You When the Water's Running* successfully defied the well-entrenched belief that a group of one-act plays could not achieve commercial success on Broadway. These accomplishments have established Anderson's reputation as a dramatist seriously interested in making stage depictions of life correspond more closely to real life.

BIOGRAPHY

Robert Woodruff Anderson was born in New York City in April, 1917, to James Hewston and Myra Grigg Anderson. His father was a self-made man who twice made his way from poverty to financial success. Perhaps as a consequence, James Anderson had great respect for the so-called "manly" virtues of self-reliance, determination, and physical courage but shared none of the aesthetic values that his wife instilled in young Robert. The resultant unhappy relationship between a husband and wife unable to appreciate each other's values has been mirrored in several of Anderson's plays, notably *All Summer Long, Tea and Sympathy*, and *I Never Sang for My Father*. The strained relationship between a father with a purely materialistic bent and a son whose artistic and literary bent embarrasses and bewilders his father forms a secondary motif in several of Anderson's plays and provides the central conflict in *I Never Sang for My Father*.

Anderson was educated in private elementary schools; at Phillips Exeter Academy, in Exeter, New Hampshire, where he wrote his first plays; and at Harvard, where he wrote plays, theater reviews, and a senior honors thesis entitled "The Necessity for Poetic Drama." He completed his undergraduate work at Harvard in 1939 and his work for the master's degree in 1940, and continued work toward a Ph.D. there until he entered the U.S. Navy in 1942. While a graduate student at Harvard, he served as a teaching assistant and also taught drama courses in several small local colleges. During his Navy service in World War II, Anderson wrote several plays, including *Come Marching Home*, which won the National Theater Conference Prize in 1945 for the best play written by a serviceman overseas and which subsequently had a very brief run Off-Broadway in New York. This prize helped him to obtain a scholarship to study playwriting under John Gassner, who later became one of Anderson's staunchest supporters among drama critics.

In 1940, Anderson married Phyllis Stohl, a woman ten years older than he, who was beloved in theatrical circles and who all of their married life was working for the theater in one capacity or another—

as teacher, director, radio scriptwriter, producer, and finally as a literary agent for playwrights. They had no children, and the last five years of their sixteen-year marriage were dominated for both by the emotional turmoil of her long, and eventually unsuccessful, struggle against cancer. The trauma of this experience and his subsequent feelings of grief and guilt haunted Anderson for many years, leaving its impact on several of his plays, until he finally exorcized it in the pages of a very autobiographical novel, *After*. In 1959, Anderson married another theater personality, the stage and screen actress Teresa Wright, who later originated the role of Alice in the stage version of *I Never Sang for My Father*. This marriage produced no children, although Wright had two children from a previous marriage.

In addition to Anderson's own playwriting, he has contributed to American drama in his organization and support of other playwrights. In 1951 he co-founded New Dramatists; for many years he served as president of the Dramatists Guild; and in 1953, as "the sixth playwright," he revitalized the Playwrights' Producing Company with the success of *Tea and Sympathy*. In December, 1990, he hosted a tea reception for New Dramatists, initiating a series of fund-raisers for this still-flourishing organization.

Only three of Anderson's plays have had any great degree of commercial and critical success: *Tea and Sympathy, You Know I Can't Hear You When the Water's Running*, and *I Never Sang for My Father*. The others have had short runs and mixed reviews. In addition to writing for the theater, however, he has produced numerous scripts for radio, television, and motion pictures, many of them highly successful in production, and has been a teacher of drama and playwriting in colleges and universities.

ANALYSIS

Robert Anderson is a heavily autobiographical playwright. His focal character is usually male, is usually a writer, often also a teacher, is misunderstood or not properly appreciated by someone close to him—most often his father or his wife—and is sometimes suffering from a tragedy associated with his wife. This character is young in the plays written when Anderson was young—in *All Summer Long*, he is only twelve, and in *Tea and Sympathy*, he is almost eighteen—but in the plays written as Anderson grew older, the focal character also is older: In *Silent Night, Lonely Night*, he is in his early forties; in *The Days Between*, he is split into two characters, both of whom are around forty; in three of the four one-act plays that make up *You Know I Can't Hear You When the Water's Running*, he is middle-aged, though in one of these he is not a writer; in *I Never Sang for My Father*, he is forty; in *Solitaire*, he is around fifty and, though not a writer since writing is obsolete in his society, a recorder of tapes in a library; and in *Double Solitaire*, he is forty-three.

Anderson's themes derive from the circumstances of this character in various incarnations. One of his most common themes is the incompatibility of a husband and wife, particularly a middle-aged couple who were once madly in love with each other. Their incompatibility may or may not be in values or goals, but its major symptom is always an unhappy sex life. In some cases, it even results in a complete cessation of any sex life within the marriage. Closely related to this theme is the theme of the importance of good sexual experiences in and of themselves, even outside marriage. Sex is seen as therapeutic, and it becomes a charitable obligation for kind and selfless people to fulfill the sex needs that they discern in lonely people with whom they have a mental or spiritual rapport. Another common theme of the plays is an unhappy father-son relationship, usually stemming from the inability of a materialistic, forceful, athletically inclined father to understand or appreciate properly the nature or accomplishments of a more sensitive, thoughtful, artistic son. Two other themes are inherent in these unhappy relationships, whether marital or father-son: the theme of guilt and hostility within the failing or failed relationship, and the theme of loneliness—the loneliness of an individual who is unable to achieve with another a sharing of values, goals and aspirations, tenderness and love.

Surprisingly for a writer so personal in theme and character, Anderson has seldom been innovative in plot, style, or technique. Perhaps because of his many years of formal education in drama, his works are

much influenced by earlier writers, particularly Anton Chekhov, John Van Druten, and Tennessee Williams. *All Summer Long*, for example, follows Chekhov's *Vishnyovy sad* (pr., pb. 1904; *The Cherry Orchard*, 1908) not only in its slow pace and in the lassitude of its ineffectual characters but also in the loss of the family home, which literally slides into a river because the adults in the family have been unable to put aside their petty personal desires and take some positive action to prevent the erosion of the soil under the house. *Tea and Sympathy* has an equally heavy debt to Van Druten's *Young Woodley* (pr. 1925), and *I Never Sang for My Father* owes several of its important elements to Williams's *The Glass Menagerie* (pr. 1944). Anderson has, however, not been wedded to any particular format or technique, but has been willing to experiment with various techniques introduced by others, using for his settings in some plays the highly realistic, conventional scene behind the proscenium arch and in others settings that are to varying degrees illusionistic and nonrepresentational. He used an almost bare stage in some of the one-act plays and a narrator-chorus figure in *I Never Sang for My Father*. His attempts to make the theater more frank and open in its treatment of sex stem from his desire to see it become more adult and honest in its treatment of human relationships, particularly the marital and extramarital sexual relationships on which his plays so often center.

TEA AND SYMPATHY

The autobiographical influences on *Tea and Sympathy* are readily apparent. The setting is a New England preparatory school similar to the one Anderson attended. Young Tom Lee has an artistic and sensitive nature and aesthetic interests that make him seem an "off-horse" to some of the other boys, to his housemaster, and to his father, who has sent Tom to this school in the hope that the housemaster will develop in Tom what the father considers a more manly character. Tom is not a writer, although in his elementary school days when his class needed a poet he was apparently the automatic choice. His real interest is in music, however, and he hopes for a career as a folksinger. Anderson's own first interest had also been music, and only after a sinus condition ruined his voice did he turn to the writing of plays. Tom falls in love with Laura Reynolds, a woman almost ten years older than he. Like Anderson's first wife, Phyllis, Laura is sympathetic to young people and eager to encourage talent in the young. Anderson's dedication of the play to Phyllis, "whose spirit is everywhere in this play," suggests that Laura resembles Phyllis in many other respects.

In addition to this strong autobiographical influence, however, there are also several strong literary influences on the play. One such influence, although a minor one, is Williams's *A Streetcar Named Desire* (pr., pb. 1947). In Williams's play, the young, sensitive first husband of Blanche kills himself when she discovers that he is homosexual. His suicide scars Blanche for life, leaving her with feelings of guilt and remorse that she attempts to expiate by having sex with teenage boys even later in life when she is much older than they. In *Tea and Sympathy*, the young, sensitive first husband of Laura, because of some incident unknown to Laura that called his courage and manliness into question, in effect kills himself by risking his life unnecessarily in battle to prove to others that he is not a coward. His death scars Laura and may lead to her desire to experience sexual love with the teenage Tom Lee.

Two more important literary influences are Van Druten's *Young Woodley* and George Bernard Shaw's *Candida: A Mystery* (pr. 1897). *Tea and Sympathy* is, in fact, so similar to *Young Woodley* that it might almost be considered an adaptation. In both plays, the young protagonist, a student at a boarding school, is disliked by his housemaster and teased by some of the students because he does not conform to their concept of manliness. Both housemasters hope eventually to become housemasters of their schools, and both are apparently projecting their own weaknesses and self-doubts on the protagonists. In both plays, the protagonist has been deprived of his mother early in life, in *Young Woodley* by her death and in *Tea and Sympathy* by the divorce of the parents. In both, the student is in love with the housemaster's young wife (in both plays named Laura), whose nature and values are far different from those of her husband. In both, Laura encourages the young man in his artistic

pursuits. In both, the young man visits the town prostitute, with resultant feelings of self-disgust, though for different reasons. In both, the young man, in a rage of frustration and despair, makes an attack with a butcher knife, Woodley an attack on another student and Tom an attempt at suicide. One important difference between the two plays is that in the last analysis, Woodley's father is far more helpful and sympathetic to his son than is Tom's father, a difference that reflects the lack of sympathetic understanding between Anderson and his own father. Another major difference is in the ending; Anderson gave his play a conclusion that, for that period in American theatrical history, was quite sensational.

This ending stems from the inspiration that Shaw's play *Candida* gave to Anderson's play. When Candida, the older married woman in Shaw's play, speculates on the effect that her rejection of the young, poetic Marchbanks will ultimately have on him, she wonders whether Marchbanks will forgive her for selfishly maintaining her own purity and chastity instead of initiating him into the mysteries of sexual love. She concludes that Marchbanks will forgive her if some other good woman teaches him about such love, but will not forgive her if he has the disillusioning experience of learning about sexual love from a "bad woman." In *Tea and Sympathy*, Tom asks Laura if she thinks Candida was right to send Marchbanks away, and Laura replies that Shaw "made it seem right." Later, when Tom, overcome by emotion, impulsively embraces and kisses Laura, she momentarily rejects his kisses, and he flees to the arms of the local prostitute, where his repulsion for the prostitute makes him unable to perform sexually and fills him with self-disgust. Laura, hearing about Tom's wretched experience, feels responsible for it, saying that she wishes she had let Tom prove his sexual prowess with her rather than sending him off to such a sordid experience. She has, thus, decided that Candida was wrong after all, and the play concludes as she is offering herself to Tom so that he will be able to prove to himself that he can indeed perform sexually as a man.

Here, Anderson is developing one of his favorite themes—the immorality and selfishness of allowing conventional mores to prevent one from offering a loving sexual experience to a kindred spirit who is lonely and in need of such love. The offering of a spirit of love and understanding is not enough in such circumstances; the truly loving person will feel the obligation to offer the full consummation of a sexual experience and will feel guilty for withholding such an offer. This theme provides the major conflict of Anderson's next play, *Silent Night, Lonely Night*, in which two lonely, unhappy people meet by chance on Christmas Eve and, though both remain committed to their own unhappy marriages, help and strengthen each other by experiencing together a full sexual communion for that night only. Each has regrets for times in the past when he or she should have offered such an experience but withheld it through mindless obedience to an inappropriate system of morality, and both are seen at the conclusion of the play as better persons because they have learned to overcome such rigid principles. In this play, the Christmas Eve setting seems intended to give a religious sanction to Anderson's thesis.

Not only the morality but also the validity of this thesis can be, and indeed has been, questioned. Gerald Weales has branded it as belonging to the "fashionable sex-as-therapy" school of drama, which he finds unrealistic, and even John Gassner pointed out the strong possibility that in reality, the awe in which Tom Lee held Laura would prevent him from performing sexually with her and would thus compound, instead of alleviating, his trauma. Others have noted the lengths to which Anderson went to make the sensational ending seem right. They note that he divided his characters for the most part along melodramatic lines into the good and the bad, with both Laura and Tom clearly in the category of the good and with the vicious housemaster clearly in the category of the bad. In addition, the housemaster is revealed as a latent homosexual, and Laura unequivocally breaks off her marriage to him before she offers herself to Tom. Even Laura's seduction of Tom takes place on his eighteenth birthday, so that she cannot be accused of contributing to the delinquency of a minor.

Tea and Sympathy thus takes up all the major themes of Anderson's later plays: the unhappy marital relationship, the unhappy father-son relationship, the feelings of guilt and loneliness deriving from the failure of such relationships, and the moral imperative of offering sexual experiences generously under certain circumstances. While derivative in plot and technique, it does break new ground in treating homosexuality explicitly rather than by innuendo and in the sexual frankness of the scene on which the curtain drops.

I NEVER SANG FOR MY FATHER

I Never Sang for My Father, though produced the year after *You Know I Can't Hear You When the Water's Running*, was written earlier and represents an earlier stage in Anderson's development. It is his most thorough and most successful attempt at exploring a difficult father-son relationship. Again, the autobiographical elements of the play are obvious. Tom Garrison, the father in the play, is like Anderson's father in many respects. He is a self-made man, and he loves athletics and athletic values. He was once a mayor (Anderson's father once ran for the office of mayor of New Rochelle), and he has never understood or appreciated the artistic and literary interests of either his wife or his son. The son, Gene Garrison, is like Anderson in being both a writer and a college professor, in having had a wife who died slowly of a lingering illness, in being much closer to his mother than to his father, and in trying unsuccessfully to establish a satisfying relationship with his father.

The most important literary influence on the play is Williams's *The Glass Menagerie*. Anderson's play was first written as a movie script, and when Anderson sought a way of giving the play version a fluidity of movement from short scene to short scene, he borrowed the narrator-chorus figure that Williams had used so successfully in *The Glass Menagerie*. In addition, the two plays are similar in that both protagonists are trying to free their lives from the claims that parents are trying to impose on them, that both do eventually reject those claims and escape their parents' domination, and that neither succeeds in throwing off the consequent feelings of guilt and remorse.

In addition to the unsatisfactory father-son relationship, *I Never Sang for My Father* develops at some length the incompatibility of the interests and values of Margaret and Tom Garrison, thus providing yet another example of Anderson's interest in the theme of the unhappy marital relationship. As in his earlier treatments of this theme, the incompatibility of values is reflected in an unsatisfactory sex life, though this aspect of their lives is barely hinted at by Margaret Garrison.

In its exploration of both the father-son and the marital relationship, *I Never Sang for My Father* is probably Anderson's best play. The characters are real, and the anguish that they experience as they try unsuccessfully to reach one another is deep and moving. Gene's reactions ring true as those of a middle-aged son who loves his mother and tries to love his father but is appalled by the inevitable dependence of both on him. Gene and his mother understand each other well, and their shared understanding of Tom intensifies their closeness. Gene and his father, on the other hand, are diametrically opposed in temperament and values, so that all Gene's efforts at reaching some rapport with his father fail miserably. Nevertheless, Gene continues to try, partly because he feels it his duty to do so, partly because his nature craves a father he can love, and partly—as his sister Alice suggests—because he has never gotten over the fact that he does not measure up to his father's idea of manliness. Tom views with contempt all Gene's accomplishments as a writer and teacher, and only once in his life, when Gene was in the Marines, has Tom felt proud of his son.

Tom is the most rigid character in the play, yet Anderson treats him fairly, showing that his character and attitudes stem from a bad relationship with his own father and from the resultant hardship of his life as a child and as a young man. His unreasonableness is believable, and his son's simultaneous desire and inability to break through it are convincing. Alice is also convincingly complex as the daughter who has succeeded in escaping Tom's domination, partly because his opposition to her marriage gave her an excuse to do so with a clear conscience, but who in one vulnerable moment unexpectedly reveals how deeply she has been affected by the lack of love from her father.

Although there is nothing new in this play—the characters, their circumstances, and their helpless and mostly ineffectual attempts to deal with those circumstances are very familiar—*I Never Sang for My Father* will probably be remembered for its complex and credible characters and for the sincerity of the emotion the play generates.

YOU KNOW I CAN'T HEAR YOU WHEN THE WATER'S RUNNING

In *You Know I Can't Hear You When the Water's Running*, Anderson returned to a form which he evidently found very congenial, the one-act play. Of approximately twenty-four plays written in his Harvard years, some twenty were one-act plays, and the one nonmusical play he wrote at Exeter was a one-act play. Of the four plays that make up *You Know I Can't Hear You When the Water's Running*, two—*The Footsteps of Doves* and *I'm Herbert*—are mere entertainments, little more than skits. The other two—*The Shock of Recognition* and *I'll Be Home for Christmas*—have much greater significance in acuteness of observation and validity and interest of characterization.

The Footsteps of Doves derives its title from a saying of philosopher Friedrich Nietzsche to the effect that major changes in one's life are not announced dramatically, with thunderous crescendos, but slip up on one almost imperceptibly, like the footsteps of doves—a saying that Anderson had used earlier, in *Silent Night, Lonely Night*, and would use again in his novel *After*. In this play, the footsteps are heard only by the husband when a middle-aged couple, George and Harriet, are buying a new bed and Harriet insists on twin beds despite all of George's arguments for the double bed. George and Harriet's sex life has deteriorated badly since the time of their youthful happiness together, and George sees the purchase of the twin beds as symbolic of an utter lack of hope that it will improve. When the younger, more vital Jill appears and makes a thinly veiled offer to share a double bed with George, it becomes apparent that he will accept this offer and thus will thenceforth accept her, rather than his wife, as his permanent sex partner.

This play expresses Anderson's oft-reiterated belief in the importance of a happy sex life to a good marriage, but it is new in its isolation of that element from all the other elements that go into making a good marriage. In his earlier plays, an unhappy sex life is seen as the result of other kinds of incompatibility in the marriage—personality clashes, value clashes, clashes in beliefs and goals—but in this play, one knows nothing about the couple except their sex life.

I'm Herbert also focuses on the sex life of a couple as the sole index of the happiness of their marriage. Some critics have found in the play that theme so common among absurdist playwrights, the lack of communication in modern society; this interpretation, however, is negated by the fact that the lack of communication in *I'm Herbert* stems neither from the specific conditions of modern society nor from the perennial human condition but solely from senility, a specific medical problem found only in some elderly people. Thomas P. Adler sees the play as almost a paean to a happy marriage that has "passed beyond physical sexuality"; this interpretation, however, is negated by the fact that the old couple in the play remember nothing at all about their former or present mates but the sexual experiences they shared, and that the sexual experiences they remember are not attached to any particular person in their minds but are remembered simply for themselves. Love is nowhere to be found in this play, which focuses entirely on the theme of the importance of sexual excitement and gratification. In the absence of any greater depth of meaning, then, it seems to be no more than an extended and tasteless joke based on a highly unfair and inaccurate stereotype of the elderly. *I'm Herbert* is, thus, the least satisfying of the plays in the quartet.

The Shock of Recognition is the first of Anderson's plays to center on the discussion of a particular theatrical issue. Jack Barnstable is an autobiographical character in that he is a writer of plays arguing for a position that Anderson supported, the acceptance in the theater of greater honesty and realism in dealing with sex. Herb Miller is a stereotype of the kind of opponent such a position often meets: a man who prides himself on his virility and who thinks of sex as the appropriate subject for dirty jokes told among men and for broad innuendoes used to embarrass naïve young women but not as something that can be discussed openly and objectively among adult men and women or can be presented in such a fashion onstage. The really interesting character in this play, however, is Richard Pawling, the actor who will sac-

rifice anything to get a part in a play. Both ludicrous and pathetic in his eagerness and determination to please, he is Anderson's most richly comic character, and the play is memorable more for this character than for any other element, even the then shocking but now passé idea of presenting male frontal nudity onstage.

I'll Be Home for Christmas, though beginning as comedy and presumably intended to maintain the comic tone to complement the tone of the other plays in this group, is at times too moving and real in its pain to be funny. Chuck's hurt and anguish, his real fear that his life has no meaning, are too strong. Like the other plays in this group, *I'll Be Home for Christmas* deals with the importance of sex, but unlike the others, it demonstrates that a healthy marriage needs more than sexual gratification. Chuck, the middle-aged husband, is appalled at the mechanical, even clinical, view that his wife Edith has of sex, which she considers an extremely important part of a wholesome married life. He is revolted as she discusses the sex education that she has been giving and proposes to continue giving to their children. He has a much more romantic view of sex and demands much more meaning, not only in his marriage but in his entire life, than he discerns around him. Unfortunately, the one-act format works against the play on this point. There has not been room to develop any notion of the values that Chuck has stood for in the past. The values of Edith are, however, both apparent and repugnant, so that as Chuck sits brooding over a letter in which his son Donny has rejected Chuck's way of life as meaningless, the audience is likely to wonder why Donny did not address the letter to his mother, rather than to his father.

SOLITAIRE/DOUBLE SOLITAIRE

The success of this quartet of one-act plays led Anderson to try the one-act format once again in two short plays on the theme of family life, *Solitaire/Double Solitaire*. The lack of success of this duet on Broadway may have helped to push Anderson in the direction of writing novels. Another very important element in his turning to novels, however, was certainly the fact that in *Double Solitaire* he had carried frankness in the discussion and portrayal of sex to the limits that it could reach on the stage. As Anderson has acknowledged, the autobiographical, even confessional, nature of the content of *After* required "so much explicit sex" and "so many interior monologues" that he had to give up his attempts to present it in the form of a play and turn to the novel instead.

OTHER MAJOR WORKS

LONG FICTION: *After*, 1973; *Getting Up and Going Home*, 1978.

SCREENPLAYS: *The Nun's Story*, 1959 (adaptation of Kathryn Hulme's novel); *The Sand Pebbles*, 1966 (adaptation of Richard McKenna's novel); *I Never Sang for My Father*, 1970 (adaptation of his play).

TELEPLAYS: *Double Solitaire*, 1972 (adaptation of his play); *The Patricia Neal Story*, 1981; *Absolute Strangers*, 1991.

BIBLIOGRAPHY

Adler, Thomas P. *Robert Anderson*. Boston: Twayne, 1978. Adler examines Anderson's life and works, providing critical analysis. Bibliography and index.

Ayers, David Hugh. *The Apprenticeship of Robert Anderson*. Ann Arbor, Mich.: University Microfilms, 1970. The first book-length study of Anderson, with a valuable bibliography of reviews and articles that appeared in *The New York Times*. Also contains a definitive account of Anderson's salad days, Navy plays, the period of his wife's cancer, the lawsuit concerning *Tea and Sympathy*, and the formation of the New Dramatists in 1951.

Gordon, A. C. *A Critical Study of the History and Development of the Playwrights' Producing Company*. Ann Arbor, Mich: University Microfilms, 1972. A thorough study of this producing organization, where Robert Anderson and Maxwell Anderson (no relation) crossed careers between 1953 and 1959. The work underlines Robert Anderson's lifelong interest in producing and developing new playwrights.

Klein, Alvin. "Giving a Theater Force His Due." *The New York Times*, October 22, 2000, p. 15. This article about Hofstra University's tribute to Robert Anderson provides some glimpses into Anderson as a person and playwright, including his influence on playwright Donald Margulies.

Sullivan, Dan. "Anderson Makes a Living: Between Killings." *The Los Angeles Times*, December 6, 1987, p. 53. In this article on the revival of *I Never Sang for My Father* at the Ahmanson Theater in Los Angeles, Sullivan talks with Anderson about his love for the theater and the difficulty of getting plays produced.

Wharton, John F. "The Sixth Playwright." In *Life Among the Playwrights*. New York: Quadrangle, 1974. Presents the story of the Playwrights' Producing Company, of which Wharton was a founding member. This chapter introduces Anderson's involvement, claiming he could have been the revitalizing force for the group in its waning years.

Lisë Pedersen,
updated by Thomas J. Taylor

LEONID ANDREYEV

Born: Orel, Russia; August 9, 1871
Died: Neivala, Finland; September 12, 1919

PRINCIPAL DRAMA

Mysl, pb. 1902, pr. 1914
Tot, kto poluchayet poshchechiny, pb. 1902, pr. 1915 (*He Who Gets Slapped*, 1921)
K zvezdam, pb. 1905, pr. 1906 (*To the Stars*, 1907)
Savva, pr., pb. 1906 (English translation, 1914)
Zhizn cheloveko, pr., pb. 1907 (*The Life of Man*, 1914)
Tsar golod, pb. 1907 (*King Hunger*, 1911)
Chyornye maski, pb. 1907 (*The Black Maskers*, 1915)

Dni nashey zhizni, pr., pb. 1908

Lyubov k Hizhmemu, pb. 1908, pr. 1909 (*Love of One's Neighbor*, 1914)

Anatema, pr., pb. 1909 (*Anathema*, 1910)

Anfisa, pb. 1909

Gaudeamus, pb. 1910

Prekrasnye sabinyanki, pb. 1911 (*The Pretty Sabine Women*, 1914)

Okean, pb. 1911 (*The Ocean*, 1916)

Chest, pb. 1912

Professor Storisyn, pb. 1912 (English translation, 1933)

Yekaterina Ivanovna, pb. 1912 (*Katerina*, 1923)

Ne ubey, pb. 1914

Korol, zakon i svoboda, pr., pb. 1914

Sobachy vals, wr. 1914, pb. 1922 (*The Waltz of the Dogs*, 1922)

Samson v okovakh, pb. 1915 (*Samson in Chains*, 1923)

OTHER LITERARY FORMS

Leonid Andreyev is best known as a writer of short fiction. In the first decade of the twentieth century, his stories and novellas gained a wide readership while arousing much controversy over their often perverse subject matter. In addition, Andreyev published two novels, generally considered to be inferior to his short fiction, and miscellaneous nonfiction.

ACHIEVEMENTS

Although his works have been largely forgotten, Andreyev, at his peak, was among Russia's most popular writers. His success rivaled that of Maxim Gorky, and his contributions to Russian drama are of great historical interest. Andreyev played a pioneering role in freeing the Russian stage from the dominance of realism, preparing the way for such theatrical innovators as Vladimir Mayakovsky. At the same time, to an extent matched by few of his contemporaries, he expressed in his plays the hothouse atmosphere of the prerevolutionary intelligentsia—a compound of decadence, diabolism, and melodramatic spiritual yearnings. The very qualities that distinguished him as a spokesperson for his age have ensured his neglect by subsequent generations.

BIOGRAPHY

Leonid Nikolayevich Andreyev was born about two hundred miles south of Moscow in the provincial city of Orel on August 9, 1871. His father, a land surveyor, died in Andreyev's early childhood, and Andreyev was reared in poverty and loneliness. Perhaps in part as a result of these deprivations, he was subject to fits of depression that led eventually to three unsuccessful suicide attempts. Many aspects of Andreyev's personality are highlighted in Max Beerbohm's parodic portrait, "Kolnijatsch" in *And Even Now* (1920), of the Russian writer who so intrigued the English at the turn of the century. According to Beerbohm, the writers of Andreyev's generation led lives "not void of those sensational details" that so interested the reading public: early alcoholism, streaks of madness, rash acts, and defiant rejection of all norms and fundamental conditions of life. This view is reinforced by the label "Decadents," popularly applied to a group of writers whose "message," according to Beerbohm, was "too elemental, too near to very naked Nature for exact definition." More than any other writer of the day, Andreyev fits this image generally held in the West of a Russian writer. Often behaviorally outside the norm, Andreyev at times seemed a savage somber soul, whose wild, barbarous, even animalistic tendencies came out in his creative heroes. With his mane of black hair, burning eyes, pale handsome face, and proud mouth, he looked and played the part of his own dark, turbulent protagonists. One characteristically sensational episode in Andreyev's life was his childhood flirtation with sudden death, when he lay down between the tracks to let an approaching train pass over him.

An insatiable reader, Andreyev read widely in the Russian classics and in foreign literature translated into Russian. He exhibited a considerable aptitude for painting and drawing, partly supporting his law studies at the University of Petersburg by portrait painting. Suffering from depression, he temporarily left his studies, enrolling again in 1893 at the University of Moscow where in 1897 he received a degree in law. After a brief and unsuccessful attempt at the practice of law, Andreyev turned first to newspaper reporting and then to feuilleton writing for the *Mos-*

cow *Courier.* In 1896, he began to devote himself to-tally to a writing career.

Maxim Gorky was among the first to encourage Andreyev as a short-story writer. He introduced Andreyev to the literary scene in 1901 by giving him the chance to read his short story "Molchaniye" ("Silence") aloud before a circle of Gorky's writer friends who had established the famous publishing house Znaniye (knowledge). The following year Znaniye brought out a small volume of Andreyev's first stories, immediately establishing his reputation. As Andreyev began to cool toward Gorky's realistic and didactic literary goals, he drew away from this group.

Having moved first to St. Petersburg in 1906, Andreyev built a spacious villa with somewhat bizarre furnishings and pretentious decor at the popular picturesque summer resort of Terioki in Finland, situated some thirty miles from St. Petersburg. Here much of the wealth brought in by his fame was dissipated by luxurious living. Andreyev spent most of the rest of his life here, purposely cut off from interruptions and the political turmoil of city life.

Indeed, Andreyev believed that political dogma and party creeds were incompatible with spontaneous artistic creativity, and the younger generation began to turn away from his increasingly apolitical writing. As a critic of society, Andreyev devoted himself chiefly to the revelation of inner mental and emotional states, ignoring for the most part the external social and political whirlwind of his time. Because of his persistent depiction of humanity's evil and perverse nature, Andreyev came increasingly under attack. His uncompromising hatred for the Bolsheviks did nothing to alleviate his stressful situation and no doubt brought on the increasing official harassment, house searches, and threats of arrest that he endured after the 1917 Revolution. During the last two years of his life, Andreyev ceased his artistic activity almost altogether, torturing himself with self-flagellation. He could not comprehend why he had risen, as he wrote in a personal letter to Sergey S. Golousev (1917), "like a rocket . . . swiftly and radiantly . . . then suddenly stopped." Finally, having stopped eating, Andreyev suffered from profound depression and constant thoughts of suicide, dying an embittered, broken man.

ANALYSIS

The major themes of Leonid Andreyev's prose carried over into his plays, where they stood out in sharper relief as he shifted from realism to allegorical symbolism. Among the Symbolists, Aleksandr Blok, in his essay "On Drama," singled out Andreyev for praise, noting his powerful dramatic technique in *The Life of Man*, in which Man from birth to death battles Fate, proving he is "no mere puppet" or "pitiful creature" but a strong being who will endure to the end in spite of the obstacles flung in his path.

Andreyev expressed his new and innovative ideas about Russian drama in "Pisma o teatre" (two letters on the theater), published in 1912-1913 in the theatrical journal *Maski* (masks) and in *Shipovnik* (the wild rose). These letters illustrate Andreyev's shift from Symbolism (as it had become known as a literary movement) to what he termed "pan-psychism." Andreyev advocated a reform of the Russian theater, rejecting large-scale productions in the tradition established by the founder of Russian realist drama, Alexander Ostrovsky. According to Andreyev, what was needed instead was a pan-psychic drama, which would correspond more closely to the mental state of the modern intellectual with his interest in such intense personalities as the "tragic" modern hero, Friedrich Nietzsche. To convey the full intensity of twentieth century people's beliefs, doubts, torments, and aspirations, Andreyev argued, drama must be symbolic, uniting the inner world with people's physical reality.

For Andreyev, real drama began not in the realm of physical activity but in silence and inactivity, whereby the dramatist must examine the innermost recesses of his mind and soul. Here a tragic struggle begins and a new Nietzschean Zarathustra speaks out. Andreyev, intensely interested in Nietzsche's views on tragedy, also looked to another German, Arthur Schopenhauer, sharing his point of view that the highest form of drama is tragedy. In a letter to the director of the Moscow Art Theatre, V. I. Demirovich-Danchenko (December 28, 1914), Andreyev wrote that "in tragedy the misery of existence is brought before us and the final outcome is here the vanity of all human striving."

Andreyev particularly looked to the Moscow Art Theatre to take up this new direction in Russian drama because it had already begun to show its unique and independent development in its productions of Anton Chekhov. While many of Andreyev's plays did indeed enjoy successful runs at the Moscow Art Theatre, the directors grew wary of the public scandals and battles with the authorities that his plays regularly provoked. All his major dramas, *The Black Maskers*, *Anathema*, *The Life of Man*, and *Samson in Chains*, remained under constant fire, and some were even banned; only the early, less provocative plays such as *Dni nashey zhizni* (days of our lives) continued to run year after year.

All Andreyev's works illustrate on a personal level his own psychological makeup, seen in the constant self-flagellation and self-aggrandizement common to all his central characters. In a larger historical context, Andreyev's plays have given the world an intense portrayal of the gloomy atmosphere and prevailing depression that seized the minds of some as political forces, both before and after the 1917 Revolution, kept an iron grip on the Russian intelligentsia.

TO THE STARS

Andreyev's first plays do not reveal the distinctive form and style of his later symbolic "tragedies." The settings of the early plays, while not overly laden with details of everyday life, still remain within the confines of realism. Andreyev's first play, written in 1906, suggests by its very title his somewhat apolitical, metaphysical bent. *To the Stars* revolves around a typical Andreyev hero, a dedicated astronomer, Ternovsky, who lives in seclusion halfway up a mountain, somewhere in Western Europe. His geographical position alone signals both his intellectually defiant attitude toward crude reality below and his own tenuous position as a mortal in relation to the heights of heaven. The theme of struggle between generations, common in Russian literature since Ivan Turgenev's *Ottsy i deti* (1862; *Fathers and Sons*, 1867), emerges in Ternovsky's debate with his children, who as political activists are involved in revolutionary activity at the mountain's base. In response to his children's claim that his scientific quest is merely a way of escaping social responsibilities, Ternovsky notes the

relative insignificance of human acts when up against the universal forces, which are embodied in the stars. Because of the play's political content, *To the Stars* was rejected by the Russian censors.

SAVVA

In *Savva*, Andreyev's second play, the young dramatist assumes an even more ambiguous political stand toward revolutionary activity. The main character, Savva, is an inventor who, like Ternovsky in *To the Stars*, is to a certain extent bound up with the powers of the intellect. As a revolutionary, he would like to destroy all old forms of culture to make way for the new. His radical act of blowing up an icon, believed to have certain miraculous powers, is his way of fighting both people's "innate servility" and their tendency to imprison themselves in superstitions, particularly religious ones. This isolated act of rebellion, however, leads only to Savva's murder, revealing Andreyev's own uncertainty about the destructive and violent results of people's attempts to liberate themselves from themselves.

THE LIFE OF MAN

Beginning with the drama *The Life of Man*, a marked shift can be noted in Andreyev's style. Although he continues to intersperse elements of realism (bits of everyday trivia) throughout the text, he increases the use of colors, shapes, pictorial metaphors, and musical tones to symbolize abstract ideas. In *The Life of Man*, the symbolism, contained at the level of allegory, is based on a revision of the old medieval mystery plays: The characters, generalizations of universal types, are Man, Man's Wife, and A Being in Gray Called He. They are surrounded by groups, or choruses, of people known only as Old Women, Friends of Man, and Drunkards. *The Life of Man*, a drama not in five acts but in five *kartiny* (pictures), depicts the unfolding of various scenes, or stages, of Man's life from his entry into the world at birth to his exit back into the "darkness beyond" at death. The backdrop, a "large massive rectangular empty room without doors or windows," gray in color, suggests no particular home or any particular social setting but is Everyman's house—that is, the physical, finite boundaries that house the mind and spirit. The symbol of the house occurs repeatedly in

Andreyev's plays and can be seen again, for example, in the image of Count Lorenzo's castle in *The Black Maskers* and in the massive temple that Samson brings down at the end of *Samson in Chains.*

The primary message throughout all Andreyev's works is expressed in *The Life of Man* at the very beginning by A Being in Gray Called He, who in a long monologue speaks about the senseless futility of Man's journey through life, his limited vision and the constant defeat of all his hopes and desires as he tragically does battle with "the iron round of destiny." From his very birth, Man is demeaned as the "Silence," so often referred to in the text, and is repeatedly interrupted by the mocking laughter of old women or their crass comments about the grotesque physicality of nature. In spite of these vulgar overtones, there remains a powerful although restrained beauty underlying Man's life, which is symbolized by a glowing candle, blazing throughout the play, until it mysteriously and tragically flickers out at the end. The symbolism is obvious, yet its simplicity and universality make it effective, for it is deeply rooted in the minds and hearts of men. As Andreyev wrote to the director of the Moscow Art Theatre, V. I. Demirovich-Danchenko, on December 28, 1914, his goal was to create "a tragedy over which Schopenhauer and his cook could have wept together."

After extremely sensational productions of *The Life of Man*, first in St. Petersburg by Vsevolod Meyerhold, who at that time was at the height of his involvement with the neo-Romantic and Symbolist Mystery Drama, and then in Moscow by Konstantin Stanislavsky, one of the directors of the Moscow Art Theatre, who swathed the old stage in black velvet for this play, Andreyev basked for some time in his success as a great Russian playwright.

KING HUNGER

Andreyev's second allegorical play, *King Hunger*, written as a sequel to *The Life of Man*, examines not the external forces of destiny that curb people but the inner force that makes them rebel against the unjust restraints placed on them by society: their haughty belief in their own power. Tsar Hunger, the dominant figure in this play, shifts back and forth between two social groups of people, serving both—as a tool of

oppression in the hands of the rich, then as a means of incitement among the poor. In the end, the barbaric revolt leads nowhere, as the workers, overcome by a destructive egocentrism inherent in all people, fight among themselves. *King Hunger* appeared at the moment when the failure of the 1905 revolution had served to reinforce the impotence of the upper-class intellectuals and the desperation of the working class. Little wonder, then, that, although a printing of eighteen thousand copies of the play sold out in one day, storms of adverse criticism came from all corners.

DNI NASHEY ZHIZNI

While his popularity continued, Andreyev's subsequent plays never achieved the wide public approval that greeted *The Life of Man*. Among the plays to follow, *Dni nashey zhizni* was the most enthusiastically received. It was first performed in St. Petersburg and then ran for seventy-four performances in Moscow and the provinces. Full of action and lively dialogue, *Dni nashey zhizni* represents a partial but temporary return to realism. Because of its social content, Andreyev sent it to Znaniye for publication: It focuses on the appalling poverty of student life. Andreyev himself regarded this work as trivia and thought that his play *The Black Maskers*, written at the same time, was more in keeping with the new direction that theater should follow. Of the many plays Andreyev was to create after *The Life of Man*, only *The Black Maskers* and *Sampson in Chains* contribute to the modern movement in Russian theater.

THE BLACK MASKERS

In *The Black Maskers*, night's void again eclipses the sun's "golden rays of dreams and hopes." This symbolic play represents the tragedy of any highly idealistic individual whose soul is a "brightly lit castle." Recalling Edgar Allan Poe's story "William Wilson," the mind of the central figure, Count Lorenzo, cracks as he tries to cope with uninvited, horrifying masked creatures who crash in on his blazing masquerade. Elements of Lorenzo's own subconscious emerge in the form of these dark monsters. Ultimately, he is confronted by his double: His cheery optimism turns out to be the real mask, from behind which looms a being intent on destroying its alter ego. Eleven years after this play was written, Andreyev saw it not only as a tragedy of the individual but also as "the tragedy of the whole revolution," which "kindled lights among the darkness" and "could not cope with the great human darkness that extinguished those torches."

SAMSON IN CHAINS

Although never produced or published in Russia, *Samson in Chains* is often considered to be Andreyev's most powerful masterpiece and certainly one of his last brilliant flashes. Looking to ancient sources, here again Andreyev uses a nonrealistic setting to remove the viewer in time and space from the externals of everyday reality. Again he attempts to convey essence instead of a social or political existence by shunning naturalistic detail in favor of a more abstract, symbolic setting. Reworking the biblical story of Samson and Delilah, Andreyev nicely illustrates his view of the new pan-psychic theater as an arena for an inner battle. This drama opens against the backdrop of a dark cave outside ancient Ashkelon. The cave, "hewn in soft rock with massive stone stairs and crude, heavy, massive furniture," conveys the sense of some grandiose personality who has withdrawn into the dark depths of his mind or soul. The recurring theme of humanity's limited vision and bestial nature is dramatically expressed in the figure of the imprisoned and blinded Samson, shown here as a wild beast with a powerful body, beard and hair in wild disorder, dragged down by heavy chains. From the outset, this Nietzschean superhero is plagued by conflicting impulses. Born a prophet, invested with divine power and will, Samson acquiesces in the carnal pleasures of a slothful existence, intoxicated by Delilah's charms, by wine and riches. This plot parallels Andreyev's own withdrawal with his second wife into luxurious living at his secluded villa in Finland. Indeed, *Samson in Chains* in part reflects what Andreyev saw as his own growing morbid desire to give up his calling as a writer and renounce the responsibility of a "cognitive and noble life" to wallow in the mire with the "lowly and the degenerate." He referred to such moments as a recurring "desire to part with . . . free solitude and to dissolve in this grey, dull mass of semi-humans."

Throughout the play, the inner dramatic tension builds, until Samson's slumbering will is finally aroused by God's voice in the desert wail of the wind and the roar of a lion. Imbued with his former strength, Samson rises up before the false, hypocritical Philistines to destroy them and himself by shattering their ancient Ashkelon temple. Samson's paradoxical triumph at the end conveys Andreyev's often repeated message that only through death can humankind ultimately escape the chains of existence.

HE WHO GETS SLAPPED

He Who Gets Slapped remains a popular play outside the former Soviet Union because the symbolism is readily accessible to the public. A film version appeared in the Soviet Union in 1922, and in 1956, Robert Varda, an American composer, based his successful opera *Pantaloon* on this Andreyev play. *He Who Gets Slapped* once again creates a dichotomy of inner and outer worlds. The central figure, bearing the name of the play's title, drops out of his former life to join Papa Briquet's Circus somewhere in an unspecified city in France. This play typifies the general antirepresentational neo-Romantic direction in Russian theater at the beginning of the twentieth century. Seeking to escape the hopelessness and colorlessness of Russian life, these Symbolist dramatists renewed an interest in the early masked theater of Oriental and Italian theater, especially *commedia dell'arte*; symbols of the circus and the clown became popular. While the "outside" or "other" world meant a society governed by cold, cultured intellect and self-satisfied bourgeois values, the circus embodied the world of emotions, intuition, beauty, and imagination. It was a place where circus performers could follow their natural inclinations.

Although *He Who Gets Slapped* is Andreyev's most symbolic play, its intent does not differ from that of either his other plays or the earlier prose: the revelation of modern people's complex psychological makeup. On the realization of society's falsity and fraud, the character He Who Gets Slapped sheds the mask of his past life to take up that of a clown, echoing the splitting of Lorenzo's mind in *The Black Maskers*. The viewer learns through conversation that He has disappeared from "that" world, purposely feigning "death" to reduce himself to a nameless nobody who will let himself be slapped for the amusement of the circus public. "A friend" on the outside has assumed the role of He's former self, taking over not only his previous intellectual career but also marrying his wife. Once inside the circus, He falls in love with Consuella, a lovely bareback rider, who embodies his ideal of physical and spiritual beauty.

As the play proceeds, escape from one world into another by means of actual death becomes the main motif. Regarding himself and Consuella as "exceptional beings" and "gods," He's only alternative is that of Samson in *Samson in Chains*: destruction of both himself and Consuella, who has consented to marry a rich baron from the outside world. Learning this, He cannot let his ideal and love be tainted by the same crass forces of greed and egocentrism that had oppressed him in his former life. (This obsession with the death of the female character may in part reflect the loss of Andreyev's first wife through death, a tragedy from which, according to the author himself, he never fully recovered.) He Who Gets Slapped dies with a defiant vow that he will continue to contest the baron for the love of Consuella in the world beyond.

OTHER MAJOR WORKS

LONG FICTION: *Sashka Zhegulev*, 1911 (*Sashka Jiguleff*, 1925); *Dnevnik Satana*, 1921 (*Satan's Diary*, 1920).

SHORT FICTION: *The Crushed Flower and Other Stories*, 1916; *The Little Angel and Other Stories*, 1916; *Seven That Were Hanged, and Other Stories*, 1958.

NONFICTION: "Pisma o teatre," 1912-1913.

MISCELLANEOUS: *Sobranie sochinenii*, 1910-1915 (16 volumes); *Polnoe sobranie sochinenii*, 1913 (8 volumes).

BIBLIOGRAPHY

Carlisle, Olga. "My Grandfather, Leonid Andreyev: Heard Again, Loud and Clear." *New York Times Book Review*, October 4, 1987, p. 15. Andreyev's granddaughter writes of the reemergence of her grandfather's works, which were suppressed after the October Revolution.

_____. "Russian Portraits: Leonid Andreyev." *The Paris Review* 37, no. 137 (Winter, 1995): 130. Andreyev's granddaughter presents a profile of the famous writer, who was being rediscovered in the 1990's.

Hutchings, Stephen C. *A Semiotic Analysis of the Short Stories of Leonid Andreyev, 1900-1909*. London: Modern Humanities Research Association, 1990. Although this work focuses on Andreyev's short stories, it provides valuable information about his life and his views of literature. Bibliography and index.

Newcombe, Josephine M. *Leonid Andreyev*. New York: Ungar, 1972. A basic biography of Andreyev that presents his life and works. Bibliography and index.

"Rare Originality, Rare Talent." *Moscow News*, August 29-September 4, 2001, p. 6. This article, written in celebration of what would have been Andreyev's 130th birthday, discusses his life and works.

Jane E. Knox

JEAN ANOUILH

Born: Cérisole, near Bordeeaux, France; June 23, 1910
Died: Lausanne, Switzerland; October 3, 1987

PRINCIPAL DRAMA

L'Hermine, pr. 1932, pb. 1934 (*The Ermine*, 1955)
Le Bal des voleurs, wr. 1932, pr., pb. 1938 (*Thieves' Carnival*, 1952)

Le Voyageur sans bagage, pr., pb. 1937 (*Traveller Without Luggage*, 1959)

La Sauvage, pr., pb. 1938 (*Restless Heart*, 1957)

Léocadia, pr. 1940, pb. 1942 (*Time Remembered*, 1955)

Le Rendez-vous de Senlis, pr. 1941, pb. 1942 (*Dinner with the Family*, 1958)

Antigone, pr. 1944, pb. 1946 (English translation, 1946)

Jézabel, pb. 1946

Roméo et Jeannette, pr., pb. 1946 (*Romeo and Jeanette*, 1958)

L'Invitation au château, pr. 1947, pb. 1953 (*Ring Round the Moon*, 1950)

Ardèle: Ou, La Marguerite, pr. 1948, pb. 1949 (*Ardèle*, 1951)

La Répétition: Ou, L'Amour puni, pr., pb. 1950 (*The Rehearsal*, 1958)

Colombe, pr. 1951, pb. 1953 (*Mademoiselle Colombe*, 1954)

La Valse des toréadors, pr., pb. 1952 (*The Waltz of the Toreadors*, 1953)

L'Alouette, pr., pb. 1953 (*The Lark*, 1955)

Ornifle: Ou, Le Courant d'air, pr. 1955, pb. 1956 (*Ornifle*, 1970)

Pauvre Bitos: Ou, Le Dîner de têtes, pr., pb. 1956 (*Poor Bitos*, 1964)

Jean Anouilh, pb. 1958-1967 (3 volumes)

L'Hurluberlu: Ou, Le Réactionnaire amoureux, pr., pb. 1959 (*The Fighting Cock*, 1960)

Becket: Ou, L'Honneur de Dieu, pr., pb. 1959 (*Becket: Or, The Honor of God*, 1960)

La Foire d'empoigne, pb. 1960, pr. 1962 (*Catch as Catch Can*, 1967)

L'Orchestre, pr. 1962, pb. 1970 (*The Orchestra*, 1967)

The Collected Plays, pb. 1966-1967 (2 volumes)

Le Boulanger, la boulangère et le petit mitron, pr. 1968, pb. 1969

Cher Antoine: Ou, L'Amour raté, pr., pb. 1969 (*Dear Antoine: Or, The Love that Failed*, 1971)

Les Poissons rouges: Ou, Mon père, ce héros, pr., pb. 1970

Le Directeur de l'opéra, pr., pb. 1972 (*The Director of the Opera*, 1973)

L'Arrestation, pr., pb. 1975 (*The Arrest*, 1978)

Le Scénario, pr., pb. 1976

Le Nombril, pr., pb. 1981

Number One, pr. 1984

OTHER LITERARY FORMS

Jean Anouilh is known only for his plays. With the exception of infrequent reviews, he wrote nothing else and was known to refuse requests for occasional pieces with characteristic truculence, professing his inability "to write."

ACHIEVEMENTS

Active as a dramatist well past the age of sixty-five, Jean Anouilh wrote nearly fifty plays in roughly as many years, among them five or ten true masterpieces that more than suffice to assure him a position of high distinction in the history of French drama.

Achieving distinction in his mid-twenties with such memorable successes as *Traveller Without Luggage* and *Thieves' Carnival*, Anouilh soon thereafter consolidated his reputation with the thought-provoking *Antigone* to become the preeminent dramatist of wartime and postwar France, reaching both a serious and a popular audience. Among the most instinctively "theatrical" of playwrights, Anouilh proved equally skillful at comedy, melodrama, near-tragedy, and satire, adopting for his efforts a new, if tongue-in-cheek, system of genre classification: In the standard collections of his theater, the pieces are duly classified as "pink" plays, "black" plays, "shining" plays, "grating" plays, and so on. During the 1950's, he added, with considerable success, a new category: "costume" plays based, if somewhat less than faithfully, on the characters and incidents of history. Both *The Lark*, which re-creates the life and death of Joan of Arc, and *Becket*, studying the tortured relationship between Thomas à Becket and Henry II, achieved great success worldwide, as did a subsequent film version of the latter, featuring Richard Burton in the title role and Peter O'Toole as the king.

Increasingly involved in the staging and direction of his plays, Anouilh wrote little new for the theater during the 1960's. A subsequent phase of his career,

Jean Anouilh (Hulton Archive by Getty Images)

beginning around 1970, brought forth several new plays deemed generally inferior to Anouilh's prior standard, with a tendency toward repetition, yet eminently stage worthy thanks to the author's personal involvement in their production.

For reasons difficult to fathom, Anouilh's plays have fared somewhat less well in English translation than might have been expected, with appreciably better success in Britain than in the United States or Canada. At times ill-served by his translators, even down to the titles of his plays, Anouilh was perhaps too irretrievably Gallic in thought and expression to reach an American audience. Even in America, however, he is destined to be remembered as the most talented, versatile, and representative French dramatist of the mid-twentieth century.

BIOGRAPHY

"I have no biography," wrote Jean-Marie-Lucien-Pierre Anouilh around the age of thirty-five to one of his earliest critics, "and am quite pleased not to have any." Going on to sketch in such bare essentials as a year of law school and two years in advertising, with

some desultory work in films, Anouilh observed that he had discovered the theater at an early age and had fortunately (he claimed) never had to resort to journalism. Thus did Anouilh drape about his life a screen of privacy that more or less protected him for the rest of his life. To an even greater degree than in the case of most prolific authors, Anouilh's work was his life, and vice versa.

Anouilh's "life in the theater" began in late 1929 or early 1930, when he succeeded the scenarist and playwright Georges Neveux as secretary to the eminent director Louis Jouvet, who had "discovered" and developed the playwriting talents of Jean Giraudoux, by then France's most eminent dramatist. Almost at once, Anouilh began to try his hand at writing plays, initially without much success; later he withdrew certain of his early efforts from circulation, and they remain to this day in a limbo perhaps well deserved. One of the few anecdotes attaching itself to the playwright's early life holds that on Anouilh's marriage in 1932 to the actress Monelle Valentin, Jouvet "gave" the young couple some opulent stage properties left over from his production of Giraudoux's *Siegfried* (pr., pb. 1928; English translation, 1930) to furnish their otherwise bare apartment; not too long thereafter, with *Siegfried* scheduled for revival, Anouilh and his wife returned home to find their flat stripped clean of furniture. Anouilh, meanwhile, was beginning to attract favorable attention with his attempts at playwriting; a sale of film rights to Hollywood around 1934 proved sufficient to assure his financial independence—despite the fact that the play, *Y avait un prisonnier*, was never filmed and has since been repudiated by its author.

Following the runaway success of *Traveller Without Luggage* in 1937, Anouilh settled into the life of the professional playwright. Divorced from Monelle Valentin, who had borne him one child, Anouilh around 1953 married an actress known professionally as Charlotte Chardon, with whom he had three more children. Soon thereafter, following the success of *The Lark*, Anouilh assumed increasing responsibility in the mounting of his plays, usually in collaboration with the director Roland Piétri.

Only after around 1968, with a cycle of generally superficial plays offered mainly as a pretext for his own involvement in their production, did Anouilh begin to inject an autobiographical element into his work. The character of Antoine de Saint-Flour, featured in several of the plays, is a successful (but harried) writer modeled clearly on the author in the manner of Neil Simon; several of these late plays also portray shabby casino orchestras similar to those in which Anouilh's mother played violin during the author's childhood. In any case, however, Anouilh appears to have been quite justified in attempting to divert public attention away from his life, all the more so as his work provides a most useful and reliable record. It is no exaggeration to say that the life of Jean Anouilh is most readily accessible through the history of the French stage in the mid-twentieth century.

ANALYSIS

The young Jean Anouilh arrived in Paris during one of the richest periods of French dramatic activity since the seventeenth century. Recently rescued from the commercial doldrums by a "Cartel" of four brilliant directors, infused with new life from abroad (German expressionism and the ground-breaking work of Luigi Pirandello), French drama in the late 1920's and the early 1930's enjoyed a genuine renaissance. Jean Giraudoux, previously known as a diplomat and a rather esoteric novelist, was charming even the crowds with his ethereal yet somehow earthy speculations on politics and love, joining such established talents as the Freudian Henri-René Lenormand, the neo-Shakespearean Jean Sarment, and the highly inventive Armand Salacrou, who was just then beginning to hit his stride as a singular interpreter of life as lived in a world of broken (and inevitably breakable) dreams. Receptive to such influences, Anouilh soon joined his perceptions to his innate sense of theater to forge a dramatic style that was uniquely and unmistakably his own, very much of its time yet destined, at its best, to prove timeless. Today, only the work of Giraudoux has achieved anything even approaching the staying power of Anouilh's finest efforts. Salacrou, at one time Anouilh's closest competitor, fell far behind him during the postwar years and never managed to regain his stride. Sarment

and Lenormand, even their best works now hopelessly dated, are all but forgotten except by students of the interwar French theater.

To a large degree, the abiding strength of Anouilh's dramaturgy resides in its basic theatricality, a polyvalent sense of play and playing that recalls and renews the most playful moments in the works of Molière and William Shakespeare. In the words of critic John Harvey, Anouilh discovered the secret early in his career, after *The Ermine*, when he ceased "toiling" at his material and began "toying" with it instead.

The Ermine, although the first of Anouilh's plays to attract widespread recognition, is perhaps the least innovative in its presentation, its originality residing primarily in Anouilh's announcement and treatment of themes that would soon come to characterize his theater. Cast in a naturalistic mold, *The Ermine* contrasts the wealthy Monime with the underprivileged, ambitious Frantz, who will stop at nothing, even murder, in order to win her hand. Monime, however, does not decide that she loves Frantz until *after* he has claimed responsibility for the crime and turned himself in to the authorities. Such hopelessness, usually polarized between rich and poor, would continue to haunt Anouilh's would-be lovers throughout the rest of his career as a playwright.

Although the masterful *Thieves' Carnival* had already been written by the winter of 1936-1937, it was *Traveller Without Luggage*, produced during that season by the illustrious Pitoëffs (Georges and Ludmilla), that truly secured Anouilh's reputation as a dramatist. In total control of his material for the first time, Anouilh moves deftly and playfully between satiric farce and near-tragedy only to conclude, with a self-mocking coup de théâtre at the end, that the concept of tragedy has long since outlived its usefulness. A similar undercutting of tragedy characterizes Anouilh's memorable treatment of time-honored classical themes in *Antigone*, whose heroine consciously gives her life in vain. Both plays, however, were among the first to be classified by their author under the heading of "black" plays, perhaps because they are too bleak and pessimistic to be considered wholly tragic.

Closely related to the "black" plays are the early "pink" plays, ostensible comedies in which, as the author has observed, there are nevertheless woven fine strands of black. Even when cast in the comic mode, Anouilh's personal vision remains profoundly pessimistic, hinting at the corrosive effects of life-as-lived and the frequently intolerable burdens of the past. *Dinner with the Family*, about a married man who rents a house for one evening and hires actors to represent his family in order to impress his would-be second mistress (or wife), is at once the most frankly theatrical and the most successful of the pink plays and remains one of Anouilh's finest achievements.

Owing mainly to the resonant, if ambivalent, success of his *Antigone*, Anouilh in the 1940's acquired a reputation as a "writer-thinker" whose plays merited serious evaluation for their "ideas" alongside the works of such consciously philosophical dramatists as Albert Camus and Jean-Paul Sartre. Anouilh, who had never made any claim to writing anything but playable theater, was miscast in such company, and his "ideas," in consequence, were frequently found wanting. His strongest plays, however, do express a worldview by no means incompatible with Sartre's existentialism or Camus's speculations on the Absurd. Like Sartre, Anouilh presents characters "in situation" and totally at the mercy of their own actions, with no deity available to rescue them (except in the most blatantly contrived of self-consciously theatrical situations). Long since corrupted by conflicting interests recalling those of Sartre's bourgeois *salauds*, the world inhabited by Anouilh's characters is a disquieting place, with communication among mortals (let alone love) as impossible as in Sartre's *Huis clos* (1944; *No Exit*, 1946), and for most of the same reasons. Dehumanized by poverty, conditioned by their aspirations to expect a world of satisfactions that simply does not exist, the have-nots among Anouilh's characters, spiritual descendants of Frantz in *The Ermine*, experience an awareness of the Absurd not unlike that of the murderous Martha in Camus's *Le Malentendu* (1944; *The Misunderstanding*, 1948).

Anouilh's work, however, differs profoundly from that of Sartre and Camus in that ideas are secondary in importance to the prime value of dramatic art; never presented solely on their own merits, the ideas to be found in Anouilh's theater are of interest to the author only insofar as they help him to present, or the audience to understand, the motivation of his characters. It is therefore more than a bit hyperbolic to see in *Antigone*, as did a number of commentators at the time, a reactionary counterpoise to the existentialist, politically liberal stance of Sartre's *Les Mouches* (1943; *The Flies*, 1946). Given Anouilh's lack of religious belief, it is wholly natural that Antigone be disabused of the faith that supposedly motivates her actions, just as the "sainthood" of Becket in Anouilh's later play will be attributed to wholly aesthetic, nonreligious, and "human" standards of behavior. A number of critics also erred in their assumption that Creon, the pragmatist, emerges somehow as the hero of *Antigone*; there are simply no heroes in Anouilh's theatrical universe, and the playwright's main point throughout the play is to stress the eventual futility of *all* human action.

During the years following World War II, Anouilh expanded his repertory to include such new categories as the "shining" or "brilliant" (*Pièces brillantes*), "grating" (*Pièces grinçantes*), and quasi-historical (*Pièces costumées*) plays. An offshoot of the prewar *Pièces roses*, or pink plays, the *Pièces brillantes* offer a particularly sophisticated form of satiric comedy, or comic satire; in the view of critic Lewis Falb, the plays resemble the diamonds recalled in their title in that they are sparkling, many-faceted, yet cold and hard at the center. Perhaps best known of the *Pièces brillantes* is *Ring Round the Moon*. Recalling the ludic wit of Oscar Wilde's *The Importance of Being Earnest: A Trivial Comedy for Serious People* (pr. 1895), *Ring Round the Moon* features twin brothers intended to be played by the same actor, with split-second entries and exits. Also notable among the "brilliant" plays are *The Rehearsal* and *Mademoiselle Colombe*.

Trenchant social satire, never far from the surface in any of Anouilh's plays, rises to a featured position in the "grating" plays, presumably so named because they are designed to set one's teeth on edge. Featuring intentionally disagreeable characters often presented in broad caricature, the "grating" plays recall such early "black" plays as *The Ermine* and *Restless Heart* in their treatment of the necessary compromise between aspirations and reality. *Ardèle* and *The Waltz of the Toreadors*, linked by common featured characters, are perhaps the most notable of the earlier grating plays; others include *Ornifle*, a generally weak reworking of the Don Juan theme, and *Poor Bitos*, a biting political satire juxtaposing World War II and the French Revolution. Anouilh's finest plays during the 1950's, however, were two of his somewhat misnamed "costume" plays, historical at least in setting, which are about as close as he ever came to writing true "plays of ideas." Both *The Lark* and *Becket* remain thought-provoking as well as highly playable, inviting the audience to speculate on what might have been going on in the characters' minds as they performed the actions now duly recorded in the pages of history.

Like Albert Camus in his *Caligula* (wr. 1938-1939, pb. 1944; English translation, 1948), Anouilh made no claim to a faithful re-creation of history, or even to writing "historical" plays. As with Camus, history serves as little more than a pretext—a fecund source of potentially fascinating theatrical characters. Earlier in his career, Anouilh, like Giraudoux and several others just before him, had appropriated the characters and setting of classical mythology to make some very contemporary theatrical statements, of which *Antigone* is the best; during the 1950's, history came to serve him much as mythology had done earlier. Devoid of faith and admittedly uncomfortable with the concept of sainthood, Anouilh in *The Lark* and *Becket* revisits the lives of two saints in order to present them in wholly human terms. As seen by Anouilh, Joan of Arc and Thomas à Becket are heroic figures, high-principled to be sure, but hardly otherworldly. Joan, offered a reprieve, pragmatically chooses martyrdom in order to provide a shining example for posterity; Thomas, denied the consolation of true belief, has adopted instead an aesthetic standard of behavior that dictates that he do the best possible job at whatever he is supposed to do, even at the cost of his life. Remarkable in their affirmation of basic human dignity, *The Lark* and *Becket* remain

among the finest of Anouilh's efforts, equal or superior in vigor to such comparable efforts as Maxwell Anderson's *Joan of Lorraine* (pr., pb. 1946) or T. S. Eliot's *Murder in the Cathedral* (pr., pb. 1935).

Some ten years after the success of *Becket*, Anouilh resumed work on a new cycle of "grating" plays that he had in fact begun even before *Becket* with *The Fighting Cock*, the latter a dark-edged comedy satirizing, among other things, the "postmodern" drama of Samuel Beckett, Eugène Ionesco, and the early Arthur Adamov. By the late 1960's, however, Anouilh had himself assimilated many of the perspectives and techniques of the newer dramatists and had begun incorporating them into his own work. *Les Poissons rouges*, generally considered to be the finest play in the new cycle, dispenses with chronology in order to present various stages in the protagonist's life, all compressed into the space of one particularly trying day. A parallel cycle of "baroque" plays, often featuring some of the same characters, has proved somewhat less successful, but the strongest of them, such as *Dear Antoine*, have been well received in production.

TRAVELLER WITHOUT LUGGAGE

Frankly derived from such sources as Giraudoux's *Siegfried*, which deals with an amnesiac veteran of World War I, and Jean Cocteau's *La Machine infernale* (1934; *The Infernal Machine*, 1936), a playful reworking of the Oedipus legend, *Traveller Without Luggage* nevertheless served notice of a new and highly innovative talent. Gleefully exploiting the conventions and resources of the stage, at times assuming the spectator's familiarity with his obvious sources, the young Anouilh both charmed and disconcerted his audiences by proving, at least in theatrical terms, that there is in life no problem too large to run away from.

In skillful parody of the Oedipus legend, Anouilh presented as his protagonist an amnesiac veteran known only as "Gaston," who is presumably in search of his own identity. Unlike Oedipus, however, Gaston will resolutely—and successfully—turn his back on the overwhelming evidence at hand.

Institutionalized for eighteen years since the Armistice, Gaston has been interviewed by nearly three hundred families in search of a missing son or brother, and even as he meets with the prosperous, respectable Georges Renaud, there are supposedly five or six other families just offstage, eagerly awaiting their turn. Considerable tension soon develops between the mounting evidence that Georges Renaud has at last found his brother Jacques and Gaston's increasing revulsion against the character of Jacques as revealed. Jacques, it seems, was for the eighteen known years of his life a most disagreeable fellow who shot birds out of trees, crippled his best friend by pushing him down a flight of stairs, and eventually slept with his brother's wife. In further parody of the Oedipus material, Gaston keeps asking questions in relentless pursuit of the hideous truth; quite unlike Oedipus, however, he will feel no constraint to live with what he has learned. Over the years, Gaston has apparently envisioned himself as a *tabula rasa* about to acquire the imprint of a joyous childhood, and he will certainly not stop now. Ironically, the cold obstinacy with which Gaston refuses to accept his identity amply proves, to the satisfaction of both the audience and his fellow characters, that he is in fact Jacques Renaud.

Crucial to the developing action is the figure of Georges Renaud's wife, Valentine, whose abiding love for the seemingly unlovable Jacques has survived the eighteen years of his absence. Anticipating by several weeks her husband's planned interview with the "living unknown soldier," Valentine entered the asylum disguised as a laundress, and she maneuvered the unsuspecting Gaston into an amorous encounter. Horrified to learn that he has thus been tricked, Gaston remains unmoved by Valentine's unquestioning love and acceptance—even after the revelation that Valentine had loved Jacques first and had subsequently married his older, established brother only for reasons of financial expediency. Georges, for his part, remains understanding, perhaps even forgiving, but for Gaston that is not enough. Oddly, the affair with Valentine appears to strike him as the least forgivable of Jacques Renaud's many recorded dastardly deeds, and he remains resolutely "pure," indeed even priggish, in her presence. Valentine, whose love for Jacques has long since been stripped of illu-

sions, urges Gaston to return to the human race, accepting both himself and her. As proof of his identity, she asks him to look for a scar on his back, the remnant of a lover's quarrel shortly before Jacques's departure for the front, when Valentine suspected Jacques of infidelity and jabbed him with a hatpin.

The device of the scar, surely the most obvious of Anouilh's allusions to the Oedipus legend, ironically becomes the agent of Gaston's eventual and unabashedly theatrical deliverance. The scar is there, and Gaston bursts into tears (offstage) when he sees it in the mirror, but it is not long before he craftily turns Valentine's love against her, using the scar as evidence to "prove" that he is in fact someone else. Like the amorous female Sphinx in *The Infernal Machine* who has told Oedipus the answers to the riddle in the hope of winning his affections, Valentine finds herself thrust aside by the machinations of an overweening masculine ego. For Gaston, though, there will be no eventual reckoning or even recognition. In place of tragedy, Anouilh seems to be saying, there is for most people only tedium, made bearable at best by a seemingly limitless capacity for self-delusion.

The controversial ending of *Traveller Without Luggage*, alternately criticized or misconstrued by observers, merely suggests that modern man, his back to the wall, will either seek refuge in daydreams or lie, cheat, and steal. Gaston in effect does both, exchanging his "real" life for one chosen after his fancy. Had Anouilh sent Gaston off to a literal castle in Spain, he could hardly have made his message more explicit; the English country house with "marvelous ponies" will surely do in a pinch. Far from being "rescued" by a deus ex machina in the person of the little English boy who needs an adult "nephew" in order to claim his inheritance, Gaston has in fact chosen the thoroughly human hell of anonymity, rejecting Valentine's promise of a life (likened to a full page of writing) "full of spots and crossed-out words, but also full of joys." Gaston's refuge, if such it may be called, is hardly preferable to that of the ostrich.

Nearly forty years after the first performances of *Traveller Without Luggage*, the play's—or Gaston's—basic premise was intriguingly and rather effectively questioned by Eugène Ionesco in a play suggestively titled *L'Homme aux valises* (pr., pb. 1975; *Man with Bags*, 1977). In Ionesco's play, the anonymous protagonist trudges through at least forty years of recent history lugging two heavy suitcases that he doggedly refuses to put down for fear of losing them, and with them his identity. Oddly replicating Valentine's appeals to Gaston, Ionesco makes the point that while identity and heredity may be cumbersome, they are all that one can confidently claim and are at the very least a point of departure for one's actions; without them, one might as well be dead.

THE ARREST

Curiously, the theatrical season of *Man with Bags*, 1975, also brought forth a new play by Anouilh titled *The Arrest*, itself a thought-provoking coda to Gaston's concept of identity. Its title no doubt an intentional double entendre embracing cardiac arrest as well, *The Arrest* expands to two hours the final moments in the life of an aging gangster, fatally wounded in a motor accident while fleeing the police. Indebted for its structure to Salacrou's *L'Inconnue d'Arras* (1935), which dramatizes the last thoughts of a suicide, *The Arrest* poses a new, pertinent, and most intriguing question: Is not the deepest (and most futile) human need that of being "understood"? Breathing his last, the hoodlum Frédéric Walter asks many questions about his life, and is fortunate enough to have them answered by the avuncular Inspector, who, like Victor Hugo's Javert in *Les Misérables* (1862; English translation, 1862), has devoted his life's work to learning the habits and lifestyle of one particular criminal. As Walter prepares to die, the Inspector helps him to "understand" himself far more effectively than any parent, child, wife, mistress, or psychoanalyst ever could. As the Prayer of St. Francis implies, it is far more human to seek to be understood than to understand, and Frédéric Walter is surely no saint. Unlike Gaston, however, he both seeks and finds the truth about himself in highly memorable theatrical terms.

DINNER WITH THE FAMILY

Written soon after *Traveller Without Luggage*, although not staged until some four years later, *Dinner with the Family* is perhaps the strongest and most memorable of Anouilh's "pink" plays, with a highly entertaining restatement of the author's characteristic themes.

Like Gaston of *Traveller Without Luggage*, Georges of *Dinner with the Family* longs for, and seeks to re-create, an idyllic life quite different from the one that he has found himself obliged to lead. A young man of some means, he has rented a charming country house for one evening in order to impress a young woman with whom he has fallen in love; to represent his parents, he has hired an aging actor and actress who at first appear to need a considerable amount of coaching in their roles.

As the action proceeds, the various threads of Georges's dream begin to unravel, if never quite completely. His parents, it seems, are very much alive and very demanding of Georges's time and money, as are his wife, Henriette, and a rather sympathetic mistress named Barbara, who happens to be the wife of Georges's best friend, Robert. It is Barbara who precipitates much of the early action by warning Georges, in a telephone call, that Henriette has threatened to rid the house of freeloaders—his parents included—if Georges does not return at once. As in *Traveller Without Luggage*, considerable tension develops between the protagonist's aspirations and the somewhat more sordid reality of his life. Georges, however, is a considerably more sympathetic character than is Jacques/Gaston; he is portrayed throughout as a fundamentally decent man whose sustained attention to the needs of other people has hampered his own emotional development.

Counterpointed by the presence of the two professional actors, who frequently offer their opinion as to how a particular scene should be played, the various levels of reality and artifice in Georges's life remain in delicate balance throughout the play. His marriage, it seems, was arranged by his parents as a solution to their own financial woes, and they have in fact been sponging off him ever since. His wife, although she professes to love him, may well be incapable of love, and Robert (with his wife) has joined the small army of freeloaders even as he has come to envy and detest his erstwhile boyhood friend. The only sane or sympathetic character in the lot is Barbara, who loves

Georges deeply and without illusion. A close spiritual descendant of Valentine Renaud, Barbara alone can see, or will admit, that Georges's life has been nearly devoured by the demands of his family and other hangers-on; in the final analysis, she loves Georges enough to grant him his right to freedom. Isabelle, the charming young woman with whom Georges has fallen in love, may well represent his last chance to "reclaim himself," and Barbara will not stand in his way.

Criticized in its time as false or at the very least incredible, the ending of *Dinner with the Family*, although frankly contrived, now seems prophetic of a later generation in which "fresh starts," if not the rule, are at least no longer the exception. Today it seems almost plausible, if still humorous, that Georges be reunited with Isabelle for their long-delayed evening meal, sometime after which they will go off to the mountains and raise bees. Georges, in fact, may well be the first member of the dropout counterculture to have been portrayed sympathetically on the stage.

ANTIGONE

The best-known and most frequently performed of Anouilh's many plays, rivaled only by *The Lark* and *Becket, Antigone* is certainly one of his strongest efforts, as relevant and resonant today as it was when it first appeared onstage.

Near the last in a long (and sometimes distinguished) line of French plays with a classical setting that began to appear in the late 1920's, including Giraudoux's *Amphitryon 38* (pr., pb. 1929; English translation, 1938) and *Électre* (pr., pb. 1937; *Electra*, 1952), *Antigone* is an even stronger and more original play than it must at first have seemed. Understatedly theatrical in presentation, intended to be played in inconspicuous modern dress, Anouilh's restatement of the Antigone-Creon debate remains one of the theater's most powerful and memorable portrayals of the inevitable conflict between youth and age, between uncompromising idealism and the weathered voice of experience.

Displaying his usual sure sense of theater, Anouilh replaces the traditional Greek chorus with a single dinner-jacketed male figure, recalling the

Stage Manager in Thornton Wilder's *Our Town* (pr., pb. 1938). The Chorus, as he is known, steps forward on a stage full of characters to explain, in urbane tones, the role and function of each character in the drama that is to follow. As the action progresses, the Chorus will continue to serve as both the narrator and commentator, with a suitable coda at the end. Given Anouilh's reluctance to make public statements, the words and thoughts of *Antigone*'s Chorus are often quoted, no doubt with some justice, as being those of the author himself.

To a somewhat greater degree than Anouilh's earlier efforts, *Antigone* expresses the author's singular, profound, but often overlooked capacity for "poetry." Eschewing the overblown rhetoric of certain of his predecessors and contemporaries in the theater, Anouilh was nevertheless highly skilled at the creation of poetic imagery, often expressed in a simple, highly memorable conceit or metaphor. In *Antigone*, particularly in the title character's dialogues with her governess and with her fiancé, Hémon, such imagery helps to establish Antigone as a character and fix her in the spectator's mind. As her language shows, Antigone combines the strength of such characters as Valentine and Barbara with the impossible idealism generally associated with the author's male protagonists, making her more than a match for the toughened, world-weary Creon.

By far the most memorable feature of *Antigone* is the stylized yet credible debate between Antigone and her uncle, whose thankless task it has been to clean up the mess created by Oedipus and his family. In one scene, anticipating numerous more modern family quarrels, Creon accuses his niece of resembling her father in her refusal to leave well enough alone; her branch of the family, he observes, tends to ask too many questions and make trouble for everyone. Politically bound to leave one of her dead brothers unburied in order to keep the peace, Creon astonishes the headstrong, idealistic Antigone by informing her that he was unable to tell the two bodies apart and that he honestly does not care which was which; after all, he concludes, both boys were venal scoundrels quite different from the heroes envisioned by their adoring younger sister. Thus disabused of any true motivation for her actions, Antigone never-theless perseveres in defying Creon's orders, telling him that her "role" is to say no to him and die. Anouilh thus casts in purely heroic terms the refusal hitherto exemplified in the attempts of Gaston and Georges to escape the sordid pettiness of life. Al-though hers will be a hollow victory, exemplified in death, Antigone at least achieves a grandeur of sorts by refusing to accept her uncle's "adult" world of smoke-filled rooms, trade-offs, and compromise.

First performed during 1944 with World War II still in progress, *Antigone* initially drew both praise and blame from both sides of the political fence. There was little doubt in anyone's mind that Antig-one represented the uncompromising, if barely visi-ble, spirit of Free France, or Creon as those who col-laborated with the Germans, if need be, in order to keep the country running. Disagreement arose, how-ever, as to which of the characters was more sympa-thetically presented, and there were those who saw Antigone's martyrdom as sufficiently "meaningless" to render Creon, by default, the true hero of the piece. *Antigone*, however, typical of Anouilh's theater in general, seeks less to make a statement than to reflect the many ambiguities of life itself. Today *Antigone* still speaks eloquently of youth and age, idealism and compromise, to spectators yet unborn at the time of its first performance.

ARDÈLE AND THE WALTZ OF THE TOREADORS

No doubt somewhat disconcerted by the freight of meaning attached to *Antigone* by numerous well-intentioned spectators, Anouilh during the postwar years appeared to turn his back on "serious" play-writing, preferring instead to occupy himself primar-ily with comedy and satire. The "shining" plays all date from this period, as do the first of the "grating" plays. Two of the more successful among the latter are *Ardèle* and *The Waltz of the Toreadors*, linked by the common, slightly ridiculous character of Gen-eral Saint-Pé. An aged version of Georges and other would-be romantic lovers in the earlier "pink" plays, the General has never quite relinquished the dreams of his lost youth, even as he has outwardly accepted all the "necessary" trade-offs, substituting assigna-tions for idylls and bottom-pinching on the stairs for

stolen kisses in the garden. In *Ardèle*, the envious General declares a family crisis when he learns that his hunchbacked sister Ardèle has fallen in love with his son's hunchbacked tutor. A "ridiculous" love such as theirs cannot be allowed to survive, he proclaims. Presumably the love itself survives, but the lovers, alas, do not, choosing double suicide as the only "rea-sonable" alternative to the corrupt perversions of "love" that they have observed in the behavior of the General himself, his deranged wife Amélie, and other members of the family. Throughout the action, Anouilh steers a tight course between broad farce and melodrama, avoiding bathos through his use of paste-board caricatures in place of more fully rounded characters. A similar approach obtains in *The Waltz of the Toreadors*, in which the General, even more cynical than before, attempts reunion with a woman who briefly crossed his path nearly twenty years ear-lier. During the years since, the General has had sev-eral more brief encounters with Ghislaine but has thus far resisted the temptation to leave Amélie and elope with her.

Arriving at long last to claim the General as her own, Ghislaine confronts him with purported evi-dence of his wife's infidelity. After much slapstick and stage business, the charges turn out to be true, but by that time Ghislaine has fallen irretrievably in love with Gaston, the General's painfully shy male secre-tary. By the final curtain, four of the characters have threatened or attempted suicide, yet all remain alive to contemplate a future fraught with compromise and disillusionment. As in *Ardèle*, Anouilh in *The Waltz of the Toreadors* avoids bathos through the judicious use of caricature; here, however, both the General and his ostensibly insane wife emerge as more fully rounded and therefore credible characters than in the earlier play. The General, very much a weathered version of Anouilh's post-Romantic heroes, elicits the spectator's sympathy as he wonders precisely what has gone wrong in his life, where and when. His wife Amélie, equally credible, has chosen to ex-press her love through jealousy, feigning invalidism for more than a decade in order to keep her basically compassionate husband from deserting her. Grim and unrelenting in its satire of contemporary marriage and morals, *The Waltz of the Toreadors* is nevertheless highly playable and has been successfully filmed.

THE LARK

With the notable exception of *Antigone*, Anouilh achieved his greatest worldwide success with two of his "costume" plays—both of them drawn, loosely and somewhat ironically, from the recorded lives of saints. Making no claim whatever to interpret history (a process that he likens to the permanent dismantling of a favorite toy), Anouilh frequently discards or distorts such data as do not happen to suit him, altering chronology if need be in order to render playable the stuff of legend. In both *The Lark* and *Becket*, Anouilh is considerably less concerned with what happened than with what the characters might be able to tell the contemporary audience about itself. His presentation of Thomas à Becket, for example, shaves at least ten years off Becket's real age and deliberately exploits the nineteenth century myth, long since corrected, of Becket's Saxon ancestry. Such distortions, however, serve in the final analysis to create highly entertaining, thought-provoking theater.

Anouilh's mature sense of the theatrical serves him well indeed in *The Lark*, in which several different characters (including Joan herself) take turns narrating (and commenting on) the action in the manner of *Antigone*'s one-man Chorus. As in the earlier play, the action is assumed complete and immutable as the curtain rises; all that remains to be seen is the particular form that the retelling will take. The characters, who at first appear to be actors rehearsing a play-within-a-play, debate among themselves as to how the action will be presented; it is Cauchon who decides that Joan's entire career must be reviewed, rather than only her trial and execution. The action then proceeds in chronological order, interrupted only by the "testimony" of the various participants and witnesses. The scene of Joan's martyrdom, although realistically portrayed, is interrupted in quasi-cinematic style to present an opulent, triumphant final scene depicting the coronation of the erstwhile Dauphin at Rheims.

For critic Lewis Falb, *The Lark* remains a weaker play than *Antigone* precisely because it lacks ambiguity. In *The Lark*, he claims, the boundaries are too well defined to allow for true dramatic tension or suspense; unlike Antigone, Joan is far too obviously right, and she seems to know as much. Nevertheless, *The Lark* remains an impressive effort, frequently revived in production and one of the more memorable plays devoted to the life and death of Joan.

BECKET

Anouilh's growing fascination with the adaptation of "cinematic" techniques for the stage, adumbrated in the final scene of *The Lark*, takes over almost completely in *Becket*, by far the longest and most technically complicated of his many plays. Indeed, the text of *Becket* often reads more like a scenario than a play, with abundant flashbacks, rapid scene changes, and highly specific instructions as to how a particular line is to be delivered. It is hardly surprising, therefore, that *Becket* has been equally successful in its well-known film version, which is extremely faithful to the play.

Ranging freely across the conventions of the murder mystery, spy fiction, and broad political satire, Anouilh in *Becket* presents a highly convincing and entertaining portrayal of a close friendship gone sour—with repercussions far beyond personal loss. Containing some of Anouilh's finest, most memorable dialogue, *Becket* shows the audience "not a saint, but a man," a character closely descended from such other demanding protagonists as Antigone and Joan. Inner-directed, secretive, at times seemingly heartless, Anouilh's Thomas is a shrewd political manipulator and pragmatist who carries both in his heart and on his sleeve the defeat of his beloved Saxon people. The defeat, it seems, has made it impossible for Becket to believe in anything except himself and in the strict code of personal conduct that has somehow ensured his survival. When asked by the king if he believes in right and wrong, Becket replies enigmatically that he believes certain actions to be more "beautiful" than others, having long since chosen an aesthetic standard of behavior in the absence of ethical or moral imperatives. When the king, irritated by the clergy, impulsively names Becket chancellor, Becket is at first awed by the responsibility but soon warms to the task, proving himself to be a most adept and manipulative politician with an instinctive sense of power. As he tells the king, his personal code dictates that he do the best—or at least most "beautiful"—job he can at whatever he is called on to do. Such apparent loyalty will eventually rebound on the king, who, seeking to control the clergy by appointing his own man—the somewhat underqualified Becket—as Archbishop of Canterbury, finds that he has unwittingly provided himself with the most formidable and indomitable of adversaries. Becket, committed as usual to performing any appointed task to the best of his ability, dedicates his skills to defending an embattled Church against the Crown. As presented by Anouilh, Becket's apparent change of allegiance is most readily understood by the audience, but not by the king.

Closely balanced between comedy and pathos (or perhaps even pathology), Anouilh's Henry II is one of his most masterful if least admirable creations. Weak, petulant, self-indulgent, and henpecked by his wife and mother, Henry emerges as a most incompetent and impulsive ruler, a compulsive womanizer with more than a trace of latent homosexuality. Trembling with rage, he responds to Becket's apparent defection with all the hysteria of an abandoned mistress, seeking mindless vengeance even as he hopes against hope for an eventual reconciliation with his erstwhile friend and boon companion. Anouilh, in whose work the lack or loss of close friendship has always loomed large, achieves remarkable results in his attribution of the king's vengeance to a friend's perceived betrayal. As the king lies almost paralyzed with unrequited love for Becket, unable even to give orders, his henchmen decide to "rescue" him by assassinating Becket, their movements eerily orchestrated by the gradually amplified "beating" of the king's heart.

Unwieldy and expensive to produce, perhaps a shade too long and discursive, *Becket* is nevertheless a superb play. Together with *Antigone*, *The Lark*, and *Traveller Without Luggage*, and perhaps the strongest

of the pink and grating plays, it secures Anouilh's international reputation as one of the century's most versatile and significant dramatists.

BIBLIOGRAPHY

Carrington, Ildiko de Papp. "Recasting the Orpheus Myth: Alice Munro's *The Children Stay* and Jean Anouilh's *Eurydice*." *Essays on Canadian Writing* 66 (Winter 1998): 191-203. Examines the way in which Munro's characters are recast from Anouilh's *Eurydice* in order to reject his conception of a pure, fated love.

Falb, Lewis W. *Jean Anouilh*. New York: F. Ungar, 1977. Explores Anouilh's life and works. Index and bibliography.

Grossvogel, David I. *The Self-Conscious Stage in Modern French Theatre*. New York: Columbia University, 1958. Explores the history and criticism of twentieth century French theater. Bibliography and index.

Guicharnaud, Jacques. *Modern French Theatre: From Giraudoux to Genet*. 1961. Rev. ed. New Haven, Conn.: Yale University Press, 1972. Examines critical playwrights and prominent themes of modern-day French theater.

Harvey, John. *Anouilh: A Study in Theatrics*. New Haven, Conn.: Yale University Press, 1964. Provides criticism and interpretation of Anouilh's works. Bibliography.

McIntire, H. G. *The Theatre of Jean Anouilh*. London: Harrap, 1981. An introductory survey of Anouilh's plays. Counters the criticism of his work and suggests a new approach to understanding his place in French theater. Bibliography and index.

Pronko, Leonard C. *The World of Jean Anouilh*. 1961. Rev. ed. Berkeley: University of California Press, 1968. Provides criticism and interpretation of Anouilh and examines his place in French theater. Bibliography.

David B. Parsell

LUDWIG ANZENGRUBER
Ludwig Gruber

Born: Vienna, Austria; November 29, 1839
Died: Vienna, Austro-Hungarian Empire; December
10, 1889

PRINCIPAL DRAMA

Der Pfarrer von Kirchfeld, pr. 1870, pb. 1872
Der Meineidbauer, pr. 1871, pb. 1872 (*The Farmer
    Forsworn*, 1914)
Die Kreuzelschreiber, pr., pb. 1872
Elfriede, pr., pb. 1873
Die Tochter des Wucherers, pr., pb. 1873
Hand und Herz, pr. 1874, pb. 1875
Der G'wissenswurm, pr., pb. 1874
Der Doppelselbstmord, pr., pb. 1876
Der ledige Hof, pr., pb. 1877
Das vierte Gebot, pr. 1877, pb. 1878 (*The Fourth
    Commandment*, 1930)
Die Trutzige, pr. 1878, pb. 1879
Alte Wiener, pr. 1878, pb. 1879
Ein Faustschlag, pb. 1878, pr. 1879
Heimg'funden, pr. 1885, pb. 1889
Der Fleck auf der Ehr', pr., pb. 1889

OTHER LITERARY FORMS

Ludwig Anzengruber's literary reputation rests on
his plays, but he also produced a prodigious quantity of prose, including two novels, *Der Schandfleck*
(1877) and *Der Sternsteinhof* (1885); numerous novellas and short stories about village life, which are
often prose sketches for his plays and which he called
"Dorfgaenge"; many calender tales that use the figure of "Steinklopferhans" from his play *Die Kreuzelschreiber* as the focal character; and many short satiric and lyric works written to support the various
magazines, notably *Figaro*, for which he served as
editor. The novel *Der Sternsteinhof* is often considered Anzengruber's literary masterpiece.

ACHIEVEMENTS

Ludwig Anzengruber was the greatest and also the
last exponent of the Austrian folk play. His social and

educational background did not favor his becoming a
playwright for the leading highbrow theater of the
time, the Burgtheater in Vienna. His thorough acquaintance with the farces and melodramas of the
traveling theater, his genuine interest in common people, and his desire to contribute to the education of
the lower classes led him naturally to take up and to
improve on the Viennese folk play and the Austrian
dialect drama. Anzengruber was appalled by the lack
of intellectual honesty and by the absence of any contemporary scientific, social, or political material in
the plays that were performed for the lower classes in
the Viennese folk theaters. This was at a time when
the very fabric of Austrian society was threatened by
the conflicts resulting from the reaction to the 1848
revolution. In a time of strict censorship, the church
and the stage were the only places where people
could meet in large numbers and hope to find the
guidance and the answers that the partisan daily press
could not provide. Unfortunately, the established
church, as Anzengruber points out in his first play,
Der Pfarrer von Kirchfeld, could not be trusted to
furnish honest answers, for the church hierarchy was
desperately trying to reestablish its political power,
which had been severely reduced during the reign of
Joseph II. The Burgtheater was content to present the
"classics," an easy way to preserve its highbrow reputation and to stay clear of the threatening pen of the
censor. "No one would come forth," Anzengruber
wrote to a friend in 1876, "who would confront his
time from the stage, and someone had to do it—thus I
had to be the one!"

In order to achieve this self-proclaimed mission,
Anzengruber instinctively and effectively picked up
the popular Viennese folk play, mainly the farce, of
Johann Nestroy and Ferdinand Raimund. Leaving its
characteristic melodramatic form (frequent songs and
musical interludes) intact, he turned its stereotyped
characters into fully developed human beings. In addition, he confronted these characters with contemporary problems, rather than with the clichéd in-

Ludwig Anzengruber (Library of Congress)

trigues of the farce, and made them speak the dialect of the inhabitants of the Viennese suburbs and of the Austrian rural population.

During his lifetime, Anzengruber's plays were not deemed worthy of performance at the Burgtheater—the contemporary problem play was not suitable company for the classics. Indeed, Anzengruber's literary reputation was more quickly and more firmly established in Germany and in Scandinavia than in his native Austria. By turning the Viennese farce and the Austrian regional folk play into the realistic problem play, Anzengruber came to represent an Austrian counterpart to Henrik Ibsen and Gerhart Hauptmann. He raised a form considered fit only for the suburban and provincial theaters to a level that made it finally acceptable for the Burgtheater. This new status for the folk play was synonymous with its demise: Once accepted at the leading theater, the folk play, transformed into a modern problem play, could not be considered a *Volksstück* any longer. Anzengruber thus represents both the zenith and the end of the Austrian folk play. No one would even consider calling the

plays of more contemporary playwrights such as Wolfgang Bauer or Peter Turrini *Volksstück*, although many of their plays use the characters, the situations, and the language of the traditional Austrian folk play.

BIOGRAPHY

Ludwig Anzengruber was born in Vienna on November 29, 1839. His father had moved to Vienna from his parents' farm to become a minor official in the Imperial civil service. At the same time, he tried his hand as a playwright and even had one of his iambic plays performed with moderate success. Anzengruber was keenly aware of his father's poetic and dramatic attempts, as well as of the fact that the elder Anzengruber never achieved any financial success with his pen. Anzengruber's early, mostly unpublished literary work refers frequently to his father's literary talent and his own hope to follow in his father's footsteps.

After the early death of his father, Anzengruber grew up in the care of his mother and his grandmother. It was particularly the mother who influenced the career of the young man; she allowed him to terminate his schooling and to take up painting and engraving for a short time, and later, after a brief apprenticeship in a bookstore, to try himself as an actor. So strong was his mother's devotion that she gave up her small business to accompany her son on all his theatrical journeys through the provinces of the Austrian Empire. Many of Anzengruber's plays have at their center the figure of the self-sacrificing and unfalteringly supportive mother; this focus is the dramatist's tribute to the woman who helped him through the bitter times of his early career and who died shortly after Anzengruber's first dramatic success.

Anzengruber had neither talent nor success as an actor: "I had little luck as an actor, and as a writer—I was diligently writing all the while—I had none." His constant contact with the stage, however lowly, provided him with a thorough knowledge of dramatic and theatrical technique, and the long days spent on the road allowed him considerable time for writing, but none of his early plays, including several librettos, brought him any financial or artistic success. At that time, when he and his mother had to pawn most of their meager possessions simply to survive, Anzengruber turned to the philosophy of Ludwig Feuerbach. He abandoned his belief in God, in any form of organized religion, and in the idea of Providence and of an afterlife. Anzengruber's plays, particularly his early ones, are dramatizations of Feuerbach's naturalistic-humanistic ethic: There is no life after death, they assert. Anzengruber, however, contrary to the traditional Viennese *carpe diem* attitude derived from this conclusion, added the injunction that one should live this life honestly, in harmony with nature, and with love and respect for one's fellow beings and for all living creatures.

In 1869, a relative was able to procure for Anzengruber a minor clerical position with the Viennese police. Most of his time was spent issuing certificates of good conduct, an activity that gave him an opportunity to study human character and to gain insight into a variety of interesting lives. At the time he took up his new position, he had already finished the manuscript of *Der Pfarrer von Kirchfeld* and, once more encouraged by his mother, submitted it to the Theater an der Wien in 1870. The play was immediately successful, and, after ten hard years, Anzengruber's dramatic apprenticeship had come to an end.

With his reputation as a dramatist firmly established, Anzengruber continued his literary output at an amazing rate until his death. *Der Pfarrer von Kirchfeld* was followed by *The Farmer Forsworn*, then by his first comedy, *Die Kreuzelschreiber.* Although his main creative period as a dramatist spanned the years between 1870 and 1877, he wrote an average of two plays per year until his death.

Although Anzengruber gained recognition in Austria, Germany, Scandinavia, and even in the United States—*Der Pfarrer von Kirchfeld* was performed as early as 1872 in Detroit—he was never able to achieve the large-scale popular success that would have allowed him to live comfortably. Thus, the playwright had to supplement his income with minor literary and journalistic hackwork until his death in 1889. The public, and therefore the producers, wanted to be entertained rather than educated, and they found this entertainment in the increasingly popular operetta rather than in Anzengruber's naturalistic folk plays.

Even after having been awarded several prestigious literary prizes, the playwright was bitter about his lack of popular appeal: "You find me a minor producer in the field of journalism and prose," he writes in a letter, "but as concerns the dramatist, you find him quite discouraged." His dramatic work in his later years was not on the same level as that of his early creative period, and the founding of the Anzengruber Theater in 1889 was somewhat of an irony.

The dissolution of his unhappy marriage of sixteen years added to Anzengruber's depression. Discouraged, overworked, and in increasingly poor health, he died in Vienna on December 10, 1889. As is frequently the case, popular recognition came soon after his death. Between 1900 and 1915, there were close to fifty-five hundred performances of Anzengruber's plays on German and Austrian stages, and his plays continue to be regular fare on both the highbrow and the popular stages of the German-speaking countries.

ANALYSIS

During Ludwig Anzengruber's formative years as a dramatist, Austria was in the grip of a cultural revolution. There was a strong reaction to the enlightened rule of Emperor Joseph II and to the policies of his circle of humanistic advisers, which had led to the revolution of March, 1848. As a consequence, there was a constant battle fought between those who would reaffirm and continue those liberal-republican policies and those who wanted a return to absolutism, strengthened by a renewed treaty between the Roman Catholic Church and the state. The intellectual exponents of this battle formed political parties and rallied around highly partisan publications, whereas the Church attempted to mobilize the still-uneducated rural population to support its conservative policies, which culminated in the declaration of papal infallibility in 1870.

Anzengruber witnessed this manipulation of the rural population with great misgiving. He believed that a group of people who had not been given the chance to acquire an understanding of the issues involved—highly complex theological issues, such as the infallibility of the pope, the celibacy of priests, and civil marriage—should not turn out to be the prime casualties of these political battles. Sympathetic to the common people both through his family background and his early experiences, he set out to "confront his time from the stage" in a way and in words that the common people could grasp. As Anzengruber intended to educate the common people, he could not hope to achieve his goal by writing plays for the Burgtheater, the stage that produced a classic repertory of William Shakespeare, Pedro Calderón de la Barca, Johann Wolfgang von Goethe, and Friedrich Schiller, as well as Franz Grillparzer and Friedrich Hebbel. Because the Burgtheater was under the personal protection and supervision of the Austrian emperor, its directors steered clear of all controversial subjects, except to support the prevailing official policies.

Anzengruber thus directed his early dramatic works at the suburban Viennese theaters, such as the Theater an der Wien, the Josefstädter Theater, and the Leopoldstädter Theater, which were the popular stages for the *Volksstück*, the popular play, mostly written in Viennese dialect. Anzengruber himself acknowledged the influence of Friedrich Kaiser, who had modified the very popular magical plays of Raimund and the caustic local farce of Nestroy into the bourgeois character play. The most attractive feature of the *Volksstück* was the couplet, a usually satiric vocal interlude, which served as emphatic commentary on the farcical action of the plays.

Anzengruber, whose bitter apprenticeship as an actor had made him painfully aware of what was effective and successful on the popular stage, shrewdly chose the form of the *Volksstück*, included popular elements of the rural tales of Eduard von Bauernfeld, and made them the vehicle for his early polemic plays.

Anzengruber contributed to the development of Austrian drama in several ways. He elevated the popular Austrian farce to the level of the serious problem play while retaining the ingredients that ensured the former's popular appeal. The musical interludes, particularly the couplet, allowed him, at least for a while, to compete with the growing popularity of the French operetta while still being able to disseminate his liberal, anticlerical ideas and his popular version of the philosophy of Ludwig Feuerbach. His easy, nonlocalized use of the Austrian dialect makes him the dramatic equal of such renowned contemporaneous Austrian prose dialect writers as Peter Rosegger and Bauernfeld. The influence of his plays, with their description of the life of the Austrian rural population, can be seen in the work of later Austrian playwrights such as Karl Schönherr, Helmut Qualtinger, Wolfgang Bauer, and Peter Turrini.

DER PFARRER VON KIRCHFIELD

Civil marriage and the question of the celibacy of Catholic priests are the main topics in Anzengruber's first play, *Der Pfarrer von Kirchfeld*. The protagonist is a sympathetic priest whose name, Hell (meaning bright, clear, luminous, in German), suggests his enlightened outlook: He is more interested in the spiritual well-being of the parishioners of the small rural community in his charge than in the finer points of dogma and canon law. Not surprisingly, the manner in which he interprets his duties as a priest incurs the displeasure both of his superiors and of his secular lord, Graf Finsterberg (again, the name is symbolic, meaning dark, gloomy, obscure). The simple people of Hell's parish are confused about the new papal directives, and Hell has no answers to their naïve questions. His humanistic approach to his duties is turned against him by Finsterberg, who has discovered that Hell has fallen in love with a girl in his employ. After the priest, in contravention to directives, has blessed the marriage of a Catholic with a non-Catholic and has given a church burial to a suicide, Finsterberg makes him officiate at the marriage of the girl he secretly loves and then orders him before a church tribunal. Hell submits to this vindictive judgment and prevents his parishioners from reacting violently when they hear that they will lose their popular pastor.

Anzengruber's discussion of church dogma is flawed, and many of his accusations against the clerics are unfounded and illogical, but he manages to create a powerful figure, which serves to enhance the popular appeal of the play. Here it is the character of Wurzelsepp, the simple, rural man who is turned misanthrope and atheist by his having been excommunicated for marrying a non-Catholic. It is he who discovers Hell's secret love and brings about the priest's downfall, but it is also he who is reconverted by Hell's magnanimity when he asks the priest to grant a church burial to his mentally disturbed wife, who has killed herself. In a sense, the true main characters of the play are Wurzelsepp and his wife, the former changed into a misanthrope by the insensitive application of church dogma, the latter driven insane by the insupportable strain between her love for her faith and for her husband.

The success of the play, described by critics as the "most genuine popular play in years," indicated that Anzengruber had chosen both the right subject matter and the appropriate form to reach his audience. In addition, the dramatist made his characters speak, not in the localized dialect of his rural Tyrolean setting, but in a supraregional conversational Austrian language, which allowed stages all over Germany and Austria to perform the play with only minor modifications.

THE FARMER FORSWORN

Anzengruber acknowledged Shakespeare as one of the few dramatists whom he had read and whom he emulated, particularly in his early plays. This influence is evident in his second play, *The Farmer Forsworn*, the main character of which is a villain in the tradition of Shakespeare's *Richard III* (pr. c. 1592-1593). Mathias Ferner has managed to gain control of his dead brother's farm by destroying the latter's will and by perjuring himself. The rightful heirs, Jakob and Vroni, his brother's illegitimate children, had to leave their father's farm, which is to belong to Ferner's daughter Creszenz and her future husband, Toni, the son of the second-richest farmer of the area. Franz, Ferner's son, is supposed to become a priest— Ferner thinks that this will, in part, atone for his own perjury—but he has studied agriculture instead. In the true tradition of the Austrian Baroque tragedy, Ferner, who believes himself safe, is brought to justice in the end. A letter, which he had believed lost and which contains proof of his perjury, is found by Vroni at her grandfather's house. Ferner's own son, Franz, prevents his father from gaining possession of the damaging document by force; Ferner, after apparently shooting and killing his son, finds refuge from a thunderstorm in the house of an old woman who is just about to tell her nieces the story of a farmer who

has perjured himself and who has finally been taken away by the devil. Ferner, who cannot help but listen to the story, dies of remorse, shock, and fear. Vroni and Franz, Toni and Creszenz are married at the end of the play.

In the figure of Mathias Ferner, Anzengruber created a tragic figure of much greater dimensions than any of the characters in *Der Pfarrer von Kirchfeld*. Abandoning topical subjects, he drew a powerful image of rural greed, but pointed out to his audience the fact that such figures were exceptional in the rural areas and that in the long run, truth, honesty, and selfless love would find at least poetic justice.

DER G'WISSENSWURM

Many of Anzengruber's plays can be grouped into pairs—two plays dealing with related topics, one in comic and the other in tragic form. *The Farmer Forsworn* deals with the problem of rural greed, the question of the rights of illegitimate children, and the attempt to buy forgiveness for past sins in the somber form of the Baroque tragedy; *Der G'wissenswurm*, Anzengruber's most frequently performed play, takes a lighthearted approach to the same subject.

Dusterer, Anzengruber's version of Tartuffe, constantly reinforces farmer Grillhofer's guilt feelings, stemming from an incident twenty-five years before, when he had driven Magdalen, a servant girl, from his farm after discovering that their illegitimate liaison was going to have consequences. Now, after a mild stroke and believing himself near death, Grillhofer finds the "worm" of his conscience stirred by his brother-in-law, Dusterer, who urges him to leave all his worldly possessions to his sister, Dusterer's wife, and to move to the city so as to have constant masses read for the salvation of his soul. Grillhofer is about ready to take the rural Tartuffe's advice, when he accidentally discovers the whereabouts of Magdalen. He finds that, far from having been ruined for life, she is a happily married shrew who gave up her illegitimate daughter soon after birth and does not even know what has become of the child. In the true tradition of comedy, the latter, a beautiful, vivacious girl, finds her way to her father's farm and absolves him from any guilt; she even thanks him for having brought her into the world.

The play emphasizes Anzengruber's anticlerical attitudes, albeit in comical form. God, the playwright asserts several times, has created human beings to enjoy life, and nobody should interfere with this enjoyment by trying to make people feel guilty for doing what is natural and enjoyable. The play is a rejection of the essentially ascetic Christian moral philosophy and reveals Anzengruber's strong indebtedness to Feuerbach.

Die Kreuzelschreiber

Die Kreuzelschreiber, Anzengruber's first comedy—it predates *Der G'wissenswurm* by two years—takes up all the topical themes of his first play, *Der Pfarrer von Kirchfeld*, and deals with them in a lighthearted way. Clearly modeled after Aristophanes' *Lysistratē* (411 b.c.e.; *Lysistratē*, 1837), the play is a satiric attack on the dogma of papal infallibility, the declaration of which increased already existing tensions between the church and state in Austria and Germany. The men of a small rural community have been persuaded to sign a petition in favor of a scholar who has come out against the new dogma—Anzengruber refers indirectly to Ignaz von Döllinger, a German theologian. All the older farmers put their name, or their "three crosses," on the petition, but soon they have cause to regret their action, as their wives are incited by the parish priest to refuse themselves to the men until the latter withdraw their signatures and repent for their sinful behavior by going on a pilgrimage to Rome.

After the usual comic complications, a tragic note enters, as the old farmer Brenninger is driven to suicide by the disturbance of his marriage. Now Steinklopferhans, Anzengruber's most famous *dramatis persona*, intervenes to settle the dispute. He arranges for the men to leave for Rome, but at the elaborate farewell ceremony, the wives discover to their chagrin that all the young girls of the village have decided to go along on the pilgrimage. In the end, jealousy, love, and common sense prove to be stronger than dogma.

Die Kreuzelschreiber succeeds in discussing a difficult theological question in a way that points out to the audience the problems of individual action in the face of abstract theological theory. It does so in a manner that is neither sententious nor ignorant of the real problems created for naïve people by such dogma. Steinklopferhans, the honest rural philosopher, has arrived at his truths not by studying dogma but by contemplating his own personal experience and by evaluating his relationship to nature and to other people. Near despair and death in his lonely quarry—the scene recalls an episode in Anzengruber's life, when he almost succumbed to typhoid fever—Steinklopferhans has his "epiphany." Suddenly, in an astonishing parallel to Ralph Waldo Emerson's "transparent eyeball" episode, he becomes aware of the only "dogma" that is to have validity for his life: "Nothing can happen to me! I am part of all this and all this is part of me! Nothing bad can ever happen to me!" Steinklopferhans is Anzengruber's spokesperson, articulating a philosophy modeled closely after Feuerbach's naturalist-humanist ideas, which, as noted above, inform Anzengruber's entire dramatic work.

The Fourth Commandment

For Anzengruber, as for Schiller, the stage was a "moral institution" more than a place for entertainment. Anzengruber is most successful in his comedies, however, which strike a delicate balance between instruction and entertainment. Thus, *The Fourth Commandment*, widely considered his dramatic masterpiece, lacks the dimension that gained for *Die Kreuzelschreiber* and *Der G'wissenswurm* both critical acclaim and popular success.

The Fourth Commandment is a social problem play that demonstrates Anzengruber's growing interest in naturalism, which emphasized the influence of milieu and heredity on the human character. The play centers on two Viennese families. In an ironic inversion of the Fourth Commandment, the well-to-do Hutterers force their daughter into a catastrophic marriage, while the working-class Schalanters contribute to their son's death in front of a firing squad and their daughter's becoming a prostitute. Only Eduard, from a family of honest and upright gardeners who sacrifice everything to allow him the necessary schooling, turns into a decent human being. As a priest, he is called on to be at Martin Schalanter's side when the latter is preparing to face the firing squad. In a moving final scene, Eduard asks the condemned man to ask his parents for forgiveness and reminds him of his duties according to the Fourth Commandment. In anticipation of the more strictly naturalist plays of Karl Schönherr and Hauptmann, Anzengruber has Martin reject this dogmatic advice: "My dear Eduard, you have no problems, you do not know that for many children the biggest disaster is to be brought up by their parents. You teach the children in school to honor their father and mother, but you should also tell the parents from your pulpit that they should be sure to lead their lives to deserve that honor."

OTHER MAJOR WORKS

LONG FICTION: *Der Schandfleck*, 1877; *Der Sternsteinhof*, 1885 (2 volumes).

BIBLIOGRAPHY

Howe, Patricia. "End of a Line: Anzengruber and the Viennese Stage." In *Viennese Popular Theatre: A Symposium*, edited by W. E. Yates and John R. P. McKenzie. Exeter, England: University of Exeter Press, 1985. This essay, from a collection on Viennese popular theater, examines Anzengruber's role in ending this genre.

Jones, Calvin N. "Ludwig Anzengruber." In *Nineteenth Century German Writers, 1841-1900*, edited by James Hardin and Siegfried Mews. Vol. 129 in *Dictionary of Literary Biography*. Detroit, Mich.: The Gale Group, 1993. A concise look at Anzenburger's life and works.

_____. "Poetry or Realism: Ludwig Anzengruber's *Die Kreuzelschreiber*." In *Negation and Utopia: The German Volksstück from Raimund to Kroetz*. New York: Peter Lang, 1993. A discussion of Anzengruber's *Die Kreuzelschreiber*.

_____. "Variations on a Stereotype: The Farmer in the Nineteenth Century *Volkskomëdie*." *Maske und Kothurn* 27, nos. 2-3 (1981): 155-162. A close look at farmer characters in the popular folk comedies of Austria.

Kuhn, Anna K., and Barbara D. Wright, eds. Providence, R.I.: Berg, 1994. A collection of essays that examines nineteenth and twentieth century Austrian and German drama. Bibliography and index.

Franz G. Blaha

GUILLAUME APOLLINAIRE
Guillaume Albert Wladimir Alexandre Apollinaire de Kostrowitzky

Born: Rome, Italy; August 26, 1880
Died: Paris, France; November 9, 1918

PRINCIPAL DRAMA

Les Mamelles de Tiresias, pr. 1917, pb. 1918 (*The Breasts of Tiresias*, 1961)
Couleur du temps, pr. 1918, pb. 1920
Casanova, pb. 1952

OTHER LITERARY FORMS

Guillaume Apollinaire's major importance as a writer lies in his poetry and his art criticism. He was part of a new age of experimentation in free verse and was closely involved both creatively and socially with the major figures in the Parisian avant-garde from 1905 to 1918. His literary career began in earnest in 1903 with a poem dedicated to a lost love and continued through the publication in 1910 of *L'Hérésiarque et Cie.* (*The Heresiarch and Co.*, 1965), a collection of twenty-three fantastical and haunting stories that have often been compared to the writings of Edgar Allan Poe. In 1911, he brought forth his first collection of poems, *Le Bestiaire* (*Bestiary*, 1978), and, in 1913, a perceptive book about cubism. In 1916, he published a novel, *Le Poète assassiné* (*The Poet Assassinated*, 1923), and the following year, he gave a lecture that anticipated the development of Surrealism.

ACHIEVEMENTS

Guillaume Apollinaire, who is considered one of France's most revolutionary and original poets as well as "the impresario of the avant-garde," never won a major award during his lifetime. He almost had enough votes to win the Prix Goncourt for *The Heresiarch and Co.* in 1910 and was proposed for the Legion of Honor in 1918 but was not made a member. From 1908 to 1909, Apollinaire gained a reputation as a leader in literary circles and as an art critic. Critics recognized the novelty of Apollinaire's inspiration and his originality of form; a few of them proclaimed him to be the "master of us all."

Apollinaire wrote many theoretical articles defining the most important trends in the visual arts while establishing his own place within the various art forms. Always ready for new experiences, he added another medium to his writings by recording three of his poems. His experimentation with new poetic forms continued from 1913 to 1916 with the creation of "lyrical ideograms," poem-drawings that were published in 1918 as *Calligrammes* (English translation, 1980).

All Apollinaire's experiments and achievements in poetry and criticism are reflected in the creation of his three major dramas. Although his involvement with the theater lasted only two years, what he achieved in that time indicates the extent of his creative imagination and the importance that he placed on experimentation, the exploring of new approaches, and the willingness to depart from antiquated formulas.

BIOGRAPHY

Guillaume Albert Wladimir Alexandre Apollinaire de Kostrowitzky was born in Rome on August 26, 1880. Mystery surrounded his birth until the publication of Marcel Adema's definitive biography in 1954. Apollinaire's birth was first reported officially in Rome on August 31, 1880, as a male child of a mother who wished to remain anonymous and whose father was unknown. His name was given as Guillaume-Albert Dulcigni. On September 29, he was baptized as Guillelmus Apollinaris Albertus de Kostrowitzky, son of Angelica de Kostrowitzky, but the father was still not mentioned. In November, Angelica officially recognized her son, although the identity of the father

was not publicly revealed until Adema established that Francesco Flugi d'Aspermont, member of a very patrician, influential Italian family, was indeed the father of Guillaume Apollinaire.

Flugi d'Aspermont was, at age forty, twenty-three years older than the unconventional Polish teenager, Angelica de Kostrowitzky. Shortly after they met, she became his mistress, eventually giving birth to two sons—Guillaume and Albert. Apollinaire knew who his father was, but he nevertheless took great delight in relating fictional, romantic stories about his parentage. To some, he declared that he was descended from Polish and Russian royalty, while to others, he represented himself as the son of a high clergyman of the Catholic Church. There was perhaps a grain of truth here: His father's family had served King Ferdinand II of Sicily and his uncle was a member of the Vatican hierarchy. Apollinaire, in creating these legends about himself, felt there was something enriching about a poet's life being as mysterious as his works often were.

Guillaume Apollinaire

After Flugi d'Aspermont abandoned Kostrowitzky and their sons, she went to Monaco and thereafter spent most of her life in France. Apollinaire, who started school in Monaco in 1887, was an excellent student, winning prizes in most subjects. He spent two years in colleges in Cannes and Nice (1897-1898), but apparently a lack of funds kept him from attending a university. He was already seriously thinking of becoming a writer, however, and prepared himself by reading widely and taking an interest in politics. With a friend, he started a newspaper in which he published his own poetry under the pseudonym of Guillaume Macabre. This early effort led to his lifelong interest and involvement in journalism.

In 1899, Apollinaire went to Paris with his brother, his mother, and her young lover, Jules Weil. Soon, financial difficulties drove Weil and the two boys to Stavelot, a small town in Belgium, while Kostrowitzky went to Spa to try her luck in the casino there. At Stavelot, Apollinaire wrote most of *L'Enchanteur pourrissant* (1909; the putrescent enchanter), inspired by local legends and folklore that combined well with his love for medieval tales of knights and Merlin the Sorcerer. Shortly after, however, Weil left the two boys in Stavelot with no money to pay their hotel bill. Appealing to his mother for help, Apollinaire received enough money for passage to Paris, with instructions to do a "midnight flit" from the hotel. Sneaking out at dawn, Apollinaire and his brother climbed steep mountain paths to the next small town, where they caught the Paris express. In 1900, Apollinaire wrote a one-act play based on this adventure. *À la cloche de bois* (the moonlight flit) was never performed or published and was his only drama before *The Breasts of Tiresias*.

Apollinaire was in Paris again but had no formal qualifications, no money, and no position. After a series of menial jobs, he began to write the first of his erotic novels. Eroticism, sexual pleasure, and love had an important part in his life and work from this time on, although many critics have implied that these writings were done solely for money. By chance, he met a German viscountess who hired him as a tutor for her young daughter, and he traveled to Germany, Austria, and Czechoslovakia with

them until 1902, when he returned to Paris as a bank clerk.

After his return, he entered into a period of intense literary activity. *La Revue blanche* published some of the poems he had written in Germany, and he acquired a circle of literary friends, Alfred Jarry, Léon-Paul Fargue, André Salmon, and Remy de Gourmont, with whom he met regularly. He began publishing his first journal, featuring some of his work as well as that of his new friends, and he also met the painters Pablo Picasso, André Derain, and Maurice Vlaminck. In May, 1905, Apollinaire wrote his first significant art review, "Picasso, peintre," examining Picasso's work, followed by subsequent reviews of the work of Henri Rousseau, Georges Braque, Henri Matisse, Giorgio De Chirico, Marc Chagall, Robert Delaunay, and many others. In 1907, Apollinaire met the painter Marie Laurencin, and they began a relationship that lasted until 1912.

The years from 1908 to 1914 were busy and productive ones for Apollinaire. He lectured on the Symbolist poets, collaborated with Jean Royere on the Symbolist review *La Phalange*, and traveled in the summer to Belgium and Holland. In 1909, after publication of *L'Enchanteur pourrissant*, Apollinaire moved to Auteuil with Marie Laurencin and edited classic erotic novels. In 1913-1914, he experimented with the new form he called *calligrammes*, a collaboration between verbal and visual language. Very much aware that revolutionary changes were about to occur in the arts, Apollinaire declared that the *calligrammes* were typographically precise at a time when typography was about to be replaced by two new methods of reproduction—the cinema and the phonograph. He predicted that the book would soon be replaced by the disc of the phonograph and the cinematographic film, with the result that literacy would no longer be based on one's ability to read and write and that a new language of living sounds that speak directly to the senses and feelings rather than to analytical reason would evolve.

When war began in Europe in 1914, Apollinaire tried to enlist in the French army. He was turned down because of his age (thirty-four) and his Italian citizenship but was eventually accepted into the artillery.

Apollinaire was deeply affected by the horror of war. His letters to friends and his poetry indicate that, for him, war was devoid of all glamour and was seen only in all its tragic futility. He was severely wounded in the head in March, 1916, and although he eventually recovered, he was much changed. In his last two years, in addition to publishing his war poems and *The Poet Assassinated*, he wrote introductions for exhibition catalogs and theater programs including one for Jean Cocteau's ballet *Parade* (1917). He also wrote and produced his own play, *The Breasts of Tiresias*, and was directing rehearsals for *Couleur du temps* (mood of the age) when he died in 1918, a victim of the Spanish flu.

ANALYSIS

Guillaume Apollinaire departed from classical features of drama such as the unities of time, place, and action and linear narrative. He insisted on the dramatist's right to exercise "poetic license" by complementing the main action of the play with secondary episodes, varying the tone of the dialogue from the pathetic to the burlesque and including many incredible episodes.

In the prologue to *The Breasts of Tiresias*, Apollinaire declared that the dramatist's universe is the stage, within which he or she is the creating god who can direct all things at will and not merely reproduce a so-called slice of life but bring forth life itself in all its truth. In the published preface, he elaborated on his conception of truth as being "true to nature" rather than being mere photographic imitation. As he defined his notion of naturalism, he also defined the avant-garde concept of Surrealism by declaring that when human beings wanted to imitate walking, they created the wheel, which does not resemble a leg. In the same way, human beings have unconsciously created Surrealism. He related this to drama by stating that the stage is no more the life it represents than the wheel is a leg. Apollinaire was proclaiming the end of illusionist theater, just as avant-garde painters and sculptors were demanding the end of illusionism in the visual arts. He made the point that illusionism had been stifling the imagination of writers and artists for a long time, and furthermore, "realistic theater" had become outdated with the introduction of the new medium of cinema, which could make realism far more palpable. Theater, then, must not be realistic, giving instead free rein to the writer's imagination.

In proclaiming his theoretical ideas, Apollinaire was not attempting to create a new set of rules to legitimize avant-garde movements such as Surrealism, Orphism, and cubism. Rather, he insisted that all artists must liberate their imaginations from the restrictions of formulas. Only then would they be free to experiment and to become more open to new ways of seeing.

THE BREASTS OF TIRESIAS

The Breasts of Tiresias was Apollinaire's only play to be performed and published during his lifetime. The theme centers on the virtue of having children in order to repopulate the country. The play opens with the heroine, Theresa, declaring that she is bored with having children and with the life of a woman and intends to become a man. She grows a massive beard and opens her dress to reveal a bosom of balloons that she tosses to the audience while declaring that she is now a man named Tiresias. She takes her husband's clothes, forcing him to don hers, and cries "no more children." He then makes an impassioned speech on the necessity for procreation, proclaiming that if she refuses to reproduce, he must take her place. In the last act, the husband has produced 40,051 children, and the country is threatened with famine. Theresa returns home, repentant, praising the virtues of fecundity.

Critical opinion was divided. Some critics insisted that the play was incoherent and accused the author of borrowing extensively from the French music hall. However, others declared that the play was a powerful demonstration of the progressive use of rhythm, imagination, and decor in the theater.

Although there have been no notable revivals of *The Breasts of Tiresias*, Apollinaire's theatrical innovations nevertheless influenced later twentieth century dramatists and directors. In the prologue to the play and the later preface to the published text, Apollinaire outlined his most original theories, including his ideas about a more imaginative architecture that included, among other features, a circular theater with two stages.

CASANOVA

Apollinaire was still working on *Casanova* when he died. He intended it to be an opera buffa, with Henri Defosse, of Sergei Diaghilev's Ballets Russes, composing the music. The score was not completed until 1920, and the play was never performed. This work is interesting mainly because of its theatrical conception. Apollinaire used an intricate device of disguise and deception in which a young girl, Bellina, is mistaken for a young boy, Bellino. There is also a play-within-a-play, wherein the boy-girl deception of the first act is now reversed to a girl-boy disguise. The third act features three duels, with Casanova killing two women disguised as Bellino. However, Casanova recognizes the third Bellino as the girl, Bellina, and the two burst into song celebrating their love. To further complicate the deception, Apollinaire planned to have the actors of the inner play perform while manipulating life-size puppets of their own characters, thus adding the reflection of a reflection that deliberately blurs the line between reality and fantasy.

COULEUR DU TEMPS

Couleur du temps was in rehearsal when Apollinaire died, with the only performance occurring on November 24, 1918. Some of his friends tried to stop the performance, feeling that the play was not daring enough. Its theme of war seemed out of date in a country now primarily pacifist. Although the text was published in 1920, documentation of the performance is scarce. It is known, however, that the sets that Maurice Vlaminck had agreed to paint were never made, and the music was not ready either.

OTHER MAJOR WORKS

LONG FICTION: *L'Enchanteur pourrissant*, 1909; *Le Poète assassiné*, 1916 (*The Poet Assassinated*, 1923).

SHORT FICTION: *L'Hérésiarque et Cie.*, 1910 (*The Heresiarch and Co.*, 1965).

POETRY: *Le Bestiaire*, 1911 (*Bestiary*, 1978); *Alcools: Poèmes, 1898-1913*, 1913 (*Alcools: Poems, 1898-1913*, 1964); *Calligrammes*, 1918 (English translation, 1980); *Il y a*, 1925; *Le Guetteur mélancolique*, 1952; *Tendre comme le souvenir*, 1952; *Poèmes à Lou*, 1955.

NONFICTION: *Peintres cubistes: Méditations esthétiques*, 1913 (*The Cubist Painters: Aesthetic Meditations*, 1944); *Chroniques d'art, 1902-1918*, 1960 (*Apollinaire on Art: Essays and Reviews, 1902-1918*, 1972).

MISCELLANEOUS: *Œuvres complètes*, 1966 (8 volumes); *Œuvres en prose*, 1977 (Michel Décaudin, editor).

BIBLIOGRAPHY

Bates, Scott. *Guillaume Apollinaire*. Rev. ed. Boston: Twayne, 1989. A chronological survey of the philosophical and aesthetic ideas of Apollinaire in relation to the facts of his life and the ideas of his time. Bibliography and index.

Bohn, Willard. *Apollinaire and the Faceless Man: The Creation and Evolution of a Modern Motif.* Cranbury, N.J.: Associated University Presses, 1991. An examination of the works of Apollinaire with emphasis on his portrayal of the face and his influence on others. Bibliography and index.

_____. *Apollinaire and the International Avant-garde*. Albany: State University of New York Press, 1997. A critical examination of Apollinaire, especially his relationship with the avant-garde artists. Bibliography and index.

Davies, Margaret. *Apollinaire*. London: Oliver and Boyd, 1964. Good critical study arranged on biographical lines.

Little, Roger. *Guillaume Apollinaire*. London: Athlone Press, 1976. Presents the essential biographical facts while placing the poet in his social and intellectual context.

Shattuck, Roger. *The Banquet Years: The Origins of the Avant-Garde in France, 1885 to World War I*. Rev. ed. Salem, N.H.: Ayer, 1984. An interesting journalistic and critical account of four artists, Henri Rousseau, Alfred Jarry, Eric Satie and Guillaume Apollinaire, and their creative age. Index.

Waggoner, Mark W., ed. *Guillaume Apollinaire: A Critical Bibliography*. Encinitas, Calif.: French Research Publications, 1994. A bibliography of critical works on Apollinaire. Contains indexes.

LouAnn Faris Culley

JOHN ARDEN

Born: Barnsley, England; October 26, 1930

PRINCIPAL DRAMA

All Fall Down, pr. 1955

The Waters of Babylon, pr. 1957, pb. 1964

Live Like Pigs, pr. 1958, pb. 1964

When Is a Door Not a Door?, pr. 1958, pb. 1967

Serjeant Musgrave's Dance: An Unhistorical Parable, pr. 1959, pb. 1960

The Business of Good Government, pr. 1960, pb. 1963 (with Margaretta D'Arcy)

The Happy Haven, pr. 1960, pb. 1964

Ironhand, pr. 1963, pb. 1965 (adaptation of Johann Wolfgang von Goethe's *Götz von Berlichingen*)

The Workhouse Donkey, pr. 1963, pb. 1964

Armstrong's Last Goodnight: An Exercise in Diplomacy, pr. 1964, pb. 1965

Ars Longa, Vita Brevis, pr. 1964, pb. 1965 (with D'Arcy)

Fidelio, pr. 1965 (adaptation of libretto of Ludwig van Beethoven's opera)

Left-Handed Liberty, pr., pb. 1965

Friday's Hiding, pr. 1966, pb. 1967 (with D'Arcy)

The Royal Pardon, pr. 1966, pb. 1967 (with D'Arcy)

The Vietnam War-Game, pr. 1967 (with D'Arcy)

Harold Muggins Is a Martyr, pr. 1968 (with Cartoon Archetypal Slogan Theater and D'Arcy)

The Hero Rises Up, pr. 1968, pb. 1969 (with D'Arcy)

The Soldier's Tale, pr. 1968 (adaptation of libretto by Charles-Ferdinand Ramuz; music by Igor Stravinsky)

The True History of Squire Jonathan and His Unfortunate Treasure, pr. 1968, pb. 1971

The Ballygombeen Bequest, pr., pb. 1972 (with D'Arcy)

The Island of the Mighty, pr. 1972, pb. 1974 (trilogy; with D'Arcy)

Henry Dubb Show, pr. 1973 (with D'Arcy)

Portrait of a Rebel, pr. 1973 (with D'Arcy)

The Non-Stop Connolly Show, pr. 1975, pb. 1977-1978 (6 parts; with D'Arcy)

The Little Gray Home in the West, pr. 1978, pb. 1982 (with D'Arcy; revision of *The Ballygombeen Bequest*)

Vandaleur's Folly: An Anglo-Irish Melodrama, pr. 1978, pb. 1981 (with D'Arcy)

Fire Plays, pb. 1991 (with D'Arcy)

Arden and D'Arcy Plays, pb. 1991

Plays, One, pb. 1994

Plays, Two, pb. 1994

OTHER LITERARY FORMS

An important work for understanding the dramaturgy and politics of John Arden is *To Present the Pretence* (1977), a collection of his essays that originally appeared in various publications over a number of years. Many of Arden's plays are also accompanied by informative prefaces, especially concerning the genesis and composition of individual plays, their production, and the dramatist's own sometimes stormy relations with the professional theatrical world. Arden's first novel, *Silence Among the Weapons*, was published in Great Britain in 1982.

ACHIEVEMENTS

Along with John Osborne, Arnold Wesker, and Harold Pinter, John Arden is one of the early leading playwrights of the so-called New Wave (or New Renaissance) of British drama. Encouraged primarily by the English Stage Company, directed by George Devine at London's Royal Court Theatre, the playwrights of the New Wave have given Britain some of the most lively drama in the contemporary world. Arden has been an important part of the movement, both through his own work and through his influence on later dramatists.

Throughout his career, Arden has been a controversial figure in his own country. None of his plays has enjoyed commercial success, and some have been attacked by critics. His best-known work, *Serjeant*

Musgrave's Dance, lost ten thousand pounds at the Royal Court Theatre; the critic Harold Hobson called the play "another frightful ordeal" and *Punch* dubbed it a "lump of absurdity." Arden's early critics complained that he sermonized and that his sermons were not clear. Audiences had trouble identifying with his central characters, and his plays were even called amoral. These confused reactions say as much about the ingrown nature of British drama at the time as they do about the plays themselves, though it is true that in his early plays the young playwright was struggling with his own uncertainties. Arden generally wrote in a mode resembling the "epic theater" of Bertolt Brecht, filling his plays with ballads, narration, emblematic actions and sets, and other "alienating" (that is, deliberately theatrical) effects. Arden's mode also draws on an older tradition in Britain: Besides Brecht, Arden has acknowledged the influence of Ben Jonson, William Shakespeare, and medieval drama. Part of Arden's achievement is that he has helped break down audience expectations of naturalistic drama to reintroduce the British to their own traditions.

Despite the initial critical reception of his work, Arden's reputation grew. Harold Hobson changed his opinion about *Serjeant Musgrave's Dance* as the play became popular with university theater groups. Eventually, it reached the status of a set text for secondary school examinations in English. Arden attained a peak of official acceptance in 1965 when the Corporation of the City of London commissioned him to write *Left-Handed Liberty* for the 750th anniversary of the signing of the Magna Carta. Thereafter, whether by choice or otherwise, Arden gradually drifted further away from the London professional theater, writing mostly in collaboration with his wife, Margaretta D'Arcy, and becoming more involved in experimental, community, and political theater.

Meanwhile, Arden's reputation spread abroad (particularly to Germany), and he has become a subject of scholarly study, including several books. This attention is deserved, even though Arden's work is uneven in quality. For example, the ambitious three-part work *The Island of the Mighty* is a disappointment, and some of the less ambitious short pieces are of minor interest. Arden's best plays seem to be several modern comedies, *The Waters of Babylon* and *The Workhouse Donkey*, and the historical parables *Serjeant Musgrave's Dance*, *Armstrong's Last Goodnight*, *The Hero Rises Up*, and *Vandaleur's Folly*. The key to Arden's best work is the same quality that appeals to university audiences: a combination of Dio-

British dramatist John Arden at the Evening Standard Drama Awards in 1960.
(Hulton Archive by Getty Images)

nysian energy with treatment of the big issues in today's world. As those issues are not likely to go away soon, probably Arden's dramatic reputation will continue to grow.

BIOGRAPHY

John Arden's development as a playwright can be explained in part by his background, which differs significantly from the London working-class background typical of fellow New Wave dramatists. The product of a Yorkshire middle-class family, Arden was educated at Sedbergh, a private boarding school in Yorkshire's remote northwest dales (where he had been sent to escape World War II bombing raids), took a degree in architecture from Cambridge University (1953), and proceeded to further his study of architecture at Edinburgh College of Art, receiving his diploma from that institution in 1955. Between Sedbergh and Cambridge, the future author of *Serjeant Musgrave's Dance* and writer for *Peace News* served in the military, mostly in Edinburgh, where he attained the rank of lance-corporal in the Army Intelligence Corps.

Arden's background in the North Country, home of medieval drama and balladry and the setting of most of his best work, is a major source of strength in his plays, as is evident from the salty language used in them. His background suggests that Arden was not born to his Socialist sentiments but arrived at them through a lengthy process of observation and deliberation. Such a process of development, involving constant challenge and considerable self-examination, would help account for the ambiguities in his earlier works and for Arden's characterizations of himself as having been a wishy-washy liberal, a sort of Hamlet of the New Wave. Possibly the young playwright also had mixed reactions to the new welfare state in Britain and to the prevailing doctrinaire atmosphere, especially in the universities, in which left-wing orthodoxy, with its assumptions and jargon, was sometimes reminiscent of Bible-belt fundamentalism: The New Jerusalem did not tolerate its sinners easily, and it found its American devils handy. Although polite and mild-mannered, Arden has always been strongly independent in his thinking. He chose,

for example, to study architecture rather than English in order to avoid compromising his creativity as a writer.

Arden's architectural study did not go to waste. It has contributed to his sense of dramatic structure and sometimes to the content of his plays. His education also gave him perhaps the strongest intellectual background of any of the New Wave playwrights. He practiced architecture in London for only two years, however, until his playwriting career was launched by the Royal Court's 1957 presentation of *The Waters of Babylon*.

That same year, Arden married Margaretta D'Arcy, an actress of Irish background. Not only have they had four sons, but also D'Arcy has been closely associated with Arden's career, first as a friendly critic/consultant and later as a collaborator. (An important distinction among their collaborative works is marked by the designations "by Arden and D'Arcy" and "by D'Arcy and Arden.") D'Arcy has influenced Arden's involvement in experimental, community, and political drama and his use of Irish material. Their travels together have also been influential, particularly two trips to the United States (Arden held guest lectureships at New York University in 1967 and, with D'Arcy, at the University of California at Davis in 1973), where they led politically controversial drama projects, and a stay in India (for the centennial celebrations of Mahatma Gandhi's birth), where they were shocked by the depth of that country's poverty. Their most controversial and effective collaboration was the six-part *The Non-Stop Connolly Show*, whose premiere in 1975 ran twenty-six hours. Critics such as Michael Cohen have called it the pair's most strident and convincing work, "probably the most ambitious attempt in English to dramatize working-class and socialist history." In 1988, the British Broadcasting Corporation aired *Whose Is the Kingdom?* (1982) in nine parts, a radio play about early Christianity.

Beginning in the 1960's, the Ardens' residence in the west of Ireland (County Galway) seemed to symbolize their distance from the London political and theatrical establishment—a distance that became manifest in their much-publicized dispute with the

Royal Shakespeare Company over its 1972 production of *The Island of the Mighty*. The Ardens ended up picketing the production. How much this unfortunate dispute affected Arden's career is hard to say, but it was certainly controversial.

Interviewed in Galway, Ireland, in 1990, Arden credited early radio plays with his success, reexamined the thematic thrust of his best-known works, commented that the "pox" of *Serjeant Musgrave's Dance* can be compared to acquired immunodeficiency syndrome (AIDS) in the 1990's, and lamented that the "epidemic" called "the use of murder to support government" is still raging, not only in Ireland but also in incidents in the Falkland Islands, Panama, and Nicaragua: "I'm thinking of the . . . rise in popularity of such politicians as [Margaret] Thatcher, [Ronald] Reagan, and [George] Bush, and I feel sickened."

ANALYSIS

The controversy accompanying John Arden's career has tended to obscure his rather old-fashioned views of the proper role of the playwright. He draws not only on an older dramatic tradition but also on an older concept of the dramatist: the playwright as burgher. Arden is an immensely civic-minded playwright, a citizen who chooses to dramatize his concern for the commonweal. This concept of the dramatist—almost antithetical to the commercial theater as it now exists—belongs to an older tradition that embraces Shakespeare, the medieval theater, and the Greek dramatists. In Arden and D'Arcy's three-part Arthurian *The Island of the Mighty*, the ancient poets are not merely entertainers but also political advisers. Arden's concept of the dramatist explains his interest in community theater; increasingly, in the global village, his concerns have become international in scope.

Arden's concept of the dramatist means that his drama has been almost exclusively political, but his politics have changed and his involvement developed over time. In his early plays, although he treated parochial issues, he tended not to take a stand; rather, like the architect he had trained to be, he was merely concerned with how people live, as indicated by such titles as *Live Like Pigs* and *The Happy Haven*. If any

stand was implied, it was likely to be anti-Socialist—for example, to condemn heavy-handed administration of the welfare state. Soon, however, through his historical parables, Arden expanded his vision. He began to connect local issues to world issues and to historical processes, and he began to deal either directly or indirectly with pacifist and Socialist concerns: militarism, colonialism, and economic and social injustice. Finally, the plays written with D'Arcy take a more militant, partisan approach toward these same issues and others (such as sexism), condemning the imperialist/militarist/capitalist/exploitative mentality and viewing the Irish situation as a prime result of this mentality.

For Arden, the development in his thinking is summed up in the crisis of the liberal: the conflict between revolution and reform and the fear that reform is only refining and strengthening an exploitative system. His thinking is influenced not only by the world scene but also specifically by Britain's past experience of empire. Also, Arden's thinking is not unique in contemporary Britain but is only one aspect of a political mood evoked by the title of the first New Wave play, John Osborne's *Look Back in Anger* (pr. 1956).

In three early social comedies, *The Waters of Babylon*, *Live Like Pigs*, and *The Happy Haven*, one sees the young dramatist struggling to find his way. All three plays are generally comic in tone, but some terrible things happen in each one. Some of the humor is undergraduate, but when these were written, the playwright had, after all, only recently been a student (and his most appreciative audience was students). Despite flashes of energy, the action drags in both *Live Like Pigs* and *The Happy Haven*, and both plays mix modes awkwardly: *Live Like Pigs* combines naturalism with the Brechtian mode, while *The Happy Haven* mixes naturalism with a Theater of the Absurd parable.

LIVE LIKE PIGS AND THE HAPPY HAVEN

Live Like Pigs and *The Happy Haven* are notable, however, for their implied criticism of the welfare state, new to Britain after World War II and hence somewhat raw. A coercive bureaucracy and pressures to conform are revealed in *Live Like Pigs* when the

Sawneys, a raffish family living in an old tramcar down by the tracks, are forced by officials to move into a public housing estate. The Sawneys turn their new house into a pigsty, offend their proper neighbors, and provoke a bloody riot. The insensitive treatment of people as objects is even more obvious in *The Happy Haven*: Here, the nursing-home setting can be seen as a satire on the welfare state, complete with a presiding doctor who performs experiments on the old people—for their own good, of course (he is perfecting an elixir of youth). Such is the bureaucratic best of all possible worlds.

THE WATERS OF BABYLON

A much better play is *The Waters of Babylon*, which sticks closer to the Brechtian mode and has a wider scope, showing postwar Britain's legacy of colonialism, militarism, and capitalism. While Britain was building a welfare state, it was being flooded by refugees and immigrants, represented in this play by the Poles, Irish, and West Indians. Their world, as the play's title suggests, is a world of dislocation and exile. Moreover, their world is the true postwar world, a world full of Sawneys, and it is impinging on the tidy British, whether they like it or not. Some do not, a group represented by the insular Englishman Henry Ginger. Others do, represented by Alexander Loap, a member of Parliament who keeps an expensive redheaded Irish mistress, and by Charles Butterthwaite, a former Yorkshire politician who finds a corrupt mate in Krank, the Polish slum landlord.

Above all, it is Krank, one of Arden's most colorful characters, who represents the soul of postwar Great Britain. His full name, Sigismanfred Krankiewicz, sums up the European history with which Britain has tried not to be involved. Krank himself wants to be uninvolved, left alone, but meanwhile he profits from his own little British empire, a run-down apartment house where he takes in immigrants and operates a prostitution ring. The chickens come to roost for Krank as they do for the British Empire: It is discovered that he spent the war in Buchenwald, all right, but as a German soldier rather than a prisoner, and he is shot by the Polish patriot Paul. Before he dies, however, Krank admits his complicity in recent

human history—a lesson, Arden suggests, that we could all learn.

SERJEANT MUSGRAVE'S DANCE

If *The Waters of Babylon* shows some aftereffects of the British Empire, *Serjeant Musgrave's Dance* goes to the Empire's heart, showing its workings. The play is Brechtian in mode, but with an elemental, mythic quality. The time is the Victorian era, around 1880. The place is a wintry North Country coal town, snowbound and starving, in the middle of a strike, the coldness of the setting suggesting the coldness of the empire's discipline. This discipline is maintained in the town by a triumvirate of mayor (who, conveniently, also owns the coal mine), parson, and constable, assisted by the distractions of Mrs. Hitchcock's pub (where a man can purchase grog and the ministrations of Annie). Abroad in the colonies, discipline is even less subtle: It is maintained by the queen's army, which collects troublemakers at home to turn them loose on troublemakers in the colonies. In an emergency, the troops can also be used against the home folks. Thus, in the name of prosperity, patriotism, and good order, blessed by religion, the ruthless forces of capitalism, colonialism, and militarism operate together in a vast but tightly enclosed system that benefits the few at the expense and suffering of the many. The ballad chorus captures the spirit of the system: "The Empire wars are far away/ For duty's sake we sail away/ Me arms and legs is shot away/ And all for the wink of a shilling and a drink."

A desperate challenge to this brutal system is mounted by four soldiers who appear in the coal town, ostensibly to recruit but in reality to bring home the truth. The truth about the system is symbolized by the skeleton of Billy Hicks, a young soldier from the town. Billy was murdered in a far-off British "protectorate," and the British army retaliated by indiscriminately wounding thirty-four natives and killing five in a bloody night raid. Now the soldiers, led by Serjeant Musgrave, hoist Billy's skeleton on a market cross in the town square, train rifles and a Gatling gun on the town's citizens (actually, on the play's audience), and proceed to lecture them about the evils of the system and their complicity in it. At first the citizens think Musgrave, who does a little dance under the skeleton, is merely balmy, but then the striking colliers heed his call for solidarity. Not unnaturally, however, they draw back when Musgrave announces plans to kill twenty-five townspeople in retaliation for the five dead protectorate natives. The final straw comes when the crowd learns that one of the four soldiers is missing, dead at the hands of his comrades. The townspeople are saved by disagreement among the remaining soldiers and by the arrival of the dragoons. The temporarily challenged system starts up again, symbolized by a dance in which all join hands and sing a mindless round, led by the grotesque Bargee, who has been Musgrave's shadow throughout the play.

The trouble is that Musgrave himself is twisted by the system. His intentions are good, but his methods are terrible. He thinks he is led by God, but he is instead moved by the military logic he opposes, as indicated by the discipline he maintains over the soldiers even after they are all deserters. Musgrave's protest takes the form of a military exercise, complete with military mathematics. As the soldier Attercliffe notes, Musgrave tries to end war "by its own rules: no bloody good . . . you can't cure the pox by whoring." Yet it is a protest that will be remembered by the townspeople—and by the people who see the play.

ARMSTRONG'S LAST GOODNIGHT

Like *Serjeant Musgrave's Dance*, *Armstrong's Last Goodnight* is "an unhistorical parable"—that is, both plays were suggested by current events: *Serjeant Musgrave's Dance* by events in Cyprus in 1958, *Armstrong's Last Goodnight* by the situation in the Congo in 1961. Setting the plays in the past provides distance from current events but at the same time raises ironic parallels. For example, *Armstrong's Last Goodnight* is ironically subtitled *An Exercise in Diplomacy*, suggesting that much diplomacy has been and is still an exercise in treachery. In *Armstrong's Last Goodnight*, it resides in early sixteenth century Scotland, a vicious land of constant feuding, plotting, and shifting alliances (rather like the early sixteenth century English court described in the play's epigraph from the poet John Skelton), a land where the biggest freebooter prevails.

In *Armstrong's Last Goodnight*, the prescribed strategy is to invite your enemy to go hunting, offer him some of the local brew, shake hands with him, swear friendship forever, and then kill him at the first safe opportunity. Johnnie Armstrong of Gilknockie, a colorful border strongman, does this to James Johnstone of Wamphray, and then James V of Scotland does it to Armstrong. To entice Armstrong, King James needs the help of his scheming ambassador, Sir David Lindsay (another poet who was involved in politics), and of Lindsay's mistress, an earthy lady who even gets used to the smell in Armstrong's castle and who describes her sexuality in terms of a hot pot of red-herring broth (boiling over, of course). This play too has its elemental, mythic qualities, qualities enhanced by the Scots dialect in which it is written, but its overriding reminder is that international relations are still conducted on the primitive level of relations among early Scotch lairds.

VANDALEUR'S FOLLY

Authored by D'Arcy and Arden, *Vandaleur's Folly* has a dialectic pattern familiar from *Serjeant Musgrave's Dance*: thesis, antithesis, fiasco. Here the exploitative system is the prototypical plantation colony of 1830's Ireland, a country of whiskey-drinking British gentry and thirsty Irish tenantry, where the absentee landlords gamble in Dublin's Hell Fire Club and visit their estates occasionally to conduct a "fox" hunt using a lively Irish lass. The play draws parallels between the treatment of the Irish, the American slave trade, and the treatment of women. For example, the slave-trader Wilberforce is the business partner of Major Baker-Fortescue, the vicious Orangeman landlord. The two are opposed by Roxana, an American abolitionist who is part black, and by Michael, an Irishman who leads the Lady Clare Boys, a peasant guerrilla group.

The most important challenge to the plantation system, however, is Ralahine, a Socialist cooperative set up by Vandaleur, an enlightened landowner. Ralahine, where landowner and tenant share equally and have equal rights, is a financial success and brings peace to the countryside, yet it drives the other landowners wild. The Commune's opponents finally destroy it by taking advantage of a fatal flaw in its makeup: Like Musgrave, Vandaleur is still infected by the system. He retains private ownership of the experimental estate and, in a fit of gambling fever, loses it to Baker-Fortescue in a faro game at the Hell Fire Club.

Subtitled *An Anglo-Irish Melodrama*, *Vandaleur's Folly* fits the description. Its one-sided characterizations result in some loss of artistic power, and the language of the play is not spiced with dialect. Yet *Vandaleur's Folly* is entertaining melodrama, and there is no trouble understanding its partisan point: Private property is wrong, and so is any arrangement that treats people as property.

Like the forthright *Vandaleur's Folly*, Arden's work generally is meant to stir people to think about the issues of today's world and perhaps to take action. One of the modern writers most attuned to those issues, Arden is very much a practical playwright: He does not merely look back in anger, but looks forward with hope. As this description implies, he is also a playwright for the young. Although his work embodies prophetic warnings, it does not reflect the despairing tone of earlier twentieth century literature, with its recurring visions of the wasteland; rather, Arden looks beyond the crisis of modern civilization toward solutions.

OTHER MAJOR WORKS

LONG FICTION: *Silence Among the Weapons*, 1982 (also as *Vox Pop: Last Days of the Roman Republic*, 1983); *Books of Bale*, 1988.

SHORT FICTION: *Cogs Tyrannic*, 1991; *Jack Juggler and the Emperor's Whore*, 1995.

TELEPLAYS: *Soldier, Soldier*, 1960; *Wet Fish*, 1961.

RADIO PLAYS: *The Life of Man*, 1956; *The Dying Cowboy*, 1961; *The Bagman*, 1970; *Keep Those People Moving*, 1972 (with Margaretta D'Arcy); *Pearl*, 1978; *To Put It Frankly . . .* , 1979; *Don Quixote*, 1980 (2 parts); *Garland for a Hoar Head*, 1982; *The Old Man Sleeps Alone*, 1982; *Whose Is the Kingdom?*, 1982 (9 parts; with D'Arcy).

NONFICTION: *To Present the Pretence*, 1977 (with Margaretta D'Arcy); *Awkward Corners*, 1988 (with D'Arcy).

BIBLIOGRAPHY

Gray, Frances. *John Arden*. New York: Grove Press, 1983. The introduction points out the inherently noncommercial "manner" and "matter" of Arden's structure, subject matter, and cast of characters, and it uses the theme as an organizational device for discussing Arden's work. Brief bibliography and index.

Malic, Javed. *Toward a Theater of the Oppressed: The Dramaturgy of John Arden*. Ann Arbor: University of Michigan Press, 1995. This study examines the plays of Arden, looking at the theory behind them and the way they were performed. Closely examines *Island of the Mighty*. Bibliography and index.

Page, Malcolm. *John Arden*. Boston: Twayne, 1984. A concise biography of Arden that examines both his life and his work. Bibliography and index.

_____, comp. *Arden on File*. London: Methuen, 1985. A compilation of facts on Arden's productions (twenty-one plays described and annotated), themes, growth as a writer, and self-evaluation through the course of his career. Easy to use, full of names and dates, and the pith of reviews. Contains a chronology and a select bibliography.

Shaughnessy, Robert. *Three Socialist Plays: "Lear," "Roots," "Serjeant Musgrave's Dance."* Philadelphia, Pa.: Open University Press, 1992. Shaughnessy looks at the political thought expressed in Arden's *Serjeant Musgrave's Dance*, Arnold Wesker's *Roots*, and Edward Bond's *Lear*. Bibliography and index.

Wike, Jonathan, ed. *John Arden and Margaretta D'Arcy: A Casebook*. New York: Garland, 1995. This casebook looks at the works of Arden and his wife, D'Arcy. Bibliography and index.

Harold Branam,
updated by Thomas J. Taylor

PIETRO ARETINO

Born: Arezzo, Republic of Florence (now in Italy);
April 19 or 20, 1492
Died: Venice (now in Italy); October 21, 1556

PRINCIPAL DRAMA

Il marescalco, pb. 1533, pr. 1535 (revised version
of the original text of 1527; *The Marescalco*,
1986)

La cortigiana, pb. 1534, pr. 1537 (revised version
of the original text of 1525; *The Courtesan*,
1926)

Lo ipocrito, pb. 1540, pr. 1545

La Talanta, pr., pb. 1542

Il filosofo, pb. 1546

La Orazia, pb. 1546 (verse play)

OTHER LITERARY FORMS

Pietro Aretino was an extremely prolific writer.
Besides his theatrical works, he is well known for his
satiric and erotic poems and dialogues. He also practiced epic and burlesque poetry, wrote several religious works, and published six volumes of letters.

ACHIEVEMENTS

Men of eminence of his day who "were not afraid
of the wrath of God" feared his pen, as Pietro Aretino
himself wrote in a letter dated December, 1552. The
readiness and soundness of his opinions, the pomposity with which he would request or acknowledge a favor, as well as the fierceness, the impudence, and the
caustic wit of his attacks, were all to become legendary, to be remembered and evoked by generations of
satirists and chroniclers.

Aretino was also to become famous—or infamous—for his works of pornography, his various
ragionamenti and *Sonetti lussuriosi* (1524; *The Sonnets*, 1926). Allusions to his licentious dialogues and
obscene poems occur so frequently, especially in English literature, as to deserve special consideration as
a separate phenomenon.

The legends that were built on his life, both the religious and secular censorship that struck his produc-

tion, along with the extent, the variety, the disparity,
and the poor editorial condition of his works, have
prevented scholars and the public from objectively
considering and appraising Aretino's personality and
achievements.

Aretino was a panegyrist, a libeler, a satirist, and a
pornographer, but he also wrote several religious
works, in keeping with the new tendencies of the
Counter-Reformation. He was the presumptuous follower of Ludovico Ariosto in *Marfisa* (1532) and
other unfinished chivalric poems, but a more effective
burlesque poet in *L'Orlandino* (1868). He was an
anti-Petrarchist, not aesthetically motivated but instinctively rebellious in regard to current poetic taste.
He was a hasty, often clumsy and ungraceful versi-
fier, a tireless epistler, and a resourceful playwright.

Aretino's admirers called him "divine," while his
detractors referred to him as "vile": Both the compliment and the insult testify to the immensity of his
fortune and influence. In his poem *Orlando furioso*
(1516, 1521, 1532; English translation, 1591), Ariosto nicknamed him the "scourge of princes," and it
has even been suggested that Aretino also, in his own
way, wrote a treatise *de principatibus*; bits of it are to
be found in his letters, in his comedies, and in his dialogues.

Aretino styled himself "the secretary of the
world." He did, indeed, seem to have his finger on the
pulse of his times. He could well be considered the
forerunner of certain modern journalists, who are always ready to guess, to sense, and to comply with
people's moods, and to take advantage of them without scruple. When Aretino decided to have his letters
published, he had anticipated the public's expectations precisely. The occasional nature of his letters involved repetitions as well as heaviness and vulgari-
ties, but also allowed him to find the most congenial
cues. In the best of moments, the very format of the
letter saved him from tediously insisting on his tricks
and inventions (something that he too often did in the
rest of his production). The way in which he always
boasted of his great influence on his contemporaries

might bother the reader, but one must certainly recognize in Aretino's writing the uncommon power of a rich and fervent mind.

BIOGRAPHY

Pietro Aretino was born in Arezzo, Republic of Florence, in 1492 into a humble family; he was the son of a shoemaker. His father abandoned the family and joined a troop of mercenaries when Pietro was a small child. His mother, Margherita (Tita) Bonci, was not of such obscure origins and, because of her great beauty, was frequently chosen as a model by the local painters. A few years after Pietro's birth, she had a love affair with the wealthy nobleman Luigi Bacci, which might have been the reason for her husband's sudden decision to leave and which continued long after he left, providing Margherita and her children (the son Pietro and two younger daughters) with all that was necessary to live. While Aretino maintained a tender relationship with both his mother and his sisters, he disowned his father's name and adopted the name of his native community.

Pietro Aretino (Library of Congress)

While still an adolescent, Aretino went to live in Perugia, where he soon became associated with men of arts and letters and was patronized by Francesco de Bontempi. The most influential among the local families seemed to appreciate him both as a painter and as a poet. In 1512, while still in Perugia, Aretino found the means to have his first book of verse printed in Venice: *Opera nova* is a collection of *facetiae*, folk songs, sonnets, and letters in rhyme in the manner of the poet Serafino Aquilano.

In 1517, after a brief stay in Siena, Aretino went to Rome to work for the Sienese Agostino Chigi, an extremely rich and powerful banker, a patron of the painter Raphael, and treasurer to the papal court of Leo X. The court was attended by other artists and prominent writers, such as Cardinal Bibbiena (Bernardo Dovizi) and Pietro Bembo. Aretino was soon able to attract the attention of the pope and Cardinal Giulio de' Medici, as well as the attention of the Roman public. His swift climb to fame and fortune reached its apex soon after the death of Leo X, in November, 1521, precisely during the conclave that resulted in the election of Adrian VI. On that occasion, Aretino displayed his talent as a fierce satirist, composing more than fifty biting sonnets that were to promote Giulio de' Medici and defame his rivals. These so-called *pasquinate* made him popular among the Roman people, who were displeased with the unexpected election of the Flemish pope. The harshness of Aretino's satire had been such that he wisely decided to leave Rome a month prior to the new pope's arrival, at the end of July, 1522.

Between 1522 and 1523, Aretino was in Bologna, Arezzo, and Florence in Giulio de' Medici's suite. Then, the latter, in order not to compromise himself further in the eyes of the pope by openly protecting one of his enemies, deemed it necessary to send Aretino first to Mantua, to the court of young Federigo Gonzaga, then to Reggio in Emilia. There his nephew Giovanni delle Bande Nere, the famous *condottiere*, whom Aretino must have met in Rome in 1519, kept his headquarters. After the death of Adrian VI and the election of Giulio de' Medici as Pope Clement VII in November, 1523, Aretino returned to Rome hoping to gain employment in the papal court as a cultural adviser. The new papal datary, Giovanni Matteo Giberti, was not, however, inclined to tolerate Aretino's defiance and his intrusions into the court's business. When Aretino succeeded in obtaining from the pope the release of Marcantonio Raimondi, an engraver who had reproduced sixteen erotic drawings by Giulio Romano, and then saucily proceeded to provide a text for the work by writing sixteen *sonetti lussuriosi*, Giberti and the pope were so outraged that Aretino had to leave the city in order to avoid imprisonment himself. He set out for his hometown, Arezzo, and then, once again, joined Giovanni delle Bande Nere in Fano, on the Adriatic, where the captain introduced him to Francis I, king of France.

Aretino was nevertheless determined to return to Rome, and he therefore composed two long odes in praise of the pope and one in honor of the datary, which proved effective. Once in Rome, however, his intolerance of the papal court's way of life—which the first draft of his comedy *The Courtesan* clearly betrays—turned into an even more open spirit of rebellion. With the *pasquinate* of April, 1525, Giberti's hostility caught fire again, and the exasperated datary tried to have Aretino slain by a hired assassin, Achille della Volta, on July 28, 1525. This attempt failed: As soon as he recovered from the wounds, Aretino left Rome, never to return.

He found shelter once again in Giovanni delle Bande Nere's camp near Mantua, where the captain was engaged in the fight against the imperial troops. After Giovanni died from injuries received during the Battle of Governolo, in Lombardy in November, 1526, Aretino wrote a famous and moving letter to Francesco degli Albizzi (Giovanni's treasurer in Florence) with the account of the hero's death. The letter, besides containing one of his many keen analyses of the historical moment, shows Aretino's capacity for deep and sincere feelings of friendship and admiration.

Aretino stayed in Mantua until March of the following year. There he sketched a poem, "La Marfisa disperata," in celebration of the Gonzaga family, which was, however, to remain unfinished (like his poems "Le lagrime d'Angelica," "Astolfeide," and

L'Orlandino). He also started to write his second comedy, *The Marescalco*, which is now known in the later, revised version of 1533. During the same period, Aretino experimented with a new genre of satire, that of the *giudizi*, or "judgments." His *giudizio* for the year 1527—which unfortunately exists only in fragments—seems to have prophesied the sack of Rome by Emperor Charles V's mercenaries, which duly occurred in May, 1527. Clement VII was obviously angered by this prophecy, and therefore the marquis of Mantua, who until then had enjoyed Aretino's presence in his court, began to feel uneasy about sheltering such an enemy of the pope.

From March 25, 1527, Aretino took his abode in the "liberal and just" Venice. He rented, from the patrician Domenico Bolani, a beautiful house on the Grand Canal, not far from Rialto, where he resided until his last few years, when he then went to live in Leonardo Dandolo's house in Riva del Carbon. In Venice, he wrote the majority of his works and lived the rest of his days honored by the friendship of great artists such as Jacopo Sansovino and Titian (who portrayed Aretino more than once), protected and feared by the greatest lords and kings of his time. Andrea Gritti, doge of Venice from 1523 to 1538, Cosimo de' Medici, duke of Florence and son of his beloved friend Giovanni, and Francesco della Rovere, duke of Urbino, always favored and protected him. In 1533, Francis I sent him a precious golden chain as a gift; in 1536, Emperor Charles V assigned him a conspicuous pension, and when, in 1543, he was passing through the Veronese territory, the emperor wanted Aretino to ride at his side while parading in Peschiera. Aretino was thus able to live in the lap of luxury and satisfy his endless thirst for pleasure. His first biographer, Giovanni Maria Mazzucchelli, diligently records Aretino's innumerable mistresses and mentions his two illegitimate daughters (Adria and Austria, born in 1537 and 1547, respectively).

Even in Venice, sorrows, troubles, and episodes of vengeance and violence occurred. In 1536, Aretino welcomed to his house Niccolò Franco, who was to help him in particular with the research for his religious works (since Aretino's knowledge of Latin was mediocre at best). In 1537, a defamatory *Vita di*

Pietro Aretino was published: The author, probably Fortunio Spira from Viterbo, declared in the preface that he had obtained most of his information from Franco. Soon afterward, Franco himself published his *Pistole volgari* (1539), with the clear intent to compete with his master's own collection of letters. An exchange of violent insults followed between the two men, and Ambrogio degli Eusebi, who was an especially loyal secretary of Aretino, disfigured Franco with a knife.

Francesco Berni had continued to cast contumely on Aretino since the time they had met in Rome, and so did Anton Francesco Doni, who had initially been Aretino's friend. There was even an attempt to take Aretino to court under the accusation of blasphemy and sodomy (a widely practiced and punishable offense). He had to flee to a villa on the Brenta, and it was only because of Francesco della Rovere's intervention and pleading with the Venetian magistrates that Aretino was able to return to Venice. Finally, also in Venice, Aretino was the victim of an armed assault by an English ambassador in search of revenge.

These episodes did not, however, seriously upset Aretino's life and career. His fame was such that, when Julius III was elected pope in 1550, he was appointed *cavaliere* of Saint Peter, and there were those who even tried to have him don the scarlet. This was not to come true: Aretino suddenly died of a stroke on October 21, 1556.

ANALYSIS

Particularly in the sixteenth century, the Italian comic theater seemed to be closely linked to the varied geographical and historical landscape of Italy in that period. One must therefore remember that Pietro Aretino first conceived and wrote his *The Courtesan* in Rome and *The Marescalco* in Mantua, even if he subsequently revised and only then published the two comedies in the safety and relative tranquillity of his Venetian abode.

THE COURTESAN

The Courtesan offers an impressive picture of the city of Pope Clement VII. In his display of the miseries and the wickedness of the papal court, Aretino introduces some fictitious characters and evokes more

than sixty historical ones. The language includes dialect, slang, jargon, foreign idioms, and both ecclesiastic and macaronic Latin. The play consists of a series of sketches. Its broken structure and continuously interrupted and resumed plot try precisely to reproduce onstage the confusion, frustration, and dismay of living in a city such as Rome, which during that period was only superficially magnificent and in reality was crumbling.

The fragile plot of the comedy interweaves two stories, that of Messer Maco and that of Parabolano. The first is a Sienese simpleton who comes to Rome to become a courtier and aims at a cardinalship. A painter, Mastro Andrea, promises to teach him how to fulfill his desire but instead makes him the object of an interminable series of mockeries. In the end, the bold Maco, confident in his new position as the perfect courtier, pays a visit to a lady's house and is chased out of it by Mastro Andrea himself, along with a friend of his, both disguised as Spanish bravos.

Parabolano is a rich Neapolitan gentleman who has fallen in love with the beautiful Roman lady Livia. One of his servants, a rascal and an exploiter, decides to make fun of his master with the help of a procuress. The latter pretends to be Livia's nurse and easily convinces the vain Parabolano that the lady is also passionately in love and would very much like for him to visit her by night. When Parabolano goes to the arranged meeting, instead of his beloved Livia he finds the uncouth wife of a baker. At this point the two plots meet, and Parabolano, who is in the end a witty person, does not avenge the jest but even tries to appease the furious Maco.

The absence of structural unity and the extreme prodigality of language and stage tricks distinguish Aretino's first comedy from the works of other contemporary playwrights, mainly from the economy of characters and words of Niccolò Machiavelli's *La mandragola* (pr. c. 1519; *The Mandrake*, 1911). Nevertheless, what appears at first to be a weakness of *The Courtesan*, and of Aretino's theatrical works in general, allows the writer greater liberty of invention and an opportunity to indulge a whimsical taste for types and situations. In *The Courtesan*, the exploitation and the subversion of theatrical patrimony is intentional and declared. In the long prologue to the original version, the author underlines the necessity for this comedy to be different with regard to the comic tradition because it represents everyday life in Rome. The reference to the crude facts of this life is accomplished by an impudent violation of the boundaries between the public and the actors: By quoting directly from the current news, the characters of the play constantly wink at the contemporary public, and this creates a sort of complicity, a singular joint liability, in the show.

The corrections made to the original text some nine years later in 1534 were conceived to give a different sense and direction to this "Roman" comedy and change it as much as possible into an "Italian" comedy. In the revised version, therefore, the original motives of Aretino's polemic as well as some of the more direct allusions and the more realistic cues have been deleted.

THE MARESCALCO

The Marescalco, written for the Gonzaga court of Mantua in 1526-1527 and published in Venice in 1533, has a more unswerving plot, derived from Plautus's *Casina* (English translation, 1774) and Machiavelli's own derivation of it, *La Clizia* (pr. 1525, pb. 1532; *Clizia*, 1961). The duke of Mantua, knowing that his blacksmith (the character of whom was modeled after a well-known homosexual at the court) is violently opposed to marriage, makes him believe that he wants him to get married at any cost. In the first four acts of the play, the audience witnesses the dialogues of the Marescalco with several characters who all announce to him the irrevocable decision of the duke. The majority approve of the decision and discuss the relative merits of marriage, while the obstinate misogynist progressively gives himself up to despair. Only after the wedding ceremony has taken place, in the last act, does the Marescalco discover to his delight that his mysterious "wife" is in fact the duke's young page in disguise.

The comedy is an excuse both to weave a plot based on the themes of misogyny and homosexuality and to offer congenial entertainment to the court during the carnival season, reproducing onstage the life of the same people for whom the work was destined to be performed. *The Marescalco* was sent from Venice to the duke of Mantua in January, 1530, and Aretino was rewarded with fifty crowns. Particularly effective are the scenes that contain the argumentation in favor of and against marriage (act 2, scene 5; act 4, scene 5; act 5, scene 6) and those in which a foolish pedagogue lays himself open to Aretino's polemic against pedantry (act 1, scene 11; act 2, scene 11; act 3, scenes 10-11). The farce is conducted with particularly lively dialogue and the usual Aretinian wealth of comic gags and situations.

LO IPOCRITO

Lo ipocrito, published in 1540, introduces a character that was unknown to the classical comedy and has been recognized as an anticipation of Molière's *Tartuffe*: a man who is generally and wrongly believed to be an unselfish and charitable person and who always succeeds in insinuating himself into his victims' homes, taking advantage of every situation. Around this original type, though, a conventional plot of love and intrigue develops and ends with an equally conventional multiple wedding and final recognition of twin brothers. In Aretino's comedies, the imitation of classical theater is, in any case, always less rigorous and consistent than in the rest of the sixteenth century Italian comic canon.

LA TALANTA

La Talanta, written in 1534 but not published until 1542, also reveals the indirect influence of ancient Roman comedy: The plot is in fact based on the common device of transvestism and the final recognition, an outline followed by many Italian works, of which Bibbiena had first taken full advantage in his *La Calandra* (pb. 1523). Aretino's fourth comedy is centered on the protagonist of the title, the beautiful courtesan Talanta, who shares her favors among four lovers. One of them is the young and impetuous Orfino, truly in love with the woman; another is the pompous and defiant captain Tinca, whose character is reminiscent of Plautus's braggart soldier Pyrgopolynices, but who also anticipates the masks of the various *Vallinferna* and *Matamoros* of the *commedia dell'arte*; a third is a quite old and tight-fisted Venetian gentleman; and the fourth is the Roman Armileo, who plays the role of *innamorato* for his own interests. All are stock characters that Aretino brings artfully up to date.

IL FILOSOFO

Il filosofo, written in ten days at the end of 1544 and published in 1546, consists of two stories that do not have much in common and develop according to completely separate plots. The protagonist of the first is a pedantic philosopher, whom Aretino facetiously named Plataristotele, comically wedding the names of the two great philosophers. His head is full of principles and theories. He is always absorbed in them and therefore neglects his beautiful wife, named (after a character in Giovanni Boccaccio's *Decameron: O, Prencipe Galetto*, 1349-1351; *The Decameron*, 1620) Monna Tessa. Like her namesake, Tessa enjoys herself with a young lover, Polidoro. When, finally, Plataristotele finds Polidoro in his house and learns of his wife's affair, he locks the young lover in a room in order to show him to his mother-in-law as proof of Tessa's betrayal. The latter frees Polidoro and puts a donkey in his place, so that when Plataristotele, in the presence of the mother-in-law, opens the door, the animal—symbol of the philosopher's own negligence and poor science—runs out of the room braying. Plataristotele mends his ways and decides, to his wife's satisfaction, never to neglect her again.

If the Italian comic theater owes much to classical comedy, it is equally indebted to the narrative tradition, to which Aretino also pays tribute. The second plot of his last comedy is based on the well-known story of Andreuccio da Perugia, from Boccaccio's *Decameron*. The name of the protagonist is, in fact, Boccaccio, a merchant of precious stones who goes to the big city with a large sum of money to make his purchases, is robbed by a shrewd courtesan, accidentally associates himself with two thieves, and, in the end, recovers more than he has lost. Of greater interest is the character of the philosopher after whom the comedy is named: His oddity and clumsiness are spicily depicted by Aretino, especially through the dialogues with the servant Salvalaglio, a clever commoner who enjoys imitating his master.

Besides the fact that they belong to the same genre and they share an interest in the spoken language of the common people and the tendency toward the most elaborated linguistic pastiches, one would attempt in vain to find a real unifying criterion of style and poetics in Aretino's comedies. Somehow, even after the revisions, the anecdotal nature of *The Courtesan* and its particular mimesis on one hand, and the corrosive and worldly nature of *The Marescalco* on the other, do not seem to be matched by the rest of the plays.

LA ORAZIA

With his last theatrical work, *La Orazia*, the "unlettered" and "natural" Aretino wanted to equal the well-read dramatists of his time and accepted the great challenge of the tragic genre. The plot of his tragedy is based on the episode of the Orazi and the Curiazi, as narrated by the Roman historian Livy. Rome and Alba have decided to settle their endless strife by means of a duel between the best three warriors of each city: the Curiazi brothers for Alba and the Orazi brothers for Rome. In the first act, the imminent combat is announced and praised by Publio, the patriotic father of the Orazi, along with his friend Spurio, while Clelia, Publio's daughter and sister to the Roman champions but also the fiancée of one of the Curiazi, confesses her sorrow to her nurse. A chorus of Virtues ends the act by commenting on the different attitudes of the characters: Publio's fortitude and Clelia's dejection.

The second act consists almost entirely of the narration of the combat given by the Roman knight Tito Tazio. Two of the Orazi and all three of the Curiazi lie dead on the battlefield. When Clelia learns the news, she begins to grieve over her betrothed's death and is quite unable to acknowledge the sacrifice of her two brothers. Harshly reproached by her father, Publio, she faints. The chorus of Virtues again concludes the act, criticizing Clelia's self-centered passion.

The triumph of the victorious Orazio opens the third act. The festive atmosphere is upset by the anguish of Clelia, who recognizes, among the clothes of the dead Curiazi, the linen tunic that she wove for her fiancé. The victor Orazio, filled with indignation for his sister's open display of despair, transfixes her before the stunned Roman public. Old Publio approves of the behavior of his son and the chorus of Virtues ends the act by commending once again his sense of duty.

In the fourth act, Publio and Spurio defend Orazio before the decemvirs, who were shocked by what they perceived as the young hero's hard-heartedness and are now calling for his execution. The judgment is finally left up to the people. In the final act, Publio discusses his son's case with the Roman people (who are represented by a single character and not by a chorus). While the people condemn Orazio's cruelty and impulsiveness, they do not sentence him to death but require him only to pass under the yoke as penance for his crime.

Critical judgments of this tragedy have always been widely discordant. One notable critic's opinion has been that *La Orazia* is the most beautiful and powerful Italian tragedy of the sixteenth century, comparable to William Shakespeare's Roman dramas and an inspiration to Pierre Corneille's *Horace* (pr. 1640, pb. 1641; English translation, 1656). Others have underlined Aretino's labored style and the awkwardness and lack of fluidity of his versification.

The choice of such a subject certainly appears symptomatic of the latter part of the playwright's career. The season of Aretino's theatrical production had begun under the sign of *Pasquino*—that is to say, the fiercest and earthiest Roman satire—and came to a close with a solemn and moralistic glorification of the ancient Roman virtues.

OTHER MAJOR WORKS

POETRY: *Opera nova*, 1512; *Sonetti lussuriosi*, 1524 (*The Sonnets*, 1926); *Marfisa*, 1532; *L'Orlandino*, 1868.

NONFICTION: *Ragionamento della Nanna et della Antonio*, 1534; *I sette salmi de la penitenzia di David*, 1534; *La passione di Gesù*, 1534; *Dialogo nelquale la Nanna il primo giorno insegna a la Pippa*, 1536; *Lettere*, 1537-1557 (*The Letters*, 1926);

I quattro libri de la humanità di Cristo, 1538; *Il Genesi*, 1538; *Ragionamento de le Corti*, 1538; *Vita di Maria Vergine*, 1539; *Vita di Caterina Vergine*, 1539; *Vita di San Tomaso Signor D'Aquino*, 1543; *Le carte parlanti*, 1543; *The Ragionamento: Or, Dialogues*, 1889 (includes all the *ragionamenti* in English translation); *The Letters of Pietro Aretino*, 1967; *Aretino: Selected Letters*, 1976.

MISCELLANEOUS: *The Works of Aretino*, 1926 (2 volumes).

BIBLIOGRAPHY

Cairns, Christopher. *Pietro Aretino and the Republic of Venice: Researches on Aretino and His Circle in Venice, 1527-1556.* Florence: L. S. Olschki, 1985. Although this study focuses on Aretino's friends and acquaintances in Venice, it helps readers understand his writings. Bibliography and indexes.

Freedman, Luba. *Titian's Portraits Through Aretino's Lens.* University Park, Pa.: Pennsylvania State University Press, 1995. Examines the portraits of Aretino done by Titian. Bibliography and index.

Lawner, Lynne, ed. and trans. *I Modi: The Sixteen Pleasures: An Erotic Album of the Italian Renaissance.* Evanston, Ill.: Northwestern University, 1988. A look at the eroticism of Aretino, Marcantonio Raimondi, Giulio Romano, and Count Jean-Frederic-Maximilien de Waldeck. Reveals some of the motives behind and themes of Aretino's works.

Waddington, Raymond B. "A Satirist's Impresa: The Medals of Pietro Aretino." *Renaissance Quarterly* 42, no. 4 (Winter, 1989): 655. This essay examines the medals of Aretino and his popularity as a writer.

Woods-Marsden, Joanna. "Toward a History of Art Patronage in the Renaissance: The Case of Pietro Aretino." *Journal of Medieval and Renaissance Studies* 24, no. 2 (Spring, 1994): 275. Analyzes the relationship between sitter (patron) and artist.

Francesca L. Savoia

LUDOVICO ARIOSTO

Born: Reggio Emilia, duchy of Modena (now in
Italy); September 8, 1474
Died: Ferrara (now in Italy); July 6, 1533

PRINCIPAL DRAMA

La cassaria, pr., pb. 1508, verse, revised pb. 1530,
pr. 1531 (*The Coffer*, 1975)
I suppositi, pr. 1509 (*The Pretenders*, 1566)
I studenti, wr. 1519 (completed by Gabriele
Ariosto as *La scolastica*, pb. 1547, and
completed by Virginio Ariosto as *L'imperfetta*,
pr. c. 1556; *The Students*, 1975)
Il negromante, wr. 1520, revised pr., pb. 1529 (*The
Necromancer*, 1975)
La Lena, pr. 1528 (*Lena*, 1975)
The Comedies of Ariosto, pb. 1975 (includes the
above)

OTHER LITERARY FORMS

As poet, Ludovico Ariosto is remembered chiefly
as the continuer and modifier of the chivalric tradition initiated at the Ferrarese court by his predecessor
Matteo Maria Boiardo (1441-1494), the author of
the incomplete *Orlando innamorato* (1483, 1495; Orlando in love). This chivalric poem in octaves treats
the passion of the paladin Orlando for the pagan Angelica. The poem was interrupted by Boiardo's death
in 1494, which coincided with France's invasion of
Italy. Because of the widespread use of artillery by
King Charles VIII in the French campaign, chivalry—
the material of Boiardo's poem—was dealt a deadly
blow. Approximately ten years later, Ariosto took up
the story where Boiardo had stopped. The composition of this epic poem became a lifelong project for
Ariosto; the third and definitive edition did not appear until 1532, the year before his death. *Orlando
furioso*, as Ariosto entitled his masterpiece, in order
to recall Seneca's *Hercules furens* (c. 40-55 C.E.; *Mad
Hercules*, 1581), is not, however, merely a conclusion
to Boiardo's unfinished opus. Rather, it is a brilliant
restaging of the entire knightly tradition, from that
portrayed in the poems and romances of the Carolin-

gian and Breton cycles to that of the Franco-Venetian
and Tuscan songs of chivalry. Ariosto wrote for a
Ferrarese court that delighted, but no longer believed,
in chivalric ideals; he mixed, therefore, illusion and
reality in the same poem. He achieved a brilliant mix
through an extensive use of fantasy and dependence
on irony, the distinguishing characteristics of his poetic art. The result is the most acclaimed poem of
Italian Renaissance literature and a work of art that
has understandably eclipsed the author's minor works
for centuries.

ACHIEVEMENTS

Ludovico Ariosto is known as both dramatist and
poet of the Renaissance court of Ferrara, where he
served the Este family. As dramatist, he is often
called the "founder of Italian comedy" but is generally esteemed less for the inherent greatness of his
five plays than for his establishment of sixteenth century *commedia erudita* (erudite or learned comedy).
Learned comedy was essentially a clever reworking
of ancient plays by Plautus and Terence. It represented, in many respects, the antithesis of the unwrit-
ten and improvised plays of the *commedia dell'arte*
that were so popular in the late Renaissance. It was
also a reaction to the sacred representations that had
been carried over from the Middle Ages. Critics have
variously described *cinquecento* learned comedy as
more spectacular than dramatic, unoriginal and lacking in vitality, much too conventional, a realistic portrayal of Italian Renaissance society, quite responsive
to contemporary cultural expectations, and, according to Douglas Radcliff-Umstead, "a vital theater
[created] from the model set by ancient Roman playwrights."

Although Ariosto was not the first to compose a
learned comedy in the vernacular, his first two plays
greatly popularized the genre. George Gascoigne's
Supposes, performed at Gray's Inn in 1566, is a translation or paraphrase of Ariosto's second play, *The
Pretenders*, and testifies to the initially widespread
influence of some of Ariosto's plays. Since the six-

teenth century, however, that influence has been almost negligible because of general critical disdain for learned comedy. That disdain, however, has been modified during the nineteenth and twentieth centuries, as a chronology of the above descriptions of learned comedy, from Jacob Burckhardt in 1860 to Radcliff-Umstead in 1969, would indicate. In addition, the appearance in 1975 of the first English translation of all five of Ariosto's plays and of Einaudi's reproduction in 1976 of the 1954 Ricciardi edition of the plays in Italian are two events that have more recently contributed to the appreciation of Ariosto's comedies in particular.

BIOGRAPHY

On September 8, 1474, Ludovico Ariosto was born in Reggio Emilia, duchy of Modena, the first child of Count Niccolò Ariosto, captain of the city's fortress, and Daria Malaguzzi Valeri. When Ludovico was about ten years old, his family moved to Ferrara. There, his father accepted the position as the general financial administrator of the dukedom. From 1489 to 1494, the younger Ariosto studied civil law, but only reluctantly and at his father's behest. During this same period, he began to manifest a pronounced preference for literary studies. In 1494, he obtained pa-

Ludovico Ariosto (Library of Congress)

ternal permission to study Latin and Greek with the Humanist Gregorio da Spoleto and, later, with Sebastiano dell'Aquila. In the meantime, between 1494 and 1500, Ludovico began to frequent the court of the duke of Este, Ercole I d'Este. He could not help but be greatly influenced by the Ferrarese court culture, where Boiardo's works were often read and discussed and where frequent dramatic spectacles were enacted with the help and participation of the youth from the Ferrarese court.

In 1500, however, the serenity of Ariosto's studies was abruptly terminated by the unexpected death of his father. As the oldest of ten children, Ludovico had to assume the responsibility for providing for his younger brothers and sisters. From that moment, there began a period of intense preoccupation with family affairs that made him long to return to his previous, relatively indolent life of literary pursuits— a wish that he realized only in his last years. In 1502, he received a commission as captain of the fortress at Canossa, but he remained there for only a short time. In 1508, he entered the service of Cardinal Ippolito d'Este, the duke's brother, and took minor vows in order to receive ecclesiastical benefices. Ariosto served the somewhat despotic and bellicose cardinal well on several diplomatic missions and began, around 1504, to plan the *Orlando furioso*. This was the period of the prose versions of his first two comedies (1508 and 1509) as well as the birth in 1509 of his illegitimate son Virginio, whom he later legitimized.

In 1509, the poet followed the cardinal into war against the Venetians and visited Rome twice on missions to Pope Julius II. He returned again in 1510 and, with Duke Alfonso, in 1512. In 1513, when Julius II died and Giovanni de' Medici was subsequently elected as Pope Leo X, Ariosto visited Rome with the hope of obtaining a position in the papal court. Such did not come to pass, however, apparently because of the poet's unwillingness to compromise his standards in order to gain favors, and Ariosto left Rome bitterly disappointed with the corruption surrounding the papacy. In Florence, during the same year, he met and fell in love with Alessandra Benucci, the wife of Tito Strozzi. His love for her remained constant until his death. Even though she was widowed in 1515, the poet waited until much later (probably 1527) to marry her, and then in a secret ceremony, so as not to lose any subsidies from the Church. In 1516, the first edition of his epic romance appeared; two other editions followed in 1521 and in 1532.

Ariosto refused, in 1517, to follow Cardinal Ippolito to Hungary, where the latter had been made bishop of Budapest. He wrote that it was out of a desire for peace and tranquillity that he chose not to travel there, but it is also possible that he did not want to be too far from his beloved Alessandra. Whatever the cause, his acknowledged reasons for leaving the cardinal's service are detailed in the first satire, which dates from 1517. The following year, Ariosto entered the service of Duke Alfonso. In 1522, the poet had to accept a position as the duke's commissioner in the destitute territory of Garfagnana; this was to be an unsavory task but one that Ariosto nevertheless successfully completed. In 1525, he returned to Ferrara, where he received public offices that allowed him to spend the remainder of his life enjoying the serenity that he had long desired and that had been denied by his heavy administrative and familial responsibilities. His final years were devoted to composing his last plays, rewriting his earlier ones, and polishing *Orlando furioso*. The poet died in his country home in Mirasole, in Ferrara, Italy, on July 6, 1533.

ANALYSIS

Although Ludovico Ariosto was a dramaturge as well as a poet, his drama has long been obscured by the well-deserved fame of his epic masterpiece. The chief reason for this traditional slighting of Ariosto's drama, however, probably lies in the five comedies' supposedly excessive reliance on Roman models for their plots, themes, and characters. (Although Virginio Ariosto wrote that his father "was not very studious and searched for few books," Ariosto's dramatic works demonstrate a thorough knowledge of Plautus and Terence; similarly, his *Cinque canti* of 1545 is proof of his extensive familiarity with Cicero, Ovid, Statius, Horace, and Catullus.) Roman comedy typically included stock characters (such as domineering and/or aged fathers, furtive young lovers,

scheming slaves, and swaggering soldiers) and love affairs (full of mistaken identities, disguises, tricks, and reversals), and employed a prologue, versification, and many monologues and asides. Unquestionably, numerous parallels to classical comedy exist in Ariosto's dramatic corpus (and, although generally unacknowledged, in much modern European comedy as well). The crucial point here is that the Italian dramatist fully intended that the classical influences should shine through his text even to the cursory reader or casual observer. His primary goal was the creation or establishment of a tradition of learned comedy. Any analysis, however, that emphasizes only classical sources and analogues invariably negates much of the originality of the comedies, regrettably neglects much of the social commentary in the plays, and usually overlooks any evolution from the first to the last play, all of which frequently discourages a close examination of the influence of Ariosto's work on the later *cinquecento* comedy. These aspects—especially the question of originality—are issues that should be considered in any assessment of Ariosto's contribution to the dramatic genre.

The view, shared by critic Franceso De Sanctis and others, that Ariosto's plays are unoriginal and lacking in freshness is a criticism not easily dismissed, but one that nevertheless misses the point of what Ariosto was attempting to achieve in his drama. It fails in large part to take into account the nature of the vernacular dramatist's task at the beginning of the sixteenth century. In the composition of erudite comedies, Ariosto was intent on re-creating a classical literary genre in his native tongue, and such a feat required him to draw extensively on popular Plautine and Terentian models. In the prologue to *The Pretenders*, he even states his desire "to imitate the celebrated classical poets as much as possible, not only in the form of their plays, but also in the content." He refers to this action as "poetic imitation rather than plagiarism"; consequently, it should be considered in the spirit of Renaissance *imitatio*. Just as Latin playwrights made use of Greek writers to create a viable Roman theater, Ariosto drew on the Latin tradition in order to initiate an Italian dramatic repertory. His role, therefore, was that of a pivotal adapter and initiator and, as such, was not totally devoid of originality. Even as he imitated, he made important modifications and innovations in order to reflect and comment on Ferrarese society and Italian courtly life. (His comments range from remarks on ducal penalties for poaching to statements on the vanity of women, the latter of which constitute a repeated theme.) Furthermore, although debts to Plautus and Terence are immediately apparent in the first two plays, they become progressively less evident in the later plays as the number of contemporary allusions increases and as ubiquitous classical prototypes are transformed into ever more realistic individuals. As Edmond M. Beame and Leonard G. Sbrocchi note in the introduction to their 1975 translation of the plays, with each successive play, Ariosto "became more daring and more original, introducing comic characters that never had appeared on the Roman stage, dealing with nonclassical themes, exploring human foibles, and placing his comedies in a contemporary Italian setting."

In his comedies, though not as skillfully as in *Orlando furioso*, Ariosto attempted to treat popular themes in classical ways. With a sympathetic ear for the life of his contemporaries, he combined a thorough knowledge of theatrical devices with a realistic depiction of human nature. Sprinkled with a liberal portion of his characteristic wit and irony, Ariosto's comedies equal any produced during his age.

THE COFFER

The Coffer, Ariosto's first play, composed originally in prose and later versified, is, as he states in the prologue, "a new comedy filled with various witticisms that neither Greek nor Latin tongues ever recited on the stage." It is, in other words, a modern comedy, even though most of its themes derive from *Phormio* (161 B.C.E.; English translation, 1598), *Heautontimorumenos* (163 B.C.E.; *The Self-Tormentor*, 1598), and *Andria* (166 B.C.E.; English translation, 1598) by Terence, and *Mostellaria* (*The Haunted House*, 1774) by Plautus. The action takes place in Mytilene, the main city on the infamously corrupt island of Lesbos, but concludes with a reference to the Moor's Inn, one of Ferrara's famous taverns. The plot revolves around a trick played by two young men,

Erofilo and Caridoro, on the procurer Lucrano in order to liberate two young ladies, Eulalia and Corisca, of whom the young men are enamored. Volpino, Erofilo's crafty servant, suggests the scheme, which suffers more than one reversal before it is accomplished. Briefly stated, the plan consists in convincing the young men's fathers that the procurer has stolen a coffer of gold brocade and must be punished. The originality of the play appears in such aspects as the transformation of the two girls from the stereotypical slaves of classical times into much more sympathetic figures. Ariosto also offers contemporary social commentary on the corruption of many Roman ecclesiastes and Ferrarese magistrates.

THE PRETENDERS

The setting for Ariosto's second play, *The Pretenders*, is the Italian city of Ferrara, but the situation derives from a favorite theme of classical comedy: the substitution of one person for another until a certain end is realized and true identities are revealed. The classical models cited in the prologue to this play are the *Captivi* (*The Captives*, 1767) by Plautus and the *Eunuchus* (161 B.C.E.; *The Eunuch*, 1598) of Terence; a tale in Giovanni Boccaccio's *Decameron: O, Prencipe Galetto* (1349-1351; *The Decameron*, 1620) may have been a closer source of the dramatist's inspiration in that both Ariosto's and Boccaccio's works feature a young lover who disguises himself in order to enter the house of his beloved. The lover, Erostrato, disguising himself as the servant of his beloved Polinesta's father, sends his own servant to school disguised as himself. Competing with an old doctor, Cleandro, who is able to offer a considerable sum of money for the hand of Polinesta, Erostrato and his fellow conspirators undergo many reverses and impersonations, which delightfully embellish the clever plot.

The play premiered in Ferrara in 1509, the year following the first performance of *The Coffer*. It was staged again a decade later in Rome, with sets by Raphael, to the great pleasure of Pope Leo X. The popularity of the comedy soon spread beyond the Alps. In addition to Gascoigne's English paraphrase in 1566, Jean Godard's *Les Desguisez* (1594) and Molière's *L'Avare* (pr. 1668; *The Miser*, 1672) are two French plays indebted to *The Pretenders*. The freshness of the play derives in no small part from the introduction of the pedantic character, Cleandro, the doctor of the law, to the Italian stage.

THE NECROMANCER

The Necromancer, the third of Ariosto's comedies to be performed, was begun during the same period as the first two, but it was not completed until 1520 and not performed until 1529. It tells the story of a swindler, or confidence man, Jachelino, who passes himself off as a necromancer or conjurer of spirits. He is able to trick many gullible people who come to him for advice, but in the end he is unmasked and forced to flee. The play, set in the city of Cremona, is quite modern and is characterized by quick dialogues and a satiric tone. The satire is directed as much against human folly as against astrology. The main plot, probably suggested by Terence's *Hecyra* (165 B.C.E.; *The Mother-in-Law*, 1598), concerns the reluctance of a young man, Cinthio, to consummate the betrothal arranged by his foster father, Massimo. Massimo hires the necromancer to discover the solution to his son's problem, not knowing that Cinthio has already married someone else. In order to be eligible for his inheritance, Cinthio has kept the former marriage a secret.

Again, coincidence and the machinations of a minor character bring about the reversals necessary for a happy ending when Cinthio is reunited with his secret love, Livinia, who turns out to be Massimo's long-lost daughter. Ariosto's careful planning and complex plot design, a carryover from his Roman models, again combines with his warmly human character portrayal to produce a clever and pleasing drama.

LENA

Lena, Ariosto's last complete play, was produced in 1528 and treats the theme of corruption. Ferrara provides the setting, and the astute protagonist provides the title for this work, which Marvin Herrick in 1960 called "Ariosto's best and most original comedy." Lena's husband assists a young lover, Flavio, in a scheme to allow him to marry his beloved, Licinia. Lena, who instructs Licinia in the ways of household tasks, is reluctant to allow the meeting, so Flavio's servant attempts to bribe her with money. Pacifico, who is little more than a procurer for his wife, Lena, who has many lovers, finally suggests to Flavio that he slip into the house hidden in a wine cask. As in *The Necromancer*, a subordinate character, here a usurer, creates insurmountable problems when he requires the wine cask in payment of a debt.

Fatio, Licinia's father, who is also Lena's landlord and one of her lovers, determines to hold the wine cask in his house until the argument over the debt is settled. As one scandal is circumvented, new ones arise. Flavio is eventually discovered in the cask, and the two young lovers, in order to avoid yet another scandal, are allowed to marry.

Repeated references to well-known Ferrarese places and personages underscore the play's satiric statement. The satire is directed at corrupt municipal authorities, incompetent officers of the law, and usurers charging exorbitant interest rates. In addition to the contemporary allusions, Ariosto based his story on a portion of Boccaccio's *The Decameron*. Although many scenes are also reminiscent of classical comedy, the play is filled with contemporary motifs.

OTHER MAJOR WORKS

POETRY: *Orlando furioso*, 1516, 1521, 1532 (English translation, 1591); *Satire*, 1534 (wr. 1517-1525; *Ariosto's Satyres*, 1608); *Cinque canti*, 1545.

BIBLIOGRAPHY

Ascoli, Albert Russell. "Ariosto and the 'Fier Pastor': Form and History in *Orlando furioso*." *Renaissance Quarterly* 54, no. 2 (Summer, 2001): 487-522. The essay looks at how Ariosto's epic poem comments on contemporary events, illuminating both the work and the times.

_____. *Ariosto's Bitter Harmony: Crisis and Evasion in the Italian Renaissance*. Princeton, N.J.: Princeton University Press, 1987. Although this work focuses on Ariosto's epic poem, it provides insight into his dramatic works.

Brand, C. P. "Ludovico Ariosto." In Vol. 2 of *European Writers*. New York: Charles Scribner's Sons, 1983. A brief biography of Ariosto that covers his life and works.

Finucci, Valeria. *The Lady Vanishes: Subjectivity and Representation in Castiglione and Ariosto*. Stanford, Calif.: Stanford University Press, 1995. Five chapters in this work examine Ariosto's depiction of women in his *Orlando furioso*. Her analysis sheds light on Ariosto's writing in general.

MacPhail, Eric. "Ariosto and the Prophetic Moment." *MLN* 116, no. 1 (January, 2001): 30-53. This essay, which looks at the historical context of Ariosto's epic poem, helps readers understand the times in which he wrote.

Murtaugh, Kristen Olson. *Ariosto and the Classical Simile*. Cambridge, Mass.: Harvard University Press, 1980. Examines the use of similes in Ariosto's works.

Madison U. Sowell

ARISTOPHANES

Born: Athens, Greece; c. 450 B.C.E.
Died: Athens, Greece; c. 385 B.C.E.

PRINCIPAL DRAMA

Acharnēs, 425 B.C.E. (*The Acharnians*, 1812)
Hippēs, 424 B.C.E. (*The Knights*, 1812)
Nephelai, 423 B.C.E. (*The Clouds*, 1708)
Sphēkes, 422 B.C.E. (*The Wasps*, 1812)
Eirēnē, 421 B.C.E. (*Peace*, 1837)
Ornithes, 414 B.C.E. (*The Birds*, 1824)
Lysistratē, 411 B.C.E. (*Lysistrata*, 1837)
Thesmophoriazousai, 411 B.C.E.
   (*Thesmophoriazusae*, 1837)
Batrachoi, 405 B.C.E. (*The Frogs*, 1780)
Ekklesiazousai, 392 B.C.E.? (*Ecclesiazusae*, 1837)
Ploutos, 388 B.C.E. (*Plutus*, 1651)

OTHER LITERARY FORMS
   Aristophanes is remembered only for his plays.

ACHIEVEMENTS
   Because the plays of his contemporaries and rivals have all been lost, it is impossible to credit Aristophanes with specific innovations in the development of Greek comedy. In his eleven surviving plays, however, one can trace an evolution in his own work. Although this evolution corresponds to a broader trend (the movement from Old Comedy to Middle and New Comedy), which in turn was influenced by changes in political and social conditions, Aristophanes' own development as an artist undoubtedly influenced such larger developments as much as it was shaped by them.

   Aristophanes was recognized as a great comic poet in his lifetime, winning many first prizes in dramatic competitions and almost never taking less than second prize. His first two plays have been lost, but his third, *The Acharnians*, displays an early mastery of comic technique and a profound unity of theme. Only later did Aristophanes develop unity of action; it was clearly not expected of Old Comedy, which had grown out of two or more heterogeneous elements (including the animal chorus and primitive forms of farce). Indeed, the unity of plot to be discerned in Aristophanes' later comedies (*Lysistrata, Ecclesiazusae*, and *Plutus*) is to some extent a compensation for the loss of certain features of the early plays—notably the freedom of the chorus to engage in wild ad hominem attacks and unbridled political satire.

   The outstanding features of Aristophanes' art are the audacity of his comic metaphors and the beauty of his choral lyrics. These are best displayed in his early and middle plays, as well as in *The Frogs*, a brilliant post mortem on Greek tragedy and the culture of imperial Athens (the Athenian defeat, marking the end of the Peloponnesian War, was imminent when the play was produced). Though Aristophanes survived his city's defeat and continued to develop as an artist, the postwar plays betray a certain weariness, a flagging of comic invention, corresponding to the political and cultural exhaustion of Athens in the early fourth century B.C.E. Perhaps the greatest single achievement of Aristophanes is the fact that his are the only plays of the Old Comedy to have survived—a tribute, surely, to his superb comic craftsmanship.

BIOGRAPHY

Very little is known of Aristophanes' life; most of what is known has been gleaned from his plays and is therefore vague or uncertain because of the comic content. The only evidence for his birthdate is the fact that he was "very young" when his first play was produced in 427 B.C.E. His first three plays were produced by another man, but it is not known whether this was because of a legal age limit, Aristophanes' inexperience, or simple preference (some of his later plays were also produced by others). He belonged to the *deme* (township) of Kudathenaion, and his father's name was Philippos. Nothing is known, however, of the family's social or economic status. A line in *The Acharnians* has been interpreted to mean that he or his father had land holdings on the island of Aegina, but these may have been acquired during the distribution of Aeginetan land to Athenian citizens after the expulsion of the islanders in 431. According to the scholiasts, the poet was indicted several times by the demagogue Cleon—whom he attacked in several plays—for usurping citizenship rights and for holding Athens up to ridicule before foreign visitors (the latter charge stemmed from his lost play *The Babylonians*, produced in 426, which portrayed the subject-allies of Athens as Babylonian slaves). Apparently Cleon was unable to make either charge stick, and Aristophanes returned to the attack. *The Knights*, presented in 424 (and which won a first place), portrays Cleon as a venal slave who flatters and cheats his master Demos ("the people" personified). The popularity of the play did not, however, have any effect on Cleon's popularity: A few weeks after it won first prize, Cleon was chosen as one of the city's ten generals for the following year.

From the lists of victors in the dramatic festivals, it can be inferred that Aristophanes was a prolific and popular playwright. The Alexandrian scholars of the third and second centuries B.C.E. knew of forty-four plays attributed to him, forty of which they consid-

Aristophanes (Library of Congress)

ered genuine. According to an early fourth century B.C.E. inscription, he also held public office (as *prytanis*, one of the presiding members of the Boulē, the council that set the agenda for the legislative assembly). His last datable play is the *Plutus*, staged in 388; two other plays were staged, perhaps posthumously, by his son Araros. All three of Aristophanes' sons tried their hand at writing comedies, but their works have not survived.

There is one further piece of biographical evidence: the vivid portrait of Aristophanes drawn by Plato in his dialogue the *Symposion* (388-368 B.C.E.; *Symposium*, 1701). As a character in the dialogue, Aristophanes delivers a brilliantly witty speech on the origin of erotic love, which he traces to the "globular" condition of the first mortals. These globular humans had two heads, four arms, and four legs apiece, and were so powerful that the gods felt threatened by them, so Zeus cut each one in half. Sexual love is thus the attraction between "halves" of formerly whole beings. What lovers really seek is indissoluble union with their other halves. This speech cannot be attributed to the historical Aristophanes. Plato was a great stylist and could easily have invented the whole. Yet the comic myth is akin to those found in Aristophanes' plays, and it sheds an interesting light on the relationship between the comic dramatist and the philosopher Socrates, whom Aristophanes satirized (unfairly, many scholars feel) in his play *The Clouds*. Socrates is also a character in the *Symposium*, and his speech, which follows and rebuts that of Aristophanes, reveals the irreducible opposition between the two men's views of the human condition. As scholar David Grene has put it, what Aristophanes most objected to in Socrates' teaching was the idea that philosophical investigation superseded all other claims on people's attention and energy, including the pleasures of food, sex, and poetry. These pleasures, together with that of competition, which Plato also deplored, are central to Aristophanes' comic vision.

ANALYSIS

Because Aristophanes has had no real literary heirs, or imitators, in subsequent European literature, some discussion of Old Comedy as a genre is in order. There are good reasons why this genre died out when Athens went into its decline and was never revived. Old Comedy was nurtured and sustained by a constellation of social and political features of imperial Athens, which never came together in quite the same way subsequently. The fifth century B.C.E. saw the height of Athenian fortunes, and the sense of limitless possibility that the times inspired is reflected in Aristophanes' early plays. Athenian democracy was also at its height. It was a limited democracy, insofar as citizenship was limited, but a direct democracy in which the citizens themselves voted on every proposed law and treaty. There were obvious analogies between the legislative assembly, the popular courts (where juries numbered in the hundreds, sometimes in the thousands), and the theater, where the people assembled in a body on a few festival days each year

to see productions subsidized by state taxes. The no-holds-barred approach prevailing in assembly and court debate spilled over into the comedies, which are filled with ad hominem attacks on individuals. Politicians and poets were favorite targets, but a man might be singled out for ridicule because of his appearance, his cowardice in battle, or even his sexual proclivities.

Two unique features of Old Comedy reflect its political and social setting with special vividness. These are the agon and the parabasis. The agon is a contest, partly physical but chiefly verbal, between the protagonist and the chorus. Its rhetoric reflects that of the assembly and law courts (and of Greek tragedy as well, which had a similar relationship to its social and political milieu). The parabasis is an address to the audience in which the comic chorus drops whatever dramatic identity the play imposes on it to speak in the first person, in the poet's own voice. The parabasis may be only tangentially related to the plot and can address any political or social issue, although always in a fantastic vein that must have blunted its political impact.

Scholars disagree considerably on the question of Aristophanes' political purpose and beliefs, though most see him as in some sense conservative—that is, supportive of moderate (as opposed to radical) democracy and of the "traditional" virtues proper to an agrarian, nonimperial economy: peace, political stability, and free trade. It is difficult, though, to elicit any specific political program from the plays, because of their essentially anarchic spirit, which tends to subvert the few sober pronouncements of individual characters. Even if it could be demonstrated from the plays that Aristophanes had such a program, the question of its impact would remain. Here again evidence is slight and ambiguous. There is no known case in which a comedy demonstrably influenced public policy. Aristophanes produced a whole series of brilliant antiwar plays during the course of the Peloponnesian War (some took first prize), but the war continued. Even the *Peace* of 421, staged the same year the Peace of Nicias between Athens and Sparta was concluded, seems more a reflection of the city's mood than a peace initiative on Aristophanes' part.

The attack on Socrates in *The Clouds* is cited by Plato in the *Apologia Sōkratous* (399-390 B.C.E.; *Apology*, 1675; which purports to be Socrates' own defense at his trial) as a source of popular hostility against the philosopher, but *The Clouds* preceded the trial by twenty-five years. What is more, to judge from the *Symposium*, Aristophanes and Socrates belonged to the same circle of friends; surely the poet had no intention of urging any action against the philosopher. Scholar K. J. Dover has pointed out that Aristophanes survived the advent of oligarchic regimes as well as the democratic backlash that accompanied their overthrow; this would hardly have been possible had he been perceived as a partisan of either. A careful reading of his plays will reveal that they take advantage precisely of the freedom from responsibility that Old Comedy permits to create a world of fantasy and wish-fulfillment. Though Aristophanes addresses real political issues, the solutions he offers are not political but poetic ones.

THE ACHARNIANS

The Acharnians, Aristophanes' earliest surviving play, deserves close consideration not only because of its intrinsic merit but also because it exemplifies two strands that run throughout his work: a celebration of the joys of peace (with its corollary, an attack on the evils of war) and a fantasy of limitless possibility for the protagonist. These two strands are intimately interwoven, for the "pacifism" of Aristophanes is by no means the selfless and idealistic stance evoked by that word in modern times. His heroes hate war not because it entails the shedding of blood but because it results in a dearth of good things: food, wine, sex, and the freedom to do what one pleases and go where one pleases. Therefore, Dikaiopolis, the hero of *The Acharnians*, after trying in vain to raise the issue of peace negotiations in the assembly, makes his own private treaty with Sparta and proceeds to enjoy the benefits: freedom to celebrate the rural Dionysia, to trade with former enemies for imported delicacies, and to stay at home and feast while General Lamachos goes off to battle with his rations of salt fish and onions. The agon in this play is a debate between Dikaiopolis and a chorus of Acharnian charcoal-burners (from Acharnai, one of the demes of

Attica), who hate the Spartans for ravaging their lands and can think of nothing but revenge. Dikaiopolis wins them over with a comic version of the war's causes (a parody of Herodotus's account of the reasons for enmity between Greece and Asia Minor) and a reminder that poor men have the least to gain from war. Like many of Aristophanes' heroes, Dikaiopolis is a "little man" of middle age or older whose triumph over the powers that be is symbolized by his rejuvenation or restored sexual potency at the end of the play. As Lamachos returns wounded from battle, Dikaiopolis returns drunk from the feast, ready for a night of lovemaking with two courtesans. Yet this play is hardly a straightforward plea for the "little man," for once he has his treaty, Dikaiopolis refuses to extend it to include another farmer whose two oxen have been seized by the enemy.

The consistency of the play lies in its imagery. On the level of dramatic action, each Aristophanic comedy is built on one or more controlling images that assume a life of their own; in the choral odes, these and other images appear in a "crystallized" form. (In Old Comedy, as in Greek tragedy, the choral poetry provides a kind of lyric reflection on the action it interrupts.) In *The Acharnians*, the central comic image is that of wine, which becomes a metaphor for peace thanks to a pun: The Greek for "truce" is *spondai*, literally the "libations" that accompanied ratification of treaties. Dikaiopolis is offered three kinds of *spondai* by the Spartans and picks the best "vintage"—that is, the longest truce. The image is appropriate in other ways as well, for peace was associated with the euphoria of drunkenness and the freedom to celebrate festivals (many of which were curtailed during the war). At the play's end, Dikaiopolis is proclaimed the winner in a drinking contest—a standard feature of the Lenaia, the festival at which the play was produced—and his victory is made to suggest (before the fact) the poet's own victory in the dramatic contest. It should be obvious that such "pacifism" as the play contains is fully compatible with the most vigorous forms of competition; within the comic universe of his plays, Aristophanes loves a good fight as much as anyone. Nor would his Greek audience have perceived this as a paradox: There was a traditional distinction, going back at least to Hesiod's *Erga kai Emerai* (c. 700 B.C.E.; *Works and Days*, 1618), between useful and destructive *eris*, "strife." Only the latter was considered hateful; rivalry and emulation were encouraged as the means to excellence and prosperity.

PEACE

This preoccupation with competition is visible, though somewhat more restrained, in the two other extant antiwar plays of Aristophanes. *Peace* is unusual in that it has no agon; instead, the members of the chorus, farmers from all the city-states, are made to "pull together" (literally and figuratively) as they raise the goddess Peace from the pit to which War has consigned her. Exhumation is only one of a constellation of images presiding over the action of this most earthy play, which opens with two slaves kneading cakes of excrement to feed a giant dung-beetle. The play's hero, Trygaios, mounts the beetle and flies to heaven, where he finds War preparing to pound the Greek cities in a mortar. No pestle is available, however (both the Athenian and the Spartan commanders in chief, Cleon and Brasidas, having recently died), and Trygaios takes advantage of the circumstance to unearth Peace, whose acolyte Opora (Harvest) he then weds. His flight to heaven notwithstanding, Trygaios has less of the entrepreneur about him than does Dikaiopolis. He is willing to share his good fortune with all who desire peace, and he even presents the goddess's other acolyte, Theoria (Ceremony), to the Council as a gift.

LYSISTRATA

In his generosity, Trygaios anticipates Lysistrata, heroine of the play that bears her name. Though she leads the women of Greece in a successful coup that leaves them in possession of the Acropolis (and the Athenian treasury), her only aim is to induce the men to make peace; she keeps nothing for herself. The motif of competition recurs in the "battle of the sexes" she so cunningly orchestrates. The agon of *Lysistrata* involves two semi-choruses, one of old men and one of old women, who at first shower one another with abuse but are eventually reconciled, forming a single chorus. The attack on the Acropolis that the old men stage, complete with battering rams

and torches, is an obvious sexual metaphor. True to their oath to resist their husbands' advances, the women repulse the attack and douse the torches. Yet once the men have signed a treaty ending the war, they are admitted for a banquet, and each goes home with his own wife, in a mass version of the "wedding" that so often closes Aristophanes' plays. Frequently in Aristophanes, and notably in Trygaios's address to the Council as he presents them with Theoria, the sexual act itself is described as a struggle, yet another form of contention. That it is an example of "good" strife should be obvious because it is also a form of union, and indeed, Trygaios compares it to various events in the athletic contests, which were among the few truly Panhellenic institutions of the fifth century B.C.E.

Despite these points of comparison, the three antiwar plays differ from one another in important ways, as might be expected from their dates of production. *The Acharnians*, fairly early in the war, allows its hero greater selfishness and irresponsibility than does either of the later plays; the mood of *Peace*, staged in 421 when peace seemed imminent, is more euphoric than that of *Lysistrata* in 411. There is even a note of pathos in Lysistrata's plea for the women left widowed and unmarried by the ongoing war, in which they have no say. The fantasy of unlimited possibility, reflected in Dikaiopolis's private treaty and Trygaios's flight to heaven, has disappeared from the latter play. Its fullest development was reached not in the war plays but in *The Knights*, and especially *The Birds*.

THE KNIGHTS

The Knights and *The Birds* are quintessentially Athenian celebrations of a quality that only the Athenians (and not all of them at that) considered a virtue: *polupragmosunē*, "doing-muchness," or "having a finger in every pie." *The Knights* is an attack on the demagogue Cleon, whom Aristophanes accuses of pandering to the people's whims for his own profit. Cleon is defeated and replaced in the course of the play (which is one protracted agon) by a man who outdoes him in pandering—a Sausage-Seller, whose qualifications for the role of demagogue are low birth, an ear-splitting voice, and the ways of the streetwise. Cleon and the Sausage-Seller compete to satisfy the appetite of Demos, "the people" personified. Although ostensibly Demos's slaves, the two panderers hold the purse strings, and what finally recommends the Sausage-Seller to Demos is the fact that he holds nothing back for himself. At the play's end, the Sausage-Seller rejuvenates his master (by "cooking" him, as Medea promised to do for the aged King Pelias), bringing back the sober and responsible Demos of the Persian War era. This miracle, however, lacks the dramatic power of his unrestrained pandering contest with Cleon. To judge from the parabasis, the poet's nostalgia is not so much for the sobriety of the old Athens as for its unchallenged supremacy.

THE BIRDS

Aristophanes' ultimate power-fantasy is *The Birds*. Two Athenians, Pisthetairos and Euelpides, leave their city and go to live with the birds, because, they say, Athens has become unlivable. They proceed to found a new city in the sky (Nephelokokkugia, or "Cloudcuckooland"), which outdoes even imperial Athens in *polupragmosunē*. With the birds' help, they build a wall between heaven and earth that keeps the smoke of burnt offerings from reaching the gods; reduced to starvation, the gods are forced to yield Basileia, a female personification of kingship, to Pisthetairos. The controlling metaphor in this play is flight, which confers not only freedom from the ordinary constraints of the human condition but also vast power—the power of one who surveys the world from a great height, the better to administer it. It is the divine power of Zeus, in short, for Pisthetairos is not content merely to become a bird; he must become a god and king of the gods. *The Birds* is the most fully realized of Aristophanes' power-fantasies, both in its dramatic coherence and in the beauty of its lyrics. It is also the one that leaves the "real world" most completely behind. Regardless of whether Aristophanes intended it as a commentary on the Sicilian expedition (which had been launched the previous year), it conveys perfectly the boundless Athenian audacity behind the expedition.

THE CLOUDS

The Clouds, although a relatively early play, deserves to be considered with the later plays for sev-

eral reasons. In the first place, it ends not with the apotheosis of the hero but with an act of violence bred of his frustration. At the same time, it places greater emphasis on the portrayal and interaction of the characters, a trait associated with the later plays (*The Frogs*, *Ecclesiazusae*, *Plutus*). The text of *The Clouds* that has survived is unfortunately not the text that was staged; it is a revision, though an incomplete one. In the revised parabasis, Aristophanes claims that he considers *The Clouds* his best play to date; he insists particularly on its subtlety and originality. Scholar Grene has suggested that he is referring to "the psychological study of human personality," which looms larger in this than in the other early plays. Though it lacks consistency and dramatic unity (perhaps because of the incomplete revision), the play features an unusually realistic hero—indeed, a sort of antihero. His name is Strepsiades (which means, roughly, "Twister"), and he is of humble country stock, like Dikaiopolis and Trygaios; unlike them, however, he is genuinely corrupt. In order to get out of paying the debts his son has incurred, he enrolls at the Thinkery, presided over by Socrates, who is here made to represent all the dubious achievements of the "new learning" (the sophistic movement of the fifth century B.C.E.). Strepsiades himself is too thick-witted to learn what Socrates has to teach, so he persuades his son Pheidippides to take the course—and thereby gets his comeuppance, for Pheidippides uses the specious reasoning he learns to justify not only defaulting on debts but also beating his parents. Strepsiades gets his revenge—by burning down the Thinkery, an act of desperation, not an assertion of comic possibility like Dikaiopolis's truce or the Sausage-Seller's trouncing of Cleon. In this play, Aristophanes came to grips with a knotty problem that has not lost its contemporary flavor: the interaction of character and values in the educational process. Perhaps because of this very complexity, the resolution, as it stands, lacks the comic release of most of Aristophanes' finales.

ECCLESIAZUSAE

In this respect, *The Clouds* resembles *Ecclesiazusae*, one of Aristophanes' two surviving fourth century B.C.E. plays. Though it lacks the wit and subtlety of *The Clouds*, *Ecclesiazusae* shares its realistic, not to say pessimistic, perspective. *Ecclesiazusae* is also a kind of anti-*Lysistrata*, for it sets up a utopia under the leadership of women but then severely undercuts it by dramatizing the chaos that results. The women's edicts are either unenforceable (when ordered to surrender their goods to the community, some citizens simply withhold them) or profoundly unnatural (the young and beautiful are forced to gratify the sexual desires of the old and ugly). The sense of realism and disenchantment is strengthened by a drastic reduction in the role of the chorus (resulting in a dearth of lyric passages) and by a more concentrated plot. The old Aristophanes can be detected, though, in the anti-philosophical stances of the play. Though the idea of pooling goods and sexual partners is attributed to the heroine, Praxagora, it is likely to have been the brain-child of a sophist or philosopher. Plato was its most famous exponent, but his *Politeia* (388-368 B.C.E.; *Republic*, 1701) came later (unless an early version of it was already in circulation in 392). Whatever its source, the idea belongs, in Aristophanes' view, to that class of abstractions ridiculed in *The Clouds* for the discomfort they cause to all but the few clever enough to manipulate them. It has been suggested that in contrast with the early plays, in which the old heroes are rejuvenated and the clock turned back to a more vigorous age, the late plays merely complete the work of destruction already in progress. According to this view, the rule of women is symbolic of the dissolution of the polity and the victory of the private over the political sphere. It is certain that politics disappeared entirely from New Comedy, the forerunner of the romance and of most modern comedy, in which the private sphere fills the foreground.

THE FROGS

The Frogs is the last surviving work of Old Comedy and perhaps the greatest. It was produced in 405, shortly after the deaths of Sophocles and Euripides and just before the Athenian defeat at Aegospotami, which ended the Peloponnesian War. The hero is Dionysus, divine patron of the theater, who undertakes a trip to Hades because he can find no good tragedians aboveground. His idea is to bring back Euripides, but once below, he finds himself called on to judge be-

tween Euripides and Aeschylus, who are contending for the "chair of tragedy." In the end, Dionysus declares Aeschylus the winner and brings *him* back to Athens. There are two choruses: one of frogs, who engage in a shouting match with Dionysus as he rows across the Stygian lake in Charon's boat, and one of Initiates to the Eleusinian Mysteries, whose life in the underworld is a joyous one of choral song and torchlight revels. The Initiates represent a kind of ideal community, warning away all who would engage in sedition or accept bribes, but they are also a true comic chorus, full of insults and bawdy jokes. This harmonizes perfectly with their dramatic identity as initiates, for the mysteries blended fertility cult with eschatological promises, and the ceremonies included the hurling of bawdy taunts.

The agon consists of the dramatic contest between the two tragedians, including hilarious parodies of each man's style and culminating in the actual weighing of their verses on a scale. Much has been made of the fact that Dionysus bases his final decision on the two men's political advice to the city. As in the finale of *The Knights*, however, the emphasis is not so much on the actual content of the advice as on the evocation of a time—that of Aeschylus's prime—when Athens was the unchallenged leader of Greece. Despite the play's premise, that the best poets are all in Hades, there is surprisingly little black comedy. The choral lyrics radiate hope (albeit an eschatological hope), and the spirit of emulation proper to Aristophanes' early plays enlivens *The Frogs* from first to last. In addition to the agon proper, there is not only a shouting match between Dionysus and the frogs but also a whipping contest between Dionysus and his slave Xanthias (to determine which of them is the god).

Aristophanes is aware, as always, of the dramatic competition in which he is himself a contestant and pulls out all the stops—just as he depicts Aeschylus and Euripides doing—in order to win. At the same time, however, there is a poignant emphasis on the need for reconciliation among the city's various factions if Athens is to survive. Therefore, the parabasis, sung by the chorus of Initiates, pleads not for Aristophanes' victory but for a general amnesty permitting exiled citizens to return. Though Aristophanes delights in competition to the very end, he recognizes that if the terms of competition are not adhered to, the city cannot stand. For later readers of *The Frogs*, the play's poignancy is increased by hindsight: Athens did fall, never to regain the eminence it enjoyed in Aeschylus's day. The fact that he chose Initiates for his chorus suggests that Aristophanes had an intimation of this and that he realized the dramatic art of Athens need not share the city's political fate—precisely because the "solutions" it offered were not political but poetic and self-sustaining visions.

BIBLIOGRAPHY

Bowie, A. M. *Aristophanes: Myth, Ritual, and Comedy.* New York: Cambridge University Press, 1993. Bowie uses anthropological techniques in comparing Aristophanes' plays with Greek myths and rituals with similar story lines in an attempt to discover how the original audiences would have responded to the plays. Includes bibliography and index.

Harvey, David, and John Wilkins, eds. *The Rivals of Aristophanes: Studies in Athenian Old Comedy.* London: Duckworth and the Classical Press of Wales, 2000. Twenty-eight essays on the other comic poets of Athenian Old Comedy, based on the fragments and citations that survive. Includes bibliography.

Lada-Richards, Ismene. *Initiating Dionysus: Ritual and Theatre in Aristophanes' "Frogs."* New York: Oxford University Press, 1999. The author uses literary and anthropological approaches in looking at how a member of Greek society would have viewed the play and Dionysus as a dramatic figure. Includes bibliography and indexes.

MacDowell, Douglas M. *Aristophanes and Athens: An Introduction to the Plays.* New York: Oxford University Press, 1995. MacDowell provides an introduction to Aristophanes' plays, including information about Athens and the political climate, essential to understanding some of the allusions in Aristophanes' works. Includes bibliography and index.

Russo, Carlo Ferdinando. *Aristophanes: An Author for the Stage.* New York: Routledge, 1994. Russo examines Aristophanes' dramatic technique in a work that is both scholarly and lively. Includes bibliography and index.

Taaffe, Laurne K. *Aristophanes and Women.* New York: Routledge, 1993. Taaffe examines the portrayal of women in Aristophanes' plays, focusing on *Lysistrata*, *Thesmophoriazusae*, and *Ecclesiazusae*. Includes bibliography and index.

Lillian Doherty

FERNANDO ARRABAL

Born: Melilla, Spanish Morocco; August 11, 1932

PRINCIPAL DRAMA

Pique-nique en campagne, wr. 1952, pr. 1959, pb. 1961 (*Picnic on the Battlefield*, 1960)

Cérémonie pour un noir assasiné, wr. 1956, pb. 1965, pr. 1966 (*Ceremony for an Assassinated Black*, 1971)

Le Labyrinthe, wr. 1956, pb. 1961, pr. 1967 (*The Labyrinth*, 1967)

Les Amours impossibles, wr. 1957, pr. 1965, pb. 1967 (*The Impossible Loves*, 1968)

La Cimetière des voitures, pb. 1958, pr. 1966 (*The Car Cemetery*, 1960)

La Communion solennelle, pr. 1958, pb. 1963 (*Solemn Communion: Panic Ceremony*, 1967)

Concert dans un œuf, wr. 1958, pb. 1965, pr. 1966

Les Deux Bourreaux, pb. 1958, pr. 1960 (*The Two Executioners*, 1960)

Fando et Lis, pb. 1958, pr. 1959 (*Fando and Lis*, 1962)

Oraison, pb. 1958, pr. 1965 (*Orison*, 1961)

Théâtre, pb. 1958-1996 (19 volumes)

Le Tricycle, pr. 1958, pb. 1961 (*The Tricycle*, 1966)

Guernica, pr. 1959, pb. 1961 (English translation, 1967)

La Bicyclette du condamné, pb. 1961, pr. 1966 (*The Condemned Man's Bicycle*, 1967)

Plays, pb. 1962-1970 (3 volumes)

Le Grand Cérémonial, pr. 1964, pb. 1965 (*The Grand Ceremonial*, 1970)

Le Couronnement, pr., pb. 1965 (revised as *Le Lai de Barabbas*, pb. 1969)

Striptease de la jalousie, pr. 1965, pb. 1967 (*Striptease of Jealousy*, 1968)

Cérémonie pour une chèvre sur un nuage, pr. 1966, pb. 1967 (*Ceremony for a Goat on a Cloud*, 1978)

L'Architecte et l'Empereur d'Assyrie, pr., pb. 1967 (*The Architect and the Emperor of Assyria*, 1969)

La Jeunesse illustrée, pr., pb. 1967

Dieu est-il devenu fou?, pb. 1967 (*Has God Gone Mad?*, 1978)

Une Orange sur le mont de Vénus, wr. 1968, pb. 1976 (*An Orange on the Mount of Venus*, 1977)

L'Aurore rouge et noire, pr. 1968, pb. 1969 (includes *Groupuscle de mon cœur* [*The Groupuscle of My Heart*, 1969], *Tous les Parfums d'Arabie*, *Sous les pavés*, *La Plage*, and *Les Fillettes*)

Le Jardin des délices, pr., pb. 1969 (*The Garden of Delights*, 1974)

Bestialité érotique, pr., pb. 1969 (*Erotic Bestiality*, 1978)

Une Tortue nommée Dostoievski, pr., pb. 1969 (*A Tortoise Named Dostoyevsky*, 1978)

Et ils passèrent des menottes aux fleurs, pr., pb. 1969 (*And They Put Handcuffs on the Flowers*, 1972)

Ars Amandi, pb. 1970 (opera libretto)

Le Ciel et la merde, pb. 1972

La Grande Revue de XXe siècle, pb. 1972

Bella Ciao, la guerre de mille ans, pr., pb. 1972

La Marche royale, pr., pb. 1973

Sur le fil: Ou, La Ballade du train fantôme, pr., pb. 1974

Jeunes Barbares d'aujourd'hui, pr., pb. 1975 (*Today's Young Barbarians*, 1978)

Le Ciel et la merde II, pr. 1976, pb. 1981

La Gloire en images, pr., pb. 1976 (ballet scenario)

La Tour de Babel, pr., pb. 1976

Vole-moi un petit milliard, pr. 1977, pb. 1978

La Pastaga des loufs: Ou, Ouverture orang-outan, pb. 1978

Punk et punk et colégram, pb. 1978

Le Roi de Sodome, pr. 1979, pb. 1981

Inquisición, pr. 1980, pb. 1982

Mon doux royaume saccagé, pr. 1980, pb. 1981

L'Extravagante Réussite de Jésus-Christ, Karl Marx, et William Shakespeare, pr. 1982

Tormentos y delicias de la carne: Homenaje à la conjura de los necios de John Kennedy Toole, pb. 1985

Les "Cucarachas" de Yale, pb. 1987

Une Pucelle pour un gorille, pb. 1987

The Red Madonna, pb. 1987

La Travesée de l'empire, pb. 1987

Comme un lis entre les épines, pb. 1996

Carta de amor, pr. 1999, pb. 2001

OTHER LITERARY FORMS

Fernando Arrabal is well known as a filmmaker; his first film, *Viva la muerte* (1971), is still considered to be his finest work in that medium. *J. L. Borges: Una Vida de Poesía* was released in 1998. He has also written a number of novels and a series of "cartas" (letters) to Spanish and International political leaders such as Francisco Franco, the king of Spain, Fidel Castro, and several Spanish prime ministers. Arrabal commissioned numerous paintings that conform to his design, published a book of photographs of New York City, and has written books as well as a regular column in *L'Express* on the game of chess. Arrabal has directed a number of his own plays around the world.

ACHIEVEMENTS

Although Fernando Arrabal's theater has consistently shocked and outraged many critics, his reputa-

Fernando Arrabal (© Miriam Berkley)

tion as an important, innovative avant-garde dramatist has been clearly established. Early negative reviews that focused on his "pornographic excesses" helped attract an audience and soon made him the most performed playwright in Paris. Combining a Spanish temperament and sense of black humor with innovative techniques reflective of the artistic ambience of Paris, Arrabal has become the first Spanish playwright since Federico García Lorca to earn worldwide recognition. His contributions to the theater were summed up by Clive Barnes in a review of *The Architect and the Emperor of Assyria* in *The New York Times*:

> Mr. Arrabal, with his perceptions, absurdities, loves and understanding, is a playwright to be honored, treasured and understood. In this play he is saying something about the isolation, the solitariness and the need of twentieth century man that, so far as I can see, no other playwright has quite gotten on stage before.

Arrabal has received a number of major awards. He received the prestigious Premio Nadal in 1984 for his novel *La torre herida por el rayo* (1983; *The Tower Struck by Lightning*, 1988) and the Espasa Calpe award in 1994 for his collection of essays *La dudosa luz del día*. He was awarded the Premio Nacional de Teatro in Spain in 2001. In 2001, when tradition dictated that the Premio Cervantes go to a Latin American writer, he received the most votes of any Spaniard.

BIOGRAPHY

Fernando Arrabal has justified his decision to write in the following terms: "I believe that I have a right to be a writer: that of possessing a biography rich in bizarre phenomena, in striking events." A brief examination of the experiences that dominated his formative years attests the veracity of his observation.

On July 17, 1936, when Arrabal was not quite four years old, the civil war broke out in Spanish Morocco, and the young boy's father was dragged out of bed, arrested, and summarily sentenced to death for his leftist inclinations. The death sentence was later commuted to thirty years' imprisonment; some years later, however, Arrabal's father escaped from the psychiatric ward of a prison in Burgos. There was more than nine feet of snow on the ground at the time, and he was dressed only in pajamas. He was never seen again.

The young Arrabal was reared in a conservative, female-dominated home that reflected the oppressive political climate of post-civil war Spain. No mention of his father was permitted; even his image was systematically excised from all family photographs. When Arrabal was seventeen, he chanced on a suitcase in the attic containing letters and photos of his father. That discovery prompted him to cease speaking to his mother for five years and provided him with the impetus for total rebellion. He began to frequent the Ateneo in Madrid, where he discovered such writers as Lewis Carroll, Fyodor Dostoevski, and Franz Kafka. An early success in a playwriting contest and a trip to Paris to see the Berlin Ensemble led him to reside in the French capital and devote himself to theater. Arrabal returned to Spain periodically until 1967, when he was imprisoned there for a blasphemous dedication in one of his novels. He was released after a month because of the pressure exerted on the Spanish government by numerous luminaries of the theater; he did not return until several years after Francisco Franco's death. The years since his traumatic experience in Spain have been highlighted by successes around the world in theater and in a variety of other genres, ranging from film to poetry, from essay to novel. In 2000 his play *The Car Cemetery* was produced by the Centro Dramático Nacional and performed with great success throughout Spain. His work *Carta de amor* was produced by that same national theater company in January, 2002.

Arrabal has produced a large number of works for the theater and continues to be productive into the twenty-first century. The quality of his work varies considerably and it appears that he will be remembered primarily for his plays written between 1952 and 1980. His most effective works generally find their inspiration in his own intensely felt experiences related to life in Spain. The number of significant works completed and the range of style, theme and dramatic conception they exhibit assure an important niche for the expatriate Spanish dramatist in any assessment of contemporary European theater.

ANALYSIS

Throughout his career as a playwright, Fernando Arrabal's finest works have been characterized by his unique ability to project memories, dreams, and obsessions onto the stage in a manner at once engaging and disturbing. The paradoxes and dualities of his own personality have formed the basis for a dialectic in his work, manifested by the clash between innocence and perversity, between Surrealist humor and lyricism and the grotesque. Despite such constants in his theater, however, a definite evolution in his technique can be identified, and it is expedient to divide his dramatic production into three periods or stages.

EARLY PLAYS

Arrabal's early plays are characterized by childlike characters who occupy a restricted area of theater space and whose innocence and naïveté clash with their own acts of amoral cruelty and with the incomprehensible, threatening macrocosmos that eventually crushes them. In some of these works, the playwright seems to be seeking the resolution of his own childhood fears and obsessions while at the same time presenting a universal vision of the oppressive nature of contemporary life. Ceremony, often deriving from Christian rituals, Surrealism, Beckettian absurdities, and humor based on the incongruous all appear regularly in these works. A circularity of structure, echoed in Arrabal's symbolic use of the wheel and the balloon, and in his predilection for the labyrinth, constitutes another important element of his early theater. Works such as *The Two Executioners* and *Fando and Lis* are obliquely autobiographical, revealing the dramatist's psychological obsessions Dreams and nightmares are re-created onstage, most notably in *The Labyrinth*, Arrabal's

Kafkaesque vision of his country's sociopolitical malaise. The basis for his mature theater, with its Artaudian conception of stage space, emphasis on the mutability of reality, and profound exploration of the realm of memory and the surreal, can be identified in some of these early endeavors, most notably *The Car Cemetery*.

THE CAR CEMETERY

The Car Cemetery, like several earlier plays, explores the nature of good and evil in the context of an oppressive, irrational world. The setting of the drama is an automobile graveyard, a microcosm of society, run by Milos and Dila. The services they provide the residents of the establishment include Dila's sexual favors, "rooms" in the remains of cars, and a urinal for those in need of one. Emanou and his fellow jazz musicians, Fodere and Topé, entertain the poor nightly. Emanou is in love with Dila, who warns him whenever the police are seeking him. Topé betrays him to the authorities, and Lasca and Tiossido, trainer and athlete, respectively, turn into police who flagellate Emanou and crucify him on a bicycle. As the play concludes, several inhabitants of the graveyard murder a newborn infant, and Tiossido and Lasca reverse their original roles and resume their campaign to set a new world record.

Much of the structure of *The Car Cemetery* is provided by the role reversals involving several pairs of characters. Milos generally dominates Dila; on several occasions he punishes her, once for not proffering sexual favors and, irrationally, another time for doing exactly that. Dila, however, aggressively threatens a cowering Milos with chastisement at another moment in the play. The drama's circular structure derives from the physical movement of Lasca and Tiossido. Those two characters begin and conclude the work by seeking a new world record, but in reverse roles. Their relationship reflects both the indomitable will of the ambitious mother and the male's need to assert himself physically in response to the feelings of inferiority he experiences when he compares himself to the female. Lasca and Tiossido also represent the oppressive nature of the state. At the play's conclusion, the absurdity of their confining, suffocating route is affirmed, and their potential

to metamorphose into police serving the system remains unchanged.

Emanou and his concept of morality constitute an essential component of the drama's thematic fiber. Like Arrabal's childlike characters in earlier plays, Emanou commits murder and performs other socially unacceptable acts. He is convinced that he will be pardoned, however, because he has memorized the meaning of goodness: "Well, when we're good, we experience a great inner joy born of peace of spirit that is revealed to us when we see that we resemble the ideal man." Emanou's resemblance to the "ideal man," which is reinforced by the miracles he performs, is all too apparent, but only seems to condemn him in the anti-Christian world in which he lives. He plays for the poor because it is impossible to put them out of their misery by killing them all, and he praises Dila for her goodness, which he equates with her willingness to accommodate all men sexually. When he does kill, Emanou always makes a point of bringing flowers to the grave of his victim. The love shared by Dila and Emanou seems to set off the social mechanism that leads to Emanou's passion and death. If Christ can be thought of as love, then both he and that emotion are abrogated by the mechanized, dehumanized world of the automobile graveyard.

The graveyard itself constitutes a central, visual symbol of the wreckage of civilization, of the moral destructiveness of modern technological society. The possibilities for staging the play evince the growth in Arrabal's conception of theater space and of the interplay between the audience and the *mise en scène*. A political note also derives from the metaphoric concept of the graveyard. Milos plays the dual role of humble servant and tyrannical oppressor to the inhabitants of Arrabal's dramatic microcosm. As José Ortega suggests, *The Car Cemetery* is a play in which Milos incarnates authoritative paternalism, aggression, and the collective neurosis of a people who, under Franco's repressive regime, have lost the ability to overcome the conflict between themselves and the "other." The murder of the infant, the crucifixion of Emanou, and the obsessive and meaningless quest of Tiossido and Lasca all contribute to the play's depiction of the repressive nature of the Fascist state in Spain.

The Car Cemetery—with its emphasis on games, its grotesque parody of religious ceremony, and its role reversals—evinces an enriched artistic vocabulary incorporating earlier motifs and anticipates the baroque aesthetic of the Panic ceremonies of the 1960's. The play's highly visual nature lends itself to a total theater approach in the Artaudian tradition (the most noteworthy example being Victor García's staging of the piece in Dijon, France, in 1966); this sort of staging came to characterize the production of Arrabal's plays throughout the 1960's. *The Car Cemetery* stands out as one of the most ambitious and noteworthy accomplishments of Arrabal's early period.

PANIC PERIOD

During the years 1959-1962, Arrabal ceased to write for the theater. In addition to writing his first novel, *Baal Babylone* (1959; *Baal Babylon*, 1961), he founded the Panic movement in conjunction with Roland Topor and Alexandro Jodorowsky. A mock-serious attempt at defining his art that burlesques the very concept of an artistic movement, Panic focuses on chance and memory as the essential components of art and life. Arrabal's work in formulating the tenets of Panic, his subsequent contact with André Breton and the Surrealists, and his collaboration with the avant-garde Argentine directors Jorge Lavelli, Victor García, and Jérôme Savary were instrumental in the evolution of his dramatic art and the enrichment of his artistic vocabulary. The plays of his Panic period were longer, more complex, and more ritualistic than his earlier endeavors. Panic ceremony, an intensified oneiricism, alchemy, the evocation of the plastic arts, and the expansion of theater space characterize his theater of the 1960's. In the two outstanding plays of this period, *The Architect and the Emperor of Assyria* and *The Garden of Delights*, Arrabal fused personal memories and concerns with archetypal psychological forces and sociopolitical elements into a complex quest for artistic and metaphysical liberation. The latter work, completed after Arrabal's release from prison in Spain, marks the transition to the final phase of his dramatic production.

While in jail in 1967, Arrabal came into contact with a number of political prisoners, immured for years for nonviolent crimes against the state. That experience caused him to identify anew with his father and to accord a greater emphasis to external reality in his theater. This shift in emphasis in his work was reinforced by his experiences as a participant in the May, 1968, rebellion in Paris. The immediate product of those traumatic events was his guerrilla theater, most notably the play *And They Put Handcuffs on the Flowers*. Subsequent endeavors varied in quality; overt pamphleteering in such political sketches and reviews as *La Grande Revue de XXe siècle* and *Bella Ciao, la guerre de mille ans* produced works of questionable merit. When Arrabal sought inspiration in his feelings about his self-imposed exile and his personal dreamlike vision of his country's past and present ills, however, the results were far more significant, as evidenced by *Sur le fil: Ou, La Ballade du train fantôme* and *La Tour de Babel*.

THE ARCHITECT AND THE EMPEROR OF ASSYRIA

The Architect and the Emperor of Assyria, generally considered to be Arrabal's finest play, develops fully such features of *The Car Cemetery* as the emphasis on games, the parody of religious ceremony, the metamorphosis of characters, and the circularity of structure. The result is a complex projection of archetypal psychological forces that combines frequent allusions to sociopolitical issues to produce a unique and original myth of contemporary humankind's quest for identity and psychic wholeness.

The Architect and the Emperor of Assyria begins with a loud explosion and flash of light, suggestive of the act of giving birth, which heralds the arrival of the Emperor, the sole survivor of a plane crash. He encounters the Architect, a primitive man of nature, who grunts in fear and hides his head in the sand. After a blackout, the action resumes several years later. The Emperor has taught the Architect to speak almost perfectly and has educated him in the ways of the Western world. The two characters, who can be viewed as different components of man's psyche, proceed to engage in a series of games. These involve domination and submission in a variety of contexts.

Underlying all of the sadomasochistic play is the figure of the mother, whose anima, in the Jungian sense, is strongly reflected by the Emperor. He drives the Architect to abandon him toward the end of the first act. Left alone onstage, he creates a scarecrow Emperor to whom he can play the Architect and continue the games. These reach a climax when the Emperor plays pinball to prove the existence of God; he also delivers a child while portraying a pregnant nun during the course of the pinball game. This grotesque act is followed by the return of the Architect, who affirms that he is hundreds of years old.

In the relatively brief second act, the Emperor is tried by the Architect for the crime of matricide. He confesses his guilt after portraying a series of witnesses derived from Arrabal's own life and then demands that he be killed and eaten by the Architect. That grotesque parody of the sacrament of Communion causes the Architect to metamorphose into the Emperor, losing all of his magic powers over the forces of nature. Just as the Architect-Emperor (now played by the actor who initially portrayed the Emperor) is exulting in his psychic self-sufficiency, the plane crash that initiated the drama is repeated. The Architect lands on the island and the Emperor babbles in fear and hides his head in the sand. The cycle has both begun and ended, just as in a chess match, in which the opponents exchange colors after each game so that the psychic struggle can be resumed.

In *The Architect and the Emperor of Assyria*, Arrabal's exploration of the interior world of his characters and his examination of the psychological and sociopolitical forces to which they are subject is elevated to the level of myth. One theme of the drama is the modern world as a corrupting force; that aspect of the work alludes to the Robinson Crusoe story. The real fascination of the play, however, results from its exploration of the human condition, of humankind's innermost fears, anxieties, and needs. Despite the humor, which is quite coarse and vulgar at times, the characters' need for one another—or metaphorically, for psychic wholeness—proves to be compelling in the theater. The grotesque and the romantic—love, blasphemy, and horror—all coalesce in the climactic scene in which the Architect devours the Emperor and assimilates his essence.

The Architect and the Emperor of Assyria is a complex work that can be approached from a number of critical perspectives. The importance of the mother figure encourages a Jungian approach; the scene in which the Emperor describes the act of matricide, where a lizard, with the son's face on it, emerges from her skull, suggests the archetype of the Mother-dragon, the devourer of her children. Grotesqueries abound: the Emperor's vision of his mother in tournedos and fillets constitutes one quintessential example of the union of the horrifying and the comic in a single image. The drama masterfully balances archetypes and universal feelings with Arrabal's personal vision and concerns. The work's rich language, Surrealist imagery, and structural rhythms all contribute to its lyric quality. *The Architect and the Emperor of Assyria* affirms the nobility of the human spirit; it does so, paradoxically, by presenting humankind's basest pretenses, needs, and drives. It is a highly poetic work that celebrates, ritualistically, the renewal of man's quest for self-understanding in today's perplexing world.

AND THEY PUT HANDCUFFS ON THE FLOWERS

Inspired directly by the author's incarceration in Spain, *And They Put Handcuffs on the Flowers* contains a number of features already associated with Arrabal's theater, but also introduced several new techniques and a heightened concern with political reality that came to characterize his work after 1968. Autobiographical events, especially the dramatist's nightmarish vision of his mother's active role in the arrest and torture of her husband, are interspersed throughout the work. Certain specific motifs and historical events contained in previous plays also recur. The demand for active participation by the audience was new, however, and the structure of the play is a great deal more complex than that of any of Arrabal's earlier works.

The stage directions at the beginning of the drama call for the audience to be accosted by the cast as they enter the theater, separated from friends and companions, and to be stripped of all sense of security in the dark foyer outside the main theater space. In that manner, the spectators should experience more immediately the pain and isolation that accompany imprisonment. A number of incidents, motifs, and dramatic techniques are then interwoven throughout the drama to provide its structure. Allusions to the first moon landing recur periodically, clashing ironically with the horrors perpetrated in the subterranean depths of Spanish prisons. This motif also functions to question the merits of space exploration while such terrible injustices and cruelties continue on earth. As in earlier works, dream sequences occur throughout, obliterating the distinction between waking reality and the oneiric. Many of these dreams are highly erotic in nature; Arrabal's penchant for what some critics consider the pornographic has never been more strongly expressed, and this element was responsible for much of the criticism that greeted the work.

The play's direct consideration of political realities is evidenced by a number of references to historical events. The prisons themselves are described in detail, and specific incidents (such as the condemnation of the man who saved his village priest during the civil war, because anyone who could do so must have had influence with the "Reds") are interspersed throughout. The title of the play is taken from a poem by Federico García Lorca, whose execution during the war is also described. The principal historical event that structures the play, however, is the trial and execution of a fictional character, Tosan, twenty-five years after his alleged crimes against the state. Based on the actual case of Julián Grimau, Tosan's story proceeds with tragic inevitability. The time that remains to him is indicated by a clock; props are of great importance in the play. The fragmentary nature of the scenes is successfully offset by the central incident of Tosan's case and by the unifying focus of the play on the total experience of incarceration in post-civil war Spain.

Arrabal utilizes a number of interesting devices in *And They Put Handcuffs on the Flowers*. Having the same actors play the roles of prisoners and jailers adds to the impact of the work. Props such as the bloodstained flag that serves to indict the military, the Church, and the wealthy oligarchy for the execution

of Tosan acquire a tremendous symbolic authority. Certain images also stand out—the most telling of these being the equation of the prison cell with the womb, through which Arrabal seems to be heralding his own rebirth into political awareness and his heightened understanding of his father's fate and its significance.

At the conclusion of the play, Tosan is garroted. He urinates out of fear before he dies, and the urine miraculously changes into blood. Arrabal had difficulty deciding on an appropriate ending for the play; in some versions, the miracle at the end is emphasized in a manner that leaves the audience with a strong feeling of hope. In at least one production directed by the author himself, however, that element of hope was deleted from the work. *And They Put Handcuffs on the Flowers*, as much as any of Arrabal's works, outraged a number of important theater critics. Its excesses, including fellatio performed on Christ, are certainly extreme and, in some cases, gratuitous, but the efficacy of the work as a total theater experience, viscerally underscoring the playwright's outrage at his country's perversity, more than compensates for its liabilities.

SUR LE FIL

Arrabal's chance discovery of a ghost town in New Mexico named Madrid provided the inspiration for *Sur le fil: Ou, La Ballade du train fantôme*, a dramatization of the theme of exile. The plot is quite simple. Tharsis has kidnapped the Duke of Gaza and taken him to Madrid, New Mexico. There they encounter Wichita, the only remaining inhabitant of the town. A former tightrope walker, he has lost his own ability to perform, but passes his art on to Tharsis. After Wichita's suicide, Tharsis returns to Madrid, Spain, to cross the Puerta del Sol on a wire in an act designed to serve as a call for freedom for the Spanish people.

Dualities abound throughout *Sur le fil*. Arrabal cleverly juxtaposes the two Madrids, suggesting parallels between the two "dead" cities. The two titles of the work underscore the dual vision of the playwright; on the wire, a literal translation of the title, suggests transcendence, while the phantom train, which descends into the depths of the deserted mines to deliver corpses that will be used to manufacture dog food, emerges as a metaphor for the exploitation of man.

Arrabal identifies with Tharsis; through that protagonist he makes a number of references to his own situation in Spain and to his feelings about having left his native country. Tharsis's talent on the wire becomes a metaphor for Arrabal's own art. Wichita, like the Architect in *The Architect and the Emperor of Assyria*, controls the forces of nature, especially the birds. The latter protect Tharsis from government planes, allowing him to complete triumphantly his walk across the Puerta del Sol. Wichita's transference of his skill to Tharsis evinces the purity and naturalness of true art. The lung disease that afflicted the miners in New Mexico parallels Arrabal's own bouts with tuberculosis and underscores the idea that he could no longer breathe, both figuratively and literally, in Spain's oppressive atmosphere. Tharsis's final triumph is accompanied by an opening up of theater space in a joyful affirmation of hope. The note of verticality is reminiscent of similar images encountered at the conclusion of Arrabal's film *¡Viva la muerte!* (1971) and subsequently reiterated at the end of the film *L'Arbre de Guernica* (1975). By returning to intensely personal feelings in *Sur le fil* and translating them into highly visual dramatic images, Arrabal managed to make an overt political statement without sacrificing the allure of his early theater.

OTHER MAJOR WORKS

LONG FICTION: *Baal Babylone*, 1959 (*Baal Babylon*, 1961); *L'Enterrement de la sardine*, 1961 (*The Burial of the Sardine*, 1966); *Fêtes et rites de la confusion*, 1967; *La torre herida por el rayo*, 1983 (*The Tower Struck by Lightning*, 1988); *La Reverdie*, 1985; *Piedra iluminada*, 1985 (*The Compass Stone*, 1987); *La Vierge rouge*, 1986 (*The Red Virgin*, 1993); *La hija de King Kong*, 1988; *L'Extravagante Croisade d'un castrat amoureux*, 1989; *El mono*, 1994; *Ceremonia por un teniente abandonado*, 1998; *Le Funambule de Dieu*, 1998; *Levitación: Novela mística*, 2000.

POETRY: *La Pierre de la folie*, 1963; *Le New York d'Arrabal*, 1973.

SCREENPLAYS: *¡Viva la muerte!*, 1971; *J'irai comme un cheval fou*, 1973; *L'Arbre de Guernica*, 1975; *L'Odyssée de la Pacific*, 1980; *Le Cimetière des voitures*, 1981; *Liberté couleur de femme; Ou, Adieu Babylone*, 1993; *J. L. Borges: Una vida de poesia*, 1998.

NONFICTION: *Lettre au Générale Franco*, 1972; *Le "Panique,"* 1973; *Sur Fischer: Initiation aux échecs*, 1974; *Les Échecs féeriques et libertaires: Chroniques de L'Express*, 1980; *Échecs et mythe*, 1984; *El Greco and Fernando Arrabal*, 1991; *Lettres à Julius Baltazar*, 1993; *La dudosa luz del día*, 1994; *Porté disparu*, 2000.

BIBLIOGRAPHY

Arata, Luis Oscar. *The Festive Play of Fernando Arrabal*. Lexington: University of Kentucky Press, 1982. Examines Arrabal's theater from the point of view of play, focusing on Piaget's concept of game playing and on episodic theater.

Berenguer, Angel, and Joan Berenguer, eds. *Fernando Arrabal*. Madrid: Editorial Fundamentos, 1979. A collection of essays in Spanish by a number of critics on Arrabal's theater as well as statements by world-renowned writers such as Samuel Beckett and Eugene Ionesco about the significance of Arrabal's theater.

Donahue, Thomas John. *The Theater of Fernando Arrabal*. New York: New York University Press, 1980. A general overview of Arrabal's theater, emphasizing the influence of the "happening," of street and guerrilla theater, and the creative use of playing space.

Glibota, Ante. *Arrabal Espace*. Paris: Paris Art Center, 1993. A coffee table work written in French with numerous color photographs and a number of essays on Arrabal's work in various genres. An invaluable source of production photos, Arrabal's paintings, and numerous other images of his life and work.

Orenstein, Gloria. "A Surrealist Theater Tractate: Fernando Arrabal." In *The Theater of the Marvelous*. New York: New York University Press, 1975. An analysis of Arrabal's theater as a manifestation of Surrealism based on alchemy. Explores the influence of André Breton, Salvador Dali, and Antonin Artaud on Arrabal's work.

Podol, Peter. *Fernando Arrabal*. Boston: Twayne, 1978. A comprehensive biography and analysis of all of Arrabal's work up to the date of publication, it is intended as an introduction to the playwright and contains brief analyses of all of his dramas prior to 1978.

Torres Monreal, Francisco. "Introducción." In *Teatro completo*. Madrid: Espasa Calpe, 1997. A lengthy introduction to the two-volume edition of Arrabal's theater in Spanish, it provides an excellent overview of the evolution of Arrabal's work for the theater.

Peter L. Podol

MIKHAIL ARTSYBASHEV

Born: Kharkov Province, Ukraine, Russian Empire;
   November 5, 1878
Died: Warsaw, Poland; March 3, 1927

PRINCIPAL DRAMA

Zakon dikarya, pb. 1912, pr. 1915 (*The Law of the Savage*, 1921)
Revnost', pr., pb. 1913 (*Jealousy*, 1923)
Vragi, pb. 1913, pr. 1917 (*Enemies*, 1923)
Voyna, pr. 1914, pb. 1916 (*War*, 1916)

OTHER LITERARY FORMS

Mikhail Artsybashev is best known for his novel *Sanin* (1907; *Sanine*, 1914). He wrote other novels and short stories in addition to plays, as well as a book of literary notes and observations, *Zapiski pisatelya* (1925). His collections of short stories were published on several occasions and his collected works in 1905-1917. Few of his works were published in the Soviet period.

ACHIEVEMENTS

Mikhail Artsybashev received no formal awards, but his contribution to Russian literature, including drama, was significant in the first two decades of the twentieth century. Although his reputation has diminished since then, there is no denying that he was a force for a while, primarily because of his bold approach to several themes that were extremely topical in Russian literature in his time.

BIOGRAPHY

Mikhail Artsybashev was born in Kharkov Province, Russian Empire, in an aristocratic family that was partially of Polish and Tartar origin. He started his higher education in art, with a talent for caricature. He moved to St. Petersburg in 1898 and, after failing to enter the Academy of Fine Arts, abandoned his first vocation and devoted his life to writing.

He published his first works at age sixteen in provincial newspapers. His concentration on the seamy side of life and bold and candid depiction of the social conditions in Russia in the first decades of the twentieth century, especially the decaying morality and the slavery to tradition among the Russian ruling class, brought him both popularity with readers and ostracism by the authorities. His first successful work was a short novel, *Smert' Ivana Lande* (1904; *Ivan Lande*, 1916), but the promising young author became extremely popular after the publication of *Sanine*, which developed a cultlike following, especially among young readers. For his candor in describing conditions, he was imprisoned briefly by the czarist government in 1912. He moved to Moscow the same year. After the Bolsheviks gained power, Artsybashev again got into trouble. This time he was accused of "immorality" in his works and of unnecessarily dwelling on the seamy side of Russian society, which was acceptable during the czarist era but "slanderous" in the reformist

Bolshevik society. He was frequently in trouble with the authorities, so much so that he emigrated to Poland in 1923. Beset by ill health and financial problems, he died in 1927, reluctant to accept help from friends.

In his last years, he edited an anti-Soviet journal, *Za svobodu* (for freedom), but for all practical purposes, his literary career ended in 1917. His popularity with readers and literary critics waned after his death, and he began to be known as a second-rate writer. However, his significance in Russian literature in the first quarter of the twentieth century was considerable, and for that reason, he cannot be ignored. He was the spokesperson for a disillusioned generation, particularly the intellectuals, during the turmoil that led to a disastrous war in World War I and the ensuing revolution.

ANALYSIS

Mikhail Artsybashev devoted the period of 1913-1916 to writing dramas. His play *War* shows the influence of the approaching world war, but his other plays continue the themes of his prose works. The most important of these themes are the relationship between men and women, mostly of a sexual nature, and their social roles not only in the society but also toward each other. In this sense, Artsybashev's works reflect the ideas dealt with in the works of leading European dramatists such as Henrik Ibsen, August Strindberg, and Frank Wedekind. Sexual explicitness, which was prevalent in his fiction and made him famous, figures prominently in his dramatic works. Employing the realism prevalent in Russian literature of the nineteenth century, he tackles the moral issues in Russian society at the beginning of the twentieth century, throwing light on some negative aspects of the human psyche, such as people's preoccupation with sex, violence, and death, the latter manifested in murder, execution, and suicide. By striving often for a shock affect, Artsybashev shows his concern for the well-being of Russian society as well as his indignation at the injustices taking place not only in the lower strata but also in the higher strata of the society. Unfortunately, he was either misunderstood or deliberately persecuted for bringing these issues into the

open, which eventually led to his leaving Russia altogether. It is not surprising that his characters are often embittered and alienated, in the best tradition of "the superfluous man" prevalent in the Russian literature of the nineteenth century.

The direct and merciless approaches of his moral criticism, most vividly in his plays, made Artsybashev very popular with readers and theatergoers, especially young intellectuals. However, because his works are so intricately connected with, and dependent on, a particular time period, they soon became period pieces and lost much of their original strength and appeal.

Technically speaking, Artsybashev's plays have considerable dramatic qualities. He knows how to build a plot and suspense. The crude naturalism of his fiction is toned down in his plays, most likely because it is easier to describe it than to show it on the stage. When Artsybashev was writing plays, the Russian theater was still somewhat puritanical. The most serious flaw in his playwriting can be found in his tendency to use long speeches, which are frequently programmatic and schematic. There is also a repetition of themes, characters, and actions, which has prompted some critics to brand Artsybashev a one-theme writer and playwright.

JEALOUSY

Artsybashev's first successful play, *Jealousy*, deals with an age-old human sentiment. The playwright juxtaposes two different views of the relationship between men and women. Journalist Andre has a rather cynical, almost nihilistic view of all women, denying their ability to feel sincere love and viewing them as nothing but self-indulgent creatures of conquest and deceit. In his view, women are rooted in the earth, from which they draw their pleasures and sensations. Their worthiness stems only from men's raising them to a pedestal of adoration, for which men pay dearly in the end. The opposite view is expressed by a member of the Douma, Simon Simonovich, who thinks that women bring beauty, poetry, romance, refinement, purity, and bliss into men's lives and that women are marvelously sensitive instruments on which men play according to their talent. It is the men who are at fault if they are unable to appreciate this beautiful gift of God, dirtying and ruining it instead.

Caught between these two extremes is author Sergey Petrovich, who loves his wife, Elena, and tends to ignore her habit of flirting while professing undying love for, and faithfulness to, her husband. When he finally finds out the truth about her relationships with other men, he strangles her in a fit of jealousy.

The somewhat inconclusive ending of the play—aside from the murder of Elena by her husband—as to who is at fault in the tragic outcome, leads nevertheless to a conclusion that the man-woman relationship is almost invariably accompanied by one of the oldest and most powerful emotions known to humankind, jealousy. Without moralizing, Artsybashev sheds light on this fact, as if to affirm that men and women will always behave this way. The only nuance derives from the duplicity found in Russian higher society, which confirms that its members behave no better than the peasants and workers.

WAR

War is centered on the Russian participation in World War I. Although the play was written at the beginning of the war, its drastic depiction of the evils of war hints of the tragic outcome for Russia three years later, manifested in its military defeat and the Bolshevik Revolution. Artsybashev personalizes the tragedy by depicting the infidelity of the woman to the crippled hero. *War* is considered the least important of Artsybashev's major plays, but as a time piece, it still bears a powerful message.

THE LAW OF THE SAVAGE

In *The Law of the Savage*, Artsybashev's views on the human condition in general and love in particular are the most drastic in all of his dramatic works. The action takes place on a country estate, where several characters are engaged in intimate relationships. An elderly country squire, Nikolai Ivanovich, clings to old-fashioned views but watches helplessly as his young wife succumbs to the advances of a prominent lawyer, Veresaev. The lawyer's wife takes revenge on him by having a relationship with a cavalry officer, which leads to a duel between Veresaev and the officer. There is also a love affair between Veresaev and his sister-in-law. All this creates a situation in which

the law of the savage, "to kill or be killed," becomes paramount. Veresaev takes full advantage of it by prematurely firing at, and cold-bloodedly killing, the officer.

At the basis of this setup lies Artsybashev's obsession with the phenomena of love and marriage. As in his other works, he lets his characters explain their (and, to a degree, his) views. Veresaev feels justified in betraying his wife because she is just a faithful wife, a good friend, and an excellent housekeeper but lacks passion. He advises his sister-in-law to lead a full life, not to be guided by reason but by instinct and the unrestrained, unleashed passion; he then promptly seduces her. However, when his wife betrays him, for revenge rather than out of passion, his vanity is so hurt that he challenges his rival to a duel and kills him.

Another character, an army physician, gives his views on the subject. He believes that women are monogamous by nature but that men cannot help but desire every woman and are justified in doing so because that is their immutable nature. Moreover, everything divine in men stems from the sex impulse; if they crush it, they lose everything—courage, ambition, and energy. Yet the physician warns against pure eroticism, which can enslave men. At the other end of the spectrum is Nikolai, who complains about the depths of dishonesty and wickedness in society, bemoaning the fact that most high-principled men consider it their right to steal the wife of their friend, even brother, regardless of circumstances and consequences. Of course, he speaks as an aggrieved husband, yet there is much sincerity and justification in his complaints. Artsybashev's sympathies are with him, not with the adulterers.

Interestingly, although Artsybashev seems to recognize the overwhelming power of passion, he creates a situation in which the law of the savage becomes necessary, thus allowing for the moral judgment concerning the necessity of controlling unrestrained instincts. He seems to tone down somewhat the earlier emphasis on the naked force of sex and unrestrained passion prevalent in his fiction works. The fact that almost all of his plays end tragically speaks in favor of this supposition.

ENEMIES

Artsybashev calls his play *Enemies* a tragicomedy. Although several couples are believed to be happily in love or trying to achieve happiness, their happiness is marred by self-doubt, infidelity, incompatibility, or jealousy. Artsybashev reveals his thoughts about love and marriage through the voice of Doctor Karnovich, who bases his observations about love mostly on anatomy and physiology. According to him, a happy marriage is impossible because men and women are so different that they cannot walk along without jostling and annoying one another. To succeed, love presupposes a complete union of body and soul, a physiological affinity and affinity of character as well as of age. A physical attraction alone is purely animal attraction. A too wide intellectual gulf leads to spiritual loneliness, which sooner or later must end in tragedy. Because it is extremely difficult to achieve such a unity, the chances of success in love are very slim.

This is borne out, as in *The Law of the Savage*, by several people who are intimately connected, through either marriage or amorous relationships. An old professor loves his wife dearly but considers her to be an impediment to his professional advancement. A physician loves both his wife and Karnovich's daughter, justifying his feelings by saying that they are just human nature and that he is too weak to resist. An officer of the Imperial Guard attracts several women. Perhaps the professor's daughter best sums up all these relationships when she wonders why these intimate partners are at the same time lovers and enemies. Therefore, for Artsybashev, the love experience is more enmity than happiness. In an article written in 1923, he expressed hope that some day men would be dominated by reason and able to distinguish love from passion, seeking spiritual intercourse independent of sex and physical nearness independent of spiritual life. Only then would jealousy, betrayal, and deceit disappear and men and women would cease to be enemies.

OTHER MAJOR WORKS

LONG FICTION: *Smert' Ivana Lande*, 1904 (*Ivan Lande*, 1916); *Sanin*, 1907 (*Sanine*, 1914); *Chelo-* *vecheskaia volna*, 1907; *U posledney cherty*, 1912 (*Breaking-Point*, 1915); *Dikie*, 1923 (*The Savage*, 1924).

SHORT FICTION: *Milliony*, 1908 (*The Millionaire*, 1915); *Rasskazy*, 1917; *Tales of the Revolution*, 1917.

NONFICTION: *Zapiski pisatelya*, 1925.

BIBLIOGRAPHY

Glicksberg, Charles I. *The Literature of Nihilism.* Lewisburg, Pa.: Bucknell University Press, 1975. Discusses the aspects of nihilism and the influence of philosopher Friedrich Nietzsche in Artsybashev's works.

Luker, Nicholas. "Artsybashev's *Sanin*: A Reappraisal." *Renaissance and Modern Studies* 24 (1980): 58-78. Reevaluates Artsybashev's main work in the framework of his philosophy and approach to literature.

_____. *In Defence of a Reputation: Essays on the Early Prose of Artsybashev.* Nottingham, England: Astra Press, 1990. In the only full-length monograph on Artsybashev in English, Luker attempts a rehabilitation of Artsybashev from a modern point of view, concentrating on his early stories but making copious references to his later works, especially *Sanine*. Excellent bibliography.

_____. "'Wild Justice': Mikhail Artsybashev's *Mstitel'* Collection." *New Zealand Slavonic Journal* (1993): 63-83. Deals with Artsybashev's later work.

O'Dell, Sally, and N. J. L. Luker. *Mikhail Artsybashev: A Comprehensive Bibliography.* Nottingham, England: Astra Press, 1983. Covers Artsybashev's works in Russian and translations in various languages, as well as critical works. Supplemented and extended by Luker's bibliography.

Pachmuss, Temira. "Michail Artsybashev in the Criticism of Zinaida Gippius." *The Slavonic and East European Review* 102 (1966): 76-87. A critical evaluation of Artsybashev by one of the leading Russian critics in the first decade of the twentieth century.

Vasa D. Mihailovich

MIGUEL ÁNGEL ASTURIAS

Born: Guatemala City, Guatemala; October 19,
 1899
Died: Madrid, Spain; June 9, 1974

PRINCIPAL DRAMA
 Cuculcán, pb. 1930, pr. 1955
 La audiencia de los confines, pr., pb. 1957
 Soluna, pb. 1955
 Chantaje, pr., pb. 1964
 Dique seco, pr., pb. 1964
 Teatro, pb. 1964

OTHER LITERARY FORMS

Miguel Ángel Asturias is best known for his novels, which combine material evocative of Guatemala's Mayan heritage with impassioned protests against social and political injustice. His theatrical works are considered an important contribution to the Latin American dramatic tradition but have not been widely translated and have made relatively little impact on the world stage. Asturias regarded his plays as a respite from writing fiction and stated that they required literary techniques with which he was not entirely at ease. It seems clear that his reputation will rest on novels such as *El Señor Presidente* (1946; *The President*, 1963) and *Hombres de maíz* (1949; *Men of Maize*, 1975).

ACHIEVEMENTS

Miguel Ángel Asturias was awarded the Nobel Prize in Literature in 1967. Although appreciative of this great honor, he publicly condemned the shoddy quality of English translations of his books and was also outraged that his work was largely unavailable in his native Guatemala. These two circumstances are indicative of the subsequent course of Asturias's literary reputation, which remains high with specialists in Latin American literature but has failed to earn him the wide public recognition enjoyed by Jorge Luis Borges and Gabriel García Márquez.

Asturias's distinguished diplomatic career was capped by the 1966 award of the Lenin Peace Prize

by the Soviet Union. Because he received it at a time when American-Soviet relations had been made particularly difficult by the Vietnam War, it is possible that this contributed to the relative neglect of his work in the United States. However, this should not obscure his remarkable achievement in simultaneously pursuing successful careers in literature and diplomacy.

BIOGRAPHY

Miguel Ángel Asturias was born in Guatemala City, Guatemala, on October 19, 1899. His father, a judge, refused to cooperate with dictator Estrada Cabrera, and in 1903 the family was exiled to the provincial town of Salamá, where Asturias first encountered the country's traditional Mayan culture. Returning to Guatemala City in 1907, Asturias grew up under a series of repressive regimes and became a prominent political activist when he entered the National University in 1917.

Asturias received his law degree in 1923 and then studied anthroplogy at the Sorbonne in Paris for the next five years. There he further developed his lifelong interest in Mayan culture while also beginning to write poetry and fiction. Asturias lived in Paris until 1933, when he returned to Guatemala to work as a journalist. The overthrow of President Jorge Ubico's dictatorship in 1944 brought in a government sympathetic to Asturias's politics, and he was offered a series of cultural attaché and diplomatic posts that took him to Mexico (1945-1947), Argentina (1947-1953), and El Salvador (1953-1954).

Asturias was now able to publish work that he had held back for political reasons. The novel *The President*, completed in 1932 but not published until 1946, was greeted with great acclaim. Its successor, *Men of Maize*, was even more rapturously received and is generally considered Asturias's masterpiece. These were soon followed by the three novels of his "banana trilogy," *Viento fuerte* (1950; *The Cyclone*, 1967; better known as *Strong Wind*, 1968), *El papa verde* (1954; *The Green Pope*, 1971), and *Los ojos de*

los enterrados (1960; *The Eyes of the Interred*, 1973),
which cemented his position as one of the finest Latin
American writers of his generation.

Asturias began another sojourn in the political
wilderness in 1954, when a right-wing coup in Guatemala forced him to flee to Argentina. In Buenos Ai-
res, he worked as a newspaper correspondent until
1962, when Argentina's turn to the political right precipitated a move to Genoa, Italy. His residency in Europe, where he became an active participant in many
writers' organizations, was undoubtedly instrumental
in his receiving the Nobel Prize in Literature in 1967.
The return of democracy to Guatemala resulted in his
being named ambassador to France in 1966, a position he held until 1970, when another military coup
led to his replacement. Asturias spent his remaining
years in Madrid, where he died on June 9, 1974, after
a career in which literature and politics were inextricably intermingled.

ANALYSIS

The dramatic works of Miguel Ángel Asturias are
distinguished by their imaginative use of material
taken from the Latin American past and the region's
indigenous cultural traditions, especially the Mayan.
Like many other Latin American writers of the twentieth century, Asturias responded to political and social turbulence with work that attempted to address
the problems of the present by invoking the cultural
achievements of his country's past.

Although Asturias's characters frequently represent historical forces or mythological phenomena,
they are never simply abstract constructs devoid of
human vitality. The highly allegorical quality of
Cuculcán's and *Soluna*'s interactions between supernatural beings and humanity exemplify his strong interest in myth and religion. The more realistic but
still heavily symbolic *La audiencia de los confines*
and *Chantaje*, contrastingly, seem to presage an activist's attack on contemporary injustices. Throughout Asturias's plays, however, the poetic and political
intermingle. While the balance between these two aspects may vary, their constituent elements, the magical and the mundane, are usually very much in evidence.

Miguel Ángel Asturias (© The Nobel Foundation)

CUCULCÁN

Although *Cuculcán* was written in dramatic form,
Asturias did not include the work in *Teatro*, the collection of his plays published in 1964. The work is,
however, generally considered to belong among his
theatrical writings. *Cuculcán* is based on Mayan religious texts and includes several episodes in which the
narrative is developed through traditional dances and
songs.

Cuculcán's three stage settings represent the
earth's relation to the Sun at morning, afternoon, and
night. The title character, a major god of the Mayas,
engages in an extended dialogue with Guacamayo, a
lesser god who asserts that only the Sun truly exists
and all else is an illusion. Secondary characters
drawn from folklore, including a dwarf grandmother,
the wind, and an inquisitive flower, look on and occasionally participate in these exchanges.

Although structured in a form that leads the audience to anticipate the resolution of its central issue

through dialogue, *Cuculcán* does not answer the question of what is real and what illusory. Asturias is more concerned with exploring the possibilities of an encounter between beings who are both real, in that they appear in embodied form, and illusory, in that they represent supernatural forces only dimly comprehended. The work is probably best understood as a theatrical exploration of Asturias's ideas about Mayan tradition and thus exemplary of one of his characteristic literary concerns.

SOLUNA

In presenting a modern version of the medieval miracle play, *Soluna* utilizes Mayan beliefs as the basis for a drama that also features sharp psychological conflicts. The title character is a sorcerer whose name combines the words *sol* (Sun) and *luna* (Moon), and these concepts of brightness and darkness, in turn symbolic of good and evil as well as the passing of time, are central to the play. Soluna himself, although never seen onstage, is deeply involved in what takes place on the estate of the wealthy landowner Mauro.

Mauro's wife, Ninica, loves him but misses the pleasures of her native city, and as the play opens she is about to return there via train. Mauro seeks solace in a magical mask given to him by Soluna. Half yellow and half orange, symbolizing the union of the Sun and the Moon, it has the power to make time pass quickly and thus lessen Mauro's pining for his wife.

Mauro then falls asleep with the mask in his arms. After a Nahual, a spirit representing the psyche of his servant Porfirión, unsuccessfully tries to steal the mask, the stage is filled with groups of peasant dancers vocally supporting either the Sun or the Moon. The tension soon escalates into stylized fighting but abruptly ceases when Porfirión appears and announces that bizarre events are happening and Judgment Day is at hand.

The terrified peasants are calmed when a vision of Ninica appears to them and states that things have returned to normal. The Nahual, however, still covets the mask and manages to steal it even though shot by Mauro. Ninica, who has in fact been injured in a train crash, now returns and tells Mauro that her beliefs

have changed and she will stay with him forever. The wounded Porfirión, who has overcome that aspect of himself represented by the Nahual, returns the mask, and the play closes with Mauro and Ninica preparing to face their new life together and the Sun and the Moon restored to their proper relation.

Soluna combines mythological and realistic elements into an effectively integrated whole, as a troubled modern marriage is saved by the intervention of supernatural forces reasserting traditional beliefs and traditions. At the play's conclusion, all has been reborn through Asturias's imaginative symbiosis of the mythological and the human.

LA AUDIENCIA DE LOS CONFINES

The title is taken from the name of a judicial court of the Spanish empire and could be translated as "the tribunals of the frontier." The protagonist is the sixteenth century Bishop Bartolomé de Las Casas, and the play tells the story of his efforts to improve the condition of Guatemala's indigenous peoples.

The villain of the piece is the incumbent Governor, who plots to incite the Indians to revolt so that Las Casas's peace efforts will fail. The Governor is also a sexual predator obsessed with native women, which has incited the anger of community leaders and provides further reason for the Governor to provoke war with the Indians. Thus he sends a priest to them on what is supposedly a peace mission but in fact provides an opportunity for the Governor to arrange the envoy's murder and so cast suspicion on his native hosts.

When Las Casas arrives, the hostility of the colonists forces him to seek refuge in a bishop's palace. The Governor's plan to have him murdered by soldiers pretending to protect him is frustrated at the last minute by Nabori, an Indian woman aware of the Governor's treachery; she helps Las Casas escape but is killed in the ensuing fighting. The play closes with the Governor under arrest and Las Casas at least temporarily triumphant in his efforts to help Guatemala's natives.

La audiencia de los confines's strong political message regarding the rights of oppressed peoples is underlined by stage directions that link its plot with an important document of the French Revolution, the

1792 Declaration of the Rights of Man. A dream sequence in which Las Casas declares his belief in overturning tyranny and realizing the will of the people indicates that in this play Asturias has directed all of his theatrical resources to the expression of his deepest political convictions.

CHANTAJE

Chantaje ("blackmail") includes more than thirty speaking parts in its chronicling of a complex urban scene that combines graphic realism with aspects of the Theater of the Absurd. Noise is an important component of the play, with traffic sounds, jukeboxes, and street musicians augmented by loudspeakers blaring commercial advertisements. A general air of frenetic activity, not all of it purposeful or even comprehensible, serves as constant background and periodic foreground to plot events.

The main characters are Carola, a prostitute; Dantés, a successful businessperson; and Atchis, a police officer who is seriously injured when hit by Dantés's car. Carola, who has been Dantés's lover and knows of his guilt, blackmails him out of $60,000 that she claims will go to Atchis. Although she then moves in with Atchis, she keeps the money and eventually goes back to Dantés when he offers her a large bribe to obtain government secrets to which she has access. Atchis then kills Dantés in a jealous rage.

Although *Chantaje*'s melodramatic plot may seem an unlikely vehicle for subtler meanings, the play is nonetheless resonant with symbolic implications. The urban chaos of its beginning is introduced to the audience with the phrase, "Let there be light!" and the noise of the city is identified with the sounds made by the creation of the universe. A character's description of the flow of traffic as a sea similarly connects apparently meaningless activity with an image of the primordial origins of life.

That this is, like *Soluna*, a drama of rebirth and reawakening is also suggested by the characterization of Carola, who is represented as transcending petty male desires and becoming a kind of eternally maternal figure whose prostitution is a sign of independence rather than immorality. Atchis, too, is refashioned as he progresses from crippiling physical debility to psychological insight into his relationships with Carola and Dantés, and his killing of Dantés is a kind of liberation over the forces that have shackled him. Although a complicated and challenging work that offers multiple interpretive possibilities, *Chantaje* clearly demonstrates Asturias's mature mastery of the possibilities of the theater.

DIQUE SECO

This comedy, whose title translates as "dry dock," takes place in the mansion of the Marquess of Alconave, whose prominent social status masks impending bankruptcy. When his friend Pichardino reveals that he is about to come into funds that he will gladly use to pay the Marquess's debts, the latter makes a major miscalculation by calling a meeting of his creditors before he has received any money from Pichardino. When the Marquess attempts to satisfy them with a game of lotto that will only partially repay whoever wins it, they tear his mansion apart in their frenzy to find something of value.

The Marquess's fortunes are eventually righted after many further bizarre plot developments, including Pichardino's incarceration in an insane asylum and a priest's acceptance of the bones of one of the Marquess's ancestors as payment for his debt to the church. These happenings are periodically interrupted by the appearances of a mysterious beauty dressed in hot pants and a white-clad jazz musician, who induces the classically trained Marquess to improvise hot jazz licks on his grand piano. When a former lover enters a convent and leaves him enough money to pay his creditors, the Marquess accepts this with the blithe assurance that he has always believed in his eventual triumph over adversity.

Dique seco is an entertaining comic farce that is completely enjoyable on its own terms but also exhibits a number of links to the more serious dramas *Soluna* and *Chantaje*. Like *Soluna*, its stage directions specify strong contrasts in lighting that emphasize the work's visual qualities; like *Chantaje*, it makes creative use of noise in constructing an unusual and effective theatrical world. On balance, however, it appears that here Asturias is taking a bit of a holiday from the essential seriousness of his other plays.

OTHER MAJOR WORKS

LONG FICTION: *El Señor Presidente*, 1946 (*The President*, 1963); *Hombres de maíz*, 1949 (*Men of Maize*, 1975); *Viento fuerte*, 1950 (*The Cyclone*, 1967; better known as *Strong Wind*, 1968); *El papa verde*, 1954 (*The Green Pope*, 1971); *Los ojos de los enterrados*, 1960 (*The Eyes of the Interred*, 1973); *El alhajadito*, 1961 (*The Bejeweled Boy*, 1971); *Mulata de tal*, 1963 (*Mulata*, 1967); *Maladrón*, 1969.

SHORT FICTION: *Leyendas de Guatemala*, 1930; *Week-end en Guatemala*, 1956; *El espejo de Lida Sal*, 1967 (*The Mirror of Lida Sal*, 1997); *Novelas y cuentos de juventud*, 1971; *Viernes de dolores*, 1972.

POETRY: *Sien de alondra*, 1949; *Bolívar*, 1955; *Clarivigilia primaveral*, 1965.

NONFICTION: *Sociología guatemalteca: El problema social del indio*, 1923 (*Guatemalan Sociology*, 1977); *La arquitectura de la vida nueva*, 1928; *Rumania: Su nueva imagen*, 1964 (essays); *Latinoamérica y otros ensayos*, 1968 (essays); *Tres de cuatro soles*, 1977.

MISCELLANEOUS: *Obras completas*, 1967 (3 volumes).

BIBLIOGRAPHY

Callan, Richard J. *Miguel Ángel Asturias*. New York: Twayne, 1970. A comprehensive treatment of Asturias's work that is particularly good on the historical and political background. Callan's argument that C. G. Jung's depth psychology is the most fruitful critical approach, however, is not entirely convincing.

Harss, Luis, and Barbara Dohmann. "Miguel Ángel Asturias: Or, The Land Where the Flowers Bloom." In *Into the Mainstream: Conversations with Latin American Writers*. New York: Harper & Row, 1967. An extensive and wide-ranging interview with Asturias that connects his work with his life experiences. An essential resource.

Henighan, Stephen. *Assuming the Light: The Parisian Literary Apprenticeship of Miguel Ángel Asturias*. Oxford: Legenda, 1999. A cogent and illuminating account of the formative years during which Asturias developed into a gifted author. Scholarly in approach, but nonetheless accessible to the general reader.

Paul Stuewe

W. H. AUDEN

Born: York, England; February 21, 1907
Died: Vienna, Austria; September 29, 1973

PRINCIPAL DRAMA

Paid on Both Sides: A Charade, pb. 1930, pr. 1931

The Dance of Death, pb. 1933, pr. 1934

The Dog Beneath the Skin: Or, Where Is Francis?, pb. 1935, pr. 1936 (with Christopher Isherwood)

The Ascent of F6, pb. 1936, pr. 1937 (with Isherwood)

On the Frontier, pr., pb. 1938 (with Isherwood)

Paul Bunyan, pr. 1941, pb. 1976 (libretto; music by Benjamin Britten)

For the Time Being, pb. 1944, pr. 1959 (oratorio; musical setting by Martin David Levy)

The Rake's Progress, pr., pb. 1951 (libretto, with Chester Kallman; music by Igor Stravinsky)

Delia: Or, A Masque of Night, pb. 1953 (libretto, with Kallman; not set to music)

Elegy for Young Lovers, pr., pb. 1961 (libretto, with Kallman; music by Hans Werner Henze)

The Bassarids, pr., pb. 1966 (libretto, with Kallman; music by Henze)

Love's Labour's Lost, pb. 1972, pr. 1973 (libretto, with Kallman; music by Nicolas Nabokov; adaptation of William Shakespeare's play)

The Entertainment of the Senses, pr. 1974 (libretto, with Kallman; music by John Gardiner)

Plays and Other Dramatic Writings by W. H.
   Auden, 1928-1938, pb. 1988
W. H. Auden and Chester Kallman: Libretti and
   Other Dramatic Writings by W. H. Auden,
   1939-1973, pb. 1993

OTHER LITERARY FORMS

Although well regarded as a playwright and librettist, W. H. Auden is known chiefly as a poet. During his lifetime, he published more than twenty collections of poetry, establishing himself as a major voice in twentieth century literature. His work includes a remarkable variety of lyric poems, notable for their range of thought and technique. Auden also wrote several longer poems, including *For the Time Being* and *The Sea and the Mirror*, both of which appeared in a 1944 collection, and *The Age of Anxiety* (1947). The shorter as well as the longer poems are in *Collected Poems* (1976, revised 1991) and *The English Auden: Poems, Essays, and Dramatic Writings, 1927-1939* (1977), both edited by Edward Mendelson.

In addition to plays, librettos, and poetry, Auden produced a substantial amount of nonfiction prose. Many of his best essays, reviews, lectures, and introductions are collected in *The Dyer's Hand and Other Essays* (1962), *Secondary Worlds* (1969), and *Forewords and Afterwords* (1973). Auden also wrote several scripts for film and radio and worked extensively as an editor and translator.

ACHIEVEMENTS

Though W. H. Auden is not regarded as a major playwright, he and his collaborators produced a body of work that is recognized today as a significant contribution to modern drama and opera. His plays with Christopher Isherwood have survived as period pieces and are well regarded as experiments in poetic, didactic drama, written at a time when the English theater offered little more than uninspired naturalism. *The Dog Beneath the Skin*, probably the most lasting of the Auden-Isherwood collaborations, contains some of Auden's finest verse written for the stage and, though often raw and uneven, remains engaging in its mixture of popular, high-spirited comedy and political satire. Michael Sidnell, while suggesting

that personal and artistic difficulties kept Auden and Isherwood from fully committing themselves to the theater, argues, nevertheless, that they "were in advance of their time in using poetry, song, dance, and fable for serious dramatic purposes in a way that did not become common on the English stage until the late 1950's, when the strong influence of Bertolt Brecht was belatedly felt."

Auden's work for the operatic stage is more difficult to assess, partly because of the complex interdependence of the librettos and their musical settings. Auden saw the librettist's role as clearly secondary to the composer's, yet his librettos with Chester Kallman are regarded by some as significant dramatic and poetic texts in their own right. John Blair, for example, treating *The Rake's Progress* as an "operatic poem," suggests that the libretto can be "seen as an epitome of Auden's mature poetic mode." As opera, the Auden-Kallman collaborations have had mixed success; *The Rake's Progress* (with music by Igor Stravinsky) is generally conceded to be their best, and, as Humphrey Carpenter points out, is apparently "one of the very few modern operas to become a permanent addition to the repertoire." In the two years following its premiere, it was staged more than two hundred times.

BIOGRAPHY

Wystan Hugh Auden was born into a middle-class English family in 1907, the son of George Auden, a medical doctor, and Constance Bicknell Auden, a nurse. Auden grew up in an atmosphere that fostered intellectual and cultural growth, and his parents, both the children of clergymen, gave him and his two older brothers a strong sense of traditional religious values. His father was the strongest influence on his early intellectual life, teaching Auden about classical and Norse mythology and encouraging his interest in science. Auden maintained this interest throughout his life, often using scientific concepts and images in his poetry.

In 1915, when he was eight, Auden went as a boarder to St. Edmund's School in Surrey, where he met Christopher Isherwood, later his close friend and collaborator. After St. Edmund's, Auden attended

W. H. Auden (Jill Krementz)

Gresham's School, an institution with a strong reputation in the sciences. During his time there, Auden began to question the religion of his childhood and to distance himself from the traditional values of his middle-class, public-school upbringing. At Gresham's, he acknowledged his homosexuality, and, by the time he left, he had abandoned his faith.

Auden's interest in writing, begun at Gresham's, flourished at Oxford, where he went to read science in 1925. He soon changed to English studies and, before finishing his undergraduate career, resolved to make poetry his vocation. While at Oxford and in the remaining years of the 1930's, Auden established a considerable reputation as a poet and experimental dramatist. In 1928, he wrote his first dramatic work, *Paid on Both Sides*, a brief "charade" that draws heavily on his English public-school experience, his fascination with the lead-mining country of his youth, and the Icelandic legends he learned from his father. Four years later, in 1932, he again turned to theater. In the summer of that year, the ballet dancer Rupert Doone and the painter Robert Medley (whom Auden had known at Gresham's) proposed to Auden

the idea of forming an experimental theater company that Doone hoped could be "self-sufficient and independent of any purely commercial considerations." The founders of what came to be known as the Group Theatre wanted to bring to the stage a combination of dance, music, and speech; they also saw in the theater a potential for left-wing social commentary, an idea that appealed to Auden, whose political leanings had become increasingly leftist during the 1930's.

At the urging of Doone and Medley, Auden produced for the Group Theatre a ballet-drama on Marxist themes. In the next several years, he collaborated with Isherwood on three more plays for the Group, the first of them *The Dog Beneath the Skin*, a work that developed out of earlier dramatic experiments by the two writers—their joint effort, "Enemies of a Bishop" (written in 1929), and two works by Auden, "The Fronny" (written in 1930) and "The Chase" (written in 1934). These plays were not published or performed, and only a few scraps of "The Fronny" survive. By the end of the 1930's, Auden and Isherwood had collaborated on a second and third play for the Group Theatre, both of them more theatrically conventional than their first one.

In 1939, Auden's life took a major turn. He and Isherwood left England for the United States, and, within two years of his arrival, Auden rejoined the Anglican communion, a reaffirmation of his childhood faith toward which he had been moving for some time. From this point in his life, his writing was informed by a Christian perspective spelled out most explicitly in the long poems he wrote during the 1940's, particularly his Christmas oratorio, *For the Time Being* (1944). Though clearly not intended for the stage, his long poems of this period make considerable use of dramatic techniques. Auden's only theatrical work of the time was a brief libretto that he wrote for the British composer Benjamin Britten; *Paul Bunyan* was performed once in 1941 but remained unpublished until after Auden's death.

Auden's dramatic career entered its second phase near the end of the 1940's, when he began the first of his several collaborations with his friend and lifelong companion Chester Kallman, whom he had met shortly after his arrival in the United States. Together, they wrote for Stravinsky a libretto for *The Rake's Progress* and, later, a briefer one called *Delia*, for which Stravinsky never provided a score. In the last twenty years of his life, Auden continued to write extensively both poetry and prose, living part of each year in New York City and part in Europe. He and Kallman continued their productive collaboration, translating a number of librettos and writing several of their own, two for the German composer Hans Werner Henze and one for the Russian-born composer Nicolas Nabokov. Their final work for the stage, written in the last month of Auden's life, was *The Entertainment of the Senses*, a brief "antimasque" commissioned for the composer John Gardiner. Shortly after completing this piece, Auden left his summer home in Kirchstetten, Austria, to return to Oxford, where he had taken up winter residence the year before. On their way to England, he and Kallman stopped overnight in Vienna. Auden died there in his sleep and is buried, as he wished, in Kirchstetten.

ANALYSIS

W. H. Auden's dramatic works—both the political plays and the librettos—are concerned at base with the exposition of ideas. In his plays, as in his poetry, he pursues a range of philosophical positions with relish and zest, and his writing for the stage is remarkable, finally, for its managing to bring dramatic vitality to political and theological concepts. His inventiveness, his willingness to experiment, and his masterful use of conventional forms (popular theater as well as opera) guarantee Auden and his collaborators a significant place in the history of modern drama.

Auden's writing for the stage falls into two distinct categories: the plays of the 1930's, written mostly in collaboration with Christopher Isherwood, and the opera librettos, all but one written with Chester Kallman after Auden's move to the United States in 1939.

The plays of the 1930's are essentially political and didactic; Auden saw them as a means of reaching a wider audience than he could with his poetry, a way to reunite, as Mendelson puts it, "the private world of the poet with the public world of the theatre." Hence, the plays set forth various psychological and political positions he adopted during the 1930's, offering audiences lessons in the history of their time and awakening them to the possibility of personal and social renewal. Written in a mixture of poetry and prose, Auden's plays borrow theatrical devices from a variety of unlikely sources: ballet, conventional melodrama, music-hall comedy, the variety show, and the cabaret sketch. He combines these devices with serious poetry (often spoken by a chorus), using a blend of popular and literary writing as a vehicle for antiestablishment political commentary. At times, the didacticism outweighs theatrical effectiveness, as it does in *On the Frontier*, a topical and technically conventional play that lacks the energy of Auden's other collaborations with Isherwood. At their best, however, the plays manage to handle political and social themes with a considerable amount of dramatic vitality.

THE DOG BENEATH THE SKIN

This vitality is best represented in *The Dog Beneath the Skin*, generally recognized as the most successful of the three Auden-Isherwood plays. An odd blend of fable and farce, the plot centers on the quest of Alan Norman to find Sir Francis Crewe, missing heir to the late squire of the English village of Pressan Ambo. Each year, the villagers gather to select by lot a young man to search for Sir Francis (whom they perceive as a sort of idealized lost leader); the ten youths who precede Alan fail in their quest, and two of them never return to the village (though both appear briefly during Alan's quest).

The first part of the play evokes the complacency of the staid and deceptively idyllic English village, whose leading citizens are the town vicar, the pompous General Hothan—a retired military man—and Iris Crewe, Sir Francis's sister, who lives at Honeypot Hall, the family estate. This trio is the object of the play's satire against the established social order. Representing religious, military, and class authority, they begin as conventional reactionaries, but by the end of the play (and in Alan's absence), they turn to fascism, establishing a militaristic youth brigade in the village. After a quest that takes up most of the play's action, Alan returns with Sir Francis to discover the altered state of affairs in Pressan Ambo. The lost heir, who had in fact been living in disguise among the villagers for the past ten years, denounces them as "obscene, cruel, hypocritical, mean, vulgar creatures." Taking Alan and a small band of villagers with him, Sir Francis leaves Pressan Ambo to "be a unit in the army of the other side," presumably a political and social order opposite the fascism now established in the village. Though some argue that Sir Francis does not speak for a specific political doctrine, others such as John Fuller see his joining of the "other side" as an explicit reference to the Communist Party. His and Alan's conversion represents, in any case, a move away from personal and political stagnation toward an active commitment to regeneration and change, an idea that Auden was working with in his poetry at the time.

Along with its explicit critique of fascist politics, the play makes a broader political statement on the entire capitalist system. The extent to which Auden embraced Marxism is not entirely clear, but he did for a time sympathize with many of its key tenets. His first play for the Group Theatre, *The Dance of Death*, is an avowedly political one, illustrating the decline and eventual death of the bourgeoisie. In *The Dog Beneath the Skin*, his intent is somewhat less overt, but the bulk of the play (and most of its vitality) comes in the quest scenes, which burlesque the moral and economic decay of European capitalism.

At the beginning of his quest, Alan is joined by a large dog that gives the play its title, provides much of its farcical humor, and, in the end, carries much of the play's thematic weight. The dog, it turns out, is Sir Francis Crewe, the object of Alan's quest. The missing heir of Pressan Ambo has been living in disguise for ten years among the villagers and is now Alan's companion. In the middle section of the play, the two of them travel together, observing the corruption of the established social order, a corruption that had previously seduced and destroyed two young men from the village. Though Alan is temporarily lured toward decadence, he manages—with the help of his dog—to escape, having learned along the way the lessons that lead to his personal salvation.

The scenes that satirize capitalist decay borrow an array of theatrical devices from the popular stage. Using slapstick, farce, burlesque, cabaret songs, doggerel, and a host of other devices, Auden and Isherwood provide a kind of comic revue of modern political corruption and personal decadence. The loosely connected comic scenes are separated by a number of choral poems that develop in a more serious fashion the implications of the play's high-spirited satire. The bulk of the satiric pieces are set in Ostnia, a decadent monarchy in Eastern Europe, and Westland, a fascist state with clear parallels to Nazi Germany. (Both of these nations reappear in the other Auden-Isherwood collaborations.) In Ostnia, Alan and the dog—accompanied by two journalists—witness a grotesquely comic execution of four workers accused of inciting revolution. The satiric point is unmistakable, as it is later in Westland, where the political system becomes an asylum that "the leader" rules by speaking to the inmates through a megaphone attached to his picture.

One of the most memorable sequences in the play occurs at the Ninevah Hotel, where Alan watches a cabaret act in the hotel restaurant, an act that, as John Fuller points out, "burlesques the sexual tyranny and . . . militant philistinism of the rich." At the end of the first sketch, which includes a crude song performed by the Ninevah Girls, one of the wealthy hotel patrons selects a willing chorus girl and orders her cooked and prepared for his dinner. This satire of wealth and sexual domination is followed by another sketch, in which Destructive Desmond uses a penknife to destroy an original Rembrandt while "a piece of third-rate Victorian landscape painting" stands unharmed beside it. The wealthy patrons applaud ecstatically at this grand entertainment, asserting their aggressive distaste for high culture.

With their "brutal, noisy vulgarity and tasteless extravagance" (as the stage directions put it), the Ninevah Hotel scenes have a comic vitality that prevents the play's didacticism from becoming ponderous. Finally, such scenes, with the chorus's commentary, allow Auden and Isherwood to illustrate pointedly the essential decadence and egotism of modern people and their inability to love and sympathize with others. This theme, which is implicit throughout the play, becomes overt in a scene at Paradise Park, where Alan meets a poet who insists that he is "the only real person in the world," a notion echoed later in the chorus's warning to the audience: "Beware of yourself:/ Have you not heard your own heart whisper: 'I am the nicest person in this room'?"

If the play finally has a significance beyond social satire, it lies in Auden's suggestion that political solutions are useless without personal regeneration. At the end of the play, Sir Francis, who is back in Pressan Ambo and revealed as the missing heir, tells the gathered villagers that for ten years he had a "dog's eye view" of them, "seeing people from underneath," observing their essential hypocrisy and their lack of common human sympathy. After he, Alan, and a few converted villagers leave for the ill-defined "other side," the chorus offers the audience a choice, suggesting that personal change must precede political action: "Choose therefore that you may recover: both your charity and your place/ Determining/ . . . Where grace may grow outward and be given praise." As in much of Auden's work of the 1930's, the exact nature of the proposed solution to personal and political ills is clouded. At the time, Auden was a diagnostician, not a healer. The ending of *The Dog Beneath the Skin* gestures toward an ill-defined "love" that is "loath to enter." Only in his later work, and after his return to Christianity, did Auden arrive at a less clouded notion of love as a means of personal and social redemption.

THE RAKE'S PROGRESS

That notion of love is defined most clearly in the long poems that Auden wrote during the 1940's, a time when his interest in stage drama subsided. Aside from *Paul Bunyan*, the brief libretto written for Britten in 1939, Auden did no writing for the stage until Stravinsky approached him in 1947 about the possibility of doing an opera based on William Hogarth's series of engravings *A Rake's Progress*. Auden agreed to the project and wrote with Chester Kallman the first of their several librettos. Auden saw in opera a logical fulfillment of his earlier interest in poetic drama. In a 1966 interview for the British Broadcasting Corporation, he suggested that "opera

is the proper place for lyric theatre, rather than the spoken drama." The "job of the librettist," he wrote in *Secondary Worlds*, "is to furnish the composer with a plot, characters and words." Clearly in a supporting role, the verbal text "is to be judged . . . by its success or failure in exciting the musical imagination of the composer."

Though Auden tended to minimize the role of the librettist, his operatic works with Kallman have considerable merit apart from their musical settings. *The Rake's Progress* is particularly well regarded both as a stage opera and as an independent poetic text. The libretto illustrates many of the central themes of Auden's mature work and suggests that several of the techniques he and Isherwood used in the 1930's plays were naturally suited for the operatic stage: the reliance on fable and myth, the use of overstatement and grand gesture, and the emphasis on idea and spectacle rather than character.

The libretto is essentially a moral fable, illustrating in religious terms the Fall and Redemption of humanity. Auden suggests that through an act of free will, humanity can choose selfless love (*agape*) and, in doing so, find grace and redemption. This theme is worked out in the fate of the opera's hero, Tom Rakewell, described by Edward Callan as "an aesthetic personality who relies on fortune and believes in his own superior destiny." Auden illustrates the folly of Tom's egotism by giving him three wishes (after the pattern of the archetypal quest hero), each of which leads him further from Anne Truelove, the libretto's symbolic embodiment of selfless love. Rakewell's first wish (for money) is, like his other wishes, fulfilled by Nick Shadow, a satanic servant who secretly aims to damn Rakewell's soul. Removed by his first wish from the redemptive powers of Anne's love, Tom makes a second wish (for happiness), which leads him to an *acte gratuit*, an existential choice to marry Baba, a bearded lady from a fair; Shadow has convinced him that such an act could bring true happiness by freeing him from the demands of necessity. According to Fuller, Auden uses Rakewell's absurd act as a critique of the existentialist view of free will; his marriage is "a grotesque parody of the true Christian choice" he will make later.

Tom's final wish (to have a magical bread-making machine he has dreamed of) brings about his final ruin. Left at the mercy of Shadow, he is offered—in a Faustian scene—a last, yet apparently hopeless, chance for salvation. Recalling Anne's love, he makes an irrational choice when Shadow asks him to name three cards: "I wish for nothing else./ Love, first and last, assume eternal reign;/ Renew my life, O Queen of Hearts, again." The choice is, in effect, a leap of faith, a genuine acceptance of love. The memory of Anne thus saves Rakewell from damnation. Denied Rakewell's soul, Shadow condemns him to madness, but in the concluding scene, Tom (imagining himself as Adonis) is symbolically redeemed from his suffering by Anne (as Venus) and dies reconciled to her.

In a sense, *The Rake's Progress* is a thematic extension of the ideas raised by the Auden-Isherwood plays of the 1930's. Auden's Christianity, his embracing of *agape*, provides a new perspective on the personal and social ills diagnosed in *The Dog Beneath the Skin*. In the later work, Auden sees human failings in personal and religious terms; social and political malaise originates, he seems to suggest, by human imperfection, in humanity's fallen nature. Only by appealing to powers outside themselves can humans find redemption.

OTHER MAJOR WORKS

POETRY: *Poems*, 1930; *The Orators*, 1932; *Look, Stranger!*, 1936 (also known as *On This Island*, 1937); *Letters from Iceland*, 1937 (poetry and prose; with Louis MacNeice); *Spain*, 1937; *Journey to a War*, 1939 (poetry and prose; with Christopher Isherwood); *Another Time*, 1940; *The Double Man*, 1941 (also known as *New Year Letter*); *For the Time Being*, 1944; *The Sea and the Mirror*, 1944; *The Collected Poetry*, 1945; *The Age of Anxiety*, 1947; *Collected Shorter Poems, 1930-1944*, 1950; *Nones*, 1951; *The Shield of Achilles*, 1955; *Homage to Clio*, 1960; *About the House*, 1965; *Collected Shorter Poems, 1927-1957*, 1966; *Collected Longer Poems*, 1968; *City Without Walls and Other Poems*, 1969; *Epistle to a Godson and Other Poems*, 1972; *Thank You, Fog*, 1974; *Collected Poems*, 1976, revised 1991 (Edward Mendelson, editor); *Selected Poems*, 1979 (Mendelson, editor); *Juvenilia: Poems, 1922-1928*, 1994, expanded 2003 (Katherine Bucknell, editor); *As I Walked Out One Evening: Songs, Ballads, Lullabies, Limericks, and Other Light Verse*, 1995.

NONFICTION: *The Enchafèd Flood*, 1950; *The Dyer's Hand and Other Essays*, 1962; *Selected Essays*, 1964. *Secondary Worlds*, 1969; *A Certain World*, 1970; *Forewords and Afterwords*, 1973; *Prose and Travel Books in Prose and Verse: Volume I, 1926-1938*, 1996 (Edward Mendelson, editor); *Prose and Travel Books in Prose and Verse: Volume II, 1939-1948*, 2002 (Mendelson, editor).

EDITED TEXTS: *The Oxford Book of Light Verse*, 1938; *The Portable Greek Reader*, 1948; *Poets of the English Language*, 1950 (5 volumes; with Norman Holmes Pearson); *The Faber Book of Modern American Verse*, 1956; *Selected Poems of Louis MacNeice*, 1964; *Nineteenth Century British Minor Poets*, 1966; *A Choice of Dryden's Verse*, 1973.

MISCELLANEOUS: *The English Auden: Poems, Essays, and Dramatic Writings, 1927-1939*, 1977 (Edward Mendelson, editor).

BIBLIOGRAPHY

Davenport-Hines, Richard. *Auden*. New York: Pantheon, 1995. This biography of the greatest English poet of the twentieth century is also a history of some of the pressing and largely unresolved human and literary problems Auden faced in this lifetime. Bibliography and index.

Fuller, John. *W. H. Auden: A Commentary*. Princeton, N.J.: Princeton University Press, 1998. A critical analysis of the works of Auden. Bibliography and indexes.

Hecht, Anthony. *The Hidden Law: The Poetry of W. H. Auden*. Cambridge, Mass.: Harvard University Press, 1993. In this learned and generously annotated study, poet-critic Anthony Hecht analyzes the poetry of W. H. Auden by highlighting the differences between Auden's public and private works.

Mendelson, Edward. *Early Auden*. New York: Viking Press, 1981. A brilliant synthesis of Auden's intellectual development and emotional history to 1939. The main movement of Auden's art was from a private to a public language. Includes notes and index.

_____. *Later Auden*. New York: Farrar Straus & Giroux, 1999. Mendelson offers a critical reading of W. H. Auden's poetry using details from the poet's life to interpret his political and philosophical verse.

Page, Norman. *Auden and Isherwood: The Berlin Years*. New York: St. Martin's Press, 1998. Examines the relationship between the poet Auden and Christopher Isherwood, looking at their friends and associates. Bibliography and index.

Smith, Stan. *W. H. Auden*. Plymouth, England: Northcote House, 1997. A general biography of Auden, covering his life and works. Bibliography and index.

Michael Hennessy,
updated by Richard D. McGhee

ÉMILE AUGIER

Born: Valence, France; September 17, 1820
Died: Croissy, France; October 25, 1889

PRINCIPAL DRAMA

La Ciguë, pr., pb. 1844 (verse play)

Un Homme de bien, pr., pb. 1845 (verse play)

L'Aventurière, pr., pb. 1848 (verse play; *The Adventuress*, 1888)

L'Habit vert, pr., pb. 1849 (with Alfred de Musset; *The Green Coat*, 1914)

Gabrielle, pr. 1849, pb. 1850 (verse play)

Le Joueur de flûte, pr. 1850, pb. 1851 (verse play)

La Chasse au roman, pr., pb. 1851 (with Jules Sandeau)

Sapho, pr., pb. 1851 (verse libretto, music by Charles Gounod; *Saffo*, 1851)

Diane, pr., pb. 1852 (verse play)

Les Méprises de l'amour, pb. 1852

Philiberte, pr., pb. 1853 (verse play)

La Pierre de touche, pr. 1853, pb. 1854 (with Sandeau)

Le Gendre de M. Poirier, pr., pb. 1854 (with Sandeau, adaptation of Sandeau's novel *Sacs et parchemins*; *Monsieur Poirier's Son-in-Law*, 1915)

Ceinture dorée, pr., pb. 1855

Le Mariage d'Olympe, pr., pb. 1855 (*The Marriage of Olympe*, 1915)

La Jeunesse, pr., pb. 1858

Les Lionnes pauvres, pr., pb. 1858 (with Édouard Foussier)

Un Beau Mariage, pr., pb. 1859 (with Foussier)

Les Effrontés, pr., pb. 1861 (*Faces of Brass*, 1888)

Le Fils de Giboyer, pr. 1862, pb. 1863 (*Giboyer's Son*, 1911)

Maître Guérin, pr. 1864, pb. 1865

La Contagion, pr., pb. 1866

Paul Forestier, pr., pb. 1868 (verse play; *Paul Forrester*, 1871)

Post-Scriptum, pr., pb. 1869 (*The Post-script*, 1915)

Lions et renards, pr. 1869, pb. 1870

Jean de Thommeray, pr. 1873, pb. 1874 (with Sandeau)

Madame Caverlet, pr., pb. 1876

Le Prix Martin, pr., pb. 1876 (with Eugène Labiche)

Les Fourchambault, pr., pb. 1878 (*The House of Fourchambault*, 1915)

Four Plays, pb. 1915

OTHER LITERARY FORMS

Émile Augier wrote a libretto for Charles Gounod's opera *Sapho*, in 1851, and published a volume of verse, *Les Pariétaires*, in 1856; with these exceptions, he devoted himself entirely to the composition of plays.

ACHIEVEMENTS

In chronological terms, Émile Augier can be credited with being the first major dramatist of the realistic school of French literature to combat successfully the excesses and extravagances of the Romantic theater. While his contemporary, Alexandre Dumas, *fils*, shared some of Augier's aversion to these excesses and extravagances, Augier preceded him in condemning the illusions of romantic love, which he removed from the center of the dramatic plot. He replaced those illusions with other motive forces: the desire for political power, the pursuit of tawdry liaisons, and, above all, the love of money. Already in *The Adventuress* and in *Gabrielle*, the anti-Romantic orientation of Augier's theater is evident. His social setting would be principally the middle class, of which he himself was a proud member, and even as he attacked the dishonesty and corruption rampant in that class, he would laud its virtues: an abiding respect for the sanctity of family life, the veneration of true love as consecrated in marriage, and a belief in the legitimacy of material success when founded on personal industry and honest dealings.

As an enthusiastic exponent of what he perceived to be the solid values of the middle class and as a playwright who saw his theater as having the utilitarian goal of seeking to preserve those values, Augier was anything but a social reformer in the revolutionary sense. His plays were almost totally lacking in any suggestion of abstract concepts or ideals relative to the creation of a new society. Nor was he concerned with any of the philosophical problems that have haunted some of the greatest dramatists. On the other hand, Augier's theater did enjoy the distinction of authenticity. Although later French playwrights, such as Henry Becque, would be more exhaustive in their realistic detail or more truculent in their denunciation of corruption, Augier offered character-types and settings that were readily recognized as being drawn directly from the world of the middle class. In this sense, he demonstrated a perceptive and, at times, profound grasp of the psychology and customs of his milieu, infusing his plays with a human interest that could result only from a keen and probing observation of bourgeois society.

Just as Augier could lay no claim to being a reformer in the domain of ideology, so he could lay no claim to being a reformer in the domain of technique or style. Although his plays are notable for their clever construction (in this he was a faithful disciple of Eugène Scribe, renowned for his *pièces biens faites*, or well-made plays), Augier lacked the fecund imagination of the truly great playwright, and often the calculated orchestration of his theatrical effects suggests more artifice than art. An example of this orchestration is the device of contrasting characters, such as in the case of his masterpiece, *Monsieur Poirier's Son-in-Law*, in which Poirier and Verdelet, Gaston and Hector, are a little too neatly set in opposition to one another. As for the language of his characters, it was prosaic to the utmost; even his early plays were composed in verse.

Nevertheless, because they were the fruits of his actual social experience, Augier's characters rang true in attitude and behavior and did not suffer from

Émile Augier (Library of Congress)

the Romantic inclination to excessive lyricism. More-over, whatever the mediocrity of his prose style, it liberated French dramatic diction from the exaggerations and histrionic abuses practiced by the previous generation's Romantic writers, reproducing, instead, the regular speech patterns of the bourgeoisie. Viewed in this light, Augier could justifiably be considered the creator of the modern comedy of manners in France. He will be remembered, however, not only for this historical distinction but also for a handful of well-crafted plays, of which *Monsieur Poirier's Son-in-Law* is the most outstanding.

BIOGRAPHY

Guillaume-Victor-Émile Augier once said that after his birth nothing had ever happened to him. Aside from his generally triumphant career in the theater, Augier's life was, in fact, largely uneventful. Augier was born at Valence, of a wealthy middle-class family, in 1820. The grandson of the celebrated writer Charles Pigault-Lebrun, who in 1831 dedicated to him his book of short stories *Contes à mon petit-fils*, Augier was not long in discovering his own literary proclivities. His father, Victor Augier, was a lawyer and hoped that his son would follow in his footsteps. In 1828, Victor took the family to Paris, where he bought a notary's practice, and Augier did embark on a law career in the offices of M. Masson after establishing a fine academic record at the Collège Henri IV.

Although he obtained a law degree from the University of Paris in 1844, Augier did not practice, preferring to write for the stage. Indeed, the very year in which he completed his law studies, Augier presented the first of nine verse plays, *La Ciguë*, to the Théâtre-Français, which rejected it. He then submitted it to the Théâtre de l'Odéon, which performed it, and successfully. From that point on, Augier, with rare exceptions, was exclusively absorbed in the writing of plays. His career as a playwright, a career whose general orientation toward social drama was already discernible in these early verse plays, developed rapidly and securely. He wrote mainly for the Comédie-Française, the Théâtre du Gymnase, the Théâtre de l'Odéon, and the Théâtre du Vaudeville.

In 1853, Augier began seriously to write plays in prose, collaborating with Jules Sandeau on *La Pierre de touche*. He had already worked with Sandeau on the composition of *La Chasse au roman* in 1851, and before that, with Alfred de Musset on *The Green Coat* in 1849. In succeeding years, he collaborated again with Sandeau and coauthored plays also with Eugène Labiche and Édouard Foussier. Influenced by the example of François Ponsard, who had become the leading advocate of the *école de bon sens*, or "school of common sense," a movement designed to free the French theater of Romantic extremes, Augier's prose plays presented both an impassioned defense of middle-class values and a close examination of the ways in which those values were subverted. The plays found a receptive audience, principally among bourgeois theatergoers, and notably in 1854 with regard to the first performance, at the Théâtre du Gymnase, of Augier's finest work, *Monsieur Poirier's Son-in-Law*, an incisive study of a bourgeois social climber. The following year, with *The Marriage of Olympe*, Augier seemed to be countering the sympathetic treatment accorded the courtesan by Dumas, *fils*, in *La Dame aux camélias* (pr., pb. 1852; *Camille*, 1856). In Augier's play, the courtesan ends up destroying the respectable family into which she has been married, proving herself, in the process, absolutely incapable of true moral regeneration.

Augier's domination of the French theater started at this time, and by 1857, he had been elected to the French Academy. During the 1860's, his would be the most prestigious name among living French playwrights, and by 1900, there would be a list of 2,656 performances of his plays at the Comédie-Française alone. The *Annales du théâtre* of 1881 would recognize Augier, along with Victor Hugo, Dumas, *fils*, and Victorien Sardou, as one of the four principal living dramatists of France.

His prestige during the 1860's notwithstanding, Augier cannot be said to have enjoyed equal favor with all segments of French society at that time. *Faces of Brass*, presented in 1861 at the Comédie-Française, provoked angry responses from supporters of the press because of its denunciation of corruption in the ranks of the journalists. *Giboyer's Son*, also produced by the Comédie-Française the following year, alienated partisans of the Catholic church by its description of the political machinations of the clergy. Nor did matters improve two years later, when, in still another first performance at thei Comédie-Française, *Maître Guérin* infuriated the legal profession with its assault on unscrupulous lawyers.

For Augier, the 1870's were characterized primarily by the unfortunate consequences of the fall of the Second Empire and by his marriage, in 1873, to a young actress, Laure Lambert. The end of the reign of Napoleon III appeared to coincide, ironically, with the end of Augier's reign in the theater. To be sure, he continued to write for the stage, as plays such as *Jean de Thommeray* and *Madame Caverlet* attest. Yet these works, while revealing Augier's concern with the decline of middle-class values rooted in the harmony and cohesion of family life, were less well received, on the whole, than those of the 1860's. The lone exception to the rule was *The House of Fourchambault*, which, in 1878, marked Augier's return to the Comédie-Française for the last time (*Madame Caverlet* had been produced at the Théâtre du Vaudeville, and another play of 1876, *Le Prix Martin*, at the Théâtre du Palais-Royal). With *The House of Fourchambault*, an arresting depiction of a bourgeois family beset with financial difficulties, Augier withdrew from the stage, still acclaimed by his public despite the partial erosion of his talent. In the very year in which *The House of Fourchambault* was presented, Augier, suffering from a nervous disease, went into retirement at Croissy, where he was to die in 1889, at the age of sixty-nine.

ANALYSIS

If the constant and predominant theme of Émile Augier's plays is money and its corrupting effect, this circumstance is not without its historical justification. The period of the Second Empire in France was marked by an enormous development of the nation's industrial potential, and with this development came a material prosperity that fostered both a wider dissemination of wealth and a more intense desire, among those not directly touched by the newfound prosperity, to share in it. So intense was this desire, in some cases, that it swept aside moral principle. Augier's self-appointed task of calling attention to this decay and noting its deleterious effects on the middle class, even as he recalled the sound values of that class, is therefore more than caprice or literary fancy.

Augier's plays are successful when he uses in a measured fashion the innovations in theme and style of the two playwrights who most influenced him, Dumas, *fils*, and Scribe. The former's tendency to expound theses in his plays, converting them into *pièces à thèse*, exerted an unfavorable influence on Augier in those instances in which Augier's dramatic apparatus becomes nothing more than a pretext for the elaboration of an idea. Scribe's propensity for overemphasizing the aspect of technical adroitness in the delineation of plot and character also exerted an unfavorable influence on Augier in those instances in which Augier appears to have sacrificed realism in the description of a social situation or individual psychology to the objective of achieving a well-made play.

In his best works, however, Augier avoids these two traps, profiting from the lessons of Dumas, *fils*, and Scribe without subverting the worthy fruits of his insightful analysis of bourgeois society. The plays in which Augier arrives at this equilibrium of art and realistic observation are *Monsieur Poirier's Son-in-Law*, *Giboyer's Son*, and *The House of Fourchambault*.

MONSIEUR POIRIER'S SON-IN-LAW

Monsieur Poirier's Son-in-Law, rightly regarded as Augier's masterpiece, is a nineteenth century reworking of a theme brilliantly treated in Molière's *Le Bourgeois Gentilhomme* (pr. 1670; *The Would-Be Gentleman*, 1675), the theme of the middle-class social climber. M. Poirier is a nouveau riche who, longing to be titled, marries off his daughter, Antoinette, to a poor aristocrat, the marquis de Presles. Underwriting the expenses of the couple, Poirier explodes in indignation when he discovers that his noble son-in-law is content to live off him and is in effect exploiting his largesse. Poirier then threatens to stop subsidizing the marquis, and this predictably provokes a crisis of major proportions for the latter, who now takes another look at the internal circumstances of his marriage and, in particular, his feelings for his wife. In so doing, he finds that he really loves her, and, happily, this discovery represents a new beginning for him, rather than a very sad end. Through the magnanimity of Poirier's friend Verdelet, the marquis is able to redress the financial aspect of the crisis and even becomes employed. At the conclusion of the play, however, Poirier, having acquired the marquis's property, is still clinging to his glorious ambition of gaining the status of a nobleman.

The particular subject of *Monsieur Poirier's Son-in-Law*, the tensions between the nouveau riche and the impoverished aristocrat, was a most appropriate one for Augier because it mirrored faithfully the social agitation of the Second Empire, with the realignments engendered by the mercantile decline of the nobility and the upward movement of the bourgeoisie. What makes Augier's treatment of this subject remarkable is his unrelenting scrutiny of the well-to-do bourgeois as typified by Poirier. Himself a bourgeois, Augier nevertheless resisted the temptation to poeticize his character. Poirier is clearly meritorious, admittedly, to the extent that he has created his wealth honestly, through hard work. Nor is he lacking in common sense, or in a kind of stubborn persistence in the pursuit of his ends, a persistence admirable by the very energy that animates it.

On the other hand, Augier has discerned Poirier's defects and does not hesitate to reveal them. This social climber borders on a caricature by the vanity and vacuity of his social ambitions. More disquieting is the fact that, once he has decided that marrying his daughter to an unscrupulous marquis was a colossal blunder, he seeks to separate her from him with a bitterness and rancor that are repugnant. Yet, if these negative qualities reduce the audience's admiration for Poirier, they reinforce the impression that his character is derived from the example of life itself. Poirier is, in fact, the model for many other representatives of the middle class in Augier's theater, such as Vernouillet in *Faces of Brass*, Maréchal in *Giboyer's Son*, and Guérin in *Maître Guérin*.

If Augier has not exaggerated Poirier's moral assets, so he has not exaggerated the marquis de Pres-les's moral liabilities. The marquis surely reflects the principal vices of his class as they were often perceived at this juncture in European history. In his own way, he too is prideful. It is only that his pride takes the form of a delight in indolence and frivolity. At the same time, however, he embodies the more traditional positive features of the aristocracy. He easily spends the money of others without question. Yet he does so with a wit, a grace, and a generosity that are the hallmarks of his aristocratic bearing at its best. What is more significant, however, is that the marquis de Presles gains in moral stature as his essential qualities are favorably mirrored in his wife Antoinette's love for him. Augier has made of her a sympathetic figure, and her adoration of her husband affects the audience's feelings toward him. The portrait of the marquis resembles that of Poirier in that both characters emerge as believable creations from the psychological as well as the historical viewpoint.

The artistic construction of *Monsieur Poirier's Son-in-Law* attests an intelligent and skillful adaptation of the precepts of Scribe. The play is well-made less in the artificial sense of perfect technical balance—notwithstanding the careful contrasting of Poirier and Verdelet, Gaston and Hector—than in the more classical sense of a rigorous economy of organization in which there is practically no padding. The nineteenth century drama critic Francisque Sarcey expressed it succinctly in his review of *Monsieur Poirier's Son-in-Law* when he observed that there was not a single scene or word in it that one would want to eliminate. When Sarcey added that the play was the masterpiece of contemporary comedy, he was asserting an opinion that the work's general excellence completely justifies.

GIBOYER'S SON

In *Giboyer's Son*, the antagonism between the aristocracy and the bourgeoisie is again a focal point of the dramatic action but in circumstances appreciably different from those of *Monsieur Poirier's Son-in-Law*, as Augier creates a larger political context for that dramatic action. The play pits the traditional aristocracy, incarnated by the marquis d'Auberville, against the Liberal Party, represented, however intermittently, by M. Maréchal. To combat the growing influence of the Liberal Party, the marquis chooses as speech writer for his Conservatives, who are aligned with the clergy, an opportunist, the journalist Giboyer. In selecting Giboyer, the marquis is well aware of the venality of the man and feels confident that Giboyer will support whatever political position will bring him the most money, especially since he is bent on educating his son, Maximilien. The latter, who does not know that Giboyer is in reality his father, becomes Maréchal's secretary, again through the agency of the marquis. Maréchal, who was formerly a member of the Liberal Party but is now under the wing of the marquis, dreams of an alliance of the "old" and the "new" aristocracy, reinforced in his expectations by the fact that his daughter, Fernande, has become the marquis's protégée and by the fact that he himself has been chosen to deliver the Conservative Party's speech in opposition to the spokesman for the Liberal Party.

Everything changes when the clerical members of the Conservative Party move to replace Maréchal. Angered and disillusioned, he bolts the party and becomes a Liberal again. His retaliatory speech is prepared by Maximilien, who now knows that Giboyer is his father because the latter, thinking his son imbued with Maréchal's earlier conservatism, has revealed himself to be the hypocritical author of Maréchal's original speech championing the Conservative ideal. Giboyer now urges his son to uphold the Liberal creed. Maréchal's revolt further disrupts the marquis's plans in that the latter, a widower with no children, had hoped to have his cousin the comte d'Outreville become heir to his title and property on condition that he marry Fernande. With Maréchal's defection, however, the marriage becomes impossible, and all the more so since Fernande's heart belongs to Maximilien, who returns her love. When the marquis discovers this, he offers to adopt Maximilien, who rejects his proposition.

Giboyer's Son is part of a trilogy (the other two plays are *Faces of Brass* and *Lions et renards*) in which all three plays treat the same political theme and two feature Giboyer. Yet *Giboyer's Son*, whose protagonist also appears in *Faces of Brass*, is the best

of the trio, both from the standpoint of thematic development and from that of technical construction. In the play, which critics of the time did not hesitate to compare to Pierre-Augustin Caron de Beaumarchais's *La Folle Journée: Ou, Le Mariage de Figaro* (wr. 1775-1778, pr. 1784; *The Marriage of Figaro*, 1784) because of the audacity of its political theme, Augier castigates the unholy alliance of the clergy and the political conservatives. Yet he does so without allowing the political content to degenerate into the kind of preachment typical of the thesis play. Despite the politics, the plot still turns primarily on the question of sentimental relationships, as the audience wonders who will win the fight for the hand of Fernande: the man whom she truly loves, Maximilien, or the husband selected for her, the comte d'Outreville.

Yet the artful subordination of political motifs to amorous ones in *Giboyer's Son* is not enough to preserve the validity of Augier's political outlook. Contemplated in the historical perspective, Augier's bourgeois biases against both Jesuits and royalists appear more glaring, and these biases necessarily call into question the ultimate fairness of his rendition of the play's politics. Moreover, even at best the radical changes in party alignments wrought by the passing of time have made much of the work's political maneuvering far less interesting.

In spite of these shortcomings, *Giboyer's Son* retains its appeal because of the penetrating analysis of Giboyer's character. The Giboyer of this play is from the very outset more fascinating than the Giboyer of *Faces of Brass* because he is now a father and, as such, is divided between his parental inclinations and the venality of his nature. That venality is all the more effectively analyzed by Augier in that, through his scrutiny, the playwright poses with unusual cogency a problem the implications of which transcend the particular case of Giboyer. The problem is both educational and moral. The son of a porter, Giboyer, in a sense, has been educated beyond the level typical of his class. Yet, while he possesses an education superior to that enjoyed by most of the other members of his class, he is still as materially poor as they and, furthermore, lacks the moral stamina to resist the temptation beckoning him to free himself from the circle of poverty by selling his journalistic talents to the highest bidder. Lured irresistibly by the prospect of making money through the opportunistic reformulation of his political views, Giboyer is anything but comic and inoffensive in his contradictions. Actually, he is a rather sinister and dangerous figure, since he is capable of journalistic blackmail. In Augier's play, he is a journalist, but one can easily imagine his counterparts in business and law. Finally, what is so troubling in Giboyer is the systematic hypocrisy that attends his activity: He is all the more to be feared because his scoundrelly nature is not obvious to the naked eye.

Yet Giboyer is illuminated by a still-vibrant paternal instinct. His corrupt behavior has one main objective, and that is to make of his son an educated man and an honorable one. While this fatherly devotion does not exonerate Giboyer entirely, it adds just that contradictory dimension to his character that renders him lifelike. The moment in the play in which Giboyer reveals to Maximilien that he is his father, act 3, scene 16, can easily be played for its pathos, but it gains a special resonance and human significance by its moving portrayal of Giboyer's genuine suffering.

Apart from the riveting complexity of its protagonist, *Giboyer's Son* recommends itself by the deft management of a variety of motifs that are melded without creating an impression of confusion and without slowing down the action. If there is the basic marriage of the political and amorous motifs, there is also abundant social commentary—all this blended convincingly because the characters do not discourse didactically on these matters but allude to them with apparent naturalness when their passions are aroused. Comic scenes alternate with near-tragic ones in a rapid movement the dramatic interest of which rarely flags.

The House of Fourchambault

The House of Fourchambault, Augier's last play, restates the fundamental position explicitly or implicitly advanced in virtually all his dramatic production—namely, that marriage must be predicated on true love and not on money. Fourchambault has had a child out of wedlock by his sister's piano teacher but has married instead a woman with a rich dowry. Given to frivolity and spendthrift ways, Mme Fourchambault has spoiled their daughter Blanche by instilling in her the ambition to marry for money and social position. Furthermore, she has encouraged her son Leopold to take as a mistress a Creole orphan from Bourbon Island, Marie Letellier, whom the Fourchambaults are sheltering until she can find a position as a schoolteacher.

Marie speaks so highly of Bernard, the man who brought her to France, that the Fourchambaults wish to meet him, not knowing that Bernard, now a successful ship owner, is Fourchambault's illegitimate son. Bernard discovers his true identity only when he tells his mother that the Fourchambaults are nearly bankrupt and she implores him to help her former lover and his family. The son not only grants his mother's wish but also acts to prevent Blanche, actually his sister, from contracting a marriage of convenience with the Baron Rastiboulois when she really loves Victor Chauvet, a bank clerk. In an even greater show of nobility, Bernard presses Leopold to restore Marie's compromised reputation, since she is thought to be Leopold's mistress, although he, Bernard, loves her himself. As their exchange becomes emotionally charged, Bernard reveals to Leopold that they are brothers, and Leopold encourages him to court Marie for his own sake.

A leading merit of *The House of Fourchambault* is, once again, that the play propounds ideas in which Augier believed very deeply, even passionately, without ever encasing those ideas in the theses of the *pièce à thèse*. If Augier holds that marriage should not exist without love, nor for that matter, love without marriage, he also holds to certain corollaries: that not one's family origins but one's character determines one's basic worth and that a sound character can be disastrously affected by a bad upbringing, as almost occurs with Blanche and Leopold. Yet these convictions are also enunciated, throughout the play, without doctrinal speechifying: They appear to result spontaneously from the interaction of the characters with one another.

This feature by itself does not, however, explain the effectiveness of *The House of Fourchambault*. A further reason for that effectiveness is the manner in which Augier depicts the Fourchambault and Bernard households. From act 1, the audience learns that Fourchambault is not an evil man, that his decision to abandon Bernard's mother was based on his father's questioning of her virtue and his own docile acceptance of that questioning. Though flawed, Fourchambault is seen in a less culpable light than his wife, whom he does not follow as she urges their son Leopold to take Marie as a mistress while waiting to meet a woman worthy of being married to him. The Fourchambaults' daughter Blanche is described in a similar fashion as being essentially a good person, but one whose outlook on life has been vitiated by her mother's insistence on a "proper" marriage.

From act 2, the audience learns that, despite its illegitimacy, the Bernard household is full of more tender loving care than is the Fourchambault household. Mme Bernard is a mother in the truest sense, and, if her son has been a success in business without sacrificing moral principle, the cause of that success is the sound education that she has given him. As for Bernard, so high is the esteem in which he holds his mother that he would not want to marry anyone who would be lacking in the apposite respect for her, and this restriction has inhibited the expression of his love for Marie. It is also in act 2 that the two families come into contact with each other, as Mme Fourchambault and Blanche, having heard so much praise of Bernard from Marie, appear at the Bernard residence. By the end of this same act, Bernard has guessed, from the emotional exchange with his mother about the Fourchambaults' financial woes, that Fourchambault is his father. Figuratively as well as literally, the stage is now set for the drama that will unfold as the Fourchambaults struggle with the consequences of their financial crisis. Augier has once again applied, and without too great a cost in natural progression, the precepts of the *pièce bien faite*.

This is not to say that all this is managed without some concession to the most recognizable forms of theatrical convention. To take, first of all, the most obvious example, Augier creates the ultimate *coup de théâtre* in scene 5 of act 5, when Bernard reveals to Leopold that they are brothers. Sarcey, usually ardent in his praise of Augier, has alluded to the artificiality of the situation that develops in act 4, scene 8, where Bernard, even as he speaks to Blanche in an effort to dissuade her from marrying the Baron Rastiboulois, is really addressing his remarks to Marie also, both a participant in and a witness to the conversation. Perhaps a more telling criticism is that, despite all his theatrical ingenuity, Augier has not created here a character who lives with the vividness and vitality of a Poirier, or a Giboyer. Ironically, the reason may be that Augier has made these characters, particularly those of the Fourchambault family, too "nice," whatever their superficial flaws, and too capable of the moral conversion that occurs once Bernard begins to exert his influence in their lives. The one character whose potential for wickedness might have been developed so as to make her a memorable creation, Mme Fourchambault, remains, rather, a case of arrested dramatic development.

These weaknesses notwithstanding, and while it is clearly inferior in artistic conception to *Monsieur Poirier's Son-in-Law* and *Giboyer's Son*, Augier's last play testifies, nevertheless, to his continued overall mastery of his craft. Émile Zola, after enumerating some of the defects of the work, acknowledged that *The House of Fourchambault* was solidly constructed and firmly written. Having seen the play when it was introduced at the Comédie-Française, Zola concluded that Augier was the master of the French stage at that time.

In any event, with *The House of Fourchambault*, Augier went out in a blaze of glory from the vantage point of popular appeal. The play's denouement in act 5, scene 5, if one is to believe Sarcey's opening-night review, caused the whole audience to explode in applause. The same critic's general assessment of the manner in which *The House of Fourchambault* was received by the public was that the play achieved one of the most outstanding first-night successes that he had ever witnessed in the theater. Sarcey's comments seem less exaggerated when one recalls that Émile Perrin, then the director of the Comédie-Française, revived *Le Fils naturel* (pr., pb. 1858; *The Natural Son*, 1879), a play by Dumas, *fils*, which treated essentially the same subject, to capitalize on Augier's immense triumph. It is clear, in the final analysis, that with the success of *The House of Fourchambault*, Augier left the theater at the very height of his popularity. It is also clear that he left the theater with a renewed expression of faith in the resiliency of the middle-class family and its values, which his decades of playwriting had in no way diminished.

OTHER MAJOR WORKS

POETRY: *Les Pariétaires*, 1856.

BIBLIOGRAPHY

Danger, Pierre. *Émile Augier: Ou, Le Théâtre de l'ambiguïté: Éléments pour une archéologie morale de la bourgeoisie sous le Second Empire.* Paris: L'Harmattan, 1998. Critical analysis and interpretation of Augier's works, with reference to the times in which he lived. Bibliography. In French.

Van Laan, Thomas F. "The Ending of *A Doll House* and Augier's *Maître Guérin.*" *Comparative Drama* 17 (1983): 297-317. A comparison of one of Henrik Ibsen's plays to Augier's *Maître Guérin.*

Norman Araujo

SIR ALAN AYCKBOURN

Born: Hampstead, London, England; April 12, 1939

PRINCIPAL DRAMA

The Square Cat, pr. 1959 (as Roland Allen)

Love After All, pr. 1959 (as Roland Allen)

Mr. Whatnot, pr. 1963 (revised version pr. 1964)

Relatively Speaking, pr. 1967, pb. 1968 (originally as *Meet My Father*, pr. 1965)

Ernie's Incredible Illucinations, pb. 1969, pr. 1971 (for children)

How the Other Half Loves, pr. 1969, pb. 1972

Time and Time Again, pr. 1971, pb. 1973

Absurd Person Singular, pr. 1972, pb. 1974

The Norman Conquests, pr. 1973, pb. 1975 (includes *Table Manners*, *Living Together*, and *Round and Round the Garden*)

Absent Friends, pr. 1974, pb. 1975

Confusions, pr. 1974, pb. 1977 (five one-acts)

Bedroom Farce, pr. 1975, pb. 1977

Just Between Ourselves, pr. 1976, pb. 1978

Ten Times Table, pr. 1977, pb. 1978

Joking Apart, pr. 1978, pb. 1979

Men on Women on Men, pr. 1978 (lyrics; music by Paul Todd)

Sisterly Feelings, pr. 1979, pb. 1981

Taking Steps, pr. 1979, pb. 1981

Suburban Strains, pr. 1980, pb. 1982 (music by Todd)

Season's Greetings, pr. 1980, pb. 1982

Way Upstream, pr. 1981, pb. 1983

Me, Myself, and I, pr. 1981, pb. 1989 (music by Todd)

Intimate Exchanges, pr. 1982, pb. 1985

A Chorus of Disapproval, pr. 1984, pb. 1985

Woman in Mind, pr. 1985, pb. 1986

A Small Family Business, pr., pb. 1987

Henceforward, pr. 1987, pb. 1988

Mr. A's Amazing Maze Plays, pr. 1988, pb. 1989 (for children)

Man of the Moment, pr. 1988, pb. 1990

Invisible Friends, pr. 1989, pb. 1991

The Revengers' Comedies, pr. 1989, pb. 1991

Body Language, pr. 1990, pb. 2001

This Is Where He Came In, pr. 1990, pb. 1995 (for children)

Wildest Dreams, pr. 1991, pb. 1993

My Very Own Story, pr. 1991, pb. 1995 (for children)

Dreams from a Summer House, pr. 1992, pb. 1997 (music by John Pattison)

Time of My Life, pr. 1992, pb. 1993

Communicating Doors, pr. 1994, pb. 1995

Haunting Julia, pr. 1994

The Musical Jigsaw Play, pr. 1994 (for children)

Plays, pb. 1995-1998 (2 volumes)

A Word from Our Sponsor, pr. 1995, pb. 1998
   (music by Pattison)

By Jeeves, pr. 1996 (music by Andrew Lloyd
   Webber)

The Champion of Paribanou, pr. 1996, pb. 1998
   (for children)

Things We Do for Love, pr. 1997, pb. 1998

The Boy Who Fell into a Book, pr. 1998, pb. 2000
   (for children)

Comic Potential, pr. 1998, pb. 1999

Gizmo, pr. 1998, pb. 1999

"House" and "Garden," pr., pb. 2000

OTHER LITERARY FORMS

Alan Ayckbourn is known primarily for his plays.

ACHIEVEMENTS

A farceur of contemporary suburbia, Alan Ayckbourn enjoys distinction not only as a prolific writer
of entertaining, well-made plays during a stage revolution when the *pièce bien faite* was out of fashion
but also as a dramatist who, beginning in 1959, has
averaged one play a year, claiming to have surpassed
even William Shakespeare in the sheer quantity of
plays written by the early 1990's. His early reputation
as a commercial dramatist, however, changed with
the times and the development of his own style and
themes, so that he has enjoyed productions of his
plays even at the prestigious National Theatre in London. A critic of contemporary society's greed, he has
increasingly honed his farce into black comedy, earning for it the label of "theater of embarrassment." In
1987 Ayckbourn was awarded a royal honor as Commander of the British Empire, and in 1997 he was
knighted for services to the theater.

In 1992 he was appointed Cameron Mackintosh
professor of contemporary theater at St. Catherine's
College, Oxford. Among other awards he has received are the Montblanc de la Culture Award for Europe and the Writers' Guild of Great Britain Lifetime

Sir Alan Ayckbourn in 1988. (AP/Wide World Photos)

Achievement Award. He has received several honorary degrees, and his work has been translated into
more than forty languages.

BIOGRAPHY

Alan Ayckbourn was born in Hampstead, London,
on April 12, 1939, to Horace and Irene Worley
Ayckbourn, his father the first violinist with the London Symphony Orchestra and his mother a novelist
and short-story writer for popular women's magazines. In 1943, when he was five, his parents were divorced and his mother married Cecil Pye, a manager
for Barclays Bank. Winning a Barclays Bank scholarship, Ayckbourn attended Haileybury School in Hertfordshire, where, during the next five years, he became interested in drama, touring in Holland as Peter
in *Romeo and Juliet* and in the United States and
Canada as Macduff in *Macbeth*.

Thus began Ayckbourn's lifelong affair with the
theater. He left school with "A" levels in English and
history and, at seventeen, joined Sir Donald Wolfit's
company at the Edinburgh Festival as acting assistant

stage manager. He also worked in summer theater at Leatherhead and then at Scarborough's Studio Theatre (under Stephen Joseph, son of actress Hermione Ferdinanda Gingold), writing plays even as he was initiated into the production rites of professional theater.

In 1959, Ayckbourn married actress Christine Roland, had a son (Steven Paul), and saw two of his plays (*The Square Cat* and *Love After All*) produced in Scarborough under the pseudonym of Roland Allen. In 1962, his second son, Nicholas Phillip, was born, and in 1964, Ayckbourn's *Mr. Whatnot* opened at the Arts Theatre in London. Thereafter, he has averaged writing at least one play per year, and he is wont to talk fondly of providing amusement for bored surburbanite vacationers on rainy Scarborough days.

Ayckbourn's early days in the theater included acting in roles such as Vladimir in Samuel Beckett's *En attendant Godot* (pb. 1952, pr. 1953; *Waiting for Godot*, pb. 1954) and Stanley in Harold Pinter's *The Birthday Party* (pr. 1958, pb. 1960). He was founder-member and associate director of Victoria Theatre in Stoke on Trent, produced dramas on the British Broadcasting Corporation's radio, in Leeds, and, after Stephen Joseph's death in 1967, returned to Scarborough in 1970. After several name changes, the Victoria Theatre became the Stephen Joseph Theatre-in-the-Round in 1996, in tribute to Ayckbourn's mentor. It became also Ayckbourn's tryout home before openings in theaters in and around London and all over the world.

In the United States, the Alley Theatre in Houston, the Arena Stage in Washington, and the Manhattan Theater Club in New York, among others, became homes for Ayckbourn's plays. Having succeeded in small English theaters such as The Arts, The Roundhouse, and The Richmond Orange Tree, and later in commercial houses in the West End, Ayckbourn's *Bedroom Farce* reached the Royal National Theatre, where both his plays and his directorship (1986) have long enjoyed a liaison. In the best of all possible theater worlds—the provincial, fringe, West End commercial, Royal National, and international theaters producing his plays—Ayckbourn not

only has survived the early critical attacks for writing the commercially profitable well-made play but also has continued writing in a long career that has no contemporary equal in quantity and consistency of experimentation. With more than fifty plays, Ayckbourn has continued to be more prolific than any of the new playwrights since the stage revolution began in 1956 with John Osborne's *Look Back in Anger* (pr. 1956, pb. 1957).

His first marriage in 1959 to Christine Allen, by whom he had two sons, led to separation and divorce some years later. In 1997 he married Heather Stoney. He has continued to live in Scarborough, Yorkshire.

Analysis

With labels flourishing during the new era in drama (Osborne's angry theater, Beckett's Theater of the Absurd, Pinter's comedy of menace, Arnold Wesker's kitchen-sink drama), Alan Ayckbourn, too, has been honored with his own label, the comedy of embarrassment, based on the increasingly black comedy in his later farces. The term derives from the unease of audiences as their laughter is deflected by the intrusion of realities underlying that hilarity. For example, the accidental murders in *A Small Family Business* and *Man of the Moment* obtrude through the farce, giving it a hollow ring. This jarring union of farce and tragedy, alien to standard farce expectations, in fact, is subtly present even in early comedies such as *How the Other Half Loves*, markedly so in *A Chorus of Disapproval*, and shatteringly so in *A Small Family Business* and *Man of the Moment*. Ayckbourn has become the hilarious tragedian of contemporary life, not unlike Ben Jonson, whose seventeenth century farces about greed seem ancestors to Ayckbourn's. Ayckbourn met the charges of early critics who faulted him for his commercially viable formula plays, commenting that one "cannot begin to shatter theatrical conventions or break golden rules until he is reasonably sure in himself what they are and how they were arrived at." The rules to which Ayckbourn is referring are the time-honored ones practiced by Greeks and Romans, Shakespeare, Jonson, Molière, George Bernard Shaw, and Oscar Wilde.

With the acknowledged influence of William Congreve, Wilde, Georges Feydeau, Anton Chekhov, Noël Coward, Terence Rattigan, J. B. Priestley, and Pinter, Ayckbourn has forged a style of old and new that has given his plays their unique quality. Using the farce conventions of his predecessors, he has experimented with the mechanics of traditional plotting by challenging its limits and extending its boundaries. One of his most noticeable changes in farce techniques is his avoidance of the linear movement of the plot and his replacing it with a sense of indefiniteness. The outcome is a circular movement, resulting in a play structure that is more akin to the static quality of Chekhov's plots than to the active one of Wilde's and Shaw's plays. His disarrangement of linear plot lines creates the illusion of a standard farce, deceiving the audience in its usual comic expectations. His technique is partly explained by the tripling, sometimes quadrupling, of the number of potentially comic couples or comic situations in the conventional farce. The standard use of the double takes what seems a quantum leap in Ayckbourn's farces.

The tripling extends to the overall architecture of plays, a number of them taking the form of trilogies. In *The Norman Conquests*, each of the three plays treats the same character and situations, one being the offstage action of what happens onstage in another. The order of performance of the three plays, thus, is of little consequence, for each is essentially repetitious of the other two. The chief difference among them is their locale: One occurs in the dining room, the second in the living room, and the third in the garden. The difference is diversionary, suggesting a traditional plot movement where there really is none. Ayckbourn's trilogy *Sisterly Feelings* goes even further in its structural inventiveness, with each play's conclusion in a given performance being determined arbitrarily by a member of the cast. Still another sometimes confusing plot invention is Ayckbourn's use of the same stage space at the same time by two or more different sets of characters (frequently couples), most prominently illustrated in *How the Other Half Loves*, *Bedroom Farce*, and *Taking Steps*. The single most famous of these scenes, in *How the Other*

Half Loves, involves two different dinner parties by two different middle-class couples (one having achieved social status and the other desperately trying to do so) seated at the same table, their only common element a third couple who are the guests at both dinners.

Ayckbourn's ingenious plotting strategies provide him ample room to comment on his favorite theme: a satire on the foibles of individuals functioning in suburbia, his chosen slice of middle-class society. His satire has its brief, unrelieved grim moments as in *A Small Family Business* and *Henceforeward*, plays in which the families' children become victims of the pervasive greed of individuals and their society and are helpless to extricate themselves. The artificially happy ending of a farce is replaced by a realistically sober ending in which the comic surfaces of the plot are maintained, even as they cannot disguise the underlying tragic realities. Thus the play stylistically satisfies the farce's requirement for a happy ending while substantively changing the genre to an ironic farce at its best and a black comedy at its most pessimistic. It is appropriate that the title of one of Ayckbourn's late plays, *The Revengers' Comedies*, derives from Cyril Tourneur's seventeenth century title *The Revenger's Tragedy* (pr. 1606-1607, pb. 1607), with the obvious parallel of the earlier era with Thatcherite England of the 1980's.

The traditional purpose of comedy has been to reveal and thereby correct the vices of the society that it portrays by exposing them (usually with a *deus ex machina* ending), thereby bringing about correction of behavior in that society. The exposure involves stereotypical characters whose mechanical behavior engenders laughter. Mere exposure is the punishment for the perpetrator of the vice, either reform or prison frequently being the result of that exposure. The vices of the age have no such corrective results in Ayckbourn's farces.

In his exposure of rampant acquisitiveness, however, Ayckbourn does realize half of the farceur's aim. At the same time, he admits to an unease about the corrective results of prevailing farces. Of the Thatcherite regime he says, "It's no coincidence that you hardly ever see members of the present Government in the theatre. . . . The arts and gentle, civilized living are rapidly being downgraded for the fast buck. It has a narrowing effect. It creates an uncaringness."

The traditional purpose of tragedy has been to cleanse the body politic of its moral stain and to affirm life through increased self-knowledge on the part of the hero, a process in which guilty and innocent alike suffer. As realistic rather than stereotypical characters who embody the values of their respective societies, characters evoke, according to Aristotelian precepts, pity and fear in the polis even as they endure individual punishments and rewards. There is no such individual or collective affirmation in Ayckbourn's plays. Again, the darker elements only continue in their nonresolution, in character-generated farces, such as Jack McCracken of *A Small Family Business* and Douglas Beechey of *Man of the Moment*. Societally, business and mass-media corrupters conspire in their lack of awareness of the morality or immorality of their actions. Individually and collectively, characters continue in a context in which punishment and rewards in a moral sense do not exist.

Ayckbourn regards *Absurd Person Singular* with its three Christmas Eve celebrations as his first "off-stage action" play, one in which two socially aspiring couples land in the thick of adversities of the most successful couple. The offstage importance increases with every play, with further inability on the part of the characters to extricate themselves from their adversities. For example, the celebratory tableaulike ending to *A Small Family Business* coexists with a tableau of the young daughter in her drug-induced pain in the bathroom. John Peter describes an Ayckbourn play as "a requiem scored for screams and laughter."

As a dark farceur par excellence of contemporary suburbia, as an ongoing reinventor of farce technique, and as the most prolific of a huge number of new dramatists in the second half of the twentieth century, Ayckbourn continues to be a force on the world stage.

RELATIVELY SPEAKING

Ayckbourn's first London success, *Relatively Speaking*, illustrates his roots in the traditional me-

chanics of the well-made farce, such as abundant coincidences, well-timed exits and entrances, complicated romantic intrigues, central misunderstandings, quid pro quos, secrets known to the audience but not to the characters, and the crucial use of an object to progress the plot. At the same time, Ayckbourn rejects the suspense-creating, teeter-totter action, the big revelatory scene, and the ending that neatly ties together the loose ends of the plot. Instead, as a keen observer and creator of character, he treats familial and marital situations whose problems are revealed rather than resolved. The results are Chekhov-like revelations of states of being, contained within the guise of farce and an increasingly bitter satire on the moral bankruptcy of contemporary society. Deceptively embodied in the local, his farce is ultimately universal in its depiction of human foibles that know no bounds of time or place.

With echoes of the exploits of Oscar Wilde's Jack and Ernest in *The Importance of Being Earnest* (pr. 1895, pb. 1899), *Relatively Speaking*, a four-character play, involves a young unmarried couple who set off for the country, each for secret reasons withheld from the other. Ginny wishes to retrieve letters from her former lover (and employer) to put a definite end to that affair. Unbeknown to her, Greg, her current lover, suspicious because of the flowers and chocolates cluttering Ginny's flat and the address he notices on her cigarette pack (like the cigarette case in Wilde's play), follows her on a different train. Ginny's lie about a visit to her "parents" begins a series of deceptions multiplied at breakneck speed, deceptions that stretch out to include an older couple, Philip and his wife, Sheila. A *sine qua non* of any farce, the seemingly unstoppable piling up of deceptions, misunderstandings, and coincidences is absurd, one of the most comical being Greg's misinterpretation of Sheila's truthful insistence that she is not Ginny's mother. To Greg, Sheila is merely eluding potential embarrassment at having to reveal the illegitimacy of Ginny's birth.

Like all farceurs, Ayckbourn bases his suspense on secrets known to only some of the characters and on not having all characters on the stage at the same time until the play's end. Consequently, all characters act on the basis of only a partial knowledge of things. While observing this convention, Ayckbourn ignores the artificial disclosure scene (also known as the big scene, obligatory scene, or *scène à faire*) in which all secrets are revealed, all misunderstandings cleared up, and a happy ending contrived. For even as Ginny and Philip depart happily, neither Greg nor Philip is fully apprised of what has happened, the former of Philip's deceptive vacation plans having included Ginny and the latter of Sheila's untruthful claims to having a lover. Thus the turning point in the conventional farce (two of the most famous occurring in Richard Brinsley Sheridan's *The School for Scandal*, pr. 1777, pb. 1780, and Wilde's *The Importance of Being Earnest*) gives way even in Ayckbourn's early farces to a Chekhovian technique of the undramatic.

HOW THE OTHER HALF LOVES

In *How the Other Half Loves*, Ayckbourn takes his technique one step further, this time in the use of stage space in a simultaneous depiction of two separate dinner parties. He superimposes the dinner party of one upwardly mobile couple (the Fosters) on that of a more affluent couple (the Phillipses) so that both couples are hosts to the same dinner guests (the Featherstones). In an eye-defying sequence of movements, the audience witnesses the two couples preparing for their guests in the same stage space, the distinctions between the relative affluence of the aspiring sets of hosts made clear only by a change in a few minor furnishings, such as pillows. The hilarious scene in which two separate dinner parties at two separate times are staged at one table is Ayckbourn's most inventive climactic scene. Their common guest, Mr. Featherstone, is the victim simultaneously of Teresa Phillips's thrown soup (intended for her husband) and the leaking upstairs toilet at the Fosters' home. Unwitting victim of the accidental physical high jinks of his hosts, Mr. Featherstone is victim in another sense, for although the fortunes of the Phillipses and the Fosters seem to be put to rights at the end of the play, the Featherstones—clearly the couple to be impressed—reveal their own marital problems, foreboding, ironically, similar problems for their younger, aspiring hosts.

TIME AND TIME AGAIN

Up to *Time and Time Again*, Ayckbourn's inventions focused on plots and staging areas. About this play, however, Ayckbourn speaks of "upsetting the balance," an upsetting involving the nature of his main character. Normally the driving force in the plot, the protagonist, Leonard, is upsettingly passive. According to Ayckbourn, he "attracts people who have an irresistible impulse to push him in one direction, but he slides out of the push." Some audiences, Ayckbourn continues, are "angered by this type," while "others get concerned." Hence, Ayckbourn himself supplies yet another basis for the label applied to him as a writer of the theater of embarrassment.

Leonard's "sliding" in the play is his refusal to be drawn into the banalities of middle-class social lunches and teas. He has developed his own system of quiet resistance. At one point, he relates the story of a telling of a tale from his former marriage. A schoolteacher at the time, Leonard arrives home one day to find his wife sampling homemade wine with a male friend. Unable or unwilling to react, Leonard spends the evening in the local jail, regaling the officers with his story and retelling it to every fresh batch of police officers as they arrive for duty. Leonard is the first of a series of Ayckbourn's passive heroes, the most humorous being Norman of *The Norman Conquests*; the most sympathetically satiric, Guy Jones in *A Chorus of Disapproval*; and the most devastating, Douglas Beechey in *Man of the Moment*.

There is an aggressive element in Leonard's passivity as he forces others to respond to his lack of involvement. From his school days, he tells yet another story of having developed a system of quoting a line or two of poetry, an "infallible system to fool all headmasters and school inspectors." He continues this pattern of behavior even as an adult. Bored by the others and interested by Leonard's erratic behavior, Joan, his current interest, joins Leonard in his game. In the meantime, Graham, a husband also attracted to Joan, pushes Peter, another admirer of Joan mistaken by Graham as her lover, into a physical fight. Leonard, as a result of the mistake, goes scot-free. The play ends with Leonard eventually leaving Joan (as he earlier had left his wife and her lover to entertain the local police officers) and walking off compatibly with Peter to the playing field, Graham and Peter still laboring under their misunderstanding.

ABSURD PERSON SINGULAR

Another Ayckbourn technique becomes more apparent with every play: his inventive use of the room. As character becomes more important than plot, Ayckbourn utilizes the room (frequently the kitchen) as a microscope under which he examines contemporary middle-class behavior in all of its acquisitiveness and sexual rituals. The kitchen, its appliances emblems of materialistic greed, is an appropriate setting for his examination.

In his *Absurd Person Singular*, structured loosely as three one-act plays, three couples celebrate Christmas Eve in three successive years in three different homes, the kitchen winding up as the room in which most of the action takes place. In the first act, the first host-couple, lowest on the social rung, aspire to the social status of their guests. In the second act, the hosts have to some extent realized their social aims. In act 3, the hosts, having played the social-status game longer than their guests, have long since been in a state of total noncommunication, a direction toward which the other two couples seem to be heading. The final scene of act 3 finds all three couples crowding the kitchen, each person in a wild frenzy of attending to chores such as replacing a light bulb, completely ignoring the suicide attempt of their hostess, with her head in the gas oven. The three couples are a variation on those in *How the Other Half Loves*.

THE NORMAN CONQUESTS

Rooms continue to be the means of Ayckbourn's microscopic examination of suburban rituals in *The Norman Conquests*. Here, Ayckbourn locates the similar actions in three different places: the dining room in *Table Manners*, the living room in *Living Together*, and the garden in *Round and Round the Garden*. The family consists of Annie, who is single and the caretaker of their sick mother, her married sister Ruth, and her married brother Reg (and the spouses of the latter two). All convene in the family's country home to provide some relief for Annie. Norman, Ruth's husband, enjoys hilariously romantic encounters with the women in each location of the three plays.

Like Leonard of *Time and Time Again*, Norman attracts female attention and finds himself in situations not of his making. A Chekhovian immobility asserts itself in Annie's abortive plans for a "dirty weekend" with Norman in East Grinstead. There is a sixth character, an outsider in the person of a slow-witted local veterinarian, played in the original stage production with exquisitely hilarious dullness by Michael Gambon, who would later become a regular actor in Ayckbourn's plays. He is a foil to Norman, whose sexual attractiveness and agility drive the women to respond to him. Each of the three plays is complete in itself, and the order in which they are performed (or seen) is more or less immaterial to the audience's understanding of each play because the action in each does not essentially depend on that in the other two and because the actions in all three are essentially the same, their different "rooms" creating different perspectives on the same situation.

TAKING STEPS AND BEDROOM FARCE

Two plays, *Taking Steps* and *Bedroom Farce*, revert to Ayckbourn's reliance on hectic physical stage business as in *How the Other Half Loves*. The action of *Taking Steps* occurs on three different floors of an old Victorian house, but one stage space is used to represent all three floors of the house. Hence the actors must take a variety of steps in imitation of stair climbing. Similarly, in *Bedroom Farce*, one stage area is occupied by three large beds to represent three different bedrooms. The potential audience confusions as to who is doing what in whose bed and the risk of actors in making false steps as they maneuver their way through time and space create suspense and keep the play's pace lively. At times, Ayckbourn's risk taking with physical matters seems its own excuse for being, an entertaining ploy to avoid the greater risk of banality potentially inherent in his repetitive marital and extramarital situations.

SEASON'S GREETINGS

In the plays of the 1960's and 1970's, Ayckbourn's ingenious strategies of plot, space, and character dominate, and laughter governs the plays' moods. In the 1980's, however, the hilarity, although remaining intact to the end of the play, is mixed with increasing audience uncertainty—to laugh or not to laugh. For example, in *Season's Greetings*, a stranger (a writer with only one book to his credit) becomes the romantic object of attention of the females. A guest of the single sister at a Christmas family gathering, he is a later version of the outsider, Leonard, in *Time and Time Again*. When the women of the household (including his hostess, the unmarried sister) are attracted to him, an angry husband shoots and almost kills him. The intrusion on farce of a potential disaster changes the nature of the laughter into the kind produced by Chekhov's *Uncle Vanya*, whose shot at his rival misfires.

Chekhov-like also in his use of a family gathering as the central event of a play, Ayckbourn has commented on that event as unimportant. It is, rather, "the response to the dinner party, not the dinner party itself." He spoke to author Bernard Dukore of the inevitable line in that response: "Wasn't that a boring dinner party?" In that line and as a consequence of it, revelations occur, not only of the problems of those couples who have succeeded but also of the pending fate of those who have not yet arrived but are on the same path. An attractive outsider acts as a catalyst to reveal the Chekhovian inner states of being that lie beneath the politely banal surfaces.

A CHORUS OF DISAPPROVAL

The outsider in *A Chorus of Disapproval* is Guy Jones, a lonely bachelor drawn into a provincial production of John Gay's *The Beggar's Opera* (pr., pb. 1728), when the leading role is suddenly vacated. A fuller version of dull Tom in *The Norman Conquests*, he rises to the occasion, though untalented and inexperienced, and becomes the hero not only of the production but also of the women who thrust themselves on him as a result of dissatisfactions in their own marriages. He is the means by which they respond to the emptiness of their suburban lives.

A SMALL FAMILY BUSINESS, HENCEFORWARD, AND MAN OF THE MOMENT

In three later plays—*A Small Family Business*, *Henceforward*, and *Man of the Moment*—the farce is increasingly ironic in Ayckbourn's progressive shift to emphasize the emotional and moral bankruptcy of

middle-class family life in Thatcherite England of the 1980's. In all three, outside forces exert pressures on family situations, pressures that the family finds difficult or impossible to control. In *A Small Family Business*, the pressure is money, involving a family furniture business in which greed corrupts completely, simultaneously involving a hilariously stereotyped, Mafia-like quintet of Italian brothers. In *Henceforward*, a gang-infested neighborhood is a refuge for a divorced composer of electronic music, who contests his wife for custody of their daughter. In a stunning move, Ayckbourn deploys a female robot, the composer's means of assuring the social worker of the presence of a maternal influence in his daughter's life. Ayckbourn compounds this bit of theatricality with the appearance of the teen daughter in full regalia as a member of one of the neighborhood gangs. In *Man of the Moment*, the theatricality takes the form of an overweight woman who accidentally kills a most repulsive character when she steps on him rather than saving him, as was her intention. Individual greed and corruption, although present, are given societal approval in the impunity and impersonality with which a television crew exploits personal tragedy in the name of a good news story. Both business and television interests conspire in a cover-up of the real story.

In these three plays, the laughter caused by coincidences and central misunderstandings is still there, but now the plays are darkened by their context of a pervasive societal hypocrisy. The problems are no longer those of innocently human complications but of socially accepted amorality. In *A Small Family Business*, the last person with any scruples, Jack, the new head of the business, cannot extricate himself from its corruption. The gang-infested neighborhood of *Henceforward* and the moral vacuum of the mass media in *Man of the Moment* remain. Ayckbourn provides no artificial resolutions to the problems, only a microscopic examination of them. Amid the farcical humor that is sustained to the end in two of the plays, two teenagers, as a result of their being ignored because of other family problems, become innocent victims, one a drug addict and the other a gang member. In the third play, an adult innocent, dull and passive

Douglas Beechey, is a subject for both hilarity and tragedy, as he is made into a mass-media hero through no attempt on his part. He belongs to a long gallery of Ayckbourn characters who have their roots in the early outsider characters such as Tom in *The Norman Conquests*.

Despite widening his settings, for example to the Costa del Sol in southern Spain in *Man of the Moment*, to ethnic restaurants, in *Time of My Life*, even to imaginary landscapes, as in *The Revengers' Comedies* and futuristic households, as in *Henceforward*, Ayckbourn's themes and theatricality have developed naturally. He has never lost sight of the little man and his desire for self-fulfillment in domesticity, even though evil may lurk abroad.

OTHER MAJOR WORKS

SCREENPLAY: *A Chorus of Disapproval*, 1989 (adaptation of his play).

TELEPLAY: *Service Not Included*, 1974.

BIBLIOGRAPHY

Allen, Paul. *Alan Ayckbourn: Grinning at the Edge.* New York: Continuum, 2002. A biography that looks at the playwright's life and works. Based on more than twenty years of interviews with Ayckbourn and of his friends and acquaintainces. Photographs. Index.

Billington, Michael. *Alan Ayckbourn.* New York: St. Martin's Press, 1990. A chronological analysis by a leading critic and scholar of Ayckbourn's plays, from his earliest unpublished works to *The Revengers' Comedies*.

Dukore, Bernard. *Alan Ayckbourn: A Casebook.* New York: Garland, 1992. A compilation of lively, analytical articles on Ayckbourn's plays in terms of their stylistic and thematic characteristics, as well as their effectiveness onstage. Includes an interview with Ayckbourn, a complete chronology, and an extensive bibliography.

Holt, Michael. *Alan Ayckbourn.* Plymouth, England: Northcote House, 1999. One of the British Council's "Writers and their Works" series, it is a sensible introduction. It contains a biography, bibliography, and commentary on the plays up to *Things We Do for Love*.

Kalson, Albert E. *Laughter in the Dark: The Plays of Alan Ayckbourn.* Cranbury, N.J.: Associated University Press for Fairleigh Dickinson University Press, 1993. The first chapter is biographical, then aspects of Ayckbourn's theater are explored, including chapters on technique; men's and women's roles; and moral, social, and political aspects. There is a separate chapter on *Absent Friends*. The best full study of the dramatist.

Page, Malcolm. *File on Ayckbourn.* London: Methuen Drama, 1989. A compilation of biographical information, production and publication data, synopses and comments on each play, interview excerpts, and a bibliography.

Watson, Ian. *Conversations with Ayckbourn.* Rev. ed. London: Faber and Faber, 1988. Unified into what seems to be an autobiography, Ayckbourn's comments range over the achievements of his entire career. Includes useful play synopses and chronology.

White, Sidney Howard. *Alan Ayckbourn.* Boston: Twayne, 1984. A chronological discussion of Ayckbourn's plays, tracing the dramatist's progress from farce to plays of character up to 1972. Includes a chronology, a bibliography, and an index.

Susan Rusinko,
updated by David Barratt

B

JOANNA BAILLIE

Born: Bothwell, Lanarkshire, Scotland; September
    11, 1762
Died: Hampstead, London, England; February 23,
    1851

PRINCIPAL DRAMA

Count Basil: A Tragedy, pb. 1798
De Monfort: A Tragedy, pb. 1798, pr. 1800
A Series of Plays, pb. 1798-1812 (3 volumes; also
    known as *Plays on the Passions*)
The Tryal: A Comedy, pb. 1798
The Election: A Comedy, in Five Acts, pb. 1802
Ethwald, parts 1 and 2, pb. 1802
The Second Marriage, pb. 1802
Constantine Paleologus, pb. 1804, pr. 1808
The Country Inn, pb. 1804
Miscellaneous Plays, pb. 1804
Rayner, pb. 1804
The Family Legend, pr., pb. 1810
Orra: A Tragedy, in Five Acts, pb. 1812
*The Beacon: A Serious Musical Drama, in Two
    Acts*, pb. 1812
The Dream: A Tragedy, in Prose, in Three Acts, pb.
    1812
The Siege: A Comedy, in Five Acts, pb. 1812
The Martyr: A Drama, in Three Acts, pb. 1826
The Bride: A Drama, in Three Acts, pb. 1828
The Alienated Manor: A Comedy, pb. 1836
Dramas, pb. 1836 (3 volumes)
Henriquez, pr., pb. 1836
Romiero: A Tragedy, pb. 1836
The Separation, pr., pb. 1836
The Stripling: A Tragedy . . . Written in Prose, pb.
    1836
The Phantom: A Musical Drama, pb. 1836
Enthusiasm: A Comedy, pb. 1836
Witchcraft: A Tragedy in Prose, pb. 1836

*The Homicide: A Tragedy in Prose, with
    Occasional Passages of Verse*, pb. 1836
The Match: A Comedy, pb. 1836

OTHER LITERARY FORMS

Though Joanna Baillie is known primarily for her
dramas, her first publication was *Poems*, which appeared as an anonymous work in 1790. Some of the
poems in this volume were reprinted in Baillie's *Fugitive Verses* (1840). During her lifetime, Baillie was
much admired for her lyrics, many of which appeared
in the collections of Scottish, Irish, and Welsh songs
brought out periodically by her friend, the music publisher and historian George Thomson. Her poetic narratives included those in the *Metrical Legends of Exalted Characters* (1821) and *Ahalya Baee: A Poem*
(1849). Baillie's prose works consisted primarily of
literary criticism, though she did publish a book on
religious dogma. Shortly before her death, Baillie
oversaw the publication of her collected works.

ACHIEVEMENTS

Although Joanna Baillie defied literary convention by publishing her plays before they were staged,
she did not intend them to be closet dramas. It was a
disappointment to her that only seven of them were
ever professionally produced. However, all major theaters in England, Scotland, Ireland, or the United
States staged a play by Baillie at one time or another;
in addition, almost all the important theater actors
portrayed one or more of her characters.

Baillie's popularity could also be measured by the
demands for new editions of her works. Critics were
not always as enthusiastic about her works as the
public seemed to be; however, Baillie always believed that her gender accounted for many of those
unfavorable reviews. Baillie counted among her ad-

mirers some of the most important writers of her day, including Sir Walter Scott, who became one of her closest friends. Baillie's achievements won her a signal honor: election as an honorary member of the Whittington Club, a prestigious London society dedicated to the advancement of culture.

BIOGRAPHY

Joanna Baillie was born to Dorothea Hunter Baillie and the Reverend James Baillie on September 11, 1762, in Bothwell, Lanarkshire, Scotland. Her twin sister died a few hours later. Joanna had an older sister, Agnes, and an older brother, Matthew. In 1772, Joanna and Agnes were sent to boarding school in Glasgow. Three years later, their father became professor of divinity at Glasgow University. After his brother-in-law's death in 1778, Dorothea's brother provided a home for the family at Long Calderwood, Scotland, and took Matthew into his medical school in London. After his uncle's death, having inherited both the school and his home, Matthew brought his mother and his sisters to London. After Dorothea died in 1806, the two sisters made their permanent home in Hampstead. Neither of them married.

Joanna Baillie had enjoyed reading plays and going to the theater in Glasgow. However, in London, her interest became a passion. Nine months after her arrival, Baillie began to write her first dramatic work. However, it was almost a decade and a half before her first volume of plays was published anonymously, arousing wild speculation as to its authorship. Not until 1800, when a third edition of that volume came out, did the public learn that the author was not an established man of letters or even a well-known woman writer but a modest Scottish spinster. Baillie was now famous.

After her third and final volume of *Plays on the Passions* appeared in 1812, Baillie turned increasingly to poetry as her primary creative outlet. In 1836, however, she did produce a three-volume set of books containing ten new plays, two of which were eventually staged, though each of them was withdrawn after opening night. This publication marked the end of Baillie's dramatic career.

In her final years, Baillie worried that her plays would be forgotten. Therefore she was delighted when a London bookseller asked her to oversee a complete edition of her works. The project was completed during the final year of her life. On February 22, 1851, she lapsed into a coma. She died the following day and was buried in the parish churchyard at Hampstead, where she lies next to her sister.

ANALYSIS

In the "Introductory Discourse" to the first volume of her *Plays on the Passions*, Joanna Baillie explained how "sympathetic curiosity" motivates people to observe others. When a writer uses this natural interest to arouse empathy for the characters he or she has created, the result can be a more compassionate society.

Baillie's belief that social reform comes from the heart, not from the head, and her fascination with psychological extremes place her clearly in the mainstream of English Romanticism, along with William Wordsworth, Lord Byron, and Percy Bysshe Shelley. However, her emphasis on the destructive power of the passions and her insistence on the need for restraint are obviously neoclassical.

Although Baillie was convinced that drama could play an important part in influencing human behavior, she felt that in her day the theater was failing in its mission. Both the tragedies and the comedies of her time were superficial, she asserted, not because they failed to recognize the primacy of emotion in human nature but because they focused on events rather than on process. Instead of showing a character already in the grips of passion, a dramatist should introduce his hero or heroine much earlier, so that the emotion could be traced from the first hint of disequilibrium to the point when it became an all-consuming force. Thus Baillie's dramas were meant to serve two purposes: Not only would they bring the audience to see how passions progressed, but they would also illustrate how plays should be written.

DE MONFORT

Unlike the other two plays in Baillie's first volume, a tragedy and a comedy both dealing with love, *De Monfort* is about a passion that is by definition evil. The tragic hero, De Monfort, is obsessed by his hatred for Rezenvelt. At first, it appears that Rezenvelt may indeed be as hypocritically wicked as De Monfort thinks. However, in the third act, Baillie traces De Monfort's hatred back to its beginning in boyhood rivalries, and from that time on, it becomes increasingly evident that Rezenvelt is not the villain De Monfort believes him to be but a decent man, worthy of the hand of De Monfort's sister Jane.

Though later critics insist that *De Monfort* is far from Baillie's best work, it has been performed on stage more than any of her other plays. When the great nineteenth century actors flung themselves into the resounding speeches Baillie had created for them, audiences insisted that she should rank with the playwright William Shakespeare. However, the play was essentially a psychological work, as the playwright had intended it to be. The dark forest in which De Monfort kills Rezenvelt symbolizes the darkness that has overtaken De Monfort's mind and soul. Baillie was true to her theory in having her hero die before trial, killed by nothing but his own poisonous hatred.

THE FAMILY LEGEND

The subject of *The Family Legend* is a feud between rival clans of Scottish Highlanders. The play was written as a result of Baillie's renewed interest in her Scottish heritage, which had been stimulated by her friendship with Sir Walter Scott. Baillie frequently consulted Scott during the composition of the play, and it was Scott who was responsible for its being accepted by the Edinburgh Theatre Royal, where it opened on January 29, 1810, with a prologue by Scott and an epilogue by another revered Scottish man of letters, Henry Mackenzie. In his letters, Scott describes the production as a triumph. For fourteen consecutive nights, the house was full and the applause deafening. The play later moved to England and to the United States. Of all Baillie's plays, only *De Monfort* was performed more often than *The Family Legend*.

Some critics argue that where stagecraft is concerned, *The Family Legend* is superior to *De Monfort* and, indeed, to the other plays in Baillie's first volume of *Plays on the Passions*. It may be that initially Baillie let her theories, not her imagination, dictate what her characters said and did; it may be simply that by the time she wrote *The Family Legend*, Baillie

was a more experienced playwright. In any case, the fact that *The Family Legend* was one of her most effective plays, as well as one of the most moving, must be attributed in part to Baillie's own feeling for Scotland and the Scottish past.

ORRA

The publication of Baillie's correspondence proved what feminist critics suspected: that one of the author's primary themes was the subjugation of women in a male-dominated society. Even though Baillie identified "fear" as the subject of *Orra*, the title character of that play is vulnerable only because she is in the power of men. After she refuses to marry his son, Orra's guardian turns her over to the villainous Rudigere, who is supposed to frighten her into compliance but in fact has his own designs on her. Although Orra is isolated, subjected to mental torture, and finally reduced to insanity, she never gives in. On the surface, the play is a warning against superstition. However, feminist critics point out that it is a celebration of a woman's strength and an indictment of the men who believe they have the right to break her.

By venturing into the field of dramatic theory, Baillie had defied the male establishment, which liked to believe women incapable of logical thought. Reexaminations of her plays in the late twentieth century have pointed to the spirit of rebellion in them and the implicit criticism of an unjust society, resulting in her being called by some scholars the most important British woman playwright of the eighteenth and nineteenth centuries.

OTHER MAJOR WORKS

POETRY: *Poems*, 1790 (published anonymously); *Metrical Legends of Exalted Characters*, 1821; *The Complete Poetical Works of Joanna Baillie*, 1832; *Fugitive Verses*, 1840; *Ahalya Baee: A Poem*, 1849; *The Selected Poems of Joanna Baillie, 1762-1851*, 1999.

NONFICTION: *A View of the General Tenour of the New Testament Regarding the Nature and Dignity of Jesus Christ*, 1831; "Epistles to the Literati: On the Character of Romiero," *Fraser's Magazine*, 14 (December, 1836): 748-749; *The Collected Letters of Joanna Baillie*, 1999.

EDITED TEXT: *A Collection of Poems, Chiefly Manuscript, and from Living Authors*, 1823.

MISCELLANEOUS: *The Dramatic and Poetical Works of Joanna Baillie*, 1851.

BIBLIOGRAPHY

Burroughs, Catherine B. *Closet Stages: Joanna Baillie and the Theater Theory of British Romantic Women Writers*. Philadelphia: University of Pennsylvania Press, 1997. Burroughs, an actor herself as well as a student of theatrical history, contends that because Baillie's purpose was to teach audiences compassion for others by expanding their imaginative powers, her plays and her theoretical writings are still relevant. Extensive analyses of the plays and of the prefaces. Includes portrait, voluminous notes, appendix, extensive bibliography, and index.

_____, ed. *Women in British Romantic Theatre: Drama, Performance, and Society, 1790-1840*. Cambridge, England: Cambridge University Press, 2000. Four of the essays in this volume deal with Baillie's works. In her introduction, the editor explains why the works of women writers such as Baillie deserve to be re-examined. Bibliography and index.

Carhart, Margaret S. *The Life and Work of Joanna Baillie*. Yale Studies in English 64. New Haven, Conn.: Yale University Press, 1923. The standard biography. Includes a chapter on stage history. Bibliography lists reviews by Baillie's contemporaries.

Carswell, Donald. *Scott and His Circle, with Four Portrait Studies*. Garden City, N.Y.: Doubleday, Doran, 1930. Carswell's section on Joanna Baillie continues to be a primary source of biographical information. Incisive and very readable. Illustrated. Bibliography, though dated, may be useful.

Donkin, Ellen. *Getting into the Act: Women Playwrights in London, 1776-1829*. London: Routledge, 1995. Points out how the double standard of the male-dominated literary establishment made it difficult for Baillie and others to gain the acceptance they merited. Illustrated, bibliography, index.

Slagle, Judith Bailey. "Joanna Baillie Through Her Letters." In *The Collected Letters of Joanna Baillie*, edited by Judith Bailey Slagle. 2 vols. Madison, N.J.: Fairleigh Dickinson University Press, 1999. An excellent biographical sketch of Baillie, including numerous excerpts from the letters, is followed by a chronology. This important scholarly work has an up-to-date bibliography and is thoroughly indexed.

Watkins, Daniel P. *A Materialist Critique of English Romantic Drama*. Gainesville: University Press of Florida, 1993. Insists that Baillie should be ranked as a major Romantic writer because of her insights into the "radical transformation" taking place in her society. A detailed analysis of *De Monfort* supports this view. Bibliography and index.

Rosemary M. Canfield Reisman

JON ROBIN BAITZ

Born: Los Angeles, California; November 4, 1961

PRINCIPAL DRAMA
Mizlansky/Silinsky, pr. 1985, revised as *Mizlansky/Zilinsky: Or, "Schmucks,"* pr. 1997
The Film Society, pb. 1987 (as a play in process), pr. 1988, pb. 1989
Dutch Landscape, pr. 1989

The Substance of Fire, pr., pb. 1991
Three Hotels, pr. 1991 (teleplay), pr., pb. 1993 (staged)
The End of the Day, pr., pb. 1992
A Fair Country, pb. 1996, pr. 1997
Hedda Gabler, pr., pb. 2000 (adaptation of Henrik Ibsen's play)
Ten Unknowns, pr. 2001

OTHER LITERARY FORMS

Jon Robin Baitz is known primarily for his plays.

ACHIEVEMENTS

Jon Robin Baitz is a dramatist who, at the age of thirty, captured national attention with only two successfully produced plays in New York. Two earlier plays, one a failure and the other a moderate success, along with a play for public television, constitute the work for which fellow playwrights such as John Guare and critics such as Robert Brustein have lauded him, the latter placing Baitz in the company of Sam Shepard and David Mamet. Baitz's not-so-fictional universe is that of unprincipled corporate wealth and private greed, monsters whose tentacles have reached out and strangled any moral sensibility in the last decades of the twentieth century. If Mamet and Shepard are artists of the inarticulate, Baitz cultivates the articulate, easily moving in a given play among a range of styles—realism, expressionism, Surrealism, naturalism. His creation of a modern Dantean myth includes references to contemporary figures such as Richard M. Nixon, Henry A. Kissinger, Margaret Thatcher, even George Bush. International mergers, corporate and private greed, Swiss bank accounts, AIDS (acquired immune deficiency syndrome), poverty, and racial bigotry are among the moral diseases that poison Baitz's stage universe. What little redemption Baitz finds in the world is, as with E. M. Forster, that of personal connection. He finds ideology becoming increasingly laughable and irrelevant. In style or theme, his plays have been likened to those of Caryl Churchill, Joe Orton, Simon Gray, and Tom Stoppard.

BIOGRAPHY

The international flavor of Jon Robin Baitz's plays, which span locales such as Southern California, South Africa, London, New York, Morocco, the Virgin Islands, and Mexico, grows out of Baitz's family life. Born in Los Angeles to a father who was an executive with the international division of Carnation Milk Company and a mother who was "a larger-than-life-Auntie Mame type," Baitz, from the age of seven to seventeen, lived in Brazil, England, and South Af-

rica. When he returned to Los Angeles, he finished high school but decided against college because being a student seemed unreal and attending college, evasive. When his parents moved to Holland, he continued his travels, using their home as a base, and worked at various odd jobs: as a short-order cook, a tractor driver on a kibbutz, and a painter of an art gallery at The Hague.

He found himself a professional eavesdropper and, as a result of his intense preoccupation with listening to other people, developed into an "elevated yenta." While deciding to be "out of the loop" and thinking of starting a small publishing company or buying a vineyard, he worked temporarily for a film producer as a "sort of" phone answerer. Out of this experience, he wrote a theater piece, *Mizlansky/ Zilinsky*, a one-act play about two seedy Hollywood hustlers, and suddenly found himself to be a playwright. Fourteen years later he turned the play into a full-length work.

Leaving the United States and then coming back to his country was a trigger to his playwriting, as though the physical distance gave "some kind of clarity to the rage I was feeling at a benumbed, becalmed, morally bankrupt country." Transferred to individuals, this moral bankruptcy or corruption is one against which Baitz's characters struggle, mostly with few or no positive results. These characters are dramatized in the South African teachers of *The Film Society*, the father and children in *The Substance of Fire*, the psychiatrist-turned-oncologist in *The End of the Day*, the American executive whose family and career destroy each other in *Three Hotels*, the diplomat and his dysfunctional family in *A Fair Country*, and the failed artist, his assistant, and the greedy art dealer in *Ten Unknowns*. Baitz admits that his global upbringing tends to keep him writing about exile.

Baitz enjoys membership in the Naked Angels, which he regards as a family of gifted actors and writers. After the devastating experience of the failure of *Dutch Landscape* (a play about Americans living abroad) at the Mark Taper Forum in Los Angeles, he credited the Naked Angels with saving his life. In fact, he wrote the first part of *The Substance of Fire* shortly after his disappointment with *Dutch Land-scape*. In 1993, *Three Hotels*, a trio of confessional monologues, was considered one of the ten best theater productions of the year, and the 1997 production of *A Fair Country* reasserted Batiz as a moralist of international relations.

Baitz became a playwright-in-residence with the New York Stage and Film Company (1986-1989) and settled in a TriBeCa loft in the SoHo district of New York. He has received a Revson Fellowship from Playwrights Horizons (1987), a Playwright USA Award (1987), the New York Newsday Oppenheimer Award (1987), a National Endowment for the Arts and Letters award (1992), a Humanitas Prize (1990) for his television play *Three Hotels*, a Rockefeller Fellowship, and a grant from the Fund for New American Playwrights for the production of *Dutch Landscape* at the Mark Taper Forum.

Jon Robin Baitz at the Eisenhower Theatre in Washington, D.C., in 1993.
(AP/Wide World Photos)

ANALYSIS

Very emphatically a social critic, Jon Robin Baitz, however, stops short of the extremity to which Mamet carries his concern with moral corruption. In Mamet's world, corruption is a given, and his characters—producers in *Speed-the-Plow* (pr., pb. 1988) and salesmen in *Glengarry Glen Ross* (pr. 1983, pb. 1984)—accept that milieu as one in which they must live. Mamet, a stylistic minimalist and the American counterpart of the English Harold Pinter, is existentially absurdist in his view of life. Baitz, on the other hand, is highly articulate, melodramatic, sometimes flamboyant in his style, and belongs to the tradition of social criticism of dramatists such as Henrik Ibsen and Arthur Miller. His characters attempt to change the total corruption of their situations but, overpowered, only sink more deeply into the system or are defeated by it. That system may be the South African English school in *The Film Society*, the publishing business in *The Substance of Fire*, or the international megacorporate world of *The End of the Day*. Social and private moralities clash, as expressed during the reunion in *The End of the Day* of two medical-school friends (now expatriate Britons living in Southern California) in their erratic recital of Matthew Arnold's poem "Dover Beach," ending with the lines: "And here we are as on a dark'ning plain/ Swept with confused armies of struggle and flight/ Where ignorant armies clash by night." One of the Britons, recently returned to California from London, describes London as genuinely sad, "so gussied up. Dolled up. Tarted up. Painted faces. But underneath," London, he continues, is like a certain type in Beverly Hills, old, rich, with stretched skin and impossibly blond hair.

Baitz's plays are searing portraits of contemporary civilization in decay. Three professions—education, publishing, and medicine—provide the context for Baitz's major plays: *The Film Society*, *The Substance of Fire*, and *The End of the Day*, respectively. The business world, diplomacy, and the art establishment are critically viewed in plays such as *Three Hotels*, *A Fair Country*, and *Ten Unknowns*.

THE FILM SOCIETY

With the production of *The Film Society* at the Second Stage on Manhattan's Upper West Side, Baitz was declared with near-critical unanimity as the new talent to watch. In the play, two teachers, Jonathan and Terry, find themselves beset on all sides by the run-down conditions in a South African English school named Blenheim, very much like the one that Baitz had attended. The decaying school, with its faded Edwardian old-boy traditions of fingernail inspections, cricket, and the discipline of caning, is obviously still a training ground for the children of those dedicated to preserving the power structure of the Afrikaners of South Africa. Jonathan dreams of changes in the financially strapped school, but in the end he opts for the comforts of the status quo. Terry, on the other hand, refusing to compromise either with his affluent family or with the school administration, is fired. His wife, Nan, also a dedicated teacher in the school, after her husband's departure gives "some sort of madwoman speech in social bloody history class," and as a result, she, too, is fired. Her firing seems doubly monstrous because it is the decision of Jonathan, who, as a result of his mother's generous gift to the school, has been appointed assistant headmaster.

All three teachers are from affluent colonial families whose political ideologies are as decayed as the school's buildings. All three are sensitive, idealistic, and intelligent, in strong contrast to the older members of the staff. Jonathan, Terry, and Nan represent different degrees of change. Terry, although doubting even his radicalism, is still the radical. Nan can work within the system but on her own terms, and Jonathan eventually capitulates to the terms of the system. Although the story is fairly simple, the relationships among the three teachers are drawn in painfully complex terms as the play works its way to the departures of Terry and Nan and to Jonathan's acceptance of his mother's verdict on his life as passivity, comfort, and loneliness. One sees him destined for the kind of human isolation found in the many schoolteachers in Simon Gray's plays.

The motif of darkness in *The Film Society* is introduced early in the allusion to the showing, at the weekly meeting of the school's Film Society, of Orson Welles's film *Touch of Evil* (1958), which was sent to the school as a result of confusion with the film that had been ordered, *That Touch of Mink* (1962). Shortly thereafter, Terry, already regarded as a leftist, angers the hierarchy with his bringing an African speaker to the school, resulting in the speaker's arrest and Terry's freeing him from prison. His wife, who at first tried to moderate Terry's radicalism, reaches her own breaking point when she lectures to her social history class on the necessity of retaining one's humanness.

The moral darkness, hotly debated in the play, is as visual as it is intellectual, as image after image of decay is evoked. According to Jonathan, herds of bats living in the mango trees attack the schoolboys; termites the size of Land Rovers scurry about the school; the swimming pool looks like a science experiment; the floor of the junior toilets is flooded, with bits of offal floating toward the showers—like the seventh circle of hell. The burning of local sugarcane fields by natives is counterpointed by the race hatred in statements about the Pakistanis and Arabs taking over London or stories of African Americans from Harlem coming en masse to South Africa. The burning of the dead by the Hindus, the funeral of an administrator, and talk of past funerals add to the dark ambience of the play.

In its straightforward movement, the action of *The Film Society* progresses rapidly in short scenes, and the characters speak with a literacy and articulateness rarely found on the contemporary American stage. Its weakness is the lack of progression necessary to make the characters convincing. They give away their positions too early and too strongly, leaving little to be proved. The two women, Jonathan's mother and Terry's wife, who are the supports, respectively, to son and husband, are a bit too obviously only that—supports—as they spell out for the audience the positions of the two men.

THE SUBSTANCE OF FIRE

Baitz's second play produced in New York, *The Substance of Fire*, continues his attacks on contemporary life, this time pitting a financially troubled publisher, Isaac Geldhart, against two sons and a daughter, who are summoned by him to discuss the fate of the family publishing firm. The daughter, Sarah, is an actress in children's television; the older son, Martin, a teacher of landscape architecture at Vassar College; and the younger son, Aaron, a partner in the family publishing business. At stake is a decision regarding the publishing of a money-losing six-volume work on Nazi medical experiments (Isaac's choice) as opposed to a money-making novel (Aaron's choice). Isaac's children own shares in the firm, Martin and eventually Sarah giving their votes to Aaron. In the second of the play's two acts, Isaac is alone, clinically depressed, in his now shabby and increasingly bare, cold apartment, where he is visited by a social worker and Martin.

As in *The Film Society*, the story and the issues of *The Substance of Fire* are clearly defined. The father is vigorously independent, intellectual, feisty, and stubborn in holding on to his past (his survival of the Holocaust). His children, with whom he enjoys little or no intimacy, stand up to his searingly caustic humor and anger. All are sympathetically portrayed and equally effective in articulating their positions, leaving in question the matter of who is right or wrong, moral or immoral. A traditionally conditioned audience tends to side with the main character, whose role in the play is of heroic dimensions. He is the kind of autocratic publishing lion for which New York is famous. His values, though financially ruinous in an age in which Japanese purchases threaten everything for which he stands, evoke the nostalgia of an irretrievable past.

The second act of *The Substance of Fire* takes place three and a half years later and brings into play a new character. A social worker, Marge Hackett, gives a new dimension to Isaac's future and at the same time expands Baitz's social criticism in the play. As she verbally spars with Isaac in much the same manner of the family gathering in act 1, her self-revelations of the past include a husband whose successful political career came crashing down as the result of a financial scandal. Her self-reinvention, after her husband's downfall, includes a college educa-

tion to prepare for her current career. She is like Isaac, who, having lost one family to the Nazis and another to New Age values, embarks on a new life, as the play ends with the possibility of future dinners with Marge and with Isaac's conciliatory walk with Martin in snowy Gramercy Park.

The closeness between Baitz's subject matter and his own experience is made clear in this play. He admits that Isaac is drawn from friends, whom he loves and thus refuses to name. He also wrote the part of Isaac for Ron Rifkin, whom he met at Williamstown, where he was impressed by the actor's performance in Arthur Miller's *The American Clock* (pr. 1980, pb. 1982).

As in his earlier play, objects take on symbolic significance beyond their realistic function. Especially striking among Isaac's collection of books and other ephemera is an old postcard with a watercolor scene painted by the youthful Adolf Hitler when he had considered becoming an artist. Isaac's emotional tie to the card is strong, yet rather than selling it, as he had done with other valuable memorabilia, he burns it, an action suggesting his stubborn refusal to capitulate and, as well, the possibility of yet another reinvention of his life.

THE END OF THE DAY

Baitz's next play, *The End of the Day*, takes gigantic stylistic leaps from the previous two plays. Retaining the brisk movement of scenes that characterizes his earlier work, Baitz indulges in an orgy of stylistic shifts, sliding easily in and out of scenes that are at one moment realistic, then, in turn, expressionistic, naturalistic, and Surrealistic. Rapidly changing locales accompany the style changes—from well-heeled Malibu Canyon to a run-down health clinic, to a vulgarly opulent London flat, and back to a Southern California art museum into which megacorporations have poured their money.

Played in its first performance with larger-than-life zest by the Welsh actor Roger Rees, the leading character, Graydon Massey, gives explicit form to Baitz's idea of reinvention in both word and deed. Now an American citizen with an American wife and a corruptly wealthy American father-in-law intent on political office, Massey opens the play with an erratic rehearsal of the Pledge of Allegiance. He feverishly interrupts his rehearsal with a long stream-of-consciousness flow of fragmented thoughts about the American Dream. The margarita-induced monologue concludes with his reason for emigrating: "The point is, in America, you can reinvent yourself. . . . In America—you can go back for seconds." In one dazzlingly fast scene, Baitz establishes the dream that has motivated emigration to the United States for centuries. From this point on, it is all morally down-hill for Massey.

In a dreamlike, expressionistic scene change, reminiscent of August Strindberg's technique in *Ett drömspel* (pb. 1902, pr. 1907; *A Dream Play*, 1907), the same set (Malibu) becomes the San Cristobal Clinic in San Pedro, described by Baitz as a "sort of vast Dantesque hell of patients just outside moaning." At this point, naturalism takes over, as Massey, a psychiatrist retrained as an oncologist, confronts an intractably impoverished clinical system and his first AIDS patient.

Complications with his Mafia-like father-in-law, the result of Massey's intention to divorce his wife, cause Massey to return to his mother, Jocelyn Massey, who lives with her brother-in-law in her vulgarly fashionable London home. To satisfy the demands of his wife and father-in-law for having funded him in his costly reeducation, Massey must wring from his mother a huge sum of money and a grotesque George Stubbs painting of a cat skeleton. This he accomplishes, but at the expense of being drawn into a huge, international, megacorporation, at the head of which is his mother. Massey's corrupted "end of the day" involves a series of oncology centers and an art museum replete with Stubbs paintings—all because of his mother's corporate generosity. Thrown into this maze of actions is an old medical-school friend, Marton, involved in a film business that has become a part of Jocelyn's empire. This second act surrealistically intensifies Massey's American Dream into the nightmare that it has become.

At one point, as Massey and Marton exchange views about politics and Massey speaks of having to vote for American "bastards," Marton reminds him of what he left behind, which was not much better:

Margaret Thatcher, "a Stalin in a wig, a cunt. A Medusa; anyone looked at her—straight to stone." The following prime minister, John Major, Marton refers to as "a concierge, a head-waiter at a provincial grill." The Iran-Contra corruption, Britons in Hollywood, the Docklands projects in London, a Kennedy-like "Ich bein un Malibuan," and, searingly, Richard M. Nixon's giving the lie to F. Scott Fitzgerald's assertion that there are no second acts in American life—all these views and many more are references to a modern Dantean world with its vividly depicted circles of sinners. William Shakespeare blends parodically with Dante in a number of references to Hamlet—particularly in a dream in which Massey's dead father appears to him and in Jocelyn's cohabitation with Massey's uncle. Baitz has said that this is "very much a play about a bad man trying to be good and ultimately becoming himself—a bad man."

THREE HOTELS

In *Three Hotels*, which appeared in an earlier version on public television two years before its stage production, Baitz carries forward the same themes and style of *The Film Society*. *Three Hotels* is about Kenneth Hoyle, an international business executive with a company that sells unhealthy baby formula to Third World countries. Kenneth, ironically, feels responsible for the death of African children, and his rise to corporate power has alienated him from his wife, Barbara, creating problems in their marriage. What is worse is that the couple's teen-age son was killed in Brazil for a beautiful watch he was wearing, which was given to him by his parents.

Consisting entirely of monologues (two by Kenneth, one by Barbara) and prohibiting any dialogue between the two characters, *Three Hotels*, of all Baitz's work, is closest to his family experience. From seven to seventeen, he observed the kind of life led by his fictional couple. International in the reaches of its corporate corruption, the play moves from Tangier, Morocco, to St. Thomas in the Virgin Islands, and then to Oaxaca, Mexico. The "end-of-the-day" fortunes of the couple parallel those of Terry and Nan in *The Film Society*.

In his mockery of an age of money, Baitz acknowledges his idols, the nineteenth century Anthony Trollope and William Makepeace Thackeray, and his twentieth century contemporaries, Martin Amis and Julian Barnes. He wants to bring their richness to his depiction of contemporary society. In his mind, he has mapped out three plays that he intends to be the American equivalent of David Hare's trilogy of dramas about English institutions: *Secret Rapture* (pr., pb. 1988, government), *Racing Demon* (pr., pb. 1990, religion), and *Murmuring Judges* (pr. 1991, justice system).

MIZLANSKY/ZILINSKY

Autobiographical influence is also evident in three later plays. Gleaned from his Los Angeles experience, the rewritten *Mizlansky/Zilinsky: Or, "Schmucks"* is about the moral comprises made to grab a buck. Two low-grade movie producers spend more time selling tax shelters, wooing investors, and avoiding litigants than making films. Mizlansky is brought down by the perfidy of his former partner in low-brow films when a tax shelter scheme of making biblical recordings for children (with Flip Wilson narrating the Last Supper) collapses, and he confronts Zilinsky with the debris of their lives. Faulted for lacking a strong narrative, the revamped comedy's 1998 New York production earned praise for Nathan Lane's portrayal of Mizlansky.

A FAIR COUNTRY

A Fair Country depicts the traumas of a minor-level diplomat stationed in Durban, South Africa, and the Faustian bargain he makes to get his family out of South Africa by releasing to his boss the names of black activists, which are then passed on to the U.S. Central Intelligence Agency and South African police. The black radicals are subsequently doomed. That betrayal quickens the breakdown of his wife and earns the reproach of his sons. Critical comments mixed praise for the writer's gifts for characterization and dialogue as well as the production's strength with criticism of flaws in story and structure. Critic Michael Feingold views this work as "the fourth of Baitz's plays to deal with a powerful, manipulative and ultimately destructive father figure countered by a truth-speaking but emotionally unbal-

anced (hence also ultimately destructive) mother." He notes that in *The Substance of Fire*, *Three Hotels*, and *The End of the Day*, the matrix is similar: father, mother, and often two sons, the younger of whom is gay and less loved, while the older often dies young in a foreign country. This recurring setup seems autobiographical.

TEN UNKNOWNS

In *Ten Unknowns*, Baitz continues his focus on corruption and moral decay by taking on the art world. The play examines an obscure, aging American figurative painter who years ago fled to Mexico when abstract expressionism hit the art world. There he drinks and paints little. However, his ambitious dealer, hoping to launch a lucrative rediscovery campaign, arranges a fifty-year retrospective at a New York gallery. To get new work out of the old painter, the dealer dispatches his former lover, a recovering addict and aspiring painter, to work as the artist's assistant. When a number of striking new paintings appear, the dealer sells them sight unseen and comes to collect them. The end of the first act reveals that the old artist is too rusty and scared to paint and that the assistant is responsible for the new works. In the second act, the two artists, after a powerful confrontation, destroy the new work. Although the first act and Donald Sutherland's performance as the older artist won commendation, critical comments pointed to shortcomings in the second act of unnecessary exposition, the characters turning into stereotypes, and unenlightened pronouncements about abstract art.

OTHER MAJOR WORK

SCREENPLAY: *The Substance of Fire*, 1996 (adaptation of his play).

BIBLIOGRAPHY

Baitz, Jon Robin. "The Substance of Robin Baitz." Interview by Porter Anderson. *Theater Week* (April 27-May 3, 1992): 20-24. This interview with Baitz is an important source of biographical information, and it shows Baitz's attitudes (resulting from his personal experiences) toward society.

Feingold, Michael. "Foreign Entanglements." *The Village Voice* 10 (March 5, 1996): 69. Includes a review of *A Fair Country*. Makes the point that Baitz's plays reveal a pattern in which a strong father figure invariably is the linchpin who either is a manipulative demon who stops at nothing to keep his family together or a hollow man who has lost all sense of what he loves and whose headlong tactics and nonstop drive destroy his family and himself. Feingold claims that the pattern is probably self-reflexive of the author who, clearly had a problem with his father.

Goodale, Gloria. "Interview/Jon Robin Baitz."*Christian Science Monitor* 92 (April 21, 2000): 20. Interview with Baitz during the premiere of the full-length version in of *Mizlansky/Zilinsky* in Los Angeles. Baitz remembers the play as an autobiographical valentine to his own days as a gofer to two seedy producers during the 1970's. He observes that playwriting in 1996 is not a vivid part of the culture and that the most difficult part of being a playwright is that you are doing work that nobody knows about. He foresees that the next generation of audiences will be smaller but more hard core, a fact of theater life that both inspires and encourages him.

Grimes, William. "The Playwright as Modern Day Moralist." *The New York Times*, May 7, 1992, pp. C1, 6. In this overview of three Baitz plays, Grimes links them with biographical information, including the author's homosexuality, not yet dealt with in a major way in his plays.

Lahr, John. "Prisoners of Envy." *New Yorker* 77 (March 19, 2001): 148. Includes a review of *Ten Unknowns*. Lahr details the story and praises much of Baitz's storytelling, as well as the production's setting, stage direction by Daniel Sullivan, and performances by Donald Sutherland and others. However, he expresses reservations about the characters' motivational lapses and melodramatic incidents in the second act.

Rasminsky, Sonya. "A Conversation with Jon Robin Baitz." *American Theatre* 10 (March, 1993): 66. Rasminsky, a Theatre Communications Group staff member, interviews Baitz, who discusses his motivation for writing plays, the effect of his global upbringing on his writing, his reaction to growing up in South Africa during apartheid, and other topics.

Rich, Frank. "Baitz's Mockery of an Age of Money." Review of *The End of the Day* by Jon Robin Baitz. *The New York Times*, April 8, 1992, pp. C17, 21. Calling attention to Baitz's possible youthful excess, Rich reviews *The End of the Day*, paying special attention to the author's flamboyant style and the unprecedented integrity with which Roger Rees plays a man with a complete lack of integrity.

_____. "Resisting the Vortex by Living a Life of Books and Anger." Review of *The Substance of Fire* by Jon Robin Baitz. *The New York Times*, March 18, 1991, p. C11. Rich analyzes the major themes of *The Substance of Fire* and sees Isaac as a harbinger of a major playwriting career.

_____. "School as a Symbol of a Society in Decline." Review of *The Film Society* by Jon Robin Baitz. *The New York Times*, July 22, 1988, p. C3. Rich's review of *The Film Society* deals with the ambiguities of Baitz's style and themes, focusing on his wit and some weaknesses as well.

Rothstein, Mervyn. "A Play Born from the Friendship Between an Author and an Actor." *The New York Times*, March 28, 1991, p. C11. Rothstein interviews both Baitz and Ron Rifkin, with emphasis on the career of Rifkin, for whom Baitz wrote the role of Isaac in *The Substance of Fire*.

Susan Rusinko,
updated by Christian H. Moe

JAMES BALDWIN

Born: New York, New York; August 2, 1924
Died: St. Paul de Vence, France; November 30, 1987

PRINCIPAL DRAMA

The Amen Corner, pr. 1954, pb. 1968
Blues for Mister Charlie, pr., pb. 1964
A Deed from the King of Spain, pr. 1974

OTHER LITERARY FORMS

Best known for his novels and essays, James Baldwin contributed to every contemporary genre except poetry. Baldwin established his literary reputation with *Go Tell It on the Mountain* (1953), a novel that anticipates the thematic concerns of *The Amen Corner*. Subsequent novels, including *Another Country* (1962), *If Beale Street Could Talk* (1974), and *Just Above My Head* (1979), along with the brilliant story "Sonny's Blues" (1957), confirmed Baldwin's stature as a leading figure in postwar American fiction. Several of Baldwin's early essays, collected in *Notes of a Native Son* (1955) and *Nobody Knows My Name: More Notes of a Native Son* (1961), are today recognized as classics. His essays on Richard Wright, "Everybody's Protest Novel" (1949) and "Many Thousands Gone" (1951), occupy a central position in the development, during the 1950's, of "universalist" African American thought. *The Fire Next Time* (1963), perhaps Baldwin's most important work of nonfiction, is an extended meditation on the relationship of race, religion, and the individual experience. *No Name in the Street* (1971), emphasizing the failure of the United States to heed the warning of *The Fire Next Time*, asserts the more militant political stance articulated in *Blues for Mister Charlie*. Less formal and intricate, though in some cases more explicit, statements of Baldwin's positions can be found in *A Rap on Race* (1971), an extended discussion with Margaret Mead, and *A Dialogue* (1975; with Nikki Giovanni). Of special interest in relation to Baldwin's drama are the unfilmed scenario *One Day, When I Was Lost: A Scenario Based on "The Autobiography of Malcolm X"* (1972) and *The Devil Finds Work* (1976), which focuses on Baldwin's personal and aesthetic frustrations with the American film industry.

ACHIEVEMENTS

James Baldwin's high-profile career, in both the literary and the political spheres, earned for him widespread recognition and a number of awards. Early in his career, he was granted the Eugene F. Saxton Memorial Trust fellowship in 1945, followed by the Rosenwald Fellowship in 1948. In 1956 he was awarded a Partisan Review Fellowship, a National Institute of Arts and Letter grant for literature, and a National Institute of Arts and Letters Award, followed three years later by a Ford Foundation grant. His magazine articles earned him a George Polk Memorial Award in 1963 and in 1964 *Blues for Mister Charlie* earned a Foreign Drama Critics Award and *The Fire Next Time* was given a National Association of Independent Schools Award. *Just Above my Head* was nominated in 1980 for the American Book Award. France honored him in 1986 by naming him Commander of the Legion of Honor. He served as a member of several organizations throughout his lifetime, including the American Academy and Institute of Arts and Letters, the Authors' League, International PEN, Dramatists Guild, Actors Studio, and the Congress of Racial Equality.

BIOGRAPHY

James Baldwin once dismissed his childhood as "the usual bleak fantasy." Nevertheless, the major concerns of his writing consistently reflect the social context of his family life in Harlem during the Depression. The dominant figure of Baldwin's childhood was his stepfather, David Baldwin, who worked as a manual laborer and preached in a storefront church. Clearly the model for Gabriel Grimes in *Go Tell It on the Mountain*, David Baldwin had moved from New Orleans to New York City, where he married James's mother, Emma Berdis. The oldest of what was to become a group of nine children in the household, James assumed much of the responsibility for the care of his half brothers and sisters. Insulated somewhat from the brutality of Harlem street life by his domestic duties, Baldwin sought refuge in the church. Following a conversion experience in 1938, Baldwin preached as a youth minister for several years. At the same time, he began to read, immersing himself in nineteenth century works such as Harriet Beecher Stowe's *Uncle Tom's Cabin* (1852) and the novels of Charles Dickens. Both at his Harlem junior high school, where the African American poet Countée Cullen was one of his teachers, and at his predominantly white Bronx high school, Baldwin contributed to student literary publications. The combination of family tension, economic hardship, and religious vocation provides the focus of much of Baldwin's greatest writing, most notably *Go Tell It on the Mountain*, *The Fire Next Time*, and *Just Above My Head*.

If Baldwin's experience during the 1930's provided his material, his life from 1942 to 1948 shaped

James Baldwin (Hulton Archive by Getty Images)

his characteristic approach to that material. After he was graduated from high school in 1942, Baldwin worked for a year as a manual laborer in New Jersey, an experience that increased both his understanding of his stepfather and his insight into America's economic and racial systems. Moving to Greenwich Village in 1944, Baldwin worked during the day and wrote at night for the next five years; his first national reviews and essays appeared in 1946. The major event of the Village years, however, was Baldwin's meeting with Richard Wright in the winter of 1944-1945. Wright's interest helped Baldwin acquire a Eugene F. Saxton Memorial Trust Fellowship and then a Rosenwald Fellowship, enabling him to move to Paris in 1948.

After his arrival in France, Baldwin experienced more of the poverty that had shaped his childhood. Simultaneously, he developed a larger perspective on the psychocultural context conditioning his experience, feeling at once a greater sense of freedom and a larger sense of the global structure of racism, particularly as reflected in the French treatment of North Africans. In addition, he formed many of the personal and literary friendships that contributed to his later public prominence. Baldwin's well-publicized literary feud with Wright, who viewed the younger writer's criticism of *Native Son* (1940) as a form of personal betrayal, helped establish Baldwin as a major presence in African American letters. Although Baldwin's first novel, *Go Tell It on the Mountain*, was well received critically, it was not so financially successful that he could devote his full time to creative writing. Returning to the United States briefly in 1954-1955, he saw the Owen Dodson production at Howard University of *The Amen Corner*. For several years, he continued to travel widely, frequently on journalistic assignments, while writing the novel *Giovanni's Room* (1956), which is set in France and involves no black characters.

Returning to the United States as a journalist covering the Civil Rights movement, Baldwin made his first trip to the American South in 1957. The essays and reports describing that physical and psychological journey propelled Baldwin to the position of public prominence that he maintained for more than a decade. During the height of the movement, Baldwin lectured widely and was present at major events such as the 1963 March on Washington and the voter registration drive in Selma, Alabama. In addition, he met with most of the major African American activists of the period, including Martin Luther King, Jr., Elijah Muhammad, James Meredith, and Medgar Evers. Attorney General Robert Kennedy requested that Baldwin bring together the most influential voices in the black community; even though the resulting meeting accomplished little, the request testifies to Baldwin's image as a focal point of African American opinion. In addition to this political activity, Baldwin formed personal and literary relationships—frequently tempestuous ones—with numerous white writers, including William Styron and Norman Mailer. A surge in literary popularity, reflected in the presence of *Another Country* and *The Fire Next Time* on the bestseller lists throughout most of 1962 and 1963, accompanied Baldwin's political success and freed him from financial insecurity for the first time. His experiences with the Civil Rights movement shaped both the narrative material and the political perspective of *Blues for Mister Charlie.*

Partly because of Baldwin's involvement with prominent whites and partly because of the sympathy for homosexuals evinced in his writing, several black militants, most notably Eldridge Cleaver, attacked Baldwin's position as "black spokesperson" beginning in the late 1960's. As a result, nationalist figures such as Amiri Baraka and Bobby Seale gradually eclipsed Baldwin in the literary and political spotlight. Nevertheless, Baldwin, himself sympathetic to many of the militant positions, would continue his involvement with public issues, such as the fate of the Wilmington, North Carolina, prisoners—an issue that he addressed in an open letter to Jimmy Carter shortly after Carter's election to the U.S. presidency in 1976. In the early 1980's, Baldwin returned to the South to assess the changes of the last three decades and to examine the meaning of events such as the Atlanta child murders.

Shuttling back and forth between France, where he felt accepted, and the United States, where he felt needed, Baldwin spent the last years of his life between two worlds. The French government made him a Commander of the Legion of Honor in 1986. At the same time, however, the Federal Bureau of Investigation (FBI) generated a 609-page investigative file on his political activities.

Although Baldwin was largely eclipsed in his role as racial spokesperson in the 1970's and 1980's, the publication of his collected essays in 1985 and his death in 1987 brought him back into the headlines and led to a reassessment of his life and work. Some critics demurred that Baldwin's celebrity derived principally from his status as a vocal African American writer rather than from great literary talent, but most observers, stressing Baldwin's passion and honesty, were more generous in their judgments. At Baldwin's funeral, Amiri Baraka delivered a eulogy that praised the late writer for making African Americans feel "that we could defend ourselves or define ourselves, that we were in the world not merely as animate slaves, but as terrifyingly sensitive measurers of what is good or evil, beautiful or ugly. This is the power of his spirit."

ANALYSIS

James Baldwin's image as an African American racial spokesperson during the 1950's and 1960's guarantees his place in American cultural history. His fiction and essays, both aesthetically and as charts of the movement from universalism to militancy in African American thought, have earned for him serious and lasting attention. Nevertheless, Baldwin's significance as a dramatist remains problematic. In large part because of Baldwin's high public visibility, *Blues for Mister Charlie* was greeted as a major cultural event when it opened on Broadway at the ANTA Theater on April 23, 1964. Baldwin's most direct expression of political anger to that time, the play echoed the warning to white America sounded in *The Fire Next Time,* the essay that had catapulted Baldwin to prominence in the mass media. Despite its immediate impact, however, *Blues for Mister Charlie* failed to win lasting support. Numerous African American critics, particularly those associated with the community theater movement of the late 1960's, dismissed the play as an attempt to attract a mainstream white audience. Mainstream critics, drawing attention to the contradiction between Baldwin's political theme and his attack on protest writing in "Everybody's Protest Novel," dismissed the play as strident propaganda. Critics of diverse perspectives united in dismissing the play as theatrically static. The play's closing, following a four-month run, underscored its failure to realize the early hopes for a new era in African American theater on Broadway.

Ironically, Baldwin's reputation as a dramatist rests primarily on *The Amen Corner*, a relatively obscure play written in the early 1950's, produced under the direction of Owen Dodson at Howard University in 1954, and brought to Broadway for a twelve-week run only in April, 1965, as an attempt to capitalize on the interest generated by *Blues for Mister Charlie*. Examining the tension between religious and secular experience, *The Amen Corner* maintains some interest as an anticipation of the thematic and structural use of music in African American plays during the Black Arts movement. Although Baldwin's drama fails to live up to the standards set by his prose, the heated public discussion surrounding *Blues for Mister Charlie* attests its historical importance as one element in the political and aesthetic transition from the nonviolent universalism of African American thought in the 1950's to the militant nationalism of the 1960's.

Baldwin's plays examine the self-defeating attempts of characters to protect themselves against suffering by categorizing experience in terms of simplistic dichotomies. Like *Go Tell It on the Mountain*, *The Amen Corner* concentrates on the failure of the dichotomy between "Temple" and "Street" to articulate the experience of the congregation of a Harlem storefront church. Like *The Fire Next Time* and *Another Country*, *Blues for Mister Charlie* emphasizes the black-white dichotomy shaping the murderous racial conflict that devastates both blacks and whites psychologically. Where Baldwin's fiction ultimately suggests some means of transcending these tensions, however, his plays frequently remain enmeshed in dramatic structures that inadvertently perpetuate the dichotomies they ostensibly challenge. Paradoxically, Baldwin's problems as a playwright derive from his

strengths as a novelist. His use of the tradition of African American folk preaching as the base for a narrative voice capable of taking on a powerful presence of its own frequently results in static didacticism when linked to a character onstage. Similarly, the emphasis on the importance of silence in his novels highlights the tendency of his plays to make explicit aspects of awareness that his characters would be highly unlikely to articulate even to themselves. As a result, conceptually powerful passages in which characters confront the tension between their ideals and experiences tend to freeze the rhythm onstage. As African American playwright Carlton Molette observed in a comment that applies equally well to *Blues for Mister Charlie*, "*The Amen Corner* is at its worst as a play precisely when it is at its best as literature."

THE AMEN CORNER

Nowhere are these difficulties seen more clearly than in Baldwin's treatment of the tension between institutionalized religion and moral integrity in *The Amen Corner*. Like *Go Tell It on the Mountain*, *The Amen Corner* challenges the dichotomy between the holy Temple and the sinful Street, a tension that shapes the play's entire dramatic structure. Accepted unquestioningly by most members of Sister Margaret Alexander's congregation, the dichotomy reflects a basic survival strategy of blacks making the transition from their rural Southern roots to the urban North during the Great Migration. By dividing the world into zones of safety and danger, church members attempt to distance themselves and, perhaps more important, their loved ones from the brutalities of the city. As Baldwin comments in his introduction to the play, Sister Margaret faces the dilemma of "how to treat her husband and her son as men and at the same time to protect them from the bloody consequences of trying to be a man in this society." In act 1, Margaret attempts to resolve the dilemma by forcing her son David, a musician in his late teens, into the role of servant of the Lord while consigning her estranged husband Luke, a jazz musician, to the role of worldly tempter. Having witnessed the brutal impact of Harlem on Luke, she strives to protect her son by creating a world entirely separate from his father's. Ultimately, however, the attempt fails as David's emerging sense of self drives him to confront a wider range of experience; meanwhile, Luke's physical collapse, which takes place in the "safe zone," forces Margaret to acknowledge her own evasions. The most important of these, which reveals Margaret's claim to moral purity as self-constructed illusion, involves her claim that Luke abandoned his family; in fact, she fled from him to avoid the pain caused by the death of a newborn daughter, a pain associated with sexuality and the Street.

As he did in *Go Tell It on the Mountain*, Baldwin treats the collapse of the dichotomies as a potential source of artistic and spiritual liberation. David recognizes that his development as a musician demands immersion in both the sacred and the secular traditions of African American music. Margaret attempts to redefine herself in terms not of holiness but of an accepting love imaged in her clutching Luke's trombone mouthpiece after his death. Both resolutions intimate a synthesis of Temple and Street, suggesting the common impulse behind the gospel music and jazz that sound throughout the play. The emotional implications of the collapse of the dichotomies in *The Amen Corner* are directly articulated when, following her acknowledgment that the vision on which she bases her authority as preacher was her own creation, Margaret says: "It's a awful thing to think about, the way love never dies!" This second "vision" marks a victory much more profound than that of the church faction that casts Margaret out at the end of the play. Ironically, the new preacher, Sister Moore, seems destined to perpetuate Margaret's moral failings. Although Sister Moore's rise to power is grounded primarily in the congregation's dissatisfaction with Margaret's inability to connect her spiritual life with the realities of the Street (Margaret refuses to sympathize with a woman's marital difficulties or to allow a man to take a job driving a liquor truck), she fails to perceive the larger implications of the dissatisfaction. Sister Moore's inability to see the depth of Margaret's transformed sense of love suggests that the simplifying dichotomies will continue to shape the congregation's experience.

Thematically and psychologically, then, *The Amen Corner* possesses a great deal of potential

power. Theatrically, however, it fails to exploit this potential. Despite Baldwin's awareness that "the ritual of the church, historically speaking, comes out of the theater, the *communion* which is the theater," the structure of *The Amen Corner* emphasizes individual alienation rather than ritual reconciliation. In part because the play's power in performance largely derives from the energy of the music played in the church, the street side of Baldwin's vision remains relatively abstract. Where the brilliant prose of *Go Tell It on the Mountain* suggests nuances of perception that remain only half-conscious to John Grimes during his transforming vision, David's conversations with Luke and Margaret focus almost exclusively on his rebellion against the Temple while leaving the terms of the dichotomy unchallenged. In act 3, similarly, Margaret's catharsis seems static. The fact that Margaret articulates her altered awareness in her preacher's voice suggests a lingering commitment to the Temple at odds with Baldwin's thematic design. Although the sacred music emanating from the church is theoretically balanced by the jazz trombone associated with Luke, most of the performance power adheres to the gospel songs that provide an embodied experience of call and response; taken out of its performance context, the jazz seems a relatively powerless expression. As a result, *The Amen Corner* never escapes from the sense of separation it conceptually attacks.

BLUES FOR MISTER CHARLIE

Blues for Mister Charlie reconsiders the impact of simplistic dichotomies in explicitly political terms. Dedicated to the murdered civil rights leader Medgar Evers and the four black children killed in a 1963 Birmingham terrorist bombing, the play reflects both Baldwin's increasing anger and his continuing search for a unified moral being. Loosely basing his plot on the case of Emmett Till, a black youth murdered for allegedly insulting a white woman in Mississippi, Baldwin focuses his attention on the unpunished white murderer of Richard Henry, who is killed after returning to his minister father's Southern home to recover from a drug addiction. Baldwin establishes a black-white division onstage as an extension of the sacred-secular dichotomy; the two primary sets are a black church and a white courthouse, both of which are divided into two areas, Whitetown and Black-town. Underscoring the actual interdependence of the constituting terms, Baldwin insists in his stage directions that the audience be aware of the courthouse flag throughout scenes set in the church and of the Cross during scenes set in the courthouse. Periodically, the dialogue brings the connections between seemingly disparate realities into the foreground. Richard's father, Meridian, responds to the liberal white newspaperman Parnell's surprise over the intensity of rage and hatred in the black community following Richard's death: "You've heard it before. You just never recognized it before. You've heard it in all those blues and spirituals and gospel songs you claim to love so much." The tentative rapprochement of Parnell, Meridian, and Richard's lover Juanita at the end of the play provides an image of a potential community capable of acknowledging the complexity of transforming both the rage and the past failures of perception into a political and moral action. When Parnell, employing a term with particularly charged meaning in the context of the southern Civil Rights movement, asks if he can "join you on the march," Juanita's tempered acceptance—"we can walk in the same direction"—represents a profound attempt not to invert the black-white dichotomy following the acquittal of Richard's murderer, Lyle Britten, an acquittal in which Parnell is implicated by his inability to challenge the underlying structure of the white legal system.

As background for this resolution, Baldwin develops three central themes: the growing anger of young blacks, the impact of this anger on the older members of the black community, and the white psychology that enables apparently normal individuals to perpetrate atrocities without remorse. The theme of anger focuses on Richard, whose experiences both in New York and in Mississippi generate an intense bitterness against all whites. Articulating a militant credo that Baldwin finds emotionally comprehensible but morally inadequate, Richard tells his grandmother,

I'm going to treat every one of them as though they were responsible for all the crimes that ever happened in the history of the world—oh, yes! They're responsi-

ble for all the misery I've ever seen . . . the only way the black man's going to get any power is to drive all the white men into the sea.

Backed up by his vow to carry a gun with him at all times, Richard's militancy comes into direct conflict with his grandmother's and his father's traditional values of endurance, hope, and Christian compassion. Ironically, Richard's compassion for his grandmother leads him to give his gun to his father, an act that leaves him defenseless when attacked by Lyle. Baldwin suggests that some adjustment between unbridled violence and naïve faith will be necessary if blacks are to put an end to their victimization without emulating the moral failures of their white persecutors.

Baldwin's comments on *Blues for Mister Charlie* emphasize the importance of the portrait of the white persecutor to his overall design. Attributing his reluctance to write drama to a "deeper fear," Baldwin stresses his desire to overcome his own dichotomizing impulses and "to draw a valid portrait of the murderer." Unfortunately, the dramatic presentation of Lyle Britten in many ways fails to fulfill this desire. Obsessed with racial honor, especially as it involves white women, Lyle seems more sociological exemplar than rounded individual. Despite the fact that he has had at least one sexual relationship with a black woman, Lyle's obsession with interracial sex, grounded in a deep insecurity that leads him to respond violently to any perceived threat to his sense of masculine superiority, dominates every aspect of his character. While sociological works such as Joel Kovel's *White Racism: A Psychohistory* (1970) and Calvin Hernton's *Sex and Racism in America* (1965) support the general accuracy of the diagnosis, Baldwin nevertheless fails to demonstrate its relation to aspects of Lyle's experience not directly involved with the obsession. Lyle's monologues on his poor white heritage and his sexual experience sound stilted and contrived, especially when juxtaposed to a generally unconvincing presentation of whites in the play. Parnell's monologue on "the holy, the liberating orgasm," for example, seems more a didactic parody of Norman Mailer's *The White Negro* (1957) than an aspect of his character.

Although in his fiction Baldwin demonstrates a profound understanding of the psychological reality and aesthetic power of silence, *Blues for Mister Charlie* veers sharply toward an overelaboration that undercuts the validity of his portrait of the white persecutors. This in turn weighs the play more heavily than Baldwin intended toward the black perspective, reinforcing rather than challenging the underlying dichotomy. The conversations among Parnell, Lyle, and Lyle's wife, Jo, concerning their attitudes toward race and sex seem wooden and static largely because they articulate attitudes that if consciously acknowledged would dictate changes in behavior in any realistic, as opposed to demoniac, characters. Although it would be possible to interpret the monologues as Eugene O'Neill-style stream-of-unconsciousness passages, the dialogue subverts the effectiveness of the technique, suggesting that Baldwin has simply failed to come to terms with the silence of his characters' personalities. Although *Blues for Mister Charlie* advances Baldwin's belief that imposing dichotomies on experience leads inexorably to emotional and physical violence, it nevertheless perpetuates a dichotomy between abstract statement and concrete experience. Baldwin's decision not to return to drama after *Blues for Mister Charlie* seems an acknowledgment that he is much more comfortable with forms in which his voice can assume a concrete reality of its own, transforming tensions that in his drama remain unresolved.

OTHER MAJOR WORKS

LONG FICTION: *Go Tell It on the Mountain*, 1953; *Giovanni's Room*, 1956; *Another Country*, 1962; *Tell Me How Long the Train's Been Gone*, 1968; *If Beale Street Could Talk*, 1974; *Just Above My Head*, 1979.

SHORT FICTION: *Going to Meet the Man*, 1965.

POETRY: *Jimmy's Blues: Selected Poems*, 1983.

SCREENPLAY: *One Day, When I Was Lost: A Scenario Based on "The Autobiography of Malcolm X,"* 1972.

NONFICTION: *Notes of a Native Son*, 1955; *Nobody Knows My Name: More Notes of a Native Son*, 1961; *The Fire Next Time*, 1963; *Nothing Personal*, 1964 (with Richard Avedon); *No Name in the Street*, 1971; *A Rap on Race*, 1971 (with Margaret Mead); *A Dialogue*, 1975 (with Nikki Giovanni); *The Devil Finds Work*, 1976; *The Evidence of Things Not Seen*, 1985; *The Price of the Ticket*, 1985; *Conversations with James Baldwin*, 1989; *Collected Essays*, 1998.

CHILDREN'S LITERATURE: *Little Man, Little Man*, 1975.

BIBLIOGRAPHY

Balfour, Lawrie Lawrence, and Katherine Lawrence Balfour. *The Evidence of Things Not Said: James Baldwin and the Promise of American Democracy*. Ithaca, N.Y.: Cornell University Press, 2001. Explores the political dimension of Baldwin's essays, stressing the politics of race in American democracy.

Fabré, Michel. *From Harlem to Paris: Black American Writers in France, 1840-1980*. Chicago: University of Illinois Press, 1991. A chapter on Baldwin's Paris experiences, "James Baldwin in Paris: Love and Self-Discovery," brings biographical details to the European experiences of the bicontinental playwright, who owed France "his own spiritual growth, through the existential discovery of love as a key to life." The notes offer interview sources of quotations for further study.

Harris, Trudier, ed. *New Essays on "Go Tell It on the Mountain."* American Novel series. Cambridge, England: Cambridge University Press, 1996. These essays examine the composition, themes, publication history, public reception, and contemporary interpretations of Baldwin's first novel.

McBride, Dwight A. *James Baldwin Now*. New York: New York University Press, 1999. Stresses the usefulness of recent interdisciplinary approaches in understanding Baldwin's appeal, political thought and work, and legacy.

Miller, D. Quentin, ed. *Re-Viewing James Baldwin: Things Not Seen*. Philadelphia: Temple University Press, 2000. Explores the way in which Baldwin's writing touched on issues that confront all people, including race, identity, sexuality, and religious ideology.

O'Daniel, Therman B. *James Baldwin: A Critical Evaluation*. Washington, D.C.: Howard University Press, 1977. A full study of Baldwin's accomplishments in all genres, with some twenty-three articles. Particularly informative are Carlton W. Molette's examination of Baldwin as playwright, Darwin T. Turner's study of Baldwin as a distinctly African American dramatist, and Waters E. Turpin's brief "Note on *Blues for Mister Charlie*." Supplemented by a classified bibliography and an index.

Porter, Horace A. *Stealing the Fire: The Art and Protest of James Baldwin*. Middletown, Conn.: Wesleyan University Press, 1989. Concentrates on Baldwin's literary output rather than his political biography and assesses his talents in the face of the necessity of social themes. Strong discussion of Harriet Beecher Stowe and Richard Wright as influences.

Scott, Lynn Orilla. *James Baldwin's Later Fiction: Witness to the Journey*. East Lansing: Michigan State University Press, 2002. Analyzes the decline of Baldwin's reputation after the 1960's, the ways in which critics have often undervalued his work, and the interconnected themes in his body of work.

Standley, Fred L., and Nancy V. Standley. *James Baldwin: A Reference Guide*. Boston: G. K. Hall, 1980. A comprehensive bibliography with more than three thousand entries, meticulously annotated, sometimes with almost essay-long commentary. A com-plicated index aids searches, once mastered. The book is divided into works by Baldwin, generically listed alphabetically, and works about Baldwin, listed chronologically and alphabetically.

Troupe, Quincy, ed. *James Baldwin: The Legacy*. New York: Simon and Schuster, 1989. A collection of essays by and about Baldwin, with a foreword by writer Wole Soyinka. Contains eighteen essays, five of which were written for this collection, and homage and celebration from many who were profoundly influenced by Baldwin, including Pat Mikell's account of Baldwin's last days in St. Paul de Vence. Brief bibliography.

Weatherby, W. J. *James Baldwin: Artist on Fire*. New York: Donald I. Fine, 1989. A portrait by a personal friend of some twenty-eight years, this study is both insightful and scholarly. The "Baldwin on Broadway" chapter covers the production of *Blues for Mister Charlie* and *The Amen Corner*, as well as Baldwin's often stormy relationship with the Actors Studio and Lincoln Center. "Down South" discusses a thwarted dramatization of *Giovanni's Room* and Baldwin's special affection for Elia Kazan. Photos and index.

Craig Werner,
updated by Thomas J. Taylor
and Robert McClenaghan

JOHN BALE

Born: Cove, England; November 21, 1495
Died: Canterbury, England; November, 1563

PRINCIPAL DRAMA

King Johan, wr. 1531(?), pb. 1538, pr. 1539(?)
Three Laws, wr. 1531(?), pb. 1547
God's Promises, wr. 1538, pb. 1547
John Baptist, wr. 1538, pb. 1547
The Temptation, wr. 1538, pb. 1547
The Dramatic Writings of John Bale, pb. 1907
    (John S. Farmer, editor)

OTHER LITERARY FORMS

A Carmelite friar and scholar turned Protestant propagandist, John Bale wrote literary history, chronicle history, and religious polemics as well as verse drama. While a Carmelite, he edited some devotional works and compiled several Latin-language catalogs of the Order's practices and history in England. His *Illustrium Maioris Britanniae Scriptorum* (famous writers of Great Britain), first issued in 1548, subsequently revised and retitled in 1557, gave biographical information about the important writers of England, Scotland, and Wales and listed the titles and dates of their works. Bale also wrote chronicles of persons he deemed noteworthy Protestant martyrs: *A Brief Chronicle of Sir John Oldcastle, the Lord Cobham* (1544), *The First Examination of Anne Askew* (1546), and *The Latter Examination of Anne Askew* (1547).

A bitter opponent of the traditional Catholicism, from which he converted in mid-life, Bale wrote polemics combining dialogue with diatribe. He interpreted the pope as the Antichrist in *The Image of Both Churches* (part 1, 1541; part 2, 1545; part 3, 1547). In *The Acts of English Votaries* (1546), Bale attacked the behavior of those in religious orders. He disputed the positions of various Catholic apologists in the verse tract *An Answer to a Papistical Exhortation* (1548), and in prose in *An Expostulation Against the Blasphemies of a Frantic Papist* (1552) and *The Apology of John Bale Against a Rank Papist* (c. 1555). Bale attacked the papacy in *Acta Romanorum Pontificum* (1558; acts of the Roman pontiffs), and he criticized opponents nearer to home in his book *A Declaration Concerning the Clergy of London* (1561).

Bale edited a work on the sacrament of Holy Communion by John Lambert, *A Treatise to Henry VIII* (c. 1548). In 1538, he translated from the German Thomas Kirchmayer's Protestant play *Pammachius*, though his translation is not extant. Bale's *The True History of the Christian Departing of Martin Luther* (1546) is a translation of German accounts originally collected by Justus Jonas, Michael Cellius, and Joannes Aurifaber.

ACHIEVEMENTS

A controversialist living in chaotic times, John Bale is known less for originality in his own work than for setting precedents that other talents brought to flower. Bale's own literary catalogs include a sprinkling of medieval trivia, such as attribution of certain literary works to the biblical Adam, yet his work provided a model for persistence in research, acknowledgment of sources, and comparative thoroughness in the entries on the writers of his own era. Modern literary biographers are still drawing on

Bale's *Illustrium Maioris Britanniae Scriptorum* and its expanded editions for information on sixteenth century writers.

In his time, Bale was known for his Protestant propaganda, which attacked various doctrines and practices of Roman Catholic tradition as well as the views of other Protestants whom Bale believed to be extreme or misguided. Hence, in all genres, dogmatic Protestant zeal motivated his writing.

Bale's chronicle on Sir John Oldcastle was intended to rehabilitate the fourteenth century nobleman's reputation. As a follower of early reformer and Bible translator John Wycliffe, Oldcastle was depicted unfavorably in traditional records. Bale's wish that Protestant martyrs be viewed sympathetically was not unique, but according to his friend John Foxe, Bale's chronicle influenced in perspective and substance the histories written by Edward Hall and Raphael Holinshed, as well as Foxe's *The Book of Martyrs* (1559). All three writers reflected to some degree a break from traditional Catholic perspectives, and the chronicles of Hall and of Holinshed were to become sources for William Shakespeare's history plays.

Although Bale recorded titles of twenty-one plays that he wrote, only five are extant. The titles of the lost works, such as *Against Adulterators of God's Word*, *Christ's Passion*, and *Simon the Leper*, imply that the lost plays share the dogmatic purpose and medieval conventions of the plays that survive.

The extant play *King Johan*, however, includes a basic innovation that later writers worked to full advantage. Among the familiar walking, talking abstractions of the morality play's virtue and vice characters, Bale placed the thirteenth century monarch King Johan (King John) and a few of his historical enemies. King Johan's ill repute easily outlasted Bale's attempt to make him a Protestant saint and hero of English sovereignty and therefore a villain to Roman Catholic historians. Still, *King Johan* is a prototype drama including historical persons and events in English theater. The history plays of Shakespeare and Christopher Marlowe display far greater sophistication in plot, characterization, and theatricality, but Bale set the precedent for the history play as a type.

He also, in perspective and substance, influenced the chronicle histories of Hall and Holinshed that Shakespeare used extensively in writing his history plays and stirred the debate over Sir John Oldcastle's true character that gave Shakespeare material for his rascal Falstaff.

BIOGRAPHY

John Bale included autobiographical notes in his literary catalogs. Beginning with those entries, then studying correspondence between Bale and his contemporaries and reviewing official records of the era, Jesse W. Harris has provided considerable background data in his book *John Bale: A Study in the Minor Literature of the Reformation* (1940), to which the following summary is indebted.

Bale was born to Henry and Margaret Bale at Cove, County Suffolk, near Dunwich, England. At age twelve, he began study with the Carmelite friars at Norwich, whose monastery had a good library. Bale learned Latin, the rites and customs of the Order, and the principles of careful study and research.

In 1514, Bale entered Jesus College in Cambridge University. College policy apparently required that he reside at Jesus College rather than with fellow Carmelites in lodgings that the order maintained at the university. When Bale arrived at Cambridge, interest in the New Learning was high and Continental Reformation influences were strong; Erasmus, the Dutch theologian and New Testament scholar, was in residence there. A number of Bale's fellow students, including Hugh Latimer, Thomas Cranmer, Stephen Gardiner, and Matthew Parker, were to become important figures in the religious and political struggles that erupted when Henry VIII assumed control of the English Church and that did not significantly subside until after the accession of Elizabeth I.

Bale took his bachelor of divinity in 1529 and his doctor of divinity not long afterward. He served briefly as prior of the Carmelite monastery in Maldon in 1530, then moved to the priory at Doncaster. In 1533, he became prior at Ipswich, not far from his hometown of Cove; by then, he had a reputation for unorthodox teaching. One William Broman, when questioned about his religious views in 1535, testified that Bale had taught him in Doncaster in 1531 that Christ was not physically present in the Eucharist.

At Ipswich, Bale grew close to Thomas Wentworth, an active Protestant who led the unorthodox friar to act more decisively on his reform convictions. Bale converted to Protestantism, left the priesthood, and married a young woman named Dorothy. On the strength of some fourteen Protestant plays already written for patron John de Vere, Wentworth recommended Bale to Thomas Cromwell, a major power in the Protestant movement. Cromwell encouraged Bale to continue writing plays and other materials to further the Protestant cause. On at least two occasions, Bale's outspoken views brought sanctions from authorities. He even spent time in Greenwich jail, but Cromwell was able to bring pressure to bear on the authorities involved, and Bale was released.

For several years, the nature of the Church in England was fiercely debated. Henry VIII's assumption of headship did not eradicate in one stroke all the centuries of Roman Catholic tradition in England, and among those who called for reform, there was no consensus on how much reform was enough. The relative influence of various factions waxed and waned. For a time, Cromwell's influence was substantial. Anne Boleyn's execution in 1536, however, set off a wave of pro-Catholic activity. By 1540, Henry VIII was less worried about the definition of the national Church than he was about the deep divisions within the body politic. He moved to solve his political problems as he had his personal problems—by execution. To be fair, he beheaded or burned three Catholic and three Protestant leaders, including Cromwell.

His patron gone, Bale fled with his wife and children to the Continent in 1540. He presumably spent time in Holland, Switzerland, and northern Germany. The publication notices in books he issued while in Europe cite places of publication such as Basle, Switzerland; Antwerp, Belgium; and Wesel, Germany. Collateral evidence indicates that he sometimes published in cities in which he lived at the time. On occasion, too, whether because of a publishing opportunity or because of concern for personal safety, his works were published in cities in which he did not reside. A few items were issued under pseudonyms.

In Europe, Bale developed further contacts with various reform leaders and continued his relationship with a number of exiled English Protestants as well. Meanwhile, his writings continued to stir controversy at home in England. In 1546, his books were banned along with the writings of several other authors, including the Bible translators John Wycliffe and Miles Coverdale. Bale's work on Anne Askew was particularly disturbing to the authorities.

In 1547, Henry VIII was succeeded by his nine-year-old son, Edward VI. The council of regents advising the boy-king was predominantly Protestant. Bishop Stephen Gardiner, who had strongly opposed Bale's writings, was imprisoned in the Tower of London. Bale then returned to England.

Through 1551, Bale continued research for his literary histories and continued writing in support of the Reformation. He was appointed rector of Bishopstoke, Hampshire, in June of 1551, and later of Swaffham, Norfolk. In August of 1552, Edward VI appointed Bale Bishop of Ossory in Ireland. Given the staunch Catholic convictions among most of the Irish clergy and laity in his bishopric, Bale provoked continually bitter conflict by attempting to limit or abolish various traditional customs and forms of worship.

Edward VI died in July of 1553 to be succeeded by Mary I, also known as Bloody Mary because of the number of executions carried out during her reign. The Catholic queen brought a return of Catholic influence to the court and to the English Church. Mary released Bishop Stephen Gardiner from the Tower to be her Lord Chancellor. Thereafter, an English translation of Gardiner's *De Vera Obedientia* (1553; of true obedience) began to circulate in England. Written in earlier days to support King Henry VIII's break with Rome, the book was a certain irritant to the older and more conservative Gardiner, in service to a Catholic queen. Bale is suspected of having done the English translation.

During 1554 and 1555, Bale lived in Frankfurt, Germany. When the English exile Church in Frankfurt split over issues of forms of worship, Bale and his friend John Foxe moved to Switzerland and stayed with a printer, Johannes Oporinus, who issued Bale's literary histories in 1557 and 1559.

Elizabeth I succeeded Mary in 1558. In 1559, Bale returned to England. Other Protestant churchmen were appointed to bishoprics. Bale was named to a prebendary, a modest position at Canterbury. He continued research and writing, though ill, and made many appeals to friends and officials for help in recovering books and manuscripts he had left in Ireland in 1553. Unfortunately, not even a letter from Queen Elizabeth could produce results. Bale died at Canterbury in November of 1563.

ANALYSIS

Discussion of John Bale's drama requires some background on the theatrical conventions of the times. At festivals, common folk enjoyed song, dance, games, and ritual skits satirizing the nobility and the clergy. Some plays were enacted, drawing from English folklore. Also in medieval England there had developed a tradition of religious instruction through drama. Certain towns presented annual cycles of plays, productions lasting three days and made up of individual plays dramatizing selected Bible stories. Such series were designed to present a Christian worldview from the creation of Adam through the life of Christ and on to the Last Judgment. The religious purpose, however, did not preclude use of humorous, even bawdy, stage business and dialogue. Depictions of saints' lives and of moral fables were also common.

Medieval religious drama, which provided a rich heritage for English Renaissance drama, included three major categories: the mystery play, the miracle play, and the morality play. The mystery play drew on liturgy and on episodes of the life of Christ, dramatizing the "mysteries" of divine intervention in the temporal world. The miracle play presented events from lives of saints or martyrs for the purpose of asserting the virtue of faith in divine power and intervention. The morality play personified abstractions such as hope and charity in conflict with vices such as pride or greed in simple stories designed to teach moral, ethical, or theological premises.

GOD'S PROMISES

Bale's verse drama *God's Promises* fits expectations of the mystery play. Although it does not focus on the life of Christ directly, it presents a pattern of biblical characters—Old Testament personalities and John the Baptist from the New Testament—as the essential preface to Christ's coming. It is understood to be a play that Bale would use as the first in a trilogy. Second and third plays would cover Christ's life, death, and resurrection and possibly the Second Coming and Last Judgment.

God's Promises consistently embodies a Christian vision of pre-Christian scriptures as the record of preparation for and prophecy of Christ's appearance on earth. Ancient and medieval theology included searches for proofs of divine order both in the natural world and in Scripture. Numerological formulas were invoked to prove the divine source of Scripture. The number one, for example, was the number of God; three represented the trinity of Father, Son, and Holy Spirit. Six was the number of mortals, while seven, combining the mortal and the divine, was the perfect number.

Bale includes himself as a commentator in *God's Promises*, but the mortal characters of this seven-act verse drama are seven in number: Adam Primus Homo (Adam, the First Man), Justus Noah (Noah the Righteous), Abraham Fidelis (Abraham the Faithful), Moseh Sanctus (Moses the Holy), David Rex Pius (David the Pious King), Esaias Prophetas (Isaiah the Prophet), and Joannes Baptista (John the Baptist).

Although one might expect a play featuring Old Testament figures to begin with material from Genesis, Pater Coelestis's (Heavenly Father's) opening is a Trinitarian self-description that seems a creedal expansion of the first chapter of the Gospel of John. Following Heavenly Father's introduction, which includes references to Adam's Fall and God's judgment on both man and woman, Adam enters to plead for mercy. The second act summarizes the era of Noah. Heavenly Father recites the evils that provoked his judgment on mortals, and Noah, like Adam, pleads for mercy. Heavenly Father, in the third act, expresses displeasure over the depravity of Noah's descendants, particularly their falling to idolatry and sodomy. Abraham, on behalf of his nephew Lot, who lives in the vicinity of Sodom and Gomorrah, appeals for mercy. He bargains with Heavenly Father until he se-

cures a promise that God will spare the cities if ten righteous citizens can be found in them. Despite the flood of Noah's era, and despite the witness of faith in Abraham, mortals continue to sin. In the fourth act, Heavenly Father gives the law to Moses for the people of Israel and for all nations. Dialogue in the fourth act reviews major events of Moses's life, such as the plagues of Egypt, the Exodus and provision of manna in the desert, and Israel's apostasy with the golden calf. For Israel's idolatry, Heavenly Father again pronounces judgment but tempers his decree with the promise of a prophet to come.

The fifth act sets Heavenly Father in dialogue with David the Pious King. Their exchanges survey the leadership of priests and prophets between the time of Moses and the accession of Saul, David's predecessor. Heavenly Father condemns David for taking the wife of Uriah the Hittite and for taking a national census (a sign of faith in mortal strength rather than in divine protection). David must choose a punishment, but again the judgment is linked with a promise. In David's case, the promise is for the greatness of his son Solomon. Heavenly Father, in the sixth act, discourses with the prophet Isaiah, recounting the infidelity of Israel after Solomon, the split into the kingdoms of Israel and Judah, the Babylonian conquest, and the Babylonian captivity of Israel as punishment for recurrent idolatry. Isaiah, continuing the pattern that Bale has set for his mortal characters in dialogue with Heavenly Father, appeals for mercy. In response, Heavenly Father cites messianic verses from the Old Testament book of Isaiah that Christian tradition has long held to be predictions of Christ's birth.

With John the Baptist, in the seventh act, Heavenly Father surveys events from the time of the Babylonian Captivity through the age of latter prophets, giving special note to the restoration of the temple in Jerusalem and to the religious renewal under King Josiah. In closing, Heavenly Father names John the Baptist the messenger to announce the coming of Christ. In a very clear paraphrase of reactions to divine call in the biblical stories of Moses, Isaiah, and others, John objects, contending that he lacks the learning and eloquence necessary for such awesome duties, but Heavenly Father prevails.

The text of *God's Promises*, then, employs close paraphrase of Scripture and creedal statements throughout. For each era in the schema, Heavenly Father is a rigorous judge, punishing idolatry yet promising some form of relief to come. The emphases in dramatizing these particular characters in dialogue with, and in service to, Heavenly Father are not only traditionally messianic but also decidedly Protestant in their management.

As a friar who left holy orders to marry, Bale offers an interesting view of the Fall of Adam and Eve. Medieval tradition includes much misogynistic coloring of the Fall. Some interpreters made much of Eve's yielding to desire and then inducing Adam to yield to desire as well. Bale, however, poses Heavenly Father attributing Adam's Fall to a failure to use reason. Such a stance might be expected from a reformer quite given to scholarship and seeing in literacy and clear thinking a means to escape what he considered decadent superstition in religion. Furthermore, keeping the responsibility with Adam rather than with Eve, Bale sidesteps a conventional argument for clerical celibacy—namely, that a married cleric would be more concerned with a wife than with his religious duties.

Bale's focus on the Sodom and Gomorrah episode from Abraham's era is a means for him to stress divine judgment on sodomy. Bale insisted that the rule of celibacy for those in holy orders simply led many to engage in homosexual or illicit heterosexual activity—observing the letter of the vow but not the spirit. Also, every act of *God's Promises* includes condemnation of idolatry. As a Protestant strongly opposed to veneration of saints and sacred relics, Bale keeps the anti-idolatry theme dominant.

In aspects of form other than the structural Symbolism mentioned above, *God's Promises* is typical of Bale's style. The lines of verse are roughly pentametric, sometimes straggling into six- or seven-beat lines. End rhymes appear in various groupings, often approximating stanzas of five, seven, or nine lines by interlocking couplets, tercets, and quatrains of sometimes exact, sometimes slant rhyme. The verse functions mainly to keep the great patches of biblical and creedal paraphrase memorable for actors

faced with long, set speeches and dialogues only occasionally relieved by some stage business. Religious songs between acts provide some variety, though the texts of certain songs do not seem wholly pertinent to the issues in the bracketing acts. The music itself may be a counter to the radical reform views that minimized or eliminated the role of music in worship.

THREE LAWS

For *Three Laws*, Bale used the morality play format. The opening is given by Baleus Prolocutor (Bale the Commentator). The first act stages the lead character Deus Pater (God the Father) calling out the three laws: Lex Naturae (the Natural Law), Moseh Lex (the Law of Moses, sometimes termed the Law of Bondage), and Christi Lex (the Law of Christ, sometimes termed the Law of Grace). At first, as in *God's Promises*, the divinity, God the Father, defines his Triune nature. He then defines each law. The Natural Law has sway in human hearts for three ages: from Adam to Noah, from Noah to Abraham, and from Abraham to Moses. The law of Moses obtains in another three ages: from Moses to David, from David to the Babylonian exile, and from the exile to the appearance of Christ. The law of Christ dominates the last age. Hence, though the characters staged are abstractions rather than biblical characters, *Three Laws* shares with *God's Promises* Bale's structural reinforcement of numerological symbols. The two sets of three eras equal the mortal number six, and the age of Christ brings the sum to the perfect seven, adding the divine number, one, to the mortal number.

The second act sets Natural Law in dialogue with Infidelitas (Infidelity). Natural Law declares, "A knowledge I am whom God in man does hide/ In his whole working to be to him a guide." Infidelity debates the very existence of Natural Law. If, indeed, God has created such an orderly world, why are there severe storms or wild animals that attack people or other extreme disruptions of order? Natural Law answers that such events are divine punishment for disregard of God. Having failed to best Natural Law in debate, Infidelity conjures the demons Sodomismus (Sodomy) and Idolatrias (Idolatry), who help him overcome Natural Law.

The third act brings the Law of Moses as a successor to Natural Law. To counter the force of the Law of Moses, Infidelity brings in Avaritia (Covetousness) and Ambitio (Ambition), who render the Law of Moses lame and blind. Evangelium (Christ's Gospel) enters in the fourth act to oppose Infidelity. The vice again produces assistants, Pseudodoctrina (False Doctrine) and Hypocrisis (Hypocrisy), and these three vice characters burn Christ's Gospel at the stake.

Vindicta Dei (God's Wrath) takes the lead in the fifth act. Infidelity offers God's Wrath a bribe to avoid conflict but is confronted and overcome. God the Father recalls the three laws for renewal and cleansing, after which the three sing praise. God the Father then announces restoration of "true faith and religion" and calls in Fides Christiano (Christian Faith) for closing doctrinal explanations.

Three Laws includes some passing references to historical figures, such as a comparison of King Henry VIII to the Hebrew reformer-king Josiah, but does not include those historical figures as active characters in the play.

While Bale's anti-Catholicism is occasionally stated outright in *God's Promises*, it runs rampant in *Three Laws*. Costuming notes at the play's end call for visual parodies. Sodomy is to be dressed as a monk, False Doctrine as a "popish doctor," and Hypocrisy as a Gray Friar. Infidelity frequently uses oaths such as "by the mass" and "by St. Stephen"; he also makes a number of coarse, offensive remarks to which the virtuous characters take exception.

Infidelity's introduction of Idolatry continues the anti-Catholic matter. Idolatry is credited with curing toothache, ague, and pox and with conjuring the Devil by saying the Hail Mary. The entrance and introduction of Sodomy carries similar attacks. Sodomy claims that clergy in Rome and elsewhere turn to him because they lack wives and do not fear divine retribution.

Bale builds a long list of Protestant propaganda charges into *Three Laws*: Veneration of saints equals idol worship; the doctrine of purgatory is a device to rob the poor; and Latin rites, Scriptures, and prayers censor the true message of the Scriptures, while English is used for those customs and practices that

bring cash to church coffers. Bale gives Covetousness a parodic creed that avers faith in the pope rather than faith in God, then continues listing various usages that Bale believed served a corrupt religious establishment while faithful parishioners were misled. Other writers and thinkers in the troubled times of the Reformation and the Counter-Reformation may have been opinionated, even bigoted. Among English writers of his day, Bale was so aggressive that he became known to succeeding generations as "Bilious Bale."

KING JOHAN

Bale's more noted play, *King Johan*, was probably written several years before 1538, its year of publication. The extant manuscript is likely two or three removes from the original, as its closing lines refer to Queen Elizabeth. The play consists of two long acts, the first with a shift of scene from England to Rome. The entrances and exits of characters, a bit of song, and various opportunities for stage business allow some relief from the steady onslaught of didactic dialogue. Formally, the play lacks the structural concern for symbolism found in *God's Promises* or for the classical convention of five acts as found in *Three Laws*. The political purpose of the drama seems its major shaping force.

The play opens with King Johan declaring that citizens should be loyal to their king, thus following the example of Christ's obedience to civil authorities. England, a widow, enters, complaining that the clergy has abused her rights and estranged her from God, her spouse, by refusing to honor God's word. Sedition derides England, then boasts to King Johan that he, Sedition, has papal authority to overcome secular rulers. King Johan confronts Nobility, Clergy, and Civil Order with the problem. Nobility says that his oath of knighthood requires that he defend the Church. Echoing Peter's denial of Christ, Nobility three times denies knowing Sedition. Civil Order declares loyalty to the king. In debate over the legitimacy of the many religious orders in a single church, Civil Order supports King Johan while Nobility sides with Clergy. The king contends that prayers and masses for the dead counter the premise that Christ's death was efficacious once for all. Nobility, Civil Order, and Clergy all submit to the king and vow to defend the realm. King Johan and Civil Order leave, and Clergy then persuades Nobility to reverse himself and believe what the Church teaches rather than reason for himself.

The scene shifts to Rome. Sedition meets Dissimulation, who, singing a litany, prays to be freed of King Johan. The two vices identify themselves as cousins, sons of Falsehood and Privy Treason, respectively, and as grandsons of Infidelity. Together they boast of various forms that the Church establishment can use for deceit. To help preserve the system, Dissimulation calls in Private Wealth. With Sedition's help, the latter two vices bring in Usurped Power, who reveals that he is Pope Innocent III in unofficial garb. Dissimulation asks the pope's blessing, then reports Clergy's complaints against King Johan of England. He has taxed the clergy, has held them accountable to civil justice rather than leaving offending clergy to ecclesiastical justice, and has forbidden bishops to appeal to Rome. Four English bishops have already pronounced the king excommunicated. He has seized church properties and has collected the revenues from salaries owed to exiled clergy. While the other characters move offstage for costume change, Dissimulation expounds on the measures that the pope will take to counter King Johan.

Returning to stage, the other vices have changed both appearances and identities. Usurped Power has become Pope Innocent III both in costume and in name. Sedition has become Steven Langton, Archbishop of Canterbury. The pope performs a ritual cursing King Johan with bell, book, and candle and declares him excommunicated. To close the first act, an Interpreter appears and summarizes the consequences in England of the king's excommunication and the interdiction of the realm (the banning of the Sacraments in the nation's churches).

In the second act, Nobility bemoans the conflict between king and clergy. Sedition, calling himself Good Perfection, offers Nobility pardon for sin in exchange for support of the Church. Nobility makes confession in rather general terms, but Sedition withholds absolution until Nobility again pledges to oppose King Johan. Met by Clergy and Civil Order, Sedition identifies himself as Archbishop Steven

Langton. Clergy kneels for absolution and is presented with parodic relics from certain saints including a louse and a "turd."

Absolution complete, Langton orders Clergy to provoke insurrection in England. Civil Order, formerly loyal to the king, now sides with the opposition. If the fortunes of the Church decline, so will the fortunes of lawyers.

Private Wealth, dressed as a cardinal, demands that King Johan restore all church property he has seized, accept Langton as Archbishop of Canterbury, and allow the return of all exiled clergy. The king insists that, in taxing the clergy, he is simply following biblical precedent. He offers to accept exiled clergy but balks at the appointment of Langton. At this, Private Wealth officially invokes the papal curse and excommunication of the king as well as the interdiction of the nation.

Nobility, Clergy, and Civil Order report the consequences of the excommunication. King Johan insists that the authority of Scripture is superior to the authority of the pope. He cites instances of Old Testament kings appointing priests. Still, he gains no support from his hearers, who reiterate their ties to the Church.

England again appeals to the king. She brings Commonality, who represents the populace and who is afflicted with poverty and blindness. As cardinal, Private Wealth orders Commonality to leave and advises King Johan to capitulate. Papal influence has raised threats of invasion from Scotland, France, and other lands. The danger is too great for King Johan. He regretfully surrenders his crown to the cardinal, submitting to papal authority and consenting to pay heavy fines.

Treason enters in chains. He recites a catalog of Catholic beliefs and practices in parody as his "crimes," then ends the list with civil felonies including "coin clipping" and counterfeiting. King Johan invokes civil justice and orders him hanged. Treason, however, is a priest. The cardinal releases him and demands that King Johan sign over a third of his realm to a sister-in-law. Widow England, in rebuttal, reports that the woman is dead. Johan confirms his submission to the pope. Sedition leaves to stir up trouble in France. Under the name Simon of Swinsett, Dissimulation concocts poison and drinks half the cup himself in order to ensure that King Johan drinks the rest. Each dies justifying himself. Dissimulation, too, relies on anticipatory pardon for his deed and on prayers and masses being said for his soul.

Verity appears to explain that in chronicles written by traditional churchmen, King Johan cannot but have a bad reputation. Nobility, Clergy, and Civil Order debate the quality of the dead king's life, then repent of their failure to support him. Next appears Imperial Majesty, who presses the trio to support their monarch, not to please the ruler personally, but on biblical authority. Sedition, threatened with hanging, also repents but, once pardoned, insists that papal supporters will continue to seek control of England. Imperial Majesty then reinstates the sentence, and Sedition is taken to be hanged. Nobility, Civil Order, and Clergy repent once more and accept the primacy of imperial Majesty. They label the pope the Antichrist.

By parody in plot and characterization, Bale offers *King Johan* as another play to declare his usual Protestant arguments and to vilify his Roman Catholic opposition. Thematically, it varies somewhat from *Three Laws* and *God's Promises*, as it raises the issue of English sovereignty to the fore. Nevertheless, by structure and dialogue, it emphasizes the familiar anti-Catholic rant apparent in Bale's other plays. In versification and style, it is no more refined. The stiff convention of keeping two characters in extended dialogue, with only occasional exchanges among three or more, is employed in *King Johan* as in Bale's other works. His reliance on paraphrase of Scripture, creeds, and traditional ceremonies is equally evident.

Although Bale seems not to have carried dramatic innovation any further in his extant plays, he did set a significant precedent by setting the thirteenth century English king and his opponents onstage to enact historical events. His interpretation is warped by his propagandistic intent, and his flair for theatricality and creative characterization, evident in certain parodic scenes, is always subordinate to his doctrinal persuasion. It therefore remained for playwrights more concerned with drama as an art form, more willing to let

their characters enact or show, rather than tell, their discoveries in life, and able to present life in its complexities onstage, rather than to reduce it to a set of foregone conclusions, to move further. Indeed, playwrights such as Shakespeare and Marlowe moved well beyond Bale's first mixture of a historical king and his enemies with the stock virtue and vice characters of the medieval morality play. They carried the history play to full development on the Renaissance stage.

OTHER MAJOR WORKS

NONFICTION: *The Image of Both Churches*, 1541 (part 1), 1545 (part 2), 1547 (part 3); *A Brief Chronicle of Sir John Oldcastle, the Lord Cobham*, 1544; *The Acts of English Votaries*, 1546; *The First Examination of Anne Askew*, 1546; *The Latter Examination of Anne Askew*, 1547; *An Answer to a Papistical Exhortation*, 1548; *Illustrium Maioris Britanniae Scriptorum*, 1548; *An Expostulation Against the Blasphemies of a Frantic Papist*, 1552; *The Apology of John Bale Against a Rank Papist*, c. 1555; *Illustrium Maioris Britanniae Catalogus*, 1557, 1559 (revision of *Illustrium Maioris Britanniae Scriptorum*); *Acta Romanorum Pontificum*, 1558 (in Latin), 1561 (in French), 1571 (in German), 1574 (in English as *The Pageant of the Popes*); *A Declaration Concerning the Clergy of London*, 1561.

TRANSLATIONS: *Pammachius*, 1538 (of Thomas Kirchmayer's play; no longer extant); *The True History of the Christian Departing of Martin Luther*, 1546 (from German accounts collected by Justus Jonas, Michael Cellius, and Johann Aurifaber).

EDITED TEXT: *A Treatise to Henry VIII*, c. 1548 (of John Lambert's work).

BIBLIOGRAPHY

Bryant, James C. *Tudor Drama and Religious Controversy*. Macon, Ga.: Mercer University Press, 1984. Bryant considers Bale's play *King Johan* as a polemic supporting Henry VIII's First and Second Royal Injunctions of 1536 and 1538, respectively. He also finds him to be a satirist of many elements of the Roman faith, including the allegorization of Scripture.

Happé, Peter. "Dramatic Images of Kingship in Heywood and Bale. *Studies in English Literature, 1500-1900* 39, no. 2 (Spring, 1999): 239-253. Happé compares and contrasts Bale's *King Johan* and John Heywood's *The Play of the Wether* (pb. 1533).

_____. *English Drama Before Shakespeare.* New York: Longman, 1999. A discussion of dramatic forms from the fourteenth to the late sixteenth century that provides a concise overview of the life and works of Bale.

_____. *John Bale.* New York: Twayne, 1996. A basic biography that covers the life and works of Bale. Happé focuses his discussion on the dramatic works. Bibliography and index.

Harris, Jesse W. 1940. Reprint. Freeport, N.Y.: Books for Libraries Press, 1970. *John Bale: A Study in the Minor Literature of the Reformation.* A look at Bale's life and works. Provides considerable background on his life.

Walker, Greg. *Plays of Persuasion: Drama and Politics in the Court of Henry VIII.* New York: Cambridge University Press, 1991. Deals with Bale's connections with Thomas Cranmer, Thomas Cromwell, and John de Vere. Sees *King Johan* as a reflection of the dangers facing the Henrician court in 1538-1539, when Bale's play was performed at Cranmer's residence, the timing suggestive of Bale's fears of the French-Spanish truce and the scheming of an English cardinal, Reginald Pole.

Ralph S. Carlson,
updated by Howard L. Ford

AMIRI BARAKA
LeRoi Jones

Born: Newark, New Jersey; October 7, 1934

PRINCIPAL DRAMA

The Baptism, pr. 1964, pb. 1966
Dutchman, pr., pb. 1964
The Slave, pr., pb. 1964
The Toilet, pr., pb. 1964
Experimental Death Unit #1, pr. 1965, pb. 1969
Jello, pr. 1965, pb. 1970
A Black Mass, pr. 1966, pb. 1969
Arm Yourself, or Harm Yourself, pr., pb. 1967
Great Goodness of Life (A Coon Show), pr. 1967, pb. 1969
Madheart, pr. 1967, pb. 1969
Slave Ship: A Historical Pageant, pr., pb. 1967
The Death of Malcolm X, pb. 1969
Bloodrites, pr. 1970, pb. 1971
Junkies Are Full of (SHHH . . .), pr. 1970, pb. 1971
A Recent Killing, pr. 1973
S-1, pr. 1976, pb. 1978
The Motion of History, pr. 1977, pb. 1978

The Sidney Poet Heroical, pb. 1979 (originally as *Sidnee Poet Heroical*, pr. 1975)
What Was the Relationship of the Lone Ranger to the Means of Production?, pr., pb. 1979
At the Dim'cracker Convention, pr. 1980
Weimar, pr. 1981
Money: A Jazz Opera, pr. 1982
Primitive World: *An Anti-Nuclear Jazz Musical*, pr. 1984, pb. 1997
The Life and Life of Bumpy Johnson, pr. 1991
General Hag's Skeezag, pb. 1992
Meeting Lillie, pr. 1993
The Election Machine Warehouse, pr. 1996, pb. 1997

OTHER LITERARY FORMS

Amiri Baraka is an exceptionally versatile literary figure, equally well known for his poetry, drama, and essays. In addition, he has written short stories, collected in *Tales* (1967), and an experimental novel, *The System of Dante's Hell* (1965), which includes numer-

Amiri Baraka (Library of Congress)

ous poetic and dramatic passages. Baraka's early volumes of poetry *Preface to a Twenty Volume Suicide Note* (1961) and *The Dead Lecturer* (1964) derive from his period of involvement with the New York City avant-garde. Other volumes, such as *Black Magic: Sabotage, Target Study, Black Art—Collected Poetry, 1961-1967* (1969) and *It's Nation Time* (1970), reflect his intense involvement with Black Nationalist politics. Later volumes, such as *Hard Facts* (1975) and *Reggae or Not!* (1981), reflect his developing movement to a leftist political position and have generally failed to appeal to either his avant-garde or his Black Nationalist audience. Baraka's critical and political prose has been collected in *Home: Social Essays* (1966), *Raise Race Rays Raze: Essays Since 1965* (1971), *Selected Plays and Prose* (1979), and *Daggers and Javelins: Essays* (1984). *The Autobiography of LeRoi Jones/Amiri Baraka* was published in 1984.

ACHIEVEMENTS

One of the most politically controversial playwrights of the 1960's, Amiri Baraka is best known for his brilliant early play *Dutchman* and for his contribution to the development of a community-based black nationalist theater. Throughout his career, he has sought dramatic forms for expressing the consciousness of those alienated from the psychological, economic, and racial mainstream of American society. Even though no consensus exists concerning the success of his experiments, particularly those with ritualistic forms for political drama, his challenge to the aesthetic preconceptions of the American mainstream and the inspiration he has provided younger black playwrights such as Ed Bullins and Ron Milner guarantee his place in the history of American drama.

Already well known as an avant-garde poet, Baraka, then LeRoi Jones, first rose to prominence in the theatrical world with the 1964 productions of *The Baptism*, *Dutchman*, *The Slave*, and *The Toilet*, which established him as a major Off-Broadway presence. Shortly after winning the Obie Award for *Dutchman*, however, Baraka broke his ties with the white avant-garde to concentrate on the creation of a militant African American theater. As his mainstream reputation declined, he gained recognition as a leading voice of the Black Arts movement, ultimately assuming a position of public political visibility matched by only a handful of American literary figures.

Baraka's many awards and honors include the Longview Best Essay of the Year award (1961) for his essay "Cuba Libre"; the John Whitney Foundation fellowship for poetry and fiction (1962); the Obie Award for Best American Off-Broadway Play of 1964 for *Dutchman*; a Guggenheim Fellowship (1965-1966); second prize in the First World Festival of Negro Arts (1966) for his play *The Slave*; a National Endowment for the Arts grant (1966); an honorary doctorate from Malcolm X College in Chicago (1972); a Rockefeller Foundation Fellowship in drama (1981); a National Endowment for the Arts poetry award (1981); a New Jersey Council for the Arts award (1982); the American Book Award (Before Columbus Foundation), for *Confirmation: An Anthology of African-American Women*; a PEN-Faulkner

Award (1989); the Langston Hughes Medal (1989) for outstanding contributions to literature; Italy's Ferroni Award and Foreign Poet Award (1993); and the Playwright's Award from the Black Drama Festival of Winston-Salem, North Carolina, in 1997.

BIOGRAPHY

Everett LeRoi Jones, who took the name Amiri Baraka in 1967, was born into a black middle-class family in Newark, New Jersey. An excellent student whose parents encouraged his intellectual interests, Jones was graduated from Howard University of Washington, D.C., in 1954, at the age of nineteen. After spending two years in the United States Air Force, primarily in Puerto Rico, he moved to Greenwich Village, where he embarked on his literary career in 1957. During the early stage of his career, Jones associated closely with numerous white avant-garde poets, including Robert Creeley, Allen Ginsberg, Robert Duncan, and Dianne DiPrima, and, with DiPrima, he founded the American Theatre for Poets in 1961. He married Hettie Cohen, a white woman with whom he edited the magazine *Yugen* from 1958 to 1963, and he established himself as an important young poet, critic, and editor. Among the many magazines to which he contributed was the jazz journal *Downbeat*, where he first developed the interest in African American musical culture that helped shape his theatrical "rituals." The political interests that were to dominate Jones's later work were unmistakably present as early as 1960, when he toured Cuba with a group of black intellectuals. This experience sparked his perception of the United States as a corrupt bourgeois society and seems particularly significant in relation to his subsequent socialist stance. Jones's growing political interest influenced his first produced plays, including the Obie Award-winning *Dutchman*, which anticipated the first major transformation of Jones's life.

Separating from Hettie Cohen and severing ties with his white associates, Jones moved from Greenwich Village to Harlem in 1965. Turning his attention to direct action within the black community, he founded the Black Arts Theatre and School in Harlem and, following his return to his native city in

1966, the Spirit House in Newark. After marrying a black woman, Sylvia Robinson (Amina Baraka), in 1966, Jones adopted a new name, "Amiri" (which means "prince") "Baraka" ("blessed one"), to which he added the honorary title "Imamu." ("spiritual leader"). Over the next half-dozen years, Baraka helped found and develop organizations such as the Black Community Development and Defense Organization, the Congress of African Peoples (convened in Atlanta in 1970), and the National Black Political Convention (convened in Gary, Indiana, in 1972). As a leading spokesperson of the Black Arts Movement, Baraka provided personal and artistic support for young black poets and playwrights, including Larry Neal, Ed Bullins, Marvin X, and Ron Milner. During the Newark riots of 1967, Baraka was arrested for unlawful possession of firearms. Although convicted and given the maximum sentence after the judge read the jury his poem "Black People!" as an example of incitement to riot, Baraka was later cleared on appeal.

Baraka supported Ken Gibson's campaign to become the first black mayor of Newark in 1970, but later broke with him over what he perceived as the Gibson administration's bourgeois values. This disillusionment with black politics within the American system and Baraka's attendance at the Sixth Pan-African Conference at Dar es Salaam in 1974 precipitated the next stage of his political evolution. Although he did not abandon his commitment to confronting the special problems of African Americans in the United States, Baraka began interpreting these problems within the framework of an overarching "Marxist-Leninist-Mao Zedong" philosophy. In conjunction with this second transformation, Baraka dropped the title "Imamu" and changed the name of his Newark publishing firm from "Jihad" to "People's War." He undertook visiting professorships at Yale and George Washington universities before accepting a more permanent position at the State University of New York at Stony Brook. In 1979, Baraka was arrested during a dispute with his wife; he wrote *The Autobiography of LeRoi Jones* while serving the resulting sentence at a halfway house in Harlem. In 1990, he was involved in a widely publicized dispute with Rutgers University officials who had denied him tenure; he compared the school's faculty to the Ku Klux Klan and the Nazi Party. Though such controversies perhaps exacerbated the difficulty Baraka experienced in finding publishers for his socialist writings, he remained an important voice in the literary world and the African American community. After teaching for twenty years in the Department of African Studies at State University of New York-Stony Brook, Baraka retired from his position in 1999.

ANALYSIS

Working with forms ranging from the morality play to avant-garde expressionism, Amiri Baraka throughout his career sought to create dramatic rituals expressing the intensity of the physical and psychological violence that dominates his vision of American culture. From his early plays on "universal" alienation through his Black Nationalist celebrations to his multimedia proletarian pageants, Baraka has focused on a variety of sacrificial victims as his central dramatic presences. Some of these victims remain passive scapegoats who allow a corrupt and vicious system to dictate their fate. Others assume the role of heroic martyr in the cause of community consciousness. Yet a third type of victim is the doomed oppressor whose death marks the transformation of the martyr's consciousness into a ritual action designed to free the community from continuing passive victimization.

The dominant type in Baraka's early plays, the passive scapegoats unaware of their participation in ritual actions, condemn themselves and their communities to blind repetition of destructive patterns. Their apparent mastery of the forms of European American cultural literacy simply obscures the fact of their ignorance of the underlying reality of oppression. Responding to this ironic situation, Baraka's Black Nationalist plays emphasize the new forms of consciousness, their roots in Africa rather than Europe, needed to free the African American community from the historical and psychological forces that enforce such blind repetition. Inverting the traditional moral symbolism of European American culture, Baraka creates rituals that substitute symbolically

white scapegoats for the symbolically black victims of his earlier works. These rituals frequently reject the image of salvation through self-sacrifice (seen as a technique for the pacification of the black masses), insisting instead that only an active struggle can break the cycle of oppression.

Because the rituals of Baraka's Black Nationalist plays frequently culminate in violence directed against whites, or symbolically white members of the black bourgeois, or aspects of the individual black psyche, numerous critics have attacked him for perpetuating the violence and racism he ostensibly criticizes. These critics frequently condemn him for oversimplifying reality, citing his movement from psychologically complex ironic forms to much more explicit allegorical modes in his later drama; the most insistent simply dismiss his post-*Dutchman* plays as strident propaganda, lacking all aesthetic and moral merit. Basing their critiques firmly on European American aesthetic assumptions, such critics in fact overlook the central importance of Baraka's changing sense of his audience. Repudiating the largely white avant-garde audience that applauded his early work, Baraka turned almost exclusively to an African American audience more aware of the storefront preacher and popular music groups such as the Temptations than of August Strindberg and Edward Albee. In adopting a style of performance in accord with this cultural perception, Baraka assumed a didactic voice intended to focus attention on immediate issues of survival and community or class defense.

THE BAPTISM

First produced in leading New York theaters such as St. Mark's Playhouse (*The Slave* and *The Toilet*), the Cherry Lane Theatre (*Dutchman*), and the Writers' Stage Theatre (*The Baptism*), Baraka's early plays clearly reflect both his developing concern with issues of survival and his fascination with European American avant-garde traditions. *The Baptism*, in particular, draws on the conventions of expressionist theater to comment on the absurdity of contemporary American ideas of salvation, which in fact simply mask a larger scheme of victimization. Identified only as symbolic types, Baraka's characters speak a surreal mixture of street language and theological argot. While the slang references link them to the social reality familiar to the audience, their actions are dictated by the sudden shifts and thematic ambiguities characteristic of works such as Strindberg's *Ett drömspel* (pb. 1902; *A Dream Play*, 1912) and the "Circe" chapter of James Joyce's *Ulysses* (1922).

The play's central character, named simply "the Boy," resembles a traditional Christ figure struggling to come to terms with his vocation. Baraka treats his protagonist with a mixture of irony and empathy, focusing on the ambiguous roles of the spirit and the flesh in relation to salvation. Pressured by the Minister to deny his body and by the cynical Homosexual to immerse himself in the profane as a path to the truly sacred, the Boy vacillates. At times he claims divine status; at times he insists, "I am only flesh." The chorus of Women, at once holy virgins and temple prostitutes, reinforces his confusion. Shortly after identifying him as "the Son of God," they refer to him as the "Chief Religious jelly roll of the universe." Given these irreconcilable roles, which he is expected to fulfill, the Boy's destiny as scapegoat and martyr seems inevitable; the dramatic tension revolves around the question of who will victimize him and why. Baraka uses a sequence of conflicting views of the Boy's role, each of which momentarily dominates his self-image, to heighten this tension.

Responding to the Homosexual's insistence that "the devil is a part of creation like an ash tray or senator," the Boy first confesses his past sins and demands baptism. When the Women respond by elevating him to the status of "Son of God/ Son of Man," he explicitly rejects all claim to spiritual purity. The ambiguous masquerade culminates in an attack on the Boy, who is accused of using his spiritual status to seduce women who "wanted to be virgins of the Lord." Supported only by the Homosexual, the Boy defends himself against the Women and the Minister, who clamor for his sacrifice, ostensibly as punishment for his sins. Insisting that "there will be no second crucifixion," the Boy slays his antagonists with a phallic sword, which he interprets as the embodiment of spiritual glory. For a brief moment, the figures of Christ as scapegoat and Christ as avenger seem reconciled in a baptism of fire.

Baraka undercuts this moment of equilibrium almost immediately. Having escaped martyrdom at the hands of the mob (ironically, itself victimized), the Boy confronts the Messenger, who wears a motorcycle jacket embellished with a gold crown and the words "The Man." In Baraka's dream allegory, the Man can represent the Roman/American legal system or be a symbol for God the Father, both powers that severely limit the Boy's control over events. The Boy's first reaction to the Messenger is to reclaim his superior spiritual status, insisting that he has "brought love to many people" and calling on his "Father" for compassion. Rejecting these pleas, the Messenger indicates that "the Man's destroying the whole works tonight." The Boy responds defiantly: "Neither God nor man shall force me to leave. I was sent here to save man and I'll not leave until I do." The allegory suggests several different levels of interpretation: social, psychological, and symbolic. The Boy rejects his responsibility to concrete individuals (the mob he kills, the Man) in order to save an abstract entity (the mob as an ideal man). Ultimately, he claims his right to the martyr's death, which he killed the mob in order to avoid, by repudiating the martyr's submission to a higher power. Losing patience with the Boy's rhetoric, the Messenger responds not by killing him but by knocking him out and dragging him offstage. His attitude of boredom effectively deflates the allegorical seriousness of the Boy's defiance, a deflation reinforced by the Homosexual's concluding comment that the scene resembles "some really uninteresting kind of orgy."

The Baptism's treatment of the interlocking themes of sacrifice, ritual, and victimization emphasizes their inherent ambiguity and suggests the impossibility of moral action in a culture that confuses God with the leader of a motorcycle gang. The encompassing irony of the Christ figure sacrificing his congregation to ensure universal destruction recalls T. S. Eliot's treatment of myth in *The Waste Land* (1922) and his essay "Ulysses: Myth and Order." Eliot's use of classical allusions and mythic analogies to underscore the triviality of modern life clearly anticipates Baraka's ironic vision of Christian ritual. Baraka's baptism initiates the Boy into absurdity rather than responsibility. If any sins have been washed away, they are resurrected immediately in pointless ritual violence and immature rhetoric. Although he does not develop the theme explicitly in *The Baptism*, Baraka suggests that there is an underlying philosophical corruption in European American culture, in this case derived from Christianity's tendency to divorce flesh from spirit. Increasingly, this philosophical corruption takes the center of Baraka's dramatic presentation of Western civilization.

DUTCHMAN

Widely recognized as Baraka's greatest work in any genre, *Dutchman* combines the irony of his avant-garde period with the emotional power and social insight of his later work. Clay, a young black man with a highly developed sense of self, occupies a central position in the play analogous to that of the Boy in *The Baptism*. The central dramatic action of the play involves Clay's confrontation with a young white woman, Lula, who may in fact be seen as an aspect of Clay's own self-awareness. In both thematic emphasis and dramatic structure, *Dutchman* parallels Edward Albee's *The Zoo Story* (pr., pb. 1959). Both plays focus on a clash between characters from divergent social and philosophical backgrounds, both comment on the internal divisions of individuals in American society, and both culminate in acts of violence that are at once realistic and symbolic. What sets *Dutchman* apart, however, is its intricate exploration of the psychology that leads Clay to a symbolic rebellion that ironically guarantees his real victimization. Clay *thinks* he exists as an autonomous individual struggling for existential awareness. Baraka implies, however, that this European American conception of self simply enforces Clay's preordained role as ritual scapegoat. As the Everyman figure his name suggests, Clay represents all individuals trapped by self-deception and social pressure. As a black man in a racist culture, he shares the more specific problem of those whose self-consciousness has been determined by white definitions.

The stage directions for *Dutchman* emphasize the link between Clay's situation and the decline of European American culture, describing the subway car where the action transpires as "the flying underbelly of the city . . . heaped in modern myth." Lula enters eating an apple, evoking the myth of the Fall. Together, these allusions contribute a literary dimension to the foreboding atmosphere surrounding the extended conversation that leads to Clay's sacrifice at the hands of Lula and the subway riders, mostly white but some black. Throughout, Lula maintains clear awareness of her symbolic and political intentions, while Clay remains effectively blind. Lula's role demands simply that she maintain the interest of the black man until it is convenient to kill him. Meanwhile, Clay believes he can somehow occupy a position of detachment or spiritual superiority. Changing approach frequently, Lula plays the roles of temptress, intellectual, psychologist, and racist. Clay responds variously to these gambits, sometimes with amusement, ultimately with anger and contempt. Consistently, however, he fails to recognize the genocidal reality underlying Lula's masquerade, unwittingly assuming his preordained role in the controlling ritual of black destruction. Much like the legendary ghost ship for which it was named, the *Dutchman*, Baraka implies, will continue to sail so long as blacks allow the white world to control the premises of the racial debate.

This rigged debate reflects Baraka's reassessment of his universalist beliefs and his movement toward Black Nationalism. Clay resembles the early LeRoi Jones in many ways: Both are articulate natives of New Jersey with aspirations to avant-garde artistic success. *Dutchman* implies that both are subject to fantasies about the amount of meaningful success possible for them in the realm of European American culture. Lula alternately reduces Clay to a "well-known type" and condemns him for rejecting his roots and embracing "a tradition you ought to feel oppressed by." During the first act, Clay stays "cool" until Lula sarcastically declares him the "Black Baudelaire" and follows with the repeated phrase "My Christ. My Christ." Suddenly shifting emphasis, she immediately denies his Christ-like stature and insists, "You're a murderer," compressing the two major attributes of the Boy in *The Baptism*, this time with a specifically social resonance. The sudden shift disrupts Clay's balance. Ironically restating and simplifying the thesis of Ralph Ellison's universalist novel *Invisible Man* (1922), Lula concludes the opening act with an ironic resolution to "pretend the people cannot see you . . . that you are free of your own history. And I am free of my history." The rapid movement from Clay as Christ and murderer—standard black roles in the fantasy life of white America—to the *pretense* of his freedom underscores the inevitability of his victimization, an inevitability clearly dictated by the historical forces controlling Lula, forces that Clay steadfastly refuses to recognize.

Clay's lack of awareness blinds him to the fact that the subway car, occupied only by himself and Lula during act 1, fills up with people during act 2. Continuing to manipulate Clay through rapid shifts of focus, Lula diverts his attention from the context, first by fantasizing a sexual affair with him and then by ridiculing him as an "escaped nigger" with absurd pretensions to cultural whiteness. Abandoning his cool perspective for the first time, Clay angrily takes "control" of the conversation. His powerful soliloquy establishes his superior understanding of his interaction with Lula, but only in the theoretical terms of European American academic discourse. Admitting his hatred for whites, Clay claims a deep affinity with the explosive anger lying beneath the humorous surface of the work of the great black musicians Bessie Smith and Charlie Parker. Ridiculing Lula's interpretation of his psychological makeup, Clay warns her that whites should beware of preaching "rationalism" to blacks, since the best cure for the black neurosis would be the random murder of whites. After this demonstration of his superior, and highly rational, awareness, Clay turns to go. He dismisses Lula with contempt, saying, "we won't be acting out that little pageant you outlined before." Immediately thereafter, Lula kills him. The murder is in fact the final act of the real pageant, the ritual of black sacrifice. Seen from Lula's perspective, the entire conversation amounts to an extended assault on Clay's awareness of the basic necessities of survival. Seen from Baraka's viewpoint, the heightened racial awareness of Clay's final speech is simply an illusion, worthless if divorced from action. Clay's unwilling participation

in the pageant of white mythology reveals the futility of all attempts to respond to white culture on its own terms. Regarded in this light, Baraka's subsequent movement away from the theoretical avant-garde and from European American modes of psychological analysis seems inevitable.

BLACK NATIONALIST PLAYS

Baraka's Black Nationalist plays, many of them written for community theater groups such as Spirit House Movers and the San Francisco State College Black Arts Alliance, occasionally employ specific avant-garde techniques. His earlier works take the techniques "seriously," but even his most experimental nationalist plays, such as *Experimental Death Unit #1*, clearly attempt to subvert the values implied by the European American aesthetic. Determined to communicate with his community through its own idiom, Baraka sought new forms in the African American aesthetic embodied in dance and music, African chants, experimental jazz, rhythm and blues, and reggae. Particularly when performed in predominantly black contexts, his work in this idiom creates an emotional intensity difficult to describe in standard academic terms, an atmosphere often extremely uncomfortable for white viewers. Even while embracing and exploiting the aesthetic potential of the idiom, however, Baraka attempts to purify and transform it. Repudiating his earlier vision of universal alienation and victimization, Baraka no longer sympathizes with, or even tolerates, passive scapegoats such as Clay and the Boy. He does not, however, remove the victim from the center of his drama. Rather, he emphasizes two new types of victims in his nationalist rituals: the clearly heroic African American martyr in *Great Goodness of Life (A Coon Show)* and *The Death of Malcolm X*, and the whitewashed black and overthrown white oppressor in *Madheart* and *Slave Ship*, portrayed as deserving their death.

MADHEART

Madheart and *Great Goodness of Life (A Coon Show)* employ different constellations of these figures to criticize the failure of the black community to purge its consciousness of European American values. Like *A Black Mass*, *Madheart* borrows the image of the "white devil" from the theology of the Nation of Islam (sometimes referred to inaccurately as the "Black Muslims") to account for the fallen condition of black awareness. Beginning with a confrontation between allegorical characters identified as Black Man and Devil Lady, *Madheart* focuses on the Devil Lady's influence over the Black Man's Mother and Sister, whose red and blonde wigs indicate the extent of their corruption. Aided by the supportive Black Woman, Black Man rejects and sacrifices the Devil Lady, symbolically repudiating white culture. Mother and Sister, however, refuse to participate in the ritual of purification. Sister loses consciousness, believing that the death of the Devil Lady is also her own death. Lamenting over her daughter, Mother calls on white "saints" such as Tony Bennett, Ludwig van Beethoven, and Batman for deliverance. Clinging to their belief in whiteness, Mother and a revived Sister descend to the level of slobbering animals. Motivated by love rather than hatred, Black Man turns a firehose on them as the play ends. His concluding speech echoes Baraka's basic attitude toward his suffering community: "This stuff can't go on. They'll die or help us, be black or white and dead. I'll save them or kill them." To avoid being sacrificed like Clay, Baraka implies, the African American community must repudiate its internal whiteness. The elimination of the white "devil," far from being an end in itself, is simply a preliminary step toward the purification of the black self-image.

GREAT GOODNESS OF LIFE (A COON SHOW)

Extending this critique of the internalization of white corruption, *Great Goodness of Life (A Coon Show)*, with its title ironic at several levels, focuses on the trial of Court Royal, a middle-aged black man accused of unspecified crimes. An offstage voice, supported by a sequence of increasingly respectable-looking Ku Klux Klan figures, echoes Lula in *Dutchman*, claiming that Court Royal has been harboring a murderer. Although Court Royal interprets the claim in concrete terms, the voice seeks primarily to bring about his repudiation of his black identity. Manipulating his fear of personal loss, the voice forces Court to preside over the ritual murder of a black martyr whose body is carried onstage to the accompaniment of projected slides showing martyrs such as

Malcolm X and Patrice Lumumba. Ordering the disposal of the corpse, the voice says: "Conceal the body in a stone. And sink the stone deep under the ocean. Call the newspapers and give the official history. Make sure his voice is in that stone too." In fact, the primary aim of the voice is to silence the African American cultural tradition by encouraging individuals to see their own situations as divorced from that of their community. Despite Court Royal's dim awareness that the "body" is that of a collective figure, the voice forces him to deny his sense that "there are many faces." After Court Royal acquiesces to this European American vision of individualism, the voice declares him "free," stipulating only that he "perform the rite." The rite is the execution of the "body."

Assuring Court Royal that the murderer is already dead, the voice nevertheless demands that he actively contribute to the destruction of the African American tradition by sacrificing the "murderer" within. To distract Court Royal from the genocidal reality of his act, the voice delivers an intricate statement on the nature of ritual action. Court, caught in the trap of European American rhetoric, ironically assumes the role of the white God and executes his symbolic son; the young black man cries out "Papa" as he dies. His soul "washed white as snow," Court merely returns to his night-out bowling. His voice sunk beneath the sea, he can only echo the white voice that commands his passive acceptance of European American rituals. Where Clay was killed by white society directly, the martyr in *Great Goodness of Life (A Coon Show)* is killed by white society acting indirectly through the timorous and self-deluded black bourgeois. Ritual murder metamorphoses into ritual suicide. Baraka clearly intimates the need for new rituals that will be capable of presenting new alternatives not under the control of the white voice.

SLAVE SHIP

Slave Ship, Baraka's most convincing and theatrically effective Black Nationalist play, develops both the form and the content of these rituals. Thematically, the play places the perceptions of *Madheart* and *Great Goodness of Life (A Coon Show)* in a broader historical perspective. Beginning in West Africa and progressing through the American Civil War, Baraka traces the evolution of African American culture, stressing the recurring scenes of betrayal in which traitors, frequently preachers, curry favor with their white masters by selling out their people. Such repeated betrayals, coupled with scenes of white violence against blacks, create a tension that is released only with the sudden ritual killing of the white voice and the black traitor. This sacrifice emphasizes Baraka's demand for an uncompromising response to the forces, inside and outside the community, responsible for centuries of black misery.

The real power of *Slave Ship*, however, stems from its performance style, which combines lighting, music, and at times even smell, to create an encompassing atmosphere of oppression that gives way to an even more overwhelming celebration. The sound of white laughter and black singing and moaning surrounds the recurring visual images that link the historical vignettes. A drumbeat reasserts itself at moments of tension and seeming despair, suggesting the saving presence of the African heritage. The drum, joined by a jazz saxophone as the black community rises to break its chains, initiates the celebratory chant: "When we gonna rise up, brother/ When we gonna rise above the sun/ When we gonna take our own place, brother/ Like the world had just begun?" Superimposed on the continuing background moaning, the chant inspires a communal dance that combines African and African American styles. Invoking the choreography of the "Miracles/Temptations dancing line," Baraka calls the dance the "Boogalooyoruba," compressing historical past and present in a ritual designed to create a brighter future. Following the climactic sacrifice, the severed heads of black traitor and white oppressor are cast down on the stage. Given ideal context and performance, the dancing of the Boogalooyoruba will then spread through the audience. *Slave Ship* thus exemplifies African American ritual drama of the 1960's; merging aesthetic performance and political statement, it marks the culmination of Baraka's black nationalist work.

PLAYS OF THE 1970'S AND 1980'S

Baraka's later plays express the Marxist-Leninist-Mao Zedong philosophy he embraced in the mid-1970's. Gauging the success of monumental dramas such as *The Motion of History* and *The Sidney Poet Heroical* is difficult, in part because they are rarely performed, in larger part because of a generally hostile political climate. The texts of the plays reflect Baraka's continuing interest in multimedia performance styles, incorporating a great deal of musical and cinematic material. Both plays comprise numerous brief scenes revealing the action of historical forces, primarily economic in *The Motion of History* and primarily racial in *The Sidney Poet Heroical*. Both present images of martyr-heroes and oppressor-scapegoats. On the page, however, both appear programmatic and somewhat naïvely ideological. The climaxes, for example, feature mass meetings intended to inspire the audience to political commitment, a technique anticipated in proletarian dramas of the 1930's such as Clifford Odets's *Waiting for Lefty* (pr., pb. 1935). The cries "Long live socialist revolution" and "Victory to Black People! Victory to all oppressed people!" that conclude *The Motion of History* and *The Sidney Poet Heroical* obviously require both a sensitive production and a politically sympathetic audience to work their desired effect. In the political climate of the late 1970's and 1980's, neither element was common, and Baraka's plays of this period could be considered closet dramas.

PRIMITIVE WORLD

In his 1984 *Primitive World: An Anti-Nuclear Jazz Musical*, he presents the money gods as the arch-fiends. Displeased at the audacity of the humans—and especially, the poor—to "want things," these money gods decide to put an end to human history. Speaking of the "grim moral" of his play, Baraka said, "we seem to be more endangered by greed and selfishness than we are by the weapons we have created to destroy each other." In this play, as in his earlier work, Baraka attempts to exorcise the demons and the demonic element within each human being that seem bent on nothing so much as the destruction of humanity—and, ultimately, of humankind.

In his speech on "Poetry and the Public Sphere" at the 1997 Conference on Contemporary Poetry, Baraka addressed more generally the recurrent theme of his work: "it is this wailing, this defiance, this resistance, this joy in the overwhelming of evil by good, that is at the base of our poetic traditions, our history, our continuing lives."

In his 1969 poem "Black Art," the poet asks that his poem "clean out the world for virtue and love"; and, bidding his poem scream, he cries, "Let Black People understand/ that they are the lovers and the sons/ of lovers and warriors and sons/ of warriors Are poems & poets &/ all the loveliness here in the world." In his still earlier drama *A Black Mass*, his black priest Tanzil speaks of reaching "back to warmth and feelings, to the human mind, and compassion. And ris[ing] again, back on up the scale, reaching again for the sphere of spheres, back to original reason. To where we always were." The exorcism of the demon oppressor in *A Black Mass* is not left to the imagination/intellect of the viewer as it is in *Primitive World*. The narrator of *A Black Mass* speaks to the audience of the need for diligence in the seeking out and in the destruction of the evil that the priests have let loose on the world in their experiment-gone-wrong—in their creation of the "soulless [white] monster." The oppressors in neither play recognize or employ the reason and the compassion possible to the occupants of this "sphere of spheres."

LATER PLAYS

When "White people. . . made [him] famous" for *Dutchman*, Baraka felt that they were making it possible for him to "continue [the] tradition" passed on to him by *his* people:

> I don't know if y'all still have that in your homes. . . . I can't speak on that, but I know that is what we as writers have to do, continue that tradition. The only way I can see that tradition being extended is through the role and function of the writer in the community.

It is not surprising that, while he was praised by such prominent African American authors as James Baldwin, Toni Morrison, Sonia Sanchez, Nikki Giovanni, Ntozake Shange, and Maya Angelou, the admittedly vengeful nature of much of his art did not afford him a sustained popularity with mainstream audiences and he found himself unable to make a living as a writer. According to Baraka, his 1982 *Money: A Jazz Opera* was even "banned in France by the United States" because it was considered "anti-American."

Baraka's 1990's plays *The Life and Life of Bumpy Johnson* and *Meeting Lillie* were somewhat less strident and, perhaps as a result, somewhat better received by mainstream critics.

Addressing a group of aspiring writers in 1998, Baraka spoke of his being readied by his parents and his grandmother for his life's work as out-of-the-mainstream writer and activist:

> It was like you had been doctored on by masters. . . . Every night at dinner, they'd be running it. . . . They would be telling you the history of the South, the history of Black people, the history of Black music and you would be sitting there. . . . My grandmother would tell me all the time about this Black boy they accused of raping this woman and they cut off his genitals and stuffed them in his mouth and then made all the Black women come there and watch. . . . Why would your grandmother tell you that story? . . . Oh, you still know the story, you still got it in your mind sixty years later. . . . Well, that's why she told it to you.

Baraka in his body of work strives to exorcise soullessness and to restore loveliness and humanity to humankind. Twentieth century African Americans, from Nobel Prize-winning author to factory worker, were influenced by the man who abandoned the title but not the role of imamu—spiritual leader. It remains to be seen whether the twenty-first century mainstream can overlook Baraka's and its own subjectivity in order that it may benefit, as well, from the spirit of his work.

OTHER MAJOR WORKS

LONG FICTION: *The System of Dante's Hell*, 1965.

SHORT FICTION: *Tales*, 1967; *The Fiction of LeRoi Jones/Amiri Baraka*, 2000.

POETRY: *Spring and Soforth*, 1960; *Preface to a Twenty Volume Suicide Note*, 1961; *The Dead Lecturer*, 1964; *Black Art*, 1966; *A Poem for Black Hearts*, 1967; *Black Magic: Sabotage, Target Study, Black Art—Collected Poetry, 1961-1967*, 1969; *It's Nation Time*, 1970; *In Our Terribleness: Some Elements and Meaning in Black Style*, 1970 (with Fundi [Billy Abernathy]); *Spirit Reach*, 1972; *Afrikan Revolution*, 1973; *Hard Facts*, 1975; *Selected Poetry of Amiri Baraka/LeRoi Jones*, 1979; *Reggae or Not!*,

1981; *Transbluesency: The Selected Poems of Amiri Baraka*, 1995; *Wise, Why's, Y's*, 1995; *Funklore: New Poems, 1984-1995*, 1996.

NONFICTION: *Blues People: Negro Music in White America*, 1963; *Home: Social Essays*, 1966; *Raise Race Rays Raze: Essays Since 1965*, 1971; *The New Nationalism*, 1972; *The Autobiography of LeRoi Jones/Amiri Baraka*, 1984, revised 1997; *Daggers and Javelins: Essays*, 1984; *The Music: Reflections on Jazz and Blues*, 1987 (with Amina Baraka).

EDITED TEXTS: *The Moderns: New Fiction in America*, 1963; *Black Fire: An Anthology of Afro-American Writing*, 1968 (with Larry Neal); *African Congress: A Documentary of the First Modern Pan-African Congress*, 1972; *Confirmation: An Anthology of African-American Women*, 1983 (with Amina Baraka).

MISCELLANEOUS: *Selected Plays and Prose*, 1979; *The LeRoi Jones/Amiri Baraka Reader*, 1991.

BIBLIOGRAPHY

Benston, Kimberly W., ed. *Imamu Amiri Baraka (LeRoi Jones): A Collection of Critical Essays*. Englewood Cliffs, N.J.: Prentice-Hall, 1978. A whole section, titled "Black Labs of the Heart," examines Baraka's drama in six essays on *Dutchman, The Slave, The Toilet, Great Goodness of Life (A Coon Show), Madheart*, and *Slave Ship*. "Baraka's theatre is one of deliverance, inexorably oriented toward liberation through confrontation," says Benston in her introduction. Contains a bibliography.

Brown, Lloyd W. *Amiri Baraka*. Boston: Twayne, 1980. Separating Baraka's literary output by major genre, Brown covers drama last, beginning with Mao Zedong's influence on the socialist perspective of such plays as *The Motion of History* and *S-1*. Even in Baraka's four early plays—*The Baptism, The Toilet, Dutchman*, and *The Slave*—Brown sees not an advocacy of revolution but "a highly effective analysis of American society" before his political views find an ideology. *Slave Ship* is a successful "ritual drama," Brown notes. Chronology, bibliography, index.

Gwynne, James B., ed. *Amiri Baraka: The Kaleidoscopic Torch*. Harlem, N.Y.: Steppingstones Press, 1985. This collection of essays hails Baraka as

torchbearer: "He opened tightly guarded doors for not only Blacks but poor whites as well, and of course, Native Americans, Latinos, and Asian Americans" (Maurice Kenny); "Baraka … stands with Wheatley, Douglass, Dunbar, Hughes, Hurston, Wright, and Ellison as one of the eight figures … who have significantly affected the course of African American literary culture" (Arnold Rampersad).

Harris, William J. *The Poetry and Poetics of Amiri Baraka: The Jazz Aesthetic*. Columbia: University of Missouri Press, 1985. In his study, Harris shows that "throughout his career, even during the . . . Marxist stage, [Baraka] has used the jazz aesthetic process to create a new black art from the artistic and conceptual innovations of the twentieth-century avant-garde." A late chapter discusses Baraka's significance to and influence on African American artists. Includes selected bibliography and index.

Hudson, Theodore R. *From LeRoi Jones to Amiri Baraka: The Literary Works*. Durham, N.C.: Duke University Press, 1973. The last chapter, "Not the Weak Hamlets," deals with Baraka's almost single-handed invention of black theater and his theory of the drama as "a device for [political] edification and motivation." Hudson states that six plays produced in 1964 and an Obie Award established Baraka as "the subject of serious critical consideration by the American theatre establishment." Index and bibliography.

Lacey, Henry C. *To Raise, Destroy, and Create: The Poetry, Drama, and Fiction of Imamu Amiri Baraka (LeRoi Jones)*. Troy, N.Y.: Whitston, 1981. Unlike other studies, which separate the works by genres, this volume divides Baraka's life into a Beat period, a transition, and a rebirth symbolized by taking on a new name. Also discusses Baraka's dramatic work in context with his writing in other genres. Supplemented by an index and a list of Baraka's works.

Reilly, Charlie, ed. *Conversations with Amiri Baraka*. Jackson: University Press of Mississippi, 1994. In the text's introduction, the editor prepares the reader for the telling of the story—"much of it told for the first time"—of "the acclaimed author who walked back into the ghetto to support his people and who never looked back." Includes chronology and index.

Sollors, Werner. *Amiri Baraka/LeRoi Jones: The Quest for a "Populist Modernism."* New York: Columbia University Press, 1978. Three chapters of this study deal with Baraka's drama. "From Off-Bowery to Off Broadway" provides a close study of *The Baptism* and *The Toilet*; *Dutchman* gets a whole chapter to itself. Good photograph section of production stills. Bibliography and index.

Watts, Jerry Gafio. *Amiri Baraka: The Politics and Art of a Black Intellectual.* New York: New York University Press, 2001. A critical appraisal of Baraka from his early Beat poetry and on. Watts argues that Baraka's artistry declined as he became more politically active, though he considers Baraka an important poet and lens through which African American political history can be viewed.

Craig Werner,
updated by Thomas J. Taylor,
Robert McClenaghan, and Judith K. Taylor

JAMES NELSON BARKER

Born: Philadelphia, Pennsylvania; June 17, 1784
Died: Washington, D.C.; March 9, 1858

PRINCIPAL DRAMA

Tears and Smiles, pr. 1807, pb. 1808

The Embargo: Or, What News, pr. 1808 (no longer extant)

The Indian Princess: Or, La Belle Sauvage, pr., pb. 1808 (libretto; music by John Bray)

Travellers: Or, Music's Fascination, pr. 1808 (adaptation of Andrew Cherry's play; no longer extant)

Marmion: Or, The Battle of Flodden Field, pr. 1812, pb. 1816 (based on Sir Walter Scott's poem)

The Armourer's Escape: Or, Three Years at Nootka Sound, pr. 1817 (no longer extant)

How to Try a Lover, pb. 1817, pr. 1836 (as *The Court of Love*; based on Charles-Antoine-Guillaume Pigault-Lebrun's novel *La Folie espagnole*)

Superstition: Or, The Fanatic Father, pr. 1824, pb. 1826

OTHER LITERARY FORMS

Although known chiefly as a dramatist, James Nelson Barker wrote some occasional verse, political poems and orations, and several newspaper essays on contemporary drama. His six biographical essays on notable Americans, including DeWitt Clinton, Robert Fulton, and John Jay, appeared in *Delaplaine's Repository of the Lives and Portraits of Distinguished Americans* (1817).

ACHIEVEMENTS

In the first half of the nineteenth century, when many American writers were struggling against a literary inferiority complex, James Nelson Barker was among the earliest of American dramatists to break new ground. His *The Indian Princess*, which took the story of Pocahontas as its central theme, was the first American Indian play ever to be performed. It began a dramatic tradition, providing a motif for American playwrights for the next fifty years. Not until the eve of the Civil War, when drama turned more toward realism, had the Pocahontas material run its course. Barker's use of the Indian as a literary motif predates by more than ten years the depiction of the Indian in the novels of James Fenimore Cooper and in the works of his contemporaries. Barker was thus among the first American writers to use native material as a corrective to what was perceived as the American writer's servile dependence on European, particularly British, literary influence.

Tears and Smiles, Barker's first play, contributed to the development of the stage Yankee, that bumbling yet shrewd New Englander whose individualism was distinctively American. Only twenty years after Royall Tyler introduced the stage Yankee in *The Contrast* (pr. 1787), Barker created the character of Nathan Yank, a major link in the chain of Yankee plays that were to remain popular throughout the first half of the nineteenth century.

Barker's crowning achievement was the last of his five extant plays. First performed in 1824, *Superstition* is one of the earliest dramas to use colonial history as its source. Dealing primarily with the bigotry and fears of a New England village in the late seventeenth century, the play is a tragedy that anticipates some of the ideas and characters later to be found in the works of Nathaniel Hawthorne. It is the most controlled of Barker's dramas, and in its fusion of historical material with convincing character motivation, it remains the best American play of its time.

BIOGRAPHY

The fourth son of John Barker, one of Philadelphia's foremost citizens, James Nelson Barker was educated in public schools and became, in his early teens, a wide reader. Though he did not go to college, he was familiar enough with some of the world's great authors to begin, at the age of twenty, his first play, based on a story by Miguel de Cervantes. This play, *The Spanish Rover*, was left unfinished and has not survived. By 1805, Barker had completed two acts of a proposed tragedy entitled *Attila*, suggested by his reading of Edward Gibbon's five-volume work, *The History of the Decline and Fall of the Roman Empire* (1776, 1781, 1788); this play has also been lost. The only knowledge of these early efforts comes from Barker's autobiographical account of his dramatic career, written for William Dunlap's *History of the American Theatre* (1832).

Though these fledgling works attest Barker's early interest in drama and indicate the scope of his reading, they also make a point about his creative imagination. The subject matter, the setting, and even the characters of both works were foreign. Attila's Rome and Cervantes' seventeenth century Spain were far removed from the bumptious America of the early Republic; the results were therefore simple false starts. In contrast, when the occasion arose for the writing of a play with an American milieu as its setting, Barker's imagination took fire.

That occasion was a hunting trip in 1806. One of Barker's companions, a theater manager, knowing of the young man's dramatic interests, asked Barker to write an American play, and a prominent actor of the day, Joseph Jefferson, who specialized in Yankee characterizations, asked that Barker include a Yankee type. Barker set to work, and in forty-three days, he completed his first play, *Tears and Smiles*, produced the following year. In his preface to the published work, Barker derides the popular opinion among critics that a successful drama had to be European in plot, setting, and character. As if poking fun at himself and his two earlier, abortive efforts, he quotes a fictitious friend who suggests that he, Barker, abandon his scheme of delineating American manners and instead "write a melodrame [*sic*] and lay [your] scene in the moon."

Having written one play, Barker, only in his early twenties, turned his youthful exuberance into more worldly pursuits. At this time, the city of Philadelphia had fallen under the spell of a sort of soldier of fortune, General Don Francisco de Miranda. Miranda wanted to liberate Venezuela and in time secure independence for all South America. In pursuit of this goal, he was seeking enlistments, promising wealth and glory to all who volunteered for the cause of freedom. Whether Barker was moved by the democratic fervor of the times or had merely surrendered to the swashbuckling Byronism of the scheme, he nevertheless left for the port of New York in August, 1806, with the idea of joining the expedition in Trinidad, West Indies. News of Miranda's defeat, however, and a series of letters from his father urging him to come home resulted in Barker's return to Philadelphia early in 1807.

This frustrated adventure can be seen as a catalyst in Barker's creative process, for his next play, first acted in March, 1808, was a political satire, *The Embargo*. Borrowing extensively from a British play by Arthur Murphy, *The Upholsterer* (1757), Barker's comedy was to be the most topical of his works. Never printed and since lost, the play was probably heavily allusive to President Thomas Jefferson's embargo of British shipping in commercial retaliation for British seizures of American vessels during this period when Britain was engaged in a war with France, led by the Emperor Napoleon I. Little else is known about what was probably Barker's least important work.

In April, 1808, Barker's third completed play was produced. *The Indian Princess* was a historically significant production, the first dramatization of the Pocahontas story. The play was enormously influential—so popular, in fact, that, by Barker's own account to Dunlap, it was eventually acted in every theater in the country. It was also the first original American play to be performed in England after its premiere in the United States.

Barker's next dramatic work was a trivial affair, an adaptation of *Travellers: Or, Music's Fascination* (pr. 1806), by British author Andrew Cherry. A kind of musical panorama, the play was never printed, and though it was a modest success when performed during the Christmas season of 1808, it was, by Barker's admission, only "a little less absurd" than its original. It has been deservedly forgotten.

After this flurry of dramatic activity, Barker began to sow the seeds of his own political future, probably at the urging and with the help of his father, who was by 1809 the mayor of Philadelphia. Becoming active in the Democratic Party of the city, Barker was sent to Washington, D.C., with letters of introduction from his father to President James Madison. There he served as his father's lobbyist and listening post; his letters to the mayor, from his arrival in the capital in December, 1809, to his departure in March, 1810, are filled with political gossip, reports of evening balls and social entertainments, and frequent pleas for more money, always postscripted by appropriately filial apologies.

Returning to Philadelphia, Barker met and married Mary Rogers in 1811, took up portrait painting as a hobby, and wrote *Marmion*. The product of his reading of Sir Walter Scott, the play was not only a dramatization of Scott's poem of the same title but also a skillful conflation of other sources relating to the subject. In particular, Barker used material from the chronicles of Raphael Holinshed. The result was a play that was fast-paced and tightly structured. *Marmion* turned out to be Barker's longest-running stage work. Interestingly, it was his first successful drama on a nonnative subject, and this on the eve of the War of 1812, when national pride and patriotism were rising.

As it did for many, the war enabled Barker to develop his political career. Appointed a regimental captain of artillery, Barker soon saw active service at Fort Erie and at Buffalo, New York. After returning to Philadelphia, he became a principal recruiting officer in the region, mustering several hundred men; served as captain in the Artillery Corps; and was appointed brevet major by 1814.

At the war's end, Barker ran for the Pennsylvania Assembly on the Democratic ticket. Though defeated, he made many political friends, who helped him a short time later to be appointed a city alderman. It was a crucial political position, for only two years later, in 1819, Barker, like his father before him, became the mayor of Philadelphia. His one-year term, from October, 1819, to October, 1820, was marked by honesty, efficiency, and courage. He trimmed the city budget, cutting his own salary first; raised money for national relief programs; and reorganized the city's police and militia during a time of civil unrest.

Defeated for reelection, Barker also suffered a deep personal loss: Over the next two years, three of his children died. Barker's loyalty to the Democratic Party was remembered, however, when Andrew Jackson became president and named Barker to the post of collector of the port of Philadelphia, a political plum, one of the choicest fruits of Jackson's spoils system. Barker held this post from 1829 to 1838.

Meanwhile, Barker's literary career continued to flourish. In the midst of his political activities leading to his post as alderman, Barker returned to a native subject for a play. *The Armourer's Escape* was a dramatization of John Jewitt's narrative of his captivity among the Nootkian Indians. Captivity narratives, real or fictional, were popular in England and in the

United States during the late seventeenth and eighteenth centuries; Jewitt was counting on such literary precedent to promote the sales of his own adventures. His book was a failure, however, and he turned to the dramatist for help. The play was never printed and is now lost.

How to Try a Lover, though written shortly after the Jewitt dramatization, was not produced until almost twenty years later, though Barker remarked to Dunlap that it was the play with which he was most satisfied. Set in thirteenth century Spain, this comedy of love forsworn and finally consummated was based on Charles-Antoine-Guillaume Pigault-Lebrun's novel *La Folie espagnole* (1801). This charming, extremely actable play is not representative of that aspect of Barker's work that is most notable—namely, his use of native material.

Barker's use of such native sources resulted in his finest work, *Superstition*. In this work, the use of history meshes with sound dramatic instinct; the drama is regarded as one of the best American plays of the period. Serious, dark, and intense, the play shows a control of plot, character, and language that few dramatists had yet attained and which gains in effectiveness when one remembers that Barker wrote the play in the years immediately following the deaths of his children and his defeat for reelection to the mayoralty.

Although *Superstition* was Barker's last play, he continued, throughout the next decade, to supply newspapers and magazines with pedestrian occasional verse, patriotic centennial odes on such themes as the birthday of George Washington and on the founding of the state of Pennsylvania.

The last twenty years of Barker's life were spent in various positions in the U.S. Treasury Department in Washington, D.C. The demands of such service effectively curtailed his literary career. He remained a respected figure in Washington until his death.

Analysis

James Nelson Barker must be considered a significant influence in the history of American drama because of his use of native material, together with his lifelong advocacy of a native American theater. His most creative period, from 1808 to 1824, coincided with a growing sense of U.S. literary nationalism, that sentiment by which American authors sought to produce a native literature that reflected the nation's character, customs, manners, and ideals. The forceful preface to his *Tears and Smiles*, for example, condemns the reverent attitude of American critics toward European standards. Denouncing these reviewers as "mental colonists," intellectually submissive to British opinion, Barker calls for a sort of declaration of literary independence, a repudiation of foreign models and an embracing of national cultural material.

Tears and Smiles

Barker's earliest play, *Tears and Smiles*, succeeds on two counts. It is, first, a quickly moving, sprightly work, filled with the youthful exuberance of an author in his early twenties. Exuberance, indeed, is a crucial ingredient, for the recipe of plot and character is otherwise spoiled by convention and claptrap. Second, the piece has some genuine historical value as an early example of the portrayal of the stage Yankee, here named Nathan Yank.

Influenced by Tyler's *The Contrast*, *Tears and Smiles* relies on traditional elements of melodrama. Louisa Campdon, the heroine, has been promised by her father to the delicate dandy, Mr. Fluttermore, whose very name is suggestive of characters from Restoration drama. Louisa, however, is in love with Sydney, a young man of recognized valor but uncertain parentage who has returned from Tripoli and the wars against the Turkish pirates to reclaim her love. The Turkish allusions show how alert Barker was to literary and theatrical trends. Tyler had used the motif in his novel *The Algerine Captive* (1797), and the Turkish or Oriental motif had been popular in the early gothic romances; in addition, operatic composers such as Christoph Gluck, Wolfgang Amadeus Mozart, and Gioacchino Rossini (Barker's contemporary) had staged Turkish operas.

By the end of the comedy, thanks to the intercession of characters such as General Campdon (Louisa's uncle) and the Widow Freegrace, the lovers are united and the fop appropriately chastened. Sydney is also reunited with his long-lost parents, who have been separated for years and suffered from pirates, slavery, and family disapproval. Such characters and situations were typical of the drama of the period, and *Tears and Smiles* is grievously weakened as art by its heavy reliance on them.

Still, the play is worthy of attention for its lively humor and satire as Barker pokes fun at Americans' seduction by European modes and manners. The opening scene quickly clears the ground for satire when Louisa's uncle protests her proposed marriage to Fluttermore, who, when he left America, was a clever, honest fellow but who has returned from his travels abroad "a puppy . . . with a pale face and a hearty contempt for everything this side of the water." Meanwhile, Barker skillfully delays Fluttermore's entrance until near the end of act 1, when Fluttermore saunters onstage with Monsieur Galliard, a combination companion and valet. The scene is humorous, with bluff Jack Rangely, the second lead, shaking hands so cordially that he knocks the powder from Fluttermore's wig. By giving Fluttermore "Frenchified" rather than Anglicized affectations, Barker provides a variation on the standard portrayal of the British fop and makes a topical point about French influence on American fashion and theater at the time. "I can't conceive what you possibly do in this corner of the globe," says Fluttermore, disparaging American manners. "No opera; no masquerade, nor *fête*, nor *conversazione*." Later, writers from Hawthorne to Henry James would seriously lament America's lack of European refinement, that sense of history and rich cultural precedent, a lack that they saw as a limiting force on the American imagination. Yet here, at the dawn of American literary nationalism, foppish Fluttermore's denigration of American culture is distinctly comic.

Of special comic interest in *Tears and Smiles* is Nathan Yank, the first stage Yankee of the nineteenth century. Introduced in Tyler's *The Contrast*, this comic figure was to be one of the most popular and enduring types on the American stage. He was generally depicted as an honest, homespun bumpkin who very often was the butt as well as the perpetrator of jokes and whose comic antics were often dramatic set pieces, independent of the main action. Actors such as Joseph Jefferson, George Handel Hill, and Joshua

Silsbee made their living playing Yankee characters. "Yankee" Hill was particularly notable for delivering Yankee monologues or yarns, a device that surely must have provided comic precedent for Mark Twain.

Barker's Nathan Yank added little to the characterization already drawn by Tyler some twenty years before. Nathan retains his predecessor's bumptiousness, for example, and holds the same status, that of servant, but whereas Tyler's Jonathan is boorish, he is also his own man. Jonathan shows a Puritan reliance on biblical precept as well as a practical sense of getting on in the world. His love scenes with Jenny, his social equal, prove him to be a man as well as a clown, a man of independent temperament, despite his status as servant.

In contrast, Nathan Yank never goes beyond the range of low comedian. He misdirects his master, Rangely, for example, by mistaking one house for another, and he indulges in a series of puns at the expense of Rangely's lover. To Rangely, who does not know her name, she is his "incognita," but Nathan henceforth refers to her as "Cognita." Inexplicably, Barker drops Nathan from the action by act 4, and Nathan is noticeably absent at the finale in act 5.

Although Nathan's shallow, one-dimensional buffoonery and his rather peripheral position in the action seem to represent a retrogression or at least a pause in the development of the stage Yankee, there is, on a closer reading of the play, an important advance in his use of dialect. Although Tyler's Jonathan used dialect inconsistently, shifting arbitrarily from formal English to homely solecism, Nathan Yank is almost always dialectical, more consistently ungrammatical. From his first "I reckon" in act 1 to his "tarnal long" in his last appearance, Yank speaks strictly homespun American. This move toward a more consistent use of dialect was an important step in the transmission of the Yankee type.

THE INDIAN PRINCESS

If *Tears and Smiles* is notable for its exuberance, *The Indian Princess* is marked by self-consciousness and a nationalistic sense of purpose. The preface to the printed edition begins with a plea to both critics and theatergoers to take American drama seriously. Barker laments the poor reception American plays have received from critics and publishers, decrying the fact that acknowledged American productions simply die, like orphans, from "total neglect." As for *The Indian Princess* in particular, he urges the public not to denigrate the play simply because it "cannot lisp the language of Shakespeare." Like all living things, he says, American drama must first creep before it can walk. Finally, in a tone that adumbrates the pronouncements of Ralph Waldo Emerson and Walt Whitman, Barker predicts that America will bring forth "a dramatic genius" once the "stagnant atmosphere of entire apathy" is dispelled.

Though Barker's remarks may be seen as a self-serving acknowledgment of his pioneering role in the development of native drama, *The Indian Princess* is far from the work of genius predicted so confidently by its author. Despite its numerous failures, however, the play has genuine merit.

The first play to use the story of Pocahontas as its central idea, *The Indian Princess* was also the first of Barker's plays based on an authentic historical text. The advertisement to the 1808 edition credits Captain John Smith's *The Generall Historie of Virginia, New England, and the Summer Isles* (1624) as being the principal source, adding that the author has preserved "as close an adherence to historic truth" as the demands of the drama allowed.

An examination of Smith's account reveals just how cannily Barker used his source material. The Pocahontas episode in Smith (which in the opinion of some historians is of questionable truth) is narrated in the third person and is quickly told in a brief paragraph. The central scene in which Pocahontas puts her own head on the block to save Smith takes only a sentence. Barker casts this somewhat fleeting, almost offhand reference into the central episode of the play. It comes in the opening of act 2, not quite halfway through the three-act drama. Some critics have suggested that this crucial scene comes too early in the play, with the result that the third act tends to be rather anticlimactic.

If the statement in the advertisement about adhering to historical truth is taken as significant of Barker's intention, then the scene is rightly placed, for it serves as the central link in the chain of histori-cal events that follow—namely, John Rolfe's love of the Indian Princess and their subsequent marriage, which cemented the bond between the English colonists and an important Indian tribe in the region, headed by Pocahontas's father, Chief Powhatan. Historically, Powhatan did seek English allies for his fight against the Susquehannocks, and in the closing scenes of Barker's play such an alliance takes place, both historically and symbolically, when all the lovers are united: Rolfe with Pocahontas; Robin (one of Smith's men) with Nima, Pocahontas's lady in waiting; and no less than three other pairs of lovers, Indian and white.

At the end of the play, Smith praises America as the new Eden, a new world "disjoined from old licentious Europe." This idea of America as a fresh start, an innocent, uncorrupted land untainted by history and therefore rich in human possibility, was a common thread in the skein of American literature during the nineteenth century. Barker's use of the idea so early in the century points out once again his pioneering sense of literary nationalism.

For all of its dramatic interest, however, the play is not without serious flaws. As in *Tears and Smiles*, Barker relies on conventional characters and situations, particularly in the scenes involving the minor pairs of lovers, such as Larry, the stage Irishman who loves Kate and who carries a potato in his pocket and commits execrable puns.

The play was originally intended as a straight drama, but Barker was persuaded to turn it into an opera—"an operatic melodrame," as the title page announces. As a result, some of the scenes are mere interludes, set pieces of vapid verse, set to music by a composer named Bray, which do little to advance the action or to discover character.

The most damaging weakness of *The Indian Princess* is Barker's inability to render effective, believable dialogue. The Indians speak, like their white counterparts, in blank verse or in orotund periods. Only on rare occasions does Barker even attempt to distinguish the speech of Indians from that of whites. These attempts often result in such rhetorical infelicities as Powhatan's exclamation at seeing Captain Smith for the first time: "Behold the white being."

The love scene between Pocahontas and Rolfe is tender, evocative, and romantic, but echoes of William Shakespeare's *Romeo and Juliet* make Pocahontas's blank verse difficult to credit:

> Thou art my life!
> I lived not till I saw thee, love; and now
> I live not long in thine absence. . . .

Barker's failure to treat the Indian in other than romantic terms (even the evil medicine man, Grimosco, and the rival, Miami, are but red-skinned gothic villains) typifies the problem faced by the early American writer who recognized the Indian as a legitimate literary property but who could not properly assimilate him into a creditable literary context because of subversive cultural differences.

SUPERSTITION

For his finest work, *Superstition*, Barker once again turned to authentic colonial records. Drawing its main outlines from Thomas Hutchinson's *The History of Massachusetts* (1795), *Superstition* is set in a New England village in 1675. Ravensworth, the minister, is a zealous but cold man who is obsessed with what he sees as "the dark sorcery" practiced by Isabella, a late arrival to the village, who "scorns the church's discipline" and holds herself aloof from the neighbors. Isabella's son Charles is in love with Ravensworth's daughter Mary, an added motive feeding Ravensworth's obsession.

To this basic plot situation, Barker successfully fuses a second motif, based also on a historical incident. A small group of Puritans who had presided over the execution of Charles I in January, 1649, were forced to flee England at the restoration of Charles II in 1660. Though the majority were later granted amnesty, some were excepted and lived under assumed identities in the New World. Barker drew on this theme of the so-called regicides for the creation of the character of the Unknown, a mysterious figure living in exile in a cave deep in the wilderness. As the play unfolds, the Unknown saves the village from Indian attack by instilling courage and leading the colonists in a counteroffensive. In the end, he turns out to be a regicide and Isabella's long-lost father, in search of whom she has come to the New World.

The melodramatic elements inherent in this character and in his discovered relationship with Isabella seriously mar the aesthetic integrity of the play. Similarly, Ravensworth, whose obsession ultimately causes the deaths of Charles, Isabella, and his own daughter, has much of the melodramatic one-sidedness of a gothic villain.

Yet the power of *Superstition* is undeniable. Its effectiveness lies in Barker's complete mastery in fusing historical event with psychological motivation. The characters' behavior and their various fates are dramatically represented as largely the results of historical forces at work; there is an inevitability to the action. Action and character, in fact, are inseparable, as in all effective tragedy. Ravensworth's single-minded determination to root out "with an unsparing hand/ The weeds that choke the soil," his conviction that "the powers of darkness are at work among us," is made clear in the opening scene, and this obsession hangs over the characters and the action as a central, remarkably sustained idea.

There is strong temptation to speculate on the influence of *Superstition* on Hawthorne, who was an undergraduate at Bowdoin College when the play was first produced. Hawthorne, indeed, would later use the theme of the regicides in his short story "The Gray Champion," and Ravensworth's obsession is anticipatory of the diabolic singleness of purpose of Roger Chillingworth in Hawthorne's *The Scarlet Letter* (1850); even the similarity of surnames is notable. It could be argued, as well, that Isabella's independent piety and relative isolation are strongly suggestive of the character of Hester Prynne.

Regardless of whether *Superstition* was a direct early influence on Hawthorne, it stands on its own as a convincing treatment of a dark episode in American colonial history and as solid evidence of Barker's legacy to the American theater.

OTHER MAJOR WORKS

NONFICTION: "Peyton Randolph," "Thomas Jefferson," "John Jay," "Rufus King," "DeWitt Clinton," and "Robert Fulton," in *Delaplaine's Repository of the Lives and Portraits of Distinguished Americans*, 1817.

BIBLIOGRAPHY

Moody, Richard. *America Takes the Stage*. Bloomington: University of Indiana Press, 1955. Reprint. Milwood, N.Y.: Krause Reprints, 1977. The author particularly notes Barker's use of native themes and characters. Though his *The Indian Princess* was the first play in which Pocahontas appeared as a principal figure, Barker relied too closely on the undramatic nature of his source, John Smith's *The Generall Historie of Virginia, New England, and the Summer Isles* (1642), and presented the famous scene too early. Much of the rest of the play is thus anticlimactic.

Musser, Paul. *James Nelson Barker, 1784-1858*. St. Clair Shores, Mich.: Scholarly Press, 1970. This definitive study, though brief, traces Barker's life and career from his early education in Philadelphia to his political career as collector of the port during the administration of President James K. Polk. Musser includes the complete text of *Tears and Smiles* and sees Barker as a writer who, by temperament and training, was a leading advocate of native material in American drama.

Richards, Jeffrey, ed. *Early American Drama*. Chapel Hill: University of North Carolina Press, 1998. This discussion of early American plays contains an analysis of Barker's *The Indian Princess*, along with descriptions of other early works.

Scheckel, Susan. "Domesticating the Drama of Conquest: Barker's Pocahontas on the Popular Stage." *American Transcendental Quarterly* 10, no. 3 (September, 1996): 231-243. The author discusses Barker's *The Indian Princess* in its historical context.

Vaughn, Jack A. *Early American Dramatists from the Beginnings to 1900*. New York: Frederick Ungar, 1981. One chapter presents a short study of Barker's five extant plays. Though noting Barker's use of melodrama and sentimentality, Vaughan also says that Barker knew how to write effective drama and could be "genuinely moving," especially in *Superstition*, probably his best play.

Edward Fiorelli

PETER BARNES

Born: London, England; January 10, 1931

PRINCIPAL DRAMA

The Time of the Barracudas, pr. 1963
Sclerosis, pr. 1965
The Ruling Class: A Baroque Comedy, pr. 1968, pb. 1969
Leonardo's Last Supper, pr. 1969, pb. 1970
Noonday Demons, pr. 1969, pb. 1970
Lulu, pr. 1970, pb. 1971 (conflation of Frank Wedekind's *Der Erdgeist* and *Die Büchse der Pandora*)
The Bewitched, pr., pb. 1974
The Frontiers of Farce, pr. 1976, pb. 1977 (adaptations of Georges Feydeau's *On purge Bébé!* and Wedekind's *Der Kammersänger*)
Antonio, pr. 1977 (radio play), pr. 1979 (staged; adaptation of John Marston's plays *Antonio and Mellida* and *Antonio's Revenge*)
Laughter!, pr., pb. 1978
Collected Plays, pb. 1981
Red Noses, pr., pb. 1985
Plays: One, pb. 1989
Revolutionary Witness, and Nobody Here but Us Chickens, pb. 1989
Sunsets and Glories, pr., pb. 1990
Plays: Two, pb. 1993
Corpsing, pr., pb. 1996
Plays: Three, pb. 1996
Dreaming, pr., pb. 1999
Jubilee, pr., pb. 2001

OTHER LITERARY FORMS

Peter Barnes is known primarily for a wide range of theater-related activities. He is an editor, adapter, and director of stage and radio plays and cabaret. He has also written many screenplays as well as worked as a story editor for Warwick Films. Barnes draws an important distinction between his film work, in which he is simply practicing a craft, and his stage plays, which are the product of an inner compulsion.

ACHIEVEMENTS

Peter Barnes is a controversial English playwright with an international reputation. His plays are all complex, seriocomic or satirical studies in opposites and extremes. For the most part, he writes highly theatrical, nonrealistic, antiestablishment plays, which employ elements of farce; alienation or dislocation effects such as the rapid succession of short, contrasting scenes or the unexpected introduction of songs and dance; and surrealistic devices. His work contains echoes of English Renaissance dramas, English music hall, American vaudeville, musical comedy, and motion pictures. His theatrical language is richly textured, full of neologisms; literary, biblical, and historical allusions; and British and American slang. In his historical plays, he creates special, eccentric languages with their own period flavor. Most of his own radio plays are more realistic, but his characters and situations are always extraordinary or disturbing. Barnes constantly attacks the corruption of the powerful, the greedy, and the obsessed, and defends the victims of society: the lonely, the old, the dispossessed, and the disadvantaged.

Although Barnes's view of the world is pessimistic, he expresses, particularly in the plays after 1978, a glimmer of hope that the world can be improved. Laughter can be used by the powerful to divert attention from their oppression of the less fortunate, but it can also be a major source of good, and Barnes's plays reverberate with irreverent laughter at social or religious pretensions and an absurd universe. Barnes's work is distinguished by its disturbing subject matter, its rough, often vulgar energy, and its spectacular stage effects. His universe is in turmoil, with no clear direction or purpose. Barnes mirrors ontological anxiety by playing on the paradoxes and ambiguities of life and by juxtaposing contrasting moods, which ultimately prevent any true comic or tragic resolution.

Barnes has also made considerable contributions to the theater and to radio drama as reviver, editor, adapter, and director of plays, both English and European, hitherto neglected in England. His own collections of radio plays for the British Broadcasting Corporation (BBC) earned for him the Giles Cooper Award for Radio Drama in 1981 and 1984. For his stage plays, he won the John Whiting Award in 1968 and the *Evening Standard* Award in 1969 for *The Ruling Class*, and the Olivier Award for Best Play of the Year, 1985, for *Red Noses*. In 1989, *Nobody Here but Us Chickens* won the Royal Television Society Award as the year's best television drama.

BIOGRAPHY

Peter Barnes was born in the East End of London on January 10, 1931. His mother, a Jew, and his father, an Anglican who converted to Judaism, later moved the family to the holiday resort of Clacton-on-Sea, Essex, where they ran an amusement arcade on the pier. He has one younger sister. During World War II, Barnes was evacuated to the county of Gloucestershire. After the war, he returned to Clacton and completed his formal education at a local grammar school, followed by a year's compulsory military service. He continued his education at night school in London while working as a civil servant for the Greater London Council and as a freelance film critic. In 1954 he was film critic for *Films and Filming*, and the following year he became a story editor for Warwick Films. From about 1958 to 1967, he worked freelance on a number of screenplays, including *Violent Moment* (1958), *The Professionals* (1960), *Off Beat* (1961), and *Ring of Spies* (1964). In 1961, he married Charlotte Beck, a secretary at the British Film Institute, who died in 1994. In 1995, he married Christine Horn.

His own first play, *The Man with a Feather in His Hat*, was produced for television in 1960. His first stage play, *The Time of the Barracudas*, was produced in San Francisco and Los Angeles in 1963, but

Peter Barnes in London in 1990. (AP/Wide World Photos)

it failed, and Barnes refused permission for any subsequent productions. In 1965, his one-act play *Sclerosis* was produced at the Edinburgh Festival and later at the Aldwych Theatre, London, directed by Charles Marowitz. In 1968, Barnes achieved considerable public success with his award-winning play, *The Ruling Class*, at the Nottingham Playhouse, later performed at the Piccadilly Theatre, London, directed by Stuart Burge. This play, more than any other of Barnes's works, has been staged all over the world, and a film version, starring Peter O'Toole, with screenplay by Barnes, released in 1972, established his international reputation.

Also in 1969, Barnes's two one-act plays *Leonardo's Last Supper* and *Noonday Demons* were played at the Open Space Theatre, London, directed by Charles Marowitz. His next full-length play, *The Bewitched*, was produced in 1974 by the Royal Shakespeare Company at the Aldwych, directed by

Terry Hands, and received mixed reviews. *Laughter!* was produced by the Royal Court Theatre in 1978, directed by Charles Marowitz, Barnes having correctly anticipated that this work would displease most critics. That same year he completed *Red Noses, Black Death*, which, thanks at least in part to the unfavorable reception of *Laughter!*, was not to be seen until 1985 in a production by the Royal Shakespeare Company at the Barbican, London, directed by Terry Hands, the title shortened to *Red Noses*.

Barnes occupied himself between stage productions by editing, conflating or adapting, and occasionally directing, plays by Ben Jonson: *The Alchemist* (pr. 1610) and *The Devil Is an Ass* (pr. 1616) at the Nottingham Playhouse, co-directed by Stuart Burge; *Bartholomew Fair* (pr. 1614) at the Roundhouse, London, under his own direction; and also plays by Thomas Middleton, George Chapman, Thomas Otway, Georges Feydeau, and Frank Wedekind, both for the stage and for radio. One notes particularly the success of *Lulu*, produced in Nottingham and London in 1970; *Antonio*, an adaptation/conflation of John Marston's *Antonio and Mellida* (pr. 1599) and *Antonio's Revenge* (pr. 1599), first heard on BBC radio in 1977 and later staged at the Nottingham Playhouse in 1979; and *The Frontiers of Farce*, produced at the Old Vic in 1976.

In an effort to refine his skills and experiment with plays employing smaller casts, Barnes worked on three sets of short radio dramas—monologues, duologues, and three-character plays—produced by the BBC in 1981, 1984, and 1986 respectively, under the headings of *Barnes' People I*, *Barnes' People II*, and *Barnes' People III*. These plays, acted by such great performers as Sir John Gielgud, Dame Edith Evans, Paul Scofield, Alec McCowen, Peter Ustinov, and Ian McKellen, were very well received in Great Britain and won two drama awards. Barnes also remained active in live theater, directing a 1987 London production of *Bartholomew Fair* and writing *Sunsets and Glories*, which was produced in 1990.

ANALYSIS

Peter Barnes's plays are a heady mixture of many theatrical forms in which the visual elements are important; the written text falls far short of offering the true effect of a good production. Barnes claims that "the aim is to create, by means of soliloquy, rhetoric, formalized ritual, slapstick, songs and dances, a comic theatre of contrasting moods and opposites, where everything is simultaneously tragic and ridiculous." Most reviewers and critics agree about the theatrical brilliance and ingenuity of his plays, but opinion is divided about the significance or depth of his views of the human condition. Barnes is concerned with the pressures of society (authority) that suppress openness of feeling and deny happiness (freedom). His plays attack class, privilege, and whatever prevents the realization of individual or group fulfillment. In his view, revolution, even anarchy, may be better than meek submission. Above all, Barnes reveals the fierce tenacity with which groups or individuals hold on to or grasp at power and make society less human. Even devotion to God conceals selfish-

ness, encourages persecution, or is a form of madness or obsession. Barnes is constantly preoccupied with people's inhumanity to others and with God's seeming indifference to human suffering. Although most of his plays suggest that the world is beyond redemption, there are small but significant gleams of hope in the darkness, especially in the plays after 1978, and the comic vitality in all of his works mitigates Barnes's anger and pessimism.

THE RULING CLASS

Barnes's first published play, *The Ruling Class*, ridicules the English upper classes, the House of Lords, the Anglican Church, public schools (expensive private upper-class institutions), the police, English xenophobia, psychiatrists, snobbery, and complacency. The play begins with the death of the thirteenth earl of Gurney. Dressed in a tutu and military dress hat and jacket, and brandishing a sword, the earl indulges in a recreational mock-hanging in order to induce intoxicating visions; he accidentally kills himself. His son, Jack, the fourteenth earl, becomes the focus of the family's efforts to marry him off to Grace Shelley, have him produce an heir, and then certify him insane. He is a threat because of his egalitarian views; he believes himself to be the God of Love reincarnated.

The loving earl is a paranoid schizophrenic with enormous energy and an eccentric verbal exuberance, but his delusions make him an easy victim. When asked why he thinks he is God, he replies, "Simple. When I pray to Him I find I'm talking to myself." His uncle, Sir Charles, persuades Grace, his mistress, a former actress and stripper, to impersonate Marguerite Gautier, the Lady of the Camelias, to whom the earl thinks he is already married. She arrives at a crucial moment dressed as the heroine of Giuseppe Verdi's *La Traviata* (1853), complete with wax camelias, singing the famous "Godiam" aria. In this splendid scene, the earl sings and dances with her.

The main focus of the play is on Jack as the New Testament God of Love and what he becomes after Dr. Herder's "cure": the Old Testament God of Wrath and Justice and Jack the Ripper. No longer open, spontaneous, and joyful, Jack becomes repressed, Victorian, and as such acceptable to the ruling class.

The pivotal scene is the confrontation arranged by Dr. Herder between the madman McKyle, the High-Voltage Messiah, and Jack, the God of Love. This scene presents the symbolic death of Jack as Jesus, and his rebirth, coinciding with the birth of Jack's son and heir, as God the Father. Jack's "change" is demonstrated by his being attacked by a surreal, apelike monster dressed in Victorian garb, a Victorian Beast who possesses him, although it is unseen by the others onstage, and Jack's pummeling seems to be an epileptic seizure. Act 2 shows Jack's successful efforts to establish his normality, dominate his family, and become a bulwark of respectability, while as Jack the Ripper he carries on a private war against sexuality by murdering his amorous Aunt Claire and, ultimately, his wife. His maiden speech in the House of Lords on the need of the strong to crush the weak receives rapturous applause: He is one of them at last.

NOONDAY DEMONS

Noonday Demons also deals with religion, this time the folly of the "saintly" anchorite's wish to purge himself of the sins of the flesh. Saint Eusebius is shown in his cave in the Theban desert, ragged and in chains, attempting to rid himself of "old style man": "In destroying my body I destroyed Space and Time," he claims. He can see into the future and communes with angelic voices. Challenged and tempted by an inner demon, he successfully resists wealth, lust, and power. When another anchorite, Saint Pior, arrives and lays claim to Saint Eusebius's cave, conflict between the two holy men quickly develops, each saint being convinced that he alone interprets God's will and that the other must be a demon. Saint Eusebius kills Saint Pior, and he is again able to commune with the angels, but the play's ending undercuts his triumph as, transported to the present, he can see how the theater audience watching *Noonday Demons* regards his life as meaningless and bizarre.

LEONARDO'S LAST SUPPER

Leonardo's Last Supper, set in the grisly Ambois charnel house to which Leonardo da Vinci's corpse has been taken, introduces the audience to the squabbling Lasca family, forerunners of modern morticians, fallen on hard times. They toast their good luck in having been sent a "golden carcass" that will restore their wealth and reputation. Yet Leonardo is not dead, although when he awakes in such a place he finds it hard to believe that he is alive. The Lascas are not interested in the gratitude of future generations for preserving "the universal man." They are the new men: "Men o' trade, o' money, we'll build a new heaven and a new earth by helping ourselves." To them, Leonardo is a luxury, as are the things he represents: beauty, truth, knowledge, and humanity. Seeing their trade being taken away from them, they seize, kill, and prepare Leonardo for burial, a family happily reunited in their business pursuits.

THE BEWITCHED

The Bewitched is long and complex, but one can recognize in it many of the themes explored in Barnes's earlier plays, with a heightened savagery and ironic intensity to them: cruelty and violence performed in the name of a God of Love; demoniac possession and angry confrontations between "holy" men; the professional pride and dedication of destroyers of people, from doctors and astrologers to torturers for the Inquisition; the absurd tenacity with which the Spanish grandees cling to their often ludicrous privileges; and the unscrupulous ways in which people behave when driven to pettiness, greed, folly, jealousy, and murder. *The Bewitched* is a concentrated attack on the madness of people's blind respect for hierarchical order.

The play deals in particular with the reign of Carlos II, the last of the Spanish Habsburgs. The end product of prolonged inbreeding, Carlos is sickly, impotent, epileptic, and the pawn of unscrupulous politicians, leaders of church and court. The play records some of the intrigues and incredible devices used to keep Carlos alive and to induce him to produce an heir to the Spanish throne and thus preserve the privileged caste. Carlos dies childless, his throne passes to the Bourbons, and the terrible War of the Spanish Succession follows: "One million dead. Two million wounded. Western Europe is in ruins." The reign of Carlos is "a glorious monument to futility." In one of his few lucid moments in the play, Carlos presents Barnes's most open attack on the system when he says,

Now I see Authority's a poor provider.
No blessings come from 't
No man born shouldst ha' t', wield 't . . .
'Twill make a desert o' this world
Whilst there's still one man left t' gi' commands
And another who'll obey 'em.

LAUGHTER!

Laughter! is the most extreme and controversial of Barnes's plays. Its thesis is voiced by the character of the Author, who introduces the play: "Comedy is the enemy," the ally of tyrants. "It softens our hatred. An excuse to change nothing, for nothing needs changing when it's all a joke." He asks the audience to root out laughter, "strangle mirth, let the heart pump sulphuric acid, not blood." This plea is accompanied by some diverting, zany stage business, including a whirling bow tie and trousers falling to reveal spangled underpants.

Part 1 deals with the reign of Ivan the Terrible; part 2 with Auschwitz. Ivan is reluctant either to wield power or to surrender it; nevertheless, in the name of authority, he slaughters thousands and kills his own son to protect him from the pain of exercising power. Finally, an Angel of Death, dressed like a seedy office clerk, confronts Ivan. After wrestling with this relentless antagonist, Ivan is petrified into a statue, befouled by bird droppings.

In part 2, the setting is Berlin, where petty bureaucrats Else Jost, Victor Cranach, and Heinz Stroop live out their working lives. It is Christmas Eve, 1942. They are visited by the snooping, fanatical Nazi, Gottleb. In spite of wartime shortages and constant fear of the authorities should they deviate from the expected norm, they manage a kind of drunken festivity, and induce an ambiguous vision of the truth behind their façade of loyalty. They rail against their superiors and intellectuals, and finally fire off a round of subversive anti-Hitler jokes. Gottleb then summons a vision of what their paperwork is really masking: the production of flues for the crematoriums at Auschwitz. Onstage, a graphic, horrible representation of the death agonies of those gassed by hydrocyanide is shown with dummies in place of human beings. Horrified, the bureaucrats cannot translate

coded office numbers into the brutal facts. They throw out Gottleb and find solace in being "ordinary people, people who like people, people like them, you, me, us." The epilogue introduces the farewell Christmas concert appearance of the Boffo Boys of Birkenau, Abe Bimko and Hymie Bieberstein, whose awful dance and patter routine comes to an end as the gas does its work.

RED NOSES

Red Noses, a most complex play, elaborates many of the themes found in *The Bewitched* and modifies some of the ideas expounded in *Laughter!* Faced with the horror of the Black Death, which has removed more than a third of the population of Europe, what can a small, bizarre group of entertainers do to improve the world? Given the facts that the Church, prayers, medicine, and wealth are helpless against the plague, Father Flote and his group of "Christ's Clowns," wearing red noses, can at least give the dying some consolation. They are sanctioned by Pope Clement VI and become agents of Church power, a distraction from the real world.

Yet Barnes also suggests that laughter can be associated with revolution and redemption. Opposed to the Floties are the Black Ravens, who see the plague as a chance to create an egalitarian society. Another opposing group, the Flagellants, seek no social change but defy the Church establishment and wish to atone for sin by self-inflicted punishment and direct appeal to God. Inevitably the Church cannot tolerate such deviations and eventually destroys both the Black Ravens and the Flagellants. The Church tolerates the Floties, however, even after the end of the plague, until Father Flote, realizing that there are valuable qualities in the beliefs of the two outlawed groups—that laughter is in fact revolutionary as well as a corrective to sin—defies papal authority and advocates SLOP, "Slow, Lawful, Orthodox Progress." Laughter will no longer be only for losers but can be a force for social and personal improvement. The Church regards Father Flote's defiance as a threat, and the Red Noses are executed. The importance of the individual, the need for social reform, and the positive power of "the laughter of compassion and joy" are at last united in a new and more positive way in a play that is highly complex and richly textured.

BARNES' PEOPLE I-III

The three collections of radio plays, too numerous to discuss here, are particularly interesting as illustrations of the transition Barnes makes from deep pessimism to a more positive view of the world. The outstanding play in *Barnes' People I* is "Rosa," about an aging, disillusioned, but still dedicated social worker. She has a brief, devastating vision of an army of geriatrics on the rampage, raging against the waste of their lives; her vision ends, however, and she knows that she must go on, working with the system, however imperfect it may be: "Slow, Lawful, Orthodox Progress." "The Three Visions," the last play of *Barnes' People III*, is a discussion between Barnes at age thirty-one, Barnes at age fifty-five, and Barnes at age seventy-four. It is clear that however little he believes he has contributed to his profession, he goes on with the struggle and never compromises.

DREAMING

Barnes's play *Dreaming* dramatizes the story of Captain John Mallory, a heroic warrior who has just taken part in the successful Battle of Tewkesbury, at the end of the War of the Roses, and who longs for home. To Mallory, home represents not a mere building but rather his family and friends. In this drama, which resembles a picaresque novel in its episodic form and its inclusion of many rogues, Mallory proceeds from scene to scene, encountering new characters and demonstrating his strength and bravery as he attempts to fulfill his dream of finding his home. He does come home and finds that his wife, Sarah, is displeased with him for having been gone for six years while fighting for the York side. He wakes up and realizes that he has been dreaming, that Sarah and their daughter, Anna, have been killed and are buried nearby. The rest of the play continues his quest to fulfill his dream of finding home. He even finds a woman who looks nothing like Sarah, Susan Beaufort, yet he initially makes himself believe—and even convinces her—that she is Sarah. He marries Susan and continues his quest to find her home—a dangerous task given that she is the last of the lucky Beauforts, the enemy of the duke of Gloucester. The

play is pessimistic, perhaps even nihilistic, in that Barnes suggests that Mallory's dream of finding a home is unattainable. The drama also concerns the importance of heroism and bravery. As Mallory pursues his dream-quest, he is aided by valorous men and women: Bess, Davy, Jack Skelton, Jethro Kell, and his new bride, Susan Beaufort. They fight for—and die for—his dream. In *Dreaming*, Barnes portrays not only the beauty of idealism but also its inherent dangers in a world filled with self-centered and ambitious people. Mallory believes that he has achieved his goal when he sees the Beaufort castle (he hopes to find the home of his new in-laws), yet what he witnesses is actually a dream, an illusion. Gloucester hopes to murder Susan Beaufort (now Susan Mallory), but she has frozen to death. Shortly before she dies, Susan, comprehending Mallory's guilt for leaving Sarah and Mallory's desire for home, claims that she is now Sarah.

Dreaming is in some respects a typical Barnes play. It is full of sharp wit, violence, and biting social criticism. Despite the dark tone of the play, the characters are quite humorous. For instance, Marie tells Mallory that her late husband was so dull that "when he masturbated his hand went to sleep." As the rogue Cobett dies, he leaves his legacy to his children: "Remember what I've taught you. Strive—reach for glory. You're murdering cut-throats. Strive to be the very best murdering cut-throats . . . Make me proud." Jethro Kell, the lucky Beauforts' chaplain, possesses a crucifix that contains a sharp dagger that he employs as a weapon. Barnes most probably is satirizing the role of the Catholic Church in fifteenth century England. Furthermore, the lucky Beauforts are being wiped out by Gloucester and are thus anything but lucky. *Dreaming*, therefore, contains humor that is reminiscent of the wit that exists in previous dramas such as *The Ruling Class* and *Laughter!* As with these two plays, and others by Barnes, the characters are not three-dimensional but rather are types, vehicles who help the dramatist get across his satire. *Dreaming* contains thirty-four characters and unusual scenes such as characters who fall in and out of open graves and characters who skate and perform triple-axles and other feats. This fact demonstrates that

Barnes continues to write plays his way—irregardless of whether they can be staged practically.

Barnes is a purist who, in many respects, writes for himself. For example, Barnes stages *Laughter!* despite his realization that it will anger some audience members. He has found success with his radio plays, *Barnes' People*. These radio plays contain one, two, or three characters; it is ironic that in some respects, such as practicality, these radio plays, although they are brief, are more stageable than *Dreaming* and other Barnes plays that have been performed onstage. Although Barnes is quite witty, it can be argued that his best plays are his earliest ones, such as *The Ruling Class* and *Laughter!*

OTHER MAJOR WORKS

SCREENPLAYS: *The White Trap*, 1959; *Not with My Wife You Don't*, 1966 (with others); *The Ruling Class*, 1972 (adaptation of his play); *An Enchanted April*, 1992 (adaptation of Elizabeth von Arnim's novel); *Voices*, 1995 (with Nicholas Meyer; in U.S. as *Voices from a Locked Room*).

TELEPLAYS: *The Man with a Feather in His Hat*, 1960; *The Spirit of Man*, 1989; *Merlin*, 1998 (with David Stevens); *Noah's Ark*, 1999; *Arabian Nights*, 2000.

RADIO PLAYS: *Barnes' People I: Seven Monologues*, 1981; *Barnes' People II: Seven Duologues*, 1984; *The Real Long John Silver and Other Plays: Barnes' People III*, 1986; *The Spirit of Man and More Barnes' People: Seven Monologues*, 1990.

TRANSLATION: *Tango at the End of Winter*, 1991 (a play by Kunio Shimizu).

BIBLIOGRAPHY

Barnes, Peter. "Theater of the Extreme: An Interview with Peter Barnes." Interview by Mark Bly and Doug Wager. *Theater* 12 (Spring, 1981): 43. Barnes talks about his relationship to Brechtian imagination and rules for the theater, as a catalyst for social change. Barnes calls for the revival of English dramatic classics and states that "comedy transcending tragedy" is a characteristic of modern times.

Dukore, Bernard F. *Barnestorm: The Plays of Peter Barnes*. New York: Garland, 1995. Dukore revises his earlier work on the playwright to create the most significant scholarship on the plays of Peter Barnes. The book is comprehensive and covers all the major plays in detail. Dukore's book contains several articles that he has published previously.

Golumb, Liorah Anne. "The Nesting Instinct: The Power of Family in Peter Barnes's *The Ruling Class* and *The Bewitched* (with additional dialogue by William Shakespeare." *Essays in Theatre* 17 (1998): 63-75. Golumb's article covers two important plays by Barnes as well as the issue of the dramatist's portrayal of family.

Hiley, Jim. "Liberating Laughter: Peter Barnes and Peter Nichols in Interviews with Jim Hiley." *Plays and Players* 25, no. 6 (March, 1978): 14-17. Barnes discusses *Laughter!*, his 1978 play at the Royal Court, dealing with "man's inhumanity to man" in the form of Ivan the Terrible and Auschwitz. "Cruelty . . . has progressed into something more systematic" than the personal affair of the feudal times, he says. Discusses his adaptation of Ben Jonson's plays and his controversy with critics over his style and content.

Hinchliffe, Arnold P. *British Theatre, 1950-1970.* Totowa, N.J.: Rowman and Littlefield, 1974. A journalistic style introduces the "rocket that came from Nottingham" with his play *Sclerosis*, produced at the Traverse Theatre. The author notes that Barnes "had been a playwright for ten years and screenwriter for fourteen" before his success with *The Ruling Class*. Also discusses *Lulu* and two one-act plays. Good midcareer assessment.

Sterling, Eric. "Peter Barnes's *Auschwitz* and the Comedic Dilemma." *European Studies Journal* 17-18 (2000-2001): 197-211. This article analyzes Barnes's ideas on comedy and how it can be dangerous and a weapon used against the vulnerable, such as during the Holocaust.

Weeks, Stephen. "Peter Barnes." In *British Playwrights, 1956-1995*, edited by William W. Demastes. Westport, Conn.: Greenwood, 1996. Weeks's section on Barnes is a very helpful tool for those interested in doing scholarship on the playwright.

Worth, Katharine J. *Revolutions in Modern English Drama*. London: G. Bell and Sons, 1972. The chapter entitled "Forms of Freedom and Mystery: Beneath the Subtext" places Barnes in the company of Samuel Beckett, Joe Orton, and Heathcote Williams. Worth describes Barnes as taking the "farce in curious new directions, mixing it with melodrama in a most unlikely and distinctive style." Contains a long discussion of *The Ruling Class*.

Worthen, W. B. *Modern Drama and the Rhetoric of Theater*. Berkeley: University of California Press, 1992. Deals with *Laughter!* at length: "To read *Laughter!* as about Auschwitz alone is crucially to misread the play's theatrical design," says Worthen, adding that the play "stages the spectator's performance as part of its critique of history." Good index.

Ian C. Todd,
updated by Thomas J. Taylor and Eric Sterling

SIR JAMES BARRIE

Born: Kirriemuir, Scotland; May 9, 1860
Died: London, England; June 19, 1937

PRINCIPAL DRAMA

Ibsen's Ghost: Or, Toole Up to Date, pr. 1891, pb. 1939

Richard Savage, pr., pb. 1891 (with H. B. M. Watson)

Walker, London, pr. 1892, pb. 1907

The Professor's Love Story, pr. 1892, pb. 1942

The Little Minister, pr. 1897, pb. 1942 (adaptation of his novel)

The Wedding Guest, pr., pb. 1900

Quality Street, pr. 1902, pb. 1913

The Admirable Crichton, pr. 1902, pb. 1914

Little Mary, pr. 1903, pb. 1942

Peter Pan: Or, The Boy Who Wouldn't Grow Up, pr. 1904, pb. 1928

Alice-Sit-by-the-Fire, pr. 1905, pb. 1919

Josephine, pr. 1906

Punch, pr. 1906

What Every Woman Knows, pr. 1908, pb. 1918

The Twelve-Pound Look, pr. 1910, pb. 1914

The Will, pr. 1913, pb. 1914

Der Tag: Or, The Tragic Man, pr., pb. 1914

The New Word, pr. 1915, pb. 1918

A Kiss for Cinderella, pr. 1916, pb. 1920

Dear Brutus, pr. 1917, pb. 1923

The Old Lady Shows Her Medals, pr. 1917, pb. 1918

Barbara's Wedding, pb. 1918, pr. 1927

A Well-Remembered Voice, pr., pb. 1918

Mary Rose, pr. 1920, pb. 1924

Shall We Join the Ladies?, pr. 1921, pb. 1927

The Boy David, pr. 1936, pb. 1938

Representative Plays, pb. 1954

OTHER LITERARY FORMS

The sheer volume of Sir James Barrie's literary output, together with the fact that his most successful and enduring works were written for the stage, tends to obscure recognition of his talent in other genres. His success as a playwright came when he was already launched as a writer. The vignettes and anecdotes of his literary apprenticeship had formed the basis for the successful *Auld Licht Idylls* (1888), and Barrie might have been content to continue drawing on his Scottish experiences in the form of articles and essays in the then popular "Kailyard" (cabbage-patch) style but for his determination to write a novel. Success in this genre came eventually with *The Little Minister* (1891), written in the same vein as the *Auld Licht Idylls*.

Barrie returned to the Scottish setting in *Margaret Ogilvy* (1896), a biography based on sentimental recollections of his mother. Questions were raised as to the genre of the work, and reviewers in Scotland were shocked by the detailed ruthlessness of his observation. No less revealing is the largely autobiographical novel *Sentimental Tommy* (1896), which, together with its sequel, *Tommy and Grizel* (1900), throws considerable light on Barrie's complex personality.

The novel *The Little White Bird* (1902) contained a blueprint for the development of the Peter Pan theme, but it was the successful dramatization of *The Little Minister* that finally channeled Barrie's literary efforts away from the novel toward the stage. The foundation of Barrie's career as a playwright was his determination to master the novel and to capitalize on his potentially limiting Scottish background and childhood experiences.

ACHIEVEMENTS

Sir James Barrie was a prolific and versatile writer who enjoyed great popularity in his day, but he tends to be remembered only as the creator of *Peter Pan*. This enduringly popular work was the most successful play of Barrie's entire career, but it is uncharacteristic of his writing in that it was aimed at a children's audience. The secret of its undiminished popularity lies in Barrie's ability to appeal on different levels to both adults and children.

The bulk of Barrie's writing has now sunk into relative obscurity. It may be that his other works, and particularly his plays, are too closely tied to the spirit of the age in which they were conceived, or that their psychology is too naïve and their characters too transparent for modern taste. Nevertheless, Barrie's achievements as a playwright should not be assessed on the merits of *Peter Pan* alone.

Taken in the context of his dramatic works as a whole, *Peter Pan* can be seen to be a natural development of an escapist tendency that frequently motivates Barrie's plays. Often his plots center on a juxtaposition of a fantasy world with the "real" world as it is represented on the stage—real for the characters themselves and accepted as such by the audience. Barrie's preoccupation with psychological escapism can be attributed to his own tendency to fantasize in his closest personal relationships. Additionally, by involving his characters in the mechanics of a fantasy

world as distinct from a theatrical representation of the real world, Barrie gives himself much greater scope for social criticism: Fantasy worlds are used to highlight the shortcomings of the real world.

BIOGRAPHY

James Matthew Barrie was of humble origins, the seventh of the eight surviving children of David Barrie, a Scottish weaver. Barrie's mother, Margaret Ogilvy, was a strict Puritan, reared in the fundamentalist beliefs of the Auld Lichts (Old Lights), a sect of the Presbyterian Church of Scotland. The unusual strength of the influence she exerted over Barrie throughout his life was detrimental to him in many ways. When he was six, his older brother David, aged nearly fourteen and his mother's favorite, died after a skating accident. Margaret Ogilvy was desolate in her loss, and the young James made a conscious effort to become a substitute for David, to help her overcome her grief. This was the beginning of the sharp divi-

Sir James Barrie (Hulton Archive by Getty Images)

sion for Barrie between home, where he was acting out a fantasy in his most intimate relationship, and the outside, real world.

Barrie entered Dumfries Academy in 1873, and while there he began to be interested in all aspects of the theater. He was a founding member of a school dramatic society and left school intent on becoming a writer. Family opposition was strong, however, and reluctantly he entered Edinburgh University, graduating in 1882. During his years as an undergraduate, he wrote as a freelance drama critic for the Edinburgh *Courant*. After an unsuccessful year spent in Edinburgh researching a book on the early satirical poetry of Great Britain, he answered an advertisement for a job as leader-writer for the *Nottingham Journal*. Editorial supervision was virtually nonexistent, and Barrie wrote extensively for the paper under a variety of names. He began sending articles to London, undaunted by frequent rejections.

In 1884, Barrie returned to Scotland, where he wrote up his mother's childhood memories. "An Auld Licht Community" was published in the *St. James's Gazette*, and the editor requested more in the same vein, which Barrie found easy to provide. The following year, he decided that to make a career of writing he would have to be in London, so he moved south. He managed to sell articles steadily and before long was making a respectable living. His first successful book, a collection of Scottish articles, *Auld Licht Idylls*, appeared in 1888; together with *A Window in Thrums* (1889), it raised a storm of protest in Scotland, but Barrie was undeterred.

Barrie was now writing furiously, working simultaneously on a novel, *The Little Minister*, and a play. The part of the second leading lady in *Walker, London* went to Mary Ansell, whom Barrie ultimately married in 1894. The marriage, apparently unconsummated, ended in divorce in 1909, their companionship having been disrupted by the extraordinary way that Barrie was attracted to the Llewelyn Davies family, initially to the children, George (born 1893), Jack (born 1894), and Peter (born 1897), but later to Sylvia Jocelyn Llewelyn Davies, their mother. Barrie met her at a dinner party in 1897 and subsequently met the children in Kensington Gardens. They were

enchanted by his stories, and he would frequently accompany them home. It was not long before he was behaving like a member of the family, despite the reluctance of their father, Arthur Llewelyn Davies, to accept this situation.

The year 1900 saw the birth of the Llewelyn Davies' fourth son, Michael, and Mary Barrie's purchase of Black Lake Cottage on the outskirts of Farnham, Surrey. Here Barrie and the three older Davies boys spent the summer of 1901 enacting adventures and fantasies in the overgrown gardens, setting the scene for *Peter Pan*. It was not until 1903, however, after the success of *Quality Street*, *The Admirable Crichton*, and *Little Mary*, that Barrie began the play that was to make him a household name.

In 1906, two years after the birth of his fifth son, Nicholas, Arthur Llewelyn Davies was diagnosed as having cancer. Unable to earn at the bar, he had no alternative but gratefully to accept Barrie's offer of financial support for his family. Barrie was by now spending almost all his free time with the Davies family, leaving his own wife, Mary, very much alone. In the three-year period between Arthur's death and her own in 1910, Sylvia Davies received continuous support and attention from Barrie, and when she died Barrie took on himself the guardianship of her sons— "My Boys," as he called them. Of the five, he seems to have been closest to George, killed in France in 1915, and Michael, drowned at Oxford in 1921. Michael's death prostrated Barrie, but he was helped over it by Lady Cynthia Asquith, who had been acting as his personal assistant since 1917. Barrie's relationship with her developed along similar lines to his relationship with Sylvia Llewelyn Davies. He frequently assisted the Asquiths out of financial difficulties with generous presents to Cynthia and became imperceptibly an extension of their family, in the face of the opposition and dislike of Herbert (Beb) Asquith, an aspiring writer.

For a shy man, Barrie was by this time a very prominent figure. Having declined a knighthood in 1909, he had accepted a baronetcy in 1913 and was awarded the Order of Merit in 1922. He was unfailingly generous with his money, and during World War I he funded and organized the establishment of a home for refugee mothers and children in France. He continued a voluminous correspondence even after being forced by pain in his right hand to train himself to write with his left.

Barrie's last play, *The Boy David*, written for the Austrian actress Elisabeth Bergner, received highly critical notices. Cynthia Asquith arranged a command performance that should have been a triumph for Barrie but ended up as an unremarkable matinee, and the playwright died shortly afterward, a disappointed man.

ANALYSIS

In his dramas, only once (in *Der Tag*) did Sir James Barrie abandon comedy as his medium of expression. His plays are known for their lighthearted whimsicality and are enjoyed for the elements of farce that even the more serious ones, such as *Dear Brutus*, contain. The majority of his characters are little more than caricatures, but Barrie nevertheless succeeds in capturing the essence of each, not least because of the careful notes about them that usually form part of the text of a given play. Comedy of character is augmented by verbal humor and a deft handling of the comic situation to put the theme of the play across to the audience with a minimum of effort. The result is that a Barrie play seems light, almost flippant, with the underlying social message only fleetingly apparent. Although the tenor and atmosphere of his plays faithfully reflect the society that filled the theaters when they were first produced, Barrie's themes and preoccupations are no less relevant today.

WALKER, LONDON

Walker, London was Sir James Barrie's third attempt at writing for the stage, but the first to meet with any real success. The idea for the setting came from a summer Barrie had spent on a houseboat on the Thames, and the play captures the lazy indolence of life moored to the riverbank. It is not by any means an outstanding work but is of interest as an early approach to the question of the relationship between fantasy and the real world, which was to become a constant preoccupation in Barrie's subsequent works.

The pleasant lethargy of the party on the houseboat is disturbed but not spoiled by an uninvited guest, an undistinguished London barber by the name of Jason Phipps. Phipps has run away from the reality of his everyday life, and for the duration of his holiday, which should have been his honeymoon, has decided to assume the identity of one of his customers, the celebrated African explorer Colonel Neil. Mrs. Golightly and the other members of the houseboat party are indebted to the newcomer for his ostensibly heroic action in saving Bell Golightly from drowning in a punting accident, and they are delighted to be able to offer hospitality to one so famous. The audience, however, is well aware that Neil is an impostor. He has bribed the only witness of the accident to support the heroic version of the episode, and he is being diligently searched for by his jilted fiancée. During the week that Phipps spends on board the houseboat, he regales the company with vivid descriptions of the adventures he has had on his explorations, drawing his listeners unwittingly into the fantasy he is building. As Neil, Phipps makes proposals to both Bell Golightly and her cousin Nanny O'Brien—proposals that they find difficult to reject, because they are caught up in the fantasy, too. As himself, however, Phipps realizes that the girl for him is the faithful Sarah, who catches up with him in the end. The last act is virtually pure farce and ends with Phipps making a quick exit into his everyday life before he can be unmasked.

Barrie had originally intended the play to be entitled "The Houseboat," but there was another work in existence by that title and thus a new one had to be found. As Phipps leaves the stage for the last time, he is asked for his address. He gives it as Walker, London, the new title of the play: "Walker" was a slang word meaning a hoaxer.

QUALITY STREET

The theme of assumed identity recurs in *Quality Street*, which was first produced in October, 1902, only one month before the equally successful *The Admirable Crichton*, enjoying a run of fourteen months. As with *Walker, London*, the definitive title of the play was a later alteration. The working title was "Phoebe's Garden," but Quality Street, the name of an actual town between Leith and North Berwick, appealed to Barrie; the final title subtly reinforces the notions of hidebound respectability with which the play deals.

The action takes place in Quality Street during the Napoleonic Wars. The heroine, Miss Phoebe Throssel, has fallen in love with a local doctor, Valentine Brown. Both Phoebe and her sister Susan, an old maid, expect that "V. B.," as they refer to him, is calling to make his declaration and ask for Phoebe's hand. Unfortunately, it becomes apparent that he has other news: He has enlisted in the army and will be leaving forthwith to join the campaign against the French. The Misses Throssel cover their disappointment admirably and, as convention demands, say nothing of love.

The second act takes place ten years later. The blue and white frilliness of the Throssel parlor has been subordinated to the requirements of a classroom. It transpires that Phoebe and Susan, having invested their money according to Brown's advice, have suffered a substantial loss and have been forced to earn their living by opening a school. Phoebe appears to have aged much more than ten years, assuming prematurely the garb and attitudes of the old maid she seems destined to become. The sisters' new way of life is highly distasteful to them, but for respectable women in their position, society offers no other choice. Their drab existence is suddenly brightened by the return of Valentine Brown and the rest of the troops. The doctor is visibly struck by the change in Phoebe when he calls on the Throssels unexpectedly, for she is at her most severe in her schoolmistress attire. Phoebe suddenly realizes that she no longer has to act older than her years. They have caught up with her, and she has come a long way from being the pretty girl that she was when the troops left for the war.

When Phoebe next appears on the stage, she has discarded her cap and drab clothes and has pulled out all her ringlets, so that she is virtually her former self, except for what she has experienced during the ten years. It is in this guise that Brown sees her next. She is inspired to pass herself off as her own niece, Miss Livvy, a ploy that her sister is pushed into supporting.

The mechanics of the deception give rise to some comic scenes, particularly when the sisters find themselves having to deceive their gossipy and envious friends, the Misses Willoughby. By wearing the same fashionable veil as her friend, which can be opened or closed at will by the wearer, Phoebe is accepted as Miss Livvy, but the ladies sense a mystery and are desperate to find out what is happening.

Phoebe daringly sets out on a round of balls given to celebrate the victory, and act 3 shows her in full swing, acting in her assumed identity in an outrageously flirtatious way and turning the heads of all the men present. She is determined to take revenge on Valentine Brown for having forgotten that he kissed her once, ten years before. For all those years she treasured both the memory of the kiss and her guilt at the impropriety of having allowed him to kiss her, only to find on his return that he does not even remember the event. The climax comes when it looks as though Brown is going to propose to Livvy, and she is preparing to reject him out of hand. Much to her surprise, however, he confesses that it is her aunt Phoebe whom he really loves; in courting her, so much like her aunt in appearance but so different in behavior, he has come to realize where his affections really lie, and where they have always lain.

The sisters now have to find a way of getting rid of the unwanted Livvy. She takes to her bed and Phoebe reappears, but the Misses Willoughby are extremely solicitous. As it seems inevitable that the deception will be discovered, the tension rises until Valentine Brown, in his capacity as a doctor, goes into Livvy's bedroom and reappears to report on the progress of the patient who does not exist. He then joins forces with the sisters to dispose of Livvy. He wraps the phantom up and takes her out to his carriage, which is sent off with the maidservant in attendance to convey the sick Livvy home. The suspicions of the watching neighbors are lulled and the way is clear for Valentine Brown to make his proposal and for it to be accepted by his beloved Phoebe.

In *Quality Street*, the assumption of a new identity is not a *fait accompli* as in *Walker, London*. It is a deliberate ploy, but it is seen to happen onstage in direct response to a development in external circumstances affecting the character. Whereas the character assumed by Jason Phipps was based on an idealization of the attributes of a person unknown to the audience, Phoebe finds her model in her own past, so her escape from her own personality is more pragmatic and less fanciful; the essence of her assumed nature has lain dormant within her. It is only in her uncharacteristic coquetry that Livvy is different from Phoebe, and in this there is a large measure of making up for lost opportunity, a foreshadowing of the development of this theme in *Dear Brutus*.

THE ADMIRABLE CRICHTON

The approach to fantasy in *The Admirable Crichton* is quite different. In this play, Barrie draws a definite line between the "real" world, where the characters originate, and the fantasy one, where they end up after the shipwreck. The desert island, however, is only fantasy to the audience; for the characters, it becomes reality, and they journey from the reality of the "real" world to the reality of the fantasy and back again in the course of the play.

The Admirable Crichton, one of Barrie's most successful plays, is a comedy with a social message. The dominant theme is the equality of all individuals. As a philosophical ideal, the concept that all human beings are naturally equal is espoused by the earl of Loam and is fashionably exploited in the peer's unprecedented declaration that one day a month all his servants will meet the other members of his household on equal terms. Thus, the first act of the play opens on one such day, when the house is in a turmoil. It is immediately apparent to the audience that both masters and servants alike find the imposition of equality frustrating and unnatural. For the daughters of the house, it is a tiresome bore to receive their servants in the drawing room and address them as social equals using a respectful form of address. When "Miss" Fisher, Lady Mary's maid, is piqued by not taking precedence over the lower-ranking Tweeny, the audience may laugh at such trivial preoccupation with position in circumstances of temporary, but nevertheless total, equality, but Barrie is reminding them how deeply ingrained in society are the distinctions of rank and privilege.

The second act takes place a short time after the first, but the setting is a remote desert island. The main characters have been shipwrecked, and they appear on the stage immediately after the catastrophe; a particular feature of the set is that unidentified objects drop at intervals from the trees to the ground, adding to the strangeness and hostility of the environment in which the castaways now find themselves. It is not long before both the audience and the characters become aware that the man best equipped to lead the castaways in their survival effort is not the earl, the socially superior and conventionally obvious candidate, but Crichton the butler. Crichton is a man who knows his place both with respect to his employers, to whom he knows he is inferior, and with respect to his fellow servants, to whom he is undoubtedly superior. His progressive assumption of authority on the island is a natural extension of his regular duties, and he is accustomed to having other people under his authority. What is unforeseen, but very humorous, is the total inability of the upper-class members of the shipwrecked party to make any practical contribution to attending to their immediate survival needs. Even with three minutes' warning of the impending disaster, they were unable to dress themselves suitably and have only one pair of boots between them. The most useful contribution the Honorable Ernest can make is to compose exasperating epigrams, and the three young ladies seem unaware of the seriousness of their predicament as they bemoan the loss of their hairpins. Such concern for trivia in the face of a desperate situation does not inspire confidence in their ability to survive.

That the relationship between master and servant is already becoming strained is apparent from the way Crichton follows the example of the peer's daughters and criticizes him for having left behind the hairpin he found on the beach. While the girls cannot see beyond the normal function of the hairpin, Crichton can visualize its use in a number of ways. The earl of Loam is quick to realize that Crichton may be stepping out of line, and a discussion of leadership develops, with the peer and the butler arguing from exactly opposite viewpoints from the ones they took in the first act. Indignantly, the upper-class members of the party decide to go it on their own, despite having saved nothing at all from the wreck. That anything was salvaged was only because of the foresight and industry of Crichton, and in due course the smell of his stew wafting along the beach brings the others crawling back to the campfire.

The events of the third act take place after a lapse of three years or so. The physical conditions of the party have taken a turn for the better, and they are comfortably housed and well fed. A number of ingenious contraptions have been devised to improve the quality of their lives, and it transpires that this is all because of the drive and ability of "the Guv." The audience may suspect that Crichton is "the Guv" but does not know for certain until he appears on the stage, a distinctly regal figure. There has been much discussion among the women prior to his appearance about who will have the honor of serving him, and the honor falls to Lady Mary, now known as Polly, who begs Tweeny to let her wear "It" for the occasion. "It" is the skirt Tweeny was prudent enough to put on the night they escaped from the wreck, the only such garment on the island.

While the audience may have admired Crichton's quiet efficiency and obvious leadership potential in act 2, the figure he cuts in act 3 is disquieting. Despite the order and efficiency he has imposed on life on the island, despite the benefits he has brought to the others who clearly would not have survived long without him, he is, nevertheless, a dictator, and it is galling to see the women courting his attentions. At a time when the Labour movement was gathering strength and the Fabians were active, Barrie may well have intended a warning to the upper echelons of society of impending social change. After all, he, himself, was nearing the top of the social ladder, having started off on its lowest rungs. It is reassuring to see the old order restored in the last act, with a return to the status quo.

Having seen a more worthy side of the upper-class characters in their newly found identities on the island, the audience might expect to see them retain some of their improved qualities, but this is not to be. When they regain their former position of social superiority, they also become subject once again to the shallow conventions and superficial moral preoccupations of society, as exemplified by the attitudes of the dowager. The distorted account that emerges of their life on the island is not a willful fabrication by the characters. It is a fantasizing of the reality of the fantasy. It is what would be expected of them by society, and in this deception it is society that should be condemned. Through the medium of humor, Barrie thus succeeds in criticizing both the philosophy that all human beings are equal and the idea that any kind of social revolution would be an improvement on the existing social order. That the existing social order is not without its defects is freely admitted, but any social critique is subordinate to the primary purpose of the play, which is to entertain and amuse.

PETER PAN

Reality and fantasy coexist in *Peter Pan*, also, but in contrast to *The Admirable Crichton*, the boundaries between the two states are fluid and indistinct. Barrie is concerned above all with the progression from the one to the other, and in most cases this is the progression from the imaginative existence of the child into the prosaic life of the adult. At first, adult reality and childhood fantasy seem diametrically opposed and mutually exclusive, but it soon becomes apparent that the degree to which the characters in *Peter Pan* are able to enter into and become part of the fantasy is directly dependent on their distance from childhood. Wendy, like her mother, will always retain a childlike streak in her nature that will ensure that her memory of Never Land will never fade completely, no matter how old she becomes, but Peter Pan will never leave Never Land because of his refusal to progress to adulthood.

The archetypal boy who never grew up, Peter Pan evolved in the stories of Kensington Gardens with which Barrie enchanted the Davies boys. The earliest literary version of these stories was a novel, *The Little White Bird*, which, contrary to Barrie's original plan, came to be dominated by Peter Pan. Barrie was increasingly attracted by this new character as his ties with the Davies family became even closer, and in 1903 he grew absorbed in writing a new play that would have Peter Pan as the central character. The scene for the play had already been set two years earlier in the gardens of Black Lake Cottage. At that time, Barrie had made a photographic record of the boys' adventures, with a preface ostensibly written by Peter Llewelyn Davies, whose name the hero of the new play assumed. Using the working title of "Peter and Wendy," Barrie offered his play to Herbert Beerbohm Tree, knowing it would entail an elaborate and expensive production, but he was not interested. It was Barrie's American associate, the impresario Charles Frohman, who grasped the play's potential and spared no effort to make it a success. He engaged the talented Dion Boucicault as producer, a recent innovation in the theatrical world, where production had traditionally been the concern of the actor-managers, and the play opened at the Duke of York's Theatre on December 27, 1904.

The plot of *Peter Pan* is calculated to appeal to the imaginations of the young. The Darling children, Wendy, John, and Michael, are induced by the intriguing, magical boy Peter Pan and his fairy acolyte Tinker Bell to abandon their comfortable nursery and savor the delights and perils of Never Land. The climax of the first act comes as they fly out the nursery window.

In the second act, the children become acquainted with the other inhabitants of Never Land. The Lost Boys, children without mothers who as babies fell out of their baby carriages, recognize Peter as their natural leader. They are permanently in danger from the Pirates, a motley crew led by the dastardly Captain Hook. The Redskins are enemies of both the Lost Boys and the Pirates until Peter and the Lost Boys rescue the belle of the tribe from death by marooning at Hook's hands. The appeal of the island is enhanced by the antics of the mermaids, the threat of the wolves and the Never Bird, not to mention the ticking crocodile that follows Hook inexorably around and around the island, waiting for the moment when it can finish making a meal of him.

In the fourth act, a great battle between the Redskins and the Pirates ends in victory for Hook, and it is then very easy for him to abduct Wendy and the Lost Boys as they prepare to leave Never Land. Only Peter can rescue them from the pirate ship before they are made to walk the plank, and this he does

with great enthusiasm. Hook meets his nemesis, the crocodile, and the Darling children return to the security of their nursery.

Peter is unique among the characters in his insistence that he does not want to grow up. The Lost Boys have no fixed opinion on the subject and are easily talked into going back with Wendy and her brothers to be adopted, and Wendy herself realizes that growing up is inevitable. It is easy to see the parallel between Peter's refusal to countenance even the thought of growing up with the singular circumstances of Barrie's own childhood. Physically, he remained a child longer than most of his contemporaries and was marked throughout his adulthood by his short stature (he was just over five feet tall); on the other hand, carefree childhood ended abruptly for him at the age of six when he embarked on the fantasy relationship with his mother, trying to live up to her expectations for his older brother.

Barrie's emphasis on the reluctance of Peter Pan to grow up is often interpreted as a disenchantment with adult life and an idealization of childhood, but Never Land offers only a temporary refuge from, and not a permanent solution to, the problems of growing up; childhood as epitomized by Peter, and to a lesser extent, the Lost Boys, is not ideal. Peter is callous and self-centered. He is illogical, inconsiderate, irresponsible, and irrepressible, but nevertheless endearing. His insouciance sets him apart from Wendy, who is already burdened with responsibilities and is happy to assume more.

If Peter Pan is a combination of Barrie himself and the characteristics that most appealed to him in the children of whom he was so fond, then Wendy must surely be a distillation of elements from the women in Barrie's life. The strongest parallel is with his mother, particularly as she emerged for him in her stories of her early childhood. Domestic responsibility came early to her, and she was already mothering her younger brother at the age of eight. The theme of motherhood is very strong in Peter Pan, and the maternal qualities of Sylvia Llewelyn Davies with her five sons must have served as a model for the scenes of Wendy and the Lost Boys. At the same time, Wendy's commonsense organization of the unpredictability of life in Never Land does not exclude her from participating in the great adventure. She is still a child and eligible to enjoy the delights of this children's preserve. She is already marked by feminine intuition, however, and if she is mother to the Lost Boys, then she expects Peter to be the father, a role of which he is particularly wary. The whole of the scene in the house underground in act 4 is built around Wendy's enactment of an adult role into which she will inevitably grow and Peter's avoidance of the parallel one that he will never accept.

Dreams are the substance of *Peter Pan*, and Barrie leaves the skeptical with the option of interpreting the fantasy on this level. On the other hand, even Mrs. Darling knows that Peter's shadow has substance: She has rolled it up and put it away in a drawer, and Tinker Bell's remarkable recovery after drinking the poison intended for Peter convinces every child in the audience, at least for the duration of the play, that fairies do exist.

DEAR BRUTUS

If Peter Pan epitomizes childhood, then Lob in *Dear Brutus* is the essence of worldly experience. He is likened, by the other characters in the play at the beginning of the first act, to Puck, or what Puck would have looked like if he had forgotten to die. He is thus at the opposite end of the age spectrum to Peter but like Peter is instrumental in strangely altering the lives of the other characters. The first act opens in a darkened room in his house, looking out onto a moonlit garden, a pertinent reversal of the usual situation. When the main characters enter the dark room, the lights go up and the ladies of the house party attempt to discover why they, particularly, have been invited. The butler, Matey, is blackmailed into giving them as much information as he knows, which is little. All he can say is to beware of the wood and not to venture out beyond the garden. His advice sounds ridiculous, because as the characters all know there is no wood for miles around, but it is Midsummer's Eve, and strange tales are told about a magic wood and its properties. When the men of the party join the ladies, they are full of enthusiasm for a project clearly suggested by Lob—namely, to go out to find the fabled wood.

During the remainder of this act, it becomes apparent that the lives of all the guests are marred in some way. Purdie, for example, cannot help being attracted to women other than his wife, and the current object of his attentions is Joanna Trout. Will Dearth is a failure and an alcoholic who is despised by his wife. Coade has achieved nothing at all in his life and even confuses his second wife with the memory of his first. Will Dearth observes that there are three things generally viewed as never returning to people: the spoken word, past life, and neglected opportunity. They would all welcome a second chance at life, and this the wood could provide. The climax to the first act is the discovery that the mysterious wood now entirely surrounds Lob's house, and one by one the characters venture out into it.

Act 2 shows how the characters react to the boon of a second chance to live their lives. It is entirely predictable that they will repeat the mistakes of their lives in the real world, and this they proceed to do. Purdie, married to Joanna, chases after Mabel, in reality Mrs. Purdie. Alice Dearth has married her other suitor, and although she is the Honorable Mrs. Finch-Fallowe in name she is now only a vagrant. Of all of them, only Will Dearth has benefited, possibly because the value of his life only declined once his wife saw him as a failure. He now delights in the daughter he wanted but never had in reality.

The third act takes place back in Lob's house. The characters drift in from the wood, leaving their fantasy existence, and in Dearth's case, his darling Margaret, behind. Their return to reality is gradual, however, and they are able to compare their two states, to arrive at some profound but depressing conclusions about the flaws in their characters that have made their lives what they are. It is Purdie, the now self-confessed philanderer, who quotes the lines from Julius Caesar that furnish the elliptical title of the play: "The fault, dear Brutus, is not in our stars, but in ourselves."

OTHER MAJOR WORKS

LONG FICTION: *Better Dead*, 1887; *When a Man's Single*, 1888; *The Little Minister*, 1891; *Sentimental Tommy*, 1896; *Tommy and Grizel*, 1900; *The Little White Bird*, 1902.

SHORT FICTION: *Auld Licht Idylls*, 1888; *A Window in Thrums*, 1889.

NONFICTION: *Margaret Ogilvy*, 1896.

BIBLIOGRAPHY

Hanson, Bruce K. *The Peter Pan Chronicles: The Nearly One Hundred Year History of "The Boy Who Wouldn't Grow Up."* Secaucus, N.J.: Carol, 1993. A study of the story of Peter Pan, from its genesis with Barrie to its many adaptations. Bibliography and index.

Jack, Ronald D. S. *The Road to the Never Land: A Reassessment of J. M. Barrie's Dramatic Art.* Aberdeen, Scotland: Aberdeen University Press, 1991. A modern critical examination of Barrie's plays. Bibliography and index.

Ormond, Leonée. *J. M. Barrie.* Scottish Writers 10. Edinburgh, Scotland: Scotland Academic Press, 1987. Ormond provides biographical information on Barrie as well as critical interpretation of his works. Bibliography and index.

Rose, Jacqueline. *The Case of Peter Pan: Or, The Impossibility of Children's Fiction.* Philadelphia: University of Pennsylvania Press, 1993. A scholarly examination of the story of Peter Pan as a fictional work for children. Bibliography and index.

Wullschläger, Jackie. *Inventing Wonderland: The Lives and Fantasies of Lewis Carroll, Edward Lear, J. M. Barrie, Kenneth Grahame, and A. A. Milne.* New York: Free Press, 1995. A study of the lives and fantasy literature of Barrie and several other nineteenth and twentieth century British authors. Bibliography and index.

Yeoman, Ann. *Now or Neverland: Peter Pan and the Myth of Eternal Youth: A Psychological Perspective on a Cultural Icon.* Studies in Jungian Psychology by Jungian Analysts 82. Toronto: Inner City Books, 1998. A psychological approach to the Peter Pan character created by Barrie. Bibliography and index.

Zia Hasan,
updated by Mildred C. Kuner

PHILIP BARRY

Born: Rochester, New York; June 18, 1896
Died: New York, New York; December 3, 1949

PRINCIPAL DRAMA

Autonomy, pr. 1919 (one act)

A Punch for Judy, pr. 1921, pb. 1925

You and I, pr., pb. 1923 (originally as *The Jilts*, pr. 1922)

The Youngest, pr. 1924, pb. 1925

In a Garden, pr. 1925, pb. 1926

White Wings, pr. 1926, pb. 1927

John, pr. 1927, pb. 1929

Paris Bound, pr. 1927 (as *The Wedding*), pb. 1929

Cock Robin, pr. 1928, pb. 1929 (with Elmer Rice)

Holiday, pr. 1928, pb. 1929

Hotel Universe, pr., pb. 1930

Tomorrow and Tomorrow, pr., pb. 1931

The Animal Kingdom, pr., pb. 1932

The Joyous Season, pr., pb. 1934

Bright Star, pr. 1935

Spring Dance, pr., pb. 1936 (adaptation of Eleanor Golden and Eloise Barrington's play)

Here Come the Clowns, pr. 1938, pb. 1939 (adaptation of his novel *War in Heaven*)

The Philadelphia Story, pr., pb. 1939

Liberty Jones, pr., pb. 1941

Without Love, pr. 1942, pb. 1943

Foolish Notion, pr. 1945

My Name Is Aquilon, pr. 1949 (adaptation of Jean Pierre Aumont's play *L'Empereur de Chine*)

Second Threshold, pr., pb. 1951 (completed by Robert E. Sherwood)

States of Grace: Eight Plays, pb. 1975

OTHER LITERARY FORMS

Philip Barry published one novel, *War in Heaven* (1938), which was dramatized as *Here Come the Clowns*, and a short story in *Scribner's Magazine* in 1922 that, along with his juvenilia and some nonfiction works, constitute his only literary output other than his plays.

ACHIEVEMENTS

Philip Barry will always be regarded primarily as a writer of superb drawing-room comedies, full of wit and sophistication and charm. Even during his own lifetime, however, critics perceived a duality in his dramatic output and were somewhat perplexed by the variety of Barry's experimentation on the stage. As easy as it would have been for him to stick to a comedic formula, grinding out comedies year after year, Barry proved an adventuresome dramatist and thereby cast confusion among the critical community. In spite of repeated failure at the box office, Barry continued with engaging persistence to write and produce serious drama in a variety of forms—tragedy in some cases—which in retrospect is of considerable interest even if it is far less pleasurable to study than are the mannered comedies.

Barry was neither as funny as George S. Kaufman nor as deeply brooding (or tedious) as Eugene O'Neill. His comedies, especially *You and I*, *Paris Bound*, *Holiday*, and *The Philadelphia Story*, attracted widespread attention when they were first produced and are still regularly revived by amateur theatrical groups. His serious dramas for the most part met with scant critical recognition and usually even less financial success, but such plays as *In a Garden*, *Hotel Universe*, *Tomorrow and Tomorrow*, *Here Come the Clowns*, and *Foolish Notion* are well within the traditions more fully exploited by such contemporaries as O'Neill, Robert E. Sherwood, Lillian Hellman, and Elmer Rice. What is often overlooked when discussing Barry's career is that he, too, was in on the beginnings of the new American drama, interested in many of the same innovations that were more highly publicized in the works of others. Partly because of his reticence, partly because his working methods eschewed the obvious, the self-consciously "serious" elements that were highlighted in the work of his contemporaries, Barry's message was often concealed by the charm of his characters and the smoothness of his dialogue.

Barry was among the earliest of American playwrights to incorporate the new Freudian psychology into his drama. Barry also did much to adapt Maeterlinckian fantasy for the Broadway stage, as in *In a Garden*. Symbolism, tragedy, realism, and poetic drama were used by Barry in his various dramatic experiments. Even social criticism forms a central part of his plays, and although he was criticized for not joining in the political movements of the 1930's, his work presents one of the most sustained and devastating critiques of the narrowness and aridity of American capitalism in the history of modern theater. All this Barry accomplished without the intellectual posing or the critical backstabbing so often associated with the theater. In spite of these credentials, however, Barry's drama has lost much of its early popularity—a fate that raises some awkward questions for

Philip Barry (Library of Congress)

anyone interested in assessing his work. In part it can be attributed to the lack of homogeneity among his plays. He skipped from one form to another and, except for high comedy, never seemed completely successful at any. He lacked the consistent vision of O'Neill, the virtuosity of Kaufman, or the social commitment of Hellman and Clifford Odets. Finally, the diffidence that allowed him social mobility denied him the passionate engagement that might have made him a great rather than merely a fascinating playwright.

BIOGRAPHY

Outwardly, Philip Barry led a charmed life: He married the right woman, made lots of money, and ran with the rich and famous. Inwardly, however, his life was not as fortunate. By the time Barry died in 1949, at the comparatively young age of fifty-three, he had experienced more failures on Broadway than successes, and he was plagued by depression and religious doubts severe enough to disrupt his otherwise disciplined and orderly work habits. In addition, all his life Barry remained on the periphery of the upper-class world he depicted in so many of his plays and emulated in his life. As Brendan Gill has perceptively noted, Barry, like such other Irish-Catholic writers of his generation as Eugene O'Neill, F. Scott Fitzgerald, and John O'Hara, spent his creative career striving for the perquisites and assurance of his Protestant "betters."

Philip James Quinn Barry was born on June 18, 1896, in Rochester, New York, to James Corbett Barry and Mary Agnes Quinn. He was the youngest of four children. His father, who emigrated from Ireland as a boy, became wealthy in a marble and granite business, and when he married Mary Agnes, they brought together two well-to-do Irish families who were obviously going to make their mark in the prospering upstate city. Unfortunately, James Barry died the year after Philip's birth, leaving his youngest son to be brought up by his sister and mother under increasingly reduced circumstances, for despite the best efforts of the two older Barry sons, the granite business gradually declined. Barry attended Nazareth Hall Academy, a Roman Catholic secondary

school, and East High School in Rochester. He attempted his first three-act play, "No Thoroughfare," in 1909, but other than a story, "Tab the Cat," which he wrote for publication in the *Rochester Post Express*, the young Philip did not show any precocious literary talent. In the autumn of 1913 he entered Yale.

The combination of East High and Yale did much to broaden Barry's world beyond the rather narrow Catholicism of his family. Especially at Yale, where he was thrown in among the Protestant elite, Barry decided to work his way into the larger, more sophisticated world of money. Because of defective eyesight, he had not been an athlete in school, so Barry turned to writing, and over the next three years he contributed poetry, short stories, and editorials to the *Yale Literary Magazine*. World War I disrupted Barry's education, and he went to work for the American Embassy in London as a code clerk after he was rejected for military service. He used the time to advantage, however, completing a three-act play, which he unsuccessfully tried to get produced. In March of 1919, he was back at Yale, his work done in London, and in June the Dramatic Club produced his only known one-act play, *Autonomy*. That September, after receiving his degree, Barry enrolled in George Pierce Baker's Workshop 47 at Harvard, and during the next year he wrote another three-act play, *A Punch for Judy*. Temporarily out of funds, Barry wrote copy for a year at W. A. Erickson, an advertising agency. During this time, he became engaged to Ellen Semple, daughter of a wealthy international lawyer, Lorenzo Semple, who with his wife lived in New York City and Mt. Kisco, New York. In the summer, Barry received word that *A Punch for Judy* would be produced by Workshop 47, would open in New York, and would go on tour. In the fall, Barry left advertising and returned to Baker's Workshop 47, where during the next few months he wrote the drafts of two plays, *The Jilts*, later retitled *You and I*, and "Poor Richard," which underwent several title changes before being published as *The Youngest*. On July 15, 1922, he married Ellen Semple, and they spent the rest of the summer honeymooning in Europe. On the return voyage, Barry, who had few prospects for employment, learned that *The Jilts* had won the Herndon Prize for the best full-length play written in Workshop 47 and that it would be produced on Broadway early in the new year. Retitled *You and I*, Barry's play became a rousing success and established him as one of the rising stars of the new American theater. Later that same year, his first son was born.

In spite of his impressive beginning, over the next few years Barry's plays were increasingly unsuccessful. *The Youngest* ran for 104 performances, *In a Garden* survived for seventy-four performances, *White Wings* ran for twenty-seven, and *John* lasted only eleven performances. During the summer of 1927, however, while Barry was living at Cannes in Southern France, his luck changed.

On the trip over, Barry and Rice had begun collaboration on a mystery play, *Cock Robin*, which Barry completed along with *Paris Bound* during his stay in France. *Paris Bound* opened in December and *Cock Robin* in January, 1928, both to good audiences. Barry followed these successes in the fall with *Holiday*, his eighth Broadway production, and it ran 230 performances at the Plymouth Theater. Thereafter, although his plays would often have a disappointing box office or receive mediocre reviews, Barry was at least financially secure. He earned increasing sums from the sale of his properties to Hollywood, and amateur performances continued to boost the revenues on each play he wrote. His second son was born in 1926. Although Barry's mother had died in 1927, his marriage, the most fortunate part of his exceptionally fortunate life, continued to provide him with sustenance. As one critic has described it, his marriage was itself "Barryesque," full of charm, intelligence, wit, and concern.

The 1930's treated Barry, professionally at least, much in the same way the 1920's had. He began strong with the successful run of *Tomorrow and Tomorrow*, slumped downward during the middle of the decade, his career reaching what was perhaps its nadir when *Bright Star* closed after seven performances, only to rise spectacularly in 1939 with the overwhelming success of *The Philadelphia Story*. The latter, starring Katharine Hepburn, ran

for more than four hundred performances and is credited with restoring to Solvency the Theatre Guild, which Barry had joined a decade earlier. Barry also published his only novel, *War in Heaven*, in 1938, and earlier in the decade he spent a brief stint in Hollywood as a screenwriter for Metro-Goldwyn-Mayer.

Barry came under increasing criticism during this period of social and political unrest. He was roundly condemned for writing frivolous plays at a time when many critics felt that all artists should be engaged in the struggle for economic and social justice. In particular, his refusal to write overtly about political causes lost him support among the younger drama critics of the period. In addition, Barry suffered two personal losses in these years: Both his brother, Edmund, and an infant daughter died.

World War II suspended the Barrys' routine of living most of the year in Southern France, but it hardly diminished Barry's output: He produced plays in 1941 (*Liberty Jones*), in 1942 (*Without Love*), and in 1945 (*Foolish Notion*). When the war was over, the Barrys returned to France. For the next three years, Barry had nothing running on Broadway, but in 1949, *My Name Is Aquilon*, his adaptation of Jean Pierre Aumont's *L'Empereur de Chine*, opened as his twentieth Broadway production and, as it would turn out, his last. After submitting the draft of his next play, *Second Threshold*, to the Theatre Guild, Barry died suddenly of a heart attack at his apartment in New York City. On December 5, a requiem mass was said at the Church of St. Vincent Ferrer, and he was buried at East Hampton, Long Island. *Second Threshold* was completed by Robert E. Sherwood in 1951 and, in the same year, it opened at the Morosco Theatre and ran for 126 performances.

Although Barry shared certain accidents of birth and background with other Irish-Catholic writers of his generation, he succeeded, unlike many of the others, in gaining acceptance into the moneyed world of the Protestant upper class. Even so, he always remained apart; the role of an observer was congenial to him. In the end, perhaps, Barry saw the upper classes clearly not only because of his proximity but also because of his restraint; by avoiding the excesses of O'Hara, Fitzgerald, and O'Neill, he was able to cross the social and financial barriers into the world that receded before the others like Gatsby's rolling prairie out into the night.

ANALYSIS

Philip Barry made his mark in American theater as a writer of high comedy and as an experimentalist, and during three decades of playwriting, he explored fully both of these artistic tendencies in his work. In the process, he came to occupy a kind of middle ground between dramatic extremes. In the words of John Gassner, Barry tried to arrive at a point of reasonableness in an unreasonable world. As a theatrical moderate, he faced a much more difficult task than did the more extreme dramatists of the period between the two world wars. Neither a social satirist nor a vacuous entertainer, a partisan politico nor a know-nothing fool, an unthinking realist nor a muddled metaphysician, Barry practiced a healing art, and his mission was to reduce the dissonance of the modern American theater. Barry's diffidence, however, made him difficult to classify, and literary history has not treated him well. Often misunderstood when he was alive, after his death he came to reside in a critical limbo in American theatrical history. As a Catholic, it is a position he would have understood and perhaps relished.

Barry became one of the United States' most financially successful playwrights, earning enough money to allow him to live in the manner of one of his own characters. He was perhaps the most accomplished writer of high or sophisticated comedy between the wars, a period notable for its witty comedies of manners. He was among the most innovative American playwrights working on Broadway during the 1920's and the 1930's. In spite of all these accomplishments, however, Barry remains largely excluded from serious discussions of American literature. The reasons for this are complex but center on Barry's need to be a maverick, an eccentric in a world dominated by corporate mentalities. Barry's plays, for all their commonality of themes, are just quirky enough to avoid easy synthesis. Both experimental and traditional, comic and serious, religious and skeptical,

Barry's work provides enough ambiguity and variety to place him in his own category, which is to say, by himself, alone. It is a position Barry would have welcomed, for like so many of his characters he eschewed easy answers and sought salvation on his own terms.

YOU AND I

Barry established his reputation with his play *You and I*, which under the working title *The Jilts* had won an award as the best play of Baker's Workshop 47. Under the terms of the award, the play chosen was to be produced on Broadway and then taken on tour. *You and I* was a resounding success, both in New York and on tour, and set the pattern for Barry's other drawing-room comedies, most notably *Paris Bound*, *Holiday*, and *The Philadelphia Story*. With witty dialogue and a modish plot, the play revealed the essentially corrupt spirit of capitalism and concluded with a realistic vision of life's limitations. The action centers on Maitland White, a fortyish businessman who decides to give up his comfortable advertising job in a soap company and return to the ambition of his youth, to become a painter. His wife rather generously agrees to give up her affluent lifestyle to help him realize his dream. His son, who is just embarking on his own life, has fallen in love with a girl and is about to give up his ambition to become an architect and go to work for the firm his father has just quit. The play concludes as the father returns to work, thereby freeing the son both to marry and to realize his dream of studying architecture in Paris. Matey realizes by the play's end that time has robbed him of any chance to become anything but a mediocre artist and that his family obligations must take precedence over his individual desires. Dreams, ambition, and talent can all die with age and obligation; such is the rather sobering resolution to Barry's witty plot.

PARIS BOUND

This pattern of hope, loss, and reconciliation (or resignation) marked all of Barry's most famous and successful comedies. *Paris Bound*, which was produced in 1927 following a series of increasingly unsuccessful dramas, also contains a cautionary ending. Jim and Mary Hutton have been married for six years when Mary learns that her husband has committed casual adultery. Deeply hurt at such a betrayal, she leaves for Paris to sue for divorce. In spite of her "modern" attitude about such things, announced on her wedding day, Mary is now prepared to forsake her liberality in favor of a more conventional morality—until she, too, is faced with temptation by Richard, a bright, attractive, young composer. Although she does not have an affair with Richard, she learns the ease of such venial sins and accepts her husband back without revealing her own involvement. She has learned that the spiritual bond within marriage should be valued above mere physical fidelity. Again, Barry's dialogue was praised by the critics, while audiences were titillated by his unconventional attitude toward extramarital affairs. A smash hit on Broadway, the play was also included in the ten best list for 1927, and screen rights were purchased by Pathé. Once again, Barry's wit and charm obscured a more serious theme, one that would surface again and again in his later plays—namely, the question of marriage and resolutions to marriages in trouble. Like that of Tracy Lord in *The Philadelphia Story*, Mary Hutton's resolution in *Paris Bound* strikes one as a little too pat for the anguish that has been expended. The problem of divorce and broken relationships was of considerable social interest during the 1920's, but Barry declined to confront it head-on.

HOLIDAY

Indeed, Barry was always able in his high comedies to skirt popular and often controversial issues by placing them in warm and sunny settings. One of the ways in which he used the upper-middle-class milieu for which he became famous was to couch radical themes in comfortable surroundings and thereby make them more palatable to his audiences. A case in point is his next broadly successful comedy, *Holiday*. Returning to the theme of a young man's dreams, *Holiday* deals with Johnny Case, who wants to risk his small fortune in order to go off and find himself, in spite of the fact that he has just met and fallen in love with the wealthy Julia Seaton. The play's plot hinges on whether Johnny, who has little prospect of earning a living and no money to fall back on, will withstand the financial and sexual pressures of Julia

in order to be true to himself. As it turns out, Johnny does break off with Julia but is followed on his travels by the less frivolous and more understanding Linda, Julia's sister. Like *You and I*, the play centers on the various pulls made on the young hero by competing value systems and by competing girls. More upbeat than the earlier play, *Holiday* seems to suggest that it is possible to have it all but that such ventures are not without risks and finally entailments, albeit not necessarily strangling ones. Barry was saying that money should not be an end in itself and that all people should have the opportunity to make life choices for themselves and to assume responsibility for such choices. His point was well taken but came at a particularly inappropriate moment. The year after the play was produced, the stock market crashed, plunging the United States into unparalleled financial decline. The ensuing Depression denied to millions the opportunities afforded Johnny, and the optimism of *Holiday* rang hollow.

THE ANIMAL KINGDOM

Barry was not to write another successful comedy of this type for four years. By 1932, the Depression was well established, with no end in sight. *The Animal Kingdom*, produced in that year, was originally written for a young Hepburn, then just beginning her stage career. For a variety of reasons, Hepburn was dropped from the cast of *The Animal Kingdom* at the last minute, but the play is now seen to be an earlier version of her hit *The Philadelphia Story*. *The Animal Kingdom* also bears a resemblance to *Paris Bound*. Tom Collier, a publisher, who has been living with Daisy Sage, a journalist, for three years, falls in love with and marries Cecelia Henry. Cecelia seduces Tom into publishing trash for a quick profit, to the damnation of his publisher's soul. Realizing the immorality of their marriage, Tom leaves Cecelia, who is more mistress than helpmate, to return to his mistress, Daisy, who is more wife than paramour. Daisy's love for Tom wins out over Cecelia's manipulation of his affection for profit. Again, Barry suggests that a marriage built only on the appetites of the animal kingdom is not a true marriage, and Daisy's pure love finally gives Tom the strength to free himself and discover who he really is. By rejecting the dictates of society, Tom is able, unlike Matey, to regain his individual integrity.

THE PHILADELPHIA STORY

For the rest of the 1930's, Barry seemed unable to write anything that would capture the imagination of his public. In 1939, however, with a second chance to work with Hepburn, Barry wrote the play for which he is probably best remembered, *The Philadelphia Story*. For Hepburn, Barry, and the Theatre Guild, which produced it, the new play was crucial. None of the principals should have worried: *The Philadelphia Story* saved the Guild financially, helped establish Hepburn's career, and rescued Barry's reputation.

As the play begins, Tracy Lord is preparing to marry for the second time, but her plans are complicated by a series of family entanglements: Her boozy former husband shows up, a reporter from a national magazine arrives to do an in-depth piece on the family, her father has developed an attachment to a lady of questionable (or perhaps "unquestionable" would be better) morals, her sister's behavior is erratic, and her uncle goes around pinching young girls. Tracy's high moral principles match the priggishness of her husband-to-be until she gets roaring drunk one night and swims nude with the journalist who is covering the family. Like Mary in Barry's *Paris Bound*, Tracy learns tolerance. Rejecting her intolerant would-be second husband, she is reunited with her estranged father and her former husband. Human warmth and understanding, Barry implies, are worth more than unthinking moral rectitude, and people with social position and wealth have no monopoly on individual morality, as the uprightness of the young reporter has proved. *The Philadelphia Story* was to be the last of Barry's high comedies and the last of his successful plays, for although two of Barry's later plays performed creditably at the box office, their success was nothing compared to that of *The Philadelphia Story*. The film version of the play, starring Hepburn as well, became one of the most successful screwball comedies of the late 1930's, while the 1956 musical film version, *High Society*, was a successful vehicle for a girl from Philadelphia, Grace Kelly.

IN A GARDEN

Although Barry will probably always be known primarily for his high comedies, he was proudest, as John Mason Brown has written, of his failures, his experimental dramas. Underneath his surface gaiety and wit, Barry was a serious student of the theater, one who was in touch with the current trends in European as well as American avant-garde drama. His so-called failures represent that audacious, unconventional side of his theatrical nature. It must be understood that in all his plays, Barry experimented. He played with dialogue, setting, character, and most of all subject matter, but those comedies that established his reputation in the American theater tended to be the least audacious stylistically. Then as now, audiences did not like to be jolted out of their complacency by too radical a form. They liked changes in the language, the plots, the themes, but not in the form of the drama. When Barry wrote a play without an intermission, when he introduced allegory or fantasy, his audiences did not respond as fully as they did to his more conservative comedies.

Barry's first obviously experimental drama, *In a Garden*, not only employed a play within a play (in itself not a radical device) but also incorporated a deliberately poetic plot and dealt in a more overt way with self-consciously "serious" topics, two elements that Barry had kept discreetly in the background of his previous plays. There is an element of Luigi Pirandello in the fey qualities of the characters, especially the girl, Lissa, and several of the critics likened Barry's work to Henrik Ibsen's *Et dukkehjem* (pr., pb. 1879; *A Doll's House*, 1880; also known as *A Doll House*). The play closed after seventy-four performances.

WHITE WINGS

Barry followed *In a Garden* with another, even more fantastic play. *White Wings* is almost totally symbolic, dealing with a family of street cleaners whose livelihood is passing with the coming of the automobile and the disappearance of the horse. Although the play intrigued the critics, it baffled the public and ran for only twenty-seven performances. Clearly, *White Wings* is concerned with modernity's impact on traditional values, but the play's symbolic manner leaves Barry's precise intentions in doubt. One critic has suggested that Barry's faith had been called into question by his rereading of the Gospels and that the "faith of the fathers" that is portrayed and undercut in *White Wings* is the Catholicism of Barry's youth. Whatever the sources of *White Wings*, Barry continued in this vein in his next play, *John*, based on the life of John the Baptist.

JOHN

John, the most serious work Barry had yet attempted, reflected the religious turmoil that he was experiencing at the time. Running for only eleven nights, the play was a disaster from the beginning; in particular, its language was too colloquial for its biblical subject matter. Still, in retrospect, the play looks better than its initial reception would indicate. The dialogue is less off-putting to the contemporary sensibility than it was to audiences in the late 1920's; indeed, *John* has affinities with Archibald MacLeish's highly successful *J. B.* (pr. 1958). Nevertheless, Barry was sufficiently discouraged by the failure of *John* to agree to collaborate with Rice on a mystery play, *Cock Robin*, which, along with *Paris Bound* and *Holiday*, managed to reestablish Barry's career at the end of the decade.

HOTEL UNIVERSE

Hotel Universe was Barry's first play of the 1930's, a play that captured the critics' fancy but was only mediocre at the box office. A parable that mixes Freudianism and Christianity, *Hotel Universe* is set in a large house that once was a hotel. Ann Field has assembled a number of guests who have in various ways rebelled against society but who have achieved only purposeless personal freedom and who now face the emptiness of their lives with increasing despair. Running without intermissions, the play is an extended psychodrama in which the various characters reenact scenes from the past, experiencing catharsis in the process. Barry's parable, however skillfully presented, did not attract an audi-

ence. Its failure with the public followed the pattern set by his earlier experimental dramas, a pattern to which most of his later serious plays were also subject.

OTHER MAJOR WORKS

LONG FICTION: *War in Heaven*, 1938.

SHORT FICTION: "Meadow's End," 1922.

NONFICTION: *The Dramatist and the Amateur Public*, 1927.

CHILDREN'S LITERATURE: "Tab the Cat," 1905; "The Toy Balloon," 1917.

BIBLIOGRAPHY

Eisen, Kurt. "Philip Barry." In *Twentieth Century American Dramatists*, edited by Christopher J. Wheatley. Vol. 228 in *Dictionary of Literary Biography*. Detroit, Mich.: The Gale Group, 2000. A short overview of Barry's life and works.

Klein, Alvin. "A *Philadelphia Story* with Social Conscience." Review of *The Philadelphia Story*, by Philip Barry. *The New York Times*, October 28, 2001, p. CT8. This review of the Hartford Stage Company's production of *The Philadelphia Story* finds the story relevant for a modern audience.

Roppolo, Joseph Patrick. *Philip Barry*. New York: Twayne, 1965. Roppolo's biographical and critical study provides the most comprehensive treatment of the playwright and his work. It includes chapters on Barry's major themes, dramaturgical techniques, and plot structure. Contains a chronology, a detailed index, and an annotated list of secondary sources.

Weber, Bruce. "Yuppies of the 1920's, Dancing with Their Demons." Review of *Hotel Universe*, by Philip Barry. *The New York Times*, May 1, 2000, p. E5. This review of the Blue Light Theater Company's production of *Hotel Universe* examines one of Barry's serious plays.

Charles L. P. Silet,
updated by Christian H. Moe

FÉLIX-HENRY BATAILLE

Born: Nîmes, France; April 4, 1872
Died: Rueil-Malmaison, France; March 2, 1922

PRINCIPAL DRAMA

La Belle au bois dormant, pr., pb. 1894
La Lépreuse, pr., pb. 1896
Ton sang, pr., pb. 1897
L'Enchantement, pr., pb. 1900
Le Masque, pr., pb. 1902
Maman Colibri, pr., pb. 1904
La Marche nuptiale, pr., pb. 1905
Poliche, pr., pb. 1906
La Femme nue, pr., pb. 1908
Le Scandale, pr., pb. 1909
La Vierge folle, pr., pb. 1910
Les Flambeaux, pr., pb. 1912
Le Phalène, pr., pb. 1913
L'Amazone, pr., pb. 1916
Notre Image, pr., pb. 1918
Les Sœurs d'amour, pr., pb. 1919
L'Animateur, pr., pb. 1920
L'Homme à la rose, pr. 1920, pb. 1921
La Tendresse, pr., pb. 1921
La Possession, pr. 1921, pb. 1922
La Chair humaine, pr., pb., 1922
Théâtre complet, pb. 1922-1929 (12 volumes)

OTHER LITERARY FORMS

Félix-Henry Bataille is known mostly for his theatrical works, but he wrote and published lyric poetry before establishing himself in the theater.

ACHIEVEMENTS

Although Félix-Henry Bataille won no formal awards for his work, he remains one of the handful of playwrights of the Theater of the Boulevard to leave a mark on French theatrical history. His career was rich, and for quite a few years, especially immediately before World War I, he distinguished himself by both amusing and moving a popular audience.

BIOGRAPHY

Félix-Henry Bataille (he is also known as "Henry" or "Henri" Bataille) was born in Nîmes, in southern France, in 1872. However, when his father, a magistrate, was named to a judicial post in Paris in 1876, the family moved there. The young Bataille studied at secondary schools in Paris and Versailles. He developed an interest in painting, especially portraiture, and in 1890, he enrolled in the Académie Julian and later at the École des Beaux-Arts, both in Paris. In 1901, Bataille published a book of lithographed portraits of well-known people of the day. Meanwhile, he continued writing poetry, something he had begun doing at the age of fifteen.

Bataille's playwriting was stimulated by friends, who speculated on his producing a fairy-tale piece. Bataille's first play was a version of "Sleeping Beauty," written in collaboration with Robert d'Humières and presented in Paris in 1894. The play was not a success, and Bataille returned, for the time being, to his painting and his poetry, publishing in 1895 a collection of poems called *La Chambre blanche* (the white room). However, influential critics and friends persuaded Bataille to try his skills in the theater once again.

His early plays were in the Symbolist vein, but he soon found his niche, with *L'Enchantement* and *Le Masque*, in the *théâtre du boulevard*. Bataille's popularity was short-lived; some observers accused him, in his later work, of writing formula plays in order to make money. His health had always been fragile, and by the time he died, in 1922, he had passed his peak as a dramatist.

ANALYSIS

Félix-Henry Bataille's work resembles, in subject matter and setting, the work of his contemporary and fellow playwright of the Paris Theater of the Boulevard, Henry Bernstein. Naturally enough, the plays of both writers appealed to the same audience—a bourgeois public looking for titillating entertainment and, perhaps, some intellectual stimulation as well. However, Bernstein's career lasted much longer than that of Bataille, who died relatively young. Even so, by some accounts, he outlived his reputation, as the French say.

Bataille called his plays *comédies*, but he used the term in its traditional French sense, inherited from seventeenth century French theater. In this tradition, a *comédie*, unlike a tragedy, has a happy ending, a positive resolution of some kind. Therefore, Bataille's plays were not necessarily lighthearted but had resolutions that were basically positive although sometimes somewhat heavy-handed or ambiguous.

Bataille's most interesting characters are women, who are his protagonists for the most part, even if they are unstable, selfish, and even cruel. His women are the catalysts of the plays' action; in some cases (in *L'Enchantement*, and *La Femme nue*, for example), the plot features a struggle between two strongly motivated women. Moreover, Bataille's plays have to do with love or passion—and focus very often on the extent to which people cannot control their feelings and the fragility of human relationships. The fundamental impact of Bataille's drama is bittersweet.

L'ENCHANTEMENT

Bataille's *L'Enchantement* sets the tone for much of his early work and presents the first two of his unconventional—even unbalanced—female characters. The "enchantment" to which the play's title refers is the strange hold that young Jeannine exerts over her doting older sister. As the play begins, Isabelle Dessandes has just married Georges, an old friend. She makes it clear to Georges and her circle of friends that this marriage simply seals a friendship—neither love nor passion has any role in the union. In fact, Isabelle confides in a close friend that she finds conjugal sex demeaning, shameful, and debasing. Her primary goal in life is the upbringing of her younger sister, something she had promised her late mother she would take care of. In contrast, Georges loves and lusts after Isabelle. However, his amorous caresses and even their nighttime lovemaking are inhibited and interrupted by Jeannine—because she has conceived a consuming passion for Georges.

Eventually, even Isabelle has had enough of her sister, whom she now rightly sees as her rival. After

Jeannine succeeds in breaking Georges's resistance, luring him into a love-anger embrace—which is witnessed by Isabelle's former suitor, Pierre—the family begins to collapse. Georges is immediately crushed by his own shame and threatens to leave the home—and Isabelle, after Pierre tells her what he saw, pulls a pistol from a desk drawer. It is unclear whether she plans to shoot Georges, herself or both. Meanwhile, Jeannine threatens to kill herself.

Georges finally asserts himself in order to put an end to this madness, as he calls it. He suggests that all three of the family members—he, Isabelle, and Jeannine—separate for a time, until they can be reasonable about the relationships among them. With the help of Pierre, who seemed treacherous only moments before, Jeannine agrees to a year of travel. Georges delivers the play's final words of reason. He attributes the chaos that he, Isabelle, and Jeannine have experienced to Isabelle's expecting too much drama from life—in effect, taking life too seriously. Georges is happy with what good things come, without overanalyzing emotions and relationships.

Unfortunately, the resolution of *L'Enchantement* seems forced. The turmoil that has driven Isabelle and Jeannine dissolves too easily with the prompting of Georges and Pierre—the latter of whom was seen early in the play not to be a real friend of Georges and Isabelle. As the play closes, however, he becomes the experienced sage.

MAMAN COLIBRI

The main character of this play, the Baronne Irène de Rysbergue, constitutes a major problem for most of the other characters. Bataille presents Irène early in the play as a very sympathetic wife and mother, respected by her husband and friends and adored by her children. Her sons, Richard and Paulot, have given their mother an affectionate nickname—Maman Colibri, "Mama Hummingbird." When Paulot explains his mother's nickname to a friend by reading a description of a hummingbird, he reads that the bird is aggressive and destructive, using its beak as a dagger with which to attack flowers. The boys do not, however, understand the multiple meanings possible in the word *colibri*.

Irène does deserve some sympathy. She was an orphan who was married off to the older Baron de

Rysbergue. He was a fine match for her: a wealthy, decent man who has been a good father. However, there has never been any question about Irène's truly loving her husband. Irène, now thirty-nine, had never known real passion until she was in effect seduced by twenty-one-year-old Georges de Chambry, an old friend of her sons. Indeed, Irène's justification of what she does is poignant: She knows she has missed something in her life and can see her youth passing quickly. She realizes that what she feels for Georges is maternal to some extent, but it is clear that she is also attracted to Georges physically. Georges is Irène's last chance at genuine romance, and she seizes the opportunity.

Although the moral hypocrisy of the social class to which the Rysbergues belong is apparent, flagrant flouting of convention will not be tolerated. Once her adultery is discovered, Irène is scorned by Richard and is almost literally thrown out of the house by her husband. Irène and Georges go to live in Algeria. However, Georges soon becomes jaded; he develops an affair with an American neighbor, and the heartbroken Irène sees that her great love has ended. She goes home.

Irène's contrition is not very convincing, but Richard, who is now married and the father of a son, forgives his mother and welcomes her home. Her husband, who has never divorced her, cannot, however, close his eyes to the past. In the play's strange last scene, Irène physically ages before us—and takes on her new role: She sees herself now as a beloved grandmother. However, this last image of Irène makes us uneasy instead of reassuring us; she is a very ambiguous figure.

POLICHE

In *Poliche*, Bataille lightens his touch. *Poliche* is farce, social satire, and comedy of morality—featuring sexual escapades and double-entendres—and, of course, a love story. Poliche, the nickname of Didier Meireuil, is the leader of a circle of pleasure-seekers who seem to have nothing to do but have a good time. As the play begins, Poliche and his group of several men and women, some of whom are married and in some cases, married to each other, arrive at a hotel in Saint-Cloud, on the outskirts of Paris. It is autumn,

and unfortunately for the group, the hotel is shutting down for the winter so there is little in the way of food and drink for the unexpected guests. A man named Saint-Vast was invited to join the group when the others met him at a party. It would appear that he is socially superior to Poliche and his friends—although he is not superior to the others morally.

No sooner has the group arrived at the hotel than Saint-Vast begins chasing the women in the party. He connects finally with Rosine de Rinck, who is also immediately attracted to Saint-Vast. What is awkward is that she and Poliche have been lovers for some time. The point of the rest of the play is that Rosine does not or cannot determine whom she really loves.

After she is abandoned—temporarily—by Saint-Vast, she and Poliche make up. In order to win back Rosine, however, Poliche thinks that he has to quit his lighthearted role and be a serious and responsible man. He soon realizes that he now bores Rosine, and what is worse, he sees that she still is drawn to Saint-Vast. In a grand gesture, Poliche sends Rosine back to Saint-Vast, claiming that his true self is the boring, narrow-minded Didier. As the curtain falls, we see Poliche in tears—again—without his beloved Rosine.

LA FEMME NUE

The first act of this play is a pleasure, expressing the joy of artistic success and the effervescence of true love between simple people. Unfortunately for the characters involved, the play's mood darkens quickly. Bataille clearly finds a good deal of *La Femme nue's* inspiration in the history and politics of Impressionist painting. References are made to paintings by Pierre-Auguste Benoir, and one character even alludes to something he heard Edgar Degas say. Within this nicely presented historical context is Bataille's hero of sorts, Pierre Bernier. Pierre is the classic hard-working but poor painter who struggles for recognition. In act 1 of *La Femme nue*, he finally achieves it: He wins the major prize at the French Salon exhibition. He and his model-mistress, Lolette Cassagne, seem to have gained everything of which they had dreamed.

Time passes between act 1 and act 2, and things have changed. Pierre has fallen out of love with

Lolette and in love with the very wealthy but arrogant Princesse Paule de Chabran. Lolette is devastated. She even goes to see the Princesse's aged husband in order to effect a kind of alliance against the divorce that Pierre and Paule want. Later, Lolette furiously confronts Pierre and Paule, collapses in despair—and attempts suicide.

In a change of heart that is abrupt and therefore barely credible, the previously hard-hearted Princesse repents of alienating Pierre's affections. She visits Lolette in the hospital and declares that she will not marry Pierre even if Lolette were to agree to a divorce. Similarly, Pierre arrives at the hospital to express his regret with what has happened. He vows to do his duty and honor his marriage to Lolette—but he does not apologize for no longer loving her. Love, says Pierre (in a speech reminiscent of Georges's analysis in *L'Enchantement*), is not something people can control: Pierre cannot, he insists, will to love Lolette and will to no longer love Paule. He promises nevertheless to return to Lolette and help create as happy a life as possible.

La Femme nue ends in true melodrama fashion. Lolette's former lover, the unpolished and unsuccessful painter Rouchard (who was introduced in act 1), appears in Lolette's hospital room. Bataille quickly draws matters to a close as Rouchard clumsily but touchingly expresses his enduring love for Lolette. As the curtain falls, one imagines Lolette finding some semblance of happiness with Rouchard—in the milieu from which she came. The spirit and humor of act 1 of *La Femme nue* are very enjoyable, but it is the *deus ex machina* arrival of Rouchard that weakens *La Femme nue* and ultimately makes it the least successful of Bataille's early plays.

OTHER MAJOR WORKS

POETRY: *La Divine Tragédie*, 1916; *La Quadrature de l'amour*, 1920.

NONFICTION: *Écrits sur le théâtre*, 1917.

BIBLIOGRAPHY

Blanchart, Paul. *Henry Bataille: Son œuvre*. Paris: Éditions du Carnet-Critique, 1922. A largely adulatory study, but Blanchart does recognize Bataille's excess in plots and style, especially in his later works. Blanchart suggests that Bataille may have been led astray by desire for financial success. In French.

Catalogne, Gérard de. *Henry Bataille: Ou, Le Romantisme de l'Instinct*. Paris: Éditions de la Pensée Latine, 1925. Focusing in detail on *La Femme nue* and *Maman Colibri*, Catalogne sees Bataille as the playwright who best represents his era in taste, subject matter, and dramatic flair. In French.

Knowles, Dorothy. *French Drama of the Inter-War Years*. London: Harrap, 1967. Knowles provides what is still perhaps the best concise history of the *théâtre du boulevard*. Moreover, the book contains indispensable information about plots, chronology, and the milieu in which French theater developed during the period.

Pillement, Georges. "Henry Bataille." In *Anthologie du théâtre français contemporain: Le Théâtre du Boulevard*. Paris: Éditions du Bélier, 1946. A detailed but harsh judgment of Bataille's work. Pillement believes that Bataille's best plays were written between 1914 and 1919 but that even before his death, his work was badly dated. In French.

Gordon Walters

PIERRE-AUGUSTIN CARON DE BEAUMARCHAIS
Pierre-Augustin Caron

Born: Paris, France; January 24, 1732
Died: Paris, France; May 18, 1799

PRINCIPAL DRAMA

Eugénie, pr., pb. 1767 (*The School of Rakes*, 1795)

Les Deux Amis: Ou, Le Négociant de Lyon, pr., pb. 1770 (*The Two Friends: Or, The Liverpool Merchant*, 1800)

Le Barbier de Séville: Ou, La Précaution inutile, pr., pb. 1775 (*The Barber of Seville: Or, The Useless Precaution*, 1776)

La Folle Journée: Ou, Le Mariage de Figaro, wr. 1775-1778, pr. 1784, pb. 1785 (*The Marriage of Figaro*, 1784)

Tarare, pr., pb. 1787 (libretto; music by Antonio Salieri)

L'Autre Tartuffe: Ou, La Mère coupable, pr. 1792, pb. 1797 (*Frailty and Hypocrisy*, 1804)

Théâtre, pb. 1966

OTHER LITERARY FORMS

Pierre-Augustin Caron de Beaumarchais is known as a literary figure only for his plays, which were the only fictional works he published during his lifetime. Although he also wrote poetry, some of which was published posthumously, none of it proved to be of enduring value. His early, unpublished works for the theater were in the form of short curtain raisers or sidewalk shows, which the French call *parades*, some of which have also been posthumously published. Beaumarchais also published *mémoires*, or legal arguments, to defend his own position in several notorious lawsuits in which he was involved, and wrote prefaces for all but one of his plays, which describe the theoretical basis of his dramaturgy and exemplify his work as a critic. A considerable amount of Beaumarchais's correspondence has also been published, most of it merely of documentary value but some of it marked by a passion for ideas and a sparkling of style that elevate it to the status of literature.

ACHIEVEMENTS

Pierre-Augustin Caron de Beaumarchais is that rarity among literary figures: a famous writer who also has solid achievements to his credit in other, nonliterary, domains. For example, at the age of only twenty-one, Beaumarchais invented a new mechanical device for pocket watches that permitted the construction of small, flat timepieces in place of the bulky, spherical ones then current. The invention made him

Pierre-Augustin Caron de Beaumarchais (Hulton Archive by Getty Images)

famous in the scientific community, earned for him the title of "Watchmaker to the King," and assured the prosperity of his father's watchmaking business for years to come. Later, in his forties, Beaumarchais made significant contributions to the French monarch as a diplomat on foreign missions, his most notable achievement being his creation of a shipping company that helped the American colonists arm themselves during the American Revolution. Beaumarchais managed to supply the arms without implicating the French crown, earning the gratitude of his own government and a permanent niche in U.S. history as well. During that same period, Beaumarchais, by then a published playwright, was instrumental in founding the Société des Auteurs and was elected its first president, thus assuring for himself a place of honor in the history of playwriting as a profession in France. Yet all of these extra literary achievements, taken together, are not the equal of his achievement as the author of the finest French comedy of the eighteenth century, *The Marriage of Figaro*, and as the creator of the modern, postclassical theater in France, which managed to take many liberties with the rigid rules of classical tradition without losing any of the aesthetic and philosophical power inherent in the nature of drama. Beaumarchais's greatest achievement was accomplished by example: He demonstrated how a play could be freed of the constraints of a prescribed form and yet be a work of art.

BIOGRAPHY

An ambitious activist by nature, Pierre-Augustin Caron de Beaumarchais, born Pierre-Augustin Caron, led a far more eventful life than is customary for a man of letters. The ups and downs of his often agitated existence, however, were seldom directly related to the literary life, resulting rather from his determined pursuit of wealth, preferment, and pleasure, from his involvement in legal wrangles, and, most honorably, from Beaumarchais's disinterested struggles against injustice.

The son of a watchmaker, Beaumarchais was apprenticed at an early age to his father's craft and mastered it so thoroughly that, when only twenty-one, he worked out a solution to one of the craft's most difficult problems in mechanics: the contrivance of a radically simplified escapement, the device that transfers the energy of a watch's spring to the network of interlocking wheels that make up its movement. The naïve young watchmaker made the mistake of showing his device to an older colleague, who promptly published a description of it as his own invention. The younger Caron complained to the Academy of Sciences, won public vindication and recognition thereby, and from that notoriety was able to establish himself as a personage of consequence at the court of Louis XV, even becoming music teacher to the king's daughters. Thus launched into the social whirl, Beaumarchais went on to a series of other activities and enterprises over the next fifteen years, increasing his fortune and prestige, while marrying and acquiring the title that enabled him to call himself Caron de Beaumarchais. In those years, he continued to encounter envy and injustice and continued to fight against those evils with courage and energy, at the same time learning valuable lessons about the human heart.

Those lessons came to fruition when Beaumarchais began his career as a playwright in 1767, at the age of thirty-five, with a tearful family drama about a young and innocent girl seduced and deceived by an aristocrat. The play, *The School of Rakes* (*Eugénie* in the original French, after its heroine-victim), enjoyed only a brief and modest success with the public. With characteristic determination, Beaumarchais tried for public success in the theater three years later, with his second play *The Two Friends*, which fared even worse with the public and was withdrawn after a very few performances. Beaumarchais was disappointed in the public failure to understand his theme of the virtues of the merchant class but was still undeterred from his theatrical ambitions. Meanwhile, he found himself embroiled in a lawsuit over an inheritance and discovered that the judge in the case had been corrupted. Again injustice brought out his best, and he turned the evil to his own advantage by publishing a brilliant *mémoire* in which he revealed the judge's corrupt dealings, thereby winning public support and acclaim. Eventually he even won his lawsuit, though it took four more years. Meanwhile, he had his first unalloyed success in the theater in 1775 with his Molièresque comedy, *The Barber of Seville*, in which the public delighted. A year later, aided by secret government funding, Beaumarchais found himself energetically assisting the American rebels in their war against the British by procuring and shipping armaments to them, having recruited a veritable fleet of ships for the purpose, from all over Europe.

Beaumarchais attained the pinnacle of his career even while engaged with his enterprise to aid the Americans. He had written a sequel to *The Barber of Seville*, called *The Marriage of Figaro*, which was ready for production in 1778 but was denied permission for public performance, by decree of the royal censor, because some of its themes struck the censor as disrespectful toward the ruling aristocracy. Not until 1784 were the objections overcome, but when the play was finally performed, it proved to be Beaumarchais's greatest triumph and one of the most successful plays of the entire century. Because the play was thought by some to be frankly revolutionary in its implications, Beaumarchais found himself in relatively good standing with the revolutionary government when it took over a few years later. Nevertheless, his last play, *Frailty and Hypocrisy*, a rather solemn sequel to *The Marriage of Figaro*, was coolly received by the public in 1792 when it was first presented. Moreover, the envy and injustice that had dogged his entire life soon emerged again, in his relations with the revolutionary government. Falsely accused of counterrevolutionary activity, he was forced into exile for several years, and all his property was confiscated. In failing health, Beaumarchais was permitted to return to Paris in 1796; he died of a stroke in the spring of 1799.

ANALYSIS

Perhaps because he was already in his middle thirties when his literary career began, Pierre-Augustin Caron de Beaumarchais showed little of the ambitious originality or inventiveness of youth in his plays—most of his plots and character-types were quite consciously derived from the work of others—but he exhibited, from the first, an exceptional understanding of the real world, which he approached with high moral seriousness. Whether somber or lighthearted in tone, whether contemporary or historical in setting, whether traditional or modern in form, the plays of Beaumarchais are all, without exception, centrally concerned with some abuse or injustice in his own society. It is true that all of his plays, even the most somber, end happily and may in that sense be called romantic comedies; yet each play, including the most cheerfully frivolous of them, has an underlying seriousness of theme which is unmistakable. Although he quickly mastered the trick of entertaining the sophisticated Paris public, Beaumarchais never allowed his moralist's impulse to be obscured by theatrical technique. In his art as in his life, he remained always the passionate and vocal opponent of injustice and fraud: His open advocacy of moral positions was perhaps his most distinctive trait as a playwright.

Through two of his plays, *The Barber of Seville* and *The Marriage of Figaro*, Beaumarchais redefined the art of theatrical comedy in France, making moral seriousness an acceptable main ingredient of the genre, and gave future generations one of the great character-types in literature with the invention of Figaro. He has had a significant and durable influence on all subsequent theatrical writing in France.

THE SCHOOL OF RAKES

Beaumarchais's outspoken advocacy of moral positions was already fully in evidence with his very first play, *The School of Rakes*. The focus of the play is a crisis in the life of a young and innocent English lady, Eugénie, who believes herself to be married to a prominent aristocrat, Lord Clarendon, only to learn, by chance, that her "husband" is about to marry someone else. The announcement of that impending marriage reveals to Eugénie that she has been deceived by Lord Clarendon, who staged a false wedding ceremony with the complicity of servants and friends in order to make her his mistress. To make her sense of shame truly complete, Eugénie finds herself newly pregnant just when the crushing truth of her plight emerges. The result is a crisis of despair, followed by a tense confrontation scene with Lord Clarendon as the play's dramatic climax. The play ends with a genuine marriage between a contrite Lord Clarendon and a forgiving Eugénie, but Beaumarchais's thrust is plain: His purpose is to attack the immoral cynicism of the powerful nobility, who prey on the innocence of decent young ladies. Surprisingly modern in its viewpoint, *The School of Rakes* is a protest against high society's double standard of sexual morality.

The theme of the social victimization of women was probably "borrowed" by Beaumarchais from Denis Diderot's novel *La Religieuse* (1796; *The Nun*, 1797), which had been written in 1760 and had made the subject popular. Beaumarchais openly claimed Diderot as his inspiration for the form of his play, at any rate, noting in his preface that he admired Diderot's invention of a new theatrical genre called *le drame sérieux*—a play neither tragic nor comic but occupying the intermediate ground between the two. It was that middle ground Beaumarchais sought to occupy with *The School of Rakes*, portraying scenes of great emotional anguish arising out of common human events, rather than events of heroic dimension, and showing the amusing side of human behavior as well, without employing the devices of excess and exaggeration that make up classic comedy. For Diderot, and for his admirer Beaumarchais, the new order of theater, *le drame sérieux*, was to be above all human, and therefore touching, rather than awe-inspiring as the classic theater had been, because it dealt with human behavior at its extreme limits.

THE TWO FRIENDS

These theories of Diderot were even more fully put into practice in Beaumarchais's second play, *The Two Friends*—more fully because, whereas *The School of Rakes* had concerned privileged members of the English aristocracy, albeit with very ordinary problems of human relationships, *The Two Friends* concerns members of the urban middle class, men engaged in commerce and finance, and a drama of bankruptcy and the sense of honor in the world of business. Diderot had advocated a focus on middle-class values in order to make the theater accessible to an increasingly middle-class audience—Diderot's preferred term was *le drame bourgeois*—but it proved difficult, after all, to find themes of compellingly high drama among the daily passions of the bourgeoisie. Diderot himself never wrote a successful play, in spite of the persuasiveness of his theory about the imperatives of a truly modern theater, and Beaumarchais had the worst disaster of his career with the play in which Diderot's theories were most faithfully followed. *The Two Friends* failed both with the public and with the critics and had to be withdrawn after a few performances in 1770. With characteristic resilience, however, Beaumarchais abandoned *le drame sérieux*, devised a play with a more frankly comic action reminiscent of Molière, and in early 1775 was represented on the Paris stage with his first genuine success, the play that made him famous, *The Barber of Seville*.

THE BARBER OF SEVILLE

The basic plot of *The Barber of Seville* derives from the ancient traditions of farce, and had its most notably successful incarnation, before Beaumarchais, in Molière's witty comedy *L'École des femmes* (1662; *The School for Wives*, 1732). The ingredients of the plot are simple. An apparently innocent young girl is the ward of a tyrannical older man who keeps her strictly isolated from the company of potential young suitors because he intends to marry her himself. In spite of the guardian's vigilance, however, the

not-so-innocent young girl finds a way to make contact with a suitable young man and so defeat the guardian's evil scheme. Beaumarchais's distinctive contribution to this ancient plot is the invention of a clever and resourceful character of the servant class—Figaro—who conducts the intrigue by which the young suitor successfully wins the girl. Moreover, as one might expect, the playwright found in the simple comic plot an underlying serious theme to which he proposed to give some prominence: the abuse of the powers of guardianship and the consequent oppression of women.

Perhaps because he feared that such criticism of the social customs of his day might run afoul of the royal censor, Beaumarchais decided to set his play in the Spain of the seventeenth century rather than in the Paris of the eighteenth. To mask the seriousness of his theme, he adopted a tone of cheerful cynicism that pervaded all the dialogue and characterized the attitudes and actions of all the principal players. This tone is precisely established in the very first scene, in which Count Almaviva, in disguise, waits in a Seville street to catch a glimpse of Rosine at her window and sees coming toward him his former valet, Figaro, now a barber and general handyman for anyone who will pay him. The dialogue which ensues is witty, disrespectful, even impudent, but always lighthearted. For example, when the Count reminds Figaro that, as a servant, he had been rather a bad lot, lazy and careless about his responsibilities, Figaro immediately replies: "Yes, my lord, but only in comparison to what is demanded of servant. . . . Considering the virtues expected of a domestic, does Your Excellence know very many Masters who have the qualifications to be Valets?"

Not only is the tone for the whole play set by this witty dialogue, but also the work of exposition is skillfully accomplished; in short order, the reader learns why the Count has followed Rosine from Madrid to Seville, why Doctor Bartholo is keeping her so carefully sequestered, and how Figaro can use his position as barber to the Bartholo household to arrange for the Count to have a private talk with Rosine. The scene that follows completes the exposition, showing Rosine in hostile conversation with Dr.

Bartholo, while contriving to drop a written message from her window to the Count in the street below without allowing her guardian to grasp what is happening. As Figaro laughingly remarks of Rosine's maneuver: "If you want to bring out the skill of even the most innocent young girl, you have only to imprison her." The rest of the play, which is constructed in four acts, simply treats the audience to the step-by-step working out of the conspiracy among Count Almaviva, Rosine, and Figaro adumbrated in the two expository scenes that begin the play.

Such a simple plot, in which Dr. Bartholo's selfish designs are thwarted and Count Almaviva wins the hand of Rosine, has the great virtue of giving the play constant clarity of direction and aesthetically satisfying unity of action, but it carries the concomitant risk of boring the audience: The outcome is predictable from the opening moments. Beaumarchais uses two devices to overcome this predictability and intensify the sense of dramatic excitement as the action unfolds. First, he tightens the time frame by having Bartholo learn, early in the second act, from Rosine's music teacher Don Bazile, that Count Almaviva is in Seville, disguised and determined to make contact with Rosine. This news causes Bartholo to make hasty arrangements to marry his ward the very next day, leaving the conspirators only a few hours in which to achieve their goal. Then, Beaumarchais contrives a series of incidents, in the second, third, and fourth acts, in which Rosine, the Count, Figaro, or all three together find themselves in danger of having their plan found out by Bartholo. Each such scene causes the tension to mount until the danger passes, at the same time forestalling any tendency on the spectator's part to become bored, since the outcome is thus repeatedly put in doubt.

It is, however, probably not the plot so much as the characters that attract and hold the interest of spectators and readers alike. Almaviva's insouciance and Rosine's native shrewdness make them an engaging couple, and their common enemy, Bartholo, is so absurdly self-centered and so maliciously jealous as a guardian that it affords the audience a positive pleasure to see his villainous intentions circumvented. The frank cynicism of Don Bazile, always ready to

serve the highest bidder, is well calculated to amuse, and nowhere more so than in his brilliant and memorable speech, in the second act, explaining the virtues of calumny as the best weapon available against one's enemies. The finest creation in the play, however, is unquestionably the character of Figaro, with his ready wit and indomitable good humor, his resourcefulness and amoral pleasure in every kind of intrigue, and above all his impudence in the face of power and his generous capacity for indignation against injustice. Nothing contributed more to the popular success of *The Barber of Seville* than the invention of this novel personality, so appealingly *sympathique* to the middle-class theater audiences of the 1770's. Beaumarchais understood, instinctively, the source of his sudden popularity, as he demonstrated by producing, almost immediately, a sequel to *The Barber of Seville* in which Figaro was even more prominently the main character. This was the sparkling masterpiece, *The Marriage of Figaro*, universally regarded as the crown jewel of Beaumarchais's theater.

THE MARRIAGE OF FIGARO

Having successfully slipped his rather strong social criticism in *The Barber of Seville* past the censor by burying it unobtrusively beneath a barrage of witty and irreverent dialogue, Beaumarchais set out, with perhaps understandable overconfidence, to make his sequel a much more explicit attack on the injustices of his time. By 1778, he was ready to present his new play, but the royal censor found it unacceptable. It took Beaumarchais six full years to overcome all the official objections and to see his new play, at last, on the boards. When it was finally performed, in 1784, it was to enthusiastic acclaim, both from the public and from the critics—not only Beaumarchais's greatest success but also probably the most successful work of the century in the theater.

The plot of *The Marriage of Figaro* is as intricate and convoluted as that of *The Barber of Seville* is simple and unilinear. It is true that, despite the complex interweaving of plots and subplots, the action of *The Marriage of Figaro* takes place within the space of a single day—but it is, as the subtitle in the original French indicates, a "mad day," full of unexpected twists and turns, arrivals and departures, disguises and deceptions, all of which transform Count Almaviva's palace into a daylong carnival. However complicated, the action is nevertheless coherently organized around one central event that lends a certain unity to the whole: the promised marriage of Figaro, now in the full-time service of Almaviva as valet and concierge, to Suzanne, first chambermaid of the former Rosine, now Countess Almaviva. What complicates the plot is that the impending marriage faces threats from several quarters: Almaviva himself, who has granted permission for the marriage, is nevertheless scheming to seduce Suzanne and make her his convenient in-house mistress, using the threat to refuse permission for the wedding if Suzanne will not cooperate; Marceline, the former mistress of Dr. Bartholo, is bent on forcing Figaro to live up to a promise he made her in writing to marry her if he failed to repay a loan by a specific date; and the Countess, suffering in the role of abandoned wife, seeks to thwart her husband's efforts to seduce Suzanne, which in turn angers Almaviva and makes him prone to go back on his promise to Figaro. Further complexities are added by the intersecting subplots involving the adolescent page, Chérubin, and the gardener's adolescent daughter, Fanchette; the old affair between Bartholo and Marceline, which turns out to have had surprising consequences when it is revealed that Figaro is their long-lost son; and the active plotting of the Countess, who suddenly decides to play an inopportune trick on her husband in an effort to win back his love. This multiplicity of events imparts to the play a magical air of movement, merriment, and surprise that keeps the reader constantly amused and attentive, as though observing the action of a new and complicated mechanical toy. It is this interlocking of so many diverse elements that has led some critics to see, in the structure of *The Marriage of Figaro*, the influence of Beaumarchais's training as a watchmaker. Certainly that intricate structure has much to do with the enchantment that the play produces in its audiences. When well staged, *The Marriage of Figaro* is a delightful kaleidoscopic spectacle.

The multiplicity of the action is matched by the variety of the comic devices used, the many rather daring shifts in tone from scene to scene, and the dizzyingly numerous reversals in fortune; the advantage seems to lie now with Figaro, now with the Count, over the matter of who will have his way. *The Marriage of Figaro* is a play that is constantly in motion: Not only are the actors required to move about a lot physically, but also they are required to exhibit a wide gamut of changing moods and emotions, and to time their entrances, exits, dialogue, and gestures with exceptional precision. Nothing is more distinctive about this play—especially in contrast to *The Barber of Seville*—than the breakneck pace at which it must be performed. There is nothing very original about the individual scenes, for as always with Beaumarchais, the dramatic ideas are quite derivative, but the intricate meshing of so many different types of scenes, without any loss of coherence or unity, is a tour de force of inventive ingenuity, the result of which was a style of comic theater that had never been seen before in France.

The Marriage of Figaro, however, is much more than a triumph of theatrical technique. For all its artificiality, which is obtrusive and undeniable, the play still manages to be memorably alive, by virtue both of the underlying truth of certain of its characters and situations and of the major themes to which it gives powerful expression. An unforgettable example of truth in characterization is the figure of Chérubin, who makes a kind of poetry out of the impulses of puberty, feeling impelled by instincts he does not understand to be constantly in the female presence and comporting himself with the strangest mixture of mischievous playfulness and exaggerated sentiment. Chérubin is not so much a realistic as an imaginative portrait of an adolescent, simultaneously child and man. Among the situations that delicately evoke emotions in the play is the daring moment, early in act 2, in which the Countess and Suzanne are trying out their scheme to disguise Chérubin as a girl so that he can be part of the wedding celebration, instead of going off to join a regiment as the Count has ordered. The situation is farcical in nature, but Beaumarchais is able to display a remarkable interplay of sensibilities as the two women react, each in a different way, to the ambiguous sexuality of the embarrassed adolescent.

The most pervasive of the play's principal themes is that represented by the struggle between Figaro and the Count, which epitomizes the eternal clash between figures of authority and privilege and the common individual longing for dignity. The nature of that clash and its basic injustice are memorably articulated by Figaro in his famous monologue of act 5, in which he complains that all the Count had to do to have so much wealth, prestige, and power was "to give himself the trouble to be born." Such words were daringly provocative to the Paris audiences of 1784, among whom the mood of revolution against aristocratic authority was already close to the surface. A second important theme is that of the systematic oppression of women, evident in the way the Count treats both the Countess and Suzanne, and the way Bartholo and Figaro deal with Marceline's wish to be legally married. Again the theme is strikingly articulated in the famous words of Marceline in act 3, which read even today as a very enlightened manifesto of women's rights. One might add that the theme of injustice is broached in a variety of forms in the play, but nowhere more pointedly than in the trial scenes of act 3, in which Beaumarchais brings off a hilarious satire of the legal system of the time. It seems inescapable that the true greatness and originality of *The Marriage of Figaro* must, in the final analysis, be defined as an extraordinary blend of technical energy in comic style and moral passion powerfully expressed. It is difficult to find its equal in that special combination of qualities.

TARARE AND FRAILTY AND HYPOCRISY

Beaumarchais himself never again reached such heights in his career. The libretto he composed for the opera *Tarare*, a few years after *The Marriage of Figaro*, was excessively simplistic and sentimental in plot, and written in flat and unimaginative verse. Poetry was not one of his talents. When he tried to revive his flagging popularity among the new postrevolutionary audiences, he turned to the material that had brought him success in the past and composed a sequel to *The Marriage of Figaro*, entitled *Frailty and Hypocrisy*, which was performed in 1792. The comic verve was gone, however, and the characters of Figaro, Suzanne, Almaviva, and the Countess

had all lost their youthful sparkle; the play seemed a self-righteous sermon on the need for compassion between spouses for the sins of youth. There was little in that final play of Beaumarchais's career to suggest the skillful theatrical technician of twenty years earlier. Only the passions of the committed moralist and the determined enemy of injustice were still in evidence, poignant reminders of past glory. Though *Frailty and Hypocrisy* was poorly received in 1792, it is interesting to note that a revival of the play in 1797 had a great success, and certainly eased the sorrow of Beaumarchais's painful last years. Nevertheless, the reputation he left behind was a major one.

OTHER MAJOR WORKS

NONFICTION: *Mémoires*, 1773-1774.

BIBLIOGRAPHY

Dunkley, John. *Beaumarchais: "Le Barbier de Séville."* Critical Guides to French Texts 86. London: Grant and Cutler, 1991. A critical appraisal of Beaumarchais's *The Barber of Seville*. Includes a bibliography.

Grendel, Frédéric. *Beaumarchais: The Man Who Was Figaro*. New York: T. Y. Crowell, 1977. An examination of the life and work of Beaumarchais. Includes a bibliography and index.

Howarth, W. D. *Beaumarchais and the Theatre*. New York: Routledge, 1995. Howarth examines six of Beaumarchais's plays and their reception by audiences, placing them within the context of prerevolutionary France. He traces the dramatist's legacy in nineteenth century vaudeville and twentieth century comic drama. Includes a bibliography and index.

Niklaus, Robert. *Beaumarchias: "Le Mariage de Figaro."* Critical Guides to French Texts 21. London: Grant and Cutler, 1995. Niklaus provides a critical examination of Beaumarchais's *The Marriage of Figaro*. Includes a bibliography

Sungolowsky, Joseph. *Beaumarchais*. New York: Twayne, 1974. A basic biography of Beaumarchais, along with criticism and interpretation of his works. Includes a bibliography.

Murray Sachs

FRANCIS BEAUMONT

Born: Grace-Dieu, Leicestershire, England;
   c. 1584
Died: London, England; March 6, 1616

PRINCIPAL DRAMA

The Woman Hater, pr. c. 1606, pb. 1607 (with John
   Fletcher)

The Knight of the Burning Pestle, pr. 1607, pb.
   1613

The Coxcomb, pr. c. 1608-1610, pb. 1647 (with
   Fletcher)

Philaster: Or, Love Lies A-Bleeding, pr. c. 1609,
   pb. 1620 (with Fletcher)

The Captain, pr. c. 1609-1612, pb. 1647 (with
   Fletcher)

The Maid's Tragedy, pr. c. 1611, pb. 1619 (with
   Fletcher)

A King and No King, pr. 1611, pb. 1619 (with
   Fletcher)

Cupid's Revenge, pr. 1612, pb. 1615 (with
   Fletcher)

Four Plays, or Moral Representations, in One,
   pr. c. 1612, pb. 1617 (with Fletcher; commonly
   known as *Four Plays in One*)

The Masque of the Inner Temple and Grayes Inn,
   pr., pb. 1613 (with Fletcher)

The Scornful Lady, pr. c. 1615-1616, pb. 1616
   (with Fletcher)

*The Tragedy of Thierry, King of France, and His
   Brother Theodoret*, pr. 1617(?), pb. 1621 (with
   Fletcher; commonly known as *Thierry and
   Theodoret*)

*The Dramatic Works in the Beaumont and Fletcher
   Canon*, pb. 1966-1996 (10 volumes; Fredson
   Bowers, editor)

OTHER LITERARY FORMS

Known almost exclusively as a dramatist, Francis
Beaumont did publish one verse satire, *Salmacis and
Hermaphroditus* (1602), and several lyrics. A collection of his verse, entitled *Poems*, was published in
1640.

ACHIEVEMENTS

Francis Beaumont's imprint on seventeenth century drama cannot be distinguished from that of John
Fletcher, since their jointly written plays secured the
reputations of both men. Indeed, the success of their
collaboration from about 1606 until 1613 was such
that later editors assumed their few solo plays to have
been joint productions. Moreover, Fletcher's many
collaborations with other writers, most notably Philip
Massinger, were widely regarded throughout the seventeenth century as the works of Fletcher and Beaumont.

Though rarely produced after the Restoration and
without critical stature since that time, the Beaumont-
Fletcher collaborations, including, among others,
Philaster, The Maid's Tragedy, and *A King and No
King*, captured large, fashionable audiences with their
blend of satire, sophisticated dialogue, and sexual titillation. These plays perfectly suited the tastes of the
more affluent theatergoers who patronized the indoor
Blackfriars playhouse, while the outdoor theaters ca-
tered to the middle-class taste for farce, romance, and
patriotic heroism. Beaumont and Fletcher's comedies
and tragicomedies expose middle-class optimism as
mere naïveté or ignorant ambition. Though never creating worlds as darkly depraved as those of John
Webster or George Chapman, Beaumont and Fletcher
nevertheless pictured society as corrupt, its rulers as
venal, its populace as stupid and conniving. Their
main characters, neither heroes nor villains, typically
represent the educated gentry. Worldly, well-spoken,
vain, they assume aristocratic privilege almost as a
virtue and thus are frequently boors, though never
unwitty ones. Good and evil have little relevance in
the Beaumont-Fletcher world. Favor is granted those
who can seduce or acquire wealth with the greatest
aplomb, the most studied indifference. Overt ambition, lack of humor, bad manners, and slow wits mark
the losers.

Though the Beaumont-Fletcher partnership ended
in 1613 and both playwrights were dead by 1625,
their collaborations stayed popular for the rest of the

century, Restoration critics regarding them as contemporary masterpieces while reducing the works of William Shakespeare and Ben Jonson to the status of mere classics. William Wycherley, Sir George Etherege, William Congreve, and, to some extent, John Dryden all wrote as followers of the Beaumont-Fletcher tradition. Those tastes in drama to which the pair had appealed at the Blackfriars were confirmed and intensified in the self-consciously fashionable audiences after 1660.

When fashions changed early in the eighteenth century, the Beaumont-Fletcher collaborations disappeared from the stage and have rarely been revived. Ironically, the least popular play in the canon, Beaumont's *The Knight of the Burning Pestle*, was increasingly performed, particularly in the twentieth century, and came to be critically regarded as one of the greatest Renaissance comedies. Structurally a daringly original play, *The Knight of the Burning Pestle* deliberately blurs the distinctions between players and audience, play and reality. In an era when taste in drama has been molded by Eugène Ionesco, Samuel Beck-

ett, and Thornton Wilder, *The Knight of the Burning Pestle* is perhaps more at home than at any previous time.

BIOGRAPHY

Francis Beaumont's life varied significantly from that of the stereotypical Elizabethan playwright, who emerged from the trade class, worked his way through Oxford or Cambridge, and struggled for an insecure living by writing for the stage, the press, and occasional patrons. As the son of a wealthy Leicestershire judge descended from the Norman nobility, Beaumont seems not to have pursued either his education or his writing out of burning ambition or necessity. Entering Broadgates Hall (later Pembroke College), Oxford, at age twelve, Beaumont left a year later, on the death of his father, and never returned to the university. He turned instead to the family profession, law, being admitted to the Inner Temple in 1600, but, again, he did not complete his studies.

During this time, Beaumont became one of the habitués of the London literary scene, befriending such luminaries as Michael Drayton and Ben Jonson. Drayton called Beaumont and his brother John, a poet, "My deare companions whom I freely chose/ My bosome friends," while the first quarto of Jonson's *Volpone* (pr. 1606) includes commendatory verses by one "F. B.," probably Beaumont. The playwright's famous association with fellow dramatist John Fletcher began in these years also, with the first of their collaborations occurring about 1606. A bishop's son, Fletcher shared with Beaumont an aristocratic heritage and Bohemian tastes. According to contemporary chronicler John Aubrey, the friends enjoyed "a wonderful consimility of phansey": "They lived together on the Banke side, not far from the Playhouse, both batchelors; lay together; had one Wench in the house between them, which they did so admire; the same cloathes and cloake, etc. between them."

Though immersed in the life of the city, Beaumont remained a member of the gentry, having inherited the family holdings on the death of his elder brother Henry in 1605. A verse letter to Jonson indicates his occasional sojourns at Grace-Dieu throughout his London years. Finally, in 1613, the same year that

Francis Beaumont (Library of Congress)

Shakespeare left London for Stratford, Beaumont ended his collaboration with Fletcher in order to marry Ursula Isley, heiress of Sundridge Hall in Kent, and return to country life. The marriage, which produced two daughters, abruptly ended three years later with Beaumont's death, on March 6, 1616.

ANALYSIS

To describe the style of a writer whose greatest body of work was done in collaboration is, to say the least, difficult. Three centuries of commentators have arrived at widely differing judgments of the contributions of John Fletcher and Francis Beaumont to the plays they are known to have written together. As nothing is known of their characteristic collaborative process, it is presumptuous to look at linguistic cues or at staging patterns as indicators of the dominant hand in certain plays or even in particular scenes. Moreover, because their collaboration produced works remarkably distinct in style from the few solo works by either man, one cannot say which characters or ideas seem typical of Beaumont and which of Fletcher.

What one can do is compare a typical work of the Beaumont-Fletcher collaboration with the single play, *The Knight of the Burning Pestle*, which is believed to be wholly Beaumont's, in order to understand his work. In these different contexts, remarkably different pictures of Beaumont the playwright emerge.

THE WOMAN HATER

Though the first version of *The Woman Hater* is considered to have been Beaumont's alone, the only extant version of the play is that revised by Fletcher in 1607, the first year of their collaboration, and it well represents the typical features of the Beaumont-Fletcher plays. Acted early in 1606 by the Children of St. Paul's, *The Woman Hater* was among those plays taken over by the King's Men when the children's company disbanded later that year. The play was acted periodically, to some acclaim, throughout the decades before the closing of the theaters in 1642. Its longevity is attested by the publication of two quartos, the first in 1607, the second in 1648-1649.

The 1607 prologue proclaims the play neither comedy nor tragedy: "A Play it is, which was meant to make you laugh, how it will please you, is not written in my part." This vagueness about form is understandable: Though the play holds together, at least somewhat, as a satire of classes and mores, the trivial plot and superficial characters make it incoherent and formless as a complete play. The pleasure it gave its audiences derives primarily from the satire—and, perhaps, from its mildly titillating dialogue between Gondarino, the misogynist, and the coquettish, though technically virginal, Oriana. The satire bites broadly rather than deeply, cutting across the ranks and occupations of society rather than exploring the corruption of a few significant individuals. One reason for the thinness of the play is that both playwrights are satisfied to have all characters function as mere caricature of familiar court and city types: the officious minister, Lucio, a would-be Machiavel; the feckless nobleman, Count Valore, who whiles away his hours with petty practical jokes; a nameless mercer, representative of the London middle class, a man easily gulled by a pimp into marrying a prostitute. Skulking through the play are also two anonymous intelligencers, courtiers of the most base and vicious sort, who feed the appetite of a decadent court for scandals and plots.

Perhaps the most extreme caricatures are the principals, Gondarino and Oriana, who embody in almost grotesque form the essential pointlessness, in the playwrights' view, of court life. In a Shakespearean comedy, the pair, a professed enemy of womankind and a clever, rich maiden, would gradually fall in love and, in the finale, marry. Beaumont and Fletcher continually tease the audience with this expectation, but the play ends with the two still mutual enemies and love nowhere to be found. At different points in the play, each professes eternal devotion to the other, but these exclamations are nothing more than tricks. There is, however, no real malice in their actions; the overwhelming impression one receives is that these deceptions are motivated merely by boredom.

The only genuine passion in *The Woman Hater* is that of the gluttonous courtier Lazarello, who gives his all in word and deed to win dinner invitations. His particular quest throughout the play is for the head of an umbrana fish, a rare delicacy, which is passed from courtier to courtier in return for favors. Though Lazarello's interest is the basest, he sparks more interest than any other character, because he seems to be the only figure who clearly attaches value to anything.

Although many commentators consider *The Woman Hater* primarily the work of Beaumont, with relatively few scenes exhibiting characteristic Fletcherian diction, the play must be considered essentially a collaboration. Its tone of cynical ennui, besides its structural emphasis on the individual scene rather than on the architectonics of the whole play, makes it very similar to *Philaster*, *A King and No King*, and other Beaumont-Fletcher tragicomedies. It is also so different in every way from *The Knight of the Burning Pestle* that one has no reason to consider *The Woman Hater* substantially the work of Beaumont alone.

THE KNIGHT OF THE BURNING PESTLE

The differences in tone and structure between *The Woman Hater* and *The Knight of the Burning Pestle* are so great that they can hardly be overstated. Where the earlier play exemplifies the typical jadedness of court life in the Beaumont-Fletcher world, the play of one year later offers an optimistic, highly original vision of human harmony. *The Knight of the Burning Pestle* is a boldly imaginative play, unconventional in some startling ways, yet fruitfully adapting conventions of the Elizabethan comic stage to Beaumont's fresh purpose. For example, the play features even more music and song than a typical Shakespearean comedy, with popular tunes and love lyrics helping to create and sustain an atmosphere of romance that would be for Beaumont's audience both idyllic and familiar. From Jonson's early comedies, such as *Every Man in His Humour* (pr. 1598, pb. 1601), Beaumont borrows a satiric perspective within which human foibles and pretensions are seen not as evil but as humbling and ironic. To Robert Greene, Thomas Dekker, and Thomas Heywood, he owes the ebullience of his middle-class characters, who carry his message of joy and harmony, even though his satire frequently makes sport of the outspoken citizen.

The Knight of the Burning Pestle is clearly Beaumont's work alone. The Beaumont-Fletcher plays have been frequently characterized as dominated by the sensational scene rather than moved forward by the plot. In plays such as *Philaster* and *A King and No King*, the plots often seem absurdly manipulated to bring certain volatile characters into confrontation; little thought seems to have been paid to the dramatic working out of a key idea or to the meaning of a conflict beyond the voltage that it can generate. In *A King and No King*, for example, the audience knows that the hero and heroine are brother and sister; the characters do not. The plot is constructed so that the two fall in love, are brought together in a passionate love scene, and then are shocked to discover the truth. There is no exploration of the moral alternatives, no facing up to the conflict between taboo and instinct; there is only the voyeuristic titillation of the audience. Conversely, *The Knight of the Burning Pestle* de-emphasizes the individual scene; all scenes are brief, with dialogues frequently interrupted by the surprising arrival of new characters. Emphasis is on movement toward resolution of the central conflict, which is nothing less than the open clash of two bourgeois ideas: romantic optimism and the virtues of industry. Through a plot that juggles two or three subplots simultaneously, so that even as one story progresses, the audience is aware of events occurring elsewhere, momentum builds to a romantic resolution that leaves all characters reconciled and the spirit of comedy triumphant.

A description of the play's movement suggests some of the complexity of its structure. The players enter, purporting to present a play entitled *The London Merchant*, presumably a typically anti-middle-class vehicle suited to Blackfriars taste. From the audience, however, comes a "Citizen," George the grocer, and his wife, Nell, who upbraid the players for their prejudice and demand that their apprentice, Rafe, be allowed to perform heroic scenes to honor the grocers of London. To humor the obstreperous pair, the players let Rafe give his speeches, similar to those that bourgeois audiences would have heard in the chivalric fantasies played at the outdoor theaters. At various points throughout the play, the intended performance is again interrupted by outbursts from the Citizens, so that Rafe can orate, sometimes alone but also in impromptu scenes hastily concocted between Rafe and one or two of the players. Surprisingly, Rafe turns out to be no ignorant blowhard, but a marvelously bright and multifaceted performer. Though the players never admit Rafe's talents, the audience observes as the play proceeds how readily they adapt themselves to meet the histrionic whims of George and Nell.

Meanwhile, the intended play also proceeds. As George had suspected, it does make "girds at Citizens," but, ironically, its hero and heroine are also middle-class; thus, the overall tone is not antibourgeois. Moreover, the satire always remains gentle. The play's most amazing character, old Merrythought, displays an utterly joyful faith in Providence that allows romantic optimism always to dominate the urge to find fault.

Simply told, *The London Merchant* begins by presenting the plan of Venturewell—the London merchant of the title—to marry his daughter, Luce, to a loyal but dull apprentice, Humphrey. Luce, however, loves Jasper Merrythought, another apprentice, who has been discharged by the merchant for his outspokenness—and for his attentions to Luce. Jasper has also been exiled from his home by his mother, who has decided to take the family belongings and leave her husband, whose carefree ways she can no longer tolerate.

With no money and in fear of the merchant, Jasper and Luce run off to be married; they, like old Merrythought, believe that things will always turn out for the best, if one does not worry. They are right. Through a surprising set of coincidences and a clever stratagem engineered by Jasper, the couple eventually wins the father's blessings, and the Merrythoughts, husband and wife, mother and son, are reconciled. Indeed, the sense of harmony is so pervasive that even the interludes by Rafe contribute to the overall effect. The players' growing acceptance of Rafe as a performer parallels the merchant's acceptance of Jasper and Luce and Mistress Merrythought's return to her husband.

It is easy to see why *The Knight of the Burning Pestle* failed in its time. For one reason, Beaumont seems to have tried the play on the wrong audience.

Romantic comedies about grocers (the pestle was the symbol of the grocers' guild) and other members of the middle class were doomed at the Blackfriars, even if they satirized tradesmen and their wives for their bluntness, ignorance, greed, and gullibility. Beaumont and the players perhaps thought, wrongly, that the sparkling good fun of this play would make the audience forget its animosities.

An equally important reason for its contemporary failure was its unconventional structure, and this might have ruined it for an audience at the outdoor theaters as quickly as it did for the viewers at the Blackfriars. Other plays, such as John Marston's *The Malcontent* (pr. 1604), include feigned confrontations between audiences and actors, but there are not any so fully instrumental to the play as those in *The Knight of the Burning Pestle*. No doubt the Blackfriars audience expected George and Nell to be harshly put down by the players when the couple first interrupted the action. When, however, their behavior was condoned and when, even worse, Rafe became a key performer, the audience was certainly confused, its dramatic expectations thoroughly thwarted. Though Elizabethan and Jacobean theatergoers tolerated many structural innovations, one does not find in this period any other play that so deeply questions the relationship between actor and spectator. One wonders indeed if Beaumont realized the originality of his venture before it was produced. Whatever the answer, one can speculate that the failure of this wonderful play led him to distrust his singular talents and to cultivate the partnership with Fletcher that won him popularity but not lasting fame.

OTHER MAJOR WORKS

POETRY: *Salmacis and Hermaphroditus*, 1602; *Poems*, 1640.

BIBLIOGRAPHY

Bliss, Lee. *Francis Beaumont*. Boston: Twayne, 1987. This readable book, medium in length, opens with a biographical sketch and continues with detailed analyses of all Beaumont's major works. This book reproduces a portrait of Beaumont and includes a thorough, well-annotated bibliography.

Clark, Sandra. *The Plays of Beaumont and Fletcher: Sexual Themes and Dramatic Representation.* New York: Harvester Wheatsheaf, 1994. An analysis of Beaumont and John Fletcher's dramatic works with an emphasis of sexual themes. Bibliography and index.

Finkelpearl, Philip J. *Court and Country Politics in the Plays of Beaumont and Fletcher.* Princeton, N.J.: Princeton University Press, 1990. An examination of the role of politics in the dramas of Beaumont and John Fletcher. Bibliography and index.

Gossett, Suzanne. *The Influence of the Jacobean Masque on the Plays of Beaumont and Fletcher.* New York: Garland, 1988. Gossett looks at the ways in which masques influenced the dramas of Beaumont and John Fletcher.

Masten, Jeffrey. *Textual Intercourse: Collaboration, Authorship, and Sexualities in Renaissance Drama.* Cambridge, England: Cambridge University Press, 1998. An examination of the collaboration of Beaumont and John Fletcher and the nature of their relationship.

Christopher J. Thaiss,
updated by John R. Holmes

SAMUEL BECKETT

Born: Foxrock, Ireland; April 13, 1906
Died: Paris, France; December 22, 1989

PRINCIPAL DRAMA

En attendant Godot, pb. 1952, pr. 1953 (*Waiting for Godot*, 1954)

"Fin de partie," Suivi de "Acte sans paroles," pr., pb. 1957 (music by John Beckett; *"Endgame: A Play in One Act," Followed by "Act Without Words: A Mime for One Player,"* 1958)

Krapp's Last Tape, pr., pb. 1958 (one act), revised pb. 1992

Act Without Words II, pr., pb. 1960 (one-act mime)

Happy Days, pr., pb. 1961

Play, pr., pb. 1963 (English translation, 1964)

Come and Go: Dramaticule, pr., pb. 1965 (one scene; English translation, 1967)

Not I, pr. 1972, pb. 1973

That Time, pr., pb. 1976

Footfalls, pr., pb. 1976

Ends and Odds, pb. 1976

A Piece of Monologue, pr., pb. 1979

Rockaby, pr., pb. 1981

Ohio Impromptu, pr., pb. 1981

Catastrophe, pr. 1982, pb. 1983

Company, pr. 1983

Collected Shorter Plays, pb. 1984

OTHER LITERARY FORMS

Samuel Beckett worked in literary forms other than drama. Although his radio plays, film script, and teleplays may be viewed as dramas that differ only in their use of various media, they nevertheless indicate his versatile and experimental approach to literary form. In prose fiction, he wrote both novels and short stories. The trilogy of novels, *Molloy* (1951; English translation, 1955), *Malone meurt* (1951; *Malone Dies*, 1956), and *L'Innommable* (1953; *The Unnamable*, 1958), written in French between 1947 and 1949, constitutes a major accomplishment in the genre. These works, like the earlier novel *Murphy* (1938), developed a monologue style of unique tone, with which Beckett had first begun to experiment in his short stories, collected as *More Pricks than Kicks* (1934). His first published literary work, however, was a poem on time and René Descartes, *Whoroscope* (1930), which won for him a prize; this work was followed by a collection of poems entitled *Echo's Bones and Other Precipitates* (1935). Beckett also turned to translations of Spanish poetry with Octavio Paz's *An*

Anthology of Mexican Poetry in 1958. In addition, he distinguished himself with his several translations of his own work, from English into French (such as *Murphy*) and French into English (such as *Malone meurt*); Beckett continued this practice throughout his career as dramatist, notably with *En attendant Godot*, which he translated into *Waiting for Godot*, and *Fin de partie*, which he translated into *Endgame*.

Achievements

Samuel Beckett is famous for his fiction and drama, which he wrote both in French and in English. *Waiting for Godot* established the Irish Beckett as a unique writer because he elected the French language as his primary means of composition and English as his secondary one. The success of *Endgame* and *Krapp's Last Tape*, as well as his trilogy of French novels, led to Trinity College's awarding Beckett an honorary doctorate in 1959. Beckett also explored ra-

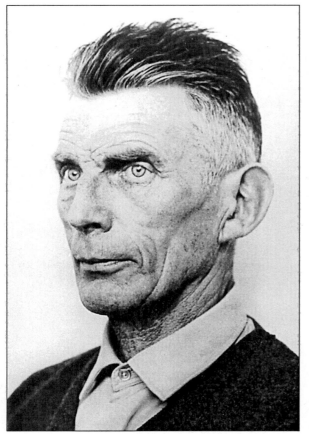

Samuel Beckett (© The Nobel Foundation)

dio, cinema, and television for his art. So conscious was he of style that people disappeared into mere voices, mere echoes, and his plays could be called, as one was, ironically, simply *Play*, performed in 1963 at about the same time as his screenplay, *Film*, was being made. In 1961, Beckett received the International Publishers' Prize with Jorge Luis Borges, and in 1970, he was awarded the Nobel Prize in Literature for artistic achievements that define the ironic stance of modern reactions to an increasingly meaningless existence.

Biography

Samuel Barclay Beckett was born at Foxrock, near Dublin, Ireland, on April 13, 1906, the second son of Mary and William Beckett. In 1920, he was sent to Portora Royal School, Enniskillen, and in 1923, he proceeded to Trinity College, Dublin, to study Italian and French. After receiving his B.A. degree in 1927, he went to Belfast as a French tutor, then to the École Normale Supérieure in Paris as a lecturer for two years, a period during which he became acquainted with James Joyce. Beckett then became lecturer in French at Trinity College and studied for his M.A. After two years, he left for Germany and returned to Paris in 1932. Doing odd jobs and writing when he could, he traveled to London, through France and Germany. This trip led to two publications: *More Pricks than Kicks* in 1934 and *Echo's Bones and other Precipitates* in 1935. Meanwhile, he had inherited an annuity after his father's death in 1933, allowing him to concentrate on his writing.

In 1937, Beckett returned again to Paris, where he began to write in French. At the same time, he was preoccupied with the English text of his first novel, *Murphy*, which was published in 1938, the same year that he was stabbed on a Paris street and nearly died. He recovered, however, and established himself in an apartment where he would live throughout World War II and long after, at 6, rue des Favorites. There, he began, with Alfred Péron, to translate *Murphy* into French. His friendship with Péron, however, was doomed by the war, which began while Beckett was visiting his mother in Dublin.

Nevertheless, Beckett returned to Paris, where he joined the French Resistance. Most of his colleagues, including Péron, disappeared, and Beckett himself barely escaped capture by the Nazis in 1942, when he fled to Free France with Suzanne Deschevaux-Dumesnil, whom he married in 1961. While in Free France, he worked on a farm for two years and began his novel *Watt* (1953). After the war, in 1945, Beckett began a remarkable period of five years during which he wrote most of his important fiction and drama. His fame began, though, with productions of *Waiting for Godot* in French in 1953 and in English in 1955, followed by productions of *Endgame* in French in 1957 and in English in 1958.

Meanwhile, other plays were produced, including his radio dramas *All That Fall* and *Embers*, broadcast by the British Broadcasting Corporation in 1957 and 1959, respectively. These productions complemented the mimes that Beckett prepared for the stage at about the same time, beginning with *Act Without Words*, which was produced on a double bill with *Endgame*, and continuing with variations to the end of Beckett's career with *Nacht und Träume* in 1983. He also prepared the script for a motion picture, *Film*, with Buster Keaton in the leading role, filmed in New York in 1964. After *Endgame*, Beckett composed two important stage plays, *Krapp's Last Tape* first produced in 1958, and *Happy Days*, in 1961. Radio and television, however, were his favorite media. From 1959, with *Embers*, and 1966, with *Eh Joe*, to the time of his death in 1989, Beckett devoted much of his talent to numerous radio and television works, testing the limits of audience understanding.

ANALYSIS

The dramatic works of Samuel Beckett reflect the evolution of his interests in various means of artistic expression, as he composed plays for stage, radio, cinema, and television. In his stage plays, he parodies traditional dramatic action and borrows the techniques used in other modes of entertainment. His themes are not constant, but they are grimly developed through a steady mood of ironic laughter if not outright sarcasm. Like the character "O" who runs from the camera's eye ("E") in *Film*, Beckett's art finds its form in a flight from conventional expectations and traditional observations. What seems meaningless and absurd is shown to be the only meaning possible in a universe where the human experience of consciousness (as subject) seems trapped by a nature and body (as object) without consciousness. Laughter is an intellectual triumph over material absurdity, and self-denial is self-affirmation. Beckett's plays are made of such paradoxes.

Whether it is in the nameless characters in *Play*, the lone and aging Krapp awaiting imminent death in *Krapp's Last Tape*, the pathetic Winnie sinking in her grave in *Happy Days*, the dying family in the masochistic *Endgame*, the monotonous life of waiting of Estragon and Vladimir in *Waiting for Godot*, or the down-and-outers in other dramatic works, Beckett demonstrates a preference for passive characters who attempt to make sense of an increasingly absurd existence and who struggle to survive in a universe that lacks love and meaningful relationships.

As a critic, a transitional thinker, an innovator, and a postmodernist who probed the human condition and sensed the absurdity of the modern world, Beckett tried to link art and life into unusual theatrical images in order to etch human beings' inner world and the human experience of consciousness. Even though his vision of life and the human predicament is discouraging, his plays are rich with clownish characters, slapstick humor, word games, irony, and sarcasm, allowing laughter to triumph over material absurdity.

Beckett is best known as the author of four intriguingly powerful stage plays; *Waiting for Godot*, *Endgame*, *Krapp's Last Tape*, and *Happy Days*. His later work has begun to receive critical attention, particularly those plays that focus on women, such as *Play* and especially *Not I*. With his first stunningly successful stage play, however, there is not a woman to be seen. Only two tramps, two strangely united male travelers, and a boy are on the stage of *Waiting for Godot*.

WAITING FOR GODOT

In this play, Beckett established his major tone of comic despair, with his characters resigned to waiting for something to happen that never happens. He also created his major dramatic style out of vaudevillian and silent-film skits by clownish characters who are determined to endure without understanding why they must. In two acts that mirror each other in language and action, *Waiting for Godot* mocks audience desire for significant form and visionary comprehension of human experience. The two protagonists are tramps by the name of Estragon (called Gogo) and Vladimir (called Didi). They seem doomed to repeat forever the experiences played out in the two acts, as they wait for the arrival of a mysterious person known to them only as Godot. This Godot never does arrive. Instead, a lordly fellow named Pozzo appears in the first act, leading his servant Lucky by a rope; in the second act, these two reappear, though Pozzo is now blind and Lucky is dumb.

The spareness of plot and scarcity of characters are reinforced by the stark setting. Only a tree (leafless in act 1, bearing a few leaves in act 2) and a lonely country road mark the location of this play's action through a day of trivial concerns by the two tramps. The interruption by Pozzo and Lucky of their monotonous life of waiting is dramatic, but it is drained of its significance by the incomprehension of the characters who participate in it. The dialogue of the four characters is, in its variety, a counterpoint to the monotony of the slapstick action: The tramps talk in short, quick bursts of verbal response to each other, Pozzo exclaims himself in bombastic rhetoric, and Lucky overflows once in a stream-of-consciousness monologue called "thinking." When they reappear in act 2, Pozzo's pomposity has been deflated into whining, and Lucky cannot speak at all. Thus does this play illustrate Beckett's intense concern for the nature and function of language itself in a world where there is so little worth communicating.

At the end of each act, Vladimir and Estragon threaten to separate, to leave—but in each act, they do not move as the curtain descends on them. The two tramps play word games to pass the time, and they entertain themselves with strategies for suicide, but they cannot kill themselves. Waiting is a part of their fate. Each act ends with the arrival of a boy to announce that Godot will not arrive this evening, but that he will come another time. The boy's claim that he is not the same boy who appeared in the first

act, that he tends sheep and that the other boy is his brother, a goatherd, constitutes allusions hinting at some religious mystery in the identity of Godot, the god who will separate sheep from goats on the day of judgment. If Didi and Gogo are denied their meeting with Godot, they are no less heroic for their waiting.

ENDGAME

Endgame is one act of waiting also, not for an arrival but rather for a departure. The servant of this play, called Clov, threatens to leave his master, Hamm, when a boy is sighted through one of the two windows in the room, or "shelter," that makes the setting for this play's action. The curtain drops without a definite commitment by Clov to move outside, and the boy is never seen by anyone except Clov. The title refers to the last phase of a game of chess, and two of the four characters move as if they were pieces in such a game. Hamm is unable to leave his chair, and Clov is unable to sit; Hamm orders Clov about, and Clov moves Hamm around. A blind ruler of his household, Hamm is a modern King Lear, blind and helpless to tend to his bodily needs. He wants his painkiller, and Clov tells him it is depleted. Hamm wants the ultimate painkiller of death but that seems elusive as well. Both Hamm and Clov wait for the end of the game of life, as all life outside their room seems at an end, except for the mysterious arrival of the boy.

On the stage are two other characters, Nagg and Nell, Hamm's parents. They have lost their legs in an accident and are as immobile as their son. They are kept by Hamm inside ash bins, pathetically reminiscing about their lives until the mother, Nell, dies and Nagg is sealed in his bin by Clov on orders from Hamm. Family values are far from the traditional ones of conventional domestic plots. Hamm tortures his father, or what remains of him, and Nagg torments his son exactly as he did when Hamm was a child. There is some remnant of affection in this play, though, just as there was in *Waiting for Godot*. The emotional tie between Gogo and Didi is repeated between Hamm and Clov, whose past binds them together even while they express a wish to separate. There is also a tie of romance holding the two parents together, though they cannot now reach each other for a kiss, and one of their most romantic adventures led to their helplessness—they lost their legs in a bicycle accident.

This play hints, through various allusions, at a meaning that transcends its apparent lack of meaning. Hamm is both an acting ham and a Prince Hamlet, calling attention to his role as a mockery of art in a meaningless universe; Hamm is also a piece of meat spiced by Clov in a world where human dignity no longer exists. The words and postures of both Hamm and Clov sometimes suggest that they are parodies of Christ on the Cross (where flesh is hammered with nails, puns on the names of the four characters), but there is no salvation for anyone in this play's world, unless it is to be in the boy waiting, perhaps contemplating his navel, beside a rock outside. Hamm is anxious for all life to end, even including that of a louse, so that the absurdity of human consciousness will cease. That boy outside is a threat, and so Hamm wants his life. Will life go on despite Hamm and evolve again, or will it finally wind down into nothingness? The play does not provide a clear sign of the answer as it concludes: Hamm replaces a bloody handkerchief over his blind eyes, and Clov, dressed as if for traveling, stands immobile watching the last pathetic moves of his master.

KRAPP'S LAST TAPE

Pathos is not the essence, however, of *Endgame*, though it may threaten to become so, as in the relationship of the tramps in *Waiting for Godot*. At the point of revealing a depth of passion that might pass for pathos, Beckett's plays pull back and laugh at the pointlessness of the possibility. Everything falls into nothing, everything dies, everything comes to a stop, though not quite, and that is the wild absurdity of it all. If the drama of entropy cannot quite come to a complete stop, that is not the fault of desire for it. In *Krapp's Last Tape*, where an ingenious use of recording tapes creates a dimension of time always present in its absence, the protagonist (and only character onstage) listens to recordings of his own voice from many years past, especially one when he was thirty-nine years old, some thirty years before. Krapp's wait for death, for an end to entropy, is supported by his

ironic dismissal of all that was meaningful at the time that he recorded the most important events of his life. In the present time of the play, Krapp is about to record the fact that the sound of the word "spool" is important, but he is drawn back to listen again and again to his recording of thirty years ago, when he described a lovemaking scene on a boat. His lust has declined, but his hunger for bananas and his thirst for wine have not, as he records his last tape.

Krapp's sense of himself, however, is threatened by the fragmented voices from his past; indeed, there is no continuous identity in this character, whose self-recording is a figure for the author's work itself. There is an irony of similarity here, for Beckett's own work may be reflected by the "plot" of *Krapp's Last Tape*. Voices are separated from the body, memories are mixed by mechanical forms, and the self is a stranger to itself. The drama of this discovery is in the encounter of one self with another, of silence yielding to voice, and voice subsiding into silence. These features increasingly preoccupied Beckett, as he moved his wit more and more into the regions of radio (all sound and voice) and mimes (no sound or voice).

HAPPY DAYS

More pathetic than all is the situation of Winnie in *Happy Days*. Entropy is visually represented by the intensifying imprisonment of Winnie, who appears in act 1 buried in a mound up to her waist and then, in act 2, up to her neck; she has become increasingly immobilized, and through it all she maintains her view of life as one of "happy days." She is happily stupid or courageously optimistic as she recounts her life's pleasures against the background of an unresponsive husband, Willie. At the end, dressed fit to kill, Willie calls his wife "Win" and seems prepared to shoot her with a pistol that she cannot seize for herself. She may be happy because she expects now to end it all with her death at last. Winnie's immobility is unchosen, and her waiting is absurdly imposed by the earth itself. As a ridiculous version of the earth-mother, Winnie is the opposite of her lethargic though "free" husband, and so she reflects the social condition of all women as well as the exploitation of that condition by men. *Happy Days*, like *Krapp's*

Last Tape, develops through monologue rather than dialogue, though in both plays the possibility for dialogue is kept alive for the sake of its ironic futility.

PLAY

The futility of dialogue, of communication, even perhaps of drama itself seems to direct the shape of the play called *Play*, which appears to have three characters who talk to one another, but in fact has three characters who talk without regard for, or awareness of, one another. The ash bins of Nell and Nagg in *Endgame* have become three gray urns in *Play*, and these contain the three characters—rather, they contain the heads of three characters who stare straight ahead, as if at the audience, but in fact only into a fiercely interrogating spotlight. Their predicament, like that of Winnie in *Happy Days*, is more frustrating for communication and self-dignity than that of Winnie or Nell and Nagg, whose memories are functional for some modicum of dialogue with another who shares those memories with them. The nameless characters of *Play* are two women and one man, once involved in a shabby conventional love tryst of a married couple and "another woman."

The drama of *Play* is a hell of isolation, regrets, emotional ignorance, and intellectual darkness. The play proceeds from a chorus of three voices in counterpoint, interrupted reminiscences without self-understanding, and a concluding chorus that repeats the opening, as if about to begin again. The urns are funereal wombs for talking heads. The emptiness of meaning from the lives of these characters is the utmost meaning they can express, and their lack of relationship is a judgment by the play on the failure of relationships in modern life generally. As in other Beckett plays of this period, the women of *Play* have a particularly painful message to deliver: Love and marriage do not exist as real possibilities for meaning for anyone anymore, especially for women, who have depended on them far more than men. The refusal to accept this predicament without a protest is dramatized in *Not I*, a play in which an apparently female character is divided between a Mouth of denial and an Auditor of silent protest. Here, Beckett has combined mime with radiolike monologue, and he has done it through a sexual pun on "ad-libbing."

ALL THAT FALL

To his achievements in stage plays, Beckett added successful accomplishments in radio and television drama, as well as one interesting script for motion pictures, *Film*. The radio plays of note are *All That Fall* and *Embers*; the teleplay deserving attention is *Eh Joe*. Communication, its failure or its emptiness, is a common theme running through Beckett's writing, and his experiments in various modes of artistic expression illustrate his search for success in communication. Radio was a challenging medium, using voice and other sounds to create imaginative shapes for audiences. *All That Fall* uses the muttering voice of an overweight old woman, Mrs. (Maddy) Rooney, making her way to a train station to meet her blind husband, Mr. (Dan) Rooney; her innermost thoughts and feelings are easily expressed in this medium, as are the concerns of those she meets along her way.

Like Beckett's other women, Mrs. Rooney has little to report that is fulfilling in her marriage; indeed, she mourns the loss of her one child, a daughter who would have been forty had she lived. Mrs. Rooney's real character is in her voice, not in her body; she can feel her self through her peculiar choice of words and sentence arrangements. This attention to vocabulary reveals Beckett's profound interest in the power of language as shaped and shaping sound. Of lesser interest is the terrible deed that lies at the center of this play's plot, the death of a child beneath the wheels of a train. Whether Mr. Rooney killed the child or not is less important than whether the audience can be moved by the mere articulation of sound to feel the horror of such a life-denying deed. *All That Fall* takes its title from a biblical verse that praises the power of a deity who protects "all that fall." The Rooneys hoot at this notion, though the child that fell beneath the train may, for all they can know, be better off than all those who, like the Rooneys, merely endure as they slowly decay with the rest of the universe.

EMBERS AND EH JOE

Like them, the narrating speaker of *Embers*, Henry, endures through a failing nature, but he uses language to explain rather than affirm failure and death. Like the waves of the sea beside which he sits while he speaks, Henry returns again and again to the same scenes of his life, trying to make them acceptable, especially his father's death and his wife's love. They are not yet coherent for him because they were experiences of futility rather than fulfillment, and so he goes on telling his story, revising as he composes, and composing as he speaks. Henry's regrets are motives for his narratives, and in *Eh Joe*, Joe's refusal to feel regret is a motive for the teleplay. As the television camera moves, like an interrogator or conscience, for an ultimate close-up of Joe's face, a voice interrupts, or propels, the camera's movement to tell a tale of suicide by a woman condemning Joe.

FILM

This technique is similar to that of *Film*, in which a male figure (played by Buster Keaton) fails to avoid self-perception, self-condemnation. In the movement of the film's narrative, the male figure is an Object ("O") for the subject of the camera's Eye ("E"); the whole action is a movement by the object of avoidance of becoming a subject. The drama of the story ends with the failure of avoidance. Art exists because of the duality narrated by the action of the film, and when the duality approaches unity, as self recognizes itself, the art ends and the object fades into a rocking subject. All that man the object, or the male figure, seems to be is an attempt to escape his consciousness of himself, including his destruction of photographs (apparently of himself) from his past. Ironically, however, in that final desperate attempt to remove images of himself, he is most fully brought to recognize himself as a subject.

The destructive deed turns out to be a constructive act, as if Beckett's film were commenting on the nature of his own art as a successful communication about failures of communication, an integration of disintegrating forms, and a discovery of meaning in meaninglessness.

OTHER MAJOR WORKS

LONG FICTION: *Murphy*, 1938; *Molloy*, 1951 (English translation, 1955); *Malone meurt*, 1951 (*Malone Dies*, 1956); *L'Innommable*, 1953 (*The Unnamable*, 1958); *Watt*, 1953; *Comment c'est*, 1961 (*How It Is*, 1964); *Mercier et Camier*, 1970 (*Mercier*

and *Camier*, 1974); *Le Dépeupleur*, 1971 (*The Lost Ones*, 1972); *Company*, 1980; *Mal vu mal dit*, 1981 (*Ill Seen Ill Said*, 1981); *Worstward Ho*, 1983.

SHORT FICTION: *More Pricks than Kicks*, 1934; *Nouvelles et textes pour rien*, 1955 (*Stories and Texts for Nothing*, 1967); *No's Knife: Collected Shorter Prose, 1947-1966*, 1967; *First Love and Other Shorts*, 1974; *Pour finir encore et autres foirades*, 1976 (*Fizzles*, 1976).

POETRY: *Whoroscope*, 1930; *Echo's Bones and Other Precipitates*, 1935; *Poems in English*, 1961; *Collected Poems in English and French*, 1977.

SCREENPLAY: *Film*, 1965.

TELEPLAYS: *Eh Joe*, 1966 (*Dis Joe*, 1967); *Tryst*, 1976; *Shades*, 1977; *Quad*, 1981.

RADIO PLAYS: *All That Fall*, 1957, revised 1968; *Embers*, 1959; *Words and Music*, 1962 (music by John Beckett); *Cascando*, 1963 (music by Marcel Mihalovici).

NONFICTION: *Proust*, 1931.

TRANSLATION: *An Anthology of Mexican Poetry*, 1958 (Octavio Paz, editor).

MISCELLANEOUS: *I Can't Go On, I'll Go On: A Selection from Samuel Beckett's Work*, 1976 (Richard Seaver, editor).

BIBLIOGRAPHY

Acheson, James. *Samuel Beckett's Artistic Theory and Practice: Criticism, Drama, and Early Fiction*. New York: St. Martin's Press, 1997. An examination of Beckett's literary viewpoint as it expressed itself in his drama and early fiction. Bibliography and index.

Birkett, Jennifer, and Kate Ince, eds. *Samuel Beckett*. New York: Longman, 2000. A collection of criticism of Beckett's works. Bibliography and index.

Essif, Les. *Empty Figure on an Empty Stage: The Theatre of Samuel Beckett and His Generation*. Drama and Performance Studies 13. Bloomington: Indiana University Press, 2001. A look at the criticism of Beckett's theatrical works over time. Bibliography and index.

Kim, Hwa Soon. *The Counterpoint of Hope, Obsession, and Desire for Death in Five Plays by Samuel Beckett*. New York: Peter Lang, 1996. An analysis of several psychological aspects present in Beckett's plays, including death and obsession. Bibliography and index.

Knowlson, James. *Damned to Fame: The Life of Samuel Beckett*. New York: Simon & Schuster, 1996. Knowlson retraces the personal development and literary evolution of Beckett, known to many as a creator of unique worlds inhabited by solitary individuals imprisoned in a world devoid of coherent communication. Bibliography and index.

McMullan, Anna. *Theatre on Trial: Samuel Beckett's Later Drama*. New York: Routledge, 1993. An examination of the later plays created by Beckett. Bibliography and index.

Oppenheim, Lois, ed. *Directing Beckett*. Ann Arbor: University of Michigan Press, 1994. This study examines the production and direction of Beckett plays. Bibliography and index.

Pattie, David. *The Complete Critical Guide to Samuel Beckett*. New York: Routledge, 2000. A reference volume that combines biographical information with critical analysis of Beckett's literary works. Bibliography and index.

Pilling, John, ed. *The Cambridge Companion to Beckett*. New York: Cambridge University Press, 1994. A comprehensive reference work that provides considerable information about the life and works of Beckett. Bibliography and indexes.

Worth, Katharine. *Samuel Beckett's Theatre: Life Journeys*. New York: Clarendon Press, 1999. A look at the production history and psychological aspects of Beckett's plays. Bibliography and index.

Richard D. McGhee

HENRY BECQUE

Born: Paris, France; April 18, 1837
Died: Paris, France; May 12, 1899

PRINCIPAL DRAMA

Sardanaple, pr., pb. 1867 (libretto, music by Victorien de Joncières; based on Lord Byron's *Sardanapalus*)

L'Enfant prodigue, pr., pb. 1868

Michel Pauper, pr. 1870, pb. 1871

L'Enlèvement, pr. 1871, pb. 1897

La Navette, pr., pb. 1878 (*The Merry-Go-Round*, 1913)

Les Honnêtes Femmes, pr., pb. 1880

Les Corbeaux, pr., pb. 1882 (*The Vultures*, 1913)

La Parisienne, pb. 1882, pr. 1885 (*The Woman of Paris*, 1913)

Madeleine, pb. 1896

Veuve, pb. 1897, pr. 1914

Le Domino à quatre, pb. 1897, pr. 1908

Une Exécution, pb. 1897

Le Départ, pb. 1897

Théâtre complet, 1909-1910 (2 volumes)

Les Polichinelles, pb. 1910, pr. 1924

Three Plays, pb. 1913

OTHER LITERARY FORMS

Henry Becque's literary career began with his writing the libretto for the opera *Sardanaple*, for which Victorien de Joncières wrote the music. This opera, atypical of Becque's literary efforts, is something he did not count in his own reckoning of his dramatic work. An imitation of George Gordon, Lord Byron's play *Sardanapalus: A Tragedy* (1821), *Sardanaple* clearly illustrates that Becque's artistic talent lay outside the realm of poetry, yet it did bring him to the theatrical world in which he would make his reputation as a controversial and innovative playwright. In addition to the controversies that his plays generated, Becque's dramatic criticism provoked controversy in an age that witnessed the birth of modern literary criticism. Becque's numerous essays and reviews for several Parisian journals, *Le Gaulois*, *La Revue illustrée*,

Le Figaro, and *Gil Blas* among them, brought him recognition as a sometimes formidable and original critic who not only championed the new, when he liked it, but also strove to demonstrate the universality and relevance of the old, particularly of the works of Molière. Many of his critical studies, along with some of his public lectures on drama, are collected in *Querelles littéraires* (1890) and *Souvenirs d'un auteur dramatique* (1895). More appear under the heading "Études d'art dramatique" in *Œuvres complètes de Henry Becque* (1924; seven volumes), edited by his grandnephew, Jean Robaglia. Robaglia's edition also contains *Notes d'album* (1898), a collection of Becque's maxims, as well as his few poems, some of his letters, and the fragments of his last and incomplete play, *Les Polichinelles*.

Although his sole operatic venture and his poetry have not exerted any influence on French literary thought, Becque's criticism still constitutes a significant chapter in the history of French theater. In his *Querelles littéraires*, for example, he considers the works of such disparate contemporaries as Giuseppe Verdi, Alexandre Dumas, *fils*, Alphonse Daudet, and Victorien Sardou. In other essays, he assesses the dramatic works and contributions of such writers as Sophocles, William Shakespeare, Molière, and Victor Hugo. Frequently and unabashedly biased, his essays reflect not only his opinions and observations but also the intensity and personal dimensions of dramatic criticism in France at that time.

ACHIEVEMENTS

Henry Becque's unquestionable literary achievement is to have given the theater two extraordinary plays, *The Vultures* and *The Woman of Paris*. An accomplished critic and the author of a dozen more plays, Becque is best remembered for the two major plays that set him squarely in the tradition of nineteenth century realism. Some have declared Becque to be the father of naturalistic drama; others, taking quite seriously his professed scorn for the cynicism and squalor of naturalistic drama, have emphasized his realism and have distinguished him from Émile Zola and his circle. Clearly, Becque's relation to naturalism remains the subject of some debate. On the

one hand, he did help to develop the dramatic subgenre *comédie rosse* that flourished at the Théâtre Libre of André Antoine: His *The Woman of Paris* served as a model that none of his imitators and self-styled disciples could quite duplicate. On the other hand, he soundly reprimanded the inadequacies of naturalism, and no matter how much he encouraged younger dramatists, they still derogated their tendencies to portray seaminess as such. A writer who took truth rather than beauty as his imperative, Becque remains closer to the art of Molière than to that of Zola. Becque's singleminded pursuit of optimum dramatic form to serve as a vehicle for intense social criticism was a noteworthy quest; he conscientiously avoided the neat formulas that the well-made play held out to him and, in his two major works, achieved unique forms of dramatic expression.

Becque's other achievements include his becoming first a *chévalier* (1886) and then an *officier* (1897) of the Légion d'Honneur as well as having been a candidate at three different times for the Académie Française. Although the honor of election to the French Academy eluded him, he was honored in various other ways. In 1893, his works were performed and his visits were celebrated in Milan and in Rome. He was also invited to lecture on drama in Liège and Brussels (1894), in Marseilles (1895), and in Holland and Denmark (1896).

BIOGRAPHY

Born in Paris on April 18, 1837, to Alexandre-Louis and Jeanne (Martin) Becque, Henry-François Becque was the second of three children in a family that always remained close. His elder brother, Charles, preceded him by three years, and his sister, Aimée, was born in 1841. As a child, Becque attended the Lycée Bonaparte (later, Lycée Condorcet) from 1848 to 1854, but he left school to seek employment without sitting for the *baccalauréat*. After a dozen years and a succession of positions with the Northern Railway Company, the Stock Exchange, the chancellery of the Légion d'Honneur, and the Polish count Alfred Potocki, Becque collaborated with Victorien de Joncières on the opera *Sardanaple*, which played at the Théâtre-Lyrique in 1867. This short-lived production may have prompted Becque to write, as his uncle Pierre Martin (Martin Lubize) had done, for the vaudeville stage and to produce *L'Enfant prodigue* (the prodigal son).

A month after Becque's second play, *Michel Pauper*, opened at the Porte Saint-Martin in June, 1870, the Franco-Prussian War began, and Becque, who enlisted at once in the French army, took part in the siege of Paris. The lack of success of *L'Enlèvement* (the elopement) drove Becque away from the theater for a time and back to the Stock Exchange for his livelihood. In 1876, he began writing for one of the many journals to which he would contribute and became drama critic for *Le Peuple*. Over the years, he also wrote for *Henri IV*, *L'Union republicaine*, *Le Matin*, *La Revue illustrée*, *Le Gaulois*, *Le Figaro*, *Revue du palais*, and *La Vie parisienne*.

Michel Pauper and some of the elements of vaudeville that he had learned helped prepare Becque to write his first major play, *The Vultures*, a work he may have begun as early as 1872, completed in 1876, and for which he spent five years seeking a producer. Between completing *The Vultures* and seeing it produced onstage, Becque had time to write *The Merry-Go-Round*, which foreshadows *The Woman of Paris*, and *Les Honnêtes Femmes* (the respectable women), a paean to feminine virtue and respectability.

In spite of the success of *The Vultures*, Becque's solitary life of poverty continued nearly unrelieved. The death of his father and mother in the early 1880's reinforced the solitude of a man dedicated to family life, a solitude that would deepen with the deaths of his sister in 1890 and of his brother in 1894. When the death of his niece, Jeanne Salva, in 1893, was followed by that of her husband, Georges Robaglia, in 1895, Becque found himself the guardian of two young grandnephews and looked after them as best he could. One of these, Jean Robaglia, would later edit the Crés edition (1924) of Becque's works and provide the most extensive firsthand biographical account of the dramatist.

With his second great theatrical success, *The Woman of Paris*, the fashionable world of the Parisian salons, especially the salon of Mme Aubernon, opened to Becque, who, by force of wit and conversa-

tional brilliance, soon became the toast of one important segment of Paris. This theatrical success, however, did not free Becque from the poverty that attended him all his life, nor did it spur him on to give other works to the theater for presentation. In fact, *The Woman of Paris* is the last play Becque offered for production and the last play he published for more than a decade.

The last fourteen years of Becque's life were spent writing for several Parisian journals, working on the unfinished masterpiece of his dramatic maturity, *Les Polichinelles* (the puppets), composing several curtain raisers and, in one case, an epilogue, while living the life of a man of the theater and a man of letters. Becque died in a nursing home in Paris on May 12, 1899, just over a month after he suffered from shock and smoke inhalation from having fallen asleep while reading and smoking a cigar.

ANALYSIS

Henry Becque's early plays, like his last plays, are not the stuff on which a theatrical reputation is made or can rest. However, both *L'Enfant prodigue* and *Michel Pauper* brought Becque a small measure of the success he sought in the theater. The former won for him some critical acclaim, and the latter was so well received that Becque felt encouraged to continue his work as a dramatist. Although both the critics and the general public recognized Becque's merits as a fledgling playwright, they took exception to the bleak, pessimistic, and brutal elements of *Michel Pauper*.

L'ENFANT PRODIGUE

In *L'Enfant prodigue*, Becque provided the vaudeville theater with a neat comedy that borrows from the traditional comedy of manners and has something in common with the work of Becque's professed master, Moliére. In his portrayal of three provincials from Montélimar who come under the amorous sway of Clarisse, the daughter of a Parisian concierge, Becque uses stock comic devices such as chance encounters and an anonymous letter and subjects the provincials to the irony and wit that would remain his theatrical trademarks. Character dominates plot in this as in all of Becque's plays, and the slight intrigue hinges on the standard element of mistaken identities and the characters' temporary inability to rectify the mistakes out of fear of self-exposure. Although each of the characters is the object of some irony, satire is reserved for the middle-class hypocrisy and manners of Bernardin, the epitome of the bourgeoisie.

MICHEL PAUPER

Becque's next play, *Michel Pauper*, far from the sort of airy vaudeville that was then the rage in the Paris of the Second Empire, is a ponderous mélange of melodrama, romantic tragedy, and *comédie larmoyante* in the vein of Victorien Sardou and Alexandre Dumas, *fils*. Full of stilted, pompous language, the play chronicles the rise and fall of Pauper as honest workman, master chemist, and gifted inventor whose idealized love for Hélène first leads him to great creative work and then propels him back to alcoholism when she confesses her guilt with the young Count de Rivailles. In some respects, one could characterize the play as being about the power of love to effect change; one could also argue that the thesis at the play's core has to do with self-hate and self-destruction in the form of alcoholism. The work has considerable potential for presenting several themes relative to the claims and expectations of situation on character; the potential, however, remains largely unrealized. Becque explored for the first time in *Michel Pauper* the situation he would use in his more important work, *The Vultures*: the consequences for a woman, and her children, of the death of her husband.

L'ENLÈVEMENT

The public was unprepared for the subject of his *L'Enlèvement*, a thesis play in favor of divorce that anticipated by several years the more popular plays of Émile Augier and Dumas on that topic. The pomposity and stiltedness of the work clearly contributed to its failure, but it failed primarily because it negated bourgeois respectability: It was one thing for Becque to satirize bourgeois values on the vaudeville stage but quite another to preach against them in an unrelievedly didactic vein.

THE MERRY-GO-ROUND

During the early 1870's, up to 1876, Becque occupied himself with writing The Vultures, but when the play was finished, he could find no theater willing to stage it. Having failed, for a time, to get *The Vultures*

before the public, he turned his hand to another play, *The Merry-Go-Round*, a one-act comedy in which he moved beyond *L'Enfant prodigue* toward a comedy of manners. Again departing from the conventional, he took as his heroine a courtesan, one of the favorite characters of the day, but treated her in a very different way from the way his theatrical colleagues had treated her. His Antonia is not sentimentalized and does not have the proverbial "heart of gold," nor, on the other hand, is she condemned for her way of life. The play's two interchangeable male characters, Alfred and Arthur, who compete for her favors, take on different roles but finally are different manifestations of the same sort of character: Both wish to enjoy Antonia without taking on the burden of financial obligations. The third man, Armand, the audience assumes, is like the other two. Becque's failure to preach against or at least to comment on the immorality he depicted caused the critics to classify this dramatic work as an example of naturalism at its worst, although even by nineteenth century standards the play is neither overtly objectionable, nor, in any important sense, a naturalist work.

LES HONNÊTES FEMMES

The public received Becque's next play, *Les Honnêtes Femmes*, with great, if undeserved, warmth. The least typical of his works, this celebration of solid middle-class virtue suggests a deliberate attempt on Becque's part to dissociate himself from the naturalists.

THE VULTURES

The Vultures, the first of Becque's masterpieces, was an innovative and controversial work that nevertheless enjoyed a great popular success. Its themes of social injustice are handled in a manner distinguishing it both from the *comédie rosse* of the naturalists and from the *pièce à thèse* of Augier and company. It is comparable rather to Henrik Ibsen's plays in seriousness, pessimism, and a sense of pathos born of deep feeling for the suffering of the innocent. On the death of M. Vigneron, his wife, son, and three daughters find themselves at the mercy of a society formed on the principle of greed. A true product of her century, Mme Vigneron cannot begin to cope with such a drastically changed circumstance; her son is, quite simply, ineffectual; her daughter Blanche, for want of a dowry, cannot marry her lover, Georges, because his mother forbids it; her daughter Judith has no prospects for making her way as an actress. Marie, the daughter destined to sacrifice herself to the chief predator for the sake of her family, marries M. Teissier, her father's former business associate and her senior by several decades, once he has agreed to give the Vignerons financial support. Teissier, in his new role as family protector, provides the ironic clue to his character and that of each of the predators who close in on the Vignerons; in the play's penultimate sentence, he tells Marie what has been painfully obvious to her and to the audience from the outset: "You have been surrounded by scoundrels, my child, since your father's death."

THE WOMAN OF PARIS

Three years after the success of *The Vultures*, Becque presented *The Woman of Paris*, his last play to be performed in his lifetime and his second major work. Unlike *The Vultures*, *The Woman of Paris* uses the comic techniques Becque had developed earlier in his career and is a comic piece of social criticism. Like its predecessor, *The Woman of Paris* won ready acceptance from the naturalists. A longer and more highly developed version of *The Merry-Go-Round*, *The Woman of Paris* is about Clotilde, a woman who drops her lover and finally takes him back once she is abandoned by a new lover and once her husband, through the influence of Clotilde's friend, Mrs. Simpson, has secured the position he sought. Like his shorter plays, this one is concerned with character development and psychological action rather than with the advance of physical action or plot. Indeed, the action of the play is minimal and serves only to reflect the aspirations and natures of the characters. This is also a highly ironic play that features the clever Clotilde keeping lover and husband off balance and the lover, Lafond, in the odd position of being jealous of Clotilde's husband while ostensibly remaining his friend. One fine ironic element that most critics note takes place in the play's first scene, when the audience witnesses a domestic quarrel between a man and a woman over a letter that the woman has received; thus the audience learns of the man's suspi-

cions that the letter will document her infidelity to him. The scene ends with Clotilde warning the man to be careful—her husband has arrived home.

One major reason that *The Woman of Paris* was so highly regarded by Zola and his followers is that Becque's play offers a slice of life without moral commentary, without much dramatic action external to the characters, without rising action, or a crisis, or a denouement. The lack of these very elements also won for Becque the scorn of the more traditionally minded critics, to whom, more than to Zola, he looked for recognition. Still, *The Woman of Paris* is significant as an innovative work that helped usher modern drama into France and as a prototype of the *comédie rosse* in the Théâtre Libre of André Antoine and his coterie.

LATER PLAYS

Having given the theater *The Vultures* and *The Woman of Paris*, Becque continued to write plays but sought to publish rather than to produce them. *Les Polichinelles*, a satire on the world of finance, remained unfinished at his death but was to have been his third major effort, one on which he worked intermittently for more than a decade. Becque published five other plays, one a brief segment from *Les Polichinelles* called *Madeleine* and another an epilogue to *The Woman of Paris* called *Veuve* (widowed), in which the recently widowed Clotilde contemplates her lover and decides she would have missed him less than she misses her husband. With the exception of *Le Domino à quatre* (dominoes for four), an interesting and relatively lively play, the rest of his late work is not inspired.

OTHER MAJOR WORKS

NONFICTION: *Querelles littéraires*, 1890; *Souvenirs d'un auteur dramatique*, 1895.

MISCELLANEOUS: *Notes d'album*, 1898; *Œuvres complètes de Henry Becque*, 1924 (7 volumes).

BIBLIOGRAPHY

Hyslop, Lois Boe. *Henry Becque*. New York: Twayne, 1972. A basic biography of Becque that examines his life and works. Bibliography.

John J. Conlon

BRENDAN BEHAN

Born: Dublin, Ireland; February 9, 1923
Died: Dublin, Ireland; March 20, 1964

PRINCIPAL DRAMA

Gretna Green, pr. 1947

The Quare Fellow, pr. 1954, pb. 1956 (translation and revision of his Gaelic play "Casadh Súgáin Eile," wr. 1946)

The Big House, pr. 1957 (radio play), pr. 1958 (staged), pb. 1961

An Giall, pr. 1958, pb. 1981 (in Gaelic)

The Hostage, pr., pb. 1958 (translation and revision of *An Giall*)

Richard's Cork Leg, pr. 1972, pb. 1973 (begun 1960, completed posthumously by Alan Simpson, 1964)

The Complete Plays, pb. 1978

OTHER LITERARY FORMS

Brendan Behan's literary reputation rests on the merits of three works: *The Quare Fellow* and *The Hostage*, his dramatic masterpieces, and *The Borstal Boy* (1958), his autobiography, published in England by Hutchinson and in the United States by Alfred A. Knopf. The two plays were performed several times before their publication, and the performance rights are still retained by the Theatre Workshop in East London. *The Borstal Boy*, set in 1931-1941, is an autobiographical narrative of Behan's adolescent years in prison. Several of the stories included in *The Borstal Boy* appeared initially in literary magazines and journals. *Brendan Behan's Island: An Irish Sketchbook* (1962) was intended by Behan to be similar in tone and structure to John Millington Synge's *The Aran Islands* (1907), but it does not stand up to this literary comparison. Unable to write for extended periods of time in his later years, Behan began taping his stories and subsequently had them edited by his publishing guardian angel and friend, Rae Jeffs. *Brendan Behan's Island, Hold Your Hour and Have Another* (1963), *Brendan Behan's New York* (1964),

and *Confessions of an Irish Rebel* (1965) are all edited results of taping sessions. *The Scarperer* (1964) was published in book form the year Behan died but had been published first as a series in *The Irish Times*, in 1953, under the pseudonym "Emmet Street." Several of Behan's works were published posthumously. Among these are *Confessions of an Irish Rebel*, *Moving Out* (1952), *A Garden Party* (1952), and *Richard's Cork Leg*, the latter of which was begun by Behan in 1960 and ultimately completed by Alan Simpson. In addition to his plays and books, Behan contributed scores of short stories and poems on a variety of subjects to journals and newspapers throughout his life. He was as renowned for his balladeering as he was for his writings, and he composed the songs for his plays. A recording entitled *Brendan Behan Sings Irish Folksongs and Ballads*, produced by Spoken Arts, provides insight into Behan's passionate personality.

ACHIEVEMENTS

Brendan Behan has been called the most important postwar Irish writer by contemporary Irish, English, and American critics. His works represent an extraordinary mixture of Irish romance, history, patriotism, and racism. All his works reflect, in some measure, the Irish Republican Army's efforts to rid Northern Ireland of the English. Paradoxically, his major literary successes came first in England, and though productions of *The Quare Fellow* and *The Hostage* met with moderate success in the United States, his most receptive audience was always in London.

Stylistically, Behan has been compared to Jonathan Swift, James Joyce, Synge, and Sean O'Casey. His treatment of the Irish in his plays and stories is simultaneously warm and biting. Clearly a social critic, Behan's writings indict law, religion, Ireland, England, and the absurdity of politics. His literary career spans barely twenty years, though the most productive of these amount to less than a decade. His

Brendan Behan in 1952. (Hulton Archive by Getty Images)

first story, "I Become a Borstal Boy," was published in June, 1942, after which he regularly contributed nationalistic essays, stories, and poems to various Irish periodicals, including organs of the Irish Republican Army (IRA) such as *Fianna: The Voice of Young Ireland* and the *Wolfe Tone Weekly.*

Behan's most productive years (1953-1959) were marked by the production of both *The Quare Fellow* and *The Hostage* and the publication of *The Borstal Boy.* During these years, Behan's fame began to wane, and his creative talent floundered in a sea of alcohol. Behan wrote principally of a world of men, yet ironically it was his association with two women that accounted for much of his artistic success. Joan Littlewood, director and manager of the Theatre Workshop at the Theatre Royal, Stratford East, London, directed *The Quare Fellow* in 1956 and catapulted Behan into the international limelight. Her production of *The Hostage* in 1958 earned for Behan equally high praise. His friend Jeffs can be credited with virtually all Behan's productivity during his final years. The publicity manager for Hutchinson's Publishing Company, she was "assigned" the obstreperous Behan in 1957. From 1957 to 1964, Jeffs's formidable task included following Behan from pub to pub, trailing and assisting him on his trips from

England to the United States to Ireland, all the while making sure he was writing or taping his work, to be edited later. Ultimately, she performed her task as a labor of love, serving as friend and confidante to both Behan and his wife, Beatrice. Without Jeffs's tenacity, Behan's literary career would have ended in 1957 in an alcoholic stupor. In his final years, Behan became a drunken caricature of himself. The early works evidence the true spark of genius that carried him through the years of honor to the dark years plagued by alcoholism and self-doubt. It is to these early works that one must turn to capture the real genius embodied in the literature of this twentieth century Irish phenomenon.

BIOGRAPHY

Brendan Behan was born February 9, 1923, in Dublin, Ireland, the first child of Stephen and Kathleen (Kearney) Behan, though his mother had two sons by a previous marriage. Born into a family with radical political leanings, Behan was reared on a double dose of IRA propaganda and Catholicism. The radical Left was part of his genetic makeup. His grandmother and a grandfather were jailed for their roles in the revolution, the former for illegal possession of explosives when she was seventy years old and the latter for his part in the murder of Lord Cavendish. Both of Behan's parents fought in the Irish Revolution and in the Troubles. Ultimately jailed for his participation in the violence, Behan's father saw his son for the first time through prison bars.

Behan was a precocious child whose reverence for writers was spawned by his father's readings of Samuel Pepys, Charles Dickens, Émile Zola, George Bernard Shaw, and various polemical treatises to his children. By Behan's own account, his home was filled with reading, song, and revolution. Juxtaposed to this violent heritage was Behan's conservative religious training. He attended schools run by the Sisters of Charity of St. Vincent de Paul, where he was a favorite, and another operated by the Irish Christian Brothers, where he found himself in constant disfavor. His militant disposition surfaced early, when at the age of nine he joined the Fianna Éireann, the junior wing of the IRA. Most of his early adult years were spent in prison. Arrested in Liverpool at the age of sixteen for participating in IRA bombings in England, Behan spent three years in the Borstal, the English correctional institution for juvenile delinquents. Released in 1941 and deported to Ireland, Behan was again incarcerated the following year for shooting at a police officer. He had served four years of a fourteen-year sentence when he was released in 1946. Additional stays in jail followed throughout his life.

The worldview projected in Behan's works recalls the environment in which he matured, one dominated by a radical family and by his prison experience. Cradled in the romance of revolution, Behan was cultured in a more traditional sense. Kathleen and Stephen Behan reared their children with a love for music and literature. Nurtured with a reverential attitude toward Kathleen's brother Peadar Kearney, a noted composer who wrote the Irish national anthem, the Behan children learned his marches and ballads in a home continuously filled with music. According to Colbert Kearney, Behan's precociousness as a child was largely attributable to the education he received at home. His father instilled in him a deep-seated respect for Irish writers and rhetoricians. He learned to read at an early age and was fond of memorizing speeches by Irish patriots such as Robert Emmet. Not as readily discernible in Behan's work is the influence of his strict upbringing in Catholicism. Behan had a love-hate relationship with the Church, and often his works condemn religion. Yet one of his most bitter disappointments came when he was excommunicated while serving time in prison. Some critics believe that this was a crisis in Behan's life from which he never recovered.

Behan began writing while in prison, and his first story, "I Become a Borstal Boy," was published in *The Bell* in 1942. The plays, poems, and short stories written during his prison terms are all autobiographical. The years from 1946 to 1956 were the most ambitious of his career. For a time he lived in Paris, but he was eventually drawn back to Ireland, where he worked as a housepainter and freelance journalist. During this hiatus from serious encounters with the law, he married Beatrice Salkeld, daughter of the

noted Irish artist Cecil Salkeld. Behan's major break came when Alan Simpson agreed to produce *The Quare Fellow* at the Pike Theatre in Dublin in 1954. The play met with critical acclaim, but, to Behan's disappointment, the more prestigious Irish theaters such as the Abbey refused to stage it. This rejection spurred in Behan an overwhelming desire to be accepted as an artist in his own country. *The Quare Fellow* was noticed by Joan Littlewood, whose 1956 London production made Behan an international sensation. He followed this success with another play, *An Giall*, which he wrote in Gaelic and later translated as *The Hostage*. Littlewood's subsequent production of *The Hostage* proved an even greater success than *The Quare Fellow*.

Critics proclaimed Behan a literary genius, but he was destroyed by his success. His notorious interruptions of his plays with drunken speeches shouted from his seat in the audience and his intoxication during interviews for the British Broadcasting Corporation enhanced the "bad boy" image he so carefully cultivated, but ultimately it killed him. The most tragic repercussion of his alcoholism proved to be his inability to sit and write for an extended period of time. *The Hostage* was Behan's last good work. When his writing sojourns to Ibiza, his favorite retreat, and the United States and Canada produced little, he resorted to taping sessions to meet his publication contracts. By 1960, after two major breakdowns as well as intermittent stays in hospitals to dry out, Behan was a shell of his former robust personality. Riding on his reputation of acknowledged artistry, he found himself incapable of writing, which led him to drink even more. Behan died March 20, 1964, at the age of forty-one. Several of his edited works published after his death created a brief, cultish interest in the man and his writing, but this adulation soon passed. What remains is the recognition that Behan was one of the finest twentieth century Irish writers. His talent will be recognized long after his colorful reputation has faded.

ANALYSIS

To understand Brendan Behan's work, one must first recognize the underlying Behan legend, which is built on paradox. Frank O'Connor, writing in the *Sunday Independent* (Dublin), said of Behan that "under his turbulent exterior there was quite clearly the soul of an altar boy." Behan was a kind, gentle man who acted violently. He was insecure and feared publicity yet perpetrated outrageous stunts to capture attention. He wrote of reasonableness and absurdity in the world yet persisted in his personal irrationality. Behan was saint and sinner, moralist and profligate, and this dichotomy is carried over into his works. Even his overriding thematic consideration, a politically divided Ireland, is complex. Gordon Wickstrom believes Behan writes of three Irelands: the Ireland of contemporary, illegal Republican fanaticism, dedicated to the destruction of everything English; the Ireland of glorious memory of the Troubles and Easter Week, needing no justification beyond the private experience of valor and sacrifice; and Ireland as it actually exists, complete with police attacks, sirens, bloodbaths, and terror.

The principal themes in Behan's works are culled from his close association with the Irish Republican Army: death, freedom, and the absurdity of humanity's impermanence in a hostile world. Behan's major plays, *The Quare Fellow* and *The Hostage*, examine these themes through the eyes of a prisoner, a character-type that figures prominently in Behan's works. As his life stands as a series of paradoxes, so, too, does his style. Behan fills his works with unsavory gallows humor and swings erratically between comedy and tragedy in a decidedly Brechtian manner. Yet the early works are tightly structured and astonishingly poetic. Songs incorporated into his plays serve as lyric Gaelic laments but can quickly turn into obscene ditties. Behan's use of vernacular and the overwhelming sense of freedom in the lines contribute to the impressive strength of his writing. An unlikely coupling of naturalism and absurdism is characteristic of his best work. His characters are drawn from the lower classes, with Irish nationalism, bordering on racism, binding them together. Ironically, Behan's genteel audiences find it easy to empathize with his murderers, prostitutes, homosexuals, and radicals, perhaps because the sordid individuals in Behan's plays and stories are presented with a depth

of compassion and understanding usually reserved for more noble literary characters.

Behan's prison years had a profound influence on him. During these stultifying periods, he became preoccupied with the two themes that dominate his works: death and freedom. In the cells and work yards of the Borstal and Mountjoy prisons, Behan mentally cataloged information about individuals, human nature, and the absurdity of the world and its systems. The examination of conflicts between gentleness and violence, a trademark of Behan's work, stems directly from his own divided nature as much as his early background. Major characters such as Dunlavin and the Warder in *The Quare Fellow*, Monsewer and Williams in *The Hostage*, or the prisoner in *The Borstal Boy* reflect various facets of his personality.

THE QUARE FELLOW

In November, 1954, *The Quare Fellow* was labeled "a powerful piece of propaganda" by A. J. Leventhal, writing in *Dublin Magazine*. This assessment of Behan's first literary and theatrical success holds true for all his works. Though his plays do not strictly adhere to agitation-propaganda techniques used by earlier European playwrights, Behan's works are obviously propagandistic. *The Quare Fellow*, the most structured of his plays, examines the issue of capital punishment. Set in a prison, *The Quare Fellow* is a series of episodes in which the prison community prepares for the execution of the unseen titular character.

Tension is deftly established on two levels: the friction maintained in the relationship between prisoners and warders and the more insidious anxiety, hidden beneath the prattle and routine of the prison, that eats at the souls of both warders and prisoners as the moment of execution draws near. Every character waits in dread for the final moment, when a man will die. Their empathetic response to ritualized, state-supported death reinforces the horror felt by the audience. The prison serves as Behan's microcosm of the world in which primal struggles of life and death as well as social struggles of promotion, acceptance, pretense, and charity are all in evidence.

The Quare Fellow opens with the singing of a man in solitary confinement, trying to keep his sanity. His haunting lament, floating over the prison grounds, becomes almost a dirge as the play progresses. The plot is moved by the institution's preparations for the day of execution. Each character fears the approach of the hour of death and manifests his uneasiness in a different way. The prisoners attempt a forced jauntiness and irreverence but are unable to call the condemned man by his Christian name, preferring instead to force on him anonymity, calling him only "the quare fellow." As the climax approaches and the moment of death is imminent, a prisoner cynically announces the offstage procession to the gallows as though it were the start of a horse race: "We're off, in this order: The Governor, The Chief, two screws Regan and Crimmin, the quare fellow between them." Yet this comic diversion is incapable of diluting the dramatic effect of the climax when the clock strikes the hour and the prisoners wail, howl, and roar in primal lamentation, as the trap drops and the quare fellow hangs. The hero of the play, the quare fellow, never appears onstage. Dunlavin, a crusty, experienced prisoner, and Regan, a compassionate warder, are the principal characters. This den of thieves and murderers has its own order, a social hierarchy based on criminal offenses and experience. Sex offenders are ostracized by the prison community, and Dunlavin bemoans his misfortune at having one placed in the cell next to his. The sex offender, for his part, is appalled that he must live among murderers and takes to quoting Thomas Carlyle.

Religion is brutally satirized in *The Quare Fellow*. The hypocritical representative from the Department of Justice is dubbed "Holy Healey" by the inmates, who paste religious pictures on their walls to curry favor during his visits. Dunlavin's friend and neighbor in the cellblock comments on the importance of the Bible to prisoners, stating, "Many's the time the Bible was a consolation to a fellow all alone in the old cell," not for its spiritual comfort, but because prisoners rolled mattress bits within its pages and smoked them. Dunlavin, in turn, recounts how in his first twelve months he smoked his way halfway through Genesis. The executioner, referred to imperially as "Himself," cannot face his job in a sober state and must be accompanied by a teetotaling, Bible-quoting, hymn-singing assistant to see him to his appointed

rounds. The incongruity of this misallied pair is obvious as Jenkinson, the assistant, sings a hymn while the hangman audibly calculates the weight of the condemned man and the height of the drop needed to kill him.

Behan's vision of the value of life and the awesome power of death is painted in masterful strokes throughout *The Quare Follow*. The dignity of humankind, the worth of an individual life, and the inhumanity of a system devised for correctional purposes are powerfully juxtaposed in this play. The 1954 Pike Theatre production of *The Quare Fellow* was well received, but it was Joan Littlewood's direction in 1956 that made it a modern classic. Although the play has been criticized as being melodramatic, Behan mixes well-developed characters with stereotypes and caricatures to provide diverse opportunities for commentary on various levels. *The Quare Fellow* is not wholly a tragedy, nor is it merely black comedy. It is an unnatural two-backed beast that violently gives birth to Behan's pessimistic worldview.

THE HOSTAGE

The music-hall atmosphere of *The Hostage* differs radically from the sterile environment of *The Quare Fellow*. From the opening jig, danced by two prostitutes and two homosexuals, to the rousing chorus, sung by the corpse, Behan jars his audience with the unexpected. Like Bertolt Brecht's *Die Dreigroschenoper* (pr. 1928; *The Threepenny Opera*, 1949), *The Hostage* is populated by a cast of societal misfits. Brechtian influences can be noticed in the play's structure as well. *The Hostage*, according to Richard A. Duprey in *The Critic*, is an indictment of law, religion, home, country, human decency, art, and even death. What is espoused within its tenuous structure is IRA radicalism, but even this cannot escape Behan's satiric barbs. The IRA officer in the play is outraged by the shoddy accommodations—a brothel—afforded him and his political prisoner, while Pat, manager of the "brockel" and a veteran of the Easter Rebellion and the Troubles, denounces the new IRA soldiers as "white-faced loons with their trench coats, berets and teetotal badges."

Thematically, *The Hostage* compares with Behan's other major works in that the protagonist is a prisoner. Leslie Williams has committed no crime except that he is an English soldier in Ireland. Taken as a hostage by IRA reactionaries, Williams is offered in trade for a jailed Irish youth sentenced to hang. The IRA cause is felt most strongly in this play, and Behan's nationalistic biases are given ample voice in the songs about the Easter Rebellion, Monsewer's senile ravings about the days of glorious conflict, and Pat's diatribes against modern Ireland. Hidden beneath the brash, gaudy, and colorful language of the play, such weighty underpinnings emerge in flashes of seriousness.

A mélange of dramatic styles pushes the plot through a series of vignettes, comedy routines, and song-and-dance numbers. Songs, jokes, and malapropisms abound in this very political play. Individually, the characters lack depth and are only one step removed from the stereotyped clowns of burlesque houses. Collectively, they champion traditional Irish Republicanism while at the same time denouncing the absurdity of its violent contemporary manifestations. This is a play about the Republican cause; it is also a play about the value of life. Leslie Williams is an apolitical character who dies needlessly, an injustice that Behan adroitly condemns. Life and death in Behan's work are never equal forces; life always triumphs. He breaks the serious mood of his final scene, in which Williams's death is disclosed, by having the corpse jump up and sing, "The bells of hell go ting a ling a ling for you but not for me. . . ."

The original Gaelic-language version of the play, *An Giall*, was a much more serious play than the version presented in the internationally acclaimed 1958 London production. The seminal version had but ten characters, whereas *The Hostage* has fifteen. Writer Colbert Kearney notes that *An Giall* is essentially a naturalistic tragedy, while *The Hostage* is a musical extravaganza. Certainly, the latter tolerates a greater degree of bawdiness than the original. Critics charged that Joan Littlewood's company substantially altered *An Giall* while in production for *The Hostage*, yet this was partially Behan's fault. During 1957 and 1958, he was committed to two projects: translating *An Giall* into *The Hostage* for Littlewood and finishing *The Borstal Boy*. He became preoccupied with the publicity and lavish promotion given the latter and neglected his commitments to Littlewood. Consequently, parts of *The Hostage* grew out of the improvisations of the Theatre Workshop and, though sanctioned by Behan, changed the play significantly from the original work. Scholar Ulick O'Connor believes several of the non sequitur scenes in *The Hostage* were invented by Littlewood and do not reflect Behan's hand in the revision. Nevertheless, the production was a hit. *The Hostage* was selected to represent Great Britain at the prestigious Théâtre des Nations festival in 1959, and it moved to the fashionable Wyndham Theatre on London's West End. Productions of Behan's plays opened in Dublin, New York, Paris, and Berlin.

The Hostage proved to be Behan's last theatrical success. His reputation sustained him as an artist for the next six years, but his talent abandoned him. He began another play, *Richard's Cork Leg*, but it remained unfinished at his death. *The Hostage* is not as neatly structured as *The Quare Fellow*, though Behan's genius for dialogue and *mise en scène* pervades the work. Behan—patriot, nationalist, and racist—is plainly seen in *The Hostage*, yet his persona, so dominant in his plays, turns to reveal Behan the humanitarian in equally sharp focus. Behan's works, like the man, are paradoxical. His legend lives on, supported by contemporary interest in Behan the revolutionary and artist.

OTHER MAJOR WORKS

LONG FICTION: *The Scarperer*, 1953 (serial), 1964 (book; as Emmet Street); *The Dubbalin Man*, 1954-1956 (serial), 1997 (book).

SHORT FICTION: *After the Wake*, 1981.

RADIO PLAYS: *A Garden Party*, 1952; *Moving Out*, 1952.

NONFICTION: *The Borstal Boy*, 1958; *Brendan Behan's Island: An Irish Sketchbook*, 1962; *Hold Your Hour and Have Another*, 1963; *Brendan Behan's New York*, 1964; *Confessions of an Irish Rebel*, 1965; *The Letters of Brendan Behan*, 1992 (E. H. Mikhail, editor).

MISCELLANEOUS: *Poems and Stories*, 1978; *Poems and a Play in Irish*, 1981 (includes the play *An Giall*).

BIBLIOGRAPHY

Behan, Brian, with Aubrey Dillon-Malone. *The Brother Behan*. Dublin: Ashfield Press, 1998. The brother of Brendan Behan writes of their lives and his brother's work.

Behan, Kathleen. *Mother of All the Behans: The Autobiography of Kathleen Behan as Told to Brian Behan*. 1984. Reprint. Dublin: Poolbeg, 1994. The mother of the dramatist and revolutionary describes her life and her family.

De Búrca, Séamus. *Brendan Behan: A Memoir*. 1971. Reprint. Dublin: P. J. Bourke, 1985. A memoir-style biography of the famous dramatist, covering his life and works.

Mikhail, E. H., ed. *Brendan Behan: Interviews and Recollections*. 2 vols. Totowa, N.J.: Barnes and Noble Books, 1982. A collection of extracts from published memoirs and interviews given by those who knew Behan. Contains fifty-one items in volume 1 and fifty-five in volume 2. Mikhail's introduction insightfully compares Behan and Oscar Wilde.

O'Sullivan, Michael. *Brendan Behan: A Life*. Boulder, Colo.: Roberts Rinehart, 1999. A biography of Behan that examines his life and works. Bibliography and index.

Witoszek, Walentyna. "The Funeral Comedy of Brendan Behan." *Études irlandaises* 11 (December, 1988): 83-91. Witoszek discusses the puzzling presence of laughter in Behan's writings in which execution is imminent. Though Death is the "central character" in all Behan's plays, there is also an orgiastic atmosphere of carnival madness, which is analyzed in terms of ritual, the Irish image of the laughing death, and Mikhail Bakhtin's theories of the carnivalesque.

Susan Duffy,
updated by William Hutchings

APHRA BEHN

Born: England; July(?), 1640
Died: London, England; April 16, 1689

PRINCIPAL DRAMA

The Forced Marriage: Or, The Jealous Bridegroom, pr. 1670, pb. 1671
The Amorous Prince: Or, The Curious Husband, pr., pb. 1671
The Dutch Lover, pr., pb. 1673
Abdelazer: Or, The Moor's Revenge, pr. 1676, pb. 1677
The Town Fop: Or, Sir Timothy Tawdry, pr. 1676, pb. 1677
The Rover: Or, The Banished Cavaliers, Part I, pr., pb. 1677, *Part II*, pr., pb. 1681
Sir Patient Fancy, pr., pb. 1678
The Feigned Courtesans: Or, A Night's Intrigue, pr., pb. 1679
The Young King: Or, The Mistake, pr. 1679, pb. 1683
The Roundheads: Or, The Good Old Cause, pr. 1681, pb. 1682
The City Heiress: Or, Sir Timothy Treat-All, pr., pb. 1682
The Lucky Chance: Or, An Alderman's Bargain, pr. 1686, pb. 1687
The Emperor of the Moon, pr., pb. 1687
The Widow Ranter: Or, The History of Bacon of Virginia, pr. 1689, pb. 1690
The Younger Brother: Or, The Amorous Jilt, pr., pb. 1696

OTHER LITERARY FORMS

In addition to her plays, Aphra Behn's literary legacy includes many noteworthy works of fiction and poetry. The three-part novel entitled *Love Letters Between a Nobleman and His Sister* (1683-1687) is both her earliest and her longest narrative effort. A fictionalized version of a notorious contemporary scandal, this novel was extremely popular at the time, but it is little read today. Of much more interest to present-day readers are the shorter novels such as *The Fair Jilt: Or, The History of Prince Tarquin and Miranda* (1688) and *Oroonoko: Or, The History of the Royal Slave* (1688). The latter is undoubtedly Behn's most enduring literary creation in any genre. Allegedly based on her own experiences in Surinam during the 1660's, the narrative relates the tragic history of a slave of African origin named Oroonoko and his wife, Imoinda, from the viewpoint of the author herself. As the story unfolds, Behn repeatedly exposes the deceitful and greedy nature of the European settlers and underscores the innate virtue of the novel's eponymous hero. He is, therefore, one of the earliest fictional manifestations of the archetypical "noble savage." Because of its implicit condemnation of slavery and colonialism, the novel is highly regarded as a harbinger of the crisis in political and social morality that was to trouble the conscience of Europeans in their dealings with the nonwhite population of the globe over the succeeding centuries.

Behn's poetry is widely diverse in character. In keeping with the convention of the time, she made it a practice to provide her plays with prologues and epilogues in verse form. She also interspersed many songs within the prose dialogue of her plays. In both instances, the quality of her poetry is usually of a high order. Two of her most successful poems, in fact, appear in *Abdelazer*. The song that begins with the line "LOVE in fantastick Triumph sat" comes at the opening of act 1, and the one commencing "MAKE haste, Amintas, come away" is to be found near the end of act 2. Both of these songs are frequently anthologized. Likewise commendable are two short narrative poems entitled "The Disappointment" and "The Golden Age." Although most of her occasional poetry consists of overly rhetorical panegyrics to illustrious personages, a few of the elegies are moving expressions of private grief. Perhaps the best of these are "To the Memory of George, Duke of Buckingham" and "On the Death of Edmund Waller, Esq."

Being fluent in French, Behn began making translations from that language as a source of income late in her career. Among the French works that she translated are the maxims of the duke François de La Rochefoucauld and two works of fiction by Bernard le Bovier de Fontenelle. More in the nature of an adaptation is her translation of Abbé Paul Tallemant's *Le Voyage de l'isle d'amour* (1663), which she published under the title *A Voyage to the Island of Love* in 1684. Tallemant's piece of fantasy is, for the most part, a prose narrative interspersed with songs, but Behn chose to render all the prose passages as rhymed couplets. In *Lycidus: Or, The Lover in Fashion* (1688), including an adaptation of Tallemant's second voyage to the Island of Love, however, she adheres to the prose and poetry distinctions of the original text. One of the songs in *Lycidus*, starting with the line "A thousand Martyrs I have made," has proved itself to be a perennial favorite with the reading public. The fact that Behn knew little Latin and less Greek did not prevent her from "translating" works written in those tongues. With the aid of French and English translations, she managed to turn

Aphra Behn (Library of Congress)

out excellent versions of Aesop's fables for an illustrated edition published in 1687. Working chiefly from a prose paraphrase, she also produced a rhymed translation of book 6 (*Of Trees*) from Abraham Cowley's poetic treatise entitled *Sex libri plantarum* (1668). The preceding five books were translated by others, and the complete text of the *Six Books of Plants* was published shortly before Behn's death in 1689.

ACHIEVEMENTS

Aphra Behn came of age during the period in English history known as the Restoration. The epoch began in 1660 with the Stuart monarchy being restored in the person of Charles II. His Royal Highness was passionately fond of the theater, and one of his first acts was to rescind the laws prohibiting the performance of plays, that had been enacted in 1642 by the Long Parliament under the domination of Oliver Cromwell. Although all forms of drama were thenceforth permitted to flourish, the best plays written in the succeeding era turned out to be comedies. The masterpieces of this genre were created by Sir George Etherege, William Wycherley, and William Congreve, among others. While it would be injudicious to claim that any of Behn's comedies should be ranked with the best of Etherege, Wycherley, or Congreve, many of her plays have withstood the test of time and are fully deserving of a contemporary readership. The same is true with respect to her novel *Oroonoko*. The dramatic vitality of *Oroonoko* and many of her other works of narrative fiction is attested by the fact that several of them have been successfully adapted for the theater by other hands. Using the novel *The History of the Nun: Or, The Fair Vow-Breaker* (1689) as the source for his plot, Thomas Southerne scored one of his greatest successes as a playwright with the tragedy entitled *The Fatal Marriage: Or, The Innocent Adultery* (pr. 1694). Two years later, in 1696, he repeated this success with a dramatization of *Oroonoko*. In the same year, moreover, Catherine Cockburn offered the theatergoing public the opportunity to see a play based on Behn's novel *Agnes de Castro* (1688). These adaptations continued to be popular into the eighteenth century.

Literary historians will always accord an honorable place to Behn for being the first Englishwoman to become a professional author and to support herself solely by means of income derived from her writings. Although it must have been a bold decision on her part to defy conventional wisdom regarding the proper mode of existence for a woman of her class, she seems not to have been seriously disadvantaged on account of her gender in pursuing a literary career and may have actually been helped by it. The only apparent adverse effect that she suffered from being a woman stemmed from the generally held belief that women are innately more virtuous than men. As a consequence of this social attitude, there was a propensity on the part of some critics, as well as the public at large, to regard her comedies as being more immoral than those of her male colleagues. This charge has been immortalized in Alexander Pope's satire *The First Epistle to the Second Book of Horace* (1737). Here, in a couplet in which he refers to Behn by a pseudonym under which she frequently published her poetry, Pope writes: "The stage how loosely does Astraea tread,/ Who fairly puts all Characters to bed." Pope's imputation is unfair, for Behn's plays are no more licentious, and frequently less so, than others written in that era. These charges, moreover, never proved detrimental to public attendance at performances of her plays. That she was one of the most popular playwrights of her age is a matter of historical record.

BIOGRAPHY

Reliable information pertaining to the first half of Aphra Behn's life is virtually nonexistent. The sparse biographical information for this period is, moreover, frequently contradictory. The earliest account of her career is to be found in the introduction to an edition of her fictional works that was published posthumously in 1696, which purports to be memoirs on her life written by a "gentlewoman" of her acquaintance. It is now believed that the "gentlewoman" in question was, in fact, Behn's personal friend and editor Charles Gildon (1665-1724). According to his account, she was born into a good family by the name of Johnson, whose ancestral roots lay in the city of

Canterbury in Kent. Her father, furthermore, was reported as being related to Lord Francis Willoughby of Parham, a man who used his good offices to secure Johnson an appointment to the administrative post of lieutenant-governor over many islands in the West Indies and the territory of Surinam. When Gildon's memoirs were reprinted a year later in an anthology devoted to the lives of dramatic poets, the text was revised in such a way as to state explicitly that Behn was born in the city of Canterbury.

Information that runs counter to Gildon's memoirs on two important issues, however, comes from the hand of another contemporary writer, Anne Finch. Finch, who is better known as the countess of Winchelsea, left a marginal note in a manuscript copy of some unpublished poems of her own in which she mentions that the place of Behn's birth was the small market town of Wye, near Canterbury, and that her father had been a barber by trade. Finch's account was first discovered by an English literary scholar in 1884, but it was not until the opening decade of the twentieth century that the pertinent entry in the baptismal registry at Wye received thorough scrutiny. It was thereupon learned that a child listed as Ayfara, along with a brother named John, was duly baptized there on July 10, 1640, but that her family name was not Johnson at all. The parents of Ayfara and her brother are, in fact, identified as a couple named John and Amy Amis. Then, in the 1950's, another English scholar perused the burial registry at Wye and found that both of these children had died a few days after their baptism: Ayfara on July 12 and John on July 16. In neither the baptismal nor the burial registries, moreover, is there any reference to John Amis's being a barber by trade. In the light of these discrepancies, it is difficult to avoid drawing the conclusion that Finch's marginal note is nothing more than a false lead.

The only other contemporary evidence pertaining to Behn's birth comes from some manuscripts now held in the British Library that were composed before 1708 by a member of the gentry named Thomas Culpepper. Culpepper reports that Behn was born at Canterbury or Sturry and that her maiden name was Johnson. He further claims that she was also his foster-sister by virtue of the fact that her mother was his nurse at one time. A subsequent check of the marriage registry at St. Paul's in Canterbury corroborated Culpepper's account insofar as a couple named Bartholomew and Elizabeth Johnson was married there on August 25, 1638. It has also been ascertained that Bartholomew Johnson was a yeoman (that is, a member of the class of small freeholding farmers) and that he originally came from Bishopsbourne, a village situated three and a half miles from Canterbury. The first of the couple's four children was, moreover, named Eaffry (Aphra), but she appears to have been born in neither Canterbury nor Sturry. The baptismal records of St. Michael's in the village of Harbledown, located just outside the walls of Canterbury, list her as being baptized there on December 14, 1640. Because Culpepper himself was born on Christmas Day in 1637, there would appear to be some question whether Johnson could have served him in the capacity of a wet-nurse.

The question of Behn's parentage is further complicated by a passage appearing in James Rodway's *Chronological History of the Discovery and Settlement of Guiana, 1493-1796*, a work first published in 1888. Here it is reported that a relative of Lord Willoughby named Johnson left his homeland toward the end of 1658 bound for Surinam in the company of his wife and children, along with an adopted daughter named Afra or Aphra Johnson. In the absence of any further corroborative evidence, however, the claim regarding Aphra's status as Johnson's foster child is still viewed with a large measure of skepticism by most literary scholars at the current time. Rodway goes on to assert that Johnson never assumed his administrative duties in Surinam because he fell ill during the voyage and died at sea. The rest of the family, according to this history, duly disembarked at Surinam and spent the next two or three years residing on one of Lord Willoughby's estates in that land.

Rodway's assertion that Johnson died before reaching Surinam is corroborated by some autobiographical remarks that Behn makes in her novel *Oroonoko*. Other statements in *Oroonoko*, however, are at variance with several items in Rodway's account of the surviving family's subsequent sojourn in the New World. For one thing, Behn herself maintains that their stay in Surinam was a matter of months rather than the two or three years mentioned by Rodway. On the basis of references made to actual events and historical personages in the course of her narrative, it is also most likely that the period of young Aphra's residence in Surinam lasted from November, 1663, to February, 1664.

Shortly after her return to England, she married a London merchant of Dutch ancestry whose surname was Behn. This marriage ended quite abruptly in 1665 or 1666, owing to the death of her husband, an apparent victim of the plague that raged throughout London during these years. At this point in her life as at several others, the widow Behn appears to have been in need of money. Whether for financial or for idealistic reasons, she chose to become a spy for the recently restored British monarchy, which was at that point engaged in a war with the states of Holland—hostilities that were soon extended to France. She was to take up residence in Antwerp (then part of Holland) for the purpose of collecting information pertaining to the activities of dissident English exiles (supporters of Cromwell) as well as the military plans of the Dutch government. Her Dutch surname must surely have been advantageous to her in this mission.

Behn is believed to have gone to Antwerp in July, 1666, and for the ensuing six months or so, she continued to send cryptographic reports back to her superiors in England, using the code name Astrea to identify herself. It is widely held that she had already adopted this pseudonym while in Surinam. Although Astrea (or Astraea) is the Greek goddess of justice, the name was quite likely suggested by Honoré d'Urfé's popular three-part novel *Astrea* (1607-1628). The eponymous heroine of this novel had a lover called Celadon, a name that came to be employed as a code name for Aphra's good friend William Scot. This individual was the son of Thomas Scot, a man who was one of the judges at the trial that ended with the execution of Charles I in 1649 and who was himself put to death as a regicide in 1660. Because William Scot was in both Surinam and Ant-

werp at the same time that "Astrea" was in these places, it is tempting to surmise that a close amorous relationship existed between them. It is, moreover, indisputable that Behn diverted much of her energies while in Antwerp to the task of obtaining a royal pardon on behalf of William Scot for political offenses that he had committed against the crown in past years.

Whether Behn received adequate financial compensation from the crown for her espionage mission on the Continent is still a debatable issue. There is no doubt, however, that she was in desperate need of money after her return from Antwerp, for she was jailed for a brief period in 1668, as a result of her inability to repay outstanding debts that she had lately contracted. On her release from debtors' prison, Behn made a bold decision to try her hand at writing for the theater as a means of achieving financial independence. Her release from confinement was probably achieved through the intercession of Thomas Killigrew. The author of several noteworthy dramas, Killigrew devoted most of his energies to managing the affairs of the Theatre Royal at Drury Lane. This organization, commonly referred to as the King's Company, was the first of two acting ensembles to be granted a monopoly over theatrical performances within the city of London. The other group, known as the Duke's Company, was managed by Sir William Davenant until his death in 1668. Both of these companies, incidentally, were the first in England to engage actresses to play the roles of women, rather than following the traditional practice of using boys and young men to perform these parts. Despite her close friendship with Killigrew, Behn's own plays were staged by the Duke's Company, under the supervision of Davenant's successors, from the time that her first play was produced in 1670 to the year 1682. The plays that she composed during this period, except for an occasional failure, proved to be popular successes, and she soon established herself as one of the public's favorite playwrights.

Behn's career as a playwright was nevertheless placed in severe jeopardy when she decided to promote the fortunes of the Stuart monarchy by using the stage to attack powerful Whig opponents of

Charles II. Her chief contribution as a propagandist for the Tory cause is to be found in the pair of plays entitled *The Roundheads* and *The City Heiress*. What precipitated a crisis in Behn's partisan political activity, however, was her composition of a sardonic prologue and epilogue for the production, in 1682, of *Romulus and Hersilia*, a play by an anonymous author. These supplementary contributions were deemed to be unwarranted aspersions on the character of the duke of Monmouth as well as other persons of quality, and a warrant for Behn's arrest was issued by the Lord Chamberlain. Subsequent events remain unclear, but she appears to have gotten off lightly in terms of actual confinement. The effect on her literary creativity was far more profound, for she ceased writing plays for a period of nearly four years. During this hiatus from the theater, she found an outlet for her literary talents in composing poetry and narrative fiction. Even though she resumed writing for the theater in the spring of 1686, most of Behn's succeeding plays never matched the success of her earlier ones, and she increasingly devoted her time to writing fictional works and to translating plays and novels of foreign authors, perhaps deeming this a superior means of earning a livelihood by the pen.

Because Behn was both beautiful and witty, she was highly successful in forming close associations with a great number of prominent persons from literary and social circles in London. The literary figures among her acquaintance included John Dryden, Edmund Waller, and Thomas Otway. The full extent of her friendship with the rakish earl of Rochester, John Wilmot, is still a matter of conjecture. It was common knowledge, however, that Behn had a variety of lovers during the 1670's and 1680's. Her most abiding romantic favor appears to have been bestowed on John Hoyle, a lawyer noted for his witty repartee and ready swordsmanship. Behn's relationship with Hoyle was greatly complicated by his unrepressed bisexual proclivities, and they parted ways several years before her death. She died after a long physical illness, the exact nature of which has still not been fully established. Behn was buried in the cloisters of Westminster Abbey. On her tombstone is a wry couplet alleged to have been written by Hoyle himself: "Here lies a proof that wit can never be/ Defence enough against mortality." These lines proved to be even more apposite in regard to Hoyle's personal fate, for his own life came to an abrupt end as the result of a tavern brawl in 1692.

ANALYSIS

Although Aphra Behn lived in an age of great intellectual ferment, her ideas on politics and society are usually commonplace and traditional. In reading her plays, one is tempted to look for connections with current feminist concerns, but except for her deep concern that marriage be entered into on the basis of mutual affection and not contracted for social or monetary reasons, there is little that Behn wished to change in the relationship between the sexes. She knew herself too well, furthermore, to attribute greater virtue to women than to men. If she did not appear to be interested in demonstrating the virtue of her sex, she at least used her plays to celebrate its power.

THE FORCED MARRIAGE AND
THE AMOROUS PRINCE

Behn began her literary career with two plays whose technique and style are based on the romantic tragicomedies written in collaboration by Francis Beaumont and John Fletcher. Plays of this type permit a serious subject to be explored while avoiding a tragic resolution of the conflict. The first of her dramas in this vein was entitled *The Forced Marriage*, a work whose theme is the conflict between love and honor. This play was followed by *The Amorous Prince*. In this play, Behn uses a double plot in which the worldly protagonist first seduces an innocent country lass and then proceeds to fall in love with his best friend's fiancée. The play thus contrasts rural innocence with urban corruption and probes the competing claims of love and friendship. The plot is resolved happily when the repentant prince agrees to marry the country lass and renounces his designs on the friend's fiancée. Neither of these plays has much to interest present-day readers, but they were received enthusiastically by London audiences at the time, and Behn's future in the theater appeared to be assured.

THE DUTCH LOVER

The performance of her third play, however, ended in failure. Despite the fact that *The Dutch Lover* is much better than either of its predecessors, the public proved unreceptive. Much of the blame for its failure, however, may justly be attributed to a poor production. Based on a contemporary novel with a Spanish setting, the intricate plot of *The Dutch Lover* involves seven sets of lovers—four of them being of earnest intent and the other three being comic in nature. One of the males who is featured in a comic pair of lovers is a Dutchman, and the play derives its name from his prominence in many of the comedic scenes. The various strands of plot mesh nicely—with the aid of multiple disguises and mistaken identities reminiscent of plays constructed in the manner of Spanish intrigue. Such comedies emphasized action and intricate plotting at the expense of character development and usually incorporated the element of spectacle. Behn's fondness for this kind of drama was an abiding one, and she persisted in writing works of this style long after its popularity with English audiences had waned.

ABDELAZER

Discouraged by the failure of *The Dutch Lover*, Behn offered the public no new plays from February, 1673, to the time when *Abdelazer* was produced in July, 1676. This work is a romantic tragedy in the grand manner, with much turgid rhetoric. The plot was derived from an anonymous sixteenth century play, and its action takes place in a Spanish-Moorish milieu. Although it met with public approbation, it is decidedly inferior to plays of this genre written by Dryden and Otway. Sensing that she lacked the temperament needed to create heroic drama, Behn did not again attempt to write tragedy.

THE TOWN FOP

For her next play, Behn turned to more congenial subject matter and for the first time composed a play whose setting lay within the city of London. Entitled *The Town Fop*, it is a marked improvement over any of her previous works for the theater. Indebted in the main features of its plot to George Wilkins's *The Miseries of Enforced Marriage* (pr. 1605), it deals with a young man whose guardian forces him to marry against his will, despite the fact that he has already promised to wed a girl with whom he is deeply in love. The girl disguises herself as a young man and feigns an attempt to make love to the wife of her former fiancé before he has had a chance to consummate their marriage. Believing that his wife has been morally compromised by this encounter, the young man divorces her and then marries his former sweetheart. The problem of forced marriage is a major theme in the works of Behn and recurs in many of her other plays.

THE ROVER

The problem of forced marriage is, in fact, the chief dramatic conflict in Behn's most famous play, *The Rover*. Like many of her plays, it is an adaptation of an earlier work by a different hand. In this case, the source was Thomas Killigrew's closet drama *Thomaso: Or, The Wanderer*. Killigrew's play has seventy-three scenes that are organized into ten acts. He wrote this work in 1654 while in exile, but it was not actually published until ten years later. Although there is no direct evidence that Killigrew granted permission to Behn to make the adaptation, it is quite unlikely that she would have done so without his express consent. Killigrew's *Thomaso* contains so much material that Behn needed two full-length plays to encompass the entire story despite her drastic condensation of certain features of the original plot. The first part of *The Rover* was produced in March, 1677, and the second part almost four years later, in January, 1681. Whereas Killigrew's entire play is set in Madrid, Behn shifted the setting for the first part of *The Rover* to Naples during the climax of its carnival season. Because mistakes in identity are rendered more credible when the populace at large is in masquerade, the change of scene has obvious advantages for a comedy of intrigue in which duels are fought based on mistaken identities.

The banished cavaliers referred to in the subtitle of *The Rover* are a group of Englishmen who are compelled to live in exile as a result of Oliver Cromwell's abolition of the Stuart monarchy in 1642. Although not as complex as *The Dutch Lover*, the plot of the first part focuses on the romantic maneuvers of three Englishmen and three Spanish ladies that eventually culminate in the matrimonial union of each pair. The central couple consists of a spirited young Spanish lady named Hellena and a witty Englishman known as Wilmore the Rover. Wilmore is believed to be a composite character based on two of Behn's close friends: John Hoyle and John Wilmot, the earl of Rochester. Wilmore is such an attractive rake that he is said to have made vice alluring to a good part of the audience. Hellena, on the other hand, was originally destined for life in a cloister. It is her sister, Florinda, who is being coerced into an arranged marriage for the sake of prestige and economic advantage. All ends well, and both sisters manage to avoid the respective forms of bondage that threaten their future happiness. There are, it must be acknowledged, many implausibilities in the plot, and some actions appear to be insufficiently motivated. These deficiencies, however, are transcended by the sparkling dialogue that flows from Behn's pen, and it is this witty repartee that constitutes the play's chief virtue. Its sequel, generally regarded as inferior to the first part, is most noteworthy for the fact that Behn introduced two *commedia dell'arte* figures into its plot: Harlequin and Scaramouche.

SIR PATIENT FANCY

Of the plays produced after the first part of *The Rover*, *Sir Patient Fancy* and *The Emperor of the Moon* are probably the most outstanding examples of Behn's dramatic craftmanship. Much of the inspiration for *Sir Patient Fancy* is derived from three of Molière's comedies—especially *Le Malade imaginaire* (pr. 1673; *The Imaginary Invalid*, 1732; also known as *The Hypochondriac*). Her play, however, should be judged on its own merits, for she borrows incidents rather than themes from the French master. Although Molière asserted that the purpose of comedy is to correct people by entertaining them, Behn herself did not ascribe any pedagogical function to the theater. She wrote her plays solely for the sake of entertaining the public. In *Sir Patient Fancy*, Behn succeeds perhaps too well, for the play is undoubtedly her bawdiest. Many women in the audience were offended by the play's overt sexual escapades, and Behn had to go to great lengths to defend herself against charges of obscenity. Had the play been writ-

ten by a man, she argued, the issue of licentiousness would never have arisen.

THE EMPEROR OF THE MOON

The Emperor of the Moon, on the other hand, is a model of decorum. This love intrigue successfully integrates a number of distinct styles, including those of grand opera and *commedia dell'arte*. Although the figures of Harlequin and Scaramouche were previously used in the second part of *The Rover*, they are incorporated much more effectively in *The Emperor of the Moon*. The plot centers on a pair of men who masquerade as the King of the Moon and Prince Thunderland as a stratagem of courtship in wooing the daughter and niece of a gullible astrologer. Before their ruse is uncovered, the two masqueraders succeed in marrying the objects of their affection. The astrologer, for his part, duly recognizes the folly of living in a world of fantasy. An immediate success when first performed in 1687, the play continued to be popular with London audiences for most of the eighteenth century.

OTHER MAJOR WORKS

LONG FICTION: *Love Letters Between a Nobleman and His Sister*, 1683-1687 (3 volumes); *Agnes de Castro*, 1688; *The Fair Jilt: Or, The History of Prince Tarquin and Miranda*, 1688; *Oroonoko: Or, The History of the Royal Slave*, 1688; *The History of the Nun: Or, The Fair Vow-Breaker*, 1689; *The Lucky Mistake*, 1689; *The Nun: Or, The Perjured Beauty*, 1697; *The Adventure of the Black Lady*, 1698; *The Wandering Beauty*, 1698.

POETRY: *Poems upon Several Occasions, with A Voyage to the Island of Love*, 1684 (adaptation of Abbé Paul Tallemant's *Le Voyage de l'isle d'amour*); *Miscellany: Being a Collection of Poems by Several Hands*, 1685 (includes works by others).

TRANSLATIONS: *Aesop's Fables*, 1687 (with Francis Barlow); *Of Trees*, 1689 (of book 6 of Abraham Cowley's *Sex libri plantarum*).

MISCELLANEOUS: *La Montre: Or, The Lover's Watch*, 1686 (prose and verse); *The Case for the Watch*, 1686 (prose and verse); *Lycidus: Or, The Lover in Fashion*, 1688 (prose and verse; includes works by others); *The Lady's Looking-Glass, to Dress Herself*

By: Or, The Art of Charming, 1697 (prose and verse); *The Works of Aphra Behn*, 1915, 1967 (6 volumes; Montague Summers, editor).

BIBLIOGRAPHY

Altaba-Artal, Dolors. *Aphra Behn's English Feminism: Wit and Satire.* Cranbury, N.J.: Associated University Presses, 1999. An examination of Behn's writings from the perspective of feminism. Bibliography and index.

Hughes, Derek. *The Theatre of Aphra Behn.* New York: Palgrave, 2001. An authoritative study of Behn's dramatic œuvre by a prominent scholar of Restoration drama. While concentrating on the playwright and her work, this study assumes the reader has a good understanding of the era and theater in Behn's day.

Hutner, Heidi. *Colonial Women: Race and Culture in Stuart Drama.* New York: Oxford University Press, 2001. Contains history and criticism of Stuart drama, including a section on Behn's *The Widow Ranter.* Bibliography and index.

Kreis-Schinck, Annette. *Women, Writing, and the Theater in the Early Modern Period: The Plays of Aphra Behn and Suzanne Centlivre.* Cranbury, N. J.: Associated University Presses, 2001. An analysis of the lives and writing of Behn and Mrs. Susannah Centlivre. Bibliography and index.

O'Donnell, Mary Ann, Bernard Dhuicq, and Guyonne Leduc, eds. *Aphra Behn (1640-1689): Identity, Alterity. Ambiguity.* Paris: Harmattan, 2000. These papers, collected from an international conference on Behn in 1999, examine the life and work of Behn. Bibliography and index.

Spencer, Jane. *Aphra Behn's Afterlife.* New York: Oxford University Press, 2000. An examination of Behn's works, including *The Rover* and *Oroonoko*, with emphasis on her influence. Bibliography and index.

Todd, Janet M. *The Secret Life of Aphra Behn.* London: Andre Deutsch, 1996. This biography of Behn delves into her spy activity while describing her life and work. Bibliography and index.

Wiseman, Susan. *Aphra Behn.* Plymouth, England: Northcote House in association with the British Council, 1996. A biography of Behn that examines her life and work. Bibliography and index.

Victor Anthony Rudowski,
updated by Ayne Cantrell

S. N. BEHRMAN

Born: Worcester, Massachusetts; June 9, 1893(?)
Died: New York, New York; September 9, 1973

PRINCIPAL DRAMA

Bedside Manners, pr. 1923, pb. 1924 (with J. Kenyon Nicholson)
A Night's Work, pr. 1924, pb. 1926 (with Nicholson)
The Man Who Forgot, pr. 1926 (with Owen Davis)
The Second Man, pr., pb. 1927
Serena Blandish: Or, The Difficulty of Getting Married, pr. 1929, pb. 1934
Meteor, pr. 1929, pb. 1934
Brief Moment, pr., pb. 1931
Biography, pr. 1932, pb. 1933
Rain from Heaven, pr., pb. 1934
End of Summer, pr., pb. 1936
Amphitryon 38, pr. 1937, pb. 1938
Wine of Choice, pr., pb. 1938
No Time for Comedy, pr., pb. 1939
The Talley Method, pr., pb. 1941
The Pirate, pr. 1942, pb. 1943 (adaptation of Ludwig Fulda's play *Die Seeräuber*)
Jacobowsky and the Colonel, pr., pb. 1944 (based on Franz Werfel's play *Jacobowsky und der Oberst*)

Dunnigan's Daughter, pr., pb. 1945
I Know My Love, pr., pb. 1949 (adaptation of
    Marcel Archard's play *Auprès de ma blonde*)
Jane, pr., pb. 1952 (based on W. Somerset
    Maugham's story)
Fanny, pr. 1954, pb. 1955 (with Joshua Logan;
    music and lyrics by Harold Rome; based on
    Marcel Pagnol's plays *Marius* and *Fanny* and
    screenplay *César*)
The Cold Wind and the Warm, pr. 1958, pb. 1959
Lord Pengo, pr. 1962, pb. 1963
But for Whom Charlie, pr., pb. 1964

OTHER LITERARY FORMS

S. N. Behrman wrote two "profile"-type biographies: *Duveen* (1952) and *Portrait of Max: An Intimate Memoir of Sir Max Beerbohm* (1960). *The Suspended Drawing Room* (1965) is a collection of (mostly) familiar essays focusing on such notables as Robert E. Sherwood, Ferenc Molnár, and A. E. Kazan. *The Worcester Account* (1954), the best of Behrman's prose works, is a collection of pieces originally published in *The New Yorker*. *The Burning Glass* (1968) is a semiautobiographical novel, and *People in a Diary* (1972; reissued as *Tribulations and Laughter*, 1972) is a memoir containing brief, often poignant essays and sketches. Behrman was also the author of numerous screenplays, including several adaptations of his own and others' works.

ACHIEVEMENTS

Although S. N. Behrman's career as a dramatist spanned several decades, his major impact on the American theater covered roughly two and a half decades, from 1927, with the great success of *The Second Man* (178 performances in New York City), to 1944, with *Jacobowsky and the Colonel*, which had a run of 415 performances, also in New York City. Excluding his earlier apprenticeship plays, written during and after studies at Harvard University, Behrman's career as a dramatist ranged from 1923, with *Bedside Manners* (in collaboration with J. Kenyon Nicholson), to 1964, with *But for Whom Charlie*. During this period, the playwright offered to the New York stage—without counting other locales—a total of twenty-two plays in full production, most of them enjoying considerable or at least moderate success. Only three plays were (relatively speaking) unsuccessful: *Wine of Choice*, *Dunnigan's Daughter*, and *But for Whom Charlie*. Even these works, however, attracted some favorable critical notice. Along with *Jacobowsky and the Colonel*, which later became a motion picture, *Fanny* (written as a musical comedy in collaboration with Joshua Logan) and *I Know My Love* enjoyed the longest runs. These works were essentially entertainments, written with a shrewd sense of the audience response yet without the writer's special touches of mannered comedy. Earlier, during the "vintage" years, as critic Kenneth T. Reed describes the period between 1927 and 1936, when the writer had seven plays in production on Broadway, a new comedy by Behrman was a special event, one eagerly awaited.

For this audience, a particular quality that marked the author's comedies was "sophistication." This term, still generally applied to Behrman, has only limited usefulness, because, among other reasons, not all his plays belong to this mode. The most significant exception is *The Cold Wind and the Warm*, a semiautobiographical work, impressionistic and poetic. Moreover, the word "sophistication" has negative connotations, perhaps carrying over from social criticism of the 1930's and 1940's. From this point of view, the word denotes, among other negative attitudes, frivolity, urbane elegance, and elitism. To be sure, most of Behrman's early comedies are set in the drawing rooms of the privileged class, with a clash between intellectuals (either true or sham), together with grasping middle-class parvenus whose special concerns are money, status, and advantageous marriage. Nevertheless, Behrman's judgment of privilege in these comedies is critical and gently satiric, not approving.

By more narrowly construing "sophisticated," the word may be applied with greater confidence to the wide range of Behrman's drama. In the general class of comic ironists such as Oscar Wilde, George Bernard Shaw, W. Somerset Maugham, and Noël Coward (also, arguably, Neil Simon), Behrman writes plays that resemble comedies of manners or polite comedies, but unlike Wilde (although he admired the Irish-

S. N. Behrman in 1952. (AP/Wide World Photos)

man's *The Importance of Being Earnest*, pr. 1895, pb. 1899), Behrman never treats frivolity or triviality as a prime theme, and unlike Coward (although he also admired Coward's *Blithe Spirit*, pr., pb. 1941), Behrman avoids sentimental fantasy. Curiously, Behrman's work more closely resembles the lighter drama of Shaw and the less farcical comedies of Maugham. Behrman's comedy does not propagandize in favor of socialistic causes, but beneath the surface banter of the American writer is a tough realistic edge, a sharp awareness of the vulgar display of wealth and the brutality of social intolerance. Also, in its satiric wit stopping short of misanthropy, Behrman's work reminds one of certain Maugham plays, such as *Our Betters* (pr. 1917, pb. 1923) and *The Circle* (pr., pb. 1921).

Judging the impact of his own work, Behrman was modest. In *People in a Diary*, he wrote: "For a time, Philip Barry, Paul Osborn, and I were the only American writers of high comedy." Of these playwrights, only the first is still remembered. By the late 1930's, Behrman had already established his reputation.

Biography

Samuel Nathaniel Behrman was the third child of Joseph and Zelda (Feingold) Behrman and was born in Worcester, Massachusetts. The first two children in the Behrman family, Hiram and Morris, were born in Eastern Europe (in or near Vilna, Lithuania). Because no official record of the writer's birth date was ever recorded in Worcester, he arbitrarily selected his own "birthday" as June 9, 1893. In *The Worcester Account*, Behrman humorously described the circumstances of his search for his true date of birth and concluded that "common sense tells me that 1893 must be reasonably close."

Readers interested in the details of Behrman's youth and schooling should turn to *The Worcester Account*, a colorful but by no means sentimentalized review of his adventures, the chapters originally written as short narratives for *The New Yorker*. From these pieces one learns that, although poor, Behrman's family enjoyed some distinction among the other Jewish residents of the neighborhood because the father was a Talmudic scholar. From him, Samuel learned "the Old Testament stories as if they had taken place recently—as if they constituted his personal past."

In 1899, Behrman entered Providence Street School, and in 1902, he heard a political speech delivered by Eugene V. Debs, then the Socialist Labor Party candidate for president. That chance occasion, as he later remarked, began in his life "an orientation it would otherwise not have had—a bias in favor of those who had suffered from cruelty or callousness." Another direction in his life was pointed by his friend Daniel Asher (who appears as the character Willie Lavin in *The Cold Wind and the Warm*). With Asher, he witnessed at Lothrops's Opera House in 1904 a melodrama entitled *Devil's Island*, and years later he still recalled the enchantment of that performance.

By 1907, when he entered Classical High School in Worcester, Behrman had begun his lifelong habit of omnivorous reading. Among his early favorites were William Shakespeare and Horatio Alger. He could, for his high school classes, recite from memory passages from *Hamlet, Prince of Denmark* (pr. c. 1600-1601) and *Macbeth* (pr. 1606, pb. 1623), and he acquired an elementary knowledge of Latin and

Greek, useful tools in his cultivation of language skills. During these years, he also deepened his friendship with Asher, who urged Behrman to write and who analyzed all the youth's fledgling manuscripts.

In 1911, Behrman toured on the Poli vaudeville circuit for some months with a skit that he had written himself, entitled "Only a Part." The circuit covered a number of theatrical points, including a New York vaudeville house on Fourteenth Street. Behrman's health, in those years precarious, obliged him to cut short the tour with two others, and he returned to Worcester. In 1912, at the family's urging, he entered Clark College. As a special student at this local school, he continued to write and act, also turning his attention to oratory. His academic work as an English major was successful, but he failed to report to physical education classes and was suspended from Clark. In the summer of 1913, he enrolled at Harvard, then reentered Clark in 1914, but was again suspended for neglecting physical education classes. The next year, he sold his first story, "La Vie Parisienne," which he wrote as a student in Charles Townsend Copeland's class at Harvard. By 1916, he had enrolled in Professor George Pierce Baker's Workshop 47, the only undergraduate admitted to Baker's famous playwriting course. Also in that year, Behrman was graduated from Harvard with a bachelor's degree. After failing to find a job in newspaper offices in several cities, he decided to continue his education at Columbia University, where he studied under Brander Matthews and other notable teachers. In 1918, Behrman earned his master's degree at Columbia. Offered a teaching appointment at the University of Minnesota, Behrman decided instead to hazard his fortune in writing. For the next two years, he worked for *The New York Times*, at first as a typist of classified ads and later as a book reviewer. Before and during this time, he sold stories and essays to several magazines. One of the most influential of them, *The Smart Set*, carried in its November, 1919, issue "The Second Man," a story that he later rewrote into the play of the same title.

For the young journalist with dreams of becoming a playwright, the early years of the 1920's were arduous, mostly frustrating, with only occasional periods of publishing success. This period came to an end in 1926, when Behrman developed a working friendship with a more established dramatist, Owen Davis, with whom he collaborated on a play entitled *The Man Who Forgot*. Later that year, *A Night's Work*, written in collaboration with J. Kenyon Nicholson, was produced on Broadway. Through these efforts and the contacts that he established with producers Ned Harris and Crosbie Gaige, Behrman was able to supplement his income with publicity work for other New York-based plays.

Finally, on April 11, 1927, Behrman's years of apprenticeship came to an end when the Theatre Guild presented *The Second Man*. After that popular and critical success, Behrman's labors were often divided between playwriting and scriptwriting for Hollywood. Also dating from this period was his long-lasting association and friendship with Harold Ross of *The New Yorker*. Over the years, Ross commissioned Behrman to write many essays, including "profiles," for his magazine—the first of which was on George Gershwin and appeared in 1929.

During the late 1920's and the decade of the 1930's, Behrman attained considerable prominence in his craft, as a playwright and as a producer-writer. In 1928, he sailed to England to oversee a production of *The Second Man* in London, with Noël Coward in the leading role. Indeed, over the years, the production of a Behrman play usually called for the talents of America's and England's most distinguished players: Alfred Lunt and Lynn Fontanne, Ina Claire, Catherine Cornell, and Laurence Olivier, among others. From 1929 to 1939, Behrman's work was produced on Broadway stages with general approval: *Serena Blandish*, *Meteor*, *Brief Moment*, *Biography*, *Rain from Heaven*, *End of Summer*, and *No Time for Comedy*. For Behrman, these years brought both regret (with the death by suicide of Daniel Asher in 1929) and personal fulfillment (including his marriage in 1936 to Elza Heifetz and the birth of their only child, David Arthur, in 1937).

In 1938, Behrman joined the Playwrights' Producing Company, an independent guild of writer-producers that included Robert E. Sherwood, Maxwell Anderson, Elmer Rice, and Sidney Howard. Until 1945, when Behrman withdrew from the company, he produced *The Talley Method*, *The Pirate*, *Jacobowsky and the Colonel*, and *Dunnigan's Daughter*. During this time, he received a significant award, as well as academic recognition: In 1943, he was admitted to the Department of Arts and Literature of the National Institute of Arts and Letters, and in 1944, his *Jacobowsky and the Colonel*, based on a sketch by Franz Werfel but almost completely reinterpreted by the playwright, won the New York Drama Critics Circle Award as the best foreign play of the season.

After 1945, Behrman divided his literary work—that is to say, writing not commissioned by Hollywood studios—between the stage and various kinds of prose. His later plays include *I Know My Love*, *Jane*, *Fanny*, *The Cold Wind and the Warm*, *Lord Pengo*, and his final production, *But for Whom Charlie*. Toward the end of his career, he turned with greater avidity to the expanded essay, which he called his "one hobby." In 1952, he published *Duveen*, a biography of Joseph Duveen, a notorious art dealer about whom Behrman had earlier written a profile entitled "The Days of Duveen" for *The New Yorker*. The autobiographical volume *The Worcester Account*, as noted above, also had its genesis in *The New Yorker*. He published *Portrait of Max* (1960), a sheaf of essays entitled *The Suspended Drawing Room* (1965), his only novel, *The Burning Glass* (1968), and a book of memoirs and appreciations, *People in a Diary* (1972). Among the awards he received during the final decades of his life were an honorary degree from Clark University (1949) and the Brandeis University Creative Arts Award (1962). In the latter year, he was also appointed Trustee of Clark University. On September 9, 1973, Behrman died in New York of apparent heart failure.

ANALYSIS

Although S. N. Behrman's plays were crafted for theatrical performance, they are also admirably suitable for reading. Modeled after the scintillating comedies of Wilde and Shaw, Behrman's plays similarly are, by turn, clever, ironic, provocative. That is not to say, however, that Behrman was an original thinker on social issues, as Shaw was, or that his plays match Wilde's sense of whimsy. Indeed, Behrman's drama

is uneven in quality. Plays such as *The Pirate* (adapted from Ludwig Fulda's play *Die Seerauber*) and *I Know My Love* (adapted from Marcel Achard) or the musical *Fanny* must be judged as entertainments, not against the highest standards of the dramatic art. Other plays are quite dated, products of their time. In particular, the comedies of the 1930's, for all their surface brilliance, resemble certain clever mating comedies of the motion pictures of that decade. During the hard years of the Great Depression, many theatergoers appreciated escapist fantasies that would carry them in imagination away from their troubles. The drawing-room settings of Behrman's plays, with furnishings opulent and refined, provided an alternative world, one inhabited by mostly clever, attractive characters whose major problem in life was to find an appropriate mate. Behrman's characters—mostly upper-class, worldly, and well-educated—fit comfortably into this world, but for modern theatergoers, the Depression-era frame of reference has vanished.

Nevertheless, Behrman's plays still appeal to audiences interested in comedy of manners. He isolates universal human traits and observes them faithfully, without exaggeration. At his best, his comedies offer the viewer (or reader) moral choices that exercise the heart. Never vulgar, rarely sexually provocative, his comedies sparkle with ample appreciation for human potentialities: for the happiness of a true marriage; for friendship based on trust; for common sense that cannot be swayed by political or social bias; for discovery of the authentic self; above all, for tolerance of others' foibles, together with the resolve never to injure innocent people through malice or ignorance.

Although Behrman was not, except in *The Cold Wind and the Warm*, basically an autobiographical playwright, many of his themes can be traced to circumstances in his life. His economically deprived youth and his years of struggle as a journalist lay behind his frequent depiction of the clash between characters emerging from deprivation and those already privileged by birth or class. At the same time, his culturally enriched childhood, one that particularly emphasized traditional Jewish values of social justice and strict moral probity, sensitized him to the contrast between superficially upright but morally corrupt people and those of genuine integrity. Finally, in his early comedies—particularly those before 1936—Behrman transformed Horatio Alger stories that he had enjoyed as a youth into moral tales concerning the Midas touch that turns gold into dross.

Typically in Behrman's variations on these ambition myths, the major (sensible) character abandons his childish illusions, discovers his limitations, and accepts in a mature way his responsibilities or potentialities. Rarely, as in *Serena Blandish*, the character is a woman; on the whole, Behrman's female leads are more astute than their romantic counterparts. For men and women alike, the tests for Behrman's pattern of discovery/initiation are through friendship or through marriage. As a youth, Behrman was not physically robust or socially assertive. Perhaps by way of compensation, he cherished throughout his lifetime generous friendships (an assumption supported by *People in a Diary*), and in his plays he established the values of supportive relationships. The greater test of maturity, however, was in the courtship clash that precedes marriage. Married late in life, at the age of forty-three, Behrman tended to view on the stage the "war of the sexes" from the vantage point of rationality, not idealistic romance. If couples in his plays achieve the promise of a satisfactory (rational) union, the credit always goes to the woman, whom Behrman—like Shaw—championed as the more sensible of the sexes. In all relationships—those of competition, of friendship, and of courtship—Behrman holds up the exemplary pattern of tolerance. Without tolerance, his characters could never come to self-knowledge, and their world of high comedy would fall apart.

THE SECOND MAN

In *The Second Man*, Mrs. Kendall Frayne, a wealthy widow whose chief asset is her common sense, and Monica Grey, a younger woman, are romantically interested in Clark Storey. Storey is a would-be poet and novelist, handsome but passionless. His counterpart is Austin Lowe, a chemist with meager social graces to match his rival's. Nevertheless, Storey wins the love of Monica; for her part, Mrs. Frayne is too worldly-wise to fall for the superficial would-be writer. By the end of the play, Storey escapes both romantic entanglements but discovers

the unsettling truth that he possesses a "second man" in his nature, one that is "calm, critical, observant, unmoved, blasé, odious." Thus, Storey attains, at the very least, the reward of painful illumination.

For Behrman's original audience, the play offered both entertainment and a moral lesson that they were prepared to accept. By challenging the playgoers' intelligence, the writer allowed them to discern, without the heavy hand of editorial intrusion, that Mrs. Frayne's "sophistication" would prevent her from choosing a poor mate. In addition to flattering the audience's urbanity, Behrman taught them a sound moral lesson. For all his protestations that he speaks honest truth, Clark Storey must—to protect his vanity—conceal his emotional shallowness and his greed to achieve status. Thus, the audience learns to reject an ambition that lacks the solid basis of integrity.

SERENA BLANDISH AND END OF SUMMER

This lesson, presented with different variations on the theme, appears in *Serena Blandish* and *End of Summer*. In both plays, fortune hunters attempt, without hiding their motives, to secure marriages that will advance their ambitions. Subtitled *The Difficulty of Getting Married*, *Serena Blandish* showcases a charming, witty young woman who has emerged from an impoverished background. Serena catches the eye of Sigmund Traub, a wealthy, middle-aged, Jewish businessman. He takes her under his wing, provides her with social advantages and money (he even lends her a diamond ring), and generally acts like a Pygmalion to her Galatea. Her ambitions, however, are never realized. The money she displays to her rich suitors she does not really possess, and at the end of the play she remains unmarried. Similarly, in *End of Summer*, Dr. Kenneth Rice pursues but fails to snare two wealthy women. A "self-made man," as he likes to call himself, he courts Leonie Frothingham and her daughter Paula for the sake of their money, but Leonie, a sensible woman in the mold of Mrs. Frayne, rejects his advances, as does her idealistic daughter. At the "end of summer," he has neither wife nor money.

MALE AND FEMALE CHARACTERS

Dr. Rice, a Freudian psychoanalyst, resembles other power-obsessive character types in Behrman's plays: Hobart Eldridge (*Rain from Heaven*), Allan

Frobisher (*Jane*), Orrin Kinnicott (*Biography*), Raphael Lord (*Meteor*), Lord Pengo (*Lord Pengo*), and Dr. Axton Talley (*The Talley Method*). Although different in certain respects, all these personalities are rigid, authoritarian, self-centered, and intolerant; most are politically conservative. They contrast with other male characters who, although less assertive, have more attractive personal qualities. Among these sensitive (but often unfocused and self-indulgent) types are a number of second-rate artists or aesthetes in the pattern of Clark Storey of *The Second Man*. They include Aaron (*The Cold Wind and the Warm*), Sasha Barashaev (*Rain from Heaven*), Daniel Chanler (*I Know My Love*), Roderick Dean (*Brief Moment*), Peter Crewe (*Jane*), Melchoir Feydak (*Biography*), Edgar Mallison (*Serena Blandish*), Derek Pengo (*Lord Pengo*), Willard Prosper (*But for Whom Charlie*), Miguel Riachi (*Dunnigan's Daughter*), and Warwick Wilson (*Biography*). Although these would-be artists range in appeal from the fragile Aaron to the radical Marxist painter Riachi, they share the qualities of self-indulgence, independence, and (to varying degrees) fecklessness.

In general, Behrman's male figures—whether petulantly dictatorial or dreamy—lack the balanced common sense of their female counterparts. Among his "strong" women in the pattern of Mrs. Frayne are Emily Chanler (*I Know My Love*), Fern Dunnigan (*Dunnigan's Daughter*), Linda Esterbrook (*No Time for Comedy*), Abbey Fane (*Brief Moment*), Marion Froude (*Biography*), Enid Fuller (*The Talley Method*), and Lael Wyngate (*Rain from Heaven*). To these may be added Leonie Frothingham (despite her naïveté) and Serena Blandish, whose good sense compensates, in large measure, for her deficiency in exaggerating the values of money and status.

TOLERANCE AND INTOLERANCE

Along with their common sense and emotional maturity, these women share a quality of tolerance. For Behrman, tolerance greatly humanizes his protagonists. To be sure, several leading males are wisely tolerant—chief among them Jacobowsky, but the "strong" women (as contrasted to frivolous types) best exemplify the virtue. In *The Second Man*, Clark Storey tells Mrs. Frayne that she possesses the two "great requirements" for marriage: money and tolerance. Running through many of Behrman's comedies is a conflict between the tolerant, blessed with habits of kindness and serenity, and the intolerant. In *Biography*, three characters hold narrowly rigid opinions: Orrin Kinnicott, Richard Kurt, and Bunny Nolan. Responding to Marion Froude's open nature, Kurt upbraids her, for "what you call tolerance I call sloppy laziness." The audience, comparing the two personalities—the woman cheerful and emancipated, the man egotistic, wrapped up in radical politics—can be expected to draw a different conclusion.

In *Rain from Heaven*, Behrman stigmatizes, in the words of Lael Wyngate, an "epidemic of hatred and intolerance that may engulf us all." Perhaps the playwright best expresses this theme in *Jacobowsky and the Colonel*. In the second act, the Nazi Colonel warns Marianne that he cannot tolerate being treated in any fashion that he believes is disrespectful. The Nazi's counterpart in this moral tale of "strange bedfellows" is Jacobowsky, the "wandering Jew" who has learned to accept life's evils with a redeeming sense of good humor. Through his example, the Colonel undergoes an initiation in the rites of true manhood. By the end of the play, the Colonel is not entirely "mature," not wholly tolerant, but he has at least learned to make compromises.

Behrman's insights into the corrosive effects of intolerance derive, at least in part, from his life's education as a Jew. Curiously, most of his apprenticeship work and the plays of the late 1920's and early 1930's avoid all mention of Jews. To be sure, Sigmund Traub in *Serena Blandish* is a Jew, a Bond Street merchant, but Behrman reveals little about the man's psychological reasons for pampering a beautiful woman not linked to him by passion. Not until 1934 in *Rain from Heaven* did Behrman create a Jewish character who functions as a spokesperson for his own ideas: Hugo Willens, who, despite his Nordic appearance, had to flee Europe because his grandmother was a Jew.

THE COLD WIND AND THE WARM AND
BUT FOR WHOM CHARLIE

Among the later plays, *The Cold Wind and the Warm* explores autobiographical themes already presented in Behrman's essays for *The New Yorker*; in this, his most touching play, Behrman comes to terms with his Jewishness, without evasion or apology. A drama of recollection, *The Cold Wind and the Warm* surprised some critics, who were accustomed to Behrman's usual "high comedy"; although reviews were mixed, the play lasted for 120 performances at the Morosco. The playwright's final stage offering, *But for Whom Charlie*—one of his least successful plays—included the minor character Seymour Rosenthal, a Jew who had once been excluded from a college fraternity because of his religion. Also in the play, however, was Brock Dunaway, a Jewish novelist seventy years old—a survivor, just as Behrman was to survive the hardships of his own past.

FRIENDSHIP AND HUMOR

Fortunately for the decent characters in the author's drama, they do not stand alone in their struggle against prejudice. For Behrman, the links of friendship, perhaps more enduring than those of romantic passion, unite men and women of goodwill. By the final act of *Amphitryon 38*, Jupiter and Alkmena move toward a deeper appreciation of each other. Jupiter asks the rhetorical question: What is the object of friendship? Alkmena's answer is probably also Behrman's: "To bring together the most totally dissimilar people and make them equal." This judgment is crucial in accepting the friendship of people as dissimilar as the Colonel and Jacobowsky. The audience must grasp the idea that they not only tolerate each other but also become friends. If social antagonists can appreciate each other's values, then people of goodwill have an even greater obligation to join forces. In *Biography*, Marion Froude's friendship with Melchoir Feydak is based on mutual respect and admiration. As decent, empathetic persons, they stand out as the only fully tolerant characters in the play. Conversely, when Behrman's characters lack a capacity for friendship, they become self-centered and obnoxious. Like Dr. Kenneth Rice (*End of Summer*), who cannot trust another person deeply enough to make him (or her) a friend, Raphael Lord (*Meteor*) and Dr. Axton Talley (*The Talley Method*) ultimately become monsters. Without meaningful attachments, Behrman believes, human beings lose their spiritual bearings and destroy themselves.

It is noteworthy that Behrman's defective characters invariably lack humor. For the dramatist, a sense of the comic, no less than a capacity for friendship, marks the true human being. In an interview with *The New York Times* in 1952, Behrman remarked: "The essence of the comic sense is awareness: awareness of the tragedy as well as the fun of life, of the pity, the futility, the lost hopes, the striving for immortality, for permanence, for security, for love."

OTHER MAJOR WORKS

LONG FICTION: *The Burning Glass*, 1968.

NONFICTION: *Duveen*, 1952; *The Worcester Account*, 1954; *Portrait of Max: An Intimate Memoir of Sir Max Beerbohm*, 1960; *The Suspended Drawing Room*, 1965; *People in a Diary*, 1972 (reissued as *Tribulations and Laughter*, 1972).

SCREENPLAYS: *He Knew Women*, 1930 (adaptation of his play *The Second Man*); *The Sea Wolf*, 1930 (adaptation of Jack London's novel); *Surrender*, 1931 (with Sonya Levien); *Rebecca of Sunnybrook Farm*, 1932 (with Levien; adaptation of Kau Douglas Wiggin's children's novel); *Brief Moment*, 1933 (adaptation of his play); *Anna Karenina*, 1935 (with Salka Viertel and Clemence Dane; adaptation of Leo Tolstoy's novel); *The Scarlet Pimpernel*, 1935 (with Lajos Biro, Robert E. Sherwood, and Arthur Wimperes); *Quo Vadis*, 1951 (with John Lee Makin and Levien; adaptation of Henryk Sienkiewicz's novel).

BIBLIOGRAPHY

Asher, Donald. *The Eminent Yachtsman and the Whorehouse Piano Player*. New York: Coward, McCann and Geoghegan, 1973. In a memoir about Asher's late, suicidal father, Daniel Asher, on whom is based a central character in Behrman's *The Cold Wind and the Warm*, the author includes a portrait of Behrman (his father's closest friend) and a vivid description of life in the tenement ghetto of Massachusetts' Worcester, where Behrman and Daniel Asher grew up.

Gross, Robert F. *S. N. Behrman: A Research and Production Handbook*. Westport, Conn.: Greenwood Press, 1992. This sourcebook provides a detailed record of Behrman's work, from the 1920's to the mid-1960's, and encompasses published and unpublished primary materials and the critical responses. Includes plot summaries and critical overviews for fifty-one plays, and an annotated bibliography. All materials are cross-referenced and indexed.

Jorge, Robert Richard. "S(amuel) N(athaniel) Behrman." In *Twentieth Century American Dramatists*, edited by John MacNicholas. Vol. 7 in *Dictionary of Literary Biography*. Detroit, Mich.: The Gale Group, 1981. A concise overview of the life and works of Behrman.

Joshi, B. D. *Major Plays of Barry and Behrman: A Comparative Study*. Jaipur, India: Pointer Publishers, 1989. Joshi compares and contrasts the dramatic works of Behrman and Philip Barry. Bibliography and index.

Klink, William R. *S. N. Behrman: The Major Plays*. Amsterdam, The Netherlands: Rodopi, 1978.

Klink lucidly evaluates Behrman's major plays excluding those adapted or written in collaboration. The study includes an introduction briefly discussing published and unpublished material about Behrman, a summary conclusion, and a bibliography. Valuable as one of few books solely on Behrman.

Reed, Kenneth T. *S. N. Behrman*. Boston: Twayne, 1975. Reed's biographical and critical study provides one of the most accessible, valuable, and comprehensive treatments of the playwright and his work. It contains a chronology, a detailed examination of Behrman's plays within the context of his life and career, an index, and a select bibliography that includes an annotated listing of major secondary sources. Reed's chapters encompass the playwright's techniques and major themes.

Leslie B. Mittleman,
updated by Christian H. Moe

DAVID BELASCO

Born: San Francisco, California; July 25, 1853
Died: New York, New York; May 14, 1931

PRINCIPAL DRAMA

L'Assommoir, pr. 1879 (adaptation of Émile Zola's novel)

Within an Inch of His Life, pr. 1879 (with James A. Herne)

Hearts of Oak, pr. 1879 (with Herne; originally as *Chums*; adaptation of Henry Leslie's play *The Mariner's Compass*)

La Belle Russe, pr. 1881, pb. 1882

The Stranglers of Paris, pr. 1881, pb. 1941 (adaptation of Adolphe Belot's novel *L'Estrangleur*)

May Blossom, pb. 1883, pr. 1884

Valerie, pr. 1886 (adaptation of Victorien Sardou's *Fernande*)

Baron Rudolph, pr. 1887, pb. 1941 (with Bronson Howard)

The Highest Bidder, pr. 1887

The Wife, pr. 1887, pb. 1941 (with Henry C. De Mille)

Lord Chumley, pr., pb. 1888 (with De Mille)

The Charity Ball, pr. 1889, pb. 1941 (with De Mille)

Men and Women, pr. 1890, pb. 1941 (with De Mille)

Miss Helyett, pr. 1891

The Girl I Left Behind Me, pr. 1893, pb. 1941 (with Franklyn Fyles)

The Younger Son, pr. 1893 (adaptation of O. Vischer's play *Schlimme Saat*)

The Heart of Maryland, pr., pb. 1895

Zaza, pr. 1898 (adaptation of Pierre Berton and Charles Simon's French play)

Madame Butterfly, pr. 1900, pb. 1935 (with John Luther Long; adaptation of Long's story)

Naughty Anthony, pr. 1900, pb. 1941

DuBarry, pr. 1901, pb. 1928

The Darling of the Gods, pr. 1902, pb. 1928 (with Long)

Sweet Kitty Bellairs, pr., pb. 1903 (adaptation of Agnes and Egeron Castle's *The Bath Comedy*)

Adrea, pr. 1905, pb. 1928 (with John Luther Long)

The Girl of the Golden West, pr. 1905, pb. 1928

The Rose of the Rancho, pr. 1906, pb. 1936 (with Richard W. Tully; adaptation of Tully's *Juanita*)

A Grand Army Man, pr. 1907, pb. 1908 (with Pauline Phelps and Marion Short)

The Lily, pr. 1909

The Return of Peter Grimm, pr. 1911, pb. 1928

The Governor's Lady, pr., pb. 1912 (with Alice Bradley)

The Secret, pr. 1913

The Son Daughter, pr., pb. 1919 (with George Scarborough)

The Comedian, pr., pb. 1923 (adaptation of Sacha Guitry's play)

Laugh, Clown, Laugh, pr. 1923 (adaptation of Fausto Maria Martini's play *Ridi, pagliaccio*)

Fanny, pr., pb. 1926 (with Willard Mack)

Mima, pr. 1928 (adaptation of Ferenc Molnár's play *The Red Mill*)

Six Plays, pb. 1928 (Montrose J. Moses, editor)

The Plays of Henry C. De Mille, Written in Collaboration with David Belasco, pb. 1941 (Robert Hamilton Ball, editor)

OTHER LITERARY FORMS

David Belasco published a number of human-interest essays and articles about stagecraft, including "How I Stage My Plays" and "Stage Realism of the Future." A serialized autobiography, "My Life's Story," was published in *Hearst's Magazine* from March, 1914, to December, 1915, followed four years later by a full-length memoir, *The Theatre Through Its Stage Door* (1919). With two of his most popular plays later turned into novels, Belasco was one of the first in the United States to capitalize on the success of dramatic works by revising them for a new reading audience.

ACHIEVEMENTS

While contemporary critics frequently criticized David Belasco's penchant for melodrama, his im-

David Belasco (Library of Congress)

mense popular success was a product of his reliance on heart-interest as well as a strict interpretation of the fourth-wall convention. Belasco paid meticulous attention to details, often rewriting extensively in rehearsal. Indeed, he is best remembered for his directing methods, his realism, and his technical effects.

Belasco was the directing genius behind many actors and actresses. David Warfield, for example, who began his career with the burlesque company Weber and Fields, under Belasco's tutelage moved from the farcical *The Auctioneer* to Belasco's own seriocomic *The Return of Peter Grimm* and later appeared in William Shakespeare's *The Merchant of Venice* (pr. c. 1596-1597, pb. 1600). Perhaps "Mr. Dave's" greatest success was Leslie Carter, a society divorcée who undertook two years of acting lessons from Belasco. Best remembered for her electrifying performance in *The Heart of Maryland*, the fiery-haired actress exemplified the sensationalism that Belasco's audiences enjoyed. Such individual triumphs by no means detracted from Belasco's attention to his entire company. On the one hand, he encouraged every expression of individual talent, no matter how slender; on the other, he held long, painstaking rehearsals commencing at least six weeks before opening night.

Belasco believed that the purpose of the theater was to mimic nature, and he attempted to immerse his actors not merely in a realistic scene but in a mood as well. As Lise-Lone Marker points out, his goal seems similar to that of the proponents of the New Stagecraft, yet Belasco saw both light and color to be as essential to dialogue as music is to a song. He is noted for his ultrarealistic stage sets—sets that seem to answer August Strindberg's objection, in the preface to *Fröken Julie* (pb. 1888; *Miss Julie*, 1912), to unstable canvas scenery. Belasco imported antique furniture and draperies for his sets, and he offered his company his collection of authentic jewelry. He even introduced a flock of sheep onstage for his production of Salmi Morse's *The Passion Play*, and *The Governor's Lady* featured an exact replica of fashionable Child's restaurant. He followed the fourth-wall convention to its logical conclusion, forcing the famous tenor Enrico Caruso to sing his arias with his back to the audience in Giacomo Puccini's operatic version of *The Girl of the Golden West*.

Belasco's stage sets were complemented by his innovations in the use of movable spots, diffused lighting, and, above all, the baby spotlight (invented by Belasco's light man, Louis Hartmann), which eliminated the harshness of the ever-present footlight. His experiments with colored silks as filters and his discovery of the scrim, which was used in staging *The Darling of the Gods*, produced the spectacular effects that earned him the nickname "The Wizard."

Biography

David Belasco was born in San Francisco, California, on July 25, 1853. His father, Humphrey Abraham Belasco, was a London actor who, with his bride, Reina Martin Belasco, had succumbed to Gold Rush fever. Once in San Francisco, however, the couple settled into shopkeeping after David's birth. Five years later, news of a gold strike in British Columbia lured them north, where David's three brothers were born and where Humphrey Belasco maintained a tobacco shop while investing in real estate and digging for gold.

Belasco's published memories of British Columbia are highly imaginative accounts, containing references to a monastic education as well as to his appearance as "Davido, the Boy Wonder," with the Rio de Janeiro Circus. More sober accounts place him first at the Colonial School and then at the Anglican Collegiate School in 1862. Two years later, he made his first professional stage appearance, as the Duke of York in Charles Kean's *King Richard III*. Belasco's other theatrical efforts took place in San Francisco, to which his family returned when he was eleven. *The Roll of the Drum*, a childhood play strongly influenced by the penny dreadfuls, and a gold medal at Lincoln Grammar School for his impassioned rendition of Matthew Gregory Lewis's poem "The Maniac" were among Belasco's early achievements.

After graduation from Lincoln, Belasco entered a self-imposed, five-year apprenticeship during which he took a touring company up and down the West Coast, deriving much of the material by copying prompt books and pirating uncopyrighted Continental works. At twenty, he began a fifty-two-year marriage with Cecelia Loverich. His subsequent career in California was furthered by Tom Maguire, an unschooled Tammany barkeeper who opened a series of successful California theaters. As Maguire's prompter at the Baldwin, a magnificent hotel/theater, Belasco oversaw Salmi Morse's *The Passion Play*, which scandalized the citizens of San Francisco. During this period, he staged his Naturalistic version of Émile Zola's *L'Assommoir* and collaborated with James Herne in such works as *Chums*, which became known as *Hearts of Oak* after its New York success under that title. Before Maguire retired in 1882, Belasco had written and directed a number of works, among them *La Belle Russe* and *The Stranglers of Paris*, an adaptation of Adolphe Belot's earlier work.

Belasco's first New York assignment was as stage manager at the Madison Square Theatre, backed by Marshall and George Mallory, who sought wholesome productions by American playwrights. The interference and parsimony of the Mallory brothers caused Belasco to leave after only a few years, in 1885. After brief stints with Steele MacKaye and Lester Wallack, Belasco was hired by Daniel Frohman to direct the Lyceum Theatre. There, he collaborated with Henry C. DeMille to produce *The Wife*, *Lord Chumley*, *The Charity Ball*, and *Men and Women*. In 1889, Belasco undertook the training of a red-haired society divorcée, Leslie Carter, for the stage. Finally, at forty, he had his first unqualified success with *The Heart of Maryland*, a Civil War drama written expressly for Carter, whose role called for her to swing on a bell clapper to keep the bell from ringing and to save her escaping Northern lover. After winning a lawsuit against N. K. Fairbank, Carter's financial backer, for withdrawing funding for another play, Belasco produced *Zaza*—inspired, in part, by Carter's determination to go on the stage—and began training another star, Blanche Bates, who initially appeared in Belasco's *Naughty Anthony*. Ironically, the afterpiece with which Belasco bolstered his slender farce—an adaptation of John Luther Long's story "Madame Butterfly"—proved the more memorable production. In later years, it became one of Puccini's best-known operas.

In 1901, Belasco produced a dramatization of the life of Madame DuBarry, the mistress of King Louis XV. In staging *DuBarry*, another Carter vehicle, Belasco imported French antique draperies and furniture. The next year, he leased Oscar Hammerstein's theater, the Republic, which was remodeled and renamed the Belasco; his first new play, a collaboration with Long called *The Darling of the Gods*, featured the back-lit scrim. Although leasing the Republic gave him relative freedom from the Theatrical Syndicate that for sixteen years controlled bookings in New York and throughout the United States, Belasco entered a 1903-1904 lawsuit charging hidden partnerships and bribery against Marc Klaw and Abe Erlanger, a lawsuit often credited with breaking the syndicate's power. Immediately after the altercation, Belasco produced his very successful melodrama *The Girl of the Golden West*, which Puccini produced as *La fanciulla del West*.

In the same year, Carter deserted Belasco by remarrying. Consequently, in 1907, it was Blanche

Bates who helped inaugurate Belasco's new theater, the Stuyvesant, whose ornamental façade hid not only the finest lighting equipment then available but also Belasco's own private studio. Shortly thereafter, Belasco shocked his public by producing *The Easiest Way* (pb. 1908, pr. 1909), Eugene Walter's play about an unreformed prostitute. Belasco recouped with a production of his own *The Return of Peter Grimm*, a play known as much for its masterly lighting as for its afterlife theme—validated, according to the program notes, by psychologist William James himself.

From 1910 to 1920, Belasco produced thirty-two plays, mostly melodramas by other authors. His masterly 1920 production of *Deburau* (Harley Granville-Barker's adaptation of Sacha Guitry's play about pantomime) and his 1922 production of Shakespeare's *The Merchant of Venice*, with David Warfield, demonstrated that he was still a powerful figure in the theater. In November, 1930, Belasco fell ill with pneumonia during rehearsals of Frederic and Fanny Hatton's *Tonight or Never* and died the following year, on May 14, in New York.

ANALYSIS

While David Belasco experimented with naturalism, an overriding number of his plays are either melodramas or farces, whose strong emotion, light wit, and happy endings appealed to his audiences. Indeed, when Belasco was not writing adaptations of foreign novels and plays, he relied on a number of well-worn themes and used his Magical Realism to disguise the similarities. Many of his well-made plays feature the trials and tribulations of young lovers. His fascination with the lives of outcast women is equally evident.

On the whole, Belasco's plays are not classics and do not even lend themselves to serious criticism. In his own day, his appeal to the emotions did as much as his wizardry in the areas of lighting and directing to guarantee his plays full houses and long runs. Today's more sophisticated audiences would judge them overly sentimental, melodramatic, and simplistic. Yet Belasco did have an enduring impact on the theater, setting an example with his imaginative approach to extending what had become the usual boundaries of staging and his meticulous attention to the details of production.

HISTORICAL PLAYS

A number of Belasco's melodramas have historical or ethnic backgrounds. *DuBarry*, set in the time of Louis XV, and *The Darling of the Gods*, set in Japan during the samurai period, exhibit the same melodramatic characteristics as *The Girl of the Golden West*—slender character motivation, a romantic plot, strong appeal to the emotions, and a denouement characterized by poetic justice. Of the three heroines, DuBarry is the only one who fails to win a happy ending. The French milliner turned king's mistress, executed by the revolutionaries as an aristocrat, does nevertheless achieve a final reunion with Cossé, her former sweetheart. Yo-San, who dies for betraying the hideout of her samurai lover's band, meets Kara in the afterlife. Of the three, the Girl—Minnie—achieves the most enduring happiness, for although she leaves her beloved Sierra Nevada mountains, she does so in the company of Johnson, a reformed thief who has become her sweetheart. *The Heart of Maryland*, perhaps the most sensational of Belasco's historical plays, features a pair of Civil War lovers divided by opposing North/South sympathies and reunited after an act of heroism on the part of Maryland Calvert herself.

NAUGHTY ANTHONY

Belasco's farces were much less sumptuous in staging and considerably lighter in plot; like *Lord Chumley*, *Naughty Anthony* relies on complicated, improbable situations for its humor. Professor Anthony Depew, a teacher of moral behavior, when caught kissing one of his patients in a darkened park gazebo, gives his landlord's name instead of his own. An incompetent lawyer, another love triangle, and a vengeful wife are coupled with what was then a mildly shocking episode in which Cora, a hosiery saleswoman, strips off her stockings onstage. Handled differently, *Naughty Anthony* might have succeeded as a satire of moral hypocrisy; as it stands, however, the tangled skeins of the well-made play are too much in evidence.

LA BELLE RUSSE

Belasco attempted to deal with the outcast woman in historical plays such as *DuBarry* and in sheer melodrama such as *La Belle Russe*, in which a notorious prostitute tries to profit from the good fortune of her innocent twin. La Belle Russe herself is saved by the love for her illegitimate child; similarly, in *Zaza*, the heroine redeems herself by becoming a great actress. Other characters, not nearly as well received, face a more realistic end.

THE HEART OF MARYLAND

A lavish and sensational Civil War melodrama, *The Heart of Maryland* made Belasco independent. The play, backed by Max Blieman, a dealer in art, opened on October 9, 1895, in Washington, D.C., and moved to the Herald Square Theatre in New York two weeks later for a run of 229 performances.

The property and light cues for the play show that Belasco paid extraordinary attention to detail, even visiting Maryland so that he could duplicate the atmosphere. The first scene opens on The Lilacs, a nostalgically reproduced mansion replete with fragrant lilac bushes and water lilies. In the near distance is a stream crossed by a rustic bridge; in the far appear the hills of Maryland. The plot interprets the conflict between North and South romantically: Maryland Calvert's Northern lover is Colonel Alan Kendrick, whose father commands the Southern forces; Nanny, a sharp-witted Yankee of sixteen, is wooed by Robert Telfair, a lieutenant in the Southern artillery unit encamped at The Lilacs. Further complications arise when Colonel Thorpe, a Southern officer in the employ of the Northern Secret Service, uses the information given to him by Lloyd Calvert—Maryland's brother, a Northern sympathizer—to further his own career rather than to warn General Hooker of General Kendrick's advance. When Alan is brought as a prisoner to The Lilacs, Maryland, despite her strong Dixie bias, passes the information to him.

In act 2, Lloyd is killed while he is carrying information, but not before he asks his sister to detain an anonymous "friend" of his—Alan. Captured while awaiting Maryland, Alan confronts his father, who keeps his military bearing with difficulty. Maryland becomes hysterical on learning of her brother's death and impulsively accuses his "friend" of spying. As the scene closes, she understands that she has accused her lover in order to save her brother's name.

At the beginning of act 3, Alan is incarcerated in an old church that serves as a prison. Maryland, crossing the lines, brings a stay of execution, but Thorpe realizes that had the letter reached the now-dead Colonel Kendrick, he himself would have been indicted for spying. He brings Alan from the prison to torment him with the sight of Maryland. Alan, bound and helpless, watches as Maryland—like the operatic heroine Tosca—stabs her attacker and urges Alan to run. The climax of the scene occurs when she races up the stairs and leaps to grasp the clapper on the bell that is rung to alert the Southern artillery. As the act closes, Maryland swings back and forth on the bell, a tour de force supposedly reminiscent of Belasco's childhood fascination with Rosa Hartwicke Thorpe's poem "The Curfew Must Not Ring Tonight."

The resolution in the fourth act finds Nanny nursing the wounded Telfair while the Northern troops, led by Alan, cannonade The Lilacs, where Thorpe has imprisoned Maryland. Thorpe negotiates a retreat to Richmond but insists that Maryland accompany him to stand trial. Alan accepts but then, given safe conduct, delivers a letter from General Lee court-martialing Thorpe for double treachery and appointing Telfair commander. The curtain closes as Maryland and Alan are reunited.

Although Belasco, in a first-night curtain speech, had said, "Now I am encouraged to hope I have proved myself a dramatist," critical praise was not forthcoming; nevertheless, the play ran for nearly nine months and had a successful season in London. Although some British critics praised Leslie Carter's histrionics as Maryland and likened Belasco to the wildly popular French playwright Victorien Sardou, George Bernard Shaw (who also disliked Sardou) made sharp-tongued fun of American melodrama while conceding that the actors themselves were better trained than their British cousins and that Carter's intensity showed her to be an actress "of no mean powers."

THE RETURN OF PETER GRIMM

One of the works that held the most personal meaning for Belasco, *The Return of Peter Grimm* is permeated not only by a sense of loss for departed family members but also by a belief in an afterlife.

During the play's first performance at the Boston Hollis Street Theatre on January 2, 1911, Belasco's younger daughter Augusta, terminally ill with tuberculosis, impressed her father with her belief that dying is another form of living—or, in Peter Grimm's words, "knowing better." Other personal facts contributed to the production of the play about the old horticulturist who returns from the dead to right his mistakes, most notably Belasco's insistence in 1898 that his mother had appeared to him in a waking dream. The next morning, news was brought during the rehearsals for *Zaza* that she had died in San Francisco during the night.

Despite rumors to the contrary, Belasco reiterated publicly that Cecil B. DeMille was responsible only for the idea of the play and not for the actual script—a script that, Belasco noted, presented the serious problem of how to make Grimm's return believable. Three factors contributed to his success in solving this problem: naturalistic stage setting, acting, and lighting. First, the props were carefully selected to suggest not only a real room but also a wealth of memories that might be evoked by a cozy, homey house; likewise, the view shown from the onstage window conveys the close tie between Grimm's sense of well-being and his thriving business. Second, Belasco instructed his other actors to look *through* the Grimm "apparition" so as to highlight the reaction of the eight-year-old child medium. Third, the complex lighting system made use of the baby lens developed by Louis Hartmann. This lens concentrated spots of flesh-toned light on all the characters but Grimm, who was bathed in a colder, bluer light; consequently, he seemed in contrast always to be shadowed. In addition, Belasco abolished the footlights and substituted bridge lights on beams above the set. The lighting schematic took almost a year to develop but was called "perhaps the most perfect example of stage lighting ever exhibited."

The melodramatic plot includes a love triangle, a villainous family member, and a child who dies young. In the long first act, the love that James Hartman, Grimm's secretary, has not only for Catherine Staats—Grimm's adopted daughter—but also for the plants themselves is juxtaposed to the money-hungry courtship of Grimm's nephew Frederick, whose dearest wish is to sell the house and nursery. Warned by his doctor that the condition of his heart may cause his death at any moment, Grimm forces an engagement between Catherine and Frederick so that he may be, he thinks, assured of the continuance of his business and of Catherine's happiness. William, the eight-year-old illegitimate son of a runaway servant, is also put under the protection of Frederick, who clearly dislikes him. At the end of the act, Peter dies.

An approaching storm, James's and Catherine's manifest unhappiness, an altercation among Grimm's old friends over their legacies—all produce a mood of suspense that builds toward the arrival of the ghost in act 2. When the ghostly Grimm does appear, however, it is very quietly; moreover, since he can make himself felt only indirectly, his efforts to save the business, to make Catherine break her engagement, and to reveal Frederick as William's father are all subtle (or else, indeed, the play would end abruptly). It is only to William, who is ill, that Grimm can speak directly. Through Grimm's influence, William points out the incriminating letter from his mother, Annemarie. Frederick's perfidy revealed and the marriage broken off, the third act centers on William's death, a scene that escapes the bathetic partly through the circus motif that carries over from the first act and partly through Peter's insistence that he is taking William away "to know better." As the curtain falls, the two dance away to the clown's tune, "Uncle Rat Has Gone to Town." The play, which moved to the New York Stuyvesant Theatre on October 18, 1911, ran for 231 performances. Critical reception was warm, citing Belasco's triumph in making the impossible appear actual by his magic of lighting and directing.

THE GIRL OF THE GOLDEN WEST

A compound of memories of California (as well as of Bret Harte, as some contemporary critics charged), *The Girl of the Golden West* opened on October 3, 1905, at the Belasco Theatre in Pittsburgh and moved to New York on November 14. Puccini adapted the play, which Belasco believed his best, under the title *La fanciulla del West* (Puccini had brought about a similar musical transformation with Belasco's *Madame Butterfly* in 1904). As Belasco

notes, teaching acting techniques to opera singers—Enrico Caruso among them—familiar only with vocal flourishes was a difficult task, considering that both he and Arturo Toscanini, the conductor, were autocratic in their methods. The December 10, 1910, premiere at the Metropolitan Opera House was, nevertheless, a success.

The melodramatic plot, which Belasco insisted was based on his father's stories, features the trusting, unlettered Minnie, owner of The Polka, a Western saloon. Most of her customers, including the gambler/sheriff Jack Rance, are in love with her. While the bartender, Nick, slyly keeps up business by encouraging her suitors, Minnie, who has fallen in love with a nameless stranger she has met on the road, cheerfully and faithfully serves as a "bank" for the prospectors' nuggets. In act 1, the stranger, Dick Johnson—in reality, Ramerrez, a bandit who has plotted to rob The Polka—appears. While Johnson is at The Polka, the Pony Express brings news that Ramerrez is in the area, and the Girl, who innocently admires Johnson, stoutly declares that she will protect the prospectors' hard-earned gold.

In act 2, Minnie welcomes Johnson to her cabin for dinner, where he becomes convinced that she is the one woman for whom he would reform. Trapped by a snowstorm, he hides when Rance and his men appear at the cabin to ascertain Minnie's safety. While there, they arouse Minnie's jealousy by mentioning Ramerrez's supposed lover, Nina Micheltorena. Minnie angrily sends Johnson out into the storm, but he is wounded by Rance and returns to take refuge in her loft. Rance is almost convinced that Ramerrez has escaped until a drop of blood from the loft falls on his handkerchief. As the act ends, Rance and the Girl play poker to win Ramerrez; during a diversion, Minnie uses the three aces she had hidden in her stocking to make a better hand, wins the right to let Ramerrez escape, and frees herself from Rance's power.

In act 3, Minnie opens the "Academy," a grammar school for prospectors, but is distracted by happiness at the thought of meeting Johnson and sadness at leaving The Polka. A crisis occurs when the Wells Fargo agent recaptures Johnson, much to the glee of Rance, who has kept his promise not to interfere but who can now take revenge. Rance proposes lynching Johnson, and the boys in The Polka are willing to follow his lead until they witness the reunion between Johnson and the Girl. Hearing her prayer, they become convinced that Providence protects Johnson. As the play concludes, Johnson and the Girl are leaving California for a new start in the "promised land" in the East.

Belasco introduced a number of special effects that enhanced the play's atmosphere. Before the first act, audiences saw a detailed panorama of the Sierra Nevada, complete with the Girl's cabin on Cloudy Mountain. The panorama, a transparency painted in evocative colors and lit from behind, slowly unrolled to the bottom of the mountain, where The Polka appeared blazing with light. The sound effects were introduced at this point; Belasco discarded the usual orchestral accompaniment, using instead a small band of concertina and banjo, playing such favorites as "Camptown Races" and "Pop Goes the Weasel," partly, Belasco claimed, in memory of Jake Wallace, the famous banjo player of the mining camp. After the houselights were dimmed and the panorama removed, the act opened on the interior of The Polka, where all props were handled with meticulous detail, from the real pineboards in the walls to the riding paraphernalia piled carelessly on the floor. In addition, even the minor characters were costumed in distinctly individualistic ways to suggest a realistic and motley selection of prospectors. Perhaps the greatest tour de force of the play was the snowstorm that trapped Johnson in Minnie's cabin. Making use of the pathetic fallacy—the idea that natural events parallel emotional and moral situations—Belasco built the suspense of the scene. Blowers, fans, rock salt, snow bags, and air tanks to reproduce the sound of the storm were operated by a cadre of thirty-two stagehands, who formed, as William Winter notes, "a sort of mechanical orchestra."

OTHER MAJOR WORKS

LONG FICTION: *The Girl of the Golden West*, 1911; *The Return of Peter Grimm*, 1912.

NONFICTION: *My Life's Story*, 1916 (2 volumes); *The Theatre Through Its Stage Door*, 1919.

BIBLIOGRAPHY

Boardman, Gerald. *American Theatre: A Chronicle of Comedy and Drama, 1914-1930*. New York: Oxford University Press, 1996. This study of Broadway dramas covers a number of Belasco's works.

DiGaetani, John Louis. *Puccini the Thinker: The Composer's Intellectual and Dramatic Development*. 2d ed. New York: Peter Lang, 2001. This biography of Puccini examines his operas, some of which were based on Belasco's plays. Contains bibliography, discography, videography, and index.

Green, Adam. "The Phantom of the Belasco: A Tale." *New York Times Current Events Edition*, July 16, 1995, p. 25. An account of a Broadway production's attempt to find Belasco's ghost in the boarded-up rooms of his apartment above the Belasco Theater.

Marker, Lise-Lone. *David Belasco: Naturalism in the American Theatre*. Princeton, N.J.: Princeton University Press, 1975. This volume is considered the standard and most scholarly biography of Broadway's most innovative producer, including Belasco's very successful collaboration with James A. Herne.

Meserve, Walter J. "David Belasco." In *Twentieth Century American Dramatists*, edited by John MacNicholas. Vol. 7 in *Dictionary of Literary Biography*. Detroit, Mich.: The Gale Group, 1981. A concise overview of the life and works of Belasco.

Meserve, Walter J., and Mollie A. Meserve, eds. *Fateful Lightning: America's Civil War Plays*. New York: Feedback Theatrebooks and Prospero Press, 2000. This anthology of Civil War plays provides a history of the American theater in the second half of the nineteenth century, providing information on Belasco as well as his play *The Heart of Maryland*.

Winter, William. *The Life of David Belasco*. 1925. Reprint. Freeport, N.Y.: Books for Libraries Press, 1970. This reprint of the 1925 edition was completed by the author's son, William Jefferson Winter, after the author's death. It discusses the history of theater in the United States as well as the playwright's long career.

Patricia Marks,
updated by Peter C. Holloran

JACINTO BENAVENTE Y MARTÍNEZ

Born: Madrid, Spain; August 12, 1866
Died: Madrid, Spain; July 14, 1954

PRINCIPAL DRAMA

El nido ajeno, pr., pb. 1894 (*Another's Nest*, 1932)
Gente conocida, pr. 1896, pb. 1906
La gobernadora, pr., pb. 1901 (*The Governor's Wife*, 1918)
La noche del sábado, pr., pb. 1903 (*Saturday Night*, 1918)
No fumadores, pr., pb. 1904 (*No Smoking*, 1917)
Teatro, pb. 1904-1931 (38 volumes)
Los malhechores del bien, pr. 1905, pb. 1912 (*The Evil of Good*, 1916)
Rosas de otoño, pr., pb. 1905 (*Autumnal Roses*, 1919)
La princesa Bebé, pr. 1906, pb. 1914 (*Princess Bebé*, 1918)
Los intereses creados, pr., pb. 1907 (*The Bonds of Interest*, 1915)
El marido de su viuda, pr., pb. 1908 (*His Widow's Husband*, 1917)
Señora ama, pr. 1908, pb. 1911 (*A Lady*, 1924)
La escuela de las princesas, pr., pb. 1909 (*The School for Princesses*, 1924)
El príncipe que todo lo aprendió en los libros, pr. 1909, pb. 1910 (*The Prince Who Learned Everything Out of Books*, 1918)
La malquerida, pr. 1913, pb. 1914 (*The Passion Flower*, 1917)
La ciudad alegre y confiada, pr., pb. 1916
Plays by Jacinto Benavente, pb. 1917-1924 (4 volumes)
Pepa Doncel, pr., pb. 1928
La melodía del jazz band, pr., pb. 1931
La moral del divorcio, pr., pb. 1932
El pan comido en la mano, pr., pb. 1934
La infanzona, pr. 1945, pb. 1958
Mater imperatrix, pr. 1950, pb. 1951

OTHER LITERARY FORMS

Although Jacinto Benavente y Martínez is recognized almost exclusively as a playwright, he also wrote poems (*Versos*, 1893), short stories (*Vilanos*, 1905), articles on the theater (*Teatro del pueblo*, 1909), newspaper articles (*De sobremesa*, 1910-1916), lectures (*Conferencias*, 1924), and memoirs (*Recuerdos y olvidos: Memorias*, 1962). He also translated William Shakespeare's *King Lear* (pr. c. 1605-1606), though the translation was never performed, and, in 1897, Molière's *Dom Juan: Ou, Le Festin de Pierre* (pr. 1665; *Don Juan*, 1755). All his works are included in the eleven-volume *Obras completas* (1952-1964).

ACHIEVEMENTS

Few modern Spanish playwrights have been as prolific as Jacinto Benavente y Martínez. The vast majority of his plays have been produced in Spain, and many have been presented abroad. Few dramatists anywhere have appeared in their own plays, as he often did, and undoubtedly his recognition in the form of tributes is difficult to surpass. The first official tribute to Benavente came when he was elected to fill the vacancy left in the Spanish Royal Academy by the death of Marcelino Menéndez y Pelayo, a seat that Benavente never occupied because he neglected to write, and hence deliver, the necessary acceptance speech. In 1946, however, the academy made him an honorary member. He was awarded the Nobel Prize in Literature in 1922, elected Favorite Son of Madrid in 1924, made president of the Montepío pension fund for widows and orphans in 1929, and awarded the Mariano de Cavia Prize for the best newspaper article published in Spain during 1947. Hence, he was recognized in universal, national, municipal, and private sectors. His greatest artistic achievement was the successful transformation of the Spanish theater from the antiquated, neo-romantic, rhetorical melodrama that had carried José Echegaray y Eizaguirre to fame, fortune, and even the Nobel Prize in Literature in 1904, to contemporary social drama in which Benavente exposed and censured the middle class. His satire, wit, and imagination brought to the twentieth century a new type of drama that opened the way for other innovations. His compassion for the victims of society made him a champion of the oppressed and an early feminist. His reproach of the middle class is so gentle, however, that this class continues to flock to the theater to see itself portrayed.

BIOGRAPHY

Jacinto Benavente y Martínez was the youngest of three sons born to Venancia Martínez, a native of Villarejo de Salvanés, and Dr. Mariano Benavente, a native of Murcia who had struggled to achieve success as a pediatrician. Among his patients were the children of prominent literary and political figures and some of their parents as well; he was director of the Hospital of the Child Jesus, a member of the Royal Academy of Medicine, and a recognized author of professional articles in whose honor a statue was erected in the Retiro Park. Hence, his family was

Jacinto Benavente y Martínez (© The Nobel Foundation)

assured a secure place in the upper-middle class of the time. He supervised the education of his children, who had in their home library a wide range of books. He was clearly the stronger figure of the two parents. Biographers of his son agree that the mother remained in the background, attending to the children's religious and social education, and that she often took her youngest son with her on afternoon visits to her friends. It was during these visits, no doubt, that Benavente was first exposed to the dialogue of middle-class ladies and the bourgeois problems that he was to portray in his plays.

As a child Benavente was quiet and studious. He was an avid reader, fascinated by the theater, who took pleasure in creating skits in which he would appear with his friends. He often dressed as a clergyman, delivering his sermons to playmates and his mother's guests. He attended the nearby Colegio San José and the Instituto San Isidro without distinction. He read William Shakespeare, Alfred de Musset, and Molière in addition to the Spanish classics. He allegedly learned English, French, and Italian during his adolescent years, and eventually he was able to translate works from those languages into Spanish. After his father's death in 1885, he gave up his law studies at the University of Madrid, traveled extensively in Europe, and for a brief period acted in the company of the prominent actress María Tubau.

Benavente was accustomed to intellectuals by virtue of his background, and he became active in the *tertulias* (gatherings) of the literati in the cafés of Madrid. In these cafés, he became friendly with the young writers who would later be dubbed by Azorín (José Martínez Ruiz) the Generation of '98. One prominent habitué of the *tertulia* that Benavente attended most frequently, held in the Café Madrid, was Ramon María del Valle-Inclán; when Benavente's conservatism clashed with Valle-Inclán's radicalism, they went their separate ways to establish *tertulias* with their own followers.

Although Benavente is traditionally considered part of the Generation of 1898, this association should be made only because of his interest in social and artistic reform. He lacked the philosophical convictions and creative genius that characterized the Generation of 1898. He initiated his literary career by publishing a volume of plays in 1892, *Teatro fantástico*, and, in 1893, one of poems, *Versos*, and another of essays, *Cartas de mujeres*. His first performed play, *Another's Nest*, was produced with little notice, but *Gente conocida*, produced shortly afterward, was widely acclaimed. At around this time he succeeded Clarín (Leopoldo Alas) as editor of *La vida literaria*, and he sporadically contributed to *Madrid cómico* and other magazines.

Benavente soon became a controversial dramatist. At one point he was so offended by adverse criticism that he swore to write no more plays. He left Spain on a tour of the United States as director of the company of the actress Lola Membrives, the most widely acclaimed interpreter of his plays. During that tour he occasionally acted and often lectured to audiences. He spent the Spanish Civil War years (1936-1939) in Valencia, where the Republican government had established its headquarters; during that period he wrote no plays. In 1949, he resumed residence in Madrid, where he continued to write and lead an active public life until his death. Although he brought to the stage the frailties of his own upper-middle class, he did not penetrate the superficiality of those problems; undoubtedly he was unable to betray his people.

ANALYSIS

Jacinto Benavente y Martínez's theater combines new forms and themes with a chronicler's account of the society in which he lived. His followers and imitators include Manuel Linares Rivas, Gregorio Martínez Sierra and María Martínez Sierra, and the Álvarez Quintero brothers, Serafín and Joaquín.

Scholars and critics have divided Benavente's work into four major categories: psychological dramas, social satires, rural plays, and fantastic plays. In his comprehensive study of Benavente, critic Marcelino C. Peñuelas distributes the plays as follows: twenty-seven satiric plays, twenty-three psychological plays, three rural plays, and seven fantasy plays. In addition to these major groupings there are, in Peñuelas's reckoning, eleven comic plays, six sentimental plays, thirty-five miscellaneous works, forty-

nine short plays, and eleven translations and adaptations, all written during Benavente's active years as a playwright. Critic Eleanor Maxwell Dial limits Benavente's plays to three categories: psychological plays (including rural dramas and character studies), social satires, and plays based on imaginary tales. Other critics tend to group Benavente's plays by chronological periods; in this case, the year normally cited as the turning point in Benavente's creativity is 1930.

By 1931 Benavente had already written his most important dramas; his work was becoming increasingly repetitious and uninteresting, lacking originality in either subject matter or form, yet still pleasing his followers in Spain and abroad. Although his new plays were staged almost exclusively in Spain, outside his native country producers relied increasingly on two early plays that have not lost their dramatic interest to this day: *The Bonds of Interest* and *The Passion Flower*. The advent of the cinema, however, gave his plays added life and allowed his works to reach wider audiences than he ever dreamed.

ANOTHER'S NEST

Benavente's first produced work, *Another's Nest*, is a psychological drama that explores the effects of a married couple sharing their home with the husband's unmarried brother, "the intruder"; this play involves multiple rivalries, jealousies, resentments, and gossip, as well as the sexual attraction on the part of Manuel for Maria, his sister-in-law. At the end of the play, the intruder announces that he will go away for the sake of restoring peace and harmony in his brother's home because "three is a crowd." He will perhaps return after the fire of youth is spent, when he no longer lusts for Maria, at which time he may share his brother's life without temptation, perhaps no longer as an intruder.

GENTE CONOCIDA

Benavente's next play, *Gente conocida* (well-known people), a social satire, was widely acclaimed by critics and the theatergoing bourgeoisie whose drawing rooms Benavente mirrored in the play. From that time until his death, Benavente's plays were sound commercial successes, although critics differed in their opinions.

The Norwegian dramatist Henrik Ibsen influenced almost everyone at this time, including Echegaray and Benavente. Indeed, both Spaniards had to defend their works from accusations of imitation and even plagiarism; both claimed that their works were authentically Spanish, although neither of them denied familiarity with the theater of Ibsen. The controversial themes of Ibsen were applied to traditional themes from the Spanish repertory. Hence, Echegaray adapted the theme of Ibsen's *Gengangere* (pb. 1881; *Ghosts*, 1884) to *El hijo de Don Juan* (pr., pb. 1892; *The Son of Don Juan*, 1895), and Benavente admitted that in writing *Gente conocida* he had merged a typical Spanish situation with some ideas that he had discovered in Ibsen. The social satires of Benavente were revolutionary because their casts were held to minimal numbers and there were recognizable personalities from Madrid's elite among the characters that he portrayed. The fact that he was known by so many of his devotees, however, limited the severity of his rebukes. His characters were drawn from real life and he did criticize their shortcomings, but he was intimidated, and the plays were little more than mild rebuffs that ended satisfactorily for all the characters. It cannot be said that Benavente was disillusioned with Spanish society; he was at most annoyed.

The setting in most of these social satires is limited to a salon or reception room, in which the characters' dialogue replaces action. The characters reveal their problems to one another, or a maid narrates to a visitor what has taken place, thus exposing the theme of the play, or the characters speak about their friends, weaving into their tales the conflicts that will lace the evening's performance. Although Benavente thus eliminates histrionic superfluity and rhetoric, he does not altogether break away from traditional Spanish themes. As in the works of Lope de Vega Carpio and Pedro Calderón de la Barca, honor is often an underlying theme in his plays. Benavente, however, does not penetrate the obviousness of the conflict. He does not analyze the reasons for a man's adulterous behavior, for example, nor does he attempt to define life itself, either in its existential sense or in its sociological sense. José Monleón superbly criticizes the morality of Benavente's characters in his observation that the mundane frivolities and preoccupations of the aristocracy are as detestable to the playwright as are the insecurities and seediness of the middle class; nevertheless, Benavente never truly juxtaposes those hollow values with other, superior values: The characters can be better than they are or they can be worse than they are, but they cannot adopt a totally new set of values.

THE BONDS OF INTEREST

Benavente's masterpiece is generally considered to be *The Bonds of Interest*, a social satire that combines fantasy, psychology, brilliant dialogue, and even aesthetics within the framework of the old Italian *commedia dell'arte*. In this play, set in an imaginary city of dual character (one for the rich, one for the poor), Benavente touches problems similar to those that plague the middle class of his other satires: honor, financial ruin, hypocrisy, ostentatiousness, even a criminal past. The characters range from the destitute Crispín, a type of picaro, and his master, Leandro, who arrive in that imaginary land with only the clothes on their backs and hope in their hearts, to a wide array of character types drawn from the *commedia dell'arte*: Harlequin, a wreck of an old soldier, Polichinela, a starving poet, a scribe, a go-between obviously reminiscent of the Spanish bawd Celestina, all motivated by materialism, all willing to compromise in order to realize their ambitions. The love story that Crispín spins around Silvia and Leandro is the only element untainted by selfishness, but the girl's parents allow the marriage only because of the interests at stake. The play moves swiftly from beginning to end with the aid of witty dialogue, exaggerated action onstage, spectacle, and intrigue. No element of society escapes criticism, and love triumphs in the end. A sequel or continuation of *The Bonds of Interest*, *La ciudad alegre y confiada* (the happy, confident city), is pitifully inferior and is now virtually forgotten.

THE PASSION FLOWER

The psychological play that has been traditionally associated with Benavente's theater is *The Passion Flower*, which also falls under the category of his rural plays. Together with *The Bonds of Interest*, it overshadows almost every other play that brought success and acclaim to Benavente. It is the only one that he wrote between 1911 and 1915 and, although it suffers from certain weaknesses, it may indeed vie for first place in public esteem. In 1923, for example, it enjoyed 750 performances in the United States and it was made into a film starring Norma Talmadge. The theme of *The Passion Flower* is an inverted Phaedra story. The mythological Phaedra falls in love with her stepson, but when refused by him, accuses him to her husband of dishonoring her; thus she has him put to death but later kills herself in her remorse. In Benavente's version, Raimunda's second husband, Esteban, is in love with her daughter, Acacia. He has caused her first betrothal to Norberto to be broken, and now, on the eve of her marriage to Faustino, he has the groom killed by his peon, Rubio. Confronted with the facts, after long interrogations that constitute enough subject matter for another play, Raimunda attempts to smooth things over. She wants to send Acacia to the home of relatives until everything is forgotten, and she tries to effect a reconciliation between Acacia and Esteban but instead of embracing Esteban as a daughter might and calling him father, as Raimunda commands, the girl embraces her stepfather passionately, and he returns her passion as they kiss, confirming the semi-incestuous attraction that had, until that moment, manifested itself in Acacia as hostility and in Esteban as devoted rejection of his paternal role. Raimunda's effort to stop her husband and Acacia from running away together ends with Esteban's shooting his wife, whose dramatic death will forever stand in the way of the lovers and, at the same time, save her daughter's honor.

The rural setting has been identified as Aldea-encabo, in Castile, where Benavente maintained a country home, and the plot is apparently patterned on a true story. One of the remarkable features of the play is the dialect; Benavente's interpretation of Castilian country dialogue dazzled the audiences of the time. The intensity of a family situation in which honor is at stake, as well as the semi-incestuous relationship between Acacia and Esteban, gives the play a compelling psychological tension. Benavente may have been acquainted with the recent psychoanalytic

theories of Sigmund Freud when he conceived *The Passion Flower*; regardless of whether he fully understood these theories, the principal characters all conform to Freudian patterns, as demonstrated by critic Harold K. Moon. Moon discusses the three main characters, treating them not as Benaventian characters but as Freudian subjects.

The play suffers from two problems: It introduces what is, to all practical purposes, a detective story, and it flirts with the traditional theme of honor without fully developing it. When the curtain falls on the first act, the question that has been raised is not "Whom does Acacia love?" but "Who killed Faustino?" The honor theme, which could inspire a different type of play, is dropped almost as soon as it is mentioned. The work, nevertheless, projects great theatrical effects in spite of the almost chaotic last scene. It restores to twentieth century drama the rural settings that Lope de Vega and Calderón had established in the Golden Age national drama, and it strongly suggests the consequences of repressed passion.

COMMONALITIES IN THE PLAYS

The plays discussed up to this point hardly reveal the range of Benavente's repertory, but they represent the best of his work; indeed, they may be the most enduring of his dramas, along with *Saturday Night* and *A Lady*. The common denominators in Benavente's work are good taste and elegant restraint. His dialogues are carefully written so that although his characters speak the truth, they are never vulgar or commonplace; there is seldom violence or unpleasant action onstage. When there is action in addition to dialogue, it is swift, as in *The Bonds of Interest*, and highly effective. There are no wasted words or deeds on Benavente's stage.

These plays share, by and large, another common denominator: The strong characters are almost always women. It is a woman who is normally sacrificed, deceived, scorned, abused, slandered, and generally mistreated. It is also a woman who sacrifices, is truthful, respectful, submissive, virtuous, and forgiving. Women's rights are normally violated by selfish husbands, brothers, suitors, or even lovers, and they respond with kindness, strength, compassion, understanding, and generosity. They go into the world to earn the family bread when it is impossible for the husband to do so, and their blood is shed as the sacrificial lamb's, to save others (as in *The Passion Flower*).

Benavente's theater portrays familiar characters drawn from his own experience: the drawing rooms or living rooms in which he was reared, the country estate where he vacationed. Even in a play such as *The Bonds of Interest* (conceived as Italian street theater of the Renaissance and set in an imaginary city that defies identification other than that it is Italian), the moral, philosophical thesis of the play differs little from the convictions that he expresses in drawing-room satires, his rural dramas, or his psychological plays.

LATER PLAYS

Benavente wrote until his death, and his last plays were produced posthumously. Nevertheless, by the end of the 1920's he had spent his talent, and although he wrote copiously, the plays of his later period reflect a stagnated talent that had lost its direction. Benavente's plays, which had initially achieved celebrity and recognition via his brilliant dialogues, had become more like long episodes with monotonous overtones. Dialogues run away from his characters so that they often lose connection with either the character who delivers them or the play in which they appear, and they tend to be repetitious without subtlety, sting, or sharpness. With few exceptions, the epigrammatic observations that had caused some critics to compare him with Oscar Wilde or George Bernard Shaw gave way to sentimentality and sermonizing. One such exception, *La melodía del jazz band*, concerning the kindness of a "bad" woman, depends for its action neither on inner passion nor on moral conflict, but on the strains of a jazz song that is played throughout.

It would be unjust, though, to dismiss Benavente's late works merely as the reflection of exhausted genius reduced to mechanical repetition. They may not be up to the standards that he established earlier in the century, but they are, nevertheless, an accurate chronicle of Republican, post-Civil War, and even contemporary Spain, particularly faithful in their portrayal of modern Spanish women, faced with new privileges (divorce, suffrage) and confronted with problems of making a livelihood.

During the monarchy and before the War, Spanish women had lived under the protection of their men. With the exception of a tiny intellectual minority, they normally did not go out into society to earn a living. In some of the plays from the 1930's, Benavente, obviously unsettled by the new wave of women, portrays some who are somewhat bewildered by their new roles. Adelina in *El pan comido en la mano* (bread eaten from the hand), for example, is so carried away by her talents as a novelist that she almost loses her marriage. The new institution of divorce ushered in briefly by the Republic comes to the stage in 1932 in *La moral del divorcio* (the morality of divorce), a rather clever exposition of Benavente's pro-divorce ideas. His awareness of new lifestyles in the years that followed his early triumphs kept him active, except for the sojourn in Valencia, and occasionally he even attempted, not entirely without success, to rekindle the spark of his genius. *La infanzona* represents a late effort to create a rural drama (similar in setting to *The Passion Flower*); once more, the theme of incest is presented carefully, and the tragic outcome of the play, like that of *The Passion Flower* is not lacking in dynamism, horror, or amazement.

Mater imperatrix is the only other play from this late period that can be considered a worthy effort. It concerns a mother's sacrifice in order to save her son from unhappiness. It portrays an American woman of questionable morals and selfish motivation, and in the course of the dialogue Benavente, through his characters, attacks a type of American womanhood. Because Benavente had spent merely a brief time in the United States, it is only logical to assume that his impressions came from his observation of American women in limited circles as well as of tourists abroad, where, far from pressures and obligations, travelers often lose perspective on propriety.

OTHER MAJOR WORKS

SHORT FICTION: *Vilanos*, 1905.
POETRY: *Versos*, 1893.

NONFICTION: *Cartas de mujeres*, 1893; *Teatro del pueblo*, 1909; *De sobremesa*, 1910-1916; *Conferencias*, 1924; *Recuerdos y olvidos: Memorias*, 1962.

TRANSLATIONS: *Don Juan*, 1897 (of Molière's *Dom Juan: Ou, Le Festin de Pierre*); *El rey Lear*, 1911 (of William Shakespeare's *King Lear*).

MISCELLANEOUS: *Obras completas*, 1952-1964 (11 volumes).

BIBLIOGRAPHY

Diaz, José A. *Jacinto Benavente and His Theatre*. Long Island City, N.Y.: Las Americas, 1972. A biography of Benavente that examines his dramatic works. Index and bibliography.

Peñuelas, Marcelino C. *Jacinto Benavente*. New York: Twayne, 1968. A basic overview of the life and works of Benavente. Bibliography.

Sheehan, Robert Louis. *Benavente and the Spanish Panorama, 1894-1954*. Chapel Hill, N.C.: Editorial Castalia, 1976. A study of Benavente's works in the context of Spanish literature of the times. Bibliography and index.

Soufas, C. Christopher, Jr. "Benavente and the Spanish Discourse on Theater." *Hispanic Review* 68, no. 2 (Spring, 2000): 13. A critical look at Benavente's work, in particular *The Bonds of Interest*.

Joseph R. Arboleda

HJALMAR BERGMAN

Born: Örebro, Sweden; September 19, 1883
Died: Berlin, Germany; January 1, 1931

PRINCIPAL DRAMA

Dödens arlekin, pr., pb. 1917
En skugga, pr., pb. 1917
Herr Sleeman kommer, pb. 1917, pr. 1919 (*Mr. Sleeman Is Coming*, 1944)
Marionettspel, pb. 1917 (includes *Dödens arlekin*, *En skugga*, and *Mr. Sleeman Is Coming*)
Spelhuset, wr. 1917, pb. 1923, pr. 1930
Ett experiment, pr., pb. 1919
Lodolezzi sjunger, pr. 1919, pb. 1954
Sagan, wr. 1919-1920, pr., pb. 1942
Porten, pb. 1923, pr. 1927
Vävaren i Bagdad, pb. 1923, pr. 1943
Swedenhielms, pr., pb. 1925 (*The Swedenhielms*, 1951)
Dollar, pr., pb. 1926
Patrasket, pr., pb. 1928
Markurells i Wadköping, pr. 1930, pb. 1957 (*Markurells of Wadköping*, 1968; adaptation of Bergman's novel of the same title)

Hans nåds testamente, pr. 1931, pb. 1968 (*The Baron's Will*, 1968; adaptation of Bergman's novel of the same title)
Four Plays, pb. 1968

OTHER LITERARY FORMS

Hjalmar Bergman wrote several important novels, many short stories, and film scripts vital to the emergence of the film industry.

ACHIEVEMENTS

It is safe to say that a Norwegian, Henrik Ibsen, and a Swede, August Strindberg, laid the groundwork for modernism in drama. They have become internationally known. The major Scandinavian playwrights in the generation to follow, Gunnar Heiberg in Norway and Hjalmar Bergman and Pär Lagerkvist in Sweden, never developed an international reputation for their drama, though Lagerkvist, who won the Nobel Prize in Literature in 1951, achieved wide recognition as a novelist. In an epoch-making manifesto, "Modern teater: Synpunkter och angrepp" (1918; "Modern Theatre: Points of View and Attack," 1966),

Lagerkvist declared that the playwright was at the crossroads: He had to choose between Ibsen's psychological realism, and Strindberg's expressionism and spiritual fantastication. This was Bergman's challenge as he wandered from one extreme to the other, testing the boundaries and exploring the ground between. Inevitably, Bergman's sense of theater put him rather closer to the spirit of Strindberg. Of the three playwrights of his generation, only Bergman developed anything like an international reputation in the theater, chiefly through Georges and Ludmilla Pitoëff in Paris. In the United States, he remains largely unproduced and unknown; in Sweden he is the only important playwright after Strindberg and an important way-station between Strindberg and Ingmar Bergman, who was no relation but felt a strong affinity for his namesake. The legacy is a peculiar blend of comedy and vision.

Taking his cue from Strindberg's chamber plays and from the Belgian playwright Maurice Maeterlinck's diaphanous mood plays, Hjalmar Bergman developed what he called marionette plays, highly stylized and symbolic, destined to cast a long shadow from their many shadows. He then proceeded to explore all the devices and strategies of the expressionism that had originated in Sweden and was flourishing in Germany.

Bergman acquired his immense Swedish popularity (a Stockholm restaurant and a theater are named for him) as a realistic novelist, in a series of genre pictures of the commercial center of Sweden's iron-ore district, the so-called *bergslag*, where he grew up, and in a study of changing social dynamics in that area. These novels were later to be turned into plays which lost something in detail but gained in dramatic situation and, in fact, emerged as farces. So, in the drama Bergman was never a pure Ibsenesque realist.

Bergman was indefatigable. He found plots everywhere. He explored everything. Sweden could scarcely have laid the groundwork in the film industry without Bergman's supplying of scripts to Victor Sjöström; in his later years, he turned his attention to radio drama and undoubtedly would have moved on to television if it had been ready for him.

BIOGRAPHY

Hjalmar Fredrik Elgérus Bergman was born September 19, 1883, in the commercial city of Örebro, the son of a bank director. From his family he derived an economic security that persisted until 1910 when he was forced to rely on his writing for sustenance. A domineering father and a propensity toward obesity made Bergman painfully sensitive in his youth. It may indeed be said that when he grew up he spent most of his life traveling from one hotel to another, writing feverishly, in flight from his accumulated neuroses.

Bergman's formal education was not extensive. On graduation from high school in 1900 in nearby Västerås, he traveled in Austria and Germany, reading in leisurely fashion Gotthold Ephraim Lessing, Arthur Schopenhauer, and Fyodor Dostoevski. One of the most influential books in Bergman's youth was Lessing's *Hamburgische Dramaturgie* (1767-1769; *Hamburg Dramaturgy*, 1889). A year at Uppsala University was largely a private discipline in philosophy and aesthetics under the tutelage of Hans Larsson. Once more Bergman's restlessness took him abroad, this time to Italy, where he was charmed and engrossed by the folkways but, most ironically, beset by an eye ailment that threatened blindness and kept him from enjoying fully the travel that his spirit required. At this time there was a passing encounter with the young E. M. Forster about which not much is known.

Bergman was early in his life attracted to drama. He never missed the engagements of traveling theater companies in Örebro. In 1903 he became acquainted with the great theater family Lindberg, of whom the father, August, was one of the eminent actors of his time (he led a company to Chicago) and the son, Per, an internationally known stage and screen director, and author of *Bakom Masker* (1949; behind masks), one of the most important critical memoirs of Bergman. Bergman's talent was thus whetted, and he wrote his first play in 1904, a lyric closet drama, a kind of folk passion play, *Mary, Mother of Jesus*, published by his father but never staged. Bergman further cemented his relations with the theater by becoming married to Stina, August Lindberg's second daughter, in 1908. That same year brought Bergman to the stage: Dramaten, the most important theater in Stockholm. The play was *Lady Vendla's Chain*, laid in the time of King Charles XII of Sweden (1697-1718), a fantasy about a powerful old man who oppresses the weak around him and turns them into puppets. Finally their fear of him is overcome and they set fire to his house and escape their servitude. The play has not survived, but the subject gave notice of things to come.

Bergman's first popular success was a novel, *Hans nåds testamente* (1910; the baron's will), which also initiated a series of works that explored the topography, social mores, and changing values of Sweden's central iron-ore district. This was Bergman's terrain, though he usually wrote about it from a safe distance. From then on Bergman lived abroad, returning to the Stockholm archipelago in the summers, and his life became his work. There were interruptions, chiefly homosexual infatuations, but he always returned to Stina, and Stina was loyal beyond the line of duty and beyond Bergman's death. For the rest of her life, she was his chief advocate, advising directors and editors, staging a series of his plays in English in the summers, always defending their marriage.

Bergman's experiments in symbolic and expressionistic theater are significant, but their failure to find an audience disturbed him. He kept coming back to the *bergslag*, the district of his youth, most notably in another popular success, the novel *Markurells i Wadköping* (1919; *God's Orchid*, 1924). In 1917, a chance viewing of Victor Sjöström's film, *Terje Viken* (1916; based on an Ibsen poem) captivated Bergman and led him into an infatuation with film, the writing of some thirty scenarios (many unproduced), and an eventual stay in Hollywood (1923-1924), when Sjöström persuaded him to take a job as script writer and assistant director. The visit was far from happy; he left after only a few months, convinced that vulgarity had reached a new stage of refinement and that America scarcely had the moral mission it assumed for itself in the world.

In 1926, in spite of an agonizing skin infection and a deterioration of the nervous system, Bergman threw his energies into a new medium, into the writ-

ing of radio sketches. By 1929, he had become Sweden's most popular radio playwright. From 1919 onward, the idea of death had never been far from Bergman's mind and in 1929 he began to write the epilogue of his life, what he knew to be his last will and testament. Characteristically, he assumed a Pagliacci role in a radio serial called *Clownen Jac* (1930; *Jac the Clown*, 1995). Bergman put his physical resources to the limit to play the clown role himself, the part of a performer who abandons his jesting and mime to read his spiritual and artistic credo to an uncomprehending audience. The work is uneven but moving, not merely as a personal statement but as a manifesto of the age. A few days later, Bergman left for Berlin, where he quietly died alone in his usual habitat, the bleak isolation of a hotel room.

ANALYSIS

Hjalmar Bergman was endlessly fecund and inventive, a source of inspiration. Drama was his life— and he was one of the great fabulists. His dramaturgy can best be summed up in these three stages: the marionette plays (1917), the expressionistic plays (1918-1923), and the realistic farces (1925-1930).

DÖDENS ARLEKIN

The focal situation in *Dödens arlekin* (death's harlequin) is the death of Alexander Broman, the personification of an authority that has dominated family, business, and community to a state of tyranny and paralysis. The stage is his office, the empty chair a symbol of his absent and declining authority. Broman never appears, but his presence is felt in a thousand ways. It is here that the children converge. Bertil, the only son and the heir apparent, is too cowed from long parental domination either to approach the bedside of his dying father or to take any kind of decisive action. The daughter Tyra arrives with her engineer husband Lerche, to whom she was married because of her father's will in the matter. She would rather have married Dr. Brising, the community doctor, who is in attendance; the relationship is, in fact, renewed. Tyra's sister Magda wanted to marry Lerche, but again parental authority had it otherwise; Magda has become a hard, even brutal woman, to whom Bertil constantly turns for support.

The intrigue of the play is realistic, but an aura of *commedia* hovers over everything. Indeed, Dr. Brising is the "death's harlequin" of the title. He calls himself a "death-doctor" because Broman's overriding authority has left him no province except that of signing certificates of death. He dances to two kinds of bells, that in the death chamber and those on Tyra's sleigh. They are not unrelated. As Brising puts it: "Death has a wonderfully stimulating effect—on the surroundings."

EN SKUGGA

En skugga (a shadow) has been called "a proverb in one act." It might as well be called a brief venture into allegory. In it, Bergman effectively fuses two themes, that of youth mated (or about to be mated) to old age, and the symbolic splitting of personality, somewhat in the fashion of Joseph Conrad's "The Secret Sharer." Erik spends the bride's last night prior to marriage with her, while the aging groom-to-be lurks suspiciously outside her door with the mother. In the morning, before a planned elopement with Vera, Erik tries to dismiss his servant, who has guarded the rendezvous. Though Erik and the servant are two separate personalities, it is clear that Bergman intends to represent man's better self dismissing his base, evil self. The evil self wins and stabs Erik, who is discovered in an ugly sprawl on the bride's bed. Vera claims him in a passionate close: "He has eyes, lips, breast, arms, hands. And you call him a shadow? He gave his life for his honor. . . . He gave me everything I asked for." Ultimately the "shadow" comes to signify sensual passion, darkly shadowing blood and violence; the real culprit is society.

MR. SLEEMAN IS COMING

The third of these "marionette plays," *Mr. Sleeman Is Coming*, opens with the interestingly contrasted dialogue of two impoverished old maids, Aunt Bina and Aunt Mina, who are about to marry off their young, lovely niece, Anne-Marie, to a desiccated old man, Herr Sleeman, the pillar of an adjoining community. In the second tableau of this almost ballet-like artifice, Anne-Marie disappears into the woods with her Green Hunter, but she is submissively back the next morning to accept the inevitable. There is real horror in the old man's arrival. The movements

of his body are grotesque; he repeats the words that the Green Hunter had spoken, turning their petals to dust. As Per Lindberg remarks, "Sleeman is the rubber stamp of that which once was life." He is a symbol of the quiet, apparently friendly power that desiccates life and turns people into will-less marionettes. None of Bergman's plays surpasses the delicate stylization of this graceful work, which has, quite understandably, become a favorite acting exercise in Scandinavia.

SPELHUSET

The immediate public response to the marionette plays was not good and Bergman, disappointed, experimented in another direction. *Spelhuset* (the gaming house) is Bergman's best effort in expressionism, which means that it was not so much a play as a charade, in spite of its exquisite theatricality. The play was in step with the advances of German expressionism and used that movement's whole bag of tricks. The presiding metaphor is not the theater or the circus, but the casino. "All the world's a gaming house," with its labyrinthine deceits, with the Manager as Ringmaster. Society has effaced character to the point of the generic: The Railroad King, First Croupier, Second Croupier, Bejeweled Beldam, First Cocotte, Second Cocotte, and so on. Much is dumb show and mumbo-jumbo. Karin and Gerhard, untainted youth, have managed to keep their identity and, hence, their names. Karin is involved in the gambling, wins a fortune at the expense of The Railroad King, but manages to make her escape with Gerhard in a lurid finale of conflagration and murder. The play did not find its way into production until 1930; Bergman himself was present, making his last public appearance in Sweden before he left the next day for Germany and early death. The play, as it turned out, was a premonition.

SAGAN

Sagan (the legend) is similarly slight in plot but rich in scenic effect. The lovely Rose would marry her doctor, Gerhard, if she had her way about it; Sune would probably marry Astrid, who worships him. Rose and Sune, however, are forced into betrothal by Family and Money, represented in a gallery of grotesques, of caricatures: the Rich Uncle, the Harridan of a Mother, the Effete Young Chamberlain, and the Heavy Aunt. Authority has its way, though just what happens at the end is not clear. Stina Bergman, who presided over the writing, says that Rose takes morphine and dies; the play says that Sune ecstatically drags her off shouting: "the sun, the sun"—perhaps a sardonic echo of the ending of Henrik Ibsen's play *Gengangere* (pb. 1881; *Ghosts*, 1885). Bergman never really resolved the play because, as he thought, "it will never get played." Nevertheless, it has been frequently staged, chiefly by Ingmar Bergman, though not yet as a film.

Though the core of the play involves Rose and Sune, the framework involves Sagan, a lovely young woman who is the mythic embodiment of unrequited love—the family curse—and also mistress of ceremonies. Invisible to the other characters, she introduces them, weaves among them, and provides the commentary and poetry of the play, like an unseen female Feste. It is a sad and lovely play that can perhaps best be described in painterly terms (Bergman was early—and briefly—a student of art): It is as if an assemblage of Rowlandson caricatures was embraced by a framework of Watteau. The nearest theatrical equivalent is Alfred de Musset's *On ne badine pas avec l'amour* (pb. 1834; *No Trifling with Love*, 1890), also the sentiment of Bergman's play, as an internal allusion makes clear. If there are ambiguities in the plot, there is no questioning the ritual power of this work, the most poetic of Bergman's plays.

PORTEN

Porten (the portal) is another dark allegory in the expressionistic mode. Henrik, a political prisoner for an unspecified crime, has been granted clemency by the government after serving only two years of his ten-year sentence. His home has been reestablished; his family awaits him with some apprehension, as do members of the community who wonder what bought off his sentence. Some feel cheated out of the martyr that he was so long as he was in prison. Henrik appears, quoting from the opening stanza of Dante's *Inferno*. He has passed through "the dark wood," so harsh that death could hardly be more so. This, however, is no midlife crisis, as in Dante, but the edge of

death. Henrik is a mass of tensions, hatreds, and suspicions of his wife's possible infidelities and of his unknown benefactor. The engineer of his release, Michael, appears halfway through the play. He, a nobleman and one-time rival of Henrik in love, lectures Henrik on the necessity of *besinning*, self-possession or acceptance of one's fate.

Bergman's play falls into two irreconcilable parts: the political and the personal. It has its dramatic moments and to a considerable degree the presiding stage symbol of the arching portal yokes all things together, whether it is the gateway from imprisonment to release, from life to death, or from social anger to self-acceptance. Bergman says that the play grew out of a "mortal peril," but such is the abstraction of the action that we may never know the autobiographical origin or the exact import of the message. It is no doubt for this reason that the play has had so little stage attention.

EXPRESSIONISTIC PLAYS

Of the other plays in this middle, largely expressionistic period (1918-1923), *Ett experiment* (an experiment) elaborates a dialectic between wealth and poverty very much under the influence of George Bernard Shaw, *Lodolezzi sjunger* (Lodolezzi sings) is an exotic bagatelle, and *Vävaren i Bagdad* (the weaver of Bagdad) exploits—and to some degree satirizes—the then current preoccupation with Eastern themes (Bergman had just translated *The Arabian Nights' Entertainments* into Swedish).

THE SWEDENHIELMS

The Swedenhielms was Bergman's first big play and his first big success. His many earlier plays were adroitly turned but slender. Though he clearly wanted to write a very Swedish drama (Stina calls it Sweden's "first classic comedy"), it has played successfully in fourteen countries (although minimally in the United States) and has had extensive exposure in film and television. So, clearly, its national character has not limited its ability to travel.

The apparent center of the play is the ebullient, extravagant, controversial Rolf Swedenhielm, an engineer who is about to win the Nobel Prize. Will he get it, will he not? His reception of the prize is resolved early enough to indicate that this is not the major tension of the play. Svante Arrhenius, who received the Nobel Prize for his work on electrolytic dissociation, is said to have been the real-life model on which Rolf Swedenhielm was based, though even more of Bergman's own father goes into the portrait. Then there are the three, apparently flighty, children: Rolf, Jr., who follows in his father's scientific footsteps; Julia, a posturing actress who is always in somebody else's play; and Bo, a light-headed lieutenant in the air force. This is essentially a family play. The boys are gamblers and high-livers in a family of aristocratic poverty. So the tension of the play, as it increasingly appears, arises in anticipation of how the father might react to the profligacy of the children and how he might ultimately be disgraced at the moment of his distinction. A creditor (right out of Ibsen) confronts the father with a handful of promissory notes that only the prize money can resolve. Most distressing are Bo's apparent forgeries of his father's name.

It develops that the real forger was Boman, the housekeeper and the play's mother figure, who was forced into such action by the extravagance of the family; she emerges the villain/heroine of the play, the sassy servant, endlessly housecleaning and keeping everybody in line, salvaging the honor of the family, the honor to which all the others merely pay lip service.

The play is classical in its compactness (everything seems to happen within twenty-four hours, though it could not). The badinage approaches that of the English comedy of manners (Bergman was infatuated with the Oscar Wilde of *The Importance of Being Earnest: A Trivial Comedy for Serious People*, pr. 1895). The character types are part of the vocabulary of classical comedy: the egocentric *pater familias* (who makes entrances with "The Toreador Song" or a thunderous snore); the irresponsible children who, it turns out, are not so bad after all; and the wily servant, though in this case the middle-aged, controlling domestic so well resuscitated as Dr. Borg's domestic in Ingmar Bergman's play *Smultronstället* (1957; *Wild Strawberries*, 1959). All in all, this is a robust, rambunctious play that works with the whole tradition of comedy.

DOLLAR

Like Honoré de Balzac, Bergman created his human comedy of interlocking characters and plots. In another greatly successful play, Julia Swedenhielm, now married to the industrialist Kurt Balzar, President of Svea, Inc., joins two other couples at a northerly resort-sanatorium to greet another Julia (namely Johnstone), the wealthy relative from America. Originally called *The American Lady*, this play came to the stage with the succinct and sardonic title *Dollar*.

Svea, Inc. is in trouble and needs all the help it can get. The same can be said of all three European marriages, where lust, distrust, boredom, and fear are rampant—clothed, however, in sophistication. Says one character, the doctor of the sanatorium: "European amorality is an old weed with manifold blossoms, endlessly mysterious in color and form."

What the American lady has to offer are money and a single-minded rectitudinous nature. With a degree in theology, she holds morning prayer in the lobby. Beyond sermonizing, however, she exposes the peccadillos of her Swedish relatives with all the assurance of one of George Bernard Shaw's virtuous ladies. So, ultimately, the play is a confrontation between American and European value systems.

Like so much of Bergman, the play skirts the edge of tragedy but always finds comic resolution. Sussi, the most high-strung of the wives, is rescued from a suicide attempt in the snow by the American Julia, disguised as a chauffeur. Julia herself, though traveling with a duke doubling (onstage) as a pedicurist, is united with the sanatorium doctor who is (not surprisingly) the *raisonneur* of the play. All three troubled European couples are brought to their senses in a traditional comic resolution.

The play's intrigue subsists not so much on action as on innuendo and a kind of badinage which has come to be called "Swedenhielmese." As film (1938), *Dollar* provided Ingrid Bergman with one of her best early roles, that of the Swedish Julia.

PATRASKET

Next to *The Swedenhielms*, *Patrasket* (the rabble) is Bergman's best-known original play. The fable of this farce is tested and infallible. A successful tradesman in a northern German city absents himself from his store to avoid poor relations who, not to be so easily sloughed off, take over the store while the owner, Rosenstein, hovers and agonizes in the neighborhood. Joe Meng, the adroit spokesman for the intruders, "the rabble," is to a degree a projection of Bergman himself. He speaks for Bergman in a notable panegyric to fantasy, a luxury for the rich but a necessity for the poor. Into the figure of Meng, Bergman concentrates everything he finds of mingled tragedy and comedy in the Jewish people: displacement, resourcefulness, business acumen, poetry, music, melancholy, and flamboyance. (The late Martin Lamm, Sweden's finest critic of the drama and for years an intimate of Bergman, believes that Meng was largely modeled after Mauritz Stiller, the renowned film director and a Russian Jew. Indeed, he suggests that the spectacular transactions Meng expects to carry out through his pretty daughter Mary have their origin in Stiller's discovery of Greta Garbo, whom he brought to Hollywood and world fame.)

Bergman compounds business and love in a double plot consciously reminiscent of Shakespeare's *The Merchant of Venice* (pr. c. 1596-1597). Meng, like Shylock, has lost a daughter, though with Meng it is a temporary loss. Bergman appears anxious to provide in Meng a sequel, perhaps a corrective, to what he believes to be the inevitably comic interpretation of Shylock. In Shakespeare's play, reflects Meng:

a Jew has been cheated, a Jew tormented, a Jew scorned! That was enough. Who wept? Wasn't there one Jew in the audience? Pah! If so, he laughed harder than the rest. . . . For Israel is like unto olives, that their virtues, like oil, must be squeezed out of them.

MARKURELLS OF WADKÖPING

Matriculation (*student examen*), or the passage from high school to profession/university (two years after an American high school graduation), looms large among Swedish rituals, enabling the successful to wear a white cap and flourish a swagger stick on festive occasions for years to come. *Markurells of Wadköping* focuses on the uncertainties and tensions of just that moment in a fictional town that is part of Bergman's territory and a conflation of Örebro and Västerås, respectively the cities of his birth and matriculation.

Markurell is the town innkeeper and entrepreneur, who with a combination of acumen, uninhibited crudity, and occasional flashes of finesse, has bought up the community, including Judge Carl-Magnus de Lorche, who represents the aristocracy (in decline) and the judiciary. Markurell is aided and abetted by Ström the barber, a sycophantic and poisonous character. Markurell's one endearing feature is his love for his son, and to ensure his son's passing his matriculation exam he stages an elaborate feast for the examiners: smoked salmon, ptarmigan, and an array of fine wines. It is hardly a subtle maneuver, though theatrical, and, typically, Markurell fails to view it as bribery. The uses of money are manifold. Young Markurell manages to pass the examination, though whether by dint of a last ditch effort or his father's maneuver is not quite clear. Evidently, the examiners are vulnerable to the good things of life since they so seldom have them.

The ultimate irony—and it is a powerful and devastating one—is that Markurell turns out not to be the father of his own son. The community has known all along that Judge de Lorche is the real father, but this shattering news comes to Markurell late in the play. Nevertheless, everything arrives at a festive close in this bittersweet drama. Late in life, Bergman adapted this play from the novel which in 1919 did so much to establish his career and gave him the added momentum to write. It lacks the amplitude and detail of the original, but it is full of vitality.

THE BARON'S WILL

Bergman came full circle: His last and perhaps his finest play, *The Baron's Will* (1931), was based on his first and perhaps finest novel, *Hans nåds testamente*. Even in his exhaustion, the old exuberance comes back. In the whole realm of drama, it would be hard to find a better and denser—if equally farcical—portrait of manor house society: indolent, self-indulgent, eccentric, busily engaging in backstairs sex.

The occasion is the seventieth birthday and the framing of the last will and testament of His Lordship Baron Roger Bernhusen de Saars (the original being Bergman's godfather). The Baron dominates everything; he runs the gamut from bowels to bombast. But he is lovable after a fashion—even to the array of retainers who, grumbling, cater to his every whim. His lovely, illegitimate daughter Ingrid gets the estate, and not the priggish Roger, son of his termagant sister Julia, who is almost a match for her brother in virtuoso flights of insult. For a time it seems that Roger and Eric, another of the estate's bastard children, will vie equally for the attention of Ingrid (they indulge in fisticuffs and there is the threat of further violence), but Ingrid and Eric, two happy offspring of healthy sexuality, are meant for each other. So love moves onward toward the new, classless society.

The retainers are marvelously portrayed; while they may defer to the aristocracy, they are outspoken and their vigor is that of the future. Bergman clearly enjoys the poetry and vulgarity of the aristocracy (in about equal proportions), but he knows that it is on the way out, whatever nostalgia he might feel. So the realism of his early novel has taken on a "story-book quality," a kind of stylization that exploits theatricality and provides the perspective of history. Realism is dull; fantasy enriches everything. This is the essence of Bergman's contribution to the stage.

OTHER MAJOR WORKS

LONG FICTION: *Hans nåds testamente*, 1910; *Markurells i Wadköping*, 1919 (*God's Orchid*, 1924); *Herr von Hancken*, 1920; *Farmor och vår Herre*, 1921 (*Thy Rod and Thy Staff*, 1937); *Chefen fru Ingeborg*, 1924 (*The Head of the Firm*, 1936); *Clownen Jac*, 1930 (*Jac the Clown*, 1995).

SHORT FICTION: *Amourer*, 1910; *Loewen-historier*, 1913; *Komedier i Bergslagen*, 1914-1916 (3 volumes); *Kärlek genom ett fönster*, 1929.

SCREENPLAYS: *Mästerman*, 1919; *Vem dömer?*, 1922; *Eld ombord*, 1922; *Karl XII*, 1924-1925; *En perfekt gentleman*, 1927.

BIBLIOGRAPHY

Bock, Sigge. *Lowly Who Prevail: Vistas to the Work of Hjalmar Bergman*. Uppsala, Sweden: Uppsala University, 1990. A critical analysis of the work of Bergman, with emphasis on religion in his writings. Bibliography and indexes.

Linder, Erik Hjalmar. *Hjalmar Bergman*. Boston: Twayne, 1975. A basic biography of Bergman that covers his life and works. Bibliography and index.

Petherick, Karin. *Hjalmar Bergman: "Markurells i Wadköping."* 2d ed. Hull, England: Orton and Holmes, 1976. This study of *God's Orchid*, one of Bergman's novels, sheds light on his dramatic works. Bibliography.

Scobbie, Irene, ed. *Aspects of Modern Swedish Literature*. Rev. ed. Chester Springs, Pa.: Dufour Editions, 1999. In addition to placing Bergman within the wider tradition, this work contains a chapter on the life and works of Bergman.

Warme, Lars G., ed. *A History of Swedish Literature*. Vol. 3 in *History of Scandinavian Literatures*. Lincoln: University of Nebraska Press, 1996. Provides information on the works of Bergman and explains his role in Swedish literature.

Richard B. Vowles

JEAN-JACQUES BERNARD

Born: Enghien-les-Bains, France; July 30, 1888
Died: Paris, France; September 12, 1972

PRINCIPAL DRAMA

Le Voyage à deux, pr., pb. 1909
La Joie du sacrifice, pr., pb. 1912
La Maison épargnée, pr., pb. 1919
Le Feu qui reprend mal, pr., pb. 1921 (*The Sulky Fire*, 1939)
Martine, pr., pb. 1922 (English translation, 1939)
L'Invitation au Voyage, pr., pb. 1924 (*Invitation to a Voyage*, 1939)

Le Printemps des autres, pr., pb. 1924 (*The Spring-time of Others*, 1939)

Denise Marette, pr., pb. 1925

Théâtre, pb. 1925-1952 (8 volumes)

L'Âme en peine, pr., pb. 1926 (*The Unquiet Spirit*, 1939)

Le Secret d'Arvers, pr., pb. 1926

Le Roy de Malousie, pr., pb. 1928

La Louise, pr., pb. 1931

À la recherche des cœurs, pr., pb. 1931

Les Sœurs Guédonec, pr., pb. 1931

Jeanne de Pantin, pr., pb. 1933

Nationale 6, pr., pb. 1935

Five Plays, pb. 1939

Le Jardinier d'Ispahan, pr., pb. 1939

Marie Stuart, reine d'Écosse, pr., pb. 1942

Louise de la Vallière, pr., pb. 1943

Notre-Dame d'en haut, pr. 1951, pb. 1952

Jean-Jacques Bernard (Ghitta Covell, courtesy of New York Public Library)

OTHER LITERARY FORMS

Although Jean-Jacques Bernard's reputation rests largely on his drama, he wrote several significant prose works. Primary among these is *Le Camp de la mort lente* (1944; *The Camp of Slow Death*, 1945), a powerful memoir of his imprisonment by the Nazis in 1941-1942 and his subsequent conversion to Catholicism. He published *Le Pain rouge*, a collection of stories focusing on the occupation of France, in 1947 and a novel, *Marie et le Vagabond*, in 1949. His memoir of his years in theater, *Mon ami le théâtre* (1958), remained popular and in print into the twenty-first century.

ACHIEVEMENTS

Along with playwright Denys Amiel, Maurice Maeterlinck, and Charles Vildrac, Jean-Jacques Bernard popularized a type of theater that has been called the Theater of the Unspoken (*l'inexprimé*) or the theater of the unexpressed for its emphasis on nonverbal communication and symbolism. This movement arose after World War I in response to the perceived verbal excesses of earlier French drama. Bernard was active in numerous theater organizations and served as president of La Société des Auteurs et Compositeurs Dramatiques from 1957 to 1959.

BIOGRAPHY

Jean-Jacques Bernard was born in 1888 in Enghien-les-Bains, France. His father, Tristan Bernard (whose real name was Paul Bernard), made a name for himself in the theater by writing farce. Jean-Jacques Bernard was Jewish by birth and was educated in Paris at the Lycée Carnot and at the Sorbonne. He wrote his first play at the age of twenty-one and finished several other short plays before the beginning of World War I. While he was in the army, he wrote war dispatches for a newspaper.

The effects of war haunted Bernard. His plays of the years immediately following World War I reveal the trauma that war inflicted on the playwright. In the early 1920's, however, he met the great director,

Gaston Baty, and entered the richest period of his dramatic career. Along with another playwright, Denys Amiel, Bernard created a vogue for what has been called the theater of silence or the Theater of the Unspoken. However, war once again changed the course of Bernard's life.

In 1941, Bernard was arrested by the Germans and was interned in Compiègne, outside Paris. He was released the following year because of poor health. The war, however, was of fatal consequence to other members of Bernard's family. His father, Tristan Bernard, was arrested by the Germans in 1944 and died, broken in spirit and in health, in 1947. Jean-Jacques Bernard's oldest son died in the Mauthausen concentration camp, where he was sent by the Nazis because of his activity in the Resistance.

Plagued by chronic illness most of his life, Bernard published little after 1950 (except for his memoir, *Mon ami le théâtre*). After the war, he worked for a time in film with his brother, and he became active in theater organizations, including La Société des Auteurs et Compositeurs Dramatiques. He died in Paris in 1972.

ANALYSIS

Some critics have noted that Jean-Jacques Bernard brought a new classicism to the French theater. Indeed, the simplicity of Bernard's plays is comparable in some ways to the French theater of the seventeenth century—the era of classicism. His plays are concise and tightly focused, and although he does not follow seventeenth century theatrical conventions of confining action to a single day and place, Bernard's theater has a spareness that creates a curious and strong impact.

Bernard is remembered as the chief member of the school of the Theater of the Unspoken or the theater of the unexpressible. In reaction to what he—and other playwrights—saw as the melodramatic and verbose theater of the nineteenth century in France, Bernard created plays in which verbal exchange is not necessarily the most important kind of communication. Instead, he believed that the real communication between people is in gesture, expression, and what is not said.

Clearly, such a theory places a great deal of responsibility on the actors of a play. Bernard wrote descriptions of his characters' actions, reactions, and expressions, but it remains up to the actors—and to the directors—to successfully express what the playwright had in mind. Therefore, one cannot fully appreciate Bernard's theater by simply reading the text of the plays. An ideal appreciation would be found in reading the text and seeing a performance of the play. This ideal approach might apply to all theater, but it is especially relevant to Bernard's drama.

INVITATION TO A VOYAGE

Invitation to a Voyage takes its title from a famous poem by the nineteenth century French poet, Charles Baudelaire. The allusions that Bernard makes by using this title serve him well. His play is about the kind of vague, quasi-mystical longing to be somewhere else, with someone else, escaping from the humdrum of one's everyday life of which Baudelaire writes. *Invitation to a Voyage* is also an excellent example of the kind of indirect communication in which Bernard's characters engage.

The setting is the Vosges section of eastern France, in particular a mountainous, forested area near the town of Épinal. The pine forests are of crucial import to Marie-Louise, the play's main character, because they surround her home and represent the imprisonment she feels in her life. Marie-Louise has been married to Olivier for several years. The couple has a young son. By all appearances, Marie-Louise and Olivier are happily married. However, in actuality, Marie-Louise hides a chronic but not explicitly articulated malaise. She feels trapped in a life that is, while peaceful and contented, confining and boring. She fears a future in which she will do the same things again and again.

Marie-Louise makes the acquaintance of Philippe, a businessperson visiting her father's factory. He gives her a copy of Baudelaire's *Les Fleurs du mal* (1857, 1861, 1868; *Flowers of Evil*, 1931), which contains the poem "L'Invitation au Voyage." This poem comes to articulate for Marie-Louise her own discontent—and her thirst for the exotic. When she hears that Philippe is leaving for Argentina, Marie-Louise is haunted by the word "Argentina" and the resonances that match her longings. Olivier rightly senses his wife's vulnerability; he is afraid that Marie-Louise will in fact run away with Philippe. He does not directly express his fears, nor does Marie-Louise express her fascination with Philippe and his life.

Time passes. Philippe returns to Épinal from Argentina for a visit. When Marie-Louise learns that he is nearby, she cannot resist the attraction; she abruptly leaves her home and goes to seek Philippe in Épinal. Olivier is terrified that she will not come back. However, Marie-Louise's adventure turns out badly. She does see Philippe, but contrary to what she had hoped, he is in no way interested in her. They talk—but about his business, not about love. Marie-Louise returns to Olivier, accepts her disappointment and her former life, as it was.

THE SPRINGTIME OF OTHERS

The Springtime of Others features one of the most memorably cruel mothers in all theater. However, the other two characters in the play, the victims of the mother's cruelty, are not entirely flawless either. This short three-act play is typical of Bernard's economy: There are only three characters (excluding a maid), and while the setting changes for each act, the plot is free of complications.

The play begins in Italy, where Clarisse and Gilberte, mother and daughter, are vacationing. Young Maurice Gardier appears and introduces himself to Clarisse, who seems deceptively absent-minded, rude, and silly. As their conversation develops, it turns out that Maurice and Gilberte had met in Paris before coming to Italy—indeed, Gilberte is the reason Maurice is here at all.

Clarisse, an aging single parent, shows herself to be rather self-absorbed and sorry for herself, and when she discovers that Gilberte is in love with Maurice, she is moved—perhaps because she fears being left alone, perhaps because she is happy for her daughter, or perhaps because she is surprised that anyone would or could fall in love with Gilberte. It becomes obvious, however, that Clarisse is taken with Maurice and sees herself as her daughter's rival for his attentions. Gilberte's devotion to her mother is strong, even childish; she suspects nothing sinis-

ter in Clarisse's actions and words. At the end of act 1, Clarisse takes a long look at Gilberte, tells her that, yes, she is in fact beautiful—then takes a table mirror and pauses at some length to look at her own image.

Maurice and Gilberte marry, and Gilberte becomes pregnant. Already given to instability, she becomes worse and begins to suspect that Maurice is having an affair with a horseback-riding friend of Clarisse, who fosters this suspicion in her daughter's mind. Through most of act 2, Clarisse seems to sympathize with her daughter. However, as the second act ends, Clarisse effects a stunning reversal: She changes sides, defends Maurice's right to have a female horseback-riding partner, and berates Gilberte, in front of Maurice, for being so touchy. Clarisse then smiles, calls Gilberte a clumsy little fool, and walks off. Gilberte dissolves into sobs.

Maurice, who was indeed unfaithful to his wife, eventually thinks the better of his actions and telephones Gilberte when she is staying with her mother. Clarisse makes a tactical error: While Gilberte stands nearby, she tells Maurice that his wife is not there and thereby loses the battle for Gilberte. Gilberte now recognizes her mother's meanness, and she and Maurice reconcile—leaving Clarisse wretchedly alone at the play's end. *The Springtime of Others* is a tour de force for an actor. There are a number of moments in the play when the meaning of words on the written page is open to several interpretations, and such richness and subtlety offer a range of opportunities for talented players.

LA LOUISE

This one-act play is based on the notion that, as nineteenth century playwright Alfred de Musset put it, "one does not play around with love." Bernard's minimalism is evident everywhere. As the play begins, the audience learns only that the scene is a war zone; no particular war is noted. The soldiers bear no weapons. The stage is barely set—except that Bernard's directions indicate a feminine presence (some prints, some flowers) in the few furnishings. What is most important in this context is that the meaning of what is happening or what is said is not always clear. This dimension of understatement, a thought-provoking subtlety, is one of the fascinating elements of Bernard's theater.

One of the soldiers, Sermain, has been foraging in the war zone for lodgings for himself and several comrades. He has struck a pranklike bargain with a young woman named Louise—or "la" Louise. The "la," the feminine word for "the," is difficult to render into English; it connotes a familiarity, even patronization or condescension on the part of the speaker. Louise has agreed to billet one of the soldiers. However, because she has only one bed, the soldier will be obliged to sleep with Louise. Such a situation does not bother Louise, whom Sermain early on characterizes as loose. She is apparently happy to have the company and sex, even with a complete stranger.

Sermain adds malicious spice to the situation. He has chosen Pierre Garbin as the comrade who will share Louise's bed—precisely because Pierre has openly declared his undying fidelity to the wife he left at home. Sermain thus wants to mock or test true love. Pierre knows only that he will spend the night in the home of a young woman; he does not know that he is to sleep with her.

Sermain's scheme fails. Pierre is exactly what he seems to be—a loving, faithful husband, the only truly upright man in a group of morally slovenly brutes. Louise understands what Pierre is; she is able to observe him without being seen as he, for example, writes a letter to his wife then breaks into sobs. As Louise learns that Pierre is a man to be admired, she too weeps, moved by such devotion in a world in which she apparently thought true love was a myth.

The play's crisis develops when it is time for bed. Instead of playing Sermain's game, Louise gives Pierre her room and her bed. She directs him to her room without even exposing Sermain's intended joke. Louise instead beds down in a closet, telling Pierre it is a second bedroom. As the curtain falls, Louise is in tears—because of her own loneliness and her admiration of Pierre's steadfastness. In some sense then, Louise is the play's heroine—her name is, after all, the title of the play. She has transcended Sermain's cheap immorality and revived her own spirit as well.

Bernard delivers only what the audience needs to know to understand the play's fundamental point— that true love exists and is a valuable commodity. Almost nothing is revealed about Louise or the soldiers other than Pierre. Even in his case, what is known is minimal: that he is married, has a baby son, and writes his wife faithfully. The play's impact resides not in the conversation between Louise and Pierre but in Louise's change in perspective, as it registers in her tone of voice, in her face, and in her final, verbally unexplained choice.

OTHER MAJOR WORKS

LONG FICTION: *Le Roman de Martine*, 1929; *Marie et le vagabond*, 1949.

SHORT FICTION: *Le Pain rouge*, 1947.

NONFICTION: *Le Camp de la mort lente*, 1944 (*The Camp of Slow Death*, 1945); *Mon père Tristan Bernard*, 1955; *Mon ami le théâtre*, 1958.

BIBLIOGRAPHY

Branford, Kester Adrian. *A Study of Jean-Jacques Bernard's Théâtre de L'Inexprimé*. University, Miss.: Romance Monographs, 1977. Criticism and interpretation of Bernard, with emphasis on the Theater of the Unspoken. Bibliography.

Coindreau, Maurice. *La Farce est jouée: Vingt-cinq ans de théâtre français, 1900-1925*. New York: Éditions de la Maison Française, 1942. This classic is an imaginative, scholarly, pioneering work on numerous groups or schools of playwrights of the period, including Bernard. In French.

Daniels, May. *The French Drama of the Unspoken*. 1953. Reprint. Westport, Conn.: Greenwood Press, 1977. An indispensable study of Bernard and other writers of *l'inexprimé* (the unexpressed)— including Maurice Maeterlinck, Charles Vildrac, and Denys Amiel. Daniels points out the positive contributions made by these writers in their plays, but she also sees the limitations of such theories.

Knowles, Dorothy. *French Drama of the Inter-War Years, 1918-1939*. London: Harrap, 1967. A widely available book that deals in literary history, including topics such as the differences between the theater of the boulevard and studio theater and the historical and cultural dimensions of French theater during this era. Contains much information regarding titles, plots, and chronology.

Surer, Paul. *Cinquante ans de Théâtre*. Paris: Société d'Édition d'Enseignement Supérieur, 1969. A history of French theater from 1919 to the Theater of the Absurd. Surer includes Bernard in a chapter titled "Le Théâtre intimiste," in which he suggests that the subtleties of the theater of the "unexpressed" may appeal only to a small, sophisticated audience. In French.

Gordon Walters

THOMAS BERNHARD

Born: Heerlen, Netherlands; February 10, 1931
Died: Gmunden, Austria; February 12, 1989

PRINCIPAL DRAMA

Die Rosen der Einöde, pb. 1959 (libretto)
Ein Fest für Boris, pr., pb. 1970 (*A Party for Boris*, 1990)
Der Ignorant und der Wahnsinnige, pr., pb. 1972
Die Jagdgesellschaft, pr., pb. 1974
Die Macht der Gewohnheit, pr., pb. 1974 (*The Force of Habit*, 1976)
Der Präsident, pr., pb. 1975 (*The President*, 1982)
Die Berühmten, pr., pb. 1976
Minetti: Ein Porträt des Künstlers als alter Mann, pr. 1976, pb. 1977
Immanuel Kant, pr., pb. 1978
Der Weltverbesserer, pb. 1979, pr. 1980
Vor dem Ruhestand, pb. 1979, pr. 1980 (*Eve of Retirement*, 1982)
Über allen Gipfeln ist Ruh: Ein deutscher Dichtertag um 1980, pb. 1981
Am Ziel, pr., pb. 1981
Der Schein trügt, pb. 1983, pr. 1984
Ritter, Dene, Voss, pb. 1984, pr. 1986 (English translation, 1990)
Der Theatermacher, pb. 1984, pr. 1986 (*Histrionics*, 1990)
Elisabeth II, pb. 1987, pr. 1989
Heldenplatz, pr., pb. 1988
Histrionics: Three Plays, pb. 1990

OTHER LITERARY FORMS

Despite an early interest in the drama revealed in an essay on Antonin Artaud and Bertolt Brecht, which he wrote while a student at the Musik Akademie in Vienna, and his experimentation with one-act plays before 1960, Thomas Bernhard achieved initial literary recognition for his poetry and prose. Only since the publication and premiere of *A Party for Boris* in 1970 did Bernhard occupy an important niche in contemporary German drama. His emergence as a playwright did not signify a radical digression from earlier philosophical or thematic concerns; in his plays, as well as in his later prose, Bernhard continued to pursue his obsession with life's theatricality and absurdity.

In addition to contributions of poems to anthologies and journals, Bernhard published four volumes of poetry. After the completion of the libretto *Die Rosen der Einöde* (1959; the roses of the desert), he embarked on a career as a writer of both long and short fiction. His *Wittgensteins Neffe: Eine Freundschaft* (1983; *Wittgenstein's Nephew*, 1986), a violent memoir consisting of one unrelenting paragraph that covers 164 pages, attests his continuing preoccupation with Ludwig Wittgenstein, given fullest expression in the novel *Korrectur* (1975; *Correction*, 1979) but apparent throughout Bernhard's œuvre. In addition, Bernhard published various autobiographical works as well as programmatic essays and speeches.

ACHIEVEMENTS

A highly controversial figure throughout his career because of his virulent attacks on society and his nihilistic and self-destructive tendencies, Thomas Bernhard emerged as one of Austria's most widely discussed modern authors. As a highly prolific writer, whose true artistic intent and radical aggressiveness vis-à-vis his audience, his homeland, and society at large remain veiled in contradiction, Bernhard elicited diverse critical reaction. Though controversial, Bernhard was recognized as a major exponent of modern German drama, yet he was justifiably acclaimed more widely for his innovative prose. The landscapes Bernhard portrayed in his prose often draw on his familiar Austria and its cities (Salzburg, Vienna). In its radical treatment of his homeland and its tradition, Bernhard's work evokes an equally strident criticism of the human condition because even the identifiable, localized settings he presents are merely paradigms of a deadly, antagonistic universe. Though the settings for his plays are not typically Austrian, they parallel metaphorically those of his prose.

Bernhard's plays have been performed in leading German and Austrian theaters, including Vienna's conservative Burgtheater, and at the Salzburg Festival. Most of them have also been broadcast on German, Austrian, and Swiss television. He received prestigious literary awards, including the Bremer Literaturpreis (1965), the Österreichischer Staatspreis für Literatur (1967), the Wildgans-Preis (1968), the Büchner-Preis (1970), the Grillparzer-Preis (1971), and the Franz-Theodor-Csokor-Preis (1972).

A contributor to the three major literary genres, Bernhard was frequently mentioned in connection with other acknowledged masters of modern literature (Ezra Pound, T. S. Eliot, Georg Trakl, Paul Éluard, Artaud, Brecht, Samuel Beckett) and with contemporary literary trends (Theater of the Absurd, Theater of Cruelty, *nouveau roman*). Despite his affinity with and indebtedness to these authors and trends, Bernhard's works remained distinctly his own creation; his plays, in particular, defy easy categorization.

BIOGRAPHY

Thomas Bernhard's characteristic ambivalence

and individual stance in regard to reality often make it difficult to distinguish fact from fiction in his various writings. The author's autobiographical works contain some reliable factual information but it is often obscured behind poetic description, as several major critics, such as Benno von Wiese and Herbert Gamper, have illustrated. The following biographical sketch can be gleaned from the primary and secondary sources available.

Bernhard was born illegitimately on February 10, 1931, to the daughter of a minor writer, Johannes Freumbichler, and the carpenter son of a farmer from the Austrian town of Henndorf. Bernhard never knew his father. His birthplace was actually a monastery near Maastricht, a refuge for young unwed mothers in the Netherlands. During his first year, Bernhard was cared for by a woman on a fishing vessel in Rotterdam while his mother worked to support herself. Bernhard's next years were spent with his maternal grandparents in Vienna and Seekirchen am Wallersee (near Henndorf). Repeatedly criticized and often rejected by a neurotic mother, Bernhard trusted only his eccentric grandfather, who could be described as an antibourgeois grumbler with an anarchistic bent. Already attending school at the age of four and a half, Bernhard was admonished by his grandfather neither to take school too seriously nor to trust his teachers blindly. This maternal grandfather, a friend of the renowned dramatist Carl Zuckmayer and an acquaintance of the provocative Ödön von Horváth, wanted his grandson to become an artist. In *Ein Kind* (1982; *A Child*, 1985), Bernhard recounts the dominant force exerted on him by his grandfather during his formative years amid these early experiences of death, rejection, and psychological strain.

In 1938, Bernhard moved with his mother and stepfather to Traunstein in Upper Bavaria, where he received his first music instruction. In 1943, he went to Salzburg to study at a boarding school that remained under Nazi control until the end of 1944. Bernhard's first major autobiographical work, *Die Ursache: Eine Andentung* (1975; *An Indication of the Cause*, 1985), deals directly with these experiences. In 1946, after the war, Bernhard's family was expelled with other Austrians living in German territory. Rejected by his stepfather and his stepfather's children, Bernhard began a commercial apprenticeship rather than attend the gymnasium. The physical demands of this labor led to pleurisy and serious lung ailments, which resulted in long hospital stays between 1948 and 1951. In 1949, Bernhard's grandfather died in the same hospital in which Bernhard himself was convalescing. Bernhard's mother died the following year. (His natural father had been killed in battle in 1943.) The trauma of these repeated encounters with death is described in *Der Keller: Eine Entziehung* (1976; *The Cellar: An Escape*, 1985) and *Der Atem: Eine Entscheidune* (1978; *Breath*, 1985), which, along with Bernhard's other autobiographical works, *An Indication of the Cause*, *Die Kälte: Eine Isolation* (1981; *In the Cold*, 1985), and *A Child*, appear together in English translation as *Gathering Evidence* (1985). Bernhard contends that his obsessive preoccupation with permanence and stability resulted from his having been denied them so decisively and consistently in his youth.

With numerous experiences of death, sickness, and rejection indelibly imprinted in his consciousness, Bernhard began to write; he published his first prose in 1950 in the *Salzburger Volksblatt*. He subsequently studied music, directing, and acting in Vienna and Salzburg. In dire physical need while in Vienna, Bernhard performed menial tasks, including the care of "an ugly, seventy-year-old deranged woman from Währing," in exchange for which he received his meals. During this period, he also served as a court reporter for the *Demokratisches Volksblatt*. After completing his studies and leaving the Akademie Mozarteum in 1957, Bernhard began his career as a writer in earnest. Thereafter, Bernhard lived primarily in Vienna and Klagenfurt but traveled extensively to Yugoslavia, Italy, Poland, and England, among other places. After 1965, he resided on a farm he purchased near Gmunden in Upper Austria.

ANALYSIS

The plays of Thomas Bernhard reflect the major thematic tendencies evident in his prose and poetry. Although the search for religious consolation so prevalent in the Austrian baroque tradition to which

Bernhard's poetry can be linked is much less apparent in his prose and dramatic work, Bernhard's writings nevertheless remain fragments of one great opus. Bernhard alludes to this fact in *Die Berühmten* (famous persons): "They make this observation with reference to all significant artists/ they all only create a single work/ and always alter it continuously within itself, imperceptibly." Writing thus assumes the function of self-assertion and constant "correction" for Bernhard, as the title of his novel *Correction* illustrates. Bernhard's private life and personal tribulations are intensely and artistically, if not factually and straightforwardly, expressed in his very individualistic writings, yet this expression symbolizes a common human suffering and malaise. Though diverse in their social backgrounds and intellectual consciousness, the characters of Bernhard's plays are subjected without exception to a consistent, destructive fate. Neither social reform nor revolution, political philosophy nor religious conviction, provide relief from the cosmic deadliness of a solipsistic universe, as a discouraging line from the novel *Verstörung* (1967; *Gargoyles*, 1970) reveals: "There are no future teachers and the prior ones are dead."

Anamnesis, the inability to forget the past, intensifies Bernhard's sense of cultural pessimism. Each individual is forced to fend for himself or herself in an attempt to escape a reality that is predicated on the recognition and confinements of a ruinous past. Tradition embodies the crimes of the past, for which only universal (and therefore pointless) culpability can be assigned. Humans are trapped in a deadly realm of antitheses from which there is no escape. Life is no longer organic but rather chaotic; humanity's experience in time and space is reduced to a circuitous hodgepodge of disjointed repetitions and illogical associations. An acknowledgment of life's absurdity becomes the only possible solution. Bernhard writes in another autobiographical work, *In the Cold*: "Artistic endeavor derives justification from its freedom, its independence from any absolute standard of judgment."

Death, lurking behind life's absurdities, is Bernhard's essential theme because it is life's universal common denominator. Life becomes an exercise in futility because death ultimately symbolizes both the greatest possible unity and the greatest possible alienation between ego and world. The process of individuation described by Arthur Schopenhauer provides as little comfort for Bernhard as humanity's eventual return to nothingness. Yet despite all of life's traumatic and absurd details, Bernhard continues to cling to it and is unwilling to allow himself to be blotted out by his own gloom and doom. His only recourse is to continue to confront life's absurdities in his art. By attempting to find words and phrases to describe personal and general experience adequately, Bernhard combats the inaccuracies of accepted social convention and opinion ("reputation") yet continues to create inaccuracies of a new kind: "When we open our mouths, we kill a reputation; we simultaneously kill a reputation and kill ourselves. But if we do not open our mouths we are soon crazy, insane, there is nothing left for us" (*Gargoyles*).

Musical qualities intensify the philosophical and thematic content of Bernhard's plays. Occasional commentary by the author on the musical structure of his plays and the actual treatment of musical themes establishes the significance of this abstract art form for Bernhard's writings. The author's language indicates especially a reliance on musical structure for his art. Statement-restatement, point-counterpoint, repetition, variation, and circular linguistic phraseology are essential elements of Bernhard's dramatic style. Such stylistic devices sustain the author's philosophical viewpoint, which *A Party for Boris* typifies: "Everything is every day, day after day, a repetition of repetitions." When viewed from a musical perspective, where the text's semantic meaning is less significant than its rhythmic, musical quality, Bernhard's language escapes the criticism of excessive repetition and thematic "overkill."

Because Bernhard nevertheless uses words and linguistic structure, his plays must also be dealt with from a semantic perspective. The monotony of his characters' language suggests a linguistic crisis paralleling that of Georg Büchner or Hugo von Hofmannsthal, yet for Bernhard, it is the essence of reality, and not linguistic inadequacy per se, which predetermines this crisis. Martin Esslin, in an essay comparing Bernhard and Gert Jonke, a contemporary Austrian writer, accurately places Bernhard in a deep-seated Austrian tradition of linguistic analysis and language skepticism, supremely expressed in the work of Wittgenstein. Esslin connects this tradition with Bernhard's toward the theater. Like Peter Handke, another contemporary Austrian writer influenced by language skepticism, Bernhard frequently adopts a hostile and even mocking stance toward the theater audience.

DIE JAGDGESELLSCHAFT

Die Jagdgesellschaft (the hunting party), which premiered at the Burgtheater in Vienna, is composed of three movements, as Bernhard explains in his appended note to the play. By structuring the last movement as the adagio, Bernhard has redefined classical sonata or symphonic form. This last movement, a funeral march marking the General's death, intensifies structurally the nihilistic denouement of the play. By varying the traditional musical form, in which a resolution would normally occur in the last movement, Bernhard ends his play decisively on a note of death and decay.

Similarly, Bernhard's motto from Heinrich von Kleist's *Über das Marionettentheater* (1810; *About the Puppet Theater*, 1950) suggests the author's view of man as a mere marionette. *Die Jagdgesellschaft*, Bernhard's third published play, described by some critics as a step toward total pessimism, reveals that death and decay extend beyond individuals and into nature itself: The infestation of the General's forest by insects parallels his own death. An atmosphere of hopelessness from which there is apparently no recourse unfolds before the viewer's eyes.

The three scenes, or movements, of the play are labeled "Vor der Jagd" (before the hunt), "Während der Jagd" (during the hunt), and "Nach der Jagd" (after the hunt). The play's limited action transpires at the General's hunting lodge over a short span of time. The General's wife, a writer, two ministers, a prince and princess, a cook, and a servant round out the cast of characters. The hunter becomes the hunted: The mortally ill General commits suicide, and his treasured forest is totally destroyed, as he is relentlessly pursued by death.

The first scene centers on a disjointed conversation between the General's wife and the writer in the cold, damp lodge. The writer is occupied with composing an aphorism for which one essential word escapes him. Language is incapable of encompassing reality, as his monologue fluctuates from one thought to another and reiterates the same key words. The General's wife is preoccupied with her husband's health (he suffers from glaucoma, has lost his left arm in the battle of Stalingrad, and was once injured by a chain saw) and with the state of his forest. In this opening scene, both characters reveal their introverted concerns; their conversation never progresses beyond mere juxtaposition of individual viewpoints. The card game in which they engage pacifies the General's wife and releases her from the unsettling consciousness of the drudgery and misery of existence; the writer acknowledges the underlying meaninglessness of the card game but nevertheless accepts its therapeutic value. This activity, like the characters' speech, is merely an attempt to "bridge the emptiness of time," an emptiness the writer intellectually comprehends but intuitively seeks to avoid. The damp cold and darkness symbolize human beings' inability to escape reality. Bernhard's characters may be mad, paranoid, and eccentric, but the world around them is equally so, and humankind is powerless to halt death's ruthless march, as the ravaging of the forest by bark beetles exemplifies. Science, too, the sum of humankind's intellectual capability to order and control its environment, is powerless in the face of nature's self-destructive rage, the rage of destruction on life itself. The deathly sickness pervading nature penetrates each and every individual human being as well. The General's wife attempts to shield him from the realization of the pervasiveness of death by hiding information from him concerning the true state of the forest. His eye disease blinds him from perceiving the approaching onslaught of death. In contrast to the somber mood of his wife and the writer, the General's cheerfulness as he enters near the end of the first scene serves as musical and thematic counterpoint. As a floundering symbol of life, power, and control, the General is at odds with the writer's pessimistic outlook.

The second scene, "During the Hunt," offers a modicum of sustained dialogue as the General's wife and the writer continue at cards. Games are won and lost, but they have no relationship to life and reality. Bernhard expresses his anti-idealistic stance concretely through the lines of the writer in the play: "Human beings are despairing human beings; everything else is a lie." The unavoidable outcome is realized as shots from the hunters' weapons ring out in the background.

The final scene, "After the Hunt," intensifies the theoretical and philosophical differences between the General and the writer. The writer views all history as nothing but an unfolding disaster. The General's various ailments all point to the gradual deterioration of his life. His stay in the hunting lodge is only a brief respite in this ongoing process; death is at work in this natural setting just as it is in the city from which he has fled. The General's attempt to shield himself from reality is further symbolized by his aversion to the writer's conception of theater, yet he cannot find consolation in the obvious deceptiveness of the Christmas plays his wife puts on. Death haunts everyone, as the writer readily recognizes. In the end, a shot resounds; the General is discovered lying dead in an adjoining room, and his forest is immediately cut down. The common denominator among human beings is the experience of death, whose sickness entirely penetrates both the physical and the metaphysical realm.

IMMANUEL KANT

In *Immanuel Kant*, which Bernhard labels a comedy, the author draws for the first time on a historical figure for a main character, although Bernhard's Kant bears only the vaguest physical or intellectual resemblance to the historical philosopher of pure reason from Königsberg. Bernhard's Kant, transposed into a contemporary setting, remains a wooden character like his predecessors; he is confused, schizoid, eccentric, diseased, and infirm. It is worthy of note that by using a quote from Artaud for the motto of the play ("that is not meant to say, that one should represent life in the theater"), Bernhard reveals a desire to transcend historical and biographical accuracy, to operate on an aesthetic plane where mimesis becomes irrelevant. What evolves is an "essence" that has as much validity as "objective" reality. Life (theater) becomes both meaningful and meaningless at the same time— meaningful because it constitutes the only means for an individual to confront destructive reality, and meaningless because no objective measure of its accuracy is verifiable. This contradiction is at the very heart of Bernhard's art.

The play begins on the front deck of an ocean-liner, as Kant, suffering continually from the cold, is being assisted by his wife, by Ernst Ludwig (the caretaker of the philosopher's beloved parrot, Friedrich), and by the ship's steward. Kant treasures and pampers this bird, which mimics his words incomprehensibly, more than he treasures human beings and their natural surroundings. The importance Kant attaches to this parrot reveals conclusively the insanity and incomprehensibility of his "philosophy," and ultimately man's inability to structure his world in any logical fashion. All that remains for Kant is the hope of arriving in the United States, where, besides receiving an honorary doctorate from Columbia University, he is to undergo eye surgery, performed by the world's best doctors. Kant's failing eyesight parallels his intellectual decline. Only sound remains as a means of representing reality. Kant is very careful to avoid damage to Friedrich's eyes, which symbolize Kant's remaining contact with the physical world. Disjointed repetition of words divorced from meaning and visual association are the only remnants of the universe that the philosopher has tried to systematize.

Life's unpredictability is revealed in Kant's unavoidable dependence on idiotic types such as Ernst Ludwig. As he exploits those around him in an attempt to preserve a position of dominance, Kant merely reveals his powerlessness all the more graphically. In the end, there is no first principle for all truths. That Kant reads only old newspapers indicates his inability to order future events. Königsberg, long the symbol of the historical Kant's stable, ordered life, floats in time and space. That Königsberg can now be found wherever Kant is reflects the growing mental imbalance, the subjectivity of human experience, and the confusion of natural limits. Kant's mental stability is further jeopardized by his confusion of

historical fact: His supposed friend Gottfried Wilhelm Leibniz actually died before Kant was even born. Kant's statement that "seasickness is the proof of everything" perfectly epitomizes Bernhard's scorn for philosophy in the face of ultimate absurdity, as does the magnificent tautology: "Everything which is not, is not; everything which is, is." The clear distinctions that existed for the historical Kant between thought and reality are shattered. Kant's dictum in the play, "The world is the opposite side of the world/ truth the opposite side of truth," admits only an unrelenting progression toward death and destruction, symbolized by his command: "Full speed ahead!" Banality has replaced the sublimity of the historical philosopher's message. For all their pessimism and despair, however, Bernhard's plays nevertheless reveal a striving toward final meaning and purpose. When the characters cease talking, life will also cease. As long as they continue to talk, death is put off. The sheer persistence of Bernhard's voice belies its hopelessness.

OTHER MAJOR WORKS

LONG FICTION: *Frost*, 1963; *Verstörung*, 1967 (*Gargoyles*, 1970); *Das Kalkwerk*, 1970 (*The Lime Works*, 1973); *Korrektur*, 1975 (*Correction*, 1979); *Ja*, 1978 (*Yes*, 1991); *Die Billigesser*, 1980 (*The Cheap-eaters*, 1990); *Beton*, 1982 (*Concrete*, 1984); *Der Untergeher*, 1983 (*The Loser*, 1991); *Holzfällen: Eine Erregung*, 1984 (*Woodcutters*, 1987; also as *Cutting Timber: An Imitation*, 1988); *Alte Meister*, 1985 (*Old Masters*, 1989); *Auslöschung: Ein Zerfall*, 1986 (*Extinction*, 1995); *In der Höhe: Rettungsversuch, Unsinn*, 1989 (*On the Mountain: Rescue Attempt, Nonsense*, 1991).

SHORT FICTION: *Amras*, 1964; *Prosa*, 1967; *Ungenach*, 1968; *An der Baumgrenze: Erzählungen*, 1969; *Ereignisse*, 1969; *Watten: Ein Nachlass*, 1969; *Gehen*, 1971; *Midland in Stilfs: Drei Erzählungen*, 1971; *Der Stimmenimitator*, 1978 (*The Voice Imitator*, 1997).

POETRY: *Auf der Erde und in der Hölle*, 1957; *In hora mortis*, 1957; *Unter dem Eisen des Mondes*, 1958; *Die Irren-die Häftlinge*, 1962; *Contemporary German Poetry*, 1964 (includes selections of his poetry in English translation).

SCREENPLAY: *Der Italiener*, 1971.

NONFICTION: *Die Ursache: Eine Andeutung*, 1975 (*An Indication of the Cause*, 1985); *Der Keller: Eine Entziehung*, 1976 (*The Cellar: An Escape*, 1985); *Der Atem: Eine Entscheidung*, 1978 (*Breath: A Decision*, 1985); *Die Kalte: Eine Isolation*, 1981 (*In the Cold*, 1985); *Ein Kind*, 1982 (*A Child*, 1985); *Wittgensteins Neffe: Eine Freundschaft*, 1982 (*Wittgenstein's Nephew: A Friendship*, 1986); *Gathering Evidence*, 1985 (English translation of the first five autobiographical works listed above; includes *An Indication of the Cause, The Cellar: An Escape, Breath: A Decision, In the Cold*, and *A Child*).

BIBLIOGRAPHY

Barthofer, Alfred. "The Plays of Thomas Bernhard: A Report." *Modern Austrian Literature* 11, no. 1 (1978). Analyzes the general themes and approaches of Bernhard's works.

Dierick, A. P. "Thomas Bernhard's Austria: Neurosis, Symbol, or Expedient?" *Modern Austrian Literature* 12, no. 1 (1979). Explores the relationship of Bernhard's plays to the sociopolitical climate of Austria.

Dowden, Stephen D., and James N. Hardin, eds. *Understanding Thomas Bernhard*. Columbia: University of South Carolina Press, 1991. Part of the series, Understanding Modern European and Latin American Literature, explores themes and approaches of Bernhard. Bibliography and index.

Finlay, Frank, ed. *Centre Stage: Contemporary Drama in Austria*. Amsterdam: Rodopi, 1999. Examines the contributions to Austrian theater by many playwrights not previously studied, including Bernhard, Fritz Hochwälder, Wolfgang Bauer, Elias Canetti, and Peter Handke. Focus is on the themes, forms, and concerns of Austria's contemporary playwrights.

Honegger, Gitta. *Thomas Bernhard: The Making of an Austrian*. New Haven, Conn.: Yale University Press, 2001. The first comprehensive biography of Bernhard in English, it examines the complex connections of Bernhard's work with Austria's twentieth century geographical, political, and cultural landscape.

Indiana, Gary. "Thomas Bernhard." *Artforum* 8, no. 3 (Fall, 2001): 17-24. Provides profile of Bernhard, a timeline of important events in his life, a reader's guide to his work, and excerpts from several pieces.

Konzett, Matthias. *The Rhetoric of National Dissent in Thomas Bernhard, Peter Handke, and Elfriede Jelinek*. New York: Camden House, 2000. Examines how these writers expose and dismantle conventions of communal consensus that work to derail the development of multicultural awareness and identity.

Sorg, Bernhard. *Thomas Bernhard*. Munich: Beck, 1992. Provides criticism and interpretation of Bernhard's works. In German. Bibliography.

Paul F. Dvorak

HENRY BERNSTEIN

Born: Paris, France; January 20, 1876
Died: Paris, France; November 27, 1953

PRINCIPAL DRAMA

Le Marché, pr., pb. 1900
Le Détour, pr., pb. 1902
Frère Jacques, pr., pb. 1904 (with Pierre Véber; *Brother Jacques*, 1904)

La Rafale, pr., pb. 1905 (*The Whirlwind*, 1906)
La Griffe, pr., pb. 1906
Le Voleur, pr., pb. 1906 (*The Thief*, 1915)
Samson, pr., pb. 1907
Israël, pr., pb. 1908
Après moi, pr., pb. 1911 (*After Me*, 1911)
Le Secret, pr., pb. 1913
La Galerie des glaces, pr., pb. 1914

L'Élévation, pr., pb. 1917
Judith, pr., pb. 1922
Félix, pr. 1926, pb. 1929
Mélo, pr., pb. 1929
Espoir, pr., pb. 1934 (*Promise*, 1936)
Le Voyage, pr., pb., 1937
Elvire, pr. 1940, pb. 1946
La Soif, pr., pb. 1949
Victor, pr., pb. 1950

OTHER LITERARY FORMS

Henry Bernstein is known exclusively for his theatrical works.

ACHIEVEMENTS

Henry Bernstein did not distinguish himself by winning awards; his notable achievement is his long, rich, sometimes even courageous playwriting career, which spanned more than a half century. One critic has said that Bernstein dominated the French stage from 1900 to 1917. Bernstein is, however, sometimes dismissed as a playwright of the Paris Theater of the Boulevard—meaning that he wrote only entertainment for a low-brow, middle-class public. However, a measured consideration of Bernstein's work proves that such a perspective is exaggerated. In fact, Bernstein's plays provide not only a fascinating record of what the French theatergoing public admired in the first forty years of the twentieth century but also a sound idea of the moral concerns of the bourgeoisie and minor nobility of the era. If Bernstein is not a playwright of profound ideas, he nevertheless intriguingly depicts an always interesting time, society, and ethos.

BIOGRAPHY

Henry-Léon-Gustave-Charles Bernstein would have been quite familiar with the social milieu that appears in his plays. Like most of his characters, Bernstein was well off. His father was a banker of Polish-Jewish origin; his mother was American, the daughter of another banker, William Seligman. Therefore, Henry was heir to a family fortune, and he added to that fortune himself.

Although he was born in Paris, Bernstein received his higher education at Cambridge, where he spent two years. In 1899, in order to avoid the last four months of his year of compulsory military service (he claimed he was a pacifist), he fled to Brussels. He was, however, pardoned for this offense.

As a writer, Bernstein took no grandiose posture. He evidently admitted that he wrote to make money. He was beyond a doubt financially successful: He made some eight million dollars during his career of writing and producing drama and selling film rights to his plays. At least a dozen of his plays were made into films. In addition, by 1900 when his first play was staged, Bernstein had acquired a reputation as a gambler and boulevardier.

A factor that would have made Bernstein something of an outsider in Parisian high society was his Jewish ancestry (he was only five years younger than the great Marcel Proust, another French—and Jewish—writer of the day). In Bernstein's early years, he, like other writers and intellectuals, came to the defense of Alfred Dreyfus in the famous Dreyfus affair, which dragged on for some twelve years. Dreyfus was a Jewish army captain accused of treason, then ultimately exonerated; rampant anti-Semitism had much to do with the persecution of Dreyfus. Bernstein's ethnic background also surfaces in his own career. His *Israël* and *After Me* both deal with anti-Semitism—which was so strong in France at this time that riots forced the closing of *After Me*. Anti-Semitic writer Léon Daudet was at least in part responsible for these riots, insofar as he openly accused Bernstein of having shirked his military service. Bernstein fought three duels with Daudet; during his career, he managed to get involved in a total of twelve duels, sometimes for professional reasons, sometimes because of his ethnic identity.

Despite what Bernstein may have done in 1899, during World War I he fought with the British in Belgium, then did duty as an observer for the French aviation service in what was then Mesopotamia. He was wounded, and while he was recovering in an Iraqi hospital, he wrote *L'Élévation* (the Elevation). After World War I, he bought his own theater in Paris, the Gymnase.

When World War II broke out, Bernstein showed that age, success, and financial stature had not diminished his courage, sense of justice, and fighting spirit. In 1940, he presented his *Elvire*, an anti-Nazi play that had only a brief run before the Germans invaded France that summer. Bernstein later escaped to the United States, where he was active in the Free France movement, but returned to France after the war. He continued his playwriting until 1953. He died on November 27 of that year, following surgery for a brain tumor.

ANALYSIS

Henry Bernstein was presented in the 1960's as an example of what French theater ought not to be. The French playwrights in vogue in the 1960's viewed the theater of Bernstein and other "popular" playwrights as anti-intellectual; writers such as Samuel Beckett, Jean-Paul Sartre, and Jean Anouilh saw theater as a vehicle for ideas, political statements, and philosophy. However, Bernstein's plays have much more substance than these writers—and critics since the 1960's—have been willing to admit.

Bernstein's theater entertains, even in the twenty-first century. His plays almost always contain some comic element—amusing characters, witty dialogue, comic situations. The real essence of his drama, however, lies in the manner in which he presents an era in French society—or at least certain elements of French society—in the first half of the twentieth century. The society he depicts is a microcosm: upper-middle-class characters and members of the hereditary nobility, as diluted as the nobility was in France at the turn of the twentieth century. The only representatives of the rest of French society are maids and valets, who for the most part perform their appointed tasks (although a maid in *Samson* takes it on herself, benevolently, to warn a mother of her daughter's misbehavior).

The upper levels of turn-of-the-twentieth-century French society, as Bernstein sees things, are materialistic, ever conscious of social status, generally superficial in any sense of appreciation of culture. This society, often referred to by Bernstein's characters as "the world," thrives on hypocrisy: It is the face one presents publicly, not one's inner passions, longings, or lusts, that matters. Therefore, when for some rea-

son one's real identity is exposed, the individual is in peril. However, in Bernstein's best plays there is always a hero or heroine—or occasionally, both, as in *Samson*—who has the courage to transcend the crowd mentality and do what is right.

THE WHIRLWIND

The world of *The Whirlwind*, like that of most of Bernstein's plays, is tightly circumscribed in more than one sense. Bernstein sets his plays for the most part in Paris, the center of French society, which, in turn, consists of a number of inner circles. *The Whirlwind* deals with insiders and outsiders (the play opens with a conversation about whether a certain man ought to be voted into an exclusive club). There is a clearly recognized distinction between those who trace their ancestry through several generations of nobility, on one hand, and those who have risen to the apex of this society on the basis of their forebears' work and have climbed the social ladder from humble origins, on the other.

At one point, Baron Lebourg, for example, is called a *parvenu*, a man who has "succeeded." This expression is usually used negatively in eighteenth and nineteenth century France. Here, the Baron accepts the characterization because his interlocutor means that the Baron has an energy for life, a joy for challenge that the old nobility no longer has. It is Robert de Chacéroy who is talking with Lebourg in this scene. Chacéroy is, in contrast to the Baron, titled but impoverished nobility, a young man driven to pay for his elegant lifestyle by gambling. He has even learned to enjoy gambling. However, Chacéroy's luck has run out. Early in the play, it is revealed that he has lost a great sum of money, and worse, he has covered his debts through embezzlement. Still, it is Chacéroy who is the focus of the love of Lebourg's daughter, Hélène. She was forced into a loveless but socially useful marriage with a boor. This, too, is a long tradition in French society, in which fathers have complete control of their families.

When the scandal of Chacéroy's dilemma becomes known in the Lebourg family, the Baron tries to buy Chacéroy off. However, Chacéroy truly loves Hélène and turns down the offer. What is more important perhaps, and the point that constitutes the last act's surprise twist, is that Robert has lost his nerve for gambling. Facing scandal, meaninglessness, and the loss of Hélène, Robert nobly kills himself—rather than ruin Hélène, who was all too willing to run away with him.

THE THIEF

The Thief is a thriller, a comedy, a love story (indeed, several love stories), and perhaps what one critic called a "comedy of character." The first two acts carry several surprises, including an exposed disguise, and the crisis of the last act is a spontaneous confession. This kind of thing is to be expected in a play in which the very title is deliberately misleading: The French title, *Le Voleur*, refers to a masculine thief, leaving the French audience no reason to believe that the play will reveal a female thief (*la voleuse*).

As is typical in Bernstein's works, the milieu is that of the wealthy but, in this case, not idle rich. Raymond Lagardes is a Paris coffee merchant; he and his second wife, Isabelle, spend a good deal of time with their old friends, thirty-five-year-old Richard Voysin and his twenty-three-year-old wife, Marie-Louise. Raymond's eighteen-year-old son, Fernand, falls madly in love with Marie-Louise, who proceeds to take advantage of him.

Raymond Lagardes discovers that money has been stolen from his house; he suspects the servants and hires a detective, who passes for a family friend. The detective, Gondoin, announces that the thief is none other than Fernand. The boy admits his guilt, to the chagrin of his father. However, in act 2, Richard Voysin finds that his wife has been hiding money in a dresser drawer in their room; after much cajoling, she confesses that it was she who took the money from the Lagardes household and that Fernand took the blame to save her honor.

The crux of the matter here is that Marie-Louise defends her theft by insisting on her love for her husband—that she spent the money on clothes so that she could be attractive for him and a credit to him in society. In addition, however, Marie-Louise, like other Bernstein characters, pleads a kind of moral helplessness: She claims to her husband that she could not stop herself from taking the money.

Surprisingly, Richard accepts his wife's explana-

tion—and forgives her, at least provisionally. He knows that what Marie-Louise did is wrong, but he understands her lapse. To some extent, Marie-Louise redeems herself in act 3: She confesses to Raymond and saves Fernand from exile in Brazil. Instead, Richard and Marie-Louise will try to start over in South America. Richard also shows his magnanimity by quietly allowing his wife to say a tender goodbye to Fernand—a scene in which she transcends her selfishness and thanks Fernand for his noble, knightly self-sacrifice.

SAMSON

Samson features a clash of social cultures and a hero and a heroine who express their courage in different ways. The Samson of the title is Jacques Branchart, a self-made man in a real sense. His past is shady: He grew up in Marseilles (a city traditionally regarded as unsavory by upper-class Parisians), mysteriously worked in Egypt, then just as mysteriously came to Paris and made a quick fortune in the stock market. In order to climb the social ladder, Jacques marries Anne-Marie d'Andeline, daughter of a marquis. Anne-Marie sees the marriage as a deal—one in which her parents have sold her like an animal.

However, Jacques, over time, falls madly in love with Anne-Marie. When she has an affair with Jérôme Le Govain, he is enraged, so enraged that he engineers a stock-market crash that ruins Le Govain—but also Jacques. Hence the play's title: Jacques, like the biblical figure, brings the roof down on himself as well as on his enemy.

Anne-Marie's parents want her to divorce Jacques, but in a surprising move, she refuses to play the game according to her parents' rules. She will not abandon her husband in his time of need; she does not, however, promise Jacques that she can make herself love him. The play ends on Jacques's likewise heroic pronouncement—that he will rise again to wealth and power.

LE SECRET

For almost two-thirds of its length, *Le Secret* plays like a bedroom farce—a love triangle, a jealous husband, and innuendo exchanged among two couples and a third man. However, in the middle of the play's third act, the situation takes a sudden and dark turn.

Constant and Gabrielle Jannelot are an apparently happy and secure couple in their thirties. Constant is a painter who, like many painters, struggles with self-doubt and hostile criticism. Gabrielle provides him with solid support in every way. The Jannelots, as well as their friends, are clearly well off: Money is not a subject of worry or conversation. Unfortunately, as is revealed at the play's crisis, the couple has suffered in their childlessness. As Gabrielle confesses, not being able to conceive hurt her a good deal.

Gabrielle's close and longtime friend, Henriette Hozleur, is in her mid-twenties. As the play begins, she is being pursued by Denis Le Guenn. After Denis seems to satisfy himself as to Henriette's virtuous past, he and she marry and are happy for a time. Not long after the marriage, the Le Guenns and the Jannelots enjoy a vacation at the Norman seaside. For reasons that remain obscure for a time, Henriette's former lover, Charlie Ponta Tulli, very much a man of the world, also appears at the resort. Eventually, Charlie attempts to engage his former mistress in at least one brief sexual encounter. Henriette is shocked—and tempted. To avoid further temptation, she asks Gabrielle to see to it that Charlie is disinvited.

Denis surprises Charlie and Gabrielle in a tête-à-tête. Denis has suspected the truth anyway—that his wife was Charlie's mistress, that she has a "past." The Le Guenn marriage is soon in jeopardy. In a fit of remorse, Gabrielle stuns her husband (and the audience) by confessing that she deliberately set out to destroy Henriette's marriage by inviting Charlie to join them all. From this point on, *Le Secret* is no laughing matter. Gabrielle is obsessively jealous: As she says, when she sees people who are happy in a happiness in which she has no part, she is enraged. In another case of her instability, she has created a serious rift between Constant and his sister—simply because Gabrielle was envious of the close relationship they had.

One of the points of *Le Secret*, as Constant says, is the sad notion that no human being can ever really know another—that everyone, in the last analysis, is alone. Even Constant and Gabrielle, formerly so happy, realize that human beings are much more complex than they know—or want to know. Denis and Henriette are reunited, but the Jannelots remain in a very uneasy state. Although Gabrielle vows to try to *learn* to be a good person, Constant is not convinced that this is possible. The Jannelot marriage is intact, but largely because Constant's name proves appropriate.

BIBLIOGRAPHY

Chandler, Frank Wadleigh. "Bernstein." In *The Contemporary Drama of France*. Boston: Little, Brown, 1920. A judgment that is all the more valuable for its contemporaneity with Bernstein's apogee. Chandler thinks that Bernstein's drama becomes more substantial with *Le Secret* and *L'Élévation*.

Knapp, Bettina L. *French Theatre, 1918-1939*. London: Macmillan, 1985. A rich presentation of the state of theater in France during part of the era in which Bernstein worked. Focuses particularly on the avant-garde theater, whose playwrights saw Bernstein as a writer of little more than cheap, unimaginative, bourgeois entertainment.

Knowles, Dorothy. *French Drama of the Inter-War Years, 1918-1939*. London: Harrap, 1967. Knowles focuses on the differences between "boulevard" theater and more serious drama, including a short discussion of Bernstein.

Smith, Hugh Allison. *Main Currents of Modern French Drama*. New York: Henry Holt and Company, 1925. Chapter 14 includes several pages on Bernstein. Smith finds Bernstein's drama superficial, too melodramatic, and formulaic.

Gordon Walters

RUDOLF BESIER

Born: Java; July 2, 1878
Died: Elmhurst, England; June 13, 1942

PRINCIPAL DRAMA

The Virgin Goddess, pr. 1906, pb. 1907

Olive Latimer's Husband, pr. 1909

Don, pr., pb. 1909

Apropos, pr. 1910

The Crisis, pr. 1910 (adaptation of P. F. Berton's play *La Rencontre*)

Lady Patricia, pr., pb. 1911

Kipps, pr. 1912 (with H. G. Wells; adaptation of Wells's novel)

Kings and Queens, pr. 1915

Kultur at Home, pr. 1916 (with Sybil Spotiswoode)

A Run for His Money, pr. 1916 (also as *Buxell*, pr. 1916)

Robin's Father, pr. 1918 (with Hugh Walpole)

The Prude's Fall, pr. 1920 (with May Edginton; originally as *The Awakening of Beatrice*)

The Ninth Earl, pr. 1921 (with Edginton)

Secrets, pr. 1922, pb. 1932 (with Edginton)

The Barretts of Wimpole Street, pr., pb. 1930

OTHER LITERARY FORMS

Rudolf Besier is noted primarily for his dramatic works, although he was also engaged in journalism and translated works from the French.

ACHIEVEMENTS

Though Rudolf Besier wrote a large number of plays, his international reputation depends on a single work, the historical drama *The Barretts of Wimpole Street*. This perennial favorite was produced for the first time at the Malvern Festival in England in 1930 by Sir Barry Jackson, following its rejection by two London producers. After twenty-seven American producers turned it down, Katharine Cornell accepted it, and the play opened in Cleveland and, shortly thereafter, at the Empire Theatre in New York.

BIOGRAPHY

Born in Java of Dutch extraction, Rudolf Besier was the son of Margaret (née Collinson) and Rudolf Besier. He was educated at St. Elizabeth College, Guernsey, England, and in Heidelberg, Germany. For several years, he was engaged in journalism, being for a time on the staff of the firm of C. Arthur Pearson. In 1908, however, Besier left journalism, having decided to devote his efforts entirely to the theater. He married Charlotte Woodward, the daughter of the Reverend J. P. S. Woodward, of Plumpton, Sussex. He wrote a large number of plays; the most famous of these plays and the one that confirmed his dramatic reputation is *The Barretts of Wimpole Street*. Critics praised the play, but it was severely criticized by members of the Barrett family, who objected to the Freudian implications in the portrayal of Edward Moulton Barrett. Later, a film version of the play was made. An extremely tall, handsome man who shunned public exposure, Besier spent the last part of his life at his home in Elmhurst, Surrey, where he died suddenly of heart failure on June 13, 1942.

ANALYSIS

Though many playgoers were surprised by the general popularity of *The Barretts of Wimpole Street*, in retrospect, the groundwork for this achievement is evident. At the beginning of his career, Rudolf Besier had demonstrated his ability to draw a portrait of a peculiar poet, and in *Secrets*, his first genuine popular success, he demonstrated his sharp and sensitive knowledge of human feelings. Further, several of his earlier plays revealed a flair for melodrama. Though *The Barretts of Wimpole Street* exhibits characteristics of a comedy (it was labeled by Besier as such), a psychological drama, and a historical drama, the play contains many of the traits of the melodrama. Above all, the intrinsic appeal of the story of Elizabeth Barrett Browning and Robert Browning has given the play its enduring appeal, yet Besier must be given full credit for realizing the dramatic potential in this well-known romance—particularly the role of

Elizabeth Barrett's father, the quintessential Victorian tyrant.

EARLY PLAYS

At start of the twentieth century, dramatic language on the English-speaking stage had increasingly tended to become dry and uninteresting, and, as a result, dialogue seemed stilted. Besier's first play, *The Virgin Goddess*, a classical tragedy written during a visit to the United States, clearly showed his eagerness to return colorful and lively dialogue to the stage. The play was greeted with mixed reviews. Three years later, Besier received considerable praise for his comedy *Don*, which centers on an eccentric and magnanimous poet. The play's formal language and heavy sentimentality have dated badly. *Lady Patricia*, a satire on English affectations, and *Kultur at Home*, which delighted audiences for the manner in which it depicted German domestic life at its worst, kept Besier before the critics and the public.

SECRETS

In *Secrets*, which Besier wrote with May Edginton, he used the device of allowing the first act to take

Rudolf Besier (AP/Wide World Photos)

shape as a prologue, commencing the main action with the second act. In the opening episode, Lady Carlton, old and exhausted from constantly tending her dying husband, falls asleep in an armchair beside his bed. The drama itself consists of a series of flashbacks presented in the form of a dream. In these, the lives of the couple are presented as they marry, endure initial poverty, and gradually attain affluence. During this time, the husband has an affair with another woman. His wife forgives him, despite her bitter jealousy, because of her realization that he needs her. Like several of Besier's earlier plays, *Secrets* is highly sentimental, but it is distinguished by its acute perceptions into the psychology of the two main characters.

THE BARRETTS OF WIMPOLE STREET

Like any work that deals with actual personages, a play demands some understanding of the lives of its characters and the times in which they lived if it is to be thoroughly appreciated. Understanding the fullness of *The Barretts of Wimpole Street* necessarily entails historical knowledge not only of Elizabeth Barrett and Robert Browning but also of the general nature of Victorian customs, manners, and class distinctions.

The oldest child in a wealthy, upper-middle-class family, Elizabeth Barrett was educated at home. As a result of a back injury at the age of fifteen, she became a chronic invalid. From her early teens until the end of her life, she read widely and concentrated on writing poetry. At the time of the play, Barrett for a number of years had been confined to her room in her father's London house on Wimpole Street. From there, she pursued her education, including the study of Greek, took frequent medication, and, with the exception of visits by her family and a few friends, remained by herself to write articles and the poetry that brought her recognition. Robert Browning, a poet then ignored by the public, one day came to pay his respects, and the celebrated literary romance began. The pair seemed ill-matched; she was six years older than he and her health was frail. Her father, moreover, had decided that none of his children should marry.

Despite such unpromising conditions, the two lovers secretly married and moved to Italy, where they lived for most of the fifteen years that remained of Elizabeth Barrett Browning's life. There, they wrote most of their now famous poems and had a son. Elizabeth Browning strongly devoted herself to the Italian struggle for independence against Austria. She wrote not only *The Cry of the Children* (1854), in which she passionately argued against child labor in England, but also *Sonnets from the Portuguese* (1850), her famous sonnet sequence celebrating her love for her husband. In 1861, she died and was buried in her beloved Italy.

The hero of Besier's play, Robert Browning, was strong, spirited, and optimistic; like Barrett, he began writing when he was young. The criticism that attended his poetry early in his career failed to discourage him, for he continued to write prolifically. His whirlwind courtship overwhelmed Barrett's initial resistance, and their romance ended only with her death, after which he returned to England. His reputation today rests primarily on his dramatic monologues, in which the speakers' own words provide psychological insights into their characters. He died in Venice in 1889, but his body was returned to England and buried in Westminster Abbey, where many of England's great poets are buried.

Set against Browning in the play is the antagonist, Barrett's father, Edward Moulton Barrett, who at the age of nineteen left Cambridge University to marry a woman more than five years older than he. The union produced twelve children; one child, a girl, died in childhood, and two boys died as adults. After his wife died, he ruled his nine remaining children like a despot, refusing to explain any of his commands and forbidding any of the children to marry. Three eventually disobeyed him, and as a result, he disinherited them and refused to see them again.

The Barretts of Wimpole Street takes place during the early years of Queen Victoria's reign. Though the living and working conditions of the lower classes were slowly improving, the poor found it difficult to make gains through their employment. The exploitation of women and child laborers was common. Putting in long hours for pitifully low wages under oppressive and unhealthy conditions, workers were barely able to survive. Then, too, the class distinc-

tions were rigidly structured and observed, with opportunities to rise to a higher class practically nonexistent. Though not of the aristocracy, Edward Moulton Barrett had inherited large sums of money and had land holdings on the British island of Jamaica. Consequently, he was able to attend Cambridge University. Supported by his own means and the wealth that came to him through his wife, he lived comfortably in a fashionable London district and reared his large family, though he was temporarily inconvenienced financially when all slaves were freed in the British Empire.

Both sons and daughters of the upper classes were dependent on their fathers for financial support. Robert Browning was himself supported by his parents until his poetry began to earn money for him. The various Barrett sons assisted their father in his office, taking orders while he attended to business in the financial quarter of London or while he was abroad supervising his land holdings. Daughters were never permitted to engage in business affairs, and, as a result, some, such as Bella, became social butterflies, while others, such as Arabel, worked in support of various social or religious causes. Certain others became little more than house decorations, awaiting the opportunity to marry. Elizabeth Barrett, therefore, stands out in contrast, for she had both a career of her own and a limited inheritance. She was fortunate also in being able to secure a respectable education. Women of the upper classes were generally encouraged to pursue only the refined graces of music, manners, and needlework. Barrett gained additional education through her own intense and varied reading and from her brothers' tutors.

Characterized by prudery, repression, and formality, the Victorian period was highlighted by a fear of outspokenness and by the evasion of facts. In *The Barretts of Wimpole Street*, for example, Arabel upbraids Bella for speaking of the birth of children and scolds Henrietta for describing their father with language she considers ugly. Houses of the wealthy were heavily and formally furnished. Women, moreover, dressed in voluminous layers of clothing, and men indulged in formal attire. When he first called on Elizabeth Barrett, Robert Browning faultlessly dressed in the manner of the times—a cape fastened around his neck, a high hat, lemon-colored gloves, and a cane. Edward Moulton Barrett, together with his sons, wore evening clothes for dinner with the family each night. The wealthy also were transported in fine carriages that were attended by coachmen and footmen wearing powdered wigs.

Besier's purpose necessitated many of the dramatic techniques he used in the play. His intention was not so much to present the love affair between Barrett and Browning as to portray a family dominated by a tyrannical, repressed father. The revolt of the most unlikely family member of the Barretts of Wimpole Street constitutes the romantic and dramatic climax, and appropriately enough, the play is set entirely in Elizabeth Barrett's room. The use of only one setting focuses audience attention on the one room that every family member visited. By this means, Besier could portray the attitudes of the various sons and daughters toward their father and, in turn, his effect on them. The play's conclusion maintains and reinforces this dramatic focus. The audience does not view Elizabeth Barrett's marriage, nor is there any scene in Italy. The play closes with the father's frustrated endeavor to destroy her dog, Flush, a final indication of his unreasoning cruelty.

Terror affects each member of the Barrett family. Elizabeth continues to drink the porter that she so detests in order not to displease her father, while Henrietta, ever rebellious, accedes to Barrett's demands and swears on the Bible that she will neither see nor communicate with her suitor, Captain Surtees Cook. Representing all the boys who, through fear of their father, are leading "a life which isn't a life at all," Octavius calls Barrett "His Majesty." The whole family is elated when informed that the father is undertaking a two-week business trip. Arabel, more placid than most of the other children, hopes that he will be detained. Elizabeth herself later declares that "our family life was one of unrelieved gloom." Besier relieves the tense, strained, family atmosphere with scenes of a lighter, even humorous, quality. The Browning story primarily supplies these brief interludes, but to a degree, the story of Henrietta and Cap-

tain Cook does so as well. Entertainment also is provided by the refreshingly frivolous Bella, whose ostentatiousness reveals an aspect of the father not brought out by any of the other characters.

Because his primary intention was not simply to dramatize the romance between two gifted poets, Besier was confronted by the problem of subordinating the literary activities and interests of his principal characters to the analysis of a family's spirit in the household of a tyrannical father. Besier's dramatic maturity is evident in the masterful manner in which he resolves the problem. He employs the play's various references to poetry either to delineate character or to move the plot forward. When Barrett, for example, is reflecting on what she perceives to be the obscure nature of Browning's poetry ("No—it's quite beyond me! I give it up!"), the audience is prepared for the tender, more intimate scene in which the shared poetic sensibilities of the lovers establish their rapport and suggest their determination to overcome the obstacles that life sets before them.

The play is divided into the classical five acts, as opposed to the more modern three, and each act is given a title: "Porter in a Tankard," "Mr. Robert Browning," "Robert," "Henrietta," and "Papa." All five acts revolve around the commanding presence (or absence) of the father: act 1, his insistence that Barrett drink porter as medicine; act 2, the appearance of his as yet unknown opponent; act 3, Browning's deepening hold on Barrett's affections; act 4, the father's cruelty to Henrietta and Barrett's realization that she must agree with Browning's wedding plans; and act 5, Barrett's final interview with her father, in which she is so revolted by his words that she becomes distraught. Indeed, the father's influence, even when he is not actually onstage, is so extensive, so tangible, that in many ways he, and not Barrett or Browning, is the main character of the play.

Much of Besier's portrayal of the father accords with the known facts of his life and personality. Not only did he terrorize his children, but also he prohibited them to marry and actually disowned three who disobeyed his injunction. In other details, however, Besier used dramatic license. He collapsed the actual time of Barrett's romance with Browning from one year to approximately four months, and he inserted into the dialogue a remark that was not to achieve acclaim until some years later. When Browning finally achieved recognition, Browning societies were established all over England for the express purpose of discussing and analyzing his poetry. Browning, after receiving a letter from a member of one of these societies asking for an explanation of one particularly obscure poetic passage, replied: "When that passage was written, only God and Robert Browning understood it. Now only God understands it." Besier felt at liberty to include the remark in a conversation between Barrett and Browning, thereby reinforcing the warmth and the humanness of their relationship.

The reader can trace in *The Barretts of Wimpole Street* the change in Barrett's feelings for her father and, at the same time, her increasing health and desire for life as she comes increasingly under the influence of Robert Browning. When the first act begins, she is "so tired—tired—tired of it all," and later she admits that she "was often impatient for the end." To Browning, she declares that love can have no place in the life of a dying woman. Three months later, however, she is miraculously revitalized, full of energy and desirous of experiencing nature's passionate embrace, all of which she attributes not to the doctors or the porter but to Browning himself: "I wanted to live—eagerly, desperately, passionately—and only because life meant you—you—and the sight of your face, and the sound of your voice, and the touch of your hand." Carried along by Browning's inspiring vitality, she nevertheless continues to resist the idea of marriage simply because of the difference in their ages. When she views her father's brutal treatment of Henrietta, however, she becomes more sure about marriage, and following her final interview with her father, when she realizes that he is "not like other men," all of her doubts disappear. With a self-assurance and determination not earlier evident, she whispers to herself: "I must go at once—I must go—I must go. . . ."

Besier raised *The Barretts of Wimpole Street* from what could have been mere sentimentalism to the genuinely dramatic. The result was a play that has continued to please audiences on stage, on television, and in film.

BIBLIOGRAPHY

Gillmore, Margalo, and Patricia Collinge. *The B. O. W. S.* New York: Harcourt, Brace and Company, 1945. A classic account of the American Theater Wing's overseas production of Besier's *The Barretts of Wimpole Street*.

Hochman, Stanley, ed. *McGraw-Hill Encyclopedia of World Drama*. 2d ed. Vol. 2. New York: McGraw-Hill, 1984. This biographical article covers the highlights of the playwright's career in the United States, including the production of *The Virgin Goddess* and *Lady Patricia*. The article features a photograph of Besier and Katharine Cornell in the first American production of *The Barretts of Wimpole Street*.

Hutchens, John. "The Actor's Month: Broadway in Review." Review of *The Barretts of Wimpole Street*, by Rudolf Besier. *Theatre Arts Monthly* 15 (April, 1931): 273-277. Hutchens reviews the original American performance of Besier's most famous play, *The Barretts of Wimpole Street*, which featured Katharine Cornell as Elizabeth Barrett Browning. He reveals that Besier's script attributes incestuous impulses to Barrett's father as the root of his tyrannical behavior. At the time, this play was considered a shocking and psychologically advanced twist to a well-known romantic tale.

Skinner, Richard Dana. "The Barretts of Wimpole Street." Review of *The Barretts of Wimpole Street*, by Rudolf Besier. *Commonweal* 13 (February 25, 1931): 469. *Commonweal* is a Catholic periodical, and its theater critic is predictably conservative. Skinner applauds the romance of Besier's *The Barretts of Wimpole Street*, yet he condemns the psychosexual abnormality of the character of Edward Moulton Barrett as "gratuitous." He calls the abnormality "a discordant note in what is otherwise one of the most beguiling stage romances of recent years."

Van Doren, Mark. "Drama: Early Victorian Father." Review of *The Barretts of Wimpole Street*, by Rudolf Besier. *The Nation* 132 (February 25, 1931): 224-225. Van Doren compliments *The Barretts of Wimpole Street* by saying that "Mr. Besier had the almost unique inspiration to make his fa-mous hero and heroine behave as if they did not know they were famous. . . . This was delightful." He states that the play's weakness lies in Besier's

characterization of the father as a perfect, predict-able monster.

A. Gordon Van Ness III,
updated by Pamela Canal

UGO BETTI

Born: Camerino, Italy; February 4, 1892
Died: Rome, Italy; June 9, 1953

PRINCIPAL DRAMA

La padrona, pr. 1926, pb. 1929
La donna sullo scudo, pr. 1927, pb. 1957 (with
   Osvaldo Gibertini)
La casa sull'acqua, pr., pb. 1929
L'isola meravigliosa, pr. 1930, pb. 1936
Il diluvio, wr. 1931, pr., pb. 1943
Un albergo sul porto, pr. 1933, pb. 1943
Il cacciatore d'anitre, wr. 1934, pr., pb. 1940
Frana allo scalo nord, pb. 1935, pr. 1936
   (*Landslide*, 1964)
Una bella domenica di settembre, pr. 1937, pb.
   1941
I nostri sogni, pr. 1937, pb. 1941
Il paese delle vacanze, wr. 1937, pr., pb. 1942
   (*Summertime*, 1956)
Favola di Natale, wr. 1940, pr. 1948, pb. 1955
Ispezione, wr. 1941, pr., pb. 1947 (*The Inquiry*,
   1966)
Notte in casa del ricco, pr., pb. 1942
Corruzione al palazzo di giustizia, wr. 1944, pr.,
   pb. 1949 (*Corruption in the Palace of Justice*,
   1962)
Il vento notturno, pr. 1945, pb. 1946
Marito e moglie, pr. 1947, pb. 1949
Lotta fino all'alba, pr., pb. 1949 (*Struggle till
   Dawn*, 1964)
Irene innocente, pr., pb. 1950
Spiritismo nell'antica casa, pr., pb. 1950
Delitto all'isola delle capre, pr., pb. 1950 (*Crime
   on Goat Island*, 1955)

La regina e gli insorti, pr., pb. 1951 (*The Queen
   and the Rebels*, 1955)
Il giocatore, pr., pb. 1951 (*The Gambler*, 1952)
L'aiuola bruciata, pr., pb. 1953 (*The Burnt
   Flower-bed*, 1956)
La fuggitiva, pr., pb. 1953 (*The Fugitive*, 1964)
Acque turbate: O, Il fratello protegge e ama, pb.
   1955
Teatro completo di Ugo Betti, pb. 1971

OTHER LITERARY FORMS

The majority of Ugo Betti's published works were written for the theater, and all but a few, including three posthumous plays, were produced during his lifetime, yet his distinctive stylistic peculiarity of jux-taposing lyric forms to stark realism in his dramas can be traced to his poetic and narrative writings.

A translation of Catullus's poem 64 as *Le nozze di Teti e Peleo* (1912; the marriage of Thetis and Peleus) was the first work Betti published. Three collections of poems followed at long intervals, witness to his lifelong interest in poetry: *Il re pensieroso* (1922; the pensive king), *Canzonette: La morte* (1932; popular songs: death), and *Uomo e donna* (1937; man and woman). Of Betti's three collections of short stories, the first two, *Caino* (1928; Cain) and *Le case* (1933; houses), were published within five years of each other, while the last one, *Una strana serata* (1948; a strange evening), as well as his only novel, *La pietra alta* (1948; the high mountain), appeared fifteen years later.

The playwright emerged naturally out of Betti's poetic and fictional activities. It was as if each of his modes of translating his artistic intuition into lan-

Ugo Betti (courtesy of New York Public Library)

guage provided an essential element to arrive at a dramatic synthesis of his aesthetic vision. As Betti himself stated in an essay on the theater, he did not believe that "those high walls which some find it convenient to imagine between poetry, narrative, and theatre, and perhaps even the movies, really exist."

Some of Betti's plays were adapted for the screen, and, after winning a competition in 1939 to write for the cinema, he was able to contribute from 1941 to 1946 to several film scenarios. From 1931 to 1952, Betti also contributed a column entitled "Taccuino" (notebook) to the newspaper *La gazzetta del popolo* (the people's gazette).

ACHIEVEMENTS

Although Ugo Betti's unusual stylistic technique was common to all the literary genres in which he engaged, his reputation rests on his plays. As a play-

wright he was best able to express his basically pessimistic vision of life, a vision he was increasingly able to define in his lifelong double role as a jurist and as a writer. In some of his notes, as well as in his final plays, he justified and illustrated his vision. His is a Christian pessimism, a logical precondition for that "final stage setting, for the resurrection of the soul and its reunion with its Creator." To arrive at that teleological culmination, Betti had to cross many thresholds as he progressed, codifying his aesthetics of antinomy both in life and in art. An extraordinary fusion of harsh cruelty and childlike innocence, naturalistic plot and literary language, pessimism and hope, Betti's dramas were subject to frequent critical misunderstanding.

When Betti's first play, *La padrona* (the mistress of the house) was selected for the prize awarded by the theatrical review *Le scimmie e lo specchio* (the monkeys and the mirror), some of the judges were astonished to learn that the author was the same man who four years earlier had published *Il re pensieroso*. It is precisely the odd combination of realistic poetic images and lyric symbolism that distinguishes Betti's finest plays.

A combative and uncompromising man, Betti himself contributed to the controversy surrounding his work. He would openly express his contempt for what he considered to be dishonest and biased criticism, and was especially sensitive to critical comparisons with other contemporary writers for whom he had little esteem.

Despite such controversy, Betti has won increasing recognition as one of the greatest Italian playwrights of the first half of the twentieth century. With such recognition, Betti has grown in stature as an interpreter of the spiritual climate of his times, and his linguistic peculiarities have also been reappraised as expressing modern human beings' utter torment. *Landslide*, a play of universal dimensions, is often regarded as a pivotal drama not only in the playwright's artistic evolution but also in the history of modern drama.

Given the philosophical thrust of his work, it is not surprising that Betti's plays were appreciated in France, where they were viewed in connection with existentialism. *Corruption in the Palace of Justice*, his masterpiece, as well as other important dramas of his maturity, was first acclaimed in Paris, then in Germany and in other European countries, as well as in South America.

In 1941, Betti received the Academy of Italy's prestigious award for the theater; in 1949, he was selected for the IDI Award of the Italian Drama Institute; and in 1950, he received the Rome Award for *Corruption in the Palace of Justice*. Betti's most significant tribute, however, is that paid to him by a new generation of dramatists, headed by Diego Fabbri, who have followed in his footsteps.

BIOGRAPHY

Ugo Betti devoted himself to the activities of a literary man while engaging full-time in his profession as a judge. This combination of roles might seem discordant at first, but in fact it holds the key to his unusual gifts as a dramatist. A native of Camerino in the Marches, a region of central Italy, Betti spent his early life, and pursued his studies, in Parma, where his father, Tullio, a country doctor, had moved his family in 1900 to become the head of the municipal hospital. Displaying from early childhood an affinity for sports, Betti first played soccer but later converted to tennis, a sport in which he engaged for the rest of his life. His inclination for poetry inspired him to compose poems from a very young age and to translate Catullus's poem 64 when he was eighteen.

Although he would have liked to pursue literary studies in Bologna, young Betti was convinced by his father that a law career would give him more security. Completing his studies in jurisprudence at the University of Parma in 1914, Betti earned his law degree, in partial fulfillment of which he wrote the thesis "Il diritto e la rivoluzione" (law and revolution). Betti's thesis revealed that, like many young people of his generation, he was not immune to the anarchical ideologies of Georges Sorel, Max Stirner, and the Italian Futurists nor to the philosophical influences of Friedrich Nietzsche and Gabriele D'Annunzio. Betti's acceptance of the necessary evils of warfare was soon to be tempered, however, by the events of World War I. Having been in favor of Italy's intervention in the

war, he volunteered and participated in it as an artillery officer. He won a medal before being captured by the Germans in October, 1917, during the disastrous Italian retreat of Caporetto, and remained imprisoned until the armistice.

It was in the trenches and then as a prisoner of war that Betti engaged in serious reading and was encouraged to pursue a literary career by two fellow prisoners, Carlo Emilio Gadda and Bonaventura Tecchi, both of whom became writers of note. The poems for *Il re pensieroso* were mostly written while Betti was in prison camp; they are in the mode of the *crepuscolari*, or decadents. From the Italian *crepuscolari*, as well as from the French Symbolists, Betti assimilated a rather precious manner. His first book of poems depicts a dreamworld; its tone is deliberately childlike and naïve. Nevertheless, these early poems already reflect his innate pessimism, pointing to the vanity of earthly life and to the ever-present mystery of death.

After the war, Betti returned to Parma, where, competing for a position as a lawyer for the National Railroads, he wrote a legal work, "Considerazioni sulla forza maggiore come limite di responsabilità del vettore ferroviario" (an act of God as a railroad carrier's limit of responsibility). Meanwhile, he was also preparing for a competition, which he won, in order to enter the legislature of the city of Parma. In 1921, he became a magistrate in the nearby town of Bedonia, and was later promoted to judge in Parma.

In 1930, Betti married Andreina Frosini and was transferred to Rome. At that time, he was already gaining attention in the world of letters, both as a poet and as a playwright. His first two plays were staged by prestigious theater companies, *La padrona* in 1926, and *La casa sull'acqua* (the house on the water) in 1929, while *L'isola meravigliosa* (wonderful island) won the Governor of Rome Prize in 1930 and was staged later that year.

After World War II, Betti became head librarian of the Ministry of Grace and Justice, so that he could devote more time to his literary activities. In 1950, he was promoted to judge of the appellate court, and served as a member of the Press Bureau of the President's Council. In the last years of his life, having returned to the fold of Catholicism, Betti found renewed strength and inspiration in his faith; his last dramas are a testimony to God's existence. At the age of sixty-one, Betti was suddenly stricken with cancer of the throat, and about three months later he died in Rome, on June 9, 1953.

ANALYSIS

Ugo Betti's theater is relentlessly preoccupied with humanity's penchant for evil. With a mixture of anguish and clinical detachment, Betti observes the human condition from the vantage point of a judge's bench, reflecting on a bitter paradox: While seeking happiness, humankind acts to destroy it.

Following Luigi Pirandello's metapsychological lead, European theater had turned a decisive corner in its treatment of the motivation of character. Modern dramatists, while drawing on naturalistic psychology, emphasized the contradictory and irrational, forces at work in human experience, forces hardly comprehended by the Darwinistic, materialistic worldview of naturalism. The question Betti poses is quite clearly stated in his notes, which he painstakingly accumulated before each play, attempting to formulate the psychological nature of his characters. If human beings want to escape anguish and sorrow, why do they cultivate vices, why do they commit crimes? Why do people so often act against their own interests?

Betti pondered on this paradox and continued to test various explanations for it throughout his life, refining, as he progressed, a metaphor he had drawn in his early notes: People, he suggested, are incapable of attaching importance to their existence as long as they look on it as "an apple ready to fall," deprived of "dignity and duration," ugly because it is transient and "soon to rot." Many of Betti's characters reflect this secret bitterness at the nature of life.

As a man and as an artist, Betti set out early in his life on a long search for God, but was able to find him in his true essence only toward the end of his journey—as a God of mercy. All his plays revolve around a single message, proclaimed in an anguished voice: Human values need revising and must be rebuilt so that humankind can rise above its destiny and freely pursue the road to justice and redemption.

LA PADRONA

Betti's basic themes are present in embryo in *La padrona*, his first play, in which the vibrancy of life is embodied in Marina, while her stepdaughter Anna, afflicted by consumption, symbolizes death. In spite of the shabby existence that is all that he can offer Marina, Pietro hopes that the child she is carrying will cement their union. It is Anna who shatters her father's dreams of building a happy life with his young and seductive second wife, revealing to him that the unborn child is not his. Cynically destroying Pietro's dream, Anna takes revenge against the stepmother she hates for her exuberance, and pushes Pietro to the brink of killing Marina. Only Anna's sudden death prevents her father from committing the crime.

Written in 1926, and still relying heavily on the tenets of naturalism, *La padrona* depicts the bleakness of the dilapidated surroundings in which the characters move, as well their inner misery. As is true for the majority of Betti's plays, the plot of this drama is rather commonplace, merely a backdrop against which the playwright can observe and analyze motives of his characters.

What was to be innovative in Betti's theater is partly previewed by the author himself in the introduction to *La padrona*. His intention, Betti explains, is to force the reader to think of those things that dismay and horrify human beings most—above all, death—to determine how humankind can be worthy of carrying that "crown of thorns" which is its conscience.

Unlike her stepmother, who is bound by her sensuality, Anna, whose life is eluding her, seeks happiness in the simple beauty of each sweet sunny day, in the garden, in the hope that fortune will lead to her path human beings who can share her joys. Yet Anna dies young, having hardly begun to fulfill her plans for living. Her father, Pietro, too, is left with his unfulfilled dream of a lasting domestic joy, which had been so close at hand. He accepts what must be, for evil, as well as good, must have its reason. Pietro repeatedly says that he "would like to know . . . who orders us about, who keeps us bound." While Pietro thus voices Betti's concept of the limitations of human liberty, it is Marina who embodies humankind's propensity to self-destruction. Her unbridled sensuality binds her and ultimately destroys her.

To deal with the universal themes of his dramas, Betti's images are both lyric and harsh in tone. In *La padrona* there are ample illustrations. The antinomy of good and evil, for example, is expressed in the metaphors of the "leafy branches shining up there," and "in the roots suffering deep down in the earth." Betti also employed unnamed characters to universalize the action in his plays. In *La padrona*, "the lame," "the neighbor," and "the relative" are commentators in the manner of a Greek chorus. Betti's characters often bear foreign rather than Italian names: They belong to no country, yet they are from everywhere.

LANDSLIDE

In 1932, with *Landslide*, Betti established his place in the world of Italian letters. Widely acclaimed at home and abroad, this play was labeled by the author "a modern tragedy." Although there are no specific political references in this or in any other of Betti's plays, the author's implicit indictment of the Fascist regime can be deduced from the characters' crimes and vices. At the same time, the foreign names and the setting in a distant city point to the universality of the theme of justice.

The characters' confession and plea for mercy is exemplified by Parsc. He is a judge unable to pronounce a sentence. He commiserates with the townspeople, who pay with their sorrow every day of their lives for the crimes they have committed. Revealing Betti's own longing for leniency, *Landslide* is a plunge into the human soul, in the deepest recesses of which are hidden unfulfilled desires, grudges, emotions, love, and hatred.

A landslide has fallen during a rainy night at the North Yard of the city, causing the death of a number of workers, driving some of the townspeople close to madness. It is up to Judge Parsc to try the case and discover who is responsible for the disaster. Accusations are whirled all across town, for, all feeling guilty, the people all become accused and accusers. In this "landslide of accusations," even the dead return to call for justice and to confess their lifelong sins, particularly those haunting them most. The Kurzes,

father and son, confront each other, the younger denouncing parental harshness as the main cause for children's unhappiness. Kurz's father acknowledges the need for a loving dialogue rather than punishment as a means to educate his children.

A frenzied young girl, Nasca, blames herself for the landslide, as does the contractor Gaucker. Even Judge Parsc feels disqualified to pronounce a sentence, publicly confessing to his sins of lust and selfishness. Pressed by Goetz, who is the most persistent among the accusers, the judge in the end opts for mercy. To fulfill the townspeople's longing for justice, divine mercy is invoked; the play ends with the word *pietà* (mercy) uttered over and over by the judge and by all those present. Anchored on a simple plot, *Landslide* is one of many of Betti's plays dealing with the theme of justice. It is an indictment of society and humankind at large for its responsibility for all the sorrows of the world.

The play derives much of its power from its subtle shifts from realistic to symbolic action. The chorus of voices rising in unison to plead for mercy introduces elements of poetic mystery and surprise. A gunshot and the blaring of a factory siren resound as echoes of doom for people's sins and for the atonement of universal guilt. The evanescent atmosphere pervading the play and its haunting quality of guilt make *Landslide* a unique masterpiece of eschatological scope.

CORRUPTION IN THE PALACE OF JUSTICE

Corruption in the Palace of Justice has been hailed as the best of Betti's great dramas. It is in fact in this play's dynamically constructed plot and for its detective-story quality that Betti best succeeds in synthesizing his stern indictment of the inadequacy of human justice, because of the failure of those who are entrusted with the administration of it.

A dubious type, Ludvi-Pol has been assassinated in one of the chambers of the courthouse, where he was called to act as a witness in a trial. Another crime takes place in the city at about the same time: A woman is killed in a fire set to destroy some documents, the location of which is known only to the judges. An inquest is conducted on request of the alarmed population of the town. A high-placed inspector, Erzi, is chosen to investigate the crimes. The judges in the courthouse are in great turmoil, as they all fear being accused of corruption through the investigation. They all become one another's prosecutors, but suspicion falls heavily on old, disease-ridden Judge Vanan through the diabolical machinations of Judge Cust.

Cust is almost outwitted by Judge Croz, who is easily his match, and who, like Cust, covets the presidency of the courthouse currently held by Vanan. Pretending to be the victim of a seizure and on the brink of death, Croz extracts a confession from Cust. When he is about to denounce Cust, Croz actually succumbs to sudden death. The only obstacle to Cust's achievement of his goal is Vanan's young daughter Elena, whom Cust must convince that her father has committed the crimes being investigated. Cust succeeds in placing seeds of doubt in Elena's heart by forcing Vanan to draw up an ambiguous memorandum. Unable to accept her beloved father's dishonor, Elena commits suicide by throwing herself down the elevator shaft.

Cust's deceit and his unrivaled corruption earn for him the presidency. His elevation to the coveted position would be unhindered, were it not for his conscience, which in the end suddenly stands between him and his victory. Incapable of bearing the burden of innocent Elena's tragic death, he is haunted by the echo of her screams as she was falling into the shaft. Suddenly it is this new obsession that prompts him to climb the staircase leading up to the High Revisor in the middle of the night. The blare of a trumpet in the distance accompanies him on his climb to unburden his guilt from his conscience.

Written in 1944 at the height of World War II, *Corruption in the Palace of Justice* is a vehement condemnation of corrupt society, but particularly of those who are entrusted with the sacred task of administering justice and who betray that trust. Elena's innocence, in contrast, counterbalances the judges' heinous crimes. Her presence in the drama is at times announced by the blare of the faraway bugle sound; Betti juxtaposes this harmony to the violent images of putrefaction and death that pollute the halls of justice. In the end, the most corrupt of men is urged by the call of innocence to recapture paradise lost.

THE GAMBLER

The Gambler of 1951 begins the final cycle of Betti's dramas, in which transcendence is the central theme. Innocence and guilt, so obsessively explored in previous dramas, are now seen from the perspective of the author's renewed Catholic faith. Emanating from God, grace lends these last works an almost religious resolution.

When Ennio, the gambler, is charged with the death of his wife, Iva, during the turmoil of the war, he pleads that he is innocent, but only of the physical crime, confessing his moral guilt for having wished for Iva's death. Absolved by human justice, Ennio, who has played a game with death, recognizes the need for Divine forgiveness. He hopes by the grace of God to be reconciled with Iva, who does in fact come back: They will be reunited for all eternity.

The Gambler, like all the plays in Betti's last phase, has been likened to a mystery play. The Functionary in *The Gambler*; the *Tizi*, or Some People, in *Acque turbate* (troubled waters); and the final chorus in *The Fugitive* play the role of commentators, while the Doctor of *Acque turbate* is a prototypical antagonist, a symbolic devil who wants Daniele to give up his struggle to gain eternal salvation.

ACQUE TURBATE

Acque turbate (alternately titled *O, Il fratello protegge e ama*; the brother protects and loves) is a drama of overwhelming universal dimensions, offering perhaps the fullest expression of Betti's credo, both as a man and as a playwright. Although good and evil coexist in the world inhabited by human beings, Betti points to the certainty of a final catharsis, at a higher level of transcendental redemption. The drama symbolizes the liberation sought in death by people—to rid themselves of the heavy burdens weighing on their conscience.

Giacomo examines his conscience as he is in the process of committing suicide, after having admitted his guilt to his friend. Gabriele had accused Giacomo of protecting his own sister Alda from a life of vice, during and after the war, because of his evil passion for her. While falling from a high rock into death's abyss, Giacomo tries to understand how such a despicable passion could have taken hold of his inner being so silently, without his knowing it.

The answer is given by the choral voice of the *Tizi*, who, embodying a universal conscience, tell Giacomo to take heart and to have faith, as everything will be explained. There is love and understanding in the Godhead, the need for whom all people feel within, where they can also know him. The ultimate message of *Acque turbate* is that, since human beings are intelligent and loving, they must emanate from a Creator who is intelligent and loving. Humanity represents God on earth as the fish represents the sea, and humanity can hope for salvation, for the choice between good and evil is within its grasp. Disorder and disharmony are brought about by humanity's failure to represent God in the world and by its yielding to the insinuation of evil.

Focusing on the torments that sin inflicts on the human soul, Betti judges humankind severely, as a professional judge should. Yet, interspersed with his stern judgments and rising above them are the poet's lyric accents of divine love and mercy. Although it is true that Betti pronounces severe sentences on all human vices and sins, his most anguished judgment is directed at the misuse of justice by those in whose trust it has been placed.

Dealing with such violent crimes as homicide, matricide, uxoricide, and fratricide, as well as with adultery, the lust of the flesh, the thirst for power and riches, theft, fraud, and gross parental neglect and misunderstanding of children, Betti the judge and playwright shows, in dramatic terms, humankind as it breaks all God's commandments. Yet even as it sins, humanity is listening to the divine voice within it.

Humankind's compulsion to sin is matched by its compelling need to return to the Godhead.

In a letter Betti wrote in the summer of 1947 to Emilio Barbetti, one of his most appreciative critics, the playwright stated that all his writings had been "various terms of a slow proof of the existence of God," and he added that seeking God is the same as finding him. No matter how dismaying their sins and vices, all Betti's heroes are "seekers after God." Betti himself continued his relentless search for God's love and mercy to the last.

OTHER MAJOR WORKS

LONG FICTION: *La pietra alta*, 1948.

SHORT FICTION: *Caino*, 1928; *Le case*, 1933; *Una strana serata*, 1948.

POETRY: *Il re pensieroso*, 1922; *Canzonette: La morte*, 1932; *Uomo e donna*, 1937; *Ultime liriche*, 1957.

TRANSLATION: *Le nozze di Teti e Peleo*, 1912 (of Catullus's poem 64).

BIBLIOGRAPHY

Arnett, Lloyd A. "Tragedy in a Postmodern Vein: Ugo Betti Our Contemporary?" *Modern Drama* 33, no. 4 (December, 1990): 543. Provides an analysis of the postmodern aesthetic in *Corruption in the Palace of Justice* and *Crime on Goat Island*.

Licastro, Emanuele. *Ugo Betti: An Introduction.* Jefferson, N.C.: McFarland, 1985. A biography of Betti that provides criticism of his major works. Bibliography and index.

Carolina Donadio Lawson

ROBERT MONTGOMERY BIRD

Born: New Castle, Delaware; February 5, 1806
Died: Philadelphia, Pennsylvania; January 23, 1854

PRINCIPAL DRAMA

The Cowled Lover, wr. 1827, pb. 1941
Caridorf: Or, The Avenger, wr. 1827, pb. 1941

'Twas All for the Best, wr. 1827, pb. 1941

The City Looking Glass: A Philadelphia Comedy, wr. 1829, pr., pb. 1933

Pelopidas: Or, The Fall of Polemarchs, wr. 1830, pb. 1919

The Gladiator, pr. 1831, pb. 1919

Oralloossa: Son of the Incas, pr. 1832, pb. 1919

The Broker of Bogotá, pr. 1834, pb. 1917

The Life and Dramatic Works, pb. 1919 (includes *Pelopidas, The Gladiator*, and *Oralloossa*)

News of the Night: Or, A Trip to Niagara, pr. 1929, pb. 1941

The Cowled Lover and Other Plays, pb. 1941 (includes *Caridorf, 'Twas All for the Best*, and *News of the Night*)

OTHER LITERARY FORMS

Robert Montgomery Bird is better known as a novelist than as a dramatist. In his dramas, Bird was clearly moving toward the subject matter that would form the basis for his two earliest novels, *Calavar: Or, The Knight of the Conquest* (1834) and *The Infidel: Or, The Fall of Mexico* (1835)—romances dealing with Mexican Indians. Yet Bird is better remembered for his novels set in indigenous North American settings—*The Hawks of Hawk-Hollow: A Tradition of Pennsylvania* (1835) and *Nick of the Woods: Or, The Jibbenainosay, a Tale of Kentucky* (1837)—than he is for his Mexican romances. In addition, Bird published a volume of short fiction, *Peter Pilgrim: Or, A Rambler's Recollections* (1838), and several works of nonfiction, including *Sketch of the Life, Public Services, and Character of Major Thomas Stockton of New-Castle, the Candidate for the Whig Party for the Office of Governor of Delaware* (1844) and *A Brief Review of the Career, Character, and Campaigns of Zachary Taylor* (1848).

ACHIEVEMENTS

How one ranks the achievement of Robert Montgomery Bird depends on the backdrop against which he is viewed. Compared with American dramatists since Eugene O'Neill, Bird must be viewed as a less than successful artist whose plays were somewhat contrived and stereotyped. Viewed against a different backdrop, that of the dramatists of the first half of the nineteenth century, Bird figures as one of the two or three most promising figures in the American drama of his time. It must be remembered that American theater audiences were unsophisticated and, at times, uncouth during this period. Bird himself called them "foolish and vulgar," and he was probably not much off the mark. Refined and cultivated Americans did not go to the theater. British audiences were not much better than those in the United States, and audiences in both countries preferred to attend performances of Shakespeare's plays rather than performances of contemporary drama. Bird knew his audiences, and if he ever forgot their salient characteristics, Edwin Forrest, the great actor of the day, was always nearby to remind him, as Forrest's notations in surviving manuscripts of Bird's dramas attest.

Robert Montgomery Bird (courtesy of New York Public Library)

Certainly, Bird's earliest plays are dramatically substandard. Some of them have never been performed, and a few had their first performances only after Arthur Hobson Quinn drew scholarly attention to Bird, in his 1916 article in *The Nation*, "Dramatic Works of Robert Montgomery Bird," and in his compendious *A History of American Drama from the Beginning to the Civil War* (1923). It must be borne in mind, however, that Bird was only twenty-one or twenty-two years old when he wrote his earliest plays and that he was then a student in medical school, which surely distracted him substantially from his literary pursuits.

Bird began to come into his own as an American dramatist in 1830 when Forrest awarded *Pelopidas*, a work surging with Romantic spirit, the prize in the annual dramatic contest sponsored by the actor. Although *Pelopidas* was never produced during Bird's lifetime, Forrest continued to hold ownership of the play. The next year, Forrest awarded the dramatic prize to Bird's *The Gladiator*, which turned out to be Bird's most popular play with audiences and which certainly vies with *The Broker of Bogotá* as his best drama. Forrest took *The Gladiator* to London in 1836, where it was received less enthusiastically than was Forrest himself as Spartacus. Nevertheless, it is significant that this was the first American drama to be transported to England. The play was performed at the Theatre Royal in Drury Lane in a run that began on October 17, and despite the less than warm reception it received, its author was elected to honorary membership in the English Dramatic Authors' Society within a fortnight of its opening. Two more of Bird's plays won Forrest's drama prizes. *Oralloossa*, one of Bird's Latin American plays, won the prize in 1832, and the following year *The Broker of Bogotá*, also set in Latin America, received the coveted award.

Bird had great literary ambitions. By the time he was twenty-two, he had a clearly laid plan for his career as a writer. He intended initially to establish himself as a dramatist and had already sketched the plans for fifty-five plays he hoped to write. Once established as a dramatist, he planned to write a series of romances, and finally he anticipated devoting the talents of his later years to the writing of history.

It is impossible to say whether Bird might have followed his plan had he not had a severe falling out with Forrest in 1837, confirming for him his earlier contention that one cannot fill one's purse with the proceeds that the writer receives from drama. Forrest was growing rich on Bird's plays, and Bird received little more than the prize money (one thousand dollars in each instance). No copyright laws, as we know them today, existed in Bird's time to protect playwrights from the sort of exploitation that Bird was experiencing.

Bird turned his efforts to writing romances, the first two of which, *Calavar* and *The Infidel*, were set in Mexico and were well received. In 1835, Benjamin H. Brewster turned *The Infidel* into a play. Bird's novels *The Hawks of Hawk-Hollow* and *Nick of the Woods*, however, had the kind of indigenous North American setting for which Americans longed and for which many American intellectuals were calling in their writings—Washington Irving in his "English Writers on America" (1820), William Cullen Bryant in his *Lectures on Poetry* (1884), William Ellery Channing in his "On National Literature" (1830), Henry Wadsworth Longfellow in his "The Defence of Poetry" (1832), and, most notably, Ralph Waldo Emerson in his Phi Beta Kappa address, "The American Scholar" (1837). These two novels established Bird as an outstanding writer capable of dealing seriously and successfully with indigenous American themes. *The Hawks of Hawk-Hollow* described the life of a Tory family in Pennsylvania a year after the Battle of Yorktown. *Nick of the Woods* told the tale of Nathan Slaughter, an Indian-hating Quaker living in Kentucky, who, because of his Quaker pacifism, refused to join his Kentucky neighbors in 1782 in taking up arms against the Indians. Given the temper of Bird's times, one would have to consider his ability to produce such writing as his outstanding literary achievement.

In the fifteen years between the publication of his last novel, *The Adventures of Robin Day* (1839), and his death, Bird, afflicted by recurrent ill health, wrote only two more significant works of any length: his sketch of Major Thomas Stockton in 1844 and *A Brief Review of the Career, Character, and Cam-*

paigns of Zachary Taylor in 1848. He also revised his dramas, hoping that he might publish them. However, Forrest would not relinquish his ownership of the works so Bird was unable to follow through on this idea.

Toward the end of his life, Bird joined forces with George H. Boker, renowned for his drama *Francesca da Rimini* (pr. 1855, pb. 1856), to agitate for a copyright law that would protect writers. It was not until two years after Bird's death, however, that the Copyright Act of 1856 was finally passed. Certainly its passage must be numbered among Bird's notable achievements, because the passage of this act made careers in writing more attractive to Americans than they had previously been.

BIOGRAPHY

Robert Montgomery Bird's father died in 1810, when Robert was only four years old. Because the elder Bird was bankrupt at the time of his death, his young son went to live in the home of his kindly uncle, Nicholas Van Dyke, who had been a member of the Council for Safety in 1776, a framer of the constitution of the state of Delaware, and president of the state of Delaware from 1783 until 1786. Bird remained in his uncle's house for ten years. The young boy led a relatively happy life with his uncle and with his uncle's family, although he was not overly happy in school and was subjected to frequent beatings. When his uncle discovered this, he withdrew Robert from the New Castle Academy, which the boy had been attending. Bird had a passion for books and for reading, and he drew heavily on the resources of the New Castle Library Company during these early years of his life. He became interested in music and in writing during this period, and by the time he moved to Philadelphia in 1820 to live with his mother and to attend a school run by Mr. Pardon Davis, he had written considerable verse. In Philadelphia, he became interested in drawing, an avocation that he continued to pursue in his later years.

Bird returned to New Castle in 1821 and enrolled in the same New Castle Academy from which his uncle had earlier withdrawn him. While there, he wrote some of his earliest descriptive pieces. He remained

at New Castle Academy until 1823, when he entered Germantown Academy to pursue courses preparatory to his entering the University of Pennsylvania as a medical student. In the summer between leaving Germantown Academy and entering the university, Bird studied medicine, as was the custom in his day, with a practicing physician, Dr. Joseph Parrish.

Bird attended the university from 1824 until 1827, receiving an M.D. degree on completion of his studies. By that time, he had published a great deal of poetry in *Philadelphia Monthly Magazine* and had begun to write plays, although they all remained fragmentary at that point. He had also laid specific plans for his literary career and had begun reading widely in classical literature, in Shakespearean and Jacobean drama, and in Latin American history, archaeology, and literature as a means of implementing his literary plans.

Life as a physician did not appeal to Bird, although in 1827 he established himself as a doctor in Philadelphia and had a substantial number of patients. After a year in medical practice, during which time he completed a comedy, *'Twas All for the Best*, and two tragedies, *The Cowled Lover* and *Caridorf*, he left the medical profession to support himself by writing.

In 1828, Bird began work on three more plays, "King Philip," "The Three Dukes," and "Giannone." He also began work on his long poem, "The Cave," and on a novel, "The Volunteers." Although none of these works was ever produced or published, within a short time Bird had also finished *The City Looking Glass*, a comedy that would finally be staged in 1933, some hundred years after it was written.

Bird was working so unrelentingly that his health began to be adversely affected, and in 1829, he sought diversion in painting as a means of regaining his health. At the end of that summer, he began a long journey to what was then considered frontier territory, Pittsburgh and Cincinnati. He spent the winter in Cincinnati with John Grimes, an artist, and his circle. During that trip, Bird visited Kentucky and imbibed some of the local color that later was to appear in his most successful novel, *Nick of the Woods*.

On returning to Philadelphia in 1830, Bird learned that Forrest was again offering an annual prize, which he had instituted in 1828, for the best play written by an American author. The prize was one thousand dollars, and Forrest, who was to act in the prize play, was to own the property in return for awarding the prize. Bird entered the contest with *Pelopidas*, a classical tragedy set in Thebes, and this play won the prize quite handily. Forrest ultimately decided against producing the play, because it did not have the sort of clearly defined central character that he required in any play that was to be a vehicle for his talent. This being the case, Bird wrote for him another play, *The Gladiator*, which was declared a prize play but for which Forrest did not give the author another one thousand dollars in prize money, reasoning that this play was a substitute for *Pelopidas*.

The Gladiator provided Forrest with the perfect role, that of Spartacus, and the play opened to enormous acclaim in New York on September 26, 1831. It soon had played in both Boston and Philadelphia, and it always played to full houses and enthusiastic audiences. By the time Bird died in 1854, *The Gladiator* had been presented more than one thousand times, and its success was to continue until the turn of the century. Forrest grew rich from the proceeds, none of which he shared with the author.

Forrest and Bird were born in the same year, and they became not only close professional associates but also close friends. Bird was to win two more of Forrest's prizes, one for *Oralloossa* in 1832 and one for *The Broker of Bogotá* in 1834. In all, Forrest awarded nine prizes for American plays, and Bird took four of them, although he was paid for only three.

In 1833, Bird and Forrest traveled together for some months. They had planned to go to Mexico but turned back at New Orleans because of a cholera epidemic. Bird went on to Nashville, Tennessee, where he had a reunion with John Grimes, with whom he went to Mammoth Cave, which the two explored fully. As a result of this exploration, Bird returned to his work on the long poem "The Cave," which had occupied him earlier. He began work on *The Broker of Bogotá*, his last drama, which he completed the next year.

By that time, Bird had concluded that he could not support himself as a playwright, and he decided to devote his time to writing romances. His explanation was that "novels are much easier sorts of things and immortalize one's pocket much sooner. A tragedy takes, or should take, as much labor as two romances; and one comedy as much as six tragedies."

Drawing on the extensive reading he had done about Latin America, Bird wrote *Calavar* in 1834, following it the next year with *The Infidel*. These novels were meticulously researched and found a ready audience, but Bird was to find his real métier in *The Hawks of Hawk-Hollow*, published in the same year as *The Infidel*, and in *Nick of the Woods*, published in 1837.

Bird set *The Hawks of Hawk-Hollow* in the area around the Delaware Water Gap on the Pennsylvania-New Jersey border, a region with which he had a particular affinity. A second edition of the novel was released in the first year of the book's publication, and that was followed by three English editions of the work by 1842. Because international copyright laws did not exist at that time, Bird did not profit financially from the English editions.

Nick of the Woods was published in 1837, the year of Bird's marriage to Mary Mayer, and was a resounding success. By 1839, the novel had been dramatized by J. T. Haines, and two other dramatizations of it were to follow, one in 1856 and another in 1940. *Nick of the Woods* was also translated into several foreign languages.

In 1837, largely at his wife's urging, Bird tried to convince Forrest to pay him some six thousand dollars that Bird believed was rightfully his. Forrest argued bitterly with Bird over this debt and stormed out of Bird's house, claiming to have complete ownership of Bird's major dramas—a claim that Forrest exercised through Bird's remaining years. Bird was never to write another play, although he revised his dramas in 1843, planning to publish them. That hope, however, was thwarted by Forrest's claim to exclusive rights to the plays.

Afflicted by a complete nervous collapse in 1840, Bird turned to farming on acreage he had bought two years earlier near Elkton, Maryland. He underwent substantial losses of his crops because of violent weather, but his health improved greatly during this interlude of intense physical activity as a farmer. In 1841, Bird was well enough to return to Philadelphia, where he had been appointed a professor at Pennsylvania Medical College, a post in which he served with high distinction until 1843, when the medical college disbanded.

Meanwhile, Bird had become active in politics. He attended the Whig Convention in Delaware as a delegate in 1842 and felt reasonably sure that he would be nominated as a representative to the United States Congress. This plan went awry when George Brydges Rodney, the incumbent, who had intended not to run for reelection, changed his mind, leaving no place for Bird on the Whig ticket. Nevertheless, Bird received a minor political appointment in 1846 when he was named to be a director of the New Castle Branch of the Farmers' National Bank. The following year, Bird was nominated for the positions of assistant director and librarian of the Smithsonian Institution but was not appointed. Using thirty thousand dollars borrowed from his close friend Senator John M. Clayton, Bird bought a one-third interest in Philadelphia's *North American*, a newspaper that thrived under Bird's editorship, although the paper's success was marred by the mismanagement of his partners. Bird gave his full energies to his newspaper work and was considered an excellent literary editor.

During the presidential campaign of 1848, Bird was a vigorous supporter of Zachary Taylor, whose biography he wrote specifically to aid the candidate in his campaign. Bird hoped for some sort of government appointment, but despite a meeting with President Taylor in 1849, Bird was not appointed to office. He spent his final years working hard on the *North American* to the detriment of his own health, as well as working with Boker to help bring about copyright laws that would protect authors from the sort of exploitation that he, Bird, had suffered at the hands of Forrest and of English publishers who had pirated his work.

Bird was in ill health during the latter months of 1853. His condition worsened in the first days of 1854, and on January 23, he died of a cerebral hemorrhage at his country residence, Kittatiny House, in Delaware Water Gap. His wife and fifteen-year-old son, Frederick Mayer Bird, survived him.

ANALYSIS

Robert Montgomery Bird's earliest plays were essentially derivative, at times suggestive of the closet drama of the Elizabethan Revival, at times recalling Ben Jonson's plays or the Restoration drama of William Congreve, with whose work Bird was well acquainted. Most of the plays of this early period are set in such romantic locations as Spain ("The Three Dukes"), Italy ("Giannone"), or other foreign places. They depend heavily on highly intricate plots in which the key characters are amply disguised; mistaken identity is central to the resolution of the plot, and coincidence is a *sine qua non* of the plays' rising action and denouement. Like many of the Restoration dramatists, Bird selected names that were either ironic—for example, "Nathan Slaughter" for a Quaker who refused to fight in *Nick of the Woods*—or descriptive—Sluggardly, the innkeeper; Ha'penny, the debtor; and Agony, the miserly uncle. These plays are no worse than much of the Restoration drama that sometimes served as Bird's model, but they can hardly be called good.

Although he cannot be classified among the greatest authors the United States has produced, Bird was a highly gifted, ambitious literary figure who had a clear sense of what he hoped to accomplish artistically. His writings brought him considerable celebrity in his own time and have won for him an enduring place in America's literary history.

'TWAS ALL FOR THE BEST

'Twas All for the Best is a complicated comedy of manners set in England. The language is stilted to the point of being painful to the modern reader. The plot revolves around Sir Noel Nozlebody, who steals his brother's daughter, rears her as his own child, and declares his own daughter to be a foundling. This play contains some scenes that are essentially tragic and that seem to have no place in a play that purports to be a comedy. In *'Twas All for the Best*, Bird was not yet in control of his medium.

NEWS OF THE NIGHT

Similarly complicated in plot is another Bird farce of the same general period, *News of the Night*, which is set in Philadelphia but follows a classical Roman story line with strong overtones of the comic spirit of Jonson. This play, with its stereotypical props of old chests, rope ladders, and women dressed as men, was first produced by the Columbia University Laboratory Players in New York on November 2, 1929.

THE CITY LOOKING GLASS

The City Looking Glass, first published in an edition by Arthur Hobson Quinn in 1933, was subtitled *A Philadelphia Comedy*. It is ostensibly about the seamy side of life in Philadelphia, but there seems to be little that is American about it. Again, the plot is reminiscent of Jonson and involves two lowlife creatures, Ravin and Ringfinger, who pursue two commonplace young ladies, only to discover that one of these girls, Emma, is really the daughter of a highly respected and wealthy Virginia gentleman. Act 4 provides small glimpses into Southern life and into the views of the times, but except for that act, the play has little relationship to anything authentically American. This drama was first performed by the Zelosophic Society of the University of Pennsylvania on January 20, 1933.

UNFINISHED WORKS

"The Fanatick," based on Charles Brockden Brown's gothic novel *Wieland* (1798), was planned but was never completed. "The Three Dukes" and "Giannone" also exist only in fragments that are a part of the Robert Montgomery Bird Collection at the University of Pennsylvania; "Giannone" is the most promising of these fragmentary plays. It is interesting to note that in these works, members of the nobility speak in blank verse while the other characters speak in prose.

Bird all but completed two tragedies, *The Cowled Lover* and *Caridorf*. *The Cowled Lover* is modeled after William Shakespeare's *Romeo and Juliet* (pr. c. 1595-1596). The ardent Raymond disguises himself as a monk in order to be near his beloved, Rosalia. Ultimately, he and Rosalia are killed by the young woman's father. The play is highly Romantic and shows the strong gothic influence of some of the authors Bird was reading at the time—Percy Bysshe Shelley and George Gordon, Lord Byron, for example. *Caridorf* suffers from having a quite unconvinc-

ing hero, a man who refuses to come to the bedside of his dying father and who first seduces Genevra, then upbraids her for having lost her chastity. The audience is asked to overlook these inhumane acts and see through to Caridorf's essential goodness, a demand that strains credulity.

PELOPIDAS

With *Pelopidas*, Bird showed signs of maturing into a significant playwright. Gone are the stereotypical plots of his earlier plays; gone are the heavy-handed props of a play such as *News of the Night*. *Pelopidas* has a typical Romantic setting, that of Thebes after the Spartans had conquered and grasped political power in the city. The tale of Pelopidas is told in Plutarch's *Bioi paralleloi* (c. 105-115 C.E.; *Parallel Lives*, 1579), which is the basic source for Bird's play. Bird, however, showing excellent critical judgment, distorted the Plutarchan version to suit his own artistic needs.

Pelopidas was a great hero of Thebes, and, with the conquest of the city by Sparta, he was forced into exile. His wife remained behind in the city, which was now controlled by four polemarchs. In Plutarch's account, these polemarchs were native Thebans who were appointed to their dictatorial positions by the conquerors. Bird, however, made two of the polemarchs, Philip and Archias, Spartan, thereby setting up an interesting contrast between them and the two Theban polemarchs, Leontidas and Philidas. Bird also established contrasts within the two pairs. Philip is the typical Spartan, businesslike, aggressive, suspicious; Archias is trusting, fun-loving, somewhat lazy. Of the two Thebans, Leontidas is a libertine whose actions really trigger the action of the plot; Philidas is a more complex character, a seeming traitor to his city who is in truth working with his fellow Thebans to unseat the Spartans.

Pelopidas leaves his exile and sneaks back into Thebes, drawn irresistibly to the city because word has reached him that Leontidas is trying to seduce his wife, Sibylla. On his return, it becomes known that Philidas, the seeming turncoat, is planning a feast with the Spartans and that he is plotting their destruction. During the very tense banquet scene, the Spartans come close to learning what is about to happen.

Bird manages to keep the suspense high until Pelopidas arrives and sees that the Spartans are dispatched. Pelopidas returns to the prison-room of his house just in time to save his wife and son from being murdered by the evil Leontidas, whom he kills.

Pelopidas is well drawn. He is a brave, rash idealist. When he first returns to Thebes, he brashly tries to rescue his wife and is captured by the enemy, only to escape and, chastened, make his more calculated and successful attempt at the rescue.

Forrest appreciated the dramaticality of *Pelopidas*, but he never allowed the play to be performed, because the role of Philidas tended to overshadow the leading role, in which Forrest would have been cast. When William E. Burton, manager of Philadelphia's National Theater, wanted to produce *Pelopidas* in 1840, Bird demurred, despite the generosity of Burton's terms, because he did not wish to enter into a disagreeable fray with Forrest, who claimed ownership of the property.

THE GLADIATOR

Had the Copyright Act of 1856 been passed twenty-five years earlier, *The Gladiator* would have made Bird an exceptionally wealthy man. As it turned out, Forrest reaped the full benefit of this play's success, while Bird received nothing for it. The story of Spartacus was well known in the early nineteenth century, and Bird adapted this popular tale to serve his purposes in *The Gladiator*. Spartacus is a Thracian, recently captured by the Romans. His fame as a fighter has preceded him to Rome, where Phasarius, one of Rome's most renowned gladiators, is plotting with the other gladiators to overthrow the city while its generals and soldiers are away. Phasarius, however, delays the planned overthrow because he wants the challenge of fighting Spartacus. Spartacus agrees to the combat because by doing so he can win the freedom of his wife and child, who have been enslaved.

The combat is arranged, and the gladiators enter the ring, but on seeing each other, they realize that they are brothers. They lay down their arms, reunite, and organize the gladiators into an army that is soon on the brink of conquering Rome. At this point, Phasarius wants to destroy Rome utterly, whereas Spartacus wishes only to take his family and return to Thrace. Phasarius, like Leontidas in *Pelopidas*, wants to seduce Julia, the daughter of a high Roman official and a captive of the gladiatorial forces. Spartacus intervenes and saves Julia. The gladiators are divided between loyalty to Phasarius and loyalty to Spartacus, and thus the Romans are able to defeat them. When Spartacus's wife and child are killed, largely through Phasarius's duplicity, Spartacus loses his will to live. Although offered a pardon from the Romans, who are grateful for his protection of Julia, Spartacus chooses to die with his sword in his hand.

Like *Pelopidas*, *The Gladiator* is concerned centrally with the human quest for liberty. Led by Spartacus as the strong, central hero, the gladiators are glorified for rebelling against their oppressors. Like many Americans of his day, Bird could appreciate the impulse toward freedom in the classical characters he idealized in this play, while at the same time supporting slavery in his own country and refusing to buy property in Philadelphia, opting instead for the eastern shore of Maryland, because he feared that Pennsylvania would soon enfranchise black people.

ORALLOOSSA

Plays about Indians were popular in America during the 1830's and 1840's. The idea of the noble savage was in the air, and Forrest had already been playing John Augustus Stone's *Metamora* (pr. 1829), which focused on these topics, for two years when he first met Bird. Indeed, in 1836, Forrest gave Bird *Metamora* to revise. Although no copy of Bird's revision is extant, it is generally thought that he in essence wrote an entirely new play, the only copy of which he delivered to Forrest. *Oralloossa* was awarded another of Forrest's drama prizes and was a resounding success when it was first performed. Forrest did not perform the play often after its initial run, partly because it was an expensive play to stage and partly because he was more at home in the role of Spartacus in *The Gladiator*.

Oralloossa bears certain surface resemblances to *Pelopidas*. In it, the Peruvian Incas are pitted against Pizarro's invading forces. Pizarro and his young compatriot Almagro are roughly comparable to Philip and Archias in *Pelopidas*, while the two Incas, Oralloossa and Manco, are roughly comparable to Philidas and Leontidas. Oralloossa serves both Pizarro and Almagro simultaneously, but he is planning the downfall of each. As in *Pelopidas*, the crucial scene is a banquet at which Pizarro's forces are to dispatch Almagro. Oralloossa, however, who has put Pizarro up to this, has also arranged that Almagro will first kill Pizarro. Only the latter event comes to pass, and Almagro, who loves Oralloossa's sister, Ooallie, survives.

Oralloossa and Ooallie are both imprisoned by the Spanish because Manco has betrayed them, but Oralloossa escapes. So infuriated is Oralloossa at his fellow Inca, Manco, that he forsakes his kinsmen and tells the new Spanish viceroy, De Castro, where Manco and Almagro are hiding. Meanwhile, Oralloossa's sister Ooallie is buried alive and dies because the priest who is supposed to save her from this fate never arrives. Oralloossa kills Almagro and then dies himself, leaving the Christian Spanish firmly in charge of the pagan Incas.

The play presents some extremely intense moments, but the climax comes so early in the action that the last act seems unbearably anticlimactic. *Oralloossa* might better have been a three-act play, ending shortly after Pizarro's murder, but three-act plays were not in vogue at the time.

THE BROKER OF BOGOTÁ

The Broker of Bogotá, Bird's last play, is better crafted than *Oralloossa*; many regard it as his finest play. It is set in Bogotá, in the Spanish territory of New Grenada, which comprised present-day Colombia, Ecuador, Panama, and Venezuela. The play's protagonist is Febro, a bourgeois moneylender who has two sons of opposite temperaments. Ramon is unbridled and unruly, although he shows regret at times when his demeanor causes his father pain. He is counterbalanced by a much more dutiful brother, Francisco, who is a comfort to his father. A daughter, Leonor, is in love with the viceroy's son, Fernando. In a plot that runs rather like that of an Italian opera, Ramon falls in love with Juana, but Juana's father will not permit Ramon, who has been disowned by his own father, to pay court to his daughter.

At this point, the villain enters in the person of the nobleman Cabarero. Having just found the key to

Ramon's father's safe, he convinces Ramon to steal a substantial sum of money that the viceroy has left with Febro for safekeeping. Coincidentally, right at this point, Febro is considering a reconciliation with his errant son, but Ramon is unaware of this. To complicate matters further, Febro is accused of the theft and is brought before the viceroy. Febro has no defense unless Ramon is willing to admit to his own guilt, and he does not have the strength of character to do this. Just at this point, the distraught Febro is told that his daughter has eloped with a suitor.

All might have ended happily because, through Juana, it is revealed that Ramon, not Febro, is the thief, and at the same time it is revealed that the lover with whom Leonor has eloped is the viceroy's son. In the tradition of Elizabethan tragedy, however, Bird cannot allow this to happen: Ramon commits suicide, and Febro dies.

The Broker of Bogotá is contrived, as were most of the plays of its period. Nevertheless, the play has a great deal to recommend it. The trial scene has much of the dramatic tension of a modern television mystery; Febro's fatherly efforts to defend Ramon when his guilt becomes known are well presented. Here, Bird's characters are multidimensional, in contrast with the relatively stereotyped figures of his earlier works. Finally, the basic conflict between the father and son, out of which the central action of the play develops, is convincing and tenable.

OTHER MAJOR WORKS

LONG FICTION: *Calavar: Or, The Knight of the Conquest*, 1834; *The Infidel: Or, The Fall of Mexico*, 1835; *The Hawks of Hawk-Hollow: A Tradition of Pennsylvania*, 1835; *Sheppard Lee*, 1836; *Nick of the Woods: Or, The Jibbenainosay, a Tale of Kentucky*, 1837; *The Adventures of Robin Day*, 1839.

SHORT FICTION: *Peter Pilgrim: Or, A Rambler's Recollections*, 1838.

NONFICTION: *Sketch of the Life, Public Services, and Character of Major Thomas Stockton of New-Castle, the Candidate for the Whig Party for the Office of Governor of Delaware*, 1844; *A Brief Review of the Career, Character, and Campaigns of Zachary Taylor*, 1848.

BIBLIOGRAPHY

Dahl, Curtis. *Robert Montgomery Bird*. New York: Twayne, 1963. Believing that earlier assessments of Bird's literary works have been too laudatory, Dahl examines Bird because of his historical significance, placing his work in the context of the literature of his time. Chronology, annotated bibliography, and index.

Foust, Clement E. *The Life and Dramatic Works of Robert Montgomery Bird*. 1919. Reprint. New York: B. Franklin, 1971. In this standard biography of Bird, Foust quickly recounts Bird's early life before discussing his major plays and subsequent association with Edwin Forrest. The majority of the book discusses Bird's life and works after the dispute with Forrest that drove him away from the theater. Genealogy, bibliography, and the complete texts of four major plays.

Hoppenstand, Gary. "Justified Bloodshed: Robert Montgomery Bird's *Nick of the Woods* and the Origins of the Vigilante Hero in American Literature and Culture." *Journal of American Culture* 15, no.2 (Summer, 1992): 51. An analysis of Bird's novel that provides insight into the author's other works.

Richards, Jeffrey H. *Early American Drama*. New York: Penguin Books, 1997. Richards presents and discusses eight pre-Civil War plays, including Bird's *The Gladiator*.

Samuels, Shirley. *Romances of the Republic: Women, the Family, and Violence in the Literature of the Early American Nation*. New York: Oxford University Press, 1996. An examination of early American literature that examines Bird's works as well as those of many others.

Wert, Justin R. "Robert Montgomery Bird." In *Nineteenth Century American Fiction Writers*, edited by Kent P. Ljungquist. Vol. 202 in *Dictionary of Literary Biography*. Detroit, Mich.: The Gale Group, 1999.

R. Baird Shuman,
updated by Gerald S. Argetsinger

BJØRNSTJERNE BJØRNSON

Born: Kvikne, Norway; December 8, 1832
Died: Paris, France; April 25, 1910

PRINCIPAL DRAMA

Mellem slagene, pr., pb. 1857 (*Between the Battles*, 1948)

Halte Hulda, pr., pb. 1858 (verse play)

Kong Sverre, pr., pb. 1861 (verse play)

Sigurd Slembe, pb. 1862, pr. 1863 (verse play; English translation, 1888)

Maria Stuart i Skotland, pb. 1864, pr. 1867 (*Mary, Queen of Scots*, 1912)

De nygifte, pr., pb. 1865 (*The Newlyweds*, 1885)

Sigurd Jorsalfar, pb. 1872

En fallit, pr., pb. 1875 (*The Bankrupt*, 1914)

Redaktøren, pr., pb. 1875 (*The Editor*, 1914)

Kongen, pb. 1877, pr. 1902 (*The King*, 1914)

Det ny system, pr. 1878, pb. 1879 (*The New System*, 1913)

Leonarda, pr., pb. 1879 (English translation, 1911)

En handske, pr., pb. 1883 (*A Gauntlet*, 1886)

Over ævne, første stykke, pb. 1883, pr. 1886 (*Pastor Sang*, 1893; also known as *Beyond Our Power*, 1913)

Geografi og kjærlighed, pr., pb. 1885 (*Geography and Love*, 1914)

Over ævne, annet stykke, pr., pb. 1895 (*Beyond Our Might*, 1914)

Paul Lange og Tora Parsberg, pb. 1898, pr. 1901 (*Paul Lange and Tora Parsberg*, 1899)

Laboremus, pr., pb. 1901 (English translation, 1901)

På Storhove, pr., pb. 1902

Daglannet, pb. 1904, pr. 1905

Når den ny vin blomstrer, pr., pb. 1909 (*When the New Wine Blooms*, 1911)

Samlede vaerker, pb. 1910-1911 (12 volumes)

OTHER LITERARY FORMS

Bjørnstjerne Bjørnson was an extremely prolific writer who, in his native Norway, is known not only as an important playwright but also as the author of a number of widely read peasant stories (short novels). He also wrote longer novels and a large number of essays, articles, and speeches. In addition, he was a prodigious letter writer; more than thirty thousand of his letters are known. His best poems were first collected in the volume *Digte og sange* (1870; *Poems and Songs*, 1915).

ACHIEVEMENTS

A public figure of great importance throughout most of his life, Bjørnstjerne Bjørnson was a creative writer, a journalist, and a politician. Even though he never ran for office, he had considerable influence on both the formation of the Liberal party in Norway and liberal politics for more than half a century. Many of his articles and speeches are political in nature.

Bjørnson was also the creator of modern Norwegian prose style, and his short novel *Synnøve solbakken* (1857; *Trust and Trial*, 1858) is considered the first modern novel in Norwegian literature. Together with Henrik Ibsen, he originated the modern drama in Scandinavia, and was regarded by his contemporaries as Scandinavia's greatest man of letters.

During his lifetime, Bjørnson was well-known both in Germany and in the English-speaking world; even today he is thought of as second only to Ibsen as a representative of Norwegian literature. In his native land, he is known by young and old both as a writer of peasant stories and as the author of Norway's national anthem.

BIOGRAPHY

Bjørnstjerne Martinius Bjørnson was born at Kvikne in eastern Norway on December 8, 1832, the oldest son of Peder Bjørnson, a rural pastor, and his

Bjørnstjerne Bjørnson (© The Nobel Foundation)

wife, Elise Nordraak. His father was the son of a prosperous farmer, and his mother came from a family of merchants.

When the boy was five years old, his father became the pastor at Nesset in Romsdalen on the west coast of Norway, and this is where Bjørnstjerne grew up. At the age of twelve, however, he was sent to school in the town of Molde and remained there until the winter of 1850, when he went to Christiania (Oslo) to prepare for his matriculation examinations. There Bjørnson attended a famous private school commonly referred to as "Heltberg's Student Factory," where Henrik Ibsen, Jonas Lie, and A. O. Vinje were also students at the time. He received his matriculation certificate in 1852 but decided against a career in theology and became a journalist instead, fighting for more realism both in prose fiction and on the stage. He also founded a periodical in which he published a number of rather immature short stories.

In the summer of 1856, however, he wrote his first play, *Between the Battles*, which was a great success when performed in Christiania. In the fall of the same year he went to Copenhagen, where he wrote the greater portion of his next play, *Halte Hulda* (lame Hulda), as well as a short story titled "Thrond," and part of his first short novel, *Trust and Trial*. This book was followed by two others, *Arne* (1859; English translation, 1861) and *En glad Gut* (1860; *A Happy Boy*, 1869).

Bjørnson's early works should be viewed in the context of contemporary Norwegian history. In 1814, Norway had become independent of Denmark and had obtained a free constitution but remained united with Sweden. Culturally, however, it was still dependent on Denmark. Bjørnson wanted to create an awareness of the heritage of his people by drawing attention to the deeds of the forefathers and by showing that contemporary farmers were not much different from their ancestors. In his writing, he therefore alternated between plays based on historical material and prose tales presenting his view of the farmers.

From 1857 to 1859, Bjørnson was the head of the theater in Bergen. There he met the young actress Karoline Reimers, to whom he was married in 1858. Bjørnson's later emphasis on the value of family life is to a great extent a result of this successful union.

While in Bergen, Bjørnson became seriously involved in politics for the first time. As the editor of a local newspaper, he was instrumental in having the city's conservative representatives in the parliament replaced by liberal politicians. His voice was also heard in national politics, and there was little time for creative writing. He therefore traveled to Italy in 1860, hoping that a stay abroad would help him concentrate on his art. *Kong Sverre* and *Sigurd Slembe*, two historical plays that established Bjørnson as Norway's greatest writer, were both written in Italy.

Bjørnson returned to Norway in the spring of 1863, and in 1865 he became associated with Christiania Theater. He also edited a paper and continued his political involvement. At the same time, he wrote his first modern drama, *The Newlyweds*, and in 1868,

he published a novel, *Fiskerjenten* (*The Fisher Maiden*, 1869), in which he discussed the place of the theater in cultural life and argued against the narrow views expressed by the leaders of Norway's influential Pietist movement. Bjørnson had strong religious convictions, but his religion was the liberal and national Christianity of the Dane, Nikolai Grundtvig.

In 1873, Bjørnson again fled to Italy in order to concentrate on his writing. The result was two plays, *The Bankrupt* and *The Editor*, which were both finished when he returned home in 1874. Now Bjørnson settled on the farm Aulestad, near the town of Lillehammer.

There had always been a close connection between Bjørnson's art and his involvement with political and social questions. This relationship became even more pronounced after 1878, when he abandoned his religious faith and actively advocated the ideas of the modern breakthrough. Having studied Charles Darwin and some of the higher critics, Bjørnson now allied himself with the radical Dane Georg Brandes and his circle. In his drama *The King*, he attacked both the institution of the monarchy itself and the social forces that traditionally have allied themselves with it, such as the state church and the military. In the short novel *Magnhild* (1877; English translation, 1883) and the play *Leonarda*, he argued for women's right to divorce, an idea to which the church was strongly opposed.

Bjørnson visited the United States during the years 1880-1881, after which he went to Paris, where he remained until 1887. The first play he finished there was *A Gauntlet*, a contribution to what has been called the great Nordic war of sexual morality. At issue in this debate was whether women ought to be given the same sexual freedom that men had traditionally enjoyed among the Scandinavian bourgeoisie, as well as what should be done about prostitution and the economic position of married women. The conservatives wanted to preserve the status quo—that is, keep wives economically dependent on their husbands, who could continue to enjoy the services of socially ostracized prostitutes—while the radicals argued to replace this arrangement with what they termed free love, which would give women the same sexual rights as men. Bjørnson was the only major Scandinavian writer who argued that men ought to be as chaste as the women had traditionally been, a view that earned for him the support of women's organizations and the scorn of both radical and conservative men.

During his time in Paris, Bjørnson wrote his finest drama, *Pastor Sang*, the first of two plays known as "Beyond Human Power," in which he both attacks the Christian belief in miracles and poignantly portrays human desire for that which goes beyond the bounds of the physical world. Then came his novel *Det flager i byen og på havnen* (1884; *The Heritage of the Kurts*, 1892) and a comedy titled *Geography and Love*, neither of which was artistically successful. After his return to Norway he wrote another novel, *På Guds veje* (1889; *In God's Way*, 1890), which is more successful as a work of art.

In 1892, Bjørnson declared that he was a socialist, and three years later came his drama *Beyond Our Might* (the second of the "Beyond Human Power" plays), the first Scandinavian drama portraying the class struggle. Its background is the rapidly progressing industrialization of Norway and a number of strikes that took place in the early 1890's. Bjørnson's next significant drama, *Paul Lange and Tora Parsberg*, has its background in the suicide of Ole Richter, the Norwegian prime minister in Stockholm and a close friend of Bjørnson. The playwright's last piece, titled *When the New Wine Blooms*, is his best comedy and expresses Bjørnson's fundamentally optimistic view of life.

Bjørnson received the Nobel Prize in 1903. His influence was great both in literature and in politics, and he was able to maintain his creative powers to the end of his life. During his last decade, he commonly spent the summers in Norway and the winters abroad. In the spring of 1909, he had a stroke that paralyzed his left side, and he died in Paris on April 26, 1910.

ANALYSIS

Bjørnstjerne Bjørnson's authorship extended from the 1850's to the beginning of the twentieth century. This was a period of great social and political upheaval in Norway, and the author was a central figure in the public debate throughout his adult life. Bjørnson did not make much distinction between art and life, and his works therefore exhibit a strong connection with the life of his nation.

This intense participation in public life caused Bjørnson to feel a need to reflect on and to distance himself from the various battles in which he took part. From time to time, he would escape from the heat of the current debate by going abroad, and his most significant works came into being during such respites from politics. His participation in public life thus gave him material for his art, and he was able to use this material by temporarily distancing himself from the various battles he fought.

Bjørnson was the son of a pastor, but he grew up in the country and always felt close to the common people. This made it natural for him to first champion liberal causes and later to consider himself a socialist. He was never a revolutionary, however, for he always placed the individual human being above theory of any kind. His concern for the individual is a common feature found in all of his works.

The Norwegian economy changed radically during the second half of the nineteenth century, a period of rapid industrialization during which trade expanded greatly. The development was cyclical rather than linear, however, and in periods of economic stagnation there were numerous business failures. During his time in Bergen, Bjørnson had closely observed a number of bankruptcies, and business conditions in the early 1870's caused him to reflect again on the subject.

THE BANKRUPT

Bjørnson was not only interested in the financial aspect of bankruptcy but also in its effects on public and private morality, as well as its consequences for family life. All these aspects are explored in *The Bankrupt*, which became a great success in both Scandinavia and Germany.

The play's main characters are the visionary and creative businessman Tjælde, his wife, and his antagonist in the bankruptcy proceedings, the lawyer Berent. Tjælde's business is diversified and includes both manufacturing and trade, and a large number of people are dependent on him for their livelihood. In his zeal to build his business, he has overextended himself financially, and a turn for the worse in the general economy has caused him to become insolvent. Tjælde refuses to face the consequences of this fact and place his firm in receivership. Instead, he continues his activities by obtaining short-term credit in the hope that business conditions will improve, and justifies his actions by pointing to the welfare of his employees.

To inspire confidence and obtain credit, however, he must project an image not merely of solvency but also of abundance. He does this by entertaining lavishly and by essentially wasting money that does not belong to him. He also refuses to reveal the true state of the firm to his wife, who nevertheless understands that there are difficulties. Bjørnson is extremely critical of the resulting weakening of Tjælde's family relationships, the strength of which the author views as fundamental to any kind of professional success. He also criticizes Tjælde for the hypocrisy inherent in his projection of an image of affluence, when in reality he is squandering the funds of numerous small savers.

The author's chief spokesperson in the play is the lawyer Berent, who confronts Tjælde with his true financial situation and exacts from him a promise that he will admit to being bankrupt. Tjælde has much difficulty keeping the promise, however, and considers both fleeing the country and committing suicide as alternatives to being dishonored, as he sees it. Support from his wife and children nevertheless enables him to live through the bankruptcy, and in the play's final act, he has established a successful smaller business and is working on repaying obligations that have no legal force but for which he feels morally responsible. The optimistic Bjørnson thus allows Tjælde to rehabilitate himself.

A GAUNTLET

The greatest issue to be debated in Scandinavia during the 1880's was that of sexual morality, and Bjørnson, like many other writers, contributed to the discussion. The conflict in the two-act play *A Gauntlet* is between Svava, a young woman of the upper-middle class, and her fiancé, Alf, the oldest son of one of the wealthiest families in the country. Svava is a firm believer in sexual abstinence before marriage, and this is a principle that she expects both men and women to follow. When, in the first act, she discovers that Alf has had an affair with one of the servant girls in his parents' home, she confronts him with the facts and asks him to explain and, if possible, defend himself. Alf appeals to the tacit understanding that exists in the bourgeoisie—namely, that women are expected to remain chaste but that the same demand is not to be made of the men. This causes Svava to slap his face with her gauntlet and to threaten to break off the engagement.

Svava is no longer willing to marry Alf because she has lost faith in him. She finds no reason to trust that he will remain faithful to her after their marriage. In the second act, she discovers that this is precisely the situation in which her own mother has found herself throughout her married life. Her mother considered leaving her husband at the time when she first discovered his unfaithfulness but decided against it for the sake of her small child, Svava. Her mother's example opens two possible courses of action to the daughter; she may resign herself to the fact that faithfulness in marriage is a rarity among people of her class and marry Alf, or she may resolve never to let herself be brought into her mother's situation. The play does not indicate which choice she finally makes.

A Gauntlet successfully presents one of the most important questions in the so-called morality debate—namely, whether men should be required to meet the same standards of sexual purity as those which were required of women. Bjørnson, the only major Scandinavian author to do so, placed himself on the same side of the issue as the emerging women's movement. For this reason he had to endure much scorn from some of his fellow writers, who were probably both more cynical and more realistic than he.

PASTOR SANG

In the late 1870's, Bjørnson abandoned his belief in Christianity, and *Pastor Sang* presents the kind of thinking that led to his decision. When discussing religion with representatives of the church, Bjørnson had been told that the miracle constitutes the decisive proof of the truth of the Christian religion. The idea of the miracle is therefore central to *Pastor Sang*. The play takes place in northern Norway, and its main character is the pastor Adolf Sang, a man of great faith who has wrought such miracles as causing a lame woman to walk and who has even brought a dead person back to life. The ultimate test of Sang's faith is the healing of his paralyzed and bedridden wife, Klara, who does not share his religious belief.

The play presents several events that are accepted as miracles by the characters onstage. The first of these is an avalanche that turns away from the church (where the pastor is praying), and, which therefore, is received as a sign from God. The audience has been prepared to view the event differently, however, for early in act 1 it is stated that there has recently been much rain and that there is danger of avalanches, and also that the church had been moved some time in the past so that it might be brought out of the avalanche's path. Through dramatic ironies such as this one, Bjørnson questions the validity of the idea of the miracle.

At the climax of the play, the pastor appears to be able actually to heal his wife, who gets up from her bed and is seen walking toward him. As they meet and embrace, however, they both die. The miracle appears to be a bona fide one, but a postscript to the play indicates that Klara's illness has a psychological not a neurological basis and that her death is the result of her having overextended herself because she has felt the pressure of her husband's religious belief. Sang's death indicates not only that a belief in miracles is vain but also that Christianity itself is literally beyond human power, in that the human mind cannot comply with the demands placed on it by religion.

The play constitutes a successful explanation of Bjørnson's rejection of the Christian religion. It is also the dramatist's finest work, for Bjørnson is able to motivate and involve the audience in a series of actions that are completely beyond the realm of reality. The strength of the drama is not that it ridicules religion but rather that it makes a faith in miracles almost acceptable to the audience. It thus brings out people's desire for that which is beyond the bounds of this physical world and poignantly demonstrates how this desire cannot be satisfied.

PAUL LANGE AND TORA PARSBERG

Written in 1898, *Paul Lange and Tora Parsberg* is the best of Bjørnson's later plays. It has its roots in the tragic suicide, a decade earlier, of Ole Richter, Bjørnson's friend and the Norwegian prime minister in Stockholm. Bjørnson had been blamed for Richter's death, for he had pressured his friend into promising not to support the Norwegian prime minister in Oslo, Johan Sverdrup, during a critical debate in the Norwegian parliament. When Richter nevertheless supported Sverdrup, Bjørnson published a private letter from Richter that made its author feel compromised and undoubtedly was damaging to him both politically and personally.

The play was in part an attempt by Bjørnson to free himself from the nagging suspicion that he was responsible for Richter's death, as well as a means of erecting a literary memorial to his friend. The drama's action basically follows the historical course of events, which are, however, somewhat simplified. Paul Lange, who corresponds to Richter, is portrayed as a gifted but weak and sensitive man. When he supports his old leader in a situation of conflicting loyalties, he is not only criticized but also scorned and ostracized because of his choice. The only person who supports him is his fiancé, the wise and proud Tora Parsberg, who loves him despite his weakness. At first she helps him cope with the situation, but when he is not given a promised diplomatic appointment which would have rehabilitated him, he is thrown into despair and chooses to die, a victim of the ugly side of politics.

Bjørnson was not quite able to realize his intentions. Lange is too concerned with the diplomatic appointment to pass for a noble man whose only flaw is that he allows himself to be destroyed by party politics. He comes across as a man who is so weak that he is unable to accept even a woman's love, and the drama becomes the story of his and Tora Parsberg's tragic relationship. As such it is well written, but it is not necessarily an appropriate memorial to an old friend.

In this later play, as in most of Bjørnson's other dramas, there is an intimate connection between life and art. This is both a strength and a weakness for the dramatist. Some of Bjørnson's plays, such as those which have been discussed above, are fine pieces of literature that also have the potential of being made into good theater. They have contributed much to making Bjørnson's literary reputation secure.

OTHER MAJOR WORKS

LONG FICTION: *Synnøve solbakken*, 1857 (*Trust and Trial*, 1858); *Arne*, 1859 (English translation, 1861); *En glad Gut*, 1860 (*A Happy Boy*, 1869); *Fiskerjenten*, 1868 (*The Fisher Maiden*, 1869); *Magnhild*, 1877 (English translation, 1883); *Støv*, 1882 (*Dust*, 1882); *Det flager i byen og på havnen*, 1884 (*The Heritage of the Kurts*, 1892); *På Guds veje*, 1889 (*In God's Way*, 1890); *Mors hænder*, 1892 (*Mother's Hands*, 1897); *Absalons hår*, 1894 (*Absalom's Hair*, 1898); *Mary*, 1906 (English translation, 1909).

POETRY: *Digte og sange*, 1870 (*Poems and Songs*, 1915); *Arnljot Gelline*, 1870 (English translation, 1917).

BIBLIOGRAPHY

Larson, Harold. *Bjørnstjerne Bjørnson: A Study in Norwegian Literature*. New York: King's Crown Press, 1945. The classic study of Bjørnson's life and works.

Naess, Harald S., ed. *A History of Norwegian Literature*. Lincoln: University of Nebraska Press in cooperation with the American-Scandinavian Foundation, 1993. This overview of Norwegian literature touches on Bjørnson and provides a context for understanding this author and his works. Bibliography and index.

Norwegian-American Historical Association, ed. *Land of the Free: Bjørnstjerne Bjørnson's American Letters, 1880-1881*, by Bjørnstjerne Bjørnson. Northfield, Minn.: Editor, 1978. The introduction to this collection of letters and speeches written by Bjørnson during his trip to the United States presents pertinent biographical information. An epilogue discusses the effect the trip had on Bjørnson's subsequent writings. Bibliography.

Sehmsdorf, Henning K. "The Self in Isolation: A New Reading of Bjørnson's *Arne*." *Scandinavian Studies* 45, no. 4 (1973): 310-323. An examination of one of Bjørnson's novels that sheds light on themes in his dramatic works.

Jan Sjåvik

LEE BLESSING

Born: Minneapolis, Minnesota; October 4, 1949

PRINCIPAL DRAMA

The Authentic Life of Billy the Kid, pr. 1979, pb. 1980

Oldtimers Game, pr. 1982, pb. 1988

Nice People Dancing to Good Country Music, pr. 1982, pb. 1983, revised pb. 1990

Independence, pr. 1984, pb. 1985

Riches, pr. 1985 (as *War of the Roses*), pb. 1986

Eleemosynary, pr. 1985, pb. 1987

A Walk in the Woods, pr. 1987, pb. 1988

Two Rooms, pr. 1988, pb. 1990

Cobb, pr. 1989, pb. 1991

Down the Road, pr. 1989, pb. 1991

Fortinbras, pr. 1991, pb. 1992

Four Plays, pb. 1991

Lake Street Extension, pr. 1992, pb. 1993

Patient A, pr., pb. 1993

The Rights, pr. 1994

Going to St. Ives, pr. 1997

Chesapeake, pr. 1999, pb. 2001

The Winning Streak, pr. 1999

Thief River, pr. 2001

Rewrites, pr. 2001 (revision of *The Rights*)

Black Sheep, pr. 2001

OTHER LITERARY FORMS

Though Lee Blessing is most widely known as a writer for the stage, he has also written more than twenty screenplays. In collaboration with Jeanne Blake, Blessing has written episodes for the television series *Nothing Sacred*, *Homicide: Life on the Street*, and *Picket Fences*. He also wrote the full-length screenplay *Cooperstown* (1993).

ACHIEVEMENTS

As a playwright, Lee Blessing has proven himself to be quite versatile—having explored everything from family dramas to historical dramas, political dramas, and message plays. Throughout this body of work, his emphasis on the exploration of contemporary issues has defined his personal style. Blessing's plays have ambitiously tackled some of the more difficult issues of the late twentieth century, including the nuclear arms race, the AIDS (acquired immunodeficiency syndrome) epidemic, modern racism, gay rights, and the Gulf War.

His most successful work to date, *A Walk in the Woods*, is a perfect example of the mirror that Blessing has attempted to hold up to the world around him. *A Walk in the Woods* received the 1987 American Theater Critics award and the George and Elizabeth Marton award, as well as nominations for 1987 Tony, Olivier, and Pulitzer awards. A simple, personalized look at Russian-American arms negotiations, *A Walk in the Woods* is his only work to have been performed on Broadway. Awards he has received for his other works include the Los Angeles Drama Critics Circle Award and the *Dramalogue* Award.

BIOGRAPHY

Lee Knowlton Blessing was born in the theatrical community of Minneapolis, Minnesota, on October 4, 1949, and would continue to call Minneapolis home for much of his adult life. After growing up in nearby Minnetonka, Blessing began his college career at the University of Minnesota before transferring to Reed College in Portland, Oregon, to complete his bachelors in English in 1971. Three years later, he began pursuing his masters of fine arts in English at the University of Iowa, where he would first begin to find success in playwriting. He went on to receive a second masters of fine arts from Iowa in speech and theater, and it was while pursuing this de-

gree that he wrote his first published work, *The Authentic Life of Billy the Kid*. This first success, staged originally as a student production at Iowa, went on to win the American College Theater Festival's National Playwriting Award in 1979 and was performed at the Kennedy Center in Washington, D.C.

Though it would be eight years before his Broadway success with *A Walk in the Woods*, Blessing was quite productive in the years following his graduation from Iowa. Between 1982 and 1985, he formed two of the more fruitful professional relationships of his career—with the Actors Theatre of Louisville and the O'Neill Theater Center. The Actors Theatre premiered his first four professional productions, and six of his plays have gone through workshop readings at the O'Neill Center's National Playwrights Conference. Also during this period, Blessing met director Jeanne Blake, whom he would marry in 1986. The couple collaborated on productions of a number of his plays, and he credits her as a major influence on his work.

The most commercially productive period of Blessing's career occurred shortly after his marriage, when *A Walk in the Woods* moved from its original production at the Yale Repertory to Broadway in 1988, becoming his first Broadway production as well as his first New York production. Critics received the play well, and the play earned him a national reputation. Soon after, another widely known Blessing play, *Eleemosynary*, would be produced off-Broadway to good response.

Blessing is one of many late twentieth century playwrights to have benefited from the decentralization of American drama. Though a minority of his works have been produced in New York—only one on Broadway—Blessing has continued to make a living as a playwright, producing his works primarily in smaller regional theaters such as the La Jolla Playhouse or the Ensemble Theater of Cincinnati. A perfect example of the working-class playwright in contemporary American drama, he has achieved moderate commercial success, and his work has been widely produced by smaller companies. His work has been timely and increasingly adventurous. He contributes to the American stage as both a writer and an educator, through his work as the head of the MFA playwriting program at Rutgers University.

ANALYSIS

Lee Blessing's off-kilter playfulness and ability to humanize contemporary issues onstage have made his latter plays popular productions in American theaters. Blessing, best known for his imaginative interpretations of factual events, has examined everything from AIDS to nuclear arms to the life of Ty Cobb. Sometimes criticized for simply skimming the surface of these issues with his work, he tends to telescope his issues into a few, key human characters. Supported by an abundance of playful wit, his strength lies in his marriage of entertainment value to substantive dialectic.

Blessing's work can be divided into two parts: his early work, characterized by realism and family drama, and his later, post-*Walk in the Woods* work, in which

he primarily takes on current events. The earlier work, which also includes his strongest emphasis on central female characters, is less adventurous and therefore less remarkable, following linear structure and internal realism more strictly. The later work becomes increasingly imaginative, playing with form, theme, and character in a way his first few works do not.

His experiments with structure most often take the form of a sort of soliloquy in the style of William Shakespeare, in which characters alone onstage directly address the audience with narratives, commentaries, or character revelations. This soliloquy device is present in one form or another in almost half of his works. Through his entire body of work, Blessing's fascination with nature as metaphor is evident, as his characters often digress into long descriptions of animal or insect behavior to illustrate certain metaphorical character points or bigger pictures. Other notable characteristics of his writing include a consistent

Lee Blessing, left, photographed with playwrights Ellen McLaughlin and Douglass Soderberg in 1985. (AP/Wide World Photos)

seriocomic cleverness and a reliance on the symbolism of light and dark.

ELEEMOSYNARY

Blessing's first play to really demonstrate his excellent command of language, *Eleemosynary* is the most successful of Blessing's family drama works, an examination of how three generations of women use language and to what end. The three women use language—specifically spelling bees—to both connect and distance themselves from one another throughout the course of the seven-scene play.

Eleemosynary was written as part of a self-assignment on Blessing's part to write plays with central female characters, as a reaction against a theatrical climate in the mid-1980's that was still less than insistent on the need to portray strong women. His most successful effort to grapple with lead female characters, *Eleemosynary* resembles his earlier *Independence* in its structural use of three central females.

The play represents Blessing's first real experimentation with structure. This modified narrative has the three women sometimes acting as storytellers and at other times as characters-in-the-moment, marking out a loose plot that spans the lives of all three. Blessing's device of having characters break the fourth wall to speak directly to the audience is used to good effect here, as he examines the relationship between cruelty and love in families.

The three women in *Eleemosynary* are, in typical Blessing form, a celebration of idiosyncrasies, each bucking the terms of society in their own quirky way. An openly eccentric grandmother, a mother who leaves her daughter to pursue research, and a daughter who memorizes the dictionary to become a spelling champion all find solace in their ability to hide behind the artifice of knowledge.

A WALK IN THE WOODS

Blessing's only work to reach Broadway, *A Walk in the Woods* achieved a level of success and popularity that the playwright has not since duplicated. This work seemed to buck the escapist tendencies of Broadway at the time, bringing to stage an honest examination of the pitfalls of Soviet-American arms negotiation.

One of Blessing's issue plays, *A Walk in the Woods* sloughs aside the complicated technicalities of arms negotiations in favor of a look at the humans behind them. The play is based loosely on an actual event in which two negotiators left the table to take a walk in the woods, only to come back with a simple agreement that both governments rejected. Blessing, though, does not hold fast to these characters, opting rather to create two fictional ones through which he can speak his wisdom on the subject.

Praised on one hand for humanizing a complicated issue and criticized on the other for oversimplifying it, Blessing does make some smart points through likable cynic Andrey Botvinik and gruff idealist John Honeyman. We see these two walking through the woods on four occasions, one to mark each season. The play's revelation—an echo of popular sentiment about the seeming endlessness of the talks—is the idea that for both sides, the quest for peace is secondary to the appearance of the quest for peace. In Andrey Botvinik, Blessing provides a character defined by his eccentricities: Botvinik is an arms negotiator who prefers to talk of Mickey Mouse rather than cruise missiles, a lovable cynic. Botvinik's wacky brand of resignation is foiled by Honeyman's American-style down-to-business optimism.

Timely and popular at the time of its opening in 1987, at the height of the arms talks, *A Walk in the Woods* has become somewhat dated because nuclear warfare has ceased to exist as a simple Russian-American dichotomy. Though the play speaks in enough generalities to still make valid political points, its fuzzy wisdom is unfortunately no longer directed toward a living target.

FORTINBRAS

One of Blessing's most successful comic endeavors, *Fortinbras* is a sort of annex to the story of *Hamlet, Prince of Denmark* (pr. c. 1600-1601), continuing where Shakespeare left off and examining the possibilities of Elsinore under Fortinbras's command. Though not blatantly so, it was written in response to the U.S. involvement in the Gulf War. The play is the story of a strong power coming in to take over a failing government, but bumbling and creating its own disaster, despite its good nature. Blessing examines whether brute force without reflection—embodied in the character of Fortinbras—is really superior to the brooding yet inactive Hamlet.

Fortinbras is a kind of man's-man character, who in Blessing's treatment, is concerned solely with acting promptly and decisively. He tramples on Horatio's desire to tell Hamlet's story and preserve his legacy, and he opts instead to blame the murder of the royal family on a Polish spy because it makes more sense, creates a common enemy for the country, and creates a necessity for Fortinbras's strong leadership. Fortinbras's tendency to miscommunicate leads to disastrous results and thwarts Horatio's attempts to exorcise past demons and, in the end, is responsible for Fortinbras's downfall as well as much of the comedy of the play. The play features the ghosts of nearly every character in *Hamlet, Prince of Denmark*, each returning in ghost-of-Hamlet style to urge revenge. The end of Blessing's play, like that of Shakespeare's, is bloodshed to a fantastic degree. *Fortinbras* is one of Blessing's funniest and most often produced works.

PATIENT A

Another of Blessing's trademark contemporary issue plays, *Patient A* was commissioned by a theater on behalf of Kimberly Bergalis, the first documented case of AIDS infection by a health care worker. Bergalis was criticized in the media for claiming to have done nothing wrong—a seeming indictment of other AIDS victims for having committed wrongdoing.

Patient A takes neither side of this issue; rather, it is an exploration of media stereotypes surrounding the AIDS crisis, a narrative of Kimberly's story, and a catalog of the experience of living and dying with AIDS. Blessing juxtaposes the extraordinary case of Kimberly, who received media attention, an invitation to address Congress, and special treatment because of how she was infected, with the ordinary case of Matthew, a gay man who received no such attention and died in anonymity. The play avoids taking sides but rather invites the audience to think about both cases and raise questions about how victims of AIDS are treated in hospitals and portrayed in the media.

Patient A marks one of Blessing's most structurally adventurous plays. He uses three actors: one to portray Kimberly, one as a utility character who plays Matthew as well as various other people who interact with Kimberly, and one to portray himself interviewing Kimberly. The characters mostly speak directly to the audience, working in tag-team fashion to relay the narrative of the story. There are short vignettes in which Kimberly and Blessing or Kimberly and Matthew interact separately, and they are woven into a continuous one-act pastiche. Blessing intersperses verses from the Andrew Marvell poem, "The Nymph Complaining for the Death of Her Fawn," throughout the play, using it as a conceit to Kimberly's story, as well as an example of how he as a playwright uses poetry to relate to—and avoid relating to—the human suffering involved in this subject matter.

OTHER MAJOR WORK

SCREENPLAY: *Cooperstown*, 1993.

BIBLIOGRAPHY

Blessing, Lee. "Accidents in a Moral Universe." *American Theatre* 18, no. 8 (October, 2001): 10. Remarks by Blessing to the 2001 graduating class of Reed College, his alma matter.

_____. "Action Versus Action." *American Theatre* 12, no. 4 (April, 1995): 64. Blessing talks about his views on the modernization of drama and the influences of television and computers on drama as a form. Talks about reaching a mass audience with live theater and how the live experience is irreplaceable.

Oliva, Judy Lee. "Blessing, Lee (Knowlton)." *Contemporary American Dramatists*. Detroit, Mich.: St. James Press, 1999. Contains a short summary of Blessing's life and catalogs his plays and awards. Analyzes Blessing's body of work, as well as his plays *Nice People Dancing to Country Music, Eleemosynary, Two Rooms, Independence, Riches*, and *A Walk in the Woods*. Comments on Blessing's idiosyncratic characters and witty dialogue.

Weber, Bruce. Review of *Two Rooms*. *The New York Times*, November 22, 2001, p. E13. A review of the Heron Theater production written just prior to the September 11, 2001, terrorist attacks on New York City.

Leah Green

ALEKSANDR BLOK

Born: St. Petersburg, Russia; November 28, 1880
Died: Petrograd, U.S.S.R.; August 7, 1921

PRINCIPAL DRAMA

Balaganchik, pr., pb. 1906 (*The Puppet Show*, 1963)

Korol' na ploshchadi, pb. 1907, pr. 1923 (*The King in the Square*, 1934)

Neznakomka, pb. 1907, pr. 1913 (*The Unknown Woman*, 1927)

Pesnya sudby, pb. 1909, revised pb. 1919 (*The Song of Fate*, 1938)

Roza i krest, pb. 1913, pr. 1921 (*The Rose and the Cross*, 1936)

Ramzes, pb. 1921

OTHER LITERARY FORMS

Aleksandr Blok was the best poet in the second wave of Russian Symbolists at the beginning of the twentieth century. His early poems are included in the collections *Stikhi o prekrasnoy dame* (1904; verses about the beautiful lady) and *Ante lucem* (1909; before light), which express his adoration of mythical Sophia, in fact his later wife. His exuberance later changed to a more somber mood, the beautiful lady being replaced by a stranger (*neznakomka*), in *Puzyri zemli* (1916; earth's bubbles), *Gorod* (1916; the city) *Snezhnaya maska* (1907; the masque of snow), and *Faina* (1916). World War I brought a patriotic fervor to his poetry, in *Na pole Kulikovom* (1908; on the field of Kulikovo) and *Vozmezdie* (1922; retribution). His masterpiece, *Dvenadtsat* (1918; *The Twelve*, 1920), expresses his reaction to the Russian Revolution, which seems to be both receptive and skeptical. Blok also wrote essays about literature, theater, music, and culture.

ACHIEVEMENTS

Aleksandr Blok received no awards for his dramatic works, but his plays were highly praised by critics and appreciated by the theater public. In addition to his plays, he wrote several notable essays about drama. His reputation will always be based on his poetry; however, even though his plays are more closet dramas than effectively staged plays, they remain significant achievements in Russian literature during the first two decades of the twentieth century.

BIOGRAPHY

Aleksandr Blok was born on November 28, 1880, into an upper-class intellectual family. His father was a professor of law at the University of Warsaw and his mother the daughter of a famous botanist at the University of St. Petersburg. His parents were divorced when he was nine, and his mother remarried, but Blok maintained close ties with his father. His mother exposed the young Blok to the arts, and he developed a taste for them. After graduating from high school with distinction, he entered the school of law at the University of St. Petersburg, mostly at his father's insistence, but soon transferred to the school of languages. He was graduated in 1906, and as he later

Aleksandr Blok (Library of Congress)

said, his truly independent life began after graduation. He had begun to write poems when he was four
years old (childish verses, to be sure), but he wrote poetry in earnest in high school and at the university. He
also wrote his first play, *The Puppet Show*, the year of
his graduation from the university, and it was published immediately. In the same year, he published
his first book of poetry, *Stikhi o prekrasnoy dame*,
featuring ninety-three poems selected from the more
than eight hundred he had written over the years.

Blok showed little interest in the events surrounding Russia's 1905 revolution, and they are not reflected prominently in his writings. He felt that he
could not become involved with liberal, revolutionary
movements, not because he did not believe in them
but because of his spiritual experience. Another reason was that he was in love with Lyubov Mendeleyeva,
the daughter of the famous chemist Dmitri Mende-
leyev. He dedicated many of his poems to her and she
became eventually "the beautiful lady" of his first
book. He built a mystical cult of her as an ideal of
pristine, spiritual beauty and love. They were married
in 1902. Unfortunately for Blok, his wife was unable
to reciprocate his adoration. When her interest in
other men, notably in Blok's close friend, the poet
Andrey Bely, became known, it thrust Blok into a desperate mood. The beautiful lady became the stranger,
which Blok was now looking for and finding in the
lower strata of the society.

Blok's reputation as a leading poet and playwright
continued to grow. He wrote poetry under the influence of the Russian Symbolists, especially Vladimir
Solovyov and Valery Bryusov, and of the French
Symbolists. He turned increasingly to theater and
wrote several successful plays, even though they
were somewhat unusual and difficult to perform. In
poetry, he tried hard to overcome his disillusionment
with the ideals of love and beauty and instead began
to depict the lives of simple people. In World War I,
he was conscripted into the corps of engineers and
later took part as an interrogator in the commission
investigating the activities of czarist ministers and
statesmen. He was also engaged in the reorganization
of the theater. When the October Revolution broke
out, Blok gave expression to his ambivalence in his

best-known work, the long poem, *The Twelve*. His
ambiguity is most obvious in the appearance at the
end of the poem of Jesus Christ leading the revolutionaries, an image that confused everyone, including
Blok himself. In reality, the figure of Christ represents Blok's fervent desire to align Christ's religion
with the popular uprising of the downtrodden. In his
final poem, *Skify* (1918; *The Scythians*, 1982), he presented Russia as both European and Asian and
pleaded with the West not to reject Russia lest it turn
against the West in all its Asiatic fury.

After the war, the new communist regime did not
trust Blok despite, and perhaps because of, *The
Twelve*. His health began to deteriorate rapidly. Attempts to gain permission for his caregivers to take
him to Europe for a cure failed repeatedly. When permission was finally granted, Blok was already on his
deathbed. He died on August 7, 1921.

ANALYSIS

Although Aleksandr Blok was primarily a poet, he
exhibited a high interest in theater. More significant,
he drew most of the material for his plays from his
poetry. He contributed plays that are either Symbolist
in nature or highly lyrical, reflecting his chief vocation of poet. Most of his plays mirror his personal
concerns and experiences, such as his love affairs or
the spirit of the time. He was highly interested in
Russian theater life, dealing with leading dramatur-
gists, even though they did not always see eye to eye
when the production of his plays was involved.

THE PUPPET SHOW

The main theme of Blok's first significant play,
The Puppet Show, underscores a discrepancy between
reality and illusions. Throughout the play, Blok indulges in an interplay between the Author as a character and Death, couched in Symbolist mysticism.
The main denouement moves along the lines of attempts at reconciling the two. In a typical *commedia
dell'arte* fashion, three couples in love at a masked
ball represent different types of love: romantic, passionate, and magical. To the Author, who frequently
interrupts the play, romantic irony concerning these
love types predominates because life is different from
Author's intentions. To solve this dilemma, Blok uses

the devices of a puppet show, borrowed from his book of poems by the same title. The three main puppets carrying on the action are Columbine, the Eternal Feminine, her lover Harlequin, and the buffoon Pierrot—all staples of Romantic comedy. Pierrot is also pursuing Columbine, in fact searching for "the beautiful life," but his pursuit turns futile. When he finally approaches Columbine, clad in white like Death, the Author intercedes, complaining that the actors have taken the play out of his hands. All actors suddenly disappear, and Pierrot is left alone on the stage. Through this, Blok pokes fun at his earlier dreams and visions, especially at his passionate love for Sophia (actually, his wife Lyubov Mendeleyeva), at his hopes and disappointments in love, wife, and friends, all of which turn into puppets or cardboard. Thus Blok, through the character Author, declares that he has been fooled by false beliefs and has trusted people who turned out only to look like people. There is no question that Pierrot represents Blok himself, Columbine his wife Lyubov, and Harlequin his friend Andrey Bely, who had an illicit relationship with Lyubov. The discrepancy between real life and illusion in *The Puppet Show* signals the beginning of Blok's turning away from Symbolism and gradually toward a more realistic approach to life and poetry.

THE UNKNOWN WOMAN

Blok's second play, derived directly from his poetry, *The Unknown Woman*, deals again with his disillusionment with love. In his poetry, he turns to a woman from the lower strata of society, a prostitute, whereas in the drama, this woman is Maria, originally a shining star. The poet sees the star falling to Earth and watches it transform into Maria. He imagines that she is the beautiful lady of his dreams and follows her to a party, where she suddenly disappears. At the end the star/Maria still shines in the sky, and the Poet derives satisfaction by gazing at it. Complex psychology and surrealist imagery make *The Unknown Woman* difficult to accept by the general public. Yet the play is appreciated for its lyricism and even social satire. The least successful of Blok's plays, it was not performed on the stage because the censor perceived in it allusions to the Virgin Mary. It was privately performed shortly before the revolution.

THE KING ON THE SQUARE

Blok's third play, *The King on the Square*, gives vent to his disillusionment with the 1905 Russian Revolution. The characters, unlike in his previous dramas, are not mythological but real. Yet they are not named but generalized as the King, the Poet, the Architect, the Clown of Common Sense, the Son, and the Daughter, each symbolizing their particular function in the play. The King, seated on his throne surrounded by water, along with other characters, expects the arrival of ships, which never come—a clear reference to the unfulfilled promises of the revolution. As in Blok's other plays, the Poet is unrealistic in his hopes for a better world and in his search for an ideal of beauty. Doomed to yearning, he fails also in his pursuit of the Architect's daughter, an embodiment of beauty. As the enraged mob, feeling betrayed, rises and destroys all the main characters, including the King, who turns out to be made of stone, the symbolical play ends on a sour and tragic note, as did the hopes of many, including Blok.

THE SONG OF FATE

Drawing again from his poetry (*Faina*) and folk tradition, Blok weaves a story of a man, Herman, leaving his wife in search of greater happiness, which he finds in Faina, a carnival singer. However, after a period in which they exchange distrust and love, Faina leaves Herman in a snowstorm so that he can return to his wife. Faina's singing and the whistling of the wind are "the song of fate," which the Russians should follow, although it is not quite clear where it may lead. The important thing is that it is the song of the people, that is, folk tradition, that will show the way through the snowstorm. This simple and somewhat romantic plot is enriched by Blok's ability to conjure up the world of dreams and combine it with the world of reality and by his faith in Russia despite all the setbacks. The play was written in 1908 and emended in 1918, at the time of cataclysmic events in Russia. With *The Song of Fate*, Blok added his voice to the call of fate in Russia.

THE ROSE AND THE CROSS

Blok's last significant play, *The Rose and the Cross*, is a drama in the style of the troubadours, unusual for the twentieth century. The setting is thirteenth century Provence, and the plot involves a countess, Izora, whom her husband accuses of infidelity, and her love quest for a knight she has seen in her dream. The knight turns out to be an old troubadour, and she rejects him, as well as a homely suitor, Bertrand. When the court is attacked, Bertrand defends his master and dies but not before warning Izora of her husband's approach while she is with another man, a page. *The Rose and the Cross* is Blok's most successful play, thanks mainly to an uncomplicated plot. Inspired by his interest in medieval literature and history, he uses Bertrand's struggle to "reconcile the Rose of Joy and the Cross of Suffering," as Blok himself stated, thus reverting to a character used often by him and representing, once again, himself in the guise of the unfortunate Bertrand.

OTHER MAJOR WORKS

POETRY: *Stikhi o prekrasnoy dame*, 1904; *Nechayannaya radost*, 1907; *Snezhnaya maska*, 1907; *Zemlya v snegu*, 1908; *Na pole Kulikovom*, 1908; *Ante lucem*, 1909; *Nochyne chasy*, 1911; *Skazki*, 1912; *Krugly god*, 1913; *Stikhi o Rossii*, 1915; *Sobraniye stikhotvoreniy i teatr v 4 kigakh*, 1916 (4 volumes; includes the poetic cycles *Puzyri zemli*, *Gorod*, *Faina*, etc.); *Solovinyy sad*, 1918; *Skify*, 1918 (*The Scythians*, 1982); *Dvenadtsat*, 1918 (*The Twelve*, 1920); *Iamby: Sovremennye stikhi, 1907-1914*, 1919; *Sedoe utro*, 1920; *Za granyu proshlykh dnei*, 1920; *Vozmezdie*, 1922 (wr. 1910-1921); *Poems of A. B.*, 1968; *Selected Poems*, 1972.

NONFICTION: *Rossia i intelligentsia*, 1918; *Katilina*, 1919; *O simvolizme*, 1921 (*On Symbolism*, 1975); *Pis'ma Aleksandra Bloka*, 1925; *Pis'ma Aleksandra Bloka k rodnym*, 1927; *Dnevnik Al. Bloka, 1911-1913*, 1928; *Dnevnik Al. Bloka, 1917-1921*, 1928; *Zapisnye knizhki Al. Bloka*, 1930; *Pis'ma Al. Bloka k E. P. Ivanovu*, 1936; *Aleksandr Blok i Andrey Bely: Perepiska*, 1940.

BIBLIOGRAPHY

Berberova, Nina. *Aleksandr Blok: A Life*. New York: George Braziller, 1996. This biography places Blok within the context of his poetic and philosophical views and of the impact of the Russian Revolution and Blok's reaction to it. Berberova, a poet who was present at Blok's deathbed, pays homage to him and to St. Petersburg in the days of the revolution.

Chukovski, Kornei. *Alexander Blok as Man and Poet*. Ann Arbor, Mich.: Ardis, 1982. An introspective essay by a respected Russian writer, a contemporary of Blok. Deals with important facets of Blok's works without going into scholarly details. Uses an impressionistic approach in evaluation, with firsthand insight into the spirit of the time.

Hackel, Sergei. *The Poet and the Revolution: Aleksandr Blok's "The Twelve."* Oxford, England: Oxford University Press, 1975. Hackel analyzes all aspects of Blok's masterpiece. Discusses the action and characters, especially the appearance of Jesus Christ. Contains relatively few references to form, so that the thematic features are brought into a sharper focus.

Kisch, Sir Cecil. *Alexander Blok, Prophet of a Revolution*. London: Weidenfeld & Nicholson, 1980. A biographical treatment combined with critical evaluation. A somewhat old-fashioned biography but still useful to a novice.

Pyman, Avril. *The Life of Aleksandr Blok*. 2 vols. Oxford, England: Oxford University Press, 1979-1980. The most exhaustive and best biography of Blok. The emphasis is on his life, but it also discusses his poetry and plays. Considers Blok to be the best Russian poet of the twentieth century.

Reeve, F. D. *Alexander Blok: Between Image and Idea*. New York: Columbia University Press, 1962. An interesting but somewhat convoluted study, with an extensive yet selective bibliography. Sees Blok as a link between Romanticism and modernism in Russian literature. The impressionistic approach reveals Reeve's admiration and his unique interpretation of Blok.

Sloane, David A. *Aleksandr Blok and the Dynamics of the Lyric Cycles*. Columbus, Ohio: Slavica, 1987. A penetrating study of Blok's poetry, with the emphasis on his tendency to write in cycles.

Vasa D. Mihailovich

ERIC BOGOSIAN

Born: Woburn, Massachusetts; April 24, 1953

PRINCIPAL DRAMA

Careful Movement, pr. 1977
Slavery, pr. 1977
Garden, pr. 1978
Heaven, Heaven, Heaven, pr. 1978
The Ricky Paul Show, pr. 1979
Sheer Heaven, pr. 1980
That Girl, pr. 1981
The New World, pr. 1981
Men Inside, pr. 1981, pb. 1994
Voices of America, pr. 1982, pb. 1994
Advocate, pr. 1983
FunHouse, pr. 1983, pb. 1994
I Saw the Seven Angels, pr. 1984
Talk Radio, pr. 1984, pb. 1988
Drinking in America, pr. 1986, pb. 1987
Sex, Drugs, Rock and Roll, pr., pb. 1990
Scenes from the New World, pb. 1993
The Essential Bogosian, pb. 1994
Pounding Nails in the Floor with My Forehead, pr.,
　pb. 1994
subUrbia, pr. 1994, pb. 1995
31 Ejaculations, pr. 1996, pb. 2000
Griller, pr. 1998
Bitter Sauce, pr., pb. 1998
Wake Up and Smell the Coffee, pr. 2000, pb. 2001

OTHER LITERARY FORMS

In addition to his prolific career as a playwright and creator of solo shows, Eric Bogosian has branched out into other written forms as well. *Notes from Underground* (1994), which takes its inspiration from Fyodor Dostoevski's *Zapiski iz podpolya* (1864; *Letters from the Underworld*, 1913; better known as *Notes from the Underground*), is a novella in journal form detailing an isolated man's attempts to connect with the outside world and his increasing tendency toward antisocial and sociopathic behavior. Bogosian also published a novel, *Mall* (2000), which focuses on the ways in which a shopping mall ties together the lives of a bizarre array of seemingly unrelated characters. The novel is part comedy and part crime thriller and contains much of the stinging social criticism found in his plays. Bogosian also wrote introductions to two books: *Physiognomy: The Mark Seliger Photographs* (1999), a collection of celebrity photographs, and *How to Talk Dirty and Influence People* (1992), the autobiography of comedian Lenny Bruce, whose standup routines laced with social criticism are an obvious forerunner to much of Bogosian's work as a dramatist. In addition, Bogosian has also written screenplays for adaptations of his work including *Talk Radio* (1988), which he co-wrote with director Oliver Stone, *Sex, Drugs, Rock and Roll* (1991), and *subUrbia* (1996), as well as the pilot episode of the television program *High Incident* (1996).

ACHIEVEMENTS

Eric Bogosian has been an active and versatile playwright since the late 1970's, crafting numerous short ensemble dramas and full-length plays, of which *Talk Radio* and *subUrbia*, which were both adapted to film, and *Griller* are the best known. However, Bogosian's greatest contribution to modern drama is his series of solo shows. These solo performance pieces—*Men Inside*; *FunHouse*; *Drinking in America*; *Sex, Drugs, Rock and Roll*; *Pounding Nails in the Floor with My Forehead*; and *Wake Up and Smell the Coffee*—consist of short monologues spoken by different characters and have led to three Obie awards. *Drinking in America* and *Pounding Nails in the Floor with My Forehead* each garnered the Obie Award for playwriting, and *Sex, Drugs, Rock and Roll* received a special citation. An outspoken supporter of the National Endowment for the Arts (NEA), Bogosian has received two NEA fellowships, and the film version of *Talk Radio* received the Silver Bear Award from the Berlin Film Festival.

Bogosian's work, more than that of most writers, has drawn particular praise for being "hip" by demonstrating a thorough understanding of contemporary culture and concerns. From his searing indictments of consumer culture to his satirical takes on morally compromised yuppies, drug pushers, Hollywood agents, and traditional tough guys, Bogosian has garnered a reputation as a devastating social critic with a biting, edgy, and oftentimes grim sense of humor.

BIOGRAPHY

Eric Bogosian grew up in the suburbs in Woburn, Massachusetts, participating in theater at his local high school and enrolling in the University of Chicago. He dropped out of college in 1973 and returned to Woburn, where he worked as an assistant manager at a Gap store in the local mall before transferring to the theater department at Oberlin College, from which he was graduated. In 1975 he moved to New York City and began pursuing a writing career. After arriving in New York, he immersed himself in the world of theater and performance art and began contributing ensemble plays by the end of the 1970's. To help make ends meet, he learned to capitalize on his talents as a performer by creating monologues that he could produce inexpensively. This work brought him to the attention of producer Joseph Papp, and Bogosian appeared in the producer's Shakespeare Festival in 1982. During the early 1980's, Bogosian continued to develop his solo work, completing his first two solo shows, and in 1984 he completed a version of his first full-length ensemble play, *Talk Radio*. He also began to land sporadic acting jobs on television in such programs as *Miami Vice* and *The Twilight Zone*.

In 1986 he completed a longer collection of monologues, *Drinking in America*, for which he received an Obie Award and which was subsequently shortened and filmed as part of a comedy special on Cinemax. A successful New York production of *Talk Radio* in 1987 led to Bogosian's collaboration with film director Oliver Stone. The two expanded on the original play by including background material and incorporating elements from the life of Alan Berg, a Colorado radio talk-show host who had been murdered. The resulting film, in which Bogosian also starred, received a good deal of attention and was honored at the Berlin Film Festival. Capitalizing on his rising visibility as a performer, Bogosian landed

Eric Bogosian in 2000. (AP/Wide World Photos)

a leading role in Robert Altman's television adaptation of *The Caine Mutiny Court-Martial* (1988), and Bogosian's next solo show, *Sex, Drugs, Rock and Roll*, was filmed by director John McNaughton in 1991.

Bogosian continued making occasional acting appearances in television programs such as *Law and Order* and *The Larry Sanders Show* in the early 1990's, and in 1994 he published his first novella, *Notes from Underground*. In 1994 Bogosian was quite busy. Theatre Communications Group published his early solo work along with *Talk Radio* in an anthology, *The Essential Bogosian*; he completed another award-winning solo show, *Pounding Nails in the Floor with My Forehead*; and he wrote his second, full-length ensemble play, *subUrbia*. The next year he accepted a high-profile acting job as the villain in the action film *Under Siege 2* (1995), and in 1996 he wrote the screenplay for director Richard Linklater's adaptation of *subUrbia*. He remained busy during the remainder of the 1990's, acting in small roles in films such as Woody Allen's *Deconstructing Harry* (1997); writing another ensemble play, *Griller*; completing another solo show, *Wake Up and Smell the Coffee*; and publishing a novel, *Mall*. A New York resident, Bogosian is married to Jo Bonney, who has also directed several of his solo shows.

ANALYSIS

Eric Bogosian's work as a performer has continued to flourish along with his writing career, and his sensibilities as an actor have heavily influenced his writing. Unlike playwrights, such as Arthur Miller, who strived to produce the well-made play, Bogosian creates character-driven works, often with little regard to formalities of plot and theme. He tries to produce an event or a happening with his plays, placing his emphasis on the performance over the text. Although this technique might seem to make his drama less accessible to literary analysis, it actually provides his work with its greatest sense of intellectual tension. Rather than carefully formulating his productions, Bogosian lets his characters bring to the stage all of their many contradictions and paradoxes, often leaving the reader or viewer with an uneasy (and highly literary) sense of ambiguity. He does not ask simple questions and does not provide direct answers. Rather, he uses the theater as a means for self-expression, particularly in his solo shows, in which he can pursue whatever thoughts are plaguing him at the moment and he can speak to his audience, whom he frequently refers to as his "tribe."

Many of those "plaguing thoughts" involve generational issues and popular culture. He often explores the ways in which his generation has moved from idealism to materialism, particularly in *Sex, Drugs, Rock and Roll* and *Pounding Nails in the Floor with My Forehead*. His view of the United States is large, and in his solo shows as well as the ensemble play, *Scenes from the New World*, he depicts a cross-section of the United States, presenting what he often describes in interviews as the "archetypes" for people that he knows. Readers of Bogosian's plays are as likely to encounter winos, prostitutes, muggers, rednecks, and drug addicts as they are to find yuppies, Hollywood agents, rock stars, family men, and business executives. In fact, although one might be tempted to point to obvious theatrical and cultural predecessors such as Bertolt Brecht and Lenny Bruce in order to place Bogosian's drama in a literary context, his affinity for such a broad range of American characters as well as his ability to juggle contradictory ideologies and personalize all the material links him as closely to the American poet Walt Whitman as to any other playwrights or performers.

TALK RADIO

Bogosian's first full-length ensemble play, *Talk Radio*, centers on the personality of Barry Champlain, a confrontational radio talk-show host, whose program, *Nighttalk*, is on the verge of being distributed nationally. The action takes place during one difficult night when Champlain wrestles with off-beat phone calls, pressures to change the show, and ultimately, a crisis of conscience. He begins to question whether going national is "selling out," and both the character, Champlain, and the writer, Bogosian, seem to question whether there is any artistic integrity in such a show at all. The play ponders whether such programs are public forums for exchanging important ideas or merely spectacle entertainments for passive listeners who derive their pleasure from hearing Champlain take on the various callers.

This play bears the hallmarks of much of the playwright's subsequent work in that it asks more questions than it answers and examines the relationship of a performer to his audience, a theme that runs as a subtext throughout much of Bogosian's solo work. *Talk Radio* amply demonstrates his penchant for being "ahead of the curve" in terms of trends in popular culture. With *Talk Radio*, Bogosian actually anticipates the arrival of such celebrity hosts as Howard Stern, but when the play was first completed in the mid-1980's, the notion of the blistering talk-show host had not yet emerged as a national phenomenon.

SEX, DRUGS, ROCK AND ROLL

In this collection of monologues, Bogosian presents another diverse array of characters, including a British rock star turned recovering drug addict, a Texas "stud" who boasts of his sexual prowess, and a cutthroat business executive. Some of the pieces are more inventive conceptually than his previous monologues, such as "Benefit," which features the rock star and establishes as its unseen context a television interview show. As he notes in his introduction, Bogosian, as a child of the 1970's, has very mixed feelings about sex, drugs, and rock and roll. For many people of his generation, "sex, drugs, rock and roll" was not merely a slogan, but actually a motto for living that defined a sense of nonconformity and rebellion, and thus, implied some vague sense of integrity. Yet, as his monologues detail, the sex, the drugs, and the rock and roll are, all three, suspect in that they have all contributed to disease, death, and debilitation for many of these characters. Bogosian's sense of contradiction and paradox is fully at work in this show as he manages to evoke the mixed feeling of a generation struggling to romanticize the values of its youth while simultaneously questioning the validity of those values.

SUBURBIA

Bogosian's second full-length ensemble play, *sub-Urbia*, focuses on a handful of young people, most in their early twenties, who spend their time hanging out behind a local 7-Eleven convenience store drinking beer, eating pizza, and discussing sex. The action focuses on one evening when an old friend of the group who has gained a small degree of fame as a member of a rock band returns home with his publicist. Although the play begins as a comedy, simultaneously reveling in and satirizing the various attitudes struck by the characters, it grows increasingly serious in tone with incidents of racism, threats of violence, betrayal, drug overdoses, and ultimately tragedy when one of the characters unexpectedly dies.

While Bogosian has suggested that the characters and events of the play emerged from his own experiences in the 1970's, the play speaks much more directly to the existentialist and nihilistic impulses of Generation X in the 1990's. Most of the characters struggle with a sense of aimlessness in which such time-killing activities as eating, drinking, and "hanging out," become an end unto themselves rather than the means to an end. The play also fits quite comfortably into the context of a mid-1990's comedy of manners, much like the television program *Seinfeld* (1990-

1998) and films such as Quentin Tarantino's *Pulp Fiction* (1994) and Kevin Smith's *Clerks* (1994) in that it provides characters who are not particularly well educated or intellectually sophisticated with what is nevertheless a highly complex and, at times, elevated rhetorical style of speech, as these young people explore the deeper philosophical implications of how they see the world.

POUNDING NAILS IN THE FLOOR WITH MY FOREHEAD

This solo show demonstrates increasing ambition and experimentation in Bogosian's work. It begins with "America," in which a nameless speaker launches into an extreme attack against anyone and anything even purporting to be politically "liberal." He follows this disturbing opening monologue with a deliberately offensive one, spoken in black dialect, by a train conductor who claims to be spreading diseases to everyone, including audience members who may be sitting in a chair in which he has urinated or leaning against a wall where he has vomited. After sufficiently numbing his audience, Bogosian then appears as "himself," attacking the audience for not applauding the previous monologue. By the end of this monologue, he winds up arguing with himself backstage about his image as an "angry" performer. This type of textual self-awareness, in which monologues segue smoothly from one to another and in which Bogosian directly draws his own character into the fray, is new to the solo shows and gives *Pounding Nails in the Floor with My Forehead* a greater sense of unity and development than its predecessors.

OTHER MAJOR WORKS
LONG FICTION: *Mall*, 2000.
SCREENPLAYS: *Talk Radio*, 1988 (with Oliver Stone); *Sex, Drugs, Rock and Roll*, 1991; *subUrbia*, 1996.
TELEPLAY: *High Incident*, 1996.
MISCELLANEOUS: *Notes from Underground*, 1994 (novella and play).

BIBLIOGRAPHY
Clements, Marcelle. "Eric Bogosian as the Man Who Won't Shut Up." *Esquire*, September, 1991, 184.

This profile attempts to see the similarities between Bogosian in private and his public persona as evidenced in *Sex, Drugs, Rock and Roll.*

Handelman, David. "A Man Under the Influence." *Rolling Stone*, June 19, 1986, 49-51. Written during the period of Bogosian's solo show, *Drinking in America*, this article connects the performance to the playwright's feelings about the death of the comedian John Belushi.

Lacher, Irene. "Bogosian Says So Long to Solo Performances: The Older and Wiser Bad Boy of Monologuists Says He Is Moving on to New Projects." *Los Angeles Times*, February 6, 2002, p. F2. Bogosian discusses his years of doing mono-logues and expresses how his interests and focus have changed since he began. He suggests that he might stop doing solo shows and devote his attention to other works.

Shirley, Don. "At His *Worst.*" Review of *The Worst of Eric Bogosian. Los Angeles Times*, February 8, 2002, p. F21. A review of *The Worst of Eric Bogosian*, a monologue taken from Bogosian's *Wake Up and Smell the Coffee* and other solo performances. Shirley finds the show, in which Bogosian portrays a series of flawed men, including an obsequious actor at an audition and a randy drug dealer, to be a sort of "best of" compilation.

Thomas Gregory Carpenter

GEORGE H. BOKER

Born: Philadelphia, Pennsylvania; October 6, 1823
Died: Philadelphia, Pennsylvania; January 2, 1890

PRINCIPAL DRAMA

Calaynos, pb. 1848, pr. 1849
Anne Boleyn, pb. 1850
The Betrothal, pr. 1850, pb. 1856
The World a Mask, pr. 1851, pb. 1940
The Podesta's Daughter, pb. 1852 (verse play)
Leonor de Guzman, pr. 1853, pb. 1856
Francesca da Rimini, pr. 1855, revised pb. 1856
The Bankrupt, pr. 1855, pb. 1940
The Widow's Marriage, pb. 1856
Königsmark, pb. 1869
Nydia, wr. 1885, pb. 1929 (early version of *Glaucus*)
Glaucus, wr. 1885-1886, pb. 1940
Glaucus and Other Plays, pb. 1940

OTHER LITERARY FORMS

Although George H. Boker is remembered primarily as a dramatist, he wanted to be remembered as a poet. To this end, he wrote hundreds of poems. *The Book of the Dead*, written in 1859 and 1860 and published in 1882, is his vindication of his father's name.

After his father, a banker, died, the Girard Bank tried unsuccessfully to sue his estate for more than a half million dollars. The emotion in these 107 poems is sincere, and the events prompting the collection are interesting, but the poems are less well crafted than those in Boker's other volumes of poetry.

After Boker ceased to write about the problems of his father's estate, he wrote many poems about the Civil War. Nearly every poem of this type is precisely dated, offering a narrative of a particular battle. Published soon after they were written in periodicals and leaflets, these poems, sentimental yet sincere and richly detailed, inspired patriotism in Northern readers. In 1864, Boker collected his Civil War verse in *Poems of the War*.

Boker's third important collection of poetry, *Sonnets: A Sequence on Profane Love*, consists of poems written between 1857 and 1887, but the work was published posthumously in 1929. Of the 313 sonnets in the sequence, the first 282 seem to be about one woman, the next thirteen about another, and the last eighteen about a third woman. Written in the Italian form, these sonnets are generally well constructed and evoke intense images. The classical allusions are forced, but the descriptions of nature are powerful.

Writing in 1927, Edward Sculley Bradley, the eminent critic who served as Boker's biographer and as editor of the sequence, argued that Henry Wadsworth Longfellow was the only American to equal Boker as a sonneteer.

Achievements

Important American literary figures of the nineteenth century respected George H. Boker as both a dramatist and a poet. He received praise from William Cullen Bryant, Oliver Wendell Holmes, James Russell Lowell, and Henry Wadsworth Longfellow. He was also elected to the Authors' Club of New York and the American Philosophical Society. Boker failed, however, to achieve comparable recognition from the American public: *Francesca da Rimini* and *The Betrothal* were his only popular plays.

Although fame eluded him, Boker was a master of the romantic tragedy. Romantic tragedy, like classical tragedy, depicts a hero or heroine, usually an admirable aristocrat, who suffers defeat or death because of fate or a fatal character flaw. For example, Leonor, the noble mistress of a king in *Leonor de Guzman*,

George H. Boker (courtesy of New York Public Library)

dies a victim of circumstances and her own determination to see her son crowned king. In *Francesca da Rimini*, Paolo and Francesca, both of royal birth, die because of their predestined love for each other and their inability to assert reason over emotion.

The conventions of romantic tragedy are less rigid than those governing classical tragedy; also, in contrast to classical tragedy, romantic tragedy emphasizes the emotions and personalities of the characters rather than the plot. In *Francesca da Rimini*, the personality of Lanciotto, Francesca's deformed and savage husband, is more interesting than the play's inevitable end. Similarly, Leonor's passionate and forceful personality is more interesting than the palace intrigue.

Other characteristics of romantic tragedy include blank verse and remote, exotic settings. Boker's two best tragedies, *Francesca da Rimini* and *Leonor de Guzman*, are both written in blank verse and take place during the fourteenth century, the former in Italy and the latter in Spain.

William Shakespeare was the finest playwright in the tradition of romantic tragedy. If Boker's works clearly do not belong in such company, he nevertheless wrote romantic tragedies superior to those of any of his contemporaries. The only other American to approach Boker's success with romantic drama was Robert Montgomery Bird, an earlier nineteenth century novelist and playwright. *Francesca da Rimini* marks the end of romantic tragedy as a viable form in the United States and stands as the best play written by an American before the twentieth century.

Biography

George Henry Boker, a lifelong citizen of Philadelphia, was born in 1823. He attended the College of New Jersey (now Princeton University), where he developed a keen admiration for Shakespeare and other Elizabethan dramatists. He was still at college when he published his first poems. When Boker was graduated in 1842, his father wanted him to be a businessman or diplomat. He tried to study law, but he could not commit himself to a business career and did not pursue law. In 1844, he married Julia Riggs, a woman he had courted for some years. They had three children, but only the first, George, survived into adulthood. This son married but did not have children.

Boker had a literary group of friends, all poets, including Charles Godfrey Leland, Bayard Taylor, Thomas Bailey Aldrich (also editor of the *Atlantic Monthly*), Edmund Clarence Stedman, and Richard H. Stoddard. Boker generously used his wealth and literary influence to help his friends become published writers.

From 1847 to 1853, Boker wrote the bulk of his work. *The Lesson of Life and Other Poems* (1848), containing several sonnets, anticipates his later sequence of sonnets. *Calaynos*, his first play, is a romantic tragedy about a man whose Moorish ancestry is not apparent. It was produced in London in 1849, apparently without the author's permission, and then produced with his permission in the United States in 1851. Angered by a playwright's lack of rights, Boker supported the Dramatic Authors' Bill, which Congress passed in 1856.

Anne Boleyn, Boker's second play, was never produced. His next two plays, which were produced, were *The Betrothal*, a comedy in blank verse, and *The World a Mask*, a social satire written largely in prose. In 1852, he published *The Podesta's Daughter*, a dramatic dialogue. That year he also wrote two more plays, *The Widow's Marriage*, a comedy that was never produced, and *Leonor de Guzman*, a romantic tragedy about two women trying to secure the Castilian throne for their sons. Boker began a sequel to this latter play but never finished it.

In nineteen intense days in March of 1853, Boker wrote his masterpiece, *Francesca da Rimini*, a reworking of Dante's account of Paolo and Francesca. It was first produced with moderate success in 1855. After writing his best play, he wrote one of his worst, *The Bankrupt*. Like *The World a Mask*, it is poorly written and shows Boker's inability to handle a contemporary setting well. Boker had it produced anonymously.

After *The Bankrupt*, Boker's dramatic production slowed down. He published *Plays and Poems* in 1856, a popular collection in two volumes that contained no new works. He labored longer than usual on

Königsmark, a dramatic sketch never produced. Boker's dramatic career was impeded by a series of events—what appears to have been a long affair with a woman from Philadelphia, a lawsuit against his father's estate, his involvement in the Civil War, and his work as a diplomat.

From 1857 until 1871, Boker apparently carried on a love affair, and during this time, he wrote almost three hundred sonnets in celebration of his love. These sonnets, along with two other short sequences probably inspired by subsequent affairs, were discovered in his daughter-in-law's house after his death and were published in 1929 with the help of his biographer, Edward Sculley Bradley. Boker was also preoccupied by a suit against his father's estate that lasted fifteen years. Soon after Boker's father died, representatives of the bank he had managed initiated a suit against his estate. Although Boker did not share his father's interest in business, he admired his father's business acumen and respected his integrity. Depressed and fearful of bankruptcy, Boker spent 1859 and 1860 writing vindictive poems against his father's enemies.

From 1861 to the end of the Civil War, Boker vigorously supported the Northern position. He wrote many poems in support of the war effort; they were published individually and were instantly successful. Boker had them published as a collection, *Poems of the War*, and they became his most widely read publication. He also helped to organize the Union League, a Philadelphia club in support of the Northern stance. Boker was its first secretary and served in that capacity until he began his diplomatic career. In 1871, Boker began an appointment in Turkey, and in 1875, he became a diplomat in Russia. He and his wife returned to the United States permanently in 1878.

Upon returning home, Boker finally achieved some of the recognition he had sought. He became president of the Union League and was elected to both the Authors' Club of New York and the American Philosophical Society. He also published previously written works—*The Book of the Dead*, comprising his poems in support of his father, and a reprint of *Plays and Poems*, in 1883. Most important, however, in 1883, Lawrence Barrett, a famous nineteenth century actor, successfully revived *Francesca da Rimini*.

Boker wrote only two more plays after his return to the United States, *Nydia*, a tragedy, and *Glaucus*, apparently a revision of *Nydia*. Neither version was produced. Ill for the last three years of his life, Boker died of a heart attack in 1890.

ANALYSIS

George H. Boker is little remembered today partly because he excelled at romantic drama, a form that modern readers, with their love of realism, seldom appreciate. *Leonor de Guzman*, with its emphasis on palace intrigue, and *The Betrothal*, with its assumption that aristocrats are better than others, understandably have little appeal for the modern American reader. *Francesca da Rimini*, however, deserves the attention of modern readers: The play's complex characterization and democratic theme can sustain interest even today.

FRANCESCA DA RIMINI

Francesca da Rimini, in spite of its imitative blank verse, is the best dramatic rendering of the love story recorded both by Giovanni Boccaccio and by Dante. The first version of Boker's masterpiece, written in 1853, was never published; the final version was published in 1856. There are important differences between these two versions. In the published version, the participants in the love triangle—Lanciotto, Francesca, and Paolo—are emphasized more or less equally. In the 1853 version, in contrast, Lanciotto is the central figure. Further, the love scenes involving Francesca and Paolo, including the one immediately preceding the consummation of their love, are largely absent in the 1853 version. These changes served not only to decrease Lanciotto's importance but also to increase the audience's sympathy for the two young lovers.

Because it is shorter, the 1853 version moves more briskly to the conclusion. For example, in the 1853 version, Boker immediately prepares the audience for the climax by having Francesca, the inadvertent cause of Lanciotto and Paolo's strife, appear in the first scene. In the 1856 version, however, Francesca does not appear until act 2, and Boker uses the

first act to reveal the personalities of the two brothers and their relationship to each other. On the other hand, the published play is generally superior to the earlier version because it allows for richer characterizations. Both versions, though, to Boker's credit, emphasize character rather than plot.

Paolo loves his brother, but, an idler, he has not the discipline necessary to ignore his feelings for his brother's wife. Francesca, while she has the audience's sympathy, is too much a victim to have their unreserved admiration. Forced to become engaged to a man she has never met, she is deceived about Lanciotto's hideous appearance by the three most important people in her life—her father, Guido; her servant and confidante, Ritta; and the man with whom she has just fallen in love, Paolo. She recognizes that Lanciotto has a more noble character than Paolo, but she is nevertheless repelled by his deformities. She displays free will in a single scene only, one not present in the 1853 version, in which she, more than Paolo, seeks consummation of their love. Francesca becomes a victim again in the last scene when Lanciotto, in an effort to force Paolo to kill him, kills her.

Lanciotto, a more complex figure than the young lovers, both repels and attracts the audience. He first appears as a hideously deformed and vicious, almost barbaric, warrior. Although his father pities the defeated citizens of Ravenna, Lanciotto wants to see the city burn and its women crying. An uncivilized man, he is also deeply superstitious. He believes a warning by his nurse that his blood will be mixed with Guido's, and later he fears doom when he thinks he sees blood on his sword. Paolo and Maletesta, the brothers' father, are more civilized than he and chide him for his superstitions, but he remains convinced that evil awaits him.

Juxtaposed to Lanciotto's savagery and superstition are his deeply felt emotions, which gain the audience's sympathy. The audience understands his desire to destroy Ravenna when he reveals the reason for such rage: His first memory is of the death of his nurse's husband at the hands of a citizen of Ravenna. Lanciotto ironically evokes the most sympathy from the audience when he discloses how much he hates his deformed body for creating fear and pity in others. He also wins the audience over when he says he will not force Francesca, who so obviously loathes his appearance, to touch him.

The last act shows Lanciotto at war with himself, fighting both his savagery and his love for his brother. When Lanciotto learns that his brother and wife have betrayed him, he, the savage soldier, feels that he cannot live with such dishonor unavenged. He races to the lovers, only to find he cannot attack his beloved brother. He asks the lovers to lie about their adultery. When they refuse, he tries to goad Paolo into killing him, but Paolo, never a fighter, remains passive. Even when Lanciotto stabs Francesca, Paolo refuses to act. Finally, Lanciotto kills his brother, too. Momentarily, he is relieved to have avenged his honor, but as the play concludes, he falls on Paolo, declaring that he "loved him more than honor—more than life." Paolo, paralyzed by his love for Lanciotto, cannot save himself or Francesca. Lanciotto, wrongly believing that his honor is more important than his love for Paolo, forces himself into violence. Thus, the play ends with two brothers—one passively, one actively—led into destruction.

Pepe, Maletesta's jester, is one reason that critics admire *Francesca da Rimini*. As Boker's own addition to the story of Francesca and Paolo, Pepe hastens the inevitable tragedy. Pepe frequently suggests to Lanciotto that Paolo and Francesca love each other, and he tells Lanciotto when their love is consummated. To assure that Lanciotto seeks vengeance, he also lies, telling Lanciotto that Paolo has hired him to kill his brother. As Pepe expects, in anger, Lanciotto kills him, but he dies glad that the two brothers will also be destroyed.

Pepe would be a completely malevolent figure except for the motivation behind his hatred for Paolo and Lanciotto. A proponent of democracy, he hates the brothers because they represent royalty. He tells Lanciotto that he would like to see marriage abolished so that everyone would be born equal. Later, in a scene not present in the 1853 version, Paolo reports that he overheard Pepe ranting about being treated as a toy. Both brothers indeed treat him like that; generally unconcerned about his desires, they expect him to do their bidding, and they fatally underestimate his

anger. Pepe is a modern antihero, supporting the cause of democracy.

Critics agree that two other plays by Boker approach the excellence of *Francesca da Rimini: Leonor de Guzman*, another romantic tragedy, and *The Betrothal*, a romantic comedy.

LEONOR DE GUZMAN

In *Leonor de Guzman*, the King of Castile and Leon dies, leaving three rivals competing for power: his wife Maria, who wants the throne to remain with her son; his mistress Leonor, who wants her son to become king; and Alburquerque, the prime minister, who wants the power for himself. The play is effective particularly because of the struggle between Leonor, the spiritually pure mistress who unwaveringly manipulates events to ensure that her son will be king, and Maria, the betrayed wife whose bitterness leads her to murder Leonor. The play ends with Leonor dead and Maria's son ill and successfully manipulated by Alburquerque. It seems that the prime minister will be victorious, but Leonor, before her death, has prophesied her son's triumph and Alburquerque's downfall so convincingly that, even as he watches her die, the prime minister already feels the sting of defeat.

Centering as it does on three strong characters, each with his or her distinctive personality, the play sustains the audience's interest. Nevertheless, it is inferior to *Francesca da Rimini*. In *Leonor de Guzman*, too many humorous scenes inappropriately distract the audience from the ensuing tragedy, and too many characters participating in palace intrigue blur the development of the three principal characters.

THE BETROTHAL

The Betrothal is a comedy about Costanza, who unhappily agrees to marry the evil Marsio to save her aristocratic father from poverty and possibly from prison. When she falls in love with Count Juranio, the count's kinsman Salvatore manipulates events so that Costanza may marry the man she loves without ruining her father. Like *Francesca da Rimini* and *Leonor de Guzman*, *The Betrothal* is written in blank verse and centers on characters of aristocratic birth, but in addition to the expected difference in tone, the differences in plot, character, and theme distinctly set this comedy apart from Boker's tragedies. Murder is plotted in *The Betrothal*, but, as is consistent with its comic tone, no death occurs. Furthermore, the romance between Costanza's cousin and Juranio's kinsman is developed into a subplot, something Boker avoids in the two tragedies.

The characters of *The Betrothal* are interesting figures, but unlike the prominent characters in the two tragedies, they are merely types—Costanza and Juranio as the virtuous lovers, Filippia and Salvatore as the loyal confidants, and Marsio as the evil suitor. Little exists in their portrayal to make them other than hero, heroine, or villain.

All three plays have a major character who is not a proper aristocrat. Pepe is a mere jester in *Francesca da Rimini*; Leonor, by becoming a mistress, has relinquished the status with which she was born; Marsio represents the nouveau riche. An important theme of the two tragedies is that those set apart from elite society may defeat the aristocracy. Pepe dies victorious, knowing that he has made royalty suffer. Leonor also dies victorious, knowing that her son, a bastard, will be king. In *The Betrothal*, however, Marsio, who is despicable partly because he lacks aristocratic graces, suffers ignominious defeat so that two aristocrats may appropriately marry each other. Boker's admiration for democracy is not apparent in this comedy.

OTHER MAJOR WORKS

POETRY: *The Lesson of Life and Other Poems*, 1848; *The Podesta's Daughter and Other Miscella-neous Poems*, 1852; *Poems of the War*, 1864; *The Book of the Dead*, 1882; *Sonnets: A Sequence on Profane Love*, 1929 (Edward Sculley Bradley, editor).

MISCELLANEOUS: *Plays and Poems*, 1856 (2 volumes).

BIBLIOGRAPHY

Bradley, Edward Scully. *George Henry Boker: Poet and Patriot*. 1927. Reprint. New York: B. Blom, 1972. A classic literary biography, examining Boker's works in conjunction with his life. Bradley concludes that Boker was the victim of nineteenth century provincials who were reluctant to praise anything American and attempts to kindle interest in Boker among early twentieth century readers. Illustrations, bibliography of Boker's writings, general bibliography, and index.

Evans, Oliver H. *George Henry Boker*. Boston: Twayne, 1984. A basic biography of Boker, with criticism of his drama and poetry. Includes bibliography and index.

Kitts, Thomas M. *The Theatrical Life of George Henry Boker*. Vol. 3 in *Artists and Issues in the Theatre*. New York: P. Lang, 1994. Kitts examines Boker's life and his dramatic works. Includes bibliography and index.

Margaret Ann Baker,
updated by Gerald S. Argetsinger

ROBERT BOLT

Born: Sale, England; August 15, 1924
Died: Near Petersfield, England; February 20, 1995

PRINCIPAL DRAMA

A Man for All Seasons, pr. 1954 (radio play), pr. 1957 (televised), pr. 1960 (staged), pb. 1960
The Last of the Wine, pr. 1955 (radio play), pr. 1956 (staged)
The Critic and the Heart, pr. 1957
Flowering Cherry, pr. 1957, pb. 1958
The Tiger and the Horse, pr. 1960, pb. 1961
Gentle Jack, pr. 1963, pb. 1965
The Thwarting of Baron Bolligrew, pr. 1965, pb. 1966 (children's play)
Brother and Sister, pr. 1967, 1968 (revision of *The Critic and the Heart*)

Vivat! Vivat Regina!, pr. 1970, pb. 1971
State of Revolution, pr., pb. 1977
Plays: One, pb. 2000
Plays: Two, pb. 2001

OTHER LITERARY FORMS

Robert Bolt began his career in drama as a writer of radio plays for the British Broadcasting Company (BBC), starting in 1953 with *The Master*, a play about the wandering scholars of the Middle Ages. He wrote sixteen scripts for the BBC, including eight for children. The first version of *A Man for All Seasons* was broadcast as a radio drama in 1954, and his very first production on the legitimate stage, *The Last of the Wine*, originated as a radio script a year earlier.

Bolt's most noteworthy achievements outside the legitimate theater, however, were as a screenwriter. He worked with the renowned British director David Lean on *Lawrence of Arabia*, creating a screenplay based on T. E. Lawrence's own writings. The film received the Academy Award for Best Picture of 1962, and Bolt's scenario received a special award from the British Film Academy. His adaptation of Boris Pasternak's novel *Doctor Zhivago*, another script written for Lean, won an Oscar for the Best Screenplay of 1965, an honor repeated in 1966 when Bolt adapted his own play, *A Man for All Seasons* (directed by Fred Zinnemann). The film version also earned for Bolt the British Film Academy Award and the New York Film Critics Circle Award in 1966. His next project was an original treatment of *Ryan's Daughter* for Lean in 1970. In 1972, he wrote and directed *Lady Caroline Lamb*, based on the life of the mistress of George Gordon, Lord Byron, the famous English poet.

In the 1980's, Bolt concentrated on screenplays, teleplays, and adaptations, notably *The Mission* (1986; starring Robert DeNiro), *Nostromo* (an adaptation of the Joseph Conrad novel, with Christopher Hampton, which was not completed), and *Without Warning* (1991), based on the life of James Brady, the press secretary to President Ronald Reagan who was disabled by a would-be presidential assassin's bullet in 1981.

Robert Bolt in 1962. (AP/Wide World Photos)

ACHIEVEMENTS

Robert Bolt earned the reputation of being a serious dramatist whose sense of stagecraft made him popular with theater audiences. Critics also recognized his talent for structure and his concern with language from the time of his appearance in the West End theaters of London with *Flowering Cherry* in 1957. This play, a popular and critical success during its 435 performances at the Haymarket Theatre, won for him the *Evening Standard* Drama Award for Most Promising Playwright of that year. Although Bolt launched his career in the heyday of the Angry Young Men, when playwrights as diverse as John Osborne, Harold Pinter, John Arden, and Arnold Wesker challenged the then reigning conventions of English theater, he was never associated with the avant-garde. In fact, Bolt deliberately rejected many features of the new drama while responding to those influences that he could accommodate to his traditional aesthetic.

Bolt's own statements about his approach to his art reflected his conviction that conventional dramatic structure, with a clearly articulated plot and an organic unity, not only satisfied the legitimate expectations of the audience but also provided an effective vehicle "for conveying delicate but immediate insights." He compared highly conventional theater, "where both sides of the footlights understand thoroughly what's going on," to a taut drumskin that resounds at the lightest tap. "Take away these conventions and you find yourself with a slack drumskin; you've got to jump up and down on it before you get even the slightest tinkle." Bolt also maintained that the slice-of-life dramatists who allow the audience to supply play endings use the theater "as a therapeutic rather than dramatic medium."

Bolt's earliest dramas were traditional well-crafted plays, largely naturalistic in approach, with a fourth-wall style of dramaturgy. Even as early as *Flowering Cherry*, however, Bolt was striving to break out of the purely naturalistic mode while maintaining a clear, unified structure. *A Man for All Seasons* realizes these ambitions. This play established Bolt as one of the most popular playwrights in the London theater, running more than nine months in London and enjoying an even longer New York run of more than a year and a half, starting in November, 1961. Despite some demurrers such as the influential critic Kenneth Tynan, the drama won widespread critical acclaim. Robert Corrigan was among those who considered *A Man for All Seasons* "one of the finest achievements of the modern theatre." Jerry Tallman of *The Village Voice* could think of no play that had surpassed it in almost forty years for dramatic tension, structure, meaning, and language. The stage version received two American drama awards in 1962: the Tony Award of the American Theatre Wing for the best play of that year and the New York Drama Critics Circle Award for the best foreign play.

BIOGRAPHY

Robert Oxton Bolt was born in 1924, the younger son of Ralph Bolt and Leah Binnion Bolt. His family lived in the small town of Sale in Lancashire, England, where his father owned a shop carrying mostly furniture, glass, and china. His mother was a schoolteacher. The playwright described his parents as loving, concerned, and not unduly strict, despite their high standards. Though Bolt described his religious

position as between agnosticism and atheism, he was reared a Methodist. He stated, "I ought to be religious in the sense that I'm comfortable thinking in religious terms and altogether I seem naturally constituted to be religious."

Despite his good home background, Bolt distinguished himself as a youngster by constantly getting into trouble and remaining at the bottom of his class in the Manchester Grammar School until his graduation in 1940. Not really prepared to enter any career or qualified to go on to a university, he became an office boy for the Sun Life Assurance Company in Manchester in 1942—a position he thoroughly loathed. Determined to escape from this whole way of life, he leaped at the opportunity to study for a degree in commerce under special wartime arrangements for admission to a university program. Through intensive preparation for his Advanced Level examinations, he gained a place in an honors school at Manchester University rather than the school of commerce. There, he began work for a degree in history in 1943. During this period, he also became a Marxist. From 1942 to 1947, he was a member of the Communist Party, inspired by youthful idealistic visions of the party's ability to change the world. He has since described himself as a Marxist with so many reservations that he would probably be scorned by a true Marxist.

After a year at Manchester University, Bolt joined the Royal Air Force and later transferred to the army, serving as an officer with the Royal West African Frontier Force in Ghana. At the end of the war, he returned to the university, where he was awarded an honors degree in history in 1949. That same year, he married Celia Ann Roberts, a painter. The couple had three children—Sally, Benedict, and Joanna—before their divorce in 1967. Bolt would later marry the actress Sara Miles, by whom he had one son and from whom he was divorced in 1976. In 1980, he married Ann Zane.

Following his graduation from Manchester, Bolt prepared for a career in education by studying for his teaching diploma, which he received from the University of Exeter in 1950. For the next eight years, he worked as an English teacher, first at a village in Bishopsteignton in Devon and then at Millfield School in Street, Devon. His desire to become a dramatist first developed in 1954 while he was searching for a Nativity play to perform with the children at the village school. Finding none of the plays he had read satisfactory, he decided to compose his own. Bolt recalled vividly "the electric tension" that built up inside him after he had composed some of the dialogue, and he remembered telling his wife, "Listen, I think I've found what I want to do." At this point, he decided to combine teaching with writing and began composing radio scripts.

An adaptation of his 1955 radio script, *The Last of the Wine*, was staged in London at Theatre in the Round in 1956. The success of Osborne's play *Look Back in Anger* that same year made Bolt feel that young playwrights might have a chance of breaking into the West End theaters, and Bolt sent his play *The Critic and the Heart* to the Royal Court Theatre, where the reader—Osborne himself—rejected it, claiming that it was a promising play but not the particular kind of drama that the theater was seeking. Although Bolt did not succeed in getting a West End showing, *The Critic and the Heart* was produced at the Oxford Playhouse in 1957 and was well received. This play represents Bolt at his most traditional. Bolt himself criticized the play for being too orthodox and completely naturalistic in form. He tells how, being inexperienced in the theater, he modeled the play on W. Somerset Maugham's *The Circle* (pr., pb. 1921), doing a detailed structural analysis and following it closely in his own play, even down to the placement of climaxes and the lengths of acts. As Ronald Hayman emphasizes, however, the content and dialogue are distinctly Bolt's own; the playwright also demonstrates his capacity for closely interweaving characters and plot. Bolt later rewrote the play as *Brother and Sister*, which was produced at Brighton in 1967; another revised version appeared at Bristol in 1968.

With his next play, *Flowering Cherry*, Bolt caught the attention of director Frith Banbury, known for his promotion of promising young playwrights. Banbury arranged Bolt's first West End production in 1957 with a stellar cast, including Ralph Richardson and Celia Johnson in the leads. The highly successful London run was followed by a New York production

in 1959; critics received it far less enthusiastically. Bolt's next work, *The Tiger and the Horse*, about the effects a petition to ban the hydrogen bomb have on a middle-class university family, is another basically naturalistic domestic drama of the same type as *Flowering Cherry*. Like its predecessor, it was directed by Banbury, beginning a successful London run in August, 1960.

A Man for All Seasons began its run at the Globe Theater in July, 1960, with Paul Scofield as Sir Thomas More; *The Tiger and the Horse*, though written first, opened a month later. Therefore, Bolt had the distinction of having two very different types of plays enjoying success at the West End theaters simultaneously. The 1960's also found Bolt branching out into screenwriting and winning distinction in that field as well. In 1961, he also went to jail briefly, along with other members of Bertrand Russell's Committee of One Hundred, for antinuclear protests that involved token breaches of the law. Bolt had been working on the screenplay for *Lawrence of Arabia* at the time, and progress on the film stopped while he was away from the scene. Finally, producer Sam Spiegel angrily pressured him into binding himself over and coming out of prison because people's jobs and thousands of dollars were at stake. Bolt spoke of this as a surrender, an action he regretted, despite the good reasons for doing it.

Bolt's next drama for the legitimate stage was *Gentle Jack*, a highly experimental drama in which he sought to move even further away from naturalism. John R. Kaiser aptly described the play as "an adult fairy tale or an allegorical fantasy" dealing with the appearance of the god Pan in the modern world. Produced in 1963, with Dame Edith Evans and Kenneth Williams in the leading roles, *Gentle Jack* is perhaps the least successful of Bolt's major theatrical works, running for only seventy-five performances. Neither the critics nor the public received it favorably. Many found it puzzling and obscure, a marked departure from Bolt's usual clarity and even from the types of drama that had made him one of the leading popular playwrights of his time.

For his next stage venture, Bolt turned to another fairy tale, but this time a highly successful one for chil-

dren, *The Thwarting of Baron Bolligrew*, first performed in December, 1965, by the Royal Shakespeare
Company at the Aldwich Theatre in London. It has
been noted that Bolt's penchant for larger-than-life
figures served him well in creating his fairy tale characters, including the stout, elderly hero, Sir Oblong
Fitz-Oblong, a knight with a strong sense of duty, and
the villainous Baron Bolligrew. The knight is a humorous version of the uncommon man of principle
who must fight against the evil and deception in the
society around him. Ronald Hayman notes that, "like
some children, he tries too hard to be good." Bolt also
makes use of a Storyteller who, like the Common
Man, provides a narrative link between episodes and
occasionally takes part in the action, such as by making the moon rise when Sir Oblong asks for it.

Bolt returned to historical subjects for the adult
dramas that he wrote after *Gentle Jack. Vivat! Vivat
Regina!*—his treatment of the rival queens Mary Stuart and Elizabeth Tudor—had its premiere at the
Chichester Festival in 1970. It then moved to the
Piccadilly Theatre in London, where it proved a major hit of the season. The play also had a successful
New York engagement in 1972. A play dealing with
the Russian Revolution and Vladimir Ilich Lenin's
central role in it, *State of Revolution*, was first produced in 1977 at the Birmingham Repertory Theatre
and later at the National Theatre.

Bolt suffered a debilitating stroke in 1981, leaving
him partially paralyzed but capable of walking with a
cane. He felt an affinity to the experiences of Press
Secretary James Brady, whose gunshot wound from
an attempt on the life of President Ronald Reagan left
him similarly paralyzed. Bolt's treatment of Brady's
life in *Without Warning* is said to incorporate much of
Bolt's own reactions to his illness. Interviewers in
1991 noted Bolt's speech difficulties but remarked on
his total clarity of thought and expression. He died in
1995.

ANALYSIS

Though Robert Bolt did not match the success of
A Man for All Seasons in his subsequent dramas, he
effectively employed the open or epic style of that
work to explore other historical subjects in *Vivat!*

Vivat Regina! and *State of Revolution*. He also continued to use the technical devices associated with a
consciously theatrical style of dramaturgy for carefully planned effects. Bolt never lost his concern for a
realistic examination of human behavior or his ability
to interweave close connections between plot and
character. He was one of the most skillful crafts-
people in contemporary British theater, a popular
playwright who took drama seriously and merits serious regard.

The full range of Bolt's achievements can be illustrated most effectively through a more detailed consideration of four major plays. *The Tiger and the
Horse* demonstrates the "uneasy straddling between
naturalism and non-naturalism" that he found in his
earlier plays. It also represents one of his attempts to
give his contemporaries the larger-than-life significance he finds appropriate in theatrical characters.
Marking a significant development in Bolt's dramaturgical skills, *A Man for All Seasons* shows how he
turned to historical settings to escape the pitfalls of
naturalism and to present individuals of significant
dramatic dimension. The play remains his most penetrating examination of the individual in conflict with
society. In *Vivat! Vivat Regina!*, he draws on the artificiality of the theater in presenting the conflict between two striking historical figures. Finally, *State of
Revolution* represents a serious attempt to explore
some decisive events in contemporary history and the
towering figure who gave them shape.

THE TIGER AND THE HORSE

The Tiger and the Horse is a well-plotted domestic drama in which a petition to ban the bomb serves
as a major catalyst in the action; its effects are skillfully interwoven with the crises of a seduction and
growing insanity to provide some intensely pitched
action.

The title alludes to an aphorism by the poet William Blake, from *The Marriage of Heaven and Hell*
(1790): "The tygers of wrath are wiser than the
horses of instruction," which suggests that the logic
of the heart can express a higher wisdom than can the
reasoning of the mind. In his review of the play, Richard Findlater aptly summarized the theme embedded
in the drama "as the relative values of commitment in

private and public life, and the balance of power between heart and head among members of the English thinking class." Through Bolt's craftmanship, public issues and private concerns are skillfully intertwined in the development of the plot.

Jack Dean, the Master of a university college who is in line for the vice chancellorship, is the horse of the play. Though a kindly, tolerant, and highly principled man, he has developed as his personal philosophy a detachment that is essentially a refusal to become involved, an emotional neutrality that he unwittingly carries over into personal relationships as well as into his approach to larger issues. Even his having abandoned astronomy to take up philosophy becomes significant in Bolt's careful delineation of his character. When his daughter Stella is looking through his telescope and taking comfort in the order she finds in nature, Dean launches into one of the "big speeches" found here and in *Flowering Cherry*: He speaks of the darkness, "ignorant of human necessities," that fills the spaces between the stars, and he adds that what appears to be a meaningful pattern in the universe is actually merely "Scribble." Thus, staid, imperturbable Dean reveals the terrifying vision of the existential void that led him to turn away from investigating the world around him and to take refuge in abstract philosophical speculation.

When Louis Flax, a research fellow from a working-class background, circulates a petition urging nuclear disarmament, Dean refuses to sign. One vote, he says, does not really matter, and he claims that he does not understand all the political and diplomatic considerations involved. The same lack of engagement is apparent in his personal life. When Stella tries to warn Dean that her mother is acting strangely and seems mentally unbalanced, he refuses to take her concern seriously. At first, too, he fends off Stella's confidences about Louis. Only when she tells her father that she is pregnant and has no intention of marrying Louis because he does not really love her does she crack that mask of imperturbability. Dean responds with natural fatherly concern for Stella and indignation against Louis, yet while he offers his daughter his firm support and expresses distress on her behalf, he still insists, "I am not involved."

Dean's wife, Gwendoline, is the tiger of the play, a woman capable of passionate intensity, though she has obviously submerged her own feelings in her role as the Master's wife. A biologist before her marriage, she is profoundly moved by the issue of the bomb, aware of the mutation that radiation can cause in unborn children. She is ready to sign Louis's petition until Sir Hugo Slade, the present vice chancellor of the university, reminds her that such an action on her part could cost her husband the vice chancellor's post. She tries to find out what Dean wants her to do, but he refuses to coerce her in any way, even offering her the pen and urging her to sign the petition. She holds back out of concern for his position, even though she continues to brood over the petition—to the point of arousing Stella's concern.

Louis Flax, like Dean, is an intellectual who is out of touch with his emotions. The general concern for humanity that underlies his petition against the hydrogen bomb does not extend itself to a genuine love for the woman bearing his child. Even though he dutifully proposes marriage to Stella, he, too, must discover the place love should occupy in his life.

The climax comes when Dean discovers that Gwendoline has gone mad and has slashed the Holbein painting belonging to the college (one that depicts a deformed child) and attached the petition to the damaged portrait. In the confrontation that follows, Dean realizes that he bears the responsibility for his wife's troubled state. His philosophy of dissociation, his unwitting failure to share anything with her, has led her to believe that he does not really love her and that he tolerated her only out of his "goodness." Her concern over the issues raised by Louis's petition finally pushed her over the edge. Though Sir Hugo Slade urges Dean publicly to dissociate himself from his wife's action, Dean accepts responsibility for what he has done to her. He expresses his love for her and refuses to dismiss her gesture as merely the aberration of an insane woman, even going so far as to add his own signature to the petition.

In many respects, *The Tiger and the Horse* is a conventional, well-made play, integrating a serious contemporary theme with the stuff of traditional domestic drama. The reservations that Hayman and others have expressed about the play are valid. In particular, the plot is so tightly developed that there is no room to develop the characters as effectively as Bolt might have done. For example, the progression of Gwendoline's madness is never really dramatized; her eccentricity and troubled behavior are only mentioned in the dialogue. Therefore, her breakdown has a certain melodramatic edge. Similarly, Louis's changed attitude after his son is born—his discovery that he really does love Stella—is not dramatized; rather, it is tacked on to provide a conventional happy ending.

A MAN FOR ALL SEASONS

With *A Man for All Seasons*, Bolt shifted to a historical subject, but one that embodies themes relevant to contemporary life. He felt that the distancing effect of a play set in past centuries would provide a way of escaping from some of the constraints of naturalism, such as an overriding concern for the skillful use of realistic plot detail.

The play's protagonist, Sir Thomas More, exemplifies the man who has realized his full potential. The historical Thomas More was a charming, urbane man, extraordinarily successful in his public and private life—happy in his family and in his friendships, accomplished as a statesman, renowned for his intelligence and wit. Unlike Jack Dean, he was intensely involved in the life of his times, yet he retained enough detachment to keep his sense of values intact. As Bolt stresses in his preface to the play, he found More's most distinctive quality to be "an adamantine sense of his own self. He knew where he began and left off, what area of himself he could yield to the encroachments of his enemies, and what to the encroachments of those he loved." Though More loved life and did not court martyrdom, he was willing to die rather than betray his deepest principles. More could not falsely express approval of King Henry VIII's divorce and subsequent marriage to Anne Boleyn, particularly when this meant swearing an oath, pledging his integrity as a guarantor of the truth. Thus, Bolt describes More as "a hero of selfhood."

Tynan objected that Bolt does not show the audience what More's underlying convictions were or why he embraced them so uncompromisingly. He notes that the playwright is not concerned with

whether these convictions are right or wrong but only that More clung to them and would not disclose them under questioning. More's speech before the death sentence is passed succinctly states his position that the act of Parliament making King Henry supreme head of the Church is contrary to divine law, but Bolt's concern is not with exploring the soundness of More's view; rather, he dramatizes More's twofold struggle—to preserve his life, if possible, but above all to preserve his soul, or essential self.

Corrigan has described the main action of the play as a series of confrontations between More and those who seek to make him retreat from that last stronghold of the self and accede to the king's behest. Bolt effectively uses the Brechtian device of a series of semi-independent scenes to develop these confrontations. The scenes show More adroitly facing powerful opponents, as well as interacting with his family, which is deeply involved with his fate. Because of Bolt's emphasis on More's domestic life, Hayman has found *A Man for All Seasons* thin on social texture, a drama focusing on personal relationships rather than showing the individual pitted against society. Yet Bolt has correctly noted that More himself attached great importance to his family life. Moreover, the conflicts Bolt presents are skillfully orchestrated to show More facing questions, opposition, and misunderstandings in the small world of his home at the same time that he is battling them in the world at large.

Perhaps the two most important foils for More are Richard Rich and the Common Man. When Rich first appears, he is arguing with More, maintaining that "every man has his price," an opinion that his own subsequent career aptly illustrates. Not adequately defined by any strong sense of personal values, as More is, he is readily tempted to sell himself in order to procure advancement. Rich undergoes something of an interior struggle when he finds himself drifting toward betrayal of his king, but he soon sheds any semblance of self-respect to become a useful tool to Thomas Cromwell. Unlike More, who will not compromise himself by a false oath that is a mere formality, Rich boldly perjures himself in a capital case to help Cromwell secure More's conviction.

The Common Man, who assumes various roles within the play, starting as More's steward Matthew and ending as his executioner, provides another foil to the man of uncommon moral courage. Bolt indicates that he used "common" in the sense of "that which is common to us all"; he intended to have the audience identify to a degree with the character. In each role, the Common Man demonstrates his overriding concern with two basic human instincts, self-interest and self-preservation. Anselm Atkins has argued that, despite essential differences, the Common Man is made to resemble More sufficiently to have the audience recognize themselves in both characters. More represents what we could be, at our best. The Common Man indicates what we all too often are—concerned finally with slipping by comfortably in life, getting what we can without too many moral scruples. Both characters are extremely rational and both seek with great care to keep themselves out of trouble. Like More, the Common Man draws a firm boundary between what he will and will not do, only in his case he draws a line where risks outweigh gains, as when Cromwell offers the jailer a dangerously large sum for information about his prisoner More. The Common Man, unlike More, is concerned with preserving his bodily life at all costs, not with the essential self, his soul.

Bolt's masterful handling of language, blending a Tudor flavor into modern dialogue and skillfully interpolating More's own words where appropriate, is a notable feature of the play. The dramatist indicated that he sought to make thematic use of images, with dry land representing society and the sea and water representing "that larger context which we all inhabit, the terrifying cosmos." These references are so naturally interwoven into the rest of the play that they generally escape notice, yet the pattern is there; such remarks as King Henry's passing allusion to *his* river, where he is playing the role of pilot, and Matthew's reference to More's fear of drowning have additional resonance when seen in this context.

VIVAT! VIVAT REGINA!

Bolt's preface to *Vivat! Vivat Regina!* makes evident his conviction that setting plays in the past is one method of giving characters the particularity they need to emerge as people rather than as archetypes while still enabling them to be "theatrical." By this the playwright meant that the characters have "a continuously high pitch of speech and action" obviously different from the pace of real life but appropriate to the heightened intensity of drama and made convincing within the dramatic framework. Bolt felt that the audience accepts theatrical speech and action more readily in characters from the past "not because we seriously think they really did continuously speak and act like that but because we don't know how they spoke and only know the more dramatic of their actions."

Certainly Bolt selected a highly dramatic subject in the parallel careers of Elizabeth I of England and Mary, Queen of Scots, and the tragic rivalry between the two monarchs. Here the tension between the individual and society emerges as a study of the conflict between fulfillment in personal relationships and the exigencies of political power. Both women are strong-willed queens. As they steer their courses through troubled political waters, each recognizing a potential threat in the other, they must make crucial choices between love and political expediency. Elizabeth, who from her youth has had to be extremely self-controlled and politically calculating, can subordinate her needs as a woman to the requirements of her office, though at great psychological cost. She suppresses part of her personality, becoming hardened and neurotic even as she achieves greatness as a monarch. By contrast, Mary refuses to suppress the emotional side of her nature. She willfully chooses love, even though she risks political disaster.

Bolt's mastery of structure is evident in his handling of complex historical events unfolding over a number of years. He employs a series of parallel scenes, with the action shifting back and forth between Mary and Elizabeth in the same type of fluid staging that characterized *A Man for All Seasons.* He also uses patently theatrical devices to advance the action and to underscore the interconnections between the two monarchs' careers. In one such scene, Elizabeth is seated aloft on the throne as the baptism of Mary's son James, heir of the Tudor line, takes place in the foreground. The most stylized piece of action occurs at the Kirk o' Field incident, where Mary is shown acting in collusion with Bothwell, the murderer of her second husband, Darnley. She is seen dancing "puppet-like under Bothwell's compelling stare," then dancing alone and frightened. After an explosion rocks the stage and scatters the dancers, John Knox steps into the spotlight vacated by Mary and denounces her. When the lights come up, the other dancers are revealed to include Elizabeth and Lord Cecil, Philip of Spain, and the pope, who remonstrate with Mary over her involvement with Bothwell.

In discussing how he gave dramatic shape to the involved story of the two monarchs, Bolt notes that he sought "to present the confused eventfulness of Mary's life as a series of single theatrical happenings, and to present the torturous complexities of Elizabeth's policy as an immediate response." Bolt draws a sharply dramatic contrast between the two monarchs in terms of sexual politics. At the beginning of the play, Elizabeth, though deeply in love with Robert Dudley, reluctantly takes Lord Cecil's advice not to marry him because of his suspected involvement with his wife's death. The queen believes him innocent but realizes that such a marriage might cost her the throne. Her decision is partially affected by the knowledge that Mary, Queen of Scots, would welcome such a move. So much has she learned to subordinate her personal feelings to concerns of state that she later agrees to let Cecil propose Robert Dudley, now earl of Leicester, as a "safe" suitor for Mary, Queen of Scots.

Instead, Mary makes a politically advantageous second marriage to Henry Stuart, Lord Darnley, which strengthens her claim to the English throne, yet even this marriage reflects Mary's determination to have a husband she can love. When Darnley proves weak and faithless, participating in the plot to kill the queen's favorite, David Rizzio, Mary falls deeply in love with Lord Bothwell. Unlike Elizabeth, she is portrayed as all too ready to risk her throne for love. Not only does she bring Darnley to Kirk o' Field under threat of otherwise losing Bothwell's love; she also refuses to repudiate Bothwell later, acting against Elizabeth's own admonition. Mary stubbornly maintains that he was tried and found innocent, de-

spite the questionable nature of the verdict. She further reveals that she has married him. Even after she has surrendered herself to the Scottish nobility on condition that they let Bothwell go, she refuses to conciliate the lords by repudiating the marriage as a forced one and thus reclaiming her throne. Passionately, she declares, "I would follow him to the edge of the earth—in my shift!" When Bothwell is driven into exile and Mary is living as a royal prisoner in England, she still clings to the hope that he will keep his promise and return. Mary's pained acknowledgment that Bothwell will not return—she learns that he has taken service with the king of Denmark and has another woman in his house—leads her to renounce love to "study policy." This "policy," however, involves her in a conspiracy against Elizabeth and leads to her execution.

Because the two queens never met historically, Bolt does not invent any scene involving a direct confrontation between them as other dramatists, including Friedrich Schiller, have done. A key scene in the latter's *Maria Stuart* (pr. 1800; *Mary Stuart*, 1801) is a meeting between Elizabeth and Mary at Fotheringhay Castle, where Mary wins a moral victory over Elizabeth that ensures her death. In *Vivat! Vivat Regina!* the monarchs exchange words onstage twice in scenes that are obviously representational of exchanges that took place in letters. In addition, Bolt gains considerable dramatic impact by emphasizing the psychological effects of the rivalry. Elizabeth's reaction to the news of Mary's escape (following the murder of Rizzio) reveals her envy of Mary's more intense involvement in life. She particularly envies the passionate response the Queen of Scots can evoke in men such as Lord Bothwell, who "raises men, half-naked men . . . and drives her enemies from Edinburgh—and for what? Why, for herself." The English queen's envy is heightened by the awareness that the child Mary is carrying will be heir to the English throne, since Elizabeth is "barren stock." When Elizabeth is thought merciful for giving Mary refuge in England, even after hearing an impassioned letter from Mary to Bothwell that furnishes proof of Mary's involvement in the plot to kill Darnley, Lord Cecil astutely observes, "I do not think that this is altogether mercy. I think our Queen sees Mary in the mirror." On the other hand, Mary signs the letter giving her approval of the conspiracy against Elizabeth after she has learned that her son, James, has never received any of the letters and gifts she has sent and that Elizabeth "has played the mother's part." Her fury against the English queen impels Mary to an action that she knows might entrap her and lead to her death.

Bolt's psychobiographical approach presents both Mary and Elizabeth in human terms while fashioning an extremely effective structure for dramatizing the intertwined careers of the two monarchs. Hayman finds that the emphasis on personal relationships, which he sees as characteristic of Bolt's dramas, prevents Bolt from mining the complexity of his subject sufficiently. Similarly, Irving Wardle has called the play "an immensely skillful piece of cosmetic surgery: adding the common touch and the free-flowing action of epic theatre, while leaving the assumptions of heroic costume drama untouched." Other critics, however, such as Samuel Hirsch, have found *Vivat! Vivat Regina!* "exciting theater" that "illuminates history by putting it in the perspective of human personality."

STATE OF REVOLUTION

When Bolt turned to twentieth century history and the Russian Revolution for the subject of his next play, *State of Revolution*, he focused on another uncommon man—this time a leader at odds not only with the capitalist society he sought to replace but also with his fellow revolutionaries. What fascinated the playwright was Vladimir Lenin's uncompromising dedication to the Marxist view of history and the Socialist Revolution as he saw it developing. Adopting the Marxist ethic that anything that promoted the establishment of the Socialist State was justified, Lenin often sanctioned extreme and brutal measures as necessary means to this great end. In an interview with Sally Emerson, Bolt stressed the paradox this man presented: "Viewed in one light, he was an indefensible monster, in another he was a great and good man. He did and said quite impermissible things but he was also selfless with no love of cruelty for its own sake."

Once again employing an episodic structure, Bolt moves from the pre-Revolutionary period in 1910,

when the Bolshevik leaders were running a school to train party activists at Maxim Gorky's villa in Capri, through the revolution and its aftermath, ending with Vladimir Ilich Lenin's death and Joseph Stalin's rise to power in 1924. In order to provide a frame for the chronicle, the playwright uses as his narrator a historical figure, Anatole Lunacharsky, an associate of Lenin who became commissioner for education and enlightenment in the Soviet State. Lunacharsky is portrayed as addressing a meeting of Young Communists around 1930, on the anniversary of Lenin's death. As critic David Zane Mairowitz has emphasized, Lunacharsky, a humane intellectual, reflects the original idealism within the revolutionary movement as well as the questioning and moral scruples that surfaced as its promise was betrayed. Mairowitz and others have also shown the basic problem with this particular framing device: The staged events purport to dramatize Lunacharsky's speech to his 1930 audience, yet such an account of the origins of Stalinism is inconceivable in that context. By 1930, the Stalinist rewriting of history was already well under way.

Nevertheless, Lunacharsky's account does present a compelling portrait of Lenin as a complex, driven man who acted with a terrible consistency in pursuing the goal of establishing a Socialist State. The play provides glimpses of the human warmth that Lenin too often suppressed in the name of revolutionary ideal, yet it also shows the cold detachment and ruthless determination he could exercise when personal feelings or human considerations seemed contrary to these greater goals. Despite his feeling of friendship for Lunacharsky, Lenin can brutally question why he is still in the party with his baggage of humanistic notions. Lenin argues that "unconditional human love is nothing but a dirty dream" at a moment in history that requires "unconditional class hatred." He further indicates that he is willing to sacrifice cultural values, even the "moral amenities," to achieve the new society that will beget its own virtue—"its own new form of love and unimaginable music." Yet Lenin's words also suggest his own brand of revolutionary idealism and his intensity of purpose.

One of the deepest ironies underscored in the drama is the contradiction that Lenin's career offers to the Marxist view of history he embraced, which postulates that history finds the individuals it needs, contrary to the doctrine that great individuals shape events. At many crucial points, it is Lenin's "overwhelming, ruthless will" that determines the course of events, prevailing over the opposition of other Bolshevik leaders. Convinced that a Russian Revolution would lead to a worldwide Socialist revolution, he argues for an end to Russian participation in World War I and the immediate pursuit of a civil war. He is also determined to use the discontent of the peasants in promoting a Socialist revolution, even though the realistic Gorky emphasizes the disparity between the goals of the peasants and the aims of the Bolsheviks; the peasants desire individual ownership of the land, not the establishment of a collectivist society. Lenin also argues for the adoption of the Brest-Litovsk Treaty with Germany despite its harsh conditions because his first priority is continuing the Revolution on any possible terms. After the Bolsheviks assume power, he continues to play the prime role in charting the development of the Socialist state. Following the Kronstadt uprising, he is the prime force shaping the New Economic Policy that permits a measure of capitalistic enterprise, because he deems this a necessary expedient. He also favors using the Cheka as a counterrevolutionary police force to root out the bourgeois elements in the party.

The greatest irony, however, is the failure of Lenin's last supreme effort to exert his will and to influence the party's choice of leader after his death. The Central Committee suppresses Lenin's "Testament" as the work of a sick man, even though its warning proves fatefully accurate. In this important document, Lenin expresses his preference for Leon Davidovich Trotsky as the next Party leader and warns that Stalin is too brutal. The irony is compounded by the fact that Stalin has been considered the ideal party functionary for years, doing what needs to be done (like Thomas Cromwell in *A Man for All Seasons*). When he hears Lenin's warning that he will not use his power as party secretary with sufficient caution, Stalin can remind the committee that he carried out all the jobs that Lenin asked him to do. He can also remind them that revolution is brutal—a statement Lenin

himself often made. Lenin's collapse takes place onstage in the background during Stalin's delivery of his triumphant speech before the Thirteenth Congress— dramatically emphasizing Lenin's unsuccessful struggle to combat the menace he sees in Stalin. Bolt's drama portrays the development of Stalinism as a perverted outgrowth of Marxism-Leninism and makes clear the dangers of a philosophy that can dispense with the "moral amenities" in seeking to establish the dictatorship of the proletariat.

State of Revolution evoked mixed responses from the critics. Although the play confirms Bolt's talent for providing a clearly developed structure in treating the complex events of the Russian Revolution and its disastrous aftermath, Mairowitz has pointed out a number of oversimplifications in Bolt's treatment of the material, such as his failure to make clear that a civil war was in progress and his focusing on the Bolshevik leaders with relatively little attention to the lower classes and their part in these historic events. Mairowitz and other critics have observed that the Bolshevik leaders tend to represent attitudes rather than fully articulated characters. Mairowitz adds that they sound like Englishmen in debate rather than impassioned Socialists. Despite such limitations, Bolt managed to construct a compelling portrait of Lenin tragically caught up in the Marxist view of history, a drama culminating in a terrifying vision of the logical consequences of the Marxist ethic as Lenin himself formulated it.

OTHER MAJOR WORKS

SCREENPLAYS: *Lawrence of Arabia*, 1962 (based on T. E. Lawrence's writings); *Doctor Zhivago*, 1965 (adaptation of Boris Pasternak's novel); *A Man for All Seasons*, 1966; *Ryan's Daughter*, 1970; *Lady Caroline Lamb*, 1972; *The Bounty*, 1984; *The Mission*, 1986.

TELEPLAY: *Without Warning: The James Brady Story*, 1991.

RADIO PLAYS: *The Master*, 1953; *Fifty Pigs*, 1953; *Ladies and Gentlemen*, 1954; *Mr. Sampson's Sundays*, 1955; *The Window*, 1958; *The Drunken Sailor*, 1958; *The Banana Tree*, 1961.

NONFICTION: "English Theatre Today: The Importance of Shape," 1958 (in *International Theatre Annual*).

TRANSLATION: *The Sisterhood: A Play*, 1989 (of Molière's play *Les Femmes savantes*).

BIBLIOGRAPHY

Carpenter, Gerald. "Robert Bolt: Drama of the Threatened Self." *American Film: Magazine of the Film and Television Arts* 14 (September, 1989): 60-62. Reviews seven films available on video, written by Bolt under several directors (he directed *Lady Caroline Lamb* himself). Carpenter finds *The Mission*, with Robert DeNiro and directed by Roland Joffe, the most successful film.

Gritten, David. "Writing for His Life." *Los Angeles Times*, June 9, 1991, p. CAL4. Written in conjunction with the presentation of the television film *Without Warning*, this essay notes the similarities between Bolt's recovery from a stroke and James Brady's recovery from the shooting.

Rusinko, Susan. *British Drama, 1950 to the Present: A Critical History*. Boston: Twayne, 1989. Rusinko places Bolt among the traditionalists, "a craftsman in the tradition of the well-constructed play middle-class audiences have come to expect." Contains a discussion of the controversy between critic Kenneth Tynan and Bolt regarding the Thomas More character in *A Man for All Seasons*.

Turner, Adrian. *Robert Bolt: Scenes from Two Lives*. London: Hutchinson, 1998. A biography of Bolt that examines his life as a dramatist and screenwriter. Bibliography and index.

Gertrude K. Hamilton,
updated by Thomas J. Taylor

EDWARD BOND

Born: Hollaway, North London, England; July 18, 1934

PRINCIPAL DRAMA

The Pope's Wedding, pr. 1962, pb. 1971
Saved, pr. 1965, pb. 1966
Early Morning, pr., pb. 1968
Narrow Road to the Deep North, pr., pb. 1968
Black Mass, pr. 1970, pb. 1971
Lear, pr. 1971, pb. 1972
Passion, pr., pb. 1971
Bingo: Scenes of Money and Death, pr. 1973, pb. 1974
The Sea, pr., pb. 1973
The Fool, pr. 1975, pb. 1976
A-A-America!, pr., pb. 1976
Stone, pr., pb. 1976
We Come to the River, pr., pb. 1976 (music by Hanz Werner Henze)
Plays, pb. 1977-1998 (6 volumes)
The Bundle: Or, New Narrow Road to the Deep North, pr., pb. 1978

The Woman, pr. 1978, pb. 1979
The Worlds, pr. 1979, pb. 1980
The Cat, pr. 1980, pb. 1982 (opera libretto; music by Henze, pb. 1983 as *The English Cat*)
Restoration, pr., pb. 1981 (music by Nick Bicat)
Summer, pr., pb. 1982
Derek, pr. 1982, pb. 1983
Red, Black, and Ignorant, pr. 1984, pb. 1985
The War Plays: A Trilogy, pr., pb. 1985 (includes *Red, Black, and Ignorant*, *The Tin Can People*, and *Great Peace*)
Human Cannon, pb. 1985, pr. 1986
Jackets, pr. 1989, pb. 1990
In the Company of Men, pr. 1989, pb. 1990
September, pr., pb. 1990
Lulu: A Monster Tragedy, pr., pb. 1992
Olly's Prison, pr. 1993 (televised), pb. 1993, pr. 1994 (staged)
Tuesday, pr., pb. 1993
Coffee, pb. 1995, pr. 1996
At the Inland Sea: A Play for Young People, pr. 1995, pb. 1997

Eleven Vests, pr., pb. 1997

The Crime of the Twenty-first Century, pb. 1999,
　pr. 2000

Chair, pr. 2000 (radio play)

The Children, pr., pb. 2000

Have I None, pr., pb. 2000

OTHER LITERARY FORMS

Edward Bond has adapted or translated classic plays, published several volumes of poetry and essays, and written a number of screenplays; he cowrote with Michelangelo Antonioni the screenplay for *Blow Up* (1967), also directed by Antonioni. Generally, Bond's essays deal with politics and the political responsibility of the artist.

ACHIEVEMENTS

Edward Bond's first major achievements occurred in the law court and in Parliament. His play *Saved* was the last British play prosecuted for obscenity; his *Early Morning*, the last banned entirely by the Lord Chancellor's office. The controversy stirred by these two plays focused attention on Britain's censorship laws and helped rally support to repeal them. Because of this notoriety and his association with London's Royal Court Theatre, long the home of experimental drama, Bond's detractors now dismiss him as an *enfant terrible* intent on shocking a complacent middle class. This view not only underestimates the excellence of Bond's early work but also denies the scope and richness of what has followed. A serious leftist, Bond has been concerned to show how social conditions generate moral ideas and how the past weighs on the present. Not surprisingly, then, Bond's later work has concentrated on mythic or historical subjects; he has written a play based on the Lear legend (*Lear*) and another about William Shakespeare in retirement (*Bingo*). *Early Morning* is set in Victoria's reign and *The Sea* in Edward's; *The Fool* is about the Romantic poet John Clare. In short, no other contemporary British playwright has explored the British past as thoroughly as has Bond in his search to find the sources of British ideas.

Bond disparages his film scripts because he believes that work in this medium cannot escape commercialism. Nevertheless, two of his screenplays, *Blow Up* (based on a story by Julio Cortázar) and *Walkabout* (1971), deserve mention. In *Blow Up*, a photographer discovers that he has accidentally taken a picture of what appears to be a murder. The film then explores the reactions of the photographer and his friends to this act of violence. This theme seems very close to those of Bond's major works. Similarly, *Walkabout*, the story of two children lost in the Australian Outback who are befriended by an Aborigine, is informed by Bond's notion that innocence is available to primitives and children in a way that it is not available to civilized adults.

His plays have won a number of awards, the earliest being the George Devine and the John Whiting Awards in 1968. However, perhaps because of his *enfant terrible* reputation, other honors were slower in coming to Bond. In 1977 he was awarded an honorary doctorate at Yale. Also that year he was appointed Northern Arts Literary Fellow of the University of Durham and Newcastle. In 1982 he became theater writer-in-residence at the University of Essex, and in the next year, visiting professor at the University of Palermo, Italy. Since the 1980's, he has gained recognition as being a major, if not the major, voice in contemporary British theater, though his refusal to join the mainstream of theater life has left him too marginalized to gain any sort of overall popularity.

BIOGRAPHY

Born into a working-class family, Edward Bond, one of four children, was evacuated to Cornwall at the beginning of World War II, after which he returned to his grandparents' home near Ely. These country experiences were important to Bond and may be the source of his exceptional ability to capture a wide variety of speech mannerisms. After the war, he returned to London for grammar school and attended Crouch End Secondary Modern School; like many of his classmates, he left school at fifteen. He later attributed his interest in playwriting to two childhood experiences: first, his early exposure to the music hall, where one of his sisters was a magician's assistant, and second, his seeing, at age fourteen, the actor Daniel Wolfit in *Macbeth* (pr. 1606). Bond says of this experience, "It was the first thing that made sense of my life for me."

After leaving school, Bond worked in a factory until he was eighteen and then fulfilled his national service obligation (1953-1955). After basic training, he found himself stationed in Vienna, where he began seriously to try to write fiction. He returned to London in 1955 and again worked in factories. After submitting some plays to the Royal Court, he was asked in 1958 to join the writers' group there and to become a regular play reader for the theater. His first produced play, *The Pope's Wedding*, was directed by George Devine, who became Bond's favorite director and a champion of his work. Since 1966, Bond has lived by his writing, although his income has come more from the cinema than the theater. In 1971, Bond married Elisabeth Pablé. He has developed a coterie following in England, Italy, and the United States and has been a popular playwright in Germany. In Italy, where Bond served as visiting professor at the University of Palermo, his continuance of the Brechtian tradition has been recognised.

Bond has become involved in Theatre in Education (TIE), a project based in Birmingham, England, called the Big Brum TIE Company. He has written a number of plays for them and has participated in tours and workshops. In 1995 he said he felt he was writing better than ever. However, despite incursions into the Royal Shakespeare Company, he has withdrawn from mainstream British theater, preferring the lesser glory of educational theater based at a provincial center.

ANALYSIS

Edward Bond's early plays, *The Pope's Wedding* and *Saved*, realistically depict the English working class. His later plays move toward mythological and historical drama, and their form seems to have been influenced by the works of both Bertolt Brecht and Shakespeare. In all of his work, Bond considers the connections of political power and violence in a society that reduces human beings to commodities.

SAVED

Bond's second play, *Saved*, created a *succès de scandale*, and much of his subsequent fame depended

on the notoriety of this first production at the Royal Court Theatre. The play tells the story of a young man, Len, who is picked up by a young woman, Pam, and taken home by her. The first scene depicts Pam's seduction of Len and his embarrassment at being interrupted by her father, Harry. Len rents a room in Pam's parents' flat, but the affair ends when Pam falls in love with another young man, Fred. All of these characters are clearly South London working class, but none is unemployed or desperate for money. The play instead examines emotional poverty and destructive relationships. Although Pam bears Fred's child, Len continues to live with her parents, who have arranged their lives so that they hardly see or speak to each other.

Fred abandons Pam, who continues to pursue him and enlists Len's aid in doing so. In scene 4, Len, Pam, Harry, and Mary, Pam's mother, studiously ignore the crying baby as the audience witnesses the emotional poverty of their lives. After a short domestic scene between Len and Pam, scene 6 provides the play's central action. It begins with Fred and Len talking to each other about Pam. Some of Fred's friends arrive and describe their rowdy activities. Pam enters, pushing the baby's carriage. She tells Fred that the baby will be quiet because she has doped it with aspirin, but eventually she argues with the men and exits. Len exits shortly afterward. More of Fred's friends arrive, and rough male joking begins. Soon, the youths notice the baby and begin pushing the carriage violently across the stage. As Fred watches passively, their actions escalate until they remove the baby's diaper and rub its own excrement on its face.

One of the men, Pete, then throws a stone to Fred, who lets it drop. There is a moment of silence, then some taunting. At last, Fred picks up the stone and throws it into the carriage. The other men then stone the child. The men run off and Pam enters and wheels the carriage away, cooing all the time to the baby, at whom she has not yet looked closely. In scene 7, the last in the first act, Pam and Len visit Fred in jail. Fred will be convicted of manslaughter, but, more important, the audience learns that Len witnessed the entire scene but did not come forward to the police. It is also apparent that Pam still loves Fred.

As Sir Laurence Olivier pointed out in his defense of the play, *Saved* is like Shakespeare's *Macbeth* and *Julius Caesar* (pr. c. 1599-1600) in that a horrifying act of violence happens in the first part of the play, with the rest of the play devoted to examining the consequences of that action. The remaining six scenes of *Saved* portray Len's continuing efforts to establish human contact and to work out his feelings about the killing. Act 2 opens with Harry and Len talking about Harry's work. The audience is unclear about how much time has lapsed since Fred's trial. Pam enters and an argument erupts. Bond uses this scene to show how Pam has not been changed by the baby's death and how Len is still searching for a viable human relationship. In the next scene, Mary and Len are alone together; she tears her stocking, which Len repairs. As he kneels beside her to work on the stocking, the audience sees that despite their age difference there is a powerful sexual attraction between them. In a clear parallel to scene 1, Harry also interrupts this scene.

Scene 10 shows Fred's return to his friends after his prison sentence. Pam and Len both go to the pub in which this reunion occurs. Several times, Len tries to find out what Fred felt during the stoning of the baby. Fred has objectified the experience and refuses to talk to Len. Indeed, his comments are all about the awfulness of prison. At the end of this scene, he rejects Pam brutally and takes up with another girl. Pam blames Len for this rejection.

Scene 11 shows a violent fight between Mary and Harry, who has accused his wife of "goin' after [her] own daughter's leftovers." Pam and Len interrupt this scene but are unable to prevent Mary from breaking a teapot (significantly, a wedding present) over Harry's head. Pam, still distraught because of her rejection by Fred, blames Len for all of her troubles.

Scene 12 is a scene of reconciliation between Harry and Len, in which Harry, among other things, tells Len that he has missed his chance because there is no war. Harry remembers killing with fondness. This scene, in which Harry and Len acknowledge their similarities, is the closest to real human contact that any of the characters come. The final scene of the play presents the entire family onstage while Len attempts to fix a chair; they sit self-absorbed and silent as he works.

This plot summary, which suggests how Bond mixes the tedious and ordinary to reveal the deeper evils in human nature, cannot convey the real power of *Saved*. His control of speech rhythms enhances the believability of the characters, revealing the depth of feeling that lies beneath the mere content of their speeches. Their very inarticulateness motivates their violence; they can only lash out.

Most of the early critics of the play were so appalled by its violence that they overlooked its devastating and insightful comments on society as well as its literary merit. Bond himself chides these critics in his introduction to the play when he writes, "Clearly the stoning to death of a baby in a London park is a typical British understatement. Compared to the strategic bombing of German towns it is a negligible atrocity, compared to the cultural and emotional deprivation of most of our children its consequences are insignificant."

The play, in fact, has two intertwined stories—the death of the child and Len's growing attraction for Mary. This second plot Bond calls an "Oedipal comedy" which is resolved by Harry's and Len's reconciliation. The death of the baby, however, must be seen in context. Scene 4, in which the baby is ignored, the personal relations within Pam's family, and the personality of Fred and his friends all suggest the bleakness of the life that would await this child if it grew up; at best, it would become like its murderers. The stoning, then, is a metaphor for the life of such children and shows in one brief, horrid moment the damage that accumulates over a lifetime.

Len constantly seeks a way out of these destructive relationships. Instinctively, he knows the importance of human contact, and instinctively he seeks it. His world offers virtually no language and no social structure to facilitate these contacts. Actions, often small and discontinuous, are thus the characters' only real means of expression. The last scene, in which Len repairs the chair, is a fitting end to the play. Len's commitment to Harry, Mary, and Pam is affirmed by this action; the others' indifference to him is affirmed by the trivial tasks they perform. The only speech in the last scene is Len's request for a hammer—a request the others ignore. Bond calls *Saved* "almost irresponsibly optimistic" because Len retains his "natural goodness." To the extent that Len survives the horrors of the play, Bond may be right in his judgment.

EARLY MORNING

In an early *Theatre Quarterly* interview, Bond suggested that *Saved* suffered from "too much realism." His next play, *Early Morning*, a political satire set vaguely in Victoria's court, suffers from no such disadvantage. The prince of Wales is portrayed as Siamese twins; Victoria is having a lesbian relationship with Florence Nightingale; and Disraeli plans a coup. Many critics, notably Malcolm Hay, see *Early Morning* as the play that holds the clue to Bond's later work. Bond's next play, *Narrow Road to the Deep North*, however—also performed in 1968—uses similar themes and techniques, won wider critical acclaim, and is more accessible to the non-British audience.

NARROW ROAD TO THE DEEP NORTH

Bond says that *Narrow Road to the Deep North* began from his reading of *Oku no hosomichi* (1694; *The Narrow Road to the Deep North*, 1933), by the seventeenth century Japanese poet Matsuo Bashō, who is a character in the play. In one section of this celebrated travel journal, "The Records of a Weather Beaten Skeleton," Bashō reports that he came across a child abandoned by a river and decided that it was fate or "the irresistible will of heaven" that had caused its abandonment. Bashō then concludes, "If it is so child, you must raise your voice to heaven, and I must pass on leaving you behind."

Bond was so shocked by this incident that he put the book down and refused to go on reading it. The memory of its festered, however, and Bond's play resulted. This genesis would suggest that Bond's play is about the social responsibility of the artist—a theme clear in two of Bond's later plays, *Bingo* and *The Fool*. Bond's Bashō, however, is a religious poet; he seeks enlightenment in his travels and therefore seeks the "Deep North." The play is thus about religion and society, and as Tony Coult observes, "Edward Bond is an atheist and a humanist. These facts are basic to what goes on in his plays. His work in-variably embodies a tough critique of the unholy alliance between religion and politics."

There are numerous formal and stylistic differences between *Narrow Road to the Deep North* and *Saved*. First, *Narrow Road to the Deep North* makes no pretense at historical accuracy: The seventeenth century poet invites nineteenth century English missionaries into Japan. The audience is firmly in the world of fable. Second, Bond is willing to address the audience directly. In the introduction, as Bond calls his prologue, Bashō says, "I'm the seventeenth century poet Bashō." Scene 1 begins, "Thirty years since I was here!," and in the next scene Bashō begins, "I've been back two years now." In short, Bond ignores the conventions of exposition and simply tells the audience directly what it needs to know and moves on. Third, Bond develops two techniques beyond their use in *Saved*. His ability to create the symbolic stage picture has increased, and he is more at home in an extended episodic structure that allows him to trace the development of a story through time. History is important to Bond, and he seeks forms that allow him to trace its consequence.

Narrow Road to the Deep North opens with a prologue in which Bashō leaves the abandoned child by the river. He returns thirty years later, having been "enlightened," to find the city ruled by the tyrant Shogo, who is discovered at the end of the play to be the child that Bashō left to die. Kiro, a young seeker after truth, wants to become Bashō's disciple, but Bashō rejects him. During this scene, prisoners are marched to the river to be drowned. Bashō is confronted face to face with Shogo's cruelty.

Two years later, Shogo summons Bashō to the palace to become the tutor of the emperor's son, the legitimate ruler of the city. On the same day, Kiro, clowning about with two other monks, gets his head stuck in a sacred pot. Bashō brings him before Shogo and challenges him to resolve this dilemma. Shogo, having no respect for the sacredness of the pot, simply smashes it. Kiro is so entranced by the power of direct action that he becomes Shogo's follower despite reservations about his cruelty. Bashō, appalled by this sacrilege, persuades the British to invade and take over.

The British are represented by Georgina, a missionary, and the Commodore, her military brother. Bashō mistakenly assumes he can control the Commodore, only to discover that Georgina is the real power and that her morality is as destructive as Shogo's barbarity. Posing as priests, Kiro and Shogo escape to the deep north, where Shogo raises an army. He retakes the city and determines that the boy emperor shall not be used against him again. When Georgina, who has been left in charge of the emperor's children, cannot tell him who is the boy emperor, he kills them all. This act drives Georgina mad. The Commodore returns with reinforcements and retakes the city, capturing Shogo in the process.

The play's last scene shows Bond's growing strength and sophistication as a playwright. Shogo has been executed offstage. A procession of cheering townspeople enters carrying parts of Shogo's mutilated body on placards. After the crowd passes, Georgina and Kiro are left onstage. Kiro opens his robe, and Georgina comically and anxiously awaits rape. Instead, Kiro performs seppuku, or ritual suicide. Two British soldiers enter and lead Georgina away. A shout is heard offstage, and a man, dripping wet, emerges from the river. Naked, except for a loincloth, he asks, "Didn't you hear me shout? I shouted 'help.' You must have heard and didn't come. . . . I could have drowned." He wrings out his loincloth and dries himself with a banner from the procession as Kiro's body pitches forward in its death spasm. Thus, Bond ends the play with a complex of rhythms and images that bring his humanist view center. The audience is left with the nude body of the bather drying himself, unaware of the corpse beside him. People must help others. Magic pots, prayers, and ritual suicide are all useless. The play echoes Brecht's heroine Joan Dark, who learns "that only men help where men are."

LEAR

Unquestionably Bond's greatest achievement is his play *Lear*, which is not an adaptation or rewrite of Shakespeare's *King Lear* (pr. c. 1605-1606) but a new play based on the Lear story. In fact, because Cordelia survives and rules in Bond's play, he claims that his play more closely follows the sources. Many of his statements about his own work must be taken

with a grain of salt; like George Bernard Shaw, Bond makes extreme statements to annoy his critics. Nevertheless, part of the power of Bond's play derives from the comparison with *King Lear*, and in many ways it forms an anti-*Lear*—that is, it acknowledges the very different social worlds that produced the two plays.

In their book on Bond's plays, Malcolm Hay and Philip Roberts describe how Bond worked and the changes he made in the manuscript during the year and a half it took him to write the play. In his notes, Bond says of *King Lear*, "As a society we use the play in the wrong way. And it's for that reason that I would like to rewrite it so that we now have to use the play for ourselves, for our society, for our time, for our problems."

Lear's plot is too complex to summarize in detail, but there are some essential similarities and differences between it and *King Lear*. Like Shakespeare's Lear, Bond's king moves from arbitrariness through insanity to understanding. Daughters rebel against their father, the kingdom is divided, and blindness and the imprisonment of father and daughter occur. Like *King Lear*, Bond's play presents its themes and characters through animal imagery.

The differences between the plays seem more important. Bond renames Regan and Goneril as Bodice and Fontanelle. Cordelia is not Lear's daughter but a guerrilla leader who overthrows Bodice and Fontanelle and finds herself condemned to repeat Lear's mistakes. The action does not start from Lear's laying down of his authority but from his arbitrary exercise of it. As Bond's play opens, Lear and his daughters are inspecting a wall that Lear is building around the entire kingdom to protect it from his enemies. Because the wall drains the local people of both land and money, they attempt to sabotage the wall. Lear executes a malingering worker without a trial; his daughters, appalled at this abuse of power, marry his enemies and lead a revolt.

All the positive characters (Edgar, Kent, Albany, Gloucester) disappear from Bond's play. Lear himself is blinded onstage. The Fool is transformed into the Ghost of the Gravedigger's Boy and functions opposite Shakespeare's fool. Instead of leading Lear to wisdom, the ghost offers Lear refuge in noninvolvement and self-pity; he is less responsible than the king.

The eighteenth century found *King Lear* too violent, and it was rewritten into a decorous tragedy. Bond seems not to have found it violent enough. Warick, Lear's counselor, is beaten onstage, and his eardrums are pierced by Bodice's knitting needle. The death of the Gravedigger's Boy is accompanied by the squeals of slaughtered pigs. A medical orderly blinds Lear with a suction device after trapping his head in a specially designed chair. Like a good doctor, he sprays an aerosol on the wound to "encourage scabbing." The play ends when Lear is shot trying to destroy the wall that Cordelia is in the process of rebuilding. Bond might not argue that human beings today are more cruel than they were in the seventeenth century, but he will not allow his audience to forget that the modern technology of cruelty far exceeds the devices of the past.

In his preface written after the first production, Bond defends himself against those critics who find his work too violent:

I write about violence as naturally as Jane Austen wrote about manners. Violence shapes and obsesses our society and if we do not stop being violent, we have no future. People who do not want writers to write about violence want us to stop writing about us and our time. It would be immoral not to write about violence.

To see and to accept humankind's role in violence leads one to see clearly, to understand. In act 2, Fontanelle, imprisoned with Lear, is executed onstage, and the medical orderly performs an autopsy on her. Lear watches with intense interest, saying: "She sleeps inside like a lion and a lamb and a child. The things are so beautiful. I am astonished. I have never seen anything so beautiful. . . ." The human body is not as it is for King Lear, "a poor bare forked thing." Bodice, the other daughter, is brought in as a prisoner during the autopsy. In their ensuing argument, Lear "puts his hands into Fontanelle and brings them out with organs and viscera." He says to Bodice:

Look! I killed her! Her blood is on my hands! Destroyer! Murderer! And now I must begin again. I must walk through my life, step after step, I must walk in weariness and bitterness. I must become a child, hungry and stripped and shivering in blood, I must open my eyes and see.

Lear's inability to shirk the violence that his world has created leads him to pity and sanity, but Bond will not stop here. At the end of this scene, Lear is blinded after witnessing the death of both of his daughters. In his blindness, he is led to insight. Bond's Lear finds no redemption; revolt, not order, is established at the end of the play. Cordelia's revolution leads to more violence because her "morality is a form of violence."

THE BUNDLE

A similar bleakness is seen in *The Bundle*, a rewriting of *Narrow Road to the Deep North*. It is as harsh and uncompromising as the earlier play had been witty and comparatively straightforward. However, it does end with a post-revolutionary state rather than despair, and thus goes further than *Lear*. Increasingly, Bond's use of alienation reminds the spectator of Betold Brecht's techniques of *Verfremdung*.

THE WAR PLAYS

The War Plays, a trilogy, is again harsh, set in a postnuclear world. Part 1, *Red, Black, and Ignorant* reveals minimalist staging, with the Monster and his wife speaking in a verse form that seems heavily influenced by Bond's contemporary, Ted Hughes, whose long poem sequences *Crow* (1970, rev. 1972) and *Gaudete* (1977) include similar verse rhythms, imagery, and surreal scenarios. The theme is not just postmodern or posturban; it seems almost posthuman.

Part 2, *The Tin Can People*, is again largely in verse with chorus. It consists of a series of little scenes. Once again, Bond is mixing forms: this time Greek dramatic form with a Hughesian verse drama, to profound effect. It represents the next stage in postnuclear drama, in scenes reminiscent of hell in Dante's *Inferno* (c. 1320; English translation, 1802).

TUESDAY

Other later plays have centered on the intrusion of the recent traumatic past on everyday domestic settings. For example, *Tuesday*, written for schools' broadcasting, begins with an English teenager, Irene, doing her homework, when events from the recent Gulf War intrude as her boyfriend arrives, having deserted from the Army when his unit is sent to the Persian Gulf. The play becomes increasingly fraught as Irene's father attempts to get Brian to hand himself over to the authorities. Irene attempts to shoot her father, and Brian is killed as he is about to be arrested.

The play's unity of time is remarkable: The one and a half hours of time elapsing in the play imitates exactly the actual performance time. The intensity of a life-changing moment is thus effectively portrayed. The ironies are rich: Brian's gun is not loaded because he refuses to kill; however, Irene uses it to try to kill her father. Brian is shot by the police. It is a domestic Vietnam scenario revisited as violently as possible.

OLLY'S PRISON

A second play involving father and daughter conflict was *Olly's Prison*. Each episode of this three-part play centers on a moment of violence. Shakespeare's *King Lear* continues to be a main subtext for Bond, and the denouement to *Olly's Prison* has a classical, even a mythological, feel to it. The prison is both literal and metaphorical. The father, Mike, the play's protagonist, wrestles with the violence within himself. He is also the victim of Frank and the younger man's violence. The irony is, typically for Bond, that Frank is a police officer.

LATER PLAYS

Other plays have included *In the Company of Men*, set in the world of big business and high finance, and, by contrast, the experimental and surreal *Coffee*, a play about the holocaust scenario of Babi Yar, in the Ukraine. In *The Children*, a disturbed mother sends her son on a bizarre errand, with fatal consequences. In *Have I None*, the setting is a ruined city in the postnuclear world of 2077: A stranger knocks on the door, and events become both tragic and yet absurdly funny. This use of farcical tragicomedy marks Bond's typical version of black comedy.

A postnuclear holocaust play, *At the Inland Sea*, was written for children and young people, a sign of Bond's growing interest in theater in education. It

uses the vocabulary of folktale, forming a story to be told to save someone's life, as in the Arabian folktales of *Scheherezade*. Bond's work with children, for example, his taking *At the Inland Sea* on tour with accompanying workshops, is reminiscent of Ted Hughes's involvement with children's verse and schools' broadcasting.

In his later plays, Bond's writing has become more and more poetic and mythological and has taken on a resonant power that marks him as one of the great modern British playwrights. His integrity and the uncompromising nature of his bleak postmodern left-wing vision make him still as uncomfortable a dramatist as in his early plays.

OTHER MAJOR WORKS

POETRY: *Theatre Poems and Songs*, 1978; *Poems, 1978-1985*, 1987.

SCREENPLAYS: *Blow Up*, 1967 (with Michelangelo Antonioni; adaptation of Julio Cortázar's short story "Las babas del diablo"); *Laughter in the Dark*, 1969 (adaptation of Vladimir Nabokov's novel); *Nicholas and Alexandra*, 1971 (with James Goldman); *Walkabout*, 1971.

NONFICTION: *Edward Bond Letters*, 1994-2001 (5 volumes); *The Hidden Plot: Notes on Theatre and the State*, 2000; *Selections from the Notebooks of Edward Bond*, 2000-2001 (2 volumes; volume 1, 1959-1980; volume 2, 1980-1995).

BIBLIOGRAPHY

Coult, Tony. *The Plays of Edward Bond*. London: Methuen, 1978. An early and important study of Bond's work. The book is designed as a companion critical reader to Bond's plays, with a valuable introductory essay. Coult takes a thematic approach, concentrating on *Narrow Road to the Deep North*, *Lear*, *Bingo*, and *The Sea*. Supplemented by a chronology.

Hay, Malcolm, and Philip Roberts. *Bond: A Study of His Plays*. London: Methuen, 1980. This definitive study single-handedly places Bond in a distinct scholarly category in which he is compared with his contemporaries. The chapters are arranged by plays, with a chronological list of plays, a strong introductory essay, and two sections of production stills. Supplemented by notes, a bibliography, and an index.

_____. *Edward Bond: A Companion to his Plays.* Rev. ed. London: Methuen, 1985. A companion volume to the preceding title, it includes a chronology, bibliography, a section on Bond on his own plays, and plays in production.

Hirst, David L. *Edward Bond.* Macmillan Modern Dramatists series. London: Macmillan, 1985. Contains three main sections: techniques of subversion, tragedy and comedy, and epic theater, including *Lear* and *The Bundle.* Hirst likens Bond to George Bernard Shaw, in that both seek a method of building a new world out of the ruins of the old. A good introduction.

Lappin, Lou. *The Art and Politics of Edward Bond.* New York: Peter Lang, 1987. The book analyses Bond's drama in relation to his left-wing political viewpoint.

Mangan, Michael. *Edward Bond.* Writers and Their Work series. Plymouth, England: Northcote House, 1998. An excellent introduction to Bond, done with his active co-operation. It stresses the interrelatedness of all his plays, and the recurrence of certain themes, images, and characters.

Peacock, D. Keith. *Radical Stages: Alternative History in Modern British Drama.* New York: Greenwood Press, 1991. In a chapter on Bond's historical allegories, and in his introductory essay, Peacock finds Bond's "alternative and . . . iconoclastic interpretation of history" at the center of his art.

Strong critical discussion of *Bingo* (on William Shakespeare) and *The Fool* (on the Romantic poet John Clare). Usable general bibliography.

Roberts, Phillip, ed. *Bond on File.* London: Methuen, 1985. An extremely valuable collection of resources relating to the plays, up to *The Tin Can People,* including reviews, excerpts from letters, interviews, and good play synopses.

Scharine, Richard. *The Plays of Edward Bond.* London: Associated University Presses, 1976. A strong study of Bond as a revolutionary, yelling "Fire!" as others "sit and watch." The first chapter, an introduction to Bond, and the last, a summary of themes and techniques, bracket six chapters on specific plays and one on "incidental dramatic works." Index.

Spencer, Jenny. *Dramatic Strategies in the Plays of Edward Bond.* Cambridge, England: Cambridge University Press, 1992. A very insightful and well-theorized study that deals with the "poetic materialism" of Bond's work up to *The War Plays.*

Stuart, Ian. "Answering to the Dead: Edward Bond's *Jackets,* 1989-1990." *New Theatre Quarterly* 7 (May, 1991): 171-183. Examines the theory and practice of "theater events" and "theater acting" and discusses a specific acting style necessary to realize Bond's plays, exploring the work in progress. The *New Theatre Quarterly* and its predecessor, *Theatre Quarterly,* began concentrating on the development of Bond's career in 1972.

Sidney F. Parham,
updated by Thomas J. Taylor and David Barratt

GORDON BOTTOMLEY

Born: Keighley, England; February 20, 1874
Died: Oare, near Marlborough, England; August 25, 1948

PRINCIPAL DRAMA
The Crier by Night, pb. 1902, pr. 1916 (one act)
Midsummer Eve, pb. 1905, pr. 1930 (one act)

Laodice and Danaë, pb. 1909, pr. 1930 (one act)
The Riding to Lithend, pb. 1909, pr. 1928 (one act)
King Lear's Wife, pr. 1915, pb. 1916
Britain's Daughter, pb. 1921, pr. 1922
Gruach, pb. 1921, pr. 1923
Scenes and Plays, pb. 1929 (includes *Ardvorlich's Wife*)

Lyric Plays, pb. 1932
The Acts of Saint Peter, pr., pb. 1933
Choric Plays and a Comedy, pb. 1939
Fire at Calbart, pb. 1939, pr. 1944
Kate Kennedy, pr. 1944, pb. 1945

OTHER LITERARY FORMS

Gordon Bottomley wrote nondramatic poetry, much of it published privately, in anthologies and in the small literary magazines of his time. Bottomley also favored minor dramatic poetry that appears in the form of monologues, "duologues" (his term), and preludes. He also wrote many one-act plays, a form fashionable in small theaters and theater festivals, religious and secular, in the early part of the twentieth century. Examples of such miniatures of dramatic experimentation include *Ardvorlich's Wife*, in *Scenes and Plays*, and the short plays with Celtic themes in *Lyric Plays* and *Choric Plays and a Comedy*.

In addition to his lyric poetry and poetic drama, Bottomley took an active interest in visual arts and the careers of colleagues in a wide range of the arts. Therefore, he introduced works by Sir James Guthrie, the graphic artist, and poetry by William Morris and Isaac Rosenberg, prominent poets of his time. He also left a lengthy correspondence with the painter and illustrator Paul Nash. It was Bottomley's conviction that serious drama must embrace music and the visual arts.

Bottomley also practiced the art of the dedicatory poem or prologue. Nearly every one of his theatrical works is dedicated in verse to a prominent artistic friend or colleague, including those mentioned above. In this practice, the playwright followed and enlivened a long-standing tradition. Often Bottomley's prologue poems contain not only the standard praise for their recipient but also a brief apologia for his work.

ACHIEVEMENTS

Gordon Bottomley was the recipient of the Femina Vie Heureuse prize, given in Paris in 1923, and three honorary degrees, from the universities of Aberdeen, in Scotland, and Durham and Leeds, in England. Perhaps, however, the playwright's achievement should be measured less by official acknowl-

edgment than by his influence on contemporaries and disciples. The intense artistic friendships that Bottomley maintained helped give momentum and focus to the efforts of the Georgian poets and to aid the movement of poetic and dramatic theme, structure, and language toward a distinctly modern mode. Bottomley was a recognized leader of his contemporaries, reading other playwrights' work in progress, writing frequent letters in response, and providing opportunities for stimulating work to designers, producers, and actors.

One of Bottomley's principal contributions to the arts was his insistence on proper vocal training and delivery of lines of verse on the stage. Seeking to reestablish verse as a proper medium for drama, Bottomley was active in the formulation of a verse-speaking society whose efforts were copied elsewhere in Britain, Ireland, and the United States. By working with this society—with John Masefield, the poet laureate, who maintained a small theater in Oxford, and with experimental groups at the theater at Dartington Hall in Devon—and by aiding in the production of his and others' works by smaller groups and amateur groups, such as the Festival Theatre in Cambridge and the Yale University Drama School, Bottomley revived emphasis on the words used by playwrights to convey their dramatic ideas. *A Stage for Poetry: My Purposes with My Plays*, published in the year of his death, encapsulates Bottomley's views on the necessity for an artistic theater, definitely not aimed at mass audiences and their tastes. Appendices in this text delineate his views on the need for the spoken word, in formal verse lines, to predominate on the stage.

BIOGRAPHY

Gordon Bottomley was the son of Alfred and Ann Maria Bottomley (née Gordon). The senior Bottomley worked as a cashier in a Yorkshire worsted mill and sent his son to Keighley Grammar School. After he left school, the young Bottomley worked as a bank clerk until illness caused him to go into near seclusion. He married Emily Burton of Arnside in 1905 and lived quietly, settling permanently in 1914 in The Shieling, Silverdale, near Carnforth in Lancashire. The Bottomleys took lengthy holidays in North Wales and often stayed with literary friends. Although Bottomley shunned the literary life of London, he was always current with literary and artistic trends, enjoying frequent communication and correspondence with such scholars as Lascelles Abercrombie, a fellow Georgian poet-dramatist; John Drinkwater, who wrote poetic plays and produced one of Bottomley's; Paul Nash, the painter, who produced sketches and studies of scenes from those plays; and Sir Edmund William Gosse, who would eventually respond negatively to the work of Bottomley and the Georgians. Perhaps Bottomley's greatest literary friend and supporter, however, was Sir Edward Marsh, the editor of several volumes bearing the title *Georgian Poetry* (1912-1922), in which Bottomley's work figured prominently.

For all of his Georgian traits, it should be noted that Bottomley was deeply influenced by the Celtic Twilight movement of the late nineteenth century, as well as by the closely related Pre-Raphaelite Brotherhood. These movements were both interdisciplinary; both celebrated an idyllic, nearly prelapsarian, era of innocence and a setting in the more remote Celtic regions of Britain. Much of Bottomley's work is set in Scotland and draws from its folklore and mythology. In this, he is seen often as imitating or paralleling the dramatic experiments of William Butler Yeats, who found his inspiration in specifically Irish material.

There is little of event to record of Bottomley's personal life, but the publication and performance of one of his plays brought him a certain notoriety. When *King Lear's Wife* was first published, it appeared as the first offering in one of Marsh's anthologies, *Georgian Poetry II, 1913-1915* (1916). The preceding volume had been published to nearly unanimous acclaim, and literary critics hailed the harder, cleaner images of the modern Georgian poets, who were self-proclaimed anti-Victorians. The young poets of the new century were successfully freeing themselves from the limitations of the past. When *Georgian Poetry II, 1913-1915* was issued, however, the general critical response was negative—in some cases outraged—by what was judged to be excessive realism. The works of Bottomley and Abercrombie in particular were singled out as being representative of

a new form of ugliness that offered violent and negative images of nature and humankind. Following productions of *King Lear's Wife* in Birmingham in 1915 and in London the next year, this negative response continued, with its focus on a corpse-washing sequence and a song, based on a child's nursery rhyme, which was considered shocking. It should be noted, however, that later critics, such as Frank Lawrence Lucas and Priscilla Thouless, have not been offended by Bottomley's harshness, generally viewing his work as transitional: He was aware of and influenced by the past, but he looked to the modern age.

Although Bottomley was in poor health for most of his life, he lived to see literary fashion change a number of times and to witness a small rekindling of interest in his drama in the 1940's, shortly before his death.

ANALYSIS

In his *A Stage for Poetry*, Gordon Bottomley, near the end of his life, gave a tidy history of his dramatic career, complete with photographs and sketches of sets and costumes. More important, he left his own record of his dramatic intentions and accomplishments. He divided his works into two parts: "A Theatre Outworn" and "A Theatre Unborn." The former includes all the major works of his early career, which are written in traditional blank verse and hold generally to the nineteenth century model of heroic drama in aristocratic settings. From this group came Bottomley's commercial, if limited, successes. The plays that constitute his "Theatre Unborn" are considerably starker, using black or white cloths as backdrops, avoiding the proscenium stage, reverting to classical choric groups in robes, and featuring not aristocrats but characters who are often only partially human—either supernatural or animalistic or both. These theatrical experiments never found a proper audience, but they were not totally alien from Bottomley's earlier works. The playwright maintained an interest in Celtic mythology that runs through his work until the very end of his career. Although he came too late to be considered a playwright of the Celtic Twilight, Bottomley's themes and their execution stay true to that late nineteenth century movement's ideals. Bottomley's plays, many of them set in Scotland, contain frequent references to humans' dealings with supernatural creatures who hold power over them. His heroes and heroines are also frequently dreamers, incapable of dealing with the rigors of the real world; such refined sensibility was the romantic legacy to the Celtic Twilight.

Although Bottomley's work has evoked little interest among critics of his own or subsequent generations, it is an excellent example of the transitional nature of the Georgian movement. Like the work of his contemporary, Yeats, Bottomley's plays bridged the Victorian and modern eras. He employed ancient Celtic folklore and mythology as subject matter, the verse form of Elizabethan drama, and combined them with the realism and clarity of language characteristic of modern drama. The more realistic content and style already being employed by Henrik Ibsen and George Bernard Shaw, however, had moved Western drama into the twentieth century, while Bottomley's work remained part of an earlier era.

THE RIDING TO LITHEND

The Riding to Lithend is, in many ways, a characteristic one-act play by Bottomley. It features a long dedicatory poem to a prominent contemporary and is based, however loosely, on saga and myth. It includes a small cast of characters, not all of which are entirely or identifiably human, and its female characters are atypically strong, if not ferocious.

The play, written in 1908 but not performed until 1928, opens with a poem to the poet Edward Thomas, who died in World War I. In the poem, Bottomley refers to a visit from Thomas in 1907 during which he encouraged Bottomley to breathe new life into the adventures of the Icelandic hero Gunnar. Bottomley also compares Thomas himself to this early type by emphasizing his Welsh heritage, likening him to one of the heroes of *The Mabinogion* (c. 1100-1200), the Welsh saga cycle.

The *dramatis personae* include Gunnar Hamundsson, the hero-warrior; his wife, Hallgerd Longcoat; his mother, Rannveig; three female servants, Oddny, Astrid, and Steinvor; and a female thrall (a slave, taken in war), Ormild. There are also three beggar-women—Biartey, Jofrid, and Gudfinn—and many

Riders, or warrior-vigilantes. The play is set in an "eating hall" in Gunnar's manor in the year 990. The female servants are combing and spinning wool and stitching a royal garment. In many of Bottomley's plays, an elaborate garment, representing its owner and symbolic of wealth and power, is prominently displayed in the opening scene.

The servant women have a sense of foreboding because all the men of the manor have been sent by Gunnar, rather unwisely it is feared, to a late harvest on the islands nearby. The abnormality of the harvest season is emphasized, and the audience learns that the seemingly capricious decision is in keeping with Gunnar's irregular hours and habits. He is an outcast from local law, and it is believed that his house is haunted by ghostly victims of his past misdeeds. Despite the foreboding occasioned by the unseasonal harvest, it is noted that Gunnar's "singing bill" (or sword) is silent, so that imminent danger seems unlikely. (The convention of the enchanted singing sword is prominent in early Northern European sagas and tales, most notably in Excalibur of Arthurian legend.) Once the concept of magic or unnatural power is introduced, there is a reference to a minor clairvoyant character who has foretold Gunnar's death. So strong is the power of this prophecy that Gunnar's brother, previously his stalwart lieutenant, has left Iceland as a result, and also to fulfill an injunction imposed on Gunnar to exile himself for three years to atone for political and other misdeeds. All of this is related by the four serving women, who conclude that Gunnar, to defy such a prophecy, must be "fey"—that is, in the power of supernatural forces.

Rannveig enters and, as mother to two sons, one in exile, wishes Gunnar would fulfill the "atonement" and thus avoid being murdered by enraged noblemen. Hallgerd, the source of the trouble, enters preoccupied and angry about her fading beauty. Gunnar and Hallgerd argue over their predicament, and as a defiant gesture she looses her hair from its covering—signifying widowhood. It is then revealed that she was a widow when Gunnar first met, wooed, and won her. Theirs has been a turbulent marriage, and in the past, when Hallgerd stole food so as not to shame her husband in time of famine and in the presence of guests, he publicly humiliated her by slapping her face. By law, he could have killed or maimed her for such an offense. In this and others of Bottomley's plays, thievery, in keeping with the era and the culture he is representing, is a crime of great import and beneath the dignity of gentlefolk. This instance of thievery was the beginning of the blood feud that has resulted in Gunnar's being under injunction of exile.

Three witchlike figures from Icelandic myth enter, posing as beggar-women. They admit to traveling by flying through the night sky in a westerly direction (which signifies death), but Gunnar nevertheless agrees to house them for the night. These crones tell of Gunnar's heroic reputation, which remains solid throughout the country, and explain that there is still one ship by which he can escape. Here it is related that he did try once to leave the country, but his horse threw him and he experienced a vision of his homeland that made him vow to stay.

The crones also engage in traditional witch behavior, taking over the spinning (which they destroy), speaking of curses, and reciting the aristocratic lineage of Hallgerd, who in many respects is a worthy wife for the heroic Gunnar. The witches incense Hallgerd, who eventually drives them out. Their true nature becomes apparent when entering characters cannot see them; they become invisible after they leave the manor.

The noblemen who have awaited Gunnar's compliance with the law arrive at his home, and a battle ensues. Gunnar fights single-handedly, while Rannveig urges prudence and Hallgerd thirsts for blood. Gunnar's bowstring is broken, and he asks Hallgerd for some of her hair to repair it. She refuses—choosing this moment to avenge the public humiliation of her that he inflicted years earlier. Gunnar dies in battle with Hallgerd laughing. Rannveig, the grieving mother, keeps Hallgerd from her son's corpse, pulling her by the hair she denied to her husband. Rannveig then tries to murder Hallgerd to avenge her son's death, and hers is the play's final soliloquy—including a lullaby that uses images of sleep and death to good effect. In a final tableau, she raises the "singing bill" aloft over the corpse of her son. It is still singing, signifying Gunnar's victory even in death.

The Riding to Lithend makes significant use of Irish references, indicating the playwright's knowledge of the early links of custom and commerce between Iceland and Ireland and thus allowing for the Celtic Twilight influence seen elsewhere in his work. Also prominent is bird imagery, especially sinister imagery of birds of prey. The witch figures resemble in appearance and powers the Morrigan, a bird-woman of Celtic mythology who is usually a figure of death or misfortune, and Gunnar is identified with a bird-god that appears on his family crest.

The play delivers a primitive message in a primitive setting, and its characters retain the necessary two-dimensional qualities of figures in saga literature, who are more important as types than as individuals. The law is irrevocable, and although Gunnar is viewed as the best of the warrior mold of his homeland, he is not above the law. Appropriately, he dies in battle.

The blank verse, in this and in nearly all of Bottomley's plays, is at times merely neo-Elizabethan, deriving from the Shakespearean model used so much in the nineteenth century theater, but it can rise to eloquence when the playwright molds an honored verse form to modern language and expression. Bottomley's servant characters often have lines of a cleaner, more precise language; unlike Shakespearean servants, they too speak in blank verse, like their masters and mistresses.

KING LEAR'S WIFE

King Lear's Wife begins with a lengthy dedicatory poem to Thomas Sturge Moore, another multifaceted artist who wrote verse plays of Bottomley's type and who also achieved distinction as an illustrator and designer of books, costumes and stage sets. The poem, written in iambic quadrameter, is composed in three stanzas of irregular length, each of which opens and closes with a triplet, while the remainder is formed in couplets. Bottomley praises *The Dial*, a literary magazine of the day, in which he had first encountered Moore's poetry from his seclusion in Lancashire. He hails Moore as "prince of poets in our time" and reminisces about conversations they enjoyed at a meeting in Surrey. Bottomley closes by offering *King Lear's Wife* as a "token . . . of admiration and loyalty."

The *dramatis personae* include Lear, king of Britain; Hygd, his queen; Goneril and Cordeil, his daughters; Gormflaith and Merryn, servants to the queen; a Physician and two Elderly Women. The setting is a primitive English castle, fitted with harsh fabrics that deny a hospitable atmosphere. Highlighted is an elaborate robe and crown that belong to the "emaciated" Queen Hygd, whose large four-poster bed dominates the stage. She is being attended by Merryn, a Cornish servant of many years' service, and it is very early in the morning—a bleak time for a bleak setting.

The immediate subject is death. Hygd wants to die, feeling unneeded in middle age, but lingers mournfully in her illness. Merryn, quite old, is characterized as superstitious and alien because of her Cornish heritage; she dreads the idea of her own death. Enter a very vital middle-aged Lear, not the old and crazed figure of Bottomley's Shakespearean model. He is accompanied by the court Physician, and he has arranged for Gormflaith, a young Scotswoman, to tend the queen.

The Physician, seeking a psychological explanation for the queen's failing health, asks what long-term bitterness nursed in secret is the cause. The king responds vituperatively, and then the Physician suggests a cure, of juniper berries, marrow of adder, and emerald dust. Only Lear has a valuable emerald, a gift from an Irish king whose daughter mothered many British kings. He refuses to destroy it to save his wife's life.

Hygd awakens alone and is joined by Goneril, who is on the edge of womanhood. Dressed in hunting garb, Goneril is described in terms associated with Diana, the Greek virgin goddess and hunter. Both Goneril and Gormflaith are representative of "life." It is Lear's belief that his wife will benefit from their presence, but Hygd is repelled by their vitality. Goneril describes a visionary encounter at a Druidic site (a holy place of the priest class that had earlier controlled Britain). In contrast, Hygd describes and dismisses the new Christian religion of Merryn. Hygd then asks about Regan (the third daughter of Lear, who appears as an important character in William Shakespeare's play but not at all in Bottomley's).

Hygd warns Goneril to enjoy her freedom now because soon she will be obliged to marry. The aging queen offers a philosophy frequent in Bottomley's work—that the domestication of fine, brave young women in marriage yields bitter results. At best, claims Hygd, women can only be venerated in age, whereas men fare better and have wider choices later in life.

They are interrupted by the child Cordeil (Cordelia in Shakespeare), who is at the door seeking her father. She is called "my little curse" and "an evil child" by her mother, who denies her access to the sickroom. Hygd claims that she conceived Cordeil to keep Lear faithful, adding that Cordeil's birth has left her an invalid. After Goneril lulls her mother to sleep, Gormflaith enters, an attractive woman, too eager to please. She reads a letter arranging an assignation with Lear, who arrives and destroys the letter for the sake of security. He then softens the blow by allowing Gormflaith to wear his emerald.

The king intends to make Gormflaith his queen after Hygd's death, despite Gormflaith's cunning observations concerning the negative effect this will have in his court and within his family. In his desire for a male heir, Lear will not hear reason. Gormflaith, in a climactic moment, asks to wear Hygd's crown, and Lear chastises her: "You cannot have the nature of a queen/ If you believe that there are things above you." Lear softens again, however, and while Gormflaith is sitting on his knee, wearing Hygd's crown, the queen awakens and sees all. Hygd tries to follow the lovers to the garden, falls, has a dying vision of Lear's mother, and dies shouting to Goneril "Pay Gormflaith."

The play rapidly becomes less poetic as Merryn discusses the need to tend the dead queen before rigor mortis sets in. The irony and bitterness increase as Goneril mockingly pays homage when Gormflaith reenters, still wearing Hygd's crown. Because Gormflaith was meant to be tending the queen, the enraged Goneril demands of her father the penalty given for servants leaving their posts, knowing fully that Lear is the cause of Gormflaith's absence. Goneril snatches the crown and places it on the dead queen.

The momentum of the play, its imagery and tone, alter greatly with the entrance of two women to minister to the queen's body. Like the gravediggers in Shakespeare's *Hamlet*, they are irreverent in the presence of death, haggling over Hygd's personal effects—traditional payment for such work. They sing a grisly work song to the tune of "Froggie's Gone a Courtin,'" preparing the reader for the equally grisly entrance of Goneril with a bloody knife. In a somewhat surprising about-face, Lear, when confronted by his murderess-daughter, disowns the dead Gormflaith and calls Goneril his "true daughter." The play ends with Lear hoping to marry off and "break" Goneril, thus bearing out Hygd's earlier fear, and the corpse washers finish by enjoying the irony of Lear's having traded one predicament—a sick wife—for another— a fearless and cruel daughter.

King Lear's Wife observes the traditional dramatic unities scrupulously. It showcases Lear against a predominantly female cast to great effect, and it develops ideas seen often in Bottomley's corpus. Beauty is power, but it is transient; death and physical violence are always near. The play rings a gender change on the classic revenge drama, because here a daughter avenges the disgrace and death of her mother. Ultimately, it affirms the sense of hierarchy and order codified in the law: Evildoers receive their just deserts.

The language of *King Lear's Wife* is not as garrulous as it is in many of Bottomley's works, and the speeches of supporting characters, such as Merryn and the two corpse washers, are effective in reinforcing the thematic message of the play. Animal imagery prevails and is well integrated. The corpse washers wear black, batlike or birdlike costumes, appropriate to their task, and the reader is prepared for Goneril's murderous role because as a huntress she has killed in cold blood and become exhilarated by the act.

Hygd, the title character, was first performed by Katherine Drinkwater, the producer's wife, and later by Lady Viola Tree, of the famous acting family. *King Lear's Wife* was the only play Bottomley wrote that provoked a significant critical response. Although that response was largely negative, it drew attention to Bottomley's work, and as a result, his plays were produced more readily in subsequent years.

OTHER MAJOR WORKS

POETRY: *Poems at White Nights*, 1899; *Chambers of Imagery*, 1907-1912 (2 volumes); *A Vision of Giorgione*, 1910; *Poems of Thirty Years*, 1925.

NONFICTION: *A Stage for Poetry: My Purpose with My Plays*, 1948; *Poet and Painter, Being the Correspondence Between Gordon Bottomley and Paul Nash, 1910-1946*, 1955, 1990.

MISCELLANEOUS: *Poems and Plays*, 1953.

BIBLIOGRAPHY

Demastes, William W., and Katherine Kelly, eds. *British Playwrights, 1880-1956: A Research and Production Sourcebook*. Westport, Conn.: Greenwood Press, 1996. This volume includes a discussion of Bottomley's life and works.

Kirkpatrick, D. L., ed. *Reference Guide to English Literature*. 2d ed. Chicago: St. James Press, 1991. This guide contains an entry describing Bottomley's life and works. Bibliographical references.

Thomas, Edward. *Letters from Edward Thomas to Gordon Bottomley*. New York: Oxford University Press, 1968. This collection of correspondence from Edward Thomas, the poet who encouraged Bottomley, to Bottomley sheds light on the relationship between the two writers. Includes bibliography.

Whitmore, Charles Edward. *The Supernatural in Tragedy*. Mamaroneck, N.Y.: Appel, 1971. An examination of the supernatural as it is used in drama. Contains reference to Bottomley.

Christina Hunt Mahony,
updated by Pamela Canal

DION BOUCICAULT
Dionysius Lardner Boursiquot

Born: Dublin, Ireland; December 27, 1820(?)
Died: New York, New York; September 18, 1890

PRINCIPAL DRAMA

London Assurance, pr., pb. 1841 (as Lee
  Moreton)
Alma Mater: Or, A Curse for Coquettes, pr., pb.
  1842
A Lover by Proxy, pr. 1842, pb. 1845(?)
The Irish Heiress, pr., pb. 1842
The Old Guard, pr. 1843, pb. 1848(?)
Woman, pr. 1843
Old Heads and Young Hearts, pr. 1844, pb. 1845
Used Up, pr., pb. 1844 (farce)
The School for Scheming, pr., pb. 1847 (comedy)
Confidence, pr. 1848 (comedy)
The Knight of Arva, pr. 1848, pb. 1868
The Willow Copse, pr. 1849, pb. 1851
    (adaptation of Frédéric Soulié's *La Closerie
    des genêts*)
The Prima Donna, pb. 1850, pr. 1852 (farce)
The Queen of Spades, pr., pb. 1851 (adaptation of
    Prosper Mérimée's *La Dame de pique*)
Love in a Maze, pr., pb. 1851
The Corsican Brothers, pr., pb. 1852 (adaptation of
    Eugène Grangé and Xavier de Montépin's *Les
    Frères Corses*)
The Vampire, pr. 1852, pb. 1856 as *The Phantom*
    (adaptation from the French)
Genevieve: Or, The Reign of Terror, pr. 1853
    (adaptation from the French)
The Fox Hunt, pr. 1853
The Young Actress, pr. 1853 (musical interlude)
Andy Blake, pr. 1854, pb. 1856 (a Gaelic adaptation
    of Jean-François-Alfred Bayard's *Gamin de
    Paris*)
Janet Pride, pr. 1854 (adaptation based in part on
    Adolphe Dennery and Julien de Mallian's
    Marie Jeanne)
Pierre the Foundling, pr. 1854 (adaptation from the
    French)

Eugenie: Or, A Sister's Vow, pr. 1855 (adaptation
    from the French)
Grimaldi: Or, The Life of an Actress, pr. 1855, pb.
    1864 (based on Théodore Barrièr and Auguste
    Anicet-Bourgeois's *La Vie d'une comédienne*)
Louis XI, pr., pb. 1855 (adaptation from the
    French)
Una, pr. 1856
The Poor of New York, pr., pb. 1857 (revised as
    The Poor of Liverpool and *The Streets of
    London*, pr. 1864; adaptation of Édouard-
    Louis-Alexandre Brisbarre and Eugène Nus's
    Les Pauvres de Paris)
Pauvrette, pr., pb. 1858 (adaptation of Adolphe
    Dennery's *Bergère des Alpes*)
The Pope of Rome, pr., pb. 1858 (revision of *The
    Broken Vow*)
Jessie Brown: Or, The Relief of Lucknow, pr., pb.
    1858
Dot, pr. 1859, pb. 1940 (adaptation of Charles
    Dickens's *The Cricket on the Hearth*)
Nicholas Nickleby, pr. 1859 (adaptation of Charles
    Dickens's novel)
The Octoroon: Or, Life in Louisiana, pr. 1859, pr.
    1861 (revised), pb. 1953 (adaptation of Mayne
    Reid's novel *The Quadroon*)
The Colleen Bawn, pr. 1860, pb. 1860?
    (adaptation of Gerald Griffin's novel *The
    Collegians*)
How She Loves Him!, pr. 1863, pb. 1868
Arrah-na-Pogue: Or, The Wicklow Wedding, pr.
    1864, pb. 1865 (in Gaelic)
Rip Van Winkle, pr. 1865, pb. 1944 (with Joseph
    Jefferson; adaptation of Washington Irving's
    story)
The Flying Scud: Or, Four-Legged Fortune, pr.
    1866, pb. 1940
After Dark: A Tale of London Life, pr., pb. 1868
Formosa: Or, The Railroad to Ruin, pr., pb. 1869
Presumptive Evidence, wr. 1869, pb. 1940 (also
    known as *Mercy Dodd*)

Babil and Bijou: Or, The Lost Regalia, pr. 1872 (with James Robinson Planché)

Led Astray, pr., pb. 1873 (adaptation of Octave Feuillet's *La Tentation*)

Belle Lamar, pr. 1874, pb. 1934 (revised as *Fin Maccoul*, pr. 1887)

The Shaughraun, pr. 1874, pb. 1880

Forbidden Fruit, pr., pb. 1876

The O'Dowd, pr. 1880, pb. 1909 (Gaelic adaptation of Eugène Cormon and Eugène Grangé's *Les Crochets du père Martin*; also known as *Daddy O'Dowd*)

A Bridal Tour, pr. 1880

The Amadān, pr. 1883

Robert Emmett, pr. 1884, pb. 1940

The Jilt, pr. 1885, pb. 1904 (adaptation of a story by Hawley Smart)

Forbidden Fruit and Other Plays, pb. 1940, 1963

The Dolmen Boucicault, pb. 1964 (includes *Andy Blake, Arrah-na-Pogue: Or, The Wicklow Wedding*, and *The O'Dowd*)

Plays, pb. 1984

Selected Plays, pb. 1987

OTHER LITERARY FORMS

Dion Boucicault's only fictional work was a collaboration with Charles Reade, *Foul Play* (1868). A short, dramatized history, *The Story of Ireland* (1881), was also published in his lifetime. *The Art of Acting: A Discussion by Constant Coquelin, Henry Irving, and Dion Boucicault* (1926) was a posthumous collection. Boucicault was a regular contributor to *North American Review* from 1887 to 1889 and had written two essays for that periodical: "The Decline of the Drama" (1877) and "The Art of Dramatic Composition" (1878). Several of his articles appeared elsewhere.

ACHIEVEMENTS

Dion Boucicault was responsible for more than one hundred plays during his lengthy career. Some have been anthologized, and the three Irish plays were published together as *The Dolmen Boucicault* (1964). The others are most accessible in the microprint series *English and American Drama of the Nine-*

teenth Century, edited by Allardyce Nicoll and George Freedley (1965-1971), which also includes prompt-book reproductions for many of the plays.

Boucicault was the mid-nineteenth century's complete man of the theater. For almost fifty years, on both sides of the Atlantic, he labored as playwright, dramaturge, actor, director, and manager. Many of his enduring contributions were in the realm of practical theater. He was, with playwright Thomas William Robertson, one of the early proponents of directed rehearsals and ensemble playing. This interest led later to his formation of touring casts to replace the traditional system in which traveling stars played virtually unrehearsed stock dramas with local companies. He improved theatrical conditions by shortening the lengthy triple bills frequently offered and by abolishing half-price admission for latecomers. As an author, he fought for changes in American copyright law and for the principle of the playwright receiving a

Dion Boucicault with his wife, Agnes, in 1860.
(Hulton Archive by Getty Images)

percentage of the receipts from his play's performance. Late in his life, he invented a method of fireproofing scenery.

As a dramatist, Boucicault was both prolific and popular. His sense of what would work on stage raised him above his contemporaries. While many of his productions were translations or adaptations of others' works, any piece was more stageworthy once he had left his mark on it. Notable examples of his talents in this area are *The Corsican Brothers*, which he adapted from a French adaptation of a story by Alexandre Dumas, *père*, and *Rip Van Winkle*, which Boucicault adapted for the actor Joseph Jefferson. The former Boucicault merely made more spectacular, but for the latter, he completely remodeled the title character. The early Rip became a young and thoughtless scamp, lovable but destructive to himself and his family. The contrast between the young and old Rip adds dramatic interest, as does the very real dilemma his early behavior creates for his wife.

Boucicault's earliest successes were original comedies of manners. With this form, he provides virtually the only link between the great comic dramatists of previous centuries and Oscar Wilde. Indeed, several of Boucicault's early plays have scenes and characters that are suggestive of *The Importance of Being Earnest: A Trivial Comedy for Serious People* (pr. 1895). *London Assurance*, his first major comedy, was revived successfully in the twentieth century.

Moving next to sentimental melodrama, the dominant form of his day, Boucicault quickly mastered the formulas that would please audiences. The plays themselves have been largely forgotten, but the spectacular scenes with which he enlivened all of them have had a more lasting effect. It was his *After Dark*, for example, that popularized the image of the hero rescued from railway tracks as a train thundered toward him. Here again, Boucicault had taken his hint from another playwright, Augustin Daly, but had doubled the atmosphere of suspense and integrated the scene into a well-made plot. His presentation of sensational scenes has been seen to have parallels with later cinematographic techniques.

Boucicault's American career had a strong effect on the development of American theater, and play-

wright-producer David Belasco can certainly be considered his follower. In England, George Bernard Shaw included him on a brief list of dramatists worth reading. It is on the Irish dramas, however, that Boucicault has had his most lasting influence. The transformation of the stage Irishman that he effected in his three best Irish plays was a clear forerunner to John Millington Synge's and Sean O'Casey's greatest characters, and both acknowledged their debt to him. Aside from grand theatricality and memorable characters, these plays were full of a gentle patriotism that only once went too far for his English audience. It was Boucicault's new version of the old ballad "The Wearing of the Green," which is sung in *Arrah-na-Pogue*, that caused that song to be banned in Britain and hence popularized it in Dublin and New York.

BIOGRAPHY

Dion Boucicault was born Dionysius Lardner Boursiquot in Dublin, Ireland, apparently in 1820, although he claimed a date in 1822. His mother, née Anne Darley, was sister to George Darley the poet and editor, and to the Reverend Charles Darley, a minor playwright. She was married to Samuel Smith Boursiquot, a Dublin wine merchant from whom she separated in 1819. Nevertheless, his will acknowledged Boucicault as his legitimate son, and the latter always referred to Boursiquot as his father—although Dr. Dionysius Lardner, who lived with Boucicault's mother from the summer of 1820 and was the boy's guardian, was probably Boucicault's actual father. Lardner was the compiler of *Cabinet Cyclopedia* and the first professor of natural philosophy and astronomy at the University of London (from 1827). Although Lardner financed young Boucicault's education in Dublin and in the London area, the affair with Boucicault's mother did not survive Lardner's relocation to England.

After a brief apprenticeship to Lardner as a civil engineer, Boucicault had embarked, by 1838, on a stage career under the name Lee Moreton. *London Assurance*, accepted for the 1841 season at Covent Garden, was a resounding success on whose proceeds Boucicault brought his mother to London. Living beyond his means, he soon exhausted the money his first few comedies and farces brought him. In 1845, he married a French widow, Anne Guiot, his elder by some twenty years. She died soon after their marriage, in the Swiss Alps, leaving Boucicault a large sum that kept him in Paris for several more years. There, he familiarized himself with the French plays that were becoming so popular in England and that were to bring him many later successes in his translated and adapted versions. Always the actor, he traveled as the Viscount de Bourcicault.

When Charles Kean took over the Princess Theatre in 1850, Boucicault, impecunious again, was hired as his literary adviser. The two learned from each other, for Kean always sought the spectacular in his productions, and Boucicault was soon presenting scenes such as the miraculous appearance of the ghost in *The Corsican Brothers*. After joining Kean, he met the young actress Agnes Robertson, the manager's ward, who was to be his companion and partner for thirty years. By September, 1853, the two were performing in New York. Boucicault was later to claim that they had never married, but all their acquaintances believed that they were man and wife. They had six children.

Having written *The Colleen Bawn* in a white heat and opened it successfully in New York, Boucicault returned with it to London in 1860, where the play ran an unprecedented 360 consecutive nights at the Adelphi. The next year, the piece opened in Dublin to enthusiastic Irish audiences. Until 1872, Boucicault was prospering in England. Then, an expensive collaboration with James Robinson Planché, *Babil and Bijou*, sent him once again to the United States in temporary disgrace. For the next few years, he toured on both sides of the Atlantic, and *The Shaughraun*, another Irish play, scored heavily wherever it played.

By then, Boucicault was often on the road without Agnes, and in 1885, while the company was performing in Sydney, Australia, he married Louise Thorndyke, a young actress in his last great success, *The Jilt*. Agnes sued for a formal divorce, which was eventually granted in England. Time was running out for Boucicault, whom William Archer had already branded "a playwright of yesterday." In 1888, his last company disbanded for lack of funds. For the next

two years, he worked for an acting school in New York, where he died after a heart attack, complicated by pneumonia, on September 18, 1890.

ANALYSIS

Dion Boucicault never had literary pretensions, but he was, and knew himself to be, a superb theatrical craftsperson. He prefaced his first publication, *London Assurance*, with an apology that answers for much of his later work as well: "It will not bear analysis as a literary production. In fact, my sole object was to throw together a few scenes of a dramatic nature, and therefore I studied the stage rather than the moral effect." He later rationalized this concentration on the individual dramatic scene by arguing the decline of an audience whose chief literary form had become the newspaper. It is also true that he had to make his living from his work, and, as he once said, "More money has been made out of guano than out of poetry."

Certainly, Boucicault did not concentrate on fine language. Indeed, when he wrote his Aristotelian essay "The Art of Dramatic Composition," he listed only action, character, and decoration as the components of a drama. Diction and thought were never an issue for him, except as they were directly applicable to the presentation of plot and character. Nevertheless, a very serviceable acting drama can be written by concentrating on plot, characters, and spectacle.

Boucicault's drama was always based on his impression, invariably correct, of what would work in the theater. At the outset of his career, this impression was founded on his reading of the masters of English comedy. Oliver Goldsmith, Richard Brinsley Sheridan, George Farquhar, Sir John Vanbrugh, and William Congreve were his sources, and he wrote well in the comic style that they had established. His best work was always in the comic vein, but as his theatrical experience grew, he perfected his skills in melodrama. His great Irish plays represent the successful synthesis of these two strains.

What Boucicault learned above all from the earlier comic dramatists was the presentation of character types. "By character," Boucicault wrote, "we mean that individuality in a person made by the consistency of feelings, speech, and physiognomy." The intricacies of character development were not for him, but in the creation of consistent comic caricature, he excelled. From the gentleman freeloader Dazzle and the befuddled pastor Rural, through the thoughtlessly alcoholic Rip Van Winkle, to the rogue heroes of the Irish plays, Boucicault forged a gallery of memorable acting parts. The essential ingredient in each is individuality. Every major role has a certain dimension of stereotype, but the successful ones are not mere stereotypes.

As in his creation of spectacle, Boucicault exploits local color to the fullest. Thus, the clever servant is given a distinctively Irish flavor; the soldiers defending the empire are also clannish Scots; and the inventory of national types in *The Octoroon* includes an American Indian, good and bad Yankees, Southern gentry, a heroine of mixed blood, and a cosmopolitan hero who cannot understand why he should not marry her. A character such as Lady Gay Spanker, a typical domineering wife, is given an extra dose of realism by being the complete English horsewoman.

Character is subordinated to plot in Boucicault's theoretical article, and plot shows the characters "suffering their fate." As in all melodrama, calamity dogs the sympathetic characters until poetic justice raises them to some form of final triumph. Financial ruin is the omnipresent threat, but there are also physical dangers to be faced by the innocent. A typical Boucicault play involves a number of threats and rescues, with a continuing major danger increasing in intensity until the final resolution. Some of his melodramas are historical, but most are set in the present. Although none of them could be called serious social drama, many do deal with real social problems: the plight of the poor, the evils of gambling and drink, even race relations. Boucicault's position is never controversial, and he is careful to balance good and evil characters in every social or national class.

The final element in the construction of a drama is decoration, which Boucicault recognized as at once the least essential and the most impressive. The realistic portrayal of locality, whether it was London, Lucknow, Louisiana, or Wicklow, was the first aim in his set design. This interest in decoration began early,

and *London Assurance*, Boucicault's first success, was also the first play in London to be staged with a box set simulating a real room. For this, he had Madame Vestris, manager of Covent Garden, to thank, but scenery was to remain of vital importance to him. He often sought out the exotic, but the representation had to be believable. His realism, however, was designed to impress rather than to probe social issues. Each play offers at least one truly sensational scene: a steamboat explosion, a near-drowning, a boat race, or a burning building. These thrilling moments of spectacle join with the dangers presented by the plot to involve the audience in a world of vicarious peril.

Boucicault's best drama discards none of the sensationalism of his more commercial melodrama. Rather, it adds a true sense of comedy and a skill in the creation of characters, particularly of Irish characters. He kept a rich brogue all his life and frequently acted parts calling for a stage Irishman. By setting plays in Ireland, he was able to exploit some traditional attributes of this stereotype without condescension. The audience laughs more *with* Myles-na-Coppaleen, for example, than *at* him. The witty dialogue of Boucicault's early comedies returns in full force in these Irish plays in such a way as to make the sentimentality of their main actions palatable even to an age unused to melodrama.

LONDON ASSURANCE

London Assurance and *Old Heads and Young Hearts* are theatrical curiosities. Boucicault took London by storm with comedies of manners, a dramatic form at least fifty years out of date. The plays are set in a time that might be the Regency (1811-1820) but draw heavily on the comic situations and characters of eighteenth century drama. Although the plots of both plays are intricate, it is their characters that make them memorable.

London Assurance offers two fine female roles: Grace Harkaway is a witty heroine in the tradition of Congreve's Millamant, while Lady Gay Spanker, "glee made a living thing," carries the last three acts with her enthusiasm. Dazzle, the man nobody knows, is essentially the clever comic servant in his manipulation of the action. He brazenly attaches himself to the company, and his discovery provides the comic conclusion to the play when he acknowledges that he himself has "not the remotest idea" who he is. The moral tag that succeeds this quip, with its tedious definition of a gentleman, is the only Victorian thing about the play.

The main action, the father-and-son opposition in a love triangle, is the stuff of traditional comedy. An interesting variation is the "disguise" adopted by the son—simply denying his identity to his own father. This barefaced lie is so improbable that it works both in the play and on the stage. In this matter, Boucicault shows a spark of the assurance that characterizes Dazzle and Charles Courtly.

OLD HEADS AND YOUNG HEARTS

Old Heads and Young Hearts was Boucicault's second well-deserved success. In this play, there are now two pairs of lovers and two fathers to be placated. The background of hunting has been replaced by that of politics, and the country retreat is run as a military post by Colonel Rocket. The family relationships of the Colonel and his daughter and of Lord and Lady Pompion are sensitively drawn. The plot is deliberately confusing, and the old heads cannot follow what is going on. Jesse Rural, a well-meaning old minister, compounds the confusion with his efforts to help the young hearts and remains baffled at the final curtain. The wit is defter than that of *London Assurance*, but *Old Heads and Young Hearts* was to be Boucicault's last effort at true comedy of manners. He would argue later that the public only thought it wanted comedy, while what it really demanded was a mixture of genres.

THE POOR OF NEW YORK

The majority of Boucicault's original plays may be classed under the general heading melodrama, of which *The Poor of New York* and *After Dark* may be considered representative. The former was suggested by the commercial panic of 1857 in New York, but with its local allusions changed, it reappeared as *The Poor of Liverpool* and as *The Streets of London*. The plot, shamelessly based on coincidence, sentiment, and sensation, was loosely borrowed from a French play. The villainous banker Bloodgood, who has cheated or ruined virtually all the other characters, is finally exposed when two men break into a burning

tenement to secure evidence against him that is about to be destroyed.

AFTER DARK

The plot of *After Dark* is incredible to an extreme that approaches self-parody. Father and daughter, husband and wife, jailer and convict, and former fellow officers are reunited by a series of coincidences, schemes, and discoveries that is utterly fantastic. The action, which is set in the lurid atmosphere of a gambling den, exploits the possibilities of the newly opened underground railway as well as provides an attempted suicide under Blackfriars Bridge.

THE OCTOROON

The Octoroon is an altogether better play than *After Dark*, although it depends on the same sort of sentimentality and coincidence. Boucicault walked a fine line between pro- and antislavery elements, and somehow managed to offend no one. Salem Scudder, a crusty Yankee who has a soft heart, is one of Boucicault's finest sentimental characters. The discovery of the murderer's identity by a self-developing photograph exploited a topical scientific discovery in a sensational manner. The ending, however, is tragic, as it must be. Zoe, the octoroon forbidden by her own society from marrying the man who loves her, had to die if the play was not to support miscegenation and offend many in the audience of Boucicault's day. The comic dialogue that was to lighten the sentiment of the Irish plays is also absent.

THE IRISH PLAYS

It is probably no coincidence that Boucicault's best plays were those with the largest roles for himself. He was a comic actor of some versatility, limited mainly by his accent, yet it was not until 1860 that he wrote a really meaty part that took advantage of this handicap. *The Colleen Bawn, Arrah-na-Pogue,* and *The Shaughraun* were his greatest successes, and Boucicault saved his best writing for them. Several other Irish plays were baldly commercial and had poor receptions.

THE COLLEEN BAWN

The Colleen Bawn drew its plot loosely from Gerald Griffin's novel *The Collegians*, but Boucicault created the characters. Drawing on his reading of Irish playwrights Samuel Lover and Charles Lever, as well as on his own skill at comic dialogue, he quickly sketched a romantic comedy with the framework of melodrama. For spectacle, he added a dramatic dive to save the drowning heroine and an elaborate series of sliding Irish backdrops. For himself, he penned the character of Myles-na-Coppaleen, the heroic vagabond, a type he would re-create as Shaun the Post and Conn the Shaughraun in succeeding plays. Yet much of the wittiest dialogue is given to Anne Chute, a strong heroine in the mold of Grace Harkaway. Danny Mann, the villain, is given unusual depth in that he sincerely believes himself to be the faithful servant of the hero, Hardress Cregan.

As in Boucicault's two other major Irish plays, the villains are homegrown and the only Englishman is a noble romantic. *Arrah-na-Pogue* and *The Shaughraun*, however, both present heroes pursued by the English simply for being patriots. The political overtones are softened in that pardons are granted in both cases, but the atmosphere of oppression has been created. In the Irish plays, the dispossessed nobility are shown as the victims of an English system administered by greedy Irish speculators. The union between Cregan and Eily O'Connor, who belongs to a lower social station, is romantically satisfying but ultimately unrealistic. In the real-life episode fictionalized by Griffin, the young gentleman did find it necessary to have his peasant mistress murdered.

ARRAH-NA-POGUE

Arrah-na-Pogue brings back many of the character types and sentiments of the earlier play. The trial of Shaun the Post, who has confessed in order to shield others, is a masterful comic scene that may well have influenced Shaw in *The Devil's Disciple* (pr. 1897). O'Grady seems symbolic of the Irish way of doing things in these plays when he asks for acquittal on the grounds of the prisoner's eloquence. Shaun's spectacular escape up an ivy-covered wall, just in time to rescue his Arrah, provides an appropriately melodramatic climax.

THE SHAUGHRAUN

The Shaughraun is certainly Boucicault's finest play. The dramatist coined the title word from the Irish *seachran*, a participle that means "wandering." Conn is at his irrepressible best when he sneaks drinks

at his own wake, after a popular Irish motif. The banter between Molineux, whose English birth was not his fault, and the spirited Claire is unforgettable. These two, however, are united in their reaction to Conn's pretended death. On that occasion, Molineux asks permission to exclaim "You Irish!" and Claire readily grants it. The playwright's confident introduction of the farcical hogshead barrel sequence into the midst of his melodramatic climax shows his complete control of the medium.

The cast of Irish characters includes the spirited heroine; the romantic heroine and her Fenian lover; the genial priest Father Dolan (once acted by Sean O'Casey); his housekeeper Moya, in love with Conn; the villainous squireen and his informer accomplice; and Conn's old mother, as well as his dog Tatthers, whose presence seems inseparable from Conn's yet who never appears onstage. This collection contains the major types from the earlier two plays, and all are handled with a surer touch. As in many comic masterpieces, only the romantic lovers seem faceless.

Boucicault did not write any great drama after *The Shaughraun*. Some would argue that he had not done so before. Nevertheless, in this fantastic blend of melodrama, genuine comic wit, and facetious Irish blarney, Boucicault concocted truly memorable theater.

OTHER MAJOR WORKS

LONG FICTION: *Foul Play*, 1868 (with Charles Reade).

NONFICTION: *The Story of Ireland*, 1881; *The Art of Acting: A Discussion by Constant Coquelin, Henry Irving, and Dion Boucicault*, 1926.

BIBLIOGRAPHY

Cullingford, Elizabeth Butler. "National Identities in Performance: The Stage Englishman of Boucicault's Irish Drama." *Theatre Journal* 49, no. 3 (October, 1997): 287-300. This study focuses on Boucicault's presentation of the stage Englishman and stereotypes.

Fawkes, Richard. *Dion Boucicault: A Biography*. London: Quartet Books, 1979. A comprehensive life and times of Boucicault. The detailed narrative draws, in part, on a number of unpublished sources. The emphasis is on theatrical history and Boucicault's place in it, rather than on the playwright's character or the wider context of his work. Bibliography.

Fischler, Alan. "Guano and Poetry: Payment for Playwriting in Victorian England." *Modern Language Quarterly* 62, no. 1 (March, 2001): 43-52. Boucicault's remark regarding payment for his works forms the basis of this essay examining compensation issues in Victorian England. Boucicault's prodigious production of plays and some of his business dealings are discussed.

Grene, Nicholas. *The Politics of Irish Drama: Plays in Context from Boucicault to Friel*. New York: Cambridge University Press, 1999. An examination of the political and social views of Boucicault and Brian Friel, among other Irish dramatists.

Molin, Sven Eric, and Robin Goodfellow, eds. *Dion Boucicault: A Documentary Life*. 5 vols. Newark, Del.: Proscenium Press, 1979-1991. An ambitious attempt to characterize Boucicault's life and times in terms of the contemporary documentary record. Each part deals with a particular phase of Boucicault's prolific and protean career and has for its centerpiece a reprint of one or more of the playwright's texts. Supplemented by memoirs, theatrical histories, and similar documentary sources.

Richtarik, Marilynn. "Stewart Parker's *Heavenly Bodies*: Dion Boucicault, Show Business, and Ireland." *Modern Drama* 43, no. 3 (Fall, 2000): 404-420. An analysis of Parker's play *Heavenly Bodies*, which is a biography of Boucicault.

Philip Oxley,
updated by George O'Brien

ROBERTO BRACCO

Born: Naples, Italy; November 10, 1862
Died: Naples, Italy; April 21, 1943

PRINCIPAL DRAMA
Non fare ad altri, pr., pb. 1886
Lui, lei, lui!, pr., pb. 1887
Un avventura di viaggio, pr., pb. 1887
Una donna, pr. 1893, pb. 1894
Infedele, pr. 1893, pb. 1894 (*Comptesse Coquette*, 1907)
Don Pietro Caruso, pr., pb. 1895 (English translation, 1912)
La fine dell'amore, pr., pb. 1896 (*I Love You*, 1913)
Tragedie dell'anima, pr., pb. 1899 (*The Tragedy of a Soul*, 1899)
Uno degli onesti, pr., pb. 1900 (*The Honorable Lover*, 1915)
Sperduti nel buio, pr. 1901, pb. 1906
Maternità, pr., pb. 1903
Il frutto acerbo, pr., pb. 1904

Notte di neve, pr. 1904, pb. 1907 (*Night of Snow*, 1915)
La piccola fonte, pr. 1905, pb. 1906 (*The Hidden Spring*, 1906)
I fantasmi, pr. 1906, pb. 1907 (*Phantasms*, 1907)
Nellina, pr., pb. 1908 (English translation, 1908)
Il piccolo santo, pr. 1909, pb. 1910 (*The Little Saint*, 1931)
I pazzi, pr., pb. 1922
Teatro, pb. 1922-1927 (11 volumes)

OTHER LITERARY FORMS
Known primarily as a playwright and a lecturer, Roberto Bracco also wrote poems, short stories, and a screenplay.

ACHIEVEMENTS
Despite his popularity in the theaters of Europe and New York from 1900 to 1920 and the firm position of respect accorded his playwriting by theatrical

and academic writers throughout the twentieth century, Roberto Bracco has not become an important influence on modern drama. Most critics, however, acknowledge the craftsmanship, psychological insight, and human sympathy found in his drama, calling for study or production of Bracco's plays based on their own merit rather than as historical curiosities or their use of the ideas of Henrik Ibsen, Gerhart Hauptmann, and Sigmund Freud.

Two reasons for Bracco's lack of influence are historical: the Fascists' coming to power in 1922 and the greatly changed attitudes toward theater and literature after World War I, which saw the rise of Luigi Pirandello as a force in Italian drama. As a deputy with decidedly liberal views in the Italian Parliament, Bracco's political and literary career was cut short by the ascendancy of the Fascists. Under Benito Mussolini, censorship was imposed, fines enforced, and prison sentences issued to offending writers. The political subjects and social issues that Bracco treated were taboo. Commenting on the American premiere of Bracco's most famous play, *The Little Saint*, in December, 1931, Walter Littlefield, theater critic for *The New York Times*, cited Bracco, besides Sem Benelli and Gabriele D'Annunzio, as "easily the most impressive dramatist on the eve of the march on Rome in the autumn of 1922. Since then he has lost his impressiveness, although now he is more secretly read than publicly played for, politically, he belongs to the Opposition."

That literary historians often make overly general comparisons among writers also has worked against recognition of Bracco's drama. For example, Lander MacClintock, a sympathetic and balanced reader of Bracco, states that *The Little Saint* "represents a point of arrival and a point of departure in the evolution of Italian theater." Oscar Brockett, a major historian of modern drama, finds time only to compare Bracco's plays with others of the period 1900-1915 and states that they are important for their imitation and popularization of Ibsen. Even though Pirandello's accomplishments, much discussed by these and other literary historians and critics, were novel, Bracco's were nevertheless solid in their own right.

Success in the theater may be highly suspect from the perspective of the scholar, discerning audience, or

Roberto Bracco (courtesy of New York Public Library)

succeeding playwright, but good plays often prove their worth by their initial reception. In the period from 1900 to 1920, only one other Italian playwright, Dario Niccodemi, had more productions than Bracco. Bracco's plays were performed from Budapest, Vienna, and Berlin to Madrid, Paris, London, and New York. English translations of some of his plays were published in Boston in the dramatic and literary magazine *Poet Lore* in 1907 and 1908, and the first part of the twentieth century saw the publication of Bracco's plays in anthologies and college texts of both modern and Italian drama. In 1966, the English theater magazine *Gambit* translated *The Little Saint*. Most academic critics, both Italian and American, cite the humane perspective of Bracco's writing.

Bracco's major achievements are general knowledge of human life in his time, reflected in a range of dramatic genres, including tragedy, comedy, both light and sentimental, and farce; his assimilation and adaptation of Ibsen's realism, especially those plays dealing with the women's issues of his day; and most important, the use of Freud's theory of the unconscious in his plots and characterizations.

In 1923, Pasquale Parisi, who wrote the first book-length study of Bracco, quoted Bracco himself on the subject of art and drama:

> Human essence is all that matters in all forms of art especially theater. One can localize ideas, atmospheres, and characters in order to obtain a greater evidence of truth. And one can generalize ideas, atmospheres, and characters to make more explicit one's vision. But human essence is always the basic element that an artist looks for, be it near him or at a distance. The results of this search constitute the intrinsic value of a work of art.

Bracco felt the necessity of observing daily life for his writing, finding in it the "chrysalis of his fantasy." Parisi stresses the natural quality of Bracco's imagination and thought, which led him past philosophy and ideas as such to the language and action of passion.

The critic Maddalena Kuitunen observes that Bracco's concern with women's issues has been overshadowed by Ibsen's. From a feminist perspective, she disagrees with Bracco's idea of the maternal instinct as a fulfillment of womanhood, but she credits him with the naturalist's accomplishment of placing characters in real-life situations of the day. Most critics, however, praise his sympathy for and understanding of women caught in a society in which, as MacClintock writes, the "woman's only defense or weapon is her astuteness, her coquetry and her powers of seduction." The tragic plays, from his early period but the work of a mature writer, are women's stories. In *The Tragedy of a Soul*, Caterina sets off a chain of tragic events as a result of the weaknesses of her husband and lover. The female protagonist of *Maternità* (maternity), on leaving her unworthy husband for her unborn child's sake, discovers that she cannot give birth, and opts to die together with her unborn child rather than save her own life. In *The Hidden Spring*, a selfish artist neglects his wife, who is his inspiration, and, having driven her mad, must accept that he has cruelly destroyed the source of his

art. The female heroine of *Phantasms* suffers the jealousy of her consumptive husband, to whom she promises fidelity after his death. Tragically, she discovers that the phantasm of her former married life, his jealousy, has made it impossible to love a man with whom she develops a relationship.

Brockett identifies the use of Freud's idea of the unconscious as perhaps the most important development in drama between 1900 and 1915, which indeed is the element most praised in Bracco's work. Even Bracco's strongest and most influential negative critic, Silvio d'Amico, praises his dramatic treatment of the subconscious. As Bracco himself explains in his preface to *The Little Saint*, he intended to trace both the conscious and unconscious of his characters: "I partially hid the soul of some characters and almost completely that of the protagonists, just as they would be hidden in real life." In an early play, *Il trionfo* (1895; the triumph), the protagonist consciously believes that his nonphysical affection for a young woman who has nursed him back to health proves that Platonic love as an ennobling force takes precedence over passionate love. He becomes jealous, however, when she and a friend develop a sexual relationship, thus proving his unconscious desire, a feeling that is stronger than the respect and gratitude he had earlier felt. When the cruel artist in *The Hidden Spring* becomes conscious of his mistreatment of his wife, she kills herself; they did not understand that the true basis of their relationship was not love but cruelty on his part and self-destructiveness on hers. Bracco's dramatization of how the unknowable aspects of the mind motivate human action is thus akin to the Greek idea of how the gods provided humankind with choices that had unforeseeable but necessarily tragic consequences.

BIOGRAPHY

Born and educated in Naples, Roberto Bracco took a job as a customs clerk at age seventeen because his parents could not afford to send him to the university. Finding such work unsuitable, he took a job as a journalist with *Corriere del Matteo*, and soon he acted on his interest in literature, publishing poems and stories in Neopolitan journals and writing one-act plays as curtain raisers for actors of the city. His first volume of short stories, *Le frottole di baby* (1881; baby's rattles), was published when he was nineteen.

Works written in his twenties, such as *Non fare ad altri* (do not unto others), *Lui, lei, lui!* (he, her, he!), and *Un avventura di viaggio* (a traveling adventure), point to his talent as a dramatist and led the way to the success of *Comptesse Coquette* in 1893, which was praised in Naples and gradually produced across Europe. Further successes established Bracco as a leading Italian playwright, allowing him to hold his position as a serious writer when foreign plays and trivial drawing-room entertainments dominated the attention of a large portion of the audience. Steadily writing plays every year or two, Bracco also lectured on the position and rights of women in Italian society, a major theme of his drama.

When the Fascists came to power in 1922, Bracco lost the position he had achieved as a liberal deputy in the Parliament, his plays were forbidden to be performed, and his books were banned. Perhaps the influence of postwar ideas and attitudes would have ended Bracco's literary career in any case, because his last play, *I pazzi*, shows his disagreement with the rationalist faith in the new psychiatry as a way to understand humanity or resolve its problems. Perhaps building on the idea of Don Fiorenzo's mysterious spiritual power in *The Little Saint*, Bracco presents the protagonist of *I pazzi* as healing people in a personal and spiritual way that involves love and understanding, characteristic of Bracco's humane sympathy for life. Living beyond his time as a writer, Bracco died in poverty in 1943.

Analysis

The plays *Comptesse Coquette*, *Night of Snow*, and *The Little Saint* are representative of the themes and attitudes most often cited in Roberto Bracco's work: his sympathetic attitude toward human predicaments, his concern for the plight of women in his society, and his successful dramatization of character based on Freudian theory (even though he himself valued the lively presentation of life rather than what he considered the tedious solutions of philosophy or psychiatry).

Comptesse Coquette

Successfully performed as *Comptesse Coquette* in New York in 1907, fourteen years after its enthusiastic reception in Naples, the play comically dramatizes how Clara, the female protagonist, resolves a conflict with her husband over the right to have a lover. With its daring and risqué subject—daring, that is, for the middle-class audiences at the turn of the century—the comedy has been misinterpreted as bitter by academic critics and "frothy" by theatrical reviewers.

At marriage, the flirtatious countess has wrung the concession of having a lover from her jealous husband. When her husband mistakenly turns up where she and her would-be lover, a friend of her husband, have met, Clara boldly sends her husband away but then laughs at the other man's attempts at seduction. When the husband returns, his jealousy stifled, she goes into the next room with him, forcing the friend to endure their happy laughter. Thus, the countess establishes comically the woman's right to sexual freedom in marriage, but Bracco has also used comedy to affirm the value of marital fidelity by exposing the husband's jealousy and lover's seduction to laughter.

The play reverses the expectation of the time, that the man might have a lover but not the woman; Bracco thus dramatized what he saw as an injustice against women. Clara's statement to her husband toward the end of the play—"I have looked and looked for the right man and in spite of myself I've been obliged to choose you"—does not reveal a cynical attitude toward women on Bracco's part but rather implies that the wife, too, can receive comic justice because she has had the opportunity but has been unable to take a lover. In *Una donna* and *Phantasms*, Bracco treats women's sexual freedom in marriage tragically, which indicates the importance of the issue to both him and his audiences.

Night of Snow

Night of Snow shows not only that Bracco's interest in women's condition went beyond sexual freedom in the upper classes but also that social attitudes affecting women had natural consequences for men. Critics have overlooked the fact that the men in relationships with women in Bracco's plays are affected by what happens to the women.

Living in the tenements of Naples, the mother and lover of Salvatore, a down-and-out man with a good education, have in the past been forced into prostitution by their poverty. Although the play shows the woman as victim of the social conditions and male attitudes of the day, Salvatore is also a victim, suffering the indignities of being illegitimate. For this he is unable to forgive his mother. During the play, he irrationally refuses the money his mother has honorably begged and earned, and sends her away. She kills herself in despair.

Because the play does not resolve what happens in the relationship between Salvatore and his lover, Graziella, it is clear that the driving force of events is not what happens to women but the necessarily terrible consequences of poverty and its effect on people's attitudes toward one another. Were Salvatore able to accept that his mother had reformed for his sake, he might have been able to see that Graziella has also given up her life of prostitution for him so that their child, which she is carrying, can be born honorably. Thus, both men and women remain the victims of social conditions, although Salvatore's male ego could be criticized as reflecting part of the problem unfairly on the women. Before the final scene, Salvatore does resolve his bitterness and resentment toward women when he recognizes that Graziella has a just claim to the money for their child's sake. Nevertheless, he must leave, unable to bear the ignominy of accepting anything from the mother who has illegitimately given him life. Her suicide shocks both Salvatore and Graziella into horror and inactivity.

When one considers that Salvatore's loss of his job and Graziella's former prostitution and present pregnancy provide the conflict in the play, the mother's suicide can be justified, because it undoubtedly will leave Salvatore and Graziella in the despair that prevented him from forgiving his mother and her from having confidence in their love. Thus, again, Bracco dramatizes the effect of social conditions and attitudes, in this play not only on women but on men as well. The play represents a more thorough use of naturalism than that with which its author has usually been credited.

THE LITTLE SAINT

Perhaps the key to apparent difficulties of motivation and dramatization in the one-act *Night of Snow* can be found by analyzing *The Little Saint*, most frequently cited as Bracco's best full-length play. To paraphrase his supporter, the critic Rudolph Altrocchi, Bracco was challenged by dramatizing the nonrational links between his characters' inner self, psyche, or unconscious mind and their acts, words, and behavior. These seemingly mysterious connections had to be imagined by him as an artist and represent "the invisible thread of dramatic development," though they imply the impossibility of knowing finally the actual sources of human motivation.

Silvio d'Amico has praised Bracco in his mastery of this form, sometimes called the "drama of silence," or the "inexpresso," as better than as handled by the French. Established by Maurice Maeterlinck and followed by Jean Jacque Bernand, the audience has to supply with its imagination important words omitted from the dialogue, ideas that perhaps cannot be expressed in words at all. From his preface to *The Little Saint*, Bracco notes:

Again my art is "vague" in this drama. In it there are never direct words because they lie at the very bottom of the existence of beings whose acts and words correspond to their mind only ambiguously. The continuous discord between my characters' mind and their behavior constitutes the invisible thread that holds the drama together and leads it, implying the absolute impossibility of telling the tragedy through the surface action.

In *The Little Saint*, Don Fiorenzo, a wise and retiring priest loved by the people he serves, is visited by his brother Giulio, who long ago departed for South America, and Annita, the daughter of a woman whom Don Fiorenzo has once loved and because of whom, spurred by her rejection, he entered the priesthood. Giulio falls in love with Annita, and Don Fiorenzo supports their marriage plans, but reluctantly. On their wedding day, Don Fiorenzo is so upset that he cannot perform the ceremony.

Don Fiorenzo's love for the girl's mother, long repressed in his unconscious, has been stirred, and he responds with a means that he consciously understands by teaching Annita his religious mysticism. Accordingly, she responds to his attention and resists Giulio's wooing, desiring only Don Fiorenzo's gentle asceticism. Giulio's love for Annita is based on a love aroused honestly by her modesty and is straightforward in representing desire seeking satisfaction.

Two months of great psychological disturbance follow, causing Don Fiorenzo's half-witted manservant, Barbarello, also to become upset. The couple decide to leave for South America, but in an instinctive attempt to preserve Don Fiorenzo's happiness, Barbarello pushes the brother to his death off a cliff. Barbarello's seemingly inexplicable act, which ends the play, corresponds, via his unconscious mind, with Don Fiorenzo's having saved him from death when he had slipped off a cliff before the action of the play begins, which resulted in Barbarello's brain damage.

The action of the play and Bracco's method are clear enough. Performed in 1909, *The Little Saint* was a major success that received unanimous praise from critics. Bracco's own words best describe his dramaturgy.

> If the characters don't explain themselves, their feelings and worries, there is no way for the spectator to know or understand them. . . . I believe that a synthesis of meaningful signs can throw on the characters enough light to make clear even what is not literally spelled out. I call this synthesis "artifice." It's the equivalent of impressions that stay in the mind of the hypersensitive observer of human behavior. Whatever emerges to the outside world is merely a synthesis of meaningful signs which contain the substantial reality hidden behind the surface.

The play ends in a way similar to *Night of Snow*, in that Graziella's and Salvatore's shocked silence is like Don Fiorenzo's state as he "stops short, thunderstruck, suffocated with horror and amazement." Only the audience, not Don Fiorenzo, can fully understand why he is so overwhelmed by the sudden rush of mixed feelings. Thus the play works like George Bernard Shaw's drama of ideas and Bertolt Brecht's epic theater in that the audience must make the synthesis of ideas required to understand the play, because the characters cannot and do not.

Bracco's use of the unconscious is also comparable to Aeschylus's use of fate, for both playwrights presuppose that human motivation cannot be fully understood and that conflicts lead necessarily to tragic consequences. Just as Agamemnon cannot know if he should sacrifice Iphigenia because the gods are divided, so Don Fiorenzo cannot comprehend the mixture of his feelings for Annita, but the tragic logic of the cycle of vengeance in the *Oresteia* (458 B.C.E.; English translation, 1777) and of the workings of the unconscious mind in *The Little Saint* ends in inevitable death. Though the reasons for human motivation vary from conflicting Greek ideas on religion and the role of the gods to the complicated modern concept of the unconscious, both playwrights find solutions in their drama for the problem of why people act the way they do.

In observing life as it really was, Bracco followed the naturalists, as the tragically realistic events of *Night of Snow* show. In bringing comedy to the issue of women's sexual freedom in marriage, a subject equally suitable for tragedy, Bracco further distinguished himself. Finally, most innovative was his dramatization of the workings of the unconscious mind, seen in *The Little Saint* as well as in many of his other plays.

OTHER MAJOR WORKS

SHORT FICTION: *Le frottole di baby*, 1881; *Smorfi umane*, 1906; *Smorfie g aie*, 1909; *Smorfie tristi*, 1909; *La vita e la favola*, 1914.

POETRY: *Vecchi versetti*, 1910.

NONFICTION: *Tra le arti e gli artisti*, 1919; *Tra gli uomini e le cose*, 1921.

SCREENPLAY: *Sperduti nel buio*, 1914.

MISCELLANEOUS: *Tutte le opere*, 1935-1942 (25 volumes).

BIBLIOGRAPHY

Carlson, Marvin A. *The Italian Stage from Goldoni to D'Annunzio*. Jefferson, N.C.: McFarland, 1981. A general study that examines Italian theater during the time in which Bracco was active.

O'Grady, Deidre. *Piave, Boita, Pirandello: From Romantic Realism to Modernism*. Lewiston, N.Y.:

Edwin Mellen Press, 2000. This study of Italian drama in the nineteenth and twentieth century sheds light on the climate in which Bracco lived and wrote. Bibliography and index.

Witt, Mary Ann Frese. *The Search for Modern Tragedy: Aesthetic Fascism in Italy and France*. Ithaca, N.Y.: Cornell University Press, 2001. This study examines the rise of Fascism and its appearance in the drama of Italy and France, a popularity that adversely affected the liberal Bracco. Bibliography and index.

John M. Lee

VOLKER BRAUN

Born: Dresden, Germany; May 7, 1939

PRINCIPAL DRAMA

Die Kipper, wr. 1962-1965, pr., pb. 1972

Freunde, wr. 1965, pb. 1971

Mink, wr. 1965, pr. 1972

Hinze und Kunze, pr. 1968 as *Hans Faust*, revised pb. 1973

Schmitten, wr. 1969-1978, pb. 1981, pr. 1982

Tinka, pb. 1975, pr. 1976

Guevara: Oder, Der Sonnenstaat, pr., pb. 1977

Grosser Frieden, pb. 1978, pr. 1979 (*The Great Peace*, c. 1980)

Simplex Deutsch, pr., pb. 1980

Dmitri, pr. 1982, pb. 1983

Lenins Tod, pr. 1983, pb. 1988

Stücke, pb. 1983-1989 (2 volumes)

Siegfried Frauenprotokolle Deutscher Furor, pr. 1986, pb. 1989

Iphigenie in Freiheit, pb. 1990, pr. 1992

Böhmen am Meer, pr., pb. 1992

OTHER LITERARY FORMS

Volker Braun is as well known for his work as a lyric poet as he is for his plays. He made his literary debut in 1965 with the collection of poetry titled *Provokation für mich* (1965; provocation for me), and in spite of his steady involvement in the theater, he has kept active as a poet throughout his career, publishing his work at regular intervals. Among the best-known volumes of his poetry are the collections *Wir und nicht sie* (1970; we and not they), *Gegen die symmetrische Welt* (1974; against the symmetrical world), and *Training des aufrechten Gangs* (1978; training of the upright posture). Numerous poems by Braun have appeared in English translation in major anthologies devoted to contemporary German poetry. He wrote some of his most remarkable poetry after German reunification in 1990, when he expressed his sense of loss of identity and apprehensiveness about the future without any false nostalgia.

Although his literary reputation is in large part based on his work as a poet and dramatist, Braun has published important prose fiction as well. The three "reports" in *Das ungezwungene Leben Kasts* (1972, 1979; the unconstrained life of Kast) are based on his experiences as a construction worker, a student, and a beginning playwright, respectively. A fourth story, focusing on the leadership role of the writer-intellectual in a socialist society and corresponding to Braun's own increased prominence in the East German literary establishment, was included in an expanded version of the book that appeared in 1979. Braun's novella *Unvollendete Geschichte* (1975; *Unfinished Story*, 1979), which offers a frank portrayal of an East German state overly prone to distrust its young people, was the center of a minor literary storm when it was withdrawn from circulation shortly after its publication.

In addition, Braun has published two prose works that draw and expand on the relationship he first explored in the play *Hinze und Kunze*. *Berichte von Hinze und Kunze* (1983; stories of Hinze and Kunze) is a collection of seventy anecdotes centering on the relationship between the worker Hinze and the party secretary Kunze. Written in conscious imitation of

Bertolt Brecht's Keuner stories (*Geschichten von Herrn Keuner*, 1930, 1958), each anecdote reveals some aspect of the complex relationship between the party leadership and working people in contemporary socialist society. The Hinze-Kunze relationship is developed in depth in Braun's *Hinze-Kunze-Roman* (1985; Hinze-Kunze novel), in which the two representative figures assume more specific fictional identities as a high-ranking party official and his chauffeur. After 1990, he published several additional volumes of short fiction.

Braun has published a collection of essays and assorted notes under the title *Es genügt nicht die einfache Wahrheit* (1975; the simple truth is not enough). Several of the essays included there, especially "Die Schaubühne nicht als moralische Anstalt betrachtet" (1968; the theater not regarded as a moral institution) and "Über die Bauweise neuer Stücke" (1973; about the making of new plays), are important expressions of Braun's views on the function and practice of theater after Brecht.

ACHIEVEMENTS

When Volker Braun's first plays were published and performed in the early 1970's, he was hailed in both the East and the West as the most promising young talent among the dramatists of his generation. He became one of East Germany's leading dramatists and a principal heir to and adapter of the Brechtian theatrical tradition in East Germany. One indication of Braun's stature as a playwright is the positive reception given his work in West Germany, where seven of his plays were published and three appeared in the repertory of major stages. Among East German dramatists, only Braun and his colleagues Peter Hacks and Heiner Müller have managed in the long term to find an audience for their work in both German states—an accomplishment made the more remarkable when one considers the political-ideological context in which inter-German cultural exchange took place. Since the early 1970's, Braun's international reputation as both a poet and a dramatist has grown steadily and has led to a following for his work outside German-speaking Europe, most notably in France, Italy, England, and the United States.

Although Braun had no direct contact with Brecht or with his historic productions at the Berliner Ensemble in the 1950's, Braun's plays clearly show the influence of Brecht and the theatrical tradition that he began. More than the work of any of his East German contemporaries, Braun's drama represents a continuation of Brecht's tradition, which he adapts to and for the situation of the socialist state in the 1960's and 1970's. Although Brecht's drama focused on the dialectic of the class struggle, Braun's theater moves to new conflicts that are to be found within socialist society itself. The dialectic tension inherent in these "non-antagonistic" conflicts—by which Braun means conflicts within one social system rather than between competing social systems—is essential to the evolution of socialism and is the focal point of Braun's dramatic method.

Braun's refusal to provide solutions to the problems he presents in his drama (that is, to suggest positive models of behavior) has been one reason for the uneven reception given his plays in his native East Germany. Especially during the early stages of his career in the 1960's, a time during which East German cultural policy encouraged affirmative theater celebrating the accomplishments of the new socialist German state, Braun's insistence on focusing on unresolved problems and unpleasant realities clearly worked against the publication and performance of his work. It would not be misleading to emphasize Braun's difficulties with cultural authorities in the East Germany. Like many critical writers in East Germany, he considered himself a committed socialist, who, in posing difficult and even unanswerable questions, sought to encourage change in the direction of a better society. His stance as a writer was one of "critical solidarity" with the cause of socialism. He did not change this stance after German reunification in 1990, but he did not indulge in naïve nostalgia about the East German past. He had been one of the severest critics of the East German state. The mixed performance history of his plays is a testimony to his critical stance. Nevertheless, he was an influential force in the East German theater, as evidenced by his nearly continuous involvement throughout his career as a dramaturge and artistic consultant for several major East German stages, including the former Brecht theater of the Berliner Ensemble in East Berlin from 1977 to 1990.

Braun's work has been recognized with three major East German literary awards: the Erich Weinert Medal for young writers, presented in 1964, and since then the important Heinrich Heine and Heinrich Mann prizes for literature, awarded in 1971 and 1980, respectively. After 1990, he continued to be recognized for his literary achievement: He also received a number of former West German literary prizes, among others, the Schiller Memorial Prize in 1992 and the prestigious Georg Büchner Prize in 2000.

BIOGRAPHY

Volker Braun was born on the eve of World War II, on May 7, 1939, in Dresden, Germany. His father was killed in the last weeks of the war, leaving his mother to rear him and four brothers alone. In 1948, the nine-year-old Braun spent a brief period of time in the care of the International Red Cross in Switzerland, where he was treated for acute malnutrition; he soon returned to his family in the Soviet Occupation Zone, which officially became the German Democratic Republic in October of 1949. In spite of the traumatic conditions under which he grew up, Braun does not generally deal with the war and its immediate aftermath in his writing. In contrast to his older colleagues, who experienced the war as adolescents or adults and whose work often returns to this experience, Braun's work, like that of many writers of his generation, has tended to focus on the postwar efforts to build a new socialist state in the void left by the defeat of fascism.

Braun finished his basic schooling in 1957 with the successful completion of the university qualifying exam, the *Abitur*; he was initially unsuccessful, however, in gaining admission to the university. Over the next four years, he worked variously as a printer in his native Dresden, then as a mine construction worker at the coal and steel cooperative Schwarze Pumpe, and finally, after completing a technical apprenticeship, as a machine mechanic at the open-pit coal mine Burghammer. His work experiences during these four years were to leave a profound mark on his early

writing and are especially apparent in the subject matter and the setting of his first several plays.

It was during this period that Braun wrote his first poetry, and in 1959 he completed the first of the four prose reports that would together make up *Das ungezwungene Leben Kasts*. More directly than in any of his other writing, the Kast stories illustrate Braun's strong personal identification with the young socialist state. The autobiographically inspired accounts reflect, in the figure Kast, important stages in both Braun's personal development and the parallel development of his country.

In 1960, Braun was admitted to the University of Leipzig, where he studied philosophy until 1964. On completion of his studies, he traveled for a time in the Soviet Union (in Siberia) before accepting an invitation from Brecht's widow, Helene Weigel, to work as a dramaturge and assistant director at the Berliner Ensemble in East Berlin. He held this position for one year before leaving to devote himself full-time to his writing.

These first years in Berlin were an especially productive period for Braun's writing. In addition to his poetry and the work on the first Kast stories, the period between 1964 and 1971 saw him work on no fewer than six plays, all but one of which (*Hinze und Kunze*) were to remain unpublished and unperformed until after a general liberalization of cultural policy in 1971. The more liberal cultural policies announced that year by new party chief Erich Honecker coincided with Braun's return to a direct involvement in theater work when he accepted a one-year position as consultant and playwright-in-residence with the civic theaters of the city of Leipzig. In Leipzig and over the next few years, Braun was able to play a part in the first successful productions of his early plays. Braun has been involved with the theater continuously since 1971, working from 1972 to 1977 with the Deutsches Theater in East Berlin, and thereafter with the Berliner Ensemble from 1977 through 1990. These two theaters were the principal proponents and producers of his work in East Germany.

In 1973, Braun was elected to the executive council of the East German Writers' Union, a post that reflected his socialist convictions and the prominence and respect that he enjoyed among his colleagues. In 1976, Braun protested the expulsion of poet and ballad singer Wolf Biermann from East Germany and questioned the cultural politics of the Socialist Unity Party. As of 1975, Braun was under observation by the East German secret police (Stasi) because of alleged "political-ideological diversion." Such observation of intellectuals, artists, and writers was typical for East German state authorities, who did not tolerate any criticism. Yet, Braun never left East Germany.

After German reunification in 1990, Braun joined a number of former West German or West Berlin institutions, such as the Academy of Arts in the former West Berlin and the German Academy for Language and Literature in Darmstadt. He also traveled to the United States in 1990 and was sponsored for a stay at the Villa Massimo in Rome in 1993. In 1994, he was a guest lecturer at the University of Wales and presented lectures at the universities of Heidelberg, Paderborn, Zurich, and Kassel. He resides and works in Berlin.

Analysis

Volker Braun's plays are concrete expressions of his dissatisfaction with the present, his unwillingness to accept the current state of things in his own society and in the world. His plays focus, therefore, on the unresolved problems and troubling contradictions of a socialist state, not so much as a criticism of its failings—although this criticism is clearly important—but as a challenge to his audience to join in the enormous task of building a new society. Braun's dramatic method is, as the critic Katherine Vanovitch has observed, to present his audience with the challenge that a socialist society in its imperfection offers and "to excite them, as individuals, to share in the poetry by grasping their opportunity to mould their own environment and, in the process, themselves."

One basic question is at the heart of all Braun's drama. It concerns the dialectical relationship between the various contradictory forces that reside within all revolutions. Braun's plays portray in manifold variation the continual struggle between utopian vision and reactionary impulse. They examine in the lives and fates of his individual protagonists the conflicts

between the desire for progress and the conservative tendency to preserve what currently exists, and between the subjective desires of the individual and the objective limitations inherent in real-life situations. In Braun's view, these conflicts are most apparent in the contradictory relationship between the political leaders of the society "who consciously orchestrate the transformation of the society or who consciously or unconsciously impede it," and those who are led and "who consciously or unconsciously put the plans into action or who criticize and resist them." Accordingly, the relationship between the political leadership and individual citizens is an important focus in his plays.

A second, related question posed in Braun's drama concerns the costs, in particular the human costs, associated with the building of the new society. Therefore, Braun's plays often examine the effect that larger political and economic issues have on the lives of individuals—that is, on the people who either willingly or under duress have taken on the task of moving the society forward.

In terms of both the choice of subject matter and their dramatic approach, Braun's plays fall into two fairly distinct periods. The first extends from the early 1960's and his first work on the play *Die Kipper* (the dumpers) through the mid-1970's and the completion of the dramas *Schmitten* and *Tinka*. During this roughly fifteen-year period, Braun's plays focused almost exclusively on the problems connected with the development of socialism in East Germany. With the lone exception of the play *Lenins Tod* (Lenin's death, written during this time but not produced until 1983), which deals with the taboo subject of the transition of power in the Soviet Union in the 1920's, all the major plays of this period are set in the German Democratic Republic of the 1950's and early 1960's, in the so-called *Aufbau*, or "building," period, in which the fledgling East German state struggled to build a new industrial economy.

Die Kipper

In his first play, *Die Kipper*, Braun focuses on the continuing existence of demeaning and dehumanizing work in the context of socialism. The case in point is the physically and spiritually ruinous work of the dumpers, who spend their entire shift dumping trainloads of sand and dirt. Although it is technologically possible to automate the dumping process, the country's fragile economy in the 1950's does not make automation feasible, and workers remain bound to the methods of production borrowed from the old system.

The play begins with a prologue in which one of the actors presents a short synopsis of the play's essential content, a synopsis that should focus the audience's attention on the play's central concerns. The play will recount one year in the life of the unskilled worker Paul Bauch, who discovers one day that "in addition to the arm that he needs for his work, he has yet another arm, and what's more two legs and even a head." Braun's point is clear: The new society does not make use of the entire person. The individual worker now, as before, is reduced to the one procedure he or she performs, and the traditional division between headwork and handwork, between the "bosses" who lead and the workers who follow, is kept intact.

In the figure of Paul Bauch, Braun embodies the energy and legitimate aspirations of the individual worker, who demands that work be meaningful and that he be involved in it completely, head and hand. Like the figures Hinze and Tinka in later plays, Bauch demands an immediate and complete change in the methods of production. He demands an ideal socialism while disregarding the very real factors that still hamper its realization. When, through an unlikely series of events, he is made *Brigadier*, the foreman of his work brigade, he throws himself into his work, driving himself and the brigade on to meet ever higher production goals. By making the tedious labor of the dump into a kind of sport, he is able to help each of his coworkers to realize the importance of the individual's contribution to the success of the whole. His innovative measures are at first successful in increasing both the level of production and the involvement of the individual brigade members in their work; they ultimately collapse, however, as Bauch's subjective demands surpass the objective reality of the young country's ability to support them. Bauch's methods culminate in an accident that destroys some

of the brigade's antiquated equipment and seriously injures one of the workers. Bauch, who is held responsible, is relieved of his post and sent to prison.

On one hand, by not being content to accept that which is "objectively possible" under existing conditions, Bauch is able to accomplish something previously considered impossible. On the other hand, his individual efforts frustrate the ultimate goal of true collective work, for the brigade members have become mere extensions of his energy. They have become his "arm," relying on his head rather than using their own. Somewhat ironically, Bauch's revolutionary energy, while contributing somewhat to the society's progress, serves to frustrate the ultimate goal of the socialist revolution. In like manner, the outdated and inadequate machinery that the dumpers must use suggests the limits within which the revolution must proceed. The young socialist state does not yet possess the objective basis for true and complete socialism, a fact that dictates the country's continuing reliance on remnants of the old social order.

Although Paul Bauch fails, the play nevertheless ends optimistically. Bauch's "unreasonable" demands have awakened a new consciousness among his coworkers, who will now proceed on their own in the direction that Bauch has pushed them—if now at a more measured and moderate pace. As foretold somewhat enigmatically in the prologue, in the end, Paul Bauch "loses a brigade, but the brigade wins." Braun's protagonists are not exemplary figures; they are not the positive heroes and heroines called for in the literary program of Socialist Realism. This fact is suggested in the title of the final 1972 version of the play, which places the dumpers as a group in the forefront, while two earlier versions of the play, entitled first "Der totale Mensch" (the total person) and then "Kipper Paul Bauch" (dumper Paul Bauch), emphasized the individual's central importance.

HINZE UND KUNZE

In his second major drama, *Hinze und Kunze*, Braun returns to some of the same issues he examined in *Die Kipper*. Like his first play, *Hinze und Kunze* went through a number of revisions and rewritings before it appeared in its final form in 1973. (An early version of the play with the title *Hans Faust* had premiered in Leipzig in 1968 but was withdrawn from production shortly after its premiere.) One significant result of the long revision process is reflected in the changing of the play's title, which in the 1973 version gives equal billing to the play's two central figures. The play follows the career and development of the construction worker Hinze, the Hans Faust of the earlier version. A figure in many ways similar to Paul Bauch, he is impatient and discouraged by the slow progress of socialism. Although he no longer goes by the name Faust, Hinze's impatient dissatisfaction with the status quo clearly links him to Johann Wolfgang von Goethe's hero, and the text is full of allusions to Goethe's masterpiece. The most obvious point of connection to the Faust theme is made in the pact between Hinze and the local party secretary Kunze. Like Mephistopheles in Goethe's play, Kunze will urge Hinze on to new experience; rather than diverting him in the manner of his predecessor, however, his Kunze will ultimately keep Hinze on track. Here, each partner is dependent on the other if their common cause is to succeed. Therefore, they agree to remain together as long as either is dissatisfied.

In the relationship between Faust and Mephistopheles, Braun has discovered a useful model with which to explore what he has termed "the most disturbing contradiction" in the socialist revolution: the contradiction between the society's leaders and those whom they seek to lead, or, stated somewhat differently, the continuing division between the subjective needs of the individual and the collective interest of the society as represented by the party. Here, as throughout his work, Braun calls attention to the disparity that exists between the goals and accomplishments so effortlessly announced in his country's newspapers and by its leaders, and the actual costs that the realization of these goals exacts in the lives of individuals. Kunze must use his best persuasive skills to win the disillusioned and skeptical Hinze for the cause; once having won him, he must push and cajole Hinze to a full commitment of himself in the slow and costly process of building the new society. As the result of their pact, Hinze develops gradually from a worker who must be manipulated by Kunze's clever arguments into carrying out the work of the new soci-

ety into one who is capable and willing to change, that is, who is capable of assuming an equal role in shaping the future of his country.

Hinze's acceptance of Kunze's challenge is not, however, without problems for his personal life. In order to pursue the work at hand and later to qualify himself through additional schooling for a leadership position, he must leave his wife, Marlies. Rather than passively accepting her abandonment, however, Marlies heeds Kunze's advice to go to work. By accepting Kunze's challenge, she, like Hinze, can make a greater contribution at the industrial plant where they later both work. To Hinze, who barely recognizes her when they meet again, she is a changed person. She is, as Kunze comments ironically, "her own man"; that is, she is no longer dependent on her husband. Although Hinze has acquired the needed education for the leadership role he now assumes at the plant, he remains the individualistic self-helper he has always been, a fact that will lead to his eventual failure as a leader. Now reunited with Hinze, Marlies provides a striking and important contrast to her husband. When Hinze's visionary plans for the future of the factory are frustrated by a decision of the party's central planners, he rebels and forsakes his agreement with Kunze. Marlies is torn between the two men who have thus far been her life, between Hinze, whose child she now carries and who wants her to leave with him, and Kunze, who urges her to stay and continue the important work she has just begun.

Marlies remains to complete the work originally undertaken with Hinze. She succeeds without him and in spite of his desertion; as Kunze later comments, however, she has progressed so far (in her socialist awareness) that she goes too far. Faced with the choice between her unborn child and following through with the work that her efforts have made possible, she chooses the latter and aborts the fetus. Through no fault of her own, she loses both husband and child because she wished to complete the tasks for which she is so desperately needed. In the broken relationship between Hinze and Marlies and in the loss of their unborn child, Braun is able to suggest the considerable human costs associated with the building of the new society. Beyond their personal tragedy, the fact that Marlies believes that she must make such a choice at all is itself a comment on the transitional and imperfect nature of the society in which such choices are, in any sense, necessary. Still, the play ends with a measure of hope. Shaken by the events that have taken place in his absence, Hinze is drawn back to the factory and to the cause it represents. As the play ends, he enters anew into his pact with Kunze and resolves to start again from the beginning.

SCHMITTEN

In the plays *Schmitten* and *Tinka*, Braun continues to examine issues related to women and to their role in the building of socialism. In the two title figures, Braun dramatizes opposite responses of women to the challenges that the new society presents. In *Schmitten*, he constructs his drama around the difficulties of workers who under all previous social systems have been the "dumb ones," those workers who have traditionally had no say in the work that they perform. Jutta Schmitten, a model worker whose example has always served to encourage others, is asked by the party to seek a higher level of qualification and responsibility by returning to school. After persuading others to do so, she refuses herself for the simple reason that she lacks confidence in her ability to learn something new. Although her coworkers attempt to shame her into compliance, the factory's chief engineer, Kolb, who is also her lover, is in the position to "spare" her. His attempt to treat her humanely, to spare her possible future embarrassment, is, however, a throwback to the thinking of the old, pre-socialist society, in which such gestures based on gender were often also a form of and an excuse for the subjugation of women. Her lover's patronizing treatment of her evokes a violent response in Schmitten and her female coworkers, who, in a mad outbreak, castrate the hapless Kolb. Ironically, it is through this act of madness that Schmitten is able to break out of the restrictive role that has limited her development.

TINKA

In *Tinka*, Braun presents the opposite case, the worker who has accepted the challenge to further her training. Tinka has just returned from three years of technical studies when the factory is informed that the planned automation for which she was trained will not take place. Tinka protests and is bitter over the passivity of her coworkers, who seem content to accept whatever decisions are handed down from above. She is especially bitter over the apparent lack of resistance by her fiancé, Brenner, who is the plant's technical director. Brenner and the local party secretary Ludwig have, in fact, begun working behind the scenes in the belief that a cautious, tactical approach will eventually restore some portion of the original automation plans. In the manner of her predecessors Paul Bauch and Hinze, Tinka is unwilling to accept less than was originally promised, and her insistent protests lead finally to her dismissal from the factory. She refuses to give in, however, and relentlessly pursues Brenner, from whom she demands complete honesty, something that his tactical maneuverings prevent him from giving. In the play's climactic final scene, the drunken Brenner kills Tinka, who has become for him a constant reminder of his own dishonesty and inadequacy.

Tinka is in part written against tactics of the kind that Brenner and Ludwig employ. Brenner's tactical maneuvering, while well-intentioned, is, in its indirectness and conciliatory avoidance of conflict, dishonest. It alienates Brenner from himself (his true beliefs) and from those around him, and it ultimately leads to violence and tragedy.

HISTORICAL THEMES

In the mid-1970's, Braun's drama entered a new, somewhat more philosophical stage. While the issues that concern him remained, in this second period, essentially the same as they were in his early work, the plays written after 1975 were no longer so narrowly focused on the specific situation and problems of East Germany. Instead, Braun turned increasingly to history and to literary sources for the material for his plays.

Revolution remains Braun's central theme in the plays of this second period, a fact that is immediately clear in his choice of material. Three of the plays, *Guevara: Oder, Der Sonnenstaat* (Guevara: or, the sun state), *The Great Peace*, and *Dmitri*, have as their central focus revolutions that fail. In spite of the fact that all three plays are based on historical events,

Braun does not intend them merely to be interesting case studies. Rather, they are parables in the Brechtian sense, which are meant to create a dialectical tension between the past and the present such that the events in the past provoke a response in the present. Each revolution portrayed is relevant to the modern audience to the extent that the past example can suggest what remains to be done.

GUEVARA

In *Guevara*, for example, Braun exposes the naive revolutionary romanticism of the title figure, who fails to recognize the real situation of the peasants whom the revolution seeks to liberate. Without their involvement, there can be no revolution, only the replacement of one set of rulers by another. Braun's reversal of the normal chronological sequence of events allows for an especially effective analysis of Guevara's failure. The play begins with Guevara's death and leads the audience back, step-by-step, to the optimistic beginnings of the ill-fated guerrilla campaign, a technique that encourages an analytical examination of the play's action.

THE GREAT PEACE

Of the plays written after 1975, *The Great Peace* stands apart as Braun's most fully realized dramatic parable. Set in ancient China, the play dramatizes the course of a "successful" peasant uprising. Having disposed of the aristocracy that tyrannized them, the peasants proclaim the "Great Peace," which, according to ancient texts, is to be more than the mere absence of war; it is a state of total equality in which there are no class differences and therefore no need for either violence or rules. The land descends quickly into chaos, however, as the absence of rules and leaders brings the normal functioning of society to an abrupt halt. At this point, the clever poet Tschu Jün takes the lead. He persuades the peasant Gau Dsu to become Emperor and then proceeds to reestablish many of the rules and distinctions that previously existed. In effect, he "saves" the revolution by subverting it. While the new reign of Gau Dsu may initially represent an improvement over that of his predecessor, the advances of the revolution remain modest. Only at the end of the play, when his reign is beset by new enemies, one of whom is the

very peasant class from which he rose, does Gau Dsu realize that his rule has in fact reestablished the structures of oppression that his revolution sought to overthrow.

In the end, it is the poet-philosopher Wang who provides the key to understanding Braun's parable. Wang is Braun's spokesperson for the utopian ideals of the revolution and is, accordingly, persecuted by both regimes in the play. His experience leads him to conclude that a revolution can preserve its ideals only if it is successful in truly changing society "from the ground up." In Braun's view, the "ground" that forms the basis for the society and its successful functioning is work; it is here, in the nature of work, that Braun sees the reason that change is so difficult to achieve. As long as there remains a distinction between headwork and handwork, between those who plan and organize the work with their heads and those who carry out the work with their hands, the structures of class oppression will continue to exist.

THE ROLE OF THEATER

While recognizing the revolution's failure, it is not Braun's intention here or in his other plays to recant his utopian view of the future. If the peasants' uprising in China failed, it was not because of the actions or omissions of Gau Dsu; it was rather because the society was not at a point in its development that would support so drastic a change "from the ground up." Similarly, in plays such as *Simplex Deutsch* (simplex German), Braun suggests that a process of human development and change must accompany any external transformation of society. The ten outwardly unrelated scenes in this play portray examples of human immaturity that continue to frustrate the process of becoming a full and autonomous human being.

Braun does not provide ready solutions to the contradictions he perceives in society. Rather, he attempts only to show his audience how both objective and subjective resistance to the achievement of revolutionary goals continues to hinder true progress toward a better society. As was the case in early dramas that examined the problems and failures of socialism in his own country, the later plays, for all their apparent pessimism, seem to suggest that what was not possible at an earlier stage in human and social development may indeed be possible in the future. As Braun notes in one of his theater essays, it is not the theater's role in his time to offer solutions to society's problems, but rather to show that solutions to its problems are possible. In the true Brechtian tradition, it is left to the audience to act on what it has witnessed on the stage and to choose for itself an alternative that will avoid the failures of the past.

IPHIGENIE IN FREIHEIT AND BÖHMEN AM MEER

After German reunification in 1990, Braun wrote two plays dealing with the new situation at the end of the Cold War, *Iphigenie in Freiheit* and *Böhmen am Meer*, both performed in 1992. They are not conventional plays with a realistic plot, but philosophical monologues deploring that nothing has changed for the better after the collapse of the Soviet Union and East Germany. In *Iphigenie in Freiheit*, Braun rewrote Johann Wolfgang von Goethe's play, releasing the protagonist, after her long stay in the Soviet Union, into the Western capitalist world with window shopping and supermarkets. Gorbachev is the new King Thoas who lets Iphigenia go, while Orestes and Pylades are two gangsters who pay for her release. The title of *Böhmen am Meer* is derived from the stage directions of William Shakespeare's comedy *The Winter's Tale* (pr. c. 1610-1611) and has the connotation of utopia. A Russian and an American who are aware of their allegorical function meet at the invitation of a Czech, but instead of peace and understanding, they continue their confrontation and blame each other for the polluted state of the world. The plot ends with a great flood. There is no room for utopia in the modern world. Both plays are short and require extensive interpretation to provide stage action for presentation in the theater.

OTHER MAJOR WORKS

LONG FICTION: *Das ungezwungene Leben Kasts*, 1972, 1979; *Unvollendete Geschichte*, 1975 (novella; *Unfinished Story*, 1979; expanded as *Die Unvollendete Geschichte und ihr Ende*, 1997); *Hinze-Kunze-Roman*, 1985.

SHORT FICTION: *Berichte von Hinze und Kunze*, 1983; *Der Wendehals: Eine Unterhaltung*, 1995; *Das Nichtgelebte Leben: Eine Erzählung*, 1995; *Die vier Werkzeugmacher: Erzählung*, 1996; *Das Wirklichgewolte*, 2000.

POETRY: *Provokation für mich*, 1965; *Vorläufiges*, 1966; *Wir und nicht sie*, 1970; *Gegen die symmetrische Welt*, 1974; *Poesiealbum 115*, 1977; *Der Stoff zum Leben*, 1977; *Training des aufrechten Gangs*, 1978; *Archaische Landschaft mit Losungen*, 1983; *Langsamer knirschender Morgen: Gedichte*, 1987; *Annatomie*, 1989; *Der Stoff zum Leben 1-3*, 1990; *Lustgarten Preussen: Ausgewählte Gedichte*, 1996; *Tumulus*, 1999.

NONFICTION: *Es genügt nicht die einfache Wahrheit*, 1975.

MISCELLANEOUS: *Texte in zeitlicher Folge*, 1989-1993 (10 volumes).

BIBLIOGRAPHY

Costabile, Carol Anne Theresa. *Intertextual Exile: Volker Braun's Dramatic Re-vision of GDR Society*. New York: Olms, 1997. Assessment of Volker Braun's works and his retrospective of the German Democratic Republic (GDR) after German reunification in 1990.

Huettich, H. G. *Theater in a Planned Society: Contemporary Drama in the German Democratic Republic in Its Historical, Political, and Cultural Context*. Chapel Hill: University of North Carolina Press, 1978. Study of the role of theater and drama in the GDR through the 1970's, including the works by Braun.

Jucker, Rolf, ed. *Volker Braun*. Cardiff: University of Wales Press, 1995. Criticism and analysis of Braun's works. Bibliography and index.

Rosellini, Jay. *Volker Braun*. Munich: Kritik, 1983. Introduction to Braun's life and work through the early 1980's. In German.

Vanovitch, Katherine. "Volker Braun." In *Female Roles in East German Drama, 1949-1977: A Selective History of Drama in the G.D.R.* Frankfurt am Main: Lang, 1982. Survey article on the female roles in Braun's plays.

James R. Reece,
updated by Ehrhard Bahr

BERTOLT BRECHT

Born: Augsburg, Germany; February 10, 1898
Died: East Berlin, East Germany; August 14,
1956

PRINCIPAL DRAMA

Baal, wr. 1918, pb. 1922, pr. 1923 (English
translation, 1963)

Trommeln in der Nacht, wr. 1919-1920, pr., pb.
1922 (*Drums in the Night*, 1961)

Die Hochzeit, wr. 1919, pr. 1926, pb. 1953 as *Die
Keinbürgerhochzeit* (*The Wedding*, 1970)

Im Dickicht der Städte, pr. 1923, pb. 1927 (*In the
Jungle of Cities*, 1961)

Leben Eduards des Zweiten von England, pr., pb.
1924 (with Lion Feuchtwanger; based on
Christopher Marlowe's play *Edward II*;
Edward II, 1966)

Mann ist Mann, pr. 1926, pb. 1927 (*A Man's a Man*,
1961)

Die Dreigroschenoper, pr. 1928, pb. 1929 (libretto;
based on John Gay's play *The Beggar's Opera*;
The Threepenny Opera, 1949)

Aufstieg und Fall der Stadt Mahagonny, pb. 1929,
pr. 1930 (libretto; *Rise and Fall of the City of
Mahagonny*, 1957)

Das Badener Lehrstück vom Einverständnis, pr. 1929,
pb. 1930 (*The Didactic Play of Baden: On
Consent*, 1960)

Happy End, pr. 1929, pb. 1958 (libretto; lyrics with
Elisabeth Hauptmann; English translation,
1972)

Der Ozeanflug, pr., pb. 1929 (radio play; *The Flight
of the Lindberghs*, 1930)

Die Ausnahme und die Regel, wr. 1930, pb. 1937,
pr. 1938 (*The Exception and the Rule*, 1954)

Der Jasager, pr. 1930, pb. 1931 (based on the
Japanese Nō play *Taniko*; *He Who Said Yes*, 1946)

Die Massnahme, pr. 1930, pb. 1931 (libretto; *The
Measures Taken*, 1960)

Die heilige Johanna der Schlachthöfe, pb. 1931, pr.
1932 (radio play), pr. 1959 (staged; *St. Joan of
the Stockyards*, 1956)

Der Neinsager, pb. 1931 (*He Who Said No*, 1946)

Die Mutter, pr., pb. 1932 (based on Maxim Gorky's
novel *Mat*; *The Mother*, 1965)

Die Sieben Todsünden der Kleinbürger, pr. 1933,
pb. 1959 (cantata; *The Seven Deadly Sins*, 1961)

Die Horatier und die Kuriatier, wr. 1934, pb. 1938,
pr. 1958 (*The Horatians and the Curatians*, 1947)

Die Rundköpfe und die Spitzköpfe, pr. 1935, pb.
1936 (based on William Shakespeare's play
Measure for Measure; *The Roundheads and the
Peakheads*, 1937)

Die Gewehre der Frau Carrar, pr., pb. 1937 (*Señora
Carrar's Rifles*, 1938)

Furcht und Elend des dritten Reiches, pr. in French
1938, pr. in English 1945, pb. in German 1945
(*The Private Life of the Master Race*, 1944)

Leben des Galilei, first version wr. 1938-1939, pr.
1943; second version wr. 1945-1947, third
version pb. 1955 (*The Life of Galileo*, 1947,
also known as *Galileo*)

Der gute Mensch von Sezuan, wr. 1938-1940, pr.
1943, pb. 1953 (*The Good Woman of Setzuan*,
1948)

Das Verhör des Lukullus, pr. 1940 (radio play),
pb. 1940, pr. 1951 (staged; libretto; *The Trial of
Lucullus*, 1943)

Herr Puntila und sein Knecht, Matti, wr. 1940, pr.
1948, pb. 1951 (*Mr. Puntila and His Hired Man,
Matti*, 1976)

Mutter Courage und ihre Kinder, pr. 1941, pb.
1949 (based on Hans Jakob Christoffel von
Grimmelshausen's *Der abenteuerliche
Simplicissimus*; *Mother Courage and Her
Children*, 1941)

Der aufhaltsame Aufstieg des Arturo Ui, wr. 1941,
pb. 1957, pr. 1958 (*The Resistible Rise of Arturo
Ui*, 1972)

Die Gesichte der Simone Machard, wr. 1941-1943,
pb. 1956, pr. 1957 (with Feuchtwanger; *The
Visions of Simone Machard*, 1961)

Schweyk im zweiten Weltkrieg, wr. 1941-1943, pr. in
Polish 1957, pb. 1957, pr. in German 1958 (based

on Jaroslav Hašek's novel *Osudy dobrého vojáka Švejka ve světove války*; *Schweyk in the Second World War*, 1975)

Der kaukasische Kreidekreis, wr. 1944-1945, pr. in English 1948, pb. 1949, pr. in German 1958 (based on Li Xingdao's play *The Circle of Chalk*; *The Caucasian Chalk Circle*, 1948)

Die Antigone des Sophokles, pr., pb. 1948 (*Sophocles' Antigone*, 1990)

Die Tage der Commune, wr. 1948-1949, pr. 1956, pb. 1957 (based on Nordahl Grieg's *Nederlaget*; *The Days of the Commune*, 1971)

Der Hofmeister, pr. 1950, pb. 1951 (adaptation of Jacob Lenz's *Der Hofmeister*; *The Tutor*, 1972)

Turandot: Oder, Der Kongress der Weisswäscher, wr. 1950-1954, pr. 1970

Der Prozess der Jeanne d'Arc zu Rouen, 1431, pr. 1952, pb. 1959 (based on Anna Seghers's radio play; *The Trial of Jeanne d'Arc at Rouen, 1431*, 1972)

Bertolt Brecht (Hulton Archive by Getty Images)

Coriolan, wr. 1952-1953, pb. 1959 (adaptation of William Shakespeare's play *Coriolanus*; *Coriolanus*, 1972)

Don Juan, pr. 1953, pb. 1959 (based on Molière's play; English translation, 1972)

Pauken und Trompeten, pb. 1956 (adaptation of George Farquhar's *The Recruiting Officer*; *Trumpets and Drums*, 1972)

OTHER LITERARY FORMS

Bertolt Brecht experimented with several literary forms, and his output in all genres was considerable. He wrote novels, short fiction, nonfiction, and screenplays. His novel *Der Dreigroschenroman* (1934; *The Threepenny Novel*) was translated in 1937; his short fiction is collected in *Geschichten von Herrn Keuner* (1930, 1958; *Stories of Mr. Keuner*, 2001); and many of his essays appeared in his three-volume *Arbeitsjournal, 1938-1955* (1973; *Bertolt Brecht Journals*, 1993). *Kuhle Wampe* (1932; English translation, 1933) is an example of his fine work in film. An exhibit of Brecht's works, on display in his final residence, includes more than thirty dramatic works, about thirteen hundred poems and songs, three novels, numerous screenplays, and more than 150 works of nonfiction.

ACHIEVEMENTS

Bertolt Brecht's influence on the contemporary theater—especially on the development of political drama—extends worldwide. In Germany, Austria, and Switzerland, his plays are the most frequently performed after William Shakespeare's. Translated into many languages, they are included in the repertoire of theater companies throughout both Western and Eastern Europe and the United States. Among the prizes that Brecht received for his works are the Kleist Prize in 1922, the East German National Prize in 1951, and the International Stalin Peace Prize in 1954. Brecht formed the Berliner Ensemble in 1949 and made it into one of the best acting companies in Europe. In 1954, Brecht's production of *Mother Courage and Her Children* was awarded first prize at the International Theater Festival in Paris. In the following year, his production of *The Caucasian Chalk Circle* received second prize at the same festival.

These two productions contributed to Brecht's international reputation as a director as well as a playwright.

BIOGRAPHY

Bertolt Brecht was born in Augsburg in Southern Germany on February 10, 1898. Between 1908 and 1917, Brecht attended Realgymnasium (high school) in his hometown, but he was almost expelled in 1916 for writing a pacifist essay (pacifism is a constant theme in his works). After leaving high school in 1917, he enrolled at the University of Munich to study medicine. In 1918, he was called for military service and worked as an orderly in the venereal disease ward of the Augsburg military hospital. After the war, he lived in Munich as a freelance writer. In 1922, he married Marianne Zoff but was later divorced from her in 1927. Brecht established himself in Berlin at the Deutsches Theater in 1924, where he worked under Max Reinhardt until 1926. That year marked the turning point in Brecht's career: He began studying Marxism and economics, and his subsequent conversion to Marxism decisively shaped his life and works. Brecht's contacts with Erwin Piscator's political theater at this time also had an impact on his dramatic theory.

As the Nazis gained power, Brecht found it increasingly difficult to have his works performed. The Nazis had long harbored resentment against Brecht. At the time of the Munich Putsch, Brecht was the fifth person on their list of people to be arrested because of his poem "Legende vom toten Soldaten" ("Legend of the Dead Soldier"), which tells how the kaiser has a dead soldier disinterred, declared fit, and sent off to the front again. In January, 1933, a performance of *The Measures Taken* in Erfurt was broken up by the police. On February 28, 1933, the day after the Reichstag fire, Brecht and his family (in 1929, he had married the actress Helene Weigel) fled from Germany. They went to Prague, Vienna, Lugano, and Paris, and finally settled in Denmark. On May 10, 1933, Brecht's works were burned in Germany. During his exile, Brecht campaigned energetically against Fascism, contributed to anti-Fascist exile journals, wrote anti-Fascist works, and maintained close contacts with other exiles. In 1935, the Nazis revoked Brecht's German citizenship. In 1939, when Denmark became unsafe, Brecht and his family moved to Sweden. From there, they went to Finland, and in 1941, they fled to California by way of Moscow and Vladivostok, settling in Santa Monica, where they remained for six years. Brecht worked occasionally for the film industry, but the only project that was actually carried out was his script for *Hangmen Also Die* (1943), which he wrote in 1942. The film, which was directed by Fritz Lang, concerns the assassination of the notorious Nazi Reinhard Heydrich by the Resistance in Czechoslovakia. On October 30, 1947, Brecht was called before the House Committee on Un-American Activities. He managed to outsmart the committee, which exonerated him of pro-communist activities. The next day, Brecht left for Zurich.

In 1948, Brecht and his wife returned to East Berlin, where Brecht was put in charge of the Deutsches Theater. In the following year, he and his wife (considered one of the most effective interpreters of his work) formed the Berliner Ensemble with the help of generous subsidies from the state. Together they received Austrian citizenship in 1950. In 1954, the Berliner Ensemble moved to the Theater am Schiffbauerdamm. Brecht's last years in Berlin were devoted mostly to directing the Berliner Ensemble. He adapted plays for the ensemble and produced model stagings of his plays. Although Brecht had an uneasy relationship with the East German government, which often criticized his plays for what it perceived to be formalism and pacifism, he did not take a public stand against the regime. In fact, during the worker uprising in June, 1953, Brecht refused to support the workers and sent a letter to Walter Ulbricht expressing his loyalty, an action that the playwright Günter Grass later criticized strongly in his play *Die Plebejer proben den Aufstand* (pr., pb. 1966; *The Plebeians Rehearse the Uprising*, 1966). Brecht died in East Berlin of a coronary thrombosis on August 14, 1956.

ANALYSIS

Bertolt Brecht's early dramas are anarchic, nihilistic, and antibourgeois. In them, he glorifies antisocial outsiders such as adventurers, pirates, and prostitutes; the tone of these works is often cynical. In the years after his conversion to Marxism, Brecht wrote didactic plays, similar in many respects to late medieval morality plays, whose style is austere and functional. These plays were intended to be performed in schools and factories by nonprofessional actors. In his later plays, Brecht combined the vitality of his early period with his Marxist beliefs to create plays that are dramatically effective, socially committed, and peopled with realistic characters. To the end of his life, Brecht thought of the theater as both a place of entertainment and of learning. By making people aware of social abuses, he believed, literature can help make the world a better place; it can help bring the Marxist goal of a classless Utopia closer to realization.

EPIC THEATER

Brecht is well known for his theories on epic theater. Although this concept did not originate with Brecht, he developed it into a revolutionary form of drama. (Toward the end of his life, Brecht wanted to change the name of his theater from "epic" to "dialectical," to stress the central role of argument in his plays.) Brecht summarizes his theories of epic theater in his notes to *Rise and Fall of the City of Mahagonny*; he later recapitulated and revised his theories in *Kleines Organon für das Theater* (1948; *A Little Organum for the Theater*, 1951) and in other theoretical writings. In his notes to *Rise and Fall of the City of Mahagonny*, Brecht lists the differences he perceives between his epic theater and the Aristotelian (or dramatic) theater. Unlike dramatic theater, in which the tightly constructed plot creates suspense, epic theater uses loosely connected scenes that are set off against one another. The loose narrative structure helps to break the suspense and makes the audience focus on the course of the play, not on how the play will be resolved at the end. Brecht is extremely critical of dramatic theater: According to him, it is static; it shows universally human, that is, fixed and unchangeable, traits. Epic theater depicts the world as it changes and shows how it can be changed. It shows that human behavior can be altered. Therefore, epic theater should make people aware of social abuses and provoke them to change social evils.

Instead of activating its spectators, dramatic theater, in Brecht's view, numbs the audience by making it identify with the characters and become involved in the action. When spectators attend such plays, he remarks caustically, they hang up their brains with their coats. Brecht satirically describes the typical audience at a dramatic play, sunk into a peculiarly drugged state, wholly passive. Brecht comments that the worst gangster film shows more respect for its audience as thinking beings than does the conventional dramatic play. If people are to learn from the theater, they should be alert, rational, and socially concerned. Instead of identifying with the characters, they should remain critically aloof—certainly a necessary attitude if they are to come to grips with the ideas that Brecht presents. In his notes to *The Threepenny Opera*, Brecht expresses his wish to create a theater full of experts like those in sporting arenas. To prevent empathy, he says, theaters should allow people to smoke: He suggests that people who are puffing on cigars (Brecht himself was an inveterate cigar smoker) would be less easily carried away by events onstage.

Nevertheless, while epic theater stresses reason, it does not dispense with all emotions. In a discussion with playwright Friedrich Wolf in 1949, Brecht noted that his theater actually tries to reinforce certain emotions such as a sense of justice, the urge for freedom, and righteous anger. Although Brecht believed that the theater should teach, he stressed that it should be entertaining as well. This emphasis is apparent in his early theoretical writings such as in "Mehr guten Sport" (1926; "Emphasis on Sport"), but it becomes even more pronounced in later writings such as *A Little Organum for the Theater*, in which he notes that if the theater were turned into a purveyor of morality, it would run the risk of being debased. The function of epic theater is not to moralize but to observe and to entertain the "children of the scientific age."

Brecht uses many so-called alienation devices to prevent the audience from becoming involved in the action. *Verfremdung* (alienation) is a term that Brecht probably borrowed from Viktor Shklovsky, the leader of the Russian formalists. Alienation makes familiar things strange. In *A Little Organum for the Theater*,

Brecht describes why alienation is important: Alienation effects are designed to free socially conditioned phenomena from the stamp of familiarity that protects them from being grasped. Brecht argues that when conditions have not been changed for a long time, they begin to seem impossible to change. One must therefore present the status quo in a new light in order to provoke understanding and change. Brecht admired the Chinese theater, with its stylized acting, masks, and anti-illusionist staging; his theater is similarly anti-illusionist. Narrators, film projections, and titles comment on the action and break the suspense by indicating what is going to occur in each scene. Brecht stresses that the titles must include the social point of a particular scene. The songs that Brecht includes in his plays are not an integral part of the action, as in an opera; rather, they comment on the action. When a character is about to sing, he steps forward to the front of the stage and the lighting changes. The songs thus interrupt the course of the action and change the mood of the play. The music itself serves as an alienation device, featuring jazz rhythms and ballad forms that are not congruent with the stage action. In epic theater, the sources of lighting and scene changes are visible to the audience, and scenes are often played simultaneously to heighten the audience's awareness that it is watching a play.

The use of historical material also plays an important part in Brecht's epic theater. Brecht believed that the distancing effect of history (or geography) can make the audience more aware of the modern world: It can show that there are no universal values, that life is impermanent, that the world can be changed. Brecht notes that historical events are unique and transitory. The conduct of people in them is not fixed and universal; rather, it includes elements that have been or may be overtaken by the course of history, and it is subject to criticism from the viewpoint of the period immediately following. As a Marxist, Brecht believed in the ultimate goal of a classless Utopia, however far in the future it may be, and this belief made him optimistic about humankind's potential and about the possibility of changing society.

Brecht also focused attention on the most effective way of acting in epic theater. He rejected Konstantin Stanislavsky's method of having the actor identify with the character that he is portraying. Brecht likens the actor to a witness at an accident: The witness explains to passersby what has happened; he does not try to cast a spell but demonstrates; he alternates imitation and commentary and acts so that the bystanders can form an opinion about the accident. The actor should be a teacher; he should make the audience understand. Brecht writes that for a scene to qualify as epic, it must have socially practical significance. Through gestic acting, social attitudes can be conveyed.

Brecht's theater is realistic, although not in conventional terms. Realism, Brecht writes, lays bare society's causal network. The realistic writer shows that the dominant viewpoint is the viewpoint of the dominators; he writes from the standpoint of the class that has prepared the broadest solutions for the most pressing problems afflicting human society—that is, from the standpoint of the proletariat. Realism, as Brecht understands it, is a Marxist critique of society. His anti-illusionist theater depicts the social problems of his age. Brecht argues that literature should give the working masses a truthful representation of life.

Indeed, the notion that art should appeal to wide audiences, rather than solely to an intellectual elite, is central to Brecht's theater. For Brecht, to be popular means to be intelligible to the masses, which can be accomplished by taking over their forms of expression and enriching them. For this reason, Brecht uses folk sayings, parables, street ballads, and other folk forms in his plays. Brecht's plays also abound in biblical allusions—Martin Luther's German translation of the Bible, he confesses, was the single most important influence on his work; he admired Luther's vigorous prose.

Many of Brecht's plays were either stimulated by existing plays or parody them. Through his parodies of classical works, Brecht hoped to make his audience question middle-class values. Brecht did not believe that classical works were sacrosanct; he wanted to reshape classical works to make them relevant to present-day society, taking over verbatim what he thought was useful and then rewriting the remainder of the play. An example of such an adaptation is Shakespeare's *Coriolanus* (pr. c. 1607-1608), which Brecht changed from a personal tragedy to a history play that reflected the viewpoint of the common man—a change of focus that he accomplished mostly by giving the plebeians a larger role.

Brecht's dramatic theories were not intended to be dogmatic. They evolved out of his practical work in the theater, and he constantly tested them, discarding them if they were not workable. This method was typical of Brecht's writing: He was always prepared to change, to adapt, to incorporate suggestions from others—even from stagehands—into his plays. The actual staging of his plays always made Brecht aware of changes that were needed to make his works dramatically effective.

LIFE OF GALILEO

Brecht's use of historical materials to illuminate contemporary problems is exemplified in one of his finest plays, *Life of Galileo*. When Brecht first became interested in Galileo, he was concerned about the fate of friends and comrades who remained in Nazi Germany and who nevertheless managed somehow to continue working. Brecht wrote three versions of the play: The first was written in 1938-1939; the second, which was an English version for the actor Charles Laughton, was written in 1945-1947; and the third was written in 1955-1956. The major difference is between the first and second versions, during which time Brecht's attitude toward Galileo changed. As in his other plays, Brecht uses many alienation devices to ensure that the audience does not identify with Galileo. He uses titles at the beginning of each scene to comment on the action. The plot is not tightly constructed. Instead, Brecht shows typical scenes in Galileo's life, beginning when Galileo is middle-aged and ending when he is an old man. Brecht's treatment of this celebrated historical figure (he sees Galileo as a pioneer of the scientific age) is intended to make his spectators see the modern world, their own world, from a critical perspective.

Like many of Brecht's characters, Galileo is a contradictory figure: He is a great scientist with a passion for the truth as well as a man with human frailties. Galileo cherishes the consolations of the flesh. He loves eating, drinking, and living a comfortable life, and he defends these habits by saying that he cannot help it if he gets his best ideas over a good meal and a bottle of wine. The pope later says that Galileo cannot refuse an old wine or a new thought. In *A Little Organum for the Theater*, Brecht remarks that Galileo thinks out of self-indulgence.

Galileo's love of good living contributes to his subsequent problems. At the beginning of the play, he is living in Venice, which pays its scientists badly but leaves them free to conduct research. To earn money, Galileo must take rich private pupils, most of whom are not intelligent. Ludovico, for example, only wants to learn about science because his mother thinks that such knowledge is necessary for conversation. Teaching such students takes away valuable time from Galileo's research. Because Galileo's request for money for his work has been refused (the Venice republic values only practical inventions), he tries to fool the government. Ludovico tells Galileo about a new invention, a telescope, that he has seen in Holland, and Galileo then pretends that the device is his own invention. Members of the government of Venice are immediately interested in the telescope because of its military implications. Galileo soon forgets about the financial rewards for his "invention" because he suddenly grasps the value it will have for his own research in astronomy. Galileo decides to move to Florence, where scientists are better paid, but where, because of the Inquisition, he will not have the freedom to publish his findings.

Galileo is excited about the dawn of a new age that, he believes, his research will make possible. For centuries, people had believed that the sun revolved around the earth; now Galileo can tell them the truth. His new cosmology will, however, have far-reaching social effects: It will destroy the old hierarchy of power. The old cosmology, as interpreted by the Church (which, in the play, represents authority in general), taught that people had to be satisfied with their destined places in society. The stars can no longer be used to justify some people exploiting others. Galileo predicts that astronomy will become the gossip of the marketplaces, and the sons of fishwives will pack the schools. To make his findings accessible to the common people, Galileo writes in the vernacular, not in the Latin of the elite. Because the Church recognized the revolutionary nature of Galileo's work, it banned his research.

In the first version of the play, Galileo is seen more positively than in the later versions. After he has recanted, he still manages to continue working. He outsmarts his inquisitors by pretending to be blind and works secretly on his major work, the *Discorsi*, which his disciple Andrea later smuggles out of the country under his coat: For Brecht, cunning is necessary for disseminating the truth in repressive societies. Through his cunning, Galileo has defended the truth and caused light to dawn in an era of superstition.

As Brecht was working on the second version of the play, the atom bomb was dropped on Hiroshima, and this event radically changed Brecht's attitude toward Galileo. He no longer viewed Galileo's recantation as a cunning plan to defend the truth but as a betrayal, as a shameful capitulation to reactionary forces. In his notes to the second version, Brecht describes Galileo as practicing his science secretly, like a vice, without any obligation to society. Instead of ushering in a new age, science has become allied with the forces of oppression. According to Brecht, Galileo's crime was the original sin of modern science. Out of a new astronomy that had revolutionary implications, he made a sharply limited special science, a pure science, and he was not concerned about the practical applications of his findings. The atom bomb, Brecht notes, as a technical and social phenomenon, is the result of Galileo's social failings and his scientific accomplishment. In the second version of the play, when Andrea praises Galileo for deceiving those who perpetrated the Inquisition, Galileo denounces himself. He insists that he recanted only because he was afraid of physical pain (he was threatened with torture). Now, he says, he sees that he has betrayed his profession. He argues that in his day astronomy emerged into the marketplaces. If someone had stood and fought then, that stand could have had wide repercussions. Instead, Galileo surrendered his knowledge to the authorities—to use, or rather misuse, as they saw fit.

The revolutionary impact of Galileo's teachings is particularly evident in the carnival scene. In this scene, the ballad singer relates how Galileo's work will destroy the social hierarchy and free people. The last scene of the play, however, contrasts with the hope and excitement of the carnival scene and shows the consequences of Galileo's cowardice. Andrea is smuggling the *Discorsi* across the border. Some children are pointing to a house where they see a grotesque shadow that looks like a witch stirring something in a cauldron. They sing "Old Marina is a witch." Andrea lifts up a boy so that he can look through the window and see that the "witch" is only an old woman cooking porridge. He tries to teach him, as Galileo had taught Andrea, to rely on observation, not superstition. Nevertheless, superstition proves to be stronger; the boy cries out that Marina is a witch, even after he has seen her with his own eyes. This scene shows that the dark ages of superstition, which Galileo's science could have changed, will be difficult to overthrow. Galileo's recantation has delayed the dawn of a new age.

MOTHER COURAGE AND HER CHILDREN

Mother Courage and Her Children also took its inspiration from contemporary events, seen from the perspective of history. Brecht finished this play in 1939 just before the outbreak of World War II. The play was loosely based on the seventeenth century novelist Hans Jakob Christoffel von Grimmelshausen's depiction of the Thirty Years' War, *Der abenteuerliche Simplicissimus* (1669; *The Adventurous Simplicissimus*, 1912). One of Grimmelshausen's characters is also called Courage, and Brecht takes from him Courage's name, her numerous husbands and lovers, and her business dealings. The play criticizes both war and business. Brecht meant to show that war is a continuation of business by other means and that it makes human virtues deadly; therefore, no sacrifice is too great to fight against war.

As her name indicates, the protagonist, Anna Fierling, is both mother and businesswoman. She is named Courage not because of an act of real courage but because she drove through the bombardment at Riga. She had to do this because she had fifty loaves of bread that she needed to sell quickly because they were becoming moldy. Mother Courage tries unsuccessfully to protect her three children, Eilif, Swiss Cheese, and Kattrin (each of whom has a different father), from the war, but her motherly instincts often conflict with her business instincts—her wagon, which is both a home and refuge for herself and her children, as well as her place of business, shows how inextricably her roles of businesswoman and mother are intertwined. Yet she does not always consider profit first. Toward the end of the play, when her fortunes are at a low point, she refuses the cook's offer to escape from the war to a small inn that he has inherited because he will not let her take her daughter Kattrin with her. In this case, Mother Courage acts against her own best interests.

One by one, Mother Courage loses her children. In the first scene, her oldest son, Eilif, is taken away by the recruiting officer, who tempts him with tales of the glory of war while Mother Courage's attention is diverted by the sergeant, who says that he wants to buy a buckle. When Swiss Cheese is arrested by the Catholic soldiers, who try to make him surrender the regimental cash box entrusted to him by the Protestants, Mother Courage bargains to free him. She is willing to pawn her wagon, hoping to find the cash box and redeem it. After she discovers that Swiss Cheese has thrown it into the river, she is faced with a dilemma: How can she and Kattrin survive without the wagon? She is actually prepared to sacrifice her wagon, but she haggles too long, and Swiss Cheese is shot. When Eilif is arrested, she is away on business and cannot help him. Kattrin is sent into town to fetch supplies for her mother and is attacked on the way back. When Kattrin is killed, Mother Courage is away at the market, taking advantage of those who are fleeing and selling their possessions cheaply. In each of these cases, she loses her children because she is involved in business activities.

Although Brecht intends the audience to be critical of Mother Courage, she is still, in many respects, a sympathetic figure, despite her negative qualities. She is cunning and tenacious and has an earthy sense of humor. Throughout the play, she debunks heroism. When Eilif is praised by his commander for his heroic deed of stealing cattle, she

boxes Eilif's ears: She tells him that he should have surrendered and not exposed himself to danger, as the peasants who owned the cattle were in the majority. Later, she argues that only poor commanders need to demand heroism of their men: Good commanders can manage without it. To survive in this world, she believes, one must be unobtrusive, not heroic. Mother Courage also sees clearly why the war is being fought. The commanders speak as though they are fighting for religion, but Mother Courage remarks that they are not so stupid; they are actually fighting only for profit.

Mother Courage's wagon symbolizes her waning fortunes: At the beginning of the play, the wagon looks prosperous and is pulled by Eilif and Swiss Cheese; at the end, it is dilapidated and pulled by Mother Courage alone. Brecht emphasizes that Mother Courage does not learn from her experiences. Only in the scene in which Kattrin is attacked does she curse the war. Usually, however, she is worried that the war could end when she has just bought supplies, which would bring about her financial ruin. After the Zurich premiere in 1941, Brecht changed parts of the play to make Mother Courage's disagreeable traits more emphatic, since the Zurich audience had seen her as a tragic figure who was simply trying to survive. In a conversation with the playwright Friedrich Wolf, Brecht defended his portrayal of Mother Courage. (He had been criticized for depicting her as unable to learn from her mistakes.) Brecht told Wolf that he was a realist, that he was not convinced that people would learn from the war he saw coming when he was writing the play. He hoped, however, that the audience could learn from watching Mother Courage. According to Brecht, Mother Courage is free to choose whether to take part in the war, yet the scope of the war, which seems to fill the whole world, suggests that she really has no viable alternative—she can either wait for the war to reach her, or she can try to earn her living from it. There seems to be no place where she could be safe to lead a peaceful life.

The deaths of her children show that virtue is dangerous. The heroic Eilif is executed for stealing cattle and killing, deeds for which he was praised in wartime. Ironically, he is executed when the war has broken out again and when his action would again have been considered heroic, but the soldiers who execute him are unaware that the war is on again. Swiss Cheese is executed for his honesty in trying to save the cash box. Kattrin is killed because she is humane. Even though Kattrin is dumb, according to Brecht, she should not be played as though she were an idiot. She is perfectly normal; it is the world that surrounds her that is abnormal. Kattrin desperately wants children but will never be able to marry because of the disfiguring scar that remains from her having been attacked. The war also made her dumb, since a soldier shoved something in her mouth when she was a child. Because of her motherliness, she is in constant danger. In the scene in which "the stone begins to speak," soldiers are preparing to attack a town where people are asleep and unaware of danger. To save the children in the town, Kattrin takes a drum and climbs up onto a roof where she beats the drum loudly to alert the town to the danger. She is shot, but she saves the town. Her positive action is contrasted with the futile actions of the peasants, whose only thought is to pray to God for help.

Brecht did not choose World War I for his setting—he thought that the war was still too recent for an audience to observe the events on the stage dispassionately and to learn from the play. The Thirty Years' War was the most destructive war in German history before World War I; in his notes to the play, Brecht writes that this was the first large-scale war that capitalism had brought to Europe. Brecht was not interested in the history of "important" people such as kings, princes, and generals (no historical character appears on the stage) but in the perspective of the common man, whom history usually ignores. Throughout the play, Brecht satirizes those who are in charge of conducting the war. The commander Tilly, who is given a hero's funeral, actually died, Mother Courage says, because he lost his way in the mist and went to the front by mistake. Brecht also shows that victory and defeat for the commanders does not always mean victory and defeat for the common people—for example, Tilly's victory at Magdeburg costs Mother Courage four shirts.

In addition to the historical setting, Brecht used several other alienation devices in the play. The titles before each scene break the suspense and are intended to encourage a critical attitude in the audience. As in *The Life of Galileo*, the scenes are loosely connected and the time span is long (twelve years). Brecht includes songs to comment on the action: The song that Mother Courage sings at the beginning and at the end of the play is an ironic commentary on this war of "religion," while her "Song of the Great Capitulation" describes life as full of broken hopes and dreams.

The mood of the play is basically pessimistic. Even after she has lost her family, Mother Courage still believes in the war: Neither she nor anyone else has learned anything by the play's end. Instead, the war continues, people continue to be killed, and some (though not Mother Courage) make profits.

THE CAUCASIAN CHALK CIRCLE

The Caucasian Chalk Circle, which was written in 1944-1945, was based on the story of Solomon in the Bible and on a thirteenth century Chinese drama by Li Xingdao, which was adapted as *Der Kreidekreis* by the playwright Klabund in 1925. As in his other plays, Brecht includes many alienation effects. The play consists of three stories: The first takes place in the twentieth century; the other two stories, those of Grusche and Azdak, take place in medieval Russian Georgia (Grusinia). Brecht also used a singer/narrator to comment on the play-within-a-play, and the actors wear masks.

The first scene takes place in Russian Georgia just after the defeat of Adolf Hitler. The owners of the land, a collective that raises goats, fled from Hitler's soldiers, while the neighboring collective stayed and fought. The members of this neighboring collective now want the land formerly used for goat-raising; they intend to grow fruit trees there and have designed an irrigation scheme for that purpose. The old owners, however, want the land returned to them. Together, the two collectives discuss the conflict peacefully and rationally and decide that the fruit growers should have the land. Goats can be raised anywhere, but only here is the topography of the land suitable for the irrigation plans. To celebrate this decision, the members of the fruit-growers' collective act the play of the chalk circle.

The first part of this play-within-a-play tells of the shrewd and good-hearted servant girl Grusche. In medieval Georgia, she works for the governor and his wife, who have an infant son Michel. At first, the mother seems to be overly solicitous about her child's welfare. She is worried when he coughs or is exposed to drafts, and she is always accompanied by two doctors. When the Revolution breaks out, however, she is so busy deciding which dresses she should take on her flight that she forgets to take her son. At first, Grusche is reluctant to take the baby—it is too dangerous to do so because the soldiers are seeking to kill him. As the singer says, however, she is overcome by the terrible temptation to goodness, and she flees with the child. Through her work and sacrifice for the child, Grusche gradually becomes more and more a mother to him. In her flight from the soldiers with him, she faces danger and hardship. She seeks refuge in her brother's house, where she claims that the child is hers and invents a husband who is fighting in the war. When the husband does not arrive to fetch her, her brother's wife, a "pious" person (always a term of criticism in Brecht's works), begins to become suspicious that the child is illegitimate; she fears that Grusche will become the object of gossip and shame the family. Grusche's brother arranges a marriage for her with a supposedly dying man, but once the "deathly ill" man hears that the war is over, he revives—he had pretended to be ill to avoid fighting. For the sake of the child, Grusche is now tied to a disagreeable husband. When Grusche's fiancé, Simon, returns from the war, Grusche again claims that the child is hers, preferring Simon to believe that she has been unfaithful to him than have the soldiers take away the child.

The Grusche story is interrupted at this point, and the Azdak story is begun. Azdak is a sort of Lord of Misrule, one of Brecht's cunning rogues. During a time of revolution, he has unwittingly given refuge to a beggar, who turns out to be the fleeing grand duke. Through an improbable series of events, Azdak is made a judge. During his tenure, he proves to be corrupt, licentious, and contemptuous of the law, yet often he turns the law upside down to help the poor. In one case, Azdak acquits a doctor who has operated free of charge on a poor patient: Despite the doctor's professional incompetence (he operated on the wrong leg), his motives were good. In another case, a landlord brings an action against a stable boy for raping his daughter-in-law. Azdak takes one look at the voluptuous daughter-in-law and declares that the stable boy is innocent—he is the one who has been raped. Another case concerns a poor widow who is accused of receiving stolen goods. She claims that Saint Banditus has given her the goods. Azdak fines the rich farmers who brought the suit against her: They do not believe in miracles; they are impious. It must be a miracle, Azdak reasons, if the poor are helped. In these decisions, Azdak intentionally disregards the actual law in order to administer a rough justice that helps the poor.

The last part of the play brings together the Azdak and the Grusche stories in a trial scene in which both Grusche and the governor's wife claim to be the mother of the child (Brecht had a predilection for trial scenes because of the central role of argument in them). The governor's wife has assembled lawyers to fight for her child, and Grusche and Simon represent themselves. It turns out that the governor's wife is only interested in her child because of what he will inherit. Without him, she is poor. Azdak listens to the arguments on both sides, berates Simon and Grusche for not having money to bribe him, and, finally, draws a chalk circle on the floor. He puts Michel in the middle and orders the two women to hold the child by the hand. The real mother, he tells them, will have the strength to pull the child out of the circle. Both times, Grusche lets go for fear of hurting the child, while the real mother pulls him out of the circle with all her strength. In a reversal of the Solomon story, Azdak decides that Grusche should have the child because she, and not the real mother, actually cares for the child. In his last action as judge, Azdak decides the case of an old couple who want a divorce. By "mistake" he divorces Grusche from her husband so that she can marry Simon, justifying his action by saying that because the old people have lived together for so long, they would be better to continue living together.

Unlike most of Brecht's plays, this play-within-a-play ends happily. Grusche is reunited with Simon and keeps the child. To be a biological mother alone is not enough, according to Azdak; one must actually love and make sacrifices for a child, as Grusche has done.

In his notes to the play, Brecht mentioned that there is an American expression "sucker," and that this is what Grusche is when she takes the child: The more she does for the child, the more her own life is endangered. The biblical allusions in the Grusche story (the birth of Christ and the flight into Egypt, for example), together with Azdak's wise and humane judgments, indicate that a new age is dawning. Azdak's decision to give Grusche the child because she is good for him brings the play-within-a-play back to the peacefully resolved dispute in the first scene. In a similar manner, the fruit growers are given the land because they will make it more productive. The promise of a new age has been fulfilled in the first scene— a Socialist Utopia has been reached.

OTHER MAJOR WORKS

LONG FICTION: *Der Dreigroschenroman*, 1934 (*The Threepenny Novel*, 1937, 1956); *Die Geschäfte des Herrn Julius Caesar*, 1956.

SHORT FICTION: *Geschichten von Herrn Keuner*, 1930, 1958 (*Stories of Mr. Keuner*, 2001); *Kalendergeschichten*, 1948 (*Tales from the Calendar*, 1961); *Me-ti: Buch der Wendungen*, 1965; *Prosa*, 1965 (5 volumes); *Collected Stories*, 1998.

POETRY: *Hauspostille*, 1927, 1951 (*Manual of Piety*, 1966); *Lieder, Gedichte, Chöre*, 1934 (*Songs, Poems, Choruses*, 1976); *Svendborger Gedichte*, 1939 (*Svendborg Poems*, 1976); *Selected Poems*, 1947; *Hundert Gedichte*, 1951 (*A Hundred Poems*, 1976); *Gedichte und Lieder*, 1956 (*Poems and Songs*, 1976); *Gedichte*, 1960-1965 (9 volumes); *Bertolt Brecht: Poems, 1913-1956*, 1976 (includes *Buckower Elegies*); *Bad Time for Poetry: 152 Poems and Songs*, 1995.

SCREENPLAYS: *Kuhle Wampe*, 1932 (English translation, 1933); *Hangmen Also Die*, 1943; *Das Lied der Ströme*, 1954; *Herr Puntila und sein Knecht, Matti*, 1955.

NONFICTION: *Der Messingkauf*, 1937-1951 (*The Messingkauf Dialogues*, 1965); *Kleines Organon für das Theater*, 1948 (*A Little Organum for the Theater*, 1951); *Schriften zum Theater*, 1963-1964 (7 volumes); *Brecht on Theatre*, 1964; *Arbeitsjournal, 1938-1955*, 1973 (3 volumes; *Bertolt Brecht Journals*, 1993); *Tagebucher, 1920-1922*, 1975 (*Diaries, 1920-1922*, 1979); *Letters*, 1990; *Brecht on Film and Radio*, 2000.

BIBLIOGRAPHY

Bodek, Richard. *Proletarian Performance in Weimar Berlin: Agitprop, Chorus, and Brecht*. Columbia, S.C.: Camden House, 1997. A study of proletarian theater and agitprop theater in Berlin, with emphasis on Brecht.

Fuegi, John. *Brecht and Company: Sex, Politics, and the Making of the Modern Drama*. New York: Grove, 1994. Fuegi is a professor of comparative literature at the University of Maryland and founder of the International Brecht Society and has published two previous books on Brecht. According to Fuegi, his newest work, dealing at great length not only with Brecht but also with a wide circle of his associates and collaborators, is the result of twenty-five years of research.

Giles, Steve, and Rodney Livingstone, eds. *Bertolt Brecht: Centenary Essays*. Atlanta, Ga.: Rodopi, 1998. A collection of essays on Brecht written one hundred years after his birth. Bibliography.

Jameson, Fredric. *Brecht and Method*. New York: Verso, 1998. A major neo-Marxist literary theorist assesses the position of one of the twentieth century's central figures in dramatic literature as a modernist and postmodernist thinker.

Thomson, Peter. *Brecht: "Mother Courage and Her Children."* Plays in Production series. New York: Cambridge University Press, 1997. An examination of the stage history and dramatic production of *Mother Courage and Her Children*, the conclusion of which was written by Viv Gardner. Bibliography and index.

Thomson, Peter, and Glendyr Sacks, eds. *The Cambridge Companion to Brecht*. Cambridge Companions to Literature series. New York: Cambridge University Press, 1994. This extensive reference work contains a wealth of information on Brecht. Bibliography and index.

Willett, John. *Brecht in Context: Comparative Approaches*. Rev. ed. London: Methuen, 1998. A comparative analysis of the works of Brecht. Bibliography and index.

Jennifer Michaels

HOWARD BRENTON

Born: Portsmouth, England; December 13, 1942

PRINCIPAL DRAMA

Ladder of Fools, pr. 1965
A Sky-Blue Life, pr. 1966, pb. 1989
Gargantua, pr. 1969 (adaptation of François Rabelais' novel)
Revenge, pr. 1969, pb. 1970
Heads, pr. 1969, pb. 1970
The Education of Skinny Spew, pr. 1969, pb. 1970
Christie in Love, pr. 1969, pb. 1970
Gum and Goo, pr. 1969, pb. 1972
Cheek, pr. 1970
Fruit, pr. 1970
Wesley, pr. 1970, pb. 1972
Scott of the Antarctic: What God Didn't See, pr. 1971, pb. 1972
Lay By, pr. 1971, pb. 1972 (with Brian Clark, Trevor Griffiths, David Hare, Steven Poliakoff, Hugh Stoddart, and Snoo Wilson)
England's Ireland, pr. 1972 (with David Elgar, Tony Bicât, Brian Clark, Francis Fuchs, Hare, and Wilson)
Hitler Dances, pr. 1972, pb. 1982
How Beautiful with Badges, pr. 1972, pb. 1989
Measure for Measure, pr. 1972, pb. 1989 (adaptation of William Shakespeare's play)
A Fart for Europe, pr. 1973 (with Elgar)
Mug, pr. 1973
Magnificence, pr., pb. 1973
Brassneck, pr. 1973, pb. 1974 (with Hare)

The Churchill Play: As It Will Be Performed in the Winter of 1984 by the Internees of Churchill Camp Somewhere in England, pr., pb. 1974
The Saliva Milkshake, pr. 1975 (staged and televised), pb. 1977 (adaptation of Joseph Conrad's novel *Under Western Eyes*)
Weapons of Happiness, pr., pb. 1976
Government Property, pr. 1976
Epsom Downs, pr., pb. 1977
Deeds, pr. 1978 (with Griffiths, Ken Campbell, and Hare)
Sore Throats, pr., pb. 1979
Plays for the Poor Theatre, pb. 1980
The Romans in Britain, pr., pb. 1980
A Short Sharp Shock!, pr. 1980, pb. 1981 (with Tony Howard)
Thirteenth Night, pr., pb. 1981 (based on Shakespeare's play *Macbeth*)
The Genius, pr., pb. 1983
Sleeping Policemen, pr. 1983, pb. 1984 (with Trude Ikoli)
Bloody Poetry, pr. 1984, pb. 1985
Pravda: A Fleet Street Comedy, pr., pb. 1985 (with Hare)
A Professional Exercise, pr. 1985 (with Hare)
Plays: One, pb. 1986
Greenland, pr., pb. 1988
H. I. D.: Hess Is Dead, pr., pb. 1989
Three Plays, pb. 1989
Iranian Nights, pr., pb. 1989 (with Tariq Ali)
Moscow Gold, pr., pb. 1990 (with Ali)
Plays: Two, pb. 1990
Berlin Bertie, pr., pb. 1992

Faust: Parts I and II, pb. 1995, pr. 1996 (adaptation of Johann Wolfgang von Goethe's play)
Ugly Rumours, pr., pb. 1998 (with Ali)
Snogging Ken, pr., pb. 2000 (with Ali and Andy de la Tour)

OTHER LITERARY FORMS

Although known primarily as a playwright, Howard Brenton has published the collections of poetry *Notes from a Psychotic Journal and Other Poems* (1969) and *Sore Throats and Sonnets of Love and Opposition* (1979). In 1989, he published *Diving for Pearls*, a novel, and in 1995, a substantial collection of his prose nonfiction was released as *Hot Irons: Diaries, Essays, Journalism*.

ACHIEVEMENTS

Howard Brenton belongs to a small group of radical English playwrights known as the "wild bunch," which includes Snoo Wilson, Howard Barker, and David Hare. Brenton's achievements in drama have been principally in openly agitprop theater in the interest of revolutionary socialism. His plays depict matters of current public interest in Great Britain, though frequently he sets the drama in a specific historical period, such as Roman Britain or nineteenth century Italy. Despite the directness of their Marxist propaganda, the plays hold their own in terms of dramatic plot and characterization. Like Edward Bond and other "fringe" playwrights, Brenton employs graphic violence and pornographic images to convey his outrage against the social complacency he detects in his country. The plot forms resemble Samuel Beckett's Theater of the Absurd and Bertolt Brecht's epic drama, but Brenton dissociates himself from both playwrights. Beckett he has criticized for being a philosophical pessimist and Brecht for lacking awareness of the theater event.

As a result of his play *Christie in Love*, Brenton won the Arts Council's John Whiting Award in 1970 and received an Arts Council Drama Bursary for the next season.

His play *Weapons of Happiness* won the *Evening Standard* Drama Award for Best Play of 1976, and he received commissions to write plays for the Royal

Shakespeare Company and the National Theatre. Frequently, his plays are collaborations with other writers, notably his friend David Hare.

BIOGRAPHY

Howard John Brenton was born in Portsmouth, England, on December 13, 1942, during the German blitzes of World War II. His parents were Donald Henry Brenton and Rose Lilian (née Lewis) Brenton. Donald Brenton retired in the early 1960's after twenty-five years as a law-enforcement officer and joined the Methodist Church, eventually becoming an ordained minister in that denomination. His avocations included the theater, in which he participated frequently as an amateur stage actor and director. Howard Brenton's interest in writing and the theater began quite early in life in imitation of his father. Traveling all over England and Wales with his family, Brenton was glum and rebellious even as a child, enjoying the nonauthoritarian environment of the stage and the privacy of writing. At age nine, he adapted a comic strip into a short play. The youthful Brenton also wrote poems and three novels, in addition to completing a biography of Adolf Hitler at age seventeen. Brenton attended grammar school and was graduated from Chichester High School in West Sussex. He initially wanted to be a visual artist specializing in abstract paintings, and with that end in mind, he enrolled at Corsham Court, an art college in Bath. Changing his mind at the last minute, he dropped art school and made plans to attend St. Catherine's College, Cambridge, to study writing. In later years, Brenton said that he hated his Cambridge years despite the fact that he was a promising student there, an unsurprising revelation, given his antiestablishment views and the place of Cambridge in the Britain's cultural life. Majoring in English, he took courses with George Steiner, the distinguished literary critic; Brenton greatly admired Steiner for his social views and for his teaching. In 1965, Brenton saw the first production of one of his plays, *Ladder of Fools*, at Cambridge and received a B.A. degree with honors.

Upon leaving Cambridge, Brenton worked odd jobs, stage managed, and acted part-time while continuing to write plays. In 1969, he performed as an actor with the Brighton Combination, for whom he also wrote the short experimental plays *Gargantua* and *Gum and Goo*. Later the same year, he worked with Chris Parr's theater group at Bradford University, which produced *Gum and Goo*, *Heads*, and *The Education of Skinny Spew* in conjunction with rock concerts given at the university. During this time, Brenton submitted a play script to the Royal Court Theatre and was invited for an interview. *Revenge*, his first full-length play, was produced at the Royal Court Theatre Upstairs, London, in September, 1969.

During the production of *Revenge*, Brenton met and befriended David Hare, a fellow playwright and director. Hare's company, the Portable Theatre, commissioned Brenton to write *Christie in Love*, which Hare directed in November, 1969, and for which Snoo Wilson (who, like Hare, was later to be professionally associated with Brenton) built the set and stage managed. The play moved to the Royal Court Theatre Upstairs early the following year and received favorable reviews. *Christie in Love* was the beginning of a long and prodigious professional relationship between Brenton and Hare. On January 31, 1970, between productions of *Christie in Love*, Brenton married Jane Margaret Fry.

As a playwright on the "fringe" in the early 1970's, Brenton wrote a number of plays to be produced in unusual spaces. His play *Wesley* was performed at the Eastbrook Hall Methodist Church in Bradford, and *Scott of the Antarctic: What God Didn't See* was produced in an ice-skating rink. These works appeared as part of the Bradford Festival in 1970 and 1971. The playwright was also involved in several collaborative efforts during this time, notably *Lay By* and *England's Ireland*. In 1972, Brenton became a resident playwright at the Royal Court Theatre. The history of the Royal Court as a theater that nurtured talented writers did much to secure Brenton's growing reputation. It was at the Royal Court that Brenton began a succession of "anti-Brechtian" epic plays, which cemented his reputation: *Magnificence*, *Brassneck*, *The Churchill Play*, *Weapons of Happiness*, and *Epsom Downs*. *Weapons of Happiness*, which took its title from a phrase spray-painted on the set of *Magnificence*, was the first play to debut at the National

Theatre's new Lyttelton Theatre. Brenton wrote *Epsom Downs* in 1977 for the Joint Stock Theatre Group.

During the same period of time, Brenton wrote three plays for television: *Lushly* (1971), *The Saliva Milkshake*, and *The Paradise Run* (1976). *The Saliva Milkshake* was also adapted for the stage and eventually was performed in New York, marking Brenton's debut in the United States. In 1973, Brenton wrote a short screenplay for the British Film Institute, *Skin Flicker*, based on a novel by Tony Bicât, who worked with him at the Portable Theatre (founded by Bicât and Hare).

In its 1978-1979 season, the Royal Shakespeare Company staged a successful revival of *The Churchill Play* at the Warehouse Theatre in London. The next year, *Sore Throats*, also performed by the Royal Shakespeare Company at the Warehouse, departed from the theatrical epics that established Brenton as an important playwright in the 1970's. The play, which the writer calls "an intimate play in two acts," occurs in a Pinteresque *mise en scène* (an empty South London flat), with only three characters: two women and a man. Brenton followed *Sore Throats* with *A Short Sharp Shock!* in 1980, a collaboration with Tony Howard. The year 1980 was to become a landmark year for Brenton with the National Theatre production of *The Romans in Britain* at the new Olivier Theatre. The play, his second for the National Theatre, provoked a strong critical reaction that did not abate during its entire run. Indeed, not since Edward Bond depicted the brutal stoning of an infant in a perambulator in his 1965 play *Saved* had London theater critics raised such an outcry against a play and a playwright. Most of the outrage was directed at the production's liberal use of male nudity and the graphic representation onstage of a Roman soldier's attempted rape of a young Celtic priest. The director Michael Bogdanov was charged with obscene behavior under the Sexual Offenses Act of 1967, and there was an effort to stop the play and withdraw the Greater London Council's subsidy to the National Theatre. Despite, or perhaps because of, all the puritan indignation over the play's visual content, *The Romans in Britain* played to full houses during its six-month run in London. Also in 1980, the National

Theatre presented Brenton's *The Life of Galileo* (1980; adaptation of Bertolt Brecht's play *Leben des Galilei*, pr. 1943), which ran for more than a year.

The Royal Shakespeare Company's performance of *Thirteenth Night* in 1981 was a little less controversial than *The Romans in Britain*. The play, a political satire loosely adapted from William Shakespeare's tragedy *Macbeth* (pr. 1606), drew criticism for its pointed, allegedly libelous references by name to prominent living British conservatives. A number of the play's offensive lines were subsequently deleted from performances. Brenton criticized academia and technology in *The Genius*, which the Royal Court Theatre produced in 1983. In the same year, the Foco Novo Theatre Company commissioned Brenton and Tunde Ikoli to write separate plays involving three black characters and three white characters. The two plays were then synthesized by the director Roland Rees into a single play, *Sleeping Policemen*. The next year, the same theater company commissioned Brenton to write *Bloody Poetry*, a play about Percy Bysshe Shelley, which the company produced at the Haymarket Theatre at Leicester. *Bloody Poetry* was subsequently moved to the Hampstead Theatre in London. In 1985, Brenton and Hare collaborated on a comedy called *Pravda*, a satire on the more commercial and sensationalistic aspects of English newspaper journalism. Presented under Hare's direction at the National Theatre, the play was both a popular and a critical success, with Anthony Hopkins's performance in the leading role being singled out for special praise.

A prolific playwright for many years, Brenton continued to generate at least one play, and often three or more, every year throughout the 1970's and 1980's. In 1989, his parody *H. I. D.: Hess Is Dead* examined the circumstances surrounding the death of Nazi leader Rudolph Hess in a Berlin prison. *Berlin Bertie*, which was first produced in 1992, demonstrates his continuing fascination with the contradictions and complexities of German social and political history, as does his 1996 adaptation of Johann Wolfgang von Goethe's *Faust: Eine Tragödie* (pb. 1808, pb. 1833; *The Tragedy of Faust*, 1823, 1828). Around this time, Brenton also began a fruitful collaboration

with writer and cultural critic Tariq Ali, with whom he has written several plays. These include *Iranian Nights*, about the Salman Rushdie affair; *Moscow Gold*, about economic and political reforms in Russia; *Ugly Rumours*, a satire on Tony Blair's "New Labour" party; and *Snogging Ken* (also with Andy de la Tour), a brief play in support of Labour candidate "Red Ken" Livingstone's (ultimately successful) bid to become London's first elected mayor. (In addition to providing artistic support, profits from this play also went to support Livingstone's campaign.) Though his productivity has somewhat slowed since the 1980's, Brenton clearly has lost neither his commitment to political reform nor his satirical edge.

ANALYSIS

Howard Brenton's plays represent an important contribution to radical and poststructuralist English drama. He belongs to the second wave of modernist English theater, the generation after Arnold Wesker, John Osborne, and Harold Pinter. His frequent, highly successful collaborations with such writers as David Hare and Tariq Ali suggest almost as forcefully as do his dramatic works Brenton's belief in theater as a social phenomenon and a social force. Though sometimes attacked for the political content of the writing, his theater is vivid and powerful propaganda. As a playwright, he has never failed to excite critical and public comment and to stir controversy.

Brenton's plays aggressively and unapologetically exploit contemporary public issues to promote revolutionary socialism and antiestablishment social causes. Whether the dramatic setting is historical (*The Romans in Britain*, *Bloody Poetry*) or contemporary (*Magnificence*, *H. I. D.: Hess Is Dead*) or futuristic (*The Churchill Play*, *The Genius*), the plays depict class struggle and the necessity of nonviolent change on a universal scale. Brenton's drama is, nevertheless, remarkably evenhanded in its treatment of the characters, sometimes critical of the radicals for their fuzzy thinking about politics and sometimes sympathetic toward the human foibles of the rich and powerful. It portrays even political conservatives, usually the villains of Brenton's stage conflicts, in the best possible light, notably in the touching dialogue between Alice and Babs in scene 4 of *Magnificence*, and in the sympathetic characterization of Captain Thompson, the physician at the English concentration camp in *The Churchill Play*. Brenton's plays frequently make the point that self-interest and misspent passion occur on all sides of a political issue, thus contributing to the general malaise in society. It is a point scored expertly in the 1969 play *Revenge*, in which opposing sides of the law are represented by a single actor.

CHRISTIE IN LOVE

Brenton's early one-act play, *Christie in Love*, demonstrates the writer's interest in the criminal mind and the banality of evil. Based on the case of the 1950's mass murderer John Reginald Halliday Christie, the play combines elements of psychological naturalism and self-conscious structuralist theater. The Constable and the Inspector, the only actors in the drama besides Christie, are intentionally flat characters, offsetting Christie himself, who is (after his initial entrance) dramatically believable and psychologically complex. In the first two scenes, the two law-enforcement officers exchange inane comments about their activity and sexist jokes that are painfully ill-timed and unfunny. When Christie appears, in scene 3, he arises slowly out of a grave of newspapers in the manner of Count Dracula, wearing a large, disfiguring fright mask. In all the subsequent scenes, Christie is maskless, revealing a quite ordinary looking and surprisingly defenseless man. The contrasting imagery suggests that the concocted tabloid image of Christie (or, for that matter, any "villain") as a monster is a false one, and that the real person who was Christie performed his heinous crimes out of love, peculiarly defined and experienced by the individual. Moreover, in the context of the play, Christie is far more genuine in his passions than his interrogators, who delude themselves with ideas of normality and morality that they enforce through violence, willful ignorance, and deprecation of sex and love.

Certain elements of the play have appeared again in Brenton's later work. Christie's theatrical resurrection from the dead is very similar to Winston Churchill's escape from the catafalque in the play-within-a-play at the beginning of *The Churchill Play*. The startling synthesis of exclamations of true love and images of brutality appears again in *Sore Throats*, in which sudden dramatic reversals and extremely contradictory actions muddle the real nature of the characters' emotions. The bleak, Cold War background and the surrealistic middle-class setting of the play recur in numerous other Brenton works, including *The Churchill Play* and *The Genius*. At the same time, *Christie in Love* is unique among Brenton's plays in the comparative subtlety of its politics and theatrical violence. In the plays most characteristic of the playwright, revolutionary socialism is openly espoused, and terrorism and violence are gruesomely reified on the stage.

THE ROMANS IN BRITAIN

Critics and reviewers frequently complain that Brenton's theater is too violent, that it is in reality only sensationalistic. A certain amount of the outcry against his play *The Romans in Britain* was directed against its graphic portrayal of torture and murder, as well as its profuse male nudity. Brenton deliberately uses shock techniques, violence, profanity, nudity, and scatology to provoke his audiences. There is a prophetic intensity about his writing, particularly in the plays of the middle 1970's and early 1980's, which are public spectacles condemning oppression and collaboration with oppression through passivity. Brenton calls this element in drama "aggro," a British slang term that suggests a mix of aggression and aggravation. Its purpose is to draw the audience together into the play's (and playwright's) outrage. Brenton has commented that his agitprop theater frequently succeeds better at agitation than at propaganda, and the usual critical and public response to his plays seems to bear him out on this point. In a much-quoted interview from 1975, Brenton commented that his plays were intended as "petrol bombs through the proscenium arch."

MAGNIFICENCE

Another aspect of Brenton's writing that draws criticism on occasion is the unevenness of his dramatic style. Scenes that are dark with pessimism and brooding alternate with slapstick comedy, and sensitive character drama intermixes with pornographic and Grand Guignol stage effects. For example, the ironically titled revenge play *Magnificence* begins with five young radicals occupying an abandoned flat in protest against the landowner's legal oppression of the poor tenants. The opening scenes center mainly on the two female members of the group: Mary, who is pregnant and whose approach to revolution is largely aesthetic, and Veronica, who formerly worked for the British Broadcasting Corporation (BBC) and who is the most intellectual (and moderate) member of the group. A sort of climax is reached in the play at the end of scene 3, when Mr. Slaughter, the landlord, in the company of a constable, breaks into the room and bodily attacks the occupants. In the process, he kicks Mary in the stomach, accidentally causing a miscarriage. The setting of the play then changes to Cambridge College, and two new characters are introduced: two men who are friends, Tory bureaucrats in government and academia, who go by the nicknames Alice and Babs. The scene, which is the center of the play, is peaceful, full of reminiscences and flirtations between the two old friends as they punt a flat-bottomed boat across the stage. In the course of the scene, Babs reveals to his friend that he is about to die, and at the scene's end, he expires quietly in Alice's arms. The final third of the play centers on Jed, a minor and mostly silent character in the opening scenes, who now seeks revenge for the death of Mary's child. The other members of the radical group have chosen a less active public course; in Jed's opinion, they have debased the principles for which they stood at the beginning. The play concludes with a riveting horror scene in which Jed attacks Alice and forces him to wear a bomb in the form of a mask on his head. When, after agonizing dramatic suspense, the explosive fails to detonate, Jed and Alice attempt to strike some sort of bargain, and then unexpectedly the bomb explodes, killing them both.

In the end, *Magnificence* leaves the audience with a sense of having watched three individual plots, each with its own impetus and tone, and—except for the obvious continuation of characters from scene to scene—little coherence is evident between the three principal parts. Brenton treats each scene on its own terms without imposing unity of action. In respect to

this professedly unconscious stylistic element, Brenton categorizes himself, along with Wilson and Hare, as a "maximalist" playwright, in contrast to the dramatic minimalism of Beckett and Pinter. Brenton's goal is to depict a situation realistically by incorporating into the play as many facets or aspects of the situation as possible. The result is a deliberate hodgepodge of styles, characters, and events.

WEAPONS OF HAPPINESS

Perhaps the quintessential Brenton protagonist is Josef Frank in *Weapons of Happiness*. Like Christie and Churchill, Frank is an actual historical figure whom Brenton "resurrects" to make a point about political activism. The real Frank was one of the twelve prominent members of the Czechoslovakian Communist Party hanged by the Stalinists in Prague in 1952. Brenton's Frank survives to 1976 by emigrating to England, where he inadvertently becomes involved in a workers' strike at a potato chip factory. Frank, a sullen and silent old man plagued with painful memories of his interrogation in the 1950's and nightmare fantasies about Joseph Stalin, is alienated not only from the factory owner and managers but also from the youthful rebels who attempt a minor coup by taking over the factory. Unable to side with the capitalists and reactionary police who want him to betray the young radicals and also unable to side with the Communists for whom violent force and half-digested Marxist ideology are legitimate tools of revolution, Frank is forced once again into a solitary position. In the end, he is able to confide in Janice, one of the young English Communists, and warns her against the utopian and terrorist tendencies that have become a part of the radical movement. He dies alone in a drain leading out of the factory. The final scene shows Janice and her comrades establishing a socialist commune in Wales, hopefully modeled on Frank's Trotskyism.

THE GENIUS

Aspects of Josef Frank's character are typical of Brenton's antiheroes—lapsed idealists who fall, at least temporarily, into inactivity because of disillusionment and embitterment about the status quo and the state of the revolution. In *The Genius*, the American physicist Leo Lehrer, perhaps modeled on

Brecht's Galileo, invents a weapon capable of destroying the whole world at once. Distressed that the U.S. military establishment has perverted his mathematical genius in the interest of power and oppression, he flees the United States for a small university in England, full of self-loathing and paranoid fears. There he meets Gilly Brown, another mathematical genius, who has accidentally completed the formula for the weapon also. In the closing scene, Gilly and Leo have left the university to camp outside the wire fences surrounding a military installation, which they, along with another student and the university bursar's wife, periodically invade in order to publicize the vulnerability of lethal military weapons to outside attack.

The Genius also presents an example of another class of Brenton character: the sideline observer who lacks the courage or will to act on his convictions. In *The Genius*, the university bursar, Graham Hay, is a liberal humanist who is initially sympathetic to Lehrer, even after, midway through act 1, Lehrer cuckolds the old man. Hay is a gentle man with somewhat rarefied academic tastes, but he is the lackey of the university vice-chancellor. In the end, Hay is interrogated by the English secret police and betrays Lehrer. Despite his right-thinking liberal humanist philosophy, Hay fails in the end for lack of moral passion.

BLOODY POETRY

Another disillusioned radical is Percy Bysshe Shelley in *Bloody Poetry*. Like Frank and Lehrer, Shelley is a refugee. He has fled from England, where his female entourage (Mary Shelley and Claire Clairemont) and he are viewed with suspicion and moral repugnance, and sets up residence in Switzerland and Italy with George Gordon, Lord Byron, a fellow radical and anarchist whose moral dissipation is portrayed in his continual drunkenness and unawareness of the consequences of his sexual liaisons. Like Frank, Shelley is haunted by the ghosts of his past life, in this case the ghost of Harriet Westbrook, Shelley's first wife, who was unable to live the life of a revolutionary (or a revolutionary's wife) and so was abandoned, eventually to go mad and kill herself. Shelley's dilemma in the play is that his wild libertarian ideology contradicts his social conscience. The puritan indignation of his countrymen and the irresponsible self-destruction of Byron do not represent his own conscience and his own concept of personal liberty, which, moreover, he cannot quite reconcile within himself. The play concludes with Shelley jubilant and adrift at sea shortly before his death. He sings about the utopian future when the men of England will rid themselves of tyrants and become free. After a blackout, Byron is seen onstage with the sail-draped corpse of Shelley and the silent, brooding ghost of Harriet. Dismayed at the unexpected death of his friend, Byron shouts, "Burn him! Burn him! Burn him! Burn us all!" thus crying down the old order in a renewed spirit of social revolution.

Bloody Poetry, like *The Genius*, also presents a sideline figure: Dr. William Polidori, whom Byron's publisher has sent to spy on the circle of radical friends in Italy. Polidori lacks the involvement in the dramatic action that would make him a sympathetic character; his moralizing commentary on Shelley's and Byron's actions is invalidated by his own lack of commitment. In his final appearance, Polidori circulates solo in the theater with a glass of wine in one hand, lying to his listeners about his close ties with the Shelley circle and supplying grisly details about Shelley's "suicide."

THE CHURCHILL PLAY

Both *The Genius*'s Hay and *Bloody Poetry*'s Polidori are part of the "vast conspiracy of obedience" Morn describes in the last act of *The Churchill Play*. It is a bureaucratic conspiracy for which everyone is and is not responsible—one which leads ultimately, so Morn thinks, to military dictatorship. The most seductive aspect of the conspiracy is its anonymity. No one needs to feel individually accountable for the atrocities that one's government (or one's private organization) perpetrates. The conspiracy of obedience absolves the individual participant from personal guilt. Polidori accepts this absolution as a matter of fact. Hay, on the other hand, has to be "taught" through intimidation not to feel responsible. The character of Captain Thompson, the concentration camp physician in *The Churchill Play*, is perhaps the best developed of Brenton's sideline observers, and the play delineates a certain progress in the ethical development of Thompson.

Thompson is the chief supporter of the seditious entertainment the prisoners of the Churchill Camp are preparing for the visiting Members of Parliament. When first seen, Thompson is defending the play to Colonel Ball, the commanding officer of the prison. Shortly thereafter, Sergeant Baxter attempts to intimidate Thompson into withdrawing his support for the play. Thompson is so shaken by the threat that he becomes deaf to the story that the new prisoner Reese tries to tell him and walks officiously away. In act 3, Thompson takes an evening walk with his wife Caroline. Their conversation reveals that their position at the camp is repulsive to their liberal humanist ideals, but at the same time, Thompson feels powerless to take a stand. He is shocked at the unjust, murderous treatment of the prisoners, but because the injustice is apparently no one person's responsibility, he does not know where he can turn for justice. Thompson and Caroline's ideology, represented by their wish for seclusion and a quiet home, tends to be obscurantist; they are unable to face the harsh reality of the camp, much less to fight against it. At the end, Thompson offers to accompany the prisoners as they attempt to escape from the camp. To the prisoners, however, Thompson is a collaborator, and despite his professed goodwill toward them, he is not one of them. They turn from him in disgust, leaving him in the company of the right-wing Members of Parliament and the camp guards.

LATER PLAYS

Brenton's focus on controversial political themes has remained constant, but a vein of satire and humor, always present in the playwright's best work, became more prominent in the 1980's and after. During this period, his plays also became, if possible, more immediately topical, dealing not only with issues but with particular current events and public figures. *A Short Sharp Shock!*, for example, was written just after Margaret Thatcher rose to power and satirizes England's leading Tory politicians. *Pravda*, written in collaboration with Hare, lambastes Fleet Street publishers who put profits ahead of journalistic truth, with a thinly disguised figure of Rupert Murdoch at the play's center.

UGLY RUMOURS AND SNOGGING KEN

One would expect such treatment of the British right from Brenton, but he also spared none of his acrimony, or his wit, when turning to his examination of the "New" Labour Party of Tony Blair in *Ugly Rumours*. This play, examining how power politics can corrupt even good intentions, made plain Brenton's view that the promise of the socialist Labour party had been sold out in an attempt to increase the party's appeal to an electorate enamored of easy solutions, slick rhetoric, and middle-of-the-road policies. Presumably because its politics were deemed a bit too sharp, the National Theatre refused a commission for the play, and Brenton and coauthor Tariq Ali had some difficulties in finding a venue for it. Their next joint effort, *Snogging Ken*, continued this attack on "New Labour" by showing the party at the heart of an attempt to keep old-style Labour candidate Ken Livingstone from being elected London's mayor.

IRANIAN NIGHTS

In addition to the public life of his native Britain, Brenton turned his attention increasingly to the international scene after the mid-1980's. *Iranian Nights* (cowritten with Ali) used humor to turn the spotlight on a deeply serious issue, the *fatwa* against the life of author Salman Rushdie issued by Ayatollah Ruhollah Khomeini after the publication of Rushdie's *Satanic Verses*. Neither the racism of the West nor the intolerance of the Middle East comes off well in this exploration of international politics and the clash between religious fervor and artistic freedom. The play also targets pseudo-intellectual liberals who defend Rushdie while admitting that they have never read the book in question.

MOSCOW GOLD

Also cowritten in 1989 with Ali was *Moscow Gold*, a play that marks a significant shift in Brenton's political development. Before the collapse of many communist regimes in Eastern Europe, Brenton, like most British leftists, felt the inevitable movement of history was toward a more communistic system. However, when many formerly communist nations began to embrace a more capitalistic model of governance in the 1980's and 1990's, this certainty was called into question. Using many of the nonnaturalistic and epic staging techniques of such earlier works as *Weapons of Happiness*, *Moscow Gold* asks its audience to cast a critical eye on history, not as it should be but as it actually is, and to consider the effect of that history on the lives of ordinary men and women.

H. I. D.: HESS IS DEAD

H. I. D.: Hess Is Dead continued Brenton's project of reassessing history in the light of the present. The play follows the movements of an investigative journalist intent on discovering whether the official story regarding the suicide of Nazi leader Rudolph Hess in Berlin's Spandau prison is really the whole story. As the play unfolds, Brenton leads the audience to question not only the truth of this individual story but also the very mechanism by which history is constructed and transmitted through an ideological framework masquerading as neutrality.

BERLIN BERTIE

Berlin Bertie, set after the fall of the Berlin Wall and the subsequent reunification of Germany, stages the reuniting of two sisters, one who remained in their native London while the other chose to live in East Germany. Disappointed by the collapse of the socialist state in which she had put her idealistic hopes, the exiled Rosa returns home, only to find herself shadowed by a mysterious member of the old East German secret police. Such plays demonstrate clearly Brenton's willingness to evolve in his thinking and tackle new subjects without ever compromising his firmly held political and ideological positions.

OTHER MAJOR WORKS

LONG FICTION: *Diving for Pearls*, 1989.

POETRY: *Notes from a Psychotic Journal and Other Poems*, 1969; *Sore Throats and Sonnets of Love and Opposition*, 1979.

SCREENPLAYS: *Skin Flicker*, 1973; *The Eleventh Crushing*, 1987.

TELEPLAYS: *Lushly*, 1971; *The Paradise Run*, 1976; *A Desert of Lies*, 1984; *Dead Head*, 1986.

NONFICTION: "The Good Between Us," 1990; *Hot Irons: Diaries, Essays, Journalism*, 1995.

TRANSLATION: *The Life of Galileo*, 1980 (of Bertolt Brecht's play *Leben des Galilei*).

BIBLIOGRAPHY

Boon, Richard. *Brenton the Playwright*. London: Methuen, 1991. Part of a series of brief volumes on modern and contemporary dramatists, intended primarily for students. Boon, a leading authority on Brenton's work, provides an accessible overview of the playwright's career.

Brenton, Howard. "Petrol Bombs Through the Proscenium Arch: An Interview with Howard Brenton." Interview by Catherine Itzin and Simon Trussler. *Theatre Quarterly* 5 (March-May, 1975): 4-20. An interview with production photographs of *Christie in Love* and other plays. Brenton discusses whether "fringe" theater has failed by 1975 and states his famous dictum "You don't write to convert. More . . . to stir things up."

Bull, John. *New British Political Dramatists*. New York: Grove Press, 1983. Contains a major chapter on Brenton, entitled "Portable Theatre and the Fringe." Bull notes the playwright's preoccupation with children in his early work and sees his characters as inhabiting an urban England, "a pintable map with the major cities flashing in multicoloured lights." Strong list of plays by, and articles about, Brenton.

Caulfield, Carl. "*Moscow Gold* and Reassessing History." *Modern Drama* 36 (December, 1993): 490-98. A brief but informative article focusing on the creation and production of Brenton and Tariq Ali's *Moscow Gold*. Caulfield argues that the play illuminates a watershed in Brenton's political thinking, the need to reassess politics and history in light of the failure of Soviet and European communism.

Mitchell, Tony. *File on Brenton*. London: Methuen, 1988. One of a series by Methuen designed for the information age. The volume is a valuable information source, organized by play title, with critical comments, review clippings, and similar short-stroke data, quickly retrieved. Strong chronology, bibliography, index.

Rusinko, Susan. *British Drama 1950 to the Present: A Critical History*. Boston: Twayne, 1989. Brenton's plays are briefly outlined chronologically, quoting as a central theme his famous comment,

"When it comes to agitprop, I like the agit, the prop I'm very bad at." Short bibliography on Brenton and other contemporary playwrights.

Wilson, Ann, ed. *Howard Brenton: A Casebook*. Casebooks on Modern Dramatists 8. New York: Garland, 1993. A collection of original essays, many

of them by well-known scholars. Each chapter focuses on a different major play or addresses a different aspect of Brenton's large body of work.

Joseph Marohl,
updated by Thomas J. Taylor and Janet E. Gardner

JAMES BRIDIE
Osborne Henry Mavor

Born: Glasgow, Scotland; January 3, 1888
Died: Edinburgh, Scotland; January 29, 1951

PRINCIPAL DRAMA

The Sunlight Sonata: Or, To Meet the Seven Deadly Sins, pr. 1928, pb. 1930
The Switchback, pr. 1929, pb. 1930
What It Is to Be Young, pr. 1929, pb. 1934
The Anatomist, pr. 1930, pb. 1931
The Girl Who Did Not Want to Go to Kuala Lumpur, pr. 1930, pb. 1934
Tobias and the Angel, pr. 1930, pb. 1931
The Amazed Evangelist, pb. 1931, pr. 1932
The Dancing Bear, pr. 1931, pb. 1934
Jonah and the Whale, pr., pb. 1932
The Proposal, pr. 1932 (adaptation of Anton Chekhov's play *A Marriage Proposal*)
A Sleeping Clergyman, pr., pb. 1933
Colonel Wotherspoon, pr., pb. 1934
Colonel Wotherspoon and Other Plays, pb. 1934
Marriage Is No Joke, pr., pb. 1934
Mary Read, pr. 1934, pb. 1935 (with Claud Gurney)
The Black Eye, pr., pb. 1935
Moral Plays, pb. 1936
Storm in a Teacup, pr. 1936, pb. 1937 (adaptation of Bruno Frank's play)
Susannah and the Elders, pr. 1937, pb. 1940
Babes in the Wood, pr., pb. 1938
The King of Nowhere, pr., pb. 1938
The Last Trump, pr., pb. 1938

The Golden Legend of Shults, pr. 1939, pb. 1940
What Say They?, pr., pb. 1939
The Dragon and the Dove, pr. 1942, pb. 1944
Holy Isle, pr. 1942, pb. 1944
Jonah 3, pr. 1942, pb. 1944 (based on his play *Jonah and the Whale*)
A Change for the Worse, pr. 1943, pb. 1944
Mr. Bolfry, pr. 1943, pb. 1944
It Depends What You Mean, pr. 1944, pb. 1948
Lancelot, pr. 1944, pb. 1945
Plays for Plain People, pb. 1944
The Forrigan Reel, pr. 1945, pb. 1949
Hedda Gabler, pr. 1945 (adaptation of Henrik Ibsen's play)
The Wild Duck, pr. 1946 (adaptation of Ibsen's play)
De Angelus, pr. 1947, pb. 1949
John Knox, pr. 1947, pb. 1949
Gog and Magog, pr. 1948
Daphne Laureola, pr., pb. 1949 (with George Munro)
John Knox and Other Plays, pb. 1949
The Tintock Cup, pr. 1949
Mr. Gillie, pr., pb. 1950
The Queen's Comedy, pr., pb. 1950
Red Riding Hood, pr. 1950 (with Duncan Macrae)
The Baikie Charivari: Or, The Seven Prophets, pr. 1952, pb. 1953
Meeting at Night, pr. 1954, pb. 1956 (with Archibald Batty)

OTHER LITERARY FORMS

Two autobiographical volumes constitute the major nondramatic writings of James Bridie. *Some Talk of Alexander*, derived from his experiences in the field ambulance unit of the British army during World War I in India, Mesopotamia, Persia, Transcaucasia, and Constantinople, was published in 1926. A second autobiography, *One Way of Living*, published in 1939, is a creative memoir written when Bridie had turned fifty. It is divided into ten chapters, each covering a five-year period of his life. There is an overlay of italicized portions in each chapter, in which an interior monologue of the author ranges freely over some imaginative, associative reflection, evoking the style of James Joyce in *A Portrait of the Artist as a Young Man* (1916). In addition to his two autobiographical works, Bridie wrote a collection of essays entitled *Mr. Bridie's Alphabet for Little Glasgow Highbrows* (1934); a collection of short plays, fragments, essays, poetry, and film and radio scripts entitled *Tedious and Brief* (1944); criticism in *The British Drama* (1945); and still another collection of essays entitled *A Small Stir: Letters on the English* (1949; with Moray McLaren). Finally, Bridie was a prolific writer of articles, described by Winifred Bannister, his biographer, as "witty, teasing admonitions usually aimed at drawing people into the theatre, and even that part of the Scottish public not interested in the theatre could hardly avoid being aware of Bridie as a personality, for almost everything he said and did in public was news."

ACHIEVEMENTS

James Bridie, like John Keats and Anton Chekhov, belongs to a long tradition of writers who were educated for a medical career but who eventually became major literary figures. The author of more than forty plays, he complemented that impressive achievement with a lifelong, active participation in the development of the Glasgow Citizens' Theatre, Glasgow's equivalent of London's National Theatre. His civic work on the Scottish Arts Council, the Edinburgh International Festival of music and drama, the film section of UNESCO, and the Scottish Community Drama Association was unflagging. He also devel-

James Bridie in 1949. (Hulton Archive by Getty Images)

oped into a more than proficient artist, for a time illustrating the *Scots Pictorial* as "O.H." His drawings and paintings have been exhibited at Glasgow art galleries.

Bridie's position in modern British drama is firmly established, and certainly he is a major dramatist in Scottish theater history. Gerald Weales in *Religion in Modern English Drama* (1961) links Bridie and George Bernard Shaw as modern religious dramatists who, at their deaths in 1951 (Bridie) and 1950 (Shaw), left religious drama "almost completely in the hands of the more orthodox practitioners," few of whom "approach Shaw and Bridie as playwrights." J. B. Priestley, a consummate crafter of the well-made play, while calling attention to some of Bridie's weaknesses, calls his best scenes "blazing triumphs." He also asserts that Bridie's "characters appear to exist more in their own right than Shaw's."

Indeed, for Priestley, Bridie is Scotland's major dramatist. In the preface to the posthumous publication of *Meeting at Night*, Priestley offers a measured evaluation of Bridie's work. He concludes his personal tribute to Bridie with the comment that since his death, "the Theatre has seemed only half the size, half the fun, it used to be."

BIOGRAPHY

James Bridie was born Osborne Henry Mavor on January 3, 1888, in Glasgow, Scotland, the son of Henry A. and Janet (Osborne) Mavor. Bridie said that in 1931, he started calling himself "James Bridie," after his grandfather James Mavor and his great-grandfather John Bridie, a sea captain. Gradually, the name Bridie—the dramatist half of Osborne Henry Mavor, the doctor—took over, so that by the time of his death, friends such as Priestley had thought of him strictly as Bridie, never as O. H. Mavor.

Near the beginning of his autobiography, *One Way of Living*, Bridie writes that on January 3, 1938, he takes pleasure, at the age of fifty, in having lived ten different lives in cycles of five years. He describes himself as a Lowland Scot who has no English or Highland blood, no Unconscious Mind, and who therefore is ill-qualified to write an autobiography. Yet he must write one, even though he makes of it a matter of mathematics rather than art, since a Lowland Scot is so ordered in his life, dividing it into three planes—intellectual, moral, and physical—that anyone out of step with it is considered disordered and abnormal. Indeed, Bridie's life was ordered, at first by a father whom he admired and who, unable to enter medicine because of financial difficulties, wished his son to become a doctor. Later, the order was of his own making.

At twenty-five, Bridie was still an undergraduate, having failed some of his medical courses, particularly anatomy. Eventually, however, he became a resident at the staff of the Royal Infirmary in Glasgow as house physician to W. R. Jack; he then moved to the eye, ear, and nose department. He served in the army field ambulance unit during World War I, returning from Soviet Russia in 1919. Joining the staff of the Victoria Infirmary in Glasgow, he led a pleasant life, and began writing, he contends, to subsidize his consulting practice. In 1923, he married Rona Locke Bremner, bought himself a car, and settled into what he describes as a happy bourgeois life. Indeed, he remarks in his autobiography that a childhood admiration for a doctor who owned a car was his reason for wanting to become a doctor. His medical career was rewarded with a doctorate of law from Glasgow University in 1939, and a C.B.E. in 1946. Of the honors conferred on him, he enjoyed most the governorship of Victoria Infirmary in Glasgow, where he had earlier served as assistant physician and honorary consulting physician.

Amid the events of a physician's life, however, Bridie's writing and theatrical interests persisted. Undergraduate productions of his plays with titles such as *The Son Who Was Considerate of His Father's Prejudices*, *No Wedding Cake for Her*, *The Duke Who Could Sometimes Hardly Keep from Smiling*, *Ethics Among Thieves*, and *The Baron Who Would Not Be Convinced that His Way of Living Was Anything Out of the Ordinary* were received with loud applause at school functions. He also wrote for the Glasgow University magazine under "unfamiliar names."

Because of his concern that playwriting, considered by some disreputable, could hurt his consulting practice, Bridie at first wrote under the pseudonym "Mary Henderson," who appears as a character in his first professionally produced play, *The Sunlight Sonata*. In addition, he feared that the hobby might become too absorbing. Another name, "Archibald Kellock" (a character in *Colonel Wotherspoon*), became the pseudonym under which he wrote other plays. In 1938, at the age of fifty, Dr. Osborne Henry Mavor and playwright James Bridie parted, and the latter devoted full time to his chosen career, one that included the development of the Glasgow Citizens' Theatre in particular and the Scottish theater in general. Bridie died in 1951 of a vascular condition at the Edinburgh Royal Infirmary, one year after the death of George Bernard Shaw, whom Bridie knew and who attended some of Bridie's plays.

ANALYSIS

At the heart of much of James Bridie's drama lies the conflict between science and religion. He explored this conflict in a variety of dramatic genres, including comedies, mystery plays, and morality plays that have interesting resemblances to those of the medieval period, and problem dramas that suggest the influence of Henrik Ibsen. In all three general groupings, one can detect a stylistic hallmark: the use of medical language, characters who are members of the medical profession or who have something to do with a member of that profession, or situations in which science is involved in either a major or minor way. In Bridie's plays, however, as in his life, science takes second place to the moral problems of his characters, even when its virtues or vices are the basis for those problems. In a general sense, then, all his dramas, including the most entertaining Shavian comedies, are morality plays.

Although Bridie's religious views were "so liberal minded, so humanitarian as to be unfixed," according to Bannister, they were, nevertheless, the driving force in his own life and in the characters of his plays. A moral fervor and rational humanism characterize his earliest performed play, *The Sunlight Sonata*, a comedy about seven characters affected by the traditional Seven Deadly Sins. Similarly, *The Baikie Charivari* is a Faustian confrontation between man and the Devil, containing seven potential evils in the form of visitors who would teach Bridie's "Faust." Indeed, Bridie's thesis resembles Johann Wolfgang von Goethe's: the necessity of never saying to the moment, "Stay, thou art fair."

Bridie's mystery plays, dramatizations of Bible stories, constitute an important part of his œuvre. In the tradition of the medieval mystery play, in which Bible stories were dramatized for "plain people," Bridie modernizes the dilemmas in which biblical characters find themselves. In fact, he wrote three versions of the Jonah story: *Jonah and the Whale*, *The Sign of the Prophet Jonah* (1942), and *Jonah 3*. Bridie's stories were drawn not only from the Bible but also from the Apocrypha and from contemporary religious events and figures.

Some of Bridie's plays have evoked comparisons with Shaw and Ibsen. Clever turns of phrase, witty dialogue, puns, and outrageous situations involving societal "outlaws" (such as the father and daughter in *Meeting at Night* who conduct a mail-order confidence racket) have earned for Bridie the label the "Scottish Shaw." Bannister records a comment that Shaw is supposed to have made to Bridie: "If there

had been no me there would have been no you." The two dramatists are dissimilar, however, in a major way, for with the exception of *Daphne Laureola*, Bridie's characterizations of women lack the strength and conviction of Shaw's. Among influences on Bridie, perhaps that of Ibsen is the strongest. It can be seen in his adaptations of Ibsen's plays but more subtly in the satiric thrusts at status-quo science and religion in plays such as *A Sleeping Clergyman*, *The Switchback*, and *The Anatomist*.

A SLEEPING CLERGYMAN

In his autobiography, Bridie claimed that *A Sleeping Clergyman* "was the nearest thing to a masterpiece I shall probably ever write." Completed at the end of 1932, before he had decided to give up medicine in order to devote himself to the theater, the play was produced in London in 1933. He had worked on the play off and on for two years, with earlier productions in Birmingham and Malvern. He stated that the play was an attempt to combine two themes with which he had dealt earlier: the scientist as dictator in *The Anatomist* and as lost sheep in the wilderness in *The Switchback*, and the relation of human beings to God in *Tobias and the Angel* and *Jonah and the Whale*.

The play is in two acts, the first preceded by a prologue and the second by a "chorus." In these two introductory portions, the framework for the story is established. At a respectable men's club in Glasgow, Dr. Cooper, a specialist in diseases of women, and Dr. Coutts, a neurologist, are relaxing with a drink. Nearby, a "huge, whitebearded" clergyman sleeps. Coutts has just returned from the funeral service of ninety-seven-year-old Dr. William Marshall, a former visiting physician at the Royal Infirmary of Glasgow. Coutts, whose father had been a friend of Marshall, represented the faculty at the funeral. The conversation then turns to another funeral attendee, Sir Charles Cameron, a noted bacteriologist. Interest in Cameron, a relative of the deceased, is aroused as the matter of his illegitimate birth is mentioned by Coutts. With a brief reference to Cameron's grandfather, a dissipated medical student, the prologue ends, and the narration shifts to a dramatization of events in the lives of three generations of Camerons. In flash-back style, the drama consists of two acts, with four scenes in each act. The action moves swiftly through more than sixty years, from 1867 to 1872, 1885, 1886, 1907, 1916, and finally to the 1930's, in a fascinating tale in which genius eventually conquers the predilection to dissipation that the latest Cameron had inherited from his grandfather.

In act 1, the first Cameron is a young medical researcher, dying of tuberculosis but, above everything else, bent on finishing the medical research project in which he is currently engaged. The efforts of Dr. Will Marshall and his sister, Harriet, to convince Cameron to spend some time with them at their shore residence are futile. After visiting Cameron in his untidy room, Will leaves, having loaned Cameron three pounds. Later, Harriet arrives to inform Cameron that she is pregnant. He agrees to her proposal of marriage, but it is later revealed, in a conversation between two relatives on the day of a birthday party for little Wilhelmina (daughter of Harriet and Cameron), that the marriage had never taken place.

The story of the second generation of Camerons is dramatized in scene 3 of act 1. Wilhelmina, now a young woman, shows the effects of heredity as she asks her Uncle Will for a cigar she wishes to try. The incident evokes the scene in Ibsen's *Gengangere* (pb. 1881; *Ghosts*, 1885) in which Oswald, an artist returning from Paris to his hometown in Norway, smokes a pipe and then recalls being sick as a child after his father had given him a pipe to smoke. Ibsen's play is about an inherited syphilitic condition; Bridie's is about inherited genius and its accompanying Bohemian lifestyle.

Wilhelmina, reared by her Uncle Will, follows in the footsteps of her mother and father in her disregard of stifling, conventional conduct. During a lovers' quarrel over her decision to marry another man, a man of her own class—even though she is pregnant by her lover, a lower-class employee of her uncle—she poisons the latter. In covering up her act, her uncle asks Dr. Coutts (father of Coutts of the prologue) to carry out the investigation of the death. In the ensuing trial, Wilhelmina is found innocent, and then, in a reversal of her earlier intentions, refuses to marry Sutherland even though he proposed. Act 1 ends on

this note. Without regard for the puritanical mores of Scottish respectability, the Camerons continue to exercise their individualism.

A "chorus" introducing the second act parallels the prologue to act 1. The clergyman still sleeps as Dr. Cooper listens to Dr. Coutts's tale of the Cameron generations. The audience learns of the trial of Wilhelmina and of the birth of her twins, Charles and Hope. The birth is followed by Wilhelmina's suicide one month later.

Act 2 continues with the third generation of Camerons, as Will Marshall once more assumes the duties of child rearing. Charles Cameron follows in his grandfather's footsteps in the sowing of his wild oats and in his genius for medical research. Like the ghosts of the past in Ibsen's plays, the present repeats the past. When Cameron cites the pressure of exams as the reason for his disorderly conduct and consequent arrest, Uncle Will provides the three pounds for his release, an amount similar to that which he had loaned Cameron's grandfather long ago.

After service in World War I, this third-generation Cameron, through both hard work and genius, eventually becomes a noted bacteriologist. At the age of fifty, he heads a medical research organization, the Walker Institute, financed by a wealthy relative, Sir Douglas Todd Walker. In his consistently blunt manner, he proposes marriage to Lady Katharine, saying that, if he wants descendants, he will have to hurry. Katharine, a worker who supplies the Institute with flowers, accepts, returning his bluntness in her acceptance.

Cameron's sister, Hope, appears on the scene from Geneva with a message from the League of Nations asking Cameron to expedite research on his cure for influenza. Both sister and brother have experienced the triumph of virtue over evil, even though it required three generations to do so. Old Will Marshall, now in his nineties, lives to see the rewards of his efforts. Vindicated, he comments to Hope at the play's end that "Charlie Cameron the First had the spark in his poor diseased body. Now lettest thou thy servant depart in peace. I did my best to keep the spark alive, and now it's a great flame in Charlie and in you. Humanity will warm its hands at you."

Bridie's view of genius as the divine force working through humankind is reflected in Katharine's comment that perhaps Cameron is a law of biology himself. God, like the sleeping clergyman in the two prologues, is removed from the immediate goings-on. Old Dr. Will Marshall, having lived ninety-seven years and having encouraged the spark of genius through three generations of Camerons, is a variation of the God principle. Like the sleeping clergyman, who is oblivious to his surroundings, Dr. Will has devoted nearly a lifetime to practicing status-quo medicine. Unlike the clergyman, however, he has nourished the genius in which he never loses faith.

In addition to the Ibsenite concern with heredity already mentioned, there is in Bridie's play the Shavian concern with a life force that works through genius, emerging in the medical breakthroughs by the Camerons in their contributions to civilization. Religious, not in the conventional doctrinaire sense but in his contribution to humankind, Cameron is the very essence of God. Bridie's God is a deistic entity that has provided human beings with laws and that has retired, like the sleeping clergyman, to a preprandial nap, to allow people to work out those laws. This working out of virtue is the personal and social morality of Bridie's plays. Weales claims that Bridie is one of the last two modern playwrights (Shaw is the other) to write religious plays based on a personal and unorthodox view of human beings' relationship to God.

The style of the play is as direct, unsentimental, and naturalistic as are the Camerons, whose disregard for the civilities of language and behavior provokes the censure of their conventional friends and relatives. Bridie's epic sweep of three generations has invited the criticism that the characters, particularly the supporting ones, are not fully developed.

THE QUEEN'S COMEDY

Two of Bridie's last plays are companion pieces that deal yet again with human beings' relationship to their God or gods. The first of the two, *The Queen's Comedy*, is a reworking of books 14 and 15 of Homer's *Iliad* (c. 750 B.C.E.; English translation, 1614). Produced in 1950, a year before Bridie's death, the play is dedicated to its director, Tyrone Guthrie, famous in both England and the United States. On the title page appears Gloucester's famous line from William Shakespeare's *King Lear* (pr. c. 1605-1606). "As flies to wanton boys are we to the gods: they kill us for their sport." The title of the play derives from the various goddesses' attitudes toward Jupiter, particularly toward his entanglement in the affairs of humankind. In a conversation with Minerva, Juno reflects on the absurdity of Jupiter changing himself into "swans and things," a reference to his love affair with Leda and, consequently, his peopling the whole world "with his little lapses—all demanding special consideration because of their remarkable parentage."

Reflecting the ravages of World War II, in which Bridie lost a son, the play modernizes Homer's view of the gods. Jupiter comments that it was "easier to make a Universe than to control it. It was full of mad, meaningless forces. I got most of them bound and fixed and working to rules and all a sudden I felt lonely. I felt that I would rather my mother had given me a puppydog or a kitten." An extension of the sleeping clergyman as a symbol for God, Jupiter feels helpless and, more to the point, is saddened by his inability to provide answers to the overriding questions of humankind's existence. It is this fact that humans discover when, slain on the battlefield of Troy, they reach Olympus. The gods in their personal habits and relationships are no better than humans. Bridie wrote this fiercely antiwar play at a time when his own deteriorating health intensified his awareness of the bleakness that pervaded postwar Great Britain.

THE BAIKIE CHARIVARI

If *The Queen's Comedy* is about the relationship between God and humankind, its companion piece, *The Baikie Charivari*, is an allegory about the relationship between human beings and the devils that besiege them during their lives. The play can be seen as Bridie's final comment on his lifelong concern with good and evil forces at work in people's lives. Produced the year after his death, the drama bears an interesting resemblance to his first professionally produced play, *The Sunlight Sonata*. Like the Seven Deadly Sins of that earlier play, seven devils confront Sir James MacArthur Pounce-Pellott, the lead-ing character, whose name is derived from that of Pontius Pilate and the comic character, Punch, of magazine fame. His wife's name is Judy, and they have a daughter whom they still call Baby, even though she is of marriageable age. Pounce-Pellott has returned to the town of Baikie on the Clyde Estuary in Scotland to retire at the age of fifty. He has spent his life in the British Civil Service in Junglipore, India.

In the surrealistic prologue, the Devil appears as a mask in the moon and speaks to a beadle, the Reverend Marcus Beadle, and to a local police officer, Robert Copper. The names of the Baikie residents, like those of the characters in a medieval morality play, symbolize their professions or qualities. In the style of the Book of Job in the Old Testament, the Devil inquires of Beadle and Copper, "Have ye considered my servant Pounce-Pellott?" When the cock crows and the Devil vanishes, Pounce-Pellott appears, a good-looking man in his fifties, announcing himself as "Knight Commander of the Indian Empire, King of Ghosts and Shadows, sometimes District Commander of Junglipore and other places."

Like Faust in his quest for wisdom, Pounce-Pellott wishes to be educated in the knowledge of the West. To this end, various neighbors (and a woman from America) appear as his teachers: the Reverend James Beadle (religion), Robert Copper (law), Councillor John Ketch (sociology, labor, and left-wing thinking), Joe Mascara (art), Dr. Jean Pothecary (psychiatry), Lady Maggie Revenant (the old aristocratic order, actually a ghost from the past), and Mrs. Jemima Lee Crowe (an American publisher who offers Pounce-Pellott money for his memoirs). These figures represent the current wisdom of the West.

In the end, Pounce-Pellott, like his predecessor Pilate, washes his hands of them all and, asking for his stick, kills them all, except Lady Maggie, whom he cannot kill because she is a ghost. The Devil reappears, announcing that only time will tell whether he has been defeated. He vanishes, and Pounce-Pellott reflects on his inability to answer the riddle of life. He does know, however, that he killed those who pretended to know. Like Cameron of *A Sleeping Clergy-*

man, he knows that he cannot know and also that he cannot stop seeking to know.

The tone of the play shifts between the surrealism of scenes such as that in which the Devil appears to Pounce-Pellott and the ironic comedy of a Punch-and-Judy world, in which the realistic antics of his wife, daughter, and the seven representatives of Western wisdom are observed by Pounce-Pellott. As the play progresses to its conclusion in the form of arguments presented by the seven teachers, the prosaic style subtly gives way to poetic and lyric passages.

As a final, highly poetic statement, *The Baikie Charivari* is a sophisticated extension of Bridie's life-long moral earnestness and a paean to the necessary effort of the human spirit to extend virtue, not in any narrow dogmatic sense or through high-flown idealism, but in the dogged persistence with which a rational humanism can create some order out of chaos, even out of the remnants of civilization left in the wake of a Trojan War or a World War II.

NO THIRD ACT

Responding to the long-standing criticism that he had difficulty in concluding a play, Bridie, at the close of *One Way of Living*, writes: "Only God can write a third act, and He seldom does." Bridie expresses his anger at "doctrinaire duds" and insists that audiences should leave the theater with their heads "whirling with speculation" and "selecting infinite possibilities for the characters . . . seen onstage." These possibilities find focus from time to time in men of genius such as Charles Cameron of *A Sleeping Clergyman* and Pounce-Pellott of *The Baikie Charivari*, who can stand alone if necessary. The miracle, mystery, and morality plays of medieval times are given contemporary significance in Bridie's theater, in that it is the miracle of individuated person that gives meaning to the existence of a Maker. As reflected in the very structure of Bridie's plays, there is no concluding "third act" to humanity's Faustian effort to work miracles on earth.

OTHER MAJOR WORKS

RADIO PLAY: *The Sign of the Prophet Jonah*, 1942 (based on his play *Jonah and the Whale*).

NONFICTION: *Some Talk of Alexander*, 1926; *Mr. Bridie's Alphabet for Little Glasgow Highbrows*, 1934; *One Way of Living*, 1939; *The British Drama*, 1945; *A Small Stir: Letters on the English*, 1949 (with Moray McLaren).

MISCELLANEOUS: *Tedious and Brief*, 1944.

BIBLIOGRAPHY

Low, John Thomas. *Doctors, Devils, Saints, and Sinners: A Critical Study of the Major Plays of James Bridie*. Edinburgh, Scotland: Ramsay Head Press, 1980. An examination of the dramatic works of Bridie. Bibliography and index.

Mavor, Ronald. *Dr. Mavor and Mr. Bridie: Memories of James Bridie*. Edinburgh, Scotland: Canongate, 1988. A biography of Bridie from a personal viewpoint. Analysis of dramatic works is included.

Tobin, Terence. *James Bridie*. Boston: Twayne, 1980. A chronological analysis of the complete multifaceted works of Bridie as a Renaissance man of the first half of the twentieth century. Includes a photograph, a chronology, a bibliography, and an index.

Susan Rusinko

EUGÈNE BRIEUX

Born: Paris, France; January 19, 1858
Died: Nice, France; December 6, 1932

PRINCIPAL DRAMA

Bernard Palissy, pr. 1879, pb. 1880 (with Gaston Salandri)
Le Bureau des divorces, pb. 1880 (with Salandri)
Ménages d'artistes, pr., pb. 1890 (*Artists' Families*, 1918)
La Fille de Duramé, pr., pb. 1890
M. de Réboval, pr., pb. 1892
Blanchette, pr., pb. 1892 (English translation, 1913)
La Couvée, pr. 1893 (privately), pr. 1903, pb. 1904
L'Engrenage, pr., pb. 1894
La Rose bleue, pr., pb. 1895
Les Bienfaiteurs, pr. 1896, pb. 1897
L'Évasion, pr. 1896, pb. 1897 (*The Escape*, 1913)
Les Trois Filles de M. Dupont, pr. 1897, pb. 1899 (*The Three Daughters of M. Dupont*, 1911)
L'École des belles-mères, pr., pb. 1898 (adaptation of his *La Couvée*)
Résultat des courses, pr., pb. 1898 (six tableaux)
Le Berceau, pr., pb. 1898

La Robe rouge, pr., pb. 1900 (*The Red Robe*, 1915)
Les Remplaçantes, pr., pb. 1901
Les Avariés, pr., pb. 1902 (*Damaged Goods*, 1911)
La Petite Amie, pr., pb. 1902
Maternité, pr. 1903, pb. 1904 (*Maternity*, 1907)
La Déserteuse, pr., pb. 1904 (with Jean Sigaux)
L'Armature, pr., pb. 1905 (adaptation of Paul Hervieu's novel)
Les Hannetons, pr., pb. 1906
La Française, pr., pb. 1907
Simone, pr., pb. 1908
La Foi, pr. 1909, pb. 1912 (*False Gods*, 1916)
Suzette, pr., pb. 1909
Three Plays, pb. 1911
La Femme seule, pr. 1912, pb. 1913 (*Woman on Her Own*, 1916)
Les Américains chez nous, pr., pb. 1920
Trois Bon Amis, pr., pb. 1921
L'Avocat, pr., pb. 1922
Pierrette et Galaor, pr., pb. 1923 (also known as *L'Enfant*)
La Famille Lavolette, pr., pb. 1926
Puisque je t'aime!, pr., pb. 1929
La Régence, pb. 1929

OTHER LITERARY FORMS

Eugéne Brieux abandoned a career as a journalist to devote himself to the writing of plays, for which he is best known.

ACHIEVEMENTS

In a preface to a volume of Eugène Brieux's plays in translation, George Bernard Shaw claimed for the dramatist the distinction of being the greatest French writer since Molière in the genre of true-to-life comedy. A lesser dramatist-critic, Ashley Dukes, taking an opposite view, considered Brieux's plays to be the work of a dullard. Shaw's extravagant praise is as wide of the mark as is Dukes's less-than-generous dismissal. Brieux's social dramas, with their focus on the stultifying and frequently destructive life of the French bourgeoisie and peasantry, evoked a sharp response from that same middle class he zealously criticized and frequently satirized. Although linked at times with the intellectual elite championed by the theatrical reformer André Antoine at his Théâtre Li-

Eugène Brieux (courtesy of New York Public Library)

bre, Brieux's works rarely verged on the bitterly cynical *comédie rosse*, the biting comedy so favored by the patrons of Antoine's avant-garde stronghold. Instead, Brieux found himself more at home in the popular theaters of the Paris boulevards, where he reached a wider audience. If that popularity was achieved by an occasional sentimentalizing of serious subject matter, Brieux nevertheless brought before his public several works that outspokenly underscored the dehumanizing effects of the dowry system in arranged marriages, a barbaric judicial system designed to benefit its practitioners rather than those unfortunates wrongly brought to trial, and the widespread ignorance concerning venereal disease.

To Brieux's credit, his works may well have played a part in social reforms of the period, most specifically in the passage of a law in several countries requiring blood tests of prospective partners in marriage. Less to his credit, a modern sensibility might well be offended by his ambiguous stand concerning universal suffrage, the employment of women, the worth of education, and the value of religion as a comfort to the masses. In an age of rapid social change, Brieux was in fact a conservative who chose to concentrate on the more obvious shortcomings of his own society. That conservatism was reflected by his election to the staid French Academy.

Like Alexandre Dumas, *fils*, Émile Augier, and Émile Zola, the writers who influenced him most, Brieux considered the theater a valid weapon for social reform. Like Eugène Scribe, on the other hand, he managed to entertain, even placate, middle-class audiences, who for a time flocked to his plays despite those works' serious intentions. Following World War I, however, Brieux's narrow concerns seemed petty compared with the universal problems of a world attempting to maintain a shaky peace and find its way toward economic recovery. He lost the obsessive reformer's drive that fueled his creativity, and his popularity waned. His plays have come to be neglected by all but the most dedicated students of the naturalistic style in the turn-of-the-century French theater. Despite a rare ability to humanize his characters of lowly station, a knack for finding genuine comedy in dramatic confrontations, and a startling honesty in depicting relations between the sexes, Brieux as a dramatist is remembered as an awkwardly moralizing clinician and outdated reformer, judged on the basis of a single play, *Damaged Goods*, which is, in fact, inferior to much of his output.

BIOGRAPHY

Eugène Brieux firmly believed that the public need know only a man's work, not the man himself. Even during the last decade of the nineteenth century and the first decade of the twentieth, the years of his greatest popularity, Brieux shunned the limelight. Typically, after his initial acclaim and good fortune enabled him to purchase a house on the Riviera, Brieux chose to move his residence as soon as a new road provided the curious with easy access to him. As a result of his retiring attitude, little is known concerning his formative years.

Brieux was born in Paris in 1858 into a working-class family, the son of a carpenter. Orphaned at the age of fourteen, he received little formal schooling. An avid reader, he attempted to educate himself, but his plan to follow prescribed school curriculum came to an end when Greek proved an insurmountable obstacle. Attempting to make ends meet as a clerk, he frequently read by lamplight or in the dimly lit hall of the building in which he lived.

A century earlier, Brieux would have become a preacher, he once observed; for a time, he decided to follow the life of a missionary. That missionary zeal Brieux eventually channeled into his writing. Interested in the dramatic literature of his time, especially the thesis plays of Augier, he believed that he could make a lasting mark as a dramatist. He submitted some of his early efforts both to Augier and to Zola but received no encouragement from either. To earn a living as a writer, he worked for various newspapers, at last settling in Rouen, where eventually he became editor of *La Nouvelliste de Rouen*.

During this period, Brieux continued to send manuscripts of his plays to theatrical producers. Only *Bernard Palissy*, a one-act verse play written in collaboration with Gaston Salandri, was accepted; it was performed once, at the Théâtre Cluny in Paris, in 1879. Brieux was unable to place another with a Parisian management for more than a decade, although a few of his plays received productions in Rouen. Finally, his *Artists' Families*, a clumsy satire exposing the hollowness of the decadent literary movement, attracted some attention in a production at Antoine's Théâtre Libre in 1890, and Brieux's career was launched.

Antoine was responsible for Brieux's first major success when he presented *Blanchette* in 1892, still perhaps his most popular work in his native country. This success enabled the dramatist to move to Paris from Rouen, but he admitted afterward that his provincial life in a small town had been the best preparation for a writing career devoted to the exploration of the life of the bourgeoisie. Soon he was presenting a loyal public with a new play almost every year under various managements, including the Comédie-Française. In 1910, he achieved one of his earliest ambitions, membership in the French Academy, having by then already been named a commander of the Legion of Honor. In 1913, he was offered the directorship of the Comédie-Française but refused the position in order to continue his own writing. In translation, some of his more forthright works ran afoul of the censors in England and the United States, but, with the aid of Shaw's energetic backing, he eventually became not merely a favorite of French theatergoers, but also a dramatist of repute abroad.

During World War I, as president of the French Committee for the Blind, Brieux devoted himself to the rehabilitation of French soldiers blinded in battle, while his energies as a dramatist diminished considerably. As a writer, he seemed no longer to be stimulated by the challenge of new causes, and his later works lack the urgency of his better plays before the war. As new plays by Brieux appeared with less frequency to diminishing acclaim, his reputation dwindled as well. His successful earlier works, however, enabled him to live comfortably during his final years. Suffering for several weeks from pleurisy and confined to a wheelchair, he asked, on December 6, 1932, to be wheeled onto the balcony of his villa overlooking the Mediterranean near Nice. Lapsing into a coma, he died shortly afterward.

ANALYSIS

With the exception of a few early plays—*Bernard Palissy* and *La Fille de Duramé* as well as *False Gods*, a later play set in ancient Egypt—all Eugène Brieux's more than thirty plays have contemporary settings, and each one focuses on a different social question. Believing in the perfectibility of humanity, Brieux attempted, through dramatization, to eradicate every social evil he encountered. As a result, the initial impulse for each of his plays was a thesis. The better works successfully dramatize the thesis by placing sympathetic and believable characters who are the victims of a particular evil in an intriguing, sometimes comic, but always highly dramatic situation. The least successful artistically are the works that remain leadenly didactic, in which the situation does not stem from characters but instead provides a platform for the espousal of an idea. Brieux's righteous indignation often overwhelms an otherwise entertaining, frequently moving drama, the point of which might have been more effective if made with greater subtlety.

BLANCHETTE

Among Brieux's least didactic plays is his first critical and popular success, *Blanchette*, but its three variant endings pinpoint the dramatist's recurring weakness. That the play can end in any of three ways underscores its arbitrary structure. The characters are well drawn, with delicacy and affection, but their actions ultimately do not dictate their fates. Blanchette may end up miserably as a prostitute, may return home a wealthy man's mistress, or may remain undefiled to become the bride of a local wheelwright. Brieux's attempt to win popular success, rather than to create a sense of logic in his heroine's inherent traits, seems to have dictated the eventual course of the play.

Blanchette affectionately depicts the lives of the Rousset family, who barely make a living from the rural tavern they run and the small tract of land they farm. They have sacrificed to send their only child, Blanchette, to school to earn a teaching certificate, but their daughter is low on the list of those waiting to be hired. The state, it seems, trains more teachers than it can use, and the waiting period may last more than a year. In the meantime, Blanchette, now educated above her station, has come to loathe the peasants among whom she lives and is even embarrassed by her parents. She spends her days reading romantic novels and dreaming about marrying a wealthy young man who will allow her to turn his elegant home into a fashionable salon. Until her daydreams come true, she plans at least to turn the tavern into a more suitable café. When her father strikes her in the midst of an angry argument over her gross miscalculation with a fertilizer that has burned their land and her deliberate breaking of a lamp, Blanchette decides that her existence has become intolerable. She goes off to make a new life for herself.

Blanchette's leavetaking, which takes place at the end of the second act, makes a suitable ending for the play. Brieux makes his point, that education ought to have some practical end, without belaboring it. Neither Antoine, who presented the work at his Théâtre Libre, nor the author himself was particularly pleased with any of the three third acts that Brieux eventually provided for the play; indeed, Antoine frequently presented only the first two acts of the play. The original third act, the most pessimistic, with Blanchette ending up a prostitute, is out of keeping with the tone of the rest, but Brieux considered it to be in line with the pessimistic view of most of the plays at Antoine's theater. His own earlier play there, *Artists' Families*, had also ended on a negative note with the unprepared-for and unlikely suicide of its protagonist. *Blanchette*, however, despite an earnest thesis, is a play of charm and humor. No audience would care to see the Roussets suffer, for they are sympathetic and sensible, good-hearted peasants, if somewhat bewildered by their moody daughter. Blanchette is at times an infuriating and unfeeling young lady, but an audience understands her frustrations and winces along with her as her father embarrasses her in front of others. Yet the play's final and best-known version, in which Blanchette accepts the marriage proposal of a young worker of equal class, is overly sentimental.

Brieux veered from an ending as dark as that of the usual *comédie rosse* of the Théâtre Libre to an ending light enough to have been dictated by a boulevard audience. The revised *Blanchette* kept playgoers happy but enabled them to overlook the very point of the play. Brieux would not make that mistake again. After *Blanchette*'s success, he had no need ever again to cater to an audience's whim.

THE THREE DAUGHTERS OF M. DUPONT

The Three Daughters of M. Dupont and *The Red Robe* represent Brieux at his best, successfully mingling satiric comedy with effective melodrama to argue a worthy thesis. A shifting focus of attention is a weakness of both plays, but intriguing character and situation hold an audience's interest throughout.

The first act of *The Three Daughters of M. Dupont* reveals Brieux as a skillful comic satirist as two sets of parents settle the terms of a dowry. The Duponts' youngest daughter, Julie, is to marry Antonin, the son of M. and Mme Mairaut. While the parents of the one pretend to know little of the financial situation of the other, the truth of the matter is that all concerned have done their homework, and each family knows exactly how much the other is worth. When M. Dupont, a printer in a provincial town, offers to add his country home to his daughter's dowry, Mme Mairaut, the wife of the local banker, immediately points out that the house in question is flooded for two months each year. M. Dupont makes outrageous statements that startle even his wife, while poor, henpecked M. Mairaut is hardly permitted by his domineering wife to enter the conversation. Brieux at first creates amusing situations at the expense of the one-dimensionally drawn parents. Both the Duponts and the Mairauts are thoroughly convinced that they have effectively swindled each other. As the play's tone changes from farce to serious drama, however, the audience is made aware that the real victim is Julie, who is being bartered as a commodity and condemned to a life of misery.

The practice of arranged marriages based on financial settlements was Brieux's target. A sensitive and intelligent twenty-four-year-old young woman is locked into marriage with an insensitive and materialistic boor who can never know her worth. Julie and Antonin share no common ground and cannot even communicate with each other. Neither makes any fruitful attempt to come to know, to understand, the other. Julie realizes that she will never love her hus-

band, whereas Antonin confuses love with his sexual desire for his attractive bride. In the play's most extraordinary and powerful scene, one which rivals in impact the final scene of Henrik Ibsen's *Et dukkehjem* (1879; *A Doll's House*, 1880), husband and wife finally speak openly to each other and admit the failure of their marriage. With daring honesty, Brieux has Julie express her revulsion at her husband's sexual advances, which gives way to revulsion with herself for accepting those advances, which in turn awaken her own animal desires. Julie's wish for children of her own has kept her at her husband's side. When Antonin, however, reveals his determination to remain childless, Julie prepares to leave him.

What slightly weakens an otherwise effective drama is Brieux's attempt to widen his scope by dramatizing the plight of other women who are victims of a constricting provincial society. Julie's stepsisters, too, suffer at society's hands. Caroline, a pathetic spinster, must work for a living, painting flowers on china, and is an embarrassment to her family. Her older sister, Angèle, was driven from their home years before for entering into an unsanctified liaison with a man and eventually, like so many unhappy heroines of French drama, drifted into prostitution. Caroline and Angèle are conventional figures of the drama. Julie, on the other hand, is a character of depth in the process of self-discovery. The action falters when the focus shifts to her sisters, whom Brieux has included so that Julie will learn from their unhappy predicaments. As the play ends, Julie comes to understand, as Ibsen's Nora does not, that she has no choice but to return to her husband. In his resolution, Brieux, undercutting his stance as reformer, displays his conventional attitudes toward marriage but tempers them with the suggestion that Julie may take a lover.

THE RED ROBE

As a journalist covering court trials in Rouen, Brieux was sometimes appalled by the slow workings and complications of the machinery of justice. Innocent and guilty alike were victims of a system that they could not fully comprehend, a system fueled at times by the greed and the ambitions of those public servants expressly appointed to uphold the laws of the state. In *The Red Robe*, Brieux exposed the inhumanity of an officialdom that could force a split between the law and actual justice. Considered by some critics to be the dramatist's best work, the play contains one of Brieux's most masterful scenes but is less cohesive than *The Three Daughters of M. Dupont* as it veers from satire to melodrama.

Set in a small town in the Pyrenees (which enabled Brieux to contrast hardworking Basque peasants, who have a language and customs of their own, with the more sophisticated men from other parts of the country, who dispense justice to them), *The Red Robe* begins in the home of the public prosecutor of a district of the third class, who has for years been denied promotion to the post of counselor in the Court of Appeal. Vagret would wear the red robe to which the higher rank would entitle him, but he has never won a trial in which the defendant has received a life sentence. He believes that his time is approaching, for an old man has been murdered and the culprit will surely be sentenced to death. Mouzon, a young man with no scruples who knows the ins and outs of political maneuvering, has been appointed examining magistrate in the case and is determined to bring to trial a local peasant who owed the victim a vast sum of money. Etchepare, the peasant, is in fact innocent, but, in order to avoid being indicted, lies about his whereabouts on the night of the murder and is caught in his lies. In the play's strongest scene, Mouzon cruelly plays cat and mouse with Etchepare and his wife, Yanetta, nearly causing the accused man to confess to the crime that he has not committed and the wife, who would protect him, to seal his doom with some damaging testimony.

At the trial itself, Yanetta's sordid past is revealed for the first time to her loving husband, and Vagret, the prosecutor, is at the point of winning a conviction against Etchepare when he is assailed by serious doubts. Realizing that he is more concerned with besting the defense attorney in a contest of orators than in seeing justice done, Vagret admits his doubts to the jury, and the peasant is acquitted. After the trial, when it is disclosed that Mouzon, despite being unfit for the post, has been made the new counselor in the Court of Appeal because of his connections, Vagret can take his disappointment in stride.

For once, he has acted as a man, not as a magistrate. Ironically, it is left to Yanetta to mete out justice in the end. Deserted by her husband, who cannot forgive her for her waywardness before their marriage, and denied her home and family, she confronts Mouzon with the wreckage of her life. When Mouzon insists that the law owes her nothing, she stabs him to death.

Once again, a structural weakness is evident in the play. The satiric comedy of the first act, when Vagret tries on the red robe that his frustrated wife has been saving for him for years, gives way to the melodrama of the scenes involving the despicable Mouzon. In addition, Vagret's change of heart, so crucial to the play's resolution, is not convincingly motivated. Brieux is also guilty of drawing his characters with overly broad strokes. Despite their acknowledged wrongdoings in the past, the peasants are men and women of integrity, whereas the officials of the court call to mind the venal cartoon figures of the French satiric painter Honoré Daumier. Nevertheless, in underscoring the discrepancies between law and justice and exposing people's inhumanity in dealing with other people, Brieux transforms social protest into viable and, at least in one scene, enthralling drama.

DAMAGED GOODS

Damaged Goods, unfortunately the play for which Brieux is best known, demonstrates a lapse in craft. Here, didacticism overpowers drama, and what results is an earnest illustrated lecture not only on the dreadful consequences of venereal disease but also on the harm caused by widespread ignorance concerning the taboo subject. The protagonist disappears after act 2, and the focus then shifts to the *raisonneur*, the author's spokesperson, a doctor whose lecture on venereal disease and its social consequence makes up nearly all of act 3. That a worldwide audience heeded what amounted to an illustrated lecture was a tribute more to the author's timeliness and daring than to his dramatic skill.

Informed by his doctor that he has contracted syphilis, George Dupont reveals that he is soon to be married. Because he intends to use the dowry to buy a notary's practice, he does not wish to delay the ceremony for the three-year period the doctor insists is necessary to be certain of his cure. Despite the doctor's warnings of the danger to his wife and the children she may bear, George postpones the wedding for only six months, under the treatment of another doctor who promises a rapid cure. He allays any concerns his bride's family might have by telling them that he is being treated, successfully, for tuberculosis.

The original doctor was correct in his diagnosis and prognosis for a cure, and the first child of George and Henriette is born syphilitic. Once George's mother learns the truth, she tries to hide the facts from Henriette and the baby's wet nurse, even though the doctor has told her of the possible consequences to the nurse and her family. To Mme Dupont, the well-being of the child is the only concern, and she refuses to allow the baby to be put on the bottle. The nurse's suspicions are aroused, however, and when she confronts George and his mother, Henriette overhears the argument and, as the second act ends, is mortified by the revelation.

In act 3, the play breaks down completely. In Brieux's most flagrant violation of logical dramatic structure, neither George nor his wife nor his mother appears. What ensues is a dialogue between the doctor and Henriette's father, a deputy of government, concerning the responsibilities not only of prospective couples but also of their parents, and even the state, which has a duty to combat the misconceptions about the diseases of syphilis, tuberculosis, and alcoholism. After pointing out to the deputy his own negligence in having investigated his son-in-law's finances but not his health, the doctor offers the hope that, should Henriette and George remain together, they may eventually be cured and bring healthy children into the world. The play, however, does not end on an entirely optimistic note. The doctor introduces the deputy to two female syphilitics and the father of an eighteen-year-old boy paralyzed by the disease. After the three have recounted their pathetic experiences, the doctor bids Henriette's father farewell, cautioning him to remember what he has just seen and heard as he takes his seat in the government chamber, so that their conversation will not have been a waste of time.

Because of its daring subject matter—treated, for once, factually and honestly, although with little dramatic skill—*Damaged Goods* became a *cause célèbre* in its time, and once the censors allowed public performances, it offered something in the nature of a religious experience. Originally banned in Paris, *Damaged Goods* was read by Brieux himself to an invited audience of public officials and doctors on November 1, 1901. In 1902, Antoine was finally permitted to produce the play in Paris. To assure audiences that they were not participating in an immoral act, he introduced the performances himself by announcing from the stage the play's serious intent and stressing the fact that it contained no obscene word or action, a practice generally continued by producers of the play in England and the United States.

The first performance in the United States took place on March 14, 1913, at the Fulton Theater in New York, before members of the Sociological Fund. Before presenting it for a regular run, the producer, Richard Bennett, arranged for a performance on a Sunday afternoon, April 6, at the National Theater in Washington, D.C., before an invited audience of Cabinet members, members of both houses of Congress, justices of the Supreme Court, representatives of the diplomatic corps, and prominent Washington clergymen. The performance was introduced by the pastor of the First Presbyterian Church, who stressed the sacredness of the occasion, likening the play to a sermon on behalf of humankind. These words were followed by a request to the audience by the pastor of the Vermont Avenue Christian Church to bow their heads in prayer. That same year, the play was made available to nontheatergoers in a faithful novelization by Upton Sinclair with the permission of the original author.

The widely proclaimed insistence on the play as a moral act led to inordinate press coverage wherever the drama was performed. As a result, it is not surprising that Brieux became known quite simply as the author of *Damaged Goods*. The translation of the play into a sermon could not, however, hide its obvious flaws. A comparison with Ibsen's *Gengangere* (pb. 1881; *Ghosts*, 1885) makes clear the shortcomings of *Damaged Goods* and the reason for the present neglect of its author's dramatic works. In *Ghosts*, a timeless play, Ibsen makes use of venereal disease as a metaphor for the constricting hold of the past on the present. Brieux's *Damaged Goods*, on the other hand, is a clinical discussion *about* venereal disease. Like so much of his work, it is a thesis play, the thesis of which is now sadly out of date.

BIBLIOGRAPHY

Cardy, Michael, and Derek Cannon, eds. *Aspects of Twentieth Century Theatre in France*. New York: Peter Lang, 2000. Provides context in which to understand Brieux's later works.

SantaVicca, Edmund F. *Four French Dramatists: A Bibliography of Criticism of the Works of Eugène Brieux, François de Curel, Émile Fabre, Paul Hervieu*. Metuchen, N.J.: Scarecrow Press, 1974. A bibliography on the criticism of Brieux, among other French writers. Index.

Albert E. Kalson

RICHARD BROME

Born: England; c. 1590
Died: England; c. 1652-1653

PRINCIPAL DRAMA

Christianetta, pr. 1623? (with George Chapman?; no longer extant)

A Fault in Friendship, pr. 1623 (with "Young Johnson"; no longer extant)

The Love-sick Maid: Or, The Honor of Young Ladies, pr. 1629 (no longer extant)

The Northern Lass, pr. 1629, pb. 1632

The City Wit: Or, The Woman Wears the Breeches, pr. c. 1629, pb. 1653

The Queen's Exchange, pr. 1631-1632(?), pb. 1657

The Novella, pr. 1632, pb. 1653

The Covent-Garden Weeded, pr. 1632, pb. 1659

The Love-sick Court: Or, The Ambitious Politique, pr. 1633-1634(?), pb. 1659

The Late Lancashire Witches, pr., pb. 1634 (with Thomas Heywood)

The Life and Death of Sir Martin Skink, pr. c. 1634 (with Heywood; no longer extant)

The Apprentice's Prize, pr. c. 1634 (with Heywood?; no longer extant)

The Sparagus Garden, pr. 1635, pb. 1640

The New Academy: Or, The New Exchange, pr. 1635(?), pb. 1659

The Queen and the Concubine, pr. 1635-1636(?), pb. 1659

The Jewish Gentleman, pr. 1636(?); (no longer extant)

The English Moor: Or, The Mock-Marriage, pr. 1637, pb. 1659

The Antipodes, pr. 1638, pb. 1640

The Damoiselle: Or, The New Ordinary, pr. 1638(?), pb. 1653

Wit in Madness, pr. 1638-1639(?); (no longer extant)

A Mad Couple Well Matched, pr. 1639, pb. 1653

The Court Beggar, pr. 1640, pb. 1653

A Jovial Crew: Or, The Merry Beggars, pr. 1641, pb. 1652

OTHER LITERARY FORMS

Besides plays, Richard Brome wrote only some brief commendatory poems attached to other writers' collections of poetry or plays. He also edited John Fletcher's play *Monsieur Thomas* (pr. 1610-1616, pb. 1639) and probably edited *Lachrymae Musarum: The Tears of the Muses* (1649), a collection of elegies, to which Brome contributed, on the death of Henry Hastings in 1645.

ACHIEVEMENTS

The reputation of Caroline playwright Richard Brome has generally been haunted by some ambiguity or doubt. During his own time, Brome was extremely popular, but even then his success was marred by criticisms that he pandered to his audience's poor tastes. Such criticisms might have been motivated to some extent by irrelevant factors, such as envy of his success and scorn for his humble background as a servant. His popularity continued during the Restoration, when his work influenced the form of Restoration comedy, and lasted into the eighteenth century. During the Victorian period, Brome was roundly condemned as the most obscene of the Renaissance dramatists and frequently contrasted with Ben Jonson—Jonson and Brome, respectively, epitomizing a "good" versus a "bad" comic dramatist. Again, irrelevant factors appear to have clouded the critical estimates of Brome.

Brome's ambiguous reputation has continued into the modern period, when he has been known as the most outstanding minor Caroline dramatist, but his status has also been on the rise. Kathleen Lynch demonstrated that Brome is an important link between Renaissance and Restoration comedy in *The Social Mode of Restoration Comedy* (1926), and R. J. Kaufmann valued Brome's work as an accurate reflection of Brome's time, a pivotal period in English history, in *Richard Brome: Caroline Playwright* (1961). Brome, however, is not merely of historical interest: His plays, particularly his best works, are still entertaining, and the social conditions he depicts bear some close resemblances to conditions today. T. S. Eliot believed that Brome should be read more, and Catherine M. Shaw, Brome's latest chronicler, in her book *Richard Brome* (1980), states that his plays could be revived onstage.

A highly professional playwright, eclectic and practical, Brome had the ability to judge public taste and had the theatrical skills to satisfy it—through his use of both satiric and romantic elements, his plotting, his characters, and his language. Of these, his characters are perhaps most appealing today, offering an engaging cross section of Caroline England. Brome's diversity of characters resembles Jonson's, but unlike Jonson, Brome seems to like his characters: His satire is tolerant rather than indignant or disgusted.

Also appealing is Brome's style. It is clear and direct, easy to follow, already anticipating the Restoration style, which T. S. Eliot called the first "modern" style. At the same time, it retains some of the old Renaissance figurative richness. Finally, Brome had an excellent ear for conversation, including cant, dialects, and speech mannerisms. The resulting blend is a particularly effective style for the theater. Brome's style is another indication that he was in tune with the theater and with his time.

Brome's success was consistent throughout his career, beginning with the early plays *The Love-sick Maid* (now lost) and *The Northern Lass*, but his art improved as he went along. To modern tastes, his best plays might include *The Covent-Garden Weeded* and *The Sparagus Garden*, written near the midpoint of his career, and *The Antipodes*, *A Mad Couple Well Matched*, and *A Jovial Crew*, written near the end. *A Jovial Crew* has generally been the favorite.

BIOGRAPHY

Little is known of Richard Brome's personal life, including date and place of birth and death. The conventionally accepted estimate of his birth date is 1590, but evidence for the date is scanty: In 1591, a Richard Brome was listed as the son of Henry Brome in the St. James Clerkenwell parish register, and depositions in 1639 and 1640 Chancery Court suits identified a Richard Brome "aged 50 years or thereabouts." Whether these records refer to Richard Brome the playwright is uncertain, since marriage and burial records of the period indicate several Richard Bromes in the London area alone. For the same reason, Brome's marriage and family relationships cannot be clearly identified, though he did apparently marry and rear a family: In 1640, he complained that the Salisbury Court Theatre's refusal to pay him caused him and his family to suffer hardship. His death can be pinned down only to the years 1652-1653.

Much more interesting information is available on Brome's career as a playwright. The most interesting fact is that, before becoming a playwright, Brome was the servant of Ben Jonson, a leading playwright and the main theorist of Renaissance English drama. The introduction of Jonson's comedy *Bartholomew Fair* (pr. 1614) refers to "his man, Master Broome, behind the arras," and Jonson wrote a commendatory poem for Brome's *The Northern Lass* that includes the following lines:

> I had you for a servant, once, Dick Brome;
> And you performed a servant's faithful parts.
> Now, you are got into a nearer room,
> Of fellowship, professing my old arts.
> And you do do them well, with good applause,
> Which you have justly gained from the stage,
> By observation of those comic laws
> Which I, your master, first did teach the age.
> You learned it well, and for it served your time
> A prenticeship: which few do nowadays. . . .

Similarly, Brome gratefully acknowledged Jonson's influence and tutelage, proud to be one of the "Sons of Ben."

How well Brome learned from his mentor is indicated by an incident that occurred in 1629. That year, Jonson's *The New Inn* failed miserably at the Blackfriars Theatre. Shortly afterward, the same company and theater presented Brome's *The Love-sick Maid*—to extraordinarily popular acclaim. Jonson was so upset that, in "Ben Jonson's Ode to Himself," he blasted popular taste in the theater, complaining that "Broom's sweepings do as well/ There as his master's meal." Other Sons of Ben seconded their master with puns on Brome's name and status and with allusions to the sweepings or dregs he was serving up. Apparently this incident ruffled Jonson and Brome's relationship only briefly, however, since Jonson left out the snide allusion to Brome when he published his ode in 1631, and in 1632, Jonson wrote his commendatory verses to Brome's *The Northern Lass.*

The coincidence of Jonson's failure and Brome's success in 1629 also indicates that Brome learned from other contemporary playwrights besides his mentor. Brome collaborated with Thomas Heywood and possibly with George Chapman, and a number of fellow dramatists, including James Shirley and John Ford, who wrote commendatory verses for Brome's works. In addition, Brome's work shows the influence of still other playwrights, such as John Fletcher, Francis Beaumont, and Philip Massinger. These collaborations, commendations, and influences confirm that, if Jonson was Brome's mentor, Brome was also widely acquainted with other dramatists and their work.

Such a view of Brome is further supported by his associations with various companies and theaters. His early play with "Young Johnson," *A Fault in Friendship* (now lost), was produced by the Prince's Company, probably at the Red Bull Theatre. In 1628, Brome was listed with the Queen of Bohemia's Players, who apparently toured the provinces and sometimes acted at the Red Bull Theatre in London (whether Brome was an actor for the company is in dispute). From 1629 to 1634, Brome wrote for the King's Men, the leading troupe in London and also Jonson's company, which produced Brome's work at court and at the Globe and Blackfriars theaters. In 1635, Brome returned briefly to the Prince's Company at the Red Bull, then signed a three-year contract to write for the King's Revels (later Queen Henrietta's Men) at the Salisbury Court Theatre. Brome found this association unsatisfactory—there was a dispute about proper payment—and did not sign a new seven-year contract with Salisbury Court Theatre when it was offered to him in 1638. Instead, in 1639 he moved over to write for Beeston's Boys at the Cockpit Theatre—a happy association that continued until the end of Brome's career.

Brome's career ended abruptly, at its height, when the English Civil War started in 1642 and Parliament closed all the theaters. A creature of the theater, Brome lived on, sadly and in poverty, until 1652 or 1653. Appropriately, his last known literary effort involved a collection of elegies entitled *Lachrymae Musarum.*

ANALYSIS

As R. J. Kaufmann observes, Richard Brome's work forms "an intelligible and complex commentary on a central phase of an historical evolutionary process." That historical process, though highly complex itself, with its many social, religious, and nationalistic side issues, can be briefly summarized as the growing challenge of the English middle class to the old aristocratic order. Although individuals did not line up neatly, the middle class as a group found its symbol of power in Parliament, while the king was the figurehead of the old order. The middle class also leaned toward the Puritan sects, while the aristocracy generally hewed to the established Anglican Church. These deep-rooted tensions and others came to a head during the ill-fated reign of Charles I, from 1625 to 1649, when Brome practiced his art, and culminated in the English Civil War and the beheading of King Charles in 1649.

As these bloody events show, Brome lived and wrote on the eve of destruction. Although his tone is comic, Brome nevertheless sets forth the conditions that led to social paroxysm. As a playwright, he sets forth those conditions in human terms, in the terms of feeling individuals. Therefore, for students of seventeenth century English history, Brome has particular significance, but there are also some strong parallels between the social conditions in his plays and those of today. For people living in unstable times, possibly on the edge of cataclysm, Brome has a message.

Brome's message centers mostly on money, which dominates the life depicted in his plays, and money's erosion of all other values. Marriages and alliances are formed on the basis of money as much as on the basis of love or friendship. Degraded aristocrats, short on cash, join with the middle class or with crooks and coney-catchers in pursuit of lucre. Groups of beggars roam the countryside. Everywhere the middle class is rampant, feeling its oats and hoping to purchase the manners and pedigrees of the aristocracy it is replacing. The world itself seems turned upside down, former values inverted. For the general theme of Mammon-worship, Brome was probably indebted to his mentor, Jonson, but Brome elaborates the social details of his theme that were apparent in the society around him. Brome might also have been indebted to Jonson for his conservative, aristocratic sympathies; with the changing makeup of the Caroline audience, Brome had to tone down those sympathies and appeared to be a more evenhanded observer.

THE NORTHERN LASS

The Northern Lass is an example of Brome's early work. The play's immediate success, combined with that of *The Love-sick Maid*, which was produced the same year, firmly established Brome's popularity in his time. These two early hits proved Brome's ability to satisfy his audience's tastes, but *The Northern Lass* makes one question those tastes and wonder whether Jonson was not right, after all, to attack them. The play's overdone intrigue and disguising become tedious, and its main attraction is its sentimental portrait of Constance from England's North Country. Yet

The Northern Lass does illustrate the typical Brome: It introduces the all-pervasive theme of money and Brome's use here, in one play, of both satiric and romantic elements.

Money's power is underlined by the play's opening scene: Sir Philip Luckless, a court gentleman, has contracted to marry Mistress Fitchow, a rich city widow. The marriage represents a common social expedient of the time, the uneasy alliance of aristocrats and members of the middle class as the aristocrats sought to replenish their funds while the middle class sought to obtain titles. Sir Philip learns how uneasy the alliance is when he meets his bride's relatives, "a race of fools," and discovers that the bride herself is a loud shrew. He regrets the marriage bargain even more when Constance, the sweet-voiced Northern lass who is in love with him, appears on the scene. Eventually, Sir Philip gets a divorce on a technicality (since he and Mistress Fitchow quarrel on their wedding day, their marriage is never consummated) and is able to marry Constance. Significantly, the conflicts between love and money, aristocracy and middle class, end in compromise: Half of Constance's rich uncle's estate comes with her hand, and Fitchow marries Sir Philip's cousin Tridewell, who rather unconvincingly falls in love with her. By Brome's time, dramatists had to give money and the middle class their due.

As the play's title suggests, it was the sentimental portrait of Constance—the romantic element—that charmed Brome's audience. Innocent and direct, Constance speaks in a fetching North Country dialect: "But for my life I could not but think, he war the likest man that I had seen with mine eyne, and could not devise the thing I had, might be unbeggen by him." Mistaking Sir Philip's courtly compliment for a marriage proposal, she pursues him all the way to London. Naïve and loving, Constance introduces another perspective into the scheming context of the play, particularly in contrast to Fitchow and the prostitute Constance Holdup. Yet even the prostitute, through confusion with Constance, takes on some of her halo, thus enabling the audience to sentimentalize both innocence and its loss. In short, Constance is a reminder that innocence exists out there somewhere—or so Brome's audience wanted to believe.

THE SPARAGUS GARDEN

A much better play than *The Northern Lass* is *The Sparagus Garden*, written around the midpoint of Brome's career. A comedy in which the satiric element predominates, *The Sparagus Garden* might well win the appreciation of a modern audience. Brome warns in the prologue that the audience should not "expect high language or much cost," since "the subject is so low." In fact, the language is sharp, colorful, and varied (including courtly and Somersetshire accents and satire of gentlemen's cant), not to mention full of sexual innuendo. The "low subject" is the Sparagus Garden, a suburban garden-restaurant with beds upstairs—the best little rendezvous for lovers in London. Here they can also sate themselves with asparagus, which is described as full of wonderful properties in both its erect and limp states.

Aside from the sexual appetites of Londoners, much else is satirized in *The Sparagus Garden*. For example, neighborly feuding is satirized in the characters of Touchwood and Striker, two rich old justices whose enmity over the years has grown into a close and sustaining relationship: They love to hate each other, and the desire of each to strike the final blow keeps them alive. Marital strife is satirized through the relationship of Brittleware and Rebecca: Brittleware fears that Rebecca will make him a cuckold, and Rebecca plays on her husband's anxiety by reciting her sexual yearnings and Brittleware's inability to satisfy them—"you John Bopeep." Anxiety about sexual promiscuity is also satirized through the figure of Sir Arnold Cautious, "a stale bachelor" and "a ridiculous lover of women" (a voyeur) who will marry no woman because he can find no virgin. Other objects of incidental satire in *The Sparagus Garden* are lawyers and poets.

The social change occurring in the Caroline period is strikingly dramatized in *The Sparagus Garden*. Not only is the Sparagus Garden a resort for gentlemen accompanying city wives, such as Mrs. Holyhock, the "precise" (that is, puritanical) draper's wife, but also its main agent (pimp/procurator/publicist) is Sir Hugh Moneylacks, a degraded knight who "lives by shifts." Having run through his own estate and that of his middle-class wife, whom he drove to an early grave, Sir Hugh is now Striker's disowned son-in-law.

A hardened hustler, Sir Hugh is not at all abashed by his father-in-law's rejection, nor is the Sparagus Garden his only money-making project. In addition, he and his confederates are instructing the Somersetshire bumpkin Tim Hoyden, who has four hundred pounds to invest in the project, on how to be a gentleman—a subject of further satire in *The Sparagus Garden*.

A JOVIAL CREW

In contrast to *The Sparagus Garden*, *A Jovial Crew* is a Brome comedy in which the romantic element predominates. The last of Brome's plays, *A Jovial Crew* is generally considered his best. It was a favorite of the Restoration and of the eighteenth century, when it was turned into a comic opera at Covent Garden—a version no doubt suggested by the play's numerous songs and dances. Performed by a jolly crew of raffish beggars, the rousing songs and dances embody the beggars' carefree philosophy, which stands in stark contrast to the middle-class ethos. The bands of beggars roaming the countryside are both an indictment of and an alternative to the emerging middle-class order. Coming from all walks of life—soldiers, lawyers, courtiers, and poets as well as peasants—the beggars turn necessity into a virtue: They form a "beggars' Commonwealth" with its own language and values, values based on fellowship rather than money. In fact, they scorn money.

The middle-class characters view the beggars' commonwealth with fear and fascination. Oldrents, an old country esquire whose home epitomizes middle-class prosperity, stability, and dullness, is vexed by a fortune-teller's prediction that his two daughters will become beggars. His friend Hearty, "a decayed gentleman," urges him to laugh at the prediction (to look on the carefree beggars and birds of the field and be as they), but to little avail. As it turns out, Oldrents has good reason to fear for his daughters—particularly since his rapacious grandfather wrested the family estate from a "thriftless heir," Wrought-on, whose own posterity became beggars. Oldrents fathered a son with one of Wrought-on's beggar-descendants, and his son, unknown to him, is his steward, Springlove, who has a yearning, each spring, to go wandering with the beggars.

Oldrents' daughters also feel the attraction of the wandering life, which promises an escape from Oldrents' dull household and worried disposition. The daughters, Rachel and Meriel, look on their begging venture as a lark, and they impose it on Vincent and Hilliard, their boyfriends since childhood, as an ordeal, a test of loyalty more significant than such childish games as "tearing of books" or "piss and paddle in't." In fact, they are all failures at alternative lifestyles, even though they have the services of Springlove, who equips and instructs them and gives them an introduction to the beggars. After experiencing the hardships of pricking their "bums" on a straw bed and waking without a mirror, they fly back to their middle-class nests.

Despite its fun and folly, its reminder of Shakespearean couples running through the forests of Arden and Athens, *A Jovial Crew* is a strong record of a deteriorating society on the verge of civil war. It was Brome's final statement. The record had been building, however, throughout his works—a record of growing middle-class dominance, of money's power, of declining loyalties and eroding values, of a vacuum at the heart of life. It is a record that the modern world might do well to examine carefully.

BIBLIOGRAPHY

Clark, Ira. *Professional Playwrights: Massinger, Ford, Shirley, and Brome.* Lexington: University Press of Kentucky, 1992. A study of the lives and dramas produced by Brome, Philip Massinger, John Ford, and James Shirley. Bibliography and index.

Gaby, Rosemary. "Of Vagabonds and Commonwealths: *Beggar's Bush, A Jovial Crew,* and *The Sisters.*" *Studies in English Literature, 1500-1900* 34, no. 2 (Spring, 1994): 401. An examination of three seventeenth century comedies revolving around money, sex, and social status and featuring country rogues: Brome's *A Jovial Crew,* John Fletcher's *Beggar's Bush,* and James Shirley's *The Sisters.*

Leggatt, Alexander. *Introduction to English Renaissance Comedy.* New York: St. Martin's Press, 1999. This work on Renaissance comedy in England contains a discussion of Brome's *A Jovial Crew.* Bibliography and index.

Sanders, Julie. *Caroline Drama: The Plays of Massinger, Ford, Shirley, and Brome.* Plymouth, England: Northcote House, in association with the British Council, 1999. An examination of the plays of Caroline dramatists Brome, Philip Massinger, John Ford, and James Shirley. Bibliography and index.

Shaw, Catherine M. *Richard Brome.* Boston: Twayne, 1980. An introduction to the life and works of Brome, with a chronology and bibliography. Chapter topics include "The Ladies Take the Stage" and "The Gentlemen: Fathers, Fools, and Fops." Gives a good sense of the contents and qualities of Brome's work.

White, Martin. *Renaissance Drama in Action: An Introduction to Aspects of Theatre Practice and Performance.* New York: Routledge, 1998. White's book delves into the staging and performance of Renaissance drama. His discussion of the difficulties of reconstructing early works features a case study of Brome's *A Jovial Crew,* which was, according to some critics, less than successfully updated for the modern stage when performed in 1992.

Harold Branam,
updated by Frank Day

ROBERT BROWNING

Born: Camberwell, London, England; May 7, 1812
Died: Venice, Italy; December 12, 1889

PRINCIPAL DRAMA
Strafford, pr., pb. 1837
Pippa Passes, pb. 1841

King Victor and King Charles, pb. 1842

The Return of the Druses, pb. 1843

A Blot in the 'Scutcheon, pr., pb. 1843

Colombe's Birthday, pb. 1844, pr. 1853

Luria, pb. 1846

A Soul's Tragedy, pb. 1846 (the seven preceding titles were published in the *Bells and Pomegranates* series, 1841-1846)

OTHER LITERARY FORMS

Robert Browning is better known as a major Victorian poet and, in particular, as one who perfected the influential verse form called dramatic monologue. His achievement in poetry, for which he forsook the theater altogether in 1846, was unquestionably much greater than what he accomplished as a writer of stage plays, yet it is difficult and unwise to distinguish the subject matter and techniques of Browning's "failed" dramas from those of his successful poems. Although he was by nature and inclination a dramatic writer, it became apparent that his peculiar interests and talent in that line were more suited to the finer medium of poetry than to the practical exigencies of stagecraft. The verse confirms his acknowledged preoccupation with interior drama ("Action in character, not character in action"). Browning's verse masterpieces in this mode include "Porphyria's Lover," "My Last Duchess," "The Bishop Orders His Tomb at St. Praxed's Church," "Andrea del Sarto," "Love Among the Ruins," "The Last Ride Together," and *The Ring and the Book* (1868-1869). A dramatic monologue by Browning typically features an incandescent moment of crisis or of self-realization in the mental life of some unusual, often morally or psychologically flawed, character. Rather like a soliloquy except in being addressed to a present but silent listener, this type of poem enabled Browning to let his speakers' personalities, motives, obsessions, and delusions be revealed—inadvertently or otherwise—in speech and implied gesture. This preoccupation with inward, psychological drama—with the springs of action rather than with action itself—is the origin of Browning's greatness as a poet and of his limitations as a stageworthy playwright.

Robert Browning (Library of Congress)

ACHIEVEMENTS

In nineteenth and early twentieth century criticism, Browning was widely considered to be the best English writer of dramatic literature (though not of stageable plays) since the Renaissance. That judgment was probably accurate enough, if only because of the remarkable dearth of fine drama during the two hundred years in question. Even today, especially if Browning's splendid dramatic monologues are included in the estimate, there can be little doubt that his achievement was, under the circumstances, extraordinary. Nevertheless, any evaluation of his plays must begin by conceding that, despite his hopes, practical theatrical craft in the ordinary sense was never in Browning's vein of genius. He was a first-rate dramatic poet, not a good technical playwright. Indeed, the very themes and methods that mark the plays' literary value are the source of their unsuitability for successful performance.

One historical explanation of this "failure" is the Romantic concept of acted and unacted drama. Browning has been associated with a widespread and consciously antitheatrical attitude among authors that resulted in plays composed with indifference to performative—as opposed to literary or expressive—criteria. If Browning did believe on principle that actual staging is not necessary to serious drama, it is less surprising that his own plays are satisfactory chiefly as reading texts. On the other hand, Browning did press persistently to see some of his work on the boards.

In any case, Browning's plays have never been popular and, with the exception of *Pippa Passes*, are not usually numbered among his most important contributions to the history of English dramatic writing. Their lasting excellence, then, is in their objective poetry and prose. As in the verse collections to which he gave titles such as *Dramatic Lyrics* (1842; in *Bells and Pomegranates*, 1841-1846), *Dramatis Personae* (1864), *Dramatic Idyls* (1879, 1880), and *Men and Women* (1855), Browning's mastery of inward action is demonstrated in the plays' delineation of moral and psychological crises and in their vivid intellectual and emotional energy. Understood as searching critiques of modern life, the psychological and moral bearings of some of these dramas—and their subversive frankness (about eroticism, for example, or respectability)—were original and significantly ahead of their time. Formal innovations in the reading plays (*Pippa Passes* and *A Soul's Tragedy*) and Browning's special gift for creating memorable female characters have also been praised.

BIOGRAPHY

As a young man, Robert Browning was tutored at his prosperous family's home near London. He spent much of a sheltered adolescence reading eagerly and eclectically in the fine library there, absorbing philosophical, artistic, and historical lore that would later emerge—sometimes rather obscurely—in his plays and poems. Devoted always to a literary career, Browning lived for many years dependent on his indulgent parents. They exerted a deep personal influence: the father intellectually, the mother religiously. In literature, the works and example of Percy Bysshe Shelley were Browning's first and most enduring inspiration, though in drama itself the constant model would be, wisely and otherwise, William Shakespeare. The privately published verse and plays of Browning's early maturity were eccentric and poorly received. Most of

the drama in particular was ill-suited to theatrical production, and in disappointment, he turned increasingly to a new type of poetry, the dramatic monologue, in order to fuse the variousness and objectivity of plays with the subtle effects of poems. Yet even after 1846, when elopement and marriage crowned his long, ardent courtship of Elizabeth Barrett Browning, she was still the better-known writer of the two. The blithe years of his wedded life were spent mostly in Italy, where Browning's fascination with the rich and enigmatic sociocultural heritage of the Mediterranean bloomed and reflected itself in the great new poems collected in *Men and Women*. Mrs. Browning's sudden death in 1861 ended this golden era and was personally devastating for her husband. Thereafter, Browning resided in both England and Italy, continuing to write poetry—notably *The Ring and the Book*—and gradually winning a wide and appreciative audience for all of his work. This late adulation, including the international Browning Society's admiration of his religious and philosophical outlook, was in striking contrast with the humiliation he had felt during the early years. In 1888, he saw the publication of the first volumes of what would become a seventeen-volume collection of his dramatic and poetic canon.

ANALYSIS

Robert Browning's best plays, whether for reading or performance, are the ones in which we are most aware of his genius for evoking "action in character": the drama of human personality in conscious or unconscious conflict with itself. Outward action and scenic spectacle are perhaps more incidental in Browning than in any other significant English playwright, though the extended implications for social morality are usually apparent. Instead, Browning concentrates on the self-articulation of minds that are devious or deviant or otherwise exceptional. One effect is to cast doubt on the normative values and impulses contending in (or generated by) such mentalities, notably in politics or love. Indeed, love of one sort or another among socially prominent characters is usually the symbolic field in which Browning's flawed or obsessive personalities perform most ineffectually or tragically. Rationalizers of selfishness, greed, hypocrisy, or cruelty are frequently presented, as are characters who let themselves and others be destroyed by the paradoxes inherent in artificial codes or standards of conduct. In particular, egomania and other faults of willful pride (including excessive shame or guilt) would appear to be Browning's diagnosis of the moral neuroses and complacencies he detected in Victorian society at large. The characters are not so much evil as inveterately and anxiously deluded.

A BLOT IN THE 'SCUTCHEON

It is easy to misconstrue the sometimes grotesque, sentimental, or overwrought behavior of Browning's characters as a lapse or compromise with popular taste on the playwright's part. In Browning, the trite or melodramatic overreaction is symptomatic—it is his subject, not his technique. The presence and perspective of intelligent, realistic, and sensible characters such as Guendolen in *A Blot in the 'Scutcheon* confirm Browning's deliberate exhibition of abnormality in others, such as the histrionic Mildred and Thorold Tresham. That contemporary readers and audiences (including Charles Dickens) could apparently value Browning's pathos for its own sake is a separate consideration. A more significant problem for Browning, and for modern readers, is the atheatricality of such refined psychological and metaphoric aims. The artistic intention may in fact be too subtle, the rendering too opaque, the intended medium too visual to elicit onstage anything like the appropriate effect. Nevertheless, as a reading text, the typical Browning play yields the same kind of dramatic significance that is to be found in his poetry.

The verse tragedy *A Blot in the 'Scutcheon*, considered Browning's best play, indicates his special effort to create something both subtle and stageworthy. In fact, he described it to the celebrated actor-manager William Charles Macready as "a sort of compromise between my notion and yours. . . . There is *action* in it, drabbing, stabbing, et autres gentillesses." Nevertheless, the observable action and strong dialogue in this drama of eighteenth century aristocratic honor remain subordinated to Browning's real interest in portraying inward conflicts and destructive ideals. Moreover, the tragic situation derives entirely from

the flawed psyches of proud, rash Lord Tresham and his guilt-tormented sister Mildred. The distraught girl and her illicit lover Lord Mertoun attempt through an elaborate charade of formal betrothal to bring their relationship within the bounds of social and class respectability. Here, then, is a combination of Browning's favorite dramatic themes: unusually heightened emotion, symbolic moments of intense individual crisis, thwarted or misdirected love and sexuality, and the inhibiting force of pride or conventionality on free feeling and action. In all of these respects, *A Blot in the 'Scutcheon* shows divided loyalties and misguidedly good intentions causing tensions that explode in impulsive and fatal choices. Mildred Tresham is visibly going to pieces throughout much of the play, her virtual derangement the price she pays for being torn between her passionate love for Mertoun and her terror of offending her imperious brother. It is her panic that has necessitated the young lovers' gamble for respectability, and she thus initiates the sequence of disastrous dissimulations, exposures, and misunderstandings. Both men are doomed when, cracking under the strain, she blurts out half the truth. Tresham and Mertoun feel bound by honor to suppress the simple word that could avert the needless catastrophe. It is the kind of situation in which Browning excelled: dilemmas in which men and women are too hampered by mixed motives to act with candor, charity, courage, or imagination.

The proud folly of Thorold Tresham is likewise responsible for the tragic denouement in *A Blot in the 'Scutcheon*. He whips himself into a rage about Mildred's "dishonorableness" and the reputation of his ancestral house, despite having seen earlier the wisdom of embarrassed concealment. In his fury, he so aggravates her already excessive shame that she is unable to reveal that her secret paramour and her formal suitor are the same person. Again in the duel scene, Tresham's selfish, intemperate anger and taunting compel the unwilling Mertoun to fight and die. Thereafter, sorrowful but still obsessed with observing the niceties of maintaining the family name, Tresham kills himself in a gesture that would seem ludicrously melodramatic were it not so poignantly in keeping with the pernicious notions of heroism and dynastic obligation he has displayed all along. Guendolen's wry epitaph confirms that one is expected to pity Tresham but by no means to admire his "perfect spirit of honor" or to condone his pointless, self-righteous suicide. Here and elsewhere, Guendolen seems to reflect the author's bemusement by what she calls "the world's seemings and realities." If the Treshams are unstable and haunted, young Mertoun seems overly casual until it is too late, at which point he overreacts in dignified fatalism. His contribution to the tragedy, apart from maintaining, all too incautiously, the liaison with Mildred and misjudging her brother, is to defy Tresham unnecessarily before the duel and to perish more or less suicidally on the latter's sword. Murders, suicides, and (as in Mildred's case) expirings under stress are almost always associated in Browning's plays with willful or simplistic escapism, albeit in the name of some illusory notion of justice. The three deaths in *A Blot in the 'Scutcheon* are good examples of this tendency.

The thematic focus of this play is on the inhumanity of what is perversely done for the sake of personal, social, and dynastic honor. In scene after scene, Tresham, Mildred, and Mertoun are either driven or betrayed by such considerations, their relationships becoming increasingly complicated, frustrated, and dangerous. At the same time, Guendolen's frank and genial perspective reminds us (and ought to have convinced the other characters) that with a little more candor and a lot less preoccupation with "name" and "blots," the whole problem could have been resolved comedically rather than tragically. She notices almost prophetically, for example, how overready the others are to announce principles for which they are prepared to die. It is also Guendolen who gaily sees through Mertoun's pretense, Tresham's gullible complacency, and Mildred's guilty secret. Her insights are ignored or come too late, but her bright and ironic personality commands the stage at the end. It is significant that Tresham, Mildred, and Mertoun apparently die uncontrite: They regret the ghastly effects, but not the causes, of their actions. Tresham's dying utterances, which he imagines to embody heroic penance and self-sacrifice, are as banal, codebound, and monomaniacal as anything he has sad

before. Mildred likewise persists in considering her own death as a just retribution and relief from anguish. Mertoun, like the others, is none the wiser for bringing on his own end. Each demise is a wholly destructive martyrdom to some abstract, overscrupulous notion of "duty" or "wrong." Moreover, these unexpected deaths are shocking. As in some of Browning's other plays (and in such dramatic monologues as "Porphyria's Lover" and "My Last Duchess"), the customary tragic effects of fear and pity are mingled with surprise and even revulsion. The conventions of drama do not easily embrace Browning's emphasis on extravagance and perversity in characters' motives and reactions. If pathology and tragedy do not mix, Browning is no tragedian. His work may nevertheless be a finer, more modern, and more disturbing criticism of life for having deviated from literary tradition.

PIPPA PASSES

Pippa Passes is Browning's most famous (though possibly least stageable) play and ranks among his best works. An early and experimental composition, the drama comprises four symbolic vignettes from Renaissance life in an Italian town. These independent scenes are structurally and thematically connected by the momentary overhearing, in each, of young Pippa's voice. The girl's innocent singing crucially affects the outcome of interviews that she unknowingly bypasses in her holiday journey. In every case, her song induces a hearer to make, at a point of personal crisis, a guilty choice in favor of just or noble action. *Pippa Passes* reveals Browning at his dramatically strongest and weakest. The situations, subtle effects, psychological focus, and tenuous framing story are quite unsuitable for theatrical performance. In reading, however, the play is successful and undoubtedly dramatic. The issues raised by the various personalities, conflicts, and resolutions of the four scenes are likewise typical of Browning at his best.

Perhaps the most memorable and evocative vignette in *Pippa Passes* is the scene that presents two adulterous lovers, Ottima and Sebald, who have just murdered Ottima's wealthy old husband. Even as the couple begin to talk, it becomes evident that their former "wild wicked" passion has become wearied and cloying. The crime designed to set them free has already started to gnaw the heart out of their love. Sebald in particular seems irritable, distracted, and resentful from the outset. He is also grimly obsessed with the man whose killing he now half regrets. Like Macbeth, he is weaker and more morbidly sensitive than his accomplice. Sebald surprises, and then alarms, Ottima by dwelling on his troubled conscience, self-disgust, and frank doubts about her value as his reward. The pace and drama intensify as Ottima grasps the seriousness of this threat to their relationship and fearfully sets out to argue and finally to seduce him back into her control. In lines of lush and powerfully sensual poetry, accompanied by indications of alluring gesture, she soon succeeds in diverting and arousing the febrile Sebald. As he excitedly begs forgiveness and names her his "queen . . . magnificent in sin," they embrace and ardently undress. At this instant, the passing song of Pippa is heard from outside the window—the famous little lyric ending, "God's in his heaven—/ All's right with the world." Grateful for being rescued by the intervention of this "miracle," a remorseful Sebald recoils at once from Ottima, bitterly repudiates her fascinations, and abruptly kills himself. It is typical of Browning that the impulsiveness and startling effect of the suicide, rather than its moral implications, are highlighted: The act's dramatic interest is in its psychology, its convincing exhibition of how that haunted mind might react, edifyingly or not, under such stress. Ottima's immediate responses—shock, envy, tender generosity, and self-recovery—are likewise rendered by Browning with skillful realism and irony. She is another of his brilliant portraits of women, and for all of her sins (a murder among them), the sanity of her final outlook underlines the strange extremism of Sebald's.

Each of the other sections of *Pippa Passes* similarly portrays two characters whose dilemma is interrupted and in some sense resolved by the passing voice of unworldly little Pippa, and, like the Ottima-Sebald scene, the others are Browningesque in their psychological verisimilitude, dramatic patterning, unusual feeling, and apparent moral opaqueness. Two parts employ a robust and naturalistic prose that con-

firms Browning's versatility and also indicates how emphatically his preference for "outmoded" verse drama was based on positive and theoretical considerations, not on any inability as a prose stylist. He never composed another play with the ingenuity and variety of *Pippa Passes*, but in the separate vignettes can be seen the germ of the great dramatic monologues to come, as well as the peculiarly psychological (or psychosocial) bearings of speeches and soliloquies in the later plays.

LESSER PLAYS

Briefer analyses of Browning's other dramas will suffice. Of these, *Strafford*, *King Victor and King Charles*, *The Return of the Druses*, and *Luria* are undistinguished. The first two are historical studies. *Luria* is a tragedy strongly reminiscent of (but much inferior to) Shakespeare's *Othello, the Moor of Venice* (pr. 1604). A convoluted romance, *The Return of the Druses* fails to integrate the politics with the love story. Features of two other plays do deserve attention. These are *Colombe's Birthday* (important as the happiest and most stageworthy Browning drama) and *A Soul's Tragedy* (very significantly the last).

COLOMBE'S BIRTHDAY

Colombe's Birthday is a fairly conventional romantic comedy about the personal feelings and minor diplomatic stir associated with a young duchess's marriage. Graceful and gently satiric, the story interestingly follows good Duchess Colombe's birthday tribulations (both a threatened insurrection and the advent of a rival claimant to the throne, followed by two attractive marriage proposals) and the sound judgment (and luck) by which she satisfies both love and public duty. There are pleasing and eloquent characters, much fine verse, a genially searching critique of "courtierways," and a satisfying conclusion in which all receive as much or as little as their behavior warrants. Moreover, as a stage play *Colombe's Birthday* is workmanlike, accessible, and sedately agreeable. There is, however, a notable scarcity of Browning's customary dramatic concerns, tensions, and techniques. Indeed, to some extent this play indicates the literary limitations of work in which he most compromises with practicality and with popular taste. It may not be coincidental, then, that *Colombe's Birthday* was the last drama Browning designed expressly for theatrical presentation and that he soon abandoned playwriting altogether.

A SOUL'S TRAGEDY

A Soul's Tragedy, Browning's most politically and philosophically serious play, has often been praised even though it is his last and his least stageable. Written in evident indifference to theatrical expectations, it dexterously traces the development and decline of a sixteenth century revolutionary's mind. The title itself seems to express the lifelong orientation of Browning's writing and the inevitability of his forsaking the theater. An entirely interior, possibly allegorical, process is being enacted in *A Soul's Tragedy*, called by its author a "wise metaphysical play." Only the inward action—defeat in the soul—is tragic, moreover; to all outward appearances the pattern and outcome are comedic.

Well-articulated theories of statecraft, and much rhetoric about public responsibility, are simply vehicles for the playwright's exploration of moral psychology. The "tragedy" lies in the latter—in the conscious and unconscious mental life underlying an individual's outward behavior and rationalized principles. As critic Trevor Lloyd has shrewdly pointed out in connection with the political dramas, Browning handles well "the frame of mind of a man undertaking an imposture for the sake of something that he can convincingly regard as a good purpose."

The mind that undergoes change in *A Soul's Tragedy* is that of Chiappino. During the first half of the play, he utters, in excellent verse, all the idealism (sincere and otherwise) of unselfish aspiration. Then, in the second part, he speaks—this time in lively prose—all the disillusionment (justifiable and otherwise) of realpolitik. That switch from "poetical" to "prosaic" thought and expression is not simply a political metaphor or an elegant gimmick on Browning's part. Both "voices" are rhetorical projections of what the self-preoccupied "soul" imagines or requires itself to believe at the moment. The touchstones against which Chiappino's development can be charted are two alter-ego characters: Luitolfo is the simple and genuine radical, while Onigben is the cynical legate whose droll Machiavellianism here is unsurpassed in

English drama. As we might expect in Browning, Onigben gets the last word.

Browning published *A Soul's Tragedy* with *Luria* in 1846 as the eighth and last issue of the *Bells and Pomegranates* series. In more ways than one, this pamphlet marked the end of an era in his artistic life. The dedication to Walter Savage Landor announced the work as Browning's "last attempt for the present at dramatic poetry." He never wrote another play.

OTHER MAJOR WORKS

POETRY: *Pauline*, 1833; *Paracelsus*, 1835; *Sordello*, 1840; *Bells and Pomegranates*, 1841-1846 (includes *Dramatic Lyrics*, 1842, and *Dramatic Romances and Lyrics*, 1845); *Christmas Eve and Easter Day*, 1850; *Men and Women*, 1855 (2 volumes); *Dramatis Personae*, 1864; *The Ring and the Book*, 1868-1869 (4 volumes); *Balaustion's Adventure*, 1871; *Prince Hohenstiel-Schwangau: Saviour of Society*, 1871; *Fifine at the Fair*, 1872; *Red Cotton Nightcap Country: Or, Turf and Towers*, 1873; *Aristophanes' Apology*, 1875; *The Inn Album*, 1875; *Pacchiarotto and How He Worked in Distemper*, 1876; *The Agamemnon of Aeschylus*, 1877 (drama translation in verse); *La Saisiaz, and The Two Poets of Croisac*, 1878; *Dramatic Idyls*, 1879-1880 (in two parts); *Jocoseria*, 1883; *Ferishtah's Fancies*, 1884; *Parleyings with Certain People of Importance in Their Day*, 1887; *The Poetical Works of Robert Browning*, 1888-1894 (17 volumes); *Asolando*, 1889; *Robert Browning: The Poems*, 1981 (2 volumes).

NONFICTION: *The Letters of Robert Browning and Elizabeth Barrett Browning, 1845-1846*, 1926 (Robert B. Browning, editor); *Intimate Glimpses from Browning's Letter File: Selected from Letters in the Baylor University Browning Collection*, 1934; *Browning's Essay on Chatterton*, 1948 (Donald A. Smalley, editor); *New Letters of Robert Browning*, 1950 (W. C. DeVane and Kenneth L. Knickerbocker, editors); *The Letters of Robert Browning and Elizabeth Barrett Barrett, 1845-1846*, 1969 (Elvan Kintner, editor).

MISCELLANEOUS: *The Works of Robert Browning*, 1912 (10 volumes; F. C. Kenyon, editor); *The Complete Works of Robert Browning*, 1969-1999 (16 volumes).

BIBLIOGRAPHY

Garrett, Martin. *A Browning Chronology: Elizabeth Barrett Browning and Robert Browning*. New York: St. Martin's Press, 2000. A chronology of the works of Elizabeth Barrett Browning and Robert Browning. Bibliography and index.

_____, ed. *Elizabeth Barrett Browning and Robert Browning: Interviews and Recollections*. New York: St. Martin's Press, 2000. A collection of interviews recalling Browning and his famous wife. Bibliography and index.

Hawlin, Stefan. *The Complete Critical Guide to Robert Browning*. New York: Routledge, 2002. A reference work that provides comprehensive critical analysis of Browning's works and information on his life. Bibliography and indexes.

Hudson, Gertrude Reese. *Robert Browning's Literary Life: From First Work to Masterpiece*. Austin, Texas: Eakin Press, 1992. Examines the critical response to the works of Browning, throughout his career. Bibliography and index.

Maynard, John, ed. *Browning Re-viewed: Review Essays, 1980-1995*. New York: Peter Lang, 1998. This collection of essays on Browning includes a critical analysis of his poems and plays as well as several on the path of his literary career. Bibliography and indexes.

Roberts, Adam. *Robert Browning Revisited*. New York: Twayne, 1996. A basic biography of Browning that examines his life and works. Bibliography and index.

Ryals, Clyde de L. *The Life of Robert Browning: A Critical Biography*. Cambridge, Mass.: Blackwell, 1993. A critical biography of the major Victorian poet which gives a fresh account of his life and analyzes his entire creative output in chronological order.

Wood, Sarah. *Robert Browning: A Literary Life*. New York: Palgrave, 2001. A biography of Browning that focuses on his literary works. Bibliography and index.

Michael D. Moore,
updated by Richard D. McGhee

FERDINAND BRUCKNER
Theodor Tagger

Born: Vienna, Austria; August 26, 1891
Died: Berlin, West Germany; December 5, 1958

PRINCIPAL DRAMA

Harry, pr., pb. 1920, and *Annette*, pr., pb. 1920 (later as *1920: Oder, Die Komödie vom Untergang der Welt*)
Kapitän Christoph, wr. 1921
Esther Gobseck, wr. 1921
Krankheit de Jugend, pr. 1926, pb. 1928 (*Pains of Youth*, 1989)
Die Verbrecher, pr., pb. 1928 (*The Criminals*, 1941)
Die Kreatur, pb. 1929, pr. 1930
Elisabeth von England, pr., pb. 1930 (*Elizabeth of England*, 1931)
Timon, pr. 1931, pb. 1932 (based on William Shakespeare's play *Timon of Athens*)
Die Rassen, pr., pb. 1933 (*Races*, 1934)
Die Marquise von O., pr., pb. 1933 (based on Heinrich von Kleist's novella)
Napoleon der Erste, pb. 1936, pr. 1937
Heroische Komödie, wr. 1942, pr. 1946, pb. 1948
Denn seine Zeit ist kurz, pr. 1943, pb. 1945
Simon Bolivar, pb. 1945 (includes *Der Kampf mit dem Engel*, pb. 1945, pr. 1957, and *Der Kampf mit dem Drachen*, pr., pb. 1945)
Die Befreiten, pr., pb. 1945
Die Namenlosen von Lexington, wr. 1946
Fährten, pr., pb. 1948
Gesammelte Werke, pb. 1948 (3 volumes)
Früchte des Nichts, pr., pb. 1952
Pyrrhus und Andromache, pr. 1952, pb. 1956
Die Buhlschwester, pb. 1954
Heulen und Zähneklappern, pb. 1954

Der Tod einer Pupper, pr. 1956, pb. 1957
Clarisse, pb. 1956
Das irdene Wägelchen, pb. 1957 (based on the
    Indian play *Mrcchakatikā*, by King Shūdraka)

OTHER LITERARY FORMS

Ferdinand Bruckner used his real name, Theodor Tagger, from 1911 to 1926 when he wrote essays, music criticism, fiction, and lyric poetry. He began in 1920 to write plays, and in 1926 he began to use the pseudonym Ferdinand Bruckner. The plays he wrote under this name are his best known.

ACHIEVEMENTS

Ferdinand Bruckner burst on the theatrical scene in Weimar Germany with the passionate intensity of a phosphorescent flame lighting up a dull, gray winter sky. When his plays first appeared, they created a sensation, for they frequently treated controversial subjects. They proved to be extremely popular with audiences, probably because of their sensational subject matter and also because Bruckner was fortunate enough to have talented directors staging the plays and energetic, talented actors performing in them. Bruckner's plays were also extremely effective theatrically; they employed numerous devices that made the performance of a Bruckner play a memorable experience.

Bruckner's plays represent a "third" direction in German playwriting after the vogue in "expressionist" styles had waned in 1924-1925. By midpoint in the decade, German audiences, especially those audiences in Berlin, were ready to accept new directions in drama. The first important direction was characterized by Neue Sachlichkeit—New Objectivity or "new matter-of-factness." Carl Zuckmayer led this new direction with folksy comedies such as *Der fröhliche Weinberg* (1925) and *Katerina Knie* (1928); these plays were actually a "neorealistic" return to formats previously employed by Gerhart Hauptmann and Johann Nestroy. Zuckmayer's masterpiece of the Weimar period was *Der Hauptmann von Köpenick* (pr., pb. 1931; *The Captain of Köpenick*, 1932), a comedy that captured the authoritarian, paternalistic spirit of Wilhelminian Germany and then made ludicrous fun

of it. Bertolt Brecht led the second direction in German playwriting during the Weimar Republic, a direction characterized by tendentiousness and an aggressive stance toward the capitalist system. His best plays of this period are *Mann ist Mann* (pr. 1926; *A Man's a Man*, 1961) and the well-known *Die dreigroschen Oper* (pr. 1928; *The Threepenny Opera*, 1949), which was based on John Gay's popular *The Beggar's Opera* of 1728. These plays espoused a specific political and socially critical viewpoint, and the direction Brecht took with them realized firmest definition in Brecht's *Lehrstücke*, or didactic plays, of which *Die Massnahme* (pr. 1930; *The Measures Taken*, 1960) is probably the best. The direction Bruckner took in the writing of his plays falls somewhere between Zuckmayer and Brecht; while his plays are socially conscious (like Brecht's), they also have a certain commercial appeal, and though they may have a sensational impact in performance, they also possess (like the plays of Zuckmayer) a highly individual and compassionate vision of the human condition.

Bruckner's plays were extremely popular during the Weimar period, but their popularity alone does not explain Bruckner's significance and achievements. His plays were significant because they treated the tormented drama that unfolded within the human psyche as the play itself progressed. A similar concern for the individual psyche was evinced in the earlier, expressionist plays, but Bruckner's plays differ from expressionist works in that the viewpoint of the plays is not nearly so distorted or subjective. Bruckner may borrow some linguistic techniques that resembled the expressionists, but his language is mainly characterized by its theatricality and by its effectiveness in performance. Many actors and directors rose to prominence while working on Bruckner's plays, and the playwright's sure sense of what "worked" in the theater is perhaps his most noteworthy trademark.

BIOGRAPHY

Ferdinand Bruckner was born Theodor Tagger on August 26, 1891, in Vienna, Austria. His father was a banker from Vienna, and his mother was French, although she herself had been born in Constantinople. The family ancestors on the father's side were Jewish, and they had been forced to leave Spain, the country of their origin. They subsequently settled in Bulgaria. Bruckner felt an allegiance to France and to the French language, and he mastered French at an early age, primarily as a result of his mother's influence. His home city, however, was Vienna; there he received most of his schooling, although he also attended schools in Graz and in Berlin. His first language, therefore, was German—even though he attributed to his mother and her interest in French literature his own interest in literary creativity. His mother also seems to have had a major impact on his work as a playwright, for most of his plays portray females as figures central to the action, and many of these figures seem to possess an energy unmatched by the males.

Bruckner also had an interest in music, and after his school graduation in 1909, he studied at the Paris Conservatory. His first published writings, in fact, were essays on composers such as Georges Bizet and Hugo Wolff. In 1911 Bruckner moved to Berlin to attend business school and also to study music with the composer Franz Streker. In 1913 he matriculated at the University of Vienna to study German philology and music history. He ceased formal study in 1914 and in that year joined the German military forces; he was released from active duty in 1915 as a result of a lung ailment.

Bruckner's experience in the military, brief though it was, served nevertheless to provoke a strong antiwar sentiment in his writing. By this time he had published pacifist essays and poems, and the wartime experience fixed in his own mind his identity as a writer. He spent the rest of the war years writing, and in 1917 he founded the literary magazine *Marsyas*. In addition to publishing this bimonthly periodical, Bruckner devoted his time to reading Søren Kierkegaard and Blaise Pascal, and to forming his own literary style. His most noteworthy effort during this period was a novella titled *Die Vollendungs eines Herzens* (1917), which had six printings and made Bruckner, then using his real name, Theodor Tagger, a well-known author throughout the German-speaking world.

In 1920 Bruckner reached a turning point in his career, for in that year he began to devote himself solely to writing for the theater. The period from 1920 to 1933 was remarkable for the German theater generally, for the level of achievement during those years has rarely been matched at any other time anywhere. Bruckner's productivity and talent also seemed to blossom during those years. In 1920 he wrote two comedies, *Harry* and *Annette*, which he subsequently incorporated under the title *1920: Oder, Die Komödie vom Untergang der Welt*. These plays were not overwhelmingly successful, but they did receive productions throughout Germany and Austria. In 1923, Bruckner became director of the Renaissance Theatre, a former cinema on Hardenburg Strasse in the Charlottenburg section of Berlin. There he learned at first hand the workings of successful theater. He was a careful observer of what made plays effective with audiences, for in 1924 he wrote *Pains of Youth*, a play that was the first of three plays that were astoundingly popular. The other plays were *The Criminals* and *Elizabeth of England*, and each of them Bruckner wrote under the name of Ferdinand Bruckner. What helped fuel the controversies surrounding *Pains of Youth* and *The Criminals* was the mystery surrounding the identity of their author. Bruckner had chosen his pseudonym as an homage to the great nineteenth century Austrian playwright and actor Ferdinand Raimund and the Austrian composer he so greatly admired, Anton Bruckner.

The playwright continued to write plays under his pseudonym for the remainder of his career, but he never again achieved the success that he had enjoyed with the aforementioned trio of plays. He emigrated to France in 1933, and from there departed for the United States in 1936; he subsequently became a United States citizen. Perhaps his most noteworthy achievement of the postwar period is a result of his life in the United States, for in 1949 he composed the translation of Arthur Miller's *Death of a Salesman* (pr., pb. 1949), which became an extraordinary triumph on German-language stages throughout the 1950's. Bruckner died on December 5, 1958, in West Berlin at the age of sixty-seven, from complications that had aggravated his lung condition.

ANALYSIS

Ferdinand Bruckner wrote twenty-six plays during a career that spanned four decades, but the plays on which his reputation rests are three that premiered in German theaters during a four-year period from 1926 to 1930. *Pains of Youth*, which had its world premiere in Hamburg in 1926, *The Criminals* (Berlin, 1928), and *Elizabeth of England* (Berlin, 1930) proved to be three of the most popular plays ever performed on stages in Weimar Germany. When World War II was over, their popularity resumed, and they sometimes still appear on German stages. They are also performed in Austria and in German-speaking Switzerland. Their popularity may be in part the result of the fact that they have served as "star vehicles" for many actors and actresses. They are popular as well because they provide multifaceted, well-developed roles for women. More than anything else, however, these plays provide startlingly good theater; their author was capable of imbuing them with an energy that intrigued and aroused audiences and that stimulated performers to do their best work.

PAINS OF YOUTH

The first of these plays, *Pains of Youth*, opened at the Hamburg Kammerspiele on October 17, 1926. The "illness of youth" referred to in the title can be variously interpreted. It may be a malady otherwise known as unrequited love, for there are numerous instances in the play of frustrated passion. It may be a kind of exhaustion that has set in after much studying: The play is set in a student rooming house, and the lead character, Marie, is about to complete her final examinations. It is most likely, however, that the "illness" of the title is a feeling of displacement and a lack of firm identity among the characters. Bruckner here portrayed the first generation to come of age in Germany after World War I, and that generation, in his dramatic view, had suffered mightily in the wake of the wholesale collapse of German society. These young people have no values; they exploit one another; they steal from one another; they attempt to murder one another; they commit suicide.

A play that dealt with the "problems of youth" was nothing new. That genre had received its best-known definition in *Frühlings Erwachen* (pb. 1891; *Spring's Awakening*, 1960) by Frank Wedekind in 1891, and Bruckner is Wedekind's debtor in *Pains of Youth*. The characters may be somewhat older than their counterparts in the Wedekind play, yet they still speak in that peculiar idiom called *aneinandervorbeireden* ("speaking past one another") that Wedekind originated. This type of speech creates a feeling of isolation and terrible longing in each character, while at the same time there is a sensation of the characters' willful desire to avoid one another. They do not really talk to one another; they speak "past" one another. They also use childish expressions which have no literal meaning; for example, the expression "Thalatala!" is used in *Pains of Youth* to express triumph or elation, much in the way a child might disclose naïve delight. One major and particularly meaningful difference between *Pains of Youth* and *Spring's Awakening* is that while the children in the Wedekind play use language in an attempt to sound grown up, the young adults in the Bruckner play use it to sound like children. The Countess Desiree is especially fond of sounding like a little girl; she tries to convince Marie at one point to come to bed with her just as the countess and her sister Marion had done as children. Later, when Marie agrees to sleep with the countess, they both jabber like schoolgirls.

The Countess Desiree represents one level of society in *Pains of Youth*; that level is the displaced nobility, nearly all of whom lost their status under the republican regime. Another level represented in the play is that of the medical student Marie, whose intelligence and hard work have brought her to the end of her medical studies after only ten semesters. She stems from hardy, upper-middle class stock. Irene is another student, but her father is a worker. Finally, there is Lucy the maid, who seems willing to be exploited by a male character named Freder. Freder succeeds in turning Lucy into a prostitute—presumably so that she will support his continued medical studies, although Freder has been studying for at least the past ten years. Other male characters include Petrell and Alt, who meander in and out of the action and serve mainly as love interests for the women. The overall character makeup of the play, however, serves to illustrate a cross section of society, and the picture that emerges from this play is indeed frightening. It portrays a society decaying from within, a society lacking all direction and motivation.

Bruckner employed the motif of youth, therefore, to make a larger social statement. These young people are not in a state of rebellion; rather, they are in a kind of daze. They are searching for no meaning or values. They are satisfied instead with any kind of momentary gratification which will allow them an escape from their despair.

The playwright also succeeded in creating fully dimensional personages on the stage, which no doubt contributed to the play's success throughout Germany. When the play first opened in Hamburg under Miriam Horowitz's direction, word soon spread about a controversial new play about students that dealt with homosexuality, drug abuse, and narcissism. Abetting the play's notoriety was the fact that no one had ever heard of the playwright Ferdinand Bruckner. The program in Hamburg described him as "a Viennese physician living abroad with a patient." Bruckner used this bit of subterfuge because as Theodor Tagger, he was still engaged as director of the Renaissance Theatre in Berlin, and he was contractually obligated there. He may also have felt somewhat insecure about his efforts as a playwright in 1926; he did not reveal his pseudonym even to his wife after *Pains of Youth* had become a success. The mystery of the playwright's true identity grew as Berlin audiences awaited the opening of the play at the Renaissance Theatre on April 26, 1928, under the direction of Gustav Hartung. Ironically, Theodor Tagger was no longer the director of the theater when *Pains of Youth* opened. He had departed for the Theater am Kurfürstendamm in 1927, and probably viewed with much amusement and pleasure the tremendously positive reception accorded the play by both critics and audiences in Berlin.

One critic asserted that the play was so popular because the playwright attempted to fuse the *theatralisch* with the *moralisch*, and such attempts had long been popular among the Germans; the dramas of Sturm und Drang in the eighteenth century had set the precedent. Another critic was closer to the mark when he stated that the play afforded actors great opportunities for bravura performances, and he singled out Hilde Koerber as Lucy the maid; that role called for the performer's understanding of a personality so self-sacrificing that it must become "the stuff

of which great heroines and great whores are made." Such performances characterized the entire production and undoubtedly added to the play's success.

THE CRIMINALS

Bravura acting performances also contributed to the success of *The Criminals* later that same year, when it made its world premiere at the Deutsches Theater in Berlin under the direction of Heinz Hilpert. Lucie Hoeflich, Gustaf Gründgens, and Hans Albers headed the cast, and the combined talents of these theater artists helped to create a production that was more popular and created even more publicity than did *Pains of Youth*. The playwright's identity continued to remain a mystery, and there were even instances of persons claiming to be Ferdinand Bruckner who presented themselves at newspaper offices across the city. Newspapers sent reporters searching through membership files of Viennese medical associations in the hope of turning up a physician who also had expertise in legal matters, for just as some observers viewed *Pains of Youth* as a veiled attack on medical education practices in Germany, so others viewed *The Criminals* as an attack on the German judicial system.

As he had done in *Pains of Youth*, Bruckner presented in *The Criminals* a cross section of society; members of this society included fallen aristocrats, sturdy burghers, and lower-class indigents who in act 2 confront criminal charges lodged against them in court. The judges in these various courts of law seem to be caricatures out of plays by Wedekind and another playwright whom Bruckner greatly admired, Carl Sternheim. *The Criminals*, however, lacks the satiric tone of a Sternheim play, and if it owes anything in its content to precedents in German drama, it is to Gerhart Hauptmann's *Die Ratten* (pr., pb. 1911; *The Rats*, 1929), which presented criminals as extraordinary figures, almost as if they formed a dynamic alternative to the static, self-satisfied society of Wilhelminian Germany. Bruckner presented a portrait of criminality within the Weimar Republic, and the criminals there form no alternative but instead reveal the numerous shortcomings of the justice system in the new Republic. Most of the characters in *The Criminals*, in fact, are not criminals at all, but merely victims of criminal circumstance who get caught in the wheels of justice and in the process are destroyed.

Bruckner's suggested staging of *The Criminals* attracted as much attention as its content. He called for a stage divided into three vertical levels, with each level in turn divided into various compartments. The result was a setting that isolated the characters in their environments, in which each was inclined to reveal some deeply personal attribute, longing, or perversion. Scenes transpired in rapid-fire order, as the stage lighting focused intermittently on one compartment and then another. Unit sets such as this, using lighting to focus on the action, were nothing new, either. Erwin Piscator had employed a unit set a year earlier in Ernst Toller's *Hoppla, wir leben!* (pr., pb. 1927; *Hoppla! Such Is Life!*, 1928), and Piscator had indeed employed variations of the technique in many of his other productions. The *Simultanbühne*, or simultaneous setting, dated at least from Johann Nestroy's *Zu ebener Erde und im ersten Stock: Oder, Die Launen des Glücks*, which premiered in Vienna in 1835. That Bruckner employed a simultaneous, compartmentalized setting to portray both the domestic and the courtroom scenes was innovative, however, and that some of the court decisions seemed simultaneously to contradict each other pointed out to audiences the contradictory, inconsistent nature of the justice system. A totally innocent youth, for example, was convicted of perjury, while the extortionist Schimmelweiss was set free.

Bruckner was also able to improve his skills as a composer of realistic dialogue in *The Criminals*. He alternated the street jargon of the younger characters with the utterances of the more educated characters, and the contrast became even more striking in act 2, when the playwright employed legalistic parlance in the mouths of the lawyers and judges. The play's strongest aspect, however, was once again the roles offered to actors. Hans Albers played Tunichtgut ("Good-for-Nothing"), and critics generally agreed that his performance alone was worth the price of admission. Other performers, such as Lucie Hoeflich as the lovesick and insanely jealous Ernestine, received praise for portrayals of "criminals of love." Some critics condemned the play as a slander against the

state; it was so controversial in Bavaria that it was banned there from public performance. In Munich, the capital of Bavaria, authorities permitted performances only before invited audiences. Despite the controversy—or perhaps because of it—Bruckner was awarded the Kleist Prize for Best Play in 1928 for *The Criminals*.

DIE KREATUR

Bruckner was by this time extremely well-known throughout the German-speaking world; *Pains of Youth* and *The Criminals* both played in every major theater to packed houses. Furthermore Bruckner's true identity was by this time well-known, for the playwright had been engaged by Max Reinhardt to compose new plays. Even in the late 1920's Reinhardt was the great theatrical impresario of Berlin. Bruckner wrote *Die Kreatur* for Reinhardt, and Reinhardt himself staged it at the Komödie Theatre in Berlin. The play was not at all well received, but Bruckner's next effort for Reinhardt proved to be his most popular success ever, and in fact it became so popular that it made Bruckner known in many non-German-speaking theatrical circles.

ELIZABETH OF ENGLAND

The play was *Elizabeth of England*, and with it Bruckner attempted to write a historical play with a psychological emphasis, paying little attention to "the sweep of history" or to the profound impact of historical events on succeeding generations. Friedrich Schiller had established such precedents for plays with historical figures, and he himself had written in 1800 a superb play featuring Elizabeth I of England, which he titled *Maria Stuart* (English translation, 1801). Bruckner consciously rejected Schiller's precedent and elected instead to follow the example of Franz Grillparzer, whose historical plays, such as *Ein Bruderzwist in Habsburg* (pr., pb. 1872; *Family Strife in Habsburg*, 1949), focus on the internal struggle of the characters. The character of Elizabeth, for example, is portrayed as one with no firm sense of royal leadership, and she wavers back and forth on the war issue. She even seems at times to be a kind of naïve schoolgirl forced to choose among members of her privy council for companionship at a high school dance. King Philip of Spain, whose character acts as a dramatic counterweight, is in contradistinction zealously decisive, and he is intent on punishing Elizabeth and all English Protestants who deviate from the "true path" of Holy Mother Church. His war against England was a result, in this play, of his religious fervor and his view of the war as a crusade.

The play is thus one built on contrasts: the Jesuits of faith on one side of the stage, the Puritans of reason on the other; in Spain, an overflow of passion, and in England a restraint of passion; and in Philip's court, a sense of security, in Elizabeth's, a sense of skepticism. These contrasts Bruckner embodied on the stage as he had done in *The Criminals*, and as he had done in that play, he employed the simultaneous setting. On stage left was located the court of Philip, and stage right found Elizabeth and her privy council. In between these courtly scenes were episodes involving Elizabeth and Essex, but those episodes served only as romantic interludes. The real action of the play centers on the issue of political leadership, and therefore the character of Philip, though he has far fewer lines, assumed a stature in dramatic and theatrical importance every bit as substantial as Elizabeth's. Political leadership was an issue very much in question during the years of this play's performance in the Weimar Republic, and Bruckner no doubt wished to submit this issue for debate.

The division of the stage into "English" and "Spanish" camps reached its climax in the "confessional scene," in which Philip and his advisers pray to their God for victory, while Elizabeth and hers pray to theirs for the same. Ornate, atmospheric organ music unified the diversity of the simultaneous setting, and director Heinz Hilpert used such devices, as he had done in *The Criminals*, to integrate action, character, theme, and setting within a unified whole. As he had also done in *The Criminals*, the director elicited superb performances from his cast. Gustaf Gründgens gave a disciplined, hard-edged rendition of Sir Francis Bacon; Agnes Straub played Elizabeth in a role that must be "sensed," in the words of one critic. The actress playing this part must have a strong personality with which to infuse the role, for the role itself remains a bare outline. The same may be said of Philip, for he essentially speaks only in aphorisms.

Hilpert was extremely fortunate to have Werner Krauss in this role, and Krauss had distinguished himself previously in dozens of other Berlin productions. Philip, however, became his masterpiece; he turned the role, said one critic, into "a Baroque monument."

LATER PLAYS

Never again was Bruckner able to create roles like Philip, Elizabeth, Ernestine, Tunichtgut, Marie, Countess Desiree, or Lucy the maid. His subsequent playwriting efforts were interesting—such as *Timon*, a treatment of William Shakespeare's *The History of Timon of Athens, the Man-Hater* (pr., pb. 1678), and *Races*, an overtly political play that attacked Nazi ideology. By 1933, Nazi ideology was firmly in place, and Nazi Propaganda Minister Joseph Goebbels swiftly began to turn the German theater into a platform for the state. Bruckner abhorred the Nazis, and he left Germany in 1933. Unlike his counterparts Carl Zuckmayer and Bertolt Brecht, Bruckner found himself unable to continue effective playwriting in exile, and his plays written while in France and in the United States lack any of the theatrical effectiveness which had characterized his earlier and most exemplary work.

OTHER MAJOR WORKS

LONG FICTION: *Die Vollendungs eines Herzens*, 1917; *Auf der Strasse*, 1920.

POETRY: *Der Herr in den Nebeln*, 1917.

BIBLIOGRAPHY

Collins, Scott. "Evidence Room's *Swell* Falters." Review of *Swell* by Ferdinand Bruckner. *Los Angeles Times*, May 26, 1995, p. 29. This review of *Swell*, an adaptation of Bruckner's *Pains of Youth*, performed by the Evidence Room in Culver City, California, criticized Director Bart DeLorenzo's adaptation of the work.

Isherwood, Charles. Review of *Race* by Ferdinand Bruckner. *Variety*, February 26-March 4, 2001, p. 52. Review of a performance of *Race* by the Classic Stage Company in New York. Analyzes the play and its relevance to modern audiences.

William Grange

GEORG BÜCHNER

Born: Goddelau, Hesse-Darmstadt (now in
    Germany); October 17, 1813
Died: Zurich, Switzerland; February 19, 1837

PRINCIPAL DRAMA

Dantons Tod, pb. 1835, pr. 1902 (*Danton's Death*,
    1927)
Leonce und Lena, wr. 1836, pb. 1850, pr. 1895
    (*Leonce and Lena*, 1927)
Woyzeck, wr. 1836, pb. 1879, pr. 1913 (English
    translation, 1927)
The Plays of Georg Büchner, pb. 1927

OTHER LITERARY FORMS

The novella *Lenz* (1839; English translation, 1963),
based on the life of dramatist Jakob Michael Reinhold
Lenz, is Georg Büchner's best-known work. A defense of Cato's suicide, a small fragment of a short
story, and some poems also exist. Büchner translated
two dramas, *Lukretia Borgia*, of Victor Hugo's *Lucrèce
Borgia* (1833), in 1909, and *Maria Tudor*, of Hugo's
Marie Tudor (1833), also in 1909. Büchner also wrote
a medical dissertation as well as several medical-
philosophical papers and, together with Friedrich Ludwig Weidig, two versions of a political pamphlet, *Der
Hessische Landbote* (1834; *The Hessian Messenger*,
1963). Some of Büchner's letters have also been translated into English.

ACHIEVEMENTS

Georg Büchner had just completed his doctoral
studies when he died during a typhus epidemic in
Zurich; he was not yet twenty-four years old. Partly
because of his short life span and partly because
his manuscripts were dispersed after his death, Büchner did not gain general recognition as one of Germany's great writers until fifty years after his death,
and his reputation outside Germany lagged behind
for an additional half century. *Leonce and Lena* was
not staged until 1895; *Danton's Death* was not produced until 1902; and *Woyzeck* had its premiere in
1913.

Büchner's political activism caused friction with
German authorities and prevented an open relationship with his parents. His medical studies paved the
way for a promising career, however, and, after completing his dissertation, he gave an inaugural lecture
at the University of Zurich in November, 1836, and
he was granted a lectureship there before his death.
His literary endeavors, undertaken originally to supplement his meager financial resources, show keen
psychological insights, an intense interest in the social injustices of the time, and an awareness of experimental dramatic techniques that place him far beyond his contemporaries in literary innovation.
Besides the historical drama *Danton's Death* and the
comedy *Leonce and Lena*, Büchner left several versions of the drama *Woyzeck* (based on an actual murder case). Another drama, *Pietro Aretino*, may have
been completed or nearly completed by January,
1837, but has been lost and is believed to have been
destroyed by his fiancé, Wilhelmine Jaeglé, who believed that the work contained indecent themes and
ideas. Many letters, manuscripts, and possibly Büchner's diary containing a wealth of information, were
also in the possession of his fiancé. Although she
had approved publication of these materials when a
Büchner edition by Karl Gutzkow was under discussion, she later withdrew her consent. The materials
were not found among her effects, and she may have
destroyed them. In 1850, Büchner's brother Ludwig
edited a collection of letters, the novella *Lenz*, and
Leonce and Lena for publication. Shortly after this
first selective edition appeared, a fire in Büchner's
house destroyed many of the remaining documents,
and Büchner's work remained obscure until 1879,
when the first critical edition of his work was published.

Because Büchner addressed himself to problems
and questions concerning the basic human condition,
his work continues to be relevant to an international
readership. A much coveted prize, originally offered
in 1923 for Hessian artists only and discontinued during the years of Nazi power, was reinstated on a

broader basis in 1951 as the Georg-Büchner Prize for Literature. Among its recipients are many of the foremost representatives of modern German poetry and prose, including Max Frisch, Paul Celan, Ingeborg Bachmann, Günter Grass, Heinrich Böll, Uwe Johnson, and Thomas Bernhard.

BIOGRAPHY

Karl Georg Büchner was born October 17, 1813, the oldest of six children of the physician Ernst Büchner and his wife, Caroline. The family encouraged wide-ranging intellectual interests—literary, political, and scientific—although the father was a reactionary conservative whose relationship with his eldest son was strained. Büchner's youngest brother, Alexander, was a writer and a political activist who took part in the revolution of 1848 and later became a professor of literature in France, where the political climate was more liberal than in Hesse. His sister Louise also became a writer and a champion of women's rights. Ludwig Büchner, a physician like his father and brother, become well-known as the author of *Kraft und Stoff* (1855; *Power and Matter*, 1870) and edited the first published collection of Georg's works. (This edition had little impact, however, because Ludwig altered and "corrected" the text extensively wherever he found Georg's linguistic expression offensive to the sensibilities of the bourgeois circle in which he lived and worked.) Another brother, Wilhelm, was a chemist, factory owner, and politician.

Georg Büchner grew up during the time of political turmoil that followed the collapse of Napoleon Bonaparte's power in Europe. As a student at the Ludwig-Georg-Gymnasium (a preparatory school for the university) in Darmstadt, which he entered at age twelve, Büchner showed not only superior intellectual and academic abilities but also an inquisitive, skeptical, and uncompromising mind that was not easily influenced by convention. In his recommendation of Büchner to officials at the University of Strasbourg, where the young man matriculated in 1831 as a medical student, the school's director noted not only Büchner's academic achievements and his keen and penetrating mind, but also what appeared to the director as imprudence in certain judgments. For the politically radical Büchner, the German-speaking French city of Strasbourg, operating after the July Revolution under the Constitutional Charter of 1830, represented a welcome liberation from the oppressive atmosphere across the Rhine River. He participated in the open political discussions that, along with rallies and demonstrations, were part of daily student life; he very likely was active also in the Société des Droits de l'Homme et du Citoyen's Strasbourg chapter. Letters to his family contain references to the necessity of throwing off the shackles that Büchner perceived as binding Germany politically. While in Strasbourg, he also became secretly engaged to Wilhelmine (Minna) Jaeglé, daughter of the pastor in whose house he lived.

The Hessian law requiring all university candidates to study for at least two years at a state institution necessitated Büchner's return to Germany in 1833. He enrolled at the University of Giessen but was incensed at the routine arrests of politically active students and at the consequent isolation he experienced when shunned and mocked by those less liberal than himself. With a small and close group of friends (August Becker, Gustav Clemm, Karl Minnigerode), he founded the secret Society for the Rights of Man in 1834. This short-lived personal engagement in revolutionary action, which engendered his incendiary flyer *The Hessian Messenger*, ended when Minnigerode was arrested with a bundle of pamphlets. Büchner attempted to warn other members of the group on the same day (August 1, 1834), reached Weidig and Becker in Butzbach, then traveled to Offenbach, where the flyer was printed. Returning to Giessen by way of Frankfurt, he found that his room had been entered and his papers searched and confiscated. In constant fear of arrest, he returned to his parents in Darmstadt in late August, and, after writing *Danton's Death* in January and February of 1835, he fled to Strasbourg in March. Becker, Clemm, and Minnigerode received long prison terms; Weidig was arrested several times, and continually harassed by the police; he committed suicide.

The remainder of Büchner's short life was spent in feverish productivity. In Strasbourg, he wrote his dissertation, read several papers to the Society of Natural History, translated two dramas by Victor Hugo to earn some income, and wrote the remainder of his literary works during a period of only a year and a half. In September, 1836, he was granted his doctorate and invited to the University of Zurich for a trial lecture, followed by an appointment there as lecturer for the winter semester, 1836-1837. He lectured on the "Comparative Anatomy of Fishes and Amphibians." His brief time in Zurich was tranquil. He spent it chiefly within a small circle of colleagues—some who were refugees like himself—and frequently with Wilhelm Friedrich Schulz and his wife, Caroline. Büchner fell ill in early February, 1837, but the nature of his condition was not determined until the middle of the month, when he was already delirious and only intermittently lucid. Wilhelmine was summoned from Strasbourg, and, on February 19, 1837, Büchner died of typhus in her presence.

ANALYSIS

Looking at *Danton's Death* and *Woyzeck* in their historical perspective, it is evident that Georg Büchner's realistic portrayal of the speech, humor, and demeanor of people from the lower classes would not have been acceptable except in comical or derogatory terms. The commoner, with his uncouth behavior, his crude jokes, his inability to express himself without resorting to his native dialect, had his place in the comedy—as a clown or fool to amuse—not as a tragic hero in a serious play. Büchner was among the first to break this basic dramaturgical rule. Where Gotthold Ephraim Lessing had made the common citizen a worthy tragic hero in plays such as *Miss Sara Sampson* (1755; English translation, 1933) and *Emilia Galotti* (1722; English translation, 1786) by pointing out that the lower classes, too, were capable of heroism and idealism, Büchner went one step further and demanded respect for the humanity of the common people, fear of their power when enraged, and compassion for their plight. In his realistic depictions of life among the lower classes, Büchner emancipated the tragedy by refusing to conform to accepted linguistic norms—for example, by using dialect and indelicate phrases within the drama—and by drawing images of human beings and their suffer-

ings from the underside of society in a manner not extensively explored until such later developments as naturalism and expressionism.

It is clear why Büchner's vision has influenced many modern writers. Thematically, he anticipated the fundamental concerns of modern drama. His theater is stark, his language forceful yet frequently colorful in its subtle, expressive shadings. His style and method bridge the centuries from the artistry in characterization and the delight in linguistic bawdiness of the Shakespearean stage to the philosophical developments in German theater of the late nineteenth and early twentieth centuries.

DANTON'S DEATH

Danton's Death is an example of Büchner's linguistic "shock therapy." Remaining essentially true to the historical occurrences in the aftermath of the French Revolution, Büchner depicts well-known political figures within an environment of sex and violence. With the expertise of a surgeon, he dissects the human animal and bares its physiological and psychological functions and drives. A world of chaos, destruction, and rebirth emerges, in which intense pain follows ecstatic pleasure and in which love and death form a close kinship to provide peace, rest, and relief: "I love you like the grave," Danton says to his wife, Julie, and explains:

> They say there is peace in the grave, and that the grave and peace are one and the same. If that is true, then I'm already lying beneath the earth when I rest between your thighs. You sweet grave; your lips are like the mourning bells, your voice is my funeral chime, your breast my burial mound, and your heart my sepulchre.

Arthur Schopenhauer's philosophy is echoed in both the insatiable instinctual drive and in the concomitant quest for peace. As macabre as this depiction appears at first, it nevertheless portrays deep devotion and personal commitment.

Interlaced with this conversation between Danton and Julie is an entirely different one—an interchange between some cardplayers nearby—which attaches eroticism to life and provides it with a lighter side. Love and sex, emotional attachment and physical pleasure, are separated in a remark about a lady who plays her cards right: "They say she offers her husband her *coeur* and others her *carreau*." A third element is introduced by one of the male players: Explaining his losing game, Hérault refers in a tongue-in-cheek manner to the political situation: "The queen was always with child, bearing jacks by the minute. I wouldn't let my daughter play games like that. The kings and queens fall on top of each other so indecently and the jacks pop up right after." In depicting the card game in sexually explicitly terms as the game of life, Hérault also expresses his disappointment at the moral depravity of society and in the fact that the execution of one type of moral degenerates (the kings and queens toppling one on the other) gave rise merely to another set of knaves from the lower classes. Here, too, life, death, and eroticism are intertwined, but with an emphasis on continued strife rather than peace. Büchner's articulation of these events in brilliant wordplay offers a concise expression of life's phenomena on different levels—realistic, philosophical, political—yet the result appeared offensive, obscene, and even pornographic to the conservative tastes of the time.

The juxtaposition of these two separate conversations (that of Danton and Julie and that of Hérault and the lady), both alive with several shades of meaning and different aspects of life, sets the tone in the very first scene for the structural composition of the drama. Using historical material as background, Büchner superimposes personal glimpses, sketches, fragments, and bits of information to form a collage effect. Gradually, characters are molded not only by the lines they speak but also by shifts in perspective, a special emphasis casting a distinctly different light on a figure, by the imagery and symbolism, and by the masterful manipulation of viewpoint that the use of the short, fragmented scene permits. Linguistic brilliance and innovative structural technique give the drama an atmosphere of stark realism and an air of modernity.

The world that Büchner depicts has moved out of the Romantic age into an era when personal alienation, human and divine indifference, and physical as well as psychological destruction threaten every individual. Nothing is certain, no one can be trusted, former values are stripped of their sentiment and revealed in their naked emptiness. Not even the most

intimate of relationships escapes this deadly scrutiny: When Danton claims to know little about Julie and she retorts that he knows her well, he insists: "We have coarse senses. To know one another? We would have to break apart our skulls and pull the thoughts from the brain's fibers." The violence that surrounds them permeates and poisons every aspect of life.

WOYZECK

In *Woyzeck*, Büchner dissects not an era but a personality, not history but science. Here he breaks apart the skull of his protagonist and pulls "the thoughts from the brain's fibers" as he examines the follies of the medical arts. Specifically, Büchner questions what he called in his Zurich lecture on cranial nerves the "teleological" or positivistic method of scientific inquiry and affirms instead the speculative, "philosophical" approach. The play is based on a real incident, the case of a mentally unstable barber, Woyzeck, who was sentenced to death after a spectacular trial for the murder of his mistress. Woyzeck had been in the care of a physician, Dr. J. C. A. Clarus, who, as Büchner believed after studying the case, did not adequately diagnose and treat Woyzeck before or after the crime. Büchner permits the doctor-figure in the play to act out the positivistic method espoused by this physician: the teleological approach. According to this view, "the organism behaves like a machine and can therefore be treated like a machine when it malfunctions" by severing the impaired part, or by treating the specific organic damage. The positivistic method seeks to ascertain the purpose of an organ and nothing further. Diseases of the mind cannot be treated in this manner, Büchner believed. He rejected the notion that all phenomena can be explained as the fulfillment of organic purpose, concluding that existence is an end in itself: "Nature does not act according to purpose. . . . All that is, exists for itself. To find the law of this existence is the goal of those who, in apposition to the teleological view, hold the *philosophical* view." This confrontation of the positivistic with the philosophical approach to science is at the basis of *Woyzeck's* plot. If *Danton's Death* could be likened to a collage because of its technique of montage, *Woyzeck* is like a fugue with contrapuntal themes and variations throughout the text.

Science and nature are depicted as antagonistic and are represented in the figures of the doctor and Woyzeck. The idea that an uneducated, poor, and powerless individual of the lower classes such as Woyzeck has the same human needs and rights as his economically, intellectually, and socially more fortunate counterpart, the doctor, is of sociopolitical significance, but Büchner's argument here is not primarily political. Rather, he seeks to show how science—the medical profession in particular—violates the fundamental principle that every form of existence has its own intrinsic value. The very crudity of the examples with which Büchner exposes the enmity between nature and science makes it impossible for the audience to miss his message. Parallels such as that between the market scene, in which a horse relieves itself onstage, and the scene at the doctor's office, in which Woyzeck is required to supply a urine sample, are abundant. To the doctor, man and beast are the same: The horse, so maintains the charlatan, is "an animalistic human being and yet a beast, *une bête*," which merely "cannot express itself, cannot explain, is a transformed human being." Woyzeck, like the horse, cannot explain himself with the eloquence of the physician and therefore is perceived by him as subhuman ("an interesting *casus*. Subject Woyzeck"). Both the horse and Woyzeck are said to be close to nature, about which the physician knows little. "Look, the beast is still nature, unideal nature!" explains the charlatan when the horse urinates. Yet when Woyzeck, too, explains his action with the words "But Sir, when nature overcomes one," the physician is unimpressed: "Nature overcomes! Nature overcomes! Nature! Have I not shown that the musculus constrictor vesicae is subject to the will?" Because he has relieved himself in the street, Woyzeck is unable to provide the doctor with a urine specimen and thereby hinders his research. Nature (natural inclination, common sense, creature instinct) is at war with science. Another animal—a cat that Woyzeck has to hand to the doctor—also refuses to cooperate with the physician's experiments: "If I throw this cat out the window, how will this entity conduct itself in relation to the centrum gravitationis and to its own instinct?" the physician asks the students and, when the cat es-

capes, explains, "Gentlemen, the animal has no scientific instinct."

As previously noted, this doctor, who conducts cruel and senseless experiments on Woyzeck and on animals, who covers his paltry, pseudoscientific findings with officiousness and Latin terminology, and whose main concerns are public recognition and personal aggrandizement, bears a strong resemblance to Dr. Johann Christian August Clarus, who was instrumental in bringing about the death penalty for the historical Woyzeck—a parallel that deepens Büchner's attack on the teleologically oriented scientific approach. Like Clarus, the doctor in the play is preoccupied with Woyzeck's physical symptoms ("Look, the man, for three months he has eaten nothing but peas, note the effect, just feel what an uneven pulse") and attributes them solely to physical causes. Like Clarus, he, too, is obsessed with gaining public recognition with the results of his experiments and thus engages in sensationalism. He totally overlooks the manifestations of potentially violent behavior in Woyzeck. Because of his erroneous perception of Woyzeck's condition, the physician not only fails to derive any useful medical information from his experiment with Woyzeck but also contributes to the latter's mental deterioration and, ultimately, to the death of Marie, who is the victim of Woyzeck's act of aggression. Such a misuse of medicine becomes a menace to those in need of help as well as to society in general.

The terms "science" and "nature," which incorporate a variety of historically antagonistic forces in their symbolic framework, are imbued by Büchner with an additional dimension. Science is identified with the callous and futile inquiry that he perceives in the teleological method. Nature becomes the symbol for the quest for answers to basic questions of existence—the less fragmented, all-encompassing approach that Büchner calls the philosophical point of view. The physician should not treat the human being like a machine whose parts may be serviced individually or replaced altogether. Rather, he should look beyond a strictly physical cause-and-effect relationship to underlying environmental factors as possible determinants for physiological and psychological dysfunctions. People are entities to themselves, with their own laws governing their own actions, not mass-manufactured products composed of interchangeable parts.

LEONCE AND LENA

Leonce and Lena, although it is a comedy, goes a step beyond *Woyzeck* in depicting the troubled human condition. Büchner wrote it to enter in a publisher-sponsored writing contest in 1836. He missed the deadline, and the manuscript was returned unopened and was later lost. The published version is taken from various unpolished drafts, which show a number of parallels to Büchner's other plays. The same correlation between love and death that appeared in *Danton's Death* is also evident in the love scene between Leonce and Lena: "Let me be your Angel of Death. Let my lips descend upon your eyes like his wings. Beautiful corpse, you are resting so lovely upon the black pall of night, that nature hates life and falls in love with death." The view of man as a machine, which Büchner denounced as scientific positivism in *Woyzeck*, also appears in *Leonce and Lena*.

As in the previously discussed plays, Büchner departs here, too, from accepted dramatic theory. If the common man was elevated to tragic hero in *Danton's Death* and *Woyzeck*, royalty and nobility are debased in *Leonce and Lena* to comic figures and fools in a plot that borrows extensively from William Shakespeare's *As You Like It* (pr. c. 1599-1600) and *Hamlet, Prince of Denmark* (pr. c. 1600-1601). This mixture of comic and tragic elements is, in itself, part of the incongruity that establishes the audience's alienation and distance from the play, and that Bertolt Brecht much later made common theatrical practice. Büchner uses an early version of the technique by willfully destroying temporal and spatial concepts. The most obvious reference to this technique is in the last scene, in which Leonce, as the new ruler, proclaims: "We shall have all clocks destroyed and all calendars suppressed." It is apparent already in the flight from the kingdom of Popo (a child's term for the buttocks), where Valerio and the prince pass through "a dozen principalities, a half dozen grand duchies, and several kingdoms" in half a day. "Here we are at the border again," Valerio exclaims. "That's a country like an onion—nothing but skins—or like

nested boxes—in the largest there's nothing but boxes and in the smallest there's nothing at all." It is obvious that the reality depicted is not genuine, and thus the question as to the meaning of this unreal world becomes paramount.

Ronald Hauser opts for the interpretation that in *Leonce and Lena* reality is shown through the eyes of the inmates in an insane asylum. It is an intriguing idea, quite reconcilable with Büchner's sense for the macabre and quite consistent with the method of inversion he applies in this play; the assumption can also be corroborated by many passages in the text. The strongest support for this reading is to be found in the fragmented scene from the first act, in which two police officers are searching for an escaped "somebody, a subject, an individual, a person, a delinquent," who, according to a warrant, is "a most dangerous individual." The prince is an escapee from the royal residence with its surrounding kingdom, whose borders are very closely drawn indeed—so close, in fact, that they are much like the confines of an asylum and its grounds. When told about Leonce's flight, the king orders a border watch. "The view from this ward permits us the most stringent surveillance," reports the master of ceremonies to the king, and the watchmen perceive only "a dog who has run through the kingdom, looking for its master" and "someone taking a walk on the northern frontier." The prince, whom Valerio calls "an imbecile," searches for his ideal woman: "She is infinitely beautiful and infinitely mindless. . . . It is a delightful contrast . . . this spiritual death in this spiritual body." King Peter shows schizophrenic symptoms when he says, "if I speak so loudly I don't know who it is—I or another. That frightens me." Only the court jester, Valerio, can portray what he really is—an idiot—and therefore he is the only character who speaks the truth. Amid all the plays on words, the witticisms, the political barbs that constitute this comedy, is the bitter nucleus—the suggestion that the entire world is nothing but an asylum for lunatics.

OTHER MAJOR WORKS

LONG FICTION: *Lenz*, 1839 (novella; English translation, 1963).

NONFICTION: *Der Hessische Landbote*, 1834 (with Friedrich Ludwig Weidig; *The Hessian Messenger*, 1963).

TRANSLATIONS: *Lukretia Borgia*, 1909 (of Victor Hugo's play *Lucrèce Borgia*); *Maria Tudor*, 1909 (of Hugo's play *Marie Tudor*).

MISCELLANEOUS: *The Complete Collected Works*, 1977.

BIBLIOGRAPHY

Chen, Jui-Min. *Inversion of Revolutionary Ideals: A Study of the Tragic Essence of Georg Büchner's "Dantons Tod," Ernst Toller's "Masse Mensch," and Bertolt Brecht's "Die Massnahme."* Studies on Themes and Motifs in Literature 33. New York: P. Lang, 1998. This study of revolutionary themes in German literature examines Büchner's *Danton's Death* as well as two other works by German writers. Includes bibliography.

Crighton, James. *Büchner and Madness: Schizophrenia in Georg Büchner's "Lenz" and "Woyzeck."* Lewiston, N.Y.: Edwin Mellen Press, 1998. A view from the medical perspective on Büchner's *Woyzeck* and *Lenz*. Contains bibliography and index.

Grimm, Reinhold. *Love, Lust, and Rebellion: New Approaches to Georg Büchner*. Madison: University of Wisconsin Press, 1985. Grimm analyzes Büchner's life and works, paying special attention to his themes of rebellion and love. Includes index and bibliography.

Hilton, Julian. *Georg Büchner*. New York: Grove Press, 1982. A concise biography examining the writer and his works. Includes bibliography and index.

Holmes, T. M. *The Rehearsal of Revolution: Georg Büchner's Politics and His Drama "Dantons Tod."* New York: P. Lang, 1995. Holmes examines Büchner's *Danton's Death* in light of its political overtones. Includes bibliography.

Mills, Ken, and Brian Keith-Smith, eds. *Georg Büchner: Tradition and Innovation: Fourteen Essays*. Lewiston, N.Y.: Edwin Mellen Press, 1992. A collection of papers from a symposium on Büchner that took place at the Institute of Germanic Studies, University of London, in 1987. Includes bibliography.

Reddick, John. *Georg Büchner: The Shattered Whole*. New York: Oxford University Press, 1994. A scholarly examination of Büchner's life and works. Includes bibliography and index.

Richards, David G. *Georg Büchner's "Woyzeck": A History of Its Criticism*. Rochester, N.Y.: Camden House, 2001. This study of Büchner's *Woyzeck* attempts to place the literary criticism of the work into perspective. Includes bibliography and index.

Helene M. Kastinger Riley

ANTONIO BUERO VALLEJO

Born: Guadalajara, Spain; September 29, 1916
Died: Madrid, Spain; April 28, 2000

PRINCIPAL DRAMA

Historia de una escalera, pr. 1949, pb. 1950 (*Story of a Staircase*, 1955)

En la ardiente oscuridad, pr. 1950, pb. 1951 (*In the Burning Darkness*, 1985)

La tejedora de sueños, pr., pb. 1952 (*The Dream Weaver*, 1964)

Hoy es fiesta, pr. 1956, pb. 1960 (*Today's a Holiday*, 1987)

Las cartas boca abajo, pr. 1957, pb. 1959

Un soñador para un pueblo, pr. 1958, pb. 1960 (*A Dreamer for the People*, 1994)

Las meninas, pr. 1960, pb. 1962 (English translation, 1987)

El concierto de San Ovidio, pr. 1962, pb. 1964 (*The Concert at Saint Ovide*, 1967)

El tragaluz, pr. 1967, pb. 1968

La doble historia del doctor Valmy, pb. 1967, pr.
    1976 (*The Double Case History of Doctor
    Valmy*, 1967)
El sueño de la razón, pr. 1970, pb. 1971 (*The Sleep
    of Reason*, 1985)
La fundación, pr. 1974, pb. 1975 (*The Foundation*,
    1985)
La detonación, pr. 1977, pb. 1979 (*The Shot*, 1989)
Jueces en la noche, pr., pb. 1979 (English
    translation, 1983)
Caimán, pr. 1981
Diálogo secreto, pr. 1984, pb. 1997
Three Plays, pb. 1985
Lázaro en el laberinto, pr. 1986, pb. 1987 (*Lazarus
    in the Labyrinth*, 1992)
Música cercana, pr. 1989, pb. 1990 (*The Music
    Window*, 1994)
Las trampas del azar, pr. 1994, pb. 1995
Una misión al desierto, pr., pb. 1999

OTHER LITERARY FORMS

Antonio Buero Vallejo is known for his articles
and books on art and literary criticism. He wrote on
the nature of tragedy, on Diego Velázquez, and on
Spanish literary figures such as Ramón María del
Valle-Inclán and Federico García Lorca.

ACHIEVEMENTS

The premiere of Antonio Buero Vallejo's *Story of
a Staircase* marked the resurgence of serious theater
in Spain after the Civil War of 1936-1939. In contrast
to the escapist fare that was then in vogue, Buero
Vallejo's play, which depicts the hopes and illusions
of families in a Madrid tenement, reflected the painful reality of the postwar period. It incorporated a
tragic portrayal of human existence generally absent
from the Spanish stage of the twentieth century. Buero
Vallejo's plays—more than twenty original works—
constitute a critical inquiry into the problem of Spain
and its destiny; at the same time, they represent an
exploration of the human condition that is universal.
Buero Vallejo was one of Spain's most acclaimed
playwrights and, perhaps, the only genuine tragedian
in the history of its theater.

In 1949, Buero Vallejo received the Lope de Vega

Prize for *Story of a Staircase*. This award was followed by the Premio Maria Rolland award in 1956
for *Today's a Holiday*, in 1958 for *A Dreamer for the
People*, and in 1960 for *Las meninas*. He won the
Premio Nacional de Teatro, Spain's national theater
award in 1957 for *Today's a Holiday*, in 1958 for *Las
cartas boca abajo*, and in 1980 for *A Dreamer for the
People*. In 1962, he was awarded the Premio Larra for
The Concert at Saint Ovide. He received the Premio
Leopoldo Cano in 1966, 1970, 1972, 1974, and 1976,
and the Medalla de Oro del Espectador y la Critica in
1967, 1970, 1974, 1976, 1977, 1981, 1984, and 1986.
In 1971, Buero Vallejo was honored as member of the
Real Academia Española. He received the Premio
Mayte and Premio Foro Teatral in 1974, the Medalla
de Oro Gaceta Illustrada in 1976, the Premio Ercilla
and Medalla Valle-Inclan de la Asociacion de Escri-
tores y Artistas in 1985, and the Preio Pablo Iglesias
in 1986. The highest honor for Spanish and Latin
American literature, the Premio Miguel de Cervantes,
was granted to Buero Vallejo in 1986. A lifetime
achievement award, the Premio Nacional de las Letras,
was also awarded in 1986. In 1994, he received the
Medalla de Oro al Merite en las Bellas Artes and the
Medalla de Oro de la Sociedad General de Autores de
Espana.

BIOGRAPHY

Antonio Buero Vallejo was born to Francisco
Buero, a military engineer, and Cruz Vallejo. He
studied art at the San Fernando School of Fine Arts in
Madrid and later served as a medical corpsman on the
Loyalist side in the Spanish Civil War. After six years
as a political prisoner, he was released in 1947 and
started to write plays. In 1949, he won Spain's major
drama award, the Lope de Vega Prize, for *Story of a
Staircase*, which he had submitted anonymously.
This prize guaranteed the play's performance.

During the era in which Francisco Franco controlled Spain, Buero Vallejo refused to make ideological concessions despite government censorship of
many of his works. From his first work, he continued
to write plays throughout his lifetime, often winning
awards. The esteem in which Buero Vallejo was held
by writers and scholars of varying persuasions was

evinced by his election, in 1971, to the Royal Spanish Academy. Buero Vallejo made several trips to the United States and lectured at major American universities in the 1960's. In 1978, he was elected an honorary fellow of the Modern Language Association of America and was honored with a special session at its annual meeting. He was also an honorary fellow of the American Association of Teachers of Spanish and Portuguese, the Society of Spanish and Spanish American Studies, and the Circulo de Bellas Artes de Madrid.

In 1994, a two-volume collection of his works appeared, and he published a collection of his essays on the theater and a play in 1999. Buero Vallejo died of a stroke in Madrid on April 28, 2000.

ANALYSIS

For Antonio Buero Vallejo, tragedy is an all-embracing quest for understanding, an intuitive investigation of an enigmatic reality. Rejecting prescriptive considerations, he considers that tragedy is the representation of human beings' struggle against their limitations, for their freedom. In their quest for

Antonio Buero Vallejo in 1986. (AP/Wide World Photos)

understanding or truth, for the light that will permit them to overcome their limitations, many of Buero Vallejo's protagonists—whose prototype is the blind Oedipus—embody the preoccupations of the dramatist. In their struggle against seemingly insurmountable obstacles, they often evince the idealism of Don Quixote. Buero Vallejo's attitude toward the struggle that tragedy implies is ultimately one of hope. Tragedy, Buero Vallejo has stated, proposes an encounter with those truths that can, perhaps, free human beings from their blindness.

The very foundation of Buero Vallejo's theater is his passion for truth. The human condition is seen as characterized by self-deception and unwillingness to face the harsher realities of life. To express this idea, Buero Vallejo often uses the symbolism of blindness and vision, of darkness and light. Indeed, this symbolism appears in the very first play he wrote: *In the Burning Darkness*, whose alienated protagonist, Ignacio, yearns to see. The new arrival in a school for the blind, he merges his desire to overcome his physical limitation with his metaphysical anguish, seeking a light that represents spiritual truth or vision. It is significant that he is the model for many of Buero Vallejo's later dreamer-protagonists. The other students, content in their world of darkness, refuse to face the reality of their limitations; they represent humankind in general, self-condemned to a spiritual blindness.

The blindness that Buero Vallejo depicts is universal. Nevertheless, it is possible to see in many of his dramas the tragedy of Francisco Franco's Spain. The school of *In the Burning Darkness*, whose students conform to its rules and deny the reality of their situation, the dark apartment of *El tragaluz* (the basement window), whose inhabitants invent fictitious versions of the tragic events that happened to them at the end of the Civil War in an effort to go on living, and especially, the prison cell of *The Foundation*, one of whose inmates deludes himself into believing he is doing research in a beneficent "Foundation"—all are microcosms of Franco's Spain.

Buero Vallejo's plays are never politically programmatic, for he does not present solutions to the questions raised. In his tragic theater, Buero Vallejo attempts, rather, to bring about, on the part of the spectators, what he calls a type of "active contemplation." There is always a delicate balance between communicative emotion and critical reflection. Identification and distancing become complementary functions of dramatic structure. It is significant that his theater is characterized by a continuous process of technical experimentation and creative innovation. Buero Vallejo has been especially interested in the problem of spectator participation and has devised a technique to achieve such a participation that constitutes one of his most original contributions to modern drama. He uses what are known as effects of interiorization, "immersion," or psychic participation, through which the spectators are brought to identify with his protagonists. In his early dramas, these effects often take the form of peculiar sense perceptions—or the lack of them—that are shared on brief occasions by the protagonist and the spectators. In his dramas of the 1970's—*The Foundation, The Shot,* and *Jueces en la noche* (judges in the night)—these effects are extended throughout a major part of the action. What the spectators see is, to a great extent, the materialization of the perceptions, thoughts, and dreams of the protagonist. The true action thus occurs within the mind of his character, and Buero Vallejo lets the audience see this action directly.

IN THE BURNING DARKNESS

In the Burning Darkness constitutes an inquiry into the mystery of life, an inquiry characteristic of Buero Vallejo's entire theater. The light, the more authentic reality for which Ignacio, the blind student, yearns, is symbolized by the distant stars. That the light for which he longs is metaphysical becomes obvious, for he states that, even if he could see the stars, he would die because he cannot reach them. The other students of the school, where an atmosphere of superficial optimism and gaiety prevails, refuse to confront the tragedy of their limitations. They refuse to acknowledge that they are blind, feigning a normality that does not exist and even referring to those who see as "sighted." The institution or school is a world of darkness and shadows that has been compared to Plato's cave. Isolated in this world of darkness, the students are ignorant of the light that shines outside.

Ignacio, however, soon turns the students' tranquil blindness into painful awareness as he points out the fiction on which their lives are based. For him, the meaning of existence is to be found only through searching for the truth, despite the suffering that this imposes. For him, there is another world, a transcendent reality to which most men are spiritually blind, a world symbolized by the distant stars for which he longs.

In the end, Ignacio succeeds in making his opponent, the leader of the students, understand his anguish. This leader, Carlos, has considered Ignacio's attitude harmful to the morale of the school and has sought to discredit him. In a pivotal scene, Buero Vallejo makes the spectators experience the same anguish that Ignacio feels by means of an "immersion" effect—a slow blackout of the stage and houselights as the protagonist describes how those who can see, close their eyes to imagine the horror of blindness. In the end, Ignacio is murdered by Carlos. His dreams, however, live on in his murderer, who repeats the dead man's words about the distant stars as the curtain falls.

On a metaphysical level, the institution represents this world, and the students, human beings in general, who are spiritually blind. Ignacio's yearning to see even though he feels it is impossible, evinces the passion for the absolute that typifies the writings of the Spanish existentialist philosopher Miguel de Unamuno y Jugo, who has strongly influenced Buero Vallejo. Ignacio's desire to transcend his limitations and to penetrate the mysteries of humankind and the universe is characteristic of many of Buero Vallejo's dreamers. Buero Vallejo's tragedy depicts the human condition, which he sees as a constant struggle between faith and doubt, with the continuing accompaniment of hope. His anguished protagonists, torn between faith and doubt, as well as the theme of physical and spiritual blindness, place the author clearly in the tradition of Unamuno. Also present in this play are echoes of the Spanish mystics, especially Saint John of the Cross, who wrote of the "dark night of the soul."

On a political level, the institution for the blind suggests any authoritarian regime that tries to convince its citizens that they are free and happy when they are not. It is a regime that does not hesitate to resort to violence when its authority is challenged. The institution has thus been seen as a symbol of Franco's Spain with its violence, injustice, and lies. Significantly, Buero Vallejo conceived the idea for the play while in prison.

EL TRAGALUZ

El tragaluz is the story of a Madrid family destroyed by the Civil War and forced to take refuge in a sordid basement apartment. The action is narrated by investigators of a future century, whose progress allows them to detect images or holograms of the past that have been mysteriously preserved. The holograms that the investigators project represent not only actions but also thoughts, and the boundaries between the two are blurred as the cameras capture the totality of human experience. At the end of the war, this family had been unable to board the crowded train that was to return them to Madrid, with the exception of the elder son Vicente, who was carrying their scant provisions. Despite his father's command to get off, he had continued to Madrid; during the following days, his baby sister had died of hunger before the family found shelter in the basement apartment, where they have lived in poverty for nearly thirty years. In order to make life bearable, they invent a fictitious version of these events that absolves Vicente of all responsibility. The dark basement apartment, like the institution of *In the Burning Darkness*, represents a refuge from the light of reality—the light that enters the narrow window projecting shadows on the opposite wall that is visible to the spectators.

The old father, traumatized by the disloyalty of his son, constantly relives the past, insisting that the basement window is the window of a train. Furthermore, he spends his time cutting out human figures from old postcards and watching the anonymous people who pass the window—just as his two sons did years ago when they pretended that they were in a theater. Contemplating these figures, the father asks a persistent question: "Who is that?" For the younger son Mario, a dreamer like Ignacio of *In the Burning Darkness*, this apparently incoherent question suggests the enigma of humankind's identity—a concern

common to both Søren Kierkegaard and Unamuno. Indeed, the father has been compared to the old madman of Samuel Beckett's *Krapp's Last Tape* (pr., pb. 1958), who is absorbed by this same enigma. Like Ignacio, Mario longs to transcend the limits of human understanding, to penetrate the ultimate mysteries of the universe.

Mario, the idealistic dreamer, chooses to remain in the basement, disdaining material success in a world in which the only way to get ahead is by deceit, precisely the means used by Vicente, who left home years ago to achieve economic prosperity and who now holds an important position. Mario has deliberately chosen poverty and obscurity. The opposition between the two brothers is heightened by Mario's concern for Vicente's secretary, Encarna, a poor country girl exploited by Vicente, who has forced her to become his mistress. For Mario, she represents the latest in a series of victims that began with his baby sister.

The opposition between the two brothers—which is not unlike that between Ignacio and Carlos of the preceding play—culminates in the "trial" scene, in which Mario accuses Vicente not only of responsibility for the death of their sister and the madness of the father but, even more important, of having victimized others ever since. Vicente "took the train" to success years ago and has never gotten off. Alone with his father, Vicente confesses his guilt. Believing, however, that change is impractical or impossible, he prepares to leave, to return to the "train that never stops." The father, reliving the past, believes that Vicente is once again about to board the real train that took him away years ago. He then stabs his son in a burst of madness—or of sanity—as the sound of the locomotive (heard whenever the characters look out the window) becomes deafening. Ambiguous and mysterious, the father is both a pitiable madman and an all-knowing judge and God figure.

El tragaluz represents a judgment on an entire generation. The investigators make clear the historical dimension of the drama when they state that "the world was full of injustice, war, and fear." Men of action (such as Vicente) "forgot to contemplate" or dream and "those who contemplated" (such as

Mario) were "incapable of action." The investigators make clear that they themselves have overcome these errors. Through them, Buero Vallejo thus expresses his hope for a time when people will have learned the lessons of history, when they will have created the more just and humane society that Mario and Vicente's generation failed to realize.

Buero Vallejo's narrators are far from being a mere Brechtian device. Their purpose is to move the spectators, to bring them to identify with the family within the frame, to understand rationally but, even more important, to feel that they themselves, like the family depicted, are being observed and judged by a sort of future conscience that is really operating in the present. Curiously enough, the spectators themselves are observed by the very characters that they are observing and on which they are passing judgment. Because the basement window is located on the invisible wall between actors and spectators, the latter are the subjects of the former's questions about the identity of the figures who pass by from the outside world. The spectators are thus led to examine their own conduct as they themselves become subjects of an investigation.

The tragedy underscores the solidarity that people must come to feel with both past and present generations. The guilt of Vicente and of Mario is the spectators' guilt. To the query, "Who is that?"—whether it is the father's question as he refers to figures who pass by the window or the investigators' questions as they observe the subjects of their experiments—the answer is, in a certain sense, that given by one of the investigators as she addresses the spectators: "That one is you, and you, and you. I am you, and you are me." The collective tragedy of Spain, *El tragaluz* is, no less, the individual tragedy of man as an ontological enigma. The play begins as a portrayal of Spanish society of the Franco era and develops into an anguished inquiry into the human condition.

THE SLEEP OF REASON

The Sleep of Reason takes place in the disastrous period following the War of Independence against the French. The years of civil discord under Ferdinand VII, with the restoration of absolutism and the accompanying terror, torture, and executions, resemble in many respects the period immediately following the Civil War of 1936-1939.

In declining health and stone-deaf for some three decades, an aged Goya lives half-hidden in his villa, in constant fear of persecution. The spectators are made to share the deafness that adds to the painter's sense of isolation and estrangement; whenever Goya is onstage, the other characters move their lips without articulating any sound at all, using only sign language or pantomime. Just as Buero Vallejo blinds the spectators for a brief period in *In the Burning Darkness*, he makes them deaf with Goya. At the same time, Buero Vallejo permits the spectators to perceive the obsessions and hallucinations of the artist, who has been driven to near madness by Ferdinand and whom the dramatist describes as living his hours of deepest darkness. Meows, owl hoots, the whirling of bat wings, and voices—often of the figures from the enigmatic and phantasmagoric "Black Paintings" that cover the walls of his villa—are revealed through sound effects. To these effects are added Goya's own disembodied voice that from time to time announces the captions of various of his engravings appropriate to the situation. Moreover, the spectators perceive, as does Goya himself, his own heartbeats, dull thuds that vary in intensity to reflect the terror that he experiences.

Buero Vallejo leads the spectators to identify with Goya, not only through having them share the painter's deafness and "hear" his thoughts, but also by having them "see" the world through his own eyes. To the vocalization of Goya's inner world, Buero Vallejo adds its visualization; slides of the "Black Paintings" are projected at opportune moments throughout the tragedy. All of these multimedia devices serve to lead the spectators into the very mind of the tormented protagonist.

"The sleep of reason produces monsters," states the inscription to Goya's "Caprice 34." Goya himself explained at the bottom of his engraving: "Fantasy without reason produces monstrosities; but together they beget true art and may give rise to wondrous things." The "Black Paintings" may thus be considered the product of a reasoned fantasy. Goya's near, but not total, madness becomes a means of apprehending reality more rigorously than it can be understood through normality. Goya, like the father in *El tragaluz*, has profoundly lucid intuitions to which the other characters cannot rise.

In his enigmatic "Black Paintings," Goya attempts to express the truth about the Spain of his time, symbolizing the irrational and absurd evil around him as monsters—half human, half animal. In "The Witches' Sabbath," for example, a mob of bestial witches and warlocks listens, in darkness, to the pronouncements of a cassocked ram, Satan. In the drama, when Buero Vallejo has Goya explain to one of his few remaining friends the meaning of his works, the painter declares that the king is a monster and his advisers, jackals. His revenge is to paint them as he sees them. Buero Vallejo thus gives to many of these paintings—products of the black mist swirling in Goya's mind—a historical and political interpretation. He believes that they represent the artist's despair over both his own personal destiny and that of Spain. The slender hope to which the artist clings is likewise seen, Buero Vallejo believes, in the painting that depicts a mythical winged woman who carries a terrified man (perhaps the artist himself) away to the mountain, far from the fratricidal rage and war on earth. When Goya is finally forced into exile, these paintings left on the walls of his villa represent his inner victory.

Shortly before his departure, Goya is beaten and humiliated by soldiers sent by the king. Their visit is prefigured by a nightmare of the artist in which the stage is filled with monsters from his imagination—masked figures with bat wings, a cat's head, pig faces, and so on—who dance grotesquely around him and attack him. This absurd dance is accompanied by nonsensical cries taken from the titles of his etchings. Using psychedelic lighting and sound effects, Buero Vallejo re-creates, in this scene, the famous "Caprice" whose inscription he uses as the play's title, letting the spectators enter Goya's tormented mind. The tragedy ends with a question as the painter abandons his villa. While a deafening din of voices repeats the title of another of his "Caprices," "If the dawn comes, we will go!"—a title indicative of his hope for the light that will drive off the demons—the

lights go down, leaving only the gigantic painting, "The Witches' Sabbath," glowing in the darkness. Among Buero Vallejo's tragedies, *The Sleep of Reason* has won for him the greatest international acclaim.

THE FOUNDATION

In *The Sleep of Reason*, Goya's near madness results in profoundly lucid intuitions and thus represents a new access to reality. In *The Foundation*, however, the protagonist's madness represents an escape from a reality too painful to face. In this tragedy, the spectators see much of the action through the eyes of a youth who suffers from a type of schizophrenic delusion. Because the spectators identify with him, they, too, become victims of a delusion; when they share, also, in his return to lucidity, their madness, like that of the protagonist, results in a clearer understanding of their own situation.

At the beginning of *The Foundation*, the action appears to take place in an elegant center for research: There is a comfortable room with a view of a sparkling landscape with majestic mountains, green forests, and a silver lake. At the end, the spectators find themselves in a prison cell and learn that the five major characters are not eminent writers and scientists who have received grants from a "Foundation," as they were led to believe, but prisoners condemned to death for political activities against the established order. This change in the spectators' perception is the result of the change in that of the protagonist, Tomás, as he gradually overcomes his alienation to perceive the same reality as his cellmates. After revealing, under torture, the name of a comrade, Tomás was incapable of facing his guilt and his sentence. He therefore created an illusionary world without pain, thus rejecting the truth for a lie.

From the beginning of the drama, the spectators see what Tomás sees—pleasantly furnished quarters and a luminous landscape whose rainbow-hued light floods the room—and hear the same music of Antonio Rossini that he hears on the stereo. Soon, however, they begin to share Tomás's perplexities at certain words of his cellmates that do not seem to correspond to the situation as he—and the spectators—perceive it; they end up by losing their faith in his and their own vision. Buero Vallejo disconcerts the spectators with the contradiction between Tomás's world and that of the other prisoners, plunging the spectators into a world of falsehood so that they may slowly emerge into a world of truth along with his protagonist.

Under the guidance of an older prisoner, Asel— one of Buero Vallejo's author surrogates—Tomás begins his slow journey to reality as he begins to demand explanations for strange occurrences that, he comes to realize, surprise only him and not his companions: the disappearance of the tobacco he thought he had, the failure of the television and the stereo he imagined, and so on. Buero Vallejo's technique has been called the visualization of an interior monologue.

The "immersion" effect in this tragedy is one of Buero Vallejo's most elaborate experiments in stagecraft. From the very beginning, the spectators share Tomás's perceptions, as illusion (the "Foundation") gives way to reality (the prison). Throughout, the set undergoes constant modifications that reflect Tomás's discovery of the stark truth. These modifications both maintain the spectators' curiosity and underscore the dialectical opposition of the two worlds presented: that of Tomás and the spectators and that of the other prisoners. The luxurious armchairs are replaced by bedrolls; wall panels descend to cover the television and stereo; the fine crystal, silver, and linens are replaced by simple metal cups and spoons; and, finally, the landscape beyond the picture window vanishes behind a portion of the wall, signaling the final triumph of reality.

The "Foundation" is an image of the world seen through the eyes of estrangement. In Tomás's rejection of reality, the spectators see their own refusal to accept the reality of their world. When the set has been dismantled, however, when Tomás's fictitious world has crumbled and reality has emerged, the spectators see their own world for what it is and always has been.

After leading the spectators to see the world through Tomás's eyes, Buero Vallejo invites them to reflect critically on its significance. For Buero Vallejo, tragedy always implies both emotive identifica-

tion and critical reflection. Once again, Asel serves as a guide. Tomás, while realizing that his "Foundation" is not real, asks himself if the rest of the world is any more real—if the prison, their death sentences, and even they themselves are not equally illusory. If so, Tomás asks, why attempt to escape, only to discover a freedom that is equally deceptive? Asel replies that, even though everything may be an illusion, an immense hologram, the fear that this may be so must not paralyze him, and no progress, however limited, must be disdained. "When you have been in prison," Asel explains, "you end up understanding that, wherever you go, you are in prison." After understanding this, Asel continues, "you have to go out into the other prison. And when you are in it, go out into another, and from that one to another. The truth awaits you in all of them." People move from one prison to another, from one illusion to another, but each step may bring them closer to reality. Only through action—represented by the difficult tunnel that Asel wants the prisoners to attempt—can truth and freedom be won.

At the end, Tomás is called from his cell to be led either to the isolation cell from which access to the tunnel may be possible, or more probably, to his execution. His fate remains undetermined. That the deceptive world of the "Foundation" continues, regardless of his destiny, is seen clearly when a guard, dressed as the hotel manager Tomás saw in his delusion, appears to welcome new inmates to the cell— which is once again transformed into the elegantly furnished room seen at the beginning of the drama. Buero Vallejo thus invites the spectators to reenter the "Foundation" together with the new occupants, as the drama begins all over again. The tragedy thus ends ambivalently, with a question that only the spectators can answer.

On the political level, *The Foundation* is Buero Vallejo's response to Franco's Spain or any other country in which people are not free. He underscores the importance of each step, each concession won from an authoritarian regime, no matter how provisional, in the struggle for freedom. The play constitutes an attack on sociopolitical systems that deceive and enslave—against the oppressive "Foundations" of the world and their ideology. Even more important, however, the play is a parable of the human condition, of the search for the truth that will enable people to be spiritually free. The work thus develops certain ideas that have their genesis in *In the Burning Darkness*. The prisons of which Buero Vallejo speaks are not only those that enslave the body but also those that enslave the soul. The playwright suggests that the obligation of human beings is to struggle for a more lucid understanding of reality, no matter how harsh and dreadful this reality may be, to struggle to overcome their human limitations. Buero Vallejo emphasizes the fact that the journey toward truth and freedom, which is the concern of all authentic tragedy, must be gradual. He suggests metaphorically that his journey must be inward (in Tomás's case to his own true past) and outward, through a series of concentric prisons from which tunnels must be opened toward an ever-brighter light.

This process has been Buero Vallejo's own. His trajectory as a playwright represents a search for truth in which, if definitive answers have seldom been found, at least the directions have become clearer. The understanding to which modern human beings aspire is tentative and precarious. It is seldom the sudden and complete illumination that finally comes to Oedipus in a blinding flash of light. This search is evident in his works from the 1980's and 1990's, *Caimán*, *Diálogo secreto*, *Lazarus in the Labyrinth*, and *The Music Window*. As these works demonstrate, the theater of Buero Vallejo is humanistic in its intent to resolve internal and external realities as the individual struggles to find a meaningful place in society. By immersing his characters in psychological conflicts, Buero Vallejo draws the audience into the experience. Hope endures despite suffering, imprisonment, and loss.

CAIMÁN

Caimán utilizes metatheater and the techniques of *mise en abîme* to define the characters both subjectively and objectively. The play is presented as a story narrated by a mother who refers to her dead daughter. As actress, she enters the scenes as they are retold and reviewed. The drama unfolds as a story that is narrated at the moment it becomes action.

DIÁLOGO SECRETO

Diálogo secreto (secret dialogue) dramatizes the tormented conscience of a protagonist afraid of confronting reality. A famous art critic, he is plagued by the burden of maintaining his image while living a lie during a lifetime of fraudulent and deceptive practices. Art in its purest form offers him hope for redemption.

LAZARUS IN THE LABYRINTH

In *Lazarus in the Labyrinth*, Lázaro creates a false memory to protect himself from the truth about an attack that killed his girlfriend more than twenty years earlier. Amnesia, visual and auditory illusions, and paranoia torment the protagonist. The dramatic tension results from the subjective versus the objective points of view, spatial confusion, and eventual liberation by searching for the truth.

THE MUSIC WINDOW

The drama *The Music Window* attempted to criticize the negative repercussions from the rapid transformation of Spanish society after the Franco era. The cost of freedom devoid of ethics is personified in the character of Javier. Materialistic and power hungry, Javier's spiraling descent into vulgarity and depravity represents the moral bankruptcy of post-Franco Spanish society.

OTHER MAJOR WORKS

NONFICTION: *Nota al programa del estreno de "La perrera" de J. de Jesús Martínez*, 1957; *Me llamo Antonio Buero Vallejo*, 1964; *Seis dramaturgos leen sus obras*, 1965; *Comentario al programa de reposición de "Historia de una escalera,"* 1967; *Tres maestros ante el público*, 1973; *Nota al catalogo de la exposición de Monsalvo dedicada a Miguel Hernández*, 1977; *Buero por Buero*, 1993; *El futuro del teatro y otros ensayos*, 1999.

MISCELLANEOUS: *Obra completa*, 1994 (2 volumes).

BIBLIOGRAPHY

Caro Dugo, Carmen. *The Importance of the Don Quixote Myth in the Works of Antonio Buero Vallejo*. Lewiston, N.Y.: Mellon University Press, 1995. Concentrates on the Don Quixote-like struggles undergone by the characters in Buero Vallejo's dramas. Bibliography and index.

Chávez, Carmen. *Acts of Trauma in Six Plays by Antonio Buero Vallejo*. Lewiston, N.Y.: Edwin Mellen Press, 2001. Focuses on the incidents of psychic trauma that occur within Buero Vallejo's plays. Bibliography and index.

Edwards, Gwynne, ed. *Burning the Curtain: Four Revolutionary Spanish Plays*. New York: Marion

Boyars, 1995. The editor introduces and translates a play by Buero Vallejo as well as three others.

Halsey, Martha T. *From Dictatorship to Democracy: The Recent Plays of Buero Vallejo*. Ottawa: Dovehouse Editions, 1994. Examines Buero Vallejo's plays from *The Foundation* to *The Music Window*. Bibliography.

Martha T. Halsey,
updated by Carole A. Champagne

MIKHAIL BULGAKOV

Born: Kiev, Russia; May 15, 1891
Died: Moscow, U.S.S.R.; March 10, 1940

Principal drama

Dni Turbinykh, pr. 1926, pb. 1955 (adaptation of his novel *Belaya gvardiya*; *Days of the Turbins*, 1934)

Zoykina kvartira, pr. 1926, pb. 1971 (*Zoya's Apartment*, 1970)

Bagrovy ostrov, pr. 1928, pb. 1968 (adaptation of his short story; *The Crimson Island*, 1972)

Beg, wr. 1928, pr. 1957, pb. 1962 (*Flight*, 1969)

Kabala svyatosh, wr. 1929, pr. 1936, pb. 1962 (*A Cabal of Hypocrites*, 1972; also known as *Molière*)

Adam i Eva, wr. 1930-1931, pb. 1971 (*Adam and Eve*, 1971)

Blazhenstvo, wr. 1934, pb. 1966 (*Bliss*, 1976)

Posledniye dni (Pushkin), wr. 1934-1935, pr. 1943, pb. 1955 (*The Last Days*, 1976)

Ivan Vasilievich, wr. 1935, pb. 1965, pr. 1966 (English translation, 1974)

Minin i Pozharskii, wr. 1936, pb. 1976 (libretto)

Rashel, wr. c. 1936, pb. 1972 (libretto; adaptation of Guy de Maupassant's short story "Mademoiselle Fifi")

Batum, wr. 1938, pb. 1977

Don Kikhot, pr. 1941, pb. 1962

The Early Plays of Mikhail Bulgakov, pb. 1972

Six Plays, pb. 1991

Other literary forms

Although Mikhail Bulgakov is regarded in the Soviet Union primarily as a dramatist, especially for the plays of the mid- to late 1920's, he is best known in the West for his novels *Master i Margarita* (1966-1967; *The Master and Margarita*, 1967) and *Sobache serdtse* (1968-1969; *The Heart of a Dog*, 1968). The fact is, however, that once Bulgakov abandoned his career as a doctor in 1920 to devote himself fully to writing, he composed works in almost all literary forms. Beginning as a hack writer, Bulgakov published more than 160 stories and *feuilletons* in periodicals, most of them appearing between 1922 and 1927, when the first part of the largely autobiographical novel *Belaya gvardiya* (1927, 1929; *The White Guard*, 1971) was published. Bulgakov's dramatic career was launched when the Moscow Art Theatre asked him to adapt the novel into a play (*Days of the Turbins*). In addition to the periodical pieces and the plays, Bulgakov wrote several novels; a number of libretti; a stage adaptation of Nikolai Gogol's novel *Myortvye dushi* (1842, 1845; *Dead Souls*, 1887); film adaptations of *Dead Souls*, Gogol's play *Revizor* (1836; *The Inspector General*, 1890) and Leo Tolstoy's novels *Anna Karenina* (1875-1877; English translation, 1886) and *Voyna i mir* (1865-1869; *War and Peace*, 1886); and a biography of Molière. Late in his life, Bulgakov also wrote his *Teatralny roman* (1965; *Black Snow: A Theatrical Novel*, 1967), a satire on Konstantin Stanislavsky and the Moscow Art Theatre.

ACHIEVEMENTS

An intellectual with a flair for showy dress and an uncompromising integrity with regard to his art, Mikhail Bulgakov clashed head-on with every form of authority with which he came into contact—the brilliant, but dictatorial director Konstantin Stanislavsky; theater critics in the Soviet press; government censors; and Joseph Stalin himself. Seemingly obsessed with the seventeenth century French playwright Molière, Bulgakov wrote both a play about and a biography of his precursor and clearly identified with him. Like Molière, Bulgakov perceived himself as a gifted writer constantly plagued and harassed by ignorant, self-serving officials who thought nothing of sacrificing art to curry favor. Like Molière, Bulgakov, despite a strong satiric bent for social criticism, alternately enjoyed the preferment and suffered the displeasure of his ruler. Bulgakov has been hailed by his American editor and biographer Ellendea Proffer as the "best Russian playwright of the Soviet period," and his plays provide an interesting and complex portrait of the Russian people in the turbulent times of the Revolution and early years of the Soviet Republic.

During the first ten or fifteen years of the Soviet period, humor flourished in several genres, and Bulgakov's early periodical stories, with their sharp wit and offbeat characters, are representative of this trend. The theater of the period was dominated by revivals of classics and an almost endless stream of revolutionary plays with the conventional plot of heroic Reds triumphing over villainous Whites. No Party writer, Bulgakov composed his revolutionary (and best-known) play, *Days of the Turbins*, along different lines and thereby gained notoriety. Drawing on the realism that characterizes the plays of Anton Chekhov, Bulgakov mixes comic and tragic modes in his play and portrays his White characters ambiguously—humans caught in turmoil, confused, silly, noble, disillusioned. Dealing with the sordid life of crime, corruption, drugs, and sex that characterized post-Revolution Moscow, Bulgakov's next play, titled *Zoya's Apartment*, is another attempt at contemporary realism, though it is much more socially critical of existing conditions. *Zoya's Apartment* also draws

attention to the government's failure to eradicate these social problems despite its cruel repression, and even to its contribution to them.

When his realistic plays were reviewed negatively, Bulgakov turned to more experimental dramatic forms. With its self-conscious theatricality and play-within-a-play structure, *The Crimson Island* resembles Luigi Pirandello's *Sei personaggi in cerca d'autore* (pr., pb. 1921; *Six Characters in Search of an Author*, 1922). *Flight*, composed as a series of eight dreams, recalls the work of August Strindberg. In his later work, Bulgakov offers social criticism by providing parallels to the past, in plays about Molière and Alexander Pushkin, or to an envisioned future in a series of science fiction satires.

If the greatest virtue of these plays is the insight provided into the people, politics, and repression of the Revolution and the Stalin regime, their greatest defect stems from their absorption in this material. Whereas Chekhov's and Molière's drama seems timeless art, Bulgakov's plays are time-bound. There

Mikhail Bulgakov (AP/Wide World Photos)

are few memorable characters, and the dramatic experiments are often flawed in design or execution. Even the conflict of ideas and values that should be the very heart of these plays falls subordinate to historical setting. Because of the scanty performance history and the delayed publication of most of his plays, Bulgakov's influence as a playwright, especially outside the Soviet Union, is negligible.

BIOGRAPHY

The son of a theology professor, Mikhail Afanasyevich Bulgakov was born in Kiev on May 15, 1891, and was reared in a middle- to upper-middle-class family among the intelligentsia of that city. Characters like the ones he must have known as a child show up in his drama frequently and are usually portrayed sympathetically, indicating, perhaps, a comparatively happy childhood in an affluent milieu that was to be radically altered during the Revolution and the following civil war. From 1901 to 1909, Bulgakov attended Kiev's Aleksandrovsky High School, where his main interest seemed to be theater. Nevertheless, though renowned in childhood as a storyteller and mimic, Bulgakov enrolled in the College of Medicine at Kiev University, from which he was graduated with distinction in 1916. Bulgakov declared a specialty in venereology and, taking his first wife, Tatiana Lappa, to whom he had been married in 1913, with him, practiced medicine in the rural villages of Nikolskoe and Vyazma, primarily curing infections and amputating limbs. Returning to Kiev, where he spent the Civil War residing in the formerly placid family apartment, he witnessed fourteen changes of government in Kiev. He later chronicled this instability and its effects on Kiev's citizens in the novel *The White Guard* and in his first major play, *Days of the Turbins*.

In 1920, Bulgakov abandoned medicine for a career as a writer, penning several no longer remembered plays for the provincial theater in Vladikavkaz, where he also did some acting. While beginning work on *The White Guard*, which in 1927 would establish his reputation as a writer, Bulgakov moved in 1921 to Moscow, the city that would be his home until six months before his death. During the next few years, Bulgakov worked on his novel and made a liv-

ing writing stories for Communist magazines and newspapers. These first stories, some clearly autobiographical, mainly depict the cruelty and violence of the Civil War and the low-life characters struggling to exist in the first years of the New Economic Policy, which went into effect in March, 1921. Among the best-known of these pieces are "Diavoliada" ("Diaboliad") and "Rokovye yaytsa" ("The Fatal Eggs"), published in the periodical *Nedra* in 1924 and 1925, respectively. In 1924, Bulgakov's marriage was dissolved, and he was married to Lyubov Belozersky. The following year marked a turning point in Bulgakov's life, witnessing the completion of the novella *The Heart of a Dog*; the publication of his first collection of stories, *Diavoliada* (*Diaboliad and Other Stories*, 1972); the publication of the first installments of *The White Guard*; and a coveted invitation from the Moscow Art Theatre to convert *The White Guard* to a play.

The story surrounding the composition and performance history of *Days of the Turbins* (the title given to the play over Bulgakov's objections) is legendary. Undergoing constant revision (by Bulgakov, Ilya Sudakov, Pavel Markov, and Stanislavsky himself) until its first public rehearsal in October, 1926, *Days of the Turbins* raised an immediate storm. As the first Soviet play to portray Whites in the Civil War sympathetically, the play caused Party members to walk out, and middle-class audiences, who may well have been thrilled to hear the old Imperial Anthem sung onstage, to line up for tickets. Despite condemnation from theater critics writing for the Communist Party presses, the play entered the repertory, becoming the Moscow Art Theatre's biggest post-Revolutionary success, and Bulgakov emerged a celebrity.

The years immediately following this controversy were good ones for Bulgakov. He had begun what was to become *The Master and Margarita*, he was active in the theater life of Moscow, and at one time, in 1928, he had three plays—*Days of the Turbins*, *Zoya's Apartment*, and *The Crimson Island*—playing simultaneously. Yet Bulgakov's next two plays, *Flight* and *A Cabal of Hypocrites*, were rejected by the party censors, and after March, 1929, all his plays were banned from the theaters. Despairing (Bulgakov burned several of his works, among them the early drafts of *The Master and Margarita*) and desperate, the playwright, on March 28, 1930, wrote a letter to Stalin, which has become famous. Bulgakov attacked the Central Repertory Committee responsible for state censorship and requested permission to leave the Soviet Union. Three weeks later, Stalin phoned Bulgakov to discuss his situation. Then, probably as a result of Stalin's direct intervention, Bulgakov was offered a position as assistant director and literary consultant with the Moscow Art Theatre, where he worked primarily on adaptations. In 1932, *Days of the Turbins* was revived and reintroduced into the repertory of the Moscow Art Theatre. Receiving several hundred rubles a month, Bulgakov was once again financially secure and began a second creative phase that produced five new plays and the biography of Molière. He also separated from Lyubov Belozersky and was married to his third wife, Elena Shilovsky.

After a rift with Stanislavsky over the production of *A Cabal of Hypocrites* in 1936, Bulgakov left the Moscow Art Theatre for the Bolshoi Theatre. He wrote several librettos for that company and began the lampoon *Black Snow*. After discovering symptoms of neurosclerosis, Bulgakov worked frantically to complete *The Master and Margarita* and wrote his final play, *Batum*, about Stalin as a young revolutionary. In late 1939, Bulgakov, now blind, moved to Leningrad, where he at last finished *The Master and Margarita*, his masterpiece, shortly before his death on March 10, 1940. He is buried in Moscow's Novodevichye Cemetery.

ANALYSIS

Like most playwrights living during a pivotal historical epoch, Mikhail Bulgakov used his artistic talents to write satires and what can only be called historical plays. His major themes recur throughout his work: a condemnation of hypocrisy and dishonesty, a depiction of individuals caught in social and political turbulence, and a portrayal of the cruelty and arbitrariness of authority. Despite the intrinsic seriousness of these issues, Bulgakov's treatment of them invariably includes humor. This humor, stemming from

several sources, is quite varied. Dominant sometimes is dialogue rife with wit, or comically mechanical caricatures, or the extreme absurdity of situation. Yet always present is the tension between the seriousness and the comedy, the tension of the ongoingness of human existence.

With the exception of plays such as *A Cabal of Hypocrites*, in which a central character is featured, Bulgakov focuses on groups of characters and the changing relationships within the group as it is subjected to external change. Examples of this kind of focus would include the family and friends in *Days of the Turbins*, who must confront a political situation that changes almost hourly, and the group of soldiers and refugees in *Flight*, who must adapt not only to a changing political climate but also to constant changes in locale. These characters are distinguished by their adaptability, their resiliency; not really heroic (there is no King Lear among them), they are prepared to compromise, for their struggle is not to maintain their individual essence in a world with which they are at odds, but merely to get by, to survive, in a world that is so mutable that comprehension of it seems to be out of the question. In this sense, Bulgakov is a modern playwright indeed.

DAYS OF THE TURBINS

It is no fluke that Bulgakov is known best as a playwright for his first major play, *Days of the Turbins*; it is his best play. Here, he has created individualized characters with whom the audience sympathizes, characters who are not merely mouthpieces for political statements or present merely for the opportunity to comment on particular situations. Though the novel on which the play is based is sweeping in scope and episodic in structure, the play itself is tightly structured, the first three acts depicting two days' action and the final act providing a kind of epilogue.

The significant plot events occur during act 2 and act 3. Here, the demise of the German-supported regime of the Ukranian nationalist Hetman is depicted from three distinct perspectives: from the general headquarters at the Hetman's palace (act 2, scene 1); from the headquarters of opposing cavalry commander Bolbotun, whose forces are closing in on Kiev (act 2, scene 2); and from the more personal perspective of Alexei Turbin's command post, as the young colonel must react to the fact that the battle is lost before it has begun (act 3, scene 1). The pervading chaos in the first of these scenes at the Hetman's palace is typically Bulgakovian. The personable Shervinsky arrives at his post to perform his role as duty officer, only to learn that the officer he is replacing has already deserted his post. Then, rapidly, the Germans announce their withdrawal, the Hetman and his commanding officers flee in disguise, Shervinsky exchanges his uniform for civilian dress, and capping the chaos, he abandons the headquarters to the comic peasant Fyodor. When the scene shifts to the opposing camp, the audience glimpses the barbarity and cruelty in store for the citizens of Kiev when the city is taken by Bolbotun. In act 3, scene 1, Alexei Turbin, who knows that his two hundred untrained troops are the final defense against this brutality and that he has already been deserted by the Germans and the Ukrainian generals, decides to disband his troops in order to save their lives. The scene is filled with mutinies, random shots in the dark, and confusion, and it ends with Alexei's death, as the transition of power is completed.

If these scenes offer events that are both historically significant and structurally central to the action, they are finally less important in the context of the play than those scenes that come before and after them, for in Bulgakov's drama, it is usually the characters' reaction to the events, rather than the events themselves, that merits full attention. Framing the military scenes are scenes in the Turbin apartment, which serves as a bulwark against the chaos of the Civil War. In the first act, the apartment is a gathering place for friends and family, and, if it has a chaotic atmosphere of its own, it is a chaos of gaiety—drinking, singing, eating, and illicit flirtation. As a succession of characters enters the apartment to escape the cold outside, it becomes clear that the apartment provides more than warmth and shelter. It provides an escape from the pending destruction outside and a preservation of the old society, with the only female character, the charming Elena, at its hub. Lariosik, a cousin visiting in search of a safe harbor, sums up the shared feeling, "the cream-colored cur-

tain . . . behind them you can rest your soul . . . you forget about all the horrors of the Civil War."

Politically, the assembly in the Turbin apartment is for Russia, a Russia that probably no longer exists outside its walls, and opposed to all the powers contesting for control. Though the men are fighting for the Hetman, they cannot drink his toast, and the only toast on which they can agree is to the health of Elena. In Bulgakov's plays, authority is nearly always presented negatively, at its best bungling and cowardly, at its worst arbitrary and brutal.

After the central political events, the characters return to the apartment, this time to hide, and the cream-colored curtains provide a different kind of refuge. With Alexei dead and young Nikolai wounded, the tone changes from gaiety to seriousness, and the men bicker over their courage and their responsibility. Yet it is significant that, though guns are heard and troops pass by, the war never actually intrudes on the apartment, which is neither stormed nor searched.

Act 4 takes place two months later. It is now Christmas, the tree is lighted, the drinking has resumed. With the Red Army poised outside Kiev, another change in power is about to occur, and the characters seem almost indifferent to it. Just as the military uniforms were exchanged for civilian clothes before, now gentleman's suits are replaced with work clothes, as the men prepare, chameleonlike, to blend into their new environment. Several of the characters declare Bolshevik sympathies, and the "Internationale" is sung, just as the old czarist anthem had been sung previously. Shervinsky and Elena announce their engagement, and there is a strong sense of a new beginning.

Doubtless, it was this positive attitude toward the Communists that permitted the original production of the play in 1926, and no doubt it was the positive portrayal of White intellectuals that provoked the uproar from party hard-liners. It is characteristic of Bulgakov, however, that the play is uncommitted politically. The focus is on the survival of these characters and of their society and values despite the turmoil that surrounds them. The celebratory feeling of the final act is not a celebration of the advent of Communism but a celebration that "we endure."

THE CRIMSON ISLAND

Based on a 1924 short story of the same title, *The Crimson Island* is at once more daring as theater and less successful as drama than *Days of the Turbins*. With unabashed references to *Days of the Turbins* and *Zoya's Apartment* and frequent inside jokes, *The Crimson Island* is, above all, a play about the theater. The action involves the casting, dress rehearsal, and censor's judgment of fictional Vasily Dymogatsky's new play, which bears the title *The Crimson Island*. This play-within-a-play, which occupies the bulk of the work, depicts a series of revolutions on a fictitious island. When the island's hereditary ruler is killed by a volcanic eruption, leadership is assumed by an upstart who solicits foreign support and who, in turn, is overthrown by a people's revolution. Farcical throughout, Dymogatsky's play is a parody of countless revolutionary plays that paraded across the boards in the early years of the Soviet regime. Clearly, Bulgakov is ridiculing the black-and-white characters and blatant dogmatism that mark these plays. At the same time, because the action allegorizes the Russian Revolution itself, it is quite possible that the historic events themselves and the historic figures who participated in them are objects of satire.

Complicating matters is the framework: the interaction of the playwright, the director Panfilovich, and the state censor Savva Lukich. Dymogatsky, though somewhat silly, displays an artistic integrity at odds with the cautious Panfilovich, who is much more interested in satisfying the whims of the censor than he is in creating an artistic achievement. Anticipating the displeasure of the absent Savva Lukich, Panfilovich frequently interrupts the action and cuts an entire scene. When Savva finally does arrive for the rehearsal's conclusion, his banning of the play is predictable. His reasons for doing so, however, point to another satiric target. He finds fault not with a farcical rendition of the heroic Revolution, but with the play's ending. The director rewrites the ending so that the English sailors, who in the original had fled in order to avoid a confrontation with the triumphant and unified "red" natives, return to the island and announce their solidarity with the revolution. The revised version ends with the entire cast joining in a chorus of revolutionary slogans. Savva at once accepts the play, and Dymogatsky is showered with congratulations.

The point is that Savva has no artistic sense at all; he is interested only in approving propagandistic works. Dymogatsky's reaction indicates Bulgakov's dissatisfaction with the state system of censorship. Dymogatsky is confused, distraught; he keeps asking, "Who wrote *The Crimson Island*?" He has lost his soul, his identity, and wanders the stage, babbling to himself. With Dymogatsky's response, one perhaps has Bulgakov's main satiric object—censorship—but one also has interpretive difficulties, for if the audience is to sympathize with the playwright and his concern for artistic integrity, what is to be made of the ridiculous farce about which he is so upset? The problem is that, in aiming at so many targets at once, Bulgakov is unable to score a direct hit on any of them. Without a true satiric norm, with all the characters appearing ridiculous, it is hard for an audience to feel much concern or even to get its bearings.

Despite these thematic shortcomings, however, *The Crimson Island* is hilarious and no doubt offers good fare for the stage; it also provides a good insider's look at the early Soviet theater and at the conditions under which authors, actors, and directors were forced to work during this troubled time. These virtues account for the play's popularity, while the play's political and satiric ambiguity account for its short stage life. Satirizing censorship and perhaps the Revolution was playing with dynamite, and the following year, 1929, seemed to fulfill a prophecy as all Bulgakov's plays were banned from the stage.

FLIGHT

Banned before it was ever performed, *Flight* nevertheless ranks among Bulgakov's noteworthy dramatic achievements. It typifies Bulgakov's work, both in the familiar subject matter (various elements of Whites in the final months of the Civil War) and in the compositional experimentation. Composed as a sequence of eight progressive dreams, *Flight* does not require a curtain; rather, in a very modern way, it employs lighting to produce fade-outs and fade-ins, an essentially cinematic technique. Additionally, the presence of lengthy stage directions and poetic epigraphs at the beginning of each dream suggests that the play is meant for readers as well as for theater audiences.

The plot depicts a group of characters on the run from an army and a way of life that are never shown. As territory after territory is abandoned to the Reds, the location shifts from a remote monastery to a railway station to Sevastopol, and as Whites become émigrés, the characters leave Russia for Constantinople and Paris. Never finding true sanctuary, the characters discover only increased poverty and misery, the fate reserved for losers. With a windfall gained in a card game and the lovers Serafima and Golubkov returning to Russia, *Flight* offers some hope at its conclusion. Yet with the most interesting character, the White general Charnota, remaining a kind of refugee, and with the pervading chaos and misery overriding the sparse comedy, the play remains one of Bulgakov's darkest.

From the outset, Bulgakov's attitude toward the events is clear. The opening dream, like the opening scene in William Shakespeare's *Hamlet, Prince of Denmark* (pr. c. 1600-1601), is filled with mistaken identities, disguises, and the repeated (and unanswered) question, "What is going on?" The treachery and disorder of the White leaders preclude any popular support, and the cause is a doomed one. The humanity and honesty of Charnota and Golubkov produce only charges of insanity, and in a Constantinople memorable for its cockroach races and fights between Italian and English sailors, the Russians are referred to as "outcasts from Hell." As in *Days of the Turbins*, the sympathetic characters endure relocation, betrayal, confusion, imprisonment, and degradation. As a result, *Flight* is much more a condemnation of the White forces than it is an endorsement of them. Doubtless, it was the positively drawn character of the White general Charnota that led to Stalin's pronouncement that the play was "an anti-Soviet phenomenon" and to its banning.

Structurally, the dream sequences are clumsily handled. Though vaguely mystical and unquestionably nightmarish, there is nothing really dreamlike about them. Certainly, they resemble only remotely the more successful dreams in plays by August Strindberg, Eugene O'Neill, and even Tennessee Wil-

liams. One question that must be asked is "Whose dreams are these?" The point of view is far too fragmented and the depicted scenes far too realistic to lend credence to the dream sequence. Consequently, the conclusion, with Serafima wanting "to forget everything, as if it hadn't happened" and Golubkov proclaiming that "it was all delirium," seems hopelessly artificial. It is, however, difficult to tell if *Flight* exists in a final version, because the play never premiered.

Indeed, such problems bedevil virtually all Bulgakov's plays, for, with the exception of *Days of the Turbins*, his plays had excessively brief stage lives and constantly underwent revision in order to get past the censors. In this regard, his central theme of people struggling against arbitrary authority and constant change reflects his own experience. Like most of his attractive characters, Bulgakov endured.

OTHER MAJOR WORKS

LONG FICTION: *Belaya gvardiya*, 1927, 1929 (2 volumes; *The White Guard*, 1971); *Teatralny roman*, 1965 (*Black Snow: A Theatrical Novel*, 1967); *Master i Margarita*, censored version 1966-1967, uncensored version 1973 (*The Master and Margarita*, 1967).

SHORT FICTION: *Diavoliada*, 1925 (*Diaboliad and Other Stories*, 1972); *Traktat o zhilishche*, 1926 (*A Treatise on Housing*, 1972); *Zapiski iunogo vracha*, 1963 (*A Country Doctor's Notebook*, 1975); *Sobache serdtse*, 1968, reliable text 1969 (novella; *The Heart of a Dog*, 1968); *Notes on the Cuff and Other Stories*, 1991.

NONFICTION: *Zhizn gospodina de Molyera*, 1962 (*The Life of Monsieur de Molière*, 1970).

TRANSLATION: *L'Avare*, 1936 (of Molière's play).

BIBLIOGRAPHY

Curtis, J. A. E. *Manuscripts Don't Burn: Mikhail Bulgakov, a Life in Letters and Diaries*. Woodstock, N.Y.: Overlook, 1992. A biography of Bulgakov that focuses on his diaries and correspondence. Index.

Haber, Edythe C. *Mikhail Bulgakov: The Early Years*. Cambridge, Mass.: Harvard University Press, 1998. A biography of the Russian writer that examines his life and works. Bibliography and index.

Milne, Lesley. *Bulgakov: The Novelist-Playwright.* Luxembourg: Harwood, 1995. A critical examination of Bulgakov's works, both novels and plays. Bibliography and indexes.

Natov, Nadine. *Mikhail Bulgakov.* Boston: Twayne, 1985. A basic biography of Bulgakov that examines his life and works. Bibliography and index.

Proffer, Ellendea. *Bulgakov: Life and Work.* Ann Arbor, Mich.: Ardis, 1984. A biography of Bulgakov that covers his literary output and life. Bibliography and index.

Smelianskii, A. M. *Is Comrade Bulgakov Dead?: Mikhail Bulgakov at the Moscow Art Theatre.* New York: Routledge, 1993. An examination of Bulgakov's dramatic works, including their performance history. Bibliography.

David Wheeler

ED BULLINS

Born: Philadelphia, Pennsylvania; July 2, 1935

PRINCIPAL DRAMA

Clara's Ole Man, pr. 1965, pb. 1969 (one act)
Dialect Determinism: Or, The Rally, pr. 1965, pb. 1973 (one act)
How Do You Do?, pr. 1965, pb. 1968 (one act)
The Theme Is Blackness, pr. 1966, pb. 1973 (one act)
A Son, Come Home, pr. 1968, pb. 1969 (one act)
The Electronic Nigger, pr. 1968, pb. 1969 (one act)
Goin' a Buffalo, pr. 1968, pb. 1969
In the Wine Time, pr. 1968, pb. 1969 (two acts)
Five Plays, pb. 1969 (includes *Clara's Ole Man, A Son, Come Home, The Electronic Nigger, Goin' a Buffalo, In the Wine Time*)
The Gentleman Caller, pr. 1969, pb. 1970 (one act)
In New England Winter, pb. 1969, pr. 1971 (one act)
We Righteous Bombers, pr. 1969 (as Kingsley B. Bass, Jr.; adaptation of Albert Camus's play *Les Justes*)
A Ritual to Raise the Dead and Foretell the Future, pr. 1970, pb. 1973
The Pig Pen, pr. 1970, pb. 1971
The Duplex, pr. 1970, pb. 1971
Street Sounds, pr. 1970, pb. 1973 (one act)
The Devil Catchers, pr. 1971 (one act)
The Fabulous Miss Marie, pr. 1971, pb. 1974
House Party, pr. 1973 (lyrics; music by Pat Patrick)
The Theme Is Blackness, pb. 1973 (collection)
The Taking of Miss Janie, pr. 1975, pb. 1981
Home Boy, pr. 1976 (lyrics; music by Aaron Bell)
Jo Anne!, pr. 1976, pb. 1993
Daddy, pr. 1977
Storyville, pr. 1977, revised pr. 1979 (music by Mildred Kayden)
Sepia Star: Or, Chocolate Comes to the Cotton Club, pr. 1977 (lyrics; music by Kayden)
Michael, pr. 1978 (one act)
Leavings, pr. 1980 (one act)
Steve and Velma, pr. 1980 (one act)
A Sunday Afternoon, pr. 1989 (with Marshall Borden; two acts)
I Think It's Going to Turn Out Fine, pr. 1990 (two acts)
American Griot, pr. 1991 (with Idris Ackamoor; one act)
Salaam, Huey Newton, Salaam, pr., pb. 1991 (one act)
Boy X Man, pr. 1995
Mtumi X, pr. 2000

OTHER LITERARY FORMS

Although known primarily as a playwright, Ed Bullins has also worked in forms ranging from fiction and the essay to the "revolutionary television commercial." His novel *The Reluctant Rapist* (1973) focuses on the early experience of Steve Benson, a semiautobiographical character who appears in several plays, including *In New England Winter*, *The Duplex*, and *The Fabulous Miss Marie*. *The Hungered Ones: Early Writings* (1971), a collection of Bullins's early stories and essays, some of which are loosely autobiographical, provides an overview of his early perspective. Active as an editor and a theorist throughout his career, Bullins has written introductions to anthologies such as *The New Lafayette Theater Presents* (1974) and *New Plays from the Black Theatre* (1969). Along with the introduction to his own collection *The Theme Is Blackness*, these introductions provide a powerful and influential theoretical statement on the aesthetics and politics of the African American theater during the late 1960's and early 1970's. *The Theme Is Blackness* also contains scripts for "rituals" and mixed-media productions, including "Black Revolutionary Commercials," which reflect the concern with electronic media visible in many of his later plays.

Ed Bullins in 1971. (AP/Wide World Photos)

ACHIEVEMENTS

Ed Bullins won the 1968 Vernon Rice Award for *The Electronic Nigger*, the 1971 Obie Award for *In New England Winter* and *The Fabulous Miss Marie*, and in 1975 both the Obie and the New York Drama Critics Circle Award for *The Taking of Miss Janie*. In 1997 he received the Living Legend Award from the Black Theatre Conference, and in 1999 he won the August Wilson Playwriting Award and the Garland Anderson Playwright Award. He has also received grants from the Guggenheim Foundation (1971, 1976), the Rockefeller Foundation (1968, 1970, 1973), the Creative Artists Program Service (1973), the Black Arts Alliance (1971), and the National Endowment for the Arts (1974).

As much as any contemporary American playwright, Bullins has forged a powerful synthesis of avant-garde technique and revolutionary commitment challenging easy preconceptions concerning the relationship between politics and aesthetics. Like Latin American writers Carlos Fuentes and Gabriel García Márquez and African writers Ngugi wa Thiong'o and Wole Soyinka, Bullins sees no inherent contradiction between the use of experimental techniques and the drive to reach a mass audience alienated from the dominant social/economic/racial hierarchy. Separating himself from the cultural elite that has claimed possession of the modernist and postmodernist tradition, Bullins adapts the tradition to the frames of reference and to the immediate concerns of his audience, primarily but not exclusively within the African American community. Although he frequently comments on and revises the philosophical and aesthetic concerns of European American modernism, he does so to clarify his audience's vision of an American culture riddled by psychological and political contradictions that intimate the need for a basic change.

Paralleling the political modernism advocated by Bertolt Brecht in his aesthetic and political debate with Georg Lukács, Bullins's synthesis takes on particular significance in the context of the Black Arts movement of the late 1960's. As a leading figure in the movement for specifically black cultural institutions and modes of expression, Bullins refuted through example the casual stereotypes of black revolutionary artists as ideologically inflexible and aesthetically naïve. Although he supports the confrontational strategies of radical playwrights committed to what he calls the "dialectic of change," he works primarily within what he calls the "dialectic of experience," which entails a sophisticated confrontation with a "reality" he understands to be in large part shaped by individual perceptions. Drawing on Brecht, Jean Genet, Albert Camus, Amiri Baraka, Eugene O'Neill, John Cage, Anton Chekhov, and Langston Hughes with equal facility, Bullins is not primarily a literary dramatist or a political agitator. Rather, he is a playwright in the classic sense, concerned above all with bringing the experience of black Americans alive onstage in a manner that forces the audience to confront its metaphorically ambiguous but politically explosive implications. His most successful plays, such as *In New England Winter* and *The Taking of Miss Janie*, demonstrate conclusively that a revolutionary artist does not need to circumscribe his vision in order to defend a preestablished ideological position. Demonstrating his affinities with Brechtian theory as opposed to Brechtian practice, Bullins creates tensions between presentation style and content to alienate his audience, white or black, from its assumptions concerning race, class, sex, and ultimately the nature of perception.

Not surprisingly, this challenge frequently disturbs mainstream audiences and critics; typical is the response of Walter Kerr, who complained in a review of *The Taking of Miss Janie* that "no one likes having to finish—or trying to finish—an author's play for him; but that's the effort asked here." Ironically, Kerr's criticism accurately identifies the reason for Bullins's success in contexts ranging from the black community theaters of San Francisco and New York to the La Mama theater in New York's Soho district. Challenging the audience to confront the experience presented rather than to accept a mediated statement about that experience, Bullins rarely presents didactic statements without substantial ironic qualification. By refusing to advance simple solutions or to repress his awareness of oppression, Bullins attempts to force the audience to internalize and act on its responses. Effective as literature as well as theater, Bullins's plays have won numerous awards and grants from both African American and European American organizations. The best of them, especially the early sections of the Twentieth Century Cycle, a projected twenty-play series, have led some critics to compare Bullins with O'Neill. Although his ultimate stature depends in large part on the development of the cycle and his continuing ability to generate new forms in response to changing audiences and political contexts, Bullins's place in the history of American and African American theater seems assured.

BIOGRAPHY

Intensely protective concerning the details of his private life, Ed Bullins has nevertheless been a highly visible force in the development of African American theater since the mid-1960's. Reared primarily by his civil-servant mother in North Philadelphia, Bullins attended a predominantly white grade school before transferring to an inner-city junior high, where he became involved with the street gang called the Jet Cobras. Like his semiautobiographical character Steve Benson (*The Reluctant Rapist*, *In New England Winter*, *The Duplex*), Bullins suffered a near-fatal knife wound, in the area of his heart, in a street fight. After dropping out of high school, he served in the United States Navy from 1952 to 1955. In 1958, he moved to California, where he passed his high school graduation equivalency examination and attended Los Angeles City College from 1961 to 1963.

Bullins's 1963 move to San Francisco signaled the start of his emergence as an influential figure in African American literary culture. The first national publication of his essays in 1963 initiated a period of tremendous creativity extending into the mid-1970's. Actively committed to black nationalist politics by 1965, he began working with community theater organizations such as Black Arts/West, the Black Student Union at San Francisco State College, and Black House of San Francisco, which he founded along with playwright Marvin X. The first major production of Bullins's drama, a program including *How Do You Do?*, *Dialect Determinism*, and *Clara's Ole Man*, premiered at the Firehouse Repertory Theater in San Francisco on August 5, 1965. At about the same time, Bullins assumed the position of minister of culture with the Black Panther Party, then emerging as a major force in national politics. Breaking with the Panthers in 1967, reportedly in disagreement with Eldridge Cleaver's decision to accept alliances with white radical groups, Bullins moved to Harlem at the urging of Robert MacBeth, director of the New Lafayette Theater.

Bullins's first New York production, *The Electronic Nigger*, ran for ninety-six performances following its February 21, 1968, debut at the American Place Theatre, where it was moved after the original New Lafayette burned down. Combined with his editorship of the controversial Summer, 1968, "Black Theatre" issue of *The Drama Review*, the success of *The Electronic Nigger* consolidated Bullins's position alongside Baraka as a major presence within and outside the African American theatrical community. Between 1968 and 1976, Bullins's plays received an average of three major New York productions per year at theaters, including the New Lafayette (where Bullins was playwright-in-residence up to its 1973 closing), the American Place Theatre, the Brooklyn Academy of Music, Woodie King's New Federal Theatre at the Henry Street Settlement House, Lincoln Center, and the La Mama Experimental Theater.

Bullins wrote *A Sunday Afternoon* with Marshall Borden and "a pseudo-satiric monster horror play, a take-off on B-movies," called *Dr. Geechie and the Blood Junkies*, which he read at the Henry Street Settlement House in New York in the summer of 1989. The La Mama theater staged *I Think It's Going to Turn Out Fine*, based on the Tina Turner story, in 1990, and *American Griot* (coauthored with Idris Ackamoor, who also acted in the play) in 1991. *Salaam, Huey Newton, Salaam*, a one-act play on the aftermath of the black revolution, premiered at the Ensemble Studio Theater in 1991.

Bullins has also taught American humanities, black theater, and play making at Contra Costa College, in San Pablo, California. He settled in Emeryville, near Oakland, and started a theater there called the BMT Theatre (Bullins Memorial Theatre, named after his son, who died in an automobile accident).

He continued his formal education at Antioch University/San Francisco, where he received his bachelor's degree in liberal studies (English and playwriting) in 1989. After he completed his master's degree in playwriting at San Francisco State University in 1994, he was appointed professor of theater at Northeastern University in 1995, where he continues to write and direct plays. In 1996 he was made acting director of Northeastern University's Center for the Arts, and his *Boy X Man*, which premiered a year earlier in Greensboro, North Carolina, was staged at the Arts Black Box Theater in Boston. Three years later many of his plays were presented at a retrospective at the Schomberg Center for Research in Black Culture in New York. An avid supporter of local drama, he has written two ten-minute plays for the Boston Theater Marathon, and works with the ACT Theater Group in Roxbury, where he mentors young playwrights and conducts workshops. In 2000 his play *Mtumi X* was produced, and his play *Goin' a Buffalo* was adapted to film and screened at the New York International Film and Video Festival in New York's Madison Square Garden.

ANALYSIS

A radical playwright in both the simple and the complex senses of the term, Ed Bullins consistently challenges the members of his audience to test their political and aesthetic beliefs against the multifaceted reality of daily life in the United States. Committed to a revolutionary black nationalist consciousness, he attacks both liberal and conservative politics as aspects of an oppressive context dominated by a white elite. Equally committed to the development of a radical alternative to European American modernist aesthetics, he incorporates a wide range of cultural materials into specifically black performances. The clearest evidence of Bullins's radical sensibility, however, is his unwavering refusal to accept any dogma, white or black, traditional or revolutionary, without testing it against a multitude of perspectives and experiences. Throughout a career that has earned for him serious consideration alongside Eugene O'Neill and Tennessee Williams as the United States' greatest dramatist, Bullins has subjected the hypocrisies and corruptions of European and African American culture to rigorous examination and reevaluation. Refusing to accept any distinctions between aesthetics and politics or between the concerns of the artist and those of the mass community, Bullins demands that his audience synthesize abstract perception and concrete experience. Providing a set of terms useful to understanding the development of these concerns in his own work, Bullins defines a constituting dialectic in the black theatrical movement that emerged in the mid-1960's:

This new thrust has two main branches—the *dialectic of change* and the *dialectic of experience*. The writers are attempting to answer questions concerning Black survival and future, one group through confronting the Black/white reality of America, the other, by heightening the dreadful white reality of being a modern Black captive and victim.

Essentially, the dialectic of change focuses attention on political problems demanding a specific form of action. The dialectic of experience focuses on a more "realistic" (though Bullins redefines the term to encompass aspects of reality frequently dismissed by programmatic realists) picture of black life in the context in which the problems continue to condition all experience. Reflecting his awareness that by definition each dialectic is in constant tension with the other, Bullins directs his work in the dialectic of change to altering the audience's actual experience. Similarly, his work in the dialectic of experience, while rarely explicitly didactic, leads inexorably to recognition of the need for change.

Bullins's work in both dialectics repudiates the tradition of the Western theater, which, he says, "shies away from social, political, psychological or any disturbing (revolutionary) reforms." Asserting the central importance of non-Western references, Bullins catalogs the "elements that make up the alphabet of the secret language used in Black theater," among them the blues, dance, African religion, and mysticism, "familial nationalism," mythscience, ritual-ceremony, and "nigger street styles." Despite the commitment to an African American continuum evident in the construction and content of his plays, Bullins by no means repudiates all elements of the European American tradition. Even as he criticizes Brechtian epic theater, Bullins employs aspects of

Brecht's dramatic rhetoric, designed to alienate the audience from received modes of perceiving theatrical, and by extension political, events. It is less important to catalog Bullins's allusions to William Shakespeare, O'Neill, Camus, or Genet than to recognize his use of their devices alongside those of Baraka, Soyinka, and Derek A. Walcott in the service of "Black artistic, political, and cultural consciousness."

Most of Bullins's work in the dialectic of change, which he calls "protest writing" when addressed to a European American audience and "Black revolutionary writing" when addressed to an African American audience, takes the form of short satiric or agitpropic plays. Frequently intended for street performance, these plays aim to attract a crowd and communicate an incisive message as rapidly as possibly. Influential in the ritual theater of Baraka and in Bullins's own "Black Revolutionary Commercials," this strategy developed out of association with the black nationalist movement in cities such as New York, Detroit, Chicago, San Francisco, and Newark. Reflecting the need to avoid unplanned confrontations with police, the performances described in Bullins's influential "Short Statement on Street Theater" concentrate on establishing contact with groups unlikely to enter a theater, especially black working people and individuals living on the margins of society—gang members, junkies, prostitutes, and street people. Recognizing the impact of the media on American consciousness, Bullins frequently parodies media techniques, satirizing political advertising in "The American Flag Ritual" and "selling" positive black revolutionary images in "A Street Play." Somewhat longer though equally direct, "Death List," which can be performed by a troupe moving through the neighborhood streets, alerts the community to "enemies of the Black People," from Vernon Jordan to Whitney Young. Considered out of their performance context, many of these pieces seem simplistic or didactic, but their real intent is to realize Bullins's desire that "each individual in the crowd should have his sense of reality confronted, his consciousness assaulted." Because the "accidental" street audience comes into contact with the play while in its "normal" frame of mind, Bullins creates deliberately hyperbolic images to dislocate that mind-set in a very short period of time.

When writing revolutionary plays for performance in traditional theaters, Bullins tempers his rhetoric considerably. To be sure, *Dialect Determinism*, a warning against trivializing the revolutionary impulse of Malcolm X, and *The Gentleman Caller*, a satiric attack on master-slave mentality of black-white economic interaction, both resemble the street plays in their insistence on revolutionary change. *Dialect Determinism* climaxes with the killing of a black "enemy," and *The Gentleman Caller* ends with a formulaic call for the rise of the foretold "Black nation that will survive, conquer and rule." The difference between these plays and the street theater lies not in message but in Bullins's way of involving the audience. Recognizing the different needs of an audience willing to seek out his work in the theater but frequently educated by the dominant culture, Bullins involves it in the analytic process leading to what seem, from a black nationalist perspective, relatively unambiguous political perceptions. Rather than asserting the messages at the start of the plays, therefore, he developed a satiric setting before stripping away the masks and distortions imposed by the audience's normal frame of reference on its recognition of his revolutionary message.

Along with Baraka, Marvin X, Adrienne Kennedy, and others, Bullins helped make the dialectic of change an important cultural force at the height of the Black Nationalist movement, but his most substantial achievements involve the dialectic of experience. Ranging from his impressionistic gallery plays and politically resonant problem play to the intricately interconnected Twentieth Century Cycle, Bullins's work in this dialectic reveals a profound skepticism regarding revolutionary ideals that have not been tested against the actual contradictions of African American experience.

STREET SOUNDS

Street Sounds, parts of which were later incorporated into *House Party*, represents Bullins's adaptation of the gallery approach pioneered by poets such as Robert Browning, Edgar Lee Masters (*Spoon River Anthology*, 1915), Melvin B. Tolson (*Harlem Gallery*, 1969), Gwendolyn Brooks (*A Street in Bronzeville*, 1945), and Langston Hughes (*Montage of a Dream Deferred*, 1951). By montaging a series of thirty- to ninety-second monologues, Bullins suggests the tensions common to the experience of seemingly disparate elements of the African American community. Superficially, the characters can be divided into categories such as politicians (Harlem Politician, Black Student), hustlers (Dope Seller, The Thief), artists (Black Revolutionary Artist, Black Writer), street people (Fried Brains, Corner Brother), working people (Errand Boy, Workin' Man), and women (The Loved One, The Virgin, Harlem Mother). None of the categories, however, survives careful examination; individual women could be placed in every other category; the Black Revolutionary Artist combines politics and art; the Harlem Politician, politics and crime. To a large extent, all types ultimately amount to variations on several social and psychological themes that render the surface distinctions far less important than they initially appear.

Although their particular responses vary considerably, each character in *Street Sounds* confronts the decaying community described by The Old-timer: "They changin' things, you know? Freeways comin' through tearin' up the old neighborhood. Buildings goin' down, and not bein' put up again. Abandoned houses that are boarded up, the homes of winos, junkies and rats, catchin' fire and never bein' fixed up." As a result, many share the Workin' Man's feeling of being "trapped inside of ourselves, inside our experience." Throughout the play, Bullins portrays a deepseated feeling of racial inferiority that results in black men's obsession with white women (Slightly Confused Negro, The Explainer) and a casual willingness to exploit or attack other blacks (The Thief, The Doubter, Young West Indian Revolutionary Poet). Attempting to salvage some sense of freedom or selfworth, or simply to find momentary release from the struggle, individuals turn to art, sex, politics, or drugs, but the weight of their context pressures each toward the psychological collapse of Fried Brains, the hypocritical delusions of the Non-Ideological Nigger, or the unfounded self-glorification of The

Genius. Even when individuals embrace political causes, Bullins remains skeptical. The Theorist, The Rapper, and The Liar, who ironically echoes Bullins's aesthetic when he declares, "Even when I lie, I lie truthfully. . . . I'm no stranger to experience," express ideological positions similar to those Bullins advocates in the dialectic of change. None, however, seems even marginally aware that his grand pronouncements have no impact on the experience of the black community. The Rapper's revolutionary call— "We are slaves now, this moment in time, brothers, but let this moment end with this breath and let us unite as fearless revolutionaries in the pursuit of world liberation!"—comes between the entirely apolitical monologues of Waiting and Bewildered. Similarly, the Black Revolutionary Artist's endorsement of "a cosmic revolution that will liberate the highest potential of nationhood in the universe" is followed by the Black Dee Jay's claim that "BLACK MEANS BUY!" The sales pitch seems to have a great deal more power than the nationalist vision in the lives of the Soul Sister and the Corner Brother, whose monologues frame the Black Revolutionary Artist-Black Dee Jay sequence.

One of Bullins's characteristic "signatures" is the attribution of his own ideas to characters unwilling or unable to act or inspire others to act on them. Reflecting his belief that without action ideals have little value, Bullins structures *Street Sounds* to insist on the need for connection. The opening monologue, delivered by a white "Pig," establishes a political context similar to the one that Bullins uses in the dialectic of change, within which the dialectic of experience proceeds. Reducing all blacks to a single type, the nigger, Pig wishes only to "beat his nigger ass good." Although Bullins clearly perceives the police as a basic oppressive force in the ghetto, he does not concentrate on highlighting the audience's awareness of that point. Rather, by the end of the play he has made it clear that the African American community in actuality beats its own ass. The absence of any other white character in the play reflects Bullins's focus on the nature of victimization as experienced within and perpetuated by the black community. The Harlem Mother monologue that closes the play concentrates

almost entirely on details of experience. Although she presents no hyperbolic portraits of white oppressors, her memories of the impact on her family of economic exploitation, hunger, and government indifference carry more politically dramatic power than does any abstraction. This by no means indicates Bullins's distaste for political analysis or a repudiation of the opening monologues; rather, it reflects his awareness that abstract principles signify little unless they are embedded in the experience first of the audience and, ultimately, of the community as a whole.

THE TAKING OF MISS JANIE

Although Bullins consistently directs his work toward the African American community, his work in the dialectic of experience inevitably involves the interaction of blacks and whites. *The Taking of Miss Janie*, perhaps his single most powerful play, focuses on a group of California college students, several of whom first appeared in *The Pig Pen*. In part a meditation on the heritage of the 1960's Civil Rights movement, *The Taking of Miss Janie* revolves around the sexual and political tensions between and within racial groups. Although most of the characters are readily identifiable types—the stage directions identify Rick as a cultural nationalist, Janie as a California beach girl, Flossy as a "soul sister"—Bullins explores individual characters in depth, concentrating on their tendency to revert to behavior patterns, especially when they assume rigid ideological or social roles. The central incident of the play—the "rape" of the white Janie by Monty, a black friend of long standing—provides a severely alienating image of this tendency to both black and white audiences. After committing a murder, which may or may not be real, when the half-mythic Jewish beatnik Mort Silberstein taunts Monty for his inability to separate his consciousness from European American influences, Monty undresses Janie, who does not resist or cooperate, in a rape scene devoid of violence, love, anger, or physical desire. Unable to resist the pressures that make their traditional Western claim to individuality seem naïve, both Janie and Monty seem resigned to living out a "fate" that in fact depends on their acquiescence. Monty accepts the role of the "black beast" who rapes and murders white people, while Janie plays the role of plantation mistress. Although these intellectually articulate characters do not genuinely believe in the reality of their roles, their ironic attitude ultimately makes no difference, for the roles govern their actions.

Although the rape incident provides the frame for *The Taking of Miss Janie*, Monty and Janie exist in a gallery of characters whose collective inability to maintain individual integrity testifies to the larger dimensions of the problem. Rick and Len enact the classic argument between nationalism and eclecticism in the black political/intellectual world; Peggy tires of confronting the neuroses of black men and turns to lesbianism; "hip" white boy Lonnie moves from fad to fad, turning his contact with black culture to financial advantage in the music business; several couples drift aimlessly into interracial marriages. Alternating scenes in which characters interact with monologues in which an individual reflects on his future development, Bullins reveals his characters' inability to create alternatives to the "fate" within which they feel themselves trapped. Although none demonstrates a fully developed ability to integrate ideals and experiences, several seem substantially less alienated than others. In many ways the least deluded, Peggy accepts both her lesbianism and her responsibility for her past actions. Her comment on the 1960's articulates a basic aspect of Bullins's vision: "We all failed. Failed ourselves in that serious time known as the sixties. And by failing ourselves we also failed in the test of the times." Her honesty and insight also have a positive impact on the black nationalist Rick, who during a conversation with Peggy abandons his grandiose rhetoric on the "devil's tricknology" (a phrase adopted from the Nation of Islam)—rhetoric that masks a deep hostility toward other blacks. Although he has previously attacked her as a lesbian "freak," Rick's final lines to Peggy suggest another aspect of Bullins's perspective: "Ya know, it be about what you make it anyway." Any adequate response to *The Taking of Miss Janie* must take into account not only Peggy's survival strategy and Rick's nationalistic idealism but also Janie's willed naïveté and the accuracy of Mort's claim that, despite his invocation of Mao, Malcolm X, and Frantz Fanon,

Monty is still on some levels "FREAKY FOR JESUS!" Bullins presents no simple answers nor does he simply contemplate the wasteland. Rather, as in almost all of his work in both the dialectic of change and the dialectic of experience, he challenges his audience to make something out of the fragments and failures he portrays.

THE TWENTIETH CENTURY CYCLE

The Twentieth Century Cycle, Bullins's most far-reaching confrontation with the American experience, brings together most of his theatrical and thematic concerns and seems destined to stand as his major work. Several of the projected twenty plays of the cycle have been performed, including *In the Wine Time*, *In New England Winter*, *The Duplex*, *The Fabulous Miss Marie*, *Home Boy*, and *Daddy*. Although the underlying structure of the cycle remains a matter of speculation, it clearly focuses on the experience of a group of black people traversing various areas of America's cultural and physical geography during the 1950's, 1960's, and 1970's. Recurring characters, including Cliff Dawson, his nephew Ray Crawford, Michael Brown (who first appeared in a play not part of the cycle, *A Son, Come Home*), and Steve Benson, a black intellectual whose life story resembles Bullins's own, serve to unify the cycle's imaginative landscape. In addition, a core of thematic concerns, viewed from various perspectives, unites the plays.

In the Wine Time, the initial play of the cycle, establishes a basic set of thematic concerns, including the incompatibility of Ray's romantic idealism with the brutality and potential violence of his northern urban environment. Stylistically, the play typifies the cycle in its juxtaposition of introverted lyricism, naturalistic dialogue, technological staging, and African American music and dance. Individual plays combine these elements in different ways. *In New England Winter*, set in California, draws much of its power from a poetic image of the snow that takes on racial, geographical, and metaphysical meanings in Steve Benson's consciousness. Each act of *The Duplex* opens with a jazz, blues, or rhythm-and-blues song that sets a framework for the ensuing action. *The Fabulous Miss Marie* uses televised images of the Civil Rights movement both to highlight its characters' personal desperation and to emphasize the role of technology in creating and aggravating their problems of perception. Drawing directly on the reflexive rhetoric of European American modernism, *In New England Winter* revolves around Steve Benson's construction of a "play," involving a planned robbery, which he plans to enact in reality but which he also uses as a means of working out his psychological desires.

Ultimately, Bullins's *Salaam, Huey Newton, Salaam* extends Bullins's vision into an imaginary future to depict the former Black Panther leader down and out in the wake of a black revolution. Bullins suggests that each of these approaches reflects a perspective on experience actually present in contemporary American society and that any vision failing to take all of them into account will inevitably fall victim to the dissociation of ideals and experience that plunges many of Bullins's characters into despair or violence. While some of his characters, most notably Steve Benson, seem intermittently aware of the source of their alienation and are potentially capable of imaginative responses with political impact, Bullins leaves the resolution of the cycle plays to the members of the audience. Portraying the futility of socially prescribed roles and of any consciousness not directly engaged with its total context, Bullins continues to challenge his audience to attain a perspective from which the dialectic of experience and the dialectic of change can be realized as one and the same.

BOY X MAN

In *Boy X Man* (the "X" means "times," as in an equation), Bullins constructs a memory play in which a young man's return to attend his mother's funeral prompts him to remember his boyhood with his mother and her "friend," who raised him as a son. The song "Blues in the Night," his first crib memory, provides the transition to scenes from the 1930's and 1940's. Ernie's mother, Brenda, is a single mom and dancer whose life improves dramatically when she meets Will, who lacks ambition but who nevertheless provides his "family" with much-needed stability. The play includes a series of highly emotional vignettes, including the following: Brenda's reliving of her discovery of her dead mother; Will's reliving of his Nazi concentration-camp experiences; and, to

provide balance, Will's attending and listening to Negro League baseball games. Bullins provides his audience with a glimpse of the problems, prejudice, and tensions that black American families encounter; but because many of the problems are not confined to the black experience, the play reflects on American life in general.

OTHER MAJOR WORKS

LONG FICTION: *The Reluctant Rapist*, 1973.

POETRY: *To Raise the Dead and Foretell the Future*, 1971.

SCREENPLAYS: *Night of the Beast*, 1971; *The Ritual Masters*, 1972.

EDITED TEXTS: *New Plays from the Black Theatre*, 1969 (with introduction); *The New Lafayette Theater Presents: Plays with Aesthetic Comments by Six Black Playwrights*, 1974 (with introduction).

MISCELLANEOUS: *The Hungered Ones: Early Writings*, 1971 (stories and essays).

BIBLIOGRAPHY

Bigsby, C. W. E. *The Second Black Renaissance: Essays in Black Literature*. Westport, Conn.: Greenwood Press, 1980. A strong chapter, "Black Drama: The Public Voice," includes a protracted discussion of Bullins's work as "a moving spirit behind the founding of another black theatre institution, the New Lafayette Theatre." Index.

DeGaetani, John L. *A Search for a Postmodern Theater: Interviews with Contemporary Playwrights*. New York: Greenwood Press, 1991. After writing more than fifty plays, Bullins still admires Samuel Beckett and still deals with the theme of "the breakdown of communications among loved ones, and misunderstanding among good intentions." Contains an excellent update of his activities and a strong discussion of the theme of rape in his work.

Hay, Samuel A. *Ed Bullins: A Literary Biography*. Detroit, Mich.: Wayne State University Press, 1997. Despite the title, Hay's "biography" contains few biographical details and really focuses on Bullins's many (more than one hundred) dramas, which he examines in some detail. The book, which was written with Bullins's approval, provides readers with the social, political, and intellectual context in which the plays were written. Hay includes an exhaustive bibliography, which helps to resolve some issues about the dates the plays were written, produced, and published. It is the only full-length treatment of Bullins's work.

_____. "Structural Elements in Ed Bullins's Plays." In *The Theater of Black Americans*. Vol. 1, edited by Errol Hill. Englewood Cliffs, N.J.: Prentice-Hall, 1980. Examines structural consistencies in *The Duplex* but adds valuable comments on earlier works. Begins with Walter Kerr's review, comparing his remarks with Bullins's structural elements, such as "desultory conversation," "unplanned and casual action," and "frequently disconnected dialogue." Compares Bullins's work with Anton Chekhov's *Tri Sestry* (pr., pb. 1901; *Three Sisters*, 1920).

Herman, William. *Understanding Contemporary American Drama*. Columbia: University of South Carolina Press, 1987. A long chapter on Bullins, "The People in This Play Are Black," details his major plays to 1984. Good biographical sketch of Bullins's New Lafayette connections, including his editorship of *Black Theatre*, the theater company's journal.

Sanders, Leslie Catherine. *The Development of Black Theater in America: From Shadows to Selves*. Baton Rouge: Louisiana State University Press, 1988. Sanders devotes a lengthy chapter of the book to Bullins. The focus is on Bullins's work for the New Lafayette productions in New York and on some of his major plays: *The Taking of Miss Janie*; *A Son, Come Home*; *The Electronic Nigger*; *In the Wine Time*; *Goin' a Buffalo*; and *Clara's Ole Man*.

Williams, Mance. *Black Theatre in the 1960's and 1970's: A Historical-Critical Analysis of the Movement*. Westport, Conn.: Greenwood Press, 1985. By concentrating on theater movements rather than on the playwright, this study underlines Bullins's strong administrative and inspirational contributions to the African American theater experience. Includes discussion of his literary style, use of music, views on street theater, and his relationship with the New Lafayette Theater. Index and bibliography.

Craig Werner,
updated by Thomas J. Taylor and Thomas L. Erskine

EDWARD BULWER-LYTTON

Born: London, England; May 25, 1803
Died: Torquay, England; January 18, 1873

PRINCIPAL DRAMA

The Duchess de la Vallière, pb. 1836, pr. 1837
The Lady of Lyons: Or, Love and Pride, pr., pb. 1838
Richelieu: Or, The Conspiracy, pr., pb. 1839
The Sea-Captain: Or, The Birthright, pb. 1839
Money, pr., pb. 1840
Dramatic Works, pb. 1841
Not So Bad as We Seem: Or, Many Sides to a Character, pb. 1851
The Captives: A Previously Unpublished Play, pr., pb. 2000 (based on Plautus's *Captivi*)

OTHER LITERARY FORMS

Edward Bulwer-Lytton was one of the most versatile and prolific writers of a far-from-laconic age. Though he held the stage during the late 1830's as the foremost contemporary English playwright, Bulwer-Lytton was more generally known in his own day for his novels, which gained an international readership. Today, what reputation remains to this once celebrated Victorian writer rests on a handful of his twenty-odd novels. Bulwer-Lytton the fiction writer was deft in many veins. Among his works are witty and elegant society novels, the best being *Pelham: Or, The Adventures of a Gentleman* (1828); the so-called Newgate novels, dealing with the dark impulses of the criminal mind, such as *Eugene Aram*

(1832); historical romances, such as the famous *The Last Days of Pompeii* (1834); metaphysical works in the *Bildungsroman* tradition of Johann Wolfgang von Goethe, including *Ernest Maltravers* (1837) and its sequel *Alice: Or, The Mysteries* (1838); and even, at the end of his life, a precursor of utopian science fiction, *The Coming Race* (1871). Bulwer-Lytton, who despite his aristocratic background was obliged to support himself through his literary labors, also wrote short stories, his best piece being "The Haunted and the Haunters" (1857), and poetry, including *The New Timon* (1846), now chiefly remembered for having provoked Alfred, Lord Tennyson; and *King Arthur* (1848-1849, 1870). His *England and the English* (1833), a multifaceted study of pre-Reform Bill England, remains one of the most insightful social histories of early nineteenth century British culture, politics, education, and manners.

ACHIEVEMENTS

Edward Bulwer-Lytton is an author whose breadth leads the public, rightly or wrongly, to undervalue the depth of his achievements. When he aimed for high seriousness in the philosophical novels devoted to such abstractions as the Ideal and the Beautiful, he proved himself superficial, but when he set his sights lower, he excelled. He produced in *Pelham* one of the earliest and finest examples of the "silver fork" novel, a genre that proved its intrinsic worth in its culminating work, William Makepeace Thackeray's *Vanity Fair* (1847-1848), and demonstrated its endurance by continuing to flourish, if only in a debased form, down to the present day. He wrote historical novels exemplary in their learning and accuracy, books that remain models for that genre, whatever one chooses to make of its worth. Finally, Bulwer-Lytton's utopian novel *The Coming Race*, though less than a finished literary achievement, prefigures in its title, theme, and format the sort of "scientific romances" produced by H. G. Wells at the beginning of the twentieth century.

Bulwer-Lytton's achievements as a dramatist are less substantial. Solidly researched, structurally sound, but inexcusably melodramatic by modern standards, his historical dramas served at best to keep playwriting

Edward Bulwer-Lytton (Library of Congress)

alive in an age when few good British writers were making the effort to do so. In *Money*, Bulwer-Lytton offered for the Victorian world what *Pelham* had given the Regency: an incisive and detailed study of the forms folly, pretension, hypocrisy, and honor take in a particular milieu at a particular time.

BIOGRAPHY

Edward George Earle Lytton Bulwer (later, on inheriting his mother's estate, to be called E. G. E. L. Bulwer-Lytton, and later still, E. G. E. L. B. L., first Baron Lytton) was the third and last son of General William Bulwer and his wife Elizabeth Barbara Lytton, the heiress of Knebworth. Both of his parents were descendants of ancient families. Bulwer's early education was erratic but intensive. He read widely and deeply in the notable library of his maternal grandfather, Richard Warburton Lytton, and instead of attending a public school, he was placed with a tutor at Ealing. In 1822, Bulwer went up to Cambridge. He earned a bachelor of arts degree in 1826 and a master of arts in 1835. His university awarded him an honorary doctor of laws in 1864.

Having finished his education, Bulwer led the life of traveler and man of fashion. He toured the Lake District and Scotland and frequented the most exclusive circles of society in London and Paris. Handsome, elegantly dressed, proficient at all the fashionable sports and pursuits, he was one of the great dandies of England's "age of cards and candlelight." Like many another literary gentleman of his day, Bulwer had been dazzled by the glamour and notoriety of the late Lord Byron, and he made the mistake of embarking on a curious romance with one of Byron's former mistresses, the mentally unbalanced Lady Caroline Lamb. This liaison led him to a yet worse error: In 1827, he married Lady Caroline's protégée Rosina Doyle Wheeler, a lovely but volatile Irishwoman, against the wishes of his mother, on whose inclinations all of his financial prospects rested.

As short of income as they were lavish in their tastes, the young couple had to rely on Bulwer-Lytton's pen to pay their bills. It proved dependable. Throughout the 1820's and 1830's, Bulwer-Lytton worked rapidly and industriously to churn out a succession of novels that gained for him a wide public and a sufficient income. This taxing labor impaired his temper and ultimately contributed to the breakdown of his marriage, however, for Rosina was suited by neither temperament nor training to suffer neglect and ill-use with composure. After traveling abroad to Naples in 1833, the Bulwer-Lyttons reached the point at which they could no longer live together. They agreed to a legal separation in 1836, but Rosina's financial dependence and monomaniacal hatred made her a recurring torment to her husband throughout the rest of his life.

Besides working hard as an author and as editor of the *New Monthly Magazine*, Bulwer-Lytton had in 1831 been elected to Parliament as member for St. Ives. A Radical Reformer, he was acquainted with the younger members of the utilitarian school. He supported liberal causes throughout his first parliamentary period, which ended when he lost his seat in 1841. The late 1830's and 1840's found him continuing his career as novelist, launching himself as a successful dramatist, and traveling, often for his health. On returning from one such trip abroad in 1849, he joined his friend Charles Dickens in forming a Guild of Literature and Art for the relief of impoverished authors. To benefit this guild, he wrote *Not So Bad as We Seem*, which an amateur troupe managed by Dickens staged in 1851. The philanthropic venture did not prosper, but the friendship of the two men of letters did. Dickens was to name one of his own sons after Bulwer-Lytton. At his fellow author's urging, Dickens rewrote the ending of *Great Expectations* (1860-1861) so that the Victorian reading public could have the affirmative sort of conclusion it tended to prefer.

In 1852, after having published his political *Letters to John Bull, Esquire* in 1851, Bulwer-Lytton was returned to Parliament as member for Hertfordshire, a position he was to hold until his elevation to the peerage in 1866. On rejoining the ranks of the Commons, he stationed himself among the conservatives, though his positions were more philosophical than were those of the usual Tory gentleman. In 1858, Lord Derby made him secretary for the Colonies. He was to raise Bulwer-Lytton to the peerage as first Baron Lytton of Knebworth in 1866.

On receiving his barony, Bulwer-Lytton retired from political life but continued his literary efforts until his death at Torquay early in 1873. His son Edward Robert Bulwer-Lytton (later the first earl of Lytton and himself a man of letters) was with him in his last days.

ANALYSIS

A combination of versatile talent and personal glamour made Edward Bulwer-Lytton a literary star of the first magnitude in his own day. His apparent brilliance has waned considerably since his death, and readers no longer see him as the literary peer of such novelists as Dickens or Thackeray—or Anthony Trollope, for that matter. Instead, he is remembered for writing a handful of works quite different from one another: an urbanely witty "silver fork" novel, an abstruse metaphysical romance, an impressively learned historical novel or two. Even though Bulwer-Lytton was more widely read and diversely educated than were many better-remembered literary figures of his day and despite the fact that his literary craftsmanship is sound, there are several reasons for his descent, if not into obscurity at least into a sort of twilight.

First, the passage of time has made the personal notoriety that surrounded Bulwer-Lytton's literary image—his violently unhappy marriage, his friendship with the "most gorgeous" Lady Blessington and the still more decorative Alfred, Count d'Orsay, his political adventures and editorial skirmishes—matters of historical curiosity rather than compelling contemporary interest. Second, the "high moral tone" so agreeable and edifying to Victorian readers sounds bombastic or bathetic to twentieth century ears. Therefore, the grandiose rhetoric to which Bulwer-Lytton, no less than most of his fellow writers, regularly resorted often blights what might otherwise be engaging books. Finally, and most important, Bulwer-Lytton's very ambition works against him for a modern audience. He was a writer who, as Sir Leslie Stephen acutely remarked, had talent enough to believe himself a genius; perpetually straining to be more of a philosopher or poet than he had power to be, Bulwer-Lytton conveyed the impression of being more superficial and insincere than he actually was. Thus, even Bulwer-Lytton's soundest literary achievements today have a smaller audience than they deserve. His plays, which are very far from being masterpieces, would no doubt have been completely forgotten had they not been written in what may be the Dark Age of British drama, that mediocre century between Richard Brinsley Sheridan and Oscar Wilde.

Bulwer-Lytton's literary detractors have accused him, both in his own day and subsequently, of being an opportunist who shrewdly gauged the reading public's desires and accommodated them. This charge is not entirely accurate—one of Bulwer-Lytton's ruling characteristics was that temperamental mobility that makes its possessor innately responsive to shifts in the climate of his milieu—but a clear sense of the

marketplace does dominate his career as a dramatist. His interest in the public theater of the day predated his writing for it. He worked in Parliament to correct or simplify certain legal abuses or complexities that handicapped the contemporary theater, and his sociocultural study *England and the English* (1833) contains a chapter assessing the state of the British stage. By the early 1830's, he had even written two dramatic pieces: a stage version of his novel *Eugene Aram* (the play, in fact, preceded the novel) and a historical drama centering on Cromwell. Bulwer-Lytton's serious theatrical career, however, dates from February, 1836, when he invited the popular actor-manager William Charles Macready, renowned for his championing of "true" Shakespearean texts and his partisanship of contemporary British ventures in legitimate theater, to meet him at the Albany. With this visit began a fruitful professional relationship that is chronicled in the two men's letters to each other. Macready's advice on dramatic affairs enabled Bulwer-Lytton to discard one embryonic play ("Cromwell") and to strengthen another (*The Duchess de la Vallière*) until it became stageable—though despite Macready's presence in a leading role, this maiden venture failed when presented in January, 1837. Bulwer-Lytton was to write a number of other mediocre and unsuccessful plays in his career, but between 1837 and 1840, he created for Macready, at this time managing a theatrical company, three plays that attained a measure of distinction and considerable popular success: *The Lady of Lyons*, *Richelieu*, and *Money*.

Three of Bulwer-Lytton's plays—*The Duchess de la Vallière*, *The Lady of Lyons*, and *Richelieu*—take French incidents for their subject matter and contemporary French drama for their inspiration: Bulwer-Lytton, a political liberal and a writer who believed in giving his politics literary embodiment, admired the early promise of France's republican revolution of 1830 and her political playwrights, particularly Victor Hugo and Alexandre Dumas, *père*. Bulwer-Lytton's own French plays, as he observes in the introductory remarks to his *Dramatic Works*, offer a trilogy that follows the passage of France's reins of power from the one (in *Richelieu*) to the many (in *The Lady of Lyons*).

THE DUCHESS DE LA VALLIÈRE

As theater, the first of these plays fails. Dealing with the career of Louise de la Vallière, one of Louis XIV's mistresses, *The Duchess de la Vallière* offers an always melodramatic and sometimes downright hysterical moral battle waged within and on behalf of the heroine. A virtuous provincial maiden, Louise goes to court, where she both falls (morally) and rises (socially) when the Sun King makes her his mistress and a duchess. Too good a woman to be continually interesting, too sincere a lover of Louis the man to be a stimulating and appreciative companion for Louis the King or the sort of intermediary courtiers find useful, Louise is soon supplanted by a more worldly mistress. After many a scene of debate, escape, pursuit, and lament, the duchess takes her leave of the king and the world and enters a nunnery.

THE LADY OF LYONS

The Lady of Lyons, based on a slight tale called "The Bellows Mender," proved more successful than had its predecessor, for a number of reasons. As the critic Charles Shattuck observes, Bulwer-Lytton the Radical selected just the sort of story—"that of the noble commoner winning out against the entrenched social prejudices of decadent aristocracy"—to please the public in an age of reform. In addition, the play is not high drama but romantic comedy: The temptations to grandiose posturing, moralizing, and philosophizing are less frequent. The lady of the play's title is Pauline Deschappelles, the beautiful daughter of a rich merchant. She inspires the love and possesses the pride that combine in the subtitle.

As the play opens, Pauline, with the encouragement of her mother, a woman as stupid and matrimonially obsessed as is Mrs. Bennet in Jane Austen's novel *Pride and Prejudice* (1813), has refused the proposal of Beauseant, *ci-devant* marquis, who bitterly states the absurdity of the lovely girl's goals in life: "Now as we have no noblemen left in France,—as we are all citizens and equals, she can only hope that, in spite of the war, some English Milord or 1-German Count will risk his life, by coming to Lyons, that this *fille du Roturier* may condescend to accept him."

To revenge himself on the proud beauty and her

family, Beauseant enlists the aid of one of "Nature's noblemen"—Claude Melnotte, the handsome and self-educated son of a gardener. Melnotte, known ironically, because of his efforts at self-improvement, as "Prince Claude," is himself a man who loves and has been brutally scorned by Pauline. Disguised as the Prince of Como and financed by Beauseant, Claude is to woo, win, and thereby disgrace the ambitious girl. Because he has been insulted by her, the gardener's son agrees, but because he truly loves her, he repents of his deception as soon as Pauline agrees to marry him, for in so doing, she reveals herself partly charmed by his title but also partly alive to his real excellence. No sooner has he wed the girl than Claude nobly offers her an annulment, which Pauline, by now seriously attached to him, is not disposed to accept. Having thus won her love, Claude goes off as a soldier to acquire a name and fortune worthy of the lady he has gained.

Two and a half years pass, and Claude, now known as the mysterious and heroic Colonel Morier, returns to Lyons to claim Pauline's hand. He is crushed to learn that the woman who vowed to wait for him is on the verge of marrying Beauseant—but relieved to discover that her apparent fickleness is only filial concern to save her now-bankrupt father's good name by giving him a rich son-in-law. Having arrived at the eleventh hour, the gardener's son, now risen to eminence in the Grande Armée, can stoop to save the little bourgeoise who once scorned him. Thus, the play's outcome is shrewdly calculated to please both republicans and romantics.

RICHELIEU

Whereas *The Lady of Lyons* offered a timely political message in a palatable comic form, Bulwer-Lytton's next play for Macready, *Richelieu*, proved more ambitious. Initially conceived as a romance set in the days of Louis XIII and only incidentally dealing with the cardinal, the play gradually changed, as Bulwer-Lytton's fascination with the complex man who was one of the great architects of the pre-revolutionary French state drew Richelieu to center stage.

Accordingly, the romantic comedy was elevated to a blank-verse drama. The love conflict—a triangular relationship whose three parties are the cardinal's ward Julie de Mortemar; her honorable admirer the Chevalier de Mauprat, at first the cardinal's foe, then his stout ally; and Louis XIII, who wants Julie for his mistress—was subordinated to a political problem: a conspiracy against the cardinal's strategies and life by a cabal allied with the Spanish powers. Bulwer-Lytton, well-read in French history, condensed a number of events occurring between 1630 and 1642 for his *Richelieu*. In one grand chain of events, the shrewd, brave, ruthless, but jovial cardinal successfully deals with the Duc de Bouillon's conspiracy, the "Day of Dupes," the apostasy of Baradas, and the treason of Cinq Mars. Not surprisingly, then, the play is full of melodramatic action. It contains an abundance of the intrigues and counterintrigues, betrayals, escapes, and pursuits admired by nineteenth century audiences. Bulwer-Lytton's chief interest, though, is in doing justice to the cardinal's character: His preface and occasional footnotes guarantee that the reader's attention remains on the cardinal's character as revealed through events, rather than on the events themselves. As statesman and private person, the Richelieu whom Bulwer-Lytton presents is a plausible mixture of vices and virtues. For a reading audience, the playwright comes close to his professed goal of "not disguising his foibles or his vices, but not [being] unjust to the grander qualities (especially the love of country), by which they were often dignified, and, at times, redeemed."

THE SEA-CAPTAIN AND MONEY

Bulwer-Lytton's third play for Macready, the piece first called "Norman," then "The Inquisition," next "The Birthright," and finally *The Sea-Captain*, failed disastrously in 1839; and Bulwer-Lytton was not immediately eager to resume his playwriting

In May, 1840, however, Macready's company was having a slow season at the Haymarket, so Bulwer-Lytton, willing to oblige a friend in need, embarked on the composition of a social comedy. He began and then abandoned "Appearances," a play conceived as "a satire on the way appearances of all kinds impose on the public." The play he then proceeded to write, *Money*, is a refinement on this theme.

In *Money*, which is the most enduring of his plays,

Bulwer-Lytton deals rather as Molière might have done with the manner in which the hypocritical world's regard for a man changes as his financial position improves or deteriorates. The play's hero is Alfred Evelyn, a high-minded but impoverished gentleman serving as private secretary to his worldly cousin Sir John Vesey, a man who lives luxuriously on the reputation of wealth, as do more than a few suave deceivers in Bulwer-Lytton's society novels. Evelyn loves and proposes to his equally poor and equally admirable cousin Clara, who, like him, is an exploited retainer of the Vesey family. Clara returns his love but knows from her parents' experience that affection without money is not enough to make a man happy. With Evelyn's best interests at heart, she refuses him. Directly thereafter, Evelyn inherits a great fortune, and Clara proves too scrupulous to confess the love she had not permitted herself to avow when he was poor. He therefore engages himself to the mercenary Sir John's charming, calculating daughter Georgina but, suspicious of her avowed attachment, pretends to ruin himself through extravagant spending, particularly gambling. As a result of this test, Georgina's insincerity and Clara's generous love become evident. The play ends with the virtuous man whom money alone cannot please gaining true wealth: As Evelyn tells his fiancée, Clara, "You have reconciled me to the world and to mankind."

As a comedy of manners, *Money* falls short of such masterpieces as William Congreve's *The Way of the World* (pr., pb. 1700) or Wilde's *The Importance of Being Earnest: A Trivial Comedy for Serious People* (pr. 1895), but it is of all Bulwer-Lytton's plays the one that proves most rewarding to twentieth century readers. *Money* demonstrates how a chronic moral disease, the avarice of the fashionable world, afflicts the denizens of a particular place and time. The Victorian symptoms of this malaise, the cold-hearted courtships, the mutual deceptions of extravagant worldlings and greedy tradesmen, the compelling drama of the gaming table, are interesting historical curiosities for a modern audience. Thus, ironically, the one play that Bulwer-Lytton chose to set in the present is the one in which posterity finds the most telling observations of a vanished age.

OTHER MAJOR WORKS

LONG FICTION: *Falkland*, 1827; *The Disowned*, 1828; *Pelham: Or, The Adventures of a Gentleman*, 1828; *Devereux: A Tale*, 1829; *Paul Clifford*, 1830; *Eugene Aram*, 1832; *Godolphin*, 1833; *The Last Days of Pompeii*, 1834; *Rienzi, the Last of the Roman Tribunes*, 1835; *Ernest Maltravers*, 1837; *Alice: Or, The Mysteries*, 1838; *Zanoni*, 1842; *The Last of the Barons*, 1843; *Harold, the Last of the Saxons*, 1848; *The Caxtons: A Family Picture*, 1849; *My Novel*, 1852; *What Will He Do with It?*, 1859; *A Strange Story*, 1861; *The Coming Race*, 1871; *Kenelm Chillingly: His Adventures and Opinions*, 1873; *The Parisians*, 1873.

SHORT FICTION: "The Haunted and the Haunters," 1857.

POETRY: *The New Timon*, 1846; *King Arthur: An Epic Poem*, 1848-1849, 1870.

NONFICTION: *England and the English*, 1833; *Letters to John Bull, Esquire*, 1851.

BIBLIOGRAPHY

Campbell, James L., Sr. *Edward Bulwer-Lytton*. Boston: Twayne, 1986. This accessible critical and biographical overview of Bulwer-Lytton's life and literary career emphasizes his fiction and pays comparatively little attention to his dramas. Bibliography and index.

Mulvey-Roberts, Marie. *Gothic Immortals: The Fiction of the Brotherhood of the Rosy Cross*. New York: Routledge, 1989. A look at the Occultism and the gothic aspects of the fiction of Bulwer-Lytton and William Godwin. Bibliography and index.

Snyder, Charles W. *Liberty and Morality: A Political Biography of Edward Bulwer-Lytton*. New York: Peter Lang, 1995. A biography of Bulwer-Lytton that focuses on his politics and social views. Bibliography and index.

Peter W. Graham

ALEXANDER BUZO

Born: Sydney, Australia; July 23, 1944

PRINCIPAL DRAMA

Norm and Ahmed, pr. 1968, pb. 1969
The Front Room Boys, pr. 1969, pb. 1970
Rooted, pr. 1969, pb. 1973
The Roy Murphy Show, pr. 1970, pb. 1973
Macquarie, pb. 1971, pr. 1972
Tom, pr. 1972, pb. 1975
Batman's Beachhead, pb. 1973
Coralie Lansdowne Says No, pr., pb. 1974
Martello Towers, pr., pb. 1976
Makassar Reef, pr. 1978, pb. 1979
Big River, pr. 1980, pb. 1981
The Marginal Farm, pr. 1983, pb. 1985
Stingray, pr. 1987
Shellcove Road, pr. 1989 (one act)
Pacific Union: The Story of the San Francisco Forty-Fivers, pr., pb. 1995
Normie and Tuan, pr. 1999

OTHER LITERARY FORMS

Alexander Buzo has written for both film and television, coauthoring the script for the television production of *Ned Kelly* (1970) and writing the screenplay for the short film *Rod* (1972). He has also contributed articles to journals and newspapers such as *The Australian Financial Review*, *National Times*, *The Sydney Morning Herald*, *The Age*, and *The Adelaide Review*.

ACHIEVEMENTS

Alexander Buzo was playwright-in-residence for the Melbourne Theatre Company in 1972-1973. During that period, his historical play *Macquarie* and a satire on big business, *Tom*, were produced. He was awarded the Australian Literature Society Gold Medal for those two plays in 1972. Buzo also received a fellowship from the Commonwealth Literary Fund in 1970 and a grant from the Literature Board of the Australia Council in 1973 and 1979. In 1972, he received the Australian Literary Society Gold Medal, and in 1998, the University of New South Wales bestowed the Alumni Award for Distinguished Achievement on him.

One of Buzo's greatest achievements has been to alter the image of the Australian theater. He belongs to the New Wave of Australian playwrights who began to come to prominence in the 1960's and whose spiritual mentor was Ray Lawler, whose *Summer of the Seventeenth Doll* (pr. 1955, pb. 1957) was the first Australian play to win international attention.

Buzo's first important play, the one-act *Norm and Ahmed*, won for him as much notoriety as fame. It was the subject of a number of prosecutions for indecency, provided by the play's obscene closing line. *Norm and Ahmed* was introduced to the public in 1968, at the Old Tote Theatre in Sydney, as part of an experimental Australian play season. It was accompanied by another one-act play, *The Fire on the Snow* (pr. 1941), by Douglas Stewart, which had been first produced as a radio play. In the original production, the closing line was delivered onstage in a Bowdlerized form, but in the play's production in Brisbane, in April and May of 1969, the final speech was delivered as written in Buzo's script. The actor playing Norm, who speaks the offending line, was arrested after about two weeks of production, having ignored warnings by the police. He was tried, convicted, and fined, but he took the case to the State Supreme Court of Queensland, where the conviction was overturned. The state authorities appealed to the High Court of Australia, which upheld the State Supreme Court's decision.

The play was produced in Melbourne, the capital of the state of Victoria, in July of 1969, and the producer and the actor playing Norm were prosecuted for indecency in that state as well. After a number of adjournments, during one of which the magistrate, counsel, and witnesses saw a special performance, the producer and actor were each fined ten dollars. They appealed, but the appeal was dismissed, and the judge decided that the line in question violated contemporary standards of decency.

Norm and Ahmed was first published as a supplement to *Komos*, the journal of drama and theater arts

of Monash University in Victoria, Australia. The publishers mentioned that they had had extreme difficulty obtaining a firm to set the type because of the obscenity charge that was then before the courts. The controversy over *Norm and Ahmed* received a considerable amount of publicity. The net effect was to liberate Australian drama from censorship, and many playwrights have followed Buzo's lead, using strong language wherever they feel it to be appropriate.

BIOGRAPHY

Alexander Buzo was born in Sydney, the capital of the state of New South Wales, on July 23, 1944, the son of an Albanian-born, American-educated civil-engineer father and an Australian mother. Buzo spent his childhood in Armidale, an inland town in New South Wales, near the border between New South Wales and Queensland, an area devoted primarily to the raising of sheep. Buzo attended primary school in Armidale and high school at the International School in Geneva, Switzerland. After completing high school, he returned to Australia. He was graduated from the University of New South Wales in Sydney.

Buzo firmly committed himself to earning a living as a writer and succeeded in doing so—no mean feat in Australia. Producing plays almost annually between 1969 and 1989, he achieved world renown as a dramatist. His plays reflect many of his personal beliefs. He detests bullies and cowards and satirizes them mercilessly, as demonstrated by his portrayal of the central character of Norm in *Norm and Ahmed* and later in *Normie and Tuan*; he is sympathetic to women's attempts to achieve equality and to make a mark in the traditionally male-chauvinist society of Australia; and, finally, he deplores the insularity of Australia and Australians, and his writings reflect his attempts to change his people's view of themselves.

Between 1978 and 2000, Buzo was writer-in-residence at six institutions, ranging from Sydney Teachers College to the University of Indonesia in Jakarta. During one of these residencies, at James Cook University in Townsville, he completed two books, a novel *Prue Flies North* (1991) and *The Young Person's Guide to the Theatre* (1998). He notes in an article written for *The Age* (Melbourne, May 28, 2001)

"As the theatre had moved more into the realm of daytime television—which made a kind of sense because its audience worked when Oprah [Winfrey] was on—I had gravitated to writing books more than plays." Buzo also published *Kiwese: A Guide, a Dictionary, a Shearing of Unsights* (1994), a guide to New Zealand's spoken English; *The Longest Game: A Collection of the Best Cricket Writing from Alexander to Zavos, from the Gabba to the Yabba* (1990), a book on cricket that he edited with Jamie Grant, and *Glancing Blows: Life and Language in Australia* (1987) a collection of prose pieces, essays, and journalism.

ANALYSIS

All Alexander Buzo's plays, which have been produced in London and the United States as well as throughout Australia, may be classified as socially pertinent and controversial. He writes to shock or at least to make his audience uncomfortable, even when they are laughing uproariously. In his earlier plays, his tone is satiric, bordering sometimes on the morbid, and in his later work, it tends to be ironic. If his plays seem to lack a definite structure much of the time, this failing is balanced by his superlative dialogue.

There is a universality of character and setting that more than makes up for the Australian idioms that Buzo employs, particularly in his early plays—idioms that will frequently baffle the non-Australian playgoer (or reader). Indeed, as Buzo has matured, his characterizations have become increasingly rich and complex. His early characters, although representing recognizable types, border on caricature. Norm, in *Norm and Ahmed*, for example, is drawn in bold strokes but with little detail. In contrast, Coralie Lansdowne, of *Coralie Lansdowne Says No*, is a fine character portrait of a troubled woman, uneasy with herself, and Weeks Brown, the protagonist of *Makassar Reef*, has a depth of character seldom met in modern drama, Australian or European, American or English.

NORM AND AHMED

As noted above, Buzo's recurring theme as a playwright is Australia's national identity. Although he has many other concerns as well, it is this theme that links plays as diverse as *Norm and Ahmed*, *Mac-

quarie*, and *Makassar Reef*. *Norm and Ahmed*, which has been called "probably the best Australian one-act play staged for many years," is primarily a study of an uncertain Australian, one who cannot come to terms with the "invasion" of his country by immigrants who have different values and different mores. Indeed, Norm is portrayed as the archetypal Australian; the attitudes he expresses are those ascribed to the conservative middle-class, median-educated "Aussie." Ahmed personifies everything that this class of Australian has come to dislike: the immigrant who is not only disturbingly "different" but also ambitious, hardworking, and self-possessed. Confronted by a "boong" such as Ahmed, the typical Aussie feels a need to reestablish his uneasy sense of superiority.

The historical background to the play, which needs no explanation for an Australian audience, will be less familiar to non-Australians. Traditionally, immigrants to Australia, of whom there were more than two million after World War II, were drawn from Great Britain and continental Europe, and for many years there was in effect a "White Australia" policy. This policy has changed, however, as the Australian government has come to realize that the country is situated in Southeast Asia, with many nonwhite neighbors. Although nonwhites have been permitted to immigrate to Australia, attitudes toward them have changed slowly, and many white Australians have retained racist tendencies.

Both Norm and Ahmed are types rather than fully developed characters. Norm, who mentions that his father was Irish, fits the stereotype of the Irish Australian: antigovernment but politically conservative, boozing, rebellious, and suspicious of foreigners. Ahmed is a leftist, unhappy with the government both in Australia and in Pakistan. He is formal, polite, and reserved.

Buzo's gift for dialogue is evident in this early play. Indeed, the play depends entirely on dialogue to hold the audience's attention. There is no plot and, with the exception of the kick to Ahmed's stomach that provides the conclusion, no action. Norm is a natural storyteller, and he keeps Ahmed engaged with tales of himself and his exploits during the war, at the same time freely expressing his attitudes toward various facets of Australian life. Norm is not only a fine raconteur but also a born actor, and he acts out many of his tales for Ahmed. His speech is glib, and he cleverly conceals his true self from Ahmed throughout the play, until the culmination. The play made a deep impression in Australia, and much has been written about why Norm kicks Ahmed.

Why indeed? Norm has received only politeness from Ahmed, but Ahmed's reserve implies a feeling of superiority, which Norm cannot tolerate. As Katherine Brisbane observes in her introduction to *Three Plays by Alexander Buzo* (1973): "His powers of reasoning may have betrayed him in the past but his prejudice he can rely on."

NORMIE AND TUAN

Normie and Tuan, based on the play *Norm and Ahmed*, could be called *Norm and Ahmed Redux*. In this one-act play, Normie and Tuan, a Chinese student from Malaysia, meet around midnight at a bus stop on a Sydney street. Normie is described as "an aging Australian," and the play demonstrates, in no uncertain terms, that even though thirty years have passed, Norm's attitude toward immigrants has not changed. He is still the white Australian, and although in the beginning of the play, he appears to pay lip service to acceptance of Asian migration to Australia, he deeply resents the path his country has taken. His parents and their progenitors referred to the United Kingdom as "home." To Normie, Tuan is the embodiment of the "Yellow Peril" that he fought against in Vietnam and his father fought against in World War II. He views the Asian immigration as a peaceful invasion of his country and an indication that Australia won the war but lost the battle.

Many of the symbols used in *Norm and Ahmed* are mirrored in *Normie and Tuan*, and these are used to reinforce the premise that the more things change, the more they stay the same. The play closes in the same manner as its predecessor, with Normie attacking Tuan and leaving him unconscious after agreeing to share a taxi with him.

MACQUARIE

Buzo's first historical play, *Macquarie*, is about one of Australia's early colonial governors, Lachlan Macquarie. The play is important in that it marks

Buzo's first foray into the roots of Australia's national identity. One must remember that the first settlement in Australia was founded in 1788. Buzo uses the historical genre to draw parallels between the past and the present. He makes his audience realize that no matter how much things have changed, certain human characteristics are constant. Greed, avarice, honesty, and high-mindedness are still as significant in maintaining societal values as they were in the nineteenth century.

The play retains a twentieth century flavor through a series of rapid changes on a permanent set—using lighting to focus on particular parts of the set, leaving other parts darkened, and employing a commentator to narrate the action. These devices, given currency by the epic theater of Bertolt Brecht, remind the audience that they are in contemporary times. Stage presentations of *Macquarie* rely heavily on technical effects of this nature, and the sparse setting that Buzo calls for compels the playgoer or reader to use his imagination to fill in the blanks. The play is not naturalistic; it does not try to present the history of the era as much as it delves into the motivations of an honorable man who is opposed by a number of self-interested factions. It stresses universal moral struggles.

Governor Macquarie is opposed by the ultraconservative, anticonvict faction of "established" Australians, among whom are his lieutenant governor and a prominent Methodist minister, Samuel Marsden, one of the wealthiest landowners of the time. The latter group wishes to maintain the status quo and violently opposes Macquarie's reform efforts.

The action opens in Sydney, in the colony of New South Wales, which, at the time, constituted all of settled Australia, except for Tasmania, then known as Van Diemen's Land. The colony extended along the entire east coast of Australia, much of which had not yet been explored. There are rapid shifts in time and place (between Sydney and London) and a lot of action. So many changes in locale occur at such a rapid pace that the audience will wonder, now and then, exactly where the action is taking place.

Considerable social commentary is included in the play, amounting almost to allegory. The clergyman

Marsden represents the evil forces in the colony, whereas Macquarie represents the forces of good, overcome by deceit, greed, and politicizing. The play dramatizes the visions of fairness and right as exemplified in a just, farsighted governor, who, although he makes errors in judgment, is basically a sincere and compassionate man. Despite his character faults, which led to his making mistakes, he was a heroic figure in early Australia.

MAKASSAR REEF

Macquarie provides audiences with an insight into the beginnings of Australia and, implicitly, a standard by which to judge the present. That judgment is made more explicit in *Makassar Reef*, a play that differs in style from *Macquarie* as much as *Macquarie* differs from *Norm and Ahmed* yet continues Buzo's investigation of the Australian experience.

The setting for *Makassar Reef* is the Celebes Islands of Indonesia. The plot concerns a no-longer-young Australian couple: Weeks Brown, a government economist in his thirties, and his fiancée, Beth Fleetwood. Other characters are Wendy Ostrow and her daughter, recently back from Geneva and now on their way to Australia, where Wendy was born but which her daughter has never seen; Perry Glasson, an Australian yachtsman-drifter, who will do almost anything to make a little money; Silver, a thief who passes as a Dutch hippie but who was really born in Australia; and two Indonesians: Karim, a corrupt government official, and Abidin, a disillusioned but still politically active journalist who earns his living as an English teacher and guide. There is also an offstage character, Madame Yu, who owns the hotel and restaurant in which much of the action takes place, and who also has a hand in prostitution, drugs, and, presumably, many other illegal affairs.

There are many parallels between this play and William J. Lederer's novel *The Ugly American* (1958). As travel has become cheaper and Australians more mobile, they have usurped the place of the American, especially in locations closer to Australia, displaying all the characteristics despised for so many years in American tourists: smug superiority, conspicuous display of wealth, and disregard for local customs.

Disillusionment pervades *Makassar Reef*. Weeks either is on vacation, has resigned, or has been fired from his post as a government economic adviser in Australia; it appears that one of the policies he advised his superiors to put into effect has had disastrous results. Almost penniless in Makassar, reduced to selling his personal possessions, Weeks is drunk through much of the play.

In this demoralized state, Weeks looks for solace in an affair with Wendy, and thus the plot is set in motion. Beth is aware of the affair but will not relinquish Weeks. Wendy's daughter, Camilla, thinks that Weeks and Beth are married; indeed, they have lived together for nine years and it would appear there is nothing left for them to do but marry. Camilla is shattered by the revelation of Weeks's affair with her mother.

Beth retaliates by having an affair with the yachtsman, Perry, who is subsequently falsely arrested in a conspiracy between the Indonesian official, Karim, and the thief, Silver. Silver, however, learns that Madame Yu, determined to rid her territory of all competition, intends to eliminate him. Needing passage from the island, he strikes a bargain with Weeks to liberate Perry, who, in return, is supposed to take Silver with him to Singapore, far from Madame Yu's influence. On liberation, however, Perry leaves the island by himself, abandoning Silver to his well-deserved fate.

At the close of the play, the audience learns that Weeks has obtained work with the World Bank in Washington, and Beth, who earlier claimed that she was pregnant by him but who casually mentions that she is now menstruating, is to go with him. Wendy and Camilla are booked on the next plane to Australia, much to Camilla's distress: She wants to return to her friends and school in Geneva, the only life she has ever known.

Makassar Reef is a dark play enlivened with occasional sparks of humor. The dialogue, as is typical of Buzo, is fast-paced, and the action shifts rapidly from point to point on the set. As noted above, there is a feeling of senselessness about life, an utter disillusionment pervading this play, a pressing-in of the world that is forcefully communicated to the audience. The mood of the play is reminiscent of post-

World War I European theater and film; it is redolent with a feeling of defeat.

The play is noteworthy for its superb characterizations, its trenchant examination of the difficulties people experience in establishing and maintaining intimacy. The stereotyped characters and broad satire of Buzo's early plays have given way to fully rounded characters and subtle irony. At the same time, Buzo has developed the theme of Australia's isolation, introduced in *Norm and Ahmed*. In *Makassar Reef*, he stresses Australia's position, geographically and economically, as a Southeast Asian nation. Thus, both stylistically and thematically, *Makassar Reef* gives evidence of Buzo's continuing growth as a dramatist.

PACIFIC UNION

Pacific Union is a full-length play about the birth of the United Nations and how tenacious Australian Dr. Herbert Vere Evatt changed the face of history. Evatt, the minister for external affairs, led the Australian delegation at the founding discussions of the United Nations in San Francisco in 1946. The play delves into Dr. Evatt's struggles to ensure that the United Nations would not be simply the tool of large nations. He helped ensure that the organization's charter became more human and larger in scope, containing provisions for the poor, the weak and the oppressed, provisions never envisaged by the major powers. Buzo's focus in this play is on Australia's relations with the world.

OTHER MAJOR WORKS

LONG FICTION: *The Search for Harry Allway*, 1985; *Prue Flies North*, 1991.

SCREENPLAY: *Rod*, 1972.

TELEPLAY: *Ned Kelly*, 1970.

NONFICTION: *Meet the New Class*, 1981; *Tautology*, 1981, revised as *Tautology Too*, 1982; *Glancing Blows: Life and Language in Australia*, 1987; *Kiwese: A Guide, a Dictionary, a Shearing of Unsights*, 1994; *A Dictionary of the Almost Obvious*, 1998; *The Young Person's Guide to the Theatre*, 1998.

EDITED TEXT: *The Longest Game: A Collection of the Best Cricket Writing from Alexander to Zavos, from the Gabba to the Yabba*, 1990 (with Jennie Grant).

BIBLIOGRAPHY

Arnold, Roslyn. "Aggressive Vernacular: Williamson, Buzo, and the Australian Tradition." *Southerly* 35, no. 4 (1975). Arnold looks at Buzo and David Williamson, focusing on the language used.

Fitzpatrick, Peter. "Alexander Buzo." In *After "The Doll": Australian Drama Since 1955*. Sydney: Edward Arnold, 1979. Fitzpatrick examines the qualities shared by Buzo and David Williamson: the fact that "they were the first to be granted the token of legitimacy," that "their developing 'professionalism' was marked by their writing for film," and that they "share a preoccupation with the values and life-styles of their own generation." Analyzes the language in Buzo's plays.

Holloway, Peter, ed. *Contemporary Australian Drama*. Rev. ed. Sydney: Currency Press, 1987. Holloway looks at modern Australian drama, including the works of Buzo. Bibliography and index.

McCallum, John. "Coping with Hydrophobia: Alexander Buzo's Moral World." *Meanjin* 39, no. 1 (April, 1980): 60-69. Analyzes the characters in Buzo's early plays (up to *Tom*), portrayed mostly as victims of an "amoral and dehumanising society." Also examines the shift in style from these early "angry" plays, as Buzo called them, to a new style of romantic comedy and witty characters. Discusses several plays, among them *Big River*, *Makassar Reef*, and *Martello Towers*.

New Theatre Quarterly 2 (February, 1986). Half the issue is devoted to Australian theater, with six articles addressing drama since 1975. Discusses Buzo throughout. Chronology from 1977 to 1983.

On the Scene 5, no. 3 (1984). The issue is devoted entirely to Buzo and the production of *Rooted*.

Rees, Leslie. *A History of Australian Drama*. Rev. ed. 2 vols. Sydney: Angus and Robertson, 1987. An outline of the history of the 1969 prosecutions arising from the language used in *Norm and Ahmed* is detailed in an appendix to Volume 2.

_____. *The Making of Australian Drama: A Historical and Critical Survey from the 1830's to the 1970's*. Sydney: Angus and Robertson, 1973. Discusses Buzo's work in chapters on university theater, on *The Front Room Boys*, on drama experimentation, and, in an appendix, on the courtroom furor over *Norm and Ahmed*.

Sturm, T. L. "Alexander Buzo: An Imagist with a Personal Style of Surrealism." In *Contemporary Australian Drama: Perspectives Since 1955*, edited by Peter Holloway. Sydney: Currency Press, 1981. Sturm's five-page essay begins by linking Buzo's drama to the "sociological pattern" of Australian "national self-consciousness" but then focuses on Buzo's rejection of such reception of his plays: "Some people regard my plays as documentaries on the Australian way of life and that disturbs me. . . . My plays are meant as works of fiction."

Includes discussions of *Macquarie* and *Coralie Lansdowne Says No*.

Thomson, Helen. "*Pacific Union* and *The Incorruptible* by Louis Nowra." *Australian Drama Studies* 29 (October, 1996). A comparison of Buzo's *Pacific Union* and a work by Louis Nowra.

Williams, Margaret. *Drama*. Australian Writers and Their Work series. New York: Oxford University Press, 1977. An examination of Australian dramatists, including Buzo. Bibliography.

C. Peter Goslett,
updated by Thomas J. Taylor

DINO BUZZATI
Dino Buzzati Traverso

Born: San Pellegrino, near Belluno, Italy; October 16, 1906
Died: Rome, Italy; January 28, 1972

PRINCIPAL DRAMA

Piccola passeggiata, pr., pb. 1942
La rivolta contro i poveri, pr., pb. 1946
Un caso clinico, pr., pb. 1953
Drammatica fine di un noto musicista, pr., pb. 1955
Procedura penale, pr., pb. 1959 (libretto; music by Luciano Chailly)
L'orologio, pb. 1959, pr. 1962
Un verme al ministero, pr., pb. 1960
Battono alla porta, pr. 1961, pb. 1963 (libretto; based on Richardo Malpiero's short story)
Era proibito, pr. 1962, pb. 1963 (libretto; music by Chailly)
La colonna infame, pr., pb. 1962
L'uomo che andrà in America, pr., pb. 1962
La famosa invasione degli orsi in Sicilia, pr. 1965 (adaptation of his story)
Una ragazza arrivò, pb. 1968
La fine del borghese, pr., pb. 1968
Teatro, pb. 1980

OTHER LITERARY FORMS

Dino Buzzati is best known as a writer of narrative fiction. He published several novels, the most famous of which is *Il deserto dei Tartari*, 1940 (*The Tartar Steppe*, 1952), and numerous collections of short stories, including *I sette messaggeri* (1942) and *Sessanta racconti* (1958). Buzzati was also an artist and illustrated some of his books, including *La famosa invasione degli orsi in Sicilia* (1945; *The Bears' Famous Invasion of Sicily*, 1947), which was later dramatized, and *Poema a fumetti* (1969). He also designed scenery for A. Lualdo's *Il diavolo nel campanile*, presented for the festival Maggio Musicale in Florence in 1951.

ACHIEVEMENTS

Most of Dino Buzzati's awards were made in recognition of his work as a writer of narrative fiction. He won the Gargano Prize in 1951 for his story *In quel preciso momento* (1950), the Naples prize in 1957 for *Il crollo della Baliverna* (1954), the Strega prize for his collection *Sessanta racconti*, and the All'Amalia prize for his narrative work in general. His play, *Un caso clinico*, won the Premio Saint Vincent in 1953. In 1958 he won the Viareggio Prize for

Literature. His work has been especially popular in France, where he was honored by the creation of a special society, the Association Internationale des Amis de Dino Buzzati, in Paris in 1976. The film adaptation of his novel *The Tartar Steppe*, directed by Valerio Zurlini, won an Italian Academy Award. He was highly regarded as a journalist and critic.

BIOGRAPHY

Dino Buzzati was born in 1906 in the village of San Pellegrino in the Dolomite mountains near the city of Belluno, where his family owned a summer home. He spent many summers there as he grew up, and he never lost his taste for hiking and mountain climbing. His father, Giulio Cesare Buzzati, was a professor of international law at the University of Pavia, and his son also took a degree in law at the University of Milan. Dino Buzzati chose another path, however, and became a journalist with the Milanese newspaper *Corriere della Sera* in 1928. Most of his life he worked with that newspaper as an editor, reporter, correspondent, and critic. He reported on warfare in Ethiopia, and during World War II, he was a correspondent reporting on several important sea battles from the deck of the cruiser *Fiume* and other navy ships. At the age of sixty, he married Almerina Antoniazzi, who edited his papers and his sixty-three diaries after his death in 1972.

ANALYSIS

Dino Buzzati's writings, both for the page and for the stage, have a distinctive aura of ominous threat and loneliness. His stories and plays often feature protagonists caught in mysterious and incomprehensible circumstances. In many cases, a character must satisfy terms that unknown forces have dictated, even if the purveyor of the terms appears as a pleasant and cheerful character whose real menace becomes gradually transparent. There is a rich sense of irony running through these works, linking Buzzati to the earlier writers of the Italian *teatro del grottesco* or Theater of the Grotesque, which emphasized the curious affinity of the horrendous with the laughable, seen in the work of such writers as Luigi Chiarelli, Pier Maria Rosso di Secondo, Luigi Antonelli, and, of course,

Luigi Pirandello. The effects Buzzati creates in this way have often inspired the adjective Kafkaesque, for his characters have a strong kinship with those hapless protagonists in Franz Kafka's *Der Prozess* (1925; *The Trial*, 1937), *Das Schloss* (1926; *The Castle*, 1930), and *Die Verwandlung* (1915; *The Metamorphosis*, 1936). Because of the surreal and metaphysical quality in his writing, some critics have associated him with E. T. A. Hoffmann and Edgar Allen Poe. The paintings of Giorgio De Chirico are often likened to the atmospheric effects in Buzzati's stories.

There is a natural theatricality to Buzzati's work, even if he favored the novel and short-story form. That sense of impending doom and frightening isolation could only be heightened in the theater, where the audience must endure the plight in the immediate moment. His association with the working theater was relatively brief and never fully comfortable. Almost all of his plays date from between 1953, the year of the production of his *Un caso clinico*, and 1968, the year of his last play, *La fine del borghese*. The famous director, Giorgio Strehler, co-founder with Paolo Grassi of the Piccolo Teatro of Milan, sensed this potential in Buzzati and urged him to write for the stage. He in fact suggested that Buzzati adapt his short story, "Sette piani," and the result was the play *Un caso clinico*, which Strehler then directed. On Buzzati's part, the theater was an intimidating form, dependent as it always is on the work of many collaborators and the vagaries of an unpredictable public. Buzzati has described in his interviews with Yves Panafieu the nerve-wracking anxiety of watching rehearsals, which on one occasion prompted him to stand up and shout "That's not it!" and storm out of the rehearsal hall when Strehler was directing his one-act play, *La rivolta contro i poveri*, only later to find that the public loved it. By contrast, watching rehearsals of Maner Lualdi's one-act adaptation of his *La fine del borghese*, everything seemed perfect in rehearsal, yet once the audience arrived, it was greeted with a great yawn. The theater, he has said, is like a drug: It sucks people in and mesmerizes them. It can be perverse and pernicious. People devote their whole lives to working this magic as actors, directors, designers, and playwrights, yet its rewards are fleeting and completely unpredictable.

Perhaps for this reason, Buzzati chose to resort to narrative rather than dramatic fiction. Certainly on the international scene he is much better known for his novels and short stories than for his plays. This is evident, for example, in the fact that none of his plays is readily available in English.

UN CASO CLINICO

Giovanni Corte, the protagonist of *Un caso clinico* (a clinical case), is a powerful industrialist, used to calling all the shots and maneuvering others into deals that yield great rewards for himself and his company. He has begun to hear the strange, hollow sound of woman singing, but no one else can hear her. After visiting a seven-story medical clinic, he finds himself admitted for observation. Professor Schroeder, chief doctor of the clinic, organizes it so that the patients are placed on higher or lower floors according to how sick they may be, the hopeless cases on the ground floor and the healthier ones on the top floor. Step by step Corte is moved downstairs from floor to floor with charming and indulgent explanations by Dr. Claretta, Schroeder's chief assistant. Corte's will is weakened with each move until he is virtually paralyzed and on the verge of death.

The play is a powerful and atmospheric piece. The settings remain virtually the same as Corte goes down from one floor to the next, but the lighting and sounds become progressively stranger and more mysterious. On one level, there is satire of the medical profession. Doctors wield such enormous power because of people's ignorance of what the diagnoses and prognoses might mean. They are powerful enough actually to make people sick. At the same time, there is something strange and metaphysical going on as Corte gradually abandons this world, weakened and summoned by the enchanting voice of the unseen woman, a siren of death.

This is by far Buzzati's most famous play. Following its success with the Piccolo Teatro in Milan in 1953, starring Tino Carraro, it played in Berlin the next year at the Knorfürstendammtheater under the direction of O. F. Schuh, then in 1955 in Paris at the Théâtre La Bruyère under the direction of G. Vitaly, using an adaptation by Albert Camus. This was a stunning success. It helped create a loyal French following of Buzzati's work, evinced by the Association Internationale des Amis de Dino Buzzati.

UN VERME AL MINISTERO

In *Un verme al ministero* (a worm in the ministry), Buzzati again mixes the satirical (bureaucracy) and the metaphysical (fear of the unknown). Office workers in a government ministry become more and more obsessed with the sounds of underground burrowing, a gnawing in the walls, that seem to be coming from some ominous excavation. Their fear grows into the conviction that they will soon face a squadron of Morzi, revolutionaries and disbelievers in God. They become paralyzed with terror. They do receive the revolutionary leader of the Morzi, and they resort to bureaucratic mumbo-jumbo in a kangaroo court trial they conduct of one of the few honest office workers, Palisierna. One of their number, Morales, rises over the tumult and chooses to take action. By resorting to chicanery, evil, treachery, manipulation, and hypocrisy, he hopes to prepare for the encounter with the Morzi. He chooses to present himself as "godless." When he then tramples and spits on the crucifix, he is suddenly struck down in a stunning *coup de théâtre* that brings the play to its end.

The play has much of the same sense of nightmarish uncertainty that often appears in Buzzati's work, although it tends to throw more emphasis on the satire of bureaucracies. The ending of the play, some critics have said, makes too clear what would be better left to provocative ambiguity.

L'UOMO CHE ANDRÀ IN AMERICA

The action of *L'uomo che andrà in America* (the man who will go to America) turns on the mystery surrounding the life of the man of the title. The author plays on people's sense of desperate waiting and their hope of achieving an authenticity that circumstance would violently deny them. America becomes an almost mythical place where their hopes can come true, where people can rise out of themselves and achieve a satisfying integrity. This far-off land, with all its prairies, deserts, mountains, and huge spaces, inspires an intense anxiety in the man, virtually a terror in the face of infinity, even as he manages to board the ship.

It is an allegory in one way on life's challenges, but it is much more than that, for it develops an interplay between circumstance and inward terror that creates a compelling psychology. The indefinite, the uncertain, and the mysterious all engage the audience with an immediate intensity. The tone is ironic, even bitter, as the situation and the characters develop, making for a subtle balance between the symbolic and the realistic.

OTHER MAJOR WORKS

LONG FICTION: *Bàrnabo delle montagne*, 1933 (*Bàrnabo of the Mountains*, 1984); *Il segreto del Bosco Vecchio*, 1935; *Il deserto dei Tartari*, 1940 (*The Tartar Steppe*, 1952); *Il grande ritratto*, 1960 (*Larger than Life*, 1962); *Un amore*, 1963 (*A Love Affair*, 1964).

SHORT FICTION: *I sette messaggeri*, 1942; *Paura alla Scala*, 1949; *Il crollo della Baliverna*, 1954; *Esperimento di magia*, 1958; *Sessanta racconti*, 1958; *Egregio signore, siamo spiacenti di . . .* , 1960; *Catastrophe: The Strange Stories of Dino Buzzati*, 1966; *Il colombre e altri cinquanta racconti*, 1966; *La boutique del mistero*, 1968; *Le notti difficili*, 1971; *180 racconti*, 1982; *Restless Nights: Selected Stories of Dino Buzzati*, 1984; *The Siren: A Selection from Dino Buzzati*, 1984; *Il meglio dei racconti di Dino Buzzati*, 1989; *Lo Strano Natale di Mr. Scrooge altre storie*, 1990; *Bestiario*, 1991.

POETRY: *Il capitano Pic ed altre poesie*, 1965; *Due poemetti*, 1967; *Poema a fumetti*, 1969; *Le poesie*, 1982.

NONFICTION: *Cronache terrestri*, 1972; *Dino Buzzati al Giro d'Italia*, 1981; *Cronache nere*, 1984; *Lettere a Brambilla*, 1985; *Montagne di vetro: Articoli e racconti dal 1932 al 1971*, 1989; *Il buttafuoco: Cronache di guerra sul mar*, 1992.

CHILDREN'S LITERATURE: *La famosa invasione degli orsi in Sicilia*, 1945 (*The Bears' Famous Invasion of Sicily*, 1947); *Il dispiaceri del re*, 1980.

MISCELLANEOUS: *Il libro delle pipe*, 1945 (with di Val MoEppe Ramazzotti); *In quel preciso momento*, 1950 (includes stories in autobiographical sketches); *I miracolirel*, 1971 (includes thirty-nine of Buzzati's paintings with his text); *Romanzi e racconti*, 1975; *Per grazia ricevuta*, 1983 (includes Buzzati's art); *Il reggimento parte all' alba*, 1985; *Opere scelte*, 1998.

BIBLIOGRAPHY

Biasin, Gian-Paolo. "The Secret Fears of Man: Dino Bussati." *The Italian Quarterly* 6, no. 12 (1962). This essay deals only with Buzzati's fiction but does explore his tone of mystery and anguish.

Esslin, Martin. *The Theatre of the Absurd*. 3d ed. New York: Penguin Books, 1983. Discusses two of Buzzati's plays in relation to the phenomenon of the Theater of the Absurd.

Rawson, Judy. "Dino Buzzati." In *Writers and Society in Contemporary Italy*, edited by Michael Caesar and Peter Hainsworth. Leamington Spa, England: Berg, 1984. Investigates the relationship between Buzzati's work and journalism and fascism.

Spinder, William. "Magic Realism: A Typology." *Forum for Modern Language Studies* (January, 1993): 75-85. Places Buzzati in the style of Magical Realism along with other European and South American authors, again concentrating on fiction.

Stanley Longman

GEORGE GORDON, LORD BYRON

Born: London, England; January 22, 1788
Died: Missolonghi, Greece; April 19, 1824

PRINCIPAL DRAMA
Manfred, pb. 1817, pr. 1834

Marino Faliero, Doge of Venice, pr., pb. 1821
Sardanapalus: A Tragedy, pb. 1821, pr. 1834
The Two Foscari: A Tragedy, pb. 1821, pr. 1837
Cain: A Mystery, pb. 1821 (with *Sardanapalus* and *The Two Foscari*)

Heaven and Earth, pb. 1822 (fragment)
Werner: Or, The Inheritance, pb. 1823, pr. 1830
The Deformed Transformed, pb. 1824 (fragment)

OTHER LITERARY FORMS

George Gordon, Lord Byron, is considerably better known as a poet than as a dramatist, and the relative importance of the poetry is quickly evident in any review of Byron's literary career. His first book, *Fugitive Pieces*, was printed at his own expense in November of 1806, and though it consisted primarily of sentimental and mildly erotic verse, it also contained hints of the satiric wit that would be so important to Byron's later reputation. The volume is also notable for having inspired the first accusations that Byron lacked poetic chastity; at the urging of some of his friends, he withdrew the book from private circulation and replaced it with the more morally upright *Poems on Various Occasions*, printed in Newark in January of 1807 by John Ridge, who had also printed *Fugitive Pieces*.

In his first attempt at public recognition as a man of letters, Byron published *Hours of Idleness* in June of 1807. The volume shows the obvious influence of a number of Augustan and Romantic poets, but despite its largely derivative nature, it received several favorable early reviews. Fortunately for Byron's development as a poet, however, the praise was not universal, and subsequent critical attacks, notably by Henry Brougham of *The Edinburgh Review*, helped inspire the writing of Byron's first poetic triumph, *English Bards and Scotch Reviewers* (1809). In the tradition of Alexander Pope's *The Dunciad* (1728-1743) but written under the more direct influence of *Baviad* (1794) and *Maeviad* (1795), by William Gifford, *English Bards and Scotch Reviewers* is the earliest significant example of Byron's satiric genius. Three more satiric poems soon followed, but none of these—*Hints from Horace* (1811), *The Curse of Minerva* (1812), and *Waltz: An Apostrophic Hymn* (1813)—attracted as much admiring attention as *English Bards and Scotch Reviewers*.

During this same period, Byron was composing the poem with which he would be most closely associated during his lifetime and which would make him

the most lionized literary figure of his day, *Childe Harold's Pilgrimage*, Cantos I-IV (1812-1818, 1819). The first two cantos of the poem, an imaginative meditation loosely based on two years of travel on the Continent, were published on March 10, 1812, and produced an immediate sensation. In his own words, Byron "awoke one morning and found myself famous." Cantos III and IV were greeted with equal excitement and confirmed the identification of Byron in the popular mind with his poem's gloomy protagonist.

In the meantime, Byron published a series of poetic tales that further exploited the knowledge derived from his Eastern travels and that continued the development of the Byronic hero, the brooding, titanic figure whose prototype within Byron's canon is Childe Harold. These tales include *The Giaour* (1813), *The Bride of Abydos* (1813), *The Corsair* (1814), *Lara* (1814), *Parisina* (1816), and *The Siege of Corinth* (1816). Illustrative of the diversity of Byron's poetic output is the publication, during this same period, of *Hebrew Melodies Ancient and Modern* (1815), short lyrics based largely on passages from the Bible and accompanied by the music of Isaac Nathan. Although Byron lacked the lyric mastery of a number of his extraordinary contemporaries, he produced well-crafted lyrics throughout his literary career, none of which is more admired or more often quoted than the first poem of *Hebrew Melodies Ancient and Modern*, "She Walks in Beauty."

Also published in 1816 was "The Prisoner of Chillon," a dramatic monologue on the theme of human freedom, which Byron was inspired to write after a visit to the castle where François de Bonivard had been imprisoned during the sixteenth century. *The Lament of Tasso* (1817), written during the following year, is a less successful variation on the same theme and, more important, an early manifestation of Byron's fascination with the literature and history of Italy. This fascination is also seen in *The Prophecy of Dante* (1821), "Francesca of Rimini" (inspired by Canto V of Dante's *Inferno*), and the translation of Canto I of Luigi Pulci's *Morgante Maggiore* (1483), which were produced in the years 1819 and 1820.

The importance of Pulci to Byron's poetic career is immeasurable. Through *Whistlecraft* (1817-1818), by John Hookham Frere, Byron became indirectly acquainted with the casual, facetious manner of the *Morgante Maggiore* and adapted the Pulci/Frere style to his own purposes in his immensely successful tale of Venetian dalliance, *Beppo: A Venetian Story*. Written in 1817 and published in 1818, *Beppo* is the directstylistic precursor of *Don Juan*, Cantos I-XVI (1819-1824, 1826), the seriocomic masterpiece whose composition occupied Byron at irregular intervals throughout the last six years of his life.

Although the final years of Byron's literary career are important primarily for the writing of *Don Juan*, several of Byron's other works deserve passing or prominent mention. *Mazeppa* (1819) is a verse tale in Byron's earlier manner that treats heavy-handedly a theme that the first cantos of *Don Juan* address with an adroit lightness: the disastrous consequences of an illicit love. *The Island* (1823) is a romantic tale inspired by William Bligh's account of the *Bounty* mutiny, a tale that possesses some affinities with the Haidée episode of *Don Juan*. The years from 1821 to 1823 produced three topical satires, *The Blues: A Literary Eclogue* (written in 1821 but first published in *The Liberal* in 1823), *The Vision of Judgment* (1822), and *The Age of Bronze* (1823), the second of which, a devastating response to Robert Southey's obsequious *A Vision of Judgment*, is one of Byron's undoubted masterworks.

Finally, no account of Byron's nondramatic writings would be complete without making reference to his correspondence, among the finest in the English language, which has been given its definitive form in Leslie A. Marchand's multivolume edition, *Byron's Letters and Journals* (1973-1982).

ACHIEVEMENTS

In his *The Dramas of Lord Byron: A Critical Study* (1915), Samuel C. Chew, Jr., makes it abundantly clear that George Gordon, Lord Byron, was simultaneously fascinated with the theater and contemptuous of the accomplishments of contemporary dramatists. He was frequently to be found in the playhouses, especially during his days as a student and during the period immedi-

ately following his Eastern travels, and on at least two occasions, he acted, with considerable success, in amateur theatrical productions. His comments on the stage suggest, however, that he was appalled by the reliance of early nineteenth century playwrights on melodramatic sensationalism and visual spectacle. His letters mention the scarcity of fine plays, and his poetry castigates modern dramatists for their tastelessness. *English Bards and Scotch Reviewers*, for example, calls contemporary drama a "motley sight" and deplores the "degradation of our vaunted stage." It cries out to George Colman and Richard Cumberland to "awake!" and implores Richard Brinsley Sheridan, who had achieved a recent success with *Pizarro: A Tragedy in Five Acts* (pr. 1799), an adaptation of a play by August von Kotzebue, to "Abjure the mummery of the German schools" and instead to "reform the stage." It asks, in indignant mockery, "Shall sapient managers new scenes produce/ From Cherry, Skeffington, and Mother Goose?" and makes sneering reference to the extravagances of Matthew Greg-

George Gordon, Lord Byron (Library of Congress)

ory "Monk" Lewis's *The Castle Spectre* (pr. 1797). It suggests, on the whole, that the once glorious English theater is in woeful decline.

Despite Byron's sense of the theater's decay, or perhaps because of it, evidence exists, in epistolary references to destroyed manuscripts and in a surviving fragment or two of attempted drama, that, as early as 1813-1814, he had ambitions of becoming a playwright, but he had completed nothing for the stage when, in 1815, he was appointed a member of the Drury Lane Committee of Management. Although he found his committee work "really good fun," it did nothing to improve his opinion of the taste of contemporary dramatists and their audiences, and when he finally finished a dramatic work, it was not intended for popular presentation.

Like the rest of his completed drama, *Manfred* was written during Byron's final, self-imposed exile from England. Begun in Switzerland and finished in Venice, the play is psychosymbolic rather than realistic and may have been inspired, as any number of commentators have pointed out, by Byron's acquaintance with Johann Wolfgang von Goethe's *Faust: Eine Tragödie* (pb. 1808, pb. 1833; *The Tragedy of Faust*, 1823, 1828). Byron appears to have known of Goethe's masterpiece through translated passages in Madame de Staël's *De l'Allemagne* (1810) and through an extensive oral translation by Monk Lewis during a visit to the poet in August of 1816. Considerable controversy has occurred, however, over the extent of *Faust*'s influence on *Manfred*, the consensus now being that *Faust* is simply one of many sources of the play's intricate materials, albeit an important one. Chew makes mention of Vicomte Françoise Auguste-René de Chateaubriand's *René* (1802, 1805; English translation, 1813), Goethe's *The Sorrows of Young Werther* (1774), Horace Walpole's *The Castle of Otranto* (1764) and *The Mysterious Mother* (1768), Samuel Taylor Coleridge's *Remorse* (1813), John Robert Maturin's *Bertram: Or, The Castle of St. Aldobrand* (1816), William Beckford's *Vathek* (1782), and Lewis's *The Monk* (1796) as other works with which *Manfred* has affinities and from which borrowings may have occurred. More important, however, *Manfred* is a cathartic projection of Byron's own troubled psyche, an attempt, which some critics have called Promethean rather than Faustian, to cope with the seemingly unconquerable presence of evil in the world, to deal with his frustrated aspirations toward an unattainable ideal, and, on a more mundane level, to come to terms with his confused feelings toward his half sister Augusta. With respect to *Manfred*'s place in theatrical history, Malcolm Kelsall, in *The Byron Journal* (1978), has made an excellent case for grouping Byron's play both with *Faust* and with Henrik Ibsen's *Peer Gynt* (pb. 1867; English translation, 1892). Kelsall states that "the new kind of stage envisaged" in these plays "is unfettered by any kind of limitation of place, and that assault, which is as much upon the conceived possibilities of stage allusion as upon unity of place, demands of the imagination that it supply constantly shifting visual correlatives for the inner turmoil of the hero's mind."

Byron's next play, *Marino Faliero, Doge of Venice*, is of an entirely different sort and ushers in a period in which Byron attempted to return to classical dramatic principles to produce plays whose themes are essentially political. He sought to counteract the undisciplined bombast and sprawling display of the drama with which he had become familiar in England by making use, without becoming anyone's slavish disciple, of theatrical techniques exploited by the ancient Greeks and Romans, the neoclassical French, and the contemporary Italians, notably Conte Vittorio Alfieri. Because he did this during a time when his involvement in Italian political intrigue was beginning to develop, Byron's decision to center his play on Marino Faliero, the fourteenth century doge of Venice who was executed for conspiring to overthrow the oppressive aristocratic class to which he himself belonged, is hardly surprising. He wrote the play as a closet drama—to be read rather than staged— considering its classical regularity an impossible barrier to its popular success, and he was furious when he learned of Drury Lane's intention of producing it. As he summarized the matter in a journal entry of January 12, 1821, how could anything please contemporary English theatergoers that contained "nothing melodramatic—no surprises, no starts, nor trap-doors, nor opportunities 'for tossing of their heads and kicking their heels'—and no *love*—the grand ingredient of a modern play"?

In *Sardanapalus*, Byron extended his experimentation with classical regularity and continued his exploration of political themes while at the same time appealing in two particular ways to popular taste. The play's setting, ancient Nineveh, accorded well with popular interest in Eastern exoticism, an interest that Byron's own Eastern tales had intensified, and the devotion of the slave Myrrha to Nineveh's troubled ruler satisfied the public's desire to witness pure, selfless love.

The Two Foscari, the third of the classically constructed political plays, again makes use of Venice for its setting. Although generally considered to be less successful than the earlier of the Venetian dramas, *The Two Foscari* contains autobiographical elements, embodied in Jacopo Foscari, that give a certain fascination to the play. Jacopo, after a youth of aristocratic gaiety, has been unjustly exiled from his native land. He had been the boon companion of the city's most promising young men, had been admired for his athletic vigor, particularly in swimming, and had drawn the attention of the city's most beautiful young women. Then the powerful had intrigued against him, and his banishment had begun. Byron's contemporaries could hardly have missed the personal significance of this situation or have overlooked the note of defiant anguish in such an exchange as the following:

GUARD: And can you so much love the soil which hates you?
JAC. FOS: The soil!—Oh no, it is the seed of the soil Which persecutes me; but my native earth Will take me as a mother to her arms.

Jacopo's persecution is carried out as an act of vengeance by an enemy of the Foscari family, an act that corrupts its perpetrator, but unlike Percy Bysshe Shelley's *The Cenci* (pb. 1819), whose theme is much the same, *The Two Foscari* is not effective theater.

Cain was published as part of a volume that also contained *Sardanapalus* and *The Two Foscari*, but it ought instead to be grouped with *Heaven and Earth*, which was written at about the same time but whose publication was delayed because of the controversy

inspired by *Cain*. In *Cain* and *Heaven and Earth*, Byron returned to the style of *Manfred*, but he derived his materials from biblical lore and from previous literary treatments of these same stories. He called the plays "mysteries," a reference both to the medieval mystery plays and to the mystified response Byron was expecting from the general public. *Cain* is a reinterpretation of the tale of the primal murder, a reinterpretation in which Cain is clearly the superior of his brother Abel and kills his brother, as Chew observes, in an "instinctive assertion of freedom against the limitations of fate." *Heaven and Earth* is based on the passage in Genesis that states that "the sons of God saw the daughters of men that they were fair; and they took them wives of all which they chose." Its plot culminates in the nearly total destruction of the flood, a destruction so general and arbitrary that the play becomes, in Chew's summary, "a subtle attack on the justice of the Most High."

Werner was much more in keeping with the literary tastes of the time than Byron's other plays, a fact that can be at least partially explained by its having been begun in 1815, during the period of Byron's closest association with Drury Lane. A surprisingly faithful rendering of "The German's Tale" from Sophia and Harriet Lee's *The Canterbury Tales* (1797-1805), *Werner* centers on the title character and his perfidious son, Ulric, an ambitious villain of the deepest dye. Making no pretense of adhering to the classical unities, the play moves with gothic ponderousness toward its dark conclusion, in which Ulric is revealed to be the cold-blooded murderer of his own fiancée's father, Stralenheim, the one man who stood between Ulric's family and their return to hereditary wealth and power.

The Deformed Transformed is one of Byron's two dramatic fragments (the other being *Heaven and Earth*). As its prefatory "Advertisement" states, Byron based it on Joshua Pickersgill's novel *The Three Brothers* (1803) and on Goethe's *Faust*. Chew points out the autobiographical significance of Byron's adding lameness to the other deformities from which his central character, Arnold, escapes by dealing with the Devil, but the play's incompleteness and incoherence make it difficult to comment further on Byron's dramatic intention. The fragment was composed in 1822 and published in February of 1824 by John Hunt.

The history of Byron's plays in theatrical production appears largely to be a tale of creative misinterpretation in the twentieth century and commercial adaptation and exploitation in the nineteenth. Margaret Howell's 1974 account in *The Byron Journal* of Charles Kean's June 13, 1853, production of *Sardanapalus* is particularly instructive. Reduced from its full length of 2,835 lines to 1,563, the play was presented almost solely as spectacle and required the approval of the local fire inspectors, because of one of its more impressive effects, before it could be performed. The production seems to have embodied everything that most disgusted Byron about London theater.

BIOGRAPHY

Born in London, England, on January 22, 1788, George Gordon, Lord Byron, who, from birth suffered from a deformed foot, was the son of Captain John Byron, nicknamed "Mad Jack" because of his wild ways, and the former Catherine Gordon. On his mother's side, the poet claimed descent from James I of Scotland and on his father's, with less certainty, from Ernegis and Radulfus de Burun, estate owners in the days of William the Conqueror. Newstead Abbey, which the poet would inherit at age ten as the sixth Lord Byron, had been granted to Sir John Byron by King Henry VIII, though the title of lord was first held by General John Byron, follower of Charles I and Charles II, the latter of whom is said to have seduced the general's wife. The poet received the title on the death, in 1798, of his great-uncle, William Byron, nicknamed "the Wicked Lord."

Because the poet's grandfather, Admiral John Byron, himself something of a rake, had disinherited Mad Jack for his even greater irresponsibility and because his father, before his death at age thirty-six, had squandered nearly all the wealth of both of the heiresses he had married, the poet's earliest years were spent in genteel poverty in his mother's native Aberdeen, Scotland, where he attended Aberdeen Grammar School. During these years, he developed his lifelong interests in both athletics and reading and

was imbued, under the influence of his nurse, Agnes Gray, and his Presbyterian instructors, with the sense of predestined evil that marked so much of his later life.

After coming into his inheritance in 1798, Byron and his mother moved to Nottinghamshire, the location of Newstead Abbey, in which the young lord proudly took up residence despite the warning of John Hanson, the family attorney, that the abbey was in such disrepair that it ought not to be lived in. During 1799, Byron's clubfoot was incompetently treated by a local quack physician, Dr. Lavender, and Byron was physically and sexually abused by his new nurse, May Gray, events that left the poet with permanent emotional scars. Later in the same year, Byron was taken to London to be treated by a more reputable physician. He was also placed in the Dulwich boarding school of Dr. Glennie, who was to prepare young Byron for admission to Harrow.

Byron entered Harrow in April of 1801, and despite an occasional period of haughty aloofness, he soon became a favorite of his schoolmates. Some of his most intense friendships dated from his Harrow days, friendships the intensity of which was probably an expression, as his biographers have pointed out, of his fundamentally bisexual nature. Nevertheless, the instances of Byron's overt amatory passion, especially early in his life, more often involved women than men. He had become infatuated with a cousin, Mary Duff, perhaps as early as age seven; had written his first love poetry for another cousin, Margaret Parker, at age twelve; and had fallen so deeply in love with Mary Chaworth during a hiatus in Nottinghamshire in 1803 that he at first refused to return to Harrow. Nevertheless, he did return, and after completing his course of studies, he enrolled in Trinity College, Cambridge, during the fall of 1805.

During his Cambridge days, Byron formed romantic attachments with two male friends, won acceptance by the university's liberal intellectual elite, kept a bear in his living quarters, and became thoroughly acquainted with the distractions of London, including the theater. He also assembled his first books of poetry, most notably *Hours of Idleness*, and, almost incidentally, earned a Cambridge master's degree, which was granted in July of 1808. After a short retirement to Newstead Abbey, during which he worked on *English Bards and Scotch Reviewers*, Byron left for London, where he became a member of the House of Lords on March 13, 1809, and where *English Bards and Scotch Reviewers* was anonymously published several days thereafter. The authorship of the scathing satire was soon discovered, and Byron had the satisfaction of being lauded for his poem by Gifford and others before his departure on July 2, 1809, for his Continental tour.

Traveling with John Cam Hobhouse and several retainers, Byron disembarked in Lisbon and made the journey to Seville and later to Cádiz by horseback. The frigate *Hyperion* then took them to Gibraltar, after which they sailed for Malta, where he managed a romantic interlude with the fascinating Mrs. Constance Spencer Smith. The brig *Spider* next delivered them to Patras and Prevesa in Greece, then ruled by the Turks, from which they set out for Janina, capital of the kingdom of the barbarous Ali Pasha, sovereign of western Greece and Albania and prototype of *Don Juan*'s piratical Lambro. Ali Pasha's court was located seventy-five miles away, in Tepelene, where Byron arrived on October 19, 1809, and where the colorful ruler flattered the young poet with an audience. The Tepelene adventure was one of the most memorable of Byron's memorable life, and when he returned to Janina, he began *Childe Harold's Pilgrimage* in an attempt to capture the poetic essence of his travels.

Following his perilous return to Patras by way of Missolonghi, where he was to die fifteen years later, Byron journeyed on to Athens, stopping first at Mount Parnassus and writing several stanzas to commemorate the event. In Athens itself, he and Hobhouse lived with the Macri family, whose twelve-year-old Theresa was immortalized by Byron as "the Maid of Athens." The two travelers explored the city and its historic surroundings from Christmas Day, 1809, through March 5, 1810. The sloop *Pylades* then carried them to Smyrna, where they took a side trip to Ephesus, after which they embarked for Constantinople aboard the frigate *Salsette*. On May 3, 1810, during a pause in the voyage, Byron swam the Hel-

lespont from Sestos to Abydos, an accomplishment about which he would never tire of boasting.

Byron's stay in Constantinople brought him further invaluable knowledge of the decadent splendors of the East and also involved him in several petty disputes over matters of protocol, disputes in which Byron's aristocratic arrogance, one of his least attractive traits, came repulsively to the fore. Such matters appear to have been smoothed over, however, by the time Byron left Constantinople on July 14, 1810.

Hobhouse returned directly to England, but Byron spent the next several months in Greece, where he added to his sexual conquests, contracted a venereal disease, saved a young woman from threatened execution, and continued his exploration of a country for whose freedom he was eventually to offer up his life. On April 22, 1811, he sailed from Greece for Malta, where he temporarily renewed his affair with Mrs. Smith, and then returned home to England, stepping ashore on July 14, 1811.

Within a month of his landing, Byron's mother died, an event that caused him considerable distress despite the uneasy relationship that had long existed between them. The year also brought news of the deaths of three of Byron's closest friends. The poet dealt with his grief as best he could and continued preparations for the publication of *Childe Harold's Pilgrimage*, Cantos I and II. He also resumed his place in the House of Lords, delivering his maiden speech on February 27, 1812, an effective denunciation of a bill requiring the execution of frame breakers (workers who violently resisted the mechanization of the weaving trade). Byron delivered two more parliamentary speeches, on April 21, 1812, and June 1, 1813, but the sudden fame that *Childe Harold's Pilgrimage* brought him after its appearance on March 10, 1812, drew his attention away from politics and changed his life forever.

The immediate effect of Byron's renown was that he became the most sought-after guest in London society and the most avidly pursued of handsome bachelors. In particular, Lady Caroline Lamb, despite being already married, descended on him with extraordinary enthusiasm. She found him "mad—bad—and dangerous to know," a description that might, with equal or greater justice, have been applied to Lady Caroline herself. Their tempestuous liaison occupied much of Byron's attention during the spring and summer of 1812 and involved indiscreet meetings, plans of elopement, threats of suicide, and a great deal of public scandal. Although they parted in September, to Byron's infinite relief, occasional storms broke out in the months thereafter.

During the years 1812 and 1813, Byron began the series of Oriental tales that would solidify his literary fame and involved himself in affairs with various other women, most peculiarly and most deeply with his half sister, Mrs. Augusta Leigh. He spent much of the summer of 1813 with Augusta, and Elizabeth Medora Leigh, born on April 15, 1814, has always been assumed to be the poet's daughter. Though Byron never publicly acknowledged her, various passages in his letters, especially those to his close confidante, Lady Melbourne, suggest his paternity.

Lady Melbourne's brilliant niece, Annabella Milbanke, also figured prominently in Byron's life during this period. Although he despised "bluestockings" (intellectual women), Byron was unaccountably drawn to Annabella, whose intelligence and wide reading distinguished her so completely from the impulsively romantic Lady Caroline and the passively maternal Augusta. Perhaps as a means of escaping the chaos of his unstable love life, Byron proposed to Milbanke on two occasions, in September of 1812 and again in September of 1813. Unfortunately for both of them, Byron's second proposal was accepted. After various delays, apparently involving visits to Augusta, Byron and Annabella Milbanke were married on January 2, 1815.

The several months of Byron's marriage were marked by continuing literary activity (especially work on the later Oriental tales and on *Hebrew Melodies Ancient and Modern*), by visits to and from Augusta, by Byron's association with the Drury Lane Committee of Management, and by fits of temper, related to the poet's marital and financial problems, which terrified both his wife and his half sister. The birth of the poet's only legitimate child, Augusta Ada Byron, in December of 1815, did nothing to improve the situation, and when mother and daughter left on

January 5, 1816, for what was purportedly a temporary visit to Annabella's parents, the marriage was effectively at an end. By March of 1816, a separation had been agreed on, and Byron affixed his signature to the necessary legal documents on April 21, 1816. A week earlier, he had spoken for the last time to his beloved Augusta, and on April 25, still experiencing financial difficulties and being roundly denounced by the press for his marital problems, Byron left England forever.

Once more on the Continent, Byron visited the Waterloo battlefield, journeyed up the Rhine Valley, crossed into Switzerland, and began looking for accommodations near Lake Geneva. Along the lakeshore, he and his traveling companion, Dr. John Polidori, were approached by Claire Clairmont, who, as a result of an affair earlier in the spring, was pregnant with Byron's child. Clairmont was accompanied by her stepsister, Mary Godwin (later to become Mary Shelley), and Percy Bysshe Shelley. The poets soon became fast friends and by early June had established households very near each other and within two miles of Geneva. Their animated conversations deeply influenced the lives of both poets, with the inspiration of their contact communicating itself, on one particular evening, to two other members of the group. During a gathering at the Villa Diodati, where Byron had taken up residence, a challenge to compose ghost stories resulted in the eventual publication of Dr. Polidori's *The Vampyre* (1819), the first English vampire tale, and Mary Shelley's classic gothic novel, *Frankenstein* (1818). During the several weeks of his almost daily talks with Shelley, Byron himself wrote "The Prisoner of Chillon" and worked diligently on *Childe Harold's Pilgrimage*, Canto III.

Although Claire had at first kept her relationship with Byron a secret from Mary and Percy, they inevitably became aware of Claire's pregnancy, after which Percy and Claire approached Byron in an attempt to resolve matters. Because Byron did not feel the same affection for Claire that she felt for him, it was decided that they should not live together. It was further decided that the child should be cared for by Byron, with Claire being addressed as its aunt. The child, Allegra Byron, was born in Bath, England, on

January 12, 1817, and died in Ravenna, Italy, on April 20, 1822.

John Cam Hobhouse arrived at the Villa Diodati with another of Byron's friends, Scrope Davies, on August 26, 1816, and following the departure for England of the Shelley household on August 29, the two toured the Alps with Byron and Polidori. Another tour, with Hobhouse only, began on September 17. Byron's combined impressions of the Alps helped inspire *Manfred*, whose composition was well advanced when the poet gave up the Villa Diodati on October 5 and journeyed with Hobhouse to Milan.

After a sojourn of less than a month in Milan, during which he met the Italian poet Vincenzo Monti and the French novelist Stendhal, rescued Polidori from an encounter with the local authorities, and came under the surveillance of the Austrian secret police, Byron left with Hobhouse for Venice, where they arrived on or about November 10. Hobhouse soon departed to see other areas of Italy, but Byron, having fallen in love with Venice and with Marianna Segati, his landlord's wife, settled in for an extended stay. In the several months of this first Venetian interlude, he completed *Manfred* and overindulged during the Carnival period.

On April 17, 1817, Byron set out, by way of Arqua, Ferrara, and Florence, for Rome, where Hobhouse showed him the local antiquities. He returned on May 28 with the completed *The Lament of Tasso* and with vivid impressions that would be incorporated in *Childe Harold's Pilgrimage*, Canto IV. Soon thereafter, he and Marianna established themselves at the Villa Foscarini in La Mira, outside Venice. There, Byron formed another liaison, this time with the beautiful Margarita Cogni; worked at what was to become the final canto of *Childe Harold's Pilgrimage*; and began the precursor of *Don Juan*, the charming *Beppo*. Late in 1817, he returned to Venice with the visiting Hobhouse and, on January 7, 1818, said goodbye to his friend after a last ride together. Byron entrusted Hobhouse with the manuscript of *Childe Harold's Pilgrimage*, Canto IV, whose publication in April brought the poet further literary fame during a time when his personal life had rendered him infamous.

In 1818, Byron's Venetian dissipations reached a level of obsessive frequency that threatened his health. Nevertheless, he continued to write, producing *Mazeppa* and Canto I of *Don Juan* and beginning Canto II. He was showing signs of physical exhaustion by April of 1819, when he became reacquainted with a woman whom he had casually encountered during the previous year. With this woman, the nineteen-year-old Countess Teresa Guiccioli, he was soon involved in one of the most long-lasting and passionate relationships of his life. In June, he followed her to Ravenna, in August to Bologna, and in September back to Venice, where they spent some of their time at Byron's quarters in the Palazzo Mocenigo and longer periods at the Villa Foscarini in La Mira. At the end of the year, when Teresa's husband cajoled her to return to Ravenna, Byron followed again.

The continuation of *Don Juan* had been one of Byron's primary literary projects in 1819, and further material was written in 1820. The year was significant for other reasons, too, including the writing of *Marino Faliero, Doge of Venice*, Byron's increasing entanglement in the revolutionary Carbonari movement, and Teresa's formal separation from Count Guiccioli. When the Carbonari movement collapsed in 1821 and Teresa's family was exiled from Ravenna, Byron accepted Shelley's invitation to move himself, his lover, and her banished relatives to Pisa, where Shelley had taken up residence. Despite this political and personal upheaval, Byron completed three plays during 1821 (*Sardanapalus*, *The Two Foscari*, and *Cain*) and wrote the magnificent *The Vision of Judgment*.

Byron became part of the Pisan Circle in November of 1821, and he remained a resident of the general Pisa area until September of 1822. These months witnessed the writing of much of *Don Juan*, which Byron had previously ceased composing on the request of Teresa and which he now resumed with her permission. The period also saw the beginnings of Byron's acquaintance with the colorful Edward John Trelawny and the less satisfactory relationship between Byron and the improvident Hunt family. Most sadly, however, these were the months in which Byron's daughter, Allegra, died in a convent at Ravenna and in which Shelley, with Edward Williams, was drowned off the Italian coast. What ultimately drove Byron from Tuscany, however, was the latest banishment of Teresa's family, this time to Genoa, where Byron joined them in late September.

In Genoa, Byron wrote his last Augustan satire, *The Age of Bronze*, and a romantic verse narrative, *The Island*, while continuing *Don Juan*. He also began making serious plans to leave for Greece, where a war of independence had recently broken out. After a traumatic parting with Teresa, he set sail from Italy aboard the *Hercules* in July of 1823, accompanied by Trelawny and Teresa's brother, Pietro Gamba. In early August, they reached Cephalonia, and in late December, they left for Missolonghi, where Byron arrived on January 4, 1824, to be greeted the next day by Prince Alexandros Mavrocordatos, the Greek military leader.

During the previous August, Byron had been taken ill after an excursion to Ithaca. At Missolonghi, on February 15, he became ill once again. His recovery was slow and was hampered by terrible weather, the disunity of the Greek leadership, and their constant demands that he supply them with money. After riding through a rainstorm on April 9, he experienced a relapse. His condition worsened during the following days, and after being bled by his physicians until his strength was gone, he died on April 19, 1824. His remains were returned to England, where they were denied burial in Westminster Abbey. Instead, he was interred on July 16, 1824, in Hucknall Torkard Church, near his ancestral home of Newstead Abbey.

ANALYSIS

Although a number of George Gordon, Lord Byron's, plays are more easily approached as dramatic poetry than as theatrical drama, the political tragedies are readily accessible to dramatic analysis. His political tragedies are literary explorations of the relationship, in an unregenerate world, of the extraordinary individual to the state. They examine the place of the almost superhumanly proud and passionate man within corporate humanity. They express the fascination with the link between earthly power and individual freedom and fulfillment that manifested itself in

Byron's first speech before Parliament and that would lead him, finally, to his death at Missolonghi. The following discussion centers on three such works, the classically constructed *Marino Faliero, Doge of Venice* and *Sardanapalus*, and the gothic, melodramatic *Werner*.

WERNER

Of Byron's dramatic works, *Werner* most closely resembles the popular theater of his day. Despite being the last play that Byron completed, *Werner* is the earliest of the plays in terms of initial composition, having been begun during the year preceding Byron's final exile from England. Byron's fascination with the story on which the play is based dates from an even earlier period. As he explains in the play's preface, he had read "The German's Tale" from the Lees' *The Canterbury Tales* at about age fourteen, and it had "made a deep impression upon" him. It "may, indeed, be said to contain the germ of much that" he wrote thereafter, an admission that suggests the importance of the play within the Byron canon, despite the play's obvious literary deficiencies.

The play's title character embodies many of the traits of the Byronic hero and has much in common, too, with Byron's father, "Mad Jack" Byron. As the play begins, Werner is a poverty-stricken wanderer, who, like Mad Jack, has been driven out by his father because of various youthful excesses resulting from the indulgence of his overly passionate nature. Although a marriage that his father considered improvident was the immediate cause of this estrangement, Werner was guilty of other, unstated transgressions before this, transgressions that prepared the way for the final severing of the parental tie. Since then, Werner has been a proud exile, burdened by a sense of personal guilt and too familiar with the weaknesses of human nature to rely on other people for consolation. His love for Josephine, herself an exile, partially sustains him, but his realization that her sufferings are a product of his own foolish actions exacerbates his gloom.

The one embodiment of hope for Werner and Josephine is their son, Ulric, who has been reared by Werner's father, Count Siegendorf, after Werner's banishment. Ulric, however, possesses his father's passions without possessing the sense of honor that would prevent those passions from expressing themselves in hideous crimes. As the play begins, Ulric is missing from his grandfather's court, disturbing rumors are circulating concerning his possible whereabouts, and the nobleman Stralenheim, a distant relation, is poised to usurp the family inheritance in the event of Werner's father's death.

The play's elements of gothic melodrama are obvious from the opening of the first scene. The play begins at night during a violent thunderstorm, and act 1 is set in "The Hall of a decayed Palace" in a remote section of Silesia. The palace is honeycombed with secret passages, which receive considerable use during the course of the play's action. The Thirty Years' War has just ended, rendering the profession of soldier superfluous and lending glamour to professional thievery, that favorite occupation of many a Sturm und Drang hero-villain. Ulric, as we eventually discover, is himself the leader of a band of soldiers turned marauders.

Ulric, another avatar of Byronic heroism, is something of a superman, possessing traits that render him capable of great good and great evil. One of the play's characters, the poor but honorable Gabor, describes him as a man

> Of wonderful endowments: — birth and fortune,
> Youth, strength and beauty, almost superhuman,
> And courage as unrivall'd, were proclaim'd
> His by the public rumour; and his sway,
> Not only over his associates, but
> His judges, was attributed to witchcraft,
> Such was his influence.

Ulric's dual nature expresses itself most clearly in his treatment of the potential usurper, Stralenheim. When Ulric is unaware of Stralenheim's identity, he courageously rescues him from the floodwaters of the River Oder, but later, when he learns that Stralenheim is a threat to his family's wealth and power, he cold-bloodedly murders him. He then conceals his responsibility for the crime and hypocritically questions his father about his possible role in Stralenheim's death. Werner has compromised his honor by stealing gold coins from Stralenheim's room, a crime that suggests the family's moral weakness, but he is incapable of murder. Freed of restraint by one additional genera-

tion of moral decay, Ulric, by contrast, is capable of almost anything.

Because of Stralenheim's murder and the nearly simultaneous death of Werner's aged father, Werner becomes Count Siegendorf and Ulric his heir apparent. All goes well for a year, although Werner, troubled by his possession of the tainted gold and by the mysterious circumstances of his rise to power, is plagued by a guilty conscience. There are manifestations of guilt in Ulric's behavior, too, but that strength of will that allowed him to rescue Stralenheim from the flood and later to cut his throat sustains him through subsequent unsavory deeds. He continues his clandestine command of the marauders who threaten the fragile peace and accepts betrothal to the loving and innocent Ida, daughter of the murdered Stralenheim. The ultimate proof of Ulric's reprobate nature occurs when Gabor, who had witnessed the hideous crime and had been unjustly branded as its likely perpetrator, comes forward to accuse Ulric. In an attempt to silence this threat to everything he has striven to accomplish, Ulric sends his minions in pursuit of the innocent man, at the same time uttering a defiant confession of his guilt before the startled Ida, who immediately falls dead in shocked disbelief.

Werner deviates from classical restraint in both content and form. In addition to relying on melodramatic plot devices, *Werner* violates the unities of place and time, a major shift in location and period occurring between acts 3 and 4. *Marino Faliero, Doge of Venice* and *Sardanapalus*, on the other hand, are much more regular, with only slight changes in setting and time taking place from one scene to the next. Like *Werner*, however, both plays center on the consequences of having men of powerful but uncertain character in positions of responsibility.

MARINO FALIERO, DOGE OF VENICE

The tenuous thread on which the plot of *Marino Faliero, Doge of Venice* hangs is the apparent historical fact that the title character, while he was doge of Venice, conspired against the tyrannous Venetian oligarchy partly because he found their rule unjust and, more important, because they failed to punish one of their number severely enough for a scrawled insult to the doge's wife. When Faliero discovers that Michel

Steno is to receive one month of imprisonment instead of death for an unsavory comment inscribed on the ducal throne, he becomes furious, although his wife, Angiolina, counsels restraint. His rage is motivated by his disgust that the oligarchy, with its facelessly diffused and inflexibly selfish power, refuses, on the one hand, to recognize the rights of the common people and neglects, on the other, to show the deference due superior spirits. His rebelliousness (like Byron's own) is simultaneously an assertion of individual, proud will and a genuine concern for democratic principles. He detests the oppressive rule of the privileged few and joins a conspiracy against them, but he maintains an aristocratic haughtiness among the "common ruffians leagued to ruin states" with whom he throws in his lot.

Ultimately, his joining the conspirators is an expression of that irrepressible, restless pride that he shares with Byron's other heroes. He exhibits not simply the temporal pride of a Coriolanus but also the everlasting, self-assertive pride of a Lucifer. Indeed, his is

> the same sin that overthrew the angels,
> And of all sins most easily besets
> Mortals the nearest to the angelic nature:
> The vile are only vain: the great are proud.

In addition to treating, with considerable complexity, the frequently self-contradictory motivations of the rebel, *Marino Faliero, Doge of Venice* explores the moral ambiguities of instigating violent actions to achieve just ends. Like the French revolutionaries, the Venetian conspirators are about to sweep away the old order in a bath of blood, but one of their number, Bertram, refuses to abandon his humanity and warns an aristocratic friend that his life is in danger. The ironic result of this humane gesture is that the rebellion is discovered and the conspirators themselves, including the proud doge, are put to death. Victory belongs to those whose ruthlessness wins out over their compassion, and he who would be kind becomes a Judas.

SARDANAPALUS

In *Sardanapalus*, this conflict between humanity and harsh political reality is again examined. Sar-danapalus is a lover of life whose mercy and whose desire for peace, love, and pleasure bring down a dynasty. As a descendant of Nimrod and the fierce Semiramis, he is expected to conduct the affairs of state by means of bloodshed and unrelenting conquest. Instead, he allies himself with the forces of vitality against those of death and thereby earns a reputation for weakness. He knows the harem and the banquet hall better than the battlefield and is judged effeminate because he prefers the paradisiacal celebration of life to the ruthless bloodletting of war and political persecution. Even when he knows that two of his most powerful subjects, the Chaldean Beleses and the Mede Arbaces, have plotted against him, he refuses to have them killed and thereby opens the way to successful rebellion. After merely banishing the two from Nineveh, he finds himself, during a symbolically appropriate banquet, beset by a usurping army.

Despite his seeming weakness, Sardanapalus, like Byron's other heroes, possesses unquenchable pride and courage. Assuming the weapons of the warrior but refusing to wear full armor, so that his soldiers will recognize and rally to him, he enters battle and temporarily staves off defeat. His lover, Myrrha, a character added to the play, significantly enough, at the suggestion of Teresa Guiccioli, shows an equally fierce courage, as do Sardanapalus's loyal troops, and for a time, victory seems possible. Still, the kingly worshiper of life is troubled in his dreams by the image of the worshiper of death, Semiramis, and there are dark forebodings of approaching catastrophe.

When it finally becomes clear that defeat is inevitable, Sardanapalus expresses regret that the fallen world in which he found himself was unwilling to accept the temporary renewal that he attempted to offer:

> I thought to have made mine inoffensive rule
> An era of sweet peace 'midst bloody annals,
> A green spot amidst desert centuries,
> On which the future would turn back and smile,
> And cultivate, or sigh, when it could not
> Recall Sardanapalus's golden reign.
> I thought to have made my realm a paradise,
> And every moon an epoch of new pleasures.

When the world refuses his great gift, he turns to the only paradisiacal sanctuary available in a universe of spiritual disorder. He unites himself with the one individual who most loves him. He has his last loyal subjects build a funeral pyre, symbolic of his and Myrrha's passion, and the lovers die amid its flames.

OTHER MAJOR WORKS

POETRY: *Fugitive Pieces*, 1806; *Poems on Various Occasions*, 1807; *Hours of Idleness*, 1807; *Poems Original and Translated*, 1808; *English Bards and Scotch Reviewers*, 1809; *Hints from Horace*, 1811; *Childe Harold's Pilgrimage*, Cantos I-IV, 1812-1818, 1819 (the four cantos published together); *The Curse of Minerva*, 1812; *Waltz: An Apostrophic Hymn*, 1813; *The Giaour*, 1813; *The Bride of Abydos*, 1813; *The Corsair*, 1814; *Ode to Napoleon Buonaparte*, 1814; *Lara*, 1814; *Hebrew Melodies Ancient and Modern*, 1815; *The Siege of Corinth*, 1816; *Parisina*, 1816; *Poems*, 1816; *The Prisoner of Chillon, and Other Poems*, 1816; *Monody on the Death of the Right Honourable R. B. Sheridan*, 1816; *The Lament of Tasso*, 1817; *Beppo: A Venetian Story*, 1818; *Mazeppa*, 1819; *Don Juan*, Cantos I-XVI, 1819-1824, 1826 (the sixteen cantos published together); *The Prophecy of Dante*, 1821; *The Vision of Judgment*, 1822; *The Age of Bronze*, 1823; *The Island*, 1823; *The Complete Poetical Works of Byron*, 1980-1986 (5 volumes).

NONFICTION: *Letter to [John Murray] on the Rev. W. L. Bowles's Strictures on the Life and Writings of Pope*, 1821; "A Letter to the Editor of 'My Grandmother's Review,'" 1822; *The Blues: A Literary Eclogue*, 1823; *The Parliamentary Speeches of Lord Byron*, 1824; *Byron's Letters and Journals*, 1973-1982 (12 volumes; Leslie A. Marchand, editor).

BIBLIOGRAPHY

Brewer, William D., ed. *Contemporary Studies on Lord Byron*. Lewiston, N.Y.: Edwin Mellen Press, 2001. A collection of essays on the works of Byron. Bibliography and index.

Chew, Samuel C., Jr. *The Dramas of Lord Byron: A Critical Study*. 1915. Reprint. New York: Russell and Russell, 1964. The first sustained analysis of Byron's plays, Chew's book is one of the best single introductory examinations of Byron's dramatic works and his career as a dramatist.

Foot, Michael. *The Politics of Paradise: A Vindication of Byron*. New York: Harper and Row, 1988. Foot's analysis of Byron's poetics as it relates to his dynamic life, which Foot divides into formative periods linked to Byron's place of residence, includes incisive analyses of *Cain, Manfred*, and *Sardanapalus*. The book also includes a pithy select bibliography that would serve as a good starting point for in-depth research on Byron. Also included are two appendices.

Franklin, Caroline. *Byron: A Literary Life*. New York: St. Martin's Press, 2000. A study of Byron's career, with some attention to the poet's neglected playwriting.

Garrett, Martin. *George Gordon, Lord Byron*. New York: Oxford University Press, 2000. A basic biography of the writer Byron that examines his life and works. Bibliography and index.

Gross, Jonathan David. *Byron: The Erotic Liberal*. Lanham, Md.: Rowman & Littlefield, 2001. A study of Byron that focuses on his political and social views. Bibliography and index.

Martin, Philip. *Byron: A Poet Before His Public*. Cambridge, England: Cambridge University Press, 1982. This fine biographical-historical analysis of Byron's plays, with chapters on *Manfred, Cain*, and *Sardanapalus*, places Byron's work within the context of his contemporaries of the second generation of Romantic poets. Bibliography.

Peters, Catherine. *Byron*. Stroud, Gloucestershire, England: Sutton, 2000. A concise biography of Byron that covers his life and works. Bibliography.

Robert H. O'Connor,
updated by Gregory W. Lanier

C

PEDRO CALDERÓN DE LA BARCA

Born: Madrid, Spain; January 17, 1600
Died: Madrid, Spain; May 25, 1681

PRINCIPAL DRAMA

Amor, honor y poder, pr. 1623, pb. 1634

El sitio de Breda, pr. 1625, pb. 1636

El príncipe constante, pr. 1629, pb. 1636 (*The Constant Prince*, 1853)

La dama duende, wr. 1629, pr., pb. 1936 (*The Phantom Lady*, 1664)

Casa con dos puertas, mala es de guardar, wr. 1629, pr., pb. 1636 (*A House with Two Doors Is Difficult to Guard*, 1737)

Los cabellos de Absalón, wr. c. 1634, pb. 1684 (*The Crown of Absalom*, 1993)

La devoción de la cruz, pb. 1634, pr. 1643 (*The Devotion to the Cross*, 1832)

El gran teatro del mundo, wr. 1635, pr. 1649, pb. 1677 (*The Great Theater of the World*, 1856)

El mayor encanto, amor, pr. 1635, pb. 1637 (*Love, the Greatest Enchantment*, 1870)

La vida es sueño, pr. 1635, pb. 1636 (*Life Is a Dream*, 1830)

El médico de su honra, pb. 1637 (*The Surgeon of His Honor*, 1853)

A secreto agravio, secreta venganza, pb. 1637 (*Secret Vengeance for Secret Insult*, 1961)

El mágico prodigioso, pr. 1637, pb. 1663 (*The Wonder-Working Magician*, 1959)

El pintor de su deshonra, wr. 1640-1642, pb. 1650 (*The Painter of His Dishonor*, 1853)

El alcalde de Zalamea, pr. 1643, pb. 1651 (*The Mayor of Zalamea*, 1853)

La hija del aire, Parte I, pr. 1653, pb. 1664 (*The Daughter of the Air, Part I*, 1831)

La hija del aire, Parte II, pr. 1653, pb. 1664 (*The Daughter of the Air, Part II*, 1831)

El laurel de Apolo, pr. 1659, pb. 1664

La púrpura de la rosa, pr. 1660, pb. 1664

Hado y divisa de Leonido y Marfisa, pr. 1680, pb. 1682

OTHER LITERARY FORMS

Although Pedro Calderón de la Barca is remembered primarily as a verse dramatist, he is also noted for his lyric poetry, some of which was not incorporated into his plays. The sonnet was the most prevalent poetic form used by Calderón. The collection *Los sonetos de Calderón en sus obras dramáticas* (1974) contains his nondramatic sonnets, those included in his plays, and the one sonnet from his long poem, *Psalle et sile* (1741).

ACHIEVEMENTS

Pedro Calderón de la Barca, whose death in 1681 marks the end of Spain's great period of literary and artistic excellence known as its Golden Age, is generally recognized as one of the most accomplished Spanish dramatists of all time. His plays differ from the plays of his predecessor Lope de Vega Carpio (the "father of Spanish theater") in several ways. Calderón's dramas are generally regarded as more polished than Lope de Vega's, and their complex structure contrasts with the seeming naturalness of Lope de Vega's works. Although Lope de Vega often seems primarily interested in capturing the essence of seventeenth century Spanish life, Calderón's dramas demonstrate the author's concern with more universal— and often abstract—questions of human existence. It is probably because of his more universal focus that Calderón's work has had a wider appeal than Lope de Vega's. *Life Is a Dream*, his most famous drama, ranks as one of the unquestioned masterpieces of world theater.

Calderón is particularly noted for his religious theater. He is the undisputed master of the *auto sacramental*—the one-act, allegorical, religious drama performed as part of Spain's celebration of Corpus Christi. This genre accounts for 74 of the 182 works included in the standard Spanish edition of his complete works, and many of his full-length plays are also about religious topics. Surprisingly, even these works continue to enjoy a wide appeal in an age in which religious faith is declining. *The Devotion to the Cross*, for example, was much admired by the agnostic philosopher Albert Camus, who translated this play into French in 1953.

BIOGRAPHY

Pedro Calderón de la Barca was born in Madrid on January 17, 1600, to an aristocratic family. Little is known about his childhood. His mother died when Calderón was ten, and his father died five years later. Calderón was educated in the Jesuit Colegio Imperial in Madrid and later in the University of Alcalá de Henares and the University of Salamanca, where he prepared himself for the priesthood. He did not, however, embark immediately on an ecclesiastical career, but preferred instead to dedicate himself to literary pursuits, participating in various poetry contests in which he won some recognition—including praise on two occasions from Lope de Vega, who at the time was Spain's leading dramatist.

In 1623, Calderón's first datable play, *Amor, honor y poder* (love, honor, and power) was performed in Madrid. At approximately the same time, the poet embarked on a military career and may have participated in the surrender of Breda, which he dramatized in his play *El sitio de Breda* (the siege of Breda). For a time, he continued to involve himself with both the theater and the military. Following the death of Lope de Vega in 1635, Philip IV appointed Calderón court dramatist and director of the newly constructed and lavish court theater at Buen Retiro. In 1637, the king named him a knight in the Order of Santiago. In 1638, he fought against the French in the Battle of Fuenterrabía, and in 1640, he helped suppress a rebellion in Catalonia (northeastern Spain). Finally, in 1642, ill health—perhaps resulting from a

wound received in battle—put an end to his military career.

Little is known of Calderón's personal life during these years, but his involvement in an altercation in 1629 affords a brief glimpse into a side of his personality not revealed by his military and artistic triumphs. In that year, one of his brothers was seriously wounded in a fight with an actor who took refuge in a Trinitarian convent, and Calderón was among the crowd that, with the legal authorities, forced its way into the convent and, when they were unable to find the man they were pursuing, subjected the nuns to insults and rough treatment. When the court chaplain, Hortensio Paravicino, later protested this conduct in a sermon, Calderón included in his play *The Constant Prince* a passage ridiculing the priest—lines that the authorities, acting on Paravicino's instigation, ultimately forced the dramatist to expunge.

Sometime after the end of his military career, Calderón became involved in a love affair and fathered an illegitimate son, Pedro José, whom he treated initially as his nephew. Following this affair and his mistress's death (perhaps as a result of it), he

Pedro Calderón de la Barca (Library of Congress)

finally realized his ambition of becoming a priest and was ordained in 1651. In an ironic reversal of customary practice, he acknowledged after his ordination that his "nephew" was actually his son. For two years following his ordination, Calderón remained in Madrid. In 1653, he became chaplain of the Capilla de Reyes Nuevos in Toledo. During this time, he continued to provide plays for the court and also busied himself composing *autos sacramentales* for Madrid's annual celebration of Corpus Christi.

In 1663, Calderón returned to Madrid to become honorary chaplain to Philip IV, and for the rest of his life, he remained in that city, where he continued to write secular dramas for the court as well as the *autos sacramentales*. His last full-length play, *Hado y divisa de Leonido y Marfisa* (the destiny and design of Leonido and Marfisa), was written and performed before the court of Charles II in 1680. Calderón's death occurred a year later on May 25, 1681, while he was working on an *auto sacramental*. The circumstances of his death caused a friend to comment that Calderón had died singing "like a swan."

ANALYSIS

Initially, Pedro Calderón de la Barca's theater seems most defined by its varied nature. The topics of his dramas are diverse, ranging from religious faith and revenge to mythological fantasy and marital fidelity. The tone of his works likewise varies from frivolity to gravity. In many respects, Calderón's theater continues to conform to the norms established by his predecessor Lope de Vega. Like Lope de Vega, he violates the classical sense of decorum by mixing humorous and tragic elements in the same play and by including in highly serious works a stock character known as the *gracioso* (funny one), usually a servant, whose lack of dignity provides occasion for laughter. Calderón also follows Lope de Vega's practice of disregarding the classical unities of time and place, which sought to limit a play's setting to a single place and decreed that its action should occur in a single day. Also, like Lope de Vega's, his plays are written in polymetric verse.

Calderón's cultured, baroque language, however, gives his plays a noticeably different tone from those of his predecessor. Because most of his plays were written for the court, he adopted a style designed to appeal to his educated audience. Thus, his characters often speak a highly complex language, rich in poetic conceits, parallelism, and classical allusions, which is intentionally artificial.

A recurrent theme in Calderón's plays is the confusion between reality and appearances. The theme is, like his style, characteristic of the baroque, and it had already been treated in various other literary works of the period, including Miguel de Cervantes's famous novel *El ingenioso hidalgo don Quixote de la Mancha* (1605, 1615; *The History of the Valorous and Wittie Knight-Errant, Don Quixote of the Mancha*, 1612-1620; better known as *Don Quixote de la Mancha*, 1605, 1615). With Calderón, however, this theme is so consistently present that it could be considered a constant that gives unity to his diverse corpus.

Another characteristic of Calderonian drama is the author's insistence—rare in Spanish Golden Age theater—on carefully "finished" pieces. Often the originality of Calderón's plays lies in the polished form in which they are presented rather than in the material treated. More than any other Golden Age dramatist, he reworked material that had already been used, and he often succeeded in transforming a mediocre work into a quite memorable one.

THE CONSTANT PRINCE

One of Calderón's early plays, *The Constant Prince*, is already illustrative of much that is characteristic of his later work. *The Constant Prince* is a reworking of an earlier play attributed to Lope de Vega, *La fortuna adversa del Infante Don Fernando de Portugal* (n.d.; the adverse fortune of Prince Fernando of Portugal). Both plays dramatize the legendary faith of a historic Portuguese prince who, when captured by the Arabs, allegedly chose to die as a martyr rather than order the surrender of the Portuguese-held city of Ceuta in order to gain his freedom. The changes that Calderón made in Lope de Vega's treatment of this story—the reduction of the cast of characters from thirty-six to fourteen and the transformation of Prince Fernando from a pious weakling to a dynamic and determined fighter, for example—illustrate the author's concern to present the material in the most effective manner.

Calderón's most significant modification of the original play, however, is his introduction of the Moorish princess Fénix (Phoenix), the daughter of Fernando's captor, the King of Fez. By incorporating into the play a subplot dealing with Fénix's persistent love for the Arab general Muley in spite of her father's wish that she marry Tarudante, the King of Morocco, Calderón establishes a parallel between Fernando and her. Like him, she is constant—in her love for Muley. Moreover, the competition between Muley and Tarudante for the beautiful Fénix mirrors the competition between Fernando and the King of Fez for the city of Ceuta (whose name corresponds to the Hebrew word for "beauty"). These parallels allow Calderón to evoke poetically the question of the true nature of beauty. When, at the end of the play, Fénix is captured by the Portuguese and returned to her people (with the stipulation that she is to marry Muley) in exchange for Fernando's dead body, it is evident that Calderón, establishing a baroque contrast between appearance and reality, wishes to communicate that the beauty of Fernando's faith is more real than Fénix's physical beauty.

Nowhere is the contrast between Fernando and Fénix more evident than in a much-discussed scene toward the end of the second act in which the two of them recite to each other sonnets on the impermanence of flowers and of stars. Fénix, who had ordered Fernando to bring her a bouquet of flowers, is horrified by the thought that their beauty is only transitory. Fernando, on the other hand, can face even the knowledge that the stars (which at the time the play was written were believed to influence human destiny) are not permanent. Unlike Fénix, he has learned to penetrate beyond appearances. Thus, he is neither captivated nor disturbed by temporary things; he recognizes that both physical beauty and misfortune will become lost in eternity, which he believes to be ordered according to a divine plan. Thus, Calderón has used Fernando's constancy in order to teach a moral lesson concerning the Christian virtue of fortitude.

CAPE AND SWORD PLAYS

The theme of appearance versus reality, which is handled seriously in *The Constant Prince*, is also present in *The Phantom Lady* and *A House with Two Doors Is Difficult to Guard*, two Calderonian plays typical of a genre referred to as *comedias de capa y espada*, or cape and sword plays. The name for this genre, which was seventeenth century Spain's equivalent of a situation comedy, derives from the costume worn by the actors playing the leading male roles. Cape and sword plays have complicated plots revolving around the courtship of one or more sets of middle-class youths who devise ingenious measures to overcome the obstacles to their love. The obstacles are usually presented by a domineering father or brother, anxious to protect the honor or reputation of a daughter or sister, and the young people frequently resort to disguises and other forms of deception, which often backfire with comic results. Duels are a frequent ingredient of these plays, but they never have grave consequences; cape and sword plays invariably have happy endings involving at least one wedding.

THE PHANTOM LADY

The Phantom Lady dramatizes the ingenuity of Angela, a bright and attractive young widow, whose brothers Don Juan and Don Luis, in a desire to protect her reputation, have confined her first to their home and then—during the visit of Don Juan's friend Don Manuel—to her room. Because the room Don Manuel is occupying is next to her own, Angela makes use of a secret door (concealed by a glass cabinet) joining the two rooms to enter their guest's quarters and play pranks on him and frighten his servant, who believes she is a ghost. As he is unaware of her existence, Don Manuel is also puzzled by Angela, but he refuses to believe that she is a phantom and eventually follows her into her room, where the two of them are discovered by Don Luis. Following a duel, which Don Manuel wins (sparing Luis's life), everyone receives an explanation of what has been happening, and Don Manuel and Angela agree to be married.

The use of illusion in the play is obvious. As a result of deceits, disguises, false entrances, and so on, all the play's male characters remain utterly confused until the final scene. As is typical of many cape and sword plays, only the female characters—Angela and her cousin Beatriz—realize what is really happening. Also typical is that the would-be deceivers (the two brothers who conceal Angela's presence from their guest) are themselves the most deceived. This is especially true of Don Luis, who, on an occasion when Angela has left the house in disguise, follows her and endeavors to seduce her, believing that she is another woman.

A HOUSE WITH TWO DOORS IS DIFFICULT TO GUARD

The stereotyped plots and characters of all cape and sword plays bear a certain resemblance to one another—though Calderón somehow manages to endow most of his with a fresh quality which makes them appealing even three hundred years after his death. Thus, many of the elements of *The Phantom Lady*—the unknown entrance, disguises, a tyrannical brother, a mysterious and beautiful lady who appears and disappears—are also present in *A House with Two Doors Is Difficult to Guard*. In this play, the appearance-versus-reality theme is even more noticeable, as when Fénix, describing (in typically baroque language) to his friend Lisardo his first encounter with the beautiful Marcela in the gardens of Aranjuez, remarks on the difficulty of distinguishing her from the carved statues of nymphs in the garden's fountains.

THE SURGEON OF HIS HONOR

Appearances produce tragic consequences in *The Surgeon of His Honor*, a play that dramatizes Don Gutierre Alfonso's murder of his wife, Mencía, because of his belief that she has been unfaithful. In the eyes of a modern audience, at least, Mencía seems to be an innocent victim of misfortune. At the beginning of the play, she is a happily married woman whose happiness is seriously threatened when a former suitor, Prince Enrique, is thrown from his horse (a typical occurrence in Golden Age drama with men who are unable to control their passions) and is brought to her house to recover. When he awakens and discovers his former fiancée, Mencía, Enrique—even after learning that she is now married—persists in efforts to resume his former relationship with her. That night, when her husband is absent, he bribes a servant to gain entry to her house. Though she rejects all Enrique's advances, Mencía does commit various indiscretions. When her husband returns unexpectedly, for example, she conceals Enrique in her room and later arranges a diversion so that he may leave. In

his hasty departure, however, Enrique leaves behind a dagger, which Gutierre discovers and which causes him to suspect his wife of infidelity. After gathering additional misleading evidence that convinces him of his wife's guilt, Gutierre arranges a bloody and startling denouement that is typical of the Senecan tragic style then popular in Spain: He engages a bloodletter, brings him to the house blindfolded, and orders him to bleed his wife to death.

The Surgeon of His Honor is thus typical of a peculiarly Spanish genre that is referred to informally as the wife-murder play. These plays have plots based on Spain's old and infamous honor code, which gave a husband (or father or brother) the legal and moral right to kill a wife (or daughter or sister) whose sexual misconduct had threatened the family's reputation. Although the plots of these plays resemble that of William Shakespeare's *Othello, the Moor of Venice* (pr. 1604), there are notable differences. In *The Surgeon of His Honor*, Gutierre—unlike Othello, who becomes aware of Desdemona's innocence and of his own blindness—remains convinced that what he did (though lamentable) was right, and the play concludes with the announcement of Gutierre's engagement to a former fiancée, an engagement arranged by King Pedro (Enrique's brother). Because the king has been informed by the bloodletter (who surreptitiously left a bloody handprint by the door of Gutierre's house so that it could be identified) of all that has happened, the king's arrangement of a new marriage for Gutierre seems puzzling. Basing their interpretation of the play on this ending, critics assumed for many years that Calderón—and other Spanish authors of similar plays—actually approved of the bloody honor code that was the basis of their dramas.

More recently, however, Calderón scholars have become convinced that this is not the case. Various elements of the play—the bloody handprint by the door (recalling the biblical account of the Passover) and the crucifix hanging above Mencía's bed when her dead body is discovered—invite the audience to examine the play's plot in a religious context and to compare the sacrifice of the innocent Mencía to the sacrifice of the innocent Christ. In this light, it is clear that Calderón has wished to show his audience how easily one may be deceived by appearances. Thus he structured the play in a way that makes the viewer participate initially in Gutierre's error, but he provided enough evidence so that further reflection would correct this initial illusion.

THE GREAT THEATER OF THE WORLD

Calderón's most famous *auto sacramental*, *The Great Theater of the World*, again emphasizes the theme of illusion. Based on the idea that, quite literally, "all the world's a stage," this play dramatizes the production of a play in which a theater manager (an allegorical representation of God) assembles a set of characters (a rich man, a king, a peasant, a poor man, Beauty, Discretion, and a child) in order to represent human life. Because the purpose of the *autos sacramentales* was to instruct the public concerning the meaning of the Eucharist, at the end of the play, the theater manager issues an invitation for some of the characters (those who have behaved appropriately) to join him at his table for a feast, but only after the audience has had ample opportunity to observe how easily some of the actors were seduced into confusing their fictional roles with reality.

THE DEVOTION TO THE CROSS

Often, Calderón's full-length plays also appear to be religious allegories. It has been suggested, for example, that one must view *The Devotion to the Cross* as an allegorical representation of the fall and redemption of humankind. The play dramatizes the fate of Eusebio, a child of unknown parents who has been reared by a shepherd and who refers to himself as "Eusebio of the Cross" because his only clue to his identity is a cross-shaped birthmark. Eusebio wins the affection of a wealthy girl, Julia, but Julia's brother Lisardo—resentful of his sister's lowly suitor—challenges Eusebio to a duel and is killed by him. Pursued by Julia's father, Curcio, Eusebio then becomes the leader of a band of outlaws. He behaves erratically, however, when he captures a priest and sees a book entitled *The Mystery of the Cross*, for he continues to be tormented by the mystery of his own origin and by the meaning of his birthmark. The mystery of his identity is resolved at the end of the play when he and the other characters discover that he is Julia's twin, Curcio's own son.

In a sense, all the principal characters of this play are as confused about their identities as is Eusebio. Like the actors of *The Great Theater of the World*, they have been trapped into playing illusory roles. In *The Devotion to the Cross*, the roles are antagonistic ones, which belie the characters' true identity as a family, and it is clear that Calderón believes that their dilemma is shared by humanity in general. He thus invites his audience to view Eusebio as a kind of Everyman—born into a confused world, uncertain of his identity. Protected by a shepherd (evoking Christ the Good Shepherd), he finally discovers the secret of his existence in the sign of the cross.

LIFE IS A DREAM

Unanimously recognized as Calderón's outstanding masterpiece, *Life Is a Dream* is again an expression of the author's favorite theme of reality and illusion, and of the almost inescapable human tendency to confuse them. Set in Poland, the play dramatizes the destiny of Prince Segismundo, who is imprisoned in a forest by his father, King Basilio, immediately after his birth. Basilio is motivated to imprison his son because—as an astrologer—he has become convinced that Segismundo will become a tyrant who will conquer his father. As is usually the case in drama, Basilio's very efforts to avoid a prophesied destiny actually cause the prophecy to be realized. Because he grows up isolated from humanity and surrounded only by animals, Segismundo quite naturally becomes a savage himself. Thus, when his father—wishing to test the accuracy of his astrological deductions before declaring his Russian nephew Astolfo heir to the Polish throne—has his son drugged, brought to the palace, and informed that he is King of Poland, Segismundo does indeed behave as a tyrant by seeking to violate an attractive woman and by throwing from the palace window a servant who gets in his way. Convinced of the accuracy of the prophecy, Basilio has Segismundo drugged again and returned to prison and proceeds with his plan to have Astolfo declared heir to the throne. The people of Poland, however, are unwilling to accept a foreign king, and, discovering the location of Segismundo's prison, they proclaim him their leader in an insurrection against Basilio. The prophecy that Segismundo would conquer his father is thus fulfilled. Its fulfillment has a rather odd twist, however, since Segismundo—who was indeed a tyrant in his first visit to the palace—is now changed. He has been told by his jailer that all that happened to him in his father's court was only a dream, that one can never distinguish between dreams and reality, but that even in dreams one has the opportunity to do good. Having learned this lesson, he pardons his father and is thus prepared at the play's close to become a wise and benevolent ruler.

Initially, it may appear that Segismundo's conversion derives from an illusion, but Calderón makes it clear that this is not really the case. Segismundo, like Fernando of *The Constant Prince*, has seen through the illusion of life and has glimpsed the reality of eternity. The soliloquy in which he proclaims that life itself is a dream is an excellent example of Calderón's poetic talent at its finest. Probably the most famous soliloquy in the Spanish language, it is as well known in Hispanic countries as Hamlet's question of existence is in English-speaking ones.

Indeed, it is clear that, in Calderón's view, Segismundo is one of the few characters of the play who has freed himself from illusion. In the author's mind, the greatest illusion of which humans are capable is the belief that they may autonomously control their destiny. It was because Basilio was a victim of this illusion at the beginning of the play that he had Segismundo imprisoned, but in the course of the drama, he also learns the nature of reality and thus kneels before his son at the play's end to ask his forgiveness. Another character, the gracioso Clarín, is not so fortunate. He tries cynically to manipulate each situation for his own gain and, during the battle between Segismundo's and Basilio's forces, hides to protect himself from harm until it is over. Ironically, an arrow lands in the very spot where he is hiding and kills him, illustrating once again Calderón's conviction that those who cling to the illusory beauty of life are inviting destruction.

SECRET VENGEANCE FOR SECRET INSULT

Like *The Surgeon of His Honor*, *Secret Vengeance for Secret Insult* dramatizes a husband's murder of his wife (and her suspected lover) in order to defend his honor, and the later play repeats many elements of the earlier one. Shortly before her wedding, Doña Leonor, like Mencía in *The Surgeon of His Honor*, is surprised by the sudden appearance of a former suitor, Don Luis. Like Mencía, she resists her former suitor's advances, but also like her, she makes the mistake of granting him an interview and is forced to hide him when her husband returns unexpectedly. Her husband, Don Lope, becomes suspicious and resolves to protect his honor by killing both Leonor and Luis. Because his goal is to protect his reputation and he believes that no one else suspects his wife's supposed infidelity, he arranges for both murders to look like accidents, but again recalling *The Surgeon of His Honor*, King Sebastián learns the true nature of what has happened and gives it his approval.

It is clear again, however, that Calderón does not endorse what his protagonist has done, and he communicates his disapproval to the audience by ironically undermining Don Lope's character. From the beginning of the play, he portrays Don Lope as an arrogantly self-centered individual who is blindly proud of his ability to control his destiny. When a friend, Don Juan, confides his sorrow at having been forced (in order to protect his honor) to kill a man who insulted a lady he was courting, Don Lope replies that Don Juan should be happy because there is no greater joy than having one's honor unstained. When Don Juan is obliged to kill yet another man (who, aware of the earlier duel, refers to him as the "offended" rather than as the "avenged" party), Don Lope decides confidently to avoid such complications by making his own vengeance a secret one. With this same air of confidence, he prepares at the end of the play to embark with King Sebastián on an expedition against the Moors in Africa—an expedition that the seventeenth century audience knew had ended in disaster. Therefore, at the conclusion of the play, Don Lope is a fine example of a tragedy about to happen—of hubris before a fall—and the audience is fully aware that the same blind pride that led him to murder two people is now leading him to his own destruction.

THE MAYOR OF ZALAMEA

The Mayor of Zalamea, which is considered by Calderón scholars to be second only to his *Life Is a Dream*, is in many ways an atypical Calderonian play. Because its protagonist, Pedro Crespo, is a wealthy peasant (unlike most of Calderón's principal characters, who are noble) and because the theme of the play is a peasant's right to defend his honor, this work bears a certain resemblance to Lope de Vega Carpio's famous "peasant plays" such as *Fuente-ovejuna* (wr. 1611-1618, pb. 1619; *The Sheep Well*, 1936), *Peribáñez y el comendador de Ocaña* (wr. 1609-1612, pb. 1614, *Peribáñez*, 1936), and *El mejor alcalde, el rey* (wr. 1620-1623, pb. 1635; *The King, the Greatest Alcalde*, 1918); indeed, *The Mayor of Zalamea* is a reworking by Calderón of another play by the same name attributed to Lope de Vega.

Initially, the plot of this play may appear to contradict Calderón's implied criticism of the honor code in *The Surgeon of His Honor* and *Secret Vengeance for Secret Insult*, for *The Mayor of Zalamea* dramatizes Pedro Crespo's utilization of his authority as the newly elected Mayor of Zalamea to order the death of Don Alvaro, a captain who, when quartered in Crespo's house, abducted and raped Crespo's daughter Isabel. Moreover, Crespo's use of this authority is of questionable legality because, as the offended party, he can scarcely be considered an impartial judge, and because the offender is a nobleman. Nevertheless, Crespo is neither blind nor arrogant. He orders Don Alvaro's death reluctantly and only after first imploring him to marry Isabel in order to repair the damage done to the family's honor. He likewise shows compassion for his daughter. A typical Golden Age father might have felt constrained by the honor code to murder a dishonored daughter, and Isabel actually expects her father to do so. Crespo arranges instead, after his efforts to have her honorably married have failed, for her to enter a convent.

Even in this play, however, Calderón makes it clear that the honor code allows no occasion for rejoicing. At the end of the play, the widowed Crespo is bereft of both his children. Isabel is in a convent, and he has reluctantly given his consent for his only son, Juan, to join the military. Although he has been honored by King Pedro II, who exonerated his execution of Don Alvaro by naming Crespo mayor for life, he faces a lonely future filled with sad memories.

THE WONDER-WORKING MAGICIAN

Because of its resemblance to the Faust legend, *The Wonder-Working Magician* has received considerable attention and praise—exciting, for example, the admiration of the English poet Percy Bysshe Shelley, who enthusiastically compared it to Johann Wolfgang von Goethe's famous treatment of the same legend. Calderón's play dramatizes the fourth century martyrdom of two saints. The protagonist Cipriano (Saint Cyprian) is enamored of the young and beautiful Justina and, like Faust, signs a pact with the devil so that he may learn black magic in order to seduce her. Though he does acquire spectacular powers, they are unable to prevail against Justina's virtuous will, and Cipriano—after embracing a skeleton that he has mistaken for Justina—recognizes, like all Calderonian heroes, that the seemingly impressive powers of evil are an illusion. The play concludes as he and his beloved, united at last, suffer death as martyrs. Ironically, the devil, who initially approached Cipriano in order to distract him from his study of theology, has been an instrument in his martyrdom and salvation. The purposes of evil have been thwarted by the purposes of good.

LOS CABELLOS DE ABSALÓN

Of all the Calderón plays based on his reworking of earlier material, the best-known is *Los cabellos de Absalón*. Its source, Tirso de Molina's *La venganza de Tamar* (wr. 1621, pb. 1634), dramatizes the biblical story of King David's daughter Tamar's rape by her half-brother Amnon and her brother Absalom's murder of Amnon in order to avenge her honor. Calderón's play condenses Tirso's into two acts (the second of which is an almost word-for-word copy of Tirso's act 3) and adds an original third act that dramatizes Absalom's own death when, in his revolt against his father, his hair becomes entangled in the low branches of a tree as he is riding through a forest.

Although Calderón's appropriation of Tirso's material may appear questionable in an age that has become accustomed to copyright laws, one should note that in the seventeenth century such practices were considered entirely legitimate. Indeed, it is quite possible that Calderón composed his play at the request of a theater manager who instructed him to write a new final act for Tirso's material.

Obviously, both dramatists found in the biblical account of David's tragic family an echo of the nefarious Spanish honor code, and both of them implicitly criticize this code by reminding their audiences that the vindication of honor may—as in the case of Absalom—be only a disguise for self-serving motives. Calderón's arrangement of the material to emphasize Absalom's hair (of which Absalom was so proud that he mistakenly understood a prophecy that he would be "elevated by his hair" to mean that his physical beauty would cause him to become king) is typical of the author's penchant for showing his villains captivated by illusion.

THE PAINTER OF HIS DISHONOR

Calderón's last famous wife-murder play, *The Painter of His Dishonor*, is perhaps his best contribution to the genre. In its rapid action, which shifts from Italy to Spain and back again, the author achieves a perfect synthesis of the themes of illusion and revenge. Many elements of its plot are familiar from *The Surgeon of His Honor* and *Secret Vengeance for Secret Insult*. The young and beautiful Serafina consents to marry Juan Roca, an old artist who attempts vainly to capture her beauty on canvas, only because she believes her former suitor, Don Alvaro, has perished at sea; Alvaro returns and, ignoring Serafina's protests that she wishes to be faithful to her husband, abducts her and hides her in his father's country house near Naples. The Prince of Naples, who has also been captivated by Serafina's beauty, discovers her presence and engages a traveling artist to paint her portrait. Ironically, the artist is Serafina's husband, who has returned to Italy to locate his wife and avenge his honor. In an action-packed final scene, Juan manages at last to capture his sleeping wife's likeness on canvas; when Serafina awakens, frightened by a dream in which she imagined her husband was killing her, she rushes for the first time to seek comfort in her abductor's arms. Alvaro and Serafina's embrace convinces Juan of his wife's guilt, and he rapidly fires two pistols, leaving both his wife and her suitor dead inside the "frame" provided by the windows that served as the standard background for the seventeenth century Spanish stage.

The painting motif that is the context for this drama suggests a number of conclusions. By emphasizing art's ambiguity, Calderón clearly suggests that Juan Roca has fallen victim to his own artistic imagination. At the same time, however, Serafina's own conduct seems equally ambiguous. While on the conscious level she remains faithful to her husband, it is clear that unconsciously she is indeed guilty of an adulterous love for Alvaro. Indeed, Serafina and Juan are similar in that both struggle in vain to exercise conscious control over a deeper self that is more real than their illusory social masks; both are examples of the inevitable human subjection to sin. Calderón's solution to this human dilemma, which is a basic theme of his work, is found in an *auto sacramental* also entitled *The Painter of His Dishonor*, in which the offended husband, Christ, pardons his wife, Human Nature, and fires instead on guilt and Lucifer.

OTHER MAJOR WORKS

POETRY: *Psalle et sile*, 1741; *Poesías*, 1845; *Obra lírica*, 1943; *Sus mejores poesías*, 1954; *Poesías líricas en las obras dramáticas de Calderón*, 1964; *Los sonetos de Calderón en sus obras dramáticas*, 1974.

BIBLIOGRAPHY

Acker, Thomas S. *The Baroque Vortex: Velázquez, Calderón, and Gracián Under Philip IV.* New York: Peter Lang, 2000. Acker compares and contrasts the works of Calderón, Diego Velázquez, and Baltasar Gracián y Morales, examining the baroque influence. Bibliography.

De Armas, Frederick A. *The Prince in the Tower: Perceptions of "La vida es sueño."* Cranbury, N.J.: Associated University Presses, 1993. Various perspectives on Calderón's *Life Is a Dream*. Bibliography and index.

Delgado Morales, Manuel, ed. *The Calderonian Stage: Body and Soul.* Lewisburg, Pa.: Bucknell University Press, 1997. An analysis of the staging and production of the dramas of Calderón. Bibliography and index.

Levin, Leslie. *Metaphors of Conversion in Seventeenth Century Spanish Drama.* Rochester, N.Y.: Tamesis, 1999. This study examines the concept of religion and conversion in the dramas of Calderón as well as those of Tirso de Molina. Bibliography and index.

Rupp, Stephen James. *Allegories of Kingship: Calderón and the Anti-Machiavellian Tradition.* University Park.: Pennsylvania State University Press, 1996. An examination of Calderón's portrayal of the monarchy in literature and of his political and social views. Bibliography and index.

Currie K. Thompson

ALBERT CAMUS

Born: Mondovi, Algeria; November 7, 1913
Died: Near Villeblevin, France; January 4, 1960

PRINCIPAL DRAMA

Caligula, wr. 1938-1939, pb. 1944, pr. 1945
(English translation, 1948)
Le Malentendu, pr., pb. 1944 (*The Misunderstanding*, 1948)
L'État de siège, pr., pb. 1948 (*State of Siege*, 1958)
Les Justes, pr. 1949, pb. 1950 (*The Just Assassins*, 1958)
Caligula and Three Other Plays, pb. 1958

OTHER LITERARY FORMS

Considered by many to have been the outstanding figure in his generation of French letters (rivaled only by his sometime friend and colleague Jean-Paul Sartre), Albert Camus is best remembered as the author of thought-provoking essays, such as *Le Mythe de Sisyphe* (1942; *The Myth of Sisyphus*, 1955) and *L'Homme révolté* (1951; *The Rebel*, 1956), and novels such as *L'Étranger* (1942; *The Stranger*, 1946), *La Peste* (1947; *The Plague*, 1948), and *La Chute* (1956; *The Fall*, 1957). *L'Exil et le royaume* (*Exile and the Kingdom*, 1958), a collection of thematically linked but otherwise widely varied short stories, appeared in 1957 to considerable acclaim.

ACHIEVEMENTS

Despite a lifelong interest and participation in the theater, frequently as actor or director, Albert Camus never achieved with his plays the success that his essays and prose fiction enjoyed. Still, the plays are valuable for their development of the themes that preoccupied him throughout his career. It was his single-minded engagement with these fundamental moral and philosophical dilemmas that won for him a reputation as the conscience of his generation—a reputation confirmed in 1957 by the Nobel Prize in Literature, which he received when he was only forty-three years old.

BIOGRAPHY

Albert Camus was born in Mondovi, Algeria, on November 7, 1913, to Lucien Camus and the former Catherine Sintès, a frail, unlettered woman of Spanish ancestry. Following the death of the elder Camus in battle during 1914, Albert grew up among his mother's family in Belcourt, a working-class suburb of Algiers. A talented scholarship student, Camus soon earned the interest and attention of various gifted teachers, including the writer and scholar Jean Grenier, with whom Camus was to maintain an often problematical friendship for the remainder of his life. At twenty, with one year left to go at the University of Algiers, Camus married Simone Hié, an attractive, brilliant, but highly unstable young woman who was also a known morphine addict. The marriage foundered within three years but did not formally end in divorce until 1940, when both parties sought the freedom to remarry.

Directed toward a teaching career, Camus was ironically disqualified from the coveted *agregation* for reasons of health. Although an accomplished athlete, he had been tubercular since childhood. Supporting himself at a variety of odd jobs, Camus joined the Communist Party during 1935 and soon found himself in charge of the propagandist Théâtre du Travail. Too resolutely proletarian of background to have had much prior exposure to the theater (which, for all practical

Albert Camus (© The Nobel Foundation)

or outline form; the collapse of *Alger-Républicain* gave Camus both the time and the need to establish his literary reputation. Meanwhile, he was engaged to marry Francine Faure, the woman who would eventually bear him twin children and still later become his widow. Reluctant to leave Francine in Algeria before he was free to remarry, Camus nevertheless departed for Paris to seek fame and fortune (or at least employment) with the help of Pascal Pia, a former editor of *Alger-Républicain*. Once there, he joined Pia in the layout department of *Paris-Soir*, a mass-circulation daily of reactionary sympathies that neither man shared or could even tolerate. After the fall of France and subsequent occupation of Paris, *Paris-Soir* relocated its offices in the city of Lyon, as did most other Paris newspapers; Lyon was still part of the so-called Free Zone. Camus, meanwhile, continued in Lyon the task of revising and polishing his extant manuscripts, in particular *The Myth of Sisyphus*.

Soon after his marriage to Francine on December 3, 1940, Camus was laid off from his job at *Paris-Soir*. The couple then returned to Algeria, to Francine's hometown of Oran—the future setting of *The Plague*—where they eked out a living as teachers. During the summer of 1942, Camus's tuberculosis recurred, and it was deemed suitable that he take the mountain air at Le Panelier, in the Massif Central not far from Lyon, where some relatives of Francine happened to own a boardinghouse. Francine, however, was obliged soon thereafter to return to Oran, where her teaching duties were both more demanding and more secure than those of her husband. Subsequent changes in the wartime political situation isolated Algeria from metropolitan France, making Francine's return to Le Panelier impossible and communication nearly so. As his health improved, Camus began finding his way to Paris to check on his manuscripts. It was there that he met Maria Casarès, a beautiful and talented Spanish stage actress. Barely twenty years old at the time, Maria was the daughter of Santiago Casarès Quiroga, an eminent anti-Franco politician then living in exile. Already established as an actress by the time Camus met her, her intelligence and talents closely matched to his own, Casarès would become the most significant woman in Camus's life as

purposes, had not hitherto existed in Algiers), Camus soon discovered what would become a lifetime enthusiasm. Through active participation in the theater as actor and director, he rediscovered much the same team spirit and camaraderie that had drawn him to participate in sports. After leaving the party in 1937, he lost little time in founding his own company, known as Le Théâtre de l'Équipe. Steady employment, however, continued to elude Camus until 1938, when a group of his friends founded the liberal newspaper *Alger-Républicain* and invited him to join its staff. The paper, with Camus as a valued contributor, survived until 1940, when conscriptions and the threat of military censorship brought operations to a halt.

Throughout his association with Le Théâtre de l'Équipe and *Alger-Républicain*, Camus had tried his hand at essays, drama, and fiction, with two volumes of essays already published by 1940. *Caligula*, *The Myth of Sisyphus*, and *The Stranger* remained in draft

an artist, although her temperament and convictions forbade any permanent disruption of Camus's marriage to Francine. Toward the end of 1943, Camus joined the resistance organization Combat and assumed an active role in the publication of its eponymous underground newspaper—once again following in the footsteps of his older friend Pascal Pia.

With the liberation of France in 1944, *Combat* became a freely circulating daily with Pia and Camus more or less at the helm. Soon thereafter, Camus was reunited with Francine, who bore him twins, a son and daughter, in September, 1945. Meanwhile, Camus's reputation as a writer was beginning to resemble fame. Public esteem for his work was sufficient, in any case, to offset the relative failure of *The Misunderstanding* during the final months of the Occupation. During the spring of 1946, Camus set off for the United States, on a lecture tour sponsored by the Cultural Services of the French Embassy. It was around this time, suggests Camus scholar Patrick McCarthy, that Camus's public utterances and perceived "image" began seriously to diverge from what the author actually thought or had written, setting in motion an insidious process that would culminate in the backlash of public opinion during the years immediately following Camus's death. Even during Camus's lifetime, the partially self-invited designation as a kind of secular saint became a burden often difficult, if not impossible, to bear.

To a large extent, the difficulty of Camus's postwar existence had to do with politics—an area in which he was temperamentally ill suited to serve as an expert, or even worse, as a sage. Although resolutely to the left of center, Camus had few unshakable convictions and even fewer proposed solutions. His approach, if such it may be called, was to study the lessons of history from a variety of disinterested perspectives, rejecting most known choices in favor of a more broadly construed if ill-defined humanitarianism. Predictably, Camus's reluctance to choose a specific political allegiance angered a number of his former left-wing colleagues in the Resistance and elsewhere, who believed that Camus had turned conservative on them. Still other former associates, such as Pia, themselves turned conservative and denounced

Camus as a mindless liberal. Camus's ruptures with Sartre and with Pia, equally (if opposingly) rooted in ideology, proved particularly bitter and lasted well beyond Camus's lifetime. Camus, meanwhile, continued rather quixotically to advocate a vaguely outlined "third choice" located somewhere between the established poles of capitalism and communism.

Following the resounding success of *The Plague*, Camus devoted himself to intensive reading in preparation for his planned political statement, a discursive essay called *The Rebel*. Reflecting broad, occasionally deep but oddly uncritical reading in history, philosophy, and literature, *The Rebel* devotes considerable rhetoric to a distinction between "revolt," the logical consequence to one's desirable awareness of "the absurd," and "revolution," the institutional manifestation of revolt that tends inevitably toward totalitarianism and a consequent reassertion of "the absurd." The fundamental question raised, quite rhetorically indeed, is whether the ends, in a political context, may be said to justify the means—the same question posed in dramatic terms by *The Just Assassins* some three years earlier. Unfortunately, the admixture of high-mindedness and careless thinking to be found in *The Rebel* sufficed to alienate such of Camus's leftist friends as remained, provoking a bitter debate that raged for several months in the pages of Sartre's review *Les Temps modernes*.

Still more political problems awaited Camus in the developing crisis of an Algerian bid for independence. His reluctance to take sides, understandable in view of his status as a *pied-noir* or North African-born Frenchman, nevertheless angered many of those who had come to see in Camus a tireless champion of human rights. Camus remained unconvinced that any proposed political solution could possibly be the proper one. Having for years advocated serious liberal reforms in the French administration of Algeria, he initially underestimated the force and convictions of the newly formed Nationalist Front, or FLN. As matters escalated, Camus lent his welcome support to the negotiation of a civil solution acceptable to both sides—characteristically expressing his mistrust of political "solutions" together with his hatred of violence and bloodshed. When a negotiated truce proved unworkable, Camus found himself condemned to inaction, torn between his pronouncements on one side, and loyalty to his own people—the French of Algeria—on the other. As a writer, he produced the enigmatic *The Fall* and the short stories of *Exile and the Kingdom* and distracted himself with the adaptation of other writers' texts for the stage. Biographical evidence suggests that Camus in his early forties may well have fallen victim to what a later generation would call the "midlife crisis." At the very least, he was severely depressed by the Algerian situation and entertained serious doubts concerning his future as a writer. The Nobel Prize in Literature awarded to him in 1957, with the war for Algerian independence still in progress, was a mixed blessing; although among the youngest of Nobel writer-laureates, Camus was all too aware of the common wisdom that the Nobel is awarded in recognition of a body of work already considered complete—or at least finished.

Unbeknown to Camus, only two years and a few months of life remained to him after his recognition by the Swedish Academy. Having recently revised (or re-revised) his extant plays in anticipation of a new American edition, with an author's preface, Camus in 1958 began campaigning in earnest to establish a theater of his own in Paris, hoping no doubt to recapture some of the spirit of Le Théâtre de l'Équipe. Now living apart from his family at Lourmarin, in the south of France, he spent most of his visits to Paris in pursuit of his new project. He had also recently finished several years' work on the stage version of Fyodor Dostoevski's novel *Besy* (1871-1872; *The Possessed*, 1913) and by mid-1959 was well launched on a new novel, set in the Algeria of his youth and tentatively entitled "Le Premier Homme" (the first man). He was killed instantly on January 4, 1960, when a car driven by his friend and publisher Michel Gallimard collided with a tree. A valid rail ticket found on his person suggested that Camus had planned to travel from Lourmarin to Paris by train, as usual, changing his mind only at the last minute; in any case, the circumstances of his death lent themselves readily to comparison with Camus's own concept of the absurd. ("After all," commented one observer, "to be killed by one's own publisher?") Gallimard himself died

several days later of injuries sustained in the wreck, although the car's two other passengers survived.

ANALYSIS

Given the depth and scope of Albert Camus's other published work, it is difficult to consider his plays without reflecting on what they might, or probably should, have been. Surely no other novelist in recent memory has been better suited or more disposed to write for the theater, and none (with the possible exception of Thornton Wilder) has been assured of a potentially more welcoming or receptive audience. Camus's ideas and pronouncements were a highly marketable commodity in the 1940's, and it is ironic that his dramatic output failed to meet the flexible standards of what was prepared to be an appreciative audience, perhaps worldwide. The key to the problem may well reside in the discrepancy, noted by McCarthy, between the public and private Camus. In all likelihood it is the private, instinctive Camus who allowed his voice to be heard through the plays, even as audiences might be expecting to hear the somewhat misconstrued author of *The Stranger* and *The Plague*. Nor do Camus's plays, like certain other works initially misunderstood, appear to have improved with age; with the possible exception of *Caligula*, they remain every bit as baffling and unworkable as they were at their first presentation and are rarely, if ever, revived in production.

It is ironic that Camus, truly a "man of the people" and proud to be one, sought to express his proclaimed "search for modern tragedy" in the accents of neoclassical kings and princes, themselves an upwardly mobile and decidedly artificial convention of seventeenth century France. People in contemporary France, regardless of class, simply do not speak in the simple past or imperfect subjunctive tenses, yet Camus's characters do, almost without exception. Indeed, the most frequent criticism leveled against Camus's dramatic characters is that they appear wooden—owing no doubt in part to the stiffness of their verbal expression—while stopping far short of true caricature, a technique that has worked for, and not against, such disparate contemporary dramatists as Jean Anouilh, Samuel Beckett, Eugène Ionesco, and even Wilder.

Nor did Camus, like Bertolt Brecht, adopt the strategy of setting his characters deliberately against the audience. Quite to the contrary, he appeared to be soliciting the identification of his audience with characters who provide no motivation for bestowing it. Even the most potentially sympathetic spectator is likely to conclude that most of Camus's characters are little more than ideas with legs—and ill-articulated legs at that.

As Ionesco, Anouilh, and others have amply proved, tragedy need not be couched in eloquent language in order to be effective. Sartre, making no claim to tragedy, nevertheless "crossed the footlights" with his often melodramatic use of street speech and occasional vulgarisms; even if certain of his plays barely merit classification as literature, Sartre achieved communication with his audience, his ideas readily accessible—a goal that continued to hover just outside the reach of Camus's dramatic talents. Only in *Caligula* did Camus achieve anything resembling credible characters; it is no coincidence that, alone among Camus's plays, it is also a rousing piece of theater.

CALIGULA

The first of Camus's plays to be written and the second to be performed, *Caligula* is unquestionably the finest of Camus's original dramatic efforts, owing in part to its genesis as a production planned for Le Théâtre de l'Équipe by its twenty-five-year-old founder and director. Although not actually staged until its author was past thirty, *Caligula* is, as Camus freely admitted, a young man's play—with all the predictable strengths and weaknesses. First performed during 1945 with the eventually famous Gérard Philipe in the title role, *Caligula* draws on the sensational accounts of Tranquillus Suetonius, today considered to have been a Roman precursor of what later would be known as yellow journalism. Unfortunately, more responsible observations concerning the reign of Gaius Caesar, alias "Caligula" (12-41 C.E.), have been lost to history; what survives is the dubious testimony of Suetonius, a publicist likely to stress the lurid aspects of any subject matter that fell beneath his hand. For Camus, less interested in sensationalism per se than in a certain perceived logic behind the emperor's behavior, Caligula emerged as a nearly ideal test case for the limits of human freedom. Strongly

influenced by recent and intensive reading in the work of Friedrich Nietzsche, Camus projected onto the documented madness of Caligula a highly lucid, logical intelligence. Here, as with the later *The Just Assassins*, Camus disclaims any intention of writing a historical play, despite his appropriation of historical characters and setting. His intention in each case is to bring forth a play of ideas based on, but not necessarily faithful to, the data of history. In Caligula's case, Suetonius's account indicates that the emperor was indeed insane, as a result of physiological causes, and had been so for years. In Camus's version, Caligula has served as the most progressive and humane of rulers until he experiences a sudden blinding vision of the absurd, rather like a religious conversion in reverse. Other characters and situations similarly undergo subtle changes, less in the interests of stagecraft than to elucidate the author's thinking. As found in Suetonius, the life of Caligula lends itself readily to dramatic presentation. Camus, as actor and director, for once had the instinct not to meddle with an otherwise sure thing. Such recorded incidents as Caligula's travesties and his awarding of military medals to the most frequent customers of the public brothel are carried to the stage pretty much intact, carefully placed so as to provide support for the author's basic premise.

As seen by Camus, the youthful emperor Caligula suddenly perceives, on the death of his sister and of his mistress Drusilla, that life has no meaning apart from the sole certainty of death. Wrongly construed as simple grief by the sycophants and nonentities in his entourage, Caligula's malaise goes far deeper than grief and is metaphysical rather than emotional in origin. From the basic awareness that "men die and are not happy," Caligula proceeds to question the discrepancy between human reality and human aspirations that Camus would later, in *The Myth of Sisyphus*, characterize as the absurd.

Traditionally, it is outsiders and social rejects such as Dostoevski's "Underground Man" who form such questions, with precious little effect on society, but in the present case the questioner is the most powerful monarch in the so-called civilized world, presumably better able than any other mortal to transform his ruminations into reality. Devoid of hope, Caligula decides instead to live in logic—using his absolute power to ensure that the rest of the world will join him. Irritated, for example, when the imperial treasurer interrupts him in conversation, Caligula chooses to take the man at his word and assumes, as he puts it, that "the treasury is of capital importance." Soon thereafter, his pun takes on added grisly significance when he orders that all private citizens rewrite their wills, designating the State as the beneficiary; when the government happens to need or want money, it will execute a citizen or two. Borrowed almost verbatim from Suetonius, the Treasury incident acquires new power and eloquence in Camus's version. In one master stroke, the seemingly mad emperor both ridicules the petty interests of self-important bureaucrats and substitutes his own logic for the incomprehensible caprice of an indifferent universe. After all, he observes, the people in question would all die sooner or later, but perhaps at an inopportune time; far better, he observes, to make their deaths serve some useful purpose.

Throughout the remainder of his reign, Camus's Caligula continues thus to turn the world on its head, curiously assured of the spectator's sympathy because he happens to make more sense than most of the characters around him. When taken to task for his atrocities, he points with justifiable pride to the fact that he has waged no wars during his reign, adding that the "smallest war" undertaken by a "reasonable ruler" would in fact have taken ten times the toll in lives exacted by his drastic measures. True, acknowledges his interlocutor, but at least people would understand, wars being a somehow more acceptable way to die. The passage in question is vintage Camus, foreshadowing both *The Stranger* and *The Plague* and resounding through the spectator's mind long after the moment has passed. Why, indeed, should wars be somehow "acceptable"? Why should death in battle or by pillage be accepted as "natural"? In Camus's terms, the ultimate tragedy of Caligula is that his single-minded pursuit of logic precludes any remnant of solidarity or fraternity with the remainder of the human race; his behavior, therefore, is presented as thought-provoking but hardly exemplary. Caligula's assassination, onstage as in life, is amply prepared throughout the action as the only logical—and doubt-less chosen—result of his bizarre experiment, which is in fact little more than a cosmic form of suicide. Unlike his historical counterpart, however, Camus's Caligula leaves in his wake an exemplary, memorable, and oddly inspiring message, exhorting the spectator to share in the best parts of his peculiarly distorted dream.

Sufficiently rich in spectacle to counteract its relatively heavy burden of thought and exposition, *Caligula*, although the first of Camus's plays, is not only his finest but also markedly superior to the routine work of dramatists who are judged to be greater than he. The dialogue, although formal, moves quickly, with frequent wit and repartee, animated by a playfulness of spirit that either deserted Camus soon thereafter or at least turned backward on itself, producing such tortured distortions of irony as those to be found in *The Misunderstanding*.

THE MISUNDERSTANDING

Presumably helped in its initial performances by the versatile Maria Casarès, generally considered to be the love of Camus's life but here cast ironically against type, *The Misunderstanding* nevertheless failed in its premiere and continually defied its author's efforts to revive it, either in text or in production. Despite several highly memorable scenes—as memorable as some of the best in *Caligula*—*The Misunderstanding* remains academic and wooden, peopled with characters who somehow fail to achieve credibility despite their frequent claims to suffering and their occasional outbursts of violence.

Enigmatically and ironically referred to in Camus's early notes as a "comedy," *The Misunderstanding* may be seen as a parody of traditional comic procedure, with clues left hanging and double meanings that fall on deaf ears. Jan, the would-be protagonist in a comedy that is of his own making, becomes a minor and expendable character in "an order . . . where no one is recognized." Totally dehumanized by the hard work and squalor from which Jan has come to rescue them, his mother and sister Martha are barely speaking the same language that he is; at any rate, all the words seem to have different meanings. Better tuned to the accents of the absurd, Martha and her mother can make little sense of the smiling traveler from warmer, sunny climes, and even less can he make sense of them. Recalling Camus's description in *The Myth of Sisyphus* of the absurd as "this divorce between the actor and his backdrop," Jan often appears as a witless comedian who has somehow stumbled into the wrong theater. Traveling under an assumed name, as if in a spirit of playfulness, he will wait in vain to be recognized; the simple truth is that his mother and sister are past caring. His death at their hands is utterly devoid of any recognition that might afford him tragic stature; oblivious to what is happening, he simply drifts off into drugged sleep before being drowned in the river.

The basic outline of *The Misunderstanding* is to be found in the novel *The Stranger*, in the form of a faded news clipping read and reread by Meursault in his prison cell. Considerably expanded for the stage, the bleak folktale nevertheless is little changed; unable to get inside the characters, the spectator is likely to agree with Meursault that "the fellow probably deserved it a little" and that "one must not play games." The only truly accessible character in *The Misunderstanding* is Jan's wife, Maria. Yet as critic Edward Freeman observes, Maria's very humanity tends to intervene between the spectator and a deeper understanding of the other characters. Even less attuned than her husband to what is actually happening, Maria somehow invites the audience to share her helplessness rather than probe more deeply, for example, into the murderous character of Martha.

A distant spiritual cousin of the homicidal Caligula, Martha is perhaps the most intriguing, if ultimately the least successful, of Camus's characters in any genre. Unlike Caligula, a man of power and some presumable education, Martha simply cannot be made much more thoughtful or lucid than she is and still remain in character. If she is to be credible at all, her instinctive awareness of, and complicity with, the absurd must appear preverbal, perhaps even preconscious—a cosmic and ultimately malevolent indifference. Unlike such other bloodstained ladies of the stage as Medea and Lady Macbeth, she must appear less villainous than simply hollow or dehumanized—even at the risk of appearing merely boring. Although to a lesser degree, the mother and Jan present a similar potential weakness, failing fully to elicit the spectators' involvement; given the spareness and austerity of Camus's exposition, spectators simply do not know enough about the characters to interest themselves in their fate.

With the possible exception of *Caligula*, *The Misunderstanding* is the most often reworked and revised of Camus's plays, and some commentators suggest that Camus was planning still another revision at the time of his death. As in the cast of *Caligula*, however, later does not necessarily mean better, and the latest extant version of *The Misunderstanding* may well be the least effective. Prepared soon after Camus's translation of Dino Buzzati's *Un Caso clinico* (1953), a truly absurdist play, the 1958 text of *The Misunderstanding* reflects Camus's exposure to the new idiom in ways that detract from his original concept of comedy parodied. In its final form, *The Misunderstanding* thus remains even more baffling than before and almost totally ineffective on the stage.

STATE OF SIEGE

Following the success of his novel *The Plague*, Camus was invited by the actor and director Jean-Louis Barrault to adapt some of the novel's premises for the stage. Working closely with Barrault, who at the time was interested in adapting some of the dramatic theories of Antonin Artaud, Camus eventually developed *State of Siege*, an elaborate, spectacular political parable set in medieval Cádiz. Despite the best efforts of Barrault, Casarès, and a number of other distinguished performers, the play was a resounding failure and is still considered the weakest of Camus's original efforts for the stage.

THE JUST ASSASSINS

Considerably more successful, and effective, was *The Just Assassins*, mounted the following year. As in the case of *Caligula*, Camus in *The Just Assassins* borrows from history, not to re-create it, but to explore the possible thoughts and motivations of historical characters.

The characters honored in the play's title are the Russian insurgents who sought to overthrow czarist rule in 1905—to Camus's view, a far more honorable group than the revolutionaries who actually succeeded twelve years later. Reflecting many of the concerns to be addressed in his essay *The Rebel*, then in progress, the play draws a fine distinction between revolution and revolt, the former being a corruption of the latter. The main historical figure in *The Just Assassins* is Ivan Kaliayev, a poet and student who renounced his first attempt on the life of a grand duke in order to spare the lives of two children, the duke's niece and nephew, who happened to be traveling with him. (His second attempt, two days later, with the children absent, succeeded, whereupon Kaliayev delivered himself up to a swift trial and certain execution.) In retrospect, it is easy to see that the figure of Kaliayev would hold particular appeal for the author of *The Plague*, in which Dr. Rieux expresses his inability to believe in a God "who allows children to suffer and die."

In Camus's play, the assassination and execution take place offstage, narrated rather than portrayed; for Camus, the real interest resides in the characters' motivations and emotions. Somewhat less stylized than the verbal barricades of *The Misunderstanding*, the debates and interactions of *The Just Assassins* produce more than their share of true dramatic satisfaction. Kaliayev, Dora Brilliant, and the others emerge as rounded characters worthy of the spectator's interest and sympathy. (The single wholly fictitious character, Stepan Fedorov, serves primarily as a terrorist counterpoise to Kaliayev's considerably more moderate views.) Indeed, in this play, Camus nearly arrived at the creation of modern tragedy.

The Just Assassins was to be Camus's last original work for the theater; for the remainder of his brief life, he would devote his playwriting talents to the adaptation of other people's work for the stage, frequently with considerable success, and to the revision of his own plays.

Other major works

LONG FICTION: *L'Étranger*, 1942 (*The Stranger*, 1946); *La Peste*, 1947 (*The Plague*, 1948); *La Chute*, 1956 (*The Fall*, 1957); *La Mort heureuse*, 1971 (wr. 1936-1938; *A Happy Death*, 1972); *Le premier homme*, 1994 (*The First Man*, 1995).

SHORT FICTION: *L'Exil et le royaume*, 1957 (*Exile and the Kingdom*, 1958).

NONFICTION: *L'Envers et l'endroit*, 1937 ("The Wrong Side and the Right Side," 1968); *Noces*, 1938 ("Nuptials," 1968); *Le Mythe de Sisyphe*, 1942 (*The Myth of Sisyphus*, 1955); *L'Homme révolté*, 1951 (*The Rebel*, 1953); *L'Été*, 1954 ("Summer," 1968); *Carnets: Mai 1935-février 1942*, 1962 (*Notebooks, 1935-1942*, 1963); *Carnets: Janvier 1942-mars 1951*, 1964 (*Notebooks, 1942-1951*, 1965); *Lyrical and Critical Essays*, 1968 (includes "The Wrong Side and the Right Side," "Nuptials," and "Summer"); *Correspondance, 1939-1947*, 2000.

Bibliography

Bronner, Stephen Eric. *Camus: Portrait of a Moralist*. Minneapolis: University of Minnesota Press, 1999. A study of Camus's life and ethics. Bibliography and index.

Kamber, Richard. *On Camus*. Wadsworth Philosophers series. Belmont, Calif.: Wadsworth/Thomson Learning, 2002. A basic look at Camus as a philosopher. Bibliography.

Lottman, Herbert R. *Albert Camus: A Biography*. 1979. Reprint. Corte Madera, Calif.: Gingko Press, 1997. A biography of Camus that covers his life and works. Bibliography and index.

McBride, Joseph. *Albert Camus: Philosopher and Littératuer*. New York: St. Martin's Press, 1992. A study of Camus that examines his philosophical views as they present themselves in his literature. Bibliography and index.

McCarthy, Patrick. *Albert Camus, The Stranger*. New York: Cambridge University Press, 1988. Provides analysis of Camus's works and biographical data.

Rizzuto, Anthony. *Camus: Love and Sexuality*. Gainesville: University Press of Florida, 1998. An analysis of the themes of love and sex in the works of Camus. Bibliography and index.

Todd, Olivier. *Albert Camus: A Life*. New York: Alfred A. Knopf, 1998. Making use of materials unavailable until after the death of the author's widow, Francine, a prominent French journalist offer a full-scale biography of the novelist, essayist, playwright, lover, and exiled Algerian.

David B. Parsell